PENGUIN BOOKS

ABE

David S. Reynolds is a Distinguished Professor at the Graduate Center of the City University of New York. He is the author of *Walt Whitman's America: A Cultural Biography,* winner of the Bancroft Prize and the Ambassador Book Award. His other books include *Beneath the American Renaissance,* winner of the Christian Gauss Award; *John Brown, Abolitionist; Waking Giant: America in the Age of Jackson; Mightier than the Sword:* Uncle Tom's Cabin *and the Battle for America;* and *Lincoln's Selected Writings.*

* * *

Praise for *Abe*

One of the *Wall Street Journal*'s Ten Best Books of 2020
A *Washington Post* Notable Book
One of *Kirkus Reviews*'s and *Christian Science Monitor*'s
Best Nonfiction Books of 2020
Winner of the Gilder Lehrman Lincoln Prize and the
Abraham Lincoln Institute Book Award

"In the realms of the frontier, education, religion, law, marriage or politics, Reynolds deepens our understanding of Lincoln's life. . . . In 1909, Leo Tolstoy observed that Lincoln's 'genius is still too strong and too powerful for the common understanding.' *Abe,* consistently learned and illuminating, goes a long way toward helping us fathom his transcendence." —*The Washington Post*

"A marvelous cultural biography that captures Lincoln in all his historical fullness . . . Using popular culture in this way, to fill out the context surrounding Lincoln, is what makes Mr. Reynolds's biography so different and so compelling. . . . Where did the sympathy and compassion expressed in [Lincoln's] Second Inaugural—'With malice toward none; with charity for all'—come from? This big, wonderful book provides the richest cultural context to explain that, and everything else, about Lincoln." —Gordon Wood, *The Wall Street Journal*

"A prodigious and lucidly rendered exposition of the character and thought of the sixteenth president as gleaned through the prism of the cultural and social forces swirling through America during his lifetime." —*The New York Times Book Review*

"David Reynolds's splendid biography is chock full of fresh information and insights about Lincoln that disprove the adage that nothing new can be said about this iconic American. Focusing on the cultural forces that shaped Lincoln and his contemporaries, Reynolds portrays the gathering storm of sectional conflict that erupted into a war over slavery and disunion in which Lincoln's commitment to freedom and racial justice was grounded in moral commitment as well as political and military exigencies. A work of literary distinction as well as sound scholarship, this biography will take its place as a classic in Lincoln studies."

—James M. McPherson, author of *Tried by War:*
Abraham Lincoln as Commander in Chief

"Before Lincoln became a man for all time, he was a man of *his* time. In this compelling, thought-provoking life of the Great Emancipator, David Reynolds reminds us that a prerequisite for leadership in a democracy is an ability to tap the zeitgeist and turn it to decisive effect, as Lincoln preeminently did."

—H. W. Brands, University of Texas at Austin

"Abraham Lincoln's America unfolds in all the nation's hope, despair, and deliverance in this monumental book. Drawing on Reynolds's unequaled knowledge and humane understanding, *Abe* is a brilliant portrait of the man and of the country he saved."

—Edward L. Ayers, winner of the Gilder Lehrman Lincoln Prize

"David Reynolds has a deeper knowledge and keener understanding of American popular culture than any other historian of the Civil War era. After illuminating studies of Walt Whitman, John Brown, and Harriet Beecher Stowe, Reynolds now brings his vast erudition to bear on our sixteenth president. This is an Abraham Lincoln at once familiar and entirely new, a man who was very much the product of his own cultural moment. No one but Reynolds could have written a book this good."

—James Oakes, author of *Freedom National: The Destruction of Slavery*
in the United State, 1861–1865 and *The Radical and the Republican:*
Frederick Douglass, Abraham Lincoln, and the Triumph of Antislavery Politics

"Reynolds' magisterial biography focuses on the dozens of different influences and experiences that fortuitously coalesced to turn Lincoln into the icon he's become . . . Even readers who think they know Lincoln's life deeply will find new insights here."

—*Booklist* (starred review)

"Reynolds is one of our most significant historians, and he is up to the enormous task of creating a cultural biography of the man who would become America's most recognizable president. A fine cultural history and biography that is accessible to all readers. . . . Consistently fun to read."

—*Kirkus Reviews* (starred review)

"Magisterial and authoritative . . . Reynolds provides a portrait rich in texture and context, not only of Lincoln but of the America he inhabited and helped redefine. The result is a must-read addition to the canon of Lincoln biographies."

—*Publishers Weekly* (starred review)

Abe

Abraham Lincoln
in His Times

David S. Reynolds

PENGUIN BOOKS

PENGUIN BOOKS

An imprint of Penguin Random House LLC
penguinrandomhouse.com

First published in the United States of America by Penguin Press,
an imprint of Penguin Random House LLC, 2020
Published in Penguin Books 2021

ISBN 9780143110767 (paperback)

THE LIBRARY OF CONGRESS HAS CATALOGED THE HARDCOVER EDITION AS FOLLOWS:
Names: Reynolds, David S., 1948– author.
Title: Abe: Abraham Lincoln in his times / David S. Reynolds.
Description: New York: Penguin Press, 2020. | Includes bibliographical
references and index.
Identifiers: LCCN 2019047287 (print) | LCCN 2019047288 (ebook) |
ISBN 9781594206047 (hardcover) | ISBN 9780698154513 (ebook)
Subjects: LCSH: Lincoln, Abraham, 1809–1865. | United States—Social life
and customs—19th century. | Presidents—United States—Biography.
Classification: LCC E457.2 .R48 2020 (print) |
LCC E457.2 (ebook) | DDC 973.7092 [B]—dc23
LC record available at https://lccn.loc.gov/2019047287
LC ebook record available at https://lccn.loc.gov/2019047288

Printed in the United States of America
1st Printing

Designed by Cassandra Garruzzo

To Suzanne, Aline, Haig, and Pat,
and to the memory of my parents,
Paul and Adelaide Reynolds,
and my sister, Carla Reynolds Coleman

CONTENTS

A Note on the Text

In this book, I have generally retained the original spelling, grammar, and usage in quotations from the era; I use *sic* only in some instances.

PREFACE

He liked to be called Lincoln, plain Lincoln, as one of his Illinois law associates reported.[1] He was Mr. Lincoln to his wife, Mary Todd Lincoln; she also called him Father—he affectionately called her Mother or Molly. He was the Tycoon to his wartime secretaries John M. Hay and John G. Nicolay. In a Civil War marching song, he was Father Abraham. He hated the formal Mr. President. As though to mediate between the different possibilities, he signed his name A. Lincoln.

But to the millions, he was Abe. Honest Abe. Old Abe. Uncle Abe. Abe the Illinois Rail-splitter.

Lincoln did not especially like the Abe nickname, but he knew that without it he would not have won the presidency in 1860. His image as Abe, the approachable everyman from what was then the West, was promoted everywhere that year, and it swept him into office. He remarked, "All through the campaign my friends have been calling me 'Honest Old Abe,' and I have been elected mainly on that cry."[2]

This book is the story of Abe—a cultural biography of America's greatest president and its central historical figure. Placing Lincoln in his rich contexts, this book explores the ways in which his absorption and transformation of roiling cultural currents made him into the leader Leo Tolstoy hailed as "the only real giant" among "all the great national heroes and statesmen of history," and whom Karl Marx called "one of the rare men who succeed in becoming great, without ceasing to be good."[3]

Among the some sixteen thousand books on Lincoln—more books than on any other historical figure except Jesus Christ—there are many biographies, a number of them superb and several that contain illuminating information about his era. From the earliest biographies, there has been an interest in Lincoln's politics; in recent times, that interest has expanded to include other aspects of the social and cultural scene. But there has appeared to date no full-scale cultural biography, which alone can capture Lincoln in his historical fullness.[4]

The limitations of standard biography are visible even in one of the finest single-volume books on the sixteenth president, David Herbert Donald's *Lincoln*. The story Donald tells is by now familiar. Born in 1809 in a one-room log cabin in frontier Kentucky, the son of undistinguished parents, Lincoln, with less than a year of formal schooling, rose to the pinnacle of power through hard work, intelligence, political shrewdness, and a good amount of luck. Donald relates the story amply and adeptly. But he doesn't go far beyond the facts of Lincoln's life. Stating that his is "a biography written from Lincoln's point of view," he writes, "I have stuck close to Lincoln, who was only indirectly connected with the economic and social transformations of the period."[5]

Convinced, surprisingly, that nineteenth-century America offered few nurturing materials, Donald presents Lincoln as the quintessential self-made man, who displayed "enormous capacity for growth, which enabled one of the least experienced and poorly prepared men ever elected to high office to become the greatest American president." Some version of this single-handed climb from primitiveness to greatness narrative informs other biographies as well.

Even the popular culture around Lincoln, in Donald's view, was tame and uninteresting—a cotton-candy sea of maudlin writing and preachy effusions, as captured in Donald's generalization about the Civil War era: "The feminine fifties were gone, but they were followed by the sentimental sixties and the saccharine seventies."[6]

It's true that there was a sentimental strain in the culture that held appeal for Lincoln. But the cultural scene was also ablaze with sensationalism, violence, and zany humor—literature, penny newspapers, music, and popular exhibits full of strange, freakish images that sometimes verged on the surrealistic. This was the bizarre, turbulent popular culture—sulfuric acid, not sap—that Lincoln participated in daily in his own jokes and stories, which were modified versions of an American humor, whose "chief characteristic," he said, was "grotesqueness."[7]

The current book reveals that Lincoln, far from distanced from his time, was thoroughly immersed in it. When he entered the presidency, he was neither inexperienced nor unprepared. To the contrary, he redefined democracy precisely because he had experienced culture in all its dimensions—from high to low, sacred to profane, conservative to radical, sentimental to subversive.

Ralph Waldo Emerson noted that genius lies in "being altogether receptive; in letting the world do all, and suffering the spirit of the hour to pass unobstructed through the mind."[8] For Lincoln, this meant traversing a culture's idioms—what Emerson called "the whole scale of the language, from the most elegant to the most low and vile."[9] In Emerson's words, "A great style of hero draws equally all classes, all the extremes of society, till we say the very dogs believe in him." The person who most fully represented this breadth of vision, Emerson wrote, was America's sixteenth president:

> Abraham Lincoln is perhaps the most remarkable example of this class that we have seen—a man who was at home and welcome with the humblest, and with a spirit and a practical

vein in the times of terror that commanded the admiration of the wisest. His heart was as great as the world, but there was no room in it to hold the memory of a wrong.[10]

Indeed, Lincoln was unusually responsive to the spirit of the hour, and this responsiveness fostered his practicality and his compassion. His close friend Joshua Speed commented, "Lincoln studied and appropriated to himself all that came within his observation. Everything that he saw, read, or heard, added to the store of his information"; nothing "was too small to escape his observation."[11] The Illinois lawyer Leonard Swett reported that Lincoln, who on the law circuit talked endlessly with average folk by day and pored over Shakespeare or Euclid by night, was the "most inquisitive man I have known," one for whom "life was a school; . . . he was always studying and mastering every subject which came before him."[12]

Lincoln believed that the surroundings shape the person. According to his law partner William Herndon, he often said, "Conditions make the man and not man the conditions."[13] But, Herndon emphasized, Lincoln also "believed firmly in the power of human effort to modify the environments which surround us." Fate and free will, then, combined in Lincoln's outlook. There were times when he felt that fate had taken over. At a trying moment during the Civil War, Lincoln wrote, "I claim not to have controlled events, but confess plainly that events have controlled me."[14] At other times, though, he took an active and aggressive stance toward the world: he became a *shaper* and a *creator*, not just an *observer* or a *receiver*. Lincoln declared, "He who moulds public sentiment goes deeper than he who enacts statutes or pronounces decisions."[15] As this book shows, Lincoln constantly molded popular opinions and language and redirected them toward what he regarded as order, justice, and fairness.

Cultural biography reveals an engaged, fully human Lincoln. It works from the premise that cultural and social surroundings infiltrate the mind and shape behavior, motivation, and expression. Every human life is culture-specific and time-specific. Outside influences saturate innermost thoughts. Although we all share virtually the same genome, as individuals our behavior and our cognition are products of the intersection of our genes and the unique environment around us. The cultural biographer's task is to describe that environment as fully as possible with the aim of revealing cross-influences between the individual and the outside world.

Cultural biography reveals not only *self-making* but also *culture-making*. Culture fashioned Lincoln; he in turn fashioned it. From a young age, he reacted creatively to the cultural materials available to him. He responded to a culture alive with subversive passions and fertile images of the sort that energized America's greatest writers—Emerson, Thoreau, Melville, Whitman, Mark Twain, and others—and that produced Lincoln's all-absorbing vision, which enabled him to guide the nation through its most turbulent period.

Political victory frequently comes to candidates who best tap into cultural attitudes. Few in American history have done so as effectively as Lincoln. Much of his greatness lay in his thoughtful response to his teeming, unstructured nation. Emerson called America "the ungirt, the diffuse, the profuse, procumbent, one wide ground juniper, . . . it all runs to leaves, to suckers, to tendrils, to miscellany, . . . formless, has no terrible & no beautiful condensation."[16] Thoreau, likewise, remarked on what he called the "confused *tintinnabulum*" of "this restless, nervous, bustling" nineteenth-century America."[17]

America's formlessness reflected a democracy that before the Civil War had few established institutions. In an era of a weak central government, the only federal agency that touched the lives of average Americans was the postal service. American Protestantism, liberated in the atmosphere of religious freedom, spawned so many new denominations, sects, and self-styled prophets that Tocqueville wrote, "In the United States there are an infinite variety of ceaselessly changing

Christian sects."[18] In the absence of organized police forces and effective crowd control, mob scenes broke out regularly from the 1830s, when Lincoln denounced the "mobocratic spirit . . . abroad in the land," right up to the second year of the Civil War, when the New York City draft riots erupted with deadly violence.[19] Periodic slave rebellions, such as those by Nat Turner in Virginia and the *Amistad* rebels at sea, created a terror in the South that turned into widespread panic when John Brown invaded Virginia in 1859 to spark insurrections.

The North and the South viewed each other as dangerously centrifugal—that is, spinning away from the center, toward the chaotic. In the eyes of antislavery Northerners, the South's intention to carry slavery into the western territories and perhaps into Cuba, Mexico, and elsewhere was an unleashed impulse that had to be stopped. For many Southerners, the North was a cauldron of wild "isms"—most perilously abolitionism—that portended social disintegration.

Accelerating these centrifugal forces were powerful assertions of individualism on each side. Among Northerners, the reformer Stephen Pearl Andrews's notion of Individual Sovereignty, Emerson's doctrine of self-reliance, and Thoreau's conviction that the individual is more powerful than the state matched the South's stubborn insistence on states' rights, which finally led to the secession of eleven slave states.

The central problem of American democracy, Walt Whitman noted, was the relation between the individual and the mass—or, on the political level, between the separate states and the Union. Whitman wrote, "There are two distinct principles—aye, paradoxes—at the life-fountain of the States: one, the sacred principle of Union, the right of ensemble, at whatever sacrifice—and yet another, an equally sacred principle, the right of each State, consider'd as a separate sovereign individual, in its own sphere."[20] Either "the centripetal law" or "the centrifugal law" alone, he emphasized, would be fatal to the nation. He tried to achieve a balance in his poetry volume *Leaves of Grass*, in which he created a powerful "I" who embraced all states, creeds, and ethnicities in the interest of promoting equality and togetherness. Trying to reconcile conflicting cultural impulses, Whitman's speaker announced himself as "one of that centripetal and centrifugal gang."[21]

Lincoln's words for these opposing forces were *despotism* and *anarchy*—real perils, he believed, that arose from secession and the slavery crisis.[22] He came closer than any other politician has done to mediate between these threats and to approach the kind of balance Whitman saw as the surest means of saving the nation. From his dual ancestry in Virginia and New England, Lincoln inherited both the code of honor associated with Cavalier culture and the moral sense attributed to bygone Puritanism. From an early age, his experiences on the frontier in Kentucky and Indiana instilled him with both powerful self-reliance and a profoundly democratic instinct linked to his immersion in nature and his reflections about mortality. Faced with the raw energies of frontier culture, he developed a remarkable ability to tame the wild, manifested later on in his measured responses to seemingly uncontrollable social and cultural phenomena. When he entered mainstream society as a lawyer and politician, he found himself in a whirl of passionate reform movements—notably abolitionism, temperance, women's rights, spiritualism, and Know-Nothingism—that he learned from even as he remained removed from them.

Witnessing reformers on all sides who took extreme positions, Lincoln stuck close to the center. Unlike many other centrists, he was neither dull nor indecisive. His liveliness owed much to the innovative performance culture of his day. Though centered, he leaned to the left, using every means possible—including, eventually, hard war—to push the nation toward equal rights and an activist federal government that promoted justice.

Like every culture, Lincoln's had its time-specific phenomena that were strongly influential at the moment but then were largely forgotten by later generations. New England Puritans versus Southern Cavaliers; the backdrop of Oliver Cromwell versus Charles I; Daniel Boone; the

Crockett almanacs; Quakerism; the new sermon style; intemperate temperance reformers; Phineas T. Barnum; popular songs like "Twenty Years Ago" and "Dixie"; British and American poetry; ministers like Theodore Parker; the higher law; John Brown; the tightrope artist Charles Blondin; the working-class figure known as the b'hoy; the drillmaster Elmer Ellsworth and his Zouaves; the military strategist and political pamphleteer Anna Ella Carroll; the humor character Petroleum V. Nasby; the retailored Thanksgiving and Christmas; the American acting style; the writings of Thoreau, Poe, and Harriet Beecher Stowe—these and other cultural markers are crucial for understanding many aspects of Lincoln's life. This book illuminates such previously neglected contexts and their relation to Lincoln.

In a letter written on April 14, 1865, the last day of his life, Lincoln said that he wanted to create "a Union of hearts and hands as well as of States."[23] That had long been his goal. As Walt Whitman, Lincoln's most sensitive observer, declared, "UNIONISM, in its truest and amplest sense, form'd the hard-pan of his character."[24]

Lincoln's UNIONISM went well beyond the restoration of the political union. It pointed to his ongoing attempt to provide unity or direction to many cultural forces in America that tended toward conflict, fragmentation, and, at times, chaos. Lincoln envisaged a nation that was both united and committed to political equality.

The following pages reveal his continual struggles to remake America—and his resounding success in doing so.

The Lincoln Tree

Lincoln said little about his ancestry or childhood. When campaign biographers approached him, he was brief. He told one of them, the journalist John L. Scripps, "It is a great piece of folly to attempt to make anything out of my early life."[1] He responded to another one, the politician Jesse Fell, by scribbling a cursory autobiography, explaining, "There is not much of it, for the reason, I suppose, that there is not much of me."[2]

Lincoln pared down his life story, sketching his ancestry, his childhood in Kentucky and Indiana, his career as a lawyer and politician in Illinois, and his emergence as an antislavery spokesman in the mid-1850s.

His public cageyness about his ancestors and his youth contrasted with his intense private curiosity about them. He told Gideon Welles, his secretary of the navy, that he had "a craving desire" to gather information about his family history.[3] He believed that one's personal and cultural backgrounds strongly shaped one's character.

Actually, he knew far more about these backgrounds than he let on. He was aware that his ancestral roots went back to early New England on his father's side and early Virginia on his mother's. This divided lineage, if widely known among the electorate, might have led different groups of voters to assign him one of these opposing sides. The Puritan-Cavalier opposition was so inflammatory at the time that exposing either of the ancestral strands could have been politically risky. Lincoln was a good lawyer, and as such, he knew how to present facts that helped his case. That's what he did with regard to his ancestors. He pruned his family tree, emphasizing facts that made him attractive to a broad spectrum of voters.

If we dig into what he left out of the public record, we find a lively tangle of ancestral and cultural roots.

PURITANS AND CAVALIERS

In an influential speech in 1886, the Georgia newspaper editor Henry Grady declared that Lincoln had combined elements of the Puritan and the Cavalier. Grady told a large dinner audience:

> From the union of colonists, Puritans and Cavaliers, from the straightening of their purposes and the crossing of their blood, came he who stands as the first typical American . . . Abraham Lincoln. [Loud and continued applause.] He was the sum of the Puritan and Cavalier, for in his ardent nature were fused the virtues of both, and in the depths of his great soul the faults of both were lost. He was greater than the Puritan, greater than the Cavalier, in that he was American.[4]

How plausible was Grady's idea of Lincoln as the unifier of warring sectional identities? To address this question, we must understand these identities and Lincoln's response to them.

Grady spoke for many who held that the Puritan-Cavalier division, not slavery, had caused the Civil War. According to this view, New England had been settled by Puritans who had fled to America to escape the persecution they suffered in England under the Anglican Church and King Charles I. When, during the English civil wars of the 1640s, Charles was overthrown and Oliver Cromwell became Lord Protector of England, the South was settled by Cavaliers expelled from England by Cromwell and his Puritan followers. Natural enemies, the New Englanders and Southerners teamed up briefly during the American Revolution to fight for independence, but in the decades after the Revolution the sectional rift reappeared and then deepened.

By the late 1850s, the North and the South were widely perceived as separate peoples—so far apart that civil war was inevitable. The nation's most widely read newspaper, the *New York Herald*, put it this way: "The people of the North and those of the South are distinct and separate. They think differently; they spring from a different stock; they are different every way; they cannot coalesce; the Puritan and the Cavalier . . . will always fight when they meet. There is nothing in common between them but hate."[5] A Tennessee-born army officer averred, "The dissimilarity of human nature between the Puritans of the North and the flathead cavaliers of the South is the foundation—the bed rock cause of our political wrangling and disputations."[6]

Each side touted what it saw as its virtues while vilifying the other. The South boasted of its stable institutions, especially slavery, and its traditions of honor, hospitality, and chivalry. Mark Twain had these values in mind when he wrote that the Civil War was caused by "the Sir Walter disease," a reference to the South's obsession with Walter Scott's historical novels, which idealized Cavalier chivalry.[7] The South viewed the North as a hotbed of anarchic reform movements, most notoriously abolitionism, which allegedly derived from Puritanism. It charged the North with fanaticism, self-righteousness, narrowness, and materialism. The Confederate president Jefferson Davis said, "Our enemies are a traditionless, rootless race. From the time of Cromwell to the present moment they have been disturbers of the peace."[8] Many Northerners, in contrast, saw themselves as worthy descendants of God-fearing Puritans who had established liberty in America. Southerners, they maintained, had created a society of oppression, decadence, and injustice.

Like most cultural myths, the Puritan-Cavalier division was based only partly on fact. Although it's true that New England was largely settled by Puritans from eastern England, while the Chesapeake colonies, Virginia and Maryland, were inhabited by Cromwell-fleeing Cavaliers from the West Country of England during the Puritan uprising of the 1640s and '50s, by the nineteenth century the US population had become far too diverse to assign a label to either section. But during the Civil War, Americans on both sides took seriously the Puritan-Cavalier split. An Ohio congressman declared in 1864 that the rivalry between the sections would never end "until you transplant the principles of the Puritans in the very heart of the Cavalier, of the New Englander in the Carolinian, a task which the conflicts of centuries have so far failed from accomplishing that they have but served to widen the breach and make the line of demarcation more palpable and distinct."[9]

Some sensed that Abraham Lincoln represented a unique fusion of cultural traits. This fusion was very different from that of the presidents who immediately preceded him, Franklin Pierce and James Buchanan. Whereas they were doughfaces—Northern men with Southern principles—he was a Southern-born man, raised in what was then the West, who came to adopt Northern attitudes. Nathaniel Hawthorne, who met Lincoln in the White House in 1863, reported, "Unquestionably, Western man though he be, and Kentuckian by birth, President Lincoln is the essential representative of all Yankees, and the veritable specimen, physically, of what the world seems determined to regard as our characteristic qualities."[10] Horace Greeley, editor of the *New-York Tribune*, wrote of Lincoln, "Coming from an old Puritan stock, and representing the faith of the Puritan intellect, as well as the strength and freedom which came from a Western education, he was the truest American we have seen for many long years."[11]

It was left to the eminent journalist Henry Grady in the 1880s to describe most forcefully the section-merging Lincoln by calling him "the sum of the Puritan and Cavalier." Reported widely, Grady's speech was remembered as a signal event in reconciling the North and South. It contributed to the growing perception of Lincoln as a bridge across the Puritan-Cavalier gulf. Eight years after Grady's speech, the Louisville editor Henry Watterson wrote that he had "encountered many startling confirmations" of Grady's point about Lincoln, who now seemed a "rugged trunk, drawing its sustenance from gnarled roots, interlocked with Cavalier sprays and Puritan branches deep beneath the soil."[12]

In his writings and conversations, Lincoln carefully avoided the sectional names Puritan and Cavalier, just as he avoided referring to the seceded states as the Confederacy without using a qualifier like "so-called." For him, the nation was *never*, by definition, two or more peoples. His vision of national unity explains why the United States, typically used as a plural noun before the Civil War (as in Walt Whitman's 1855 statement "the United States need poets"), became commonly used as a singular noun after it.

Although Southerners like Grady and Watterson used Lincoln's example to challenge the Puritan-versus-Cavalier schism, they didn't appreciate how he had crafted his public image so that he could nurture boldly progressive forms of social justice. He presented himself and his ancestry in such a way that they might make a powerful statement about a unified nation devoted to human equality.

CULTURAL GENEALOGY

Lincoln's attitudes toward his ancestors can be best understood if we consider his era's ideas about heredity. The perennial debate over nature versus nurture was played out in Lincoln's time. On the one hand, there were those who, following in the wake of the post-Lockean European thinkers Comte Georges-Louis Leclerc de Buffon (1707–1788), Pierre-Jean-Georges Cabanis (1757–1808), and Johann Friedrich Blumenbach (1752–1840), maintained that environment was the main factor in shaping humans. On the other hand, the case for inborn characteristics had its defenders as well. This argument had been made forcefully by the German phrenologist Franz Gall (1758–1828), who described many different brain "organs," determined by heredity, that individually controlled religiosity, benevolence, combativeness, sexual desire, language, and so on. Later phrenologists modified Gall, making room for human variability according to culture.

This was the view of America's leading popularizer of hereditarian science, the phrenologist Orson S. Fowler. In his often-reprinted 1843 book *Hereditary Descent,* Fowler argued that one's physical and mental make-up came from one's ancestors, reaching back "four, five, and more generations; and probably many more."[13] Fowler pointed out that like-minded people tended to settle in certain locales, creating distinct cultural identities that shape individuals from there, even when they move elsewhere. He connected New England, for instance, with morals and religion. In a chapter titled "Descendants of the Puritans," Fowler wrote, "New England was settled by the moral sentiments. . . . This hereditary law being true, what could reasonably be expected of their descendants but that religious zeal seen wherever New England has settled?"

For Fowler, there was no clear boundary between nature and nurture. Both heredity and cultural environment were prime movers. Lincoln felt the same way. He frequently declared that "conditions make the man," as his law partner and friend William Herndon reported; at the same time, he believed in "heredity—transmission—pre-natalism and the like."[14] Herndon writes, "Lincoln believed that men are the children of Conditions—of circumstances & of their environments which surround them, including a hundred thousand years or more of education with acquired habits & the tendency to heredity, moulding them as they are & will forever be." Lincoln thought that he was shaped by *both* his immediate contexts and his ancestral past.

He was deeply curious about that past, and he learned more about it as time went on.

His famous statement "All that I am or hope ever to be I got from my mother, God bless her" reportedly came during a discussion of "*hereditary qualities of mind—nature*" that he had with William Herndon during a carriage ride on the Illinois law circuit court in 1850.[15] The date is important, for there was great excitement then over Orson Fowler's bestseller *Hereditary Descent*. Fowler popularized the phrenological view that the mental capabilities of men came mainly from their mothers. "Men distinguished for their native strength of intellect," Fowler wrote, "have always been descended from mothers of strong powers of mind."[16] Lincoln shared this view. He said that his mother, Nancy Hanks, despite her modest education, was "highly intellectual by nature, had a strong memory, acute judgment and was cool and heroic," an assessment confirmed by others, who used words like "beyond all doubts an intellectual woman," "a woman known for the extraordinary strength of her mind," and "very smart, intelligent, . . . naturally strong-minded."[17] Lincoln, who accepted contemporary ideas about heredity, attributed his own powers of mind largely to his mother.

But his debt to his mother ran deeper than her own character; it reached back to her father, who Lincoln believed—with justification, according to scholars—to have been a Virginia settler.[18] Lincoln described this Southern grandfather as "a Virginia planter or large farmer" who took sexual advantage of a "poor and credulous" young woman, Lucy Hanks, the daughter of a plantation overseer.[19] Although Lincoln was reportedly ashamed that his mother was born out of wedlock, he saw positive dimensions in his supposed maternal grandfather. Lincoln told Herndon he believed that through his mother he had inherited from the Virginian "his power of analysis, his logic, his mental activity, his ambition, and all the qualities that distinguished him from the other members of the Hanks family," a clan that was otherwise, in Lincoln's words, "a lecherous family—a family low even among the poor whites of the south" (a reference in particular to his reputedly promiscuous maternal grandmother, Lucy Hanks).[20]

Lincoln was proud to have been descended from a man who appears to have been a Cavalier. As far as we know, Lincoln never used that word in connection with his maternal grandfather, nor was he likely to have done so, given his distaste for sectional labels. But Lincoln's words about the Virginia planter showed his interest in the Cavalier type. In his words, "my mother . . . was the daughter of a nobleman—so called of Virginia."[21] Dennis Hanks recalled that the young Lincoln was cheered by his mother's assurances that "Abe had jist as good Virginny blood in him as Washington."[22] Lincoln described his planter grandsire as "a Virginia aristocrat" and his mother as "a great noble woman—a woman of a very fine cast of mind—was broad-minded—liberal—generous-hearted— quickly sympathetic woman."[23] These qualities—nobility, generosity, geniality, a "liberal" nature—are ones that were typically associated with the Cavalier bloodline.

Also, Lincoln exhibited what was considered a defining Cavalier trait: honor.[24] An Indiana neighbor declared, "Men would Swear on his Simple word—[he] had a high & manly sense of honor."[25] He displayed honor throughout his life, as when he accepted a duel challenge from the politician James Shields or when he kept true to his promise to wed Mary Todd despite his second thoughts about her. In marrying her, he was joining a Cavalier-like Kentucky family, with a distinguished line of Southern landowners often referred to as aristocrats.

If Lincoln derived certain Cavalier traits from his mother, he can be said to have inherited Puritan ones from his father's side, in terms of his era's understanding of heredity. Lincoln knew the history of Puritanism, and he could relate to it through his paternal ancestors. Lincoln was fascinated by the record of rebellions on the part of ultra-Protestants.

One of his favorite books in childhood was *Pilgrim's Progress* by John Bunyan, the Puritan dissenter who had joined Oliver Cromwell's New Model Army in 1642 and served in it for three years. When Lincoln was older, he favored history books that dealt with Protestant upheavals. According to his Illinois friend Joseph Gillespie, "Lincoln never I think studied history in connection with politics with the exception of history of the Netherlands and of the revolutions of 1640 and 1688 England and of our own revolutionary struggle."[26] Gillespie was referring to Lincoln's interest in major religious rebellions: the Dutch Revolt from the 1560s to the 1640s, in which seven Protestant low countries overthrew the rule of the Roman Catholic king Philip II of Spain; the Glorious Revolution of 1688, in which the Protestant William of Orange deposed his Catholic father-in-law, James II; and the English civil wars of the 1640s, when the Puritan Oliver Cromwell overthrew Charles I and his Cavaliers.

If, as Gillespie reported, Lincoln did explore Cromwell and his Puritan Roundheads, he found much food for thought. The Cromwellian revolution spearheaded, among other things, the notions of personal liberty and self-ownership that contributed to the antislavery impulse. While proslavery Americans insisted that the Constitution supported the right of property in man, the antislavery side held that self-ownership and control of one's own labor were rights that preceded the Constitution. James Oakes finds roots of this view in the Puritan-led English civil wars, which, he writes, generated the radical premise that "the right of property itself originated in the universal, natural right of freedom—freedom defined as self-ownership. . . . Freedom, not slavery, was the normal condition of every human being."[27]

This, exactly, became Lincoln's view. In an 1858 speech he insisted that "the universality of freedom" was based on the principle that all humans had "God-given rights to enjoy the fruits of their own labor"—an idea he repeated, with Puritan emphasis, in the Second Inaugural Address, where he declared, "It may seem strange that any men should

9

dare to ask a just God's assistance in wringing their bread from the sweat of other men's faces."[28]

Self-ownership is just one concept Lincoln may have noticed when he reflected on the Puritan revolution under Cromwell. Another is the importance of taking a moral position on perceived social evils. Orson Fowler noted that New England was "settled by the moral sentiments" and that Puritanism was "enthroned upon our Republic."[29] For anti-slavery Northerners, the New England Puritans had left as one of their main legacies a righteously moral position on social issues. Southerners and Copperheads agreed but insisted that this Puritan-inspired mixture of morality and politics betrayed the Constitution and caused the Civil War. The Copperhead Samuel S. Cox, in his 1863 speech "Puritanism in Politics," said that the Constitution was a mound that had once protected the nation but "a reptile had been boring that mound" and let loose "the deluging ocean of war." "Puritanism," Cox declared, "is that reptile." He explained, "Abolition is the cause of the war. It is the offspring of Puritanism. The history of Puritanism shows that it always sought to introduce the moral elements involved in slavery into politics."[30]

Lincoln, however, showed that one could adhere to the Constitution without sacrificing the devotion to morality that was then widely considered a vestige of Puritanism. The slavery issue, he said, "reduced to its lowest terms, is no other than the difference between the men who think slavery a wrong and those who do not think it wrong."[31] It's likely that Lincoln, as a believer in cultural influence and heredity, would accept Fowler's argument that "the descent of the moral affections from generation to generation" was "hereditary fact" that could be seen most commonly among "the descendants of the Puritans."[32] In this context, it's notable that Lincoln expressed his opposition to slavery in moral terms: he called it "a great moral wrong," and he attacked "the absence of moral sense about the question."[33] He drove his point home with a personal reference: "I have always hated slavery, I think as much as any Abolitionist."

This "always" takes us back to Lincoln's childhood. It is commonly known that there was an antislavery element in the Baptist community immediately surrounding the young Lincoln in northeastern Kentucky. But the familial and cultural roots of his specifically *moral* antislavery stance have been neglected.

Lincoln's father, the barely literate Thomas Lincoln, has generally been given short shrift by biographers. But it's important to recognize that those who knew Thomas well attested to positive qualities, including an ethical sense. John Hanks, a first cousin of Abe's mother, reported that Thomas was "a good quiet citizen, with moral habits, had a good sound judgment, kind husband and father."[34] Others close to Lincoln in Kentucky or Indiana testified that while Thomas was neither ambitious nor intellectual, he was virtuous and pious—he was described by various people as "strictly a moral man, never used profane or vulgar language," "a plain unpretending and scrupulously honest man," one whose "inflexible honesty, truth, humor, and good nature . . . were his son's direct heritage from him, . . . transmitted from his early New England ancestors."[35]

Lincoln took an interest in his father's Puritan past. Even his use of Lincoln as his surname harked back to early New England, for on the Kentucky frontier, where he spent his first years, the name was commonly spelled as Linkhorn or Linkhern. As Henry C. Whitney remarked about the name, Lincoln "seems always to have spelled it after the manner of his remote English ancestry."[36]

When in 1848 a distant relative, Solomon Lincoln of Hingham, Massachusetts, heard then-congressman Lincoln give a campaign speech on behalf of presidential candidate Zachary Taylor, he expressed pride in the idea that the Puritan zeal for human liberty was being carried on by this New England–rooted relative from the West. Praising "the able speech of honorable Mr. Lincoln of Illinois," Solomon wrote that it was "a source of gratification to those bearing his name that the old stock has not degenerated by being transplanted. On the contrary it exhibits fresh vigor in the fertile soil of the West."[37] Solomon was a historian and genealogist with a deep knowledge of Hingham, the Massachusetts town (on the Atlantic coast south of Boston) where Lincoln's first American ancestor, Samuel Lincoln, had lived. Having written a history of Hingham, Solomon was curious about the ancestry of Abraham Lincoln, who wrote Solomon saying that he knew "little of our family history" but that biblical names like Abraham, Mordecai, and Isaac were "common names in our family."[38] Solomon replied that "the names which he gave me . . . are all family names here and I hope yet to link you to a New England ancestry."[39]

Lincoln may have already known of this ancestry. When in September 1848 he spoke in Dorchester, Massachusetts, and was introduced as "one of the Lincolns of Hingham," Lincoln "said, playfully, that he had endeavored in Illinois to introduce the principles of the Lincolns of Massachusetts."[40] By 1859 he had gained enough knowledge of his New England past to tell the Chicago author James Grant Wilson, "I believe the first of our ancestors we know anything about was Samuel Lincoln, who came from Norwich England, in 1638, and settled in a small Massachusetts place called Hingham, or might have been Hanghim."[41] (The wordplay was a bit of Lincoln-esque humor that spoofed Southern jibes about Puritans who hanged Quakers and witches.) Lincoln's interest in his Hingham forebears was sincere, for in 1860 he told a British visitor, the detective George Hartley, that he hoped one day to travel to England to explore their environment.[42]

Had he ever gotten the opportunity to take that trip, he would have visited a region with a deep history of Puritan revolt. Samuel Lincoln, who came to America in 1637 (a year earlier than Lincoln told Wilson), had been born and raised in the village of Hingham, near Norwich in Norfolk County, a rural area in eastern England.[43] That part of Norfolk was a seedbed of Puritan resistance to the English church and the king. Among those associated with the area were the Reverend John Robinson, who preached in Norwich for five years before becoming the spiritual leader of the Separatist Puritans of Scrooby, who migrated to the Netherlands before some of them sailed on the *Mayflower* to the New World; Robert Browne, known as the father of Congregationalism, who was imprisoned in Norwich for his religious beliefs; and Oliver Cromwell, who raised many troops from the Puritans who populated the region.

Hingham's minister, the Reverend Robert Peck, who baptized the infant Samuel Lincoln in 1624, was, like Cromwell and Robinson, a Puritan arch enemy of the Anglican Church, whose rituals and icons seemed to Peck to be profane holdovers from the Roman Catholic Church. Brought before the Anglican authorities three times for heresy, Peck was excommunicated and fled to America in 1638, months after Samuel Lincoln had immigrated there. Samuel, who lived briefly in Salem, Massachusetts, moved sixty miles south to Hingham, where he met up with Peck and his protégé Peter Hobart, another Puritan minister from England. Peck and Hobart served as copastors in the Massachusetts village until 1641, when Peck returned to Norfolk County to participate in Cromwell's resistance movement against Charles I. Hobart stayed in Massachusetts, where he became a thorn in the side of the religious establishment of the Massachusetts Bay Colony by demanding greater local rule and relaxing regulations for church membership.

Hobart's parishioner Samuel Lincoln, a weaver who turned to farming, had followed two brothers, Thomas and Daniel, who had previously immigrated to America. Around 1649, Samuel was married to a minister's daughter, Martha Lyford. They had eleven children, eight of whom survived to adulthood. Altogether, some sixty Lincolns were residents of Hingham in the first generation of immigrants. Samuel Lincoln appears to have been a devout Puritan; he helped to fund and build the Old Ship Church, which since its opening in 1681 has stood as the longest-running continuously used church in America. Heavily timbered with ceiling planks that look like the ribs of a ship, this squat, modified-Gothic edifice preceded the more familiar white, spired New England churches by more than half a century.

The Old Ship Church, Hingham, Massachusetts. Samuel Lincoln, the fourth great-grandfather of the president, helped to build this church in which he and his family worshipped.

In 1921, a commemorative article on Samuel Lincoln described "the Puritan lineage of Lincoln, the idealist, the liberator, the very spirit of that democracy which we celebrate this month on Lincoln day." The article affirmed that it was "historically proved and internationally ratified the greatest descendant of Puritan lineage is Abraham Lincoln."[44] Installed two years earlier, in St. Andrew's Church in Hingham, En-

gland, was a bust of Abraham Lincoln, which hailed the "many generations" of Lincolns who had lived in the parish, ancestors of "Abraham
Lincoln . . . greatest of that lineage."[45] In 1937, Hingham, Massachusetts, celebrated the three hundredth anniversary of the arrival of Samuel Lincoln by installing a tablet in the town in his honor.

CULTURAL MIGRATION

The liberty-nurturing Puritanism of the earliest American Lincolns
came filtered to Abraham through the forward-moving, expansionist
Lincolns of the intervening generations. William Dean Howells, in his
1860 campaign biography of Lincoln, connected the migrations of Lincoln's forebears with the same spirit that had originally impelled many
Puritans to come to America. Howells wrote that "the backwoods-man
of today corresponds to the Puritan two centuries ago. The same work
which the Pilgrim Fathers had to do is now set for the settlers of Illinois
and Wisconsin." Howells emphasized that Lincoln "finds his greatest
strength from that which he sprang," meaning the frontier, which made
him seem to many the heroic backwoodsman who would rescue the nation with his sterling American values, inherited from his adventurous
ancestors.[46] These mobile Lincolns were on a migratory cusp that kept
some of them in frontier conditions for extended periods.

Among the president's ancestors, only Samuel Lincoln's son Morde-
cai (1657–1727) remained in the state he was born in. A Hingham, Mas-
sachusetts, native, Mordecai in adulthood relocated to a nearby town,
Scituate. Exhibiting technological savvy of the sort that anticipated
Lincoln, the only president who has held a patent for an invention,
Mordecai, a blacksmith and miller, introduced smelting furnaces to
New England and powered a trip hammer in his forge by damming a
brook that ran between Scituate and Cohasset. Here he produced iron

products—tools, nails, hinges, shovels, kitchen utensils, and so on—that were necessities in his community. He also built two other dams that powered a sawmill and a gristmill.[47]

Mordecai's first son, also Mordecai (1686–1736), initiated the migration westward or southward carried on by later generations of Lincolns. Mordecai Jr. was born in Hingham and died in Pennsylvania. In between, he lived for a number of years in Freehold Township, New Jersey, where he married Hannah Saltar, the daughter of a prominent landowner. All of his six children were born in New Jersey, where he and his brother Abraham ran an iron-producing business. Mordecai bought tracts of New Jersey land that eventually reached six hundred acres. Attracted by the rich ore available in the Schuylkill Valley west of Philadelphia, Mordecai moved in 1722 with his family to Chester County, Pennsylvania, where he became a junior partner in an iron-works. He sold his share in the company in 1725 with the plan of moving back to New Jersey, but his wife soon died, leaving five living children, and he decided to stay in Pennsylvania. He was married to Mary Robeson in 1729. The couple bought and settled on a one-thousand-acre tract in Exeter, Philadelphia County (later known as Berks County), building a farmhouse near the Schuylkill River.

A neighboring Exeter family, the Boones, were destined to have a strong influence on the Lincoln line. Squire and Sarah Boone bought their farm, a few miles away from Mordecai's land, in 1730. Four years later their sixth child, Daniel Boone, was born. The Lincolns and Boones grew close to one another.

When Mordecai Jr. died at fifty in 1736, Squire Boone appraised Lincoln's estate, which included two enslaved men, Negro Will and Negro John.[48] The great-great-grandfather of the Great Emancipator, then, was apparently a slaveholder.

THE QUAKER BOND

Was Lincoln aware of slavery or other skeletons in his ancestral closet? If so, did he intentionally doctor his past when giving information to campaign biographers?

He was especially reserved about his ancestors. Even though he knew about the Puritan-Congregationalist and Baptist lineage of his father's side, he told campaign biographers that he was descended from Quakers. Of his paternal grandfather, also named Abraham Lincoln, he wrote, "His ancestors, who were quakers, went to Virginia from Berks County, Pennsylvania."[49] He repeated this story to others.[50]

Actually, it's probable that *none* of his direct male ancestors on his father's side were Quakers. The Pennsylvania ancestor Lincoln highlighted, Mordecai Jr., appears to have carried on the Congregationalist Puritanism of his grandfather Samuel.[51] Mordecai's first wife, Hannah Saltar, was a Baptist who was descended from two New England Baptist preachers, Obadiah Holmes and William Bowne. Hannah Saltar's Baptist faith was passed on to her oldest son, John Lincoln, the president's great-grandfather.[52]

Although the woman John married, Rebecca Flowers Morris, came from a family of Pennsylvania Quakers, her religious beliefs are unknown. At any rate, when John and Rebecca in 1768 moved from Berks County, Pennsylvania, to the Shenandoah Valley in Virginia, he became active in the Linville Creek Baptist church. All of their six children were Baptists, including Abraham, the president's grandfather. The Baptist faith came down to Abe's father, Thomas Lincoln, who along with his wife Nancy Hanks, joined Baptist churches in Kentucky and, later, Indiana.

With all these Baptists in his background, why didn't Lincoln mention that religion anywhere in his autobiographical sketches, especially because, as we'll see later, Baptist preaching contributed powerfully to his development? And because he knew about his original American ancestor, Samuel Lincoln the Puritan, and had a strong suspicion of a Cavalier strain on his mother's side, why did he not mention them either?

Lincoln wanted, above all, to avoid associating himself with any divisive cultural currents that might accelerate the nation's movement toward war. The Puritans, the Cavaliers, and the Baptists all signaled division. The Puritan-Cavalier gulf seemed unbridgeable, and the Baptist Church was a stark reminder of the divide over slavery. When in 1845 America's great evangelical churches, the Baptists and the Methodists, separated into Northern and Southern branches, several politicians predicted civil war. The Kentucky senator Henry Clay said, "[T]his sundering of the religious ties which have hitherto bound our people together, I consider the greatest source of danger to our country."[53] Senator John C. Calhoun of South Carolina, in his last major speech before the Senate, declared that once the large Protestant churches broke apart, "nothing will be left to hold the States together except force." By the late 1850s, nearly all Protestant denominations had been torn apart, as had other religious organizations. In his debates with Stephen Douglas, Lincoln asked rhetorically of slavery, "Does it not enter into the churches and rend them asunder?"[54] He pointed to ever-deepening rifts not only in the evangelical churches but also in Presbyterianism, Unitarianism, and the American Tract Society, which distributed vast quantities of religious literature.

There was one cultural current, however, that was *not* a source of intense sectional tension: Quakerism. The Quakers, once a persecuted minority, had become widely viewed as a mediating influence in America. Many Quakers had settled in the mid-Atlantic region, forming a buffer between New England and the South. While Quakers opposed slavery, appealing to Northerners, they also held attraction for many Southerners because of their tolerant outlook. As pacifists, they were not about to go to war over slavery. A contributor to the pro-Southern *DeBow's Review* highlighted the Quakers in summarizing the settlement of America: "Three great elements enter into the character of the American people derived from the colonization of three distinct classes of society. These are, the Puritan, the Quaker, and the Cavalier." The essayist said that while the Puritan and the Cavalier remained perennial enemies, the Quakers stood for reconciliation. In their geographical location and their mild faith, the Quakers promised, the essayist wrote, "to unite in an indissoluble bond the jarring interests of the Puritan and the Cavalier."[55] Southerners gave Quakers slack on their antislavery position, attributing it to their ethical stance on a number of social issues. Another *DeBow's* essayist wrote, "It is consistent for a rigid sect like the Quakers to oppose slavery, because they proscribe war and luxury and all other evils."[56]

For Lincoln, therefore, presenting himself as the descendant of Quakers helped identify him with a group that won sympathy in both the North and the South. Quakerism furthered his goal of national unity. Why bring up his Puritan, Cavalier, or Baptist ancestors when he knew that Quakerism had broad cultural appeal? Besides, he was genuinely attracted to aspects of the Quaker faith, especially its dismissal of creeds and its opposition to slavery.

Small wonder, given these inclinations, that when running for the presidency in 1860, he released facts about his family background that emphasized Quakerism. Readers of the some twenty campaign biographies of Lincoln that appeared in 1860 would have thought that the candidate was solely of Quaker background. The very first biography, known as the Wide Awake edition, began by stating: "The ancestors of Abraham Lincoln were of the good old stock by whom the State of Pennsylvania was founded. Members of the Society of Friends, they lived in Berks County, Pennsylvania, and emigrated from thence to Rockingham County, Virginia."[57] The next biography, by Reuben Vose, said the Lincoln forebears "were respectable members of the Society of Friends."[58] The popular Wigwam edition described Lincoln's grandfather, Abram [sic] Lincoln, as "the old Friend," a Quaker born in

Pennsylvania (actually, he was a Baptist born in Virginia) and influencing "all the descendants" of the Lincoln clan.[59] The biographies by those closest to Lincoln, John Locke Scripps and Joseph H. Bartlett, reported that his ancestors were "members of the Society of Friends" (Scripps) and were notable for "their adherence to the Quaker faith" (Bartlett).[60] Another biography was cheeky in its evasiveness, using a joke about Adam and Eve to forestall all inquiry beyond the candidate's Quaker background:

> His earlier ancestors came to Virginia from Berks County, Pennsylvania. Farther back than this we do not choose to trace his lineage. Those interested in genealogical researches will doubtless find that he is descended in a direct line from Adam and Eve. These ancestors were distinguished only for honesty and industry. To say that they were Quakers is to say this much.[61]

Did Quakerism have the potential, as *DeBow's* maintained, "to unite in an indissoluble bond the jarring interests of the Puritan and the Cavalier"? If so, that may explain why Lincoln brought Quakerism to the fore of his family past, in order to mollify contentious forces. In dealing with his ancestry, Lincoln, in Hawthorne's view, was at once crafty and sincere—crafty in his effort to sculpt his public image, and sincere in his bedrock instinct to foster national unity. He saw that his country was threatened by a storm that could destroy it. He wanted to avert the storm or, should that prove impossible, to be the tree that best withstood the blast and sheltered a reunified, improved nation when it was over.

That he managed to become that sturdy tree attests not only to his artful shaping of his ancestral history but also to the strength and creativity he gained as a boy growing up on the Kentucky and Indiana frontier.

Child of the Frontier

Lincoln biographers have long been challenged to explain his apparently miraculous transformation from an ill-educated frontier youth into a wise statesman. Ever since William Herndon and Jesse Weik in their 1888 biography wrote that Lincoln rose from a "greater depth" than any other great person, starting out from "a stagnant, putrid pool," Lincoln's life has been seen as a climb from extremely adverse conditions to the height of power.[1] How could someone with barely literate parents, little access to books, and less than a year of schooling become a deeply informed, tactful political leader?

Lincoln played up his image as the self-made man. To a campaign biographer, he generalized that his youth could be summed up in Thomas Gray's phrase "the short and simple annals of the poor."[2] It was, after all, advantageous for him to claim that he came from a very lowly background, for it confirmed his image as the true democratic American—one of the people, like such national icons as Benjamin Franklin or Andrew Jackson. The difficulty of his childhood has been exaggerated by a number of commentators, including one who claims that he was "reared in gripping, grinding, pinching penury and pallid poverty, amid the most squalid destitution possible to conceive."[3]

If publicly Lincoln talked down his childhood, privately he could speak well of it. According to his friend and law colleague Leonard Swett, he "told the story of a happy childhood. There was nothing sad nor pinched, and nothing of want, and no allusions to want, in any part of it. His own description of his youth was that of a joyous, happy boyhood."[4]

Although this glowing statement doesn't match other evidence, Lincoln's formative influences shaped him more positively than is usually thought. The frontier culture around Lincoln was crude and chaotic, but he, with the aid of his parents and his reading, developed special gifts for controlling and reshaping its powerful energies.

ABE'S FATHER AS FRONTIER GUIDE

Woodrow Wilson wrote, "Abraham Lincoln came from the most unpromising stock in the continent, the 'poor white trash' of the South."[5] Lincoln's father has been subject to especially severe criticism. It is commonly said that Thomas Lincoln was a shiftless, impecunious rube who kept the young Abe from his books and hired him out so regularly that, as Lincoln later said, "I used to be a slave."[6]

Although this oft-told story helps to explain the development of Lincoln's antislavery views and his ambition to escape his rough past, it should be recognized that Thomas Lincoln, despite his shortcomings, served as a guide to Abe through tumultuous frontier culture and highly uncertain economic conditions.

One element of his guidance was his physical sturdiness—a great boon on the frontier. At five feet ten inches, his weight varying from 175 to 195 pounds, Thomas was compact and brawny. Dennis Hanks, who said that he could never find points of separation between Thomas's ribs, called him "A muscular man[;] his equal I never saw."[7] With coarse black hair, gray-blue eyes, a strong nose, and a swarthy complexion,

THOMAS LINCOLN

Thomas had a robust appearance borne out by his extraordinary strength and his powers of endurance. Known as "a tremendous man in a rough-and-tumble fight," he once quickly thrashed a "monstrous bully" in Kentucky in a tussle from which Thomas emerged without a scratch.[8]

A "rough-and-tumble" was, in frontier slang, the equivalent of a "gouging"—an all-out fight in which plucking out an eye was a goal. Thomas apparently proved himself "the best man" in his region without resorting to this gruesome maneuver. In fact, A. H. Chapman, an Indiana neighbor who witnessed the momentous battle, reported that "this is the only fight [Thomas] ever had. . . . No one else ever tried his manhood in a personal combat, he was a remarkable peaceable man."[9] This statement points to what may have been one of Thomas's bequests to his son: a nature that inclined to peace rather than violence. Like his father, Abe was extraordinarily powerful and good at fighting. But also like Thomas, Abe was kindly and left no record of having maimed an opponent, as he apparently restricted himself to "scientific" fighting, in which physical injury was not the aim.

Thomas Lincoln was known as an amiable man—in various accounts, "Exceedingly good humored," "unpretentious," "kind," one who "never appeared to be offended" and "loved Company—people & their Sports very much."[10] A relative said that Thomas "took the world easy" and "never thought that gold was God."[11] Similarly, an Indiana neighbor reported that he "was happy—lived Easy—& contented. . . . He wanted few things and Supplied them Easily."[12]

Though not concerned with accumulating wealth, Thomas Lincoln nonetheless managed to do surprisingly well, given the adverse conditions he faced. Having witnessed at ten his father's murder by a Native American, Thomas, along with his four siblings, was taken by his widowed mother, Bathsheba Lincoln, to live near relatives in Beech Fork, Washington County, Kentucky.[13] Because of the law of primogeniture, the substantial estate of Thomas's father, amounting to more than 4,000 acres of Kentucky land and much personal property, went to Thomas's older brother, Mordecai. Thomas started working in his teens, and from that time forward he was employed at various times in several lines of work: primarily as a carpenter and a farmer but also as a manual laborer, a soldier in the Kentucky militia, a prison guard, and a road surveyor. By 1803, at twenty-seven, he had enough money to buy a 238-acre farm for cash near Mill Creek in Hardin County, where he lived for three years with his mother and his sister and brother-in-law.

Early in 1806 he was hired by Kentucky store owners to build a flatboat and take goods down the Mississippi River for sale in New Orleans. In June, shortly after returning from Louisiana, he was married to Nancy Hanks. According to the prevailing belief among historians, Nancy Hanks was born out of wedlock in 1784 in what is now West Virginia. At a young age, she was taken to live in Kentucky by her grandparents, Ann and Joseph Hanks, who raised her until she was twelve, when she moved in with her aunt and uncle, Betsy and Thomas Sparrow. For a time in her late teenage years, she was evidently under the guardianship of Richard Berry and his wife Polly Ewing Berry, neighbors of Thomas Lincoln in Kentucky. It was in Richard Berry's cabin that Thomas Lincoln and Nancy Hanks were married.

After the marriage, Thomas took Nancy to live in a small home in Elizabethtown, Kentucky, that he built on a lot he bought there; he soon purchased a second lot. Busy as a carpenter, he was a respected member of the Elizabethtown community and a regular customer at the town's main store, Bleakley & Montgomery. On February 10, 1807, less than eight months after their wedding, Thomas and Nancy welcomed to the world a daughter, Sarah, who came to be known as Sally.

After two years in Elizabethtown, Thomas took his family to live on a 348-acre property he bought on the South Fork of Nolin Creek, about three miles south of present-day Hodgenville. On this land, commonly known as the Sinking Spring Farm, Thomas moved into a log cabin that was typical of the frontier. Measuring sixteen by eighteen feet, it had a dirt floor, a large fireplace, and one window of greased paper that allowed in diffused light. Here Abraham Lincoln was born on February 12, 1809.

The red clay soil at Sinking Spring proved to be barren, and the title to the property came under dispute. In 1811, Thomas bought a more fertile lot near Knob Creek, twelve miles to the northeast. Moving with the family there in November 1811, Thomas successfully farmed a section of that 230-acre property, located in a beautiful area noted for its unusual hills, so sharply defined that they were called knobs. He also sometimes accepted carpenter jobs. By 1814, he was ranked fifteenth among the ninety-eight residents listed in the Hardin County tax roll

A re-creation of Lincoln's birthplace cabin,
Hodgenville, Larue County, Kentucky.

in terms of the value of the property he owned.[14] Of the 104 families
living in that area of the county, only 6 owned as many horses as he
did.[15] His carpenter tools were said to be the finest in the region.

In fall 1816, Thomas took his wife, the nine-year-old Sally, and the
seven-year-old Abe across the Ohio River to live in southern Indiana in
Perry County (soon renamed Spencer County).

Considering his success in Kentucky, why did Thomas leave the state?

The move, Lincoln later explained, "was partly on account of slavery."[16] Thomas and Nancy Lincoln belonged to an antislavery sect of the
Baptist church; their negative views of slavery, along with competition
from slave labor in Hardin County, where nearly half of the adult population were enslaved, helped motivate the relocation. Under the Northwest Ordinance of 1787, Indiana, which became a state in 1816, was part
of the territory designated by the Founders to be free of slavery.

An even more important reason for the move was the uncertainty of

Kentucky real estate. Lincoln noted that his parents moved "chiefly on account of the difficulty in land titles in Ky." Despite his smart real estate investments, Thomas ended up losing money on his Kentucky properties because of the confusing land policies there. Originally a western extension of Virginia, Kentucky had long been exploited by eastern land speculators who laid claim to large parcels, many of them poorly surveyed or overlapping. The situation did not improve when Kentucky became a state in 1792. Land ownership remained hazy due to faulty surveys and what was known as shingling: the layering of claims on the same property by different owners. Henry Clay as a young Lexington attorney handled many cases of competing land titles; he found that the "same identical tract was frequently shingled over by a dozen claims."[17] Humphrey Marshall, the cousin of Chief Justice John Marshall, affirmed that "the face of Kentucky was covered, and disfigured by a complication of adverse claims to land, not less on an average than four fold." The great Kentucky explorer and surveyor Daniel Boone had to leave the state due to a suit over prior claims on his property. As a Boone biographer writes, "The lawyers and land speculators were too shrewd for the pioneer," who became "a houseless, homeless, impoverished man"; he eventually died in poverty in Missouri.[18]

Thomas Lincoln's experience with Kentucky land was almost as unlucky as Boone's. The Mill Creek property had been improperly surveyed—its area was actually 200 acres, not 238—so that when Thomas sold the parcel in 1814, he lost money on it. As for the Knob Creek farm, he lost it (and nine neighbors also lost their properties) as a result of an ejectment suit filed by the heirs of an eighteenth-century title holder, the Philadelphian Thomas Middleton, who as a Revolutionary War veteran had been awarded 10,000 acres of Kentucky land.

Land shingling also cost Thomas the birthplace farm at Sinking Spring. In 1783, the Commonwealth of Virginia had granted to one William Greene thirty thousand acres of land in what later became Hardin County, Kentucky. Half of this land was sold to Richard

Mather, a New York speculator. In 1805, Thomas Vance bought three hundred acres from Mather, who took back a lien on the land to secure the unpaid purchase price. Vance sold the farm to Isaac Bush, who then sold it to Thomas Lincoln. Meanwhile, the lien had not been satisfied with Mather, who in 1813 sued Vance, Bush, and Lincoln for title to the property. Bush by then had disappeared, leaving Vance and Lincoln responsible for the debt. Lincoln wanted to settle the matter by paying off Mather, but Mather rejected the offer and in 1816, after a court battle, resumed ownership of the land.

In light of the quicksand-like conditions of Kentucky real estate, Thomas Lincoln's decision to move to southern Indiana, where property was surveyed and sold by the federal government, was a sound one. This move from risky to secure land ownership seems to have had a lasting impact on Abraham Lincoln, many of whose later activities, as we shall see, related to his desire for justice in land policy, from his precise mapping of lots as a surveyor, through his demands as a congressman for James Polk to name the exact place where the Mexican War broke out, through to his dedication as president to providing western homesteads for the poor.

In Indiana, Thomas Lincoln proved that he was capable of navigating unpredictable economic conditions. Congress had divided Indiana land into 160-acre subdivisions cheaply priced for settlers. In October 1817, Thomas, after "squatting" for a year on property near Pigeon Creek, went on a 120-mile round-trip trek to the United States Land Office in Vincennes and purchased the land he had been farming, taking advantage of an installment plan whereby he agreed on the price of $2 an acre for 160 acres, paying only $16 as an initial down payment. Economic hard times left him cash poor and unable to complete his payments, and he returned half his acreage to the government, reducing his total debt to $160, which he paid. Later, Thomas shrewdly leveraged another Indiana property, some forty miles to the west. He managed to add 20 acres to the Pigeon Creek property, which he sold at a profit just before moving with his family to Illinois.

He handled other difficulties adeptly, too. Establishing himself on the Indiana frontier—"a wild region, with many bears and other wild animals still in the woods," as Lincoln later described it—was a severe challenge.[19] On a knoll at Pigeon Creek, Thomas built an eighteen-by-twenty-foot cabin, initially windowless and floorless, which housed the Lincolns for thirteen years. Nancy's aunt and uncle Betsy and Thomas Sparrow, along with her eighteen-year-old cousin Dennis Hanks, arrived from Kentucky in 1817 and moved into a shelter on the property that Thomas had built before the house-raising. Like the Lincolns, the Sparrows had been driven from Kentucky by an ejectment suit due to prior claims on their land. In September 1818, the Sparrows died of milk sickness, caused by drinking milk from cows that eat the poisonous white snakeroot.

Even greater tragedy for Abe came when the same illness took the life of his mother, Nancy Hanks Lincoln, who died on October 5 at thirty-four. Nancy suffered from the debilitating effects of milk sickness—trembling, vomiting, and abdominal pain. Aware that she was dying, she called Abe and his sister to her side and told them to revere God and to be good to their father and to each other.[20] Thomas Lincoln placed her body in a plain coffin he had built and buried it without a marker on a knoll near the Pigeon Creek cabin.

After Nancy's death, Dennis Hanks moved into the Lincoln cabin, where he and Abe, ten years his junior, slept in a small loft reached by climbing wooden pegs. Within a year Thomas took a trip back to Elizabethtown, Kentucky, where he proposed to an early acquaintance of his, Sarah Bush Johnston, now a thirty-year-old widow with two daughters and a son, who ranged in age from eight to thirteen. On December 2, 1819, Thomas and Sarah were married in Elizabethtown. Thomas returned to Indiana with Sarah and her children, and Sally and Abe had a new mother and three stepsiblings. The modest cabin now housed eight people, including the Lincolns, the Johnstons, and Dennis Hanks.

In spite of his increasingly heavy family responsibilities, Thomas remained moderately prosperous, even though the economy took a six-year tumble in the wake of the Panic of 1819, the first of several downturns, followed by deep recessions that would make the nineteenth century an economic roller coaster.[21] Lincoln later recalled to Leonard Swett: "It was pretty pinching times, at first in Indiana, getting the cabin built, and the clearing for the crops; but presently we got reasonably comfortable."[22] Actually, farmers like Thomas Lincoln were in a strong position during hard times, for they adopted a subsistence lifestyle. They lacked money but not provisions. As James Hall described the situation in Indiana: "The whole population trembled on the brink of ruin. . . . Yet it is not to be inferred that the people were destitute, or desperately poor; far from it. They were substantial farmers, surrounded with all the means of comfort and happiness."[23]

Far from being hopelessly mired in poverty, Thomas Lincoln was sometimes in a position to be generous to others, especially to relatives he hosted or housed. As the granddaughter of his second wife recalled, "He made a good living and I reckon would have gotten something ahead if he hadn't been so generous. He had the old Virginia notion of hospitality. Liked to see people set up to the table and eat hearty and there was always plenty of his relations and grandmother's [*sic*] willing to live on him."[24]

He kept his company in good humor, for he was an excellent raconteur who "loved fun—jokes and equalled Abe in tel[l]ing Stories," according to John Hanks, who lived with the Lincolns in Indiana for four years.[25] One of his jokes was later recalled by a family member. When his second wife, Sarah, asked which of his two wives he preferred, Thomas said the question reminded him of a Kentucky friend, John Hardin, who owned two fine horses and was asked which one he liked the best. Hardin's reply: "I can't tell, one of them kicks and the other bites and I don't know which is wust."[26]

Both Thomas and his son shifted between humorous sociability and melancholy. Thomas "often got the 'blues,' had some strange sort of spells" of sadness, much like Abe, whose mood shifts were noted by many who were close to him.[27] It may well be that, for both, death and other forms of loss were sources of gloom. Another blow came in 1828, when Abe's sister, Sally, who had married an Indiana neighbor, died in childbirth. Thomas also felt painfully the vicissitudes of Kentucky land ownership and the post-1819 depression in Indiana. He is sometimes accused of self-pity for his oft-repeated comment "why everything that I ever teched either died, got killed or was lost," but for someone who witnessed at close hand his own father's murder and who was later severely buffeted by life, the statement is perhaps understandable.[28]

If Thomas and his son both experienced depression, there also was a healthier bond between them: temperance. The first three decades of the nineteenth century, when Abe grew up, was a period of astoundingly high alcohol consumption in America. In 1820, Americans spent $12 million on liquor, an amount that exceeded the total expenditure of the US government.[29] By the mid-1820s, the average American consumed more than seven gallons of alcohol annually (about three times today's per capita average). Liquor was used as a medicine from early childhood and onward, and it was served at work, at virtually all social functions, and after sports and games. In an 1842 temperance speech, Lincoln recalled that during his youth "we found intoxicating liquor, recognized by every body, used by every body, and repudiated by nobody. It commonly entered into the first draught of the infant, and the last draught of the dying man."[30] People of all callings and classes, he noted, drank.

Thomas Lincoln's family saw alcohol production, sale, and consumption up close. Distilleries were fixtures on the Kentucky scene. Early in their marriage, Thomas and Nancy lived near a distillery in

Elizabethtown. When the Lincolns moved to Sinking Spring, there was a distillery on an adjoining farm. The move to Knob Creek brought them to one of the leading centers of whiskey production in the United States. What was then the nation's largest distillery was within two miles of the Lincoln home and within sight of Abe Lincoln's school. Other stills were within a forty-mile radius of the Lincoln property in a region now known as the bourbon capital of the world, where whiskeys like Jim Beam, Heaven Hill, and Maker's Mark are produced.

There was also liquor production and consumption in the extended Lincoln family. Thomas's uncle, also named Thomas Lincoln, who ran a distillery in Fayette City, had a serious drinking problem.[31] When in 1810 Uncle Thomas was sued for spousal abuse by his wife, Elizabeth, his violence was attributed to "intemperance and intoxication."[32] During the trial, it came out that his wife also suffered from alcohol dependence. Another relative with drinking issues was Mordecai Lincoln, Abe's uncle on his father's side. Wealthy and talented, Mordecai nonetheless was so addicted to liquor that he froze to death in a snowstorm after an evening binge made him pass out in his carriage while he was driving home.

Many political leaders were bibulous. The Kentucky-bred Henry Clay was a heavy drinker who once got so inebriated that he leaped onto a sixty-foot table at a party and danced wildly down its whole length, smashing crockery and glasses as he cavorted. Other alcoholic politicians of the era included Daniel Webster, Franklin Pierce, John Randolph, and Lincoln's arch opponent Stephen A. Douglas. In alcohol-laced America, it seemed at times that, indeed, liquor was "repudiated by nobody," in Lincoln's words. Even two Baptist preachers the Lincolns often heard in Kentucky, David Elkin and William Downs, were known to be dissipated.

Given the flood of alcohol around them, it is notable that Thomas and Abe Lincoln were restrained in their drinking. A relative testified that Thomas "would take his dram, [was] not a habitual drinker—never drank on Christmas[;] had one or two apple toddy."[33] Abe rarely touched alcohol; occasionally he nursed a drink in social situations for the sake of appearance. He said of liquor, "I hate the stuff. It is very unpleasant and always leaves me flabby and undone."[34]

Abe kept a close watch on the ever-growing temperance movement, which went through several phases between the 1820s and 1850s. Early in this period, Lincoln wrote temperance articles for newspapers, and later he gave temperance addresses and joined the Sons of Temperance, a group opposed to alcohol abuse. But he never became a rabid temperance advocate; he avoided the extremes of total abstinence, Washingtonian Society confessionalism (the precursor of Alcoholics Anonymous), and prohibitionism. The moderation he showed foreshadowed his approach to slavery. His involvement with the temperance movement became an important factor in his political rise.

He learned to be moderate during his youth. His refusal to drink at many social events must have raised some eyebrows, but it kept him on a steady course. Here again, his father led the way in avoiding extremes. Thomas "was temperate in his Habits, never was intoxicated in his life," said a friend.[35]

Also exemplary was his father's honesty. Lincoln's famous honesty as a lawyer and politician had a personal precedent in his father, who was widely described as truthful. Thomas's stepgranddaughter recalled, "Uncle Abe got his honesty and clean notions of living and his kind heart from his father."[36] A minister who interviewed Thomas's nieces and nephews similarly concluded that the president "received from his father certain qualities of mind, . . . above all, his proverbial honesty and truthfulness."[37] Others who knew Thomas concurred that he was "a Strictly honest and hard-working Man," "a sturdy, honest God-fearing man whom all the neighbors respected."

Like other rural Americans of the time, Thomas needed all members of the family to help out around the house and farm. Lincoln later recalled that an axe was put in his hands when he was eight, and that instrument remained there for much of his youth and early manhood. He felled trees, split rails, and built fences. He also did farmwork such as planting seeds, sowing crops, taking grain to mills for grinding, and tending animals. During the 1820s he worked successively as a supplier of wood for steamboats, a ferry operator on the Ohio River, a carpenter, and a riverboat steersman on two trips that he took by flatboat down the Mississippi to New Orleans.

The fact that his father often hired him out to neighbors has been called oppressive or exploitative, but this practice was common. As Sara Quay notes, "If families were to be successful on the frontier, they depended on contributions of every member of the family unit, regardless of age, size, or interest in doing so."[38] Children as young as five were given chores, and a father could claim a son's wages until the son was twenty-one. Therefore, Thomas Lincoln was doing nothing unusual when in the mid-1820s, under financial pressure after a friend defaulted on a loan Thomas had endorsed, he hired out Abe to neighbors doing various jobs (as ferry operator, farmhand, wood chopper, butcher, store clerk, and others) that paid between ten cents and thirty-one cents a day. Like other frontiersmen's sons, Abe worked at his father's behest.

Did Thomas impede his son's education? The image of Thomas as an ignorant taskmaster who scolded the studious young Abe for reading instead of doing his farmwork is a staple of books and films, based mainly on Dennis Hanks's comment that Abe "was a Constant and I m[a]y Say Stubborn reader, his father having Sometimes to slash him for neglecting his work by reading."[39] To the extent that this is true, it should be noted that hostility to education prevailed on the frontier. Most country folk of the time considered schooling a frivolous distraction or a threat to the rural lifestyle. The education historian Mark Friedberger explains, "Unlike middle-class urbanites, farmers did not regard education favorably. Parents wanted their children to remain on the farm, to look after them in their old age, and then to inherit the Homestead land."[40] Parents knew that children who did receive education tended to leave their farms and move to cities, where better jobs were available.

Also, Thomas Lincoln's Baptist faith inclined him against education. The Baptist religion was simple and pietistic, and frontier preachers, most of them uneducated, denounced "book larnin'," which they regarded as useless in gaining God's grace.[41] These frontier ministers stood opposed to public schools, regarding them as part of an elite urban conspiracy to spread false religion and destroy local control.[42]

But Thomas Lincoln managed at times to rise above this widespread mistrust of education. Sarah Bush Lincoln, Lincoln's stepmother, declared, "As a usual thing Mr. Lincoln never made Abe quit reading to do anything if he could avoid it. He would do it himself first. Mr. Lincoln could read a little & could scarcely write his name: hence he wanted, as he himself felt the uses & necessities of Education his boy Abraham to learn & he Encouraged him to do it in all ways he could."[43] Abe himself reportedly said, "My father had suffered greatly for the want of education, and he determined at an early day that I should be well educated. And what do you think he said his ideas of a good education were? We had an old dog-eared arithmetic in our house, and father determined that somehow, or somehow else, I should cipher clear through that book."[44] It makes sense that Thomas would value ciphering, because measurement and proportion were important tools in his work as a carpenter and cabinetmaker.

THE ANGEL MOTHER
AND FRONTIER RELIGION

Lincoln idealized his mother, Nancy Hanks Lincoln, who died when he was nine. He once called her "my angel mother," not only to distinguish her from his stepmother but also to sanctify her as "all that I am or ever hope to be."[45] Because so little is known about Nancy—about her unidentified father, the details of her childhood, or even her looks, which were contrastingly reported—we can't fully say what Lincoln meant by these words, except perhaps to express his pride over her supposedly aristocratic Virginia bloodline. From what we do know about her, he may also have been referring to her strong mind and her participation in frontier religion.

Whether or not Nancy was ashamed of her premarital reputation as a "loose" woman, or of the fact that her mother, Lucy, had been indicted by a jury for fornication, and Lucy's daughter Sarah bore six illegitimate children, we may never know.[46] Nor can we be sure of the accuracy of William Herndon's report that Lincoln expressed shame over his mother's illegitimacy and called some members of her family "*lascivious—lecherous*—not to be trusted."[47]

We can, however, glean certain characteristics of Nancy's from those who knew her. While she was sometimes described as sad and quiet, her mental strength and goodness shine through in virtually all contemporary commentary. An Indiana neighbor, Nathaniel Grigsby, declared that she was known for "Extraordinary Strength of mind among the family and all who knew her: she was superior to her husband in Every way. She was a brilliant woman—a woman of good sense and Modesty."[48] Others called her "highly intellectual by nature," "a great noble woman—a woman of a very fine cast of mind," "a gentle, kind, smart—shrewd—social, intelligent woman."[49]

She was also reputed to possess courage and physical strength—perhaps extraordinarily so, if there's validity in the comment by two of Lincoln's friends that she was "one of the most athletic women in Kentucky. In a fair wrestle, she could throw most of the men who ever put her powers to the test," including a law clerk who "had frequently wrestled with her, and she invariably laid him on his back."[50]

Like her husband, Nancy accepted the simple faith preached at the Baptist churches she joined in Kentucky and Indiana. She was called both "resolute, fearless, . . . cool and self-possessed amidst all exposures and dangers" and "a *pious* heroine" whose heart was filled "with thoughts of Him who watched over them by night and day."[51]

Because no American president used religion to unify the nation as effectively as Lincoln, it's important to recognize his mother's role in establishing his religious frame of mind. Although Lincoln never joined a church and rejected creeds, he was clearly influenced by the nondogmatic faith of his parents. His mother in particular served as his main instructor in what became one of his early texts, the Bible, which he once called "the best gift God has given to man."[52] Abe in his youth was not a constant Bible reader. Dennis Hanks said, "Lincoln didn't read the Bible half as much as [is] said"—testimony confirmed by Abe's stepmother, who remarked, "Abe read the Bible some, though not as much as is said."[53] But he read it enough to learn a technique he regularly used in his own expression: adding resonance and suggestiveness to his stories and speeches. He seems to have learned the technique especially from hearing his mother read the Scriptures aloud. A relative commented that his mother taught him "to read the Bible—study it & the stories in it and all that was moraly [sic] & affectionate in it. . . . Lincoln was often and much moved by the stories."[54] As this comment suggests, it was specifically the imaginative narratives and the moral themes of the Bible that struck home with Lincoln. The Bible for him was both entertaining and instructive.

He also found this combination of diversion and instruction in the Baptist preachers he witnessed. The remarkable variety of religious expression in pre–Civil War America is a testament to what was a distinguishing feature of American religion: radical creativity fostered by religious freedom. Emerson caught the free religious spirit of America when he wrote: "The Protestant has his pew, which of course is only the first step to a church for every individual citizen—a church apiece."[55] The famous British tourist Frances Trollope wrote of Americans: "The whole people appear to be divided into an almost endless variety of religion factions. . . . Besides the broad and well-known distinctions . . . there are innumerable others springing out of these."[56] Religion, in short, hit the fan.

The Baptist faith of Lincoln's parents was, among all American religions, the most varied in its manifestations. No other religious body yielded so many different branches as the Baptists. There were Primitive Baptists, Free-Will Baptists, Hard- and Soft-Shell Baptists, Particular Baptists, General Baptists, Six-Principle Baptists, Anti-Mission Baptists, Two-Seed-in-the-Spirit Baptists, German Seventh-Day Baptists, Close-Communion, General, Sabbatarian, and Foot-Washing Baptists—all with different emphases in doctrine: so many, in fact, that a nineteenth-century historian of the religion remarked, "The term 'Baptist' has ceased to become a distinguishing name if used without a prefix."[57]

One Baptist offshoot was the Little Mount Church, the small church in Hardin County, Kentucky, whose members included Thomas and Nancy Hanks Lincoln.

This was a very special offshoot. The fifteen people who in 1809, the year of Lincoln's birth, broke off from the regular Baptists to form the Little Mount Church, believed that the Bible stood opposed to slavery—a highly unusual view for that day, especially in Hardin County, where in an adult population of some 2,600, nearly half were enslaved persons.

The Little Mount Church's minister, William Downs, whom Louis Warren calls "the first preacher whom Abraham Lincoln heard, and the preacher he heard most often in his childhood,"[58] was an ardent emancipationist, as was the church's other minister, David Elkin. Lincoln would later declare that he could not remember a time when he did not loathe slavery. Today such religious opposition to slavery may seem natural, but in the early nineteenth century it was not, except among Quakers. Southern ministers were confident that the Bible supported slavery, and even in the North, outspokenly abolitionist clergymen were sparse before 1820. For a Kentucky church in a slaveholding area to organize so early on an antislavery basis was extremely uncommon—a chance mutation, indeed. Lincoln's ethically based hatred of the South's peculiar institution, then, was nurtured by a rare, fortunate development in the rapidly dividing Baptist Church.

If Lincoln's Baptist background opened the way to his antislavery convictions, it also cultivated creativity in religious matters. The splintering of the Baptists immersed him in an environment that was constantly yielding fresh faiths. A relative heard Lincoln say "that if he could take the best parts from all the churches, he could make a new church better than any of them."[59] During his childhood and teenage years, Lincoln was so taken by colorful sermons he heard that he became an expert in imitating them. The Baptists were the most influential denominations in popularizing what I elsewhere identify as the new religious style: a sermon style based not on the bygone Puritan formula of Text, Exposition, and Proof (or Application) but rather on free-flowing, usually extemporaneous strings of inspirational passages, vernacular speech, anecdotes, and sometimes humor.[60]

A historian of the Baptist church in Kentucky explained that "the advantage possessed by the Baptists, was the greater popularity of their preaching compared with that of their rival sects." Unlearned but powerful, the preachers "mingled constantly with the masses of the people," "understood the force of their local dialect," and delivered "literally extemporaneous" sermons in which "they drew their illustrations from the daily habits of their hearers."[61] The Baptists' vivid sermons strongly affected Lincoln. John Locke Scripps, Lincoln's earliest authorized biographer, wrote in 1860 that Lincoln as a boy had been strongly shaped by "the early backwoods preachers." Scripps wrote, "Many of these early pioneer preachers . . . [were] freed from conventional restraint" and "were gifted with a rare eloquence" that "wrought upon the imagination of their hearers."[62] As Lincoln later told a friend, "I don't like to hear cut-and-dried sermons. No—when I hear a man preach, I like to see him act as if he were fighting bees!"[63]

The young Lincoln was so attracted to the new religious style that he imitated it whenever he could. Endowed with a wonderful memory, he would attend a service, go home, and regale friends and neighbors by repeating the sermon. Dennis Hanks recalled that Lincoln would stand "on a stump or log, . . . mimacing the Style & tone of the old Baptist preachers."[64] Hanks said Lincoln would "repeat the sermint [*sic*] clean through from text to doxology. . . . I heerd him do it many a time."[65] Another relative reported that not only would Lincoln "repeat almost word for word the sermon he had heard the Sunday before," but if he didn't attend church, "Abe would take down the bible, read a verse—give out a hymn—and we would sing—we were good singers . . .—he would preach & we would do the Crying—sometimes he would join the Chorus of Tears."[66]

Lincoln's sermonizing signified his penchant for *performance*. The religion of his youth and young manhood was, above everything, performative. So was virtually everything else he participated in. Many neighbors later recalled his attending political speeches or trials and returning home, mounting a stump, and repeating what he had heard. The same applied to stories he read or jokes he heard or songs he learned: he loved to perform them in front of an audience. To call such behavior impersonation is not strong enough. It was rather a Whitman-esque, omnivorous absorption and recycling of cultural materials. Sermons, speeches, courtroom arguments, hymns, popular jokes, stories, and poems: Lincoln appreciated all of them for their performative value.

Lincoln's proclivity toward mimicry extended even to the Bible. At twenty, he wrote the "Chronicles of Reuben" (1829), a secular variation on an Old Testament story that was part of the cultural trend toward fictionalizing the Bible, a trend that eventually produced religious bestsellers like *The Prince of the House of David*, *Ben-Hur*, and *The Robe*. But whereas these inspirational novels were intended to buttress Christianity, Lincoln's biblical poem was a jeu d'esprit that pointed a Bible story toward the sensual and the bawdy.

Lincoln allegedly wrote the "Chronicles of Reuben" after he learned that he was not invited to a wedding party celebrating the dual marriages of the Grigsby brothers Reuben Jr. and Charles, Indiana neighbors. Written in a faux-biblical style, the poem describes a sexual mishap that occurs after the party, when the two grooms are led in the dark to the wrong rooms; each brother finds himself in bed with the other's wife. Based on the Bible story of the prophet Reuben, repudiated by his family for having slept with his father's concubine, Lincoln's coarse poem titillated some and outraged others, including a woman who called the poem "Smutty" and a twentieth-century Christian biographer of Lincoln who dismissed it as "a rude backwoods joke, written . . . in full accord with the standards of humor current in the time and general environment."[67]

Today what seems unorthodox about the poem is not its lewdness but its startling secularity. The poem shows that the young Lincoln was thoroughly at ease in adapting the Bible for personal use—in this case to pillory an unfriendly neighbor. In doing so, he aped the cadences and imagery of the Bible, as indicated by some of the poem's opening lines:

> It came to pass when the sons of Reuben grew up that they were desirous of taking to themselves wives, and, being too well known as to honor in their own country, they took a journey into a far country and there procured for themselves wives.
>
> It came to pass also that when they were about to make the return home they sent a messenger before them to bear the tidings to their parents. . . .[68]

Behind Lincoln's youthful gamboling with sermons and the Bible lay a suspicion of organized religion, which over time came through in his jokes and stories, a good number of which were about religion or preachers. He loved telling one about a Millerite couple who agree to share their secrets with each other in advance of ascending to heaven. The wife confesses that their son was sired by a one-eyed shoemaker in town. The husband, though outraged, says that at least their other children are his. The wife replies, "No, they belong to the neighborhood."

The husband shouts, "I am ready to leave. *Gabriel, blow your horn!*"[69] Another Lincoln story involved a Baptist preacher who announces to his congregation, "I am the Christ whom I shall represent today." As he gives his sermon, a lizard runs up his pants, across his back, and to his neck, causing the preacher to flail wildly and disrobe, impelling a woman to stand up in her pew and cry, "Well, if you represent Christ, I am done believing in the Bible."[70] Lincoln also told of an African American boy he once met who was using street mud to build a miniature church, with steeple, pews, pulpit, and so on. When Lincoln asked the boy where the preacher was, the boy grinned and said, "Laws, I hain't got *mud* enough!"[71]

Lincoln's humorous and performative treatments of religion cloaked a struggle with doubt. His questioning of faith was darkened by his lifelong preoccupation with the brevity of life. He was obsessed by the impermanence of earthly things, and in his writings there are few references to an afterlife.

Abe's heaviest early loss was the death in 1818 of his mother, when he was nine. His grief over his mother's death evidently instilled in him a sense of transience that would disturb him throughout his life and that he tried to leaven with poetry and humor. We see his mournful, poetic, and puckish sides in the earliest extant writing in his hand, lines he jotted in a copybook in the early 1820s:

> Abraham Lincoln his hand and pen he will be
>   good
> but god knows When Time What an em[p]ty vaper
> tis and days how swift they are swift as an indian arr[ow]
> Mete[o]r
> fly on like a shooting star the presant moment
>   Just [is here]
> then slides away in h[as]te that we [can] never say
>   they['re ours]
> but [only say] th[ey]'re past

Abraham Lincoln is my nam[e]
And with my pen I wrote the same
I wrote in both hast and speed
and left it here for fools to read.[72]

Grammatically flawed like much schoolboy scribbling, these lines are nonetheless suggestive, even in their disorder, rather like free verse. The passage begins and ends with short poems about "Abraham Lincoln," the first one telling us that he will be good "when god knows when," the last one saying he has hastily penned words "for fools to read." While writing his full name twice suggests self-assertion, the playful naughtiness of the closing couplet of each poem radiates self-deprecation and fun, exhibiting Lincoln's trademark humility and humor.

The lines connecting the opening and closing poems are in a completely different mood. Copied from an Isaac Watts hymn, they deliver a powerful message about time and mortality. Here are Watts's opening stanzas:

> Time, what an empty vapor 'tis!
> And days, how swift they are!
> Swift as an Indian arrow flies,
> Or like a shooting star.
>
> The present moments just appear,
> Then slide away in haste;
> That we can never say, they're here,
> But only say, they're past.

It is telling that the adolescent Abe copied verses from Isaac Watts, whose resonant rhythms influenced a number of nineteenth-century American poets. Significantly, Abe included only the hymn's doleful opening verses, omitting its joyful second half, which pictures the bliss of heaven. The dark verses he selected typified many of the songs and poems that stirred him for the rest of his life. Transience, the disappearance of the present moment, the impermanence of all earthly things— these themes haunted Lincoln, so much so that he eventually settled on a favorite song (the wistful ballad "Twenty Years Ago") and a favorite poem (William Knox's "Mortality") that are about loss and death.

Lincoln seemed here to be on the cusp of a discovery about language. Poetry became his favorite genre; he memorized poetic lyrics and recited them often. For him, poetry organized and crystalized experience as no other type of language did. "To President Lincoln poetry was the fairest side of truth," remarked a journalist who met with Lincoln several times during the Civil War.[73] Poetry gave order and meaning to life experiences that tended toward the chaotic or uncontrolled. If, as Mikhail Bakhtin suggests, language is a centripetal force that helps regulate centrifugal reality, we can say that Lincoln found in poetry, the most structured form of language, a means of arranging and giving meaning to his experience.[74] In turn, he gave structure and meaning to the national experience in pithy, poetic speeches that had the cadences and resonant imagery of poetry.

Before he reached the point that he could do so, he went through a process of maturation that broadened his vision and engaged him with the cultural and political world around him. This process was sped by his stepmother, Sarah Bush Lincoln.

FAMILY RELATIONS AND
TEENAGE ROMANCES IN INDIANA

The period Abe lived in Indiana in his stepmother's presence, from 1819 to 1830, was a crucial time in his formation. Many of the traits and convictions that later flowered in him were seeded during these years. Sarah Bush Lincoln helped cultivate them.

Abe and his stepmother loved and respected each other. Sarah testified that "Abe was the best boy I Ever Saw or Ever Expect to see," adding that "I can say what scarcely one woman—a mother—can say in the thousand and it is this—Abe never gave me a cross word or look and never refused in fact, or Even in appearance, to do anything I requested him."[75] Abe called Sarah Mama and told an Indiana neighbor that "she had been his best Friend in this world & that no Son could love a Mother more than he loved her." They bonded psychologically and intellectually. "His mind & mine," Sarah recalled, "seemed to run together—move in the same channel." Lincoln, for his part, remarked that he appreciated "the encouragement he always had received from his Step Mother."[76]

The granddaughter of a Dutchman who had emigrated from Rotterdam to New York, Sarah Bush was born in 1788 in Hardin County, Kentucky.[77] When she was two, she was taken to live in Elizabethtown, where she grew up. Her father, Christopher Bush, was a slave patrol leader and landholder who owned more than two thousand acres in Kentucky by the time Sarah was fifteen. Sarah had eight siblings, including six brothers locally known as rough-and-tumble fighters. "There was no backout in them," a family friend observed; "they never shunned a fight where they considered it necessary to engage in it, and nobody ever heard them cry 'enough.'"[78] (One of them reportedly refused anesthetics when doctors made a nine-inch incision in his back to remove a bullet.) Sarah developed into a strong yet gentle woman, described as "quick and strong-minded," "kind," and "a woman of great energy, of remarkable good sense, very industrious."[79] Tall, ringleted, and fair-complexioned, she had an erect posture and a sprightly personality.

In 1806, at eighteen, she married Daniel Johnston, a hard-luck man of obscure background who was constantly in debt. The Johnstons had three children: John, Elizabeth, and Matilda. After eight years of financial struggle, Daniel was hired as the keeper of the Hardin County jail in Elizabethtown. The family of five moved into an area in the forty-two-by-twenty-two-foot stone jail, where Sarah served as cook and cleaning woman.

After her husband's death from cholera in 1816, Sarah lived as a single mother until her marriage in December 1819 to Thomas Lincoln, whom she had known from a young age when they lived near each other in Kentucky. There are various accounts of Thomas's proposal to Sarah shortly after he arrived in Elizabethtown after his trip from Indiana. A popular one is that he showed up one day and told her, "I have no wife and you no husband. I came a-purpose to marry you. I knowed you from a gal and you knowed me from a boy. I've no time to lose; and if you're willin' let it be done straight off."[80] He paid her small debts, and their marriage ceremony, conducted by a Methodist minister in an old log house on Elizabethtown's main street, took place on December 2. Thomas loaded the wagon with Sarah's possessions—a bureau, a table, a set of chairs, kitchenware, and some books and clothing—and the couple and her children made the 140-mile trek westward to the Lincoln cabin in Little Pigeon Creek, Indiana.

Ten-year-old Abe and his sister Sally, twelve, must have been excited by the arrival of their stepmother and three stepsiblings. Sarah's belongings added luxury to the bare cabin, which profited from her oversight. She persuaded Thomas to improve the cabin by laying down a wood floor, fixing the roof against the elements, and adding a sleeping loft for the three boys (Abe, John Johnston, and Dennis Hanks) and a feather bed beneath it for the three girls (Sally and her stepsisters). Sarah attended to the orphaned Abe and Sally. Dennis Hanks recalled "she Soaped—, rubbed, and washed the Children Clean. . . . She sewed and mended their Clothes & the Children once more looked human as their own good mother left them."[81]

By 1820, the family living in the Pigeon Creek cabin included the forty-two-year-old Thomas and his wife Sarah, ten years his junior, along with Dennis Hanks, twenty-one; the thirteen-year-old stepsisters Sally Lincoln and Elizabeth Johnston; the eleven-year-old Abe and his stepbrother John D. Johnston, ten; and stepsister Matilda Johnston, nine.

The relationship between Abe, his sister, and the three stepsiblings was affectionate. His sister Sally—short, somewhat heavyset, with dark eyes and chestnut-brown hair ("just as pretty as Abe was homely," said a neighbor)—was described as "a quick minded woman & of extraordinary Mind," not just "intellectual & intelligent" but also eminently practical. She was "a gentle, Kind, smart—shrewd—social" woman, always ready with a friendly laugh.[82] In 1823 she became a member of the Little Pigeon Creek Baptist Church, as did her father and stepmother, but not her brother, who never joined a church. Three years later, at nineteen, Sally married a fellow Baptist, Nathaniel Grigsby. Tragically, she died a year and a half later after giving birth to a stillborn child. When Abe received the news of her death, he "sat down on a log and hid his face in his hands while the tears rolled down through his long bony fingers. Those present turned away in pity and left him to his grief."[83] He blamed the Grigsby family for not summoning a doctor in time to save her; his anger helped fuel his satirical attack on the Grigsbys in his biblical poem the "Chronicles of Reuben."

Among his stepsiblings, Abe formed a special bond with Matilda, known as Tilda. She recalled that he was "good to me, good to all. . . . Abe seemed to love Everybody and Everything; he loved us all and Especially mother."[84] Tilda noted his studiousness, commenting that "Abe was not Energetic Except in one thing—he was active & persistant [sic] in learning—read Everything he Could—Ciphered on boards—on the walls."[85] She said that she and Abe "grew up loving one another as brother and sister."[86]

Abe once gave Tilda a memorable lesson in honesty. Her mother had warned her against following him into the woods when he went to fell trees. One day she sneaked away from the cabin, followed him, and surprised him from behind by leaping on him, grabbing him by the neck and kneeing him in the back, causing him to tumble on the ground. While falling, she was cut badly by his axe. As he staunched her wound with pieces of his shirt, he advised her to tell her mother the truth about the incident, instead of covering it up, as she intended to do.

Tilda's brother, John D. Johnston, was a problematic figure in Abe's life. On the one hand, he was a kind, generous, and frank person who grew close to Abe. The two worked together on canal building in Louisville, Kentucky, and later on the construction of a flatboat that they and two other men navigated down the Mississippi in 1831. However, John was temperamentally very different from Abe. Shiftless and unintellectual, he became a favorite of Thomas Lincoln, while Abe was preferred by his stepmother. John made few efforts to get ahead in life and at times became a financial drain on Abe, who lent him money to the point of exasperation. "You are not *lazy*," Lincoln wrote him in December 1848, "and still you *are* an *idler*."[87] Warning John to stop "uselessly wasting time," Abe generously offered to match any earnings John made over the succeeding five months. Despite Abe's frustration with his stepbrother, he spoke of him "in the Most affectionate Manner," saying that he and John "were raised together, slept together, and liked each other as well as actual brothers could do."[88]

Although Lincoln was shy and awkward around girls, some of whom laughed at his odd looks and ungainliness, he had several romances in Indiana. After his death a number of women reported having had a relationship with Abe, including Elizabeth Tully, who called herself Abe's "first regular company" and said that he signaled his marriage intentions to her; Elizabeth Ray, who kept in her possession a pair of earrings she reported to have received from him; Caroline Meeker, a Kentucky girl he visited and flirted with at a corn-husking bee; Elizabeth Wood, the daughter of a good friend of Abe's who rejected him because of "his awkwardness and large feet"; the beautiful, well-to-do Hannah Gentry, who insisted she would have been Mrs. Lincoln if Abe had not been "too fond of onions, as she could not endure them"; and Julia Evans, "a very beautiful girl. . . . My heart was in a flutter," Abe reportedly said of her after meeting her while working in Princeton, Indiana.[89]

What are we to make of such claims of romantic attachments to the young Lincoln? Surely several of them reflected wishful exaggeration on the part of women to whom the ungainly, reticent Abe took on romantic charm when viewed through the retrospective lens of national hagiography. Most of these relationships appear to have been passing teenage crushes. Taken cumulatively, however, they were the early signals of what later was described as Lincoln's strong passion for women.

That said, while living in Indiana, Lincoln was far less interested in romance than in improving his mind. As John D. Johnston said, Abe didn't take much truck with girls. "[H]e was too busy studying at the time."[90]

And that studying paid off handsomely.

Foundations of Presidential Character

At an early age, Lincoln set off on a quest for meaning. His stepmother stated that as a boy he "must understand Every thing—even to the smallest thing—Minutely & Exactly— he would then repeat it over to himself again & again."[1] Lincoln, when asked in 1860 by the Connecticut minister John P. Gulliver how he achieved his clear, powerful way of speaking, explained that ever since childhood he had sought ceaselessly for clarity. He recalled that the one thing that made him angry as a child was when he could not fully understand the conversations of neighbors who visited the cabin. He described to Gulliver going to his loft and "spending no small part of the night . . . trying to make out what was the exact meaning of some of their, to me, dark sayings. . . . I was not satisfied until I had repeated over and over, until I put it in language that was plain enough, as I thought, for any boy I knew to comprehend."[2]

Lincoln's faith in language developed during a cultural journey that began with the books he read in his youth. William Herndon once remarked that Lincoln read deeply but not widely. In this respect, Lincoln was equidistant from two of his famous predecessors: John Quincy Adams, an omnivorous reader who knew six languages, and Andrew Jackson, about whom it was said that the only book, other than the

Bible, that he ever read through was Oliver Goldsmith's novel *The Vicar of Wakefield*. In childhood, Lincoln read the small number of books that were available to him on the frontier. He read them closely and remembered them later on. When we look at his reading, at school and at home, we see that it planted the seeds for many of his adult traits.

FRONTIER SCHOOLS AND FORMATIVE BOOKS

The schools on the Kentucky-Indiana frontier were single-room log structures, usually windowless and dirt-floored—or, if adapted to the angle of a hillside, floored with rough planks, beneath which hogs gathered, emitting into the schoolroom swarms of fleas that students fended off by laying pokeweed on the planks.[3] Also annoying were the plentiful splinters on the logs on which students sat. Because paper was scarce, answers were frequently scratched with charcoal on slate or wood. Much of the school day was devoted to individual and group recitation. The idea behind these "blab" or "vocal" schools was that information could be best imprinted on the memory if spoken aloud—a habit that stuck with Lincoln, who later irritated colleagues in his Springfield law office by constantly reading aloud from newspapers or books.

A school term customarily lasted two or three months and was scheduled not to conflict with the planting and harvesting seasons, when children were needed for farmwork. Because of the unpredictable terms and the sporadic appearance of teachers, schooling for most frontier children was often brief.

Lincoln's experience was typical. His total time in school, as he reported, was less than one year. He attended five schools for short terms, two in Kentucky before he turned seven and three in Indiana at the ages of eleven, thirteen, and seventeen. His first teacher was Zachariah Riney, whose schoolhouse was located about three miles north of the

Lincolns' Knob Creek home. A Maryland-born Catholic who had moved to Kentucky in 1795, Riney mainly taught Abe spelling, using Thomas Dilworth's popular *Dilworth's Spelling-Book: A New Guide to the English Tongue*. Abe's next teacher, Caleb Hazel, lived close to the Lincolns and attended the same Baptist church. The son of a tavern keeper, Hazel was briefly trying his hand at teaching. He was a large man who severely punished naughty students. Four years later, after the Lincolns moved to Indiana, Abe attended a school run by Andrew Crawford, a former justice of the peace in Spencer County who taught his students good etiquette along with the three *R*s. Next came the school of James Swaney (aka Sweeney), which was four and a half miles away from the Lincolns' Pigeon Creek home. The distance precluded Abe's regular attendance at this short-lived school, but Swaney is credited with teaching from Lindley Murray's *English Reader*, among the best literary anthologies of the time. Abe's last teacher, Azel W. Dorsey, was a former election clerk, coroner, and local politician. A man of wide interests, Dorsey was Abe's best teacher and is especially credited with training the seventeen-year-old Lincoln in basic algebra.

When recalling his frontier education for an 1860 campaign biographer, Lincoln had little positive to say. "There were some schools, so called," he wrote, "but no qualification was ever required of a teacher, beyond '*readin, writin, and cipherin,*' to the Rule of Three [that is, basic algebra]. If a straggler supposed to understand latin, happened to sojourn in the neighborhood, he was looked upon as a wizzard [*sic*]. There was absolutely nothing to excite ambition for education."[4] Showing his customary tendency to underplay his background, Lincoln made it seem as if he had little education—an image he also projected in a short autobiography he wrote for a congressional directory in June 1858, where he stated, "Education defective."[5]

However, as shown by the experiences of Frederick Douglass, who had no formal schooling yet became one of the century's most eloquent communicators, or Walt Whitman, a great poet despite having left school at eleven, in nineteenth-century America, as today, a sound education could be found outside the classroom. This was the case with Lincoln. He absorbed the cultural energies of the frontier, and he read books that helped shape his character.

When we survey these eclectic influences—to which can be added newspapers, which he began reading in Indiana in the 1820s—we see that his mind was fed early on by all kinds of sources, high and low, sacred and secular. Absorbing the new religious style of preachers at the same time as crude frontier humor, he was integrating culture in an extraordinarily wide-ranging manner.

His openness to his cultural surroundings laid the basis for his character, which was described by the Illinois attorney John W. Scott:

> When you come to analize [sic] his character, the elements that entered into it, you will find that he possessed no one element of character in any higher degree than many of his co[n]temporaries. His greatness sprang from a strange combination of all the essentials of character entering into and forming a grand and heroic character, independent of any one great essential—And such a character is always Self-reliant—[6]

Scott recognized what Emerson and Whitman stated eloquently—in democratic America, the highest individualism lay in the greatest representativeness: the ability, in Whitman's phrase, to "contain multitudes."[7]

He was an attentive reader, and little was lost on him, especially because he repeated passages aloud and wrote them down whenever he could. The books the young Lincoln read broadened him immeasurably.

In the 1860 campaign biography by John Locke Scripps, authorized by Lincoln, seven books from Lincoln's early years are highlighted as having been especially formative: Thomas Dilworth's *Spelling-Book*, the Bible, Aesop's *Fables*, Bunyan's *Pilgrim's Progress*, Mason Locke Weems's *The Life of Washington*, Benjamin Franklin's autobiography, and James Riley's *Narrative of the Loss of the American Brig Commerce*. Other books important to the young Lincoln included William Scott's *Lessons in Elocution, The Kentucky Preceptor*, Noah Webster's *The American Speller, The Seven Voyages of Sinbad*, Daniel Defoe's *Robinson Crusoe*, and Lindley Murray's *The English Reader*.[8]

One of the earliest books he read, Thomas Dilworth's *Spelling-Book,* was heavily didactic; it taught reading and spelling through preachy poems, biblical passages, and fables followed by interpretations. Each virtue points humans in a definite direction (lying and atheism lead toward hell, honesty toward heaven, and so on). But its didacticism sometimes contains seeds of radicalism. The first lesson in the book reads: "No man may put off the laws of God; / My joy is in his law all the day"[9]—a seemingly tame statement, yet one that presaged what for Lincoln and many other Americans would become one of the most controversial concepts of the pre–Civil War decade: the higher law, by which disobedience to human laws was deemed justified or even required if these laws were found to be in violation of God's law.

Other textbooks Lincoln read were more far-reaching than Dilworth's. For example, William Scott's *Lessons in Elocution* included literary passages such as the soliloquy of Hamlet's uncle on the murder of his brother ("Oh! My offense is rank; it smells to heaven"), which Lincoln would spontaneously recite during his presidency. Another source of memorable passages was Lindley Murray's *English Reader*, which Lincoln later called "the best school-book ever put into the hands of an American youth."[10] This encyclopedic volume contained a range of poetry and prose selections as well as speeches by Cicero, Saint Paul, and others.

Aesop's *Fables* proved a fertile source for him. The story about the strength of bundled sticks prompted Lincoln to use the image later in a political circular when encouraging his fellow Whigs to act in unison rather than separately.[11] The fable about the lion who surrenders his teeth in order to win the woodman's daughter and then is beaten to death by the woodman was cited by Lincoln when he refused to make concessions to the Confederacy that he knew would weaken the North.[12] Aesop's tale about two whites who futilely tried to rub away a black man's skin color reminded Lincoln of Northerners who coldly de-emphasized the African American as a consideration in the war.[13]

Lincoln's early reading exposed him to the core values of American democracy.

Take one of his favorite books, James Riley's *Narrative of the Loss of the American Brig Commerce*. First published in 1817, Riley's book went through twenty-four editions and enjoyed a lively sale. It was one of the last—and among the most famous—of the so-called Barbary captive narratives that had been written regularly since 1680.[14] These narratives, some fictional and others, like Riley's, based on fact, involved American or British sailors who were captured off the Barbary Coast in northern Africa, taken captive, and held in slavery by their Muslim captors.

Riley makes strong statements against American slavery. Although he portrays the Barbary masters as frequently harsh toward their white slaves, whom they call "Christian dogs," he points out the inconsistency of America, supposedly the land of equality, holding more than a million black people in slavery. While Riley expresses appreciation for "the blessings of my native land, where political and moral institutions are in themselves the very best of any that prevail in the civilized portion of the globe," he adds, "and yet, strange as it must appear to the philanthropist, my proud spirited and free countrymen still hold a million of the human species in the most cruel bonds of slavery, who are kept at hard labor and smarting under the savage lash of inhuman mercenary drivers," and enduring "the miseries of hunger, thirst, imprisonment, cold, nakedness, and even tortures."[15]

Riley's dual message—America has the world's finest political system, but its democratic ideals are betrayed by the worst form of oppression—came to be shared by Lincoln, who would famously hail his nation as "the last best hope of earth" and yet loathed slavery so much that he chose civil war over tolerating its spread.[16]

Lincoln also encountered antislavery passages in other books he read in his youth. *The Kentucky Preceptor* contains a grim story, "The Desperate Negro," about an enslaved man who slashes his own throat to avoid being whipped by his master. William Grimshaw's *History of the United States* indicts slavery as "the climax of human cupidity and turpitude" and cites the pronouncement of human equality in the Declaration of Independence—later to become Lincoln's favorite text—to predict confidently that slavery would someday be abolished in America.[17]

It is likely that the young Lincoln, weaned in an antislavery Baptist sect, already had intimations of his later antislavery interpretation of the nation's founding documents, which he appears to have read in his midteens. *The Statutes of Indiana* (1824), a law book he borrowed from his friend David Turnham, included as prefaces the Declaration of Independence, the Constitution, and the Northwest Ordinance of 1787. One of Lincoln's main achievements as a politician would be to combine the spirit of these three founding texts in a way that convincingly positioned the antislavery argument within the boundaries of the American system. Crystallizing the arguments of other antislavery politicians, he merged the concept behind the Northwest Ordinance—which forbade the extension of slavery in the Western territories north of the Ohio River—with the Declaration's pronouncement of human equality and the Constitution's protection of human rights. This antislavery constitutionalism, which he presented most persuasively in the Cooper Union Address in 1860, was grounded in his meditations on the Founders and their ideals as a teenager in Indiana.

DISCOVERING THE FOUNDERS

His interest in the Founders was fanned by *The Life of George Washington* by the Maryland-born preacher and bookseller Mason Locke Weems. In February 1861, when addressing the New Jersey Senate on a stop on his trip east to assume the presidency, he recalled that "a way back in my childhood the earliest days of my life being able to read, I got hold of a small book, . . . 'Weems's Life of Washington.' I remember all the accounts there given of the battlefields and struggles for the liberties of the country, especially 'the crossing the river' and the contest with the Hessians"[18] First published in 1800, Weems's *Washington* appeared in expanded form in 1806, containing some new "very curious anecdotes," including the apocryphal story about the cherry tree. This revised book went through many editions before Weems's death in 1825. Lincoln read the 1809 edition, with its "curious anecdotes" and its illustrative woodcuts. Lincoln could not know that Weems had made up the story about the young George confessing to his father that he was responsible for cutting down the cherry tree.

But patriotism and candor were not the only virtues Lincoln found in Weems's book; another was the kind of toughness and athletic prowess that were prized greatly in Lincoln's frontier region. Weems's Washington, tall and sturdy, is superlative at sports and fighting. He can throw a stone across the Rappahannock River below Fredericksburg— a feat rarely equaled, Weems informs us. And he is known locally as an athletic champion: "George, like a young Greek training for the Olympic Games, used to turn out with his sturdy young companions '*to see*,' as they termed it, '*which was the best man*,' at running, jumping, and wrestling"—activities they pursued into the night.[19] Lincoln, too, was known for his strength and sports skills. He could lift heavier weights, throw objects farther, and jump longer than any of his companions. He once mused about who would be the victor if he wrestled with

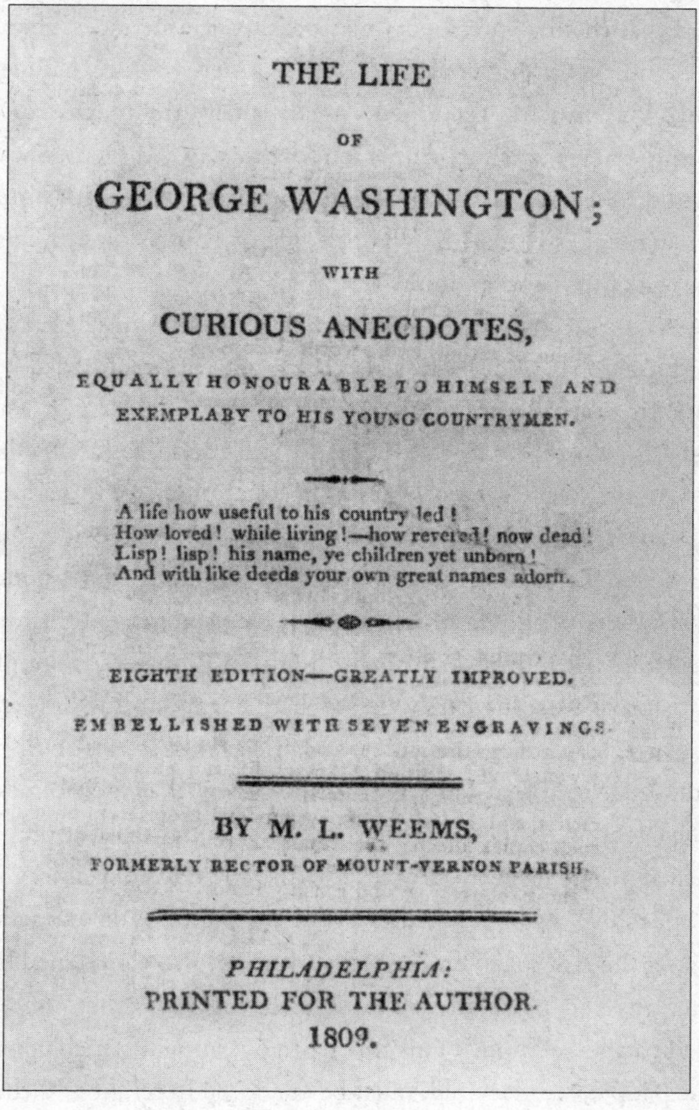

THE LIFE

OF

GEORGE WASHINGTON;

WITH

CURIOUS ANECDOTES,

EQUALLY HONOURABLE TO HIMSELF AND
EXEMPLARY TO HIS YOUNG COUNTRYMEN.

A life how useful to his country led !
How loved ! while living !—how revered ! now dead !
Lisp ! lisp ! his name, ye children yet unborn !
And with like deeds your own great names adorn.

EIGHTH EDITION—GREATLY IMPROVED.

EMBELLISHED WITH SEVEN ENGRAVINGS.

BY M. L. WEEMS,
FORMERLY RECTOR OF MOUNT-VERNON PARISH.

PHILADELPHIA:
PRINTED FOR THE AUTHOR.
1809.

Mason Locke Weems, *The Life of George Washington*

Washington. When reminded that a descendant of Washington's had reported that the first president "was perhaps the strongest man of his day. . . . And that in his youth he was a frontier wrestler, having never been thrown," Lincoln remarked, "I can outlift any man. . . . When I was young, I never was thrown." He added wryly: "If George was loafing around here now, I should be glad to have a tussle with him, and I rather believe that one of the plain people of Illinois would be able to manage the old aristocrat of old Virginia."[20]

The aristocrat of old Virginia may have been a muscleman, in the view of biographers, but he was also the model of evenhandedness—an attribute Lincoln aspired to. Another bestselling biography of Washington that Lincoln read was the 1807 book by David Ramsay, who portrayed the Founder as the epitome of equanimity. "He had religion without austerity," Ramsay wrote, "dignity without pride, modesty without diffidence, courage without rashness, politeness without affectation, affability without familiarity. . . . [He was] a lover of order, systematical and methodical."[21] Another bonus of Ramsay's biography was the inclusion of Washington's will, in which he manumitted his enslaved workers on the decease of his wife—an antislavery gesture on the part of the First American that fed into Lincoln's view that the Founders desired the eventual extinction of the South's peculiar institution.

Washington's Farewell Address was also included in Ramsay's book. In his speech, Washington emphasized the paramount importance of preserving the American union, which, he saw, was threatened by warring factions and party divisions. A unifying force that Washington appealed to was religion. "This unity of government which constitutes you one people," he declared, must be anchored in religion. Otherwise, he asked, how could oaths taken in courts or public hearings have credence? How could checks and balances work if amorality reigned? "Of all the dispositions and habits which lead to political prosperity," he said, "religion and morality are indispensable supports."

The Washington that Lincoln and his contemporaries read about did not only promote religion publicly; he observed it privately as well. Ramsay writes of the first president: "The friend of morality and religion, he steadily attended on public worship; encouraged and strengthened the hands of the clergy; and in all his public acts made the most respectful mention of Providence. In a word, he carried from private life into his public administration the spirit of piety, a dependence upon the supreme governor of the universe."

Weems's Washington is even more pious than Ramsay's. In Weems's biography, the young George is taught to believe in God by his father, who in a crucial scene teaches him that all the beautiful and useful things in the world did not come by chance but were of divine origin. It was "at that moment that the good Spirit of God ingrafted upon [George's] heart that germ of *piety*, which filled his after life with so many of the precious fruits of *morality*."[22] As president, Weems's Washington never misses church, no matter how pressing the national business is. As for the Farewell Address, that, Weems writes, was "about the length of an ordinary sermon" and "may do as much good to the people of America as any sermon ever preached, that DIVINE ONE on the mount excepted." Washington's death elicits from Weems a gush of piety even more rapturous than Harriet Beecher Stowe's description of the death of the young Eva St. Clare in *Uncle Tom's Cabin*. Washington is escorted heavenward: "Swift on angels' wings the brightening saint ascended; while voices more than human were heard (*in fancy's ear*), warbling through the happy regions, hymning the great procession, towards the gates of heaven."

Weems's and Ramsay's readers could not know what historians have discovered: Washington was not nearly as devout as many Americans of that time wanted to believe. Although he was an Episcopalian, his church attendance was irregular, and he rarely, if ever, took communion. He was extremely private about his religious views, which seem to have been closer to deism than to Christianity. On his deathbed, he did not call for a member of the clergy. It is unclear if he believed in an afterlife.[23]

But he did believe in the utility of religion as a means of fostering morality and unity in America. He saw the need of the religious spirit for supporting democratic institutions, and he did not privilege one religion or denomination over another.

In this regard, he was like another Founder with whom Lincoln was deeply familiar, Benjamin Franklin. In Indiana, the twelve-year-old Lincoln, at his father's request, reportedly read aloud to the family sections of *The Life of Dr. Benjamin Franklin, Written by Himself*, a 1793 version of Franklin's classic autobiography, which appeared in 1818 in a longer form as the multivolume *Memoirs of the Life and Writings of Benjamin Franklin*, which Lincoln also apparently read. Franklin, raised a Calvinistic Congregationalist, as a young man became a thoroughgoing deist—that is, one who puts Christianity on the same level as Islam, Judaism, and all other religions. Dismissing established churches as oppressive human inventions, deists believed in God's laws—scientific principles controlling the physical universe—as written in the Book of Nature. Reason apprehends these laws, and conscience leads humans to choose between right and wrong and follow the path of virtue. Franklin wrote a deistic pamphlet and won over two close friends to his newfound philosophy. However, he soon discovered that deism opened him up to sharp criticism, and he decided that, as he put it, "this doctrine, though it might be true, was not very useful."[24] After giving out some copies of his freethinking pamphlet, he destroyed the remaining ones and said little overtly about deism for the rest of his life.

Although Lincoln, like the Founders, was a rationalist who viewed church religion skeptically, he could look to them for moral and spiritual guidance. After all, Franklin, Jefferson, and Thomas Paine had performed good works and had founded a mighty nation. And they

BENJAMIN FRANKLIN

were religious, in their own way. Although Jefferson as president care-fully respected the separation of church and state, even he invoked "a benign religion, . . . acknowledging and adoring an overruling provi-dence" in his 1801 inaugural address, which was included in an anthol-ogy that the young Lincoln read, *The Kentucky Preceptor*.[25] And Washington, despite his guardedness about his own faith, nonetheless insisted on religion as a necessary support for democratic institutions. Lincoln, in this respect, was like Washington—secretive about his own religion, but innovative and insistent on the uses of religion in Ameri-can public life. Like a deist, he rarely took sides among religions, and his tolerance of many faiths was remarkable. For him, as for Washington, the religious spirit held the potential of stabilizing and unifying a fragmented nation.

Lincoln also resembled Franklin, who rejected the Calvinistic faith of his childhood, turned for a time to deism, and then espoused a pragmatic religion based on good deeds. In one of the rare moments that he discussed his private beliefs, Lincoln declared he would join a church if he found one whose only requirement was to follow the Golden Rule.[26] This was essentially the view of Franklin and the other Founders, who escaped the confines of a single church without abandoning religion altogether.

SELF-MAKING AND VIRTUE

Franklin, who had risen from humble beginnings to the highest realms of achievement, established in his autobiography the self-made man stereotype that by Lincoln's time had become part of the nation's cultural fabric. Franklin's autobiography stood as a how-to guide for Americans who wanted to advance, including the young Lincoln, who must have taken notice of the famous list of thirteen virtues that Franklin observed. How did Lincoln measure up to these virtues? Six of them—Moderation, Temperance, Tranquility, Humility, Sincerity, and Justice—were ones for which Lincoln undeniably deserved high marks. Franklin's statement about Moderation, "Avoid extremes," defined Lincoln more clearly than any other conceivable phrase.[27] As a Northerner from a Southern background who could claim both Puritan and, in his mind, Cavalier roots, Lincoln was by nature prepared to take a middling course that, in the end, proved to be the salvation of the nation. He could take his place securely in the center because he had a genuine understanding of both antislavery and proslavery extremists that led him to see that radical militancy could, if carried through, destroy the Union.

Industry, another of Franklin's virtues, was demonstrated in Lincoln's youth. Lincoln once said that his father taught him how to work but not how to enjoy it. The work he referred to here was manual labor—the kind of work frontiersmen and farmers did. But felling and mauling trees had a positive impact on Lincoln's career, for these frontier jobs fed the popular image of Lincoln as the Illinois Rail-splitter, which helped get him elected president. Even when he shirked manual labor in his youth, Lincoln was preparing for the future. Dennis Hanks declared, "Lincoln was lazy—a very lazy man—he was always reading—scribbling—writing—ciphering—writing poetry &., &."[28] In his account of Industry, Franklin advises, "[B]e always employed in something useful: cut off all unnecessary actions." But the activities that Hanks saw as signs of laziness were actually very useful to Lincoln in the Franklinian sense. Just as learning to read was Frederick Douglass's path to freedom and influence, so the young Lincoln's pursuit of reading, ciphering, and writing poetry lay behind his later success in redefining the nation through eloquent, well-reasoned language.[29]

His reading spurred his precocious ambitiousness. In Dilworth's *Spelling-Book* he would have read, "He that will not help himself, shall have help from nobody."[30] In Scott's *Lessons in Elocution*, he received similar counsel: "Whatever you pursue, be emulous to excel." Lincoln took such advice to heart. When he was a teenager in Indiana, a neighbor, Elizabeth Crawford, scolded him for teasing girls and asked, "What do you Expect will become of you?" She recalled his confident reply: "'Be Presdt of the US,' promptly responded Abe . . . He said that he would be Presdt of the US told my husband so often—Said it jokingly—yet with a Smack of deep Earnestness in his Eye & tone."[31] William Herndon confirmed, "He was always calculating, and always planning ahead. His ambition was a little engine that knew no rest."[32]

Lincoln's record on Franklin's virtue of Tranquility was mixed. Periodically, Lincoln erupted in anger—as a lawyer against churlish or ungrateful clients, as president against visitors who pressured him too hard for favors, and so on. What was most remarkable, however, was how he kept calm in situations that would have traumatized the average person. "Through all his life, and through all the unexpected and stirring events of the rebellion," his private secretaries Hay and Nicolay noted, "his personal manner was one of steadiness of word and act."[33] Had Lincoln been emotionally unstable, Herndon added, he "would have lost—*lost*, all, *all.*"[34] Fortunately for the nation, he was practical, patient, and cool.

Humility, another of Franklin's virtues, became one of Lincoln's signature qualities. In his first speech as a fledgling Illinois politician, as a friend recalled, the ungainly, simply attired Lincoln announced, "Gentlemen and citizens. I assume you know who I am. I am humble Abraham Lincoln."[35] Like Franklin's self-effacing Poor Richard, the roughhewn Lincoln appealed to the American masses because he seemed to be on their level.

Lincoln was also honest in the sense of Franklin, who wrote of Sincerity: "Use no hurtful deceit." Lincoln's sincerity, in a pragmatic Franklinian sense, cannot be denied. Lincoln seemed like an anomaly: a frontiersman, lawyer, and politician with an indisputable air of honesty. The Illinois attorney Samuel C. Parks, identifying as Lincoln's major trait "*integrity* in the longest sense of that term," noted, "I have often said that for a man who was for a quarter of a century *both a lawyer & a politician* he was the most honest man I ever knew."[36] And he was honest from an early age, as was testified by his stepmother, who recalled, "He never told me a lie in his life—never Evaded—never Equivocated never dodged."[37] It was no surprise that the masses came to know him as Honest Abe.

In heeding justice whenever he could, Lincoln revealed his debt to the Scottish Common Sense philosophy to which he was exposed in his youth. Having emerged from Edinburgh in the early eighteenth century and having spread to England, the Continent, and America, Scottish

Common Sense taught that every person is born with a conscience—a knowledge of the distinction between right and wrong—and that through reason and the exercise of virtue one could follow that conscience. The young Lincoln got a heavy infusion of Common Sense philosophy from his early reading, not only from Franklin but also from William Scott's *Lessons in Elocution* and Lindley Murray's *Reader*, which contain pieces by the Edinburgh thinker Hugh Blair (1718–1800) and others of the Common Sense school. A typical passage in Scott's book reads: "Let fame be regarded, but conscience much more. It is an empty joy to appear better than you are; but a great blessing to be what you ought to be."[38] Murray's book is equally insistent on the moral sense, as in this statement: "Listen with reverence to every reprehension of conscience; and preserve the most quick and accurate sensibility to right and wrong."

What was truly unusual about Lincoln was that he firmly distinguished between right and wrong without maintaining that he was following direct commands from God. He realized that the idea that God takes sides leads to narrowness and, at worst, bloodshed. It was important, in his view, for humans to believe in a Divine Being but equally important for them not to pretend to understand God's purposes.

Lincoln has often been called a fatalist—an accurate assessment, as long as we understand that he was not a pessimistic one. His was not the fatalism of, say, Jonathan Edwards, who insisted that most humans were predestined to hell—a notion Lincoln found repulsive—nor was it the gloomy determinism of later American authors, such as Frank Norris or Theodore Dreiser, who saw humans as pawns amid material forces.

Lincoln's view was more in line with the optimistic fatalism he found in Alexander Pope's "An Essay on Man," a poem that was included in his childhood anthologies and that long remained a touchstone for him. As president, Lincoln once told a British visitor that he thought "An Essay on Man" "contained all the religious instruction which it was necessary for a man to know." The president asked the visitor if they knew any wiser lines than the concluding ones of the poem's First Epistle, which Lincoln recited from memory:

> All Nature is but art, unknown to thee;
> All chance, direction, which thou canst not see;
> All discord, harmony not understood;
> All partial evil, universal good:
> And, spite of pride in erring reason's spite,
> One truth is clear, whatever is, is right.

When the visitor praised the beauty of the passage, Lincoln smiled and said, "Yes, that's a convenient line, too, that last one. You see, a man may turn it, and say, 'Well if whatever is is right, why then, whatever isn't must be Wrong.'" Lincoln laughed heartily, and his visitor joined in.[39]

Beneath the humor lay Lincoln's sober recognition that right and wrong were, after all, relative. The best one could do, he realized, was to attempt to align good works with one's sense of justice, without ever being assured that one knew God's plan. In Pope's terms, that plan was "unknown to thee," "not understood," something "thou canst not see." Nonetheless, in Pope's view, "direction," "harmony," and "universal good" were there, even though they were hidden from "erring reason."

Charity and benevolence were also well instilled in him in his youthful reading. The famous last paragraph of the Second Inaugural Address, which extends charity to all—including the widow, the orphan, and all nations—echoes the all-compassing benevolence recommended in Lindley Murray's *Reader* ("We should cherish sentiments of charity towards all men") and in William Scott's *Lessons in Elocution*: "From charitable and benevolent thoughts, the transition is unavoidable to charitable actions . . . toward nations, communities of men, and individuals," including "the dying parent and the weeping orphan."[40]

The compassion promoted in these books extended to animals as well. Scott includes a piece in which Hugh Blair writes, "Never sport with pain and distress in any of your amusements, nor treat even the meanest insect with wanton cruelty"—a sentiment Lincoln also found in Noah Webster's *Spelling Book*, which advises: "It is wrong to give needless pain even to a beast. Cruelty to the brutes shows a man has a hard heart, and if a man is unfeeling to a beast, he will not have much feeling for men."[41]

Whether from the influence of such passages or from the promptings of his own nature, Lincoln from a young age took a stand against cruelty to animals. Like most Americans of the time, he considered eating meat necessary, but he treated the animals he encountered with respect and avoided killing them for sport. His attitude toward animals—and toward nature generally—merits discussion on its own, for it powerfully influenced his politics, his language, and his philosophy.

4

The Powers of Nature

Lincoln grew up in the kind of physical and cultural environment that American thinkers often turned to for inspiration. Many easterners looked to the West for the vigor and creativity that they considered authentically American. Walt Whitman was hardly alone when he fantasized that a sturdy, western "blacksmith or boatman" would rescue America politically.[1] Emerson urged American writers to turn their eyes "westward" and take lessons from "the Kentucky stump-oratory, the exploits of Boone and David Crockett, the journals of the western pioneers, agriculturalists," which Emerson called the nation's "genuine growths."[2] Emerson's friend Thoreau, who lived for two years near Walden Pond to get close to nature, extolled the untamed vigor of the West. He wrote, "The West of which I speak is but another name for the Wild; and . . . in Wildness is the preservation of the World."[3] Later, the aristocrat-turned-outdoorsman Teddy Roosevelt formed the nationwide Boone and Crockett Club, designed to foster frontier values such as "energy, resolution, manliness, self-reliance, and a capacity for self-help"—qualities he saw in Lincoln, whom he called "my great hero."[4]

Lincoln did not have to join a club or spin fantasies about the West. Nor did he have to leave town to adopt a life in nature by building a cabin in the woods. Close to nature from the beginning, he was immersed in the Boone-Crockett culture Emerson and Roosevelt praised. Like David Crockett, Lincoln was a backwoodsman who became a Whig politician. Not only had Lincoln's ancestors befriended and intermarried with the Boones, but Daniel Boone had also played a large part in the emigration of the Lincolns from Virginia to Kentucky—an interfamily affiliation highlighted in William Thayer's 1863 book *The Pioneer Boy*, the bestselling contemporary biography of Lincoln.

Growing up on the frontier, the future president experienced American life in its crudest forms. He was not what the popular adventure writer Thomas Mayne Reid denigrated as a "closet-naturalist" (a mere spectator of nature) or what Teddy Roosevelt called a "parlor reformer" or what Lincoln himself dismissed as a "silk stocking" politician.[5] He had a vital, organic closeness to nature that formed the bedrock of his politics and his presidential policies.

HUMAN AND NONHUMAN

In September 1846, as twenty-nine-year-old Henry David Thoreau was descending Maine's Mount Katahdin after a failed attempt to reach the summit, he came upon an area so savagely beautiful that he had a virtual meltdown. He wrote: "This was that Earth of which we have heard, made out of Chaos and Old Night. . . . Man was not to be associated with it. It was Matter, vast, terrific,—. . . rocks, trees, wind on our cheeks! the *solid* earth! the *actual* world! the *common sense! Contact! Contact!*"[6] The rugged Katahdin scene, so different from what Thoreau called the "tame, cheap" landscape of his rustic town, Concord, fed his passion for the wild that lay behind his nature writing in the remaining sixteen years of his life.[7]

Lincoln's life followed an altogether different trajectory. It began with immersion in nature, later followed by town life and entry into law and politics. Lincoln did not have to experience anew contact with harsh nature, for he'd had it from the beginning. Nature-anchored philosophy led Thoreau to live deliberately outside the whirl of society, while it spurred Lincoln's efforts to change society and government. Thoreau, rebelling against mainstream American culture, rejected the technological improvements associated with capitalism; for him, they represented the intrusive "machine in the garden" that threatened to disrupt his private meditation on higher truths.[8] Politically, Thoreau believed that the principled individual was greater than the government— which explains his public championing of the vigilante abolitionist John Brown. Lincoln, in contrast, took the Whig view that the government should promote improvements such as the railroad, the telegraph, canals, and roads, which bound people together and stimulated commerce.[9] If a deep awareness of nature ushered Thoreau toward self-absorbed philosophizing, it prompted Lincoln to seek ways to control nature's powers and put them to practical use.

One of Lincoln's earliest recollections was of the power of nature. Although his native Kentucky wasn't the "howling wilderness" that Daniel Boone had encountered on his first exploratory trip in 1769, it was still developing when Lincoln lived there.[10] Most Kentuckians were farmers and hunters, and many of them lived in log cabins and got by on barter or subsistence living.

He had no memories of the birthplace farm, which his family left when he was two, but he did recall Knob Creek, where he worked as a boy on the three fields that had been cleared for farming. One day he helped out by placing pumpkin seeds on small mounds while others planted corn. A few days later, a hard rain in the surrounding hills caused the fields to flood, washing away the seeds. Vibrant matter, in the form of an unexpected flood, squelched human effort, teaching the young Abe a lesson about nature he would not forget.

Even more vivid exposure to untamed nature came when the family moved to Indiana. Nearly as large as Kentucky, Indiana was far more sparsely settled; in 1821 its population was only 147,178, compared to Kentucky's 564,317.[11] Southern Indiana was truly a frontier—"a wild region," as Lincoln recalled it, "with many bears and other wild animals still in the woods."[12] A diarist wrote, "Indiana is a vast forest just penetrated in places by backwoods settlers who are half hunters, half farmers."[13] Countless varieties of trees, some of them enormous, covered the land, their branches and tops often enveloped in lush, serpentine vines. The undergrowth was so thick that "a man Could scarcely git through on foot," a Lincoln neighbor wrote; Dennis Hanks reported the brush was matted together so tightly that "as the old Saying gowes [*sic*] you could Drive a Butcher Knife up to the Handle in it."[14] Swarms of insects—mosquitoes, black flies, and poisonous yellow flies—filled the air, as did many kinds of birds, notably clouds of pigeons that darkened the sky when they flew overhead.[15] The region was alive with animals: wildcats, panthers, bears, raccoons, grouse, and wild turkeys.

In February 1817, just before Abe turned eight, a flock of wild turkeys approached the cabin while Thomas was away. Spotting the fowls, Abe seized his father's rifle, pointed it through a crack in the wall, and fired, killing one of the turkeys. A terrible feeling overcame him at what struck him as a senseless murder of a living being. As he later reported through a campaign biographer, "He has never since pulled a trigger on any larger game."[16]

This simple statement opens vistas on Lincoln that are appreciated only when we consider its cultural contexts. Abe's animus against hunting placed him among a small group of environmentally conscious Americans who recoiled from the killing of animals. The animal that aroused Abe's emotion was of central interest to his contemporary John James Audubon, a progenitor of environmental awareness. Audubon praised "the great size and beauty of the wild turkey," which he called "one of the most interesting of the birds indigenous to the United States of America."[17] Audubon's esteem for the bird led him to feature his painting of the wild turkey as Plate I in his landmark volume *Birds of America*.

At the time Abe killed the bird, the Haitian-born Audubon lived in Henderson, Kentucky, forty miles from Pigeon Creek. Audubon can be credited with preserving in art hundreds of birds, six of them now extinct, including two breeds then common in Indiana, the passenger pigeon and the Carolina parakeet. Unlike Abe, however, Audubon had no qualms about killing birds, no matter how beautiful. Hunting aided his ornithology; he killed birds to examine them. Here he differed not only from Lincoln but also from Thoreau, who abandoned the killing of animals because of his growing sympathy for them. Thoreau admitted that for a while he killed "new and rare birds" in order to analyze them, but he gave up the practice. And as he explains in *Walden*, "I am now inclined to think that there is a finer way of studying ornithology than this. It requires so much closer attention to the habits of the birds that, if for that reason only, I have been willing to omit the gun."[18] There was a more basic reason Thoreau dropped the gun. "To be serene and successful we must be at one with the universe," he noted. "The least conscious and needless injury inflicted on any creature is to its extent a suicide. What peace—or life—can a murderer have?"[19]

Remarkably, Lincoln felt this way at seven. He was a skilled marksman, and he sometimes joined family members on hunts for raccoons, deer, or other animals. But he did not hunt enthusiastically. Here he differed from his father, who found "no small amusement and pleasure" in killing all kinds of game, which the family needed for food, skins, and material for barter.[20] He also differed from most American boys, for whom hunting was a popular pastime.[21] Dennis Hanks recalled, "We all hunted pretty much all the time," with the exception of Abe.[22] He "was not so fond of the gun or the sport as I was," said an Indiana neighbor.

Lincoln's reluctance to hunt was especially remarkable in his frontier environment. From Daniel Boone onward, frontiersmen were literally defined by the rifle. Hunting was more than a sport, more even than a source of food or a tool of survival—it was integral to frontier manhood. This remained true right up to the late 1880s, when Teddy

Roosevelt formed the Boone and Crockett Club "to promote manly sport with a rifle."[23] The club's constitution stipulated that "No one shall be eligible for membership who shall not have killed with a rifle in fair chase . . . at least one individual of one of the various kinds of American large game."

Lincoln disliked hunting because, like Thoreau, he felt a kinship with animals. He often bore sad witness to the cruel treatment of animals. One of the most popular activities at frontier events like logrolling and militia musters was the gander pull, a blood sport in which galloping horsemen tried to seize and pull off the greased head of a suspended live goose. Whoever tore off the head received a small prize, usually the goose for cooking. Another source of entertainment was burning small animals alive. Men would "round up a chip-munk, a rabbit, or a snake, and make him take refuge in a burning log-heap and watch him squirm and fry."[24]

During his Indiana years, Abe intervened a number of times when he witnessed friends inflicting tortures such as pouring live coals on the backs of turtles or poking toads with sharp sticks. His stepsister Matilda Johnston recalled an incident when her brother John caught a turtle and "brought it to the place where Abe was preaching—threw it against the tree—crushed the shell and it suffered much—quivered all over—Abe preached against cruelty to animals, contending that an ant[']s life was to it, as sweet as ours to us."[25] This proanimal declaration was one of several times that Abe spoke out on the topic in his youth. At both Swaney's and Dorsey's schools, he composed "short sentences against cruelty to animals" and "essays on being kind to animals and crawling insects."

He did not go as far as some, then and now, who oppose all killing of animals. He ate meat, and parts of his clothing were made of animal skins. In the mid-1820s, he worked for a time butchering hogs. He wielded the club and assisted in dumping the hogs' carcasses in scalding water and scraping off the bristles. But he never lost his sympathy for animals. Ward Hill Lamon explained that Abe "could not endure to witness the needless suffering even of a brute."[26] Joshua Speed summed up Lincoln's empathetic nature when he generalized that "Lincoln had the tenderest heart for anyone in distress, whether man, beast, or bird."[27]

Abe knew the power of nonhuman forces well. In his youth he twice almost lost his life to them. As a seven-year-old in Kentucky, he and a friend, Austin Gollaher, tried to cross a stream by walking on a narrow log. Austin safely crossed, but Abe lost his footing and fell into the water, which was seven or eight feet deep. Neither boy could swim. Abe floundered in the water until Austin managed to pull him out with a long stick. Austin later recalled, Abe was "almost dead. I got him by the arms and shook him well, and then rolled him on the ground, when the water poured out of his mouth."[28]

Another near-death experience caused by a nonhuman power came three years later, when Abe was a ten-year-old in Indiana. One day he rode to a mill two miles away from the family cabin, carrying a sack of corn to be ground into meal. He had to wait in line to do his work, and it was sundown before his turn came to attach his mare to the rotating beam that drove the grindstone. As the horse walked round and round, Abe whipped it, crying, "Get up—you lazy old divil."[29] He did this a number of times before the horse, irritated by the goading, kicked Abe in the forehead. Abe had just said, "Get up" before he was knocked out by the horse's hoof. Abe was taken home, where he lay unconscious until early the next morning, when he awoke and finished his command: "you lazy old divil." In his many retellings of this story, Abe attributed his completion of the spoken command to physical forces. He told William Herndon that he believed "that the mental energy— forces had been flash[e]d by the will on the nerves & thence on the muscles; and that that [sic] the energy—force or power had *fixed* the muscles in the exact shape . . . to utter those words" automatically.

The nonhuman affected Abe strongly not only in such dramatic episodes but at every turn on the frontier. When he was young, his father made him and his sister toys made out of corncobs, twigs, and corn silk. His clothing consisted of animal hides—buckskin pants and a coonskin cap—and a rough linsey-woolsey shirt. His chores and jobs brought him into direct contact with nature. He cut and sold firewood to steamboats on the Ohio River, served as a ferryman by rowing a boat back and forth across the hundred-foot mouth of Anderson Creek, plowed, killed hogs, made fences, and took two trips hauling goods by flatboat down the Mississippi to New Orleans—the kind of extended experience in river life that Mark Twain would immortalize in *Life on the Mississippi* and *The Adventures of Huckleberry Finn.*

Payments for goods or services on the frontier were often made by barter. Legal mediums of exchange included corn, wheat, whiskey, wool, hogs, venison, coonskins, or other natural items. Preachers were paid by whiskey, corn, or smoked meat.[30] For example, when Thomas Lincoln contributed to his Baptist church, he gave corn, not cash, as indicated in the church records: "Thomas Lincoln, white corn, manufactured pounds 24."[31] One could improvise exchanges, as Abe did when he traded a cord of wood for fine cloth from which he "had a shirt made, and it was positively the first white shirt . . . which he had ever owned or worn."[32]

Abe wrote with a pen made of turkey buzzard feathers, using pokeberry ink.[33] When he had no paper, he wrote on walls, fences, or floors. He was so eager to learn that, as a neighbor said, he wrote words and sentences "with charcoal, he scoured them in the dust, in the sand, in the snow—anywhere and everywhere the lines could be drawn."[34]

Given his interest in words and his closeness to the nonhuman world, it's understandable that he would create stories or jokes that brought together people and animals, the human and the nonhuman. He spent so much time spinning yarns and telling jokes—from his Indiana youth to his many years on the Illinois law circuit through his two terms as president—that storytelling and humor stand out as preferred modes of public communication for him.

He frequently used nonhuman images. At different times, he compared political opponents to ticks, a dog, a lost pig, and a corncob. He was just as likely to use nonhuman images on allies as on opponents. When someone advised him to dismiss all seven members of his cabinet, he said he was reminded of a western farmer who, trying to get rid of skunks on his property, laid a trap and caught a skunk that made "such an infernal stench that he thought he had better let the rest go."[35] Aware that his treasury secretary Salmon Chase was scheming to run against him for the presidency, Lincoln laughed and said, "I suppose he will, like the bluebottle fly, lay his eggs in every rotten spot he can find."[36]

He often compared his generals to animals. Battlefield commanders were like bulls crowding a farm, and sending more and more troops to demanding generals like George McClellan was like "shoveling fleas across a barn floor—half of them never get there."[37] In another of Lincoln's jokes, the timid McClellan was a scared rooster who fled a cockfight. [38] Praising the toughness of his two greatest generals, Lincoln declared, "Grant has the bear by the hind leg, while Sherman takes off the hide."[39]

Lincoln even applied nonhuman imagery to himself. After the defeat at Chickamauga he confessed that he felt "confused and stunned like a duck hit on the head."[40] A joke that he used on himself and others involved chickens whose legs were tied so often to a wagon when they were transported that whenever the birds saw wagon sheets, they turned over and held up their legs for tying. He said he felt like that when he was inundated by requests or advice from visitors; if he listened to everyone, he said, "I had just as well cross my hands and let you tie me."[41]

RING-TAILED ROARERS
AND FEMALE SCREAMERS

Lincoln understood American humor well, especially one of the most popular genres, frontier humor. Besides hearing this humor delivered orally on the frontier, he read comic almanacs, jest books, humorous newspaper columns, and anthologies of humor. He told the journalist Noah Brooks that "the grim grotesqueness and extravagance of American humor were its most striking characteristic."[42] Indeed, from the appearance of James Kirke Paulding's fictional *Letters from the South* (1817) and Paulding's long-running play *The Lion of the West* (1831) to the magazine tales about the boatman Mike Fink (introduced to readers in 1828) through the immensely popular Davy Crockett almanacs (1835–56) and William T. Porter's humor columns in *The Spirit of the Times* (1831–61), Americans feasted on backwoods humor of the most violent, bizarre variety.

This humor was, in effect, the American frontier on steroids. Lying, bragging, rough-and-tumble fighting, and all the rest were taken to sensational extremes. A common narrative thread in the popular stories, the fight scene, was based on a pattern that Lincoln witnessed often at the frontier events he attended.[43] Many of these fictional scenes involved two or more muscular frontiersmen, fired up by alcohol, who get into a bragging match about who is the best man; the boasting escalates into a rough-and-tumble fight that ends in a maiming, with the victor gaining the respect of spectators and the defeated combatant. Sometimes women fighters were involved, as in the memorably titled piece "A Desperate Fight Between Two Women, One Man, and Two Bears" (the women save the man by killing the bears with an axe and boiling syrup).[44]

References to scalping, blood drinking, and cannibalism abounded in the popular humor. Gouging out eyes became a source of mass entertainment, especially in the Crockett almanacs, where screamers—wild, boastful men and women of the frontier—collect eyeballs. In one episode, a man courts a woman by giving her two eyeballs he has gouged out; she dries them and wears them as earrings to church. In another story, a female screamer dons a long necklace of eyeballs she has won in her rough-and-tumbles with women. Not only are the screamers sadistic and bloodthirsty, they are superhuman: Crockett, finding the earth

A typical Crockett almanac

and sun frozen in place, kills a huge bear and squeezes its blood over the sun and the world's axis, freeing up both.

The language of this humor combines the human and the nonhuman: frontier screamers, also known as ring-tailed roarers, advertise themselves as "half-horse, half alligator, part earth-quake, and a little of the steamboat."[45] In one exchange, a screamer declares: "I can whip my weight in wild cats and ride straight through a crab apple orchard on a flash of lightning. Clear meat-ax disposition!"—answered by, "I can tote a steam boat up the Mississippi and over the Alleghany mountains. My father can whip the best man in Old Kaintuck and I can whip my father."[46] A female screamer can "laugh the bark off a pine tree, swim straight up a cataract, gouge out alligators' eyes, dance a rock to pieces, sink a steamboat, blow out the moonlight . . ."[47]

Both the negative and positive aspects of the frontier are taken to weird extremes in this humor. The self-reliance and courage of the frontiersman becomes the unleashed braggadocio of the ring-tailed roarer. Closeness to nature becomes a complete merging of the human and nonhuman: a man or a woman is simultaneously a horse, a meat-axe, an alligator, a rooster, a streak of lightning, sired by a hurricane or an earthquake.

Lincoln, who knew his era's culture from top to bottom, tapped into the kind of bawdy or scatological humor that was common on the frontier. He was sometimes called a "smutty" or "dirty" jokester, a label he didn't reject. Once when someone suggested that he collect his humor in a volume, he held his nose and said, "Such a book would stink like a thousand privies."[48] A friend said, "Lincoln had 2 characters—one of *purity*—& the other as it were an insane love in telling dirty and Smutty Stories."[49]

Because only a fraction of his jokes have survived, it's impossible to say how many of them were coarse. But the ones that have been passed down appear to be relatively tame by current standards. He told a story about a sleepy boy who went to bed, his cat curling up beside him, when his fawning mother begged him to come show her house guests what a "fine, pretty and moral boy" he was. The boy growled, "Mother— damn it—let me alone till I f—k this damned old she cat and get her with kitten."[50] Another of Lincoln's favorite jokes had him climbing a tree while a friend fell asleep below; for fun, Abe defecated into what he thought was his friend's hat on the ground, not knowing that the friend had put Abe's hat in its place.[51] In another tale, Lincoln put a patriotic spin on scatology: he said that after the Revolutionary War, when the American hero Ethan Allen was visiting England, he used an outhouse and was asked by his hosts if he had seen the picture of George Washington they had hung there in mockery. Allen replied that he had not seen it but thought it was an appropriate place for the picture, because "nothing . . . Will Make an Englishman Shit So quick as the Sight of Genl Washington."[52] Lincoln also loved telling the story of a man who, while cutting a turkey at a dinner party, "expended too much force and let a fart—a loud fart so that all the people heard it distinctly." The company fell silent, but the man bravely went on with his task, announcing, "Now by God I'll see if I can't cut up this turkey without farting."[53]

Herndon noted that Lincoln told the latter story "to show the power of audacity, self-possession, quick-wittedness, etc.," explaining that "the nib of the thing was what Lincoln was after."[54] Like the often vulgar frontier humor Lincoln knew well, his dirty jokes flouted the prudish conventions of bourgeois society. There were important differences, however, between Lincoln's storytelling and frontier humor. None of his extant stories possess the structurelessness of frontier humor. Mark Twain once called the tall tale—the frontier exercise in hyperbole and lies rendered in a disconnected, rambling fashion—the one truly indigenous form of American humor.[55] A typical hero of frontier humor, George Washington Harris's Sut Lovingood, boasts, "I ladles out my words at random like a calf kicking at yaller jackets," while another one, Joseph Glover Baldwin's Ovid Bolus, endlessly "lied from a delight of invention and the charm of fictitious narrative."[56]

Lincoln used images from frontier humor and other sources—so much so that he called himself "a retail dealer," explaining that only about one out of six of his stories were original with him.[57] Despite this heavy debt to popular sources, he *was* original as a storyteller. He did not string together directionless exaggerations, as did authors of tall tales. In most of his stories, he replaced disconnection with structure, obfuscation with meaning, and a message based on aggression with one envisioning democratic togetherness and human equality.

Whereas tall tales rambled without reaching a climax, Lincoln's stories, even when lewd, were typically brief and purposeful. As his secretary John Nicolay said, "They were always short. Lincoln's worst enemy never accused him of telling a long story. And they never lacked point . . .—told not for themselves alone, but in illustration of some point he saw and wished to make clear to others."[58] Actually, he sometimes intentionally dragged out stories to stall for time or divert attention, but he kept their message in mind. Lincoln's friend David Davis testified, "He used them for a purpose, and learned to use them because he could accomplish in a few minutes by one of his inimitable stories what would have exhausted hours to clear away by argumentative appliances."[59] William Herndon pointed out that "he loved a story however extravagant or vulgar, if it had a good point. . . . [I]f it exposed no weakness or pointed no moral, he had no use for it either in conversation or in public speech; but if it had the necessary ingredients of mirth and moral no one could use it with more telling effect."[60]

THE FRONTIER CARNIVAL

By the mid-1820s, Abe was eager to move beyond the raw life of the Indiana frontier, but he could not go out on his own without reaching the legal age of twenty-one. Meanwhile, he learned much from frontier culture, which was crude and chaotic.

Lincoln was raised in what has been called a carnival culture: a folk society, aligned with nature's rhythms, that brought together the high and the low, the sacred and the profane, the conventional and the subversive. Gatherings at frontier militia musters, elections, revivals, and court days were extraordinarily varied and cacophonous. Mingled together were prostitutes and maidens, gamblers and preachers, peddlers of fake and real products, all engaged in some kind of pitch, con, sport, or fight.[61] This was the frontier carnival: the rawest expression of American democracy.

Lincoln knew the carnival well. As a youth he participated in logrollings, cornhuskings, weddings, court days, elections, house-raisings, dances, and other frontier events. Logrolling referred to the communal gathering and burning of logs a settler had cleared from the land, house-raising to the construction of a cabin with the aid of neighbors, house-warming to the party held in a house once it was built, cornhusking to the stripping of corn by competing groups. Most of these activities took place between the late fall and the spring. Several lasted for days. A house-raising could involve three days' work by thirty neighbors. Elections typically stretched out over three days. At weddings, the marriage service was followed by all-night dancing and, within the next couple of days, by a party at the groom's house known as the infare. There was also the frontier custom of the delayed funeral, whereby a funeral service was deferred until long after burial (sometimes up to a year) to allow for a "decent" time for grieving.

These and other frontier festivities were attended by people of all classes. Farmers and manual laborers mixed with judges, doctors, lawyers, clergymen, and teachers. Not only were these events democratizing; they fostered a sense of cultural unity, too. Hospitality on the American frontier—both to neighbors and to complete strangers—became legendary. Mutual aid, enlivened by festivities and games, was a way of life.

All kinds of games and competitions took place at social events. Abe was almost always welcome there, as his strength was considered valuable in competition: "Whenever he appeared at logrollings, a joyous whoop went up, for his great strength was an asset to any team. . . . The team which enrolled Abe Lincoln usually defeated the other."[62]

The negative side of these social activities was that they regularly involved drunkenness and violence. Liquor flowed freely. As Lincoln later recalled, "[T]o have a rolling or a raising, a husking or a hoe-down, any where without [alcohol] was *positively insufferable*."[63] It was considered bad manners not to offer liquor and just as impolite to refuse it. At elections, ten-gallon barrels of whiskey, positioned near polling booths, were provided by candidates.

Then there were the fights. Friendly games often deteriorated into fights so savage that today's extreme fighting, with combatants punching and kicking each other in cages, seems tame by comparison. The only restraint on the frontier was that if an opponent cried "Enough!" the fight was over; other than that, there were few rules. A foreign visitor touring the Midwest observed that combatants "tear one another's hair, bite off noses and ears, gouge out eyes, and, in short, endeavor to destroy or mutilate each other."[64] The western traveler Timothy Flint met many one-eyed people in "the region of gouging," his name for the frontier, where, in his words, "Fights are characterized by the most savage ferocity. Gouging, or putting out the antagonist's eyes by thrusting the thumbs into the sockets, is part of the *modus operandi*. . . . Kicking and biting are also ordinary means used in combat; I have seen several fingers that had been deformed, also several noses and ears, which have been mutilated, by this canine form of fighting."[65] Victors gained the respect and friendship of both their opponents and the community. Flint, for example, saw "a tall, profane, barbarous, and ruffian like looking man" who was "emphatically pronounced the 'best' man in the settlement" because he had "whipped" all the rest and had gouged out the most eyes.[66] A diarist in Kentucky reported that "all the country round stood in awe" of a fighter who "was so dexterous in these matters that he had, in his time, taken out five eyes, bit off two or three noses and ears and spit them in the faces" of his opponents.[67]

How did Lincoln fit in with this raucous frontier culture? This was his natural element, said some, such as an acquaintance who said that "the young Lincoln of Pigeon Creek, like all his Indiana cronies, was pretty much of a rowdy," and another who called him "nothing more than a wild *harum scarum boy*, and jumping and wrestling were his only accomplishments."[68]

Jumping, wrestling, and other sports, yes; rowdy or harum-scarum activity, probably not. As well suited to the frontier carnival as Abe was, he was actually very different from most of its participants. Because he drank only moderately, drunkenness was not an issue for him. As for strength contests and rough-and-tumble fighting, he thrived on the former but shunned the latter.

He avoided fights when he could and, like his father, fended them off with a show of unusual toughness when he couldn't. An example from the Indiana years was when Abe had a spat with his Pigeon Creek neighbor William Grigsby. The date and cause of the conflict are disputed—some say it occurred in 1826 over the ownership of a puppy; others date it three years later, caused by bad feelings over the "Chronicles of Reuben," Abe's satirical poem about the Grigsby family. William Grigsby challenged Abe, who refused the challenge, explaining that the fight would be unfair due to Abe's greater strength and size. In his place, Abe offered his stepbrother John D. Johnston. In most versions of the story, Johnston was getting the worst of the fight when Abe stepped in, grabbed Grigsby, tossed him aside, and then confronted a crowd of Grigsby's supporters who were present, announcing that he was "the big buck of the lick," adding, "If any one doubts it, he has only to come on and whet his horns." There was some scuffling, but no one wanted to tangle with the tall, powerful Abe, and the crowd dispersed.[69]

We see Abe's unusual response to frontier culture when we look at his two trips by flatboat to New Orleans.[70] The trips, the first beginning in Rockport, Indiana, in April 1828 and the second in New Salem, Illinois, in March 1831, occurred when rivers were swollen due to post-winter melt and spring rains—a customary time to transport northern produce for sale or barter in the slave states. Abe made his first 1,276-mile journey with Allen Gentry (the son of a local storekeeper) and the second 1,627-mile one with his stepbrother John, his second cousin John Hanks, and the businessman Denton Offutt. Abe helped build the flatboats—the first measuring fifteen feet by forty feet, the second, eighteen feet by fifty feet, each navigated with long oars called sweeps and a rear rudder—which were dismantled and sold as lumber in New Orleans before the return trip north by steamboat. The trips south took three to four weeks, the return trips about two weeks.

Vast stretches of wilderness interspersed with river towns—among them Memphis, Walnut Hills (Vicksburg), Natchez, Fort Adams, Baton Rouge, Donaldsonville, and Convent—made the trips both an extended frontier journey and a southern tour culminating in the cosmopolitan experience of New Orleans, with its creole population of French, Spanish, and Germans mingled with numerous free and enslaved blacks, the latter visible everywhere—at the pier, on the streets, and in auction houses.

Did Abe have a life-altering revelation about the horrors of slavery in New Orleans? That dramatic story, once common in Lincoln biographies, has been modified in recent times due to fragmentary evidence. On the first trip, Abe allegedly told Allen Gentry upon seeing an enslaved girl being examined on the auction block, "Allen, that's a disgrace."[71] On the second trip, John Hanks recalled, "[W]e Saw Negroes Chained—maltreated—whipt & scourged. Lincoln Saw it—his heart bled— . . . I Can say Knowingly that it was on this trip that he formed his opinions of Slavery: it ran its iron in him then & there—. . . . I have heard him say—often & often."[72] Lincoln, though, recalled that Hanks didn't make it to New Orleans, having returned home from St. Louis. But whether or not Hanks or Lincoln misremembered details of the trip, William Herndon also reported that Lincoln talked of witnessing slavery in New Orleans. This certainly makes sense, given the inescapable presence of the South's peculiar institution in that city.

However, it is doubtful that the trip south reshaped Lincoln's opinions on slavery. Lincoln's statement that he hated slavery as long as he could remember takes us back long before New Orleans, to his earliest childhood years in Kentucky, where he probably witnessed slavery firsthand and heard it denounced in the pulpit. At any rate, it's difficult to identify a transformative moment in Abe's feelings about slavery, which seem to have been negative from the start. As Leonard Swett noted: "He believed from the first, I think, that the agitation of Slavery would produce its overthrow, and he acted upon the result as though it was present from the beginning."[73]

Actually, what may be the most striking aspect of the New Orleans trips is how *little* they changed Abe, who returned from the trips as resistant to the excesses of frontier life as when he'd embarked on them. As in his quarrel with Grigsby, he used toughness to escape, rather than engage in, a fight. One night when he and Allen Gentry were tied up below Baton Rouge, they were assaulted by club-wielding blacks. As Lincoln related the incident in his third-person account to a biographer, he and Gentry "were attacked by seven negroes with intent to kill and rob them. They were hurt some in the melee, but succeeded in driving the negroes from the boat, and then 'cut cable,' 'weighed anchor' and left."[74] This brief recollection played down an extremely violent episode, one that left Abe with scars above his right eye and left ear. It says much about Abe's fighting skills that he and Allen drove away seven attackers, even if we accept the story that the blacks were frightened off by Allen's call for Abe to fetch the guns on board. Also notable is the fact that evidently there was no follow-up to the fight, no effort on Abe's part to go to the local authorities or to wreak vengeance on his attackers. Violence or vindictiveness did not come naturally to him.

Nor did the ways of the riverboat men, who were, by and large, caricatures of crude frontiersmen. The phrase "half horse, half alligator" was first used around 1808 by western travelers in reference to Mississippi boatmen, whom Mark Twain described as "rough and hardy men; rude, uneducated, brave, . . . heavy drinkers, coarse frolickers in moral sties like the Natchez-under-the-hill of that day, heavy fighters, reckless fellows, every one, elephantinely jolly, foul-witted, profane, prodigal of their money, bankrupt at the end of the trip, fond of barbaric finery, prodigious braggarts."[75]

Abe shared none of these qualities, except bravery and hardiness. He was light-years distant from the archetypal riverboat man, Mike Fink. Born in 1770 in Pittsburgh, Fink moved steadily westward, eventually settling near St. Louis, Missouri. He spent three decades hauling goods on flatboats on the Ohio and the Mississippi Rivers. Like Daniel Boone and Davy Crockett, he was an expert marksman—so skilled that he was supposedly banned from some frontier shooting contests. He was also a legendary braggart, brawler, and drunkard; he died in a gun fray in 1823, a lonely alcoholic. Oral folk myths blossomed around him, and in 1828, the year of Abe's first New Orleans trip, Fink appeared in print in Morgan Neville's story "The Last of the Boatmen." Soon he was famous in popular culture as a fictional ring-tailed roarer, spouting bizarre boasts and racist rants. Scores of tales about him were published, featuring passages like this one in Emerson Bennett's 1848 novel *Mike Fink*:

> Hurray for me, you scapegoats! I'm a land-screamer—I'm a water-dog—I'm a snapping turkle—I can lick five times my own weight in wild-cats. I can use up Injens by the cord. I can swallow niggers whole, raw, or cooked. I can out-run, out-dance, out-jump, out-dive, out-drink, out-holler, and out-lick any white thing in the shape o' human that's ever put foot

within two thousand miles o' the big Massassip! Whoop! Holler you varmints! Holler for the Snapping Turkle![76]

In light of such extravagance, Lincoln during his trips down the Mississippi may be said to have defined himself *against* the image of the boisterous riverboat man. After his first trip, which earned him eight dollars a month—wages that he probably turned over to his father—he returned to menial work in Indiana.

But his mind was set on improvement, starting with *self*-improvement. The subsistence living and menial jobs that constituted a large part of his Indiana experience did not allow him to improve. He told Elizabeth Crawford, "I don't always intend to delve, grub, shuck corn, split rails, and the like."[77] His friend Joseph Gentry similarly recalled that he "often told me he never intended to make his living that way—he often said he would get some profession, in fact his whole mind seemed bent on learning and education."[78]

Driven by an interest in social issues, he felt the impulse to write. In the late 1820s he showed new pieces to his Indiana friend William Wood, who proved responsive to them. One of Abe's political essays, on the necessity of preserving the American Union and respecting the Constitution, so impressed Wood that he showed it to a local judge, John Pitcher, who declared that "the world couldn't beat it" and who reportedly had the essay published in a newspaper.[79] Another of Abe's compositions, on temperance, also won favor with Wood, who showed it to a Baptist preacher, Aaron Farmer, who sent it to an Ohio paper that printed it. Wood recalled, "I saw the printed piece—read it with pleasure over and over again." Abe also wrote a lot of poetry, Wood reported. One poem that stood out in Wood's mind was "The Neighborhood Broil."

Although these writings haven't survived, their topics tell us about Abe's mind-set in the late 1820s. His mind was reaching well beyond the confines of southern Indiana, which seemed increasingly provincial to him. The two pieces on temperance and a local fight suggest his effort to assert literary control, through prose and poetry, over two of the wilder aspects of frontier culture: excessive drinking and rough-and-tumble fighting.

We've seen the forces he faced on the Indiana frontier. He would soon confront similar ones—and numerous others—in Illinois, where he moved when he was twenty-one. There he found himself cast into a dialectic of occasionally losing control of such forces and then struggling to regain it.

Several factors contributed to the move to Illinois in 1830. John Hanks and his family had moved there two years earlier and had written glowing letters about the fertility of the soil there. In the fall of 1829, milk sickness struck the Pigeon Creek region, and Dennis Hanks wanted to leave before the illness affected his family, which consisted of his wife, Elizabeth Johnston Hanks (Abe's stepsister), and their four children. The Pigeon Creek cabin was cramped and crowded, and Abe had joined his father in cutting lumber in preparation to build a new home. But the plans quickly changed because his stepmother wanted to stay close to her daughter Elizabeth, Dennis's wife, and her other daughter, Matilda, who was also moving with her husband, Squire Hall, to Illinois. And so the whole clan prepared to make the 225-mile move to Macon County in central Illinois. Thomas Lincoln sold his land and livestock, and his wife sold a parcel of land she still owned in Elizabethtown, Kentucky. They both received letters of dismissal from the Pigeon Creek Baptist church, providing them with church records they could use in Illinois.

In March 1830, the Lincoln, Johnston, and Hanks families—thirteen people, including eight adults and five children—traveled northwest for two weeks over roads that were nearly impassable due to the spring thaw. They rode in wagons—probably three of them, the Lincoln wagon pulled by oxen and the other two by horses.[80] They arrived at Decatur,

Illinois, a two-street town then just nine months old consisting of ten or twelve cabins and an unfinished courthouse. From there they proceeded about ten miles west to a plot on a knoll above the north bank of the Sangamon River that John Hanks had staked out for them. John, the twenty-one-year-old Abe, and others cleared fifteen acres of land and fenced it with rails they cut from the lumber they felled. (These rails, or ones like them, were key props at the Republican nominating convention in May 1860, when John Hanks thrilled the crowd by carrying them onstage in support of the Illinois Rail-splitter's candidacy.)

After the land was cleared and a cabin, barn, and smokehouse were built, Abe lived there with his father, stepmother, and stepbrother for a year, beginning in late March 1830. He spent the summer and fall working for Macon County farmers, raising crops, driving teams, breaking prairie, reaping, and splitting rails. He and John Hanks chopped hundreds of cords of wood and made thousands of fence rails that they sold in Macon and Sangamon Counties, dividing the proceeds equally.

December brought what became a landmark event in Illinois history: the winter of the deep snow. Settlers in the region marked important dates in their lives by the winter. Those born before it were called Snow Birds; some of them wore memorial badges.[81] Sleet began to fall on December 20 and turned to a soft snow on Christmas Eve that left half a foot, making for a pleasant holiday. Ten days later, a roaring blizzard arrived, bringing blinding snow and frigid cold. Frequent storms and high winds swept Illinois for the next sixty days. Temperatures stayed below freezing for much of the time and hovered below zero for at least two weeks. Snow levels in many areas rose as high as six feet, with drifts reaching twenty feet. Intermittent sleet storms created a treacherous coating of ice. The weather, as Eleanor Atkinson describes it, was "a wonder at first, and then a terror, a benumbing horror, as it became a menace to life of men and animals. . . . It was beyond human power to do more than keep at bay the twin specters of cold and starvation."[82] Livestock stranded in the fields froze to death, and humans hunkered down in their cabins. Those who ventured out risked their lives, including Abe.

In February 1831, he set out for the cabin of William Warnick, the sheriff of Macon County for whom he split rails. While crossing the Sangamon River, Abe fell through the ice.[83] The shallowness of the river at that point saved him from drowning, but his feet became badly frost-bitten as he trudged through deep snow two miles to the Warnick place. With the aid of home remedies applied by Mrs. Warnick, he slowly recovered, but he had to remain with the Warnicks for three weeks. The upside of the incident was that he spent much of his time reading an Illinois statute book owned by Warnick that helped stimulate his interest in the law.

Late in the winter, Abe and John Hanks were hired by Denton Offutt to build a flatboat so that the three of them could take produce—pork, corn, and so on—downriver to New Orleans. The first leg of the journey took them on the Sangamon River to the small Illinois town of New Salem. Riding the flatboat on water produced by melt from the snow made Lincoln feel like "a piece of floating driftwood," a phrase he often used to describe his first arrival in New Salem, where he would spend the next six years of his life.[84]

Upon their departure from New Salem, the boat got stuck on a mill-dam, and Lincoln had to use some ingenuity to free it. He fetched an augur from a cooper in New Salem, drilled a small hole in the boat's bow to release water that had accumulated there, and transferred some cargo to another craft. The lightened craft made it over the dam. Denton Offutt was so impressed by Abe's abilities that he offered the young man a job at his New Salem store upon their return from the South.

That job, it turned out, was long in coming. Upon their return from New Orleans in June, Offutt and Lincoln would have to wait months for the arrival of goods that were to be sold in the store. In the meantime, Abe served as an election clerk in the area.

He spent the month of July 1831 staying in the family home in Coles

County, in southeastern Illinois, where his father now lived. During the visit, Abe had another memorable fight. Daniel Needham, a tall, powerful man, approached him with a "rough and peremptory" challenge to wrestle him at Wabash Point. In the fight, which attracted many spectators, Abe easily handled Needham, throwing him twice. His pride hurt, Needham remarked, "You have thrown me twice, but you can't whip me." Abe replied, "Needham, are you satisfied that I can throw you? If you are not and must be convinced through a thrashing I will do that too for your sake."[85] Realizing that wisdom was the better part of valor, Needham backed out gracefully, and he and Abe became friends.

Besides showing once again both Lincoln's strength and his compassion, the incident revealed the political uses of fighting. A year earlier, Lincoln had impressed an Illinois crowd when he stood on a stump and gave a political speech about navigation on the Sangamon River. Now he impressed the locals with his physical prowess and sense of fair play. As a witness reported, the fight made him "forever popular with the boys of that neighborhood."[86]

This initial political speechifying and audience-pleasing fighting presaged far more daring and significant forays into politics that Abe would make over the next decade as he rose to prominence in Illinois.

5

The School of Events

The year that the twenty-two-year-old Lincoln floated like driftwood into New Salem, 1831, brought two major events that pushed the nation toward a precipice. The slavery crisis, which had been presumably resolved a decade earlier by the Missouri Compromise, intensified exponentially when the slave rebel Nat Turner terrorized Virginia and the abolitionist William Lloyd Garrison announced in his new newspaper, *The Liberator*, "I *will be* as harsh as truth, and as uncompromising as justice. . . . AND I WILL BE HEARD."[1]

Thus began a decade of mobbing, lynching, and vigilante violence, much of it related to the growing conflict over slavery. In 1835 alone, America saw 141 recorded riots in which seventy-one people were killed.[2]

This was the turbulent backdrop to Lincoln's ascent into Illinois politics, leading to his excoriation of what he called "this mobocratic spirit" sweeping the nation.[3] His demand for a strict respect for laws had been strengthened during his early Illinois years. Central Illinois, where he settled, offered a unique mix of settlers from the East and from the South, and offered a model of unity for an increasingly divided nation.

These years brought intellectual enrichment; we know that Abe avidly read the works of Thomas Paine, Robert Burns, and William Shakespeare, among others, during this time. They also brought valuable lessons in what Abe called the "school of events."[4] His victorious fights against local ruffians and his command over rough troops in the Black Hawk War gave him practice in dealing with the wildest types, while his friendship with lawyers and other professionals saw him bridging the gap between classes. There was an organic unity between his various jobs—store clerk, postmaster, surveyor, and part-time laborer—and his entrance into politics and the law. Politically, his promotion of canals, roads, and other improvements grew from his experience making nature useful to humans, while his push to move the state capital to central Illinois reflected his awareness of the importance of place. The Springfield Young Men's Lyceum address, his first major speech, fused national ideals with his keen observations of current events.

BOTH SIDES NOW

One of Lincoln's remarkable statements in the Second Inaugural Address describes the religious views of the North and the South: "Both read the same Bible, and pray to the same God. . . . The prayers of both could not be answered; and that of neither has been answered fully."[5] These deceptively simple words contain a world of wisdom. Religion was a main driver of the Civil War. Each side was convinced of God's favor. Very few participants in the war could detach themselves sufficiently from their convictions to grasp the paradox Lincoln perceived: Northerners and Southerners were going at one another's throats with similar prayers in their hearts and similar hymns on their lips. While vowing to pursue the war against slavery with unshrinking firmness, Lincoln in the Second Inaugural made a dramatic move beyond destructive partisanship.

His unusually broad perspective was nurtured during his years living in New Salem and, from 1837 onward, in Springfield. Twenty miles apart, New Salem and Springfield were located near the center of Illinois. Their mixed populations merged the state's two main cultural strains. The state's northern half was settled largely by people from the northern and eastern United States, many of whom immigrated to Illinois through the Erie Canal and the Great Lakes. The lower section of Illinois, known as Egypt, was settled mainly by people from Kentucky, Virginia, North Carolina, and other Southern states. The doubleness that Lincoln sensed in his ancestry—Puritan and Cavalier—was reflected by the state's two cultures. An early historian of Illinois noted:

> It was the soil of the Northwest, of which Illinois formed an integral part, that witnessed, virtually for the first time, the union of the descendants of those first colonists, so diverse in aims and religious faith, who landed respectively at Jamestown and Plymouth Rock, two hundred years before. In other words the progeny of the Roundhead and the Cavalier here met on common ground.[6]

Common ground, yes, but it was hotly contested because of real and perceived cultural differences between the state's two sections. Northern Illinoisans prided themselves on being industrious, temperate, shrewd, and restrained; they regarded the southern citizens of the state as indolent, hotheaded, and sybaritic. The southerners, for their part, viewed the "Yankees" to the north as fanatical, intrusive, and tricky, while they considered themselves hospitable, dignified, sociable, and frank. There were sharp differences on slavery, with the southerners tending toward conservatism and northerners tending toward a more progressive view.

With its conflicting populations, Illinois was a microcosm of the divided nation. Lincoln's New Salem, located near the center of the state, was a different kind of microcosm: it represented a mixing of Northern and Southern views. Founded in 1828 when the Reverend James Cameron and his relative by marriage James R. Rutledge built a sawmill and a gristmill on the Sangamon River, New Salem at its height, around 1833, consisted of about twenty-five families, most of whom lived in log cabins on a single dirt street that intersected at one end with a road that led to Springfield, to the southeast. The majority of New Salem's residents were, like Lincoln, from the South, but there were a number of settlers from the eastern states, including the Vermont-born, Dartmouth-educated Dr. John Allen, Dr. Jason Duncan (another Vermont native), the New Hampshirites Charles J. F. Clark and Matthew S. Marsh, the New Yorker Samuel Hill, and John McNeil, also from New York.[7]

Dr. Allen exerted the strongest New England influence on the village. A reform-minded Presbyterian, Allen was a thin, consumptive man with a clipped white beard whose physical debilities, including a lame leg, were belied by his energetic efforts to tend to his fellow New Salemites both morally and physically. Initially looked on with suspicion as a "Yankee," he vocally opposed slavery, and he founded a temperance society and a Sunday school in New Salem. Antislavery activism, Sabbatarianism, and temperance were identifiably New England reforms—all were promoted by the East's leading preacher, Lyman Beecher, the head of the so-called Benevolent Empire, a nationwide network of eastern-based reform movements. John Allen, a kind of mini-Beecher, influenced Lincoln's views on slavery and temperance.

Several of the Southern residents of New Salem also felt a kinship with Lincoln, in part because their backgrounds resembled his. Take the town's schoolteacher, Mentor Graham. Graham's ancestors had fled religious persecution in the British Isles and had immigrated to Massachusetts, much like Samuel Lincoln.[8] Successive generations of Grahams followed a movement, like that of Lincoln's forebears, through New Jersey and Pennsylvania, down to Virginia and North Carolina, then west to Kentucky, where Mentor Graham was born in Nolin County, not far from one of Lincoln's childhood homes. In Kentucky, the Grahams, like the Lincolns, were "emancipation Baptists" whose church broke off from the regular Baptist church over slavery, just as Thomas and Nancy Lincoln's Little Mount Church had done. Besides hating slavery, the young Mentor, like the young Abe, preferred reading

A reconstruction of New Salem, where Lincoln lived from 1831 to 1837 (photographs of the New Salem State Historic Site, Menard County, Illinois). *Top, left to right*: a mill where wool was prepared for spinning; a doctor's home and office; the first Berry-Lincoln store, also used as the village post office. *Middle, left to right*: a cooper shop, where casks, barrels, and buckets were produced; oxen pulling a Conestoga wagon; the second Berry-Lincoln store. *Bottom, left to right*: shelves with goods for sale in the Hill-McNamar store; interior of Jack Kelso's cabin; James Rutledge's tavern, where Lincoln slept in the loft.

to hunting and trapping. Mentor had an ecological bent—he was "a near-worshiper of trees," according to his biographers—and he revered the Kentucky politician Henry Clay, as did Abe.[9]

In 1826, attracted by the rich soil and the absence of slavery in Illinois, Mentor moved to Sangamon County, Illinois, settling on acreage about a mile outside of what soon became New Salem. He established a subscription school in a sixteen-by-eighteen-foot log cabin. He charged each student five cents a day because few parents had money; in the early phase they paid him in butter, eggs, meat, and other produce. Tall, with red hair and bushy red eyebrows, Graham was a serious, sometimes harsh and temperamental teacher, recalled by students for his readiness with the whip. Well read, he knew his Shakespeare and his Thomas Paine.

Graham was joined in New Salem by a number of his relatives, most of them from the South, and several of them with ancestral histories like his and Lincoln's. In fact, nearly half of New Salem—the Greenes, the Herndons, the Abells, the Potters, the Goldsbys, the Onstots, the Elmores, and the Raffertys—were related to Mentor Graham.[10]

Lincoln, therefore, found himself in congenial company in New Salem. He also found intellectual stimulation there. He learned a lot from Mentor Graham and from one of Mentor's cousins, William G. "Billy" Greene. Exactly what he learned from whom is unclear. Mentor later insisted that he trained Abe in grammar and in the math skills he needed as a surveyor. Lincoln, on the other hand, told his secretary of state, William H. Seward, that Billy Greene had taught him grammar and math.[11] Greene, however, confessed that he didn't know grammar and only held a book while Abe recited rules. Another twist is that Billy's college-trained brother, Lynn McNulty Greene, claimed the honor of being Abe's grammar instructor. The likeliest scenario is that Mentor Graham suggested the book *A Compendium of English Grammar*, by the Maryland teacher Samuel Kirkham, and Abe studied it on his own, with occasional quizzing by the Greenes.

Kirkham's book had a marked impact on Lincoln. Published in 1823, Kirkham's *Grammar* went through more than a hundred editions. Abe, always seeking clarity of expression, was doubtless inspired by Kirkland's prefatory statement: "Without the knowledge and application of grammar rules, it is impossible for anyone to think, speak, read, or write with accuracy."[12] Without good grammar, Kirkham continued, expression could become either nonsensical or the exact opposite of what one intended to say. Kirkham reminded his American readers that they lived "in an age of light and knowledge" and "in a land of liberty;—a land on which the smiles of Heaven shine with uncommon effulgence." One had no excuse "to grovel in ignorance" when one could "enjoy the rich boon of freedom and prosperity which was purchased with the blood of our fathers." Grammar, as Kirkham presented it, was an avenue to exact meaning and to fulfilling the goals of the Founders: it was both precise and patriotic. Abe labored over the book's expositions of syntax, etymology, orthography, rhetoric, and prosody, spurred by Kirkham's reminders that "knowledge is power" and that "an enlightened and virtuous people can never be enslaved." For Abe, learning grammar was liberating.

DEBATING AND REFLECTING

Another instructive experience for Abe in New Salem was participating in debating societies. In 1830–31 a debating club was founded by James Rutledge that Abe, Mentor Graham, the lawyer Bowling Green, and a number of others joined. According to Rutledge's son Robert, Abe, when he spoke, initially prompted smiles from his listeners, who were expecting to hear jokes from him, but he pursued the topic at hand "with reason and argument so pithy and forcible that all were amazed."[13] Gesturing awkwardly and sometimes stuffing his hands into his pockets, Lincoln looked odd, but he impressed his hearers, including one who remarked "that there was more in Abe's head than wit and fun, that he was already a fine speaker, that all he lacked was culture to enable him to reach the high destiny which he knew was in store for him."

Among the lessons that Abe could have learned from the debates was that virtually anything could be argued persuasively if supported by plausible evidence. Because the minutes of Rutledge's society have not survived, we don't know the topics under debate, but the minutes of another group, Thomas Nance's Tyro Polemic and Literary Club, suggest the content and style of such discussions. Nance, born in 1811 in Green County, Kentucky, moved to Illinois in 1830, settling outside New Salem. He taught school in the area and started his literary group in 1833. Lincoln seems to have attended some of the group's meetings because he reported having walked several miles to participate in a debating society. If he did so, he got exposure to reasoned arguments made about many issues, ranging from the outlandish to the deeply serious. One of the more bizarre topics was: If you are in a life-and-death emergency on a boat and you have to choose a loved one to throw overboard, which "bespeaks the most prudence" to get rid of, your wife or your mother?[14] More meaningful questions included "Should females be educated and have the right to vote?"; "Should a wife promise to obey her husband?"; "[H]as slavery been beneficial to the W[estern] continent, or not [?]" For the twenty-two-year-old Lincoln to be meditating on such issues, which were debated from both conservative and radical perspectives, was an exercise in careful thinking on controversial topics.

Nance's society had many rules, including one saying that all discussions must be strictly secular, with no mention of God. Debating without reference to God would have strengthened Lincoln's argumentative powers; it also matched his philosophical outlook during the New Salem years, which leaned strongly toward deism. Because the opening decades of the nineteenth century witnessed the Second Great Awakening—with its religious revivals, rising church membership, and charismatic preachers—it is sometimes forgotten that deism was still widely discussed, especially on the frontier. A historian of the time noted, "Deistic and atheistic belief flourished on the frontier among even the better classes."[15] This was true of New Salem, where, as William Herndon reports, "A good deal of religious skepticism existed, . . . and there were frequent discussions at the store and tavern, in which Lincoln took part."[16] Thomas Paine's *The Age of Reason* and Constantin-François Volney's *The Ruins of Empires*, Herndon explained, "passed from hand to hand . . . Lincoln read both these books and thus assimilated them into his own being."

Most Americans of the time had mixed feelings about deism. On the one hand, they were aware that it had been espoused by several of the Founders, including Jefferson, Franklin, and Paine. On the other hand, they equated it with wicked infidelity. In New Salem, Lincoln found himself in an environment of rational discussion where he could voice his skeptical views. He had sidelined church religion throughout his youth. In Indiana, his stepmother recalled, "Abe had no particular religion—didnt think of that question at the time, if he ever did—He never talked about it."[17] The relaxed intellectual atmosphere of New Salem permitted him to discuss his doubts openly. Even a devout Baptist like Mentor Graham candidly explored free thought with him. Graham recalled a series of sessions in which he set Abe to "parsing every word in Paine's *Age of Reason*."[18]

In Paine's work, Abe encountered searing commentary on religion. Paine argues that all religions are human creations, produced by a fear of the unknown or by a desire to terrify, enslave, or gain power and profit. Every religion, Paine notes, boasts an inspired prophet, a messiah figure who had announced God's word, allegedly gained through direct revelation. Islam, Judaism, Christianity, and all other religions were based on bygone miracles. Paine reports that he has never seen direct evidence of such miracles, which he regards as hearsay upon hearsay. Every church, he points out, accuses other churches of unbelief. "For my part," Paine writes, "I disbelieve them all."[19] This does not mean that Paine dismisses God. He avers that God's laws are inscribed on the physical universe. Scientific principles are the one demonstrable, universal truth. By learning these principles through the exercise of reason, one gains an appreciation of the Divine Architect behind nature. In sum, Paine writes, science is the "true theology," and "my own mind is my own church."

Lincoln confirmed his acceptance of Paine and other deists in conversations with friends in Illinois. James H. Matheny recalled that Lincoln "would talk about Religion—pick up a Bible—read a passage—and then Comment on it—show its falsity and its follies on the ground of *Reason*—would then show its own self made & self uttered Contradictions and would in the End—finally ridicule it and as it were Scoff at it."[20] Abe did more than just talk. While living in New Salem, he wrote what was called "a little Book on Infidelity"—his own version of *The Age of Reason*.[21] In this unpublished manuscript, he attacked the supernatural underpinnings of the Bible, such as the Virgin Birth, the miracles of Christ, and the Resurrection. In essence, he did what Jefferson had done when he used a sharp blade to remove supernatural references from the Bible, or what Franklin did when he laid out six simple precepts of a universal religion, which retained God, moral rules, and the afterlife but omitted the Bible.[22]

Like Franklin, however, Lincoln soon learned that deism, while perhaps true, was not useful. The New Salem store owner Sam Hill, though a disbeliever himself, read Lincoln's skeptical book and knew at once that it must not be published. Hill "had an eye to Lincoln's popularity—his present and future success; and believing that, if the book were published, it would kill Lincoln forever, he snatched it from Lincoln's hand" and tossed it into a stove, where the flames devoured it.[23] Nonetheless, Lincoln's reputation as a deist spread locally, hampering his political ambitions. He ran for the Illinois state legislature four times—in 1832, 1834, 1836, in 1840—and, tellingly, lost the first election to the Democratic preacher Peter Cartwright, who made deism an issue then and raised it again later, when he ran against Lincoln for the US Congress in 1846. Lincoln managed to win the latter election after he published a carefully worded handbill saying that though "I am not a member of any Christian church, . . . I have never denied the truth of the Scriptures: and I've never spoken with intentional disrespect of religion in general, or of any denomination of Christian in particular." He added that he could never support a political candidate who openly criticized religion.[24]

This denial of religious infidelity reveals the political Lincoln who feared he would lose the religious vote if he openly avowed deism. He was right. For instance, James Matheny's father, a devout Methodist, loved Lincoln "with all his soul" and yet "hated to vote for him because he heard that Lincoln was an Infidel." Matheny added, "Many Religious—Christian Whigs hated to vote for Lincoln on that account."[25] With such potential loss of a major voting bloc, Matheny maintained, Lincoln, in the years after his reentry into politics in 1854, "played a sharp game here on the Religious world . . . well Knowing that the old infidel, if not Atheistic charge would be made & proved against him," and to fend it off, he presented himself as "a seeker after Salvation" in an effort to win Christian voters. For Matheny, Lincoln "often if not whol[l]y was an atheist," but "as he grew older he grew more discrete— didn't talk much before Strangers about his religion, but to friends— close and bosom ones he was always open & avowed"—a conclusion shared by William Herndon, who called Lincoln "an Agnostic generally, sometimes an Atheist."[26]

It's more accurate, however, to place emphasis on Matheny's term "seeker." If Lincoln was on a quest for the meaning of words, he also sought a higher meaning to life.

A distinction must be made between private and public religion as they relate to Lincoln. Privately, Lincoln's religion adapted to circumstances and was secret. Several of Lincoln's closest friends confessed that they knew nothing about his religious views. From the slim evidence we have we can say that while he placed little faith in doctrines or churches, he believed in a powerful, unknowable God, in moral standards, and in the Bible, which he saw as a repository of wisdom, despite what he regarded as its inconsistencies. Although he evidently never experienced a life-altering religious conversion, there were times, as after the death of his son Willie, that he gratefully received the consolation offered by Christian ministers.

He saw clearly the practical uses of religion in the public sphere, not only for politicians but in the American population at large, for whom religion was a source of unity and uplift. But he was loath to identify a particular religion as being worthier than another. Like Emerson and Whitman, he admired a general, nondenominational religious spirit that he hoped as president to disseminate through his religious proclamations.

Personally, Lincoln was in a period of rebellion against organized religion during his early years in Illinois. In 1831, shortly after arriving in New Salem, he discovered what became his all-time favorite poem, "Mortality," by the Scottish author William Knox. This bleak poem, all fifty-six lines of which Lincoln committed to memory, delivers, in verse after verse, the point that life is short, happiness is fleeting, and power and glory, no matter how great, are doomed to disappear. Lincoln once said that he would give everything he had to be able to write a poem like "Mortality." His love of the poem became so well known that it was sometimes mistakenly attributed to Lincoln himself. The poem's anxious opening line, "O why should the spirit of mortal be proud!," leads to the repeated message that there is no reason for pride because all human achievements—indeed all humans—are short-lived. In rolling anapests, the poem mentions people of different phases and stations—infants, mothers, fathers, maidens, beggars, priests, kings—all of whom are soon "hidden and lost in the depths of the grave." And as the last verse reminds us, it all happens quickly:

> 'Tis the wink of an eye,—'tis the draught of a
>   breath—
> From the blossom of health to the paleness of
>   death,
> From the gilded saloon to the bier and the
>   shroud—
> O why should the spirit of mortal be proud![27]

"Mortality" is close in theme to another poem Lincoln memorized, William Cullen Bryant's "Thanatopsis," which Lincoln encountered in the 1840s on a visit to his wife's family. Like Knox's "Mortality," Bryant's poem emphasizes the shortness of life; everyone, Bryant writes, is destined "to be a brother of the insensible rock / And to the sluggish clod," to be tossed by the worker's shovel and pierced by tree roots. In picturing the earth as "one mighty sepulchre," "the great tomb of man," Bryant underscores the sheer physicality of death.[28]

In Lincoln's attraction to such gloomy poems we see a mind stoically confronting the possibility of nothingness after death. In this respect, he was distant not only from the era's evangelical religion, which centered on one's eternal prospects, but also from mainstream liberal Protestantism, which increasingly emphasized the so-called Good Death: the assurance of a comfortable passage to heaven and a reunion with loved ones there. The Good Death had many manifestations in nineteenth-century popular culture, including Eva St. Clare's joyous flight heavenward in *Uncle Tom's Cabin*, in efforts to meliorate the deaths of Civil War soldiers, and in bestselling novels about a blissful afterlife, such as Elizabeth Stuart Phelps's trilogy about heaven, *The Gates Ajar*, *Beyond the Gates*, and *The Gates Between*.[29] Lincoln himself was not immune to the appeal of the Good Death, as evidenced by the adornments surrounding Willie's open coffin during the White House funeral in 1862.[30]

In reflective moments, however, Lincoln considered honestly the possibility of death succeeded by dissolution. It would seem that in the New Salem years he reached a point where, as Hawthorne reported of Melville, "he had pretty much made up his mind to be annihilated."[31] When a New Salem neighbor, Parthena Hill, asked Lincoln, "Do you really believe there isn't any future state?" he replied soberly, "Mrs. Hill, I'm afraid there isn't. It isn't a pleasant thing to think that when we die that is the last of us."[32]

His obsession with death explains his passion for works by the Graveyard Poets, especially Thomas Gray, and the Dark Romantics, Byron in particular. One of his favorite Byron poems, "Darkness," is a chilling picture of lifelessness. The poem's speaker reports "a dream, which was not all a dream" about an immense space in which everything is rotting, burning, or bloody—and, finally, empty. In the dream, stars "did wander darkling in the eternal space, / Rayless, and pathless," while "the icy earth / Swung blind and blackening in the moonless air,"; "The world was void, / . . . Seasonless, herbless, treeless, manless, lifeless"; the ocean was dead, the winds "were wither'd in the stagnant air." The poem ends in blackness: "Darkness had no need / Of aid from them—She was the universe!"[33]

To think of Lincoln enjoying such all-nullifying poetry seems, on the surface, at odds with his reputation for humorous storytelling and his alignment with Whig politics, which was dedicated to actively improving society physically and morally. Actually, though, his taste for literature that verged on the nihilistic reveals his impulse to take what neurophilsophers call a ruthlessly reductive approach to the world— that is, he considered its most basic features.[34] To strip away all familiar things and gaze into the void, as he did when reading a poem like Byron's "Darkness," was to risk losing one's philosophical bearings and to make one vulnerable to depression. Indeed it would seem that philosophical angst, produced by a perception of life's meaninglessness in the vast scheme of things, contributed to his repeated spells of melancholy, which he called "the hypo."[35] He was at times akin to Melville, who, in Hawthorne's words, could "neither believe, nor be comfortable in his unbelief" and was "too honest and too courageous not to try to do one or the other."[36]

On the other hand, facing the void had positive effects as well. It generated in Lincoln a cosmic democracy. If all humans were on the same level in the face of death—we all disappear and, probably, resolve into nothingness—then social distinctions, hardened religious views, and the instinct to domineer over or enslave others are in vain. As Knox's poem insistently declares, "Why should the spirit of mortal be proud!" Universal equality mocks false pride and narrows views. We all end up with the "insensible rock" and the "sluggish clod." Walt Whitman famously proclaimed this ruthlessly reductive democracy: "For every atom belonging to me as good belongs to you."[37] In this cosmically egalitarian scheme, we must strive to put aside petty differences that lead to oppression and, in the worst case, war.

Given this outlook, it is understandable that Lincoln during his time in New Salem took a special liking to William Shakespeare and Robert Burns. Lincoln enjoyed reading and reciting these authors in the company of John (Jack) Kelso, who arrived in New Salem in 1831 from Kentucky with his wife and two of her relatives. Reportedly an ex-schoolteacher, Kelso, stout at five feet ten and two hundred pounds, got by on odd jobs in New Salem, preferring fishing and hunting to regular work. Kelso has been harshly treated by some Lincoln biographers. David Donald calls him "fat, lazy," Carl Sandburg depicts him as a genial drunkard, and Albert Beveridge characterizes him as "utterly worthless."[38] Such dismissals do a disservice to Kelso, who was close to Lincoln and had a notable influence on him. "Kelso and Lincoln were great friends," recalled the New Salemite Hardin Bale, "always together—always talking and arguing."[39] Lincoln boarded with Kelso and his family for a time. William Greene found that Kelso was "an excellent *reliable* man." Other neighbors saw Kelso and Lincoln sitting on the bank of the Sangamon River, Jack casting for fish while both of them were engaged in conversations about Shakespeare and Burns.

Lincoln had encountered snippets of Shakespeare in school anthologies, but under Kelso's influence he expanded his knowledge, which eventually became quite broad: on the Illinois law circuit, as Henry Whitney testified, "he read Shakespeare through, and much of it over and over again"; John Hay, his White House secretary, said, "He read Shakespeare more than all other writers together."[40] He was especially drawn to *Macbeth*, *Hamlet*, and *King Lear*, but he was familiar with a range of other tragedies, the history plays, and comedies like *A Midsummer Night's Dream* and *The Merry Wives of Windsor*. In light of his temperament and his cultural tastes, we understand why he was drawn to Shakespeare, who takes the wildest, most disruptive aspects of human experience—madness, violence, perversity, malicious jealousy, greed, vindictiveness—and renders them in exquisitely calibrated lines whose rhythms are subtly adapted to human emotion and whose wonderful images turn even horror into a form of beauty. If Lincoln in daily life swung between humorous performance and gloomy meditation, so did Shakespeare in his plays, some comic and others tragic, with constant tonal shifts in individual works, as in his use of the Fool in his tragedies.

ROBERT BURNS

Lincoln found similar variety in another of his favorite authors, Robert Burns. This eighteenth-century Scottish poet and songwriter, known as the Ploughman Poet because of his rural background and working-class themes, drew widespread interest in America, along with controversy over the eroticism and sacrilege of his poems. Lincoln may have responded to Burns enthusiastically for reasons similar to those of Walt Whitman, who was fascinated by the combination of pessimism and humanism, iconoclasm and democracy in Burns. Whitman noted "the black and desperate background" in several of Burns's poems, with their passages about "hypochondria, the blues."[41] At the same time, Whitman loved Burns's "steel-flashes of wit, home-spun sense, or lance-like puncturing," as well as his fundamental sympathy for lowly creatures of the animal kingdom, such as the field mouse, and average workers on farms and in small villages. "He had a real heart of flesh and blood beating in his bosom," Whitman wrote; "you could almost hear it throb." This intensely human quality in Burns made him for Whitman a symbol of democracy and union. In Whitman's words, Burns was "the essential type of so many thousand—perhaps the average . . . of the decent-born young men and the early mid-aged, not only of the British Isles; but America, North and South, just the same."

Lincoln loved Burns so much so that he learned by heart many of his poems—in the original Scottish dialect, no less. If we look at a couple of Burns poems Lincoln memorized we see the combination of gloom and optimistic humanism that he, like Whitman, enjoyed. "Tam O'Shanter," which Lincoln often recited, is a bacchanalian poem about a drunken worker, with his long-suffering wife waiting at home, who gallops through a storm and has both horrific and erotic visions in a weird fantasy interrupted by lines about the ephemerality of pleasure. Burns writes: "But pleasures are like poppies spread, / You seize the flower, its bloom is shed: / Or like the snow falls in the river, / A moment white then melts forever."[42] This pungent reminder of life's transience interrupts an otherwise adventurous poem about working-class life and marital discord, adding the kind of "black and desperate background" that Whitman found in Burns's poetry—and that Lincoln, with transience always on his mind, appreciated. Another of Lincoln's favorites, Burns's "Holy Willie's Prayer," is a humorous, trenchant satire on religious hypocrisy and Calvinistic theology. The speaker, a self-righteous orthodox Christian, is a callous seducer who denounces a card-playing, bibulous friend whom he judges will be damned by a God who "sends one to heaven and ten to hell"—a slap at the Calvinistic doctrines of election and predestination, which appalled Lincoln.

Milton Hay testified that "He could very nearly quote all of Burns' Poems from memory." William Greene commented that Lincoln "knew all of Burns by heart."[43]

While it's virtually impossible that Lincoln could recite *all* of Burns's long, idiosyncratic poems, Hay's and Greene's statements that he did so raise the issue of Lincoln's astonishing capacities for memorizing poems or prose passages. Multiple other witnesses also attested to his skill in spontaneous recitations. Oliver Wendell Holmes's poems "The Last Leaf" and "Lexington"; Byron's "Childe Harold's Pilgrimage"; Poe's "The Raven"; Constance's speech to the Cardinal in Act 4 of Shakespeare's *King John*; Claudius's soliloquy "Oh! my offense is rank, it smells to heaven" (*Hamlet,* act 3, scene 3); King Richard's speech "For God's sake, let us sit upon the ground / And tell sad stories of the death of kings" (*Richard II,* act 3, scene 2)—these are just a few poems or passages Lincoln is said to have recited from memory. No other president— indeed, few people, other than trained actors—have matched Lincoln's reciting ability.

Lincoln did not recite poems to show off. The journalist Noah Brooks testified that when Lincoln quoted poems in conversation, he did so "always with the air of one who deprecated the imputation that he might be advertising his erudition."[44]

In any case, Lincoln was *not* erudite in the sense of, say, the multilingual polymath John Quincy Adams or the learned Thomas Jefferson, with his library of more than five thousand volumes. "The truth about Mr. Lincoln," William Herndon opined, "is that he read less and thought more than any man in his sphere in America."[45] This statement is misleading. Lincoln actually read quite a lot, especially in the New Salem years. But he read selectively, and he memorized even more selectively. And, yes, he thought deeply about what he read. He chose to memorize pieces that were truly meaningful to him, and he recited them when they matched his emotions of the moment. In the truest sense, these were, for him, *lived* poems. They projected his innermost feelings. Because the authors he recited were characteristically subtle, Lincoln felt that the complexity of his emotions was beautifully captured in their lines. Of Burns's poignant elegy "Lament for James, Earl of Glencairn," Lincoln remarked, "Burns never touched a sentiment without carrying it to its ultimate expression and leaving nothing further to be said."[46] Poetry, for Lincoln, ushered emotion to the outer limit of expression.

But poetry did not only *express* emotion; it *channeled* it and *shaped* it. No other form of language is as structured as poetry, especially in the metered, carefully phrased forms that he preferred. For Lincoln, reading poets like Burns and Shakespeare was a master class in the redirection of the amorphous or the uncontrolled.

LIFE LESSONS

Lincoln also learned such lessons in his personal experiences in New Salem, where from the start he found himself engaged in channeling the powerful energies of his cultural, natural, and political environments. It was by regulating these energies that Lincoln developed talents he later used to direct the passions of the Civil War toward national unity.

Lincoln's talents for fostering unity were strengthened in New Salem, where he experienced life in dizzying variety. His jobs there nurtured flexibility and confidence of the sort that Emerson describes in his essay "Self-Reliance." Emerson complains, "We are parlor soldiers. We shun the rugged battle of fate, where strength is born." He points out that if a young college graduate miscarries in his early jobs— if he "is not installed in an office within one year afterwards in the cities or suburbs of Boston or New York"—people say that he is "ruined" and "that he is right in being disheartened and complaining the rest of

RALPH WALDO EMERSON

his life." Emerson adds, "A sturdy lad from New Hampshire or Vermont, who in turn tries all the professions, who *teams* it, *farms* it, *peddles*, keeps a school, preaches, edits a newspaper, goes to Congress, buys a township, and so forth, in successive years, and always, like a cat, falls on his feet, is worth a hundred of these city dolls. . . . He feels no shame in not 'studying a profession,' for he does not postpone life, but lives already. He has not one chance, but a hundred chances."[47]

Emerson was protesting against the formulaic predictability of those who got on a rigid professional track instead of plunging into real-life situations that helped them find their priorities. In New Salem, Lincoln became an Emersonian man, adventurous and resilient. A summary of his experiences during the New Salem years yields a record of occupations even more varied than Emerson's imaginary list. After returning to New Salem from his summer of 1831 visit to his father in Coles County, Lincoln served successively as an election clerk, the navigator of a raft, a clerk at Denton Offutt's store, a militiaman in the Black Hawk War (first as a captain and then as a private), a store owner with William Berry, the postmaster of New Salem for three years, and an assistant to the county surveyor John Calhoun, for whom Lincoln laid out townships, home sites, school districts, and roads. During this period, Lincoln also ran for state congress from New Salem, winning on his second try, which led to his serving in the state legislature. He had part-time jobs as a rail-splitter, a millworker, a farmhand, the keeper of a still, and a worker at Samuel Hill's store. His success was irregular, but like the cat in Emerson's essay, he always landed on his feet. That was because there was an organic connection between many aspects of his life in New Salem: between his work, his reading, and his accomplishments as an athlete and a militia captain.

His jobs, as varied as they were, actually lent themselves to establishing continuity between different areas of his life. There were two common denominators among his occupations: they were physical but they gave room for socializing and for intellectual growth, and they bonded him with the two main classes in New Salem, the roistering roughs and the social elite. Just as his daily conversation swung between crude frontier jokes and recitations of Burns or Shakespeare, so his human encounters made him adept in traversing social barriers and appealing to people of different backgrounds.

In New Salem, Lincoln did not work, read, and socialize separately. Lincoln's jobs tending stores—with Offutt, with Berry, and with Hill—included slow periods that he filled with reading. It was at Offutt's store, where he clerked with Billy Greene, that he studied Kirkham's *Grammar*; Billy quizzed him from the book. Lincoln's other positions in stores allowed similar time for reading. His personal library was small, consisting mainly of eighteenth-century poetry, but he borrowed books from others in the area, including the well-to-do Bennett Abell, the justice of the peace of Bowling Green, and the merchants John Mc-Neill (aka McNamar) and Isaac Chrisman. He was thrilled to be appointed postmaster in 1833, because many newspapers arrived at the post office, and he had ample time to read them. "Mr. Lincoln's education was almost entirely a newspaper one," a friend recalled—an exaggeration, to be sure, but nonetheless a testament to Lincoln's attentiveness to the news of his day and to contemporary popular culture.[48] In New Salem, among his favorite newspapers were the *Louisville Journal*, the *St. Louis Republican*, and the *Sangamo Journal*. He also read the *Congressional Globe* and the Acts of Congress.

But it wasn't just in the stores or in the post office that he did his reading. His postal work took him on lengthy journeys around the region to deliver mail. On these trips, whether by foot or on horseback, he often carried books or newspapers that he read on the way. On the streets in New Salem, he was often seen holding a book and reading it. Robert B. Rutledge described him walking through the village, absorbed in a book, then stopping for a while to socialize, and "when the company or amusement became dry or irksome," continuing on his walk.[49] He enjoyed reading aloud—a vocal expression of the written word that was a holdover from the "blab" schools of his youth. The fact that he could recite from memory passages that he'd read impressed others. But as Robert Rutledge pointed out, the memorization did not always come automatically. When Lincoln wanted to remember something he would write it down. Rutledge recalled, "I . . . have known him to write whole pages of books he was reading."

If Lincoln's reading helped him win favor with the area's intelligentsia, his physical prowess made his reputation among a completely different set—the rough, happy-go-lucky frontiersmen who were often at odds with more respectable types.

Within a few miles of New Salem, there were small communities,

Clary's Grove and Little Grove, with gangs that had names like the Gums, the Watkinses, the Dowells, the Arnolds, the Bonds, and the Kirbys.[50] Anticipating later groups of American young men Lincoln would deal with, including the b'hoys and gangs of American cities and the torch-bearing Wide Awakes of the 1860 presidential campaign, the frontier roisterers around New Salem were fundamentally good-hearted. They helped people in trouble, and they gave themselves to Jesus at religious revivals. But they were also a tough lot who loved to flout respectability. They got drunk, whooped furiously, and had all-out brawls on the streets of villages or towns. For fun, they would cut the manes and tails off horses or loosen a cinch strap and put a pebble under a saddle just to see a rider thrown. When Baptist preachers were dunking converts in the Sangamon River, they disrupted the ritual by tossing dogs or logs into the river. At frolics they would grab a wild pig and throw it alive into a fire, eating it when it was cooked. The blood sport of gander pulling was one of their favorite pastimes. Once in New Salem they forced a rotund, drunken man into a barrel and pushed it down a steep bank; the man was saved when the barrel was stopped by a tree.

Lincoln witnessed the ravages that these frontiersmen were capable of. The Clary's Grove Boys, the dominant roughneck group, drove a New Salem store owner, Reuben Radford, out of business with their wild behavior. The group's members demanded that Radford liberally serve them whiskey. At the time, stores like Radford's sold alcohol by the barrel, but if they wanted to serve individual drinks, they had to get a license. Radford did not have one, but he agreed to give the Clary's Grove Boys two drinks apiece. That did not satisfy them, and they became so worked up that they trashed his store. The disheartened Radford wanted to sell off his inventory and vacate the store. He found a buyer in Billy Greene, who in turn quickly sold Radford's goods to Lincoln and his partner, William Berry. When Lincoln and Berry started their own store, offering for sale Radford's goods along with other supplies, Lincoln protested when Berry, an alcoholic, pressed him to sell drinks individually. The Lincoln-Berry store soon "winked out," in Lincoln's words. When Berry died in January 1835, Lincoln owed creditors a hefty amount—what he and his friends called "the national debt"—that he did not fully pay off until 1848.[51]

If the Clary's Grove Boys set off the string of events that drove Lincoln into debt, they had far more positive effects on him as well. They were key players in launching his political career. They had remarkable political sway. As the Illinois governor Thomas Ford explained, "The candidate who had the 'butcher knife boys' on his side was almost certain to be elected" in many of the state's precincts.[52] Personal loyalty was crucial to the backwoods roughnecks, who followed the frontier tradition of testing a stranger by seeing if he might qualify as "the best man" in the region.

Lincoln passed the test in tried-and-true frontier fashion. One of the most popular folk legends surrounding Davy Crockett was his winning the friendship and the vote of a man he whipped in a rough-and-tumble fight. Far from provoking continued hostility, the battle led to sincere friendship and political support. The same thing happened to Lincoln. He started working at Dennis Offutt's store in October 1831, and it was not long before Offutt, noting his clerk's unusual physical strength, offered to pay ten dollars to anyone in the area who could beat Abe in a fight. A swaggering, bibulous eccentric—dubbed by one historian "the Barnum of New Salem"[53]—Offutt spread news of his bet, and he was answered by the Clary's Grove Boys, who put up their strongest champion, Jack Armstrong, to challenge Offutt's tall, powerful employee, who at the time weighed more than two hundred pounds. Before the fight, Abe specified that he wanted no "wooling & pulling"—meaning that he wanted to wrestle cleanly, without the hair-pulling, eye-gouging, and biting that were standard in rough-and-tumbles.[54]

On the day of the fight, many people from New Salem and its environs gathered in front of Offutt's store, where the contest took place. Whiskey, money, and knives were staked on the outcome. Jack Armstrong, described as "a man in the prime of his life, square built, muscular and strong as an ox," was a formidable opponent, but Abe met the challenge.[55] The details of the fight are unclear. In one version, Abe was getting the better of Jack, at which point Jack committed a foul that enraged Abe, who seized Jack by the throat, held him straight out, and shook him like a doll. A different rendering had Abe getting the better of Jack and provoking the anger of Jack's friends, who en masse threatened to attack Abe, who faced them and declared that he was ready for all comers. The most likely story is that the two fighters came to a draw and broke off the fight, perhaps because of a foul committed by Jack.

At any rate, what really matters is that Abe endured a frontier initiation ritual that aided his political ambitions. Whether or not he emerged as "the best man" that day, he won the deep loyalty of the Clary's Grove Boys, who thereafter supported him at political rallies and at the polls. As an early commentator noted, Lincoln now had on his side "'the barefoot boys,' 'the huge-pawed boys,' or 'the butcher knife boys,' who in the elections of those days so often held the balance of power."[56]

He gained the respect of the Clary's Grove Boys not only as a political candidate but also as their leader in the Black Hawk War, which he and they participated in during the spring and summer of 1832. This short-lived war was one of many results of the United States' ongoing occupation of the ancestral lands of Native Americans. The story of Black Hawk, a leader of the Sauk and Fox tribes, was sadly typical. Through unfair treaties, William Henry Harrison in 1804 had wrested fifty million acres of land in northwestern Illinois and parts of Wisconsin and Missouri from the Sauks and Foxes, who were promised a federal annuity and the right to continue to occupy their land until the US government sold it to settlers. Pressured by encroaching whites, the natives finally moved west to Iowa. But in early April 1832, a food shortage induced Black Hawk, along with about a thousand men, women, and children, to move back into a small portion of their former Illinois lands, evidently to raise crops there. His reentry into Illinois alarmed state leaders like Governor John Reynolds, who called up troops to drive out the Indians. At the time, all men between the ages of eighteen and forty-five had to do militia duty. Among those called up were sixty-eight men from the New Salem area, including Lincoln and the Clary's Grove Boys. Now a person of stature among the frontiersmen, Lincoln was elected captain of a company in the Fourth Regiment of Mounted Volunteers. Jack Armstrong, his wrestling opponent, was his first sergeant. The rest of the unit struck observers as "the hardest set of men he ever saw," "the wildest company in the world," but Lincoln, though inexperienced militarily, gained his troops' respect and affection.[57]

In the Black Hawk War, Lincoln also befriended several future lawyers or politicians, including John Todd Stuart, John J. Hardin, Edward D. Baker, Joseph Gillespie, and Orville Hickman Browning, all of whom later became important to his career.

That Lincoln was popular with both the wild set and the professionals showed again that he was capable of bridging social groups. For the roughs, his physical strength and mental toughness made him stand out. As J. Rowan Herndon explained, Lincoln "Became very Poupular [sic] in the army" because "he could throw Down any man that took hold of him," "outjump the Best of them," "outbox the Best of them," and tell the best stories and jokes.[58] Actually, the throwing down part was not completely true. When Lorenzo Dow Thompson, the leader of another militia unit, competed with Lincoln for a campsite by engaging him in a wrestling match, Lincoln had a surprise. "You see," Lincoln recalled later, "I had never been thrown. . . . You may think a wrestle, or 'wrastle,' as we call such contests of skill and strength, was a small matter, but I tell you the whole army was out there to see it."[59] Thompson threw him twice, but Lincoln's supporters admired his courage in taking on the powerful Thompson. Lincoln had more success with "the champion of the Southern companies," who was taller and heavier than Abe. "I reckoned that I was the most wiry," Lincoln said, "and soon after I had tackled him I gave him a hug, lifted him off the ground, and threw him flat on his back. That settled his hash."[60]

Lincoln appealed to different types because of his flexible personality. A fellow militiaman said that Abe was "always cheerful, and his spirit and temper such as would engender the like cheerfulness in all surrounding minds: in fact the whole company, even amid trouble and suffering, received Strength & fortitude, by his buoyancy & elasticity."[61] John Todd Stuart explained that Abe was "exceedingly popular" because he was "so good natured, genial, upright."[62] Upright, perhaps, but capable of escapades. Stuart recalled that Abe, General James T. Henry, and he "went to the hoar houses" in Galena, in northern Illinois. "All went purely for fun—devilment—nothing Else."[63]

Although Lincoln saw no military action during his fifty-one days of service in the Black Hawk War, he encountered gruesome scenes. In mid-May 1832, he witnessed the bloody aftermath of the Battle of Stillman's Run, in which an outnumbered Indian band had defeated 275 Illinois militia under Major Isaiah Stillman. Lincoln's company was part of a force that found the corpses of eleven soldiers, all of them scalped, some with their heads cut off, and others with the throats cut or genitals scooped out.[64] Lincoln helped bury the dead. Later his unit came upon an old woman the natives had slaughtered, her scalp hanging on a ramrod, with a young woman lying nearby, her belly ripped open and her infant hanging from a tree branch.[65]

The Black Hawk War, ironically enough, brought out Lincoln's sympathy for ethnic others. Discussion of Lincoln and race usually neglect to mention that, while his public racial pronouncements were sometimes conservative, on a personal level he showed compassion toward people of color. One evening an Indian came into the army camp bearing a signed letter from Lewis Cass saying that he was "a good & true man."[66] Lincoln's men wanted to kill the guest. Lincoln announced that he would fight or duel anyone who tried to do so. No one took up the challenge.

While performing his militia duties, Lincoln must have been grati-
fied that he did not have to wage battle against the natives. But other
militiamen did, and like most white-Indian encounters in the nineteenth century, the brief Black Hawk War ended wretchedly for the
Indians. Black Hawk tried to surrender under a flag of truce, but his
envoys were slaughtered. By early August, the defeated chief tried to
move with his remaining party west across the river to Iowa, but hundreds of women, children, and warriors were massacred during the retreat. More than half of the original Indian party were killed during the
war. Black Hawk was captured and taken on a tour of the eastern states
so that he could witness the power of white civilization. He was finally
released to his tribe in Iowa. He recalled his former lands in Illinois as
"a beautiful country. I loved my towns, my corn fields, and the home of
my people."[67] All of northern Illinois, as a historian of the time noted,
"was now ready for white possession."

During his first year in Illinois, Lincoln had experienced firsthand
the kind of violence and sensationalism that most Americans of the day
only read about. Frontier humor, with its ring-tailed roarers and bloody
Indian battles, became so popular that the leading example of this
humor, the Crockett almanacs, would be featured in a 1946 exhibition
by New York's Grolier Club among the "One Hundred Influential
American Books Published Before 1900," along with *Huckleberry Finn*,
the Declaration of Independence, *Uncle Tom's Cabin*, the Gettysburg
Address, and other classics.[68] As the cultural historian Franklin J.
Meine writes, "Through the medium of the Almanacks, the fantastic
tales of the Davy Crockett myth mushroomed like an atom-bomb
cloud" in nineteenth-century America, and for more than fifty years
"the fabulous Davy reigned more or less supreme as the popular symbol
of the American frontiersman." Lincoln for a time virtually inhabited a
real-life Crockett almanac; he engaged in repeated contests of frontier
manliness and witnessed the bloody ravages of Indian warfare. That
he did so without indulging in the typical vices of real and fictional

frontiersmen—drunkenness, tobacco chewing, eye gouging, cruel pranks, and blood sports—made him a notably *improved* version of the frontier rough, one with the energy of a Crockett or a Clary's Grove Boy but without the excesses.

POLITICS AND GEOGRAPHY

Abe returned to New Salem from the Black Hawk War just two weeks before the August 1832 election. Before joining the war in the spring, he had entered his name as a candidate for the Illinois state legislature. That he ran for office after having spent only a short time in Illinois, at the young age of twenty-three, attests to his already vigorous political ambition. He appealed to both respectable and rough types in a short speech he gave at Papsville, a now-defunct village outside Springfield. The speech appealed to anti-Jackson voters who would soon consolidate locally and nationally as the Whig Party. Lincoln's words, as reported by a witness, were:

> Fellow citizens, I presume you all know who I am—I am humble Abraham Lincoln. I have been solicited by many friends to become a candidate for the legislature. My policies are short and sweet, like the old woman's dance. I am in favor of a National Bank, I am in favor of the internal improvement system, and a high protective tariff. These are my sentiments and political principles. If elected I shall be thankful; and if not, it will be all the same.[69]

It would be hard to find a more condensed statement of what was emerging as Whig Party doctrine, most famously advanced by Lincoln's political idol, Henry Clay. When Lincoln proclaimed support for the national bank, he was placing himself in opposition to President

Andrew Jackson, who was running for reelection in 1832 on a platform that highlighted his plan to dismantle the Second Bank of the United States. The Hamiltonian national bank, anticipating the Federal Reserve Bank, centered monetary policy in the federal government instead of distributing it to the states, as Jackson and the Democratic Party aimed to do. The protective tariff, another Whig priority that Lincoln mentioned, was designed to shield American industry from unfair foreign competition while encouraging the manufacture of goods in the United States. Internal improvements, a third part of the Whig program, referred to the canals, railroads, roads, and other advances in the movement of goods and people.

Just as significant as the Whig message of Lincoln's "short and sweet" speech was his bullish behavior that day. One of his supporters in the audience, J. Rowan Herndon, got into a fight with a gang of roughs just as Lincoln was preparing to speak. Upon spotting the melee, Lincoln went to Herndon's aid; he charged the attackers and, in Herndon's words, "threw them about like boys."[70] This aggressive action quieted the roughs, and Lincoln delivered his speech.

In March 1832, Lincoln issued a "Communication to the People of Sangamon County" in which he announced his main motive for running for state office: to promote internal improvements. He supported a central railroad in Illinois but called its $290,000 price tag too high to make it immediately feasible. His "Communication" (presumably a handbill) grew from his immersion in the natural environment of New Salem and Springfield. He announced that he had a unique knowledge of the Sangamon River, having observed it closely as a flatboat navigator and a mill worker. "From my peculiar circumstances," he wrote, "it is probable that for the last twelve months I have given as particular attention to the stage of the water in this river, as any other person in the country."[71] He showed the same kind of sensitivity to changes in water levels that Thoreau later would observe in Walden Pond, but unlike the Concord naturalist, Lincoln wanted to put his knowledge of nature to economic use. The Sangamon River was a twisting stream, clogged with debris and snags, that, Lincoln argued, could be made navigable by large boats, perhaps all the way to Springfield, if a channel was cut through the prairie to reduce its bends. The straightened river would not only become shorter, but areas of floating timber would be avoided. "I believe the improvement of the Sangamon River," Lincoln announced, "to be vastly important and highly desirable to the people of this county." If elected, he promised, he would push for this project.

The election that took place just after his return from the war was a chastening experience. His popularity with local people of all types led to his winning all but twenty-three of New Salem's three hundred votes cast in the August 1832 election. But he fared less well countywide, and he came in eighth among the twelve candidates from Sangamon County who were vying for four seats in the Illinois General Assembly.

Among those who defeated him that year was Peter Cartwright, an early nemesis of Lincoln's who would later run against Abe for the US Congress. A Methodist revivalist of immense personal magnetism, Cartwright, twenty-three years older than Lincoln, had successfully run for state office in 1828 and had served in the legislature. Born in Virginia to poor parents who migrated west after the Revolution, Cartwright was raised in Logan County, Kentucky. He moved to Illinois in 1823 and settled in Pleasant Plains, eight miles southwest of the future New Salem. Like Lincoln, he was morally opposed to slavery and yet also mistrusted Garrisonian abolitionism, which he considered disruptive. He was wonderful at telling stories and jokes, skills he memorably used in the pulpit.

He was a pioneer of the new religious style—the anecdotal, pungent sermon style that influenced many nineteenth-century Americans, including Lincoln, who made his own innovative uses of religious images. Cartwright, in his twenty years as a traveling Methodist minister, baptized more than twelve thousand converts and gave more than eight thousand extemporaneous sermons brimming with entertaining lines

PETER CARTWRIGHT

and vivid warnings of God's judgment. At religious camp meetings, a witness reported, "his wild, waggish, peculiar eloquence poured forth, splashing and foaming, like a mountain torrent. Glancing arrows of wit, the most galling satire, well-directed shafts of ridicule, and side-splitting anecdotes were hurled in every direction with such wonderful effect, that in a very short time the whole encampment was in a perfect uproar of laughter." This "torrent of indescribable humor" was followed by descriptions of hell and heaven that overwhelmed his hearers.[72] At revivals, it was not unusual for scores of his listeners to fall senseless to the ground or have visions or trances that made them jerk, dance, run, bark, or laugh hysterically. Some would be taken home and would lie motionless for days, without eating or drinking, and awake to describe their visions. A middle-size, muscular man with thick black hair and a rugged head on which perched a furry white-beaver hat, Cartwright was the quintessential frontier preacher, as ready with his fists as with his stories. He was known to go into his audience, seek out scoffers or drunkards, threaten them, and, in some cases, pummel them.

Lincoln, we may surmise, envied Cartwright's talents in entertaining and controlling audiences, but he was repelled by the preacher's efforts to mix zealous evangelical Christianity with social issues. When Cartwright wrote a newspaper piece calling for Methodist-controlled schools in Illinois, Lincoln responded with an article (published under the name of his then-employer Samuel Hill) charging Cartwright with being "a most abandoned hypocrite" and insisting that it was impossible to tell whether Cartwright "is greater fool or knave" and that "he has but few rivals in either capacity."[73] Thus began a period, which lasted until the late 1840s, when Lincoln frequently resorted to the kind of slashing rhetoric that Cartwright himself helped popularize and that became common among orators, penny-newspaper writers, and sensation novelists during this period.

Lincoln's commitment to internal improvements was evident in his role in what at the time was a huge event in the county: the much-ballyhooed voyage of the *Talisman*, a 136-foot steamboat loaded with 150 tons of freight that left Cincinnati, Ohio, on February 2 and headed, via several rivers, including the Sangamon, toward Springfield, Illinois. A successful voyage would open up substantial new trading possibilities between Springfield and eastern and Southern markets, because transportation by river was much cheaper than over land. Excitement rose to a fever pitch when the *Talisman* reached Beardstown, about a hundred miles downstream from Springfield. Lincoln joined many others from the area who used their axes all along the shore of the Sangamon River to clear away overhanging branches so that the *Talisman* could complete its voyage. Cheering crowds swarmed on the riverbanks as celebratory banners flapped on trees and whiskey-fueled parties raged.

When the boat made it to a mill just below Springfield on March 24, the festivities grew even more joyous. Long poems hailing the *Talisman* were published locally, and a tremendous ball was held to honor the skipper, who was accompanied by his beautiful "wife" (it was soon learned, to widespread dismay, that she was actually a prostitute). After a week's holdover in Springfield, the *Talisman* tried to head on a return voyage, but the river's level had sunk, and the boat could not turn around. Lincoln was hired, along with J. Rowan Herndon, to navigate the boat back to Beardstown—a challenging task indeed, especially because at New Salem the vessel got stuck on the dam, part of which had to be torn away to allow for downstream passage. Although the *Talisman* made it to Beardstown, and Lincoln earned forty dollars for his efforts, the voyage was deemed a failure. Four years later, another steamboat, the *Utility*, attempted a similar voyage to Springfield but got stuck at Petersburg, where it was dismantled and sold as lumber. That was the end of the steamboat plans for Springfield—plans that in 1842 became moot when the Northern Cross Railroad reached the town.

Between the *Talisman* fiasco and the railroad's arrival, Lincoln was a vocal promoter of internal improvements. He backed the Illinois and Michigan Canal, a project initiated in 1824 but in quiescence until the early 1830s, when Lincoln arrived on the political scene. Upon its completion in 1848, the canal, which nearly bankrupted the state at a cost of more than $6 million, would connect the Great Lakes to the Mississippi River via a number of rivers in Illinois that were connected to Chicago by a thirty-six-mile waterway. For Lincoln, the canal was an ideal project, for it meant utilizing nature to improve society. His aim was to become "the DeWitt Clinton of Illinois"—a reference to the New York politician behind the construction of the nation-changing Erie Canal.[74]

Lincoln got the opportunity to push the canal project when he was elected to the legislature in 1834. The canal met with stiff opposition among southern Illinoisans, who believed that the canal would spur the emigration of ex–New Englanders from the northern part of the state to the lower sections. Southern legislators spoke out against the canal "for fear it would open the way for flooding the state with Yankees." A common saying in southern Illinois was "Why, a Michigan Canal would wash Gawd's country clean down to the Gulf," because it would inundate the land with "damn Yankees."[75] The Southerners preferred the plan for a railroad running from Peru, on the Illinois River about a hundred miles southwest of Chicago, to Cairo, on the Mississippi River in the extreme southern part of the state. Not only did Peru seem safely distant from the Yankee-producing Great Lakes, but the Illinois River was a boundary between the state's two sections; below it, the state became increasingly dominated by Southern-born settlers. Cairo, at the confluence of the Ohio and Mississippi Rivers, connected with the markets and people of the South.

Lincoln had his own section-specific plans for canals and railroads. In his "Communication" he generalized, "There cannot justly be any objection to having rail roads and canals, any more than to other good things." Besides calling for the straightening of the Sangamon River, he joined other Whigs in backing the Illinois and Michigan Canal. He saw value in railroads as well, despite their high cost. He advocated a rail line from some northern point on the Illinois River down to Jacksonville and then thirty-five miles east to Springfield. "This is, indeed, a very desirable object," he wrote. "No other improvement that reason will justify us in hoping for can equal in utility the rail road."[76]

By supporting a railroad whose terminus was Springfield, Lincoln was quietly dispensing with the idea of a terminus in a deep-southern Illinois town like Cairo. He was laying plans for the development of his area of the state—plans also integral to the hoped-for work on the Sangamon River and the *Talisman* experiment. He seemed to sense that the Yankee-Southern merging that was already occurring in his central region would be economically strengthened by the internal improvements he had in mind.

Although his loss in the 1832 race temporarily stymied his plans, his success in 1834 paved the way for their realization. By 1834, when he was supplementing his meager salary in the post office with his work as an assistant surveyor, he had little time for official campaigning, but he met many people in the region during his mail deliveries and his trips as a surveyor. He won people over with his personality and his integrity. Despite his Whig affiliation, influential Democrats, including Judge Bowling Green and many roughs, came to his support. They appreciated his friendliness and leadership qualities. His physical strength again had an impact. When a punch-out erupted while he was giving a speech at Mechanicsburg, he rushed into the audience and broke it up. We don't know if the free-for-all was alcohol generated, but we can be sure that the temperate Abe did not follow the usual custom of plying voters with liquor. A citizens' meeting of the time said that the typical candidate treated audiences "with ardent spirits, for the purpose of influencing their votes"; many political rallies degenerated into carousals in which "a large portion of the voters would be drunk and staggering about town, cursing, swearing, hallooing, yelling, huzzaing for their favorite candidates, throwing their arms up and around, threatening to fight, and fighting"; "hundreds of them" would mount horses and gallop through towns "screeching like so many infernal spirits broke loose from their nether prison."[77]

It was this kind of irrational behavior—brawls, sprees, Cartwright-like religious frenzy—that the rationalist Abe avoided or stopped. But had he taken rationalism too far, he would have alienated Illinois voters, who recoiled from stiff, proper candidates. William Butler voted for him "because he told good stories, and remembered good jokes—because he was genial, kind, sympathetic, open-hearted."[78] Some were even drawn to him despite his reputed irreligiousness, such as Russell

Godbey, who confessed that a friend warned him "not to Vote for him—because Abe was a Deist," but "I did vote for him nonetheless."[79]

He also had the advantage of his distinctive appearance, which had entertainment value. "Not only did his wit, kindliness, and knowledge attract people," observed his friend Coleman Smoot, "but his strange clothes and uncouth awkwardness advertised him, the shortness of his trousers causing particular remark and amusement. Soon the name 'Abe Lincoln' was a household word."[80] This was the decade when Barnum, the great peddler of the bizarre, and the Crockett almanacs, with their proudly ugly hero, won over large, sensation-seeking American audiences. James Matheny remembered that the idea of Lincoln running for office was at first "regarded as a joke; the boys wanted some fun; he was so uncouth and awkward, and so illy dressed, that his candidacy afforded a pleasant diversion for them."[81] Aware of his listeners' tastes, Lincoln brought attention to his physical oddness. During his first race, just after the Black Hawk War, he joked, "Gentlemen I have just returned from the Campaign. My personal appearance is rather shabby & dark. I am almost as red as those men I have been chasing through the prairies & forests [and] on the Rivers of Illinois."[82] Critics maintained that he went too far with his self-deprecatory humor. "Mr. Lincoln," a Democratic newspaper charged, "has . . . a sort of *assumed clownishness* in his manner which does not become him. . . . It is *assumed*—assumed for effect."[83]

The effect, assumed or not, took hold in the 1834 election. The clownish, ill-dressed, honorable Lincoln won the second highest number of votes of all candidates competing for the four Sangamon seats in the General Assembly. Among the other winners was John T. Stuart, the Springfield attorney Lincoln had met in the Black Hawk War. The slim, handsome Stuart had been recommending the study of law to Abe, who followed his advice and read law books that fall. Politically, Stuart was a thoroughgoing Whig known especially for his advocacy of internal improvements. Stuart and Lincoln roomed together that winter in Vandalia, the state capital, located seventy-five miles south of Springfield. A primitive town with a population of between six hundred and eight hundred, Vandalia had a dilapidated two-story brick state house, where the House of Representatives met on the first floor and the Senate on the second.

Lincoln played second fiddle to the experienced Stuart in the General Assembly's term, which ran from December 1, 1834, to February 13, 1835. But the young legislator made his mark. Although he didn't speak up much, he regularly attended the Assembly's sessions, and he pursued his two main priorities: internal improvements and the promotion of the Springfield/New Salem area. He chaired two committees that looked into the possibility of incorporating the Beardstown and Sangamon Canal Company, designed to improve the Sangamon River and connect it by a canal with the Illinois River. A bill was passed, and Lincoln, in a move toward what today would be called insider trading, bought stock in the new canal company; he encouraged others to do so as well. When it was learned, however, that the cost of improving the river would be more than $800,000, the plan was dropped. Lincoln's other pet project, the Illinois and Michigan Canal, to connect the Great Lakes to the Illinois River, got a boost when the legislature passed a $500,000 appropriations bill that he voted for.

But his chief concern remained advancing the cause of central Illinois. To this end, he submitted to the house a petition from "sundry citizens of the counties of Sangamon, Morgan and Tazewell, praying the organization of a new county out of said counties."[84] Had this petition led to legislation, it would have made Lincoln's region by far the most important in the state at the time. By combining Sangamon County with Morgan (to the west) and Tazewell (to the north), such a bill would have created a megacounty that would become, literally, the center of Illinois.

In his very first foray into politics, then, Lincoln was trying to establish a place between the opposing sections—a place where Northerners and Southerners, Yankee Puritans and Southern Cavaliers, could come together. His goal was to draw both sides toward the center. Unable to do this through his current strategies—the citizens' petition failed, the local canal company never happened, and the Illinois Central Canal was slow in coming—he set his sights on moving the state capital from Vandalia to Springfield, where the merging of Yankees and Southerners was already happening. After the Black Hawk War, many settlers from the northern section of the state moved into the growing town. As Paul Angle notes, "Where before the great majority had come from Kentucky and Tennessee, there were now large numbers from Ohio and New England as well."[85]

The relocation of the capital to Springfield preoccupied him during his next two terms in the Assembly, in 1836–37 and 1838–39. In these sessions he was the leader of the so-called Long Nine, Whigs from Sangamon County whose average height was about six feet. The relatively subdued Lincoln of the 1834–35 session was replaced by a shrewd politician who aggressively pursued his goal of moving the state capital. This was no easy matter, because Springfield had six competitors: Vandalia, Peoria, Decatur, Alton, Jacksonville, and an uninhabited site, later the village of Illiopolis, twenty-five miles east of Springfield. (Chicago, a fledgling town with a population of five hundred, was out of the running.)

Springfield's spokesman was Lincoln, who had behind him the power of the Long Nine—seven representatives and two senators. Stephen T. Logan recalled that Lincoln "was at the head of the project to remove the seat of the government" to Springfield.[86] Much later, during his presidency, Lincoln sometimes used patronage to achieve his goals. His canny strategizing was on display during his third term in the state assembly. Internal improvements still mattered to him, but he knew Springfield would get them anyway if it became the capital. And so improvements became a carrot he could use to draw various parts of the state to his side: he reportedly promised to support this or that city's request for a rail line, a canal, or a road in exchange for a vote for Springfield. He threw his earlier caution about high costs to the winds in supporting various kinds of improvements, along with compensation to counties that would not be getting them, with the stratospheric price tag of $14 million, which, after the Panic of 1837 devastated the economy, left Illinois with a long-standing debt. Critics accused him and others in the Long Nine of corruption. One said "the whole state was bought up and bribed" by the Sangamon legislators, who resorted to "chicanery and trickery"—a distortion of what was actually the standard practice of logrolling.[87] "Legislation in our Western States," Judge David Davis explained, was "generally based on barter. . . . 'You vote for my measure & I will vote for yours.'"[88]

Whatever trade-offs were involved, Lincoln felt very strongly about the issue. One of his most dramatic encounters—a near duel with General William L. D. Ewing—arose over it. After the Springfield relocation was approved, Ewing, a muscular, pugnacious promoter of Vandalia, used "cutting and sarcastic" arguments against the Springfield junto, targeting its leader, Lincoln. "Gentlemen," Ewing exclaimed, "have you no other champion than this coarse and vulgar fellow to bring into the lists against me? Do you suppose that I will condescend to break a lance with your low and obscure colleague?" Outraged, Lincoln leaped up and gave a scathing reply that "tore the hide off Ewing." A duel seemed imminent, but friends of both men intervened and prevented a deadly encounter.[89]

Why was Springfield so important to Lincoln that he came close to risking his life in its defense? The main reason came down to the city's central position in the state. The *Sangamo Journal*, in an article probably written by Lincoln, denied that he had "miserable motives" such as dispensing favors in exchange for votes, explaining, "It was from the fact that the great population [of Illinois] being North, that a more central location was desired, and this it could not be doubted was the governing consideration with the Legislature."[90]

His ambition to see the state government moved to the center of the state was related to his feelings about slavery. Not only did some of the New England settlers bring antislavery views with them, but Putnam County, to the north of Springfield, had firmly established itself as the antislavery nexus of the state. Putnam, which at the time took up a large portion of northern Illinois, "had so solid an anti-slavery base that it remained a stronghold of thought and action throughout the ante-bellum decades."[91] Lincoln knew of the county's antislavery importance. He wrote a Putnam resident, "I was not aware of your being what is generally called an abolitionist: ... Though I well knew there were many such in your county."[92] By promoting Springfield, therefore, Lincoln was helping to usher the state government closer to an antislavery region.

THE CULTURAL WORK OF REASON

The General Assembly approved the relocation bill on February 28, 1837. Two months later, the twenty-seven-year-old Lincoln moved from New Salem to Springfield. He had been studying law for three years, and he had often attended court sessions run by Bowling Green, the rotund, jovial judge in New Salem who became a kind of surrogate father for him. Just before moving to Springfield, Lincoln earned his law license. His political colleague John T. Stuart, opening an exciting door, had invited him to be a junior partner in his Springfield law firm. Lincoln anticipated a fresh start in the future capital and rode on a borrowed horse to Springfield.

On April 15, he arrived at a general store near the town's main square. With his saddlebags on his arm, he went inside and asked about buying materials for a single bed. When the store's proprietor, Joshua F. Speed, told him that the price of the items would be seventeen dollars, Abe said that he couldn't pay now but hoped to do so by Christmas. He told Speed about his new law job and added glumly, "If I fail in this, I do not know that I can ever pay you." Speed later recalled, "I never saw a sadder face." But Speed told Abe that he need not worry, for he had a large room above the store where he slept in a double bed, and Abe could sleep there too. Abe went upstairs and, after checking the room, put his saddlebags on the floor and then returned to the store, his face beaming. "Well, Speed," he said, "I am moved!"[93]

Lincoln lived nearly four years with Speed, who would become a lifetime friend—probably the closest one he ever had. Five years younger than Abe, the blue-eyed, dark-haired Speed had been born in 1814 Kentucky to a wealthy slaveholding family that lived on a plantation near Louisville. In 1835 he moved to Springfield and took up storekeeping. His friendship with Lincoln grew quickly. They had shared intellectual interests that led to the creation of an informal literary and debating club. They also had similar temperaments, swinging between cheerfulness and depression. In the late 1830s, they briefly shared a love interest, Matilda Edwards, and they served as mutual advisers at anxious moments during later relationships that, for each of them, led to marriage.

Springfield, with a population of about 1,600 when Abe arrived, was a formerly raw town that was becoming vibrant and respectable. Not that it completely shed its rawness. It had a serious problem with dirt and roaming hogs. In dry periods, its unpaved streets produced nostril-clogging dust; in wet weather, they became virtually impassable quagmires. The "dirt and discomfort" that William Cullen Bryant complained of when he visited the town in 1832 had, if anything, worsened when Emerson lectured there in January 1853. "Here I am in the deep mud," he wrote home; "it rains, & thaws incessantly, &, if we step off the short street, we go up to the shoulders, perhaps, in mud."[94] Untended privies and manure piled near stables emitted noxious odors. Hogs roved about, foraging on the garbage tossed on the streets and digging holes to wallow in. According to the historian John J. Duff, "Hog holes, filled with filth and mud, met one at every turn. The smell, so positive and unequivocal, and the orchestration of the nonstop grunting, were a constant source of irritation."[95]

In this regard, however, Springfield was no different from most grimy, animal-infested towns of the day. In 1837 there were more than twenty stores in Springfield that sold groceries or dry goods, four hotels, shops for clothing and shoes, coffeehouses, and drugstores. Log structures were steadily being replaced by ones built with brick or boards.[96] In the town square, a large Greek Revival state house was constructed to host the operations of the state government, whose official transfer to Springfield came in 1839. Cultural offerings came from the Thespian

Springfield in 1860. This is Fifth Street, on the west side of the public square where, from 1852 onward, Lincoln and Herndon's law offices were located above a store.

Society, which put on plays, and the Young Men's Lyceum, which offered public lectures and discussions. Two Bible societies and two temperance societies addressed moral and religious issues, and several Protestant denominations established churches there. A colonization society, devoted to sending free blacks to Africa, had been established in 1833, with John T. Stuart serving as one of its officers.

Promoting colonization was tolerated, but anything more radical than that met with stinging rebukes. Illinois as a whole had a notably mixed record on race and slavery. Before Illinois entered the Union as a free state in 1818 under the antislavery terms of the Northwest Ordinance, slaveholding had existed in the territory for a century. The territorial governor of Illinois, Ninian Edwards, the father of Mary Todd Lincoln's brother-in-law, was a slave owner who in 1815 advertised for sale twenty-two enslaved persons along with two cattle, "a full-blooded stud horse, a very large English bull, and several young ones."[97] Although slavery was supposedly abolished when Illinois became a state, a version of it survived in the form of indentured servitude, by which blacks signed a contract to work for long periods—often twenty years, sometimes for life—for a white person in exchange for food and shelter. Even slavery itself did not fully disappear; it was, as one historian notes, "winked at" in the state.[98] In the 1830 census, the Springfield resident Dr. John Todd, the uncle of Mary Todd, was listed as holding five black people as slaves. By 1840, in the town's population of 2,579 there were 115 African Americans, six of whom were listed as "slaves."[99]

As for free blacks, they had few rights under the state's draconian black laws, which prohibited African Americans from serving on juries, testifying in court, or voting. An 1848 amendment to the state constitution forbade free blacks from settling in Illinois, a prohibition implemented by a law of 1853.[100]

Antislavery sentiment waxed and waned in Illinois. In the early years, proslavery forces pushed for a convention to amend the state constitution to legalize slavery. In 1822 the convention was prevented by a popular ballot, thanks to a challenge by antislavery spokespersons. Thereafter, antislavery sentiment languished until the early 1830s, when certain antislavery groups—Christian ministers, freethinkers, Quakers—began to speak out against slavery. Radical abolitionists, however, were rare. Even most of the antislavery figures who lived in Putnam County were racists who believed that free blacks should emigrate to Liberia. As an observer of Putnam County noted, "There is a most unparalleled prejudice here, among the people generally, against the Blacks."[101]

Anything resembling extreme abolitionism received harsh criticism. After the Reverend Jeremiah Porter gave an abolitionist speech in Springfield in mid-October 1837, a citizens meeting passed resolutions stating that "Abolition . . . can be productive of no good result" and that "the leaders of those calling themselves Abolitionists are designing, ambitious men, and dangerous members of society" whose effect was "to breed contention, broils, and mobs."[102]

Two weeks after the passage of these resolutions, the antislavery editor Elijah P. Lovejoy died at the hands of a racist mob in Alton, Illinois. Mobs had previously destroyed several of Lovejoy's printing presses. On the evening of November 7, 1837, a screaming crowd surrounded his warehouse in Alton. When he came out to confront the people, he was shot. His murder was one of many antiabolitionist incidents that shook the nation during that decade. In October 1835, Boston's mayor had to imprison William Lloyd Garrison to protect him from raucous opponents who threatened to lynch him. In Cincinnati, a mob destroyed the establishment of the antislavery editor James G. Birney, hauling away his printing press and heaving it into the Ohio River. In St. Louis, a black sailor, Francis McIntosh, was chained to a tree and burned to death by a mob after he had killed a policeman who had threatened his friends. In New York, mobs damaged stores and churches associated with antislavery leaders, and a race riot broke out in the Five Points. Similar outbreaks occurred in New Jersey and Connecticut. In the South, the dissemination of abolitionist literature fueled paranoid reactions among those who feared a massive slave insurrection. Amos Dresser, a New Englander who went south to distribute antislavery writings, barely avoided being lynched in Nashville, Tennessee; a group of prominent citizens publicly whipped him and expelled him from the state. In July

1835, rumors of an imminent slave rebellion in Mississippi led to the hanging, without trial, of many African Americans and several whites suspected of being involved in the plot.

The panicked response to the slavery issue appalled Lincoln. He had remained publicly silent on slavery until his second term in the Assembly, when he and a fellow congressman protested against proslavery resolutions passed by the Illinois legislature. The resolutions said that the US government had no right to interfere with slavery in the Southern states or in the District of Columbia; this would amount to "an interference with the rights of property in other States." The legislators added "that we highly disapprove of the formation of abolition societies, and of the doctrines promulgated by them."[103]

Seven weeks later, Lincoln and another Long Nine member, Dan Stone, issued a written protest against these resolutions. Lincoln and Stone argued that while Congress could not abolish slavery in the states, it had the right do so in the District of Columbia if it had the backing of voters there. Lincoln and Stone wrote that they believed "that the institution of slavery is founded on both injustice and bad policy; but that the promulgation of abolition doctrines tends rather to increase than to abate its evils."[104]

Although this last statement seems conservative, it is understandable in context. Lincoln here reacts against the inflammatory moralizing of the Garrisonians, just as he would soon protest against similar rhetoric used by temperance reformers. In 1837, it was bold of him and Stone to declare in the conservative Illinois political arena that slavery was unjust. And they didn't reject abolitionism; they just said that the way it was being promoted stirred up unnecessary acrimony.

Lincoln was alarmed by mobs provoked not only by the slavery dispute but also by other issues. In Charlestown, Massachusetts, an anti-Catholic mob burned a convent and threatened to kill nuns. The Charlestown affair showed that even staid New Englanders could give themselves over to mass frenzy. The same applied to transplanted New Englanders in northern Illinois, where disputes over land claims prompted recently arrived easterners to battle over land. As Thomas Ford wrote:

> The old peaceful, staid, puritan Yankee, walked into a fight in defence of his claim, or that of his neighbor, just as if he had received a regular backwoods education in the olden times. . . . The readiness with which our puritan population from the East adopted the mobocratic spirit, is evidence that men are the same everywhere under the same circumstances.[105]

Lincoln, too, saw that "the staid, puritan Yankee" was as likely as the Southerner to resort to mob action. Anarchic behavior by Americans of different sections led him to denounce it in a lecture he gave at the Springfield Young Men's Lyceum, where on January 27, 1838, he talked on "The Perpetuation of Our Political Institutions." He announced that the country was beset by "this mobocratic spirit, . . . now abroad in the land," which, he feared, threatened to destroy American democracy.[106] He declared, "Whenever the vicious portion of population shall be permitted to gather in bands of hundreds and thousands, and burn churches, ravage and rob provision stores, throw printing presses into rivers, shoot editors, and hang and burn obnoxious persons at pleasure, and with impunity; depend on it, this Government cannot last."

Revolutionary passion, he emphasized, had been necessary in the time of the Founders, who galvanized revolt through the stirring language of the Declaration of Independence. But those days had passed. The revolutionary energies fostered by the Declaration must now be tempered by strict observance of the law. "As the patriots of seventy-six did to the support of the Declaration of Independence," he said, "so to the support of the Constitution and Laws, let every American pledge his life, his property, and his sacred honor." To be sure, some laws were bad. But the Constitution provided the means of replacing bad laws, and the justice system demanded due process in dealing with alleged malefactors. "Let reverence for the laws," he insisted, "be breathed by every American," from young to old; "let it become the *political religion* of the nation." Revolutionary emotions must yield to reason. He concluded, "Passion has helped us; but can do so no more. It will in future be our enemy. Reason, cold, calculating, unimpassioned reason, must furnish all the materials for our future support and defence."

This was Lincoln the rationalist trying to cap the political and social turmoil around him. It was also pure Lincoln (that is, the twenty-nine-year-old Lincoln, given to rhetorical flourishes) because the language was rooted deeply in the natural world. Throughout, Lincoln projected his major points in images of nature, which he tied directly to the national experience. Americans, he announced, occupy "the fairest portion of the earth, as regards extent of territory, fertility of soil, and salubrity of climate." The Founders' task was to "possess this lovely land; and upon its hills and valleys" build the edifice of liberty. Americans faced no "transatlantic military giant" who could "step the Ocean, and crush us at a blow." If we fail, we must "die by suicide," which would happen if we let lawless passions control us. Mobs, he said, were "common to the whole country," from New England to Louisiana. In Mississippi, whites and African Americans "were seen literally dangling from the boughs of trees upon every road side," almost as profuse as "the native Spanish moss of the country, as a drapery of the forest." In this bleak environment, self-aggrandizing individuals, with little regard for the American system, were frighteningly capable of taking control of the nation and tyrannizing over it; "*but such belong not to the family of the lion, nor the tribe of the eagle.*" As for the Founders, "They *were* a forest of giant oaks; but the all-resistless hurricane has swept over them, and left only, here and there, a lonely trunk, despoiled of its verdure, shorn of its foliage." Now was the time for "we, their descendants, to supply their places with pillars, hewn from the solid quarry of sober reason."

The natural world—ocean, trees, a quarry, birds, snow, sun, and so on—here solidifies Lincoln's ideas. The earth yields a political message: rebuild the edifice of liberty on solid ground by obeying the law, or else the hurricane of revolutionary passions will tear it down.

The message of Lincoln's address at the Young Men's Lyceum reflected not only his experiences with nature but also his preparation for the law, especially his study of the eighteenth-century English jurist William Blackstone. For Lincoln, Blackstone's *Commentaries on the Laws of England* was the essential text for all lawyers.[107] We find in Blackstone several principles that reappear in Lincoln's lyceum address. Blackstone established civil law as a crucial defense against two extremes: anarchy and tyranny. Mob action posed so great a danger, Blackstone argued, that riotous groups numbering up to eleven people should be punished by fine and imprisonment, while the penalty for larger groups should be very harsh—even, in some cases, execution.[108] Lincoln, of course, did not go that far, but he said that without due process, the basis of American society might snap apart; some will seek the "total annihilation" of the government, while others will become "disgusted with a government that offers them no protection."[109] What was needed, in the view of both Blackstone and Lincoln, was a strong government that produced clear laws that were faithfully observed by all citizens. Lincoln here followed Blackstone in placing highest value on civil law, rather than on natural law.[110] Following natural law, or the dictates of one's inborn moral sense, could lead in any direction. Natural law, then, must be harnessed—it must be debated in legislatures and courts; it must be held up to the tests of evidence and experience. Then, if it proved desirable, its dictates would be enacted in new civil laws.

Staking a middle ground between tyranny and mob action had political implications for Lincoln. When in the lyceum speech he warned about "men of ambition and talents" who "burn for distinction" and longed to be an American Caesar or Napoleon, he probably had in mind Stephen A. Douglas, the stentorian, self-aggrandizing Democratic legislator who had already emerged as his main political opponent. Also, while Lincoln saw mass violence among different groups, he associated it mainly with rabble-rousing Democrats. Whigs noted that Democrats—nicknamed Locofocos, after lighted matches—were the most frequent inciters of riots, driven by their hatred of abolitionists.

For the Whig *Sangamo Journal*, Lincoln stood out as the state's leader in quelling such politically motivated violence. In an article that appeared in the wake of the lyceum speech, an essayist (probably the paper's editor, Simeon Francis) charged that "wherever the Loco Focos have been predominate of late years, . . . they have had their seditious assemblies, their mobs, their destruction of property, their violations of the law, their attempts to intimidate and overawe its functionaries." The essayist asked, to whom do we owe the salvation of "our present government"? The answer highlighted the Whigs and their leader: "To whom but to those with arms in their hands, with Lincoln at their head, repressed the first open treason of the progenitors of Loco Focoism."[111]

In time, Lincoln would face the problem of suppressing truly nation-shaking treason and mass violence. For now, he was honing his mob-suppressing abilities in Illinois. He was also learning basic parameters—natural law versus civil law, democratic abstractions versus earth-based politics—that would guide his political thinking all the way up through the Civil War. He would eventually tip the balance toward natural law and centripetal power, but he would never surrender his faith in the Constitution, in a compassionate central government, and in the earth as a symbol of stability. He would also retain his respect for reason, which was especially strong in the lyceum speech.

Reason must subdue wild passion. That was his public position in the 1830s. Reason, however, proved hard to maintain when he was faced with severe personal loss and the vicissitudes of romantic relationships. Even resolutions of social problems that seemed staid and moderate, such as the temperance reform, could, he discovered, prove resistant to reason.

Rationalism was his ideal, but there were times in these years, both privately and publicly, when the irrational took over.

Turmoil and Sensations

Lincoln may have hailed "cold, calculating, unimpassioned reason" in his 1838 lyceum address, but he had harrowing encounters with the irrational, both personally and culturally. His doomed love for Ann Rutledge and his painful second thoughts when he was on the verge of marrying Mary Todd drove him at times to near-suicidal depression.

Simultaneously, dramatic cultural changes occurred in the nation. When the French diplomat Alexis de Tocqueville visited America in 1831, he noted anarchic forces that created disorder in the young American democracy.[1] Popular culture exploded during that decade. Mass newspapers dropped dramatically in price, purveying news filled with crowd-pleasing sensational stories about crimes, sex scandals, duels, and the like. Emerson generalized that Americans were "reading all day murders & accidents in the newspapers," and Thoreau spoke of the "startling and monstrous events as fill the daily papers."[2] When real-life sensations weren't available, editors made them up, as in the famous Moon Hoax, a hugely popular newspaper story of 1835, widely accepted as true, about a powerful telescope that revealed a society on the moon with purple unicorns, brown man-bats, and golden palaces. This decade saw the rise of alleged cure-alls like Brandreth's Pills, and of P. T. Barnum, who first earned big money when he hoodwinked the public by presenting the aged African American Joice Heth as a 161-year-old ex-nanny of George Washington.

In some respects, Lincoln fit into this sensational culture. His odd appearance and folksy speech gave him novelty appeal on the hustings. If popular culture was often sensational, so was his rhetoric, which during this period tended toward the slashing and the startling. But he refused to surrender himself to the surrounding rush toward sensation and disorder. He gained his unique talents for control through his private struggles with romantic passion and his public encounters with the turbulent culture of Illinois.

THE THROES OF ROMANCE

Lincoln's three main romances—with Ann Rutledge, Mary Owens, and Mary Todd—are usually treated separately, with the women placed in competition with one another. Victory in the competition has been differently assigned over the years. The idea that Ann Rutledge was the great love of Lincoln's life originated in an 1866 lecture by William Herndon, who believed that Lincoln, trapped in a marriage with the "*female wild cat of the age*," was haunted by the memory of Ann Rutledge, the lovely, kind New Salem woman whose death at twenty-two in 1835 had devastated Lincoln.[3] Ann Rutledge's reputation among Lincoln commentators peaked in the 1920s and '30s, when scholars, authors, and filmmakers invested her with saintlike qualities. She became, in the eyes of the poet Edgar Lee Masters, the virtual mother of the nation, the woman whose tragic passing inspired Lincoln's charity. Masters has Ann's spirit announce, "Out of me the forgiveness of millions toward millions, / And the beneficent face of a nation, ... / Bloom forever, O Republic, / From the dust of my bosom!"[4]

Ann tumbled from her heights when the respected Lincoln scholar James G. Randall challenged the story about her relationship with Abe, pointing out that Herndon's evidence consisted of hearsay and decades-old recollections.[5] Since then, Ann Rutledge's reputation has wavered. For example, Randall's University of Illinois student David Herbert Donald at first rejected the story about the romance, then included it in his Lincoln biography, and eventually doubted it again. Thanks to the spadework of Douglas L. Wilson, John Y. Simon, and others, the Ann-Abe relationship has been restored to credibility, though it is now generally seen as formative rather than life defining.[6] Mary Todd Lincoln's image has improved, as scholars such as Jean Baker and Catherine Clinton have brought attention to positive qualities in her, though her neuroses and quirks have kept alive serious questions about her character.[7]

Mary Owens, meanwhile, has rarely been considered a key player in Lincoln's love life. The indifference about her is understandable, because her brief relationship with Lincoln ended in their breakup. But it is useful to include Mary Owens in discussing Lincoln's romances, which can be best understood when placed against their cultural background.

To call early-nineteenth-century American culture sexist or patriarchal is an understatement. Women could not vote, and discussing politics was considered unladylike. When a woman married, she surrendered her right to hold property separately from her husband. American law followed the era's leading law text, William Blackstone's *Commentaries*, which stated, "The very being or legal existence of the woman is suspended during the marriage, or at least is incorporated and consolidated into that of the husband."[8] The legal disappearance of women took the form of coverture, by which married women were economically dependent and civilly dead. If a woman found herself in an unhappy or abusive marriage, gaining a divorce was extremely difficult in many states. A husband, in contrast, could respond to unorthodox or disagreeable behavior on his wife's part by having her committed to an asylum. Job opportunities for women were limited. Middle-class society was largely controlled by the cult of true womanhood, with its emphasis on piety, passivity, and purity for women.[9] In light of these restrictions, some bold women dared to defy convention, as witnessed by the emerging women's rights movement and by female-authored novels and poems that featured a variety of sturdy, sometimes rebellious character types. Women who stepped out of conventional roles and became reformers or authors were subject to mockery, insult, or ostracism.

Lincoln was well aware of injustice against women. In a handbill from 1836, the twenty-seven-year-old Lincoln announced, "I go for admitting all whites to the right of suffrage, who pay taxes or bear arms, (by no means excluding females)."[10] He wrote this at a time when women in most states were banned not only from voting but also from many other public roles. For him to promote women's suffrage twelve years before the famous Seneca Falls women's rights convention—and eight decades before the Nineteenth Amendment gave the vote to all American women—was remarkable, especially because he was a political aspirant who risked losing his reputation in a state where coverture was law. Actually, he may have been more progressive on the issue than his handbill indicated. William Herndon wrote, "Seeing that Woman was denied in *free* America her right to the elective franchise, being the equal but the other side—the other and better half of man—he always advocated her rights—*yes, rights.*"[11]

Did these rights include the right of sexual choice? According to the prudish mores of the day, a woman who had premarital sex was regarded as "fallen" beyond redemption. One reason prostitution rates were high for women between the ages of fifteen and thirty was the common view that single women known to be sexually active had no future in polite society. Lincoln saw the hypocrisy and one-sidedness of this attitude. He vented his feelings in "Seduction," a poem he wrote for James Matheny's literary group in Springfield in the late 1830s. The poem argued that men were just as culpable in illicit sexual activity as women. Lincoln drove the point home in a creatively rhymed verse:

> Whatever Spiteful fools may Say—
> Each jealous, ranting yelper—
> No woman ever *played* the *whore*
> Unless She had a man to help her.[12]

These lines exposed the "spiteful fools" who cast sexually active single women into social hell without recognizing the complicity of their seducers. Lincoln also opposed the double standard whereby adultery was acceptable if committed by the husband but not by the wife. Lincoln held "that a woman had as much right to violate the marriage vow as the man—no more, no less."[13]

The period's free-love movement advocated free choice of romantic partners for both men and women, governed by so-called passional attraction, or desire unconstrained by social convention. Although Lincoln did not advocate free love, he did recommend freedom of romantic choice for women.

He made his attitude clear in his relationship with Mary Owens. Initially, this romance seemed the opposite of free. In 1836, Lincoln's New Salem friend and admirer Elizabeth ("Betsy") Abell invited her sister, Mary Owens, to travel from Kentucky to Illinois in order to marry Lincoln. As he later recalled, he had met Mary during an earlier visit to Illinois and found her "intelligent and agreeable." He saw no objection "to plodding through life hand in hand with her."[14] When he saw her again in 1836, however, he was repelled by her looks: she was now extremely overweight—"a fair match for Falstaff," he said—and was remarkable "for her want of teeth, and weather-beaten appearance in general." But he was willing to go forward with the marriage. He left the decision in her hands. "What I do wish," he wrote her, "is that our

MARY OWENS

further acquaintance shall depend upon yourself." She should do whatever made her happy. Her choice, as it turned out, was to reject him, at which point, in his words, "I . . . for the first time, began to suspect that I was really a little in love with her."

What explains Lincoln's willingness to marry Mary Owens, despite his reservations about her? Part of the answer surely lies in her intelligence and expressiveness. Those who knew her well called her "a very intellectual woman—well educated," "the most intellectual woman I Ever Saw," "quick & strong minded," a "good conversationalist and a splendid reader."[15] She was not the retiring, submissive type of woman associated with the cult of domesticity. Nor was she averse to hearing about politics, a topic usually reserved for males. In a letter to her from Vandalia, Lincoln described at length the political deliberations of the state legislature there.

She could make bold statements, as when she initiated a correspondence with the New Salemite Thomas J. Nance by writing, "You are well aware, Thomas, that in writing you this letter, I am transgressing the circumscribed limits laid down by tyrannical custom, for our sex."[16] Perhaps her characteristic confidence led Abe to think she could handle even small things on her own. Once when she and Abe were riding in a group that came upon a creek, she was offended that Abe did not follow the example of the other men, who helped their female companions to cross it. She recalled that when she scolded him for not caring "whether my neck was broken or not," he laughingly replied "that he knew I was plenty smart to take care of myself."[17] She also got upset when he failed to help Bowling Green's wife carry a baby up a hill. She told Betsy Abell, "I thought Mr. Lincoln was deficient in those little links which make up the great chain of woman[']s happiness." Lincoln may have thought that attending to such "little links" was unnecessary for sturdy women like Mary Owens and Mrs. Green. At any rate, his moments of self-absorbed abstraction frequently made him disregard everyday niceties.

Although we can't be sure how Mary might have changed if she had married Abe, one wonders if they would have been happy in the long run. Her political views turned out to be very different from his. She had been raised in a family of wealthy Kentucky slaveholders, and when the slavery crisis deepened, she became intensely pro-Southern, to the extent that she and Abe "differed as widely as the South is from the North," in her words.[18] In 1841 she married her sister's brother-in-law, Jesse Vineyard, who moved with her to Missouri, where the couple had enslaved workers. Jesse tried to ensure that the neighboring territory, Kansas, became a slave state. He crossed over into Kansas and cast illegal votes for a proslavery legislature there. His stated goal was to "vote on all occasions" in Kansas in order to help make it "a slave State at all hazards."[19] Mary Owens's husband did what he could to further the westward expansion of slavery—the very thing that Lincoln would devote himself to preventing.

There was no such discrepancy between Abe Lincoln and Ann Rutledge. Their backgrounds were similar. Lincoln's paternal ancestors, as we have seen, had escaped Anglican persecution in England and fled to Massachusetts, moving over generations through Pennsylvania, Virginia, and then Kentucky, leading to the relocation of Thomas Lincoln's family to Illinois. Ann's grandparents were Scottish-born Presbyterians who settled in Ireland, where Anglican persecution drove them to immigrate to Pennsylvania.[20] From there they moved to Virginia and then South Carolina, where James Rutledge, Ann's father, was born in 1781. After the Revolution the Rutledges took advantage of free government land offered near Augusta, Georgia, where the family relocated and where James was raised. In the fall of 1807 the Rutledges and other Scots-Irish in the Augusta area moved north to Henderson County, Kentucky. There James Rutledge married Mary Ann Miller in 1808. Anna Rutledge (known as Ann), the third of their ten children, was born in 1813. Ann was only three months old when her parents took her and her siblings to live in Illinois. They left Kentucky because of threats from Native Americans and for reasons similar to those behind Thomas Lincoln's departure: disputes over land titles and opposition to slavery. The Rutledges settled in White County, Illinois, before moving in 1826 to Sangamon County, where two years later James founded New Salem along with his Scots-Irish friend John M. Cameron.

James Rutledge not only opposed slavery but also had progressive views on women's issues, stimulated, perhaps, by his witnessing the success of Sarah Porter Hillhouse, who in 1803 had become Georgia's (and possibly America's) first woman newspaper editor and publisher. He believed in a sound education for his children, including Ann, who by her early teens enjoyed reading Shakespeare's plays and sonnets. By eighteen, Ann was a comely, good-natured woman with light auburn hair, blue eyes, and a "Mouth well Made b[e]autiful," in the opinion of her teacher, Mentor Graham.[21] She stood five feet four inches and weighed about 125 pounds. She was courted first by William Berry, a preacher's son who later became Lincoln's store partner. After rejecting Berry because of his heavy drinking, Ann also snubbed another suitor, the crude, homely storekeeper Samuel Hill. She was more receptive to John McNeil, an enterprising New York–born businessman who accumulated an impressive estate of some $10,000 to $12,000 while living in New Salem. He and Ann became engaged, but in 1832 he told her that before marrying her he had to return to New York to retrieve his parents and bring them back to Illinois. She learned that his real surname was McNamar; he used the name McNeil as an alias to dodge inquiries from his eastern relatives. He left for the East but soon stopped writing letters to Ann and did not come back for three years. During this time Abe pursued Ann. He had met her while boarding in James Rutledge's tavern, and he studied grammar with her under Mentor Graham.

Evidently, Abe and Ann intended to get married, although whether there was a formal engagement is unclear. Whatever plans they had were shattered when the twenty-two-year-old Ann became gravely ill of typhoid in the summer of 1835. She died on August 25. Abe fell into depression.[22] His friends kept watch over him and made sure that he didn't carry a knife in his pocket. Having long pondered the controlling power of nature over human life, he now regarded nature as a hostile force. Obsessed by the sheer physicality of Ann's death, he said, "I can never be reconcile[d] to have the snow—rains & storms to beat on her grave."[23] Although Lincoln's grief over Ann's passing is understandable, one wonders why he became so depressed that some of his friends seriously feared that he would kill himself.

His vulnerability to deep gloom in the 1830s was worsened by mournful songs and poems. Reportedly, one of his and Ann's pastimes was singing songs from *The Missouri Harmony*, a compilation of nearly two hundred hymns and secular songs presented in shape notes, a simple form of notation for amateur singers.[24] First published in 1820, *The Missouri Harmony* was among the shape-note books that the composer Virgil Thomson has called "the musical basis of almost everything we make, of Negro spirituals, of cowboy songs, of popular ballads, of blues, of hymns, of doggerel ditties, and all our operas and symphonies."[25] One of the main themes of the lyrics in the book was death, as in the lines "How feeble are our mortal frames, / What dying worms are we," or "Death, what a solemn word to all! / . . . We just arise, and soon we fall, / To mix with earth again."[26] Besides *The Missouri Harmony*, among the popular songs Lincoln was known to have sung were doleful ones about doomed lovers, broken romances, and the death of loved ones.[27] In "The Shoemaker's Daughter," a pair of lovers who become separated later find themselves together on a boat at sea whose starving passengers are forced to draw straws to see who will be cannibalized; the woman pulls the shortest straw, and her lover is chosen to kill her, a fate avoided only when a rescue ship arrives. In "Barbara Allen"—a classic folk song later recorded by Bob Dylan, Johnny Cash, Dolly Parton, and others—a man dies of grief because he thinks he has been rejected by his lover; it turns out that he misunderstood her, and on his passing the woman dies of sorrow, too. "William Riley," another standard folk song, depicts a man who is jailed after being wrongly accused of stealing his lover's jewels.

Taken together, these songs form a dismal portrait of ill-fated love. We should also recall that Ann died at a moment when the twenty-four-year-old Lincoln was questioning religion and was reading dark-themed poetry. His favorite poem, William Knox's "Mortality," may have come to his mind in connection to Ann's death. An early biographer ventured that in the weeks after her death "he muttered these verses as he rambled through the woods; he was heard to murmur them as he slipped into the village at nightfall; they came unbidden to his lips in all places."[28] Although this story is probably apocryphal, it points to Lincoln's fixation on writings about the brevity of life and the physicality of death. His gloom was mirrored in Knox's lyrics, especially in lines like these: "The maid on whose cheek, on whose brow, in whose eye, / Shone beauty and pleasure, her triumphs are by; / And the memory of those who loved her and praised, / Are alike from the minds of the living erased."[29] Culture, in the form of disturbing songs and poems, reflected Lincoln's depression.

How would Ann Rutledge have been as a life partner for Lincoln? She combined the qualities of domesticity and firm-mindedness that he sought in women. She was, as Herndon relates, "an excellent housekeeper" and was locally known for her fine needlework.[30] She was also so intelligent that the New Salemite William Greene said that "her intellect was quick—Sharp—deep & philosophic as well as brilliant."[31] Lincoln himself described her as "natural & quite intellectual, though not highly educated." He confessed, "I loved the woman dearly & sacredly. She was a handsome girl—would have made a good wife."

A good wife, perhaps, but a motivator to political greatness? There's no evidence that she took an interest in public issues or sympathized with Lincoln's ambitions.

Four years after Ann's death, Abe met a different kind of woman, Mary Todd, whose ambition matched his. Like Ann Rutledge and Mary Owens, she was both domestic and bright, but she also possessed strong ambition. Born into a wealthy Lexington, Kentucky, family in 1818, she was the fourth child of Robert and Elizabeth Parker Todd. In girlhood Mary predicted to family members that she would someday marry a man who would be elected president. She knew Henry Clay, the eminent senator and perennial presidential candidate, who was a Lexington neighbor and a close family friend. In Lexington she attended school for nearly ten years—remarkable in a day when only a tiny fraction of American women received more than four years of formal education.

MARY TODD LINCOLN

At the Reverend John Ward's Shelby Female Academy she learned many subjects and became fluent in French. She continued her education, in French and other fields, at a local boarding school run by Parisian émigrés Augustus Mentelle and his wife, Charlotte. By the time she reached adulthood, Mary Todd was a cultured, attractive woman. She moved to Springfield, Illinois, in October 1839 to live with her sister Elizabeth Todd Edwards, whose husband, Ninian Edwards Jr., was a leading politician and a member of the Whig Long Nine from Sangamon County. At parties held at the Edwards's large home on Springfield's "Aristocracy Hill," the vivacious Mary Todd was wooed by a number of up-and-coming lawyers and politicians, including two who would later compete against each other for the presidency, Stephen A. Douglas and Abraham Lincoln. Politics influenced Mary's choice of the gangly, homely Abe over the slick, magnetic Stephen. In the late 1840s she reportedly declared that Lincoln "is to be President of the United States some day; if I had not thought so I never would have married him, for you can see he is not pretty."[32]

Mary's ambitiousness was a key catalyst to Lincoln's rise. Her sister Elizabeth said, "She was an Extremely Ambitious woman and in Ky often & often Contended that She was destined to be the wife of some future President—Said it in my presence in Springfield and Said it in Earnest."[33] During her marriage, she was, according to Elizabeth, "the most ambitious woman I ever saw—spurred up Mr. Lincoln, pushed him along and upward—made him struggle and seize his opportunities." Had he married someone else, said his friend Joshua Speed, he "would have been a devoted husband and a very—*very* domestic man"; he "needed driving." John T. Stuart went so far as to say, "His wife made him Presdt: She had the fire—will and ambition—Lincolns talent & his wifes ambition did the deed." Even William Herndon, who crossed swords with Mary, credited her with putting him on the path to the presidency. "Mrs Lincoln was a stimulant to Lincoln in a good sense," Herndon wrote; "she was always urging him to look up—struggle—conquer and go up to fame by becoming a big man: she coveted place—position—power— wanted to lead society and to be worshipt by man and woman: . . . She was like the toothake—kept one awake night and day."[34]

Five feet two inches tall, Mary Todd had wide-set blue eyes, a small nose, a straight mouth, and a round face encircled by brown hair. She struggled with her weight, calling herself a "ruddy *pineknot*" with "periodic exuberances of flesh."[35] She had shapely shoulders that she showed off by wearing dresses that exposed them.

Like Mary Owens, Mary came from a rich slaveholding Kentucky family. But in her case, the slaveholding background did not translate into support of slavery. She was descended on both sides from

Scots-Irish Covenanters, Presbyterians who had immigrated to America, escaping Anglican tyranny in search of religious freedom. In the British Isles, the Covenanters had fought against both the Cavaliers under the Stuart kings and the Congregationalist Puritans under Cromwell. In America, the Covenanters became outspoken critics of slavery, which they opposed on the basis of both natural law and the Bible.[36] This antislavery sentiment took different forms, according to social context. In the North, Covenanters espoused abolitionism. Southern Covenanters began with a similarly urgent antislavery agenda but in time settled into a more moderate advocacy of colonization, which called for gradual abolition followed by the relocation of African Americans in Liberia or elsewhere.

Mary Todd's family and its forebears reflected the evolution of Covenanter antislavery feeling in the South. Mary's uncle, John Todd, while serving in the Virginia legislature in 1777, had called for the abolition of slavery in Kentucky County. Although his descendants did not repeat this demand, some of them, including Mary's father, Robert Smith Todd, supported colonization, then considered radical in the South. Though a slaveholder, Robert Todd desired the eventual extinction of slavery and the shipping of emancipated blacks out of the country. To that end, he supported a colonization society in Lexington and in 1833 voted to ban the importation of additional enslaved people into the state.[37]

The antislavery viewpoint of Robert Todd and his first wife, Elizabeth "Eliza" Parker Todd, explains why their four daughters, including Mary, opposed slavery. By contrast, eight of the nine children that Robert had by his Episcopal second wife, Elizabeth ("Betsy") Humphreys Todd, supported slavery. During the Civil War, four half brothers and three brothers-in-law of Mary Todd Lincoln fought for the Confederacy. She did not publicly express grief when four of them died in battle, because she wholeheartedly supported her husband and the Union cause. Mary became "a more ardent abolitionist than her husband," a biographer notes.[38]

As a Southern woman with Northern principles, Mary was a living embodiment of the union of sections that would be the driving force of Lincoln's politics. This union of cultural opposites was mirrored in a marriage between personal opposites. Herndon noted that Mary was "the exact reverse" of Abe "in figure, in physical proportions, in education, bearing, temperament, history—in everything."[39] Mary, when discussing her marriage, referred to "our opposite natures."[40]

But the opposition can be overstated. Not only were Mary and Abe born Southerners who held similar views on slavery, but she had also been close to his beau ideal, Henry Clay. She was, like Abe, an excellent mimic, and she loved discussing politics and enjoyed his favorite poets, particularly Robert Burns. Their physiques, of course, were very different, but their temperaments had commonalities. If Abe shifted between entertaining storytelling and meditative abstraction, she swung between exuberant social chatter and private paranoia. It's tempting to call both of them manic-depressive, but it's risky to assign psychological labels in retrospect. Whatever their psychological conditions, they avoided being incapacitated for long periods by mental illness. Both had a keen eye on Abe's advance in the public sphere.

Like many marriages, Abe and Mary's had its turbulent times, but in their case the turbulence must be seen in context. While somewhat unusual for a woman, Mary's biting style was consistent with the sensational culture. A relative testified that she was "quick at repartee and when the occasion seemed to require it was sarcastic and severe."[41] She had "an unusual gift of sarcasm," according to another relative, and "now and then indulged in sarcastic, witty remarks, that cut like a Damascus blade."[42] Lincoln, too, was a master of sarcasm during the period when he met and married Mary. As a politician, he was locally famous for his "slasher gaff" rhetoric—caustic attacks on political opponents. But he worked hard at balancing the sensational and the rational in his speeches and writings, just as he struggled mightily to maintain an equilibrium between powerful emotions and reason in his personal relationships.

SENSATIONALISM AND SARCASM

The popular turn toward sensationalism that occurred during the 1830s and '40s brought not only mob violence but also physical fights between journalists or politicians. The New York *Evening Post* editor William Cullen Bryant took a cow whip to a rival, who seized the whip and thrashed Bryant in front of City Hall. In 1836 the New York editor James Watson Webb, who was involved in two duels against politicians, publicly whipped James Gordon Bennett for twenty minutes as crowds cheered. Bennett, the editor of the immensely popular *New York Herald*, was said to invite such whippings because he knew that reports of it would sell newspapers. A foreign observer quipped that Bennett would "bend his back to the lash and thank you; for every blow is worth so many dollars."[43]

Violence and sensationalism had a strong effect on the style of popular literature and oratory. Walt Whitman, then a young journalist, described a rival as "a reptile marking his path with slime wherever he goes, . . . a midnight ghoul, preying on rottenness and repulsive filth."[44] The author and reformer George Lippard began his career by writing the lurid Gothic thriller *The Ladye Annabel* and the stinging literary satire "The Spermaceti Papers," leading to his nightmarish, politically subversive city-mysteries novel *The Quaker City*, in which ruling-class types are mocked from a working-class standpoint.[45] Lippard was the most famous of numerous American urban novelists who combined Gothic excess and trenchant social commentary. Lippard's close friend Edgar Allan Poe extracted terror and perversity from popular sensational genres. Poe's literary satires enraged his enemies so much that one of them pummeled him badly, and he spent several days in bed recovering.

The speeches of President Andrew Jackson, as Kenneth Cmiel shows, marked the transition toward sensational political expression, as in his assaults on "aristocrats" who made the "monster bank" a "Hydra of Corruption."[46] Reading Jackson's attacks on the bank, the diarist Philip Hone remarked, "The language . . . is disgraceful to the President and humiliating to every American." It smelled "of the kitchen" and was produced by "the scullion," not "the gentleman."[47] Others who specialized in shocking public language were James Gordon Bennett, Horace Greeley, Benjamin Butler, and Andrew Johnson.

The rough-and-tumble spirit of American public life permeated Lincoln's immediate political world in Illinois. Springfield's sheriff, Garrett Elkin, responding to attacks on him in the *Republican*, horsewhipped the paper's editor, George R. Weber, whose brother stabbed Elkin and another man with a knife. The brother's assault provoked a duel challenge against Weber. Lincoln witnessed a fracas at a political meeting in July 1836, when Ninian Edwards leaped on a table and called a Democratic opponent, the Reverend Jacob Early, a liar. A duel was barely averted; during the back-and-forth, Edwards drew a pistol, and "the whigs & democrats had a general quarrel then & there."[48] Two years later, while running against each other for Congress, Lincoln's friend John T. Stuart and Stephen Douglas engaged in fisticuffs in a local tavern. A witness said, "They both fought till Exhausted—grocery floor Slippery with Slop." Another time in the campaign, when the hotheaded Douglas again angered Stuart, the latter seized the diminutive man by the neck and pulled him around until Douglas bit his thumb, scarring him for life. Douglas was so upset by a piece in the *Sangamo Journal* that he used his cane to attack the paper's editor, Simeon Francis, who jammed the Little Giant against a cart before being pulled away by spectators. What Douglas lacked in physical power he made up for in rhetorical vigor. His speeches were savage, often alcohol-fueled denunciations meant to humiliate opponents. In Sidney Blumenthal's words, his speaking style "resembled that of a frontier fighter, spitting, shooting, and gouging," filled with "ranting, illogic, and invective, peppered with frequent use of the word 'nigger.'"[49] Douglas's bludgeoning style, Lincoln saw, was hard to combat because many audiences willingly accepted absurdities if they were delivered with enough force. As Lincoln later wrote of Douglas, "A neatly varnished sophism would be readily penetrated, but a great, rough *non sequitur* was sometimes twice as dangerous as a well polished fallacy."[50]

Early in his political career, Lincoln tested out the popular sensational style, mastering invective and abrasive humor. In the legislative races of 1832 and 1834 he was restrained, but in 1836 he unleashed his caustic wit. During the campaign he "used the weapons of sarcasm and ridicule, and always prevailed," an observer noted.[51] When a Democrat wrote a piece falsely charging him with opposing repayment of a state loan, Lincoln in a handbill stated that "the author is a *liar* and a *scoundrel*, and that if he will avow the authorship to me, I promise to give his proboscis a good wringing."[52] A decade before George Lippard and other popular writers used Gothic images to unmask their opponents, Lincoln did so with such force that the *Sangamo Journal* likened him to a tomb raider: "The Van Buren men . . . are taking shelter like ghosts under the rotten bones and tombstones of the dead acts of the administration. Mr. Lincoln, however, lifted the lid, and exposed to the eye the wretched condition of some of the acts of the Van Buren party."[53] Lincoln contributed to "Sampson's Ghost," a six-part newspaper series partly in the Gothic style in which a ghoulish "unearthly visitant" terrorizes James Adams, an attorney whom Lincoln charged with forgery and fraud in depriving the heirs of Joseph Anderson of their rightful inheritance.[54]

He made innovations on the sensational style, using animals and things in ways that typified his humor and storytelling. He compared a Democrat who greatly exaggerated the expenses of internal improvements to a Hoosier bachelor who fired at what he thought was a distant squirrel that was in fact a louse on his eyelash. Lincoln said of his opponent, "He imagined he could see squirrels every day, when they were nothing but *lice*."[55] In an 1837 speech on Van Buren's subtreasury system, he compared Democrats who absconded with public funds to a man in an Irish folk song who had a cork leg that ran faster the more he tried to stop it. In the same speech, he used his awareness of vibrant matter and the overwhelming power of nature to expose what he saw as corruption streaming out of the Van Buren White House:

> I know that the great volcano at Washington, aroused and directed by the evil spirit that reigns there, is belching forth the lava of political corruption, in a current broad and deep, which is sweeping with frightful velocity over the whole length and breadth of the land, bidding fair to leave unscathed no green spot or living thing, while on its bosom are riding like demons on the waves of Hell, the imps of that evil spirit, and fiendishly taunting all those who dare resist its destroying course, with the hopelessness of their effort; and knowing this, I cannot deny that all may be swept away.[56]

This spiraling sentence reaches gloomy depths of the sort we find in what I describe elsewhere as dark reform literature: popular writing that exposes social abuses in sensational images so graphic that the images themselves, rather than the abuses, seize our attention.[57] In this passage, Lincoln ostensibly addresses corruption, but what we see is an evil spirit and all-destroying lava alive with devils who mock everyone. Such post-Calvinist images anticipated the dark reform writing of George Lippard, whose 1845 novel *The Quaker City*, one of the era's huge sellers, features a nightmarish scene in which massive corruption creates a dystopic America that heaves and then explodes like a volcano.[58] Herman Melville, who praised the Calvinistic "power of blackness" in his contemporary Nathaniel Hawthorne, extensively used dark reform images in his early fiction that set the stage for his vast, appalling white whale, relentlessly pursued by the "grand, ungodly, god-like" Captain Ahab, who is a kind of overreaching dark reformer intent on piercing the greatest "whited sepulcher" of all, Moby-Dick.[59] Other Lincoln contemporaries influenced by dark reform were Whitman, whose 1842 temperance novel *Franklin Evans* emphasized the aberrant results of alcohol abuse, and Poe, who in stories like "The Black Cat" and "The Cask of Amontillado" probed the psychology of alcohol-crazed murderers.

Did Lincoln hope to follow the path of others and become an author? He certainly tested his literary abilities in the 1830s and '40s. He wrote an uncounted number of pieces for Springfield's Whig paper, the *Sangamo Journal*, which he virtually coedited during this time. The paper printed "The Suicide's Soliloquy," the first of his three published poems (later to include "My Childhood Home I See Again" and "The Bear Hunt").[60] In "The Suicide's Soliloquy," Lincoln tried to gain poetic control over private tensions that were evidently left over from Ann Rutledge's death. "The Suicide's Soliloquy" was a means for him to imaginatively purge and simultaneously gain literary control over his self-destructive impulses. Like his two later published poems, "Soliloquy" regulates a melancholy theme with steady iambic meter and regular rhymes. Like Lincoln's stories, it is filled with nature images. The poem is the last utterance of a wretched man, alone at midnight in the woods as an owl hoots, who imagines wolves eating his carcass, buzzards picking at his bones, a raven cawing, and so forth. He also has a vision of leaping off a precipice into the burning waves of hell, where screeching devils surround him. The moment of suicide is described physically: the "sweet steel" of the dagger "rip[s] up the organ of my breath / And draws my blood in showers." "I strike!" he cries. "It quivers in my heart," as he draws out the dagger and kisses it, "my last, my only friend."

The poem channels not only desperate personal passion but also dark cultural energies. The newspapers of the time were filled with reports of suicides—the more sensational the better. The *Sangamo Journal* published many such stories, including "Most Melancholy—Double Suicide," about lovers, depressed by opposition from their parents, who hang themselves; "Singular Suicides," about four sisters who separately kill themselves days or weeks apart; the report of an "extremely prepossessing" girl, falsely charged with robbery, who swallows arsenic; and what is, understandably, called "the most extraordinary suicide in the world's record," about a German woman whose husband is so depressed that she stabs herself after hearing doctors say that only a "real misfortune" will shock the man back to sanity—indeed, the man recovers nicely after her suicide, prompting the doctors to say that "no medicine could have worked with such potency on either mind or body."[61]

Compared with such tawdry sensational news stories, Lincoln's "The Suicide's Soliloquy" brings poetic control and resonance to a popular theme that had particularly strong meaning for him in the aftermath of the loss of Ann Rutledge. Three years after he published this poem, he fell into another depression that again produced suicidal thoughts. He called himself "the most miserable man living," and those close to him described him as "Crazy as a Loon," in peril of becoming "a lunatic for life."[62] The occasion this time is murky, but it was believed on all sides to be related to his recent breakup with Mary Todd.

Biographers have identified a number of factors that contributed to Lincoln's break with Mary and his subsequent melancholy. They include his doubts about his love for Mary, to whom he nonetheless felt committed; the opposition of her family to the marriage; his sudden infatuation with the lovely eighteen-year-old Matilda Edwards; his attraction to an even younger teenager, Sarah Rickard, who was half his age; his financial uncertainty as a junior lawyer and a low-paid legislator; his sorrow over the impending departure to Kentucky of his friend and bedmate, Joshua Speed; and Mary's reported flirtation with other men. There were exterior factors, too, including the embarrassing episode in December 1840 in which Lincoln and two Whig colleagues jumped out a state house window to prevent Democrats from having a quorum on a disputed bill. Also disconcerting for Lincoln, who had championed ample funds for internal improvements in Illinois, was the resulting financial default of the state on January 1, 1841, a date known locally as "the fatal first."[63]

It's mistaken to isolate any single factor in his withdrawal from Mary and his psychological tailspin. Lincoln himself, if asked, probably could not have explained why the "hypo" came over him with devastating force.

What really matters for history is that he soon recovered and went on to marry Mary Todd, who helped push him along the path to the presidency. The relevant questions are: How did he recover emotional stability, and what made him change his mind about marrying Mary? The standard explanation is that sometime in late summer or early fall of 1842 Eliza Rumsey Francis, the wife of the newspaper editor Simeon Francis, reintroduced Abe and Mary, who had some private meetings that led to a rapprochement. Such encounters rekindled the romance, and Lincoln's sterling sense of personal honor impelled him to fulfill the promise of marriage he had previously made to Mary Todd.

There were also significant cultural factors at work that have been ignored. One is the lessons he learned from political conflicts over class issues, which put him at risk of death a few times in the 1836–42 period. Another is his relationship to the era's most popular reform, the temperance movement. A third is his and Mary's participation in progressive ideas about gender and marriage that emerged around the time they reunited.

Only by exploring these cultural phenomena do we understand Lincoln's psychological rehabilitation and his life-defining commitment to Mary Todd.

FIGHTING OVER PARTY AND CLASS

In a memorable political episode of 1840, Lincoln dealt with an issue that was becoming highly sensitive for him and for America at large:

the relationship between political affiliation and social class. At a public rally that summer, the Democrat Richard Taylor criticized Whigs as the party of the rich, whose aristocratic airs distanced them from average Americans. Enraged at this representation of his party, Lincoln, who was standing to Taylor's side, slowly edged up to the speaker and, when he got close, jerked open his vest. Out tumbled shirt frills "like a pile of Entrails" and "gold chains—gold watches with large seals" that "hung heavily & massively down."[64] The audience roared in mockery of the hypocritical Taylor. Lincoln told the crowd that not long ago he had been a flatboat man wearing buckskin pants that shrank so much that they exposed his lower legs and left a purple mark on them. "If you call this aristocracy," Lincoln declared, "I plead guilty to the charge."

Politics and class were vexing issues for Lincoln at a time when he was mingling with Springfield's social elite on Aristocracy Hill and simultaneously campaigning for the Whig presidential candidate William Henry Harrison, a large landowner and scion of a wealthy family who was being sold to the public as the quintessential common man, one who purportedly occupied a log cabin and drank hard cider. This was neither the first nor the last time that image trumped substance in American elections, but it was among the most significant instances of such distortion. One might think that Lincoln, with his genuinely humble background, would not have to prove his working-class credentials, but he did, because Whigs were commonly dubbed "aristocrats" or "ruffled-shirt gentry."[65] And so he followed the example of others involved in Harrison's Log Cabin campaign, which in its populist hoopla anticipated the image-filled promotion of the Illinois Rail-splitter in the 1860 presidential race.

The Democrats in 1840 were still riding the coattails of the immensely popular Andrew Jackson, whose successor, Martin Van Buren, had kept some of Old Hickory's policies alive in his first term and was running for reelection. The Whigs did what they could to make Van Buren, the self-made farmer's son, seem aristocratic, charging him with living in decadent opulence in the White House. It is no wonder that the political parties struggled vigorously over the issue of class. With the rise of a market economy, class divisions deepened during the antebellum era, creating social tensions. Between 1774 and 1860, the percentage of total assets owned by the richest 1 percent of Americans increased from 12.6 percent to 29 percent, while that controlled by the top 10 percent rose from less than half to nearly three quarters.[66] The rich lived in mansions in areas, like Springfield's Aristocracy Hill, that seemed distanced, economically if not geographically, from the humbler, more crowded neighborhoods of the working class or the poor. Class anxieties fostered popular novels that contrasted the so-called upper ten—the "idle" rich who lived off the labor of others—and the "lower million," the underpaid workers and the oppressed poor. It was to no politician's advantage to be associated with the upper ten, especially at a time when voter participation was extremely high; it reached 80.2 percent of eligible voters in 1840.[67]

Lincoln began fighting publicly over social class in the 1836 state election, when he "skinned" opponents by emphasizing their upper-class associations. His most famous critique that year was aimed at the political turncoat George Forquer, a former Whig who had become a Democrat, apparently to win favors from President Jackson, who appointed him as the high-salaried land register of Illinois. Forquer owned Springfield's largest house, on which he installed a lightning rod, a device new to that region. At a political meeting, Forquer, calling Lincoln a "young man" who had to be "taken down," gave a speech so severe that the Clary's Grove Boys, Lincoln's ardent supporters who were among the audience, squirmed with rage.[68] When Forquer was done, Lincoln took the platform and, in a coolly sarcastic riposte, admitted that he was too inexperienced to know political tricks, but, "live long or die young, I would rather die now than, like the gentleman, change my politics, and with the change receive an office worth three thousand dollars a year, and then feel obliged to erect a lightning rod over my house, to protect a guilty conscience from an offended God." This statement caused a sensation, and Forquer was humiliated.

This was the first of many public situations in which Lincoln used what the Illinois governor Thomas Ford called "the little big man" technique—that is, posing as humble or inferior for political effect.[69] Lincoln would use this technique for the rest of his career, and he honed it in his early Illinois races. In January 1837, he used it against Usher Linder, a noted politician who wanted to divide Sangamon County and launch an investigation of the Illinois State Bank. Linder had a reputation, as a contemporary observed, as "the greatest orator of this State."[70] Lincoln began his speech by admitting that he knew Linder did not like "wasting ammunition on *small game*" such as himself. But he praised Linder only to damn him, for in the next breath, he said that Linder's "decided superiority" lay in his faculty of "entangling the subject, so that neither himself or any other man can find head or tail to it."[71] In the rest of the speech, Lincoln gave a stinging, if not always logical, discussion of the bank issue in which Linder came off as ignorant, elitist, and possibly corrupt.

The most notorious of Lincoln's little-big-man skinnings occurred in the 1840 legislative race, when he took aim at the Democratic opponent, Judge Jesse B. Thomas. In the Springfield courthouse, Thomas spoke against Lincoln and accused Whigs of forging letters related to Stephen A. Douglas, the state's leading Democrat. In his reply, Lincoln put on his little-big-man pose, saying that he was "a humble member of the 'Long Nine,' so that he could not swell himself off to the great dimensions of his learned and eloquent adversary." If he tried to do so, he feared he would "be attended with the fate of the frog in the fable, which tried to swell itself to the size of an ox." But, he added, he could prick pinholes in his adversary and "bring him down to size."[72] What followed was a scathing ad hominem attack in which Lincoln, an excellent mimic, not only blasted the judge but imitated his distinctive speech, gait, and mannerisms. The mimicry caused real pain. As the audience cheered Lincoln on, Thomas began to "blubber like a baby, and withdrew from the assembly." He cried for much of the rest of the day. Deeply ashamed, Lincoln soon apologized to Thomas.

As far as we know, none of these skinnings put Lincoln in physical danger. The same cannot be said of other hostile encounters. With his athletic skills and his rough frontier background, Lincoln was always ready for combat. Once when his Whig friend Edward Baker provoked Democrats in the audience, Lincoln seized a heavy pitcher and threatened to smash anyone who tried to attack Baker. Another time, he and Baker protected a colleague from hecklers by assuring him that "we both think we can do a little fighting, so we want you to walk between us until we get you to your hotel."[73]

Some of Lincoln's political battles led to life-threatening moments when the subjects of his attacks called for a duel. Although dueling had been outlawed since 1810 in Illinois, when it was still a territory, someone who wanted to engage in a duel got satisfaction by facing his opponent out of the state—a favorite spot was the no-man's land called Bloody Island, between Illinois and Missouri. That evasion of the law became less attractive in 1848, when Illinois's new constitution stipulated that no dueler could hold a position of honor or power in the state. Before then, challenges were common, though rarely did they result in a duel, because typically the parties reached a settlement. That was the case in 1837 when friends intervened to settle the dispute between Lincoln and the Democrat William L. D. Ewing, who appeared to be ready to have a duel over the issue of moving the state capital to Springfield.

In his next potentially fatal encounter, Lincoln became his own mediator. In late October 1840, while he was wrapping up the Harrison campaign in southern Illinois, Lincoln got into a verbal contretemps with William G. Anderson, a Democratic politician. Evidently, both men charged each other with falsifying party records. Lincoln's remarks were abrasive enough that Anderson wrote a note saying that Lincoln's words "imported insult," adding, "I think you were the ag-

TURMOIL AND SENSATIONS

gressor."[74] The note was clearly a challenge, but Lincoln defused the situation in a cautiously worded letter in which he told Anderson, "I entertain no unkind feeling to you, and none of any sort upon the subject, except a sincere regret that I permitted myself to get into such an altercation."

THE VICTORY OVER DARK REFORM

Lincoln's address to the Springfield Washington Temperance Society before a packed house in the town's Second Presbyterian Church on February 22, 1842, was a key moment in his career as a public speaker. The dark reform rhetoric that characterized some of his earlier speeches—such as the devil-infested lava of corruption or the slashing sarcasm of the skinnings—was absent from his temperance address. A main argument of the speech was that American reformers had been too sensational and that a new, more rational way of addressing reform was needed. He saw that temperance, like abolitionism, was a well-meaning movement but that the dark images and hyperemotionalism of many of its proponents were self-defeating. Persuasive appeals to reason, he argued, must replace irrationalism and denunciation. The speech signaled his rational treatment of a hotly debated public issue.

Lincoln had long experience with the temperance movement. In Indiana he had written a temperance article that was published in an Ohio newspaper. In Springfield in 1838 he formally pledged "never to drink ardent spirits" (redundant in his case because he hated the taste of alcohol) and signed the constitution of the Sangamon Temperance Society along with 185 others, including his friend Simeon Francis.[75] In the 1840s he rode by horse and buggy around central Illinois giving temperance talks.[76] In 1853 he signed a group letter congratulating Springfield's Presbyterian minister James Smith for a temperance speech he had given.[77] During the Civil War, he greeted a delegation of the Sons of Temperance by declaring, "Intemperance is one of the greatest, if not the very greatest of all evils amongst mankind." He added, on a note of caution, "The mode of cure is one about which there may be differences of opinion."[78]

He knew those differences well. He recognized that the noble aim of combating alcoholism had been hindered by contests between various approaches to temperance reform and behavioral lapses on the part of reformers. He also knew that temperance, like other reforms, could be taken to an extreme. He had developed a relaxed, tolerant view of drinking that freed him of narrow views of alcohol consumption. Those who drank, he recognized, were fallible and yet basically as good as those who abstained. To win drunkards to sobriety through reasonable persuasion, he insisted, should be the temperance reformer's goal.

In making this point, he was reacting against a tradition of dark temperance oratory and literature. He chastised "uncharitable" and "feelingless" reformers who excoriated drinkers as "the authors of all the misery and crime in the land," whose "houses were workshops of the devil," and who "should be shunned by all the good and virtuous, as moral pestilences."[79]

He had ample exposure to this kind of gloomy rhetoric. One of his main schoolbooks, William Scott's *Lessons in Elocution*, included a story about Death, a grim king, who seeks a prime minister among many diseases—gout, asthma, palsy, and others—and decides to choose a woman named Intemperance, who asks the other illnesses, "Am I not your parent? The author of your beings?"[80] As a teenager in Indiana, Lincoln sang the dark temperance song "John Anderson's Lamentation" (aka "John Adkins' Farewell"). In this bleak song, an alcoholic who is about to be executed for murdering his wife tearfully gives moral messages to other inebriates and to his own poor, parentless children. "Oh sinners! Poor sinners! Take warning by me," the man cries. "The fruits of transgression, behold now and see." The temperance message is stark:

Much intoxication my ruin has been.
And my dear companion I've
    barbarously slain; . . .
A whole life of sorrow can never
    atone,
For that cruel murder that my hands
    have done;
I am justly condemned, it's right that I
    should die,
Therefore, let all drunkards take
    warning hereby.[81]

The song typified the popular dark temperance genre, which yielded countless poems, short stories, novels, and tracts. Mason Weems, one of Lincoln's favorite authors, wrote the popular *Drunkard's Looking Glass*, in which a preacher, lured by the devil, gets drunk and murders his father, rapes his sister, and hangs himself. The Reverend George B. Cheever's *Deacon Giles' Distillery* (1835) pictures a still in which devils produce barrels of rum emblazoned with labels like "Sickness," "Poverty," "Death," "Hell," and the like. Dark temperance fiction crowded newspapers and achieved bestselling status in Timothy Shay Arthur's 1854 novel *Ten Nights in a Bar-room*, which traces the collapse of a once-respectable community after the introduction of a saloon and a distillery.

Lincoln had exposure to temperance reform in both New Salem, where John Allen founded a temperance society in 1831, and in Springfield, which had three temperance societies when Lincoln moved there in 1837. The Presbyterian Allen had founded the New Salem group because he found the village "a notoriously wicked and intemperate place."[82] Within two years of its founding, Allen's society counted seventy-six members. By 1835, the group's work had taken effect: New Salem had become largely a temperance town. Those who wanted to drink without

Dark reform. Illustration from George B. Cheever's sensational
temperance novel *Deacon Giles' Distillery* (1835), showing devils
producing barrels of rum, which have labels such as "Sickness,"
"Poverty," "Death," and "Hell."

inhibition moved to Petersburg, two and a half miles away, where "you
could drink yourself to death and no one would interfere."[83]

Although the records of Allen's society have not survived, we get a
sense of the group's approach to temperance from an 1834 address given
by one of its members, Thomas J. Nance.[84] The speech begins by advocating total abstinence, which, Nance says, cultivates reason in humans.
While this part of the talk anticipated Lincoln's praise of reason in the
Washington Temperance Society speech, Nance makes the kind of dark
turn that Lincoln avoids; he describes the disease, despair, broken
homes, and crime that come from drinking. Nance tells a sensational
story of the kind told endlessly by his contemporaries about a man who
begins as a moderate drinker but who becomes a sot who loses his family and dies a miserable, lonely death.

If the temperance message of New Salem Society was typical of the era, so was the conflict between different approaches to drinking. When the town's schoolmaster, Mentor Graham, joined John Allen's society, he was expelled by his hard-shell Baptist church, which considered temperance reform a sacrilegious meddling with human character that must be left solely to God. At the same time that Graham was kicked out, so was a member of the congregation who was perpetually drunk. The church's inconsistent response to alcohol use gave rise to a humorous predicament when a third congregant stood up in church, waved a half-filled flask of whiskey, and declared, "Brethering, you turned one member out because he did not drink, and another because he got drunk, and now I want to ask you, how much of this 'ere critter does a man have to drink to stay in full fellership in this church?"[85] Another twist came when Mentor Graham got drunk and was expelled from Allen's temperance society, at which point he rejoined the church.

Backsliding like Graham's was so common that the figure of the "intemperate temperance reformer"—the person who advocated temperance but resumed drinking—became a standard figure of ridicule in popular culture. The overwhelming majority of those who pledged total abstinence eventually returned to the bottle.[86] Lincoln had been familiar with such inconsistent behavior since early childhood. Three of the preachers who were most influential on his family—William Downs, David Elkin, and Jesse Head—had serious drinking problems, as did Father William de Rohan, a Catholic priest who had contact with the Lincolns in Kentucky. The Reverend Jesse Head was a bundle of contradictions: "Though an Abolitionist, he owned slaves. Though a temperance advocate, in common with the majority of the backwoods preachers, he would not refuse an occasional 'dram.'"[87] William Downs was bibulous, "disorderly, indolent, slovenly, and self-indulgent," while David Elkin was "uncultivated" and "somewhat sullied" by "too free a use of strong drink."[88]

The intemperate temperance reformer remained a standard figure in Lincoln's experience. William Herndon, his longtime law partner, was an ardent temperance advocate from the early 1840s onward. He joined several temperance groups and, as mayor of Springfield in the mid-1850s, led the failed effort to institute prohibition there. But he was an alcoholic whose frequent drunkenness often tested Lincoln's patience. (Mary Todd Lincoln, for her part, labeled Herndon a *"wretched drunken madman."*)[89] Other intemperate temperance men in Lincoln's circle included the lawyers and politicians Usher Linder, Richard Yates, and Kirby Benedict. Linder eloquently advocated prohibition and yet was too inebriated to perform his lawyerly duties three times. Once he was reportedly so drunk at a dinner that when a platter of chicken was handed to him he dumped all the meat on his own plate and then handed the empty platter to Lincoln, saying, "Abe, have some chicken."[90] Lincoln's friend Richard Yates, another fervent promoter of temperance, was so drunk at his inauguration as governor of Illinois in 1860 that he arrived late at the ceremony, where Lincoln and others had waited for him for half an hour, and he slumped on a chair while a clerk read his inaugural speech.[91] The Decatur, Illinois, attorney Kirby Benedict was yet another temperance advocate—as a judge in New Mexico he enforced strict laws against drinking, gambling, and swearing on the streets—who drank heavily. When during his presidency Lincoln got complaints that Benedict was failing in New Mexico due to his tippling, Lincoln replied, "I know Benedict. We have been friends for thirty years. He may imbibe to excess, but Benedict drunk knows more law than all the others on the bench in New Mexico sober. I shall not disturb him."[92]

The truth is that, unlike other promoters of temperance, Lincoln had a relaxed and charitable view of those who drank. After all, his ideal politician, Henry Clay, was a heavy drinker, as was one of his finest generals, Ulysses S. Grant. A binge drinker, Grant was an intemperate temperance man: before the war he had joined a temperance society after hearing a lecture by John Bartholomew Gough (himself a notorious backslider who preached temperance but was once found passed out in a brothel after a week of carousing). Grant was usually sober in important situations but periodically returned to the bottle. Shortly before Grant took Vicksburg, two temperance men approached Lincoln in the White House urging the removal of Grant because "he drank too much whiskey." "Ah!" Lincoln said. "By the way, gentlemen, can either of you tell me where General Grant procures his whiskey? Because, if I can find out, I will send every general in the field a barrel of it."[93]

Behind such a joke was Lincoln's realistic recognition that while excessive alcohol use could be destructive, those who drank must not be rejected as a class. He was less bothered by drinkers or backsliders than by the damning rhetoric used by many temperance advocates. The intemperate temperance he objected to was the extremely harsh rhetoric used by reformers.

In making this argument in his Washington Temperance Society speech, he joined a backlash against extreme reformers that had been gathering force for a decade. In an 1835 piece on "The Intemperate Temperance People," a correspondent for a Massachusetts newspaper wrote, "The sober and rational part of the community are tired and disgusted with the violence, fury, and persecuting spirit of those who call themselves *Reformers*."[94] The *New York Times* ran an article titled "Intemperate Temperance Men" that denounced "the extravagancies of these crazy reformers, . . . whose enthusiasm in every cause they undertake soon becomes *monomania*." This was true not only of temperance promoters, the writer maintained, but of diet reformers, antiprostitution activists, and abolitionists who demanded immediate emancipation. The "blind and intemperate zeal" of these extreme reformers could only arouse "the distrust and contempt of the public."[95] Another newspaper essayist averred, "We can tell these intemperate temperance zealots that they do the cause infinitely more harm than even the drunkards themselves." The reformers would succeed, the essayist argued, only if they used "more *honey* and less *vinegar*" in their language, if they remembered that "'soft words turn away wrath'" while "harsh ones 'stir up strife,'" and that they should "aim, not to *drive*, but to '*win*' man."[96]

Lincoln amplified these arguments in his 1842 Washington Temperance Society speech by presenting a capsule history of the tactics that had been used to combat intemperance. Temperance reform in America, he noted, originated in an earlier generation when alcohol consumption was widespread among people of all classes and ages: "Universal public opinion not only tolerated, but recognized and adopted its use."[97] Since then, alcohol abuse had been fought by preachers, lawyers, or agents—all well intentioned but mistaken in their strategies. "The warfare heretofore waged against the demon of Intemperance," he said, "has, somehow or other, been erroneous. Either the champions engaged, or the tactics they adopted, have not been the most proper." These reformers resorted to "thundering tones of anathema and denunciation," not recognizing that "it is not much in the nature of man to be driven to any thing" and that "the conduct of men is designed to be influenced by *persuasion*, kind, unassuming persuasion." To win someone over, he insisted, you must be compassionate: "Therein is a drop of honey that catches his heart, which, say what he will, is the great and high road to his reason, which, when once gained, you will find but little trouble in convincing his judgment of the justice of your cause."

Drunkards, he continued, are no worse than other people. By telling them that they are doomed to poverty, crime, and death, they inevitably go downward. The Washingtonian movement, Lincoln declared, offered a wholly new approach to temperance reform. Founded in 1840 by six alcoholics in Baltimore who grouped together, shared their stories, and pledged themselves to temperance, the Washingtonians represented for Lincoln a reform that sprang from the people themselves, not from preachers or other establishment types. As "friends and companions," the self-reformed Washingtonians "know that they are not demons" but generally are "kind, generous and charitable, even beyond the example of their more staid and sober neighbors."[98] And so, "*They* teach *hope* to all—*despair* to none." Even those who do not drink should join the movement, Lincoln maintained, because the drunkard "needs every moral support and influence, that can be possibly brought to his aid," with everyone "kindly and anxiously pointing him onward." This movement, Lincoln predicts, will prove "a noble ally . . . to the cause of political freedom," portending a time "when there shall be neither a slave nor a drunkard on the earth." Lincoln's vision of universal liberty leads to his ecstatic peroration:

> Happy day, when, all appetites controled, all passions sub-dued, all matters subjected, *mind*, all conquering *mind*, shall live and move the monarch of the world. Glorious consum-mation! Hail fall of Fury! Reign of Reason, all hail!

The enthusiasm of this declaration, unparalleled in his writing, goes far beyond his response to the temperance movement. Actually, despite his contributions to the movement, including this speech, he was not a persistent supporter of temperance reform. A friend said that in 1854 he joined the Sons of Temperance, a secret reform group, but never at-tended its meetings.[99] He did not get involved with the prohibition movement that swept the nation in the wake of the Maine Law of 1851, a movement that attracted William Herndon, Simeon Francis, and sev-eral other associates.

Lincoln's Washingtonian speech was less a plug for a particular movement than it was a fresh means of bringing about social change, one that tapped into what he later called "the better angels of our na-ture" and a politics "of the people, by the people, and for the people."[100] His 1842 statement of this hopeful theme was ahead of its time, as evi-denced by the criticism of his address by church members, who were offended by its sympathy toward drunkards and its praise of reason, unaided by religion.

But for Lincoln, the speech had both cultural and personal implications. Culturally it pointed away from vicious demonizing and divisive fanaticism toward compassion and common humanity. Personally, it announced Lincoln's newfound control over destructive irrational impulses. When Lincoln sang praise to the "Reign of Reason"—with appetites and passions controlled by "all conquering *mind*"—he was expressing anew his impulse to tame the wild that had previously produced his physical battles against frontier bullies and his arguments against "mobocracy." During his period of depression, friends said, Lincoln had been overtaken by confused, irrational thoughts. The Washingtonian address was his public proclamation of his return to reason.

He hoped that the speech would help his close friend Joshua Speed, who had left Springfield and moved back to Kentucky. A month after he delivered the speech, Lincoln sent a copy of it to Speed, asking him and his wife Fanny to read it aloud to each other. This unusual request may have at first seemed out of place to Joshua, who, like Lincoln, had no alcohol-related issues. But if he read the speech, it surely comforted him. He and Lincoln had fought together against depression and had lifted each other to a healthier mental place. Their mutual assistance grew from their sincere affection for each other. If Lincoln found in the Washingtonian movement an example of how marginalized drunkards could rehabilitate through mutual support and companionship, he believed his speech could have a healing effect on Joshua Speed, who, like himself, had been isolated by depression and who recovered through friendship.

REGAINING EQUILIBRIUM

The relationship between Lincoln and Joshua Speed has sometimes been characterized as homosexual. The strongest statement of this interpretation comes from the AIDS activist Larry Kramer, who quotes from what he calls Speed's long-lost diary, which was supposedly discovered under the floorboards of Speed's store in Springfield. However, there is no evidence that such a diary ever existed outside of Kramer's imagination. (At any rate, a diary probably would not have survived the fire that destroyed Speed's store in 1855.) C. A. Tripp, who joins Kramer in sexualizing the Lincoln-Speed relationship, points to the fact that the two slept in the same bed for more than three years and for a year thereafter sent letters to each other with affectionate phrases like "Yours forever."[101]

This reading of the Lincoln-Speed relationship falsely imposes today's ideas of sexuality on the past. As is true with everything, his friendships must be placed in their cultural contexts. Lincoln lived in an era that did not know clear sexual categories; the word "homosexual" was not used in English until 1892 and wasn't widely known to the public until the 1920s. Before then, intimacy between people of the same sex was not typically associated with a sexual predilection.[102] Men regularly slept with men, and women with women—often because of the exigencies of space or available bedding. To "sleep with" someone did not have the sexual connotation that it has today. Lincoln slept in his youth with his stepbrother and in New Salem with a number of economically struggling young men. When he traveled on the law circuit, he often found himself in the situation of Melville's Ishmael and Queequeg, forced to sleep together in an inn due to insufficient accommodations. Lincoln stayed in places so small that as many as twenty people slept in the same room, up to three to a bed, with the rest squeezed sardinelike on blankets on the floor.

According to his friends, Lincoln was ardently heterosexual. He was, David Davis said, "a Man of strong passions for woman—his Conscience Kept him from seduction—this saved many—many a woman."[103] To Whitney, Lincoln "over & over again" described "sexual contact" as "the harp of a thousand strings." Herndon confirmed that Lincoln was "a man of terribly strong passions for woman" and "could scarcely keep his hands off them." Herndon learned of two visits to prostitutes Lincoln made when he was single in Illinois, including one in which Lincoln stripped, got into bed with the woman, and found that her fee was five dollars. When he told her he had only three dollars, she offered to work on credit, but ever honorable, Lincoln refused the offer, put on his

JOSHUA FRY SPEED (C. 1842)

clothes, and left.[104] Herndon also recalled that Lincoln once told him he had caught a disease from a Beardstown prostitute "during a devilish passion."[105]

That said, Lincoln's intimacy with Joshua Speed was unusually close. In their years together in Springfield they not only slept together but also had most meals together. They usually dined at the home of William Butler, who had generously offered to feed Lincoln for free. (Speed paid Butler for his meals.) After dinner, Speed was generally part of the crowd that gathered in the back room of Speed's store to discuss literature or politics with Lincoln. Speed also attended many court sessions in which Lincoln served as an attorney. As Speed wrote to a Lincoln biographer, "No two men were ever more intimate."[106]

Intimacy in their case almost certainly did not involve sex. William Herndon, who was scrupulously observant of every aspect of Lincoln's behavior—even to the extent of inventing scandals in order to demystify Lincoln—never reported a physical relationship between Speed and Lincoln, which he would have known of because he slept in the same Springfield room with them for two years. (A fourth man, Speed's clerk Charles R. Hurst, also slept in the room.) During the Civil War, Lincoln recalled, "I slept with Joshua for four years, and I suppose I ought to know him well."[107] Speed and Lincoln joined other nineteenth-century heterosexual same-sex couples—among them, Emerson and Martin Gay, Daniel Webster and James Hervey Bingham, or, in fiction, Cooper's Leatherstocking and Chingachgook, Melville's Ishmael and Queequeg, and Mark Twain's Huck Finn and Jim—whose relationships were loving without being sexual.

Carl Sandburg commented that both Lincoln and Speed had "a streak of lavender" and "spots soft as May violets."[108] This ambiguous description, which relies on rhapsody rather than analysis, rightly points to Lincoln's and Speed's sensitivity but ignores the fact that both men instinctively keyed into the fluid ideas about gender of their era, as expressed, for instance, by the thinker and activist Margaret Fuller, who wrote in 1843, "There is no wholly masculine man, no purely feminine woman."[109] Lincoln exhibited a gentleness and tenderness then associated with womanhood. With all his physical strength and mental toughness, he had a mild side. As the Massachusetts senator Henry Wilson said, "Mr. Lincoln is a man of *heart*—aye as gentle as a woman's and as tender—but he has a will as strong as iron."[110] Lincoln's friend Joseph Gillespie confirmed, "He was gentle as a girl and yet as firm for the right as adamant. He was tender hearted without much shew of sensibility."

As president, Lincoln's tender side would make him quick to pardon deserters and to help out the family members of imprisoned or missing soldiers. As a bachelor in Springfield, it generated a symbiosis with Joshua Speed. If we follow Lincoln's life from his mental turmoil in January 1841 to his Washingtonian speech in February 1842 (which was also the month of Speed's marriage), we see how same-sex love could facilitate mental recovery. During Lincoln's breakdown, Speed was one of the few people who had access to the isolated, suicidal Lincoln. In that dark moment, Speed may have saved Lincoln's life. He recalled that "Lincoln went Crazy—had to remove razors from his room—take away all Knives and other such dangerous things—&c—it was terrible."[111] Another savior was Lincoln's friend Dr. Anson Henry of Springfield.

The attention of Speed and Dr. Henry was instrumental in Lincoln's recovery, as was the cognitive repair resulting from Lincoln's active resumption of his law practice. Just as pursuing law books had helped him regain mental equilibrium after his post–Ann Rutledge collapse in 1835, his new law partnership, established in May 1841 with the prominent attorney Stephen T. Logan, ushered him into full-time legal activity and permitted him to exercise his reason in practical ways. In the late summer, Lincoln seems to have suffered a mild depression, but that was allayed by a three-week visit to Farmington, Joshua Speed's family plantation in Louisville, Kentucky. One of the largest plantations in the state, Farmington featured a white-columned brick mansion modeled after Jefferson's Monticello, on 550 acres of fields where hemp and other produce were cultivated. Lincoln's visit there was comforting for him. He was with Joshua, and he became close to Joshua's half sister Mary, a forty-two-year-old single woman, and to Joshua's mother, Lucy Speed, who gave Lincoln a Bible, which she hoped would comfort him. Many years later, Lincoln sent her a photograph with the handwritten inscription "For Mrs. Lucy G. Speed, from whose pious hand I accepted the present of an Oxford Bible twenty years ago."[112] Reading this Bible did not change Lincoln's religious views, but it had a positive effect, visible in his speeches from then on, which had far more references to God than had his earlier ones.

Also at Farmington, Lincoln aided in Speed's courtship of Fanny Henning, a brown-eyed, pious woman who lived in Lexington, eighty miles to the east. Lincoln twice accompanied Speed to the Henning home, where he diverted Fanny's father by conversing with him while Speed was wooing Fanny. After that, Lincoln served as a close participant in Speed's developing romance, which was as tortured as had been Lincoln's court-ship of Mary Todd the previous winter. This time it was Speed who drifted in and out of depression, while Lincoln acted as the rational counselor. When Speed in December 1841 confessed to having serious doubts about his forthcoming marriage, Lincoln specified three possible reasons for his anxieties: the winter weather, an inactive social life, and Speed's underly-ing "nervous debility."[113] In advising Speed, Lincoln pursued the same kind of balance between reason and passion that he did in his speeches on mobs and on the temperance movement. On the one hand, he assured Speed that physical and emotional attraction, not reason, had originally guided his choice of Fanny. "What had reason to do with it, at that early stage? . . . All you then did or could know of her, was her *personal appear-ance and / deportment*; and these, if they impress at all, impress the *heart* and not the head." He added, "Say candidly, were not those heavenly *black eyes*, the whole basis of your easily *reasoning* on the subject?"[114]

While reminding Speed of the emotional basis of his relationship with Fanny, he also bolstered the relationship rationally. Whatever fears Speed had, Lincoln argued, would soon disappear, as had his own gloom the previous year. In five long letters around the time of Speed's marriage, he gave reason after reason why Speed should be happy with Fanny. Then in October 1842, eight months after Speed's marriage and a month before his own, Lincoln wrote his friend, asking, "Are you now, in *feeling* as well as *judgement*, glad you are married as you are?"[115] This question, along with his other interchanges with his friend, had as much to do with his own state of mind as with Speed's.

A balance between reason and passion was what he was trying to establish in himself, a balance he projected outward onto the turbulent American culture around him. In the Washingtonian speech, as in the lyceum address four years earlier, he offered reason and calmness as the counterweights to unbridled passions. Drinking and mob action suspended reason, he pointed out, while sobriety and observing the law restored it. Both speeches described the intense emotions behind the American Revolution as necessary for their time but unwanted today. The revolution of '76, he said, introduced liberty to the world, but "it had its evils too," because it "breathed forth famine, swam in blood and rode on fire," and for years "the orphan's cry, and the widow's wail" were heard.[116] In contrast, the Washingtonian reform leaves "no orphans starving, no widows weeping." Proclaiming the "Reign of Reason" was Lincoln's way of asserting both social control and personal control of combating cultural chaos and private demons.

Around the time he gave his Washingtonian speech, he confirmed his mental recovery in letters to Speed in which he wrote, "I have been quite clear of the hypo since you left,—even better than I was along in the fall" and "I have been quite a man ever since you left."[117] Notably, in explaining why Speed felt anxious just before his marriage, Lincoln says that "nervous debility" was what distinguished Speed and him from most people. This trait, Lincoln writes, "though it *does* pertain to you, *does not* pertain to one in a thousand. It is out of this, that the painful difference between you and the mass of the world springs."[118] A shared anxiety during premarital wooing, in short, united them.

Lincoln soon found relief from such anxieties in his second try with Mary Todd. Direct information about the postdepression courtship that led to their marriage is sparse. Although Lincoln recovered psychologically, he did not apparently reenter the social whirl on Aristocracy Hill, as is indicated by the fact that Mary in June wrote a friend, Mercy Levering, that he "deems me unworthy of notice, as I have not met him in the gay world for months." She added that if "'Richard [that is, Lincoln] should be himself again,' much, much happiness it would afford me."[119]

Abe and Mary reunited after they teamed up against the Irish-born Illinois politician James Shields by writing installments of what have come to be known as the "Lost Townships" letters in the *Sangamo Journal*. Shields, the state auditor, issued an announcement that Illinoisans must pay all debts in gold or silver, not in the paper currency issued by the Bank of Illinois, which had failed as a result of the economic depression. Although this order sprang from economic necessity rather than personal motives, Lincoln took the opportunity to launch a very personal attack on the Democrat Shields, a self-important, highly sensitive man who was close to Stephen A. Douglas. Lincoln did so in a satirical article published in the *Sangamo Journal* on September 2, 1842, followed a week later by a similar piece written by Mary Todd and her friend Julia Jayne.

Three previous installments of the "Lost Townships" letters, written by someone else, had appeared in earlier issues of the newspaper, but the ones written by Abe and Mary are completely different from those. Abe introduces a female narrator, Rebecca, a gossipy, brash widow who visits a recently married friend, Ned, who expresses outrage over Shields and the currency issue.

By using a female narrator, as opposed to the omniscient narrator of the former "Lost Townships" satires, Lincoln did something rare. Only a few other male writers before 1860 used female speakers effectively. In the eighteenth century, the sixteen-year-old Benjamin Franklin had published sketches in which he impersonated Silence Dogood, a scolding widow who commented on social issues; later, as Polly Baker, he wrote a fictional speech to a court objecting to the sexual double standard. Among male writers of the antebellum era, Poe was the only major figure who took on a female persona; he did it twice, in his literary satires "How to Write a Blackwood's Article" and "A Predicament." From 1847 onward, the humorist Benjamin Shillaber utilized a female speaker, Mrs. Partington, who became a popular favorite in the 1850s. Among women writers, Frances Whitcher introduced her comic female narrator, Widow Bedott, in 1846; Marietta Holley popularized her humorous speaker, Betsey Bobbet, in the 1850s.

All of these nineteenth-century women narrators avoided serious involvement with politics. The feeble-minded Mrs. Partington attacked women's suffrage. The Widow Bedott and Betsey Bobbet were submissive types who aimed desperately to get married and enter "wimmens spear."[120]

Rebecca, the female speaker that Lincoln created, and that Mary and Julia developed, was far more unconventional than these narrators. She was brazen, bawdy, witty, and politically involved. In Lincoln's installment, she begins by making what would then be considered a dirty joke: she suggests that the child of her neighbor Jeff has been fathered by another man because the infant's hair appears to be the wrong color. She then enters into a political discussion with Jeff, who is appalled by the fact that he cannot pay his taxes in paper money, thanks to James Shields's proclamation. For the rest of the sketch, Lincoln does his little-big-man act, this time in the guise of a woman. Sarcastically playing the humble person, Rebecca mouths the excuse Shields gave for imposing the currency restriction, saying, *"there is danger of loss to the 'officers of State,' and you know Jeff, we can't get along without officers of State."*[121] Jeff grumbles that Shields and other state officers thrive on their high salaries while other Illinoisans are driven into poverty. Rebecca questions Jeff, who has had dealings with Shields, who comes off as both a political turncoat and a person of amorphous gender. Jeff assumes that the preening Shields is a Whig, though the knowing Rebecca insists he is a Democrat. Jeff declares that "Shields is a fool as well as a liar. With him truth is out of the question, and as for getting a good bright passable lie out of him, you might as well try to strike fire from a cake of tallow." Jeff tells of a fair where he saw "Shields floatin about on the air, without heft or earthly substance, just like a lock of cat-fur where cats had been fightin." Here Lincoln suggests that Shields is an absolute nullity, politically and personally. At the fair, the vain, dandy-ish Shields paraded among adoring women and said that he was sorry that he could not marry them all, explaining, "Too well I know how much you suffer; but do, *do* remember, it is not my fault that I am *so* handsome and *so* interesting."

The Rebecca sketch by Mary Todd and Julia Jayne, published a week after Lincoln's, was even more daring than his. In the course of Lincoln's piece, Jeff's voice largely replaces Rebecca's, so that Shields is mocked mainly from a male perspective. In the Todd-Jayne version, in contrast, Rebecca holds center stage throughout. The mockery of the proud Shields now comes wholly from a crude, rough-spoken woman who is unafraid to move well outside the limits of genteel female behavior. This defiance of gender roles is accomplished with boldness and aplomb. At the beginning of the sketch, Rebecca is in the process of making butter when she is approached by Jim Snooks, who tells her that Shields, furi-ous at being compared to cat's fur, demands satisfaction (that is, he wants a duel). Rebecca replies that a duel is fine with her, but there is another alternative: Shields can come to her and see what satisfaction he can get out of squeezing her hand. If satisfied, he can marry her. With ersatz bashfulness, she offers herself: "Really Mr. Printer, I can t help blushin— but—it must come out—I—but . . . well! if I must I must—wouldnt he— may-be sorter, let the old grudge drop if I was to consent to be—be—h-i-s w-i-f-e?"[122] She boasts of her attractions: she is under sixty, four feet three inches tall, and about that much around the middle. If Shields doesn't accept her marriage proposal, she is ready for a duel. As the one being challenged, she gets to choose the weapons: she suggests either a broomstick, hot water, or a shovelful of coals. She wonders if she should dress as a woman or a man for the duel, leaving the decision to him. As she says, "I'll give him choice . . . in one thing, and that is whether, when we fight, I shall wear breeches or he petticoats; for I presume that change is sufficient to place us on an equality."

As a follow-up to this satire, Mary and Julia wrote a poem about Shields, signed "Cathleen," that was published a week later in the *Sangamo Journal*. In the poem, Cathleen announces the forthcoming marriage of Shields and Rebecca:

> Ye Jew's-harps awake! The Auditor's won:
> Rebecca the widow has gained Erin's son;
> The pride of the North from Emerald Isle
> Has been wooed and won by a woman's smile. [So on for fourteen more lines].[123]

In these pieces Mary and Julia broke all kinds of nineteenth-century taboos. Middle-class women did not make marriage proposals to men, especially in aggressively physical terms; nor did they offer to fight duels or to cross-dress.

Given the sharpness and unconventionality of the Rebecca satires, it is understandable that Shields was roused to action by the women's sketch. To preserve his honor, he requested a duel. He asked Simeon Francis, the editor of the *Sangamo Journal*, for the identity of the author of the Rebecca letters. Learning of Shields's inquiry, Lincoln assumed full responsibility for the satires. He refused to apologize to Shields, who sent an official challenge through his friend General John D. Whiteside. Lincoln replied that he was opposed to dueling, but when Shields pressed the issue, he accepted the duel, which was to take place on Bloody Island on September 22.

As the challenged party, Lincoln could select the weapons, and he chose large military broadswords, which he thought would give him an advantage over Shields, who was seven inches shorter than he. Abe explained, "I did not want to kill Shields, and felt sure that I could disarm him . . . ; and furthermore, I didn't want the d—d fellow to kill me, which I rather think he would have done if we had selected pistols."[124] He bragged, "If it had been necessary I could have split him from the crown of his head to the end of his backbone."[125] The boast, however, underestimated Shields, who was an expert with both the sword and the pistol. While growing up in Ireland and England, he had taken fencing lessons from ex-soldiers of the Napoleonic wars. Shields's biographer reports, "He learned fencing or sword exercise and became so expert in the art that few men of any size or experience could surpass him."[126] He became so proficient that when he first came to North America he was for a time a fencing instructor in Canada. It's quite possible that Shields would have defeated Lincoln, and America would have been deprived of its greatest president.

Fortunately, when the dueling parties convened on Bloody Island, friends on both sides intervened, and the fight was called off. Shields went on to become the only person in history to be elected to the US Senate in three different states. During the Civil War he served as a brigadier general in the Union army under Lincoln.

The whole situation had brought Abe and Mary back together. Abe learned that Mary Todd was not a conventional woman like Ann Rutledge, Mary Owens, or Matilda Edwards (who eventually married a wealthy older man). He saw that Mary was ready to step outside accepted gender roles and experiment with alternative views of womanhood and manhood. If he took on feminine qualities in his Rebecca sketch, she tested out dueling, proposing marriage, and cross-dressing in the installment she wrote with Julia. Unlike other women he had known, Mary seemed to have exceptional capaciousness and flexibility.

That flexibility also related to her own family past. On this point, she differed greatly from Joshua Speed, who, like her, was from a wealthy Kentucky family of slaveholders but, unlike her, did not surrender his acceptance of slavery. He defended the institution when Lincoln confronted him about it in a letter of 1855. Although Speed remained loyal to Lincoln during the Civil War—indeed, as Lincoln's main personal contact in Kentucky he helped keep that border state in the Union—he continued to hold black people in bondage right up to the ratification of the Thirteenth Amendment. Mary, in contrast, did an about-face on slavery, eventually rejecting it completely and giving her unconditional support to Lincoln and the Republicans.

In the end, Abe discovered that what he most sought in American culture—the unity of diverse attitudes and voices—was what Mary embodied. At a time when there was already talk of war between the North and the South, she was a Southern woman open to Northern views. At a moment when different spheres for men and women were being defined, she embraced domesticity but also ventured bravely into politics and other male realms.

UNCONVENTIONAL DOMESTICITY

They were aware that their marriage would distance them from their immediate families. Abe was increasingly alienated from his father. His rare visits to Coles County were mainly to see his stepmother. Although he occasionally sent his father money, he stayed aloof from him. When in 1849 he was notified that his father was dying of heart disease and had asked to see him, Abe went for a visit only to find that it was a false alarm. His father was recovering from lung congestion. Two years later, Abe got a similar message. He wrote a consolatory letter to his stepbrother John D. Johnston, assuring him that Thomas would soon be with loved ones in heaven but adding, "Say to him that if we could meet now, it is doubtful whether it would not be more painful than pleasant."[127] He soon learned that his father had died. He did not attend the funeral. Although he intended to install a stone and a fence at his father's grave, he never did more than scratch the letters "T. L." on an oak board that he stuck into the ground at the grave site; the board was later stolen by curiosity seekers.[128]

What explains Lincoln's estrangement from his father? A common interpretation is that he was distanced from his father from an early age and became more so over time. But his memories of what he called his "joyous, happy boyhood" and Thomas Lincoln's sound record in Kentucky and Illinois argue against this view.[129] The real rift between the father and son came after their first year together in Illinois, when Thomas moved to Coles County, where he ended up in Goosenest Prairie, and Abe went to New Salem. Abe's experiences there broadened him greatly and prepared the way for his social and professional rise after his move to Springfield in 1837. The surviving evidence about Thomas Lincoln suggests that he made no advance at all in Illinois. Maintaining a subsistence lifestyle, he lived hand to mouth. A neighbor described him as "an excellent spec[imen] of poor white trash," "[a] rough man—never drank but lazy & worthless—had few sheep—poked around behind them talked an[d] walked slow."[130] John D. Johnston, who continued to live with his wife and children with Thomas Lincoln, was so indolent that Abe sharply reproved him in an 1851 letter, calling him "an idler" given to "uselessly wasting time."[131] Abe's growing distance from his father and stepbrother reflected his core belief that humans were distinguished from other animals by their capacity to improve their lot. This belief nurtured his Whig commitment to improving infrastructure through government spending and his dedication to improving himself intellectually and professionally. Perhaps here lies the explanation of his increasing alienation from his father and John D. Johnston, who remained notably *un*improved.

Mary was also separating emotionally from her family. While her resentment of her stepmother and stepsiblings in Kentucky can be overstated, there is no doubt that after her move north she felt closer to her relatives in Illinois than to the ones who remained in the South. Then tensions arose with the Illinois clan once her interest in the lowborn, ungainly Abe Lincoln became known. Mary's sister Elizabeth Todd Edwards, who reportedly tried to break up the relationship for two years, recalled, "I warned Mary that she and Mr. Lincoln were not suitable. Mr. Edwards and myself believed they were different in nature, and education and raising. They had no feelings alike. They were so different that they could not live happily as man and wife."[132]

With all these family conflicts, Abe and Mary decided to have a low-key wedding. Abe did not invite his Coles County relatives; in fact, his father never met Mary because he never got an invitation to Springfield. Mary, for her part, failed to invite her father and stepmother to the wedding—a highly unusual omission for a woman in that era. On the morning of November 3, 1842, Abe asked an Episcopal priest, Charles A. Dresser, to hold a simple ceremony in his home that night. Dresser agreed, but on the street Abe met Ninian Edwards, who, on hearing the plan, insisted on holding the service at his house because he was Mary's guardian. Abe, thirty-three, and the twenty-three-year-old Mary were married in the parlor of the Edwards home on the evening of November 4; Reverend Dresser read from the Book of Common Prayer. Abe gave Mary a ring that bore the inscription "Love is Eternal." About thirty relatives and friends, invited at the last minute, attended. There was a light reception. A week later Abe wrote a friend, "Nothing new here, except my marrying, which to me, is matter of profound wonder."[133]

Surveying the span of cultural and personal events leading up to Lincoln's wedding, we can better understand his mental collapse and his subsequent recovery. The issues he had tussled with publicly for years—internal improvements, class divisions, and the handling of social reform—may be said to have imploded in January 1841, when the state nearly went bankrupt due to the expensive improvements plan he had backed and when his prospect of marrying someone from Aristocracy Hill clashed with the little-big-man persona he had been cultivating. Devoted to improvement on every level, he could not seek solace in his backward father or stepbrother, and yet a commitment to the society woman Mary Todd frightened him. His relationship with his fellow sufferer Joshua Speed provided a much-needed balm, as did his reflections on the Washingtonian movement, which for him was a model of comradely healing and rational self-control.

One would think that after calling for restrained rhetoric in his temperance speech he would avoid the kind of vitriolic language that had characterized his skinnings, but the Rebecca letters proved otherwise. They were, in fact, far more caustic than anything he had previously produced. And yet the Rebecca episode, though it put him at risk of death in a duel, solidified his relationship with Mary. Her participation in the Rebecca gambit showed that she could venture beyond the boundaries of class and gender. If their collaborative rebellion against conventions widened the gap between them and their families, it made possible their marriage.

Shortly after the wedding, Abe and Mary moved into the Globe Tavern, a boardinghouse just west of Springfield's public square, where Mary's sister Frances and her husband William Wallace had recently lived. Room and board came to eight dollars a week. In the eighteen-by-fourteen-foot room, a son, Robert Todd ("Bob" or "Bobby") Lincoln, named after Mary's father, was born on August 1, 1843.

After spending the early winter of 1843–44 in a rented house on Springfield's South Fourth Street, the Lincolns sought a permanent domicile. In January 1844, Abe bought a one-and-a-half-story, five-room frame house from the Reverend Charles Dresser for $1,200 plus a town lot worth $300. Located at the corner of Eighth and Jackson Streets in Springfield, the house had a sitting room, a parlor, a kitchen on the ground floor, and two cramped bedrooms upstairs. In the backyard was a latrine, a water pump, a carriage house, and a small barn for animals. A few blocks away, farms began, their broad fields stretching into the distance. This choice of a home reflected not only Abe's modest finances at the time but also the couple's impulse to keep a distance from Mary's relatives, who lived several blocks away on Aristocracy Hill. The Lincolns lived in the Jackson Street house for seventeen years. On March 10, 1846, a second son, Edward ("Eddie" or "Eddy") Baker Lincoln was born. That year the Lincolns added a bedroom and a pantry.

During their early years in the Jackson Street home, the Lincolns

The Globe Tavern, Springfield, Illinois, where the Lincolns boarded during the first year of their marriage and where Robert Lincoln was born.

The Lincoln house on Eighth and Jackson Streets, Springfield, Illinois (a lithograph based on a photograph). This is how the house appeared when the Lincolns bought it in 1844. Between then and 1860, the couple enlarged the home a few times, most notably in 1856, when they created a full second story and made other major changes. This is the only house Lincoln ever owned. Three of his children—Eddie, Willie, and Tad—were born here.

Abraham Lincoln in 1846 or 1847
(photograph attributed to Nicholas H. Shepherd)

lived a life that outwardly fit the cult of domesticity. In line with the split-spheres custom of the day, he was away for several weeks a year, traveling the Eighth Judicial Circuit and practicing the law in small-town courthouses, while she stayed at home, tending to the children. Mary wrote, "A nice home—loving husband and precious child are the happiest stage of life," a period when "you are a happy, loving Mama."[134] Mary got household training from books like *Miss Leslie's Cookery* and *Miss Leslie's Housekeeper*. She spoke of her "years of very very great domestic happiness—with my darling husband & children."[135]

The Lincolns had an unusual attitude toward parenting. Their boys had free run of the house (except for the parlor) and the law office.

Having been raised in an atmosphere of rote learning and harsh discipline, Abe wanted to loosen the parental bonds. As Mary recalled after his death, "He was very very indulgent to his children—chided or praised for it he always said 'It is my pleasure that my children are free—happy and unrestrained by paternal tyranny.'"[136] One of Lincoln's political friends remarked, "He was the most indulgent parent I ever knew[.] His children litterally [*sic*] ran over him and he was powerless to withstand their importunities." Lincoln himself admitted, "We never controlled our children much."[137] Although Mary occasionally used the lash to punish misbehavior, as when two of her boys dismantled a clock she had bought or when Tad fell in a mud puddle, she was also forbearing. Jean Baker notes, "Usually she was more indulgent than even her permissive husband, once berating Lincoln for what must have been his own feeble effort to discipline the 'codgers.'" Mary conceded, "If *I* have erred, it has been, in being too indulgent."[138]

The Lincolns' lenient attitude can be linked to an emerging view of education and parenting that was radical for its day. Their distaste for overly harsh discipline owed an allegiance to the so-called Pestalozzian system of education, based originally on the Romantic theories of Rousseau and Locke, that was advanced by progressive teachers like Bronson Alcott, whose Temple School discouraged flogging or reprimands on behalf of allowing children the freedom to play, roam, and learn by free association instead of by memorization. Alcott believed that children could learn to heed the inner voice of conscience if liberated rather than punished. Lincoln evidently believed that his sons could best tap into their highest potentiality if largely left to their own devices.

As the Lincolns' views of child-rearing suggest, their outward acceptance of conventional marital roles was deceptive. In the decades after Lincoln's death, some commentators questioned his marriage, taking special aim at Mary Lincoln. William Herndon led the way by calling the marriage a "policy match" that became intolerable for Abe because of Mary's "avaricious," "mean," "insulting," and "imperious" nature.[139] These were overstatements made by Herndon in hindsight, fueled by slurs she had made about him and by his mission of debunking falsely rosy Lincoln biographies. We cannot, however, ignore Herndon's comments altogether. Mary did sometimes behave oddly or violently.

But the extremes of complete vilification and falsely rosy descriptions of Mary miss the basic fact that she chafed under the gender restrictions of her era, as did many other women. Cultivated and strong-minded, she was faced with what was then the extremely patriarchal institution of marriage. Even before marrying, she was skeptical of the institution. She spoke half jokingly of "the *crime of matrimony*" and asked, "Why is it that married folks always become so serious?"[140] The fact is, for most women of that era marriage was what Emily Dickinson called a "soft Eclipse"—that is, an arrangement that, with all its promised comforts, threatened to snuff out a woman's independence and her legal rights. As a newspaper article of the time explained, "Men have a thousand objects in life—the professions, glory, ambition, the arts, authorship, advancement, and money-getting, in all their ramifications, each sufficient to absorb their minds," whereas a woman has the "sole hope" of marriage, and "the future presents nothing but careless desolation." If she steps outside her assigned role, "she is proclaimed a scold, a shrew," and "calumny dogs her footsteps, hissing at her with a thousand tongues, and spitting out lies and poison from every one."[141]

Mary was too idiosyncratic and determined to fit easily into a normal middle-class marriage. At the same time, however, she could not identify with women reformers. And so she sought outlets for her trapped energies, which were vented not only in the Rebecca satire but also in her giddy socializing and her free-flowing letters to friends and, later, in her angry outbursts, her migraines, her excessive shopping sprees, and, in the White House years, her behind-the-scenes financial dealings with men.

Her unpredictability created some difficulties for Lincoln and aroused the hostility of men in his circle, but it was undergirded by her genuine love of him and her fierce loyalty to what he stood for. Ultimately, she was a positive force in his life.

Just as Lincoln got home training in handling conflict, he constantly mediated over conflicts as a lawyer. Virtually every cultural theme that affected him personally—issues of gender, class, marital discord, violence, and so on—became grist for his professional mill in the over five thousand law cases he was involved with.

The law also forced him to think deeply about slavery and the meaning of America. Was there a higher law than human law? It was a question Lincoln debated inwardly, one that led eventually to his startlingly simple answer, which changed American history.

Law and Culture

Call it the Lincoln phoenix story, after the mythical bird that rises from its own ashes. Abe Lincoln takes up the practice of law in 1837, settles into domestic life in Springfield, and spends two years in Washington as an undistinguished US congressman. Frustrated by not getting a government appointment he wants from President Zachary Taylor, he abandons politics and resumes the law in Illinois. In 1854 he emerges as a new being: an astonishingly eloquent antislavery politician.

This tale, often recycled in the Lincoln literature, ignores important factors that made this a period not of political flameout and sudden resurrection but rather of steady growth toward antislavery flowering. Between 1837 and 1854, Lincoln became engaged with American culture on a number of vital levels in ways that would shape him into the Lincoln of history.

As a lawyer and a politician, he demonstrated an unusual ability to corral dizzying cultural forces at a time when national unity, his highest goal, was threatened by the growing tensions over slavery. His nearly twenty-five years as a lawyer enriched him by exposing him to both popular culture and elite culture. Party politics—including, during these years, three terms in the Illinois state legislature, campaigning for two Whig presidential candidates, and a term in the US House of Representatives—stabilized him until the early 1850s, when the Whig Party disintegrated and the Democratic Party aligned with conservatism. By then, Lincoln was prepared to offer a cohesive antislavery vision that would become the bulwark of the Republican Party, a vision distilled from cultural and political phenomena he had witnessed during this crucial interregnum.

AN UNLAWERLY LAWYER

Biographers have long sought ways of integrating Lincoln's long law career into his political evolution. It is often said that his courtroom appearances honed his persuasive skills, which he put to use in his major political speeches. Also frequently mentioned are the many contacts he made—with Illinois lawyers, politicians, and potential voters—who later proved instrumental to his political rise.

All of this is true, but the law influenced him in other ways that were even more important than these. To understand how, it helps to look at his successive law partnerships with John Todd Stuart (1837–42), Stephen T. Logan (1841–44), and William H. Herndon (1844–61). The three partnerships are usually said to have followed a pattern of decline, from the suave, savvy Stuart to the brilliant but idiosyncratic Logan to the inexperienced, volatile Herndon.

Actually, though, the path from Stuart to Herndon steadily opened vistas on culture that contributed to Lincoln's maturation. His association with Stuart nurtured his self-reliance, while that with Logan cultivated his negotiating skills and ethical sense, and the Herndon connection sharpened his awareness of social injustice. All three partnerships created a relaxed atmosphere that allowed Lincoln to escape the confines of standard law practice and maintain contact with vibrant American culture.

JOHN TODD STUART

The Kentucky-born, college-educated John Todd Stuart, who was Mary Todd's first cousin, was a tall, handsome man described as "the soul of southern courtliness—the 'compleat gentleman,'" the essence, that is, of Southern chivalry: the Cavalier.[1] He had met Lincoln, two years his junior, during the Black Hawk War, and they subsequently served together as Whigs from Sangamon County in the state legislature. Stuart had helped tutor Lincoln in the law before inviting him to join him as his partner. Their partnership lasted from April 1837 to April 1841. Their office, on Hoffman's Row just west of Springfield's public square, was cramped and sparsely furnished, with a table, a couch, a few chairs, and a small bookcase.

They were both unmethodical, and papers tended to disappear after being tucked away in random places, including in Lincoln's hat. In a note from 1839, Lincoln reported to his partner that "Old Mr. Wright... is teasing me continually about some *deeds* which he says he left with you, but which I can find nothing of. Can you tell where they are?"[2] In the same letter, playing on Stuart's pro-Southern sympathies, Lincoln wrote, "A d—d hawk billed yankee is here, besetting me at every turn I take, saying that Robt Kinzie never received the $80. to which he was entitled. Can you tell any thing about the matter?"

The partners' looseness paralleled Lincoln's open attitude toward the law. A skilled case lawyer, he studied legal writings and precedents for the cases he handled but otherwise relied mostly on common sense. He developed a strong sense of independence during his affiliation with Stuart, who was busy pursuing a political career. In 1838 and 1840, Stuart was elected to the US House of Representatives, and he spent the better part of his time in Washington as a Whig representative from Illinois. His absences left Lincoln virtually on his own for much of the term of their partnership.

Lincoln had a grueling schedule that cultivated his ability to adapt to quickly changing situations. For example, on November 23, 1839, he handled eleven different cases in Sangamon Circuit Court at a time when he was coming off a hectic political season that saw him running, successfully, for a fourth term in the state legislature and campaigning for the Whig presidential candidate, William Henry Harrison.[3]

Lincoln's largely single-handed pursuit of the law fostered what many said was one of his major attributes: self-reliance. At the same time that the Concord, Massachusetts, philosopher Ralph Waldo Emerson was developing his notion of self-reliance, to be expressed in his famous 1841 essay of that name, Lincoln gained mental independence as an Illinois lawyer. Just as Emerson called for readers to reject traditions and authority, Lincoln, as a friend noted, "could act no part but his own. He copied no one either in manner or style"—an assessment seconded by a fellow attorney, who said that Lincoln "pursued his own independent course."[4] Other lawyers similarly testified that they "never knew him in trying a law-suit to ask the advice of any lawyer he was associated with" and that there was not "a single circumstance tending to show that he was influenced in his judgment or conduct by any of his associates."[5]

When Stuart was reelected to Congress, Lincoln realized he could not carry on the firm's burdensome duties alone. The partnership was dissolved on April 14, 1841. Lincoln had already begun collaborating on law cases with Stephen T. Logan, and after he split with Stuart, he began a partnership with Logan. Their first office was on Fifth Street across from Hoffman's Row; after two years, the pair moved into a third-floor office in the Tinsley Building, an imposing new structure on Sixth and Adams Streets that also housed a store, a post office, and the US District and Circuit Court.[6] Lincoln's knowledge of the law grew markedly during his affiliation with Logan. Born in Franklin County, Kentucky, in 1800, Logan had worked for ten years as a lawyer in his native state before moving in 1832 to Springfield, Illinois, where he continued as an attorney and served for two years as a circuit court judge. A short, wizened man, Logan had a shrill voice, nervous mannerisms, and a sweeping mane of light hair. Unlike Stuart, he was a master of the law and was nitpicking in its application. He had admired Lincoln ever since he saw him give a political speech in 1834. On the platform, Logan reported, Lincoln appeared "very tall and gawky and rough looking," with "pantaloons that didn't reach his feet by six inches," but he gave "a very sensible speech."[7] Logan had witnessed Lincoln's rise as a politician and lawyer, and asked him to join his law office in 1841. "Lincoln's knowledge of law was very small when I took him in," he later recalled. But "Lincoln was growing all the time," and through careful study of individual cases, "he got to be quite a formidable lawyer." Logan found that Lincoln was especially effective with juries, as he "seemed to put himself at once on an equality with everybody."

STEPHEN T. LOGAN

Besides helping Lincoln become a more knowledgeable lawyer, Logan trained him in an area that would have lasting importance for the future president: negotiating between conflicting points of view and pursuing honesty. Logan, while adept at challenging opponents in court, preferred to resolve disagreements between warring parties outside the courtroom. A fellow attorney said of Logan, "He was not a promoter of litigations. He settled more controversies than he brought suits. He was a peace-maker."[8] Lincoln adopted the same attitude. In notes for a lecture on the law that he wrote in 1850, he advised, "Discourage litigation. Persuade your neighbors to compromise whenever you can."[9] There was no one, he wrote, who was "more nearly a fiend" than a lawyer who was wont "to stir up litigation."

Logan's ethical practice of the law also influenced Lincoln. Weaned, like Lincoln, in the British common-law tradition, Logan accepted Blackstone's fundamental axiom that human law is based on moral rules. "He understood that all just laws recognize and enforce moral principles," a eulogist said of Logan, and that "the common law, constitutional law, and statute law—all justice and all equity—are expressions of the moral sense of the law-makers." The eulogist added, "The appeal was always to [Logan's] sense of right—his conscience."[10]

This emphasis on ethics clearly appealed to Lincoln, who wrote that "a moral tone ought to be infused into the profession" of law.[11] In making this point, he directly challenged a widely held animus against lawyers. There was a "common, almost universal" belief, Lincoln wrote, "that lawyers are necessarily dishonest," and this "impression of dishonesty is very distinct and vivid" among most Americans. He was right. A journalist of the time generalized, "There is a strong prejudice against lawyers as a class."[12] There was a popular antilawyer story, reprinted in many nineteenth-century newspapers, that had originated with the pioneering Methodist clergyman Jesse Lee, who told of once walking between two lawyers and telling them of a verbal mistake he had made in a recent sermon. He had intended to say, "The devil is the father of liars" but had instead said "the father of lawyers." He let the error stand because "it was so nearly true, I didn't think it was worthwhile to correct it." Insulted, the two lawyers wondered aloud whether Lee was a greater fool or knave. Turning from one lawyer to the other, Lee said mischievously, "Neither; I believe I'm between the two."[13]

To counteract this widespread mistrust of lawyers, Lincoln put great emphasis on honesty. He went so far as to advise against taking up the law if it meant sacrificing one's honesty. "If in your own judgment you cannot be an honest lawyer, resolve to be honest without being a lawyer. Choose some other occupation" rather than "consent to be a knave."[14]

Several factors contributed to the breakup of the Lincoln-Logan partnership in December 1844: the irritable Logan and the humorous Lincoln were constitutionally different; there may have been tension over pay, with Logan getting an unfair share of the firm's earnings; and the political ambitions of the men may have clashed.[15] Logan, however, gave a benign explanation for the split: "I wished to take my son David with me who had meanwhile grown up, and Lincoln was perhaps by that time quite willing to begin on his own account. So we talked the matter over and dissolved the partnership amicably and in friendship."[16]

Lincoln now had the opportunity to assume a senior position in a partnership. He took on the twenty-six-year-old William Herndon, nine years his junior. Lincoln and Herndon remained in the Tinsley Building until 1852, when they moved diagonally across the public square to an office at 103 South Fifth Street.

Many have wondered why Lincoln invited the young, inexperienced Herndon, who had been studying in the Lincoln-Logan law office, to become his partner. Not only was Herndon given to bouts of heavy drinking, but he was temperamental and sometimes querulous.

Why, then, the choice of Herndon? On a basic level, Herndon respected Lincoln without falsely idealizing him. In the chaotic time just after the Lincoln assassination, Herndon would brush away the mists of hagiography and seek the "real" Lincoln. He interviewed scores of people who had known Lincoln and contributed his research to the biography penned by another of Lincoln's attorney friends, Ward Hill Lamon. Lamon's controversial book was attacked because it raised questions about the president's religious faith and his marriage. A mixed reception also greeted Herndon's 1889 biography, cowritten with Jesse Weik, which resisted portraying Lincoln as a saint. Intent on being clear-eyed about the president's flaws, Herndon still found no evidence of intentional dishonesty on Lincoln's part. Canniness, yes, and secretiveness,

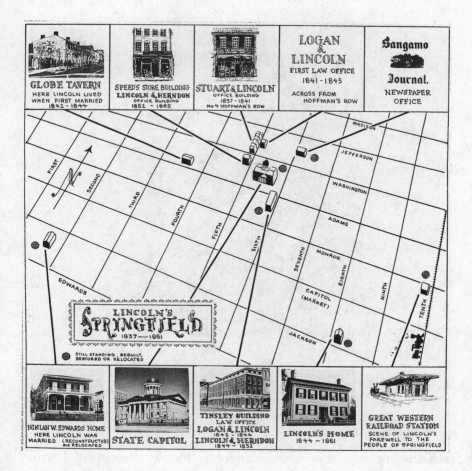

Lincoln's Springfield. As this street grid shows, Lincoln's successive law offices were located near Springfield's public square, the site of the Illinois State House. Lincoln worked with John Stuart from 1837 to 1842 in Hoffman's Row, just north of the square. He then worked with Stephen Logan, at first (from 1841 to 1843) across the street from Hoffman's Row and then (1843 to 1844) in the new Tinsley Building, southeast of the square. He and his third partner, William Herndon, worked initially (1844 to 1852) in the Tinsley Building, and then in 1852 they moved to an office above a store on South Fifth Street, which bordered the west side of the square. Also indicated on the grid are the *Sangamo Journal* newspaper offices, just northeast of the square; the Globe Tavern, a block west of the square on Adams Street; farther to the southwest, Ninian Edwards's home, where Lincoln and Mary Todd were married; seven blocks east of there, Lincoln's home on Eighth and Jackson Streets; and, close to the home, the railroad station where Lincoln said his emotional farewell to Springfield before his trip east to assume the presidency in 1861.

WILLIAM H. HERNDON

self-absorption, and occasional coolness—but not dishonesty. Lincoln had "some defects & a few positive faults," Herndon wrote, but "he was an intensely sincere and honest man"—so much so, Herndon added in italics, *"I would rather doubt any man's simple word than to doubt Lincoln's honesty."*[17] In fact, "nothing but demonstration of dishonesty or vice could shake him." Herndon gave a number of examples from Lincoln's law practice, including one in which, believing that a client involved in a lawsuit had overestimated the size of a disputed piece of land, Lincoln measured her property with surveyor's instruments, found a small error, and made her revise the terms of her suit accordingly.

With regard to politics, Lincoln's selection of Herndon after his previous law experiences is analogous to his choice of Mary Todd in the wake of his romances with Ann Rutledge and Mary Owens. If Mary Todd espoused Northern views that complemented her Southern background (unlike the proslavery Owens or the politically neutral Rutledge), so did William Herndon, who said, "I was a southerner—born on a southern soil—reared by southern parents, . . . but I have always turned *New Englandwards* for my ideas—my sentiments—my education—."[18] He continued turning in that direction. Throughout his partnership with Lincoln, Herndon kept up with the cutting-edge antislavery thought that emanated from New England.

Here he stood in sharp contrast to Lincoln's previous law partners. Though John Todd Stuart remained fairly close to Lincoln, they parted ways politically over the issue of slavery. Lincoln would later join the emerging antislavery Republican Party, while Stuart went with the proslavery Democrats. During the Civil War, Stuart denounced the Emancipation Proclamation and joined the Copperhead opposition to Lincoln. Also, he envied his former law partner's success on the national scene. Herndon concluded that "Stuart in his heart hated Lincoln."[19]

Lincoln's second law partner, Logan, was more supportive than Stuart; he remained politically loyal to Lincoln and, as a delegate to the 1860 Republican Convention, assisted in the choice of Lincoln as the party's candidate for the presidency. However, Logan was quite conservative on the issues of race and slavery. As a state legislator in 1847–48 he played a large role in the passage of the new Illinois constitution, which barred from the state free blacks as well as enslaved persons accompanying their masters. One also wonders about Logan's active participation in the national Peace Conference of February 1861, in which representatives from twenty-one states met in Washington, DC, in a futile effort to prevent civil war by giving major concessions to the South, including allowing slavery to spread west to the Pacific under a restored Missouri Compromise.

The partnership with the antislavery Herndon, in contrast, put Lincoln in daily interchange with a man who shared his hatred of slavery. It also made the atmosphere of his everyday operations as a lawyer even looser than they had been previously.

Both Lincoln and Herndon loathed the drudge work of the law. An Ohioan of the time noted that the "business of a lawyer's office, generally has as little interest as a merchant's accounting room. Declarations, pleas or demurrers, bills or answers in chancery, petitions in dower or partition, conveyances, depositions, the collection of notes, engross the time of an attorney."[20] Gibson W. Harris, who apprenticed with Lincoln and Herndon, remarked, "except to a peculiarly constituted mind, the law is a dry and uninteresting study."[21] Lincoln wrote about "the drudgery of the law" and especially "detested the mechanical work of the office." Herndon explained, "A law office is a dull, dry place, so far as pleasurable or interesting incidents are concerned."[22]

The dryness of law work that the partners complained of was memorably captured in Melville's 1853 short story "Bartleby, the Scrivener." The story's provincial, middle-class narrator is a lawyer of deeds and mortgages who does "a snug business" in "a snug retreat"; his urban office looks out on blank walls, symbols of his dull, confining Wall Street existence.[23] Tedious office work is done by the lawyer's copyists, one of whom, Bartleby, is described as "pallidly neat, pitiably respectable," and who at first is amazingly efficient at copying long documents. This task, today accomplished by photocopying, was, in the lawyer's words, "a proverbially dry, husky sort of business," which, in Bartleby's case, leads to depression and death. Saying that he "prefers not" to copy or obey other commands, Bartleby drifts into a completely passive state and finally is taken to a prison, appropriately named the Tombs, where he dies, curled up before a wall in the prison yard. The soul-deadening work of the law office has sapped the humanity out of Bartleby and has led to alienation and death.

Both Lincoln and Herndon were aware of the perils of losing one's soul to repetitive drudgery. They managed to avoid much of the boredom that came with the work. Lincoln had done a good amount of copying documents early on in his time with Stuart, and Herndon performed such tasks under Logan and Lincoln and then as Lincoln's junior partner. But the atmosphere of the Lincoln and Herndon South Fifth Street office, located above a store on the west side of the public square, was anything but Bartleby-like. Herndon's relaxed attitude gave Lincoln plenty of opportunity to behave in an unlawyerly way. Lincoln typically showed up at around nine at the modest office, which was usually a mess. Plants sprouted from the dirty floor because of seeds that leaked from envelopes sent by farmers Lincoln represented. The windowsill was filthy, and the door panels were broken. A colleague of Lincoln's said, "No lawyer's office could have been more unkempt, untidy, and uninviting."[24] Lincoln often stretched out on the small couch, with one of his long legs on the sofa and the other extended to the table or a chair, spending an hour musing over a book or newspaper, often reading aloud. He meditated for a time, then broke out with a joke or story. Sometimes one story led to another, the result being, as Herndon recalled, "Nothing was done that morning. Declarations—pleas—briefs & demurrers were flung to the winds. It was useless to attempt to read anymore that morning."[25]

When Lincoln's sons Willie and Tad visited the office, they romped about and created a chaos of papers, overturned inkstands, and scattered pens and coal ashes. "Lincoln would say nothing," Herndon noted, "so abstracted was he and so blinded to his children's faults. Had they s—t in Lincoln's hat and rubbed it on his boots, he would have laughed and thought it smart." Even his approach to the law was casual. Herndon testified, "Lincoln knew no such thing as order or method in his law practice."[26] He scribbled notes and stored them, along with letters from clients, in his hat, sometimes losing them.

Lincoln's tendency to be distracted by reading, storytelling, or his boys interfered with his law work. He never became a deep student of the law. Herndon noted that although Lincoln studied closely on a case-by-case basis, he "was a second rate lawyer," adding rhetorically, "What—make a *great* lawyer of a man who never read [law books] much!"[27] Lincoln knew his own shortcomings as an attorney. A colleague confirmed that he was "aware of his inferiority as a lawyer" and would admit it "with a smile or a good natured remark."[28] In notes he wrote toward a lecture on the law, he wrote, "I am not an accomplished lawyer. I find quite as much material for a lecture in those points wherein I have failed, as in those wherein I have been moderately successful."[29]

But if he failed, he can be said to have lapsed in the positive sense of Thoreau, who said that his aim was to "fail" in business, or Melville, who wanted to write novels that were said to "fail" commercially.[30] Although Lincoln was an ambitious lawyer whose annual income reached $4,500 in the 1850s, he had little interest in pursuing money for its own sake.[31] Sometimes he could earn a lot for a single case—he once sued a railroad company to collect a fee of $5,000—but he was known, and sometimes ridiculed, for keeping his fees low. The money he earned while working with Herndon was divided equally, even if, as was often the case, Lincoln worked more than his partner on a certain case. In general, personal fulfillment was his main objective, and in that sense he succeeded. Far from allowing himself to become a walking corpse like Bartleby or a "safe" lawyer like Bartleby's employer, he allowed his lawyer's life to contribute to his cultural and social development. Spending part of the day reading Byron or Burns and telling stories or jokes strengthened his connections with all levels of culture.

LESSONS OF THE LAW CIRCUIT

He greatly improved these connections when he traveled on the law circuit. Twice a year, for several weeks in the spring and several more in the fall, he trekked by horseback or buggy—then, from the mid-1850s, by railroad—from courthouse to courthouse in counties included in the Eighth Judicial Circuit. The towns on the circuit had few lawyers and thus depended on itinerants to handle disputes or crimes. At its peak, between 1843 and 1853, the Eighth Circuit included fourteen counties covering ten thousand square miles—about twice the size of Connecticut. Lincoln usually traveled with other lawyers and judges, who stayed in inns together, socialized with one another, and joined or challenged one another in court.

Among his traveling companions, at various times, were men who would become active in his political life. The brilliant Bloomington attorney Leonard Swett became a leading Republican operative in Illinois who backed Lincoln in his 1860 presidential run. Henry Clay Whitney of Urbana also campaigned for Lincoln and wrote a book about the law circuit as well as a two-volume biography of the president. Kirby Benedict, a Decatur lawyer, traveled sixteen years on the circuit with Lincoln, who liked him so much that as president he refused to replace the alcoholic Benedict as chief justice of New Mexico. The Springfield judge Samuel Hubbel Treat, who served as a judge on the Eighth Judicial Circuit from 1839 to 1848, presided over at least nine hundred circuit cases in which Lincoln was involved. Lincoln received from Treat a 1739 joke book, *Joe Miller's Jests*, and, in Treat's words, "evidently learned its entire contents, for he found Lincoln narrating the stories contained therein around the circuit, but very much embellished and changed, evidently by Lincoln himself."[32] In 1862, Lincoln thanked Treat for a "very patriotic and judicious letter" containing information about the Mississippi River.[33]

The two law circuit companions who became closest to Lincoln were David Davis and Ward Hill Lamon. Like William Herndon (and Lincoln himself), both were Southern-born men who came to adopt antislavery views. Davis, destined to become Lincoln's campaign manager in 1860 and, in 1862, Lincoln's first appointee to the Supreme Court, was a Maryland-born graduate of Kenyon College and Yale Law School who moved to Illinois in 1835 and served in politics and the law before being appointed as a judge on the Eighth Circuit in 1848. An imposing man, Davis weighed around three hundred pounds and cloaked his heft with natty suits. Intent on establishing himself as a prominent Illinoisan, he bought so much real estate that he eventually became the largest landholder in the state. His approach to the law was almost as unconventional as Abe's. He had little interest in legal precedents or technicalities. Henry Whitney noted that Davis "did not know, or care for, the philosophy of the law, but he was the incarnation of common-sense and sterling judgment."[34] Leonard Swett recalled that "he never relied on his knowledge of authorities and never allowed his legal lore to smother his common sense."[35]

Ward Hill Lamon, known as "Hill," was a tough, whiskey-swigging lawyer who became one of Lincoln's most trusted associates. Born in Virginia and trained in law at the University of Louisville, Lamon was admitted to the Illinois bar in 1851 and practiced law in Danville and, later, in Bloomington. He traveled with Lincoln on the circuit in the 1850s. Despite his Southern background, he hated slavery, though he also loathed abolitionism of the Garrisonian variety, which he saw as divisive. Gifted with a fine voice, Lamon entertained the other lawyers by singing popular songs and playing the banjo. He loved telling off-color stories. Tall and powerful, he was wont to get into fights, sometimes with unexpected results. He once tore the seat of his pants while wrestling outside a courthouse. When he entered the court, a fellow lawyer jokingly passed around a sheet requesting contributions to buy

DAVID DAVIS   WARD HILL LAMON

him new trousers. The paper at last reached Lincoln, who said dryly, "I can contribute nothing to the end in view."[36]

Along with other circuit companions, Lamon helped boost Lincoln into the presidency. At the 1860 Republican convention in Chicago, held in the hall called the Wigwam, Lamon printed three hundred counterfeit tickets to maximize the number of Lincoln's supporters, who out-screamed their opponents. Armed with pistols, a bowie knife, and brass knuckles, Lamon served as the president-elect's bodyguard in dangerous situations. Lincoln appointed him as the US marshal of the District of Columbia. Lamon hosted the ceremonies dedicating the soldiers' cemetery at Gettysburg on November 19, 1863, and sat near Lincoln on the platform while the president delivered his address.

It was while traveling on the law circuit that Lincoln developed the quality that Emerson said made him unique: his ability to encompass the entire range of experience. On a rudimentary level, riding on the circuit immersed him in raw nature to a degree he had not known since his frontier childhood. The distance he and his fellow lawyers covered between the various towns averaged around thirty-five miles and stretched as far as fifty. Known as the mud circuit, the Eighth Circuit led David Davis to write in exasperation, "Bad roads, broken bridges, swimming of horses, & constant wettings are at the main incidents of Western travel."[37] Lincoln got wetter than the others, for his height and long legs made him the chosen tester of streams, into which he waded with his pants legs rolled up in search of shallow areas for crossing.

Traveling the circuit was like revisiting precivilized America. The Illinois countryside, as one of Lincoln's companions remarked, "was then quite as desolate and almost as solitary as Creation's dawn, . . . And the broad prairies were in the same condition of virginity and desolation that they had been since Columbus saw the welcome light of San Salvador."[38] Another traveler in Illinois reported: "For miles and miles we saw nothing but a vast expanse of what I can compare to nothing else but the ocean itself. . . . The tall grass seemed like the deep sea. . . . It seemed as if we were out of sight of land, for no house, no barn, no tree was visible, and the horizon presented the rolling waves in the distance."[39]

The inns or farmhouses where the lawyers stayed were of the crudest variety—cramped, bug infested, with leaky roofs, few beds, wretched food, and no indoor plumbing. Lincoln's friend Judge David Davis reported, "every thing [was] dirty & the eating horrible," with "the table greasy—table cloth greasy—floor greasy," and with the typical bedroom "a dirty place—plenty of bedbugs &, &."[40] Most of the travelers, Herndon noted, "would growl—complain— . . . And whine about what they had to eat—how they slept— . . . And how disturbed by fleas, bedbugs, or what not."[41] Traveling on the circuit, Davis said, involved "being eaten up by bedbugs and mosquitoes."[42] But Lincoln didn't gripe. For someone who had been weaned in the most primitive conditions in childhood, the rough environment was familiar, even bracing. The closest he came to complaining was when he joked about the food at inns, as when he once looked at his plate and said, "Well—in the absence of anything to eat I will jump into this Cabbage."[43] Another time, he allegedly told his host, "If this is coffee, please bring me some tea, but if this is tea, please bring me some coffee."[44] Despite these minor issues, he loved the circuit. As David Davis testified, Lincoln was "as happy as he could be when on this Circuit. . . . This was his place of Enjoyment."[45]

Part of the enjoyment came from his invigorating experiences in the towns he visited. Court sessions in the circuit towns, which lasted from three days to a week, were reminiscent of the raucous frontier gatherings of his youth. Because people living in isolated Illinois places had few sources of entertainment, they swarmed to town on the court days. They traded horses, shot craps, bought goods from peddlers and quack doctors, engaged in wrestling matches, danced to fiddlers, and drank copiously. And they loved witnessing trials. The typical courtroom scene involved spectators, often drunk and puffing cigars or chewing tobacco, crowding onto benches and reacting noisily to the proceedings.

Lincoln became an attention-grabbing favorite on the law circuit. He would arrive in a town with saddlebags and some books draped over his horse, on which he sat holding an oversize greenish-brown umbrella on which his name was sewn in white thread. Although he was a fine horseman, he made what a witness called "an eccentric picture," with his umbrella and "his feet not far from the ground."[46]

In court, as in his political speeches, Lincoln used his Barnumesque awkwardness—his assumed clownishness, as it was then called—to draw in sensation lovers and then allowed his nobler qualities to emerge through his potent reasoning and expressive language. When speaking before a jury, Lincoln at first appeared, in Herndon's words, "awkward,

Lincoln on October 27, 1854
(print from a daguerreotype taken in Chicago)

angular, ungainly, odd," with his voice "shrill, squeaking, piping" and his head jerking back and forth for emphasis. But in the course of his address, his voice became melodious and "his form dilated, swelled out, and *he rose up a splendid form*, erect, straight, dignified."[47]

If his exterior oddness attracted attention, so did his unusual kindness. In his years on the circuit, Lincoln became a welcome presence among Illinois townspeople. A reporter who traveled with him was struck by the fact that he "knew, or appeared to know, every body we met, the name of every tenant of every farm-house, and the owner of every plat of ground. Such a shaking of hands—such a how-d'ye-do. . . .

He had a kind word, a smile and a bow for every body on the road, even to the horses, and the cattle, and the swine."[48] Everywhere he went, Lincoln exhibited the openness that led Emerson to note that he "draws equally all classes, all the extremes of society, till we say the very dogs believe in him."[49] David Davis observed that Lincoln preferred the "simple life" on the circuit to practicing law in a city, "where, although the remuneration would be greater, the opportunity would be less for mixing with the great body of the people, who loved him, and whom he loved."[50] Wherever he went on the circuit, another law colleague wrote, "he brought sunshine. All men hailed him as an addition to their circle. He was genial; he was humorous."[51]

Lincoln knew how to use stories or jokes to sway a jury. "In court," Herndon noted, "he was irrepressible and apparently inexhaustible in his fund of stories."[52] One story, adapted from an anecdote in the 1739 jest book Samuel Treat had given him, was effective in the trial of a client charged with assault who had merely been defending himself against an attacker. Lincoln compared his client to a farmer carrying a pitchfork who used its prongs to fend off a fierce dog, killing the animal. When asked by the dog's owner why he didn't use the other end of the pitchfork, the farmer replied, "Why did [the dog] not come after me with his other end?"[53] Lincoln drove the point home by holding an imaginary dog in his hands and shoving it hindmost toward the jury.

In another trial, where his client was being sued for $10,000 for having assaulted a newspaper editor, Lincoln stared at a paper in his hand and started laughing, at first softly and then wildly. His laughter was contagious, for the entire courtroom was soon in hysterics, though no one knew what the joke was. In a lull, Lincoln brought himself under control and explained that the plaintiff had originally wanted $1,000 but, believing that Lincoln's client was wealthy, had multiplied the amount tenfold. Laughter, Lincoln said, was the only response to the absurd demand. His theatrics won the day, for the plaintiff was awarded only $300. The judge in the case said of Lincoln's "peculiar laugh" and "wonderfully funny facial expression" that "a comedian might well pay thousands of dollars to learn them."[54]

Another time Lincoln got the courtroom in stitches when he compared the plaintiff to a hog walking under a fence so crooked that it kept coming up on the same side. He made the plaintiff seem ridiculously confused.

As a storyteller, Lincoln really got going when the workday was over. After dinner, he either entertained a small group in Judge David Davis's room or joined large storytelling sessions in a local barroom or parlor. The gatherings in Judge Davis's room were boisterous but exclusive. The jovial Davis responded heartily to Abe's storytelling. Frequently on the circuit he invited a few to his room to hear Lincoln tell stories.

For Lincoln's public storytelling fests, in contrast, everyone was welcome. In a large room filled with noisy spectators, he and other storytellers regaled a mixed group that included lawyers, plaintiffs, defendants, and townspeople. In these public sessions, which often stretched into the early morning hours, Lincoln honed his skills in reaching the popular mind. He had a friendly competition with two other lawyer raconteurs he often traveled with, William Engle of Menard County and James Murray of Logan County. The three riffed on one another's tales. Abe would tell a story, and then someone would cry out to William Engle, "Now Uncle Billy, you must beat that or go home." Engle would respond, "Boys, the story just told by Lincoln puts me in mind of a story that I heard once as a boy." When Engle finished, someone would say to James Murray, "Now is your time. Come on, Murray, do your level best or never come here again to tell your stories."[55] Murray performed, and then it was Lincoln's turn again, then Engle's, and so on for hours in front of listeners who applauded, hurrahed, and laughed until their sides ached. Because rural folk had few sources of fun, some followed the three jesting lawyers from county to county, much like groupies of a later era who followed their favorite band from gig to gig.

Lincoln, for his part, found on the circuit cultural enrichment while remaining relatively free of immediate domestic concerns. Those with him were delighted that they could enjoy him all week long. In the words of David Davis, "Why, he kept us all from dying of what the French call ennui! We would all have been dead long ago but for Lincoln! He is a whole show by himself, the drollest man on earth, full of humor and anecdote, and a whole magazine of knowledge besides."[56]

By calling Lincoln "the drollest man on earth" and "a whole magazine of knowledge besides," Davis paid homage to both Lincoln the Barnumesque entertainer and Lincoln the knowledge seeker. The law circuit not only opened up for Lincoln fresh avenues to popular language through creative storytelling; it also provided intellectual stimulation. Those who gathered in Judge Davis's room sometimes discussed serious topics. Henry Whitney recalled, "We frequently talked philosophy, politics, political economy, metaphysics and men; in short, our subjects of conversation ranged through the universe of thought and experience."[57]

It was Lincoln, in particular, who "ranged through the universe of thought and experience." Davis and the others, while they enjoyed discussions, had an equally strong penchant for small talk. Lincoln, though sociable, was uninterested in directionless chatter. When superficial conversation broke out, he frequently headed in either of two directions: toward popular culture or toward high culture.

By embracing both, he opened his vision in ways similar to some of the era's major authors: Emerson, Thoreau, Whitman, Hawthorne, Melville, and Poe. The richness of their writings stemmed from these authors' democratic embrace of all levels of culture, from the sensational to the sublime, from the ephemeral to the timeless. "I contain multitudes," says the speaker of Whitman's *Leaves of Grass*. So, too, did Lincoln.

Lincoln on February 28, 1857
(print from a photograph by Alexander Hessler)

HE HEARD AMERICA SINGING

Lincoln grew close to the popular mind by attending local performances in towns on the Eighth Circuit. A fellow lawyer said Lincoln
would go by himself to "any little show or concert"—even to "a small
show of magic lanterns &c. really for children."[58] Most of the towns
didn't offer much in the way of serious theater. The culture Lincoln
found in his travels usually came in the form of musical performances,
sometimes concerts and sometimes impromptu sing-alongs. In music, a

friend noted, "his tastes were simple and uncultivated, his choice being old airs, songs, and ballads"—"of a style," a law colleague explained, "to please the rustic ear."[59]

Like Walt Whitman, he enjoyed attending concerts given by family singers—groups of four or more performers, usually close relatives, who sang popular songs and played instruments. During the Civil War, he became a big fan of the Hutchinson Family Singers, who performed all types of songs, including political ones like "Lincoln and Liberty," the 1860 campaign song that became so popular at rallies that it helped him win the election.

On the law circuit, Lincoln frequently went to hear the Newhall Family, a traveling troupe consisting of the parents, two sisters, a brother, and a brother-in-law. One of the songs the family sang that especially appealed to him was "Ben Bolt," a nostalgic ballad whose narrator tells a childhood friend that many of the people and things he once loved are now gone. In a hotel on the circuit, Lincoln had a memorable encounter with the teenage Lois E. Newhall, one of the sisters in the group. The Newhalls had been performing in town that week, and several lawyers encouraged Lincoln to repay them by singing "some of the songs for which you are already famous." Lois offered to strike up a tune on her melodeon so that he could give a solo performance. He replied, "Why, Miss Newhall, if it would save my soul, I couldn't imitate a note that you would touch on that instrument. I never sang in my life; and those fellows know it. They are simply trying to make fun of me!" He offered to recite from memory a poem; it was his favorite, William Knox's "Mortality," which, with its emphasis on death and transience, was a kind of literary version of "Ben Bolt." Lois was brought to tears by his delivery of the poem, and she asked him to write it out for her. The next morning, while she was eating pancakes, he handed it to her.[60]

A particularly telling incident from that period shows the breadth of Lincoln's exposure to popular music. The pianist and singer Jane Martin Johns had arranged for a fine Gilbert piano to be shipped from

Boston to Decatur, one of his stops on the circuit. When the wagon carrying the piano stopped at the front steps of the Macon House Hotel in Decatur, Mrs. Johns asked men nearby to move the piano into the parlor. The tall Lincoln stepped forward, taking off his gray shawl and saying to Leonard Swett, "Come on, Swett, you are the next biggest man." Lincoln went to the hotel's basement and returned with two long boards, which the two men used as a ramp to maneuver the piano inside. After dinner that evening, Lincoln attached the legs of the piano and positioned the instrument against the wall. Jane Johns seated herself at the piano and played a medley of songs. She began with instrumental pieces, including "Washington's March" and "The Battle of Prague," and then launched into popular ballads, with which her listeners sang along. She recalled:

> For tragedy, I sang Henry Russel[l]'s "Maniac" and "The Ship on Fire," then made "their blood run cold" with the wild wail of the "Irish Mother's Lament." For comic, we sang "The Widdy McGee" and "I Won't Be a Nun," topping off with "Old Dan Tucker," "Lucy Long," and "Jim Crow," the crowd joining in the chorus. These were followed by more serious music, . . . "Moonlight, Music, Love and Flowers," "Rocked in the Cradle of the Deep," "Pilgrim Fathers," "Bonaparte's Grave," and "Kathleen Mavourneen." . . . As a finale, I sang "He Doeth All Things Well" after which Lincoln, in a very grave manner, thanked me for the evening's entertainment and said: "Don't let us spoil that song by any other music tonight." Many times afterwards I sang that song for Mr. Lincoln and for Governor [Richard J.] Oglesby, with whom it was also a favorite.[61]

It would be hard to find a brief summary that covered as wide a range of pre–Civil War popular music as the songs Mrs. Johns mentions here. The songs mirrored Lincoln's eclectic interests. Mrs. Johns created categories for her songs (tragic, comic, serious, and so on) but from today's perspective, we can assign more specific ones: sensational, sentimental, religious, humorous, and patriotic. Lincoln embraced them all.

Among the sensational songs played by Mrs. Johns that evening were "The Irish Mother's Lament" (about a woman who curses her three sons for disobeying her orders and then goes mad with grief after they drown in a lake), Henry Russell's "The Maniac" (about a delusional man chained in an asylum), and Russell's thrilling "The Ship on Fire" (a burning vessel is sinking, and all aboard are terrified). These songs are in line with several other sensational ballads Lincoln is known to have enjoyed, including "Fair Ellender" (in which a bride-to-be kills her fiancé's ex-girlfriend, and then the fiancé kills the bride-to-be and himself), "Lord Randall" (about a man poisoned by his sweetheart), and "The Oxford Girl" (in which a man bludgeons his partner to death and throws her corpse into a river). These and similar songs gave musical life to the kind of sensational themes found in penny newspapers and pulp novels of the day.

The sentimental genre is typified by another song Mrs. Johns performed that night, the Irish ballad "Kathleen Mavourneen," designed to draw tears with its portrait of the death of a loved one. In the song a man repeatedly asks his somnolent lover, Kathleen, to wake up; she cannot, because she is dead. Sentimentality is also prominent in other songs Lincoln loved, such as "The Inquiry" and "Twenty Years Ago." In "The Inquiry," the speaker asks the wind, the ocean, and the moon if there is any place "where weary man may find / The bliss for which he sighs," "'Where miserable man may find a happier lot," "Where free from toil and pain, / The weary soul may rest?" The answer given by the natural elements, thrice repeated is, "No." The song makes an upturn at the end, when Faith, Hope, and Love answer, "Yes, in Heaven."[62]

Nostalgia floods "Twenty Years Ago," which Hill Lamon often sang for his friend. Lamon wrote:

One "little sad song"—a simple ballad entitled "Twenty Years Ago"—was, above all others, his favorite. He had no special fondness for operatic music; he loved simple ballads and ditties, such as the common people sing, whether of the comic or pathetic kind; but no one in the list touched his great heart as did the song of "Twenty Years Ago." Many a time, in the old days of our familiar friendship on the Illinois circuit, and often at the White House when he and I were alone, have I seen him in tears while I was rendering, in my poor way, that homely melody.[63]

The song's poignancy lies in its contrast between the dour theme that everything is fleeting and the optimistic one that death is part of the world's natural rhythm and that friendship and joy make life worth living. The song's speaker tells his friend Tom about visiting his childhood home and seeing old sights: a familiar tree, a school playground, a sledding hill, a river flanked by willow trees, a bubbling spring, a grapevine swing where the youths formerly "played the beau / And swung our sweethearts 'pretty girls,'" a tree on which they inscribed their names, and an old churchyard where the speaker's sweetheart now lies. Everything has changed: the tree is bigger, the stream is narrower, the swing is ruined, the initials carved on the tree have been removed by "some heartless wretch," and so on. But life goes on and nature is eternal, symbolized in the song (as in Whitman's "Song of Myself") by the ever-sprouting grass. The contrast is caught in the second verse:

> The grass is just as green, dear Tom, barefooted
>   boys at play
> Were sporting just as we did then, with spirits
>   just as gay;

But the Master sleeps upon the hill, which,
    coated o'er with snow,
Afforded us a sliding place just twenty years
    ago.[64]

The song doesn't mention an afterlife. The last verse simply says, "Few are left of our old class, excepting you and me; / And when our time shall come, dear Tom, and we are called to go, / I hope they'll lay us where we played just twenty years ago." Offering no image of heaven or spiritual reunion with loved ones, the song is closer in spirit to Bryant's poem "Thanatopsis" than to heaven-directed works like Stowe's *Uncle Tom's Cabin* or Elizabeth Stuart Phelps's *The Gates Ajar*.

This is not to say that religious songs did not resonate with Lincoln. Quite the contrary. The song that Lincoln asked Mrs. Johns to make her finale that night, "He Doeth All Things Well, or, My Sister," doubtless moved him deeply because of the pious glow it cast around deceased loved ones. The song must have made him think of people he had lost—his mother, his sister, and, perhaps, Ann Rutledge. The song's speaker follows a beloved sister's life from the cradle to the grave, chiming in after several of life's successive phases, happy or tragic, with the phrase "He doeth all things well." The speaker blesses the sister as she lies in the cradle, and as years pass, "a wild idolatry" of her overcomes the speaker, who worships "at an earthly shrine" and forgets "He who doeth all things well." For a time, the sister "obscure[s] the light, which round His throne doth dwell." But then she dies. The speaker cries, "And oh! That cup of bitterness—*let not my heart rebel*, / God gave— He Took—He will restore—'He doeth all things well.'"[65]

Despite Lincoln's materialist bent, he did not surrender the hope that, in the song's words, "He will restore." At Baptist services in Indiana, the Lincoln family had sung hymns from Starke Dupuy's hugely popular compilation *Hymns and Spiritual Songs*, including "O, When

Shall I See Jesus," "How Tedious and Tasteless the Hour When Jesus I No Longer See," "Jesus, My All, to Heaven Has Gone," and "Alas! And Did My Savior Bleed."[66] During the 1850s, Lincoln reportedly visited a dying woman who wanted him to write her will. He comforted her by reading Bible passages and reciting the words of the hymn "Rock of Ages." A Springfield printer who accompanied him that day remarked, "Mr. Lincoln, I have been thinking that is very extraordinary that you should so perfectly have acted as pastor as well as attorney." Lincoln paused and replied, "God, and eternity, and heaven were very near to me to-day."[67]

Faith was a comforting resource for Lincoln, a sometime church-goer though never a church member. But he could also break into a playful parody of religion. His law circuit companions guffawed when, on a difficult carriage ride between Urbana and Danville, he walked ahead on the muddy road and, in exasperation, bellowed out a twisted version of a Methodist hymn. He sang, "Mortal man with face of clay, / Here to-morrow, gone to-day!"—adding, as Whitney notes, "verses even more ridiculous: verses which he improvised and sang without regard [to] / time, tune or metre."[68]

Lincoln liked to joke about erring or ignorant preachers. Judge Davis once turned to him in court complaining about some lawyer's tediously long document, and Lincoln drawled, "It's like the lazy preacher that used to write long sermons, and the explanation was, he got to writin' and was too lazy to stop."[69] Lincoln adopted a raspy squeal to imitate an illiterate Ohio preacher who, having failed to interest his "Bretern and sistern" in the Bible story of Noah's "three sons—ahem—namelie, Shadadadarack, Meshisick, and Belteezer," said, "Dear perishing friends, ef you will not hear on toe me on this great subject, I will only say this, that Squire Nobs has recently lost a little bay mare with a flaxy mane and tail amen!"[70] Another of his jokes involved a minister who declared that God made a perfect man, Jesus, but no perfect woman. A lady in the congregation stood up and said she disagreed, insisting that she had been hearing about a perfect woman for the past six years. When the minister asked who that ideal woman was, she replied, "My husband's first wife!"

If Lincoln managed to both respect religion and parody it, the same can be said of his wry attitude toward other social conventions.

Here is where his affection for humorous music comes in. A song Mrs. Johns sang at the Decatur jamboree, "I Won't Be a Nun," speaks to his taste for erotic humor. He evidently enjoyed off-color songs. Dennis Hanks reported that Lincoln liked "Little Smuty Songs I wont Say any thing a Bout would Not Look well in print"—though Hanks did mention a song about a "turban'd Turk" who keeps "a hundred wives under lock and key / . . . Yet long may he pray with his Alcoran / Before he can love like an Irishman."[71] Like that song, "I Won't Be a Nun" is suggestive rather than explicit—but it was still risqué for the era. It tells of a woman who declares that she is too pretty and too wild to be sent off by her mother to be a nun. "I'm sure I cannot tell what's the mischief I have done," the woman says coyly, but "I'm so fond of pleasure that I cannot be a nun."[72]

If such songs raised eyebrows in polite society, the other humorous songs Mrs. Johns sang that evening tickled ribs. One of them, "The Widdy McGee," mocks middle-class courting rituals. The song is about a timid man who tells himself, day after day, to go court a certain widow, but each time he embarks, some bird flying about—a crow, a starling, a magpie, etc.—makes him think it's bad luck to court on that day, until the last day of the week, when he shows up to woo her at a church only to find that it's her wedding day. We can surmise that Lincoln saw in the song a comic version of his own nervousness over wooing Mary Todd, not to mention his superstitiousness (a believer in prophetic dreams, he grew up among frontier folk for whom "the flight of a bird in at the window, the breath of a horse on a child's head, the crossing by a dog of a hunter's path, all betokened evil luck in store for some one").[73]

Whatever his response was to the song, we can be sure that he reacted enthusiastically to other of Mrs. Johns's humorous choices that night—"Old Dan Tucker," "Lucy Long," and "Jim Crow." These were minstrel standards: songs introduced onstage by whites in blackface who caricatured the language, appearance, and behavior of black people. Today, the inherent racism in minstrel shows is widely understood, which has made it difficult for Lincoln biographers to talk about his love of "darky" performances. But in Lincoln's cultural context, minstrel songs could at times have a subversive edge. Dan Tucker, the protagonist of the song of that name, is a prankster who flouts mainstream white conventions and boasts about his toughness and sexual prowess. He disrupts normal language, too, because much nonsense is mixed in with his boasts and his threats of violence. "Lucy Long" is at points misogynistic, as when the narrator says he will trade her for corn if she proves to be a shrewish wife, but elsewhere it is daring, as in the chorus, which enjoins Lucy to "take your time," and in verses that invite her to "tarry"—both of which suggest that she may be inclined to delay marriage until she can enjoy a sexual affair beforehand.[74] "Jim Crow," which later became the sobriquet of racial segregation, was T. D. Rice's famous song that, in its original version, spoofed black people and yet imagined extraordinary powers for them. Like the backwoods superman Davy Crockett of frontier humor, Jim Crow brags of immense feats: "I wip my weight in wildcats / I eat an Alligator, / And tear up more ground / Dan kiver 50 load of tater."[75]

The cloaked progressiveness of minstrel music is especially visible in a song that Lincoln often asked Lamon to sing to him: "De Blue Tail Fly." Lincoln called it "the buzzing song."[76] It is about an enslaved man who protects his master from flies until one bites a horse that throws the master, who dies from the fall. As in many minstrel songs, the black speaker wears a submissive mask—he waits on "massa" and tries to ward off the flies—but after his master dies, he says indifferently, "Ole

Massa's gone, now let 'im rest, / Dey say all tings am for de best." The constantly repeated chorus shows that the man is glad his master is gone: "Jim crack corn I don't care, / Ole Massa gone away."

Minstrel music sometimes got political, as in another song Lincoln loved, "Zip Coon." The song's black speaker mentions Andrew Jackson's assault on the Bank of the United States, which has been "blone to the moon," and says that Zip can now replace Jackson: "An de bery nex President, will be Zip Coon." And who will be his vice president? None other than that wild figure of popular humor, Davy Crockett:

> Zip shall be President, Crocket shall
> be vice,
> An den dey two togedder, will hab de
> tings nice.[77]

In the topsy-turvy political world of humorous songs, then, an African American—or, at least, a pretend one—can become president, and a frontier screamer can be his vice president. Through to today, Americans are accustomed to seeing the subversive impact of popular music. Blues, jazz, rock, punk, rap, and so on—popular music has been like the prow of an icebreaker, bursting through the frozen sea of convention. The same was true in Lincoln's time.

The typical popular song of that era was flexible and variable: the tune remained the same, but the words were constantly revised by different performers—so much so that in some cases no "original" version can be identified with certainty. Virtually all minstrel songs appeared in different versions, as did many other songs, including several Mrs. Johns sang that evening. Two of them, "Old Dan Tucker" and "Rosin the Bow," have special relevance to Lincoln. The lilting melody of "Rosin" provided the music for the Hutchinson's campaign song "Lincoln and Liberty," in which Lincoln appears as the potent "rail-maker statesman," skilled in "felling and mauling" trees, the "good David," with his "unerring" sling, who slew "the Slaveocrat's giant" (that is, Stephen A. Douglas, known as the Little Giant).[78] Among the many versions of "Old Dan Tucker" were the Hutchinsons' "Get Off the Track," which warned people to get out of the way of the train of Emancipation, and another Lincoln campaign ditty in which Abe becomes the Crockett-tough destroyer of political opponents:

> Old Abe is coming down to fight,
> And put the Democrats to flight;
> He's coming with the wedge and maul
> And he will split 'em one and all.
> Get out the way, you little giant
> You can't come in, you're too short
>   and pliant.[79]

Although the image of Abe as a rail-splitting ironman who fought his way to victory was a favorite among songwriters and the Northern public, Lincoln himself saw music as a unifying force, not a divisive or competitive one.

The nation as a whole, after all, was what was chiefly on his mind. He doubtless got special pleasure out of the patriotic songs that he knew from childhood on. "Hail Columbia," which was the unofficial national anthem of the United States until "The Star-Spangled Banner" took its place in 1931, was regularly played at events during his presidency. In this musical tribute to the heroes of the American Revolution, there is no sectional strife, only a united effort against a common enemy. The watchword of the song is unity, as promoted in the chorus:

> Firm, united let us be,
> Rallying round our liberty,

As a band of brothers joined,
Peace and safety we shall find.[80]

Chief among this Revolutionary "band of brothers" were the founding fathers, especially George Washington. "Hail Columbia" makes a ringing proclamation—"Let Washington's great name / Ring through the world with loud applause"—followed praise of Washington's "God-like pow'r." Lincoln, with his love of humor, couldn't resist taking so high-flown a song off its pedestal, as he did, according to Dennis Hanks, when he joined in singing, "Hail Columbia, happy land, / If you ain't broke I will be damned."[81]

SOARING HIGH

If Lincoln's musical experiences broadened his knowledge of popular culture, his reading during the law years enriched his knowledge of high culture and science. He didn't read widely in fiction; his preference was for poetry or nonfiction. In the latter area, he profited from his partnership with Herndon, who read widely and had one of the largest private libraries in Springfield. A bookseller there said that "Mr. Herndon read every year more new books in history, pedagogy, medicine, theology, and general literature, than all the teachers, doctors, and ministers in Springfield put together."[82] Herndon reported that Lincoln took advantage of his book collection. "I had an excellent private library," he recalled, "probably the best in the city for admired books. To this library Mr. Lincoln had, as a matter of course, full and free access at all times."[83]

Among the "admired books" that Herndon said that Lincoln had access to were ones by Immanuel Kant, Ralph Waldo Emerson, Theodore Parker, Thomas Carlyle, Henry Ward Beecher, David Strauss, Joseph Ernest Renan, and Ludwig Feuerbach. Because Herndon said only that these were "the kind of books which Lincoln had access to and sometimes peeped into," we cannot know the extent of Lincoln's familiarity with them.[84] If we imagine that he looked into the authors just mentioned, we can say that he got doses of idealist philosophy (Kant and Emerson), liberal Protestantism and antislavery sentiment (Parker and Beecher), higher criticism of the Bible (Strauss and Renan), and materialist humanism (Feuerbach).

He was also interested in science. He perused Robert Chambers's *Vestiges of the Natural History of Creation*, which anticipated Darwin in its denial of special creation and its argument that life forms evolve over time. He was especially excited when in the mid-1850s Herndon brought to the law office *The Annals of Science: Being a Record of Inventions and Improvements.* Lincoln looked it over carefully and remarked, "It's got up on the right plan; because it gives the successes and failures of experiments. The history of the successes of life & experiment shows what can be done in art, science—philosophy; & economizes time and expense. The history of failures shows what cannot be done, as a general rule and puts the artist—scientist & philosopher on his guard & sets him a thinking on the right line."[85]

Scientific advance was more than merely a passing interest of Lincoln's. Six times in the late 1850s he gave an expanding lecture, in two successive parts, on discoveries and inventions in which he argued that humans were fundamentally different from other animals, because they had the capacity to *improve* their condition. Lincoln's advocacy of the Whig Party's agenda of internal improvements (what we would call infrastructure) and technological advance is well known. What has not been pointed out is that Lincoln traced this agenda to its primitive origins.

"All creation is a mine, and every man, a miner," he announced in his April 1858 "Lecture on Discoveries and Inventions." "The whole earth, and all *within* it, *upon* it, and *round about* it, including *himself*, in his physical, moral, and intellectual nature, and his susceptabilities, are the infinitely various 'leads' from which, man, from the first, was to dig out his destiny."[86] Especially significant here are phrases "all creation" and "whole earth." Lincoln extended his vision backward in time, returning to the earliest reaches of history. What he found was a key difference between the human and nonhuman world. In his words, "Fishes, birds, beasts, and creeping things, are not miners, but *feeders* and *lodgers*, merely." For example, beavers build houses, and ants and bees provide food for the winter, exactly the way they did five thousand years ago. Humans are different. "Man is not the only animal who labors; but he is the only one who *improves* his workmanship. This improvement, he effects by *Discoveries*, and *Inventions*."

Human history, Lincoln points out, has been a succession of discoveries: first came clothing, then spinning and weaving, followed by iron tools, the wheel, wagons and boats, and aids to agriculture such as farm animals and the plow. In the second part of his lecture on discoveries and inventions, which he gave the next year, he went on to discuss history's other important advances, including speaking, writing, printing, steam power, the railroad, and the telegraph.[87]

As an Illinois state politician and later as president he promoted Henry Clay's American system of federally funded internal improvements. But, for him, improvements were not just a political program; they were a defining feature of humankind. Unlike other animals, he maintained, humans are able to reflect upon their physical environment and perform experiments which, over time, can lead to remarkable improvements in communication, transportation, and food production. Lincoln traced an archaeology of discoveries because he wanted to tie human inventions directly to the natural world.

Lincoln continued his informal program of intellectual enrichment on the law circuit. During off hours, when he wasn't telling stories or enjoying local musical or theatrical performances, he usually went somewhere alone and read. John T. Stuart recalled Lincoln "Carrying around with him on the Circuit—to the various Courts, books such as

Shakespear[e]—Euclid . . . He loved Burns."[88] Stuart also remembered that Lincoln loved a particular poem by Fitz-Greene Halleck—probably, as Douglas L. Wilson notes, Halleck's moving eulogy to Burns.[89] Lincoln later wrote that he had not recently "met with anything more admirable than Halleck's beautiful lines on Burns," and one can understand why.[90]

Not only does Halleck present Burns as the quintessential democratic poet, with "A love of right, a scorn of wrong, / Of coward, and of slave," but he used language that seems to have stayed with Lincoln. Regarding Burns's grave, Halleck writes of "the mute homage that we pay / To consecrated ground," emphasizing: "And consecrated ground it is, / The last, the hallowed home of one / Who lives upon all memories, / Though with the buried gone." Halleck's word choice struck home with Lincoln, who in one of his poems said that memories "will hallow all" and "Seem hallowed, pure, and bright, / Like scenes in some enchanted isle, / All bathed in liquid light."[91] When commemorating the dead at Gettysburg, he declared, "we can not consecrate, we can not hallow this ground," because soldiers, living and dead, "have consecrated it far above our poor power to add or detract."[92]

If Halleck stimulated Lincoln's thoughts about hallowing and consecrating burial grounds, Euclid, another author he read on the circuit, anticipated the opening words at Gettysburg about the nation "dedicated to the proposition that all men are created equal." Lincoln had been studying Euclidian geometry since his early Illinois years, and he continued to do so on the circuit, where he mastered the propositions—all 173 of them—contained in the first six books of Euclid's *Elements*. As Lincoln later explained, he had often encountered the word "demonstrate" in his law reading, but he wondered how it differed from "reason" or "prove."[93] Euclid taught him what demonstration was. Lincoln declared that "Euclid, well studied, would free the world of half its calamities, by banishing half the nonsense which now dilutes and curses it." If published and distributed by the Tract Society, he insisted, "it would be a means of grace."

Why was geometry sacred? We can glean the answer from David Davis's comment that on the circuit Lincoln "studied Euclid—the exact sciences—his mind struggled to arrive at moral & physical—mathematical demonstration."[94] Davis's juxtaposition of the moral, the physical, and the mathematical is telling. Lincoln's search for exactness, both physical and moral, was also noted by Henry Clay Whitney, who observed that at farmhouses on the circuit Lincoln would closely examine some farm implement—turn it over, stoop down, stand off, shake it, and find "every quality and utility which inhered in it"—and that he was equally inquisitive about moral matters: "He would bore to the center of any moral proposition, and carefully analyse and dissect every layer and every atom of which it was composed, nor would he give over the search till completely satisfied that there was nothing more to know, or be learned about it."[95]

In his studies, Lincoln tried to connect the certainty of Euclidian geometry with morals and politics. Euclid had especially powerful meaning for him, because, time and again, his geometric propositions gave irrefutable evidence of equality. Euclid's propositions about triangles, quadrilaterals, parallelism, and other geometric shapes or lines are full of rules about equal angles, equal sides, equal degrees, and so on. It was understandable that Lincoln would have sought Euclidian support for the "proposition" that "all men are created equal."[96] On this point he shared the view of the black reformer William Hamilton, for whom Euclid was a potent teacher of abolitionism, because, in Hamilton's words, any American who refused to accept human equality "does not agree with axioms in geometry, that deny that things can be equal, and at the same time unequal to one another."[97]

Lincoln's rationalist impulse also explains his interest in Poe, another of his law circuit favorites. He appears to have been fascinated by the genre Poe virtually invented, the detective tale. According to a campaign biographer, William Dean Howells, Lincoln's "mathematical and metaphysical" mind was "pleased with the absolute and logical method of Poe's tales and sketches, in which the problem of mystery is given, and wrought out into everyday facts by the process of cunning analysis." Howells added, "It is said that he suffers no year to pass without a perusal of this author."[98] Stuart said that Lincoln "Carried Poe around the Circuit—read and loved the Raven—repeated it over & over."[99] Another companion testified that Lincoln would habitually rise earlier in the morning than the other lawyers, sit by a fireplace, stir up the coals, and muse, "inspired, no doubt, by that strange psychological influence which is so poetically described by Poe in 'The Raven.'"[100]

EDGAR ALLAN POE

But Poe also saw the *limitations* of reason. On this point, Poe trumped Euclid. In one of his signature detective stories, "The Purloined Letter," Poe includes a digression on the shortcomings of mathematical reasoning. "Mathematical axioms are *not* axioms of general truth," says Poe's detective, C. Auguste Dupin, who points out that they do not apply, for example, to morals, to chemistry, or to motive.[101]

Lincoln on some level agreed with Poe, for during his law circuit years he wrote a poem, "My Childhood Home I See Again," that plunged into the irrational and suggested that there was no reasonable explanation for it. Penned in 1844 when Lincoln was visiting Indiana while campaigning for the presidential candidate Henry Clay, the poem, which was published three years later in an Illinois newspaper, begins as a typically Lincolnesque meditation on mortality—many of the people and homes of his youth are now gone—and then becomes a Poe-like effort to limn the irrational. Halfway through the poem, Lincoln describes an Indiana neighbor, Matthew Gentry, who had tried to kill his parents and himself. As Lincoln explained in a letter, Gentry "is an insane man, rather a bright lad and the son of the rich man of our very poor neighborhood," who at nineteen "unaccountably became furiously mad, from which condition he gradually settled into harmless insanity." In the poem Lincoln writes of "Poor Matthew! Once of genius bright— / A fortune-favored child— / Now locked for aye, mental night, / A haggard mad-man wild." Lincoln vividly recounts how this "howling crazy man" had assaulted his family, wounded himself, and writhed and shrieked "with maniac laughter" when he was chained.[102]

In his other major poem of this period, "The Bear Hunt," Lincoln uses another childhood memory—in this case, his father's hunt for a bear who had killed one of his swine—to put the human-animal association to sharply satirical use. At the start of the poem the bear hunt is an episode of "glorious glee" for a "merry *corps*" of hunters, but by the end the hunters prove to be cruel and blindly self-interested.[103] Lincoln wins our sympathy for the animals—both the chased bear and his canine pursuers. Lincoln adopts the perspective of the bear, who runs furiously, then tires and slows down, and finding himself surrounded by dogs who bite him, fights desperately but then is riddled with bullets. Blood flows from the bear as it dies. Lincoln then makes his satirical point. Custom dictates that a bear's skin is awarded to the one who drew first blood in the hunt. A bitter argument over the award breaks out among the hunters. Lincoln writes:

> But who did this, and how to trace
> What's true from what's a lie,
> Like lawyers, in a murder case
> They stoutly *argufy.*

However, the one who deserves the prize, we learn, is not human. Up to the fallen bear runs the dog that had first sunk its teeth into the bear during the chase. The dog now bites into the animal again, growling and shaking, and he "swears, as plain as dog can swear, / That he has won the skin." And so, Lincoln suggests, if justice were true, the dog would be recognized as the winner. But, naturally, the men snicker at the dog. In the final verse, Lincoln drives home the point about the insensitivity of "two-legged dogs," who say,

> Conceited whelp! we laugh at thee—
> Nor mind, that now a few
> Of pompous, two-legged dogs there be,
> Conceited quite as you.

EXPANDING WITH THE LAW

Lincoln's pursuit of the law led him to consider rationally a remarkable variety of topics. The expansiveness of his vision was influenced by the sheer variety of his legal practice. His 5,173 law cases covered a tremendous range, from sexual aberration to white-collar crime.[104] The practice of law broadened him in several ways: it exposed him to the full gamut of idioms in American popular culture; it saw him team up with lawyers in some cases and oppose them in others; and it forced him to argue both sides of the same issue in different cases. Taken together, these factors freed him of narrow views and fostered good judgment and compassion.

Unlike the typical lawyer today, who has a specialty—family law, or criminal law, or bankruptcy law, or personal injury law, etc.—attorneys on the Illinois law circuit dealt with virtually every kind of legal situation. More than half of Lincoln's cases related to debt litigation, another fifth to inheritance matters or mortgage foreclosures, about 15 percent to cases involving crimes, divorce, or slander, 5 percent to railroads, about 1 percent to medicine, and 8 percent to miscellaneous matters.

These cases ranged from the trifling to the momentous. Lincoln carefully considered each case on its own, no matter how trivial. As Whitney noted:

> It is strange to contemplate that . . . Mr. Lincoln's whole attention should have been engrossed in petty controversies or acrimonious disputes between neighbors about trifles; that he should have puzzled his great mind in attempting to decipher who was the owner of a litter of pigs, or which party was to blame for the loss of a flock of sheep, by foot rot; or whether some irascible spirit was justified in avowing that his enemy had committed perjury; yet I have known him to give as earnest attention to such matters, as, later, he gave to affairs of State.[105]

There was no theme or idiom of American culture that Lincoln's law experience did not encompass, from the sensational to the sentimental, from the crudest vernacular to the most sophisticated technical language.

On the sensational side, he handled topics that in the hands of popular writers gave rise to lurid works aimed at titillating a wide readership. Herndon, who gave up the law in his later years, looked back on his experiences with Lincoln: "If you love the stories of murder—rapes—fraud &c. a law office is a good place—but good Lord let me forget all about a law office."[106] Elsewhere, Herndon called the law office the place to learn "stories of fraud, deceit, cruelty, broken promises, blasted homes."[107] Although only a small percentage of Lincoln's and Herndon's cases related to homicide, assault, spousal abuse, divorce, or sexual misconduct, we can understand why such cases lingered in Herndon's memory. Some of the cases went well beyond the scandals treated in the penny newspapers or pulp fiction of the day.

In an era avid for what a conservative critic called "public poison"—racy fiction about crime or illicit sex—Lincoln dealt with such topics judiciously in court. He handled situations that were even more shocking than those portrayed by sensationalists such as Poe, George Lippard, or George Thompson.[108] There is nothing in the period's popular literature, for example, as bizarre as the bestiality cases Lincoln handled. In 1847, he and Herndon represented William Torrence, who claimed that Newton Galloway had slandered him by accusing him of impregnating a pig. Galloway claimed that Torrence "caught my old sow and he fucked her as long as he could," and now the pig was "bellying down and will soon have some young bills" (a reference to Torrence's first name). Lincoln argued that this "false, scandalous, malicious" charge severely damaged Torrence's reputation.[109] In another case, a client of Lincoln's was charged with copulating with a neighbor's dog and, in two others, with cows.[110]

Other forms of illicit sex, such as adultery and extramarital fornication, were also then a crime. Lincoln defended Nancy M. Martin, who claimed that Achilles M. Underwood slandered her by saying publicly that he had copulated with her and that she "has been *fucked* more times than I've got fingers and toes for damned if it aint so big I can almost poke my fist in[.]"[111] Lincoln won $237 for Martin. Emily Cantrall hired Lincoln and Herndon to represent her in a slander suit against John Primm, who reportedly said that "William King screwed Charles Cantrall's wife twice while he was gone, and before that he crawled in bed with her and her husband and screwed her."[112] James Mitchell hired Lincoln to defend him in a slander suit after he allegedly called Missouri Mitchell, the wife of Elijah Mitchell, "a base whore" and "a nasty stinking strumpet" and said he could "prove it by the Nances. They have rode her in the corner of the fence many a time."[113]

The language used in these and other of Lincoln's sex cases was more explicit than what can be found in the American-made pornography that has survived from that era. By the same token, the murders Lincoln handled resembled episodes in the period's violent pulp fiction.

The canard that Lincoln was an ineffective criminal attorney has been convincingly challenged in recent times. He handled seventeen homicide cases, fifteen as a defense attorney and two as a prosecutor. Ten of the trials went to jury verdict, of which Lincoln was, by a conservative estimate, on the winning side five times. Counting the cases that were settled by plea bargain, one could say that he won or satisfactorily resolved 70 percent of his homicide cases.[114] Granted, his performances were not always the result of brilliant legal arguments. In an effort to save a client found guilty of murder, he once filed a request for arrest of judgment so nitpicking as to be called spurious.[115] Another time, he was preparing to defend a woman accused of murdering her husband when she slipped out of the state and was never caught—possibly a deliberate lapse of attention on his part, giving rise to the legend that he joked in court, "She wanted to know where she could get a good drink of water, and I told her there was mighty good water in Tennessee."[116]

The biographical and cultural meanings of his criminal work have been overlooked. As we've seen, Lincoln emerged from violent cultures: the frontier, with its rough-and-tumble fighting; the riverboat culture of "half-horse, half-alligator" men; the gangs of New Salem, where the Clary's Grove Boys reigned supreme; and contentious Illinois politics, which saw Lincoln clashing with opponents and nearly having a duel to the death. He was also alarmed by nationwide mobocracy—group vigilantism—and the fierce, denunciatory language of reformers, which he wanted to be replaced by milder, more logical forms of persuasion.

His murder cases gave him the opportunity to revisit all these cultural arenas. He reexperienced frontier violence when he defended William Fraim, a volatile riverboat man who stabbed to death the ferryman William Neathammer in a Frederick, Illinois, saloon on February 17, 1838, after a fight erupted when the latter blew tobacco smoke in the former's face.[117] A later case, *People v. William Duff Armstrong* (the celebrated "Almanac Trial"), came directly out of Lincoln's fighting past.[118] The accused murderer, Duff Armstrong, was the son of the late Jack Armstrong, the champion wrestler of Clary's Grove whom Lincoln had fought to a draw and who came to respect Lincoln so much that the two became fast friends. Duff had allegedly crushed the skull of James Preston Metzker during a brawl in a "whiskey camp" on the outskirts of a religious revival. In defending Duff without charge for Jack's widow, Hannah, Lincoln gave one of his best courtroom performances, winning a not-guilty verdict.

Another murder case, *People v. Truett*, grew out of the turbulent Illinois political culture that had put Lincoln in potentially deadly situations.[119] A politician who had threatened violence against him, William L. D. Ewing, was involved in the case, as were several other of Lincoln's opponents, including Jesse Thomas (whom Lincoln had famously "skinned") and Lincoln's perennial foe Stephen A. Douglas. The murder resulted from a power struggle within the state Democratic Party. In 1837, Douglas seized leadership of the state party from former boss William L. May. At the party's convention, a committee of Douglas supporters, including Jacob Early, dismissed May's son-in-law Henry B. Truett as register of the land office in Galena. In March 1838, Truett took revenge against Early. While Early was sitting in a hotel parlor, Truett talked with William Ewing, who was walking out of the hotel. Evidently, Ewing provided information about Early that angered Truett. Armed with a pistol, Truett approached Early and charged him with being involved in the land office decision. Early replied that he would say nothing unless Truett revealed his source, at which point Truett yelled vehemently at Early, calling him a "damned liar," "damned coward," "damned scoundrel," and the like.[120] When Truett pulled out his pistol, Early rose and picked up a chair. Truett circled him and, when Early stumbled, shot him. Early died three days later, and Truett was charged with murder. The judge in the trial was Jesse Thomas, who appointed Stephen Douglas to the prosecuting team. The defense lawyers included Lincoln and Stuart, with the assistance of Edward Baker. Though Truett seemed clearly guilty, Lincoln won the case by arguing that Truett was defending himself from an attack by the chair-wielding Early. Lincoln's friend Dr. Elias Merryman and his future brother-in-law Dr. William Wallace provided medical evidence. Douglas's prosecution team performed listlessly at the trial, and Truett walked free.

Lincoln's murder cases taught him how cases such as Truett's could be evaluated rationally through the careful marshaling of evidence. "When I have a particular case in hand," he explained, "I . . . love to dig up the question by the roots and hold it up and dry it before the fires of the mind."[121] Herndon, who knew as much about Lincoln's law practice as anyone, identified reason as Lincoln's chief trait. Herndon wrote, "His reason ruled despotically all other faculties and qualities of his mind. His conscience and heart were ruled by it. His conscience was ruled by one faculty—reason. His heart was ruled by two faculties—reason and conscience."[122]

Lincoln's rationality was visible in his public telling of a famous murder trial he was involved with, one that his lawyer friend James Matheny called "probably the most remarkable trial that ever took place in Springfield, and beyond a doubt one of the most dramatic trials that ever took place in the whole county."[123] *People v. Trailor & Trailor* is the only murder case where we have lengthy records by Lincoln, who described the case in detail in a letter to Joshua Speed and in an 1846 newspaper story, "Remarkable Case of Arrest for Murder."[124]

This was the kind of case that popular sensational writers of the day feasted on. Three Trailor brothers—Archibald, Henry, and William—had accompanied Archibald Fisher from Clary's Grove to Springfield. Somewhere on the journey Fisher disappeared. Later, in a coerced confession, Henry Trailor told authorities that his brothers had murdered and robbed Fisher, dumping his corpse into a pond. Search parties drained the pond, dug up fresh graves, and scoured the countryside but failed to find the body. Archibald and William Trailor were tried for murder, with Lincoln on their defense team. During the trial, Dr. Robert Gilmore testified that the mentally challenged Fisher, ill and dazed, was actually at his home. The accused murderers were freed, and soon thereafter Fisher arrived in Springfield.

In his newspaper write-up, Lincoln used the case to warn of the dangers of emotionalism in assessing alleged criminality. Several times in his narrative Lincoln describes the rising excitement of Springfield residents who, carried away by their feelings, were ready to rush to judgment. When the story of the Trailors' alleged guilt became known, Lincoln writes, "excitement became universal and intense."[125] When further evidence of their guilt surfaced, "excitement rose to an almost inconceivable height." Lincoln saw that the public thirsted for a guilty verdict and an execution. As he wrote Speed, when it was revealed that Fisher was living, "Some looked quizical, some melancholly, and some furiously angry." The man who had led the search for Fisher's body "looked most awfully wo-begone; he seemed the '*wictim of hun-requited haffection*' as represented in the comic almanac [sic] we used to laugh over," while another member of the search party "said it was too *damned* bad, to have so much trouble, and no hanging after all."

Lincoln here parodies the disappointment of sensation lovers by quoting from a comic almanac of the sort that abounded in sensation. He noted, "Thus ended this strange affair; and while it is readily conceived that a writer of novels could bring a story to a more perfect climax, it may well be doubted, whether a stranger affair ever really occurred." For Lincoln, the Trailor case underscored the need for careful examination of evidence, which here prevented two people from being wrongly sent to the gallows.

Mob passions of the sort that he witnessed in the Trailor case, if repeated on a large scale, threatened to cast both the innocent and the guilty into a whirlpool of anarchy. As he had stated in the 1838 Springfield Lyceum address, "the innocent, those who have ever set their faces against violations of law in every shape, alike with the guilty, fall victims to the ravages of mob law; and thus it goes on, step by step, till all the walls erected for the defence of the persons and property of individuals, are trodden down, and disregarded."[126] The end result, he insisted, was the "total annihilation" of government and the rise of tyranny.

Lincoln witnessed the perils of mob law up close in his law practice. Thomas Delny, suspected of raping a seven-year-old girl, was hauled to a river by a mob that tied a rope around his neck and fixed it to a heavy weight with the aim of drowning him; he escaped death only by confessing to the crime before the mob and begging for a fair trial, which he got, with Lincoln serving as the chief prosecutor, and was found guilty.[127] Henry B. Truett, whom Lincoln had successfully defended for the alleged murder of Jacob Early, had nearly been lynched by aroused citizens around the time of the killing. Duff Armstrong came close to being lynched while awaiting trial in jail. The evidence against Armstrong seemed so strong that the public saw him as "as a fiend of the most horrible hue." Rumors of his past immoral behavior came to be accepted as "gospel truth, and a feverish desire for vengeance seized upon the infatuated populace, whilst only prison-bars prevented a horrible death at the hands of a mob."[128]

Lincoln's brilliant defense of Armstrong, reported nationwide during his presidential run in 1860 and later immortalized in John Ford's film *Young Mr. Lincoln* (in which Lincoln faces down a lynch mob, then goes on to win freedom for his client), shows that his courtroom success came not only from applying reason and assembling scientific evidence but also from appealing to domestic feelings of the sort popularized by sentimental genres of the day. He cleverly used natural science to dismantle the testimony of the prosecution's chief witness, James Allen, who claimed to have seen Armstrong strike Metzker with a slung-shot (a heavy, leather-wrapped lead ball attached to a cord). When asked how he could see Armstrong at night from 150 feet away, Allen declared that the moon was high and bright, giving him a clear view of the crime. Having committed Allen to this story, Lincoln entered as evidence an almanac that, as he later demonstrated to the court, showed that the moon at the time was, in fact, on the horizon and emitted little light. Allen looked like a perjurer—even more so when later testimony revealed that Nelson Watkins, Armstrong's cousin, owned the slung-shot and had it in his pocket that night.

In his summation to the jury, Lincoln made devastating use of these facts while putting on a masterly sentimental performance. The prosecuting attorney, J. Henry Shaw, recalled,

> He told the jury of his once being a poor, friendless boy; that [Duff] Armstrong's parents took him into their house, fed and clothed him, and gave him a home. There were tears in his eyes as he spoke. The sight of his tall, quivering frame, and the particulars of the story he so pathetically told, moved the jury to tears also, and they forgot the guilt of the defendant in their admiration of his advocate. It was the most touching scene I ever witnessed.[129]

Lincoln made no mention here of his historic "wrassle" with Duff's father, which had initiated him into the Clary's Grove Boys' violent culture, nor of Duff's own rowdy history. Also, he had strategically confined his direct examination of Nelson Watkins to the slung-shot issue, ignoring any further knowledge Watkins might have had (in fact, Watkins had seen Duff strike Metzker with a wagon hammer). Instead, he conjured up a time when Duff's parents had taken him, a "poor friendless boy," into their home. Newspapers reported that he appealed to the jurors "as fathers of sons who might become fatherless, and husbands of wives who might be widowed," drawing tears from many who were present, including Duff's mother, who sobbed under a sunbonnet that hid her face.

If Lincoln combined sentimentality with science in the Armstrong trial, he mixed it with patriotic paeans to the founding fathers in another of his famous performances, his defense of a Revolutionary War widow in *Rebecca Thomas v. Erastus Wright*.

Reimagining the Revolutionary War was a major strain in popular culture, from Parson Weems's semifictional biographies of Washington and Franklin through Walt Whitman's tale "The Last of the Sacred Army" to bestsellers of the 1840s and '50s, such as George Lippard's *Legends of the American Revolution* and Joel Tyler Headley's *Washington and His Generals*. These works not only revisited history; in some cases, they made it. For instance, Lippard's legend that the Liberty Bell was rung shortly after a group signing of the Declaration of Independence on July 4, 1776, was reprinted as fact in schoolbooks until the early twentieth century. (Actually, the Declaration was approved by Congress on July 4 but probably was not signed until August 2, 1776, and the Liberty Bell may have been among the bells rung on July 8, not July 4.) Such legends resurrected the democratic past with an eye to critiquing what was regarded as the undemocratic American present, when an oppressive ruling class allegedly cheated the humble working class.

Lincoln tapped into this subversive-patriotic strain in his defense of

Rebecca Thomas, who, he argued, had been overcharged for winning a pension by the agent Erastus Wright. If in the Duff Armstrong trial Lincoln performed emotionally in order to draw tears, in this trial he poured forth righteous anger. His jottings for his speech to the jury included notes about the Revolution that would be worthy of one of Lippard's legends: "Not professional services.—Unreasonable charge . . . —Revolutionary War.—Describe Valley Forge privations.—Ice—Soldier's bleeding feet.— Pl[ainti]ffs husband.—Soldier leaving home for army."[130] The "bleeding feet" and "privations" of soldiers had little to do with the legal problem at hand, but Lincoln, like Lippard, Whitman, and Headley, knew well how to push patriotic buttons for emotional effect. He won the case for the widow.

How does his rhetorical use of culturally popular themes jibe with his mandate that lawyers must be honest? Lincoln's job as a lawyer was to make his case as persuasively as possible, using whatever tools he had. There was a time when some maintained that Lincoln would not defend bad people or ones with unsavory claims.[131] It is wrong, however, to pretend that Lincoln only defended clients he believed in. Had he done so, he would have violated due process, based on the bedrock principle of innocent until proven guilty. The United States was founded on the powerful version of presumed innocence affirmed by Blackstone, who wrote, "It is better that ten guilty persons escape than that one innocent suffer"[132]—a formula magnified by America's founders, such as Franklin ("[I]t is better 100 guilty Persons should escape than that one innocent Person should suffer")[133] and John Adams ("It's of more importance to community, that innocence should be protected, than it is, that guilt be punished.)"[134] The guilt of alleged murderers such as Henry Truett and Duff Armstrong had to be *proved* by evidence presented in court. As we know, such evidence doesn't always assure victory, as in cases where venue can be a deciding factor in a jury's decision. Nonetheless, it is up to a lawyer to request a change of venue, as Lincoln wisely did in the Armstrong case. Sometimes a lawyer profits from a lackluster performance by the opposing side, as in the Truett trial. And sometimes the unexpected happens, as when Fisher turned up alive.

Part of due process, as practiced in the United States, is understanding both sides of a case: seeing issues in a nuanced way and anticipating objections by examining the opponent's argument. Lincoln was especially skillful in this regard. He told a fellow lawyer that "he habitually studied the opposite side of every disputed question, of every law case, of every political issue, more exhaustively, if possible, than his own side. He said that the result had been that in all his long practice at the bar he had never once been surprised in court by the strength of his adversary's case—often finding it much weaker than he had feared."[135] The sheer volume and variety of his law practice expanded his vision notably.

Part of this expansion resulted from the fact that he often partnered with lawyers who at other times opposed him in court. For example, after he left John Stuart, with whom he had served as cocounsel on 487 cases, he challenged him in court 308 times.[136] The balance with his next partner, Stephen T. Logan, was 667 cases with him and 306 against him. Of the nearly 1,500 cases in which he participated with his third partner, William Herndon, he challenged Herndon 15 times. He faced off against his close friend Edward Baker, after whom he named his second son, in 72 percent of 178 cases—about the same percentage of times he opposed another close friend, James Matheny, in the 87 cases they were both involved in. Ward Hill Lamon, later Lincoln's bodyguard and his appointee as the marshal of the District of Columbia, took the opposing side 4 out of 158 times. Lincoln even worked on both sides with the lawyer who became his political nemesis, Stephen A. Douglas. The two teamed up on 3 cases and opposed each other in 28 cases.

SEEING BOTH SIDES

If serving as both cocounsel and adversary was revealing, so was taking different sides in different situations. There were few sides in the law that Lincoln did not defend in the more than 5,000 documented cases he participated in during his two-plus decades as an attorney. Of the 133 railroad cases that he and his partners took on, he defended railroad companies 71 times and opposed them 62 times. His flexibility on the temperance question was reflected in the fact that he took the side of the liquor dealers in 32 cases but defended prohibition or temperance in 7 cases. In cases of spousal disagreement, mostly he represented abused wives, but he also defended a number of men taken to court by their wives.

The latter topic was something of a special case for Lincoln. As a lawyer supporting a growing family and working in a competitive field, he took on a number of cases in which he defended husbands accused of misbehavior, among them a man whose wife charged him with giving her venereal disease, another who was a drunkard who consorted with prostitutes, a third who was having adulterous relationships with three different women, and so on. Lincoln also defended a number of men who had been cuckolded by their wives.

But he seemed to have strongly preferred to defend wronged women. Like other Illinois lawyers, he had a lively practice in divorce, because the states in the Northwest were far more liberal in their divorce laws than were most of the eastern states, where the requirements were, in general, stiff for procuring separation from one's spouse. States with conservative divorce laws, such as New York, typically permitted divorce only in cases of adultery. Illinois, in contrast, allowed it as well for drunkenness, cruelty, or desertion. Due in large part to its highly mobile population, Illinois by 1857 had the highest divorce rate in the nation.

For these reasons, Lincoln and his partners handled a wide variety of divorce cases. Virtually any situation found in the sensational newspapers and novels of the day appeared for consideration by Lincoln the lawyer. He had particularly extensive experience with women who went to court. Women were plaintiffs or litigants in a full 20 percent of the cases he handled between 1837 and 1860.[137] A large percentage of the 131 divorce cases he took on involved women who claimed to have been abused by drunken, cruel husbands.

In litigating such cases, Lincoln unwittingly found himself at the forefront of a progressive movement that was rapidly becoming of central importance to advocates of women's rights. Reformers like Elizabeth Cady Stanton and Susan B. Anthony were active in both temperance and women's rights. Closely associated, these movements grew in tandem, which accounts for the fact that both the Eighteenth Amendment, enforcing Prohibition, and the Nineteenth Amendment, which gave women the vote, were ratified the same year, 1920. The correspondence between the movements came from the fact that many American women found themselves trapped in marriages with abusive, alcoholic men. A whole genre of dark temperance literature traced the inexorable decline of once happy families after the husband took to the bottle. As early as 1831, a temperance pamphlet, *Address to Females*, demanded new divorce laws that would make it easier for abused women to separate from drunken husbands—only then "shall woman achieve her true rank and no longer be a slave, but companion, of man."[138] The 1844 novel *Letters from the Alms-House, on the Subject of Temperance* describes an alcoholic who descends into poverty while maltreating his wife and children, whom he leaves desperate and penniless after he dies in a drunken stupor. In *The Autobiography of a Reformed Inebriate* (1845) the narrator has nightmarish visions of inebriated husbands terrorizing those around them: one man drives his family outdoors with a club, another drags his wife by the hair, a third assaults his wife with tongs. Melville, in *Moby-Dick*, gave his version of dark temperance in his portrait of

Ahab's harpoon maker, the wretched blacksmith Perth, whose formerly blissful family had been destroyed by the "Bottle Conjurer! Upon the opening of that fatal cork, forth flew the fiend, and shriveled up his home."[139]

Lincoln dealt with alcohol-ravaged families as a lawyer. Eliza Lloyd hired him and Stuart in her divorce suit against Peter Lloyd, who habitually drank and who "left her in a hopeless condition with a new-born infant."[140] Ann McDaniel retained Lincoln and Logan to pursue her divorce from Patrick McDaniel, who took her earnings and spent them on "reveling and drunkenness."[141] In a case in which Lincoln was involved (in an unknown capacity), Martha Jones charged that her drunken husband beat her, choked her, and said he would slit her throat.[142] Cynthia Klein retained Lincoln and Herndon to sue for divorce from John Klein, an alcoholic who punched and whipped her, threatened to shoot her, and spent time in "every house of ill fame in Springfield."[143]

The examples could be multiplied of family cases Lincoln handled, any of which could have produced a popular dark temperance tale. But alcohol-fueled cruelty was not the only family controversy Lincoln considered. Some women cited impotence, desertion, or verbal abuse as reasons for divorce. His overall success in family cases is extraordinary, even in light of the relatively relaxed divorce laws of Illinois. Among his many cases of women suing for divorce, he won an extraordinary 82 percent of the time. He helped Sarah Hill get a divorce from a husband who was "not a natural and perfect man" (that is, he was sexually inadequate).[144] He and Herndon successfully represented Sarah Hook, who had been drugged and kidnapped by a man who forced her to marry him.[145] Elzena Ray claimed that her husband was still married to another woman, by whom he had two children; represented by Lincoln and Herndon, she won a divorce on the grounds of bigamy and desertion.[146]

A case that reportedly stood out for Lincoln was that of "a very pretty refined & interesting woman" who sued for divorce on grounds of cruelty from a husband who was "a rather gross, morose, querulous, fault finding, cross, & uncomfortable person," who showered her with "very offensive & vulgar epithets."[147] With no evidence of physical injury, all but one of the jury members favored the husband. But as in the film *Twelve Angry Men*, one member swayed the rest of the jury, holding fast to the belief that the husband's verbal abuse was itself valid reason for divorce. The juryman announced, "[G]entlemen, I am going to lie down to sleep, & when you get ready to give a verdict for that woman, wake me up, for before I will give a verdict—against her, I will lie here until I rot, & the pis-mires carry me out of the Keyhole." Indeed, the jury found for the woman, much to Lincoln's delight. He "always regarded this as one of the most gratifying triumphs of his professional career."

The abuse of women was a bête noire for Lincoln. During the Civil War, though known for his clemency toward erring soldiers, there was a crime he could not forgive: rape. A judge said of him: "There was only one class of crimes I always found him prompt to punish—a crime which occurs more or less frequently about all armies—namely, outrages upon women."[148] In reviewing Lincoln's law cases related to abused women, one feels a distinct favoritism toward such women that was at odds with the objectivity he generally tried to maintain in the law.

That objectivity was also tested in the twenty-four cases in which he dealt with African Americans. His antislavery side impelled him to defend the rights of blacks, but he recognized that the law often limited these rights. Two law cases of the 1840s, *Bailey v. Cromwell* and *In Re Bryant et al.*, illustrate Lincoln's conflicting loyalties to the higher law—that is, the natural law view that slavery is unjust and immoral—and positive law, or man-made laws, that condoned slavery.

These differing approaches to slavery had been played out before a national audience in two previous cases, handled by other lawyers, involving slave ships: the *Antelope*, a Spanish-licensed ship transporting nearly three hundred enslaved Africans that was intercepted off the coast of Florida by a US federal cutter in 1820; and the *Amistad*, a Cuban-bound vessel that in 1839 became the scene of a revolt by enslaved blacks who were later captured and taken into custody in the United States. The natural-law-versus-positive-law debate raged when these cases went through the legal system and reached the US Supreme Court. In the *Antelope* case, at issue was the fate of the enslaved people aboard the ship: should they be freed or held in bondage? Lawyers including Francis Scott Key (of "Star-Spangled Banner" fame) and William Wirt argued that the *Antelope* blacks were free under the law of nations, or natural law. Lawyers for the opposing side, notably John M. Berrien, held that slavery was determined by human laws in individual locales, and because the *Antelope* blacks had been originally enslaved by Spanish captors, they should be treated as property. Chief Justice John Marshall agreed with the latter claim. He argued that although slavery was "contrary to the law of nature," natural law did not trump human law. And so, Marshall declared, "This Court must not yield to feelings which might seduce it from the path of duty, and must obey the mandate of the law."[149] Some of the *Antelope* blacks were sold into slavery in the United States; the remainder were shipped to Liberia.

The *Antelope* case was on the mind of the ex-president and congressman John Quincy Adams when in 1841 he defended the *Amistad* rebels before the Supreme Court. Pointing to a copy of the Declaration of Independence on the wall of the court chamber, Adams said, "In the Declaration of Independence the Laws of Nature are announced and appealed to as identical with the laws of nature's God, and as the foundation of all obligatory human laws."[150] Adams's eloquent appeal to natural law was effective, and the *Amistad* rebels were set free.

The conflict between positive (or statute) law and natural law framed Lincoln's attitudes toward slavery. On the one hand, he knew that the Constitution could be interpreted as a proslavery document, with its clauses about three-fifths representation and the return of fugitives

JOHN QUINCY ADAMS

from labor. The latter clause explains why he reluctantly accepted the Fugitive Slave Act during the 1850s. At the same time, he was strongly attracted to the argument of antislavery politicians that the natural law of human equality, grounded in the Declaration, was enforced by the Constitution, with its advocacy of justice and human rights.

This antislavery view of the Constitution was promoted vigorously by politicians like Adams and Salmon P. Chase, who would become Lincoln's first secretary of the treasury. In his legal practice during the 1830s and '40s, Chase became known as the Attorney General of Fugitive Slaves. Chase used law to preach morality and justice, as in the 1846 case of the Ohio abolitionist John Van Zandt (the model for John Van

Trompe in Stowe's *Uncle Tom's Cabin*). Van Zandt was brought to trial for helping nine fugitives from Kentucky to flee north. Chase, serving as cocounsel with another future Lincoln cabinet member, William Henry Seward, used the case to promote natural law. In a speech before the Supreme Court, Chase declared, "No legislature can make right wrong, or wrong right."[151] The Supreme Court, however, did not accept Chase's argument that the Constitution embodied antislavery natural law. Van Zandt lost his case.

In time, Lincoln as a politician would make these kinds of moral pronouncements on slavery, but as a lawyer he avoided generalizations about the institution. The closest he came to promoting natural law was when he argued for the freedom of Nance Legins-Cox in the 1841 case *Bailey v. Cromwell*. Nance was an enterprising black woman who in 1827 had been purchased as a servant by the wealthy Illinoisan Nathan Cromwell but who thereafter sued several times for freedom. By 1836, she was still considered the property of Cromwell, who left Illinois that year on a trip and quickly arranged to sell her services to David Bailey, who gave him a promissory note of $376.48. Cromwell died during the trip, and his son, Dr. William Cromwell, sued Bailey for payment on the promissory note. Bailey, an abolitionist from New England, refused to pay, insisting that Nance was now a free woman. After losing his case in a lower court, Bailey hired Lincoln to represent him in the state supreme court.

Lincoln argued that before being purchased by Cromwell, Nance was a free black, which made the sale illegal. The court agreed, and ruled that Nance was free. In support of this argument, Lincoln cited the Northwest Ordinance of 1787, which barred slavery and involuntary servitude in territories northwest of the Ohio River, and the Illinois state constitution of 1818, which also prohibited slavery and involuntary servitude. Lincoln also cited an obscure 1705 British decision in *Smith v. Brown and Cooper*, which posited that an enslaved person brought into a free country automatically earned freedom. This principle underlay the antislavery arguments of William Blackstone in his *Commentaries* and the Somerset decision of 1772, which made natural law the antislavery basis of English common law. For Lincoln to cite the little-known 1705 ruling shows that he had dug deep to find sources of antislavery thought.

More than a century after *Bailey v. Cromwell*, Supreme Court justice William O. Douglas commented on the case: "Thanks to Lincoln, the courts had been supplied with a mass of data supporting the principle of freedom. Certainly this was one of the most far-reaching of the nearly 250 cases in which Lincoln was to appear before the state's highest tribunal."[152] In the case, Lincoln won a ruling that anticipated the Thirteenth Amendment, whose language mirrors that of the antislavery documents he cited in his address to the court, including the Illinois constitution. Illinois would be closely connected to the Thirteenth Amendment in other ways as well: one of the US senators from the state, Lyman Trumbull, sponsored the amendment in the Senate, while the Illinois representatives Isaac Arnold and Owen Lovejoy cosponsored it in the House. After the Thirteenth Amendment was passed by Congress, it was sent to Illinois governor Richard Yates, who promoted it so persuasively that the state became the first to ratify it.

Lincoln continued to help African Americans when he could in court. Twice he successfully defended operators of the Underground Railroad who had been arrested for assisting fugitives. He periodically provided legal help to William de Fleurville (known as William Florville), his African American barber in Springfield. Not only did Lincoln represent Florville in court, he voluntarily paid his taxes for a number of years.[153]

This problack lawyerly activity on Lincoln's part contrasts with his performance in the 1847 trial of the Kentucky slaveholder Robert Matson in *In Re Bryant et al.*[154] Matson had brought five of his enslaved people—Jane Bryant and her four children—to live for a time in Illinois. The family, upon hearing that Matson planned to sell several of its

members into the Deep South, had fled for protection to the abolitionists Hiram Rutherford and Gideon M. Ashmore. Matson sued to retrieve the family, hiring the lawyer Usher Linder, who in turn took on
Lincoln as counsel.

Although it is unclear why Lincoln accepted Linder's offer to join
him in representing Matson, he apparently had second thoughts about
doing so. After joining Linder, he was approached to represent the enslaved blacks by Hiram Rutherford, who said, "I had known Abraham
Lincoln several years, and his views and mine on the wrong of slavery
being in perfect accord, I determined to employ him; besides, everyone
whom I consulted advised me to do so."[155] Rutherford noticed a tense,
perplexed look on Lincoln's face when he pondered the request. Lincoln initially refused Rutherford's offer, seemingly out of deference to
the "cab rank rule," by which a lawyer remains committed to the party
that first approached him. But Lincoln soon decided to switch sides. He
informed Linder that he would prefer to represent the blacks, and he approached Rutherford. However, Rutherford's pride had been wounded
by Lincoln's initial rebuff, and he rejected the offer.

The trial saw the spectacle of the African American family being
defended by two proslavery lawyers, Orlando B. Ficklin and Charles
Constable, with the antislavery Lincoln on the side of the slaveholder.
Some of the same sources Lincoln had cited in representing Nance
Legins-Cox—British common law, the Northwest Ordinance, and the
Illinois state constitution—were used by Ficklin and Constable in the
Matson case. Lincoln, according to one report of the trial, "winced"
when he heard the antislavery statements made by Ficklin and Con-
stable.[156] The statements were persuasive to the court, for the five blacks
were awarded freedom.

Lincoln's arguments for Matson differed significantly from that of
his cocounsel. In addressing the court, Linder used the Matson case to
make a generalization about slavery; the enslaved were property, Linder
said, and Matson had been deprived of what he rightfully owned. In

effect, Linder was voicing a proslavery higher law, which viewed slavery as a natural, justified institution. Lincoln, in contrast, stuck to the technicalities of positive law. Because Matson had made clear from the start that he brought the Bryant family to Illinois for only a temporary stay, he was protected by Illinois law, which provided that enslaved workers who stayed briefly in the state were deemed to be "in transit" and were thus still the property of their owners.

The Matson trial occurred just a week before Lincoln left Illinois on his trip east to Washington, where he would assume his seat in the US House of Representatives. The Mexican War, which was then approaching its end, had fanned the controversy over slavery, which had been intensifying for decades. Lincoln's clinging to positive law in the Matson case was not out of keeping with his trepidation over opposing versions of the higher law, which on the national scene was already breeding predictions of civil war.

If positive law was a stabilizing influence for Lincoln, so was the political position of the Whig Party, which struggled to maintain national unity at a time when the nation seemed on the verge of fragmenting.

8

Economy and Politics

The rational skills Lincoln was honing on the rambunctious Illinois law circuit proved extremely useful when he applied them to the surrounding economic and social turbulence that confronted him as he entered national politics in the 1840s.

The American market economy veered between boom and bust. The Panic of 1837 initiated a recession that was one of the worst in US history. Economic instability gave Whigs like Lincoln an opportunity to attack the Democrats' policies of free trade, hard currency, and the depositing of federal funds in state banks. Lincoln branded the Democratic program as dangerously decentered and corrupt. He and his fellow Whigs called for a restored central bank, a national currency, a protective tariff, and government funding of internal improvements.

This program attracted many new voters in the 1840s. The party won the White House with William Henry Harrison in 1840 and Zachary Taylor in 1848, and came close in 1844, when Henry Clay lost to the Democrat James K. Polk. In these hard-fought elections, which saw tremendous voter turnouts, both parties faced the challenge of appealing to an unruly electorate that included large numbers of young men casting what was called their virgin vote.[1]

The battle for the youth vote was waged in circus-like political campaigns and raucous election days filled with drinking, brawling, screaming, and bonfires. Whigs created folk symbols—from the log cabins and raccoons of the William Henry Harrison campaign to the "monster" torchlight demonstrations of the Zachary Taylor one—that had huge appeal for the masses. However, even as Lincoln witnessed the political power of popular symbols, he felt a strong need to bring under control the often anarchic energies of what he called the "shrewd wild boys" who made up a large segment of voters.[2]

He knew that these voters were, in the main, opposed to extreme stances on the most divisive issue of the day: slavery. Although he was appalled by the threatened westward spread of slavery, as a US congressman from December 1847 to March 1849 he carefully avoided radical statements on slavery, choosing instead to remain publicly restrained. In Congress he learned how, as a left-leaning moderate from central Illinois, he was well positioned to address the nation's deepening divisions.

SEEKING SHELTER FROM ECONOMIC STORMS

The ravages that the Panic of 1837 inflicted on the nation had a special impact on Lincoln. As a Whig legislator in Illinois, he ardently promoted government spending on internal improvements. Just before the recession struck, he had helped pass a bill, the Internal Improvements Act of 1837, that called for more than $10 million to be invested in railroads and canals. The subsequent recession drove Illinois to near bankruptcy. The Whig program seemed to be in disarray. While Lincoln's psychological breakdown in early 1841 resulted mainly from romantic difficulties, the bottoming out of the Illinois economy appears to have contributed to his suicidal depression.

Lincoln also witnessed the destructive effects of the financial crisis as a lawyer. A full 55 percent of his law cases—more than 2,800 in all—were related to debt litigation. In the brief period when the federal bankruptcy law was in effect (1842–43), he and Stephen T. Logan handled 72 bankruptcy cases.[3]

Witnessing the economic downturn drove Lincoln to fresh political action. One of his most prominent early political speeches was his May 1839 assault on President Martin Van Buren's proposal for a subtreasury system (which, despite opposition like Lincoln's, went into effect the next year). In the aftermath of Andrew Jackson's dismantling of the Bank of the United States, Van Buren called for the establishment of "pet banks" in states that would become repositories of federal funds in the form of hard currency. The system, in the view of Lincoln, fostered inefficiency and corruption. Taking paper money out of circulation and demanding specie (hard money), he declared, would cause "distress, ruin, bankruptcy and beggary."[4] Putting federal money under the watch of minor government officials invited criminality. He gave facts and statistics to back his claim that the typical subtreasury director would be constantly tempted to pilfer funds and abscond with them as fast as the Irishman in a popular song whose cork legs ran away with him. Lincoln's speech culminated in his sensational image of "the lava of political corruption," alive with devils, that flowed from the Van Buren White House in the form of the subtreasury plan.

Lincoln continued his attacks on the Democrats' economic policies throughout the 1840s. Those policies, however, actually gave a boost to him and his fellow Whigs. Michael Holt affirms that the Panic of 1837 "was the pivotal episode in the growth of the Whig Party."[5] The Whigs charged that the successive Democratic presidents—Andrew Jackson for two terms, followed by Martin Van Buren—had caused the American economy to unravel. Whigs offered alternatives to Jacksonian economic principles: free trade would be replaced by a protective tariff, the insistence on specie by an openness to paper money in the form of a national currency, and the subtreasury system by a restored national bank.

Lincoln's economic philosophy was close to that of America's leading economist, Henry C. Carey. It appears that Lincoln was familiar with Carey's landmark book *Principles of Political Economy* (1837).[6] Carey was an unofficial economic adviser to Lincoln during the Civil War, sending him letters of advice. One of Carey's fundamental ideas was the necessity of a protective tariff to stimulate the growth of American industries. Carey noted that American industrial production faltered at times when tariff protection was weak and revived when it was strong. Free trade, Carey insisted, created waste, because paying the costs of transporting goods from abroad resulted in higher prices on those goods when they were sold in the United States. The tariff, by increasing the price of foreign goods, provided an incentive to American mining and manufacturing.

Lincoln aired similar views in a note on the tariff that he wrote in 1846. He argued that only goods that were impossible or expensive to produce in America, such as coffee, must be imported from abroad. Most products, he argued, could be produced at home. The cost of these American products, in his view, would be far lower than foreign ones, to which the cost of shipping, storage, insurance, and so on must be included. Even more strongly than Carey, he emphasized the labor theory of value—that is, the idea that the value of a product should be tied as closely as possible to the actual labor that went into making it. Lincoln wanted to reduce the role of the middleman in the production and sale of goods. He applied the term *useless labour* to "all *carrying*, & incidents of carrying, of articles from the place of their production, to a *distant* place for consumption, which articles could be produced of as good quality, in sufficient quantity, and with as little labour, at the place of consumption, as at the place carried from." He identified three types of work: "*useful* labour, *useless* labour and *idleness*." Because only the first of these has merit, he wrote, the aim should be to "drive *useless* labour and *idleness* out of existence."[7] Some have noted that Lincoln's statements about labor move beyond standard Whig economics. Actually, these statements put him in the company of radical labor reformers of the 1840s, such as George Lippard, who contrasted the "upper ten" and the "lower million"—that is, the so-called "idle" rich who make money off the work of others, and the mass of toiling Americans, who do the actual work.[8] Whitman in the 1855 *Leaves of Grass* made the same distinction: "Many sweating, ploughing, thrashing, and then the chaff for payment receiving, / A few idly owning, and they the wheat continually claiming."[9]

Lincoln gave his customary spin on the notion of work. His long-time habit was to trace ideas to origins—pull them up, in his metaphor, by the roots and illuminate them by the fires of the mind.[10] His ideas behind labor were no exception. In this case, he seemed to have been influenced by another leading economist, Francis Wayland, whose book *Political Economy* "Lincoln ate up, digested, and assimilated," according to Herndon.[11] Wayland, to support his point that "Labor has been made necessary to our happiness," cites Genesis 3:19. Wayland writes, "The universal law of our existence, is, 'In the sweat of thy face shalt thou eat thy bread, until thou return to the ground.'"[12] Similarly, Lincoln, in describing labor, writes, "In the early days of the world, the Almighty said to the first of our race 'In the sweat of thy face shalt thou eat bread.'"[13]

Lincoln went on to give this passage a distinct antislavery meaning. He memorably paraphrased it in the Second Inaugural Address, his antislavery masterpiece.[14] He emphasized it to a Baptist delegation to the White House, saying, "To read in the Bible, as the word of God himself, that 'In the sweat of *thy* face shalt thou eat bread,['] and to preach there-from that, 'In the sweat of *other mans* faces shalt thou eat bread,' to my mind can scarcely be reconciled with honest sincerity."[15]

His fixation on the passage marks a difference between him and

Henry Carey. Both men connected antislavery arguments with economics, but in different ways. Carey was a hardheaded pragmatist who ignored the humanistic or moral issues surrounding slavery and focused solely on financial ones. In his view, slavery would disappear when a strong tariff was in place for a sustained time. His idea was that the reason the South had become so dependent on trade with England and other foreign powers was that the slave system tended to exhaust its lands, forcing it to sell as much cotton and tobacco abroad as possible in order to buy foreign cloth and metal products. With the implementation of a tariff, Carey argued, the South would be spurred to tap into its rich iron reserves and produce metal products and textile factories on its own. Manufacturing would grow, and the South's slave-dependent culture would eventually be replaced by self-sufficient communities where slave labor would be de-emphasized. Early in the Civil War, Carey wrote Lincoln, saying that the war was due to the mismanaged US economy. Carey explained: "Had the policy of Mr Clay, as embodied in the tariff of 1842, been maintained, there could have been no secession, and for the reason that the southern mineral region would long since have obtained control of the planting one." By restoring a high tariff, Carey continued, "we may retrace our steps and secure the permanent maintenance of the Union"; but "if the British free trade system be readopted—the Union must, before the lapse of many years, be rent into numerous fragments, mere instruments in the hands of foreign powers."[16]

Lincoln's antislavery interpretation of the tariff idea was more humanistic than Carey's. By maintaining that one should earn the rewards of sweat from one's own brow, he was invoking an image of labor that he would later apply to slavery. Lincoln came to pity the unrewarded labor and physical and mental suffering endured by the enslaved.

In his writing on economics during the 1840s, however, he did not explicitly link the "sweat from the brow" trope to slavery. Indeed, he shied away from making extended statements on slavery, and when he did, as in his proposal in Congress for the gradual abolition of slavery in the District of Columbia, he did so in a moderate way.

Given his lifelong hatred of slavery, why did he recoil from making any long antislavery speech early on? The answer lies partly in his role as a politician trying to appeal to a largely young American electorate. Before he would dare to raise the controversial issue of slavery with American voters, he had to learn how to appeal to these voters, who were often rowdy—and racist—young men.

THE BATTLE FOR YOUNG AMERICA

"We have all heard of Young America. He is the most *current* youth of the age."[17] So Lincoln declared in 1860 in the second part of his continuing lecture on discoveries and inventions. He devoted most of the lecture to contrasting the young American—smart, cosmopolitan, eager to spread freedom, up to date on modern inventions and fads—with the "old fogy," stodgy and looking backward. He traced Young America to the youngest of all humans, as recorded in Genesis: Adam. Lincoln pointed out that Adam came up with the first invention, a fig leaf apron to cover his nakedness. From there, Lincoln followed the long trail of subsequent discoveries and inventions: speech, writing, printing, steam power, and others, each of them a leap forward.

Lincoln here aligned Young America with Whig-Republican principles. Just as in the earlier part of his lecture on inventions he had defined humans as improving animals, so his linkage here of Young America with progress through inventiveness reflected his effort to summon American youth—a large part of the voting population—to the Whig-Republican vantage point. He had been trying to do so for years. His chief competitor in the struggle was the Democrat Stephen A. Douglas.

STEPHEN A. DOUGLAS

The conflict between Lincoln and Douglas is normally seen as one of warring political ideas. Douglas, indifferent about slavery, championed popular sovereignty, or the right of states carved out of western territories to decide for themselves about slavery; Lincoln, morally opposed to slavery, wanted to halt its expansion. This contrast, discussed endlessly by historians, speaks to the ideological distance between the two men. However, there were many politicians of the time who were at loggerheads over slavery. Why did the slavery debate crystallize in the memorable verbal showdown—at some moments close to an old-time rough-and-tumble fight—between the two politicians on the hustings in Illinois in 1858? And why did Douglas get under Lincoln's skin to the degree that he did? In the mid-1850s, Lincoln wrote a note in which he compared himself to Douglas. He remarked that he had known Douglas for more than two decades, but "With *me*, the race of ambition has been a failure—a flat failure; with *him* it has been one of splendid success."[18]

Lincoln's sense of insufficiency came from the political prominence Douglas had gained, largely by appealing to young voters. The Vermont-born Douglas had moved to Illinois in 1833 and met Lincoln there two years later while serving in the state legislature. He had little formal education and worked his way up as a lawyer, judge, and politician. He successfully ran for the US House of Representatives in 1843 and 1844 and then in 1846 for the Senate, where he served from 1847 until his death in 1861, making a big mark on the national scene. He helped push the Compromise of 1850 through Congress, and he authored the Kansas-Nebraska Act, the 1854 law that left future decisions on slavery to voters in newly admitted states.

Douglas's national visibility partly explains Lincoln's envy of his longtime rival. But there was another dimension to the competition: the battle for Young America. From 1840 onward, winning the youth vote was a chief aim of American politicians. In the years that followed, several political factions courted Young America—including nativists and supporters of the 1856 presidential candidate John Frémont—but no one did so over the long term with the effectiveness of Stephen Douglas. Five feet four, stocky, with a broad face and a determined look, Douglas earned his nickname "the Little Giant" by giving pugnacious speeches filled with slick reasoning and sensational invectives that appealed to young voters. By the early 1850s, he was, as a journalist noted, "the favorite son of Young America."[19]

In the early going, Douglas had a step up on Lincoln in the battle for young voters because of his political loyalties. Originally, Young America emerged from the expansionist spirit of the Democratic Party, forcefully verbalized in the *Democratic Review* by its editor John L.

O'Sullivan (who coined the phrase *Manifest Destiny*) and pushed by the Democratic president James K. Polk, the main force behind the Mexican War, which led to America's acquisition of more than half a million square miles of territory, all the way to the Pacific. Douglas rode the wave of Young America's enthusiasm for westward expansion.

The challenge of politicians was to channel the barely controllable energies of the young toward party loyalty. Rival political clubs often brawled. In 1844 the *New York Herald* reported that "it is notorious that the fighting men—the bullies—the 'sporting men'—the 'gentlemen of the fancy'—as they are called in their own slang" were "hired and paid by both parties, as the leaders and managers of these political clubs." Armed with bowie knives and revolvers, these club leaders were "producing a state of affairs which now threaten us with riot, bloodshed, conflagration, and we know not what terrible disorders."[20]

In his autobiographical book *A Boy's Town*, William Dean Howells re-created the youth culture of his native Ohio in the 1840s. From a young man's perspective, Howells recalled, political campaigns were forms of mass entertainment. Each party had its popular campaign songs and rustic symbols, and young people, whether of voting age or not, went crazy with enthusiasm. Election days were filled with drinking, fights, yelling, and setting bonfires. Howells had especially vivid memories of boys hurling fireballs—turpentine-soaked rag balls that were lit, picked up gingerly, and thrown in high arcs that left trails of flame.[21]

It was important for politicians to exploit this frenzied enthusiasm because one's virgin vote usually signaled one's political future. Once committed to a party, the young voter, like a faithful partner in a monogamous marriage, typically stayed loyal to the party in subsequent elections.[22] Although the Democrats had the populist heritage of Andrew Jackson to draw from (hickory poles, first used in 1828 to boost "Old Hickory" Jackson to the presidency, remained a staple for Democratic candidates in later races), the Whigs became skilled at concocting attractive folk myths and organizing on the ground-roots level.

The 1840 Whig campaign for William Henry Harrison was an effective charade. The Whigs turned what was intended by Democrats to be an insult—the jeering suggestion that Harrison should return to his log cabin and drink hard cider—into a badge of honor. No Harrison rally was complete without a log cabin—usually many log cabins, some small and toted about on wagons, others pictured on badges or flags, and yet others large structures covering hundreds of square feet. In some of the large cabins there was a plain-clad woman at a spinning wheel, a rifle-toting frontiersman at the front door, and outside, a canoe, a horned owl, and a chained raccoon—all reminders of the woods. As we know, image often trumps reality in political campaigns. In reality, Harrison, who was descended from Virginia's ruling class, lived in a sixteen-room mansion in Ohio. He was a temperance advocate who didn't touch liquor. But barrels of spiked cider were on hand at Whig rallies to add a giddy buzz to the homespun atmosphere. Attracting "grocery" voters (in a day when saloons were called groceries) was part of political strategy, as Lincoln recognized. In the midst of the Log Cabin campaign, he wrote a friend, "A great many of the grocery sort of Van Buren men, as formerly, are out for Harrison. Our Irish Blacksmith Gregory, is for Harrison. I believe I may say, that all our friends think the chance of carrying the state, verry [sic] good."[23]

Whigs piled on other popular symbols, too. To represent Harrison's momentum, a large ball was rolled from town to town. Also, Harrison's inglorious engagement with Native Americans at Tippecanoe River in 1811—he burned an Indian village to the ground after repulsing a surprise attack by the natives—was hailed as a victory on a level with Andrew Jackson's at New Orleans. Thus was born "the hero of Tippecanoe," who would march to victory with "Tyler too."

March he did, to a structured rhythm. The Whigs proved adept in organizing.[24] Lincoln, as casual as he may have been in his law office, approached the Harrison campaign with militaristic discipline. In a pro-Harrison newspaper, the *Old Soldier*, he and his Whig cowriters insisted that Van Buren's "double-drilled army" must be defeated. The writers recalled how in the War of 1812, American forces, "on learning that an organized foe was invading their land, they, too, organized— met—conquered—killed and drove the foe beyond the 'world of waters.'" And so "We justify—we urge—organization on the score of necessity. A disbanded yeomanry cannot successfully meet an organized soldiery." The Whigs addressed their readers: "Organization must again be had. We . . . will form the rank and file; you shall be the generals, and commanders-in-chief. Thus organized, we will meet, conquer and disperse Gen. Harrison's and the country's enemies, and place him in the chair, now disgraced by their effeminate and luxury-loving chief."[25]

Lincoln wrote a circular that gave precise directions to Whig organizers. "Captains" should be appointed on various levels—county, precinct, and section. Each captain must "pledge to perform promptly all duties assigned to him." All these duties were designed to create a substantial Whig turnout at the polls. In an era before mass advertising and robocalls, this get-out-the-vote drive was intensely personal. The duty of the section captain, Lincoln wrote, was "to see each man of his Section face to face, and procure his pledge that he will for no consideration (impossibilities excepted) stay from the polls on the first monday in November; and that he will record his vote as early on the day as possible."[26]

What did it matter if voters cast their ballots early or late in the day? Lincoln evidently wanted to secure as many Whig votes before wildness and distraction took over. Young party operators plied voters with drink, coaxed them with entertainment, or foisted ballots on them (in those days, each party printed its own colored ballots and handed them out). As Jon Grinspan notes, "Young Americans spent their times buttonholing neighbors, manufacturing ballots, and intimidating voters in hidden locations where smart dealings verged on hidden tricks."[27] Howells recalled the turbulence of election days in what he called "that barbarous republic of boys." The Whigs yelled, "Democrats eat dead rats!"—answered by, "Whigs eat dead pigs!" Alcohol-fueled fights were a ritual. Howells recalled:

> There were always fights on election-day between well-known Whig and Democratic champions, which the boys somehow felt were as entirely for their entertainment as the circuses. . . . The fighting must have come from the drinking, which began as soon as the polls were opened, and went on all day and night with a devotion to principle which is now rarely seen.[28]

Lincoln saw the crucial importance of winning over young male voters. As we've seen, he was not above fighting to gain control, as in his historic battle against Jack Armstrong, which jump-started his political career by winning over the Clary's Grove Boys to his side, or his threats of physical reprisal against opponents in the state legislature. He continued to reach out to young men. Here Lincoln faced a special challenge because of his marriage to Mary Todd. In a decade when voters bought into populist symbols, Lincoln knew the price of being married to a woman who had lived among the wealthy on Springfield's Aristocracy Hill. He wrote a friend in 1843, "It would astonish if not amuse the older citizens of your County, who twelve years ago knew me a strange, friendless, uneducated, penniless boy, working on a flat boat—at ten dollars per month to learn that I have been put down here as the candidate of pride, wealth, and arristocratic [sic] family distinction. Yet so chiefly it was."[29]

He would later be wildly successful in overcoming any taint of aristocracy when he swept to victory as the Illinois Rail-splitter in 1860. But a pressing issue for him in the 1840s was how to woo the youth vote. He knew that the future for any politician was in the hands of young voters whose behavior could be erratic and whose energies must be guided. In the midst of campaigning for Zachary Taylor in 1848, he gave advice about attracting young voters in a letter from Washington to his Springfield law partner William Herndon:

> Now as to the young men. You must not wait to be brought forward by the older men. For instance do you suppose that I should ever have got into notice if I had waited to be hunted up and pushed forward by older men. You young men get together and form a Rough & Ready club, and have regular meetings and speeches. Take in every body that you can get, Harrison Grimsley, Z. A. Enos, Lee Kimball, and C. W. Matheny will do well to begin the thing, but as you go along, gather up all the shrewd wild boys about town, whether just of age, or little under age—Chris Logan, Reddick Ridgely, Lewis Zwizler, and hundreds such. Let every one play the part he can play best—some speak, some sing, and all hollow. Your meetings will be of evenings; the older men, and the women will go to hear you; so that it will not only contribute to the election of "Old Zach" but will be an interesting pastime, and improving to the intellectual faculties of all engaged. Dont fail to do this.[30]

Lincoln drives his point home emphatically—"Dont fail to do this"—because he sees the absolute necessity of directing the political loyalties of "hundreds" of Springfield's young people in a Whig direction. Songs, speeches, any "interesting pastime," as long as it is "all hollow" (presented with great energy), must be used to pull in young voters. The letter reveals his perception of Herndon as his connection to the young: "You young men get together and form a Rough & Ready club." In other letters to Herndon, he referred to "you and others of my young friends at home" and advised, "Go it while you're young!"[31]

Here, then, is another reason for Lincoln's selection of Herndon, nine years his junior, as his third law partner—and, later, of Ward Hill Lamon, a decade younger than Herndon, as his political enforcer. They were hot-blooded, smart young men given to bouts of drinking and thus close in spirit to the "shrewd wild boys" Lincoln competed for.[32] Lincoln knew that some of these youths could not yet vote, but "whether just of age, or little under age," they were immensely valuable. They were either virgin voters or future ones, and Lincoln wanted to channel them toward his party.

TIPTOEING AROUND SLAVERY

In urging Herndon to form Rough and Ready clubs to attract the young, Lincoln revealed that at this point in his career he was interested more in preserving the unity of his party and his nation than he was in forcefully asserting his antislavery principles.

He saw that antislavery reform was riddled with divisions. In 1840, the New York–based followers of Lewis and Arthur Tappan broke off from William Lloyd Garrison's Boston-centered American Anti-Slavery Society because of the latter's advocacy of women's rights and nonresistance. The Garrisonians, already on the fringe, became especially unpopular in the 1840s, when they advocated disunion (the separation of the North from the slaveholding South) and rejected churches and the government, both of which they regarded as corrupted by the South's peculiar institution. Both groups had only tangential connections with Unitarian/transcendentalist antislavery figures such as Theodore Parker, Ralph Waldo Emerson, and Henry David Thoreau.

While Lincoln hated slavery as much as anyone, he was alarmed by divisions within the antislavery ranks. He came to dismiss Garrisonian abolitionists as "those who would shiver into fragments the union of the states; tear to tatters its now venerated Constitution; and even burn the last copy of the Bible, rather than slavery should continue a single hour."[33] Moral persuasion, advocated by the Tappanites, or individual resistance, championed by transcendentalists like Thoreau, he considered inadequate to combat the Southern slave power.

He was ideologically in line with the Liberty Party and its successor, the Free Soil Party, which challenged slavery through political channels.[34] These parties' goal of halting the westward spread of slavery later became the centerpiece of the Republican Party. In the 1840s, however, these nascent forms of antislavery politics struck him as well-intentioned but futile. He observed that in 1844 the Liberty Party unwittingly helped the spread of slavery because it swung the election from the antiextensionist Henry Clay to the expansionist James Polk. Had the Liberty Party not been in the picture, he noted, Clay almost certainly would have won New York and the White House, which would have given antislavery voters what they wanted: a president reluctant to wage war on Mexico in the interest of seizing western territories, where slavery could find root.[35] By the same token, in the 1848 race, Lincoln criticized the Free Soil Party as a sectional, one-idea party that jeopardized the chances of the Whig candidate Zachary Taylor, whom Lincoln saw as an electable figure who as president would not stand in the way of the Wilmot Proviso, which called for barring slavery from the western territories.

The fact that he could support two slaveholders—Clay and Taylor—shows how far he would go in the interest of Whig Party unity. In his own political campaigns of the 1840s he appears to have largely avoided the highly contentious slavery issue. Having been defeated in the race for a seat in the Illinois General Assembly in 1832, he was elected to the Assembly four times: in 1834, 1836, 1838, and 1840. He became increasingly attentive to party unity. In the state races during the 1830s, the Whigs followed the system of multiple candidates running against one another. By the end of the decade, the Whigs had seen the need to put aside this system of competing candidates and adopt the convention system, whereby party members met and decided on a single candidate for a particular office. This was how the Democrats had chosen their presidential candidates ever since 1832 and their state candidates in Illinois since 1835.

The Whigs succeeded on the national level by holding their first convention in 1839, when they nominated Harrison for the presidency. Soon they outdid the Democrats in organizational strength. Lincoln attended the first Whig Party state convention on October 7, 1839. In 1840 he not only contributed to the programmatic Whig circular outlining various levels of officers to corral voters, but he was ready to put party loyalty above personal ambition. In March 1840 he wrote Stuart, "I do not think my prospects individually are very flattering, . . . But the party ticket will succeed triumphantly."[36] As it turned out, he was elected to his fourth term in the General Assembly that August, even as he worked to advance the cause of William Henry Harrison. He promoted the distribution of the Harrison newspaper the *Old Soldier* and listed names of former Democrats who, in his words, "have come out for Harrison." He also helped write a flyer instructing voters about the locations of local ballot boxes.

At times his party zeal seemed to overwhelm his antislavery views. Harrison's opponent, Martin Van Buren, had, nineteen years earlier as a New York legislator, voted for suffrage for free, property-holding blacks. Lincoln, with an eye on discrediting Van Buren, denounced "the political course of Mr. Van Buren, and especially his course in the New York convention in allowing free Negroes the right of suffrage." Lincoln got "spontaneous bursts of applause" and "convulsed the house with laughter" with his "highly amusing anecdotes," leading to his concluding praise of "the civil and military reputation of the hero of Tippecanoe."[37]

Lincoln's disparagement of black suffrage here is reprehensible but unsurprising, given the ban against African American political participation in most states in 1840, when he made these remarks. His racial attitudes would evolve, and he became the first American president who called openly for the vote for African Americans. Actually, it was the Democrats who were most given to public race-baiting. Stephen Douglas's speeches often became racist rants, and in his 1858 debates against Lincoln he aligned white supremacy with the nation and its founders. The N-word was commonly used by Democrats who wanted to tar their opponents with advocacy of abolitionism and amalgamation (miscegenation). Democrats branded even a conservative Whig like William Henry Harrison—the descendant of slaveholders who had once tried to open the way for slavery in both Indiana and Ohio—as a dangerous abolitionist who would bring about an appalling racial reversal as president. Harrison was an "Abolitionist of the first water," the Democrats charged, who would "make slaves of White men" while making "free men of black slaves."[38] The Democrats' views came through in a satirical poem, "Jim Brown—The Politician," whose black speaker, a Whig loyalist, boasts that when Harrison becomes president, he will win a congressional seat and will marry a white woman. "I am a good Whig nigger," he announces, "and my name is Jim Brown." He says he has been campaigning hard for "Hard Cider, Abolition," and "dear Massa Harrison, de friend ob de nigger." He predicts that he will rise so high socially that he will be able to purchase white people and hold them as slaves. He concludes: "Stan back and let de darkie come, he go de whole figger, / For Harrison, White Slavery, and free rights ob de nigger."[39]

Harrison's victory was *not* followed by the advance of black people. Harrison died after just thirty days in office, and his successor, John Tyler, took a conservative course on race. A Virginia gentleman, Tyler was attended by enslaved workers in the White House. Blacks lost legal ground under Tyler. In *Prigg v. Pennsylvania* (1842) the Supreme Court ruled that the fugitive slave law of 1793 invalidated the personal liberty laws that several Northern states had passed. Tyler set the stage for virulent controversy when he called for the annexation of Texas. Opponents and supporters of annexation vocally aired their views on what rapidly became the prelude to a momentous struggle over slavery's role in westward expansion.

Lincoln, despite his hatred of slavery, at first showed little concern with the proposed annexation of Texas. "I never was much interested in the Texas question," he wrote in October 1845. "I never could see much good to come of annexation; . . . on the other hand, I never could very clearly see how the annexation would augment the evil of slavery."[40] His opinion would change after he heard admonitory speeches on the Mexican War as a Whig politician from 1846 to 1848. For the time being, maintaining party unity was chiefly on his mind. In March 1843 he wrote a Whig declaration, "Address to the People of Illinois," that called for more extensive use of the convention system in the selection of the party's candidates. Lincoln delivered a loud and clear message of unity. He declared, "That 'union is strength' is a truth that has been known, illustrated and declared, in various ways and forms in all ages of the world." To illustrate the point, he mentioned the fable of the bundle of sticks told by "that great fabulist and philosopher, Aesop." He also cited "he whose wisdom surpasses that of all philosophers," Jesus, who "has declared that 'a house divided against itself cannot stand'" (Matthew 12:25; Mark 3:25; Luke 11:17).[41]

Later, Lincoln would famously apply the house divided image to the nation as a whole, but for the time being he concentrated on the Illinois Whig Party. In areas of the state where Whigs did not hold conventions, he noted, candidates were "'on their own hook,' . . . not contending shoulder to shoulder against the common enemy, but divided into factions, and fighting furiously with one another." In the name of unified action, he wrote, "we urge the adoption of the Convention System."

Lincoln's party loyalty was put to the test that spring when a convention was used to select a Whig candidate for the US Congress from the state's seventh district. Lincoln wanted the nomination. "The truth is," he wrote, "I would like to go [to Congress] very much."[42] Lincoln, thirty-four years old, was competing for the nomination against John J. Hardin of Morgan County and Edward D. Baker of Sangamon County, both of whom were fellow lawyers and friends of Lincoln's since the time of the Black Hawk War. But in a preliminary election in Sangamon County, Baker beat Lincoln, reportedly because of Lincoln's reputation as a skeptical deist and his association with Aristocracy Hill due to his marriage into the wealthy Todd family. Lincoln reluctantly accepted an appointment as a county delegate representing Edward Baker at the Whig Party convention, held in Pekin, Illinois, on May 1. "In getting Baker the nomination," Lincoln remarked, "I shall be 'fixed' a good deal like a fellow who is made groomsman to the man what has cut him out, and is marrying his own dear 'gal.' "[43] As it turned out, the convention chose Hardin, not Baker. Though disappointed, Lincoln reported to Joshua Speed, "So far as I can judge from present appearances, we shall have no split or trouble about the matter; all will be harmony." Lincoln assured Hardin that he would push to get tremendous Whig support for him in Sangamon County. "We make it a matter of honor and pride to do it; . . . because we love the whig cause; [and] . . . we like you personally."

The show of good feelings at the Pekin convention benefited Lincoln, who proposed at the meeting a resolution for a rotation arrangement by which Hardin would serve out his congressional term and Baker would be the next nominee for Congress. The resolution passed, and the rotation began. Hardin served in Congress from 1843 to 1845 and was followed by Baker, whose term lasted from March 1845 until he resigned from Congress in December 1846 to serve in the US Army.

Lincoln's turn for a congressional run came next. In 1846, he competed against an old foe, the Democrat preacher Peter Cartwright, in the race to succeed Baker. In the campaign, Lincoln skillfully circumvented one of the Methodist Cartwright's main charges against him: that he was a nonbeliever. His July 1846 "Handbill Replying to Charges of Infidelity," published in local newspapers, is a masterwork of equivocation. Instead of directly admitting to his doubts about church religion and the literal truth of the Bible, Lincoln wrote that, while not a member of a Christian church, he had never spoken disrespectfully of religion. He added that he could never support a political candidate "whom I knew to be an open enemy of, and scoffer at, religion."[44] The key word here was "open." Privately, Lincoln had often scoffed at religion. Publicly, he knew that it was a valuable tool for political ascendancy.

In the August 1846 election against Cartwright, Lincoln won by a large margin. But he was not entirely comfortable with the prospect of going to Washington. In October he wrote Speed, "Being elected to Congress, though I am very grateful to our friends, for having done it, has not pleased me as much as I expected."[45]

His trepidation may have been due in part to the exigencies of building a middle-class lifestyle in Springfield, developing his law practice, and providing for his growing family, which by the spring included the three-year-old Bob and the newly arrived Eddie. Lincoln described Eddie as "very much such a child as Bob was at his age—rather of a longer order." As for Bob, he seemed "quite smart enough," but, Lincoln wrote, "I some times fear he is one of the little rare-ripe sort, that are smarter at about five than ever after." He was also wild. Lincoln reported, Bob indulged in "a great deal of that sort of mischief, that is the offspring of much animal spirits." Earlier that day, for example, he had run off and was lost, and then retrieved. His mother "had him whip[p]ed," Lincoln said, but "by now, very likely he is run away again."[46]

As a doting parent, Lincoln observed his son's wildness with amused detachment. It was far more difficult to know how to deal with a national crisis that threatened to spin out of control. That crisis was the escalating battle over slavery. By going to Congress, Lincoln knew he would find himself in the thick of the slavery debate.

The crisis seemed especially severe to Whigs like Lincoln who were strongly committed to programs for government funding of internal improvements. In the mid-1840s, these defining Whig programs collided with the aim of the Democratic president James K. Polk to pursue aggressively the war against Mexico. The Whigs were furious that Polk had vetoed a bill calling for internal improvements, which he dismissed as a waste of money, while he poured huge sums into a war that Northern Whigs saw as an illegal takeover of western territory, where slavery could spread.

The conflict between support of internal improvements and pursuit of the Mexican War was made vivid to Lincoln at a national convention he attended in July 1846, four months before he went to Washington, and stayed with him until his term in Congress ended two years later. The conflict led him to think deeply about the role of the federal government in addressing social problems. He emerged with the conviction that the government must be an activist in a positive direction: it must materially benefit citizens, not lead them into bloody wars of aggression.

He now faced two main political crises: the intensifying debate between Northerners and Southerners over slavery—a debate that already produced talk of disunion and civil war—and the military takeover of lands formerly controlled by Mexico. There was, however, a source of hope for him: the fact that Midwesterners, positioned centrally geographically and politically, could help to resolve escalating tensions and maintain national unity.

A WATCHFUL POLITICIAN

On the sweltering morning of July 5, 1847, a brilliant sun shone on the milling thousands who had come from around the nation to Chicago for the three-day River and Harbor Convention. In the crowd was the thirty-seven-year-old Whig politician from central Illinois, Abraham Lincoln, who had been recently elected to serve in the Thirtieth Congress, which would convene in December. Lincoln had taken a four-day carriage ride north from Springfield to attend the convention. He cut an odd figure. "Tall, angular and awkward," an observer noted, "he had on a short-waisted, thin swallow-tail coat, a short vest of the same material, thin pantaloons, scarcely coming down to his ankles, a straw hat and a pair of *brogans* with woolen socks."[47] Some law associates of his were sitting under a hotel veranda when they spotted him. One of them, the attorney S. Lisle Smith, cried, "There is Lincoln on the other side of the street. Just look at 'Old Abe.'" Another lawyer, Elihu B. Washburne, was taken aback by the remark: "Old Abe, as applied to him, seems strange enough, as he was then a young man." Though new to Washburne, the nickname had been previously used for Lincoln. It would never suit the physical Lincoln, even when, during the Civil War, his face became furrowed and sunken. With his dark hair and youthful body, he did not look elderly when he died at fifty-six. But to many, he was "Old Abe": avuncular, trustworthy, familiar.

Old Abe must have been delighted by the River and Harbor Convention. More than ten thousand Americans traveled to Chicago—the flat, spread-out city of sixteen thousand inhabitants whose streets were mud or dust, according to the weather—to celebrate what had long been one of his priorities: internal improvements. The convention offered the buoyant prospect of national unity. People of all political viewpoints were there, from proslavery types to abolitionists. A Chicago journalist noted: "Old Babel never witnessed more discordant tongues than there were sentiments . . . among the crowd. . . . We had the Boston differences, the New York differences, the Missouri differences, and the sectional differences everywhere. Then we had our differences here at home." For the moment, though, all were "members of one great party actuated by one impulse and with the same great end in view": the development of midwestern harbors, rivers, and railroads that would increase the commerce of the nation.[48]

Attendees were determined to persuade the federal government to fund improvements, wherever they were needed. A journalist affirmed

that the convention would be recalled as a time "when party predilections were obliterated; when sectional interests were forgotten," when nineteen states came together "in one grand harmony" in the interest of "common humanity."[49]

There was even the promise that the growing divide between the North and the South would be healed by the work of the convention. The meeting, held under a huge tent, began with addresses hailing the Midwest as the site of a salubrious mingling of competing cultural elements. In his opening speech, "The Relation of New England Puritanism to the Growth and Prosperity of the West," the Massachusetts minister William Allen declared that the Midwest was populated by "swarms from the New England hive, who led the march of emigration towards the setting sun." The "descendants of Yankees," he said, were founding colleges, plowing prairies, and building cities like Chicago. By teaming up at the convention with people from different sections with the same goal, "the descendants of the Puritans ... find themselves associated with many others, in whose veins flowed different blood, and sprung from different sources all uniting here, and forming one *Great Brotherhood*."[50]

The next speaker, Senator Tom Corwin of Ohio, drove home the message. Not only Puritans, he declared, but Pennsylvanians, and Kentuckians, and "*huge swarms* from Ohio" are settling the Midwest and today are "here united, forming a Congress of the American People." Corwin argued that the convention challenged centrifugalism, as indicated by the presence of a Georgia delegate who is "to learn here whether our glorious republic is destined to be composed of widely disjointed fragments, or whether it is to become, and remain united until the 'last syllable of recorded time.'" Let there be no section or party here, Corwin demanded—no Whig, no Democrat, "nothing but American."

Such declarations, repeated frequently during the convention, affirmed the ideal of "UNIONISM" that Walt Whitman later identified as the foundation of Lincoln's character.[51]

But the appearance of unity was deceptive. Shadows were cast over the convention by President James K. Polk and the Mexican War. The convention had been originally planned in reaction to Polk's August 1846 veto of a river and harbor bill that appropriated $500,000 to internal improvements. Polk insisted that funding rivers and harbors drained money from the Treasury that was needed for the war against Mexico. He stated, "It would seem the dictate of wisdom under such circumstances to husband our means and not waste them on comparatively unimportant objects."[52]

Opponents of Mr. Polk's War, which eventually cost the nation more than $100 million, were infuriated by his attitude. The president, they insisted, was diverting funds away from projects that would bind the nation to a war that was dividing it. Polk's veto was "an insult to the country," one critic wrote: "'Husband our means,' forsooth. Are not millions being squandered by this same James K. Polk for the invasion of Mexico and the extension of slavery? . . . Are not the Treasury doors unbarred whenever the 'open sesame' is whispered by the slave-driver? And yet Mr. Polk outrages the intelligence of the people, his masters, by claiming . . . that the object for which we ask is comparatively unimportant!"

There was also the issue of the constitutionality of improvements. The Constitution gives Congress the power "to regulate commerce with foreign nations, and among the several states, and with the Indian tribes." Polk put a strict-constructionist spin on the clause, which, he said, covered international and interstate commerce but not local improvements. For instance, since the Illinois River and Chicago harbor were in only one state, they did not qualify for federal funding under the commerce clause. And, he insisted, "regulate" did not mean "create"; the government's job was to oversee intrastate commerce, not to create new canals, harbors, or river passages in particular states.[53]

At the Chicago convention, Lincoln addressed the constitutional question. The crowd called him up to respond to a speech given earlier by a Polk ally, the lawyer David Dudley Field. To Field's contention that the government should not fund rivers in individual states, Lincoln asked "how many states the lordly Hudson ran through"—a reference to the fact that Congress had funded the improvement of the New York river.[54] Lincoln generalized that Congress should indeed provide money whenever individual states needed it because "the accomplishment of such improvement was for the general good, although local points received the immediate advantage."[55]

Already Lincoln was outlining the big-spending, activist government he would call for in the 1850s and would put into operation during the Civil War. But he wanted government spending to be directed toward useful projects such as infrastructure and, later on, toward preserving the Union and freeing the enslaved. In President James Polk, he saw the government directing funds in an ill-considered direction.

In the fall of 1847, he did not yet vocally make the connection between expansionism and the spread of slavery. Actually, he seemed to retreat to conservativism on slavery for the moment, if his willingness to serve as an attorney for the Kentucky slaveholder Robert Matson that October is an indication.

Soon enough, on his trip east to Washington, DC, to take his seat in Congress in December, he would gain full exposure to antislavery interpretations of the Mexican War.

Before leaving Springfield, he rented the Jackson Street house to a brick contractor for ninety dollars a year. On October 25, he, Mary, and the two boys set off on a trip by steamboat and train to Lexington, Kentucky, where they had arranged to stay for three weeks with her family. A local paper reported:

> Mr. Lincoln, the member of Congress elect from this district, has just set out on his way to the city of Washington. His family is with him; they intend to visit their friends and relatives in Kentucky before they take up the line of march for

the seat of government. He will find many men in Congress who possess twice the good looks, and not half the good sense, of our own representative.[56]

On one stretch of the journey, the four-year-old Bobby and eighteen-month-old Eddie got so boisterous in a railroad car that they upset other passengers. A nephew of Mary's stepmother, who accompanied the Lincolns part of the way, declared on arriving at Lexington, "I was never so glad to get off a train in my life. There were two lively youngsters on board who kept the whole train in a turmoil, and their long-legged father, instead of spanking the brats, looked pleased as Punch and aided and abetted the older one in mischief."[57]

Lincoln had the opportunity to witness slavery firsthand in Lexington, with its auction block and whipping post in the public square, its slave jails, the coffles that were led along the road in front of the Todd house, and the operations of firms like Bolton, Dickens and Co., one of the largest slave traders in the South.

And surely he got food for thought when, on a dark, rainy November day, he went to hear a speech given by his political idol, Henry Clay. In his speech, Clay, who was launching his fourth run for the White House, described the Mexican War as a war "of offensive aggression, . . . actuated by a spirit of rapacity," which "might have been averted by prudence, moderation, and wise statesmanship."[58] Though a slaveholder himself, he declared, "I have ever regarded slavery as a great evil, a wrong; . . . I should rejoice if not a single slave breathed the air or was within the limits of our country." But he opposed immediate emancipation, which, he said, would cause "collisions and conflicts between the two races, shocking scenes of rapine and carnage, [and] the extinction or expulsion of the blacks." For this reason, radicals who demanded immediate abolition "have done incalculable mischief even to the very cause which they espoused, to say nothing of the discord which has been produced between different parts of the Union." He recommended gradual abolition and colonizing freed blacks abroad, but he insisted that, according to the Constitution, slavery must be left alone in the states where it already existed.

If we omit Clay's prediction of a racial war that would supposedly follow immediate emancipation, his message that day—antiextensionism, permitting slavery where it already existed, and gradual emancipation followed by colonization—pretty much defined Lincoln's position on slavery until the early part of the Civil War.

Lincoln was not yet ready to express openly this position in 1847. But Clay's words doubtless stayed in his mind as he witnessed the congressional debates over the Mexican War and slavery.

THE CONGRESSIONAL CAULDRON

Lincoln's term as a Whig representative in the Thirtieth Congress (1847–49) is commonly seen as unremarkable. He emerged from it as "Spotty Lincoln," the "Ranchero Spotty of one term"—nicknames assigned to him by contemporary journalists because of his Spot Resolutions, in which he discredited the Mexican War by demanding that President James Polk identify the geographical spot where American blood had been shed that had launched the conflict.[59] If it was in the United States, as Polk insisted, the war could be justified, but if, as Lincoln suspected, it was in land that was rightfully Mexico's, then Polk was guilty of unprovoked aggression. Although Lincoln later emphasized that he voted for troop supplies despite his opposition to the war, it was hard for him to escape criticism for what seemed to be unpatriotic nit-picking. He returned to Springfield as a frustrated politician, to be roused to meaningful action again only in 1854, when the passage of Stephen Douglas's Kansas-Nebraska Act threatened to spread slavery westward.

Omitted from this oft-repeated narrative is the fact that Lincoln's two years in Washington were immensely valuable to his development. They saw him witnessing for the first time on a national scale the potentially crippling paradoxes of the American democratic experiment.

They also saw him discovering ways he might deal with these paradoxes, which were embedded in the very environment Lincoln and his family entered when on December 2, 1847, they arrived by train in Washington, DC. The city was an assemblage of grand buildings, scattered houses, and broad avenues crisscrossed by roads (most of them dirt) that stretched away indefinitely. For the visiting Charles Dickens, it was a "City of Magnificent Intentions," with "spacious avenues, that begin in nothing, and lead nowhere; streets, miles-long, that only want houses, roads, and inhabitants; public buildings that need but a public to be complete."[60]

Like the nation, the city was a paradox. It had been designed, as the architect Pierre Charles L'Enfant wrote to George Washington, to be the seat of a "vast empire," but by 1847 that empire, expanding westward in the spirit of Manifest Destiny, seemed headed toward fracturing over slavery.[61] The tension between the nation's egalitarian ideals and its unjust practices was reflected in the contrast between the Capitol Building—the august center of democracy, constructed largely by free and enslaved blacks—and the city's dozen or so slave pens, jails, and auction blocks, including the ever-crowded Williams Slave Pen and the busy Franklin and Armfield slave-trading firm, both of them near the Capitol.

The paradoxes of Washington played out in Congressman Lincoln's private and political lives. After a short stay in the modest Indian Queen Hotel, he and his family moved into a boardinghouse across from the Capitol run by Mrs. Ann G. Sprigg and owned by the Democratic journalist Duff Green. Congressmen formed "messes" in such boardinghouses. Lincoln joined a Whig mess whose members differed in their views of slavery. Mrs. Sprigg's was known as the Abolition House because of its antislavery heritage. It had served as an unofficial station on the Underground Railroad, and radicals like Theodore Dwight Weld and Joshua Leavitt had lived there. One of Lincoln's fellow boarders was Joshua Giddings, the representative from Ohio who had become an antislavery icon when in 1842 he had broken the congressional gag rule on slavery. Giddings boldly voiced his abolitionist views, was censured by Congress, and resigned in protest but was soon reelected by a large margin. He returned to Washington and remained a thorn in the proslavery side until his congressional service ended in 1858. A Whig turned Republican, he supported Frémont in 1856 and four years later campaigned for Lincoln, who appointed him as the US consul to Canada in 1861.

Discussions over the long dinner table at Mrs. Sprigg's often turned into debates over slavery. Along with Giddings and Lincoln, boarders strongly opposed to slavery included the Pennsylvania congressmen Abraham McIlvaine, a vehement critic of the Mexican War, and John Strohm, who presented antislavery petitions to Congress from Pennsylvania Quakers and called for the abolition of slavery in Washington, DC. Three other Pennsylvanians—James Pollock, John Blanchard, and John Dickey—took moderate positions, while Elisha Embree of Indiana was a conservative and Patrick Tompkins of Mississippi supported slavery. Often joining the conversation was Duff Green, who lived nearby and dined at the Sprigg establishment. A cantankerous Calhounite who criticized abolition, Green staunchly defended Southern rights.

Faced with these conflicts, Lincoln proved to be a skilled mediator. In his law practice, as we've seen, he discouraged litigation and recommended compromise. In politics, he esteemed, above all, Henry Clay, the Great Pacificator, whose biographer Nathan Sargent boarded at Mrs. Sprigg's. Lincoln's efforts to defuse hostility at the dinner table were highly successful. As another boarder, Dr. Samuel C. Busey, observed,

Lincoln "may have been as radical" in his abolitionism as anyone present "but was so discreet in giving expression to his convictions on the slavery question as to avoid giving offence to anybody, and was so conciliatory as to create the impression, even among the proslavery advocates, that he did not wish to introduce or discuss subjects that would provoke a controversy." Instead, he used his time-tested escape valves: storytelling and humor. Full of "amusing jokes, anecdotes, and witticisms," Busey reported, Lincoln, when a discussion got hot, would "lay down his knife and fork, place his elbows upon the table, rest his face between his hands, and begin with the words 'that reminds me,' and proceed. Everybody prepared for the explosions sure to follow." Provoking "a hearty and general laugh," he would "so completely disarrange the tenor of the discussion that the parties engaged would either separate in good humor or continue conversation free from discord. This amicable disposition made him very popular with the household."[62]

He continued the storytelling elsewhere. He often went to the busy mail room of the House of Representatives, where he told so many yarns that he was soon regarded as "the champion story-teller of the Capitol."[63] He carried on the performance at a nearby bowling alley. His comically awkward bowling style did not interfere with his enthusiasm for the game. In fact, it may have increased it, for his ungainly efforts at bowling, combined with his incessant storytelling, attracted crowds of spectators as he bowled—satisfying for one who thrived on assumed clownishness.

It was difficult to maintain clownishness—or seriousness, for that matter—in Congress, where even getting heard was a challenge. Sessions of the House of Representatives were chaotic. The House, which would not have its own chamber until a wing was added to the Capitol in 1857, met in a ninety-five-foot hall (later Statuary Hall) with green marble columns and a high, domed ceiling that reverberated with the representatives' ceaseless chatter. As John J. Hardin, one of Lincoln's Illinois predecessors in the House, lamented, "Of all the places to speak or to try & do any business, the Hall of the House is the worst I ever saw. I would prefer speaking in a pig pen with 500 hogs squealing . . . or talk to a mob when a fight is going on, . . . than to try to fix the attention of the House. Not one man in fifty can make himself heard on acc[oun]t of the construction of the Hall."[64] To make matters worse, Lincoln was assigned a poor seat—number 191—in the rear row of the Whig section, off to the left of the Speaker.

Despite the adverse conditions, Lincoln observed and learned from the congressional proceedings. He took his seat in the House on December 6, 1847, and maintained steady attendance throughout his term, making all but 13 of 456 roll calls. Lincoln "was attentive and conscientious in the discharge of his duties," a fellow politician noted, "and followed the course of legislation closely."[65] He served industriously on two committees: Expenditures in the War Department and Post Offices and Post Roads.

Though he sat in the rear row, his height enabled him to see his colleagues. He was likely present when on February 21, 1848, the eighty-one-year-old antislavery congressman John Quincy Adams collapsed in the House chamber from a massive cerebral hemorrhage. Adams died two days later. Lincoln helped organize his funeral and attended the service in the House on February 26.[66]

Lincoln's experience in the House was unsettling in other ways as well. Just nine days after Lincoln took his seat, President Polk sent a message to Congress explaining why he had vetoed a bill, passed on March 3 (the last day of the previous congressional term), which had appropriated more than half a million dollars for harbor and river projects in several states. Polk had studied the report of the House Committee on Commerce and the Memorial of the Chicago Harbor and River Convention, which called for increased federal funding for rivers and harbors so that Congress could better regulate commerce, and found in them "a good deal of partisan bitterness, better suited to an irresponsible newspaper than to an official document."[67] In his veto message, an eight-thousand-word screed he worked on for several months, he laid out in detail his argument against federal funding of local improvements. Such funding, he insisted, was unconstitutional and, given the large expenses of the Mexican War, wasteful and deficit-increasing. The national government was under no obligation to support improvement projects that gave special benefits to particular states while excluding others.

And so the Chicago convention's dream of national unity fostered by federally backed improvements was shattered by the president whose earlier veto of a similar bill had prompted the convention in the first place. Lincoln mulled over Polk's message. His response came six months later in a June 8, 1848, speech before the House. Arguing that government-funded improvements were constitutional, he pointed to the redoubtable jurist Chancellor James Kent, who had unequivocally decided that, according to the Constitution, Congress, not the president, was responsible for regulating improvements. More important, amending the Constitution must not be taken lightly. Lincoln advised, "[L]et it stand as it is. New hands have never touched it. The men who made it, have done their work, and have passed away. Who shall improve, on what *they* did?"[68] As for Polk's contention that certain states received excessive benefits from federal funds, Lincoln said that was, to some degree, true of all federally backed improvements, even ones for seacoasts. At any rate, there was no separating local development from the national scene. Every meaningful improvement, even if confined to an individual state, benefited all Americans.

What's notable about this speech was not only its typically Lincolnian message of unity—local improvements help the whole nation—but also its stylistic restraint. One could not tell from the speech that government funding of improvements was a core issue for Lincoln, one that had long stirred his deepest emotions and that was a main reason for his loyalty to the Whig Party. In the speech Lincoln listed his main topics, numbered one to six, and then addressed each of them rationally. As usual, he returned to origins, going back to early investment in improvements by John Quincy Adams, and then moved forward through the presidents to Polk, who had twice vetoed river and harbor bills, and then dwelled on the constitutional and local-versus-national issues. Nowhere did he voice the common Whig complaint about Polk's funneling money away from improvements toward a war that might extend slavery. And by saying the Constitution was fine the way it was, he rejected the radical abolitionist position that the Constitution was a proslavery document.

Indeed, he mentioned slavery only in passing in his congressional speeches, even when directly addressing the war. Here he contrasted sharply with other representatives of both parties, between which there was constant friction over slavery—so much so, as Joanne B. Freeman shows, that brawls, pummelings, stabbings, and duel threats were common in Congress.[69] One all-night quarrel over the Wilmot Proviso on the House floor involved Southern Democrats and Northern Whigs. A Kentucky representative described the mayhem: "Imagine 230 tom cats fastened in a room, from which escape is impossible, with tin cans tied to their tails—raging and screaming, and fighting, and flying about from 6 P. M. to 6 A. M., twelve hours—and you will have some idea of the last jubilee in the House."[70] At three o'clock in the morning a fistfight erupted between Lincoln's Illinois friend Orlando B. Ficklin and Jacob Thompson of Mississippi. Both were drunk. Another fight broke out between the Virginian Richard K. Meade and Lincoln's messmate at Mrs. Sprigg's, Joshua Giddings of Ohio.

Known as the Lion of Ashtabula, Giddings was six feet two, heavyset, and fearless. He took pride in his status as an antislavery martyr who had been forced to resign because of his views but was then triumphantly reelected by his Ohio constituents. "I allways [sic] make the fur fly," he boasted. Once, when another congressman threatened him with a pistol and a sword cane, he declared, "Come on! The people of Ohio don't send cowards here!"[71] His denunciations of slavery and the

Mexican War were brash. In a speech in support of the Wilmot Proviso he announced: "I would rather see this Union rent into a thousand fragments than have my country disgraced, and its moral purity sacrificed, by the prosecution of a war for the extension of human bondage." Slavery, he continued, was an institution worthy of pirates and highwaymen—"It is founded in violence, and maintained by crime."[72] Giddings went so far as to suggest that there should be a separation between the "Puritans" of the North and the criminals of the South—he said that he did not want "the people of New England, the descendants of the Puritan fathers, [to] be transferred from the union formed in 1787, to a political fellowship with blacklegs and slave-mongers of Texas, in order to sustain African servitude in that government." Giddings's moral distinctions were absolute: "I rejoice that this is a question which admits of no compromise. Slavery and freedom are antagonists. There can be no compromise between right and wrong, between virtue and vice."

Giddings was voicing opinions in the kind of language Lincoln would later use—slaveholders were like highwaymen, slavery was all about violence, there was a clear distinction between right and wrong. But it would take time for Lincoln to air such views openly, and never would he call for disunion. Indeed, he may have been thinking of Giddings's vision of "this Union rent into a thousand fragments" when, in 1852, he attacked those who "would shiver into fragments the Union of these States" rather than see slavery continue.[73]

While Giddings raised the specter of the disintegration of the Union, Lincoln anchored his criticism of the war in an eternal constant: the soil, Mother Earth. His Spot Resolutions, widely derided in his day and seen as an impediment to his career, in fact show him returning to origins in a new way.

That his later speeches were grounded in nature is presaged in the Spot Resolutions. Lincoln expanded on the trope President Polk used when he attributed the war to Mexican soldiers "invading the ter-

[r]itory of the State of Texas, striking the first blow, and shedding the blood of our *citizens on our own soil*."[74] Was this true? Lincoln asked. In his youth, he had witnessed how competing land claims had affected his father, who lost hundreds of acres due to shingled properties in Kentucky. He saw a similar problem with conflicting claims over territory at the start of the Mexican War, but this time the conflict had serious implications for the nation and its future. Lincoln agreed with Polk that "title—ownership—to soil" was the key to the Mexican War, but it was incumbent on the president "to present the facts, from which he concluded, the soil was ours, on which the first blood of the war was shed." The land in question was the disputed territory between the Nueces River and the Rio Grande in Texas. Lincoln pointed out that Polk had begun the war under the assumption that this territory was part of Texas, when in fact Mexico plausibly laid claim to it. Lincoln summarized the history of the Texas revolution of 1835–36 and the subsequent annexation of Texas by the United States to argue that this land did not, in fact, belong to America, which had therefore engaged in the war of aggression against a foreign power.

Lincoln charged Polk with a confusion of aims. He said Polk hoodwinked the nation by "fixing the public gaze upon the exceeding brightness of military glory, that attractive rainbow, that rises in showers of blood—that serpent's eye that charms to destroy."[75] Lacking credible facts to support his explanation for the war, Polk was utterly lost. He "now finds himself, he knows not where," giving speeches that are "like the half insane mumbling of a fever-dream." And so, Lincoln declared, "his mind, tasked beyond it's [*sic*] power, is running hither and thither, like some tortured creature, on a burning surface, finding no position, on which it can settle down, and be at ease."

Lincoln here uses nonhuman images—a snake's eye, showers of blood, an animal scurrying on a burning surface—to deflate the patriotic pretensions of Polk's imperialist version of Manifest Destiny. Lincoln sees the centrifugal forces unleashed by the war, and he hurls them right back at Polk. He channels these forces into a centripetal center—a spot, an exact place—and he argues that Polk, who cannot describe that spot correctly, represents the lies behind irresponsible American expansionism, an uncontrolled animal rushing about in aimless confusion. Lincoln concludes that Polk is "a bewildered, confounded, and miserably perplexed man."

Notably absent from Lincoln's harangue is direct mention of slavery. Unlike Giddings, he did not dwell on slavery, because he did not want to alienate fellow Whigs who were Southerners or had Southern sympathies.

However, he learned in Congress how to use Whigs of different sections to advance his antislavery views palatably. He joined the Young Indians, a group of seven representatives, five of them Southerners, who supported the Whig Party's 1848 candidate for the presidency, Zachary Taylor. A no-party general who had never cast a vote in a presidential election, Taylor was virtually a blank canvas onto which one could project one's preferences. Even though he was a Mississippi slaveholder, Lincoln painted him as a Northern-leaning Whig. He did so in a way that proved irresistible to his fellow congressmen.

On July 27, 1848, he gave a pro-Taylor speech that made clever use of humorous techniques he had honed over the years: nonhuman images, little-big-man satire, and physical clownishness. Nonhuman images peppered the speech. In answer to a Democratic representative's charge that "we have deserted all our principles, and taken shelter under Gen: Taylor's military coat-tail," he pointed out that "his own party have run the five last Presidential races" under "the ample military coat tail of Gen: Jackson."[76] Every recent Democratic campaign, trying to exploit Jackson's record as a tough military leader, had used "never ending emblems" associated with Old Hickory: hickory poles and hickory brooms, James K. Polk as "Young Hickory," Lewis Cass as "of the true 'Hickory stripe,'" and so on. All such Jackson claptrap exposed the Democrats as "a horde of hungry ticks" who "have stuck to the tail of the Hermitage lion [that is, Jackson] to the end of his life; and . . . are still sticking to it, and drawing a loathsome sustenance from it, after he is dead." This leechlike Jackson dependence reminded Lincoln of the story of someone who said he could make a new man out of an old one and still have enough left over to make a little yellow dog. The Democrats, likewise, had twice made presidents out of Jackson and "have had enough of the stuff left, to make Presidents of several comparatively small men since; and it is your chief reliance now to make still another."

The current Democratic candidate, Lewis Cass of Michigan, was being hailed by biographers who, Lincoln said, were "tying him to a military tail, like so many mischievous boys tying a dog to a bladder of beans."[77] Lincoln mocked Cass's performance in the War of 1812, in which he had served under an officer who invaded Canada and then retreated, with Cass reportedly breaking his sword and spending part of the time picking huckleberries. Combining the mock heroic and the nonhuman, Lincoln summoned up his own less-than-stellar performance in the Black Hawk War. He asked, "By the way, Mr. Speaker, did you know I am a military hero? Yes sir; in the days of the Black Hawk War, I fought, bled, and came away." Lincoln could not say that he broke a sword, for he had none, but he had accidentally bent a musket. He boasted: "If Gen: Cass went in advance of me in picking huckleberries, I guess I surpassed him in charges upon the wild onions. If he saw any live, fighting indians, it was more than I did; but I had a good many bloody struggles with the musquetoes." Lincoln turned from onions and mosquitoes to hogs. In response to Democrats who pointed to divisions among the Whigs, he asked, "Some such *we* certainly have; have *you* none, gentlemen democrats? Is it all union and harmony in *your* ranks?—no bickerings?—no divisions?" The competing groups of Democrats in a state like New York reminded him of a drunken man, indicted for stealing "ten boars, ten sows, ten shoats, and ten pigs," who exclaimed, "Well, by golly, that is the most equally divided gang of hogs, I ever did hear of." Lincoln's punchline: "If there is any *other* gang of hogs more equally divided than the democrats of New York are about this time, I have not heard of it."

In delivering the speech, Lincoln outdid himself in physical clownishness. He walked up and down the aisles of the House, gesticulating, varying his voice for comic emphasis, and jiggling his coattails at key moments. A reporter called him "a tremendous wag" and noted that "his style [was] so peculiar, that he kept the House in a continuous roar of merriment."[78] Another witness joked that he hoped Lincoln wouldn't "charge mileage" for his peripatetic wanderings about the House floor."[79]

But the clownish Lincoln had a strategy. If, in general, he aimed to add meaning to the nonsensical humor of his era, here he made an antislavery point. As he saw from Giddings and others, to speak out sharply in Congress against slavery was to risk alienating conservatives. And so, amid the jokes and comic gestures on that hot July day, he genially turned the slaveholding Zachary Taylor into a moderately antislavery Whig. Lincoln felt certain Taylor would follow the Whig policies on improvements, the tariff, the currency, and other matters. Would he also back the Wilmot Proviso? Lincoln couldn't say for sure, but he was confident that Taylor was a man of the people who would respond to growing popular support for the proviso and would do the right thing by not vetoing it if it came to his desk. One thing was certain, Lincoln said. Taylor's opponent, Cass, if elected, would definitely obstruct the proviso and follow "a course of policy, leading to new wars, new acquisitions of ter[r]itory and still further extensions of slavery." And because "one of the two is to be President," he asked, "which is preferable?"[80]

By packaging his antislavery message in other Whig policies and enlivening it with humor—and projecting it all onto the popular Taylor—Lincoln made his antislavery point without offending Southerners or doughfaces.

But the truce between the Northern and Southern congressmen would not last. Lincoln could lampoon the Democrats as a divided gang of hogs, but the Whigs were equally divided, despite their joining up over Taylor.

Driven by his instinct for unity, Lincoln throughout the 1840s reached out to supporters of slavery. But it was not long before the futility of his efforts became clear. Take his friendship with the Springfield lawyer Albert Taylor Bledsoe. Bledsoe, according to his biographer, "had more to do with molding Lincoln's intellect than any man who ever touched it."[81] This is an overstatement, but doubtless the multifaceted Bledsoe—he was an Episcopal priest, an attorney, a Whig journalist, and, later, a professor of mathematics—was initially a positive example for Lincoln. At the time Lincoln was acquainted with him, Bledsoe shared Lincoln's devotion to the unity of the Whig Party in Illinois. However, after he left in 1848 to teach in Southern universities, Bledsoe became increasingly attached to the South's institutions. By the time of the Civil War, Bledsoe described the North as representing "brute force, blind passion, fanatical hate, . . . [of] constitutional law and human rights," and Lincoln as "the talented but the low, ignorant and vulgar, rail-splitter of Illinois."[82] Bledsoe is best remembered today as one of the main architects of the Lost Cause, that nostalgic idealization of the Confederacy that became an underpinning of Jim Crow.

Fractures also arose among Lincoln's pro-Taylor group, the Young Indians. The group originally consisted of two Northerners (Lincoln of Illinois and Truman Smith of Connecticut) and five Southerners (William Ballard Preston, John S. Pendleton, and Thomas S. Flournoy of Virginia, and Robert Toombs and Alexander H. Stephens of Georgia). The latter three were ardent Southern-rights men who later became linchpins of the Confederacy. Flournoy in 1861 participated in Virginia's secession convention and served as a cavalry officer in the Confederate States Army. Toombs helped lead Georgia out of the Union and was the first secretary of state of the Confederacy. Alexander Stephens became the Confederacy's vice president.

Stephens is an especially intriguing case, for he developed a genuine

Alexander H. Stephens

friendship with Lincoln in Congress, and the two later had important contacts during the Civil War. "I knew Mr. Lincoln well and intimately," Stephens later recalled.[83] He considered the Illinoisan as one of the best orators in the House. Lincoln, for his part, admired the brilliant Stephens. A friend of Lincoln reported that "of all the men in the South (of those who differed from him on the slavery question) Mr. Stephens of Georgia was his favorite . . . I have frequently heard him speak in very respectful terms of Stephens."[84]

The political chemistry among Whigs during the Thirtieth Congress put the two in the same camp. The thin, sickly Stephens was bold in his opposition to Mr. Polk's War. After two months in Congress, in early February 1848, Lincoln wrote to William Herndon saying that the "little slim, pale-faced, consumptive" Stephens had "just concluded the very best speech, of an hour's length, I ever heard. My old, withered, dry eyes, are full of tears yet."[85]

In the speech, Stephens attacked the Mexican War much the way Lincoln had in his Spot Resolutions. Polk had launched a war of aggression on soil that didn't belong to the United States, Stephens said. The Nueces, not the Rio Grande, was the southern border of Texas; the land in between, where Americans first went on the attack, belonged to Mexico. Polk had acted despotically instead of following the Constitution, which assigns to Congress the power of declaring war. Therefore, patriotic Americans like Henry Clay's son had died in a war that had been unwisely started by a power-hungry president. Like Lincoln, Stephens drew from the biblical story of Cain killing Abel. Lincoln had said "that [Polk] is deeply conscious of being in the wrong—that he feels the blood of this war, like the blood of Abel, is crying to Heaven against him."[86] Similarly, Stephens declared, "The mark is fixed upon [Polk] as indelibly as that stamped upon the brow of Cain by the finger of God. His friends may say 'out, foul spot,' but I say it will not 'out.'"[87] In an emotional appeal against this "disgraceful and infamous" war, Stephens said, "I have very little hope for the country until the people begin to *feel*; they will then reflect, they will then speak, and they will then act."

If this speech brought tears to Lincoln, the one Stephens gave ten days later surely alarmed him. Stephens declared that the nation, faced with "difficulties of no ordinary magnitude," had entered a "night of storms and tempests—of gloomy and appalling darkness, with no light to cheer the heart, and no star to guide a hope." A tyrannical president had caused a war that might very well divide the nation. Will the Union be destroyed? Stephens asked. That would be tragic because "The Union is not only the life, but the soul of these States." The Wilmot Proviso did not bode well. The South would never tolerate the North's insistence on forbidding slavery's extension. "Will the South submit to this restriction?" Stephens asked. "Will the North ultimately yield? Or shall these two great sections of the Union be arrayed against each other? When the elements of discord are fully aroused, who shall direct the storm?"

Who, indeed, *would* direct the storm? Surely not a radical Northerner like Giddings, who was prepared to see the Union fragment if his antislavery goals were not met. And not a Southerner like Stephens, for whom the Union, while precious, was not as sacred as his section's right to preserve slavery. Stephens had supported Taylor as the only electable Whig candidate, but when Old Rough and Ready assumed office, he turned out not to be as pro-Southern as Stephens had imagined. By early 1850, when Taylor had been in office less than a year, Stephens viewed the president as a mere tool in the hands of Northern abolitionists. "The North is insolent and unyielding" in its pursuit of the Wilmot Proviso, Stephens fumed. "My Southern blood and feelings are up."[88] Announcing that he was "prepared to fight at all hazards and to the last extremity" to defend slavery, he wrote, "Everything I see around me augurs the approach of anarchy . . . I see no prospect of the continuance of this Union long." During the Civil War, Lincoln would have a recurrent dream of being on a boat moving without direction on a foggy ocean. For Stephens in 1850, America itself was already lost at sea. "Everything here is uncertain," he wrote. "We are like a set of fellows at sea, trying to make port in a fog. There is no seeing a rod before you, and no one pretends to know where we are drifting." Compromises, like the one being proposed in Congress by Henry Clay and Daniel Webster, would only delay what Stephens saw as the inevitable dissolution of the Union. Stephens noted, "The temper of the country is fretful. The *centrifugal* tendency in our system is decidedly in the ascendant."

With "the *centrifugal* tendency" in the ascendant, a Free Soil journalist in Brooklyn, Walter Whitman, in 1850 responded to the crisis by writing political poems in a loose yet balanced style that augured the 1855 *Leaves of Grass*, in which he announced himself as "one of that centripetal and centrifugal gang," the "equalizer of his age and land"—the Answerer for the distracted nation, which, he was confident, would be healed when it absorbed him affectionately.[89] But when it did *not* absorb him, he declared he would be "much pleased to see some heroic, shrewd, fully-inform'd, healthy-bodied, middle-aged, beard-faced American blacksmith or boatman come down from the West across the Alleghenies, and walk into the Presidency."[90] His geographical specificity was telling. A Brooklynite, Whitman sensed that the nation's savior would not come from the Northeast or the South, which were divided politically and culturally, but from what was then the West, beyond the Alleghenies. Only a westerner could mediate between the conflicting sections.

Lincoln, who lived in the central section of a western state, also knew the importance of geography. In his 1848 pro-Taylor speech he paused to identify correctly his home locale: "I am a Northern man, or rather, a Western free state, with a constituency I believe to be, and with personal feelings I know to be, against the extension of slavery."[91] He got added confirmation of geography's importance from a speech before the House given by the Indiana representative William Wick in late April 1848. Lincoln wrote a Washington printer requesting three hundred copies of the speech for distribution. He was stirred by Wick's message: Midwesterners were crucial to the survival of the Union. Wick said that he had heard talk of "the dissolution of the Union" from extremists in both the North and the South, but "in the Middle and Western states a very different feeling prevails. In the West, we consider the Union our ALL."[92] The West's function was to "keep the peace of the antislavery sons of the Pilgrims and the Cavaliers, to each of whom this subject [slavery] is one on which they like 'to pile up the agony.'" To the warring sections, Wick announced, "Divide the Union you will not! WE SWEAR IT! . . . And if you talk about a fight, I give you notice that you cannot make the territory of the Middle States your battle-field." Both sides shared the burden of guilt: the South for enslaving people, the North for participating in the triangle trade. But the Puritans and

Cavaliers had better beware: there was an "impassable barrier" between them—the middle and western states. Wick warned, "The Western States hear the Union being threatened, and are feeling 'wolfy.' So look out Mssrs. Pilgrim and Cavalier, or you will hear thunder."

Although Lincoln never got this militant in his defense of the Middle West, he resembled William Wick in promoting the political role of his area of the nation. In a time when the opposing sections drew the nation toward separation, geographical centrism bolstered Lincoln's political centrism.

"IS THE CENTER NOTHING?"

Centrism was hard to maintain in the contentious Thirtieth Congress, which may in part explain Lincoln's frustrations with his Washington experience. Within a few months of the Lincolns' arrival in the capital, Mary and the boys returned to her father's home in Lexington. Since most congressmen were not accompanied by their families in Washington, Mary may have been lonely there. Also, evidence suggests that her erratic behavior irritated some of the boarders at Mrs. Sprigg's. In early April 1848, Lincoln wrote her glumly, "In this troublesome world, we are never quite satisfied. When you were here, I thought you hindered me some in attending to business; but now, having nothing but business—no variety—it has grown exceedingly tasteless to me. I hate to sit down and direct documents, and I hate to stay in this old room by myself."[93] Affectionately, he shared small news: he had been looking for plaid stockings for "Eddy's dear little feet," and he had bought shirt studs. Delighted to hear that Mary was free of her usual spring migraines, he joked, "I am afraid you will get so well, and fat, and young, as to be wanting to marry again." By midsummer, he missed her terribly. On July 12, he wrote, "Come on just as soon as you can. I want to see you, and our dear—*dear* boys very much."[94] She came with Bobby and Eddie later that month.

In August, he was asked to campaign for Taylor in New England, where the Whigs feared they would lose voters to the Free Soil Party, which was organized that month in Buffalo. After his congressional session ended, he and his family traveled north to New York and then to New England.

Perhaps inspired by William Wick's promotion of the Middle West as the potential savior of the Union, Lincoln put on his best midwestern performance when in September he toured Massachusetts, the center of New England abolitionism. In Worcester, he addressed slavery, saying that "the people of Illinois agreed entirely with the people of Massachusetts on this subject, except perhaps that they did not keep so constantly thinking about it." He associated the Midwest with a sensible view of slavery, which, he said, should be prevented from spreading but not tampered with in states where it already existed. He also pointed out that the Whig agenda under Taylor addressed far more issues than slavery, which was the Free Soil Party's only concern. Tapping, as usual, into popular humor, he remarked that the Free Soil Party's single-issue platform reminded him of "the pair of pantaloons the Yankee pedler offered for sale, 'large enough for any man, small enough for any boy.'"[95] Voting for Van Buren, the Free Soil candidate, was, he said, like voting for the Democrat Cass, since the new party had no chance for victory. The best choice for antiextensionists, then, was Taylor. The Taunton crowd was geographically specific when it applauded Lincoln: "At the close of this truly masterly and convincing speech, the audience gave three enthusiastic cheers for Illinois, and three more for the eloquent Whig member from that State."

His midwestern identity stood out to Massachusetts audiences. In describing Lincoln, some reporters used the word *Sucker*, vernacular for Illinoisan (a term apparently derived from a state fish). "Mr. Lincoln . . . is a capital specimen of a 'Sucker' Whig, six feet at least in his stockings," remarked a Cambridge journalist—seconded by a Taunton one, who commented, "Mr. Lincoln is a genuine Sucker, and is well versed in the po-

ZACHARY TAYLOR

litical tactics of the Western country. His speech was full of humor. . . ."[96] A Worcester politician reported, "His style and manner of speaking were novelties in the East."[97] The assumed clownishness he had developed on the Illinois hustings struck an observer who wrote, "His awkward gesticulations, the ludicrous management of his voice and the comical expression of his countenance, all conspired to make his hearers laugh at the mere anticipation of the joke before it appeared."[98]

New Englanders also linked his good sense with the Midwest. In Boston, he gave a speech "replete with good sense, sound reasoning, and irresistible argument, and spoken with that perfect command of manner and matter which so eminently distinguishes the Western orators."[99]

However, one wonders how comfortable Lincoln was in promoting Taylor at the expense of the Free Soil Party, whose antislavery agenda was close to the Republican Party agenda he would later champion. He argued that Taylor, as a centrist who followed the popular will, was positioned to resolve the slavery issue. But Taylor, after all, was a Southerner. A Taunton reporter plausibly questioned Lincoln's idea that Taylor would do more than any other candidate to get the Wilmot Proviso passed. For that to happen, the proviso must first get through the Senate, which was virtually impossible due to the strong Southern presence there. And could effective antislavery leadership come from "the unrepentant slaveholder, Zachary Taylor"? What was needed, the reporter noted, was to break up the current parties and rally the North around antislavery principles.[100]

This reshuffling of the parties, indeed, happened over the next six years, which saw the collapse of the Whigs and the rise of the antislavery Republicans. But in 1848, Whig Party unity was still foremost in Lincoln's mind. His reasoning that Taylor was the only *electable* candidate with antislavery potential that year proved accurate. In the November election, Taylor gained the White House by winning 47 percent of the popular vote and 163 electoral votes. The Free Soil candidate, Van Buren, won 10 percent of the popular vote but did not carry a state. The time was not yet ripe for a national antislavery party.

On their return trip to Illinois, via Albany, Buffalo, and the Great Lakes, the Lincolns stopped to see Niagara Falls. For Lincoln, the sight of the Falls took him far beyond political centrism to the perennial center: nature, the earth. He would later quip, "The thing that struck me most forcibly when I saw the Falls was, where in the world did all that water come from?"[101] But his written response to Niagara in 1848 was rhapsodic; it anchored unity in nature and historical origins. The Falls, he noted, have universal appeal. He began by asking: "By what mysterious power is it that millions and millions, are drawn from all parts of the world, to gaze upon Niagara Falls?" In a purely physical sense, he noted, there was little mystery. With the specificity of a natural scientist, he explained that five hundred thousand tons of water, fed by two or three hundred thousand square miles of rain on the earth's surface, cascaded a hundred feet, crashed, and exploded upward. But, he continued, the "great charm" of the sight was its "power to excite reflection, and emotion." The air absorbed the rising mist and later sent it back to the earth as rain. This cycle of water tumbling, rising, and returning was timeless. The origins of the Falls reached back to earliest history:

> When Columbus first sought this continent—when Christ suffered on the cross—when Moses led Israel through the Red-Sea—nay, even, when Adam first came from the hand of his Maker—then as now, Niagara was roaring here. . . . The Mammoth and Mastadon—now so long dead, that fragments of their monstrous bones, alone testify, that they ever lived, have gazed on Niagara. In that long—long time, never still for a single moment. Never dried, never froze, never slept, never rested[.][102]

For Lincoln, Niagara Falls represented nature's corralling of chaotic energy: millions of gallons of water, from all over, were channeled to a powerful center that was forever present, forever alluring, and always fresh—a true constant over time.

If explaining the Falls scientifically and philosophically gave Lincoln intellectual control over wild nature, so did his reflections on an experience he had on a steamboat while returning to Illinois. When the boat got stuck on a sandbar, the captain ordered that planks and empty casks be put under the hull in order to lift the craft. The incident led to Lincoln's invention of "buoyant chambers" for boats—inflatable bladders designed to float vessels over obstacles. When he reached Springfield, having given Whig speeches in Chicago and Lacon, he got the assistance of a local mechanic to design a wooden model of his invention, which he whittled in his law office. In early December, Lincoln was back in Washington for the second session of the Thirtieth Congress, and by March he had filed a patent for "An Improved Method of Lifting Vessels over Shoals," with long, exact specifications for producing and installing his "adjustable buoyant chambers." Nothing came of Lincoln's patent, which was destined to fall into history's trivia bin as the only one ever filed by an American president.[103]

Another idea Lincoln proposed that winter in Washington—the abolition of slavery in the District of Columbia—had a brighter future, though it was frustrated in the short run. Abolitionists had long brought attention to the incongruous presence of slaveholding and slave trading in the District. Proposals by antislavery congressmen like John Quincy Adams to abolish slavery there had come to naught. Passions over the issue flamed up in April 1848, when seventy-six fugitives were spirited away from Washington on the schooner *Pearl* and recaptured before the vessel made it out of the Potomac River. Lincoln's messmate Joshua Giddings drew national attention when he defended the enslaved people (most of whom were sold to the Deep South), faced down a proslavery lynch mob, and gave a withering speech in the House about the irony of the existence of slavery in the nation's capital.

In January 1849 Lincoln drafted a bill that called for the gradual emancipation of the District's enslaved people. He softened the bill by stipulating that emancipation must be approved by voters in the District and that slave owners must be compensated for giving up their chattel. Lincoln showed his proposal to some local officials, who supported it. But Southern congressmen subsequently expressed displeasure over the idea, and Lincoln dropped it.

It would not be until April 1862, under Lincoln, that slavery would be abolished in the District of Columbia. But the effort in 1849 by the forty-year-old Lincoln was a turning point for him. Not only was it the first time that he came up with antislavery legislation, but his bill signaled the progressive centrism that later became his trademark.

Tellingly, his proposal won support from both Joshua Giddings and Duff Green; it was one of the few things that the abolitionist congressman and the Southern-rights champion agreed on. In his first major foray against slavery, then, Lincoln mediated effectively between Northern and some Southern interests. He proposed abolition without threatening the Union. On the slavery issue, he had inched toward effective political centrism.

He may have seen his bill as a means of testing the antislavery credentials of that quintessential centrist, Zachary Taylor. In the unlikely scenario that the bill passed Congress, would Taylor sign it and thus live up to his billing as the people's president, averse to using the veto power? Lincoln did not get the chance to find out. But he did have other expectations of the president.

Among them was patronage, which for Lincoln was closely related to geographical centrism. Lincoln tried to persuade Taylor to award important government posts to Whigs from his central section of Illinois. In the spring and summer of 1849, a battle grew over the position of commissioner of the US General Land Office. This plum position, which paid $3,000 a year, held high importance for Lincoln because it involved supervising the surveying and sale of public lands. He had long put a priority on land use. He promoted the Whig agenda that the states should receive a portion of the moneys raised by the federal government from the sale of public land. Also, he doubtless saw an opportunity to help secure the Mexican Cession for freedom. A Whig from central Illinois, Lincoln believed, would be in an ideal position to regulate land use in a way that avoided the extremes of sectionalism. Lincoln reported to friends that, initially, he was considered for the Land Office position. Soon, however, he threw his weight behind Cyrus Edwards, the brother of his brother-in-law Ninian Edwards (and the father of his former love interest Matilda Edwards). However, the Chicago attorney Justin Butterfield soon emerged as Taylor's favored candidate. Lincoln respected Butterfield but insisted that his appointment would be "an egregious political blunder" that would "give offence to the whole whig party here."[104]

Why this hostility toward Butterfield? Lincoln later explained, "I opposed the appointment of Mr. B. because I believed it would be a matter of discouragement to our active, working friends here, and I opposed it for no other reason."[105] "Here" meant central Illinois. In appointing the Chicagoan, President Taylor had said, "I think the commissionership should go north."[106] Not only was Butterfield from the northern section of the state, but among his main backers were easterners, including the Massachusetts senator Daniel Webster.[107]

Once it was clear that Cyrus Edwards was not going to win the commissionership, Lincoln eagerly sought the job for himself. He solicited recommenders and, in June 1849, wrote President Taylor. He described his fitness for the position in geographical terms, declaring that "I am as strongly recommended by Ohio and Indiana, as well as Illinois"—indeed, by "the whole Northwest." He complained that Illinois appointments had all gone to the southern or northern sections of the state. What was needed was someone from the center. "I am in the center," Lincoln wrote. "Is the center nothing?—that center which alone has ever given you a Whig representative?"[108]

Butterfield got the appointment, and Lincoln supported him; at least the new land commissioner was an Illinoisan. But the patronage job Lincoln truly wanted had eluded him. He subsequently turned down offers of two positions in Oregon Territory: first, as secretary to the governor and then the governorship itself. The high salary that came with the latter job was tempting, but going to the Far West would sacrifice his geographical centrality and would confront him and his family with harsh living conditions.

If Lincoln felt shortchanged by the patronage system, others, it turned out, were frustrated with his own performance as a political patron. He expressed a willingness to run for reelection to the House, but Illinois Whigs had expected more governmental favors from him and instead nominated Stephen T. Logan, who lost a close election in August 1848 to a Mexican War hero, the Democrat major Thomas L. Harris, who would lose his seat two years later to the popular Whig, Richard Yates.

For now, Lincoln was satisfied to be back in central Illinois, which had more lessons to teach him. The Eighth Judicial Circuit now covered fourteen counties, and he was the only Illinois lawyer who consistently traversed its 440 round-trip miles each year. During the 1850s, he continued to learn much as a traveling lawyer. As tensions over slavery intensified during that decade, he also reentered politics. Extreme positions, antislavery and proslavery, hardened on both sides, widening political polarization and raising the possibility of civil war. When the threatened westward expansion of slavery drew Lincoln back into politics in 1854, he made a determined effort to avoid extremes.

"Is the center nothing?" he had asked President Taylor. As a political candidate and then as president, Lincoln would teach the world that in a deeply divided time, the center is *everything*—the center, that is, with an eye always trained on pushing the nation in a strongly progressive direction.

As Lincoln entered the 1850s, America responded to the growing slavery crisis by finding answers to political conundrums by looking beyond human laws to what was called the higher law, which caused wildly unpredictable actions on both the abolitionist and the proslavery sides. Lincoln reined in this higher-law trend by arguing convincingly that the founding fathers themselves had provided the most inspiring higher law of all.

9

Antislavery Emergence

In 1855 Lincoln confided to his best friend, Joshua Speed, that the sight of the chained blacks the two had seen on the Ohio River steamboat fourteen years earlier haunted him. "That sight was a continual torment to me," he wrote; "and I see something like it every time I touch the Ohio, or any other slave-border." Slavery, he confessed, had "the power of making me miserable." He insisted that Speed, a slaveholder, should "appreciate how much the great body of the Northern people do crucify their feelings, in order to maintain their loyalty to the constitution and the Union."[1]

What had happened to Lincoln? When he had first seen the enslaved group on the boat in 1841, he had acted distanced. At the time, he had written Joshua's sister Mary that although the blacks were being torn from loved ones and sent "into perpetual slavery" in the Deep South, they were singing, cracking jokes, and playing cards. Chained like "so many fish on a trot-line," they were nonetheless "the most cheerful and apparantly [sic] happy creatures on board." Tailoring his language for the slaveholding Speed family, who had recently hosted him for three weeks in Kentucky, Lincoln commented, that the group's carefree behavior showed that showed that God "renders the worst of human conditions tolerable, while He permits the best, to be nothing better than tolerable."[2]

In 1841, then, Lincoln had described the blacks as strangely contented despite their confinement.

In 1855, in contrast, he remembered the same group with a depth of anguish that the most fervent antislavery Northerners would feel.

To mention antislavery Northerners is to point to a cultural shift that fed into Lincoln's altered response to those enslaved people on the steamboat. The Northern people as a whole had turned in an antislavery direction. Lincoln, with his politician's eye ever trained on public opinion, felt freshly emboldened to promote his antislavery attitudes vigorously. As he told Joshua Speed, "the great body of the Northern people" now opposed slavery.[3] Lincoln had always opposed it, but he had done so in public only intermittently. By the mid-1850s, he was forthright and persistent in his assault on slavery.

A number of interrelated factors—political, social, and cultural—caused the sea change in the North's attitude, which in turn contributed to Lincoln's boldness on the public stage. The political ones—the debates over the Wilmot Proviso, the Fugitive Slave Act of 1850, and the Kansas-Nebraska Act—have often been discussed. Less frequently mentioned, yet equally important, are key social and cultural changes.

The 1845–55 decade is recognized by literary historians as the American Renaissance, which produced masterpieces by Poe, Melville, Hawthorne, Emerson, Thoreau, and Whitman. The complexity of their writings reflected the darkening political landscape. Some works contain interesting portraits of race and slavery, as in Melville's 1855 story "Benito Cereno," in which the slave problem is presented as a knot that cannot be untied, or in Thoreau and Emerson, who challenged slavery through civil disobedience and by promoting the violent abolitionist John Brown.

This decade also witnessed what could be called the *Antislavery* Renaissance. Landmark slave narratives—by Frederick Douglass, Henry Bibb, William Wells Brown, Josiah Henson, and others—gained widespread visibility with their searing first-person accounts of slavery. The Fugitive Slave Act of 1850 provoked an outpouring of antislavery writing, notably Harriet Beecher Stowe's 1852 bestseller *Uncle Tom's Cabin*, which acted like a force of nature on popular attitudes.[4] In politics, the antislavery spark set by the Liberty Party in 1840 and the Free Soil Party in 1848 became the fire in the 1850s that swept the North in the form of the Republican Party, which came close to winning the presidency with John Frémont in 1856 and then won it with Lincoln in 1860. The activism of reformers like William Lloyd Garrison, Wendell Phillips, and Gerrit Smith and preachers such as Henry Ward Beecher, Theodore Parker, and George B. Cheever, along with notorious fugitive slave episodes, added fuel to the antislavery conflagration. By 1855, Frederick Douglass could say of the antislavery movement, "Its auxiliaries are everywhere. Scholars, authors, orators, poets, and statesmen give it their aid."[5]

Three main themes became the focus of the Antislavery Renaissance: history, humanity, and the higher law. History refers to the invoking of past examples—either the *Mayflower* landing or the British civil wars of the 1640s or the American Revolution (or some combination of the three)—that antislavery advocates held up as precedents of their argument. Humanity refers to seeing enslaved blacks not as things, brutes, or inferior people, but as fully human. The higher law refers to the law of morality and justice that transcends human law, including what some regarded as proslavery passages in the Constitution. Antislavery politicians and some progressive reformers had long argued that antislavery principles were actually embedded within the Constitution, which, "interpreted as it *ought* to be interpreted," Frederick Douglass declared in 1852, "is a GLORIOUS LIBERTY DOCUMENT."[6]

While these antislavery themes won increasing sympathy in the North, they provoked a strong reaction among Southerners, who promoted their view that the right of holding people as property was guaranteed by the Constitution.

Throughout the 1850s, Lincoln treated the heated arguments over slavery in the same way he did other divisive or turbulent forces: he controlled and channeled them. One of his chief means of control was his compelling melding of history, humanity, and the higher law in his first major antislavery speech, at Peoria, Illinois, in October 1854.

LESSONS FROM STOWE, LESSONS FROM DEATH

"Is this the little woman who made this great war?"[7]

The words sound like Lincoln. Did he really say them when he greeted the diminutive Harriet Beecher Stowe in the White House in November 1862? We may never know for sure, but we do know that the meeting was cordial between him and the woman whose 1852 antislavery novel was a catalyst for the Civil War. When Lincoln was working on a draft of the Emancipation Proclamation, he checked out of the Library of Congress Stowe's *A Key to Uncle Tom's Cabin*, which described the sources of characters and scenes in her landmark novel.[8]

He knew of Stowe's famous antislavery siblings as well, notably the popular minister Henry Ward Beecher. In 1860, shortly after his nomination for the presidency, Lincoln had met with a family friend who reported, "He knew much about all [the members of] the talented Beecher family; showed me a well worn copy of Harriet Beecher Stowe's *Uncle Tom's Cabin*, and some clippings of Henry Ward Beecher's sermons and speeches."[9]

It says much that Lincoln was familiar with the antislavery Beecher family, including Henry Ward Beecher, who not only denounced slavery from his Brooklyn pulpit but held an auction among his parishioners to win freedom for the two enslaved Edmonton sisters, victims of the 1848 *Pearl* incident in which more than seventy fugitives were recaptured in Washington, DC. Later, Beecher sent to the Kansas Territory boxes labeled "Beecher's Bibles" containing guns he wanted to be used by free state settlers there to fight against slavery. Beecher

Harriet Beecher Stowe with her father, Lyman Beecher,
and her brother, Henry Ward Beecher

supported Lincoln during the Civil War and eulogized him eloquently
after his death.

The Beecher family included other antislavery clergymen as well,
including Edward Beecher, the St. Louis minister who was close to the
abolitionist martyr Elijah Lovejoy, whose death at the hands of a proslavery mob had occurred in Illinois in 1837, when Lincoln was a rising
politician in the state.

There was an emotional connection between Lincoln and Harriet
Beecher Stowe: their shared experience of witnessing slavery firsthand
while losing close family members. In both cases, grief deepened their
awareness of the horrors of slavery.

As a housewife in Cincinnati in the 1830s and '40s, Stowe met
fugitives who came across the Ohio River from Kentucky. She heard

their life stories, and she befriended Ohioans who helped them flee north on the Underground Railroad. The loss of her beloved young son Charley to cholera in 1849 contributed to her sympathy for the enslaved. She wrote of Charley, "It was at *his* dying bed, and at *his* grave, that I learnt what a poor slave mother may feel when her child is torn away from her."[10] Two years later, she penned her antislavery bestseller *Uncle Tom's Cabin*, which moved millions with its portrait of the deaths of Eva St. Clare and her enslaved companion Uncle Tom.

HARRIET BEECHER STOWE

The emotional deepening of Lincoln's response to slavery between 1848 and 1854 was also influenced by personal tragedy. Death struck the Lincoln family three times in seven months at a moment when

Lincoln traveled south, where he had the opportunity to witness directly the horrific effects of slavery.

First came the passing of Mary's fifty-eight-year-old father, Robert Smith Todd, who in July 1849 fell victim to the nationwide cholera epidemic that had taken Stowe's Charley a year earlier. Todd's unexpected death, in the midst of his campaign for a seat in the Kentucky Senate, was surely extremely painful for Mary. She had identified with her father, whose emotional nature, taste for fine things, and ambitiousness had shaped her. She appreciated his having provided her with an excellent education. He had also been a buffer between his first wife's children, including Mary, and his second wife, Betsey, whom they held suspect as the replacement and rival of their sainted mother.

Lincoln must have also been saddened by Robert Todd's sudden death. Although the two men had not been close, they had respected each other—not the least because of their shared admiration for Robert Todd's friend Henry Clay. After the birth of his namesake, Robert Todd Lincoln, Mary's father had visited Springfield—something he never did for his three other married daughters in Illinois. He gave the Lincolns $200 a year until his death, and he supplied Mary an additional $120 annually for her own use. He bought a large land lot for the couple south of Springfield that Mary sold in 1854 for $1,200, and he had his son-in-law represent him in recovering a small debt and let him keep the amount he collected.[11]

Lincoln continued to represent him after his death. Todd left the bulk of his estate, including his enslaved workers, to his second wife, Betsey; the remainder was divided among his fourteen children. He also left behind an unfinished lawsuit he had filed against Robert Wickliffe, whom he charged with illegally confiscating the estate of a wealthy relative, Mary Todd Russell. In September 1849 Lincoln procured a bill of revivor and filed a suit for Robert Todd's heirs against Robert Wickliffe in Fayette County court in Lexington, Kentucky.

The case was rooted in a long-standing dispute in the Todd family.[12]

John Russell, Mary Todd Russell's only child by her first marriage, had had a son, Albert, by an enslaved woman. After John's death in 1822, Mrs. Russell purchased the woman and her child with the idea of freeing them. But Mary's second husband, Robert Wickliffe, would not allow her to do so unless she transferred to him her properties, worth half a million dollars (nearly fourteen million dollars today). In 1827, she made the transfer and soon emancipated the enslaved woman and the teenage son, sending them to Liberia. Later, Robert S. Todd claimed that Wickliffe had stolen Mary Russell's estate, which, he said, rightfully belonged in the Todd family. The suit lapsed after Robert Todd's death, but Lincoln revived it. In late October 1849, he traveled to Lexington to work on it. In court, Wickliffe insisted that Mary Russell had acted out of love for him, not coercion—an argument that eventually won Wickliffe the case, which dragged on until 1858. While Lincoln lost the case, he could not but have been moved by the powerful example of the emancipationist Mrs. Russell, who paid the extraordinary price of the equivalent of fourteen million dollars to free two enslaved females, her son's lover and their child.

Although Lincoln did not leave a detailed record of his three weeks in Lexington, his stay there could have exposed him to slavery in some of its harshest forms. On the grounds of the Fayette County courthouse, where he went regularly, was a three-pronged poplar tree used as a whipping post where the enslaved were lashed for even the most minor infractions, such as appearing on the streets after 7:00 p.m. Also on the courthouse grounds was an auction block where men, women, and children were sold. The Lincolns spent a lot of time with Mary's brother Levi Todd and her maternal grandmother Elizabeth Parker, both of whom lived on Short Street, a center of slave activity. Within sight of their homes was the slave mart owned by William A. Pullum and leased by Lewis C. Robards, a notorious slave dealer. Robards crowded enslaved people into pens, eight feet square and seven feet high, with small barred windows, heavy iron doors, and damp brick floors covered with vermin-infested straw. Robards specialized in buying people who were sick or aged and disguising their infirmities in order to sell them at a profit. Across the street from the Parker and Todd residences, Robards had a two-story building, formerly a theater, that he had converted into a luxurious holding place for young mulatto "fancy girls"—destined to be the concubines of Southern masters—who sold for high prices. Robards generated sales by stripping the women in front of would-be buyers.[13]

Lincoln must have also been aware of the discussion of slavery taking place in the Kentucky legislature. Proslavery legislators were alarmed over a rising abolitionist spirit in the state, signaled by a large emancipationist meeting, led by Henry Clay, that was held in Frankfort earlier that year. To counter such antislavery activities, a constitutional convention was organized with the goal of protecting slavery in Kentucky. The convention began on October 1, 1849, holding its sessions at the statehouse in Frankfort, some of which Lincoln probably attended. If he did, he could not have been pleased by the deliberations, which led to the approval of a new state constitution that banned free Negroes from entering Kentucky and made emancipation very difficult. A clause in the state constitution read: "The right of property is before and higher than any constitutional sanction, and the right of an owner of a slave and its increase is the same, and as inviolable as the right of the owner of any property whatever."[14] A historian of the Kentucky constitution notes, "With the ratification of the convention by a substantial majority all hope of emancipation in Kentucky vanished for many years."

The intensification of Lincoln's emotional response to slavery appears to have been influenced not only by his witness of the institution in Kentucky but also by two other deaths in the family—that of Mary's eighty-year-old grandmother Elizabeth Parker on January 20, 1850, and most devastating of all, that of Lincoln's three-year-old son Eddie two weeks later.

Widow Parker had provided solid support for Mary and her siblings after the death of their mother (her daughter) in 1825. A bond developed between Mary and her grandmother that lasted through the Lincolns' 1849 visit to Lexington, when they spent much time with her. Though the death of the aging widow was not unexpected, it cannot have been easy for them. She may have seemed especially admirable to them in retrospect, for she had arranged to have her enslaved workers freed upon her death.

The worst blow for the Lincolns came when their second son, Eddie, died. A sickly boy, Eddie was apparently afflicted with consumption (pulmonary tuberculosis), the leading cause of death in mid-nineteenth-century America. Due to the primitive nature of medicine in the era before germ theory, around a quarter of American children died before reaching the age of five.[15] The symptoms of Eddie's final illness, fever and coughing, arrived in early December. He lingered for fifty-two days and died on February 1, 1850. Overwhelmed by grief, Mary fell into periods of sobbing and refusing food. Lincoln was alarmed for her health. "Eat, Mary, for we must live," he said.[16]

Eddie's death had a permanent impact on the Lincolns. The erratic behavior commonly attributed to Mary dates mainly from the post-Eddie period. The subsequent deaths of two other sons and her husband would traumatize her further. Given her extreme sensitivity to life's vicissitudes and her instability, it is surprising that, until the last months of her life, she did not become so depressed that she disengaged from society entirely.

As for Lincoln, his mournful moods, which Herndon noticed in the law office in the 1850s, were connected, on some level, with Eddie's death. Lincoln had always been haunted by mortality, and the passing of his innocent child seemed especially cruel. "We miss him very much," Lincoln wrote to a relative.[17] He had loved Eddie deeply. In the letter from Washington in which he mentioned looking for socks for "Eddy's dear little feet," he had written, "Dear Eddy thinks father is 'gone tapila' ['gone to the capital']"; he also asked after "dear Bobby" and wrote,

"What did he and Eddy think of the little letters father sent them? Dont let the blessed fellows forget father."[18]

In February 1850, one of the "blessed fellows" was gone. The grieving father would not forget him.

A week after the boy's death, a poetic eulogy, "Eddie," appeared in the *Springfield Journal*. The poem was long thought to have been written by Mary Todd Lincoln, in part because its last line—"Of such is the kingdom of Heaven"—appeared on Eddie's tombstone in Hutchinson's Cemetery in Springfield. Actually, the poem was written in 1849 by the St. Louis poet Ethel Grey and appeared in her volume *Sunset Gleams from the City of the Mounds*.[19] The *Springfield Journal* published Grey's poem "By Request," which suggests that the Lincolns may have known of the poem and submitted it to the paper. The poem bathed its deceased subject in images of the Good Death, which was nineteenth-century America's way of making death meaningful and consoling.[20] The Eddie of the poem is now "the angel child, / With the harp and the crown of gold, / Who warbles now at the Saviour's feet," a "blossom of heavenly love," who "Dwells in the spirit-world above."[21]

Did the rationalist Lincoln take this pious attitude toward Eddie's death? The Springfield minister who conducted Eddie's funeral, the Reverend James Smith, claimed that Lincoln at this time began an exploration of religion that led him to embrace Christianity. A native of Glasgow, Scotland, Smith had been a deist in his youth who later experienced a religious conversion and became the pastor of Springfield's First Presbyterian Church. Mary Todd Lincoln, raised a Presbyterian, had been attending the Episcopal church in Springfield but was so impressed by Smith that she joined his church in 1852. Although Lincoln never became a member of the church, he rented a family pew there and sometimes attended services with Mary.

Smith based his claim about Lincoln's alleged religious turn on discussions he had with Lincoln, who reportedly read Smith's book *The*

Christian's Defence, a detailed rebuttal of atheism, deism, and polytheism. As the story goes, while visiting Lexington, Lincoln found the book in his father-in-law's library, read it, and consulted with Smith about religion when he returned to Illinois.[22] Perhaps this was true, but we cannot tell how seriously Lincoln took *The Christian's Defence*. Herndon recalled that he brought the book into the law office, "threw it down upon our table—spit upon it as it were—and never opened it to my knowledge."[23] Robert Bray, an authority on Lincoln's reading, gives *The Christian's Defence* a "C" ("Somewhat unlikely") among the books Lincoln read.[24]

Nonetheless, the 1850–51 period did see at least a temporary upswing in Lincoln's religious faith. This becomes clear when we look at a letter he wrote in January 1851 to his stepbrother John D. Johnston in which he offered religious comfort to his dying father. He explained that he could not come to Coles County because he was occupied with, among other things, Mary's postnatal illness (she had given birth to William Wallace Lincoln on December 20, nearly eleven months after the death of Eddie). He also said that seeing his father would not be good for either of them—a sign of the distance that had grown between father and son. But he wrote in a pious tone, asking Johnston to tell his father "to remember to call upon, and confide in, our great, and good, and merciful Maker; who will not turn away from him in any extremity. He notes the fall of a sparrow, and numbers the hairs of our heads; and He will not forget the dying man, who puts his trust in Him. Say to him that . . . if it be his lot to go now, he will soon have a joyous [meeting] with many loved ones gone before; and where [the rest] of us, through the help of God, hope ere-long [to join] them."[25]

The Good Death couldn't be described more succinctly: God watches over us, cares for us, and ushers us to an afterlife where we will be with lost loved ones, soon to be joined by those left behind.

Lincoln here identifies with the sentimental culture of his day—the culture that yielded the inspiring death of Stowe's angelic Eva, ornate gravestones, and novels about the daily life in heaven like Elizabeth Stuart Phelps's bestseller *The Gates Ajar*. One could argue that the disruptions of the 1846–52 period—the polarization in Congress, the direct exposure to the harshness of slavery, the succession of deaths in the family—shook him and impelled him to seek solace in a higher power.

As with Stowe, his personal grief, coupled with his concern over the social crisis, led him to embrace an attitude toward slavery that was at once human and spiritual, allied with both feeling and the higher law. She swayed a large portion of the Northern public by projecting these impulses in *Uncle Tom's Cabin*, the most popular work of the age.

Although we don't know for certain if Lincoln read *Uncle Tom's Cabin*, his "well worn" copy of it suggests that he did. At any rate, his law partner William Herndon bought the book when it appeared in 1852 and surely talked about it in the law office.[26] Also, newspapers in central Illinois, as everywhere else in the North, ran regular ads and stories about the novel, which became an inescapable cultural presence.

HUMANITY, SLAVERY, AND POLITICS

Uncle Tom's Cabin vivified the humanity of enslaved people, a theme that became an underpinning of Lincoln's approach to slavery. Southerners' treatment of the enslaved as nonhuman was a standard object of criticism among abolitionists, from Theodore Dwight Weld through Charles Sumner, who frequently quoted Judge George Stroud's 1827 dictum that "the cardinal principle of slavery,—that the slave is not to be ranked among *sentient beings*, but among *things*—is an article of property—a chattel personal,—obtains as undoubted law in all of these [slave] states." A Maryland law, for example, stipulated that "personal property shall consist of specific articles, such as SLAVES, WORKING BEASTS, ANIMALS OF ANY KIND, stock, furniture, plate, books, and SO FORTH."[27] In the words of a proslavery politician, the enslaved "were just as much *property* as horses, cattle or land."[28] Frederick Douglass made a tremendous impact while giving antislavery lectures when he stood tall, expanded his arms wide, and declared, "I am one of the *things* of the South! *Behold the thing!*"[29]

Stowe's exposure to this principle came from many sources, including the case of the Underground Railroad conductor John Van Zandt, the prototype of the heroic John Von Trompe in her novel. In his plea on behalf of Van Zandt before the US Supreme Court, the lawyer Salmon Chase (Lincoln's future secretary of the treasury) emphasized the humanity of blacks. Chase declared, "No legislature can make right wrong, or wrong right. . . . No legislature can make men, things, or things, men."[30] An early subtitle of a draft of *Uncle Tom's Cabin* was the ironic *The Man That Was a Thing* (eventually changed to *Life Among the Lowly*). The novel exposes the cruelty of slavery's dehumanization of blacks. Its enslaved characters express a range of human emotions— family loyalty, devotion to God, joy, pain, bitterness, revenge, and hope—but are treated like animals or other property.

The book's characters represented the kind of suffering Lincoln could have witnessed during his Lexington visits. The whipping of an enslaved man for minor offenses provides the climax of Stowe's novel, in which the kindly Tom dies at the hands of henchmen of the slave owner Simon Legree. The novel centers on the forced separation of slave families, a phenomenon that Lincoln had witnessed on the steamboat in 1841 and, most likely, on the auction block in Lexington. The sexual exploitation of enslaved women, one of Lewis Robards's business practices in Lexington, is dramatized in Stowe's portraits of the kept woman Cassy and the breeder Prue.

Despite these and other correspondences between Stowe's novel and Lincoln's experience with slavery, it's important to note that Lincoln departed in important ways not only from her but also from other reformers.

The response to *Uncle Tom's Cabin* was notably mixed. In the North, it pushed popular attitudes in an antislavery direction. It was a main

UNCLE TOM'S CABIN;

OR,

LIFE AMONG THE LOWLY.

BY

HARRIET BEECHER STOWE.

VOL. I.

FIFTIETH THOUSAND.

BOSTON:

JOHN P. JEWETT & COMPANY.

CLEVELAND, OHIO:

JEWETT, PROCTOR & WORTHINGTON.

1852.

Title page of *Uncle Tom's Cabin* (1852)

reason why Lincoln could report in 1855 that "the great body of the Northern people" opposed slavery. In the South, the book was excoriated and, in some places, criminalized. "The wide dissemination of such dangerous volumes [as *Uncle Tom's Cabin*]," a Richmond newspaper announced, could lead to "the ultimate overthrow of the framework of Southern society amid circumstances of tragic convulsion from which the imagination starts back with horror!"[31] A black minister in Maryland was sentenced to ten years in the state penitentiary for having the book in his house.[32] Stowe received hate mail, including an envelope from the South containing an ear cut from the head of an enslaved person, sent in payment, as a note explained, for her defense of "D—n niggers."[33]

The very vividness of *Uncle Tom's Cabin*—its emotional intensity and sensationalism—made it divisive. Lincoln, who regarded slavery as "an apple of discord" that threatened the Union, in his public statements avoided the kind of melodramatic passion that made Stowe's novel so captivating to some and so hateful to others.[34]

Here he differed not only from Stowe but also from other antislavery figures of the day. Herndon was his main conduit to radical reformers. "I was the abolitionist," Herndon wrote, "and kept on my table such speeches as Theodore Parker's, Giddings's, Phillips's, Sumner's, Seward's, etc. . . . I purchased all the anti-slavery histories, biographies, etc., and kept them on my table, and when I found a good thing, a practical thing, I would read it to Lincoln." He and Lincoln read the prominent antislavery newspapers, including the *Liberator*, the *National Era*, the *Chicago Tribune*, the *New-York Tribune*, and the *Anti-Slavery Standard*.[35]

When Lincoln said that he "hated slavery . . . as much as any Abolitionist," therefore, he was making a well-informed comparison.[36] He had a wide-ranging knowledge of antislavery activism. He shared the loathing of slavery that was the common denominator among all its varieties, including Garrisonian radicalism, the evangelicalism of the Beechers and Finneys, Transcendentalist individualism, and the political approach of the Liberty and Free Soil Parties. Of the varieties, he strongly preferred the latter, which remained within the confines of the democratic system established by the Founders in the Constitution. But he had not campaigned for antislavery third parties in the 1840s because they drew votes away from the Whig Party, which he then saw as the best means for bridging the sectional divide and fending off what his fellow Whig Alexander Stephens called "the *centrifugal* tendency."[37]

In the early 1850s, however, this tendency overtook the Whig Party, which fragmented due to the very sectional tensions it had tried to heal. In 1852, Lincoln campaigned for Winfield Scott, who turned out to be the Whig Party's last presidential candidate. As America's leading army general, Scott appeared to have the potential for attracting Southern votes for his exemplary record in the Mexican War and Northern ones because of his antislavery leanings. But he was a weak presidential candidate. Old Fuss and Feathers, as he was called, was a stickler for discipline who was known for military prowess and physical heft (he weighed more than three hundred pounds) but not for political acuity.

Lincoln was hard-pressed to defend him. If the Whig Party was spinning apart, Lincoln's speech before Springfield's Scott Club in late August 1852 was itself centrifugal. In contrast to his finest efforts, the Gettysburg Address and the Second Inaugural Address, which were tightly focused on social justice, the Scott speech was slashing, meandering, and crassly humorous. In this partisan diatribe, Lincoln spent most of his time attacking Stephen Douglas's arguments on behalf of the Democratic candidate Franklin Pierce while offering little positive support of Winfield Scott or the Whigs. He decimated many Democratic arguments but replaced them with virtually nothing. To expose Franklin Pierce's "ludicrous and laughable" record as a brigadier general in the Mexican War, he told an anecdote about Pierce and his horse rolling in the mud, which he compared with a mock-militia story borrowed from frontier humor.[38] Caricaturing Pierce's waffling on the slavery issue, he repeated racist lines from a sea shanty in Frederick Marryat's *Diary in America*: "Sally is a bright Mullatter, / Oh Sally Brown— / Pretty gal, but can't get at her, / Oh, Sally Brown." Lincoln added, "Now, should Pierce ever be President, he will, politically speaking, not only be a mulatto; but he will be a good deal darker one than

Sally Brown." These are odd words, indeed, coming from one destined to become the Great Emancipator.

The speech's randomness was uncharacteristic of Lincoln, but it reflected the political atmosphere of the early 1850s. The parties reshuffled due to the Compromise of 1850, a bipartisan settlement of the slavery issue that made certain concessions to the North (the admission of California as a free state and the abolition of the slave trade in the District of Columbia) and others to the South (notably the Fugitive Slave Act).[39] As Lincoln said in his Scott speech, "the compromise measures were not party measures— . . . for praise or blame, they belonged to neither party to the exclusion of the other."[40] He noted that Whigs like Henry Clay and Daniel Webster had forged the Compromise along with Democrats like Stephen Douglas. By coming together in what was touted as a permanent resolution of the slavery crisis, the two parties lost the sharp edge of competition that had separated them in the previous decade. Compromise yielded flaccidness. Both parties equivocated on slavery; in Lincoln's metaphor, both were Sally Browns. The lack of political electricity in 1852 dampened voter turnout, which was the lowest, percentage-wise, of any presidential race between 1840 and 1904.[41]

The absence of sharply defined issues had the positive effect of contributing to the literature of the American Renaissance. The masterpieces of the 1850–55 period—*The Scarlet Letter*, "Bartleby, the Scrivener," *Moby-Dick*, *Leaves of Grass*, and *Walden*, among them—reflected the party turmoil, which unleashed a whirl of social and cultural images, unattached to fixed political programs, that became free for recombination and transformation in literary art.[42]

The political disorder also opened the way to unique achievements of the Antislavery Renaissance, including such groundbreaking novels as Stowe's *Uncle Tom's Cabin* (1852), Frederick Douglass's *The Heroic Slave* (1852), and William Wells Brown's *Clotel: or, The President's Daughter* (1853).

But the same conditions that fostered cultural expression stymied forceful political leadership. The election of 1852 brought to power Franklin Pierce, the charming, weak-kneed alcoholic from New Hampshire who bowed to the Southern slave power during his presidency. Pierce's successor, the Pennsylvanian James Buchanan, another heavy drinker, also proved to be a lackey of the South's. Walt Whitman branded the presidencies just before Lincoln as "our topmost warning and shame."[43] Historians rank Pierce and Buchanan in the lowest tier of American presidents.

The dialectic of party collapse and cultural flowering also yielded the Abraham Lincoln we venerate. The conditions that drove lesser politicians to turpitude and ineptness turned him into a significant moral presence on the political scene.

His development was sped by his meditation on the deaths of two Whig leaders: Zachary Taylor and Henry Clay.

The death in 1850 of the sixty-six-year-old Taylor, after just sixteen months in office, shocked the nation. On July 4, he had attended festivities at the site where the Washington Monument was to be built. He spent hours in the hot sun and returned to the White House at 4:00 p.m. Famished, he consumed large quantities of iced milk and cherries. That evening he felt ill, and over the next few days he suffered from nausea, vomiting, diarrhea, and dehydration. At times he appeared to respond to calomel treatment, but he died on July 9. His doctor identified the cause of death as cholera morbus, an intestinal illness (unrelated to Asiatic cholera) that was probably gastroenteritis.

Two weeks after Taylor's death, Lincoln delivered a eulogy for the president in Chicago. Lincoln described Taylor's record as a battlefield leader who succeeded against overwhelming odds. Unflappable courage and doggedness in pursuit of victory—these qualities, which he saw in Taylor, were ones he would later seek in his Civil War generals, discovering them in Grant and Sherman. "His rarest military trait," Lincoln said, "was a combination of negatives—absence of *excitement* and absence of *fear*. He could not be *flurried*, and he could not be scared."[44]

Taylor was fair to his soldiers and officers; though a strong leader, he never behaved like a tyrant, and he avoided vindictive behavior. Was he a great president? Lincoln backed off from that question by saying the presidency is "not a bed of roses," and Taylor did not "escape censure." But Old Zack had "the confidence and devotion of the people" to a rare degree.

Above all, Taylor made viable a centrist position that, Lincoln thought, could alone bring about slavery's demise without disrupting the Union. Although Taylor held some 140 people in bondage, Lincoln viewed him as a noncontroversial Southerner who would not veto the Wilmot Proviso and who thus would prevent slavery from spreading. Lamenting that Taylor's death lessened the chances of resolving the conflict over slavery, Lincoln said: "I fear the one *great* question of the day, is not now so likely to be partially acquiesced in by the different sections of the Union, as it would have been, could Gen. Taylor have been spared to us." Lincoln missed the moderation of Taylor, who had denounced the "intemperate zeal" of "fanatics" on both sides—that is, Northern abolitionists and Southern fire-eaters.[45]

Moderation and centrism, the two virtues Lincoln highlighted in Taylor, also characterized Henry Clay, who died in 1852. In his eulogy of his political hero, Lincoln emphasized that Clay had put the Union above all else. Lincoln quoted approvingly from a journal that said of Clay, "He knew no North, no South, no East, no West, but only the Union, which held them all in its sacred circle."[46] As a stabilizing force, Clay had few parallels in American history. He had taken "the leading and most conspicuous part . . . in those great and fearful crises"—the Missouri question of 1819–20, the nullification controversy of 1832, and the debates over the Mexican Cession that led to the Compromise of 1850. Far more clearly than Taylor, Clay stood morally opposed to slavery and its extension. Though a slaveholder, he had said, in a speech Lincoln had attended, "I have ever regarded slavery as a great evil, a wrong."[47]

HENRY CLAY

Like Taylor, Clay denounced extremists. Clay was a "truly national man," Lincoln declared, who had moderated between "extremes on the subject [of slavery]."[48] On the one hand, he had opposed radical abolitionists who, in Lincoln's words, "would shiver into fragments the Union of these States; tear to tatters its now venerated constitution; and even burn the last copy of the Bible, rather than slavery should continue a single hour." On the other hand, Clay had lambasted Southerners who rejected the Declaration of Independence's words about human equality. Lincoln quoted Clay's remark that to deny the ideal of equality we "must blow out the moral lights around us, and extinguish that greatest torch of all which America presents to a benighted world. . . . [We] must penetrate the human soul, and eradicate the light of reason, and the love of liberty." Noting that Clay had worked for the gradual abolition of slavery in Kentucky, Lincoln supported Clay's vision of the gradual, peaceful extinction of slavery.

SENSATIONALISM AND THE HIGHER LAW

This hopeful prospect, however, seemed increasingly unlikely, as sectional tensions flared stronger than ever. The Compromise of 1850 did little to allay the tensions, and the Kansas-Nebraska Act, which opened the West to slavery, and the Dred Scott decision, which denied citizenship to blacks, fanned them further.

Antislavery writings intensified the polarization by portraying the enslaved as wronged, suffering human beings and by looking beyond proslavery laws and affirming the higher laws of justice and equality.

The prototype for the depiction of the suffering of enslaved people had been established in Theodore Dwight Weld's landmark book, *American Slavery as It Is* (1837). Drawing from an array of Southern sources, Weld presented a dreary litany of horrors: the enslaved, he reported, are routinely flogged and, "have red pepper rubbed into their lacerated flesh, and hot brine, spirits of turpentine, &c., poured over the gashes to increase the torture"; "they are often stripped naked, their backs and limbs cut with knives, bruised and mangled by scores and hundreds of blows with the paddle, and terribly torn by the claws of cats, drawn over them by their tormentors"; they are hunted by bloodhounds, torn in piece by dogs, suspended and beaten mercilessly; they eyes are cut out, their ears cut off, they are branded with hot irons; "they are maimed, mutilated and burned to death over slow fires"; and so on.[49]

Few major antislavery works omitted scenes of whipping, ear cropping, or other forms of torture. To prove that the enslaved were human, the antislavery authors presented scene after scene demonstrating that slaves felt exactly the same pain that whites would under such circumstances. The sexual exploitation of enslaved women was also a common topic. Antislavery writings from George Bourne's *Slavery Illustrated in Its Effects Upon Woman and Domestic Society* (1837) onward gave examples of sexual misconduct by masters that varied from the graphic to the nauseating. Bourne generalized that the whole South was "one vast brothel, in which multiform incests, polygamy, adultery, and other uncleanness are constantly perpetrated—and there is not a man, or woman, or boy, or girl, or any who has arrived at the age of puberty, that is not acquainted with nearly the whole mass of abominations."[50] Other abolitionists made similar points. Wendell Phillips declared, "The South is one great brothel."[51] William Lloyd Garrison branded slave owners as "monsters who have . . . given over to prostitution and ravishment, with all possible impunity, a million and half of helpless females."[52] The black abolitionist David Nelson declared, "Of the grown females belonging to more than two millions of our race, nearly every one is either a prostitute or an adulteress, and every grown male is either a fornicator or an adulterer."[53]

Antislavery writers who harped on such themes were often charged with what Carol Lasser calls voyeuristic abolitionism and what I have termed immoral reform: that is, the practice of describing vice so graphically that sensationalism obscures social message.[54] This opportunistic sensationalism extended to many other movements as well, including anti-Catholicism, anti-Mormonism, labor reform, and antiprostitution. There was no reform, in fact, that did not come under attack when some of its promoters went beyond exposing vice to wallowing in it and providing gratuitous details.

Although Lincoln had sometimes used such sensational reform rhetoric early on, he never allowed it to dominate his discourse, and he saw its shortcomings. In his 1842 Washingtonian speech he had decried temperance reformers' "thundering tones of anathema and denunciation"—their obsession with the evils resulting from alcohol abuse.

He advocated rational persuasion. By the 1850s, some of the radical abolitionists whose writings Herndon shared with him had alienated many Americans with their uncompromising language. William Lloyd Garrison conceded in 1854 that "a 'Garrisonian' abolitionist [is] the most unpopular appellation that any man can have applied to him."[55] The same year, Wendell Phillips noted that mainstream antislavery politicians distanced themselves from radical abolitionists because they wanted to avoid being "soiled by too close contact" with those "rough pioneers."[56]

Politically, popular sentiment in the North was definitely moving in an antislavery direction, as indicated by the strong run for the presidency waged by the Republican candidate John Frémont in 1856. The widespread anger caused by the Fugitive Slave Act and the popularity of works like *Uncle Tom's Cabin* and Richard Hildreth's *The White Slave* had contributed to the sea change in opinion. For Lincoln, the main impetus for taking up the antislavery cudgel in earnest was the passage of the Kansas-Nebraska Act.

He was, of course, one of many Northerners who argued against the extension of slavery. But he introduced a language that was uniquely forceful, for it projected all the passion and principle of the Garrisonian abolitionists while avoiding their sensationalism.

He also avoided their extreme interpretation of the higher law, which contributed to their view of the Constitution as a proslavery document. The phrase "higher law" had been around for some time and was ushered into the cultural mainstream by Senator William H. Seward in his 1850 speech "Freedom in the Territories." In answer to the proslavery argument that the Constitution sanctioned slavery even in the western territories, Seward insisted that the western lands were protected by "a higher law than the Constitution"—the law of natural justice, supported by God and morality.[57] Actually, Seward was not rejecting the Constitution; rather, he was making a rhetorical point. Unlike the Garrisonians, who dismissed the Constitution as "an agreement with hell" because of what they regarded as its proslavery message, Seward was part of a long line of antislavery politicians, reaching back to the founding era, who considered the Constitution an antislavery document because of its guarantees of due process and other rights. But his "higher law" statement, intended to quash proslavery readings of the Constitution, sparked widespread discussion and numerous attempts in the North to interfere with enforcement of the Fugitive Slave Act.[58] It also fed into Stowe's portrayal in *Uncle Tom's Cabin* of blacks and whites who heroically resisted proslavery laws. This virtuous lawbreaking, fused in Stowe's novel with tributes to the heroes of 1776, led Frederick Douglass to write, "We doubt if abler arguments have ever been presented in favor of the *'Higher Law'* than may be found here [in] Mrs. Stowe's truly great work."[59] Another reviewer described "the tears which [*Uncle Tom's Cabin*] has drawn from millions of eyes, the sense of a 'higher law,' which it has stamped upon a million hearts."[60] Southern reviewers, meanwhile, denounced the novel as a "portentous book of sin" that enforced "the doctrines and practices of the higher-law agitators at the North"—"all the enemies of the constitution."[61]

But abolitionists, Lincoln insisted, were *not* enemies of the Constitution, which he and similar-minded Northern politicians regarded as an antislavery document—an argument he pursued during his political rise over the next decade. He greatly admired Seward but regretted that the senator's higher-law speech had yielded misinterpretations that could prompt lawbreaking. In the margin of a newspaper article on slavery, he jotted, "I agree with Seward in his 'Irrepressible Conflict,' but I do not endorse his 'Higher Law.'"[62] He realized that the higher law could be appropriated by anyone to defend any position. He pointed to the irony of proslavery Democrats attacking Seward's higher law while promoting their own versions of a higher law. Regarding the "proclamation of a 'higher law,'" Lincoln declared that "in so far as it may attempt to foment a disobedience to the constitution, or to the constitutional laws of the country, it has my unqualified condemnation." He added, "But this is not the true ground of democratic hatred to Seward; else they would not so fondly cherish so many 'higher law' men in their own ranks."

His perception of the malleability of the higher law was shrewd. Southern fire-eaters and filibustering agents of slavery were just as prone to anchor their cause in God and morality as were abolitionists. Alexander Stephens, one of slavery's most visible defenders, averred that the higher law supported the South's peculiar institution. In a speech of 1856, he declared, "Let no man . . . say that African slavery as it exists in the South, . . . is in violation of either the laws of nations, the laws of nature, or the laws of God!"[63] Five years later, in his famous Cornerstone Speech, Stephens boasted that the Confederacy was the first society in history based on the "great . . . moral truth" that "the Negro is not equal to the white man, that slavery, subordination to the superior race, is his natural and normal position."[64] During the Civil War, Southerners boasted that God fully supported them. A Southern author typically hailed Confederate president Jefferson Davis as "a Christian of the Robert E. Lee type" and said that the South would be revered through the ages for having had *a Christian President! A Christian General! A Christian soldiery!"*[65]

Lincoln saw that the higher law was, potentially, the most centrifugal force in the culture because it could be pointed in any direction. Indeed, it *was* pointed in all directions in the 1850s. For Stephens and other Southerners, slavery represented the ideal form of ethics: it accorded with the laws of nature and God, which mandated racial hierarchy, with whites in the superior position. The Northern sage Emerson, in contrast, denounced the proslavery Fugitive Slave Act by declaring that "no forms, neither constitutions, nor laws, nor covenants, nor churches, nor bibles, are of any use in themselves; the devil nestles comfortably into them all."[66] William Lloyd Garrison, enforcing his higher-law principle of immediate emancipation, burned the Constitution publicly because he thought it supported slavery. Stephen A. Douglas said that to reject the Fugitive Slave Act while pretending to be loyal to the Constitution was hypocritical. He declared, "I know not how a man reconciles it to his conscience to take that oath to support the Constitution, when he believes that Constitution is in violation of the law of God."[67] Douglas called those who disobeyed the Fugitive Slave Act "crazy fanatics" and traitorous "conspirators" who must be given harsh jail sentences.[68] His dedication to it was as passionate as was his devotion to two other proslavery enactments: his own Kansas-Nebraska Act and the Supreme Court's Dred Scott decision.[69]

Lincoln, in contrast, rejected Dred Scott, vilified Kansas-Nebraska, and accepted the Fugitive Slave Act only with great reluctance. He denounced the latter law as "very obnoxious," declaring it "ungodly! no doubt it is ungodly!"[70] But he held that the law must be observed because of Article IV, Section 2 of the Constitution, which mandated the return of fugitives from labor. "We are under legal obligations," he lamented, "to catch and return their runaway slaves to them—a sort of dirty, disagreeable job."[71] As he wrote, "I confess I hate to see the poor creatures hunted down, and caught, and carried back to their stripes, and unrewarded toils; but I bite my lip and keep quiet."[72] He was in the position of Walt Whitman, who in his poetry democratically embraced fugitives but in a prose piece said that they must be returned to their owners out of respect to the Constitution.[73]

On the hated Fugitive Slave Act, Lincoln had to bite his lip and keep quiet many times. He also had to quell his impulse to express publicly his private sympathy for blacks. The issue of Lincoln's racial attitudes is hotly contested. Because of his occasional use of the N-word and certain hidebound statements he made in speeches, some argue that he was actually a racist. One historian generalizes that "racism was the center and circumference of his being."[74] We realize the utter falsity of this statement when we place Lincoln's attitudes toward race in their cultural contexts.

When he reentered politics in the 1850s, Lincoln found himself in a sea of racism. Laws aimed at restricting the settlement of black people in Illinois reflected popular racial attitudes, according to a Chicago journalist who wrote, "[There] is in the great masses of the people a natural and proper loathing of the negro, which forbids contact with him as with a leper." The journalist bragged that Illinois "for many years has wisely kept her soil for white men alone; she has inhibited the negro from coming within her limits for settlement, and reserved her broad prairies for her white citizens, for her white farmers, laborers and mechanics."[75]

Such attitudes were most frequently expressed by proslavery Democrats, but they were also aired by some antislavery figures, creating the ironic phenomenon that Frederick Douglass described as "opposing slavery but hating its victims."[76] Cassius M. Clay, the outspoken abolitionist whom Lincoln heard speak in Springfield, generalized that black people "lack self-reliance—we can make nothing out of them. God has made them for the sun and the banana!"[77] Lincoln's antislavery Illinois colleague Senator Lyman Trumbull, destined to be a major force behind progressive enactments, including the Thirteenth Amendment, the Freedmen's Bureau Acts, and the Civil Rights Bill of 1866, declared, "There is a very great aversion in the West—I know it to be so in my State—against having free negroes coming among us. Our people want nothing to do with the negro."[78] The *New York Times* remarked that Republicans had always "aimed at the good of the *white men* of the country, and had nothing to do with negroes."[79] The famous antislavery editor Horace Greeley described blacks as "indolent," "vicious," "generally ignorant," "dissipated," and "groveling in their tastes and appetites."[80] Greeley wrote, "[W]e make no pretensions to special interest in or liking for the African Race. We love Liberty, Equality, Justice, Humanity, . . . but we do not like negroes, and heartily wish no individual of that race had ever been brought to America."[81]

To be sure, there were notable exceptions to this record of racism among white antislavery spokespersons. One thinks especially of John Brown, Lydia Maria Child, Wendell Phillips, and numerous Quaker reformers, particularly Sarah and Angelina Grimké. William Lloyd Garrison, though accused of condescension in his treatment of blacks in the American Anti-Slavery Society, also showed racial openness, as did an increasing number of Republican politicians.

Then, too, abolitionism emerged among African Americans, from the seventeenth century onward. To mention the African American contribution, however, is to point again to racism, for in the 1850s some of the loudest calls for emigration from the United States came from blacks—James Theodore Holly, Martin Delany, Mary Ann Shadd, and Samuel Ringgold Ward, to name a few—who advocated fleeing racial prejudice in the United States by relocating abroad. Among the points of destination mentioned were Africa, Canada, Central and South America, and the West Indies, particularly Haiti.[82] Even some former antiemigration blacks, including Frederick Douglass, William Wells Brown, and William Watkins, briefly supported removal to Haiti. Martin Delany explained that free blacks in the North "occupy the very same position politically, religiously, civilly and socially (with but few exceptions,) as the bondman occupies in the slave States"; he added, "there is no species of degradation to which we are not subject."[83] His answer was emigration. He announced, *"Africa for the African race, and black men to rule them,"* and "Self Reliance and Self-Government on the Principle of African Nationality." (Delany dropped the emigration idea during the Civil War, when he recruited black troops for the Union army and became one of the nation's few black field officers; he had a warm relationship with Lincoln, whom Delany eulogized passionately after the president's death.)

Theodore Parker, an abolitionist who has special relevance to Lincoln, manifested typical contradictions on slavery and race. A Boston Unitarian minister who championed progressive causes, Parker was known to Lincoln through William Herndon, who corresponded with

THEODORE PARKER

the preacher throughout the 1850s and bought copies of his writings that he shared with Lincoln. The paean to "government of the people, by the people, and for the people" in the Gettysburg Address echoes a similar phrase—"Democracy is Direct Self-government, over all the people, for all the people, by all the people"—in Parker's 1858 talk "The Effect of Slavery on the American People," which Lincoln marked with pencil in the copy he read.[84] On religion, Lincoln said that he identified with Parker's liberal, creedless views more strongly than with those of other preachers.[85]

After the passage of the Fugitive Slave Act in 1850, Parker dedicated himself to the antislavery cause. A vigorous champion of the higher law, he declared, "It is my duty to resist a wicked law by all the expedients that are naturally just. . . . Who gave us the right to do wrong? I am bound to obey every natural law of God writ in the Universe."[86] In Boston he protected the fugitive William and Ellen Craft and served as the minister at their wedding before sending them to safety in England. He and other members of his Committee on Vigilance also aided other runaways, including George Latimer, Shadrach Minkins, Thomas Sims, and Anthony Burns. Parker lectured throughout the nation in the 1850s, reaching more than a hundred thousand Americans annually by averaging one hundred lectures a year, many of them directed against slavery.[87] Believing that violence alone could liberate America's enslaved millions, Parker joined the Secret Six of Northern radicals who helped fund and promote the militant abolitionist John Brown.

Inspired by this antislavery activism, William Herndon wrote Parker in 1854 that he had read all of Parker's writings. Herndon confessed, "I am *pulled* to them. . . . You are my ideal—strong, direct, energetic & charitable."[88] In their correspondence, which lasted until Parker's death in 1860, the two radicals shared news about the ongoing antislavery struggle, waxing passionate in their denunciations of the South's peculiar institution. As the decade progressed, Herndon kept Parker abreast of the doings of Illinois's rising antislavery star, his gangly, eloquent law partner. He sent Parker speeches by Lincoln and Douglas, lavishing praise on the former while anathematizing the latter. The freedom fighter Parker supported, John Brown, became one of Herndon's heroes.

But neither Parker nor Herndon shared John Brown's egalitarian views on race. Whereas Brown believed that blacks should be integrated into American society and treated equally with whites, Parker and Herndon espoused the more prevalent view that black people, while they deserved freedom, were inferior beings. "No doubt the African race is greatly inferior to the Caucasian in general intellectual power,"

Parker wrote, "and also in an instinct for liberty which is so strong in the Teutonic family."[89] The reason he supported John Brown was that he thought that the enslaved were too passive to fight for freedom on their own. He stated, "The African is the most docile and pliant of all the races of men; none has so little ferocity: vengeance, instinctual with the Caucasian, is exceptional in his history."[90] Weak and passive, blacks were like children who need protection from the aggressively competitive Anglo-Saxon race, which took advantage of them and would eventually crush them. Parker accepted the ethnological view that blacks and other "inferior" races would disappear, a view espoused by many nineteenth-century figures.

William Herndon also appears to have considered the idea of racial extinction. Just as his alcoholism ran counter to his promotion of prohibition, so his antislavery activism was larded with racism. On the one hand, like Parker, Herndon selflessly assisted fugitives from slavery—in his case, as a lawyer who defended them in court. On the other hand, he was not above making repellent remarks about African Americans and the Irish. In a letter to Parker, he wrote, "The poor miserable Irish . . . will perish from the [stink?] of humanity, and men of grander type will take their place. Poor fools." In the same letter he stated, "I am for cutting out the nigger, and as I now see it, it is self defense for the *white man.* . . . The cause [of conflict] must be eradicated before the *white* men are safe."[91]

It is to Lincoln's credit that he avoided such generalizations about race. While running for state office in the 1850s, he sometimes made conservative-sounding statements, but they were brief, perfunctory ones intended to appeal to certain groups of Illinoisans whose votes he needed. Actually, he loathed the race-baiting that his Democratic opponents utilized to whip up the public. Exasperated by Stephen Douglas's racist diatribes, Lincoln wrote, "Negro equality! Fudge!! How long, in the government of a God, great enough to make and maintain this Universe, shall there continue knaves to vend, and fools to gulp, so low a piece of demagougeism [sic] as this."[92] As Lincoln's political speeches of the 1850s reveal, he was far from being the thoroughgoing racist that some claim he was.

"MY FIRST IMPULSE WOULD BE
TO FREE ALL THE SLAVES"

By 1854, the year of Lincoln's political reemergence, Illinois enforced harsh legalized discrimination. Like Indiana and Oregon, Illinois had passed laws that forbade free black people from entering the state. Its first black law was approved in 1819. In 1848, while Lincoln was in Washington serving in Congress, Illinois voters had approved an amendment to the state constitution banning black people from entering the state. The amendment took effect in 1853, when the legislature passed An Act to Prevent the Immigration of Free Negroes into This State, which stipulated that any black person entering Illinois must leave within ten days or face a misdemeanor charge and a stiff fine. This was one of the most severe black laws passed by any Northern state before the Civil War.

The prevalence of such race-based restrictions in his state impelled Lincoln at times to advocate colonization—the transporting of free blacks to foreign places such as Liberia. Like many prominent Americans, from Jefferson and Madison through Monroe, Jackson, Clay, and Harriet Beecher Stowe, he talked of the departure of free blacks because of racial prejudice that, he thought, made coexistence in America difficult for both blacks and whites.[93] Lincoln joined the Illinois Colonization Society in the 1840s and by 1857 was one of its managers. He also joined the Springfield branch of the American Colonization Society.

But he perceived the extraordinary difficulty of colonization, and during the Civil War he abandoned the idea. On the matter of race, he seems to have profited from his contact in Washington with antislavery politicians who, as Richard H. Sewell points out, managed "to transcend the racism of the age" sufficiently to recognize the humanity of blacks and fight for their "most basic freedoms."[94]

Lincoln never reveled in white supremacy, as did his opponent Stephen Douglas. Privately, Lincoln wrote that slavery on the basis of a difference in color or intelligence made no sense, because that would mean that people could enslave anyone who was darker or less smart than they.[95] Moreover, he did not display prejudice in his private encounters with black people. When he made comments on race publicly, they were typically short, almost mechanical, as when, responding to Douglas during the 1858 debates, he gave a terse list of certain political and social rights for blacks he did not favor. Also, he carefully regulated his word choice to leave open the possibility that he would promote such rights in the future.

He cunningly surrounded his racist-sounding pronouncements with phrases that pointed in a radically abolitionist direction. He thus participated in what I call the "benign subversive" style that characterized the writings of Hawthorne, Melville, Whitman, and other writers of the American Renaissance—that is, packaging rebellious or progressive themes in conservative stylistic containers.[96]

Consider his October 1854 speech at Peoria, Illinois, on the Kansas-Nebraska Act, which marked his reentry onto the political stage. The speech contains one of his longest, most measured public expressions on slavery and race.[97]

In a central passage in the speech, he admitted that he had no clue as to how slavery could be abolished constitutionally. "If all earthly power were given me," he declared, "I should not know what to do, as to the existing institution." He then considered several courses of action:

> My first impulse would be to free all the slaves, and send them to Liberia,—to their own native land. But a moment's reflection would convince me, that whatever of high hope, (as

I think there is) there may be in this, in the long run, its sudden execution is impossible. If they were all landed there in a
day, they would all perish in the next ten days; and there are
not surplus shipping and surplus money enough in the world
to carry them there in many times ten days. What then? Free
them all, and keep them among us as underlings? Is it quite
certain that this betters their condition? I think I would not
hold one in slavery, at any rate; yet the point is not clear
enough for me to denounce people upon. What next? Free
them, and make them politically and socially, our equals? My
own feelings will not admit of this; and if mine would, we
well know that those of the great mass of white people will
not. Whether this feeling accords with justice and sound
judgment, is not the sole question, if indeed, it is any part of
it. A universal feeling, whether well or ill-founded, can not be
safely disregarded. We can not, then, make them equals. It
does seem to me that systems of gradual emancipation might
be adopted; but for their tardiness in this, I will not undertake to judge our brethren of the south.[98]

The outward message here is a conservative one adapted to a general
audience in Illinois, with its strong prejudice against blacks. After con-
ceding that he has no solution to the slavery question, Lincoln weighs
different possibilities: freeing the enslaved and returning them to Africa; freeing them and having them live as the underlings of whites;
freeing them and making them the political and social equals of whites.
None of the plans, Lincoln says, are feasible. Most of the blacks taken
to Africa would die there; besides, America's shipping resources could
not come close to accommodating such massive numbers of passengers.
Freeing blacks and making them a permanent underclass in America
did not improve their condition, while trying to grant them equal rights
would be prevented by the prevailing racism.

Couched in this conventional passage are radical themes. Lincoln begins with an abolitionist declaration—"My first impulse would be to free all the slaves"—and he doesn't surrender the idea: he repeats, "free them all" and "free them," and he also mentions gradual emancipation. He betrays real frustration over his inability to find a workable solution to the slavery problem. Although he says that "my own feelings will not admit of" making blacks "politically and socially, our equals," he adds the conditional clauses "and *if mine would*," "Whether this feeling accords with *justice and sound judgment*," and "whether *well or ill-founded*," along with concessions to public opinion: "we well know that those of *the great mass of white people will not*" and *"A universal feeling . . . can not be safely disregarded"* (italics added). In these clauses, Lincoln hints that he leans strongly toward granting rights to enslaved workers. By saying that he defers to a "universal feeling" on race among "the great mass of white people," he is subsuming his progressive leanings to majority opinion.

He was, therefore, muzzled by a locally biased public to whom his political fortunes were tied. Public opinion was vital to him. To win the votes, he could not be as progressive in public as he was in private. As for the Constitution, he wanted to show that it had an antislavery message, despite its obligatory concessions to slavery. How could he make this case without alienating conservative Illinois voters?

The Peoria speech, which initiated his dramatic political rise, showed the tools he would use to refashion antislavery language. His three basic tools—history, humanity, and the Declaration of Independence as the nation's higher law—were standard antislavery ones. Lincoln used them with special skill at Peoria.

In history, he found evidence of antislavery sentiment among the Founders—sentiment grounded in a dedication to self-government that reached back to the seventeenth-century British civil wars. In humanity, he identified fundamental characteristics that bridged the racial gap and negated the proslavery views of blacks as mere chattel. The higher law posed a special problem, because it was a loose cannon. Eloquently expanding on the arguments of previous antislavery politicians and authors, Lincoln transformed the higher law, potentially anarchistic and omnidirectional, into a force for renewed patriotism. He did so by demonstrating that the nation itself originated in a higher law: the ideal of human equality announced in the Declaration of Independence and codified in the Constitution.

Although these ideas were not original, his mixing and calibration of them were. He cautiously avoided the extremes of sensationalism and sentimentality that marked other uses of them. He also avoided sectionalism. Trying "to convince and persuade," in his words, rather than denounce or exaggerate, as he saw other reformers doing, he built his case rationally, with winning touches of emotion, poetry, and sarcasm.[99]

The lawyer Henry Whitney witnessed the tall, rawboned Lincoln, who looked like "a rough intelligent farmer," deliver the speech on the portico of "a dingy, dirty courthouse" in Peoria on the evening of October 16, 1854. The speech, a reply to Stephen Douglas's oration in defense of the Kansas-Nebraska Act given earlier that day, drew cheers, long applause, and handkerchief waving from the crowd, which filled the courthouse grounds. Whitney recalled, "I have never heard that speech equalled before or since except by Lincoln himself."[100]

We can understand the speech's appeal. For the first time in his career, Lincoln verbalized publicly the antislavery feelings he had long harbored, feelings shared by many in his Illinois audience who, whatever their feelings on race, were appalled by proslavery legislation and were hungry for a convincing attack on slavery by a politician.

Why did he delay until October 1854 before coming out full throttle against slavery? It's well known that the Kansas-Nebraska Act roused him from political torpor and made him a dedicated champion of the antislavery cause. Less understood is his alarm over proslavery centrifugalism. In Lincoln's mind, Kansas-Nebraska did far more than open up the western territories to slavery; it threatened to lead to the unchecked expansion of American slavery throughout the Western Hemisphere. Upon the passage of the bill, he declared, "We were thunderstruck and stunned; and we reeled and fell in utter confusion."[101] Seeing that slavery, "the genius of Discord himself," was now free to spread, he realized that "shocks, and throes, and convulsions must ceaselessly follow." His aim at Peoria, he announced, was to show that Douglas's bill was not only "wrong in its direct effect, letting slavery into Kansas and Nebraska" but also "wrong in its prospective principle, allowing it to spread to every other part of the wide world, where men can be found inclined to take it.[102]

The "wide world" meant, primarily, nations to the south eyed by proslavery expansionists. As he put it in one of his 1858 debates with Douglas: "If Judge Douglas' policy upon this question succeeds, and gets fairly settled down, until all opposition is crushed out, the next thing will be a grab for the territory of poor Mexico, an invasion of the rich lands of South America, then the adjoining islands will follow, each one of which promises additional slave fields."[103] The spread of slavery, he wrote during the secession crisis in February 1861, would put America "on the high-road to a slave empire." He said of the Southern states, "If we surrender, it is the end of us, and of the government. They will repeat the experiment upon us *ad libitum*. A year will not pass, till we shall have to take Cuba as a condition upon which they will stay in the Union."

How justified was his fear of slavery's hemispheric expansion? Very justified, if we consider the stated goals of slavery's defenders.

Douglas proclaimed neutrality on slavery, which, he maintained, would take root only where it was established by a territory's voters and enforced by local police regulations. But as Lincoln noted, Douglas's "*declared* indifference" was, in fact, "covert *real* zeal for the spread of slavery."[104] Douglas's proslavery colors came out when he said of Central America, "the time will come when our destiny, our institutions, our safety will compel us to have it," and of Cuba, "I do not care if you want it or not . . . we are compelled to take it, and we can't help it."[105] In his debates with Lincoln, Douglas declared, "The time may come, indeed has now come, when our interests would be advanced by the acquisition of the island of Cuba. (Terrific applause.) When we get Cuba we must take it as we find it, leaving the people to decide the question of slavery for themselves, without interference on the part of the federal government, or of any State of this Union. So, when it becomes necessary to acquire any portion of Mexico or Canada, or of this continent or the adjoining islands, we must take them as we find them, leaving the people free to do as they please, to have slavery or not, as they choose."[106]

Douglas feigns fairness here, leaving the decision on slavery to the people in America's future colonized nations, but he well knows that Cuba, Mexico, and the Caribbean islands would decide for slavery, while an American takeover of Canada, which was controlled by England, was highly unlikely. Areas to the south were common targets of proslavery expansionists such as Senator Jefferson Davis, who declared, "Cuba must be ours" to "increase the number of slaveholding constituencies"; he envisioned a slave empire that would also include the Yucatán, Panama, and other Latin American countries.[107] The North Carolina congressman Thomas Clingman concurred. "I should like to see Cuba a part of this Union," he said, adding that "the natural increase of slaves would, in less than a century, justify the extension of our territory, until we should occupy that portion of Mexico which bordered the Gulf, and ultimately Central America and the West Indies islands."[108] The desire to add Cuba as a Southern state led to the Ostend Manifesto, which stated that if Spain refused to sell the island, America had justification to take it by force. The manifesto, issued in October 1854—the month of Lincoln's antislavery speech at Peoria—came to naught, as did most other Southern schemes for expansion. But an eagerness for new slave territory drove the South right up to the Civil War.

It is not surprising, given Lincoln's apprehension over the South's goals, that one of his most sweeping denunciations of slavery came at Peoria. About the "zeal for the spread of slavery," he declared:

> I hate it because of the monstrous injustice of slavery itself. I hate it because it deprives our republican example of its just influence in the world—enables the enemies of free institutions, with plausibility, to taunt us as hypocrites—causes the real friends of freedom to doubt our sincerity, and especially because it forces so many really good men amongst ourselves into an open war with the very fundamental principles of civil liberty—criticising the Declaration of Independence, and insisting that there is no right principle of action but *self-interest*.

Lincoln's loathing of slavery comes through as strongly here as it does in any work by the most radical abolitionist. And yet the terseness of the passage distinguished it sharply from much antislavery writing of the era. He emphasizes the "monstrous injustice" of slavery but omits the whips, gore, rapes, and other horrors that characterized sensational antislavery writing. He avoids the dark-reform rhetoric that permeated much political speech in the 1850s, as in Senator Charles Sumner's blistering "The Crime Against Kansas," which describes the slave power as "the great Terrestrial Serpent" with its "loathsome folds ... coiled around the whole land" and mocks a proslavery politician as a "chivalrous knight" whose mistress was the ugly "harlot, Slavery"—or in Frederick Douglass's "What to the Slave Is the Fourth of July?," with its images of slavery as "a horrible reptile, . . . the venomous creature" that is "nursing at the tender breast of your youthful republic," while "YOUR HANDS ARE FULL OF BLOOD."[109]

Lincoln points out the hypocrisy of America's slaveholding democracy but doesn't go to the subversive extreme of the dark-reform orators, or the the Constitution-burning Garrison, or the violence-condoning Parker.

In some ways, the Peoria speech is a prose version of Stowe's *Uncle Tom's Cabin*. Both works criticize slavery without demonizing Southerners. In Stowe's novel, two of the main Southern characters—Emily Shelby of Kentucky and Augustine St. Clare of Louisiana—are good people who want to free their slaves, while the savage, whip-wielding plantation owner Simon Legree is a transplanted New Englander. Lincoln notes a similar phenomenon: "We know that some southern men do free their slaves, go north, and become tip-top abolitionists; while some northern ones go south, and become most cruel slave-masters."[110] Announcing that he has "no prejudice against the Southern people," Lincoln takes this attitude to a new level when he declares, "They are just what we would be in their situation." If in his law practice he studied his opponent's case just as closely as his own, so as an antislavery politician he opened himself up to the Southern point of view. His tolerance led to his outreach to the South in the First Inaugural ("We are not enemies, but friends. We must not be enemies") and the Second Inaugural ("With malice toward none; with charity for all").[111]

If both Stowe and Lincoln avoided attacking Southerners in general, they did pillory the slave dealer. In *Uncle Tom's Cabin*, the coarse trader Haley, who views slavery as "just business" and blacks as "critters" who "ain't like white folks . . . ; they gets over things," buys Uncle Tom and sells him into the Deep South.[112] Also, he and his slave-catching sidekicks Marks and Tom Loker pursue the fugitives Eliza and George Harris as they flee north with their child, whom Haley wants to buy. The Shelbys do not want to sell their chattels to Haley, but they must do so to pay off debts. Lincoln in his Peoria speech describes the Southerner's predicament: "[Y]ou have amongst you, a sneaking individual, of the class of native tyrants, known as the 'SLAVE-DEALER.' He watches your necessities, and crawls up to buy your slave, at a speculating price. If you cannot help it, you sell to him; but if you can help it, you drive him from your door. You despise him utterly. You do not recognize him as a friend, or even as an honest man."[113]

It did not satisfy either Lincoln or Stowe merely to comment on Southerners and slavery; they must also consider the historical roots of the antislavery impulse. In *Uncle Tom's Cabin*, the runaway slave George Harris invokes the founding fathers and the Hungarian revolutionary Lajos Kossuth when he takes up a gun against his pursuers—a controversial scene of slave rebellion that for many years thrilled Stowe's readers and the audiences of the numerous plays and films based on the novel.

When revisiting history, Lincoln was interested not in drama but in accuracy. We tend not to think of him as a historian, but his knowledge of the history of slavery was remarkable. Fascinated by origins, he privately recorded key historical dates: 1434, when the enslavement of Africans began in Spain (he recognized race-based slavery as purely a social construction, referring wryly to "the invention [in 1434] of negroes, or, of the present mode of using them"); 1501–3, when Spain transported enslaved people to its American colonies; 1516–17, when Spain's Charles V escalated the African slave trade; 1620, when a Dutch ship brought enslaved Africans to Virginia [it was not known in Lincoln's time that a British ship had brought more than twenty Africans to Virginia a year earlier];[114] 1626, when slavery was introduced in New Amsterdam; 1776, when there were some six hundred thousand enslaved persons in America; and 1855, when the number had soared to 3.4 million.[115]

He knew that the history of the nation's founders was largely a construct of the contemporary viewer. Looking at the founding generation, Southerners saw a group of leaders—Jefferson, Washington, Madison, Monroe, and others—who themselves held people in bondage and who produced a Constitution that condoned slavery.

Although Lincoln understood this proslavery view, he also saw a strong antislavery impulse among the Founders.[116] It was clear to him that they anticipated the eventual extinction of slavery. In the Constitution, they established basic human rights that had been previously announced in the Declaration of Independence. In the Ordinance of 1787, as he told the Peoria audience, they registered their animus against slavery's expansion by reserving vast expanses of land northwest of the Ohio River for freedom. In the three decades after 1790, they took increasingly harsh action against the slave trade, which was punished in 1808 by corporal and pecuniary penalties and, when those proved insufficient, by the death penalty, imposed in 1820, the year that saw the passage of the Missouri Compromise, intended to quell tensions over slavery. Slavery had always been something that America's political leaders (mainly Northern ones, but also some Southerners) had wanted to retard and restrict.

The Kansas-Nebraska Act, which left the decision on slavery to voters in the territories, betrayed this antislavery impulse and defied the intentions of the Founders.

The Peoria speech was Lincoln's first full presentation of this history of antislavery politics. His later speeches, especially the one at Cooper Union in 1860, enriched this narrative. Recounting history alone, however, would not draw many to the antislavery side. Essential to his argument was an emphasis on humanity. To demonstrate that blacks were humans was to take a major step toward affirming their rights. But he had to be extremely careful. Many white Americans, as seen, regarded blacks as inferior or subhuman—a view bolstered by ethnology and by reactionary interpretations of the Bible. To enter into the subjectivity of blacks and dwell at length on their suffering was to risk being dismissed as overly radical.

Uncle Tom's Cabin again provides a point of comparison to the Peoria speech. Although many readers were so moved by Stowe's portraits of African American emotional life that they embraced the antislavery cause, the novel struck conservative reviewers, including some Whigs in central Illinois, as an example of disruptive abolitionism. An essayist for the *Quincy Whig* (a paper that had published one of Lincoln's poems) argued that while Stowe successfully portrayed "the evil, the wretchedness, the crime, the degradation, the sin of slavery," she went too far in expressing empathy for blacks. The essayist explained, "Sympathy for suffering, and oppression, is a natural, and noble characteristic of the human heart, . . . but African slavery is a peculiar case," and whites must "suffer their sympathies to be governed by their judgment, and guided by their discretion." Stowe lacked such judgment. By suggesting that blacks had the same feelings as whites, she ignored "those insuperable feelings of aversion and disgust entertained by a great majority of the people of the Northern States towards the Africans." She therefore exhibited the "insane fanaticism" of extreme abolitionists, who were responsible for "the years of trouble, discord, and dissension" that had made America "a scene of ceaseless strife and turmoil."[117]

To avoid such censure, Lincoln had to perform a deft maneuver. Privately, he could say that the memory of chained blacks was a "continual torment" in his mind, with the power to make him "miserable," but if in the political arena he dwelt at length on the suffering of the enslaved he risked being dismissed as a flaming radical. And so in the Peoria speech he swiftly and pungently highlighted the humanity of the enslaved people without depicting individual anguish. He pointedly used the kind of nonhuman imagery that produced humor in other contexts. If in his everyday jokes and stories he exploded pretension by comparing people to animals or things, at Peoria he made similar comparisons to expose slavery as utterly dehumanizing. He mentioned the slave pen near the Capitol, where, he said, "droves of negroes were collected, temporarily kept, and finally taken to Southern markets, precisely like droves of horses."[118] He said that Southerners' desire to take their enslaved workers to Nebraska just as they took their hogs was "perfectly logical, if there is no difference between hogs and negroes," but, he added, "you thus require me to deny the humanity of the negro."

He used nonhuman comparisons to point out contradictions in the South's racial attitudes. Why had many Southerners in 1820 supported the law passed that year which made the slave trade punishable by death? After all, they "never thought of hanging men for catching and selling wild horses, wild buffaloes or wild bears." And how about the fact that more than four hundred thousand free blacks lived in the United States and the territories? If sold into slavery, they would be worth around $200 million. "How comes this vast amount of property to be running about without owners? We do not see free horses or free cattle running at large. How is this?"

His most controversial use of nonhuman images at Peoria—one cited by those who cast him as an incendiary—came in his devastating assault on Douglas's views on race. Douglas, he declared, "had always considered this government was made for the white people and not for the negroes." This was "the key to the great mistake" behind the Kansas-Nebraska Act. "It shows," Lincoln declared, "that the Judge has no very vivid impression that the negro is a human; and consequently has no idea that there can be any moral question in legislating about him. In his view, the question of whether a new country shall be slave or free, is a matter of as utter indifference, as it is whether his neighbor shall plant his farm with tobacco, or stock it with horned cattle."[119] Horned cattle, tobacco, hogs, horses, wild buffaloes, and bears— Lincoln at Peoria implemented his antislavery political ecology.

If he accentuated the humanity of blacks, he also fused the higher law doctrine with patriotism—a tricky task because the higher law was appropriated for both anti- and proslavery uses. The problems surrounding the higher law become clear in the *Quincy Whig* review of *Uncle Tom's Cabin*. The reviewer, while impressed by the novel, complained that Stowe endorsed lawbreaking by making heroes of those who defied the Fugitive Slave Act. She thus placed herself among those who "raise their eyes to Heaven, and with an impious hypocrisy worthy of [the Puritan leader] Cromwell, talk of 'a higher law!'" For the reviewer, this made her an anarchist who "would excite her countrymen to the disobedience of the laws!" And such law flouting could breed civil war. In the reviewer's words, "[Stowe] would, for the

---

---

accomplishment of her purpose, risk the creation of the most terrible of all conflicts, a civil war:—and, with a disregard of consequences worthy of an Abolitionist, would lead the poor objects of her compassion on to liberty, and happiness, through an ocean of blood and tears!"[120]

Lincoln, fully aware of conflicting interpretations of the higher law, followed the lead of previous antislavery politicians by channeling this potentially anarchistic cultural current into two documents treasured by most Americans: the Declaration of Independence and the Constitution. Those documents, he knew, were not free of controversy. There was the ongoing quarrel over whether the Constitution was proslavery or antislavery. As for the Declaration of Independence, some, like the Indiana congressman John Pettit, branded it as "a self-evident lie," a statement for which, Lincoln said at Peoria, Pettit would have been hung by the Founders.[121] The phrase Pettit rejected, "all men are created equal," was exactly the one that Lincoln seized upon as the resolution of clashing uses of the higher law. The Declaration overrode distinctions between people and granted life, liberty, and the pursuit of happiness to all. Blacks, as humans, deserved these fundamental rights. The highest of higher laws—what Lincoln at Peoria called "my ancient faith"—was the doctrine of human equality announced in the Declaration of Independence and preserved by human rights passages in the Constitution.

Why, then, not free all the enslaved people immediately? Because the Constitution, as a concession to the South, protected slavery where it already existed, just as it mandated the recovery of fugitives from labor. To deny these facts was to retreat into sectionalism, which could lead to civil war. Lincoln, following the example of his cynosure Henry Clay, devoted himself to the nation as a whole. As he announced at Peoria, "I . . . wish to be no less than National in all the positions I may take," avoiding any position that was "narrow, sectional and dangerous to the Union."[122]

Preserving the Union while demonstrating its antislavery foundations, then, remained his highest goal. He had shown at Peoria that he possessed all the weapons necessary to combat centrifugal cultural forces that swirled around him. Over the next five years, these forces continued to assail him, more strongly than ever. His chief opponent, Stephen Douglas, made sure that he felt the full brunt of them. Lincoln battled back valiantly, using the weapons he had unsheathed at Peoria.

The Isms and the Woolly Horse

A n 1860 political cartoon, *The Republican Party Going to the Right House*, shows the party's presidential candidate, Lincoln, being carried on a rail by the party's most famous newspaper editor, Horace Greeley, into a lunatic asylum. Mop haired and awkward, his shirt sleeves rolled up, Lincoln looks back at a miscellaneous crowd of followers and says, "Now my friends I'm almost in, and the millennium is going to begin, so ask what you will and it shall be granted." His acolytes call for social change: a free-love couple argues for "passional attraction" and the banishment of marriage; a Mormon promotes polygamy; a bearded socialist advocates the distribution of property; a spinsterly suffragist predicts woman's ascendancy over man; a tramp asks for a free hotel room; a street tough demands the firing of all policemen so that "the bohoys [*sic*] can run with the machine" and engage in "a muss"; and a dandified African American declares, "De white man hab no rights dat cullud pussons am bound to spect. I want dat understood."[1]

The cartoon is misleading but telling. Actually, Republicans had little tolerance for radicalism or social disruption. They denounced free love, dismissed Mormonism along with slavery as "relics of barbarism,"

The Republican Party Going to the Right House
(New York: Currier & Ives, 1860.) Political cartoon by the lithographer Louis
Maurer that shows Lincoln being carried into a lunatic asylum by the antislavery
newspaper editor Horace Greeley. Lincoln looks backward at reformers who
represent various "isms," including socialism, women's rights, Mormonism,
free love, and the advocacy of equal rights for black people. Lincoln promises
that once he is in office he will fulfill all the demands of the reformers and usher
in the millennium.

preferred free enterprise to socialism, and did not call for women and
African Americans to strip white males of power.

But the cartoon accurately reflects virulent anti-Republican hostility on the part of Democrats and Southerners, who criticized Lincoln's
party for its alleged association with subversive "isms" that, in their
view, threatened to ruin the nation.

The cartoon also points out a very real problem that Lincoln and
others faced in the mid-1850s: political and social fragmentation. The
collapse of the Whig Party let loose an array of factions. In June 1858,
looking back at the formation of the Republican Party four years

earlier, Lincoln declared, "Of *strange, discordant*, and even, *hostile* elements, we gathered from the four winds, and *formed* and fought the battle through, under the constant hot fire of a disciplined, proud, and pampered enemy."[2] The Republicans stood to the left of Democrats on many issues, and if you squinted at them from an unfriendly viewpoint, as the Democrats did, their components blended into many other unconventional isms that bubbled up in the cauldron of antebellum culture.

Seeing that his party had burst into fragments that were often mistaken for radical isms, Lincoln took an active role in shaping a new fusion party that was appealingly moderate and yet firmly devoted to antislavery principles.

Lincoln correctly described the shattering of the old party system and the "hot fire" of insults that were hurled at Republicans. The epithet "Black Republicanism"—the worst ism of all, in the Democrats' view—raised the specter of racial reversal that the Republicans would supposedly bring about. A Democratic journalist wrote that the Republican Party, ranging from members "who can go a little nigger" to ones "who can go the whole nigger," championed "the various isms and fanaticisms that have infected our country . . . ; forsooth, witchism, foolism, mesmerism, abolitionism, knownothingism, spiritualism, &c., &c."[3]

Such denunciation by Democrats prompted New York's Robert Emmet, the lead-off speaker at the first national Republican convention in Philadelphia in June 1856, to confront the isms charge. "They may call us Black Republicans and Negro-Worshippers," he said. "They may say that we mean to concentrate and gather under our wings all the odds and ends of parties, all the isms of the day. Be it so. Let them come at us with all their isms. We will merge them all in that great ism: patriotism. [Rapturous and prolonged cheering.]"[4]

Some Republicans, especially the mercurial Horace Greeley, did champion passing isms. Lincoln had a different approach to the isms. He observed them and channeled their energies in ways that combatted two specific ones: sectionalism, which he tried to challenge at every turn, and what he called "Douglasism"—that is, the Democratic Party's effort, under Stephen A. Douglas, to open the way for the spread of slavery.[5] His refusal to get caught up in other isms in spite of constant charges of being their defender is not adequately appreciated. His reaction against such charges helps explain the doggedness of his pursuit of what in 1854 he called America's *central idea . . . the equality of men.*"

WOOLLY HORSE, WOOLLY PARTY

Stephen Douglas pounced quickly and hard. In 1854, the year that saw the passage of his Kansas-Nebraska Act, he declared the Whig Party dead. (In a wry comeback, Lincoln announced himself at a political rally as a ghost.) Soon Douglas was insisting that the fusion party being rebuilt on its ruins was an amalgam of wild isms. In the 1856 presidential campaign, which pitted the Democrat James Buchanan against the Republican John Frémont, Douglas repeatedly delivered a stump speech that, he hoped, would kill off the fledgling Republican Party. To raucous audiences, he declared:

> The black republican army is an allied army, composed of Know Nothings, Abolitionists, Free Soilers, Maine Liquor Law men, (laughter,) woman's right men, (increased laughter,) Anti-renters, Anti-Masons, and all the isms that have been sloughed off from all the honest parties in the country, and have made a combination against the Democracy. We have got to fight this allied army. . . . Our business is to bury all the isms and all their allies in one common grave in November next.[6]

The anti-ism argument was repeated by many other Democrats who wanted to present Frémont and the Republicans as troublesome radicals. One journalist, insisting that only the Democrat Buchanan could save the nation, lambasted Frémont as "a strictly sectional candidate for the Presidency, nominated by the North, sustained by an abolition conglomerate of all the *isms* at war with the rights of the States and the perpetuity of our blessed Union."[7] Governor Henry Wise of Virginia told a cheering crowd at Richmond that if Frémont was elected, isms would rule the land, and civil war would surely follow. Wise announced, "It [the Republican Party] is all the isms, I say, combined in the superlative ism, which I denounce as demonism." He asserted that the choice of "slavery or abolition, Frémont or Buchanan, democracy or demonism . . . are fearful issues; they are issues of peace or war—of civil war, of blood, disunion and death. [Tremendous cheers.]"[8]

Civil war, blood, death. Surely, this was an overreaction to Frémont, the reserved western explorer and former California senator who had been chosen by the Republicans because, while opposed to slavery, he came without the controversial reputation of more outspoken candidates such as Salmon Chase and William Henry Seward. But for Democrats, Frémont was like any other Black Republican—vilely antislavery and overly sympathetic to blacks.

To highlight his supposedly Negrophile tendencies, Democrats seized on an unusual symbol associated with him: the Woolly Horse. In 1847, the showman Phineas T. Barnum, always on the lookout for curiosities, purchased a brown, curly-haired horse, without a mane or a tail, and waited for the right moment to put it on exhibit. The moment came in 1850, after Frémont, who had been lost for weeks while exploring the snow-bound Rockies, emerged from his trek unharmed. Barnum seized the public excitement over the adventure by claiming that Frémont in his travels had captured an "extremely complex" beast, "made up of the Elephant, Deer, Horse, Buffalo, Camel, and Sheep," that "easily bounds twelve or fifteen feet high."[9] A legend arose about Frémont and his men in the wilds having chased this creature as it flew along, leaping many yards at a time. Frémont's father-in-law, Thomas Hart Benton, sued Barnum for his chicanery, but the lawsuit only increased interest in the Woolly Horse and its alleged connection to Frémont.

In the 1856 race, Frémont, said his political enemies, was the Woolly Horse—woolly in the sense of being an abolitionist who defended black people. A Democratic reporter branded Frémont as the "merest tool" of "Northern fanatics" like Seward and Giddings. "The 'Woolly Heads' at Philadelphia," the reporter wrote, "have mounted the Woolly Horse and are now going strong for *wool*. It is their pretended love for wool which induced them to nominate Fremont.... Oh, their love [is] for any thing that wears *wool*, from a black sheep down to a nigger."[10] An Ohio paper averred that "The genuine Woolly Head Republicans think the day is not far distant when they can say, 'nigger ahead, white man behind.' ... Freemen of Ohio! Choose to-day—Fremont and Nigger Supremacy or Buchanan and a government for white men!"[11]

A political cartoon pictured Buchanan as an antlered buck whose rear legs kick the woolly horse, Frémont, over a cliff. Frémont cries, "O I shall never get to the White House. Why did Barnum sell me to Greeley & Seward?"—which elicits Buchanan's command: "Carry this Woolly Horse back to Barnum, if he's not too much injured ... The Union forever!"[12]

By 1856, Lincoln was a known antislavery politician. The previous year, he had almost won a seat in the US Senate from Illinois. The state legislature gave him forty-five votes on the first ballot—just five shy of the number needed for victory. In later ballots, maneuvering by the opposition chipped away at his lead. Alarmed at the growing support for the proslavery Democrat Joel Matteson, he told his backers to shift to the antislavery Democrat Lyman Trumbull, who won the seat. Lincoln's rising visibility resulted in the Republican Party nearly choosing him as Frémont's running mate at its first national convention, held in Philadelphia in June 1856. The spot went instead to the New Jersey politician William L. Dayton. In the fall, Lincoln campaigned widely in Illinois for the Frémont/Dayton ticket.

During the campaign he gained valuable practice in representing a "woolly" party. In one speech, replying to the charge that "Mr. Lincoln and the woolly party are working to endanger if not dissolve the Union," Lincoln said that that he "would go for Fremont . . : —would go for the woolly horse itself, if necessary to secure congressional prohibition of slavery in the territories."[13] In another speech, responding to a Democrat in the audience who shouted that Frémont was "a woolly head," Lincoln insisted that the Republican Party was actually right in step with Washington, Jefferson, and Clay and thus walked in "old paths." Clueless as to how to refute Lincoln's historical argument, the heckler said that Frémont "found the woolly horse and ate dogs." Lincoln retorted, "*That* aint true—but if it was, how does it prove that Fremont is a *woolly head*—how?" No answer came from the heckler. Lincoln: "You're *treed*, my friend. [Loud laughter.]"

But opponents of the Republicans made sure that "woolly" stuck to the party. Lincoln himself was accused of woolliness. In the 1860 presidential race, Stephen Douglas's running mate, Herschel V. Johnson of Georgia, said of the Republican Party that you might "simmer it down, and then dissolve it in a fluid, and all you could find would be 'WOOLLY-HEAD, WOOLLY-HEAD,'" and that America should be "ready for disunion in the case of Lincoln's election."[14] The *New York Herald* printed a poem that associated Lincoln with a sick, lame Woolly Horse, meant to symbolize his party's advocacy of futile ideas about racial equality:

> Oh, the Woolly Horse has got the ails,
> And up Salt River [that is, toward oblivion]
>   started,

Where Old Abe is splitting rails
All sad and broken hearted.[15]

For the Democrats, the Woolly Horse was the unsightly mascot of Black Republicanism.

NAVIGATING THE ISMS

Among the other isms commonly used to denounce Lincoln's party were Maine Lawism, Know-Nothingism, and women's rights. It's understandable that Republicans were accused of an association with these isms. Many Republicans supported the 1851 Maine Law, which prohibited the sale of alcohol, in their conviction that slavery to the bottle was akin to chattel slavery. Know-Nothingism—the secret anti-Catholic movement so called because its members pledged to say nothing about it to outsiders—held appeal for conservative Protestants and nativists in the party who feared the influx of foreigners in America. Women's rights, while not a popular movement, joined hands with the Republican Party in the 1856 race, when, for the first time, women turned out in great numbers to support the wife of a presidential candidate, Jessie Benton Frémont.

Lincoln learned how to turn these issues to his advantage by avoiding narrow association with any of them while directing their supporters to his main project of stopping slavery's spread.

That he did so is remarkable because he was surrounded by partisans of these issues. Prohibition was a key cause for several people close to him, including his law partner William Herndon, his former partner John T. Stuart, and the newspaper editor Simeon Francis. Lincoln joined these men in signing a letter requesting the publication of a temperance lecture given in January 1853 by the Reverend James Smith before a convention of the Sangamon County Maine Law Alliance.[16] We can surmise that Lincoln gave his signature, which was last on the list, reluctantly—to go along with his Republican friends, perhaps—since Smith's speech used the kind of uncharitable language he frowned upon. Smith described the drunkard as "a miserable being with bloated face and shabby appearance, frequenting the lowest haunts of vice . . . forever under the influence of strong drink, stretched senseless in the gutter; or rolling in the mud on the highway; or staggering into the midst of his unhappy family, besmeared with blood and dirt."[17]

Maine Law fever struck William Herndon especially hard. Though he was a tippler whom Lincoln once had to bail out of jail after he and some hooligans drunkenly trashed a building, Herndon joined several temperance groups, including the Washingtonians and the Temple of Honor, and served as president of the Maine Law Alliance. After being elected as Springfield's mayor in April 1854, Herndon went door to door to liquor sellers, urging them to close down. He pushed for a prohibition law and was thrilled when the Illinois legislature passed one in February 1855, subject to a referendum. Did Lincoln write this law? In the early twentieth century, promoters of the Eighteenth Amendment (the Prohibition Amendment) spread the story that Lincoln was the bill's author. A bald effort to put his imprimatur on prohibition, the story was either an intentional fabrication or a case of old-age misremembering on the part of the ailing temperance advocate James B. Merwin, who claimed to have been "an intimate friend" of Lincoln's (a highly dubious claim: Lincoln's son Robert reported that he had no recollection at all of Merwin).[18]

At any rate, when the Illinois prohibition bill was brought to a popular vote in June 1855, it was defeated. Herndon glumly wrote Theodore Parker, "We got badly beaten in our temperance move. . . . It is very hard to overcome interest, appetite, habit and the low demagogue who rules the synod in the grocery [that is, the saloon]."[19] Herndon may well have drowned his disappointment in liquor, as he did at many other difficult moments in his life. As one historian writes of Herndon:

"A leader in the temperance movement, his greatest failing was his addiction to alcohol."[20]

Lincoln shared neither Herndon's zeal for prohibition nor his addiction; on this point, he was also distant from other intemperate temperance men he knew, such as Usher Linder and Richard Yates. Although Lincoln joined the Sons of Temperance, he must have done so in the spirit of his 1842 temperance address, in which he urged nondrinkers to team up with drinkers in fighting addiction. Of course he had no such problem himself. In answer to Stephen Douglas, who asked about his attitude toward the temperance movement, he replied, "I am temperate in *this*, that I don't drink anything."[21] As a lawyer, he was flexible on temperance—in the courtroom, he sometimes defended prohibition advocates and at other times liquor sellers.[22] As a politician, he aligned himself with temperance mainly because he knew it would attract Republican support. For instance, when running for the Senate in 1854 he received assurance that a certain legislator would back him "if he finds you safe, as I assure him he will, on Anti-Nebraska, Maine Law, Good Whig &c &c—."[23] However, Lincoln did not want to push the temperance cause too zealously, which might have alienated would-be Democratic fence jumpers or the increasing number of German and Irish émigrés in Illinois, groups that were repelled by the temperance movement. On temperance, Lincoln sought a middle point between extremes, positioning himself carefully in the center.

He performed a similar maneuver with regard to Know-Nothingism. The Know-Nothings became a significant force in the mid-1850s, just when Lincoln was rising to political prominence. Stirred to xenophobia over the surge of European immigrants in America, many of them Irish or Germans escaping poverty or persecution in their native countries, the Know-Nothings (soon renamed the American Party) sent candidates to office throughout the nation, aiming to introduce nativist legislation.

By 1854, they numbered one million nationally and elected eight governors and hundreds of congressmen, as well as the mayors of Boston, Chicago, and Philadelphia.[24] They were especially successful in the Northeast, as in Massachusetts, where in 1854 they won the governorship and all but three of the state legislature's four hundred seats. They clashed with Democrats and immigrants in major cities, including Chicago, Baltimore, Cincinnati, and New Orleans, in political riots that killed more than seventy people and wounded several hundred.[25]

Initially, Lincoln treated the Know-Nothings dismissively. When in 1854 Douglas accused him of being connected with the group, Lincoln quipped in a speech that "he *Knew Nothing* in regard to the Know-Nothings." If the group "had for its object interference with the rights of foreigners," Lincoln said, "he was unqualifiedly against it; and if there was anything good in it, why, he said God speed it! [Laughter and applause.]" He turned the tables on Douglas, joking that if the group's "members were bound by such horrid oaths as Judge Douglas told about, he would really like to know how the Judge found out his secrets? [Renewed laughter.]"[26]

By 1855, when Know-Nothingism was in full flush, Lincoln took it seriously. Viewing nativism as a form of hateful prejudice, he redoubled his commitment to human equality. One of his fullest condemnations of ethnic and religious bias came in his August 1855 letter to Joshua Speed, in which he wrote:

> I am not a Know-Nothing. That is certain. How could I be? How can any one who abhors the oppression of negroes, be in favor of degrading classes of white people? Our progress in degeneracy appears to me to be pretty rapid. As a nation, we began by declaring that "*all men are created equal.*" We now practically read it "all men are created equal, *except negroes.*"

When the Know-Nothings get control, it will read "all men are created equal, except negroes, *and foreigners, and catholics*." When it comes to this I should prefer emigrating to some country where they make no pretence of loving liberty—to Russia, for instance, where despotism can be taken pure, and without the base alloy of hypocracy [*sic*].[27]

This paragraph, written to his closest friend in the same letter in which he confessed his "continual torment" over slavery, would prove to be a key one in Lincoln's career. His denunciation of America's "progress in degeneracy" toward racism and nativism matched the deep bitterness expressed in the mid-1850s by Walt Whitman, who wrote that recent political and social developments showed how "villainy and shallowness . . . are just as eligible to These States as to any foreign despotism, kingdom, or empire."[28] Whitman responded to the surrounding intolerance and prejudice by writing poetry in which he democratically announced himself as "pleas'd with the native and pleas'd with the foreign," asserting that he did not separate "the white from the black, or the native from the immigrant just landed at the wharf."[29] But he quickly learned that his poems would not have immediate social impact. He wrote in 1856 that only a new kind of leader—a shrewd, beard-faced "American blacksmith or boatman" who would "come down from the West across the Alleghenies, and walk into the Presidency"—could save America.[30]

Unbeknownst to him, the kind of president he imagined was in the making in Illinois. During the first half of 1856, Lincoln worked to push the Republican Party, already dedicated toward containing slavery, toward a more egalitarian position on immigration and religion. In his turn away from Know-Nothingism, Lincoln pointed himself and the nation toward the democratic embrace of people of various nationalities and faiths that would characterize his presidency.

Promoting sympathy for foreigners—especially Roman Catholic or

WALT WHITMAN IN 1855

Jewish ones—was not easy for a Republican, because antislavery and nativism often went hand in hand. Lincoln did not want the Republican Party to lose the loyalty of so-called Old Line Whigs—conservatives who opposed both the extension of slavery and the unrestricted admission of immigrants. In late 1855 he rejected the invitation from the abolitionist Owen Lovejoy to join the new antislavery fusion party because he recognized the popularity of nativism among leftover conservative Whigs. He wrote the notoriously radical Lovejoy: "Not even *you* are more anxious to prevent the extension of slavery than I; and yet the political atmosphere is such, just now, that I fear to do any thing, lest I do wrong. . . . I have no objection to 'fuse' with any body provided I can

383

fuse on ground which I think is right; and I believe the opponents of slavery extension could now do this, if it were not for this K. N. ism." He insisted that the new fusion party could not succeed "until we can get the elements of this organization [that is, the Know-Nothings]." He added, "Of their principles I think little better than I do of those of the slavery extensionists. Indeed I do not perceive how any one professing to be sensitive to the wrongs of the negroes, can join in a league to degrade a class of white men."[31]

He was genuinely repelled, therefore, by the intolerance of the Know-Nothings. And so, on the immigration issue, he worked for progress tactfully, often behind the scenes. He undertook this delicate maneuver in two state political conventions that he attended in 1856: the convention in Decatur, Illinois, in February and the one in Bloomington, fifty miles north of there, in June.

At the conventions, which led to the formation of the Illinois Republican Party, Lincoln's revulsion against Know-Nothingism moved him toward an especially broad interpretation of the Declaration of Independence. The Decatur meeting of state anti-Kansas-Nebraska Act newspaper editors saw him collaborate with Georg Schneider, editor of the Illinois *Staats-Zeitung*, to provide an anti-nativist plank for the emerging party.

Born in Bavaria in 1823, Schneider had been condemned to death after participating in the revolution of 1848 but escaped to America, where he edited a St. Louis newspaper before establishing the *Staats-Zeitung* in Chicago. He and many other German Forty-Eighters who joined the antislavery ranks of the Republican Party felt threatened by the suddenly potent Know-Nothings. In Schneider's words, the Germans "were in a most unpleasant and critical position, and their political future seemed dark." To combat the Know-Nothing surge, he proposed at Decatur a plank that challenged nativism. His proposal at first aroused "a storm of protest" at the convention, and he was overcome by "utter despair." But Lincoln intervened and mollified the convention's attendees. He announced that Schneider's ideas were "already contained in the Declaration of Independence and you cannot form a new party on proscriptive principles."[32] "This declaration of Mr. Lincoln's," Schneider remarked, "saved the resolution and, in fact, helped establish the new party on the most liberal democratic basis." The convention, swayed by Lincoln, adopted a plank in its platform forbidding discrimination "on account of religious opinions, or in consequence of place of birth."

The antinativist precedent having been established, the major Republican convention in Bloomington adopted a similar plank, as did the Republican National Convention held in Philadelphia in June.

In the presidential race that year, Lincoln vehemently opposed the candidacy of the Know-Nothing Party's candidate, the ex-president Millard Fillmore. He attacked Fillmore's position on slavery and added that he "could not go for Fillmore for another reason": Lincoln "did not like the Know Nothings." He assured his audience, "They were, however, an ephemeral party, and would soon pass away."[33] But nativists had broad appeal, as he learned that November, when Fillmore won 22 percent of the popular vote—enough to tilt the key states of Illinois, Indiana, Pennsylvania, and New Jersey away from Frémont to Buchanan. That Lincoln in 1860 would win these states owed much to his success in reacting to Know-Nothingism as he did to other controversial isms: he avoided taking a partisan stance and making extreme statements.

On the one hand, he made known his opinion that prejudice against foreigners resembled prejudice against blacks, and that both biases subverted the nation's central idea of human equality. Having made this point in his 1855 letter to Speed, he went public with the argument four years later when his letter on the topic, addressed to the German-born journalist Theodore Canisius, appeared in the *Illinois State Journal*. Lincoln agreed with Canisius's criticism of a stiff naturalization law in Massachusetts, and he went on to argue that the whole idea of America was the elevation, not degradation, of immigrants. "I have some little notoriety," Lincoln wrote, "for commiserating the oppressed condition of the negro; and I should be strangely inconsistent if I could favor any project for curtailing the existing rights of *white men*, even though born in different lands, and speaking different languages from myself."[34] Shortly after writing this, Lincoln bought a printing press and appointed Canisius as the editor of a German-language newspaper in Springfield, the *Illinois Staats-Anzeiger* (the *Illinois State Advertiser*), which promoted the Republican Party throughout the 1860 race. Lincoln also gathered around him skillful German American operatives, including Gustave Koerner and Carl Schurz. During the Civil War 216,000 troops—about 10 percent of the total Union army—were German-born.

Lincoln's remarkably open attitude toward different religions and nationalities extended to one of the most ostracized groups in America: Jews. Immigration from Europe swelled the US Jewish population from around 4,500 in 1830 to 40,000 in 1845 and 150,000 by 1860.[35] Moving to America in search of opportunity and relief from the persecution they experienced in Europe, Jews succeeded economically, mainly as shopkeepers or peddlers, but they found acceptance into American society difficult. As one rabbi noted, "Suspicion and contempt met [the Jew] at every step, and forced him not seldom, to hide his origin and bury his faith in his bosom." Ulysses S. Grant, who had briefly joined the Know-Nothings in the 1850s, took typically harsh action in December 1862, when he ordered Jews to be expelled from his military department in Tennessee. Lincoln quickly revoked Grant's order—a signal of his warm feeling toward Jews. The feeling was not in all cases mutual, as indicated by the some 2,000 Jews who supported the Confederacy, among them Jefferson Davis's secretary of state, Judah P. Benjamin. But for the large majority of American Jews who supported Lincoln, he was "Rabbi Abraham, . . . one of our nation—the seed of Israel," whose "entire nature," one rabbi opined, was "truly Judaic and truly Jewish in spirit."[36]

In 1862 Lincoln signed into law a bill that provided the nearly seven thousand Jews who served in the Union army with chaplains, and during the war he awarded some fifty military appointments to Jews. He had high regard for his Jewish podiatrist, Issachar Zacharie, whom he appointed as a special envoy to the South. The Jewish photographer Samuel G. Alschuler took two important pictures of Lincoln: one of the beardless lawyer in an ill-fitting, borrowed black coat in 1858, and the other of the bearded president-elect two years later. Lincoln befriended and collaborated politically with a number of Jews.[37] Closest to him was the Illinois haberdasher Abraham Jonas, whom Lincoln called "one of my most valued friends."[38] Born in 1801 in England, Jonas immigrated to the United States in 1819, settling first in Cincinnati and then in Williamstown, Kentucky, before moving to Quincy, Illinois, where he became a lawyer and a Whig politician. He met Lincoln in Whig circles and, like him, joined the Republican Party and campaigned for Frémont in 1856. He became one of Lincoln's most ardent boosters, promoting him both before and after Lincoln's nomination for the presidency in 1860.

During the 1860 presidential campaign, Jonas gave Lincoln a crucial warning about the Know-Nothings. Jonas informed Lincoln that the Democratic congressman Isaac N. Morris was about to go public with the story that Lincoln had been spotted leaving a Know-Nothing lodge in Quincy. Lincoln denied the story and told Jonas not to publicize his denial. As was often true on controversial issues, Lincoln took the cautious route. He wrote Jonas: "Our adversaries think they can gain a point if they could force me to openly deny the charge, by which some degree of offence would be given to the Americans. For this reason it must not publicly appear that I am paying any attention to the charge."[39]

After all, despite his compassion for immigrants, he did not want to alienate holdover Old Line Whigs in the Republican Party who leaned toward the "American" (that is, the Know-Nothing) view of foreigners. He had learned a lesson about party conservatives as early as 1844, when he called a Whig meeting in Springfield to protest against nativist riots in Philadelphia. At the meeting, he expressed deep sympathy for foreigners, but a reporter noted that his was not the typical Whig attitude. The reporter wrote, "Lincoln expressed the kindest, and most benevolent feelings towards foreigners; they were, I doubt not, the sincere and honest sentiments of *his heart*; but they were not those of *his party*."[40]

The truth was that as a Whig and then as a Republican, he had to be careful not to lose the backing of nativists. His experience with A. M. Whitney, the father of his Illinois law colleague Henry C. Whitney, showed how the Know-Nothing movement held sway among conservatives even after it had died as a party. During the 1860 presidential race, Lincoln got word that Whitney was taking steps to win him the nativist vote in Illinois, including contacting the state's former leader of the American Party, John Wilson. Three years later, in the middle of the Civil War, confident that he had saved the state for Lincoln, Whitney approached the president, asking for political favors for Chicago. Whitney reminded Lincoln that he had "worked faithfully" for him in the 1860 campaign as "one of the representatives of the American party."[41]

In the end, religion rather than nationality was a better predictor of how Christian European immigrants cast their vote in the 1860 race: Republicans won the majority of the Protestant vote, while Catholics, in the main, went Democratic.[42] (Jews did not tend to vote as a bloc, as indicated by the editor of New York's *Jewish Messenger*, who wrote, "there is no 'Jewish vote.'")[43] During the Civil War, Lincoln faced the special challenge of generating support among Catholic immigrants. He was able to do so in large part because the war itself stirred patriotic spirit among recently arrived immigrants who saw military service for the Union as a means of gaining respect while earning an income.

One group that took advantage of this trial by fire was the Irish, who before the war had been the favorite targets of the Know-Nothings.[44] Of the some 175,000 Irish who participated in the Civil War, 85 percent fought for the Union. Many were inspired by Irish-born revolutionary leaders who had immigrated to America, including Thomas Francis Meagher, who rallied Irish troops at the beginning of the war, and

Michael Corcoran, who became a Northern hero when he was captured at Bull Run and was treated harshly in a Confederate prison before being freed in an exchange. Lincoln knew these leaders and also consulted with Archbishop John Hughes about appointing Catholic army officers and chaplains for military hospitals. Although many Catholic priests disapproved of abolitionism, most Northern ones supported the Union war effort. The war did not do away with nativism, but it dampened it. Like African American troops, Irish soldiers earned widespread respect for their courage on the battlefield. Although the draft riots in New York in 1863 caused an anti-Irish reaction, Irish priests and soldiers were among the harshest critics of the rioters.

All in all, Lincoln's pivot away from Know-Nothingism toward toleration made possible his productive relationships with foreigners. He had expressed this broadmindedness while on the hustings in Illinois in the 1850s. He mocked the Democrats' supposed regard for foreigners by taking Stephen Douglas to task for saying that when the Founders affirmed human equality, "they were speaking of British subjects on this continent being equal to British subjects born and residing in Great Britain." By this logic, Lincoln said, "not only negroes but white people outside of Great Britain" including "the French, Germans and other white people of the world" were "all gone to pot along with the Judge's inferior races." Lincoln insisted that ethnic and religious difference must foster unity, not division, because people of all nations and faiths who came to America were bonded by its central principle that "all men are created equal."[45]

GIVE 'EM JESSIE!

All men; but how about women? In July 1848, at Seneca Falls, New York, the world's first women's rights convention rewrote the Declaration of Independence to assert that "all men and women are created equal."[46] The approximately 260 women and 40 men who gathered at the two-day convention laid out an ambitious program calling for suffrage, property rights, employment opportunities, and fair marriage laws for women. Similar conventions met regularly over the following decades. Gains in property rights came steadily, as did advances in employment and marriage laws. Woman suffrage, though granted in certain states, did not become enforced nationally until the ratification of the Nineteenth Amendment in 1920.

In the 1850s, women's rights figures were caricatured as manlike oddities. The Republican Party, the alleged home of the isms, was associated with women's rights. To a certain degree, this was true. Leaders of the women's rights movement such as Susan B. Anthony and Elizabeth Cady Stanton, though not always convinced that the Republican Party moved fast enough toward social change, generally aligned themselves with the party. Though the party leaned in a protofeminist direction, it did not openly embrace women's rights, which was considered secondary to the slavery issue.

In 1856, Republicans found in Jessie Benton Frémont an attractive combination of political forthrightness and conventional womanhood. The well-educated daughter of the Jacksonian politician Thomas Hart Benton and the wife of the dashing Republican presidential candidate John Frémont, Jessie was unafraid to express her political opinions and yet remained devoted to her husband and children—a merging of independent thinking and domesticity that Republican voters found irresistible. A Jessie cult arose. (By a happy coincidence, her name corresponded with "Give 'em Jessie!," a slang expression that meant, roughly, "Give 'em hell!") Groups called Jessie Circles, Tribe of Jessie, Sisters of Jessie, and Jessie Clubs sprouted throughout the North. Women turned out at political rallies in unprecedented numbers, gaining a sense of empowerment by shouting, "Our Jessie!"[47] A banner at a New Hampshire rally delivered the bold message "Jessie for the White House." Popular campaign songs included "Oh, Jessie Is a Sweet Bright Lady" (to the tune of

JESSIE BENTON FRÉMONT

"Comin' Through the Rye") and "We'll Give 'Em Jessie" (to the tune of "Wait for the Wagon"). Should Jessie Frémont "preside over the White House," asserted the popular *Frank Leslie's Weekly*, "we may look for a new era of glory," and "we doubt not that she would do much to soften the asperities of sectional strife, and thus quietly, but not the less firmly, exert her influence beyond the circle of her home."[48]

Democrats, on the other hand, saw Jessie as a Republican virago who planned to foist women's rights on the nation. A Boston paper fumed that Jessie's supporters "are looking forward to the nomination of a Woman's Rights Ticket, with one of their noble champions as standard bearer.— The hour of triumph for Abby Folsom and Lucy Stone is at hand. The auspicious day when strong minded women will take their places in the Cabinet and the Senate house is about to dawn."[49] In Pittsburgh, a journalist warned, "When women leave their quiet, happy home, neglect their domestic duties, and participate in public affairs, they become objects of pity, make the judicious grieve, and cause the virtuous to lament their degradation." A Richmond paper declared that Jessie Circles were just "the old Amazonian phalanx, of which [feminist/abolitionist] Abby Kelly is Generalissimo."[50] The *New York Day-Book* went so far as to say "that if Frémont is elected, Jessie is to be president."[51]

Actually, Jessie was neither the heroine idolized by Republicans nor the radical suffragist castigated by the Democrats. She was an intelligent, ambitious woman who had long been exposed to politics but who faced severe private struggles that periodically generated mood disorders and complicated her marriage.

She bore similarities to an emotionally erratic Springfield, Illinois, woman whose presidential ambitions for her husband would, unlike Jessie's, soon reach fruition.

Jessie Benton Frémont and Mary Todd Lincoln had much in common. Though born into slaveholding families, both women envisaged the end of slavery and ended up marrying leading Republicans who represented the North. Both were well educated for their day: Mary had a decade of schooling in Lexington, Kentucky, and was fluent in French; Jessie, according to her biographer, "learned to read by the time she was four years old, and by her teens . . . spoke five languages, read Latin and Greek, and was well versed in history, geography, literature, and science."[52] Both grew up in a political atmosphere. Mary as a child knew Henry Clay and his circle, while Jessie lived much of the time in Washington, DC, and met many prominent associates of her father, the Missouri senator Thomas Hart Benton. Both women became estranged from family members upon marriage. Senator Benton distanced himself from Jessie after she eloped at sixteen with the illegitimate, reputedly Catholic John Frémont; members of the Todd family frowned upon Mary marrying a seeming rube, and Mary in turn snubbed Abe's family. Both women directed great energy toward promoting their husbands. Participating in politics vicariously, each came to be known as her spouse's "kitchen cabinet." Both dealt with money in ways then atypical for women. After John had lost his mining fortune, Jessie provided the family's income by writing books about John and his experiences. Mary, as first lady, overspent government funds and engaged in backroom deals in order to redecorate the White House; after Lincoln's death she used various means to augment the already substantial Lincoln estate, including pilfering White House furniture, selling her dresses, and pleading poverty to win a government pension.

And both women were unafraid to speak their minds to powerful men. In September 1861, Jessie, outraged when Lincoln revoked General Frémont's military order in Missouri emancipating enslaved people there, visited the president in Washington to defend her husband's position. Lincoln rebuffed her, calling her "quite a female politician."[53] But he was married to such a woman. As first lady—a term used regularly for the first time in relation to her—Mary became known for giving political advice to her husband and was dubbed "the lady President" and "the presidentess."[54] She became close to leading politicians, such as Charles Sumner, and she lashed out when one of them crossed her, as in the case of Thaddeus Stevens, who in 1867 opposed awarding her a widow's pension and received her curses in return.

But neither Mary nor Jessie strayed far beyond the appearance of conventional womanhood. They didn't want to ruin their own reputations or their husbands'. Dynamic and independent-minded, they nonetheless disapproved of women's rights reformers and projected a traditional image. Jessie, who supervised a household that included three children and a teenage niece, was praised as "so feminine, . . . attractive as a woman, . . . devoted as a wife."[55] Mary also aligned herself with true womanhood. She assured James Gordon Bennett, whose paper had published the "lady President" comment, that "My character is wholly domestic."[56]

Outwardly Mary honored the cult of domesticity. But she and Abe forged their own kind of marriage.

The Springfield Family

In March 1850, shortly after the death of little Eddie, Mary discovered that she was pregnant. On December 1, 1850, William ("Willie") Wallace Lincoln was born, followed on April 4, 1853, by Thomas Lincoln, nicknamed Tad by his father, who thought the infant's large head made him look like a tadpole. Although advice manuals recommended breastfeeding for ten months, Mary nursed her children for up to two years.[1]

The Lincolns' child-rearing resembled the Romantic view of the Reverend Horace Bushnell, who advised that *"religion loves too much the plays and pleasures of childhood, to limit or repress them by any kind of needless austerity"* [italics in the original][2] The Lincoln children developed at their own pace, with little pressure or interference. Of course reprimands or brief spankings were sometimes called for. But, generally, strict oversight was avoided. Mary told Herndon that her husband said, "'It is my pleasure that my children are free, happy, and unrestrained by parental tyranny. Love is the chain whereby to lock a child to its parents.'"[3]

Bob and Willie were normal learners, but Tad was not; he could not read until he was twelve. Born with a cleft lip and palate, he had a vocal impediment that made him difficult to understand. He became a temperamental boy who in the White House ignored his tutors, ran around, and played. "Let him run," his father would say; "there's time enough yet for him to learn his letters and get poky. Bob was just such a little rascal, and now he is a very decent boy."[4]

Lincoln was right about Bob's rascality. As a youth, Bob came to be known as the "head of pranks."[5] Once he and a few friends tried to reproduce animal tricks they saw at a circus by going into the Lincoln barn and attempting to train dogs to stand on their hind legs and bark, the way the circus lions roared. When all else failed, the boys looped ropes around the dogs' necks and suspended the animals from rafters. A neighbor heard a ruckus and ran to Lincoln in his law office. He rushed to the barn, scattered the boys, and cut down the dogs, two of which had died.

But Bob had a sober side, and he had to endure ridicule from his peers, who called him Cockeye or Cross-eyed Bob because of his condition of right esotropia, a form of strabismus in which the right eye turns inward (his father had left hypertropia, or an upward-turning left eye). In 1853, he entered the preparatory academy of Springfield's newly formed Illinois State University and two years later became a freshman at the university. Although he got better grades in math and science than in the humanities, he was, like his parents, an avid reader. In 1859, he took the entrance exam for Harvard but failed it, upon which his parents sent him to Phillips Exeter Academy in Exeter, New Hampshire. After a year there, he was accepted into Harvard, where he graduated in 1864. He had become a reserved, rather stuffy young man.

Willie was a happy mix of Tad and Bob, combining the former's zest with the latter's intelligence. When he and Tad weren't playing soldier in the White House—setting up a fort on the roof, wearing colorful Zouave uniforms, or playing with the president's guards—they were riding their pony in the backyard or being hauled by their pet goats, which they tied to a wagon. Willie was curious and sensitive, much like his father. He wrote out an accurate timetable of a railroad route from Chicago to Washington, and he precociously composed poetry.

FAMILY POLITICS

If the Lincolns' attitude toward parenting was out of the ordinary, so were their separations. Lincoln's most famous phrase about the slavery-riven nation—"a house divided against itself cannot stand"—makes us reconsider his marriage. Over the years, Abe and Mary were divided in two senses: they were separated from each other for much of the time; and when they were together, emotional outbursts, mainly on Mary's part, frequently drove Abe to go elsewhere, especially his law office. Their marriage was a metonym of the divided nation. And it carried a lesson: a house divided *could* stand if the two sides were thoroughly devoted to the union. Just as Walt Whitman in his poetry offered comradeship and affection as the panacea for the shattered America, so the Lincolns remained devoted to each other and their children despite strains on their relationship.

The strains were real. Abe and Mary had very long spaces in their togetherness. Throughout the 1850s, Abe was on the law circuit or the political hustings for months at a time. In 1850, he was away 175 days and in Springfield 190 days; 1852 saw him traveling 155 days and staying home 200 days—and so on for the rest of the decade.[6] Robert Lincoln recalled that his father "was almost constantly away from home."[7] Lincoln himself conceded in 1858, "I am [away] from home perhaps more than half my time."[8] Understandably, the separations took a toll on the marriage. According to a Springfield neighbor, Mary said that "if her husband had Staid at home as he ought to, that She could love him better."[9] But she was devoted to him and his career as a lawyer and, most of all, as a politician.

Actually, the separations gave both spouses freedom to enjoy other kinds of relationships. Both took advantage of becoming close to different people during the times of separation. For Lincoln, traveling for weeks at a time with his lawyer friends—eating and sleeping with them,

MARY TODD LINCOLN

spending evenings, trading jokes and stories—provided a release into a casual, homosocial environment.

Mary, although she missed Abe when he was away, was to some extent liberated by the arrangement. She formed strong bonds with women friends whom she often addressed with affection and yearning. To Mercy Levering, she wrote, "You know the deep interest I feel for you. . . . [Y]our kind & cheering presence has beguiled many a lonely hour of its length."[10] In another letter, she called her friend "my dearest Merce, the sunlight of my heart." Levering returned Mary's affection, and the two inhabited a female world of intimacy and love.[11] Even as they confessed their love for each other, they happily discussed their marriages. Mary sustained her affectionate language with other woman friends, like Mrs. Hannah Shearer, "I can *never cease* to love you. . . . I shall never cease to miss you."[12] These outcries of love are interspersed with joyful words about her Springfield friends and a forthcoming trip. A later friend, Eliza Slataper, received similar words from Mary, who wrote, "I shall feel lonely beyond expression without you—*come to me.* . . . Do come if you love me."[13]

In an era when such passionate expression of love between women was common, Mary could use such language without raising bourgeois eyebrows. What *did* raise eyebrows was sex radicalism, popularly known as free love. The free-love movement, advocated by reformers like Mary Gove Nichols and Thomas Lake Harris, regarded marriage as an oppressive institution that entrapped women. Marital entrapment was, in fact, widespread in an era when Anglo-American common law still treated the wife as legally, economically, and physically subject to the husband, who had the right to chastise her to the point of physical punishment. According to law, the husband must not inflict permanent physical injury, but this rule was often disregarded in practice, especially in the case of drunken husbands who became uncontrollably abusive. Several of the isms—including free love, women's rights, temperance, spiritualism, and radical abolitionism—protested against the virtual enslavement of women in marriage. Women's rights leaders, in their 1848 Declaration of Sentiments, said of the wife: "In the covenant of marriage, she is compelled to promise obedience to her husband, he becoming, to all intents and purposes, her master—the law giving him power to deprive her of her liberty, and to administer chastisement."[14] More than thirty utopian communities were formed in the United States in the 1840s and '50s. A number of them practiced free love. In communities such as Modern Times on Long Island, the Berlin Heights Community in Ohio, and Ceresco in Fond-du-Lac, Wisconsin, conventional marriage, which was viewed as a prison for women, was replaced by an open arrangement in which women and men followed so-called passional (aka passionate) attraction in choosing sexual partners.

Predictably, free love was attacked in mainstream newspapers, including the ones in central Illinois that the Lincolns read. The Lincolns' local paper, the *Illinois State Journal*, condemning "the Free Love leprosy" at Ohio's Berlin community, described a Love Cure building, where people paired up casually, and a free-love screed that announced "MARRIAGE IS THE SLAVERY OF WOMAN: *Free love is the freedom and equality of woman and man: Polygamy is marriage multiplied:* FREE LOVE IS MARRIAGE ABOLISHED."[15] Another central Illinois paper, the *Ottawa Free Trader*, reported a free-love event in Ohio where a woman said that "altho' she had one husband in Cleveland, *she considered herself married to the whole human race. All men were her husbands, and she had an undying love for them.*" She asked, "*What business is it to the world if one man is the father of my children or ten men are?*"[16] The same paper fumed that the Ceresco, Wisconsin, community observed "the most vile" doctrines, based on "the lowest sensuality." At Ceresco, women could change sexual partners at will, fornication was deemed "holy," and adultery was considered "the highest and truest relation of which two people are capable." Were these principles universally accepted, the paper argued, the world would become "a vast brothel," and nothing would be left but "a prospective generation of bastards and strumpets."[17]

How did the free-love movement influence the Lincolns? While their marriage may have been a house divided saved by mutual devotion, they certainly did not go so far as to accept free love, an idea that willfully flouted the marriage institution and replaced it with individual desire. In Lincoln's eyes, free love provided an anarchic analogue of Southern states that left the American Union. Addressing a crowd in Indianapolis on his trip east in February 1861, he said of the seceding states, "In their view, the Union, as a family relation, would not be anything like a regular marriage at all, but only as a sort of free-love arrangement,—[laughter,]—to be maintained on what that sect calls passionate attraction. [Continued laughter.]"[18]

Beneath the joking was his bedrock belief in union and mutual respect, both nationally and personally. On a personal level, he bore witness to great suffering produced by the marital inequities that generated the women's rights and free-love movements. As we've seen, as a lawyer, he participated in more than twenty cases involving battered wives. In most of these cases, a woman hired him to represent her in a divorce suit against a violently abusive, often alcoholic husband. Lincoln must have argued these divorce cases persuasively, because he had a stellar record in representing such wives. Of the twenty-one cases I've reviewed, his team secured a divorce for the female plaintiff nineteen times; two cases were dismissed. Without overtly endorsing free love or women's rights, Lincoln represented women who had the kinds of husbands who inspired these movements.

It may well be that his close attention as a lawyer to the abuse suffered by many wives influenced his response to his own wife's irregular behavior. His laxness as a parent was matched by his tolerance as a husband. Allegedly, Mary once threw a piece of wood at him when he failed to respond to her appeals for him to tend to the fire. She was known to chase him out of the house, wielding a broomstick, club, or knife.

While such moments pained Lincoln, he also could view them as a healthy letting off of steam, then a rare option for women. He told the story of a henpecked husband, Jones, whose wife drove him out of the house. When asked how he could stand her behavior, Jones replied, "Why, it didn't *hurt* me any; and you've no idea what a *power* of *good* it did Sarah Ann!"[19] Mary's half sister Emilie Todd, who visited Springfield in the winter of 1854, remarked that Mary "had a high temper" and "did not always have it under complete control," but it "was soon over, and her husband loved her none the less, perhaps all the more, for this human frailty which needed his love and patience to pet and coax the sunny smile to replace the sarcasm and tears."[20] A Springfield neighbor, James Gourley, said, "Lincoln & his wife got along tolerably well, unless Mrs L got the devil in her: Lincoln paid no attention—would pick up one of his Children & walked off—would laugh at her—pay no Earthly attention to her when in that wild furious Condition."[21]

It's difficult to say what caused Mary's mood swings. Her problems were in part physical. She reported having near-hemorrhagic menstrual periods. With striking openness in a time when such statements were tabooed, she wrote to Abe, "I have had one of my severe attacks. . . . Some of *these periods* will launch me away."[22] Other of her symptoms were headaches, fatigue, rapid heartbeat, eye problems, mouth swelling, and irregular gait. In light of these symptoms, commentators have hypothesized about illnesses she may have had, including pernicious anemia (vitamin B12 deficiency), diabetes, or even syphilis.[23] Mental illness has been attributed to her, particularly bipolar disorder, more commonly known as manic-depressive illness.[24]

Diagnoses of physical and mental conditions have also accumulated around Abe. His lanky frame has been associated with Marfan syndrome, and his long limbs and asymmetric, lumpy lower lip with multiple endocrine neoplasia, type 2B, a rare, cancer-causing genetic disorder.[25] It has been suggested that the irritability, insomnia, tremor, and the rage attacks he sometimes experienced were caused by the "blue mass" pills that he took for constipation until 1861, when he quit them because, he said, they made him "cross."[26] The pills contained large amounts of mercury, which, as we now know, can damage the nervous system and internal organs. Some have linked his habitual melancholy to chronic depression.[27]

Such diagnoses are merely informed guesswork. To continue with conjectures, we may wonder if Mary occasionally experimented with free love. We know that she eventually found consolation in spiritualism (contact with the dead), one of the isms closely allied with free love. Spiritualism held that the choice of sexual partners was determined by magnetic "affinities." When Abe was away, did Mary feel affinities for other men? Uneasy about being alone and terrified of storms, she frequently hired local boys or men to stay with her. She said to James Gourley, "Mr Gourly—Come—do Come & Stay with me all night—you can Sleep in the bed with Bob and I."[28] Gourley, the man she reportedly told that she would love her husband better if he stayed home, remarked cryptically, "She is no prostitute—a good woman. She dared me once or twice to Kiss her, as I thought—refused then—wouldn't now." Gourley's comment that Mary was "no prostitute" and yet offered to kiss him suggests at least some sexual freedom on her part, as does her rumored behavior on shopping trips during the White House years with government worker William S. Wood, with whom she stayed in hotels in New York. When an anonymous correspondent in June 1861 wrote Lincoln about "the scandal of your wife and Wood," the exposure of which would "stab you in the most vital part," the president reportedly spoke harshly to Mary and barely communicated with her for several days.[29]

However, the idea advanced by some biographers that the marriage was dysfunctional overlooks the firm devotion between Mary and Abe. That devotion superseded other relationships. Take Mary's rejection of Julia Jayne Trumbull. Having helped reunite Mary and Abe after their 1841 breakup, Julia was a bridesmaid of Mary's and one of her closest friends. But the friendship ended during the Senate race of 1855, when Julia's husband, Lyman Trumbull, emerged victorious after Lincoln swung his supporters to Trumbull because of Democratic scheming. In Mary's view, Trumbull should have given Lincoln his votes, not the other way around. Lincoln was relieved that at least the senatorship had gone to the like-minded Trumbull, whom he congratulated and continued to befriend. Mary, in contrast, turned the cold shoulder to Lyman Trumbull and never talked to his wife again.

HOME WORK

Mary's complete devotion to her husband did not dampen her self-reliance. She assumed a large role in family decisions, such as the education of the children and the refurbishing of the Jackson Street home. A legend grew that she supervised single-handedly the expansion of the house in 1856. While Abe was away on the law circuit, the story goes, Mary, using $1,200 that she earned from the sale of eighty acres she had inherited, added downstairs rooms and a second story to the house. She

The Lincoln home in Springfield after its expansion (photo of 1860).
Lincoln and his son Willie are standing behind the fence on the porch.
The two figures standing in the foreground are unidentified.

made the house look so different that when Abe returned to Jackson
Street, he asked a neighbor, "Wilkie, can you tell me where old Abe
Lincoln lived around these parts?"[30]

The reconstruction of the house that year, however, was a husband-
wife collaboration, as were the lesser remodelings in 1849–50 and in
1859–60. Mary and Abe transformed the modest one-and-a-half-story
home into a spacious structure with an entry hall flanked on the left by
a double parlor, a dining room, and a kitchen and, on the right, by a family room and bedroom. Upstairs were the bedrooms of Mary and Abe (it
was customary then for genteel couples to have separate bedrooms) plus
a bedroom for Willie and Tad and an extra room used as a maid's room.

There was great competition for servants among middle-class families. Mary was not well positioned to compete because she was both temperamental and penny-pinching. Women who served the Lincolns occasionally remarked about her dictatorial manner. Harriet Hanks, the daughter of Lincoln's second cousin Dennis Hanks, lived with the family for a year and a half in the 1840s and was so annoyed by Mary that she later refused to talk about her.[31] Another hired girl complained, "She always talked to us as if we had no feelings, and I was never so unhappy in my life as while I was living with her."[32]

Doubtless Mary, who had grown up attended by enslaved people, was a demanding employer. Her attitude, however, was not unusual for the time. A domestic guidebook she consulted, *Miss Leslie's House Book or Manual of Domestic Economy for Town and Country*, emphasized that servants tended to be lazy and inefficient unless they were strictly supervised. A housekeeper, Miss Leslie advised, "unless she is blessed with excellent servants, . . . will find herself unable to depend upon them . . . without frequent personal inspection from herself."[33] Mary seems to have had trouble with a teenage Irish girl, Catherine Gordon, who frequently left her bedroom window open, evidently to allow boys into the room. Not all servants, however, had a bad relationship with Mary. One said, "If you are good to her, she is good to you and a friend to you."[34]

It's unclear how many live-in servants the Lincolns employed. Catherine Gordon was listed in the 1850 Springfield census as living at the Jackson Street house, as was a female between ten and twenty in 1853 and Mary N. Johnson in 1860. Mariah Vance, a married black woman who lived in Springfield, came to the house on a regular basis for several years to help with the laundry, cooking, and other chores.

Due to the lack of modern conveniences, such chores were onerous. Laundry involved heating water from an outdoor pump in kettles over an open fire, soaking the laundry in the hot water mixed with home-made detergent (a concoction of lye, hickory wood, vinegar, salt, starch, coffee, or bran, depending on the material), scrubbing it on a serrated board, and hanging it out to dry on lines made of horsehair or twisted seaweed. For the typical American family, laundry was especially demanding because it was usually done once a week, as opposed to the European custom of doing it every one to three months. About the only household duty that bore resemblance to today was rodent control, which involved setting out poison, patching up holes in walls, and owning cats, several of which were among the boys' pets at Jackson Street along with their pet dog, Fido. Abe did some chores, such as chopping up logs from the backyard woodpile; stoking the fire; milking the family cow; currying the horse, Old Bob; and helping with shopping.

At least twice weekly Mariah Vance came to the home—sometimes, probably, with one or more of her youngsters in tow (she eventually had thirteen children). The presence of African Americans in the Lincoln home brings up the issue of Mary Lincoln's view of race, which was connected to her politics. Mariah Vance seems to have been happily employed by the Lincolns, as was her sister, Elizabeth, in the household of Mary's uncle, John Todd, who also lived in Springfield.[35] Mary's close relationship with black women continued in her White House years, when her servants included Rosetta Wells, who praised her warmly, and Elizabeth Keckly, the formerly enslaved and seamstress who became Mary's closest friend.

We can trace the liberalization of Mary's politics by noting her response to her servants. In the mid-1850s her frustration with Catherine Gordon—and perhaps with other Irish servants—helps explain her attraction to Know-Nothingism. In 1856, just when Lincoln was campaigning for the Republican John Frémont, Mary endorsed the American Party's presidential candidate, Millard Fillmore, explaining her choice with an ethnic reference. She wrote her half sister Emilie, "My weak woman's heart was too Southern in feeling, to sympathize with any but Fillmore. I have always been an admirer of his, he made so good a president & is so just a man & feels the *necessity* of keeping foreigners, within bounds. If some of you Kentuckians had to deal with the 'wild Irish' as we housekeepers are sometimes called upon to do, the South would certainly elect Fillmore next time."[36]

Not only did she support the nativist Fillmore, but she also de-emphasized her husband's support of Frémont's presidential run. She wrote Emilie in 1856 that though Lincoln "was a Frémont man, you must not include him with so many of those, who belong to *that party*, an *Abolitionist*. In principle he is far from it—All he desires is, that slavery shall not be extended, let it remain, where it is—'."

At this point Mary represented Abe's conservative side, the Old Whig part of him that nodded to nativism and eschewed radicalism. Over time, she shifted to the left. During his presidency she drew close to the Radical Republican view of slavery. By 1863, an antislavery journalist found that she was "more radically opposed to slavery" than her husband and had "urged him to Emancipation, as a matter of right, long before he saw it as a matter of necessity."[37]

LINCOLN, SPRINGFIELD'S BLACKS, AND THE UNDERGROUND RAILROAD

While this comment sheds light on Mary's political progress, it minimizes Lincoln's antislavery commitment, which was always strong. The cultural and social environment of Springfield buttressed this commitment.

Some twenty-one black people lived within a three-block radius of his Jackson Street home.[38] He saw blacks on the streets regularly, and he came to know several of them well. He treated African Americans with respect and helped them when he could. For example, he rescued his valet, William H. Johnson, from a difficult situation in the White House. Johnson had begun working for Lincoln in Springfield and had accompanied the president-elect on his trip east to Washington in February 1861.[39] A very black man, he found himself ostracized by lighter-skinned African Americans who worked in the White House. Sensitive to Johnson's predicament, Lincoln, shortly after his inauguration, wrote to his navy secretary, Gideon Welles, whom he asked to find a position for Johnson. Describing him as "honest, faithful, sober, industrious and handy as a servant," Lincoln explained, "The difference of color between him & the other servants is the cause of our separation."[40] When Welles proved unable to find a place for Johnson, Lincoln approached his treasury secretary, Salmon Chase, who appointed Johnson as a laborer and messenger. All the while, Johnson continued to do part-time work for Lincoln, such as shaving him and tending to his wardrobe. He accompanied the president to Gettysburg in November 1863. On the trip, Lincoln came down with smallpox but recovered, attended by Johnson. But Johnson himself came down with the illness and died of it in January 1864.

The closeness between Lincoln and African Americans was especially pronounced in the case of William Florville. Born in Cap-Haïtien, Haiti, about 1806, Florville, a free black, was taken by his godmother to live in Baltimore, where he lived in a Catholic orphanage before moving first to New Orleans, then St. Louis, and in 1831 to Springfield, Illinois.[41] He served as Lincoln's barber there for twenty-four years. Lincoln loved going to his barbershop and entertaining the locals with stories or listening to Florville play the violin. Witty and entrepreneurial, Florville ran a mock-royal ad in local papers announcing himself as the "Emperor and Autocrat of all the Barbers of Sangamo," who was "making known to all my subjects, that I continue to *nullify* beards at my Tonsorial Palace," and requesting contributions to "my treasury." His business acumen enabled him to accumulate Springfield real estate; at one point he owned almost a whole city block between Eighth and Ninth Streets along Washington Street. Lincoln aided him substantially by representing him in court.[42] Once he secured for Florville a payment of $100 that was owed to him. In another court case, Lincoln won titles of several Springfield lots for him. During the 1850s, Lincoln paid Florville's property taxes when needed. He grew so close to Florville that the *Illinois State Journal* noted, "Only two men in Springfield understood Lincoln, his

WILLIAM DE FLEURVILLE (AKA WILLIAM FLORVILLE)

law partner William Herndon, and his barber, William de Fleurville." It was an emotional day when Florville accompanied the Lincolns to Springfield's railroad station in February 1861 for their trip east. Even more affecting was when word came in 1862 of the death of eleven-year-old Willie Lincoln, which prompted a heartfelt letter of condolence to the president. Florville included the consoling news for Tad that his dog, Fido, was in safe hands with a neighbor. In the letter, Florville hailed Lincoln as a "truly great Man" and confessed to "having for you, an irrisisteble feeling of gratitude for the kind regards Shown, and the manifest good wishis [*sic*] exhibited towards me."[43] Florville served as an honorary pallbearer at Lincoln's funeral in Springfield in May 1865.

A grim footnote to Florville's life is that his grandson, George Richardson, was falsely accused of raping a white woman in an incident that sparked the deadly Springfield race riot of 1908. This experience of violent white supremacy during the Jim Crow era was shared by another African American from Lincoln's Springfield days, William K. Donnegan. For years, Donnegan, a cobbler, had made Lincoln's size fourteen shoes. He lived just five blocks north of Lincoln in Springfield. Donnegan worked hard, made wise investments, and accumulated a substantial estate. He became the best-known black person in Springfield. However, his thirty-year marriage to a white woman spelled his doom during the 1908 Springfield riot. On August 14, a mob of whites hauled him out of his home, cut his throat, hung him on a nearby tree, and stabbed him several times. The militia arrived and cut down his body, but he died the next morning. The incident was a catalyst for the formation of the National Association for the Advancement of Colored People (NAACP).

There is a common misconception that Lincoln's Springfield contained few black people who vocally protested against slavery. David Donald, for instance, claims that the blacks in Springfield "were not people who could speak out boldly to say that they were as American as any whites."[44] Benjamin Quarles alleges that Lincoln's lack of awareness of radical African Americans in Springfield accounts for the fact that he went to Washington lacking a "rounded knowledge" of African Americans, about whom he knew only "the Negro of dialect story, minstrel stage, and sea chantey."[45] Actually, Springfield was a lively venue for African American activism. Each year, many of the city's black population gathered to celebrate the anniversary of the 1834 emancipation of some eight hundred thousand enslaved people in the British West Indies. Periodically, Springfield's blacks held other antislavery meetings as well. At one, in 1858, those present issued a striking resolution. Printed in its entirety in the *Illinois State Journal*, the resolution vigorously denounced slavery and the Dred Scott decision. The resolution hailed "the great charter of liberty, the Declaration of Independence" and called boldly for African American suffrage: "We also claim the right of citizenship in this, the country of our birth. We were born here, and here we desire to die and to be buried. We are not African. . . . Why then should we be disfranchised and denied the rights of citizenship in the north, and those of human nature itself in the south?"[46]

WILLIAM K. DONNEGAN

Some African Americans in Springfield were active on the Underground Railroad. Among them was William Donnegan, who claimed that he hid "scores" of runaways in the garret of his home on Jefferson Street, five blocks north of the Lincoln home. In one dramatic incident, three white men with a bulldog pursued him while he was on a

Springfield street helping a runaway girl escape. When the men set their bulldog on him, he shot the animal and shouted that he would "kill any four-legged or two-legged dogs that bothered me much more."[47]

Also active in aiding fugitives was Jamieson Jenkins, a black drayman who lived a block south of Lincoln's home. Born in South Carolina, Jenkins moved to Springfield around 1848. In February 1861, he gave Lincoln his last carriage ride in Springfield when he drove the president-elect and his family to the railway station. A dauntless protector of runaways, Jenkins, in an especially dramatic incident in 1850, helped seven fugitives travel sixty miles on the Underground Railroad from Springfield to Bloomington.[48]

The participation of blacks Lincoln knew in the Underground Railroad raises the issue of his relationship to the Fugitive Slave Act. His grudging acceptance of the law raised doubts about his antislavery commitment among abolitionists such as Wendell Phillips, who called him "The Slave-Hound of Illinois."[49] Most Northerners were outraged by the law, by which the federal government mandated the return of fugitives to masters who provided an affidavit of ownership. The law subjected those who protected runaways to a $1,000 fine and six months in jail. Harriet Beecher Stowe swayed millions of readers with her moving portrait of three fugitives—George and Eliza Harris and their small son Harry—who struggled their way north to Canada along the Underground Railroad. Vivid scenes such as Eliza's perilous dash to freedom across the ice floes of the Ohio River and George's shootout with slave catchers in the rocky pass became stamped on Northern hearts, not only by Stowe's novel but also by countless theatrical versions of *Uncle Tom's Cabin*, which, in its many avatars over the next eighty years, became the most popular play in American history.

Lincoln was in a position like that of Stowe's John Bird, an Ohio politician in the novel who recognizes the Constitution's mandate to return fugitives from labor but who sympathizes deeply with runaways. Lincoln's comment to Joshua Speed about biting his lip and keeping silent over his torment at seeing the capture of fugitives speaks to his real feelings.[50] On the one hand, he had in mind the Constitution's clause about returning fugitives. At the same time, his emotions and his principles were on the side of the fugitives.

It was risky in Illinois to vent open repugnance to the Fugitive Slave Act. The closest Lincoln came to doing so publicly was taking the side of fugitive blacks in court. Two of his colleagues in law and politics, John Stuart and Edward Baker, avoided taking on fugitive slave cases for fear of damaging their reputations. Lincoln, in contrast, several times defended runaways or their protectors. In 1845, Joseph Warman, an African American traveling in Illinois, was jailed on suspicion of being a fugitive because he did not have freedom papers on him. The court discharged Warman when Lincoln helped him secure a writ of habeas corpus.[51] Also that year, Lincoln won a not guilty verdict for Marvin Pond, who was charged with harboring a fugitive from slavery (it was later revealed that Marvin's abolitionist brother Samuel Pond had been the one who helped the man). In 1847, Lincoln represented John Randolph Scott, also accused of sheltering a runaway. Lincoln got the case dismissed on the technicality of Scott's first name not being included on the indictment. The same year, Lincoln successfully defended another accused Underground Railroad conductor, George Kern, by arguing that there was no proof that the black man Kern assisted was in fact enslaved. This argument became the linchpin of an 1857 case handled by Lincoln's partner William Herndon in which the Kentucky slave owner John McElroy went to court to take possession of a black man in Illinois who, he insisted, was his property. Herndon lost the case, but he boldly told the court, "The presumption, when a negro is arrested in a free State, is that he is free, and the arresting agent must show his authority."[52]

As an attorney, then, Lincoln bucked the proslavery trend of the national government. Federal actions from the Fugitive Slave Act through the Kansas-Nebraska Act to the Dred Scott decision increasingly diminished the rights of blacks, who, Lincoln said in 1857, were trapped behind "heavy iron doors" and "bolted in with a lock of a hundred keys, which can never be unlocked without the concurrence of every key."[53] At the same time, however, he knew that a large proportion of Northerners detested the Fugitive Slave Act and also opposed the extension of slavery. His comment to Joshua Speed that "the great body of the northern people do crucify their feelings" about slavery pointed to his awareness of the widespread antislavery impulse. This impulse surfaced in various ways: in the personal liberty laws, granting varying degrees of rights to African Americans, that were passed in fourteen Northern states;[54] in the near-victory of John Frémont in 1856; in the groundswell of support for John Brown, the warrior for freedom in Kansas; and in the surging popularity of antislavery literature—not just *Uncle Tom's Cabin* but also slave narratives and antislavery plays, sermons, poems, and songs.

In Illinois, Lincoln's conscience was stimulated by three radicals: the Chicago newspaper editor Zebina Eastman, the Springfield businessman and educator Erastus Wright, and the Princeton, Illinois, clergyman politician Owen Lovejoy. These three came out strongly against the Fugitive Slave Act and put their beliefs into practice by serving on the Underground Railroad. They launched attacks on slavery from a moral and religious standpoint. Lincoln was slow to admit having an alliance with these men, and for good reason. To have done so would have surely alienated the conservative Whigs who maintained a strong presence in central Illinois. But in keeping contact with the three men, whom he openly honored later on, he prepared the way for his own future as the Great Emancipator and the facilitator of the Thirteenth Amendment.

Zebina Eastman, born in 1815 in Amherst, Massachusetts, moved in 1838 to Illinois, where he worked with Benjamin Lundy on the antislavery newspaper the *Genius of Universal Emancipation*, which, after Lundy's death in 1839, became Eastman's the *Genius of Liberty* and then the *Western Citizen*, renamed the *Free West* before being integrated into the *Chicago Tribune*. Eastman was an unabashed champion of the Underground Railroad. In 1844, he published an announcement in his paper of the "LIBERTY LINE," whose "improved and splendid Locomotives" ran "Night and Day" to "Libertyville, Upper Canada," with "SEATS FREE, Irrespective of color" and overcoats for those "afflicted with the protracted chilly-phobia."[55] Chicago, the hub of Illinois abolitionism, was a key stop for runaways, whom Eastman was always eager to assist. Lincoln at first seemed too conservative to Eastman, who came out against Lincoln during his 1854 run for the Senate. But by the time of the Civil War, he had gained respect for Lincoln, who in turn praised Eastman as "one of the earliest, and most efficient of our free-soil laborers, . . . more than a common man, in his sphere."[56] Lincoln appointed him as consul to Bristol, England. Eastman worked hard to represent the North's antislavery position in England, and in 1864 he sent a letter congratulating Lincoln for his reelection, declaring that his note came from "one of the humblest, who hopes to be one of the truest, of the fr[i]ends of the Author of the Proclamation of Emancipation."[57]

A mutual friend of Eastman's and Lincoln's, Erastus Wright was another antislavery enthusiast. Another transplanted Massachusetts man, with a deep Puritan background, Wright was one of thirty Springfield residents who in 1837 left the town's First Presbyterian Church and formed the radical Second Presbyterian Church, whose members were mainly antislavery New Englanders. A teacher, school commissioner, and businessman, Wright hired Lincoln to represent him in several debt cases. The two found themselves on opposite sides in a case in which an elderly widow hired Lincoln to represent her in a suit against Wright, who, she claimed, had overcharged her for his services

OWEN LOVEJOY

in procuring for her a Revolutionary War widow's pension. Lincoln's passionate defense of the widow, punctuated by jingoistic Revolutionary War images, persuaded the jury to award her thirty-five dollars and costs.[58] But Wright and Lincoln remained friends and political allies. Wright referred to Lincoln as "my near neighbor and fast friend," and in 1860 Lincoln reported to Wright's daughter, "your father calls on me every day."[59] It is telling that Lincoln was so close to the radical antislavery visionary Wright, a busy Underground Railroad agent and a strong advocate of the antislavery higher law.

Owen Lovejoy was cut from the same cloth as Wright. In May 1864, shortly after Lovejoy's death, Lincoln wrote that "every step" in their relationship "has been one of increasing respect and esteem."[60] The key word here was "increasing." At the start, when they first met at the Springfield state fair on the rainy afternoon of October 4, 1854, there was tension between them. Although both viewed slavery with equal loathing, Lovejoy, along with his radical friend Ichabod Codding, was eager to establish the emerging Republican Party as the proper platform for gathering together the antislavery factions in the North. Lincoln resisted the rush to the new party. When Codding invited him to join the Illinois Republican Central Committee, Lincoln testily replied that, while he opposed slavery as much as any Republican, "the *extent* to which I feel authorized to carry that opposition, practically; was not at all satisfactory to that party."[61] For a time he remained cagey about a connection with Codding, Lovejoy, and other Republicans, but while visiting Lovejoy's congressional district in 1856 and, as Lincoln wrote, "seeing the people there—their great enthusiasm for Lovejoy," he sensed a swelling antislavery fervor among average Illinoisans.[62] Owen Lovejoy served as the party's sharp prow, bursting through the ice of moderation and the choppy sea of prevarication and evasions. He made no bones about his hostility to the Fugitive Slave Act and his activity as an operative in the Underground Railroad. In 1859 he declared on the floor of Congress, "Proclaim it then upon the house tops. . . . Owen Lovejoy lives at Princeton, Illinois, three quarters of a mile east of the village, and he aids every fugitive that comes to his door and asks it."[63] He became an unflagging supporter of Lincoln, who eventually called him "my most generous friend."[64]

Lincoln's friendship with several black and white leaders of the Underground Railroad brings into question his reputation among some historians as having been merely a moderate antislavery spokesman.[65] As president, after all, he would oversee the repeal of the Fugitive Slave Act in June 1864. Previously, he had made clear that he disliked the way the Fugitive Slave Act was being carried out—particularly the enforcement of provisions in the law that violated due process, such as not permitting a captured black to testify that he was in fact a free man, not a runaway. In the First Inaugural Address, he would concede that the Constitution demanded that fugitives must be returned, but would ask, "[I]n any law upon this subject, ought not all the safeguards of liberty known in civilized and humane jurisprudence to be introduced, so that a free man be not, in any case, surrendered as a slave? And might it not be well, at the same time, to provide by law for the enforcement of that clause in the Constitution which guarranties [*sic*] that 'The citizens of each State shall be entitled to all privileges and immunities of citizens in the several States?' "[66]

In carefully chosen language, Lincoln comes very close here to affirming citizenship rights for African Americans. He makes no mention, at this point, of voting rights—he would not publicly make that radical appeal until after Appomattox. But already, in March 1861, he is calling for blacks to enjoy one of the most fundamental rights in a democracy—that of habeas corpus and trial by jury. The fact that he would soon suspend habeas corpus for Northerners suspected of disloyalty, even as he was opening doors for black people, perhaps shows that his abhorrence of rebellion was so great that he could advocate due process for blacks while being willing to suspend it for Southern sympathizers.

IMPROVING SPRINGFIELD, IMPROVING POLITICS

Wherever Lincoln looked in Springfield he saw improvement. African Americans like Florville and Donnegan were getting ahead, as were many of the Germans, Irish, and Portuguese immigrants who had settled in the blocks around the Lincolns' home. Springfield as a whole was prospering. Its population grew from 2,600 in 1840 to 9,400 by 1860, a gain of more than 350 percent.[67] The economy was robust, led by the sale of farm products. It flagged during the downturn of 1853 and the recession of 1857, but it weathered even those rough times fairly well. The value of land in Springfield leaped from $1 million in 1847 to well over $4 million in 1858.

To a man who had progressed from the backwoods to middle-class respectability, Springfield's economic advance could only be encouraging. It confirmed his core belief in the labor theory of value, American style: the idea that anyone could make it through hard work. When approached by a law student who asked about the key to success, his advice was simple: "Work, work, work, is the main thing," said Lincoln.[68] He wrote in notes toward a lecture, "The leading rule for the lawyer, as for the man, is *diligence*. Leave nothing for tomorrow, which can be done to-day."[69]

This, of course, was the national formula, rooted in the Protestant work ethic and put to use by Americans from Benjamin Franklin through Horatio Alger to modern-day workers. For Lincoln, the formula had special meaning. It gave him an answer to the South's so-called mudsill theory, which held that the North's poor were stuck in their low position—they were "slaves without masters"—and as such, they lacked the care and protection that the South provided to its enslaved blacks.

The mudsill theory, Lincoln said, inaccurately depicted workers as "fatally fixed for life." In fact, they could rise. "This," he declared, "is *free* labor—the just and generous, and prosperous system, which opens the way for all—gives hope to all, and energy, and progress, and improvement of condition to all."[70] Freedom gave all Americans, regardless of color, opportunity. "One of the reasons why I am opposed to Slavery is just here," he said in an 1860 speech. "What is the true condition of the laborer? . . . I want every man to have the chance—and I believe a black man is entitled to it—in which he *can* better his condition—when he may look forward and hope to be a hired laborer this year and the next, work for himself afterward, and finally to hire men to work for him!" (Notably, he here envisages a black man as a business leader—remarkably progressive for that era.)

His vision of improvement included advances in technology. In an 1858 lecture he said, "Man is not the only animal who labors; but he is the only one who *improves* his workmanship."[71] Around him in Springfield he saw the improving animal at work. Not that other animals were out of the picture. Hogs still crowded Springfield's streets: odorous, grunting flea carriers, they were, at the same time, excellent consumers of street garbage and a ready source of meat for the needy.[72] Mud and dust continued to be problems, but they were greatly alleviated by a drainage system and planking for the sidewalks and streets installed during the 1850s. By the middle of the decade, gas lamps illuminated the streets, fed by pipes from the Springfield Gas Light Company that also brought lamp fuel into the homes of the well-to-do. (The Lincolns, like most residents, continued to use candles and lard oil.)[73] By 1853, two railroads ran into Springfield, facilitating travel and the distribution of goods.

City services expanded. Springfield's single law officer was supplemented in 1854 by five policemen, who six years later received uniforms (though they groused about having to pay for them). In the absence of a fire department, citizens were virtually powerless to handle the fires that periodically broke out. The worst one, a conflagration in 1855 that wiped out half a block near the public square, led to the creation of Fire Company No. 1. Nicknamed the Pioneers, the company held festivals attended by notables, including, in July 1858, Abraham Lincoln, who delivered a toast to "'The Pioneer Fire Company.' May they extinguish all the bad flames, but keep the flame of patriotism ever burning brightly in the hearts of the ladies."[74] Soon came Sangamo Fire Company No. 2, Hook and Ladder Company No. 1, and Young America Hose Company No. 1. As in the cities of the Northeast, volunteer fire departments raced to fires in a fierce competition among groups of colorfully uniformed b'hoys, for whom running with "the masheen" (the hand-drawn fire engine) to a fire was as important as actually fighting the flames—a losing endeavor anyway in towns like Springfield that lacked a central water supply.

The town saw a cultural quickening. Visiting lecturers in the 1850s included such eminences from the East as Ralph Waldo Emerson, Horace Greeley, Horace Mann, and (at William Herndon's invitation) Theodore Parker. Controversy surrounded Parker's lecture in October 1856, the month before the presidential election. Herndon had been prodding his favorite philosopher to lecture in Springfield, and he and his law partner must have been satisfied with Parker's talk, "The Progressive Development of Man," which argued that humans were distinguished from lower animals by their ability to improve their lot through inventions—the theme Lincoln would develop in his two lectures on discoveries and inventions. But Parker's reputation as a radical abolitionist had preceded him. Springfield's Democratic paper, the *Register*, reported that "Theodore Parker, the great disunion and abolition speaker of Massachusetts," had in his talk "preached disunion and nigger supremacy after the most approved mode, and pointed to Fremont's election as the great end to be achieved to secure these desired results."[75] Clearly, the reporter had not attended the talk; actually, Parker had given what the *Illinois State Journal* called a "purely literary lecture." But Parker, notorious as a protector of fugitive blacks and a supporter of isms such as women's rights, stood as an example of the danger of open radicalism in the highly charged political atmosphere of the 1850s. The *Register*'s response showed that any association with the isms could provoke the anathema of Democrats.

This helps explain why Lincoln was slow in joining the new Republican Party and why he associated himself intermittently with a plan for colonization. The position that blacks and whites could not live on equal terms in America reflected an environment hostile to integration. Take, for example, Illinois's draconian law of 1853 that stipulated that a black person from another state who stayed in Illinois longer than ten days was subject to arrest, imprisonment, a fifty-dollar fine, and removal from the state. "In looking at the recent black law of Illinois," Frederick Douglass declared, "one is struck dumb with its enormity."[76] The law stayed in effect for twelve years. Such attitudes were felt elsewhere in America. Racial discrimination led to a surge of emigration plans made by African Americans in the 1850s.[77]

Lincoln, however, was far from being an unqualified supporter of colonization. In subtle ways, he actually subverted the program from within. He spoke about the virtual impossibility of transporting millions of black people, and he held that emigration must be voluntary, not forced. He was developing a strategy he had introduced at Peoria in 1854 and that he would perfect in the late 1850s in his political battles against Stephen A. Douglas: that is, using a conservative cover to appeal to moderates while delivering a fundamentally radical message.

The House Divided and the Lincoln-Douglas Debates

W hat were Lincoln's core convictions as he entered the slavery debate in earnest in the late 1850s? All humans are equal. Freedom—a respect for individual liberty—must merge with a belief in human equality, or justice for all. Slavery and other forms of oppression are wrong. Indifference toward them is de facto support for them.

For Lincoln, these were the real issues of the slavery controversy. But how could he present his radical ideas about them to an electorate that included a substantial number of conservatives and moderates? His answer, in effect, was that of Walt Whitman, who declared, "Be radical, be radical, be radical—be not too damned radical."[1] Observing the political and cultural conditions of the 1850s, Lincoln learned how to be radical without sounding too damned radical. He retreated from extremist isms that were said to be grounded in New England Puritanism. In his speeches and his debates against Stephen Douglas, he summoned liberty, associated by many with Puritanism, into the vision of human equality proclaimed in the Declaration of Independence. The American Revolution, which had brought Northerners and Southerners together against a common oppressor, became for him the touchstone for the unified struggle for human rights.

PURITAN LESSONS

He was cautious not to get too close to a movement that attracted many antislavery advocates in the 1850s: the veneration of the nation's Puritan forefathers. Despite his fascination with his own New England roots, he avoided publicly associating himself with Puritanism.

Other leading antislavery figures, in contrast, brandished such an association. The clergyman politician Owen Lovejoy, the brother of the antislavery martyr Elijah Lovejoy, as a fellow politician remarked, "hated slavery with the animosity of a regular Puritan," and insisted that the nation's founders derived their democratic principles "from the old puritan stock."[2] Other antislavery Illinoisans who were proud of their deep New England heritage included Zebina Eastman, Erastus Wright, Ichabod Codding, and Edward Beecher.[3]

In Illinois and throughout the nation, December 22—known as Forefathers' Day, because, as was generally thought, the Pilgrims landed at Plymouth Rock on that day in 1620—was a major holiday, led by the New England Society, which had many branches in the North and even a few in the South. Several politicians who became members of the Lincoln administration, including William Henry Seward, Gideon Welles, Salmon P. Chase, Francis P. Blair, and Hannibal Hamlin, spoke at Forefathers' Day celebrations. Extolling the *Mayflower* and Plymouth Rock provided a platform for linking antislavery passion with America's early history. Antislavery orators compared the Pilgrims' rebellion against British aristocratic institutions to the struggle against the Southern slave power. Puritanism, the speakers argued, had fostered self-government, clear moral distinctions, and the antislavery higher law.

Self-government referred to the Puritans' rejection of the age-old doctrine of the divine right of kings. In this view, the 1649 beheading of King Charles I by Oliver Cromwell's Parliamentarians ushered in a spirit of self-rule. The argument for the natural rights of the individual, in opposition to the divine right of kings, was first made in detail by the seventeenth-century British politician Algernon Sidney, who has been called "Puritanism's greatest political philosopher."[4]

Sidney and other Puritan rebels, such as John Lilburne, paved the way for John Locke by arguing that the most valuable property was oneself and the highest goal was self-government. This Puritan spirit in turn contributed to the founding fathers and, later, American antislavery reformers.

To govern one's self and one's own labor subverted the rationale for slavery. As the antislavery clergyman Henry Ward Beecher announced at a Forefathers' Day event, "Only give the whole of man to himself and he is made to be prudent, virtuous, orderly and self-governing. This is the molecule, the atomic cell of Puritanism."[5] Or, as Theodore Parker expressed it, "The dreadful axe of Puritanic Oliver Cromwell shore off the divine right of kings, making a clean cut between the vicarious government of middle ages and personal self-rule of modern times."[6]

Another characteristic that antislavery reformers attributed to Puritanism was a tendency to make absolute moral distinctions and enforce them in the public arena. Americans generally considered the terms *Yankee*, *Puritan*, and *Anglo-Saxon* "virtually synonymous in their connotations" and that all were dedicated to morality in politics.[7] The nation's leading thinker, Emerson, noted that "our position, of the free states, [is] very like that of the [Calvinistic] covenanters against the cavaliers."[8] He wrote: "The moral peculiarity of the Saxon race,—its commanding sense of right and wrong, the love and devotion to that,—this is the imperial trait."[9] "Few bodies or parties have served the world so well as the Puritans," Emerson wrote. Everything "of vigorous sense, or practical genius this country shews, are the issue of Puritan stock," including moral movements such as abolition, which was "but the continuation of Puritanism."[10] For the Puritan-Yankee, slavery was wrong.

To oppose its abolition was like trying to stop nature. In Emerson's words, "As well complain of gravity, or the ebb of the tide. Who makes the Abolitionist? The Slaveholder."[11]

Similarly, Lincoln's friend Owen Lovejoy, who traced his antislavery principles to the Pilgrims, appealed to nature's laws. Addressing Congress, he asked whether it is possible to send a river back to its source or calm the waves of a storm-tossed ocean. "Much less can you annul the eternal distinction between right and wrong," Lovejoy said. "Before all law and above all law, human and divine, is the idea of right and wrong, eternal, indestructible."[12]

The appeal to morality bred the antislavery higher law, which also was thought to come from Puritanism. The Puritan Algernon Sidney was commonly accepted as the principal ancestor of the higher law. He famously wrote, "That which is not just, is not Law; and that which is not Law, ought not to be obeyed."[13]

This is how many antislavery Northerners saw proslavery laws. At a typical Forefathers' Day ceremony held in Plymouth in 1855, William Henry Seward, Lincoln's future secretary of state, attributed his antislavery principles to Puritanism. While admitting that he had no Puritan ancestors, he declared, "I know no better rule of conduct than that of the Puritans," who appealed to "a law, broader, older, and more stable" than human law, "a law universal in its application and in its obligation, established by the Creator and Judge of all men, and therefore paramount to all human constitutions." "The Puritan principle," he said, was "the absolute equality of all men" and "the spirit of Freedom, which is the soul of the Republic itself."[14]

Another speaker that day, the abolitionist Wendell Phillips, said that Seward, the "great apostle of the higher law," lied when he said "he is not descended from the Mayflower." "There is such a thing as pedigree of mind, as well as of body," Phillips explained, "and he knows as much about the Mayflower, that I am sure, as a Western man would say, 'I was *thar*.' [Cheers and laughter.]" Knowing about the *Mayflower*, for

Phillips, meant standing for antislavery principle. In reference to the antislavery battles in the western territories, Phillips declared, "The Pilgrims, had they lived in 1855, would not be in Plymouth, but in Kansas." Their creed would be "the Underground Railroad, and a thousand of Sharpe's rifles, addressed 'Kansas,' labelled 'Books'" (a reference to weapons, disguised as Bibles, that were boxed and sent west by the antislavery minister Henry Ward Beecher). As for Plymouth Rock, Phillips said, the antislavery warrior Elijah Lovejoy had "leveled his muzzle across it at Alton, Illinois."

Moving words. But also, from Lincoln's vantage point, sectional ones. The kind that could inflame hostilities between the North and the South, between Republicans and Democrats. Antislavery radicals claimed to have a corner on the Puritan spirit. Among those who addressed Forefathers' Day events were the controversial reformers William Lloyd Garrison, Frederick Douglass, Charles Henry Remond, and Lucy Stone. At one Forefathers' Day celebration, Garrison said: "Nothing is more clear than that the Abolitionists are the only people in this country who have a right to celebrate the Landing at Plymouth."[15] Frederick Douglass declared that America's conflicting societies were seeded by the 1619 arrival of a slave ship in Virginia and the 1620 landing of the liberty-seeking Puritans in Massachusetts.[16]

Predictably, such praise of the New England Puritans aroused the ire of slavery's supporters. One proslavery essayist bitterly proposed in 1858 that New England leave the United States, join England, and allow the South to take over Jamaica in order to reenslave and civilize its black population. In proposing "New England for Jamaica," the writer expressed the aim of the Southern-controlled US government to extend slavery by taking over the West Indies.[17] Insisting that "New England has been the source of all the evils" in America, the essayist explained that "there was a principle of evil in Puritanism from which, when it ripened into rottenness, was propagated all the isms that have since swarmed over the land. There is not a false religion, a false philosophy, a false literature, or a false system of politics in the country, of which the origin may not be traced to New England Federalism, Abolition-ism, Know-Nothingism, Emersonianism—these, and a thousand other kindred impostures, have all the same prolific womb, in which a brood of unborn devils are now struggling for development and delivery." From this perspective, Puritanism's self-rule led to anarchistic individ-ualism, its political morality to fanatical persecution, and its higher law to defiance of the Constitution. The only worthy product of New En-gland, the writer added, was the author Nathaniel Hawthorne, who criticized the Puritans, mocked Transcendentalism and other isms, and supported the Democratic president Franklin Pierce, his chum since college days.

Slavery's defenders charged that Puritanism generated horrible isms. After the election of Lincoln, a political cartoon titled *Worship of the North*, by the Confederate caricaturist Adalbert Johann Volck, pic-tured Lincoln's bust atop an antislavery Republican altar whose base is labeled PURITANISM. Above the base are stones labeled WITCH-BURNING, SOCIALISM, FREE LOVE, SPIRIT RAPPING, ATHEISM, RATIONALISM, and NEGRO WORSHIP.[18] Northern politicians and reformers swarm around the altar, on which lies a bleed-ing white man who has been stabbed by the knife-wielding abolitionist clergyman Henry Ward Beecher, who kills whites sacrificially in idola-trous reverence for black people. Above the devilish-looking bust of Lincoln and the words CHICAGO PLATFORM is seated the idolized black man, who holds a spear that has been given to him by John Brown, a statue of whom, labeled ST. OSAWATOMIE, is in the background to the right. Other figures include Senator Charles Sumner, who holds a torch to help Beecher take aim at his white victim; the antislavery editor Horace Greeley, who swings incense in the left corner; and Harriet Beecher Stowe, who kneels in prayer on the right-center side of the picture.

The cartoon's main message was clear: New England Puritanism

WORSHIP OF THE NORTH

Worship of the North (etching by Adalbert Johann Volck, 1863). Anti-Republican cartoon that shows Northern politicians and reformers crowding around an antislavery altar that is built on the bedrock of "PURITANISM."

had bred the Republican Party and John Brown. How true was the message? In the case of John Brown, very true. He was a Calvinist who believed God had chosen him to eradicate slavery; he revered his Puritan lineage and was regularly compared to Oliver Cromwell, the seventeenth-century Puritan warrior. Brown also believed that African Americans should share equal rights with white people—what slavery's proponents called "negro worship." The cartoon pertained as well to a number of other antislavery figures who, to varying degrees, traced their views to the Puritan tradition of liberty and freedom fighting.

To include Lincoln in the picture, however, was deceptive. Despite his connections to Puritanism through his New England ancestry and his association with the Republican Party, he was careful to deemphasize these connections.

He was well aware of the political implications of Puritanism. On December 22, 1856, he went with fellow attorney James H. Matheny to the annual meeting of the New England Society of Illinois held in Springfield, presided over by his friend Simeon Francis, editor of the *Illinois State Journal*. Toasts were raised to the landing "at the rock of Plymouth, 230 years ago this day," to New England, "the birthplace of political and religious liberty," and so on.[19] A more suggestive toast went, "In the establishment of our national independence, the Puritan and Cavalier marched shoulder to shoulder. May their successors never forget that 'all men are created free and equal.'"

This idea pointed to a route out of sectionalism for Lincoln. New Englanders and Southerners had fought together against a common enemy in the American Revolution. Lincoln concentrated on this idea. He *fused* ideas derived from the Puritans with those established by the Revolutionary War generation. As the toast said, "The Puritan and Cavalier marched shoulder to shoulder" in the Revolution—the key moment of national unity. During the Civil War, Lincoln would decline an invitation to attend a Forefathers' Day celebration. He focused neither on the Puritans nor on the Cavaliers but rather on restoring the nonsectional spirit of the founding fathers.

THE NAKED QUESTION, THE CENTRAL IDEA

Lincoln's improvement upon Revolutionary-era ideals shaped his response in the 1850s to Stephen A. Douglas, culminating in the famous debates during their competition for the US Senate in 1858.

In the landmark debates, Douglas accused Lincoln of having worked as early as 1854 "to abolitionize the Old Whig party all over the State" and to "bring old Democrats handcuffed and bound hand and foot into the Abolition camp." Douglas said Lincoln followed a prearranged plan "to bring into the Abolition camp the old line Whigs, and transfer them over to [Joshua] Giddings, [Salmon] Chase, [Frederick] Douglass, and Parson [Owen] Lovejoy, who were ready to receive them and christen them in their new faith. (Laughter and cheers)."[20]

The record shows that, in a literal sense at least, Douglas was completely wrong. Actually, Lincoln was slow in joining the emerging antislavery fusion group that became the Republican Party. In October 1854, he kept away from an antislavery meeting in Springfield organized by the antislavery radicals Owen Lovejoy and Ichabod Codding. A month later, he bristled when he learned that Codding had added his name to the Illinois Republican Central Committee without consulting him. Lincoln wrote Codding saying that while he hated slavery, he was not yet ready to take political action to oppose it. He explained, "I suppose my opposition to the principle of slavery is as strong as that of any member of the Republican party; but I had also supposed that the *extent* to which I feel authorized to carry that opposition, practically, was not at all satisfactory to that party."[21]

At this point, he didn't want to ruffle the sensibilities of Old Line

Whigs in central Illinois, who recoiled from any sign of abolitionism. He lost his 1854–55 run for the Senate mainly because key antislavery leaders like Zebina Eastman refused to back him. In February 1856, he did not go to the important Republican convention held in Pittsburgh, attended by Codding, Lovejoy, Giddings, Greeley, and others. Lincoln instead chose to attend the milder anti-Nebraska editors' convention in Decatur, Illinois.[22]

The fact that in May he participated in the more militant antislavery convention in Bloomington, fifty miles north of Decatur, exemplifies his dictum that events shaped him. In the opening months of 1856 the slavery crisis intensified greatly. In January, President Franklin Pierce endorsed the bogus proslavery legislature in Kansas that had been elected by gun-toting, knife-wielding Border Ruffians from nearby Missouri who crossed into Kansas and cast ballots for proslavery candidates. The conflict over slavery in Kansas erupted into open warfare. In 1855, Lincoln had prophetically written of Douglas's Kansas-Nebraska Act, "I look upon that enactment not as a *law*, but as *violence* from the beginning. It was conceived in violence, passed in violence, is maintained in violence, and is being executed in violence."[23] By early 1856, Kansas had become the scene of proslavery atrocities committed against free state settlers, prompting John Brown's violent reprisal in May at Pottawatomie Creek, where he supervised the slaughter of five proslavery settlers. The same month, on the floor of the US Senate, Charles Sumner's antislavery speech "The Crime Against Kansas" earned him a near-fatal pummeling at the hands of the South Carolinian Preston Brooks. "Bleeding Kansas" and "Bleeding Sumner" became the watchwords of the North.

The violence in Kansas haunted the May 29 antislavery convention in Bloomington, which turned out to be one of Lincoln's peak moments. He reached oratorical heights just when America seemed poised in the balance, with Kansas seemingly capable of tipping the nation toward slavery or away from it. The Lawrence, Kansas, editor James S.

Emery, whose newspaper press had been destroyed by a proslavery mob on May 21, talked about Kansas, a theme taken up by Lincoln in his speech. The awkward-looking, plainly dressed Lincoln gripped the audience with his eloquence—so much so that reporters forgot to write down his words. From the patchy reports we have of the so-called Lost Speech, we glean that he began with the history of American legislation on slavery, leading to the Kansas-Nebraska Act. Reportedly, he mentioned two violent incidents in Kansas. But he did not dwell on violence, nor did he resort to sensational rhetoric. He strained toward unity. He was speaking before a varied audience, which included, on the conservative side, Old Line Whigs and Democrats and, on the radical side, higher-law Republicans. He rallied this mixed group around the goal of arresting the spread of slavery. As one listener reported, "Mr. Lincoln planned and perfected this union of widely diverse elements as no other man could have done. His 'Lost Speech' welded together these elements."[24] Similarly, the journalist John L. Scripps wrote that Lincoln's speech "fused the mass of hitherto incongruous elements into perfect homogeneity."[25]

In calling for a stop to slavery's expansion without demanding the repeal of the Fugitive Slave Act or interference with slavery where it already existed, Lincoln can hardly be said to have "abolitionized" the parties, as Douglas claimed. Not only had Lincoln postponed active engagement in the antislavery fusion movement, but he was not among the thirty-three Illinois delegates to the first national Republican Convention, held in Philadelphia on June 17, 1856. Even though a substantial segment of the convention voted for his candidacy as vice president, he did not attend the convention "for fear that he would be 'platformed'— that is forced to accept some more extreme antislavery platform position, such as the repeal of the Fugitive Slave Act."[26] It is telling, however, that he preferred as the Republican Party's presidential candidate the Supreme Court justice John McLean, an antislavery radical, to the more moderate John Frémont.

Lincoln supported the 1856 Republican platform, which opposed the extension of slavery without venturing into the controversial territory of interfering with slavery itself or with the Fugitive Slave Act. Lincoln kept nonextension front and center in his vision, refusing to be diverted by the growing chorus of complaints about the abominable isms supposedly associated with the Republican Party and the North as a whole.

The chorus grew very loud in the mid-1850s, when not only Douglas's Democrats but also the South's leading social theorist, George Fitzhugh, cried out against the isms. In his book *Cannibals All! Or, Slaves Without Masters*, Fitzhugh discussed what he called "the philosophy of the isms," which, he said, dominated the Northern mind. Fitzhugh asked: "Why have you Bloomers and Women's Rights men, and strong-minded women, and Mormons, and anti-renters, and 'vote myself a farm men,' Millerites, and Spiritual Rappers, and Shakers, and Widow Wakemanites, and Agrarians, and Grahamites, and a thousand other superstitious and infidel isms at the North?" "This unsettled, happy demented state of the human mind," he wrote, proved "that free society is a failure."[27] For Fitzhugh, the fractured, frantic cultural climate of the North had been prepared for by "the Pilgrim fathers" in the "unctuous days of Knox and Cromwell," whose individualistic ethos bred persecution and such horrors as the execution of witches.[28]

Lincoln refused to be sidetracked by the outcry against the isms. Slavery, he declared in August 1856, "should be not only the greatest question, but very nearly the sole question." Noting the diversionary tactics of the proslavery side, he stated, "Our opponents, however, prefer that this should not be the case." He again drove home his main point: "The question is simply this:—should slavery be spread into the new territories, or not? This is the naked question."[29]

Along with the naked question went a central idea. "Our government rests in public opinion. . . . Public opinion, on any subject, always has a '*central idea*,' from which all its minor thoughts radiate. That 'central idea' in our political public opinion, at the beginning was, and until recently has continued to be, 'the equality of men.'"[30]

By laying down his main question and his central idea, Lincoln helped to pull the disparate elements of the Republican Party together. That unifying mission continued to dominate his mind, even when on June 16, 1858, he introduced the provocative image of the house divided in a speech in Springfield. Quoting Jesus's words, he declared:

> "A house divided against itself cannot stand."
> I believe this government cannot endure, permanently
>   half *slave* and half *free*.
> I do not expect the Union to be is dissolved—I do not
>   expect the house to *fall*—but I do expect it will
>   cease to be divided.
> It will become *all* one thing, or *all* another.[31]

The house divided metaphor, though ostensibly divisive, in fact simplified the national situation. America was *not* divided in the 1850s; it was fragmented—terribly so. Numerous isms made antebellum culture an ever-changing kaleidoscope, as projected in Herman Melville's 1857 novel *The Confidence-Man*, a disjointed, premodernist literary masterpiece whose shape-shifting hero assumes various cultural guises. And there were the competing factions within the Republican Party. By unifying the Republicans, Lincoln hoped he could heal the fragmented nation. Faced with "old differences, prejudices and animosities," in his words, the party's "members were drawn together by a paramount common danger"—the westward spread of slavery.[32]

The way Lincoln expressed the house divided message enforced his ideal of unity. He did not predict a civil war, nor did he follow William Henry Seward in proclaiming an irrepressible conflict. Instead, he repeated a passage from the Bible and put it in quotation marks. The house divided passage previously had circulated widely in many contexts.

Lincoln himself had used it in his 1843 effort to unify the Whig Party. A dozen years later, in a letter to the Kentucky lawyer George Robertson, he asked, "Can we, as a nation, continue together—*permanently*—*forever*—half-slave, and half free?"[33] The *Richmond Enquirer*, in an 1856 article he mentioned in several speeches, expressed this idea from a militantly proslavery perspective, with the dire statement that "the war between the two systems rages everywhere, and will continue to rage until the one conquers and the other is exterminated."[34] Lincoln, in contrast, expected the nation to turn wholly to freedom. Far from a naive belief or mere dream, this intuition was based on his faith in human improvement and his devotion to public opinion. The central idea of America—the equality of all humans—was threatened by proslavery enactments, most recently the Dred Scott decision, which asserted that black people had no rights that whites had to respect. What was needed was a forceful antislavery political leader who could express the nation's central idea with special eloquence and tap into the antislavery instincts of the Northern public.

FIGHTING THE LITTLE GIANT

By the summer of 1858, Lincoln wanted to be that leader. He secured a public forum that, as it turned out, gave him national visibility. Selected by the Illinois Republican Party as its candidate for the US Senate, Lincoln challenged his Democratic opponent, Stephen A. Douglas, to a series of debates over two months to be staged in various locations throughout the state. The debaters started out on August 21 in the upper middle of the state at Ottawa, proceeded to the nearby town to the northwest, Freeport, then went five hundred miles south to Jonesboro, in the section of the state known as Egypt; then on to the east-central town of Charleston, and then counterclockwise in a circle up to

Galesburg, down to the center-west Quincy, ending up on October 15 in the southwest river town of Alton.

It was a taxing schedule for the debaters, especially given the fact that both of them made many other campaign appearances that fall as well. Lincoln, traveling by railroad, carriage, or boat, gave more than 60 speeches and covered some 4,500 miles. The well-heeled Douglas, who moved about in a lavish private train fitted out with a booming cannon labeled "Popular Sovereignty," reportedly gave 130 speeches and spent $50,000 on the campaign, as opposed to Lincoln's modest $1,000.[35]

STEPHEN A. DOUGLAS

Map of the 1858
debates in Illinois

ABRAHAM LINCOLN

For the huge crowds that turned out for the debates—from around 1,200 to 1,500 in Jonesboro to nearly 20,000 in Galesburg and Ottawa— the verbal sparring between Douglas and Lincoln was part political discussion and part slugfest. The contrast between the short, stocky Little Giant and the tall, angular Long Abe made the debates a Barnumesque curiosity show—"the best circus in town," as one reporter called it.[36]

Applause, cheering, laughter, and shouts of "Hit him again!" erupted throughout each speech. Newspapers slanted their reportage of the debates according to their political loyalties: stenographers from the Republican *Chicago Press and Tribune* tried to put Lincoln in a good light (for example, by giving him longer cheering and applause than his opponent), while the Democratic *Chicago Times* favored Douglas (by replacing his oft-repeated term "nigger" with "negro," and so on).

Douglas and Lincoln each tried to appear moderate without losing touch with his base. Douglas's right-leaning, racist base was indifferent about slavery; Lincoln's left-leaning followers tended to oppose slavery on moral grounds without wholly surrendering the notion that black people were inferior to whites. Both men reached out to centrist voters while catering, as much as possible, to their more extreme party members.

For Douglas, the task was especially delicate because he had alienated many Southern-leaning Democrats by opposing the Lecompton Constitution, the 1857 proslavery state constitution in Kansas that had been supported by the administrations of Franklin Pierce and James Buchanan. Douglas had used Lecompton as a means of suggesting that he was fair on slavery—that is, he supported its expansion only when a territory or state followed a lawful election process, not a corrupt one, as Kansas had. His position won over some antislavery figures, including, for a time, the Republican editor Horace Greeley.

But Lincoln saw through the ruse. He knew Douglas didn't care if slavery was voted up or down. His indifference was made clear by his unwavering support of the Dred Scott decision, which barred black people from citizenship. From a moral standpoint, Douglas was on the same page as Chief Justice Roger Taney and presidents Franklin Pierce and James Buchanan. These figures were so similar in their views that Lincoln had come up with the metaphor of an intricate structure built collaboratively by a team of four carpenters: Stephen, Roger, James, and

Franklin. He had introduced this image in two speeches leading up to the debates, where he again used it.

Douglas, prepared for Lincoln's accusation of a proslavery conspiracy, went on the attack immediately in the opening debate, offering his own conspiracy story, which blamed Lincoln for taking the lead in 1854 in abolitionizing the Illinois parties. Douglas repeated the story in later debates. Lincoln denied the charge and told how, in fact, he had rejected appeals to join the emerging antislavery party. Douglas's repeated falsifications elicited different responses from Lincoln: anger, as when he leaped from his seat and advanced while Douglas was speaking, until he was pulled back by a colleague; feigned indifference ("I hate to waste my time on such things"); and exasperated humor ("I don't know how to meet this kind of an argument. I don't want to have a fight with Judge Douglas, and I have no way of making an argument up into the consistency of a corn-cob and stopping his mouth with it at all. [Laughter and applause].")[37]

Douglas, for his part, tried to shrug off Lincoln's idea of his having conspired with Taney, Pierce, and Buchanan to advance slavery. Regarding Lincoln's "beautiful figure . . . about the building of a house," Douglas said, "I am not green enough to let him make a charge which he acknowledges he does not know to be true, and then take up my time in answering it, when I know it to be false and nobody else knows it to be true. (Cheers.)"

Actually, neither conspiracy theory was accurate literally, but each had a large amount of truth in spirit. Although Douglas did not actively collude with the other "carpenters" to protect slavery, there was no need to. The four were similarly engaged in twisting the Constitution to lend support to slavery. By the same token, Lincoln did not participate in the plans of the antislavery radicals. But as he had said at Peoria in October 1854, he hated slavery as much as any abolitionist. And he saw that the Little Giant's pose of neutrality was a mere cover for racism and amorality.

A clue to the different strategies of the debaters lies in the politicians and reformers Douglas associated Lincoln with in order to smear him. Those figures included Owen Lovejoy, whom Douglas mentioned thirty-seven times in the debates, Frederick Douglass (twenty times), Joshua Giddings (sixteen), and Ichabod Codding (four). Among others whom Douglas mentioned were Lyman Trumbull, Salmon P. Chase, William Lloyd Garrison, and Wendell Phillips.

Mentioning Garrison, Phillips, and Frederick Douglass was Douglas's way of associating Lincoln with disruptive isms. These reformers supported not only abolitionism but also other movements held suspect by moderates, including women's rights. The problem with bringing up these figures, however, was that Lincoln had never had any known contact with them before 1858. Also, he had carefully controlled his antislavery rhetoric to avoid appearing to be in the radical camp. During the Frémont campaign he had denounced slavery but had struggled not to sound like a radical abolitionist. A hostile newspaper suspected that "his niggerism has as dark a hue as that of Garrison or Fred Douglass" but noted that Lincoln "softened his remarks to a supposed palatable texture, . . . laboring under much restraint" to keep "within moderate bounds" in order to avoid alienating "the old whigs about him."[38]

In the debates, Douglas, tossing facts aside, made a straight connection between Lincoln and the radicals. He found that referring to Frederick Douglass was a forceful way of tapping into his listeners' racism.[39] He received supportive cheers when he mocked Lincoln for having the African American leader among his team of advisers—a straight-out lie, but one so effective that he told other stories intended to cater to racial prejudice. Frederick Douglass, he said, had been seen, shockingly, sitting with a white woman in a carriage driven by a white man. Even worse, he had given a lecture in Chicago arranged by Lincoln's supporters. (Shouts of "Shame on them" came from the audience.) And Lincoln, Douglas insisted, was, despite his show of Whiggish moderation, as much a Black Republican as Douglass or any other radical.

Sneering at Lincoln's position that people of all races were equal under the Declaration of Independence, Douglas said, "Did old Giddings, when he came down among you four years ago, preach more radical abolitionism than that? ('No, never.') Did Lovejoy, or Lloyd Garrison, or Wendell Phillips, or Fred. Douglass, ever take higher abolition grounds than that?"

Frederick Douglass once said that no one in that era did more than Stephen Douglas "to intensify hatred of the negro."[40] He may have been right. In a typical speech just before the debates, Douglas said that Lincoln, who "thinks the nigger is equal to the white man by Divine law," wanted to eliminate the law forbidding African Americans from settling in Illinois. "When he lets down the bars," Douglas said, then "the floods shall have turned in upon us and covered our prairies thick with them till they shall be as dark and black as night in mid-day," and Lincoln "will apply the doctrine of nigger equality."[41] Lincoln, in response, quoted Douglas's statements about blacks: "'They are an inferior race.' 'Between the white man and the negro, he goes for the white man; but between the negro and the crocodile, he goes for the negro.'"[42] What Douglas was really saying, Lincoln declared, was that "the white man may rightfully treat the negro as a beast or a reptile." By this pernicious doctrine, he pointed out, "the negro is no longer a man but a brute," and a "man, with body and soul, is a matter of dollars and cents."

Douglas brandished his racism in the debates:

> I am opposed to negro citizenship in any and every form. (Cheers.) I believe this government was made on the white basis. ("Good.") I believe it was made by white men, for the benefit of white men and their posterity for ever, and I am in favour of confining citizenship to white men, men of European birth and descent, instead of conferring it upon negroes, Indians and other inferior races. ("Good for you." "Douglas forever.")[43]

Lincoln's comments on race in the debates had a completely different tone. Although he made some racist statements, especially before the Southern-leaning audiences at Charleston and Jonesboro, he did so reluctantly and briefly, in response to Douglas's incessant race-baiting. He told the Charleston audience that a man in his hotel had asked him if he really favored "producing a perfect equality between the negroes and white people." Lincoln explained, "While I had not proposed to myself on this occasion to say much on that subject, yet as the question was asked me I thought I would occupy perhaps five minutes in saying something in regard to it." He did not even devote five minutes to the topic. On the subject of citizenship for black people, he said, "I am not nor ever have been in favor of making voters or jurors of negroes, nor of qualifying them to hold office, nor to intermarry with white people." We should notice his deft use of verb tense here. To say "I am not nor ever have been" is very different from saying "I never will be."

Had he spoken differently, he would have had little chance of attracting a large number of voters in a state that had some of the harshest black codes in the nation. He would have also seemed out of touch with what was then considered cutting-edge science. The nation's leading scientist, Louis Agassiz of Harvard, opposed slavery yet maintained that "the brain of the Negro is that of the imperfect brain of a seven month's infant in the womb of a White."[44] Such theories about racial inferiority would only intensify in the course of the nineteenth century. As respectful of black people as Lincoln was when he dealt with them personally, while running for office in 1858 against a man who railed endlessly at his "Black Republicanism," he sometimes aired hidebound racial views.

His concessions to racial conservatism were counterbalanced by surprisingly progressive statements. He declared that "there is no reason in the world why the negro is not entitled to all the natural rights enumerated in the Declaration of Independence, the right to life, liberty and the pursuit of happiness. [Loud cheers.] I hold that he is as much entitled to these as the white man. . . . [I]n the right to eat the bread, without leave of anybody else, which his own hand earns, *he is my equal and the equal of Judge Douglas, and the equal of every living man.* [Great applause.]"[45]

This pronouncement and others like it by Lincoln showed how far apart he and Douglas were in their views of race and self-government. For Douglas, black people were incapable of self-government because of their innate inferiority. For Lincoln, they were fully as capable in controlling themselves and making a living as whites. Self-government for Douglas meant the right of white citizens of each state to decide on that state's institutions, including slavery. Self-government for Lincoln meant majority rule in communities, as established by the Constitution, but also self-rule for individuals, which stemmed from both the Founders and the early Puritans.

In respecting both types of self-government, Lincoln resembled the Illinois politician Owen Lovejoy. Although early on Lincoln had kept a distance from Lovejoy because of his bold antislavery politics, the two had grown closer over time, and by 1858 they were virtually political twins. Or, rather, Lovejoy was Lincoln's radical alter ego; he often said explicitly what Lincoln couched in more moderate language.

A bluff, large man with striking blue eyes, Lovejoy loved telling jokes but saw slavery as no joking matter. He approached the institution with all the seriousness of his brother Elijah Lovejoy, the editor who had been killed while confronting an antiabolitionist mob in 1837.

And Owen Lovejoy valued his Puritan roots. Born and raised in Maine, he moved to Illinois and trained for the Congregational ministry. He preached for years in a Princeton, Illinois, church that was described as "purely an offshoot of Massachusetts," made up of "men direct from Plymouth Rock and many of whose ancestors came over in the Mayflower, and nearly all of whom were of the purest Puritan stock."[46]

After leaving the ministry and turning wholly to politics in 1856, Lovejoy directed his Puritan intensity against slavery. In his famous speech "Human Beings Not Property," delivered before Congress in February 1858, he declared that the divine right of kings had oppressed humankind for ages until God inspired the Puritans to found a nation built on self-rule. "America was the theatre where this manifestation was to be made," Lovejoy said. "The old Pilgrim barks, borne as by a miracle over the angry ocean, came freighted with the elements of a new political life, and the germ of a new national organization." This idea of self-government spread until it inspired many Americans. "Then came the crisis of our fate!" Lovejoy declared. "Our ancestors, Cavalier and Roundhead . . . met that crisis manfully, heroically." The joint Northern and Southern effort in the Revolution toppled tyranny and enacted Jefferson's immortal words about equality in the Declaration. Jefferson, Lovejoy noted, did "not say that all *English* men are born equal, or all *French* men, or all *Scotch* men, or all *Dutch* men, or all *white* men, or all tawny men, or all *black* men, but ALL MEN."[47]

Lincoln promoted this broad interpretation of human equality so persistently that Douglas charged him with merely imitating Lovejoy. "Mr. Lincoln," Douglas said, "is very much in the habit of following in the track of Lovejoy in this particular, by reading that part of the Declaration of Independence to prove that the negro was endowed by the Almighty with the inalienable right of equality with white men," when, in fact, Douglas said, the Founders meant "white men, men of European birth and European descent, and had no reference either to the negro, the savage Indians, the Fejee, the Malay, or any other inferior and degraded race, when they spoke of the equality of men."[48]

Douglas saw that Lincoln was influenced by Lovejoy in other ways as well. In the opening debate, he said, "Lincoln has evidently learned by heart Parson Lovejoy's catechism. (Laughter and applause.)"

Douglas was right. Several of Lincoln's arguments were a virtual gloss of statements made by Lovejoy.

Take the relationship between the American economy and slavery. Douglas defended popular sovereignty by saying that just as different farm products and businesses prospered in different states, so slavery was a state decision and would grow only where it was enforced by local police regulations. Lincoln replied that slavery was wholly different from the production of goods. The "variety in the industrial pursuits and productions of a country," he noted, "produces commerce, brings us together, and makes us better friends. We like one another the more for it."[49] Slavery, in contrast, created discord. Every time it had come up for national discussion, from the Missouri crisis of 1820 to the fight over Kansas-Nebraska in the 1850s, sectional tensions escalated and murmurings of civil war were heard.

Lovejoy had made the same point six months earlier in his congressional speech. All sections of the nation, he pointed out, were bound by economic relations. Commerce fostered cohesion. Only slavery disrupted the national scene. "The territorial extent of our country," Lovejoy said, "the variety of its productions, and the range of its climate, are, if left to their natural operation, elements of strength, union, prosperity, and harmony." Slavery had the potential to "hurl us . . . into ruin and chaos."[50] Like Lincoln, Lovejoy thought that abolishing slavery could be a gradual process. Calling for the "ultimate extermination" of slavery, Lovejoy announced to the South: "We shall not push you. If you say that you want a quarter of a century, you can have it; if you want half a century, you can have it. But I insist that this system must ultimately be extinguished."[51]

Ultimate extinction became Lincoln's mantra in 1858. He aired it publicly in July in the "House Divided" speech and repeated in other addresses, including the debates with Douglas. He anchored the idea firmly in the goals of the Founders, who, he said, had tolerated slavery but had regarded it as an evil that must disappear over time. As he said in the Ottawa debate, "I believe if we could arrest the spread, and place [slavery] where Washington, and Jefferson, and Madison placed it, it *would be* in the course of ultimate extinction."[52]

Lovejoy had estimated it would take twenty-five to thirty years for slavery to disappear. Lincoln guessed it could take twice that long: "I do not suppose that in the most peaceful way ultimate extinction would occur in less than a hundred years at the least; but that it will occur in the best way for both races in God's own good time, I have no doubt."

It's difficult today to imagine slavery lasting in America until 1958, but that's how intractable the institution seemed when Lincoln spoke these words, in the fall of 1858. Douglas insisted that Lincoln's House Divided statement meant "boldly and clearly a war of sections, a war of the North against the South, of the free states against the slave states—a war of extermination—to be continued relentlessly until the one or the other shall be subdued."[53] Lincoln's reply was simple: "Not war." He discounted any other than a peaceful solution. There was no chance that Kentuckians would "shoulder their muskets and . . . march into Illinois," and "no danger of our going over there and making war upon them."[54] Change would have to come slowly, through the electoral process.

But—and this was the key point for Lincoln—change *must* come, no matter how long it took. There was no retreat. Slavery was a wrong that must be obliterated.

"IT IS THE ETERNAL STRUGGLE BETWEEN THESE TWO PRINCIPLES–RIGHT AND WRONG–THROUGHOUT THE WORLD"

Wasn't this something like the higher law—the loose cannon that Lincoln denigrated? If so, in Lincoln's view, it was a higher law advocated by the Founders, who had envisaged the end of slavery because it conflicted with the Declaration's doctrine of human equality. On the issue of law, Lincoln made sure that Douglas was hoist on his own petard. Douglas had attacked Lincoln for not respecting the Supreme Court's ruling in the Dred Scott case, but Lincoln reminded listeners that Douglas himself renounced Dred Scott by promoting popular sovereignty, which hailed local rules—what Douglas called "police regulations"—as the final arbiter of slavery, whereas Dred Scott in fact superseded local rules by requiring states, even those that had voted to be free soil, to respect ownership of blacks who had been enslaved elsewhere. Douglas, in short, was adrift in moral relativism and illogic.

Lincoln's choice of a Bible quotation as his symbol of the slavery conflict was a gesture toward the higher law of religion. When Douglas criticized Lincoln for saying that a house divided could not stand, Lincoln asked, "Does the Judge say it *can* stand? [Laughter.] . . . If he does, then there is a question of veracity, not between him and me, but between the Judge and an authority of a somewhat higher character. [Laughter and applause.]" Lincoln here reminded Douglas of the sacred text from which the house divided image came.[55]

Lincoln was now ready to follow Owen Lovejoy by emphasizing publicly the dictates of morality. Lovejoy, the brashly open Underground Railroad conductor whose antislavery vision was grounded in Puritanism, declared that all the forces of civilization and nature stood in opposition to slavery.

Throughout the debates, Lincoln publicized his moral opposition to slavery in the most unequivocal terms. Two years earlier, at the Republican National Convention in Philadelphia, party leaders, while they voiced their strong opposition to slavery, had been wary of making moral pronouncements, perhaps in an effort to avoid sounding like incendiary Garrisonians. Robert Emmet, the president of the convention, declared, "We come to treat Slavery not as a moral question. . . . Slavery is, so far as our functions are concerned with it, a political evil; and we do not come here to discuss the great abstract principles of right and wrong, the laws of God and the behests of the Bible, Slavery be right or wrong."[56]

Lincoln, in contrast, now equated the Republican Party with the

Lincoln on October 1, 1858, two weeks before the final
Lincoln-Douglas debate (photograph by Calvin Jackson)

law of justice and morality. His boldest statements came during the
final debate, at Alton, where Owen Lovejoy's Puritan-fired abolitionist
brother had been murdered two decades earlier. Lincoln declared that
there was a sharp difference in America between "one class that looks
upon the institution of slavery as a wrong, and of another class that
does not look upon it as a wrong. The sentiment that contemplates the
institution of slavery in this country as a wrong is the sentiment of the
Republican party. It is the sentiment around which all their actions, all
their arguments, circle, being a moral, social, and political wrong"—an

echo of Lovejoy's statement months earlier that slavery was "an evil, social, moral, and political—a wrong to the slave."[57]

Then Lincoln delivered a full-scale Lovejoyan declaration:

> That is the real issue. . . . It is the eternal struggle between these two principles—right and wrong—throughout the world. They are the two principles that have stood face to face from the beginning of time; and will ever continue to struggle. The one is the common right of humanity and the other the divine right of kings. It is the same principle in whatever shape it develops itself . . . , whether from the mouth of a king who seeks to bestride the people of his own nation and live by the fruit of their labor, or from one race of men as an apology for enslaving another race, it is the same tyrannical principle.[58]

Lincoln here combined the major themes that antislavery advocates traced to Puritanism: self-rule versus the divine right of kings, absolute moral decisions, and the principles of liberty and equality. Right and wrong, Lincoln declared, have been rigidly distinguished from the beginning of time. They are a part of the natural order and the divine plan, as deeply entrenched as the difference between "the common right of humanity" and "the divine right of kings."

No Forefathers' Day orator could have expressed the idea more strongly than that.

There's evidence that the public bought his argument. In the November elections, the Republican candidates for office, the most visible of whom was Lincoln, won 53 percent of the popular vote statewide, as opposed to 46 percent for Douglas and the Democrats. But Douglas won the election, because, at the time, the Illinois legislature chose the US senator. And the districts represented in the legislature were weighted to the Democrats.

Lincoln and his associates suspected foul play in the election results. Because of flexible voter registration laws, tampering with elections was commonplace, especially by manipulating the immigrant vote. Democrats, in particular, were known to "colonize" swing districts with Irish railroad workers who were rapidly naturalized so that they could vote. David Davis, who had high praise for Lincoln's speeches in the Senate race, remarked, "There would be no doubt of Douglas' defeat if it was not from the fact that he is colonizing Irish votes."[59] William Herndon, likewise, was confident that "there is nothing which can well defeat us but the elements, & the wandering roving robbing Irish, who have flooded over the State."[60]

Lincoln, also suspicious of Democratic hijinks, was prepared to fight fire with fire. On October 20, five days after his last debate with Douglas, he wrote the Republican operative Norman Judd saying that while he felt confident about his chances in the election, he feared being "over-run with fraudulent votes to a greater extent than usual." He said he had recently spotted fifteen Irishmen going around with bags (presumably containing money to be used to bribe voters). He wrote Judd: "I have a bare suggestion. When there is a known body of these voters, could not a true man, of the 'detective' class, be introduced among them in disguise, who could, at the nick of time, control their votes? Think this over. It would be a great thing, when this trick is attempted upon us, to have the saddle come up on the other horse."[61]

It's unclear what Lincoln expected this disguised agent to do to control votes, but he seemed ready to go to the limit to defeat Douglas and the Democrats.

As it turned out, he fell victim to the malapportionment of the Illinois legislature. Legislative seats still followed districting based on the 1850 census, before the population explosion that occurred in the northern, largely Republican portion of the state. And so, though Lincoln and the Republicans won the statewide popular vote, the legislature on January 5, 1859, elected Douglas to the Senate by a vote of 54 to 46.

Despite his stellar performance in the debates, Lincoln was left with the reality of the loss to Douglas. By one account, he had moments of depression. On the evening of Douglas's victory, the lawyer Henry Whitney found Lincoln alone in his law office "gloomy as midnight, . . . brooding over his ill-fortune" and murmuring, "I expect everybody to desert me.'"[62] But as usual, humor helped him deal with the loss. He told a journalist "that he felt like the Kentucky boy, who, after having his finger squeezed pretty badly, felt 'too big to cry, and too badly hurt to laugh.'"[63]

He had lost a battle, but he had a better chance than before of succeeding in the long run. He had stood toe to toe with the most magnetic speaker of his day and had expressed the Republican Party's positions on slavery with striking acuity and moral urgency. Talk of his running for president in 1860 began to circulate. When he told his friend Anson Henry that the Senate race "gave me a hearing on the great and durable question of the age," even "though I now sink out of view, and shall be forgotten," Henry assured him that the people "will bear you on their memories until the time comes for putting you in possession of their House in Washington."[64]

It was not just his principled, logical defense of the Republican program people would remember; it was also his common touch, his genuine identification with the popular heart.

Even his demeanor radiated egalitarianism. We get a sense of what the forty-nine-year-old Lincoln was like in the fall of 1858 from a reminiscence by the Ohio journalist David Ross Locke, who interviewed him in Quincy, the venue of the sixth debate with Douglas. Locke would prove a significant figure for Lincoln during the White House years. Adopting the persona of Petroleum V. Nasby, a bigoted, loutish Copperhead, Locke wrote devastating satirical newspaper sketches and books that Lincoln read avidly and shared with others.

When Locke interviewed Lincoln in a Quincy hotel room, Lincoln took off his coat, tie, and shoes and tilted back on his chair, with one of his large feet perched on another chair. "I like to give my feet a chance to breathe," he explained.[65] Locke noted, "He seemed to dislike clothing, and in privacy wore as little of it as he could." Lincoln's face was in its default look—sad and abstracted—but it came alive when the talk turned to a recently deceased politician who had been an extremely vain man. Lincoln joked that if the man had known how many people would attend his funeral, "he would have died years ago."

As a journalist and political humorist himself, Locke appreciated Lincoln's ability to tell jokes that weren't just exercises in random rib-tickling or pointless exaggeration, as was most of the era's popular humor. Locke noted, "He said wonderfully witty things, but never from a desire to be witty. His wit was entirely illustrative. . . . He never cared how he made a point so that he made it, and he never told a story for the mere sake of telling a story. When he did it, it was for the purpose of illustrating and making clear a point."[66]

This potent storytelling ability of Lincoln's annoyed Douglas, who said, "Every one of his stories seems like a whack upon my back."[67]

Locke found that Lincoln's joke about the egotistical man who would have died years ago to attend his huge funeral fit the immediate context. When Locke saw Douglas speak at the Quincy debate the next day, he saw nothing but self-importance. Douglas was "so full of self that there was room for nothing else"; he championed conservative views just to get ahead.[68]

Lincoln had once warned that America could be taken over by a despotic leader who served himself, not the nation. Locke sensed that possibility when he saw the speech by Douglas, who "fed upon applause till he fancied himself a more than Caesar."[69] The scene was ominous: "He suppressed facts, twisted conclusions, and perverted history. He wriggled and turned and dodged; he appealed to prejudices; in short, it was evident that what he was laboring for was Douglas and nothing else." For Lincoln, in contrast, "his personal interests did not weigh a particle. He was the representative of an idea, and in the vastness of the idea its advocate was completely swallowed up." Lincoln was "absolutely honest—honest all the way through—and in face and manner satisfied all men that he was so."

The little-big-man humor Lincoln had utilized for so long found a natural target in the pretentious, egotistical Douglas. Lincoln said that many who wanted the famous Douglas to be president "have seen in his round, jolly, fruitful face, post offices, land offices, marshalships, and cabinet appointments, chargeships and foreign missions, bursting and sprouting out in wonderful exuberance ready to be laid hold of by their greedy hands," whereas "in my poor, lean, lank, face, nobody has ever seen that any cabbages were sprouting out. [Tremendous cheering and laughter.]"[70] Douglas's constant insults and evasions led Lincoln to compare him to a cuttlefish, "a small species of fish that has no mode of defending itself when pursued except by throwing out a black fluid, which makes the water so dark the enemy cannot see it, and thus it escapes. [Roars of laughter.]" Popular sovereignty became so attenuated in Douglas's contradictory explanations that it was "as thin as the homoeopathic soup that was made by boiling the shadow of a pigeon that had starved to death." One of Douglas's repeated stories about antislavery radicals was such "stale fraud" that it reminded Lincoln of "the fisherman's wife, whose drowned husband was brought home with his body full of eels." When asked what to do with the corpse, she replied, *"Take the eels out and set him again."*

By the late 1850s, Lincoln was well positioned to unify the Republican Party as a political candidate with unique popular appeal. Not only did he transform politics, but he also stood poised to transform a key political base that Stephen Douglas had once controlled: Young America.

His success in corralling the enthusiasms and spirit of young Americans would sweep him into the presidency and into the early phase of the Civil War.

13

Blondin, Barnum, and B'hoys

There are clear takeaways from America's greatest president. To be an effective leader in a deeply divided time, keep to the center while clinging to the nation's core principle of human equality. Make the center lively—even, at times, shocking. Don't insult your opponents. And don't forget young voters.

During the 1850s, Lincoln took a middle position on the isms of his day. He didn't fully embrace any of them, but he didn't distance himself from those who did. He kept his eye trained on the one ism that really counted. In September 1859, he urged the Ohio politician Salmon Chase to do all he could to stop Douglasism—the threatened westward spread of slavery. "That ism," Lincoln wrote, "is all which now stands in the way of an early and complete success of Republicanism."[1] He explained that "the chief effect of Douglasism" was to change the "moral tone and temper" of the American people by inviting them to become indifferent about human rights. All of Douglas's "reasoning and sentiments," Lincoln declared, "spring from the view that slavery is not *wrong*."

But in arguing that slavery *was* wrong, Lincoln did not join those who gathered under the moral banner of New England Puritanism. He was notably absent from the grand ceremony for the laying of the cornerstone of the National Monument to the Forefathers in Plymouth,

Massachusetts, on August 2, 1859. Completed in the 1880s, the eighty-one-foot monument, featuring symbolic statues of Faith, Morality, Liberty, and the like, rooted public morality in the Pilgrims. "Our life is their life," one speaker announced to the crowd of five thousand. "From their oppression springs our freedom."[2] Among the orators that day were the antislavery leaders Salmon Chase, Henry Ward Beecher, John Parker Hale, Henry Wilson, and Francis P. Blair. Letters of support came from other notables. But not from Lincoln.

Nor did he participate in the widespread celebration in the North of the quintessential latter-day Puritan, John Brown, who was executed in Virginia on December 2, 1859, after he and a band of followers raided Harpers Ferry in a bold but doomed effort to spark a slave rebellion that they hoped would lead to the fall of American slavery.

He resisted overpraising John Brown because he saw that any violation of the Constitution, real or perceived, threatened the Union. He carefully honed the Republican Party's argument that the Founders themselves realized the wrongness of slavery and anticipated its ultimate extinction. As shall be discussed, he presented this argument most fully in the landmark Cooper Union Address of February 1860, which Harold Holzer calls "the speech that made Abraham Lincoln president."[3]

Often overlooked cultural factors also contributed to his election. The most important ones can be summed up in three words: Blondin, Barnum, and b'hoys. Charles Blondin was a tightrope performer to whom Lincoln was compared by many, including Lincoln himself. Just as Blondin symbolized Lincoln's effort to remain centered between radicals and conservatives, so Barnum, the master showman of the age, represented the kind of theatrics that helped lift him to the nation's highest office. Another huge boost came from Lincoln's success in winning over the b'hoys, a large body of young Americans who had formerly been loyal to his opponent, Stephen Douglas.

BALANCED OVER THE FALLS

In the summer and fall of 1859 the touring thirty-five-year-old French acrobat Charles Blondin (né Jean-François Gravelet) dazzled Americans with his tightrope walks, the most famous of which were his repeated crossings of Niagara Falls. Poised on a hemp rope 200 feet above the roaring, mist-bellowing falls—five hundred thousand tons of water plunging per minute, Lincoln had once calculated[4]—Blondin traversed the 1,100-foot span between the American and Canadian sides as thousands of spectators gasped and cheered. Advancing across the rope, which was steeply sloped because it sagged some 60 feet in the middle, he steadied himself by a balancing bar and performed amazing tricks: somersaults, flips, headstands, monkey crawls, and balancing on a chair. He walked backward, at night, blindfolded, in chains, and on four-foot

CHARLES BLONDIN   BLONDIN ABOVE NIAGARA FALLS

457

stilts. One of his most famous feats was walking across with his agent, Henry Colcord, on his shoulders. Another involved his pushing a stove in a wheelbarrow to the middle of the rope, cooking an omelet, and lowering the meal to passengers on the *Maid of the Mist* below.[5]

Lincoln found in Blondin a symbol for his centrist position on major issues. Before the Civil War and during it, Lincoln balanced himself between extremes: between popular sovereignty and the demand for immediate abolition, between Southern and Northern views, between ungoverned higher laws and what he and other Republicans saw as the antislavery higher law within the Constitution. He thought that if he leaned too far in any direction, the nation could fall into anarchy or despotism. With the political and cultural forces around him spinning toward the centrifugal, he provided a solid centripetal counterweight.

He identified strongly with Blondin. In the summer of 1862, a group of radical antislavery Bostonians visited him in the White House and urged him to aim the war more directly toward the abolition of slavery. He greeted the group cordially and listened while its leader read an address that said "the government must have a policy" on slavery. After the speech, Lincoln sat back and threw a leg over the corner of a table. He thought for a moment, then asked, "Do you remember that a few years ago Blondin walked across a tight rope stretched over the falls of Niagara?" Suppose, he said, that all the nation's goods and achievements were crammed into a wheelbarrow, and the security and safety of everyone's home depended on Blondin's guiding it successfully over the falls. He continued, "As he was carefully feeling his way along and balancing his pole with all his most delicate skill over the thundering cataract, would you have shouted to him 'Blondin, a step to the right!' 'Blondin, a step to the left!' or would you have stood there speechless, and held your breath and prayed to the Almighty to guide and help him safely through the trial?"[6] The Bostonians got the point and left.

What he did not tell them was that he had in his drawer a draft of the Emancipation Proclamation, which he would announce publicly in

September in the Preliminary Emancipation Proclamation and issue in its final form the following January. He had already put into writing the sort of antislavery policy they called for.

The artist Francis Carpenter, who called the Emancipation Proclamation "an act unparalleled for moral grandeur in the history of mankind," heard Lincoln make a similar remark to a delegation of westerners in 1864. Complaining hotly about the progress of the war, the westerners heard the same story the Bostonians had. Lincoln invited them to imagine all their property transformed into gold and given to Blondin to transport across the Niagara River. "Would you shake the cable," he asked, "or keep shouting out to him, 'Blondin, stand up a little straighter—Blondin, stoop a little more—go a little faster—lean a little more to the north—lean a little more to the south.' No, you would hold your breath as well as your tongue, and keep your hands off until he was safe over."[7]

Political cartoonists often made the Blondin comparison. In June 1860, shortly after Lincoln was chosen as the Republican Party's presidential candidate, the humor magazine *Vanity Fair* published *Shaky*," picturing a costumed, scared-looking "Mr. Abraham Blondin De Lave Lincoln" walking precariously on a narrow, crooked log, barely keeping his balance because he is holding a pole weighed down by a bag holding a black man, with Horace Greeley in the background yelling, "Don't drop the carpet bag."[8] The message? Lincoln, as a Republican, faced the challenge of keeping centered on the controversial issues of race and slavery. The same theme informed *The Coming Man's Presidential Career, a la Blondin*, in which Lincoln crosses Niagara with an African American on his shoulders while holding a pole inscribed with the word "Constitution."[9]

Lincoln's Blondin-like centeredness galled some radical abolitionists. In 1864, Wendell Phillips complained that Lincoln, who was slow to come out in support of the vote for black people, must be pushed off his tightrope (that is, he must not be reelected). Frustrated by the

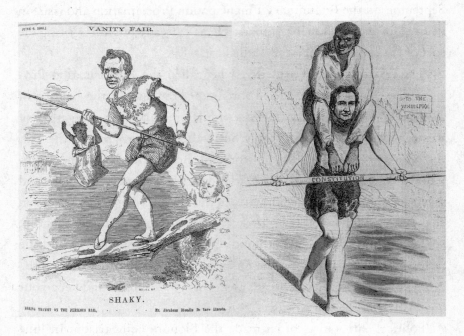

Shaky ... Mr. Abraham Blondin De Lave Lincoln (Vanity Fair, June 9, 1860)

The Coming Man's Presidential Career, a la Blondin (Harper's Weekly, August 25, 1860)

president's public silence on African American suffrage, Phillips declared in a speech that "the franchise for the slave" was "indispensable" and "inevitable," but "there is Blondin—don't speak to him! He may go over—take care! Mr. Lincoln stands there balanced, with the pole, on a rope. Keep mum, nation!" Impersonating Lincoln, Phillips said, "'Don't think I shall go over! Oh, no; I am balanced—balanced even!'" "But the question," Phillips continued, "is whether he *is* well balanced with his eye fixed upward. . . . The Abolitionist says to Lincoln—'Look up—to justice, of God, to the rights of every man under the law!' He is looking down at Kentucky, and I tremble for him."[10]

Phillips had a point. Lincoln focused on keeping border states like Kentucky in the Union, and he was publicly silent on black suffrage until after Appomattox, when he recommended it in a speech (to the disgust of the actor John Wilkes Booth, who was in the audience). Unbeknownst to Phillips, Lincoln had already promoted the African American vote in a private letter to the Louisiana governor Michael Hahn.[11] Also, he was waging a hard war that would lead to a Union victory and the passage of the three Reconstruction Amendments, which emancipated and gave citizenship rights to black Americans.

Lincoln, therefore *was*, to use Phillips's words, looking up "to justice, . . . to the rights of every man under the law!" But he was cautious about expressing his abolitionist sympathies too strongly, which, he knew, would inflame the border states and Copperheads.

He had been training for years to be a political Blondin, one who carefully mingled progressive public statements with moderate ones. His 1837 announcement that slavery was unjust but that vituperative abolitionists used the wrong means of fighting it; his 1854 Peoria speech, which coupled abolitionism with colonization; his debates with Stephen Douglas, in which he repeated the common idea that blacks were not equal to whites while saying that they merited fair treatment under the Constitution—these are a few of the many instances in which Lincoln tempered radical declarations with conservative ones.

This balanced, Blondin style drew criticism. In 1858 there appeared a pamphlet, *Abraham Lincoln! And His Doctrines, Examined and Presented in a Concise Form, from His Own Speeches,* which juxtaposed passages from various Lincoln addresses to suggest that he often contradicted himself. In the sarcastic words of the pamphlet, his speeches revealed "Mr. Lincoln an Advocate of Negro Equality and Negro Citizenship" and, simultaneously, "Mr. Lincoln Opposed to Negro Equality" and "Opposed to Negro Citizenship"; "Mr. Lincoln Will Not Vote to Admit a State with Slavery" and he "Will Vote to Admit a State with Slavery"; he was "Not in Favor of Interfering with Slavery Where It Now Exists" and he wants it "To Be Put on a Course of Ultimate Extinction."[12]

Such apparent incongruities in Lincoln make one think of Walt Whitman, who in 1855 wrote, "Do I contradict myself? / Very well then . . . I contradict myself; / I am large . . . I contain multitudes."[13] Whitman's contradictions reflected a democratic poet's expansive goal of putting all of American experience onto the page. Lincoln's, in contrast, show him hovering around the center in an effort to keep himself and his nation in balance in a politically unstable time. Just as a tightrope artist, responding to natural conditions like wind, leaned slightly one way or the other to keep on the rope, so Lincoln tilted right or left according to the demands of the moment. During the debates with Douglas, for instance, he made his most conservative statements on race and slavery while speaking in the Southern section of Illinois and his most forward-looking ones in the state's Northern section.

His Blondin approach to politics helps explain his rise to the leadership of the Republican Party. In the jockeying among possible candidates for the party's 1860 presidential run, he stood for moderation. When Ohio Republicans drafted a platform calling for the repeal of "the atrocious Fugitive Slave Law," Lincoln advised Salmon Chase to oppose it, explaining that such a plank would "explode" the forthcoming Republican National Convention, where its supporters and its opponents would "quarrel irreconcilably."[14] As much as Lincoln hated the Fugitive Slave Act, he reminded Chase of Article IV, Section 2, the Constitution's so-called fugitive slave clause. Lincoln had similar advice for Schuyler Colfax of Indiana, whom he warned to avoid "apples of discord" that might disrupt the party. Lincoln counseled, "We should look beyond our noses; and at least say nothing on points where it is probable we shall disagree."

The period between the fall of 1858, when he had the debates with Douglas, and November 1860, when he was elected president, saw him accomplishing an especially difficult Blondin feat. He was both self-reliant and, to use his words, controlled by events. He exercised aggressive individual effort while responding sensitively to outside forces.

The strongest force was the nation's response to the militant abolitionist John Brown. Brown had taken on mythic proportions in much of the North because of his antislavery activities in Kansas Territory, where in 1856 he and his small band of followers had defeated larger military units that tried to turn Kansas toward slavery. Brown's slaying of five proslavery settlers on Pottawatomie Creek in May 1856, in response to numerous atrocities committed by the proslavery side, was part of the spiraling cycle of violence in Bleeding Kansas.

Among some antislavery Northerners, Brown rose to virtual sainthood after his October 1859 assault on Harpers Ferry, Virginia, when Brown and eighteen followers invaded the arsenal there in a bold attempt to spark a slave rebellion that he hoped would lead to the fall of slavery. After a battle in which a total of seventeen were killed, Brown and six followers were captured, tried, and hanged. Though found guilty of treason, murder, and inciting a slave rebellion, Brown, during his weeks in jail while awaiting execution, exhibited a selfless devotion to the nation's millions of enslaved blacks that won the admiration of some leading Northerners. Henry David Thoreau compared Brown to Jesus Christ.[15] Emerson, similarly, called him "that new saint" who would "make the gallows glorious like the cross."[16] William Herndon averred that Brown "was good and great and is immortal—will live amidst the world's gods and heroes through all the infinite ages."[17]

John Brown worship swept the North, leading to the stirring "John Brown's Body," the Union army's favorite marching song, reworded by Julia Ward Howe as "The Battle Hymn of the Republic."

The veneration of John Brown put Republicans in a tricky position. If they praised him without qualification, they lay themselves open to the charge of supporting an armed invader of the South who observed his own higher law. But to reject him altogether was to alienate the

JOHN BROWN

growing number of Northerners who followed cultural leaders like Emerson and Thoreau in revering him. And so most Republicans took an ambivalent position, praising Brown's antislavery motives but disapproving of his violent tactics.

Despite their caution, Republicans could not escape being accused of Harpers Ferry. Shortly after the raid, one of Lincoln's advisers, Charles H. Ray, recognized the vulnerability of the Republicans. Ray wrote Lincoln, "We are damnably exercised here about the effect of Old Brown's wretched fiasco in Virginia, upon the moral health of the Republican party! The old idiot—The quicker they hang him and get him out of the way, the better."[18]

Actually, John Brown had distanced himself from Republicans, whom he viewed as all talk and no action. To Southerners, however, he and the Republicans were coconspirators. A Virginia newspaper announced that "Harper's Ferry is just a manifestation of the horrific and wrong-headed doctrines of Black Republicanism," which should now be called "Brown Republicanism after John Brown."[19] A proslavery pamphlet generalized, "The principle upon which John Brown and his allies acted, is the same which has been proclaimed by nearly all the leaders of the Republican party."[20]

William Henry Seward, then the Republican front-runner for the presidency, was often singled out for blame, even though in fact he had no connection with John Brown. "With his avowed doctrine of the 'higher law' and the 'irrepressible conflict' doctrines," one Southern newspaper announced in an article on Brown, Seward would instigate "anarchy, blood and revolution" were he in the White House.[21] Another paper reported that the main lesson of Harpers Ferry was "that Mr. Seward is the arch-agitator who is responsible his elevation to the Presidency would stimulate servile insurrections all over the South." The Mississippi senator Jefferson Davis declared, "We have been invaded, and that invasion, and the facts connected with it, show Mr. Seward to be a traitor, and deserving of the gallows." If Seward was not punished, Davis argued, "then John Brown, and a thousand John Browns, can invade us, and . . . the Black Republican government will stand and permit our soil to be violated and our people assailed and raise no arm in our defense."[22]

The vilification of Seward put Lincoln in an unexpectedly strong position to win the Republican nomination for the presidency. Lincoln's friend Jesse Fell had previously brought up the idea of Lincoln's casting his hat in the presidential ring, but at the time Lincoln thought he was not prominent enough to run. "Oh, Fell," he said. "What's the use of talking of me for the presidency, whilst we have such men as Seward, Chase, and others, who are so much better known to the people and whose names are so intimately associated with the principles of the Republican Party. Everybody knows them; nobody, scarcely, outside of Illinois, knows me."[23]

But in the wake of Harpers Ferry, his unfamiliarity actually increased his chances to be nominated. Unlike well-known figures like Seward, Chase, and Greeley, he did not have a controversial reputation. Jesse Fell remarked that Seward and Chase had "said radical things which, however just and true, would seriously damage them, if nominated." What the Republicans needed was a candidate "who has no record to defend and no radicalism of an offensive character."[24]

With no widely known radical tendency that could link him to John Brown, Lincoln seized the opportunity to capture the center of the party. Between November 1859 and early May 1860, he established himself as the Republican Party's Blondin.

He began his centrist positioning in earnest in the place where John Brown had first gained fame: the Kansas Territory. Invited by a Kansas politician, Lincoln gave two speeches there in early December 1859, around the time of John Brown's execution in Virginia. In his speeches, Lincoln was guarded about Brown. Just when the eyes of the nation were fixed on the scaffold in Virginia, Lincoln delayed mentioning John Brown until the end of his speeches. His comments were brief. He said that Brown had shown "rare unselfishness, great courage," and "he agreed with us in thinking slavery wrong." But, he added, Brown's effort had been futile and lawless, and nothing could "excuse violence, bloodshed, and treason."[25]

He pointed out that violence like Brown's, if responded to correctly, could actually lead Americans toward a renewed respect for the governmental system established by the founding fathers. The history of Kansas, Lincoln said, was one of "strife and bloodshed" in which "both parties had been guilty of outrages."[26] Such violence flew in the face of the Founders, who had created a representative democracy based on elections. Ballots, not bullets, were the weapons of the American people. Moreover, Lincoln noted, if not for Douglas's Kansas-Nebraska Act, violence would never have arisen in Kansas, where slavery had once been banned by the Northwest Ordinance and the Missouri Compromise. The Republican Party, far from promoting violence, kept alive the vision of the Founders, who treated slavery as an evil that eventually would disappear.

Over the next several months, he determinedly avoided any open association with extreme political positions.

In the autobiographical sketch he sent to Jesse Fell in December 1859, he made no direct mention of slavery. Discussing his ancestry, he dismissed any connection with Puritanism, which was linked in the popular mind with antislavery radicalism—a linkage recently enforced by the ultimate Puritan, John Brown, the Cromwellian warrior who prized his New England roots. Lincoln publicly disavowed his New England past, writing in the Fell sketch that "efforts to trace my ancestors to New England were vain" (even though privately he was deeply curious about his fourth great-grandfather, the Puritan Samuel Lincoln of Hingham, Massachusetts).[27] In the Fell autobiography, Lincoln described his humble frontier background, his lack of formal education, and his service in the Black Hawk War and in the US Congress. But he mentioned neither his hatred of slavery nor the Republican Party. He announced himself "always a whig in politics, and generally on the whig electoral tickets"—a coded way of proclaiming himself a moderate. He even cloaked his prized policy of the nonextension of slavery in a euphemism. With a feigned rhetorical yawn, he wrote, "I was losing interest in politics, when the repeal of the Missouri Compromise aroused me again. What I have done since then is pretty well known."[28]

The autobiography was intentionally tame. It contained nothing inflammatory—nothing about the house divided, about the injustice of the Dred Scott decision, or about his disgust over the brutal treatment of enslaved blacks or their permanent imprisonment in slavery, all of which he had spoken of in his 1850s speeches.

While softening his public posture, Lincoln simultaneously took active steps to advance his own cause. His self-reliance shone brightly in his landmark Cooper Union speech, which he delivered in New York City on February 27, 1860.

Invited to speak by a New York Republican club that had been hosting antislavery lectures, Lincoln originally was scheduled to appear at Henry Ward Beecher's church in Brooklyn, but the venue was subsequently changed to the Cooper Institute in Manhattan.

Lincoln prepared for the speech by doing careful historical research. To rebut a recent article in *Harper's Magazine* by Stephen Douglas, who argued that the founding fathers favored popular sovereignty, Lincoln perused documents related to the early development of the nation: the five-volume *Debates on the Adoption of the Federal Constitution* by Jonathan Elliot, the *Annals of Congress*, and the *Congressional Globe*. As Herndon recalled, "He searched through the dusty volumes of congressional proceedings in the State library, and dug deeply into political history."[29] Lincoln and a woman related to his wife left Springfield on February 22 by train to Jersey City, then by ferry across to New York. The newly built Cooper Union building had a large auditorium, the Great Hall, whose columns and arches made it one of the most elegant halls in the United States. On the day before the speech Lincoln attended Beecher's church to hear the famous preacher. On the twenty-seventh, after going to Mathew Brady's studio to have his picture taken, he worked on his speech, which he delivered in the evening to an audience of some 1,500 people, who paid twenty-five cents apiece to hear him.

His speech was a triumphant political performance in a prominent eastern venue.

Like the Kansas speeches, the Cooper Union Address contained no controversial or alarming images: it made no reference to the House Divided or the like. The three main ingredients of his 1850s speeches— history, humanity, and the higher law—were still there, but with a very different emphasis. Lincoln at Cooper Union channeled humanity and the higher law through the history of the nation's Founders.

He did this by recounting in detail the Founders' attitude toward slavery as expressed in different documents, from the Northwest Ordinance and the Constitution through the Bill of Rights to the Missouri Compromise. He made a head count of antislavery votes among the Founders, showing that a majority of them—twenty-one of thirty-nine—had treated slavery as an evil that would eventually disappear.[30] The Founders had subtly recognized the humanity of black people; they never used the word "slavery" or "slave" in the Constitution, in which blacks are referred to as "persons." They had made antislavery natural law an organic part of the Constitution by treating slavery as an evil that must be abolished over time.

Aligning the antislavery Republican Party with the vision of the Founders, Lincoln challenged the canard that the party was radical or destructive. The opposite, he said, was true. The party did not introduce novel or unsettling ideas. Far from fostering violence, it opposed it. As for John Brown, he had nothing to do with Republicans. Lincoln dared his audience to name any associates of Brown's who were Republican. Not a single Republican, he noted, was with John Brown at Harpers Ferry. "John Brown's effort was peculiar," he said.[31] Obsessed by the injustice of slavery, Brown believed that God had commissioned him to end it. His effort at Harpers Ferry had failed, partly because of a lack of enthusiastic response by the liberated blacks and partly because a general insurrection was impossible due to the lack of communication networks among the enslaved population.

Those who charged the Republican Party with producing John Brown were exactly wrong, Lincoln said. Republicans shared Brown's antislavery passion but expressed it in the voting booth. The Republican Party had no intention of interfering with slavery where it already existed, as Brown had done. The party, then, was a powerful *restraint* on the kind of anarchistic violence Brown had resorted to. What would happen, Lincoln asked, if you directed the North's antislavery sentiment "out of the peaceful channel of the ballot-box, into some other channel? What would that other channel probably be? Would the number of John Browns be lessened or enlarged by the operation?"

Republicans responded rapturously to the Cooper Union speech. The influential antislavery editors Horace Greeley of the *New-York Tribune* and William Cullen Bryant of the *New York Evening Post* called it one of the greatest political addresses they had ever heard. The day after the speech, four New York newspapers circulated 170,000 copies of it.[32]

Hasty arrangements were made for Lincoln to go on a tour of New England to lend support to Republican candidates there. First he went to New Hampshire, where he visited his son Robert, who was attending Phillips Exeter Academy. He then gave speeches in various towns and cities in New Hampshire, Rhode Island, and Connecticut. Most of the speeches resembled the Cooper Union Address so closely that he wrote to Mary that he was nervous about appearing before "reading audiences, who have already seen all my ideas in print."[33]

On his eastern trip, Lincoln had given 11 two-hour speeches in ten days—a burst of oratorical activity by a man who delivered some 175 speeches from 1854 to 1860.

He emerged from his eastern tour a viable candidate for the presidency. For more than a year, he had been corresponding with political associates about the choice of a Republican presidential candidate in the forthcoming 1860 race. Senator William Henry Seward of New York was the politician mentioned most often. Other names included Governor Salmon Chase of Ohio, Senator Simon Cameron of Pennsylvania, Supreme Court justice John McLean, and the Missouri lawyer politician Edward Bates. These men represented a range of antislavery intensity, from the perceived radicalism of Seward (of "higher law" and "irrepressible conflict" fame) to the conservatism of Bates, a former slaveholder who had been an Old Line Whig.

Lincoln found himself positioned midway between the Seward and Bates wings of the Republican Party. A typical comment came from Mark W. Delahay, a Kansas Republican who wrote Lincoln, "The Radical stand point of Mr Seward renders our defeat certain if he is nominated—and the Extreme Radical wing would not rest quiet if Mr Bates could be nominated." Hence the need for a centrist like Lincoln. "The Republican Party has a head and a tail to it, and a middle." Seward was the radical head, Bates the conservative tail, and if the convention chose either, the other would drop off. "I say you represent the middle," Delahay told Lincoln, "and if nominated you could hold the head and tail on and beat the Democracy."[34]

Joseph Medill, the editor of the *Chicago Press and Tribune*, similarly saw Lincoln as ideally positioned between Seward and Bates. More and more politicians, he noted, "are convinced that 'Old Abe' is the man to win the race with" because of his principled centrism. Medill asked, "Does not common sense whisper in every man's ear that the middle ground is the ground of safety?"[35]

Lincoln, meanwhile, grew confident about his prospects nationally but was nervous about his situation in Illinois, where, he feared, he might not get past the state nominating convention, to be held in Decatur in May. He had met in January with Jesse Fell and other party leaders who assured him of their backing at Decatur. But an intraparty quarrel among Illinois Republicans had left him vulnerable to being bypassed as the state's presidential choice. Both radical supporters of Seward in the state's Northern section and Bates advocates in Southern Illinois had concocted a false controversy between Lincoln and Norman Judd, the head of the Illinois Republican Committee. In February, Lincoln wrote Judd, "Your discomfitted assailants are most bitter against me; and they will, for revenge upon me, lay to the Bates egg in the South, and to the Seward egg in the North, and go far towards squeezing me out in the middle with nothing."[36]

Judd, however, was determined to prevent Lincoln from being

squeezed out of the middle. With Lincoln in mind, Judd used his position as a member of the Republican National Committee to secure Chicago as the site for the national convention, scheduled for May 16–18. Other cities under consideration—New York, Cleveland, and St. Louis— lost ground in the competition for hosting the convention because they were in states with front-runners for the nomination (Seward, Chase, and Bates, successively) who might then be unfairly privileged in the choice of a candidate. Chicago won the competition largely because of Lincoln's relatively low profile.

Lincoln's political fate was now in the hands of political operatives like Judd, who worked devotedly on his behalf. Others included David Davis, Leonard Swett, Ward Hill Lamon, Gustave Koerner, Stephen Logan, Joseph Gillespie, Richard J. Oglesby, and some fifteen other men who had long known Lincoln in Illinois's legal and political circles. This supportive group proved to be the principal outside force that lifted him to the presidency.

Among the canniest of the group was Richard J. Oglesby. A Kentucky-born lawyer and Mexican War veteran, Oglesby went on to become a major general in the Civil War, a US senator, and a three-term governor of Illinois. But perhaps his greatest achievement was to invent the rail-splitter image that became indelibly associated with Lincoln. Recalling the Log Cabin campaign of 1840, Oglesby, who presided over the Illinois Republican nominating convention at Decatur, devised a way to make Lincoln irresistibly attractive to the average voter. He sought out Lincoln's cousin, the elderly John Hanks, and asked what type of work Lincoln excelled in. Hanks replied, "Well, not much of any kind but dreaming, but he did help me split a lot of rails when we made the clearing twelve miles west of here."[37] Oglesby and Hanks rode a buggy into the country and found rail fences, made of black walnut and honey locust trees, that Lincoln had helped build.

On May 10, thousands of Illinois Republicans, including Lincoln, gathered in a makeshift structure covered with a circus tent, called the

RICHARD J. OGLESBY

Decatur Wigwam, to nominate candidates for the state governorship and the US presidency. During a lull in the discussion of gubernatorial candidates, Richard Oglesby announced that there would be a presentation. Into the convention walked John Hanks and a friend, each carrying a wood rail and a placard that read, "Abraham Lincoln, The Rail Candidate for President in 1860."[38] The men held a banner that said the rails were from a lot of three thousand that Lincoln had split on his father's farm when he first settled in Illinois in 1830.

Cheering and applause erupted. Hats, canes, and books tossed in the air nearly brought down the canvas ceiling. Lincoln, who had been hauled by the crowd to the stage, looked at the rails and said that maybe they were his, "but whether they were or not, he had mauled many and many better ones since he had grown to manhood."[39] More cheering, mixed with laughter. The enthusiastic attendees adopted a resolution naming Lincoln as Illinois Republicans' first choice for the presidency, to be promoted by the state's delegates to the national convention.

The Illinois Rail-splitter was born. *Abe* was about to emerge on the national scene.

But for the Abe image to have an impact, Lincoln first had to secure the Republican nomination. Reaching that goal was sped by a group of Lincoln supporters, led by his campaign manager David Davis, who attended the Republican National Convention from May 16 to May 18. Because no building in Chicago was big enough to house the convention, a 100-by-180-foot wooden structure was built at the southeast corner of Lake and Market Streets. Dubbed the Chicago Wigwam, the building could hold more than ten thousand people. Four hundred and sixty-six delegates represented twenty-four states, including the slave states of Maryland, Virginia, Delaware, Kentucky, Texas, and Missouri, whose presence at the convention signaled the Republican Party's effort to prove itself nonsectional.[40]

The air buzzed with excitement when a mass of politicians and spectators gathered in the Wigwam on May 16. Before long, the floor was slippery with saliva and tobacco juice, and the air reeked of whiskey guzzled by the raucous crowd.

The Republican platform passed by the convention supported the nonextension of slavery and denounced the recently revived slave trade. To reach out to the South, the platform promised to protect slavery where it already existed. One plank lambasted armed invasion of a state, such as John Brown's raid, as "the gravest of crimes."[41] Other planks endorsed federally funded river and harbor improvements, the transcontinental railroad, and a homestead act. If Lincoln at this time was pulling back from the overt radicalism of the Peoria and "House Divided" speeches, so the Republican platform struck a moderate tone at a divided moment, when a radically worded provision could provoke disunion or civil war.

The temperately phrased but firmly antislavery party platform favored Lincoln. So did his team of operatives, who played the politicians and the onlookers at the Chicago Wigwam masterfully. An expert organizer, David Davis delegated team members to approach representatives of the various states in order to sway votes by promising certain political rewards if the states went for Lincoln. Even though Lincoln had written, *"Make no contracts that will bind me,"* Davis doled out promises of patronage, regardless of whether or not they could be fulfilled.[42] When the Chicago lawyer Wirt Dexter later remarked that Davis must have prevaricated at the convention, Davis declared, *"Prevaricated. Prevaricated, brother Dexter? We lied, lied like hell."*[43]

Among the most active Lincoln boosters at the convention was Ward Hill Lamon. The burly, hard-drinking Lamon had no scruples about using any means of advancing Lincoln's cause. Lamon went to a Chicago printer and had hundreds of counterfeit convention tickets issued. Early on May 18, he handed out the tickets to Chicagoans who supported Lincoln. His strategy was to fill the Wigwam with as many Lincoln backers as possible before a large contingent of Seward supporters could enter the building. He instructed the Lincolnites to outshout Seward's backers.

Davis and his team had expected Lincoln to win on the third ballot, and they were right. On the first ballot, Seward had 173.5 votes, Lincoln 102, with Cameron, Bates and McLean far behind. The second ballot saw Seward at 184.5, Lincoln at 181, and Salmon Chase in the mix with 42.5 votes. A shouting match between the various candidates' supporters developed in which the artificially inflated Lincoln contingent became especially uproarious. After the Sewardites let loose with wild yelling, Lincoln's name was announced. His supporters exploded with a sound compared by one observer to "all the hogs ever slaughtered in Cincinnati giving their death squeals together" and by another to "a thousand steam whistles, ten acres of hotel gongs, a tribe of Comanches, headed by a choice vanguard from pandemonium."[44]

A combination of the noise, Davis's strategizing, and insufficient support for Seward led to the selection of Lincoln on the third ballot.

Lincoln, meanwhile, was back in Springfield, doing law work and checking the convention results as they came over the telegraph wires. He relaxed for a time by playing handball against a wall with some boys. When the news of his nomination arrived at the law office, he accepted the exuberant congratulations of those around him and then excused himself by saying, "I must go home; there is a little short woman there that is more interested in this matter than I am."[45]

The next day, a Republican committee led by the Massachusetts congressman George Ashmun appeared at the Lincolns' Jackson Street home to deliver the official results of the convention. Friends of Lincoln had sent bottles of brandy and champagne to be served with cakes and sandwiches to the committee. Hours before the committee arrived, Gustave Koerner and Judge Ebenezer Peck visited the Lincolns and saw brandy decanters set out on a table, with a basket of champagne bottles on the floor below. The sight disturbed Peck and Koerner, who warned the Lincolns that there could well be some temperance men among the visitors, and the liquor should be removed. Mary, recalling the mint-julep political receptions in her childhood home, remonstrated vigorously, but Lincoln said, "Perhaps, Mary, these gentlemen are right. After all is over we may see about it, and some may stay and have a good time."[46]

When the committee arrived at the home that evening, the liquor was out of sight. Ashmun delivered a brief notification speech in the front parlor as Lincoln, looking solemn as though carrying a new weight, listened. Expressing his "profoundest thanks," for this "high honor," Lincoln said he was "deeply, and even painfully sensible of the great responsibility" that went with it.[47] After the interchange, the committee was served ice water from a silver pitcher. When the committee left, a number of them joined the carousals that were going on in the saloons and the streets of Springfield, which exploded with wild celebration of Lincoln's nomination.

Two weeks later, in response to a reporter's inquiry about the cold-water reception, Lincoln wrote in a letter, "Having kept house sixteen years, and having never held the 'cup' to the lips of my friends then, my judgment was that I should not, in my new position, change my habit in this respect."[48]

Self-reliant action, carefully regulated rhetoric, and the machinations of political friends had brought Lincoln to the cusp of the presidency.

Now popular culture took over, sweeping Abe into the presidency.

BARNUM, SPECTACLE, AND THE 1860 CAMPAIGN

In February 1863, a low point in the Civil War for the Union, the Lincolns held a reception in the White House for Charles S. Stratton and his new wife, Lavinia Warren. Known to the world as General Tom Thumb, Stratton stood two feet eleven inches and weighed twenty-one pounds; his wife, eight pounds heavier than he, was two feet six. At the reception, attended by many Washington luminaires, the six-foot-four Lincoln warmly greeted the couple. "It was pleasant," one of the guests that evening wrote, "to see their tall host bend, and bend, to take their little hands in his great palm, holding Madame's with especial chariness, as though it were a robin's egg, and he were fearful of breaking it."[49] The widely reported event became a subject of public interest and genial commentary.

The Tom Thumb reception was just one of many points of convergence between Lincoln and the culture of spectacle promoted with incomparable verve by the age's master showman, Phineas T. Barnum. Four months before the Tom Thumb event, Lincoln had held a reception

P. T. BARNUM AND TOM THUMB

for Barnum and another famous little person, George Washington (aka Commodore) Nutt. Tom Thumb and Commodore Nutt were among the curiosities exhibited at Barnum's five-story American Museum on New York's Broadway. Visited by millions each year between its opening in 1842 and its destruction by fire in 1865, the museum featured human, scientific, theatrical, and historical exhibits. Under the guise of offering rare information and instructive entertainment, Barnum catered to the sensation-hungry American public, exploited to the hilt by what I call the -est factor: America's fascination with the tallest, the shortest, thinnest, fattest, strangest, and so on.[50] The exhibits at his museum included Joice Heth, allegedly the 161-year-old black nanny of

George Washington; the seven-foot-eleven-inch Anna Swan, billed as the Nova Scotia Giantess; the Siamese twins Chang and Eng; and the Feejee Mermaid.

The American public feasted on the bizarre or grotesque. It gobbled up crime pamphlets, sensation-filled penny newspapers, and lurid urban novels like George Lippard's *The Quaker City* and George Thompson's *City Crimes*, whose villainous protagonists—Devil-Bug and the Dead Man, respectively—are among the most physically repulsive figures in American literature. Davy Crockett of the humorous Crockett almanacs boasts that he is so ugly that he sometimes doesn't get up in the morning for fear of scaring the sun away.[51]

To many, Lincoln fit in with such crowd-pleasing curiosities. His cragged face, with its cavernous eyes, large mouth and nose, and swarthy complexion; his wide ears and unruly black hair; his huge hands and feet and overly long arms and legs—these features, along with his ill-fitting clothes and awkward gait, made him seem almost as unusual as a Barnum exhibit. "To say that he is ugly," a journalist wrote, "is nothing; to add that his figure is grotesque, is to convey no adequate impression."[52]

The novelist Nathaniel Hawthorne, who visited Lincoln in the White House in 1862, pointed out that Lincoln's ordinary appearance was part of his Uncle Abe persona, exaggerated in a calculating way, with the intent of winning over the American audience. Here was Hawthorne's description of the president:

> [I]n lounged a tall, loose-jointed figure, of an exaggerated Yankee port and demeanor, whom, (as being about the homeliest man I ever saw, yet by no means repulsive or disagreeable,) it was impossible not to recognize as Uncle Abe. . . . There is no describing his lengthy awkwardness, nor the uncouthness of his movement; and yet it seemed as if I had been in the habit of seeing him daily, and had shaken hands with

him a thousand times in some village street; so true was he to the aspect of the pattern American, though with a certain extravagance which, possibly, I exaggerated still further by the delighted eagerness with which I took it in.[53]

Hawthorne captures the performative Lincoln, whose aim was to appear as the plainest American: what Hawthorne calls "the pattern American." Just as Benjamin Franklin had won great popularity by posing publicly as the bumpkin Poor Richard, so Lincoln performed as the lowly Uncle Abe. He was the humble American as political spectacle. His homely averageness was, in Hawthorne's words, "exaggerated" and "extravagant."

Lincoln joked about his appearance because he knew it was salable. He had his own version of the -est factor: he enjoyed playing the ugliest man. He often told a story, adapted from frontier humor and jest books, about meeting a horrible-looking stranger with a gun who had been instructed to shoot someone uglier than himself. Lincoln's eyes sparkled when he delivered the punchline: he opened his shirt and told the man, "If I am uglier than you, then blaze away."[54] During the Civil War, when he heard that a cabinet member, Edwin Stanton, in an angry moment cried, "We've got to get rid of that baboon at the White House," Lincoln was asked how he could endure such an insult. "Insult? insult?" the president said; "that is no insult; it is an expression of opinion; and what troubles me most about it is that Stanton said it, and Stanton is usually right."[55]

Baboon, ape, gorilla: such epithets were used to describe him by adversaries and even by some allies. The Union general George McClellan, for instance, called him "the original gorilla."[56]

Small wonder that he was sometimes compared to a Barnum exhibit. When riding on the law circuit, with his tall hat, long umbrella, and spindly legs that nearly reached the ground, he was, in Herndon's words, "a sight—beat anything that Barnum ever had or could by any possibility."[57] The only thing more bizarre was Lincoln's all-elbows-and-knees, clomping attempts at dancing, about which Herndon wrote, "Barnum could make more money on Lincoln's dancing than he could on Jumbo."

When Lincoln wanted to communicate a message, he knew how to use his physical differences to draw people in. Many contemporary observers noted that at first he came across as plain or awkward, even bizarre, but in the course of speaking, his manner and arguments won over his listeners, and his appearance even seemed to change, creating an aura of humanity and genuineness. A lawyer who was in the audience at the Cooper Union Address initially felt "pity for so ungainly a man" as the "angular and awkward" Lincoln, who at the start of his speech thanked "Meester Cheerman," fiddled with his suspenders, and spoke in "a low, monotonous tone" that tended "to dwindle into a shrill and unpleasant sound." But as the speech progressed, his "face lighted as with an inward fire; the whole man was transfigured." He "held the vast meeting spellbound" as "his trenchant and convincing arguments confirmed the soundness of his political conclusions."[58] His striking looks and manner proved to be effective lures to many who subsequently heeded his words. The New York lawyer George Templeton Strong remarked that Lincoln initially seemed like "a barbarian, Scythian, yahoo, or gorilla," but proved himself "most sensible, straightforward, honest, . . . clear-headed and sound-hearted," a man of "evident integrity and simplicity of purpose."[59]

Lincoln's supporters made political capital of his physical oddness, which attracted attention to his superior qualities. A Boston journalist, reporting that there was "so much curiosity to learn the personal appearance and bearing of Mr. Lincoln," described him as "a tall, lank man, awkward," but with "a grandeur in his thoughts, comprehensiveness in his arguments, and a binding force in his conclusions, which were perfectly irresistible."[60] The Illinois Republican Lyman Trumbull described him as "a giant in stature, six feet three inches high, every inch a man, and a giant in intellect as well as in stature."[61] Backers at the Chicago convention explained, "Honest Old Abe is the homely but expressive phrase," the "rude designation . . . invented by unerring popular instinct, [that] expresses the entire and confident affection which the heart of the masses feels for Mr. Lincoln wherever he is known."

The very first Lincoln campaign biography of the 1860 presidential race stated: "His features are not handsome, but extremely mobile; his mouth particularly so. He has a faculty of contorting that feature in a style excessively ludicrous, and which never fails to provoke uproarious merriment." But his typical speech is "an expression of great impressiveness, all the more remarkable from the contrast with the extremely humorous air it sometimes assumes"; it reveals such "profound earnestness" and "sure evidence of thought" that it sways the audience. With its combined ludicrousness and good sense, his oratory is "eminently addressed to the popular mind."[62]

Lincoln's true character also came out in his speeches, in which he exploited the showman-like energies that Barnum represented but channeled them in a serious direction: toward communicating the bedrock principles that mattered to him. Barnum was above all interested in effect, Lincoln in message. Among Barnum's exhibits were General Santa Anna's wooden leg, pilfered during the Mexican War, and a knife-headed pike taken from John Brown's raid on Harpers Ferry. For Barnum, these items were valuable only for their impact on curiosity seekers. For Lincoln, in contrast, Santa Anna and John Brown related to issues he cared about deeply: the Mexican War and the fight against slavery.

Many of Barnum's marvels were frauds. Joice Heth, advertised as more than a century and a half old, was, as her autopsy revealed, in her seventies when she died in 1856. The Feejee Mermaid, who appeared lovely in Barnum's posters, was nothing more than a monkey's torso sewn to the bottom half of a fish. Barnum had no qualms about fooling the public as long as he kept it entertained. Known as "the prince of humbug," he wrote the popular book *Humbugs of the World*, in which he argued that "humbug is an astonishingly wide-spread phenomenon—in fact almost universal"; he showed that it permeated virtually all aspects of culture and society.[63]

When Lincoln used the word *humbug*, in contrast, he had in mind the bogus reasoning behind proslavery laws and arguments. The Kansas-Nebraska Act was, in his words, "a naked humbug, a foul wrong, perpetrated under false pretences, sustained by weak inventions and afterthought."[64] "All this talk about the dissolution of the Union," he declared, "is humbug—nothing but folly." Douglas's popular sovereignty idea was "the most errant humbug that has ever been attempted on an intelligent community." Lincoln repeated the idea so often that he elicited the word in call-and-response fashion. In his debates with Douglas, he said, "Let us talk about Popular Sovereignty! [Laughter.] What is Popular Sovereignty? [Cries of 'A humbug,' 'a humbug.']"

THE 1860 PRESIDENTIAL CAMPAIGN AND THE REIGN OF IMAGE

Such Barnumesque interchanges with audiences had served Lincoln well during the 1850s, but when the 1860 campaign came, he was faced with a new reality. Public silence replaced speeches. In that era, it was considered unseemly for a presidential candidate to campaign for himself. One of Lincoln's opponents in the four-way 1860 race, Stephen Douglas, was ridiculed for going from state to state on his own behalf. Under the pretense of visiting his mother in Vermont, he traveled throughout the northeast and then elsewhere, promoting himself. Journalists and cartoonists mocked him as a wandering child looking for his mother. A typical cartoon, *Honest Old Abe and the Little Boy in Search of His Mother—A Sensation Story*, showed Lincoln leaning on an axe and towering over the diminutive Douglas, who looks confused and fatuous in his frilly child's garment, as the White House looms in the distance.[65]

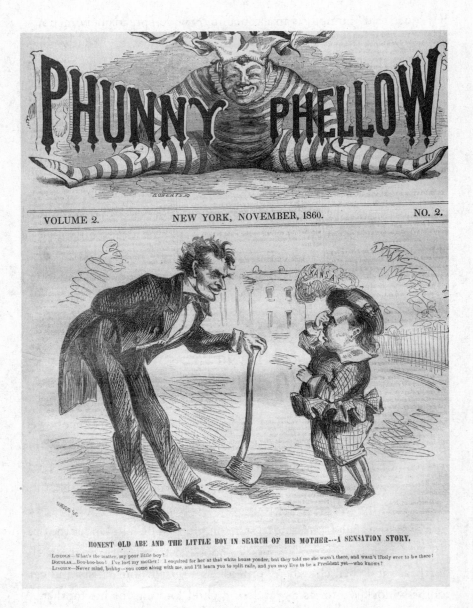

Honest Old Abe and the Little Boy in Search of His Mother—A
*Sensation Story (*Phunny Phellow*, November 1860)*

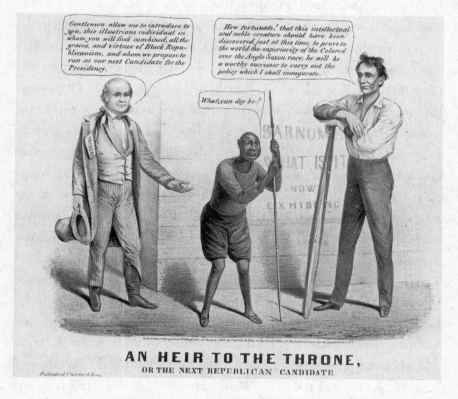

An Heir to the Throne, or the Next Republican Candidate
(New York: Currier & Ives, 1860). This lithograph by Louis Maurer pictures
Lincoln extolling Barnum's "What Is It?" as an "intellectual and noble creature"
who proves the "superiority of the Colored over the Anglo Saxon race."

By giving no major speeches between the Cooper Union Address in
February 1860 and his inaugural address in March 1861, Lincoln was
not only following the custom of the day but also remaining guarded at
an extremely volatile time. Even with his compassionate centrism, he
was, after all, an antislavery Republican whose election raised the possibility that Southern states would secede—which eleven of them did,
despite his ongoing efforts to remain moderate. During the campaign,

he stayed in Springfield. He spent much of his time in an office in the state capitol, meeting with visitors and keeping up correspondence.

His withdrawal from the public did not signal a rejection of the Barnumesque culture that had aided his political rise. To the contrary, he was more influenced by that culture than he had been previously. Opponents caricatured him as a freak who threatened to change the nation for the worse. Barnum's prize exhibit that year was "What Is It?," an eighteen-year-old African American, William Henry Johnson, whose tapering cranium indicated microcephaly but whom Barnum presented as a creature discovered in Africa who was the connecting link between the human and the monkey. Political cartoonists made a racist connection between Barnum's African and Lincoln's supposedly unnatural attitude toward black people. A Currier & Ives cartoon called *An Heir to the Throne, or the Next Republican Candidate*, pictured Barnum's misshapen black man standing bent between Horace Greeley and Lincoln. Greeley introduces the man as an "illustrious individual in whom you will find combined, all the graces, and virtues of Black Republicanism, and whom we propose to run as our next Candidate for the Presidency." Lincoln, leaning on a rail, says, "How fortunate! that this intellectual and noble creature should have been discovered just at this time, to prove to the world the superiority of the Colored over the Anglo Saxon race, he will be a worthy successor to carry out the policy which I shall inaugurate." The black man looks at the two whites and wonders, "What, can dey be?"[66] The racism was glaring.

"What Is It?" and other Barnum oddities would continue to be used negatively by Lincoln's enemies to pillory him during the Civil War. Being portrayed in political cartoons as freakish or ugly apparently did not significantly damage his reputation in the atmosphere of spectacle and sensationalism Barnum had helped create.

At the same time, however, now that he was on the national stage, he had to appear plausibly presidential. Photographers aided him in this regard. On the morning of the Cooper Union Address, Lincoln had

The great American WHAT IS IT? chased by Copper-heads (Boston, 1863). Anti-Lincoln lithograph by E. W. T. Nichols that shows Lincoln ripping up a paper that says "Constitution & the Union as it was" and dropping a paper that reads "New Black Constitution [signed] A. L. & Co." Lincoln tells African Americans who are pursuing him to "Go back to your masters, don't think you are free because you are emancipated." The blacks say, "Take us to your Bussum," "FADDER,r,r,r ABRUM," and similar endearing words. The snakes are Copperheads (Peace Democrats in the North); one snarls that Lincoln has "nigger on the brain"; others yell, "Hit him again," and so forth. On the right, a devil has brought the skeleton of John Brown from hell to witness the chaos Brown created through his armed attacks on slavery before the war.

gone to the studios of Mathew Brady, who took pictures of him that were later reproduced and distributed during the presidential campaign. Brady adjusted Lincoln's collar to cover his unusually long neck and added other elements that suggested solidity and dignity. In Brady's portrait, the beardless Lincoln, with his pronounced cheekbones, broad forehead, and eyes looking at the viewer, stands tall next to a column, with his left hand resting on two books. In his dark two-piece suit, bow tie, and white shirt, he is the picture of calm respectability. While many cartoon caricatures portrayed him as an ugly bumpkin, the Brady photograph—which, after all, presented the flesh-and-blood Lincoln,

Abraham Lincoln in February 1860
(photograph by Mathew B. Brady)

not an artist's rendition—remained a realistic reference point for those who wanted to see his true character. Reproduced in popular magazines, lithographs, posters, and cartes de visite, the Brady picture was one of history's most significant pieces of political propaganda. Lincoln reportedly said, "Brady and the Cooper Union speech made me president."[67]

If pictures of him in a suit and tie presented him as serious and decent, ones of him less formally dressed (wearing jeans, with his shirt open and his sleeves rolled up) projected the image of the Illinois Railsplitter, of Abe in all his variations.

In the 1860 campaign, frontier images were everywhere. At the Chicago convention, an Ohio delegate rose to "put in nomination the man who can split rails and maul Democrats, Abraham Lincoln. [Great applause.]"[68] The door to the *Chicago Press and Tribune* office was framed by rails, and Chicagoans carried rails on the streets.

Frontier fever swept the nation. Throughout the North, Republican parades and rallies featured rails, rail makers, log cabins, blacksmiths, and flatboats. Rail-splitter clubs proliferated. Wigwams, patterned after the structures at Decatur and Chicago, were built and used as campaign headquarters. Newspapers titled *Rail Splitter* were published in Chicago and Cincinnati. Songs, especially those written and performed by the popular Hutchinson Family, hailed the candidate whose opponents would "find what, by felling and mauling, / Our rail-maker statesman can do."[69] Among his accomplishments, according to his supporters, was to divide his rivals. One cartoon showed the muscular Lincoln swinging a maul and splitting a rail labeled "Democratic Party"—a reference to Lincoln's challengers, who, at odds over slavery, split into the Northern Democrats, represented by Stephen Douglas; the Southern Democrats, headed by John C. Breckinridge; and the Constitutional Union Party, led by John Bell.[70] (During the Civil War, a Union song, sung proudly by Tad Lincoln, went, "Old Abe Lincoln a rail splitter was he, / And he'll split the Confederacee.")[71]

The Last Rail Split by "Honest Old Abe."

The Rail-splitter (a life-size oil portrait painted for Lincoln's presidential campaign in 1860). In the background is a flatboat like the ones that Lincoln had worked on as a youth. In the distance is the White House.

The Last Rail Split by "Honest Old Abe" (*Momus*, June 2, 1860). Lincoln is pictured causing the split of the Democratic Party into Northern and Southern factions.

Republicans sent Lincoln frontier-related gifts: axes, mauls, wedges, pieces of rails and cabins, and the like—so many that his Springfield office became, in the words of John Nicolay, "a perfect museum" of curiosities.[72] Robert Lincoln became known as a Prince of Rails—a triple pun, referring to his father's erstwhile occupation, the 1860 visit of the Prince of Wales to America, and the fact that Robert was on the railroad train that carried Lincoln eastward to the presidency. The division of the Democrats into a proslavery wing under John Breckinridge and a popular sovereignty one under Stephen Douglas was attributed by Republicans to Honest Abe, shown in political cartoons splitting the rail labeled "Democratic Party" with his maul.

This masthead image of a Chicago campaign newspaper (*The Rail Splitter*, September 15, 1860) shows Lincoln splitting the Democrats; below that is a mock ad for a play titled *The Wandering Minstrel, or Douglas in Search of His Mother.*

The populist symbols of previous presidential campaigns paled by comparison with those that surrounded the Illinois Rail-splitter. The hickory sticks and hickory brooms of the 1828 campaign were metaphors for Andrew Jackson's toughness. The log cabins, hard cider, and raccoons of the 1840 race were resonant images, but they had little connection to the wealthy William Henry Harrison. In 1860, the symbols fit the candidate. Lincoln *had* split rails, he *had* lived in frontier cabins, he *had* piloted flatboats, and so forth.

Moreover, "Honest Abe" was not merely a persona. Lincoln was, of course, a canny politician who pulled strings, but those closest to him attested to his fundamental honesty. William Herndon's description of him as "an intensely sincere and honest man" matched that of Mary Todd Lincoln, who called her husband "almost a monomaniac on the subject of honesty"—an opinion shared by many others.[73] It was chiefly as Honest Abe that he appealed to the Northern electorate. An Indiana journalist wrote, "There are to-day more of the elements of universal popularity in the character and personality of 'Honest Abe Lincoln of Illinois' than any other man on the American continent."[74]

Coming after the administration of James Buchanan, which, in Michael Holt's words, "was undoubtedly the most corrupt before the Civil War and one of the most corrupt in American history," candidate Lincoln stood out for his integrity.[75] A five-member Select Committee of Congress led by John Covode of Pennsylvania issued a report in June 1860 that revealed extensive bribery, graft, and electoral fraud under Buchanan. Horace Greeley, who denounced this "wholesale executive corruption, legislative bribery, and speculative jobbery," asserted that "we recognized in Honest Abe Lincoln the right man to lead us."[76] Another journalist noted "a feeling that corruptions have grown frightfully rank at Washington, and that it is high time that the honest masses should interfere . . . and the great watchword will be not antagonism to slavery, but 'honest Abe Lincoln.'"[77]

The honest masses did interfere. And a large majority of them were young.

CONQUERING YOUNG AMERICA

Among the followers of Lincoln pictured in the satirical cartoon *The Republican Party Goes to the Right House* is a street tough who says that he wishes all police stations could be destroyed "so that the bohoys [*sic*] can run with the machine and have a muss when they please."[78]

The connection made here between Lincoln and the b'hoys is telling. The b'hoys, or Bowery Boys, were working-class men—butchers, wagon drivers, day laborers, and so on—who were always in a "muss" (a brawl) and ever ready to run with their "masheen" (a hand-drawn fire engine) to fight fires in fierce competition with other b'hoy companies. Dressed in colorful shirts and stovepipe hats (like Lincoln's hat) and with hair cut short in back and waxed long in front (hence the nickname Soap Locks), the b'hoy, generically called Mose or Sikesey, was unruly but good-hearted, loyal to his friends and to his g'hal, the working-class woman who walked with confidence and defiance. Although unlearned, the b'hoy and g'hal were 'cute (acute). They aped the tastes and manners of the upper class, and they enjoyed Shakespeare as much as they did melodramas or minstrel shows.

Originating in New York street culture and popularized in plays such as Benjamin Baker's *A Glance at New York in 1848*, the b'hoy became a national figure when he merged with other masculine types. The journalist George Foster wrote in 1850, "The 'b'hoy of the Bowery, the rowdy of Philadelphia, the Hoosier of the Mississippi, the trapper of the Rocky Mountains, and the gold-hunter of California are so much alike that an unexpected hand could not distinguish one from the other."[79] When Walt Whitman sought a national type from which to fashion the persona of the quintessentially democratic *Leaves of Grass*, he chose the b'hoy, a figure he knew well from the streets of Brooklyn and New York. Whitman's description of himself as "one of the roughs"—a swaggerer, idler, boaster—is patterned after the b'hoy, which explains why early reviewers dubbed him "Walt Whitman the b'hoy poet," "the Bowery B'hoy in literature," a writer who "would answer equally for a 'Bowery boy,' 'Mose' in the play . . . or the 'Bhoy that runs with the engine.'"[80] But Whitman's speaker is very much a transformed b'hoy, one brought under poetic control and given a philosophical dimension. As a journalist, Whitman had written, "It is too common among

A B'HOY AND A G'HAL

supercilious people to look on the Firemen as turbulent noisy folk, 'bhoys' for a row and a 'muss' only. This does the great body of them a prodigious injustice."[81] In his poetry, Whitman invested the b'hoy with depth and compassion.

If Whitman tried to redirect the energy of the b'hoy in poetry, Lincoln did so in politics. When Lincoln said that he wanted to lure what he called the "shrewd wild boys about town" to the Whig side while campaigning for Zachary Taylor in 1848, he sensed what historians have confirmed: young voters, especially first-time ones, were then a large element of the voting population, and their loyalty must be gained if a candidate hoped to succeed.[82]

In the early going, the Whigs were at a disadvantage in attracting these voters. The movement known as Young America arose around the Democratic journalist John L. O'Sullivan's notion of Manifest Destiny. The Democrats promoted Young America as fresh, patriotic, and forward-looking, as opposed to the Whigs, who were dismissed as "old fogies."

In the competition for the b'hoys and their ilk nationwide, Stephen Douglas took an early lead. His success resulted largely from his combative style, which was immensely attractive to the male voters who made up Young America. Feisty yet genial, the whiskey-swigging, tobacco-chewing Douglas used words as if he were engaged in a bare-fisted brawl or in an eye-gouging fight. Known as "the favorite son of Young America," Douglas was described by a Chicago reporter as "a rowdy. He is of the class of barroom politicians. He is at home with the low and the vulgar."[83] Another journalist used similar words: "He appeals to the rowdy element, the wild types. Mr. Douglas and the b'hoys are similarly matched."[84]

By and large, the working-class voters attracted to Douglas shared his reactionary racial views and his indifference about slavery. But a sea change in the political attitudes of rowdies and roughs occurred in the 1850s. The 1856 Republican candidate John Frémont had natural appeal to young men who admired his record as a fearless western explorer. Although it's unclear to what degree young working-class voters shared his antislavery commitment, there are signs that they were becoming more progressive on slavery. The stage version of Stowe's *Uncle Tom's Cabin*, shown in Barnum's American Museum and in many other venues throughout the nation, was a tremendous draw for working-class playgoers.

Rowdy types who in former times had mobbed abolitionists, chased down fugitives from slavery, or harassed free blacks were suddenly caught up in Stowe's action-packed, moving story, which invited viewers to sympathize with fugitives and hiss at a brutal slave owner. The

New-York Tribune reported of a New York performance of the play: "The 'b'hoys' were on the side of the fugitives. The pro-slavery feeling had departed from among them. . . . They believed in the higher law."[85] A Philadelphia journalist commented, "One may infer a hopeful change in public sentiment, when they see three thousand persons unconsciously accepting anti-slavery truth; hundreds of boys—incipient rowdies, growing up to become the mobocracy of another generation, but preparing unwittingly to '*mob on the right side.*'"[86]

The proslavery phenomena that spurred Lincoln's return to politics—the Kansas-Nebraska Act, the Dred Scott decision, and the federal government's endorsement of Kansas's proslavery Lecompton Constitution—also contributed to the antislavery turn in the Northern working class. The 1856 Republican presidential candidate John Frémont, the famed Path-Finder of the Rocky Mountains, projected a rough hardihood that young voters found attractive; Young America clubs proliferated, and newspapers, including the *Young America Fremont Journal* of Boston, spread the antislavery slogan "Free Soil, Free Labor, Free Men, Fremont."[87] By 1860, Harriet Beecher Stowe was astounded to notice that antislavery sentiments that a decade earlier would have been considered "rank abolition heresies" were spoken of approvingly by many workers she encountered on the streets.[88]

Lincoln welcomed Young America, formerly Democratic, to the Republican side. In his second lecture on discoveries and inventions, given in Springfield in February 1859, he began by declaring, "We have all heard of Young America. He is the most *current* youth of the age."[89] Without mentioning either political party, he went on to associate Young America with a rage for the new, a desire for westward expansion, and a rejection of old fogies. All of these attitudes had defined the Democrats' Young America in the 1840s, but Lincoln presented an updated Young America, one "very anxious to fight for the liberation of enslaved nations and colonies." He showed how Young America was different now in other ways, too. The Republicans, like the Whigs before them, were the party of technological and social improvement. Lincoln in his lecture harked back to earliest history to show that improvement was endemic to humans, revealed in the discovery of clothing, language, iron, printing, and, more recently, the power of steam. He sarcastically identified the early fifteenth century as the time of "the invention of negroes, or the present way of using them," and suggested that thoughtful Americans had passed beyond such old fogyism. He used antislavery metaphors to describe the dramatic advance of humanity caused by printing. It is difficult to realize, he said, "how strong this slavery of the mind was [before printing]; and how long it did, of necessity, take, to break its shackles." America was the site of the world's greatest progress, because "a new country is most favorable—almost necessary—to the immancipation [sic] of thought, and the consequent advancement of civilization and the arts." Freedom of the mind, he subtly suggested, must lead to an end to old-fashioned ideas like slavery.

Between the 1859 lecture and the early months of the Civil War in the spring of 1861, Lincoln got a close look at—and a deep appreciation for—the new version of Young America, which now leaned Republican.

He was, like Whitman, a b'hoy writ large. If, as George Thompson wrote, the b'hoy had proliferated nationally as the Indiana Hoosier, the western trapper, and other male types throughout the nation, Lincoln was, in the words of a campaign song, the rail-splitting "son of Kentucky, / The hero of Hoosierdom through; / The pride of the Suckers [Illinoisans] so lucky." If the b'hoy loved both Shakespeare and minstrel shows, so did he. If the b'hoy was ill educated yet shrewd, he brandished his lack of education. In his autobiographical sketches, he not only emphasized his lack of formal schooling, but he once wrote "Education defective" and another time highlighted his primitive background by erasing the g in his phrase about learning "Reading—writing—ciphering to the rule of three."[90] When Stephen Douglas in a debate derided him by recalling the time when Lincoln was "a flourishing grocery-keeper [that is, saloon keeper] in the town of Salem" who "could beat any of the boys wrestling, or running a foot race, in pitching quoits or tossing a copper, [and] could ruin more liquor than all the boys of the town together (uproarious laughter)," Lincoln went with the joke, saying that while he never ran a saloon, he "did work the latter part of one winter in a small still house, up at the head of a hollow. [Roars of laughter.]"[91] He earned great political capital from his identification with average Americans. His uncle Charles Hanks tried to shock the public when during the 1860 campaign he recalled Abe as "nothing more than a wild *harum scarum boy*," and lazy to boot, but this combination of disorder and idleness held great attraction for young roughs.[92]

And the roughs were ready to channel their energy into tightly focused action when he ran for president. The young Wide Awakes who backed him during the campaign originated in Hartford, Connecticut, where he spoke on March 3, 1860, during his post–Cooper Union tour of New England. His audience that evening consisted mainly of young men who were thrilled when the city's twenty-nine-year-old mayor introduced Lincoln as one who had done "yeoman service" for the Republicans, and when Lincoln announced himself as a "dirty shirt" Republican—words confirmed that night by his "gaunt, homely figure, unpretending manner, conversational air, careless clothing and dry humor"—it made him seem "a man of the people." After making an antislavery speech, he entered a carriage. Quickly the vehicle was surrounded by scores of young men who spontaneously arranged themselves in military order. They escorted the carriage to the hotel. Lincoln remarked to the mayor, "The boys are wide awake. Suppose we call them the Wide-awakes."[93]

When Lincoln, momentously, won the presidential nomination in May, inquiries poured into Connecticut from all over the North about the procedures of the Wide Awakes. The name had gotten out, and soon a pro-Lincoln Wide Awake club formed in Hartford and, before long, in many other Connecticut towns as well. There was the nighttime parade, in which the Wide Awakes wore long oilskin coats and carried torches along with placards and banners that read "Lincoln Against Slavery," "Free Soil and Free Men," and the like. Mass demonstrations by the Wide Awakes became a defining feature of the campaign to elect Lincoln and his running mate, Hannibal Hamlin of Maine.

These demonstrations were very different from the turbulent rallies for Stephen Douglas. The difference was noted by John Hay, a young Springfield law apprentice who, along with his journalist friend John G. Nicolay, worked for the Lincoln campaign in 1860; the two "boys," as Lincoln called them, became his private secretaries in the White House.[94]

Describing a tremendous Lincoln rally held on August 8 in Springfield, Hay wrote, "There was none of that . . . rowdy plebeianism which outcrops in all Douglas crowds . . . no pandering to the vile ground-swell of ruffian passions; no barefooted rangers; no hangings in effigy," and none of the "yelling diabolism that spiced the Douglas turnout of July."[95] Twenty Wide Awake clubs from different parts of Illinois poured into Springfield in horse- or oxen-drawn wagons that carried log cabins, rail-splitters who mauled logs, blacksmiths who made horse-shoes, weavers who spun jeans, carpenters who hammered nails, and so on. Trains from all over the state brought more Lincoln supporters. At the Fair Grounds, Lincoln showed up in a carriage and was carried to a platform, where he stood as the crowd cheered for ten minutes, after which he confessed he had nothing to say but he was glad to see the crowd. With the help of an efficient Wide Awake, he mounted a horse and rode away. That night, thousands of Wide Awakes paraded by torchlight through Springfield as fireworks blazed above them—a scene that looked like "the onward march of a vast conflagration." The whole affair, Hay wrote, came off with "intense decency and tremendous cohesion"—an assessment seconded by a local reporter who noted that "the most admirable order was preserved," with the Wide Awakes marching "in a very gentlemanly manner, [and] dispersing in a becoming way."[96]

The Wide Awakes channeled the enthusiasm of young voters, which

A procession of Wide Awakes in New York City, 1860

became wild under Douglas, into disciplined campaigning. This was the new Young America, pro-Lincoln and pro-Republican. The clubs that backed Lincoln had names in which "Wide Awake, "Young," and "Young America" were used interchangeably, as in a rally represented by the Young Men's Lincoln Club, the Upper Alton Wide Awakes, and the Young America Lincoln Club of Alton.[97] At another event, "the German Republican Wide Awakes turned out in full force, assisted by about three hundred of the Lincoln and Young America Wide Awakes, for escort duty."[98]

The fate of the nation seemed to be in the hands of Republican Young America. The popular magazine *Harper's Weekly*, which was supportive of Lincoln, printed in its September 1, 1860, issue a cartoon of *Young America Rising at the Ballot-Box and Strangling the Serpents*

Disunion and Secession. Based on the legendary story of the infant Hercules killing two snakes sent by Queen Hera to kill him, the cartoon shows America's symbolic goddess Columbia assuring her snake-murdering baby, Young America, that only he can save the Union. "Well done, Sonny!" Columbia says. "Go it while you're young, for when you're old you can't."

Young America Rising at the Ballot Box and Strangling the Serpents
Disunion and Secession (Harper's Weekly, September 1, 1860)

Young America indeed helped elect Lincoln, but killing the serpent of secession would be far from easy.

On November 6, Lincoln spent the day in his office at the State House. He created a scene when at 3:30 p.m. he went to a polling booth to cast his ballot. Admirers mobbed him, shouting his nickname. "The cheers were perfectly deafening," a journalist wrote. "'Old Abe,' 'Uncle Abe,' 'Honest Abe,' . . . and other remarks abounded, and altogether the scene was one of rare interest."[99] At 5:00 p.m., he went home for dinner, and at 7:00 p.m., went to Springfield's telegraph office to keep track of the election results. The news was positive until 10:30 p.m., when silence came from New York. But soon notice came that he had not lost New York City and Brooklyn by as great a margin as had been expected and had won the state. The telegram read, "We tender you our congratulations upon this magnificent victory."[100]

Nationally, Lincoln had won nearly 40 percent of the popular vote, with about 30 percent going to Douglas, and the remainder divided between Breckinridge and Bell. Lincoln won 180 electoral votes to his opponents' combined 123.

At the news of his victory, he was calm. Others were not. "The Springfield boys had heard it, too," an observer recalled, "and the great crowd which had filled the State House surged into the street and began cheering, yelling and shouting like a thousand madmen suddenly let loose from their keepers."[101] Lincoln said that a little woman was waiting at home to hear from him, but as he was leaving the telegraph office, supporters insisted that he go with them to a nearby restaurant, where in an upstairs room the wives and daughters of Republicans wanted to congratulate him. He said that because he had been "in the hands of his friends for the past five months he might as well make it one night more." At the reception, mothers and their daughters filed by him, kissing him—not always on the cheek. At first their affection made him uneasy, but then he cheerfully surrendered to it, calling it "a form of coercion not prohibited by the Constitution or Congress." He went home at around midnight and found Mary asleep. When he told her the news, she at first stirred groggily without responding. Raising his voice, he exclaimed, "Mary, Mary! *we are elected!*"[102]

The next morning, cannon boomed all over town, and crowds

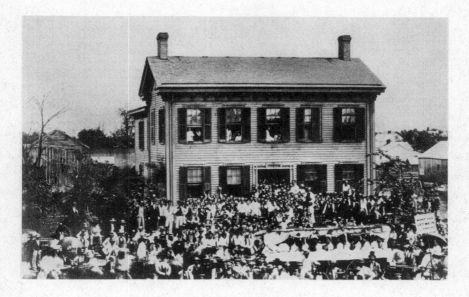

Lincoln's Springfield home during the 1860 campaign. A political procession is gathered outside. Lincoln, in a white shirt, stands to the right of the front door.

flocked to see him in his State House office. Always ready to greet the people, he held a levee—the kind of welcoming event that he would hold regularly in the White House during the Civil War.

Despite the victory, visitors noticed that he looked sad. To several groups of callers, he said, "Well, boys, your troubles are over now, but mine have just begun."[103]

Blondin was now walking on the rope, and the roar of the falls below was growing ever louder.

Challenging Secession

During the 1860 presidential race, a leading Southern magazine remarked sourly that if Lincoln won the election, the White House would be soon occupied by "a vulgar partisan of John Brown."[1] Lincoln's public distancing of himself from Brown prior to the election had failed to impress Southerners. They sensed that he hated slavery just as much as John Brown had. They were right, although he wanted to combat it through the electoral process, not through violence. His victory on November 6, 1860, meant that an antislavery Republican would take office in March. Southern states opted for secession, starting with South Carolina on December 20, 1860. By February 1861, seven states had formed the Confederate States of America, with its own constitution, which protected slavery and its extension into the territories. The provisional Confederate States Congress chose as the Confederacy's provisional president the ex–US senator from Mississippi Jefferson Davis, who was inaugurated on February 18. His presidency was confirmed in a Southern general election on November 6. His vice president was Alexander H. Stephens of Georgia.

Stephens, Lincoln's former Whig friend and fellow member of the congressional Young Indians in 1848, initially resisted secession and gave a speech before the Georgia legislature on November 14, 1860, calling for the South to remain in the Union. Stephens at first assured his fellow Southerners that Lincoln was a safe choice for the presidency, for he had no intention to interfere with slavery where it existed. On November 30, Lincoln wrote Stephens asking him to send him a copy of the speech. After reading it, Lincoln assured Stephens that the North had no designs on slavery. Stephens asked Lincoln to make some public statement that would cool sectional tensions, but Lincoln said the issue stood on a firm moral distinction: "You think slavery is *right* and ought to be extended; while we think it is *wrong* and ought to be restricted."[2]

It all came down, then, to moral judgment: your higher law versus my higher law.

So Stephens soon made clear his higher law: slavery was a God-ordained institution, and the South was right to separate from the Union in order to protect it. The Confederacy's "cornerstone," he announced in a landmark speech of March 1861, "rests upon the great truth, that the negro is not equal to the white man; that slavery—subordination to the superior race—is his natural and normal condition. This, our new government, is the first, in the history of the world, based upon this great physical, philosophical, and moral truth."[3]

In response, not once did Lincoln waver from his belief in the wrongness of slavery. Not once did he lose faith in the absolute sanctity of the Union. Many of those around him were willing to compromise on principles that for him provided a firm backbone. Lincoln demonstrated an unyielding adherence to the nonextension of slavery in the face of politicians who wanted to sacrifice this principle in order to save the Union.

Those over the years who have argued that the Civil War could have been avoided if a solution to the crisis had been reached beforehand ignore the fact that between December 1860 and the outbreak of the war in April 1861 some two hundred efforts at compromise were proposed.[4] All proved futile.

For Lincoln, any attempt to compromise that permitted the spread of slavery raised the possibility of unchecked centrifugalism—the ever-extending reach of the slave power. The compromise plan introduced to Congress in December 1860 by Lincoln's old Whig friend from Kentucky John J. Crittenden included six proposed constitutional amendments and four congressional bills, most aimed at appeasing the South. Crittenden called for a restoration of the Missouri Compromise, stipulating that the 36 degrees 30 minutes parallel, dividing free from slave territory, be extended to the Pacific. Other parts of the compromise toughened the Fugitive Slave Act and promised the permanent protection of slavery where it already existed through a constitutional amendment. Lincoln took special umbrage at the 36 degrees 30 minutes proposal, which allowed for the expansion of slavery. If Southerners were granted this concession, he wrote, they would demand possession of Cuba within a year and soon thereafter would be "filibustering for all [territory] South of us, and making slave states of it."[5] He was hardly alone in his feelings about the Crittenden measures, which failed to pass in Congress.

He also responded negatively to the peace conference held in Washington on February 4, 1861. One hundred thirty-one delegates from twenty-one states gathered to discuss possible solutions to the national crisis. The convention agreed on seven proposals that resembled the Crittenden compromise and, like it, went nowhere.

It was clear that compromise on slavery of the type reached in 1820 over Missouri and in 1850 over the western territories was now impossible. Lincoln remained intent on curbing the expansion of slavery, and he knew that the South was equally determined to protect and expand slavery, even to the extent of destroying the American Union. How was he, as incoming president, going to deal with the seceded Southern states, whose number increased as the months passed? He pondered the question while in Springfield in the months between his election in November and his departure for Washington in February 1861. His long train ride east, with many stops along the way, gave him the opportunity to test out various strategies for confronting the secession crisis.

TESTING, HEDGING, AND PERFORMING

During the weeks before his trip to Washington, DC, Lincoln wrapped up personal and business matters in Illinois. In late January, he visited his seventy-three-year-old stepmother, Sarah Bush Lincoln, who lived near Charleston in Coles County, Illinois. The farewell was emotional. She predicted (correctly) that she would not see him again. A friend of Lincoln's reported, "She embraced him when they parted & Said she would never be permitted to see him again that she[']d felt that his enemies would assassinate [him]. He replied No No Mama (he always called her Moma) they will not do that trust in the Lord and all will be well. We will See each other—again."[6] While in Coles County he also met other relatives, visited his father's grave, and gave directions for a stone marker.[7]

Returning to Springfield on February 1, he settled his finances and arranged to appear at towns and cities along his route east. On the evening of February 6, he and Mary held a reception at their home, which was "thronged by thousands up to a late hour."[8] Having arranged to rent out their house during their time in Washington, the family moved on February 8 into rooms at a hotel, the Chenery House. Two days later Lincoln went to his law office, where he discussed unfinished law cases with his partner and told him to leave up the sign "Lincoln and Herndon" until he returned after his presidency.

In the early morning of a stormy February 11, he gave a farewell speech to a thousand people who had gathered at Springfield's small railroad station to bid him goodbye. In the wind and sleet, trembling with feeling as he stood on the platform of the train's rear car, he told

SARAH BUSH LINCOLN

the crowd that he had lived in Springfield for more than a quarter of a century and had raised sons there, one of whom had died. He might never return to Springfield, he said prophetically. He was now about to take on a burden greater than even Washington had faced. Without God's help, he said, he could not succeed, but with it, he could not fail.

He had arranged with Mary that he would go by train to Indianapolis, where she and their sons would join him the next day. Those traveling with him included David Davis, Ward Hill Lamon, Norman B. Judd, his secretaries John Hay and John G. Nicolay, the drill instructor Elmer Ellsworth, and other friends, associates, and guards.

The thirteen-day trip, covering nearly two thousand miles and making dozens of stops in seven states, witnessed Lincoln by turns testing, hedging, and making a spectacle of himself.

At various stops, he tested out different approaches to addressing the national situation. In his first important speech, at Indianapolis, he tried combining topical humor with seriousness. He jokingly said the South was as devoted to the Union as was a free-love spouse to fidelity or a sick person who took homeopathic pills to getting cured. He then became firm. He emphasized the federal government's obligation to keep control of US forts, collect import duties, and regulate the mails in the South. Despite the current talk about "coercion" and "invasion," he said, no coercion was involved in the government carrying out its normal functions throughout the nation.[9] As for secession, it was by definition illegal. A state had the same right to secede from the Union as a county from a state: that is, no right at all. Since when, he asked, does a minority have control over the majority? The whole is greater than the part. The Union is greater than the individual state.

The Indianapolis speech, which was printed in newspapers nationwide, proved divisive. Lincoln received telegraphs from Washington reporting "both strong approbations and remonstrations" of it.[10] The Northern press, in general, praised it. The *New-York Tribune* called it "skillful, judicious, and adapted to give encouragement and hope to those who heard it."[11]

But the South viewed the speech very differently. "This speech will be read throughout the South to-day with the greatest alarm," one paper announced. "The Cotton States will look upon it as a tocsin of war, and will take immediate measures to resist the shock." All "peace measures . . . are knocked into a cocked hat by this war speech," as Lincoln's proposed retaking of US forts in the South "will take any amount of hard fighting and a large draft upon the blood and treasure of the country."[12]

Southern papers took the moral high ground, connecting Lincoln's images with the crude isms of the North. In an article titled "A Good Prospect of War," a Georgia newspaper intoned, "With the characteristic vulgarity of his party, he compares the old doctrine of States Rights to 'free love,' one of the *isms* of his own clime, only less detestable than Abolitionism, and sneers at the idea of a free people exercising the rights of self-government in any other form than as the vassals of the Federal— i.e., Black Republican—government."[13] A Richmond journalist pilloried Lincoln as "a canting, ill-bred, indecent old man," whose "want of all dignity must disgust all Americans," with his "illustrations drawn from '*free love, passional attraction,*' and *homeopathic pills!*"[14] A Charleston, South Carolina, paper insisted that "Lincoln's vulgar, insidious, and unmistakable coercion speech," with its "filthy allusion to free love," meant that the South must seize Forts Sumter and Pickens now instead of waiting for them to surrender.[15]

Lincoln a fanatical devotee of Northern isms who was proclaiming war on the South? This was exactly how he did *not* want to be viewed. Therefore, for the remainder of the trip, he steered clear of controversial statements. Instead, he offered reassurances. At his stops in Cleveland, Pittsburgh, and Philadelphia, he said, "[T]here really is no crisis," only an "artificial" one that would disappear "if the great American people will only keep their temper, on both sides of the line."[16] Southerners were still citizens under the Constitution, he said. Their rights were protected. The North returned their runaways to them. "Why all this excitement?" he asked. "Let it alone and it will go down of itself."

He sometimes dispensed bromides. At Columbus, he said, "There is nothing going wrong. It is a consoling circumstance that when we look out there is nothing that really hurts anybody. . . . [N]obody is suffering anything. This is a most consoling circumstance, . . . all we want is time, patience and a reliance on that God who has never forsaken this people."[17] In Pennsylvania he proclaimed himself in line with that state's Quaker heritage, founded on "peaceful principles." He declared that "no one of the Friends" who originally settled there or have since lived there "has been or is a more devoted lover of peace, harmony and concord than my humble self."

At most stops he hedged, evading direct political statements altogether. He had been publicly silent during the campaign and since the election. He had feared that anything he said might disrupt the national situation. Overtures to the South of the kind that Crittenden was making would betray his basic beliefs and his party's platform. On the other hand, overly harsh words about the South could alienate the border states and push them into the Confederacy. His safest tactic now was silence. As he told an audience at one stop, "I have been occupying a position, since the Presidential election, of silence, of avoiding public speaking, of avoiding public writing. I have been doing so because I thought, upon full consideration, that was the proper course for me to take."[18]

At most of his train stops, he did not comment on politics. He gave excuses. He was tired. His voice was hoarse (actually, he did have a cold during part of the trip). And a line that got many laughs: if he spoke at all the stops, he would not reach Washington until after the inaugural.

If he hedged or was silent, how could he make an impact on Northerners whose loyalty he counted on? Through much of the trip, he relied on the kind of spectacle that Barnum had popularized.

In effect, he put himself on exhibit. At several stops, he successfully performed his ugly man act. Typical were his remarks to "a large crowd of ladies." Addressing them, he said, "I am glad to see you; I suppose you are glad to see me, but I certainly think I have the best of the bargain. (Applause.)"[19] Sometimes he put himself and his wife on comic display. The six-foot-four-inch Lincoln and his five-foot-two-inch wife made a kind of giant-dwarf show, as when they appeared at a Pennsylvania depot, where he told his viewers that they now saw "the long and the short of it!"; this caused "a loud burst of laughter, followed by enthusiastic cheers as the train moved off." In Cleveland, where he wearied of shaking hands and decided to bow as the crowd filed by, he felt that he was "on exhibition," while the people acted as though "they were assisting at an animal show" or "were engaged in a grotesque ceremony of mock adulation."[20]

He made a spectacle of expressing public thanks to Grace Bedell, the twelve-year-old upstate New York girl who had written him four months earlier suggesting that he would look better with a beard. When the train stopped at her town, Westfield, he asked about the "young lady" who had encouraged him to grow whiskers. Grace, "a beautiful girl, with black eyes," was pointed out to Lincoln, who met her and "gave her several hearty kisses, . . . amid the yells of delight from the excited crowd."[21]

In Manhattan, Lincoln engaged in a different kind of spectacle. Walt Whitman was present when Lincoln arrived in front of his hotel, the Astor House. The president-elect emerged from his carriage, stretched his long limbs, and gazed casually at the thousands of spectators who had come to see him. "There were no speeches, no compliments, no welcome—as far as I could hear, not a word said." The "sober, unbroken silence," Whitman surmised, reflected the fact that Lincoln was not popular in Manhattan, a city with commercial ties to the South that had recently considered seceding from the Union. Whitman sensed that "many assassin's knife and pistol lurked in hip or breast-pocket there." Nevertheless, Whitman wrote, "there was a dash of comedy, almost of farce," as Lincoln looked curiously at his viewers and they looked curiously at him. Cool and relaxed, Lincoln walked slowly up the Astor House steps and disappeared through the entrance, "and the dumb-show ended."[22]

While in New York, Lincoln and his family became directly associated with P. T. Barnum, who sought out Lincoln at the Astor House and said, "Don't forget, you 'Honest Old Abe'; I shall rely upon you and I advertise you."[23] A notice was published saying that Lincoln would visit his Broadway Museum. He didn't go, but Mary went with Robert, who reportedly found special fascination in "What Is It?," the alleged link between humans and simians that cartoonists liked to compare with his father.

Lincoln made a spectacle of patriotism when he spoke at Trenton, New Jersey, where he recalled Washington's crossing the Delaware and making his famous surprise attack on the Hessians, and at Philadelphia's Independence Hall, the site of the nation's founding, where he praised the Declaration of Independence and raised a flag.

There was something far deeper in his Philadelphia appearance than patriotic spectacle. For Lincoln, the Declaration signified, above all else, human equality. Should the nation ever lose touch with that ideal, then it was not worth saving. There was a dark edge to his words that day. He said that he often had thought about "the dangers" the Founders faced in forging the Declaration, and "the toils" endured by the officers and soldiers who fought for it. They fought not just for separation from England but for "something in that Declaration giving liberty, not alone to the people of this country, but hope to the world for all future time"—for the "promise that in due time the weights should be lifted from the shoulders of all men, and that *all* should have an equal chance. (Cheers.)"[24]

The Revolutionary generation had fought for that principle, and many died for it. He, too, was ready to die for it. Twice in the speech, he mentioned his own death. "I will consider myself one of the happiest men in the world," he said, if as president he could preserve that principle. But "it will be truly awful," he declared, if that principle were lost. Then the shocker: "I would rather be assassinated on this spot than to surrender it." In closing: "I may, therefore, have said something indiscreet, but I have said nothing but what I am willing to live by, and, in the pleasure of Almighty God, die by."

Why the references to death? And why did Lincoln apologize for saying "something indiscreet"? We get a clue from a negative response to the speech by a Democratic journalist who commented that Lincoln at Philadelphia "declared he would 'rather be assassinated on the spot' than abandon his idea of negro independence and negro equality."[25] What the journalist recognized was the radical egalitarianism—a belief in the equality of *all* people, regardless of race or nationality—that Lincoln's reading of the Declaration implied.

Was Lincoln making an unusually radical statement on race as a kind of existential outcry, being fully honest when faced with the prospect that he was just about to die? The journalist thought so; he wrote that the death imagery Lincoln used in asserting the rights of black people was connected to his fear of imminent assassination.

The possibility of assassination haunted Lincoln. He predicted to several of those close to him that he would meet a sudden and violent end. There was justification for his fears. His private secretary John Nicolay wrote, "His mail was infested with brutal and vulgar menace, and warnings of all sorts came to him from zealous or nervous friends."[26] One anonymous missive came to him early in 1861 that read, "May the hand of the devil strike you down before long—You are destroying the country. Damn you—every breath you take."[27] About the same time, a grammatically challenged A. G. Frick threatened an unusual mode of assassination: "[I]f you don't Resign we are going to put a spider in your dumpling and play the Devil with you you god or mighty god dam sundde of a bit[c]h go to hell and kiss my Ass suck my prick and call my Bolics your uncle Dick goddam a fool and goddam Abe Lincoln who would like you goddam you excuse me for using such hard words with you but you need it you are nothing but a goddam Black nigger."[28]

During the White House years, few days went by without Lincoln receiving a threatening letter.[29] He generally ignored the threats. He considered most of them hot air, and he had the fatalistic view that there was no effective defense against a determined assassin.

But during his Philadelphia visit, the threat seemed real, and defense was available.

On the evening before the speech at Independence Hall, he was informed that there was a plot to assassinate him in Baltimore during his trip between Philadelphia and Washington. The detective Allan Pinkerton, who had been spying with five operatives in Baltimore for weeks, reported to Lincoln that secessionist thugs led by an Italian barber, Cypriano Ferrandini, would try to kill him after he emerged from his train to travel between depots in Baltimore. A separately verified warning of a Baltimore plot came from Washington, sent by William Henry Seward through his son Frederick.[30]

Baltimore, known as Mobtown because of gangs like the Plug Uglies and the Blood Tubs, had often been the site of political violence, as in 1857, when the visiting James Buchanan had been hissed at and pelted with stones by roughs, and in 1860, when marching Wide Awakes were assaulted with eggs and brickbats. Baltimore's police chief, George P. Kane, said, "The Plugs on the one hand were determined on giving [Lincoln] a rousing reception, and the Tubs [a Democratic organization] were equally determined to prevent the Plugs from giving the president elect any reception at all."[31]

Lincoln accepted the news of the death threat but wished to carry out his plan of participating in the Independence Hall ceremony and then going in the afternoon to the state capital, Harrisburg, to address the state legislature. At Harrisburg, he took precautions. Instead of waiting to take his scheduled train south on February 23, he went by a special train on February 22 from Harrisburg to Philadelphia. There, posing as an invalid, he bent over and was led to a semiprivate sleeping car of a passenger train by detective Kate Warne, who pretended to be his sister. He was disguised in an old overcoat, a shawl, and a soft wool hat. On the journey, he was accompanied by Warne, Pinkerton, and the burly Ward Hill Lamon, who was armed with pistols, a knife, a slungshot, and brass knuckles. The train left Philadelphia at 10:50 p.m. and arrived four and a half hours later at Baltimore, where, after an agonizing delay, Lincoln switched trains in the quiet of early morning and went on to Washington, where he arrived at 6:00 a.m. on Saturday,

February 23. Mary and the boys came down later in the day on the regular train.

When news of Lincoln's surreptitious trip got out, the press exploded in derision. The president-elect was a coward. If he was scared of some Baltimore roughs, how was he going to stand up to the Confederacy? He had proved himself a fool. An Indiana paper, in a piece on "Lincoln's Flight," fulminated, "The whole thing was a disgrace to the man, and a stigma upon the character of our people. We hope never to hear of such a miserable and disgusting spectacle again. Every rational man is heartily ashamed of it."[32]

A *New York Times* reporter, Joseph Howard, disgruntled that he had been left off the inaugural train in Harrisburg, concocted the story that Lincoln had sneaked into Washington disguised in a military cloak and a Scottish cap. Satirists had a field day with the image. A *Vanity Fair* cartoon showed Lincoln dancing in a kilt and feathered cap: *The MacLincoln Harrisburg Highland Fling.* A St. Louis paper said the report of Lincoln dressed in "a military cloak and Scotch plaid" was "the first literal example of Presidential masquerading"; it was so "mixed up with the ludicrous" that "posterity will regard the extraordinary hegira as the hugest joke the Presidential joker ever perpetrated."[33]

A Southern wag penned a song, "The Lincoln Dodge," set to the tune of "Yankee Doodle," with verses such as:

> They went and got a special train
> At midnight's solemn hour,
> And in a cloak and Scotch plaid shawl,
> He dodged from the Slave Power.
> *Refrain*—Lanky Lincoln came to
>   town,
> In night and wind and rain, sir,
> Wrapped in a military cloak
> Upon a special train, sir.[34]

The MacLincoln Harrisburg Highland
Fling (*Vanity Fair*, March 9, 1861)

Lincoln on February 24, 1861
(photograph by Alexander Gardner)

This was Barnumesque spectacle at its most embarrassing. How was Lincoln to recover his image as a solid, trustworthy leader?

Once again, Mathew Brady helped. Brady, who had a photography studio in Washington run by the young Alexander Gardner, had arranged to provide *Harper's Weekly* with a photograph of the newly bearded Lincoln that would become the basis of a lithograph to appear in the magazine around the time of the inauguration. Lincoln sat for a portrait in the studio on Sunday, February 24, the day after he arrived in Washington. The Scots-born Gardner, a stout, bohemian-looking man with a dark beard and long hair, had Lincoln sit on a chair beside a table on which was an inkwell and Lincoln's signature stovepipe hat—a reminder to viewers that his customary headwear was *not* a Scotch cap. This was one of seven times Lincoln would sit for Gardner.

Although the five photographs Gardner took that day were not as striking as the 1863 Gettysburg portrait (a frontal close-up of Lincoln looking directly at the camera) or the 1865 one of the gaunt, weary Lincoln (the last known studio picture of him), the inaugural portrait restored dignity to the much-caricatured Lincoln. In the picture, Lincoln appears calm, unexcited to the point of boredom, as though neither the national crisis nor the uproar over his recent trip has flustered him. The photograph, which was reproduced and widely disseminated, lent visual support to his statements during the trip east that the crisis was artificial and would go away on its own.

"WE MUST NOT BE ENEMIES"

The crisis, of course, was *not* artificial, and Lincoln knew it. A report came that an attempt on his life would be made during the inaugural parade on March 4. With several government officials promoting conciliation, on the day before the inaugural Lincoln said he was open to having a convention of all states to work out differences between the North and South.

But a repeat of the previous month's failed Peace Convention was not to be. Nor did anything come of a constitutional amendment proposed by Thomas Corwin of Ohio, which would have prohibited Congress from interfering with slavery in a state—an exercise in redundancy because this provision was already in the Constitution.[35]

The morning of March 4 was cold and overcast. Lincoln spent the morning meeting with friends and cabinet appointees and looking over his speech. At noon he rode in an open carriage in a procession that led to the Capitol. Rooftop riflemen watched windows, while soldiers guarded the procession. Lincoln entered the Capitol through a boarded tunnel built for the occasion. In the Senate chamber, he witnessed the swearing in of his vice president, Hannibal Hamlin. By the time Lincoln emerged on the portico of the Capitol, a bright sun was shining.

With the unfinished Capitol dome and an extended crane above him, he stood on a temporary platform and surveyed the thousands who had come to hear him. Adjusting his spectacles, he opened his manuscript and delivered a thirty-five-minute address that he hoped might heal his torn nation.[36]

Lincoln's inaugural address, though conciliatory in parts, did not yield on the principles he held dear, principles that he believed had defined the nation from its founding. He had worked on the address for several weeks before leaving Springfield. Documents he studied while writing the speech, in addition to the Constitution, included George Washington's Farewell Address (1796), Daniel Webster's Second Reply to Hayne (1830), Andrew Jackson's message to Congress on nullification (1833), and Henry Clay's 1850 speech on South Carolina's threat to secede.

The common denominator of these classic American texts was their insistence on the absolute inviolability of the Union. Washington, warning Americans to resist "every attempt to alienate any portion of our Country from the rest, or to enfeeble the sacred ties which now link together the various parts," declared that "a government for the whole is indispensable" to the "permanency of your Union."[37] Webster averred that the federal government is not the agent of state governments but rather is "the People's Government; made for the People; made by the People; and answerable to the People."[38] Union, Webster said, was just as sacred as liberty. Jackson declared that secession by a state "can not be acknowledged."[39] Clay insisted that the federal government must respond militarily should a state leave the Union.

While he was inspired by these previous leaders, Lincoln faced a crisis that for them had been only imaginary. By the time of his inauguration, seven Southern states had seceded; soon thereafter, four more followed, and the border states hung in the balance. The inaugural address, he knew, must be very cautiously worded. It must affirm the federal government's resolve to save the Union without pushing the South so hard that reunion became impossible.

Wishing to fine-tune the speech, Lincoln had about a dozen copies of it printed and distributed to friends for their comments. Several of them—David Davis, Carl Schurz, and Francis P. Blair—made no substantive changes, but two, Orville Browning and William Seward, softened his tone. Browning thought Lincoln's declared intention to "reclaim" US forts taken over by the rebels made the federal government sound too aggressive. Lincoln removed the word, saying, more mildly, that the federal power would be used "to hold, occupy, and possess the property, and places belonging to the government, and to collect the duties and imposts."[40] Seward suggested thirty-three changes, twenty-seven of which Lincoln accepted, some in modified form. By far the most important was Seward's suggestion to replace the militant closing line of the original, in which Lincoln left the question of "peace, or a sword" up to the South, with a charitable final paragraph that, in Lincoln's reworking, became one of the most memorable passages in American oratory, as we'll see.

On the trip east he had had a scare when the satchel containing the speech was left with a hotel clerk by seventeen-year-old Robert. Uncharacteristically furious with his son, Lincoln rushed to the clerk's office, clambered over a counter, and sorted through a pile of bags until he found his satchel.

The inaugural address was in some ways a pastiche of the themes he had tested out in his speeches at the railway stops. His moments of hedging or silence were paralleled in the opening lines of the address, where Lincoln said he would not repeat political points laid out in the Republican Party's platform. The inaugural's main theme—the impossibility of secession—expanded upon the Indianapolis speech, where he said that a minority cannot overrule the majority. The inaugural's assurance that the North would not invade the South without provocation recalled Lincoln's praise of Quakerish "peaceful principles" in Pennsylvania.[41] His promise in the inaugural to leave slavery alone where it existed and to enforce the Fugitive Slave Act if the suspected runaways received due process was one he had made at Cleveland.

But the inaugural was far more than the sum of his rail-stop speeches or of arguments made by former presidents. It succeeded as an original statement whose parts were held together by cultural elements that have been largely overlooked.

A main element of the speech, as it turned out, was a dramatic form of the higher law: one that affirmed national unity, preexistent to the Constitution and integrated into it. Lincoln's answer to Southerners who used states' rights to defend secession was that there is a higher law than any human law—what he called in the inaugural the "universal law" or "organic law," "the fundamental law of all national governments."[42]

Lincoln summarized this universal law concisely: no nation was formed with its own destruction in mind. Perpetuity was the goal of any nation. "It is safe to assert," he said, "that no government proper, ever had a provision in its organic law for its own termination."[43] In America, Lincoln said, national consolidation originated with the Articles of Association (1774), was made perpetual by the Declaration of Independence (1776) and the Articles of Confederation (1781), and then was enacted by the Constitution (1787). The Constitution proclaimed that the aim of the people of the United States was "*to form a more perfect union.*" Secession, which creates a Union that is "*less* perfect than before," was thus "absurd."

In affirming permanent union as the higher law behind the nation, Lincoln rejected not only the South's states' rights argument but, implicitly, the many individualistic versions of the higher law that had appeared in the 1850s. Transcendentalists like Thoreau, who believed that the individual was greater than the state; reformers like Stephen Pearl Andrews, with his doctrine of Individual Sovereignty; John Brown, who resorted to individual violence to dislodge slavery; filibusters like Narciso López and William Walker, who invaded nations to the south—these and other figures had used their own higher laws to defend their actions.

While emphasizing the broader law of nations, Lincoln in the inaugural did not lose sight of the moral law that motivated him and other antislavery reformers. He said, "One section [of the nation] believes slavery is right, and ought to be extended, while the other believes it is wrong, and ought not to be extended."[44]

His unwavering view that slavery was wrong qualified the concessions to the South that he made in the inaugural. When he declared that the Constitution let slavery alone where it already existed—which accounted for his nod to Corwin's amendment, just passed by Congress—listeners were surely aware of his oft-stated belief that slavery was an evil on the path to extinction. They also must have sensed the tenuousness of his endorsement of the Fugitive Slave Act, which he undercut in the inaugural by saying that "the moral sense of the people is against the law" and that free blacks were often illegally captured and enslaved.[45]

To subvert the South's position, he deployed clever rhetorical weapons, some devised by himself, others derived from the general culture. "Physically speaking," he said, "we cannot separate. We cannot remove our respective sections from each other, nor build an impassable wall between them." The United States was not, he added, like a husband and wife, who could decide to go their separate ways. The continent—the very earth itself—bound the parts of the nation together. Separation violated the law of nature.

He also appealed to divine law, though in an unusual way. His religious images in the inaugural were more nuanced than those he had used during his trip. In his farewell remarks at Springfield he had said that he could succeed only with God's help—a banal statement that he repeated in his remarks at Buffalo and Newark. At Lafayette, Indiana, he made the equally trite comment that Americans "are bound together, I trust in christianity, civilization and patriotism" (a statement that offended some American Jews).[46]

In the inaugural address, he fused religion with democracy: "In our present differences, is either party without faith in the right? If the Almighty Ruler of nations, with his eternal truth and justice, be on our side, or on yours, that truth and that justice will surely prevail, by the judgment of this great tribunal, the American people." The North and the South, he was saying, each believed that its view was supported by God. Which side was correct must be finally decided by the "great tribunal": the people. In the 1860 election, the people had decided against slavery. In democratic America, the people's judgment was equivalent to God's judgment.

The address achieved a balance between the centripetal and the centrifugal of the sort Walt Whitman considered the highest aim of American democracy. Lincoln named two great dangers to the nation: despotism and anarchy. Despotism would result from an excess of centripetalism: that is, from an overbearing federal government that ignored constitutional rights of states or individuals. Anarchy, on the other hand, resulted from secession, or an overemphasis of states' rights. "Plainly," Lincoln declared, "the central idea of secession, is the essence of anarchy."[47] If a group of states separates from the Union, why cannot one or two states, by the same principle, separate from the newly formed Confederacy? Other divisions would follow. Centrifugalism would reign. Centrifugalism, in turn, invited despotism. The more confused a society is, the higher the risk of a despot seizing power under the guise of bringing things under control. It was a vicious circle. Division in a nation breeds anarchy, which in turn invites despotism.

A respect for majority rule, Lincoln argued, can hold the sections of the nation together. "Whoever rejects it," he declared, "does, of necessity, fly to anarchy or despotism."[48]

An appreciation of shared cultural values could also foster the spirit of union, he indicated. His broadest foray into culture in the inaugural address comes in its famous peroration. Consider his revisions of Seward's suggested final paragraph, which reached out to the South.

Here is Seward:

I close. We are not we must not be aliens or enemies but
["countrym" deleted] fellow countrymen and brethren. Although passion has strained our bonds of affection too hardly
they must not ["be broken they will not" deleted], I am sure
they will not be broken. The mystic chords which proceeding
from ["every ba" deleted] so many battle fields and ["patriot"
deleted] so many patriot graves ["bind" deleted] pass through
all the hearts and ["hearths" deleted] all the hearths in this
broad continent of ours will yet ["harmon" deleted] again
harmonize in their ancient music when ["touched as they
surely" deleted] breathed upon ["again" deleted] by the ["better angel" deleted] guardian angel of the nation.[49]

Here is Lincoln:

> I am loth to close. We are not enemies, but friends. We must
> not be enemies. Though passion may have strained, it must
> not break our bonds of affection. The mystic chords of mem-
> ory, stre[t]ching from every battle-field, and patriot grave, to
> every living heart and hearthstone, all over this broad land,
> will yet swell the chorus of the Union, when again touched,
> as surely they will be, by the better angels of our nature.

Lincoln's transformation of Seward's imagery and style is striking.
Seward's abrupt "I close" became Lincoln's emotive "I am loth to close."
Lincoln transformed Seward's labored line about aliens, countrymen,
and brethren into the concise "We are not enemies, but friends. We
must not be enemies." In a similarly graceful revision, Lincoln used
parallelism to streamline Seward's bumpy description of the broken
bonds of affection.

Seward's passage had cultural resonances that became especially em-
phatic in Lincoln's final sentence, which called for national unity on the

basis of common culture. The "mystic chords" connecting the dead with the living evoked spiritualism, the influential movement that deeply affected Mary Todd Lincoln and millions of other Americans, North and South. The connecting "chords" would remind many of Lincoln's hearers of the electromagnetic forces that were then thought to form "spiritual telegraph" between the living and the dead. The joining of every "patriot grave" to "every living heart and hearthstone" drew from other sources of cultural unity: the shared worship of the founding generation ("every patriot grave") that negated sectional categories such as Puritan and Cavalier; and the imagery found in popular domestic literature ("heart and hearthstone"), which had a nationwide readership. "This broad land" utilized political ecology in its suggestion of the American continent. "The chorus of union" referenced music, which Lincoln considered a key unifying cultural force. "The better angels of our nature" not only humanized Seward's rather distant "guardian angel of the nation," but it also drew from what was a common trope in sentimental literature of that era: the angelic nature of good people—exemplified by the heroine of the era's most popular novel, Stowe's Little Eva, who is repeatedly called a human angel and who is bound by goodness to her black companion, the enslaved Uncle Tom.

Lincoln's revised version of Seward's paragraph was a culturally representative passage offered to a divided nation in what was a massive rhetorical effort to repair the Union.

The effort failed. Although Northern journalists generally saw the inaugural as a sensible, compassionate peace offering, Southerners took it as coercive declaration by a Black Republican president. Extremists on both sides raved. For radical abolitionists, the speech was a dough-faced sellout to the South. For rabid fire-eaters, it was a declaration of war by the North.

Thomas Nast captured the divided response to the speech in one of

This is the way the North receives it.   THE PRESIDENT'S INAUGURAL,   And   This is the way the South receives it.

Thomas Nast, *The President's Inaugural* (*New York Illustrated News*, March 23, 1861). A caricature of the divided response to the First Inaugural Address, which was seen by some as too dovish and by others as too hawkish.

his earliest political cartoons, *The President's Inaugural*.[50] One side of the cartoon shows the North's response: Lincoln appears as a gentle woman holding a palm branch in one hand and the scales of justice in the other, with the word *PEACE* in the background. The other half of the cartoon, representing the South, pictures Lincoln as a saber-wielding, helmeted soldier with *WAR* blazing near him and his foot crushing a Southerner.

Lincoln had done his best to save the nation by affirming cultural and political union, but as he assumed office he faced irreparable division. After the inaugural ball that evening, in the early morning hours of March 5, he got word from Major Robert Anderson, the Union commander at Fort Sumter in Charleston Harbor, South Carolina, that he needed provisions. Lincoln was determined to resupply Fort Sumter, over the initial objections of six of seven cabinet members and the aged general Winfield Scott. He notified the governor of South Carolina that he was sending a ship to deliver supplies to Fort Sumter.

Before the ship reached Charleston, at 4:30 a.m. on April 12, 1861, the Confederate guns began bombarding Fort Sumter. During the battle, the US flag was torn and fell down. After thirty-four hours of shelling, Major Anderson evacuated the fort. On April 15, President Lincoln issued a proclamation calling up 75,000 militia for ninety days' service.

The Civil War had begun.

REMEMBER ELLSWORTH!

Calling up 75,000 militia sounds simple enough in retrospect, but it was complicated in 1861. The regular army of the United States was then small, consisting of some 16,000 career soldiers who were on duty on the western frontier, the Canadian border, and installations on the Atlantic Ocean.[51] The paucity of federally controlled troops resulted from the nation's long-term animosity against standing armies.

Lincoln wanted to centralize control of a large army, but he was under constitutional restraints. On March 18, anticipating a civil war, he wrote his attorney general, Edward Bates, asking him to appoint the twenty-three-year-old drill instructor Elmer Ellsworth as the chief clerk of the War Department and inspector general of militia for the United States in a new government department to be dedicated to "promoting a uniform system of organization, drill, equipment," for "the Militia of the several States."[52]

Bates thought hard about the president's proposal. In a month, he sent a detailed answer. Lincoln's proposed appointment of Ellsworth was unconstitutional for three reasons, he wrote. First, the president had no control over state militias. He could call for volunteers, but as Bates wrote, "since the State militia are not now in the actual service of the national government, . . . the President has no power over them by virtue of his office." Second, the creation of a new military department was the responsibility of Congress, not the executive branch. Finally, according to law, Lieutenant Ellsworth must serve three years in the military before he could be released for government service.[53]

Lincoln's response to Bates's rejection of Ellsworth is unrecorded, but surely he was disappointed. For Lincoln, Ellsworth promised great improvements to a US military system that was disorganized, inefficient, and demoralized.

Elmer Ellsworth has largely been minimized in works on Lincoln; one historian dismisses him as "a parade-ground warrior, ignorant of combat."[54] Actually, without knowing about Ellsworth, we do not fully understand either Lincoln or the Civil War. Ellsworth was a major source of inspiration to the president and to the Union army.

Born in 1837 in Malta, a hamlet near Mechanicsville in Saratoga County, New York, Ellsworth was raised in humble circumstances. His father, Ephraim Ellsworth, was a tailor who struggled to make ends meet. His mother, Phoebe Denton Ellsworth, was a pious Presbyterian. Both parents had New England ancestors; the father was descended from a Revolutionary War soldier. Elmer attended local schools and loved reading books, especially ones about war and battles. As a teenager, he organized a local military company, the Black Plumed Riflemen. He learned the manual of arms and became a good shot and a fine swordsman. He developed strict temperance habits, having heard a lecturer say that the devil dwelled in a barrel of hard cider.[55]

At fifteen Elmer became a clerk in a linen goods store in nearby Troy, New York. He then moved to New York City, where he worked at a dry goods store. In 1854, he relocated to Rockford, Illinois, where he found employment in a patent agency, and then he moved to Chicago to work as a law clerk.

But his heart was in military matters. While in Chicago he met Charles A. DeVilliers, who had served in a French Zouave regiment in the Crimean War. Under DeVilliers's guidance, Ellsworth became an expert fencer and adept at the intricate military exercises of the Zouaves. Originally a group of Berber warriors associated with the Zouaoua, a mountain tribe in Algeria, the Zouaves by the 1850s were composed mainly of French soldiers and officers known for their ferocity and rapidity in battle. The Zouaves wore uniforms that were partly Eastern—with billowing trousers, short coats, and Oriental caps—while retaining the bright colors of the French army.

Fascinated by the exotic Zouaves, Ellsworth studied them and decided to create a Zouave unit of his own. The United States Zouave Cadets of Chicago conducted their first drills under their young leader in April 1859. He aimed to improve his men "morally as well physically" and "to place the company in a position second to none in the United States."[56] Abstemious to the point of avoiding tobacco, tea, and coffee, he forbade his men from entering barrooms, gambling halls, or houses of prostitution. His Zouaves, striking in their Oriental uniforms, performed publicly before crowds who were thrilled by their precise coordination and quickness. Ellsworth trained them to perform exercises that combined acrobatics with military moves such as running in double quick-step, firing as skirmishers while advancing or lying down, parrying for the head, and so on.[57] Soon Ellsworth took the Zouaves on the road, appearing before tremendous crowds in many cities throughout the North.

After the tour, he returned to Illinois and resumed his study of the law. Sometime that year, he became an apprentice in the law office of Lincoln and Herndon. He read law books and gained enough experience to earn entrance to the Illinois bar.

But his mind remained fixed on the military and on Republican politics. He spent much of 1860 campaigning for Lincoln and other Republicans. Lincoln grew to admire him, calling him "the greatest little man I ever met!"[58] By the time Lincoln was ready to take his trip east to Washington in February 1861, he asked Ellsworth to come along and take care of crowd control.

Ellsworth not only fulfilled this function but also raised new possibilities for military organization that appealed to Lincoln, who declared, "That young man has a real genius for war!"[59] Ellsworth, concerned about the disorganized condition of the regular army, discussed with Lincoln a plan to coordinate the militias of the various states through a department in Washington. His goal was to reorganize "the militia . . . of the whole country; to unify and bring the entire system more completely under the control of a central authority."[60] Lincoln liked the idea so much that he proposed it to Bates, whose objections based on the Constitution thwarted the plan.

But Bates's interference did not spell the end of Ellsworth's influence. After the fall of Fort Sumter, Ellsworth became the chief actor in a series of events that were a key part of the initial phase of the Civil War.

On April 29, Ellsworth was in New York City organizing a regiment to fight for the Union. For recruits, he sought none other than the original b'hoys: Manhattan firemen, known to be brave, tough, and skilled with firearms because of their pastime of going on target excursions.

For Ellsworth, the b'hoys had the mettle for being good soldiers, ready for the most arduous situations. Within a week, Ellsworth had selected 1,100 men, taken from New York's fire companies. He organized them as the Eleventh New York Volunteer Army. They were known alternately as First Fire Zouaves, Ellsworth Zouaves, and the First Regiment New York Zouave.

The young men quickly fell into line under Ellsworth. A slight man who stood five feet five inches tall and had flowing black curls and a mustache, the handsome Ellsworth had a magnetic, no-nonsense

COL. ELMER E. ELLSWORTH

presence that made even the b'hoys, given to disorder and insouciance, act in a disciplined way. The puritanical Ellsworth prohibited drinking, swearing, and unruly behavior among his troops, who became known as his "pet lambs," ready to obey his every command and aware of the punishment that was forthcoming if they did not.

The departure from New York of Ellsworth's regiment on April 30 was a grand affair, witnessed by cheering thousands who waved flags and hailed the troops of b'hoys, each attired in a modified Zouave uniform: a blue-trimmed gray jacket, red shirt, loose gray trousers, a red

The Departure of Col. Ellsworth's Zouaves from New York
(*Frank Leslie's Illustrated Newspaper*, May 11, 1861)

cap with a blue band, and a regulation overcoat. The Zouaves, aka the New York Eleventh, marched through the city to a wharf on the Hudson, where they left on the steamship *Baltic*, on which they went to Annapolis and thence by rail to Washington, DC. They arrived in the capital on May 2.

Lincoln had been waiting for them. He had feared that Confederate forces could move on the capital at any time. Within days of the Fire Zouaves' arrival, he reviewed the troops, shaking hands warmly with all of them. Tad and Willie loved watching Ellsworth lead the Zouaves in their acrobatic drills.

For lack of housing, the Zouaves camped out for a few days in the Capitol building. A journalist reported, "We visited the quarters of Col. Ellsworth's Zouave regiment in the capitol on Saturday, and found the b'hoys in undisputed possession of the rotunda and the new and old House of Representatives." These men "of herculean proportions, with massive shoulders and chests" lounged about with their feet on desks, chatting and laughing, and having fun, since "no one is given to more 'mad pranks' than 'these 'bold soger b'hoys' from New York." For instance, "We saw one of the b'hoys with bare legs and feet," gleefully squirting hose water at his comrades.[61]

Within a week, Ellsworth moved his troops to a military camp on high ground near the Potomac southeast of Washington.

The Zouaves could not stifle their unruliness. When some of them went on a drunken spree, Ellsworth had the miscreants confined in a jail. Other soldiers aggressively approached women on the streets. John Hay noted that many Washingtonians "persist in believing Ellsworth's 'pet lambs' to be the most graceless *mauvais sujects*. Girls who were never kissed before, complain dolefully of rude salutes."[62]

Not all the women, however, resisted the men's advances. Looking from a hotel window, a reporter saw Ellsworth's men in action:

> They are in every respect emphatic representatives of that peculiar element of city life, popularly classed as "b'hoys." They are I-don't-care-a-dammish set of fellows, whose quaint dress, slushing manners, and questionals [*sic*] have proven sadly alluring to our neighborhood young ladies, some of whom are a little distinguished for not being "slow." . . . [The typical Fire Zouave] is a type of his fellows, loves a glass, a girl, or a row, don't care for expenses, and is "bound to be a hero, by jingo, or die!"[63]

The boisterous Zouaves became local heroes when they put to use their firefighting skills in a dramatic incident. Willard's Hotel, where the Lincolns had stayed between their arrival to Washington and their move into the White House, caught fire in the early morning of May 9.

An alarm sounded. Ellsworth's b'hoys swarmed to the conflagration, which they fought bravely and doused.

An aura of mythic fearlessness surrounded the firemen soldiers. A common saying had it that if a battle was raging against the Confederates and you rang a fire bell behind it, Ellsworth's Fire Zouaves would rush forward and scatter the enemy in order to reach the fire on the other side.[64]

Anti-Confederate fever seized Ellsworth's soldiers. The rebel flag became a symbol of the detested "traitors" who were trying to destroy the Union. John Hay noted that every member of the regiment was eager to bring home a Confederate flag. Hay reported soldiers who declared, "We boys is goin' to fight for these pieces of cloth till we die!" and "It'll be the flag o' secession, nailed on to the bottom o' this flag staff!"[65]

Lincoln shared their hatred of the flag. He was appalled when he looked out of the White House and saw the Confederate flag flying from the Marshall House Hotel in Alexandria, Virginia, across the Potomac River from Washington.

That flag, as it turned out, had a key role in elevating Elmer Ellsworth to virtual sainthood in the North.

On May 23, Ellsworth gathered his troops and told them they would move the next day across the Potomac to take Alexandria. The Zouaves, champing at the bit, prepared for the attack, priming their weapons and loading their knapsacks. On the evening before the attack Ellsworth wrote his parents, saying that "whatever may happen" in the battle tomorrow, they should recall that he was "engaged in a sacred duty." At the end of the note, he wrote, "My darling and ever-loved parents, good-bye." He also wrote his fiancée, Carrie Spafford, proclaiming his love for her and asking God to "grant you a happy & useful life & us a union hereafter."[66]

Early in the morning of May 24, Ellsworth and his troops crossed by boats and bridges from Washington to Virginia. As they entered

Alexandria, Ellsworth saw the rebel flag suspended on a pole from a high dormer in the Marshall House. He thought of sending a small detail to remove the flag but then decided to retrieve it himself. Along with a corporal, Francis Brownell, he entered the hotel and went upstairs, where he found narrow stairs leading up to the dormer. Once there, he hauled in the flag and started with it downstairs along with Brownell. When he reached the second floor, he was met by the hotel's owner, James W. Jackson, who leveled a shotgun at Ellsworth and blasted him in the chest, killing him instantly. In the next moment, Jackson himself was sprawled on the floor, killed by Brownell's carbine.

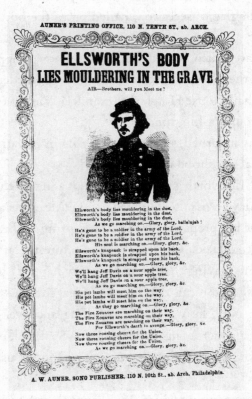

Song sheet about Elmer Ellsworth, to the tune of the "John Brown Song"
(Philadelphia: A. W. Auner, 1861)

Murder of Col. Ellsworth of the Fire Zouaves and the Death of Jackson, His Assassin,
by the Hand of Frank Brownell, at Alexandria, Virginia, May 24, 1861
(Philadelphia: J. Magee, 1861). In this lithograph, the dying Ellsworth, wearing his
loose Zouave uniform, clings to the Confederate flag he has just stolen from a
dormer window in James W. Jackson's hotel in Alexandria.

The news of Ellsworth's death shook the entire North. Ellsworth had attracted widespread admiration during his prewar tour with the United States Zouaves, and he was revered for having helped protect the capital from invasion with his Fire Zouaves. He had chosen the rowdiest elements of the American population—the b'hoys—and turned them into disciplined, obedient soldiers ready to direct their energy toward the defense of the Union. He persuaded all but only a handful of them to sign on for military service, not for the required ninety days but for the entire length of the war. For Ellsworth to become the first Union officer killed in battle was both gut-wrenching and inspirational. He suddenly was a martyr to the Northern cause.

The South regarded him as a demon. A typical Southern journalist wrote, "A band of execrable cut-throats and jail-birds, known as the Zouaves of New York, under that chief of all scoundrels, Ellsworth, broke open the door of a citizen, to tear down the flag of the house—the courageous owner met the favorite hero of the Yankees in his own hall, alone, against thousands, and shot him through the heart."[67]

Ellsworth's passing deeply affected Lincoln, who thought of the young man as a family member. Reporters arrived at the White House for an interview and found the president unable to speak. He was in tears. He had just learned of Ellsworth's death. As he dried his face with a handkerchief, he said, "I will make no apology, gentlemen, for my weakness; but I knew poor Ellsworth well, and held him in great regard."[68]

He and Mary went to the Navy Yard, where Ellsworth's body had been brought. He arranged for a public viewing of the body in the East Room of the White House. Thousands streamed by the coffin, of solid iron, with glass showing Ellsworth's body from the head to the waist. When Lincoln leaned over the coffin, he cried, "My boy! My boy! Was it necessary that this sacrifice should be made!"[69] The coffin subsequently was taken by train north for burial in Ellsworth's upstate New York village. On the way, the train stopped in Manhattan, where hordes of people turned out to see the fallen soldier. The coffin was taken by boat to Albany, where a funeral service was held. Ellsworth was buried in Mechanicsburg.

Lincoln wrote a heartfelt letter to Ellsworth's parents. "Our affliction here," he wrote, "is scarcely less than your own." He praised Ellsworth highly: "His power to command men, was surpassingly great—This power, combined with a fine intellect, an indomitable energy, and a taste altogether military, constituted in him, as seemed to me, the best natural talent, in that department, I ever knew. And yet he was singularly modest."[70]

A friend of the Lincolns wanted to share with them a happy memory involving the fallen hero but, in her words, "I was told the President wept at the mention of Ellsworth and I was afraid it would make him grieve."[71] The bloodied Confederate flag Ellsworth had captured ended up in the possession of Mary, who put it in a drawer, for she couldn't bear to look at it. (More than once, the mischievous Tad removed it and displayed it outside the White House, to the shock of visitors.)

Also distraught was Lincoln's secretary John Hay, who had been close to Ellsworth ever since the two had worked together in Lincoln's law office. "No man ever possessed in a more eminent degree the power of personal fascination," Hay wrote. "He has left a void which is not to be filled."[72] Three months after Ellsworth's death, Hay wrote to his Rhode Island friend Hannah Angell: "When Ellsworth was murdered all my sunshine perished. I hope you may never know the dry, barren, agony of soul that comes with the utter and hopeless loss of a great love."[73]

The reaction of most Northerners to the killing of Ellsworth was anger and a desire for revenge. Ellsworth's death, predicted the *New York Herald*, will create "a deep feeling of indignation in our community, which will spread throughout the loyal States, inspiring a patriotism that will not expire until full justice is meted out to the rebels who have put the constitution and law at defiance."[74]

By July, those signed up for Union military duty had swelled to 187,000.[75] In Lincoln's hometown a company formed called the Springfield Zouaves, who resolved to "establish as our *war cry 'Ellsworth,'* and our motto 'Death to all *traitors and rebels.'*"[76]

"Remember Ellsworth!" was a popular Union slogan throughout the war, shouted by soldiers and hailed in poems like this one:

> Before he found a martyr's crown
> In Freedom's cause, O bright renown!
> He tore the flag of Treason down.
> Remember Ellsworth, boys!
> *Remember Ellsworth*—this shall be
> The rallying cry of all the free
> Who would our flag still honored see.
> Remember Ellsworth, boys![77]

After Ellsworth's death, the New York Eleventh was taken over by Colonel Noah L. Farnham, an ex-fireman who, like Ellsworth, was small, wiry, and a tough disciplinarian.

Farnham and his Fire Zouaves met with a harsh reckoning at the First Battle of Bull Run (aka First Manassas) on July 21, 1861. They served under General Irvin McDowell in the attack on a railroad junction at Manassas, where Confederate troops under P. G. T. Beauregard were trying to halt the Union army's march south toward Richmond.

Northerners were so excited about the battle that they expected an easy victory as a prelude to a quick war. Civilians and politicians arrived from Washington, some with picnic baskets and blankets, in order to watch the battle from Centreville Heights, several miles from the battlefield. What they saw was unexpected, to say the least. Although the initial skirmishes went well for the Union, a Confederate reinforcement under Joseph E. Johnston changed the tide of the battle. Also crucial was the performance of brigade commander Thomas J. Jackson, who earned his nickname "Stonewall" by closing a gap in the Confederate line just when it had begun to give way under a heavy Union assault.

The battle turned into a rout in which many Union soldiers and officers ran away. During the battle, Noah Farnham received a head wound from which he later died. His men suffered more than one hundred casualties, with an additional sixty-eight men missing and presumed captured.

Confederates believed that God had punished the North for Ellsworth's flag-stealing escapade at the Marshall House. A Southern newspaper stated, "A terrible retribution has fallen upon the brutal regiment known as ELLSWORTH Fire Zouaves. . . . The *Fire Zouaves* [at Manassas] . . . threw themselves upon their knees and pleaded for mercy. But mercy there was none. No quarters were shown, and only a scanty remnant of the famous Fire Zouave saved themselves by flight. So has the death of [James W.] JACKSON been avenged at last!"[78]

But in the North, Ellsworth quickly became a martyr whose death must be violently avenged. Popular songs about the fallen hero included

"Ellsworth's Avengers," "Death of Col. Ellsworth," and "Ellsworth, the Gallant Zouave." The vastly popular John Brown marching song, with its rousing "Glory, glory, hallelujah!" chorus, was often sung as a tribute to Ellsworth, with lines such as:

> Ellsworth's body lies mouldering in
>   the dust, . . .
> Ellsworth's knapsack is strapped upon
>   his back, . . .
> His pet lambs will meet him on the
>   way . . .
> The Fire Zouaves are marching on
>   their way
> For Ellsworth's death to avenge.

Ellsworth's Fire Zouaves, as a contemporary journalist noted, became "the nucleus of other extensive bodies of men whose mode of warfare would soon strike terror in the enemy."[79] Two regiments were formed in honor of Ellsworth: the New York Seventeenth Regiment, called Ellsworth's Avengers, which consisted of volunteers from every county in New York State; and the Seventy-third New York Volunteer Infantry Regiment, called the Second Fire Zouaves, which mustered in July 1861 and served in many major battles, including Chancellorsville, Gettysburg, Antietam, and Appomattox Court House.

Ellsworth's influence lived on in other ways, too. Soldiers sent letters home in envelopes decorated with an engraving of Ellsworth standing in his colorful Zouave outfit, his sword drawn as he holds a flagstaff crowned by a miniature fireman's axe, with a Confederate flag on the ground below his boots.[80] Cartes de visite, lithographs, and broadsides kept Ellsworth's image before the public.

The Fire Zouaves nickname was adopted by several units. There were Baxter's Fire Zouaves, the Philadelphia Fire Zouaves, the Boston

Tiger Fire Zouaves, and others. Tad and Willie Lincoln received as a gift a Zouave doll, which they summarily court-martialed for a military crime, executed, and buried in the White House rose garden.[81]

Fire Zouaves became a source of fun for popular humorists, including one of Lincoln's favorites, Robert Henry Newell, who as Orpheus C. Kerr (a pun on "office seeker," the bane of Lincoln's early presidency) wrote about a mythical army unit, the Mackerel Brigade. According to a contemporary source, "Lincoln . . . seized eagerly upon everything Orpheus C. Kerr wrote, and knew it all by heart."[82] In one of Kerr's sketches, a Fire Zouave named Private Shorty takes a comically long time to die. When he is shot in the head by a Confederate sniper, he asks his comrade, "Is any of my brains hanging out?" "No, Shorty," answered the other, bursting into tears; "you never had any to hang out." The narrator describes Shorty calmly taking out a pipe and, while smoking it, giving "a history of Nine's [Fire] Engine and the first 'muss' he was ever engaged in. After finishing the pipe, and requesting me to wrap him up in the American flag, he spit on one of my boots, and then died." The narrator adds, "His remains will be taken to the first fire that occurs."[83]

While funny, such portraits of working-class bravery and patriotism had serious meaning for Lincoln. Early in the war, he found himself distrustful of officers. A third of commissioned officers in the regular army and navy went over to the Confederacy. These included several whom Lincoln tried to woo for the Union. He appealed to Colonel John B. Magruder, saying, "You are an officer of the army and a Southern gentleman, and incapable of any but honorable conduct." Lincoln explained he was constitutionally obliged to challenge secession, but he "bore testimony to the honor, good faith, and high character of the Southern people, whom he 'knew well.'" Magruder's defection was devastating. Lincoln said, "When I learned that he had gone over to the enemy and I had been so completely deceived in him, my confidence was shaken in everybody, and I hardly knew who to trust anymore."[84]

Also shattering was the defection of Robert E. Lee, to whom

Lincoln offered command of the Union army. Even though Lee objected to secession and said he would, if he could, surrender the South's enslaved millions to the Union, he declared that he could not take up weapons against his native state, Virginia. On April 20, three days after Virginia seceded, Lee resigned from the regular army, went to Richmond, and was soon in command of Virginia's state forces.

Although Lincoln was reassured by the fact that Virginians such as Winfield Scott, George H. Thomas, John W. Davidson, and several other officers remained loyal to the Union, his bitterness over the resignation of more than three hundred regular officers after Fort Sumter led him to place special value on the loyalty of average Northerners. In his July 4 message to Congress, he thanked the officers who had remained loyal but excoriated their "treacherous associates" who chose the Confederacy. "It is worthy of note," he said, "that while in this, the government's hour of trial, large numbers of those in the Army and Navy, who have been favored with the offices, have resigned, and proved false to the hand which had pampered them, not one common soldier, or sailor is known to have deserted his flag." "This is essentially a People's contest," he declared, and the "most important fact of all, is the unanimous firmness of the common soldiers, and common sailors."[85]

The South, unsurprisingly, looked down on the Northern army as vulgar and lowly while extolling its "chivalrous" troops under Cavalier leaders like Lee and Magruder. A Raleigh, North Carolina, paper stated, "The army of the South will be composed of the best material that ever yet made up an army; whilst that of Lincoln will be gathered from the scum of the cities—the degraded, beastly off-scouring of all quarters of the world."[86] One Virginia journalist noted "the rapid enlistment at the North of 'Dead Rabbits,' 'Plug Uglies,' 'Blood Tubs,' 'Jakies,' 'Soap Locks,' 'Bar-room Loungers,' 'Loafers,' 'Wharf-Rats,' 'Thieves' and 'Pick-Pockets,'" while another said the Union military consisted of "*barbarians* who compose the lower orders of the Northern cities, and who are *much inferior in humanity and refinement to African negroes.*"

But Ellsworth had made the b'hoys and their ilk the pride of the North. The respect for the common-man soldier Lincoln showed in his message to Congress was captured in a Northern song that blamed the South for starting the war by invading forts, which prompted Ellsworth's Fire Zouaves to lead the fight against the South:

> So then we called the Volunteers the
>   Country for to save,
> And show the Southern Chivalry that
>   Northern men were brave;
> And then our gallant Firemen formed
>   a regiment of Zouaves
> And under Colonel Ellsworth
>   expressed the Country's cause,
> But they lost their young Commander,
>   for the Union he did die,
> But they'll make the South pay
>   dearly.[87]

Ellsworth had not only enhanced Lincoln's appreciation of the common soldier; he had also made the president think deeply about the relationship between the federal government and the states in the control of the armed forces.

This issue was in turn part of a larger question. In a time of civil war, how large and powerful was the federal government permitted to grow while remaining within constitutional limits? Lincoln's answer, as time proved, was: very large. He expanded the power of the central government—and especially the executive office—more dramatically than had any previous president. He did so, not because of personal aggrandizement or "socialist" leanings, but to repair the Union and restore harmony to the American people, now engaged in a terrible civil war.

The Higher Laws of War

The three amendments to the Constitution ratified by the states just after the Civil War—the Thirteenth, Fourteenth, and Fifteenth—changed the nation dramatically. They abolished slavery, increased the power of the federal government, and gave the vote to black males. These amendments were important hallmarks on the path to civil rights.

But what about during the Civil War? What was the state of the Constitution then?

Views of it were in radical flux. At the beginning of the war, Lincoln, who had always been a stickler for respecting the Constitution, found himself confronted with a national emergency that led him to take extremely strong executive actions, some of which violated the letter of the Constitution. He increased the size of the regular armed forces, twice called up militia volunteers, imposed a naval blockade on Southern ports, and suspended habeas corpus in certain regions—all without congressional approval.

His suspension of the writ of habeas corpus—the right of an arrested person to compel the government to justify the arrest—was especially controversial. As his critics pointed out, the Constitution clearly puts the suspension of habeas corpus among the powers of

Congress. Lincoln explained his suspension of the writ as an emergency measure taken because the South's secession threatened the very life of the nation. His attorney general, Edward Bates, provided a legal rationale for suspending habeas corpus during a civil war. Anna Ella Carroll, a largely forgotten Maryland pamphleteer, cited historical precedents for Lincoln's aggressive action, arguing for a greatly strengthened executive branch in wartime. At the same time, the liberation of enslaved people by the Union armies and calls for permanent emancipation by antislavery spokespersons pushed Lincoln toward radical action. At the end of the war, when praised for freeing the enslaved, he replied, "I have only been an instrument. The logic and moral power of [William Lloyd] Garrison, and the Anti-slavery people of the country and the army, have done all."[1]

The antislavery people and the army. Crediting them was not merely Lincoln being humble. It was his way of recognizing the powerful influence that abolitionists and the military had on emancipation. In 1861, Garrison issued a pamphlet that presented arguments by leading antislavery figures, from John Quincy Adams through Charles Sumner, who held that the war power embedded within the Constitution gave the president extraordinary authority.

Lincoln had pledged to leave slavery untouched where it existed because of the proslavery clauses in the Constitution. But within the first two months of the war, enslaved blacks were liberated by the advancing Union army, leading to the military liberation of tens of thousands well before Lincoln issued the Emancipation Proclamation.

The Puritan-versus-Cavalier conflict played a prominent role in both the debate over civil liberties and the war effort. For the North, the Puritan heritage represented a noble battle for God and principle. For the South, it stood for Northern Constitution busting and fanaticism.

With bloody war now raging between the two sections, Lincoln remained Blondin, poised on his tightrope above the raging falls.

CIVIL LIBERTIES IN WARTIME

At 2:00 a.m. on May 25, 1861, the Maryland cattle breeder John Merryman was sleeping soundly at his farm in Cockeysville when he was awakened by loud knocking. Groggy and confused, he walked to the door, opened it, and found himself confronted with military officers who told him he was under arrest for treason against the United States.

The officers took Merryman immediately to Fort McHenry in Baltimore, where he was held under the supervision of General George Cadwalader. Days passed, and Merryman received no formal charges. He demanded a writ of habeas corpus from the US Circuit Court for Maryland, led by Roger B. Taney, who was also the chief justice of the Supreme Court. Taney issued a writ of habeas corpus, ordering Cadwalader to bring Merryman to court the next day to determine the legal basis for his detention. Cadwalader refused, explaining that President Lincoln had suspended habeas corpus in the region between Philadelphia and Annapolis because of the threat posed by Maryland secessionists who were trying to lead that state into the Confederacy.

In the wake of the deadly Pratt Street Riots in Baltimore on April 19, in which a mob of toughs attacked Union regiments that were traveling to the nation's capital, Merryman, who served in the Baltimore County Horse Guards, was suspected of but not charged with training Confederate soldiers, cutting telegraph wires, and destroying bridges on which Union troops passed. Maryland had not yet voted to remain in the Union, and secessionist sympathizers kept up their attacks on the travel routes of Northern soldiers. Judge Taney—tall, gaunt, tousle haired, and stooped with his eighty-four years—ruled that Merryman's arrest without charges was illegal. The president had no right under the Constitution to suspend habeas corpus. Only Congress could do that. Nor could a military officer under the president's command suspend the writ. If military power were allowed to reign, Taney wrote, then "the people of the United States are no longer living under a government of laws, but every citizen holds life, liberty and property at the will and pleasure of the army officer in whose military district he may happen to be found."[2]

Lincoln, who had disagreed sharply with Taney's racist decision in *Dred Scott v. Sandford*, which ruled that black people were not US citizens and had no rights whites were bound to respect, ignored his ruling on habeas corpus in *Ex Parte Merryman*. Lincoln defended his suspension of the writ in his message to Congress on July 4. The Southern states were attempting to destroy the Union. He asked, "Are all laws, *but one,* to be unexecuted, and the government itself to go to pieces least one law be violated?"[3] The Constitution stipulated that habeas corpus "shall not be suspended unless, in case of rebellion or invasion, the public safety may require it." Lincoln stated, "Now it is insisted that Congress, not the executive, is vested with this power. But the Constitution itself, is silent as to which, or who, is to exercise this power."

Actually, this was literally true—but not entirely accurate. The Suspension Clause appears in Article I of the Constitution, under the powers and limits of Congress. Lincoln strengthened his position somewhat when he explained that he had suspended the writ only when faced with a national emergency while Congress was not in session. However, he was on constitutional thin ice.

He now appealed to what he called organic law. The issue of secession, he declared, "presents to the whole family of man, the question, whether a constitutional republic, or a democracy—a government of the people, by the people—can, or cannot, maintain its territorial integrity, against his own domestic foes. It presents the question, whether discontented individuals, too few in number to control the administration, according to organic law" can "arbitrarily, without, any pretense, break up the government, and thus practically, put an end to free government on earth."[4]

This was the issue of national self-preservation that he had talked about in Cincinnati on his trip east and had raised again in the inaugural address.

Edward Bates made similar points in a July 5 letter in which he defended the president's suspension of the writ. In the letter, Bates avoided mentioning the Merryman case, evidently because he could not rebut Taney's argument that the Suspension Clause applied only to Congress. Nor could he refute the legal precedents Taney cited. Instead, Bates admitted that Congress held sway over the writ in normal times but that "in case of a great and dangerous rebellion like the present," the president became the "sole judge of the emergency" that required his action to preserve the public safety. In times of peace, Bates wrote, Congress could "repeal all power to issue the writ," but the president might permit "the arrest and confinement of persons implicated in the rebellion."[5]

Few scholars over the years have accepted Bates's reasoning. By single-handedly suspending the writ, Lincoln indeed had contradicted the letter of the Constitution. How about its spirit? That's more complicated. One of Bates's main points is that the president, under the Constitution, must "take care that the laws be faithfully executed," and that he "will, to the best of his ability, preserve, protect, and defend the Constitution of the United States." For both Lincoln and Bates, secession was equivalent to anarchistic lawbreaking and an attempt to destroy the government. If we take account of "the whole family of man" and "organic law," Lincoln said, we see that no nation designed its own destruction—least of all a democratic republic grounded in a just Constitution. The rights of dissenting individuals were far less important than the perpetuation of the Union.

Lincoln continued in this vein through the early part of the Civil War. He infringed on the right of free speech when he permitted the arrest and imprisonment of Southern-leaning newspaper editors in the North. When a Baltimore journalist editorialized against the president's dismissal of Taney's ruling, federal troops arrested the writer, who was imprisoned without charge or trial for fourteen months. During the summer of 1861, in what Harold Holzer calls "the 'Salem Witch' hunt of the Civil War," some two hundred newspapers and their editors were subjected to menacing by federal agencies, civilian mobs, or Union troops.[6] A number of editors were imprisoned in Brooklyn's Fort Lafayette, which came to be known as the American Bastille. Although the suppression fever ebbed during the war, it did not disappear. In May 1864, Lincoln ordered the arrest and imprisonment of two New York editors who issued in their papers a fake proclamation calling up 400,000 troops.

A scathing, comprehensive appraisal of Lincoln's relationship to the Constitution came in a July 1861 speech before the Senate by John C. Breckinridge, the Kentucky lawyer and politician who had run as the Southern Democratic presidential candidate in 1860. The criticism of Lincoln's so-called despotism, which had been mounting for several weeks, reached new intensity in Breckinridge's address. Lincoln, Breckinridge charged, was guilty of "high crimes and usurpations."[7] He had violated "the right of every citizen to be arrested only by warrant, and his right to have his body brought before a judge, . . . a right of rights, . . . the respect of which is the measure of progress and civilization." Breckinridge added that Lincoln had defied the Constitution in other ways, too. Without the sanction of Congress, he had blockaded Southern ports and rivers, increased the size of the army and navy, ordered unreasonable searches and seizures, and used public money to fund these acts. With Lincoln having seized the powers of Congress and the judiciary, Breckinridge declared, "We are rushing, and with rapid strides, from a constitutional government to a military despotism," substituting "the will of one man for a written constitution."

How was Lincoln to respond to such charges? The avenue he most consistently took thereafter was the constitutional one of procuring congressional approval for his actions. However, he had breached the Constitution early on, and he was in unknown legal territory in some of his actions during the war. He would never fully escape the charge of being a despot, even as late as February 1865, when the Confederate commissioners at the Hampton Roads peace conference compared him to King Charles I, or indeed two months after that, when he was assassinated by a Southern actor who regarded him as a hateful tyrant.

ANNA ELLA CARROLL AND THE DEFENSE OF PRESIDENTIAL POWER

The most eloquent defense of Lincoln against these charges of despotism and Constitution breaking came from a surprising source: Anna (aka Anne) Ella Carroll, a Southern journalist, railroad lobbyist, and pamphleteer. One historian remarks that Carroll "essentially wrote the textbook on presidential war powers" and another calls her writings "the best and most persuasive contemporary rationalizations of the theory upon which Lincoln acted."[8] Nevertheless Anna Ella Carroll has gone unmentioned in Lincoln biographies, perhaps because she was a woman who worked anonymously and behind the scenes. Born in 1815 in Baltimore, she was descended from the distinguished Charles Carroll of Carrollton, a signer of the Declaration of Independence, and from Thomas King, a Puritan dissenter who had fled from Northern Ireland to America in 1683. Her father, Thomas King Carroll, was a Maryland politician who served as the state's governor in 1830–31. Although Anne grew up in a slaveholding family, she turned against slavery as a young adult and, upon Lincoln's election, freed the enslaved workers she had inherited. Know-Nothingism attracted her in the 1850s, but the deepening rift over slavery led her to become a propagandist for the Republican Party and its leader. Her powerful pro-Union editorials and pamphlets helped prevent her home state, Maryland, from joining the Confederacy. She wrote anonymously published pamphlets on habeas corpus, presidential powers, and secession that proved convincing to many readers, including Lincoln. In late 1861, when the military prospects of the Union flagged, she promoted a successful approach to the western theater on the Tennessee River that was in sync with similar plans by Lincoln and his generals. In light of her accomplishments, Lincoln told a group of congressmen: "This Anna Ella Carroll is the head of the Carroll race. When the history of this war is written she will stand a good bit taller than ever old [Declaration signer] Charles Carroll did."[9]

ANNA ELLA CARROLL

Her most effective pamphlet was the one she wrote in reply to John C. Breckinridge. In it, she substantiated, through historical research and persuasive rhetoric, Lincoln's argument that preserving the nation demanded an unprecedented exercise of presidential power. She pointed out that Breckinridge's claim that Lincoln defied the Constitution was fundamentally wrong. The South, not the North, had flouted the Constitution and had started the war. Southerners had hatched secessionist plans as early as 1831 and had expanded them under John Calhoun in 1849. In 1850, Jefferson Davis sketched a Confederate constitution that called for secession and the South's takeover of Cuba and Central America. Mississippi governor John A. Quitman rallied others to the secessionist cause. Proslavery forces infiltrated the Democratic Party, resulting in the election of presidents Pierce and Buchanan, and then divided the Democrats in 1860 with the goal of putting Breckinridge and his followers in a position to take control of the nation.

In light of this nefarious Southern conspiracy against the government, military law must temporarily replace legislative and judicial rule. Anne argued that Lincoln, as commander in chief, had the right to use "every instrument known to the law of war:—To annoy, to weaken, to destroy the enemy until its armies are overthrown and the civil authority is re-established."[10] He needed "no statute law," she wrote, "to enable him, in the absence of Congress, to defend the assault on the nation's life; because his right rests on the supreme or universal law of self-defense, common to nations as individuals—everything that has life, every being that has existence, has the right to resist, and slay the assailant when an attack is made on that life."

Previous American leaders, she noted, had prepared the way for Lincoln by placing this universal law of self-defense above statute law. During the American Revolution, habeas corpus was suspended in some regions to facilitate the arrest of groups, such as Quakers, suspected of disloyalty to the American cause. George Washington had ordered the imprisonment of thirteen men suspected of complicity with the enemy. At Germantown, he had destroyed a noncombatant's house, and during the siege of Yorktown "he levelled the suburbs, feeling that the law of property must be postponed for the safety of the nation." Carroll said she could "cite instances where Tories were shot and hung, and their properties confiscated without the form of law, during the American Revolution."

At the end of the war of 1812, Andrew Jackson in New Orleans had jailed three men, suspended habeas corpus, and ordered the execution of two deserters. Thomas Jefferson also valued the nation more than individual rights. Anne Carroll quoted from an 1810 letter in which Jefferson wrote: "A strict observance of the written laws is doubtless *one* of the high duties of a good citizen: but it is not *the highest*. The laws of necessity, of self-preservation, of saving our country when in danger, are of higher obligation. To lose our country by a scrupulous adherence to written law, would be to lose the law itself, with life, liberty, property & all those who are enjoying them with us; thus absurdly sacrificing the end to the means."

Given the national emergency Lincoln faced, Carroll argued, he was fully justified in taking extreme steps. On habeas corpus, Carroll gave Lincoln virtual carte blanche, saying that "it might be his duty . . . to arrest traitorous Senators and members of Congress, Judges of Courts, & c., who are in complicity with the rebellion, and treat them as public enemies. Instead of suppressing one press, he may extend it to all presses engaged in exciting and stimulating the treason. Instead of arresting a few traitors he may arrest all traitors, and deprive them of the means of warring on the Government."

Her reply to Breckinridge made an impact on the Lincoln administration. Attorney General Bates wrote Anne thanking her for presenting "so much sound constitutional doctrine and so many valuable historic facts in a form so compact and manageable." Bates added, "The President received a copy left for him and requested me to thank you cordially for your able support."[11]

Anne became a major publicist for Lincoln's view on the need for dramatically strengthened executive powers in a time of war. She wrote several papers on the topic, including "The Constitutional Powers of the President to Make Arrests and to Suspend the Writ of *Habeas*

Corpus," "The War Powers of the Government," and "The Relation of Revolted Citizens to the National Government." The latter paper, which she wrote at Lincoln's request, developed his argument that the so-called Confederacy was still part of the Union, not a separate nation. She was, in the words of the journalist and reformer Mary Livermore, "one of the advisers of President Lincoln. She was admitted to his presence at all times, and he reserved a special file for her communications."[12] He read her writings and learned from them. He wrote her a note in August 1862 in which he mentioned one of her recent pieces and praised her previous ones. Lincoln wrote, "Like every thing else that comes from you I have read the address to Maryland with a great deal of pleasure and interest. It is just what is needed now and you were the one to do it."[13] His openness to aggressively argumentative women like Anne Carroll puts the lie to historians who charge Lincoln with male chauvinism, such as one who speaks of his "discomfort with accomplished women."[14]

On the issues of free speech and habeas corpus, however, Lincoln was not prepared to exercise as much power as Anne Carroll said that he could. He was especially careful to protect freedom of religious expression. When a provost marshal in Missouri ordered the Presbyterian Samuel B. McPheeters to leave the state because he had expressed sympathy with the South, Lincoln intervened, insisting "the U.S. government must not . . . undertake to run the churches . . . ; let the churches, as such take care of themselves."[15]

But pro-Southern politicians demanded a stronger reaction, he thought. When the Ohio Democrat Clement Vallandigham was arrested in May 1863 for urging an immediate end to the war and restoring the Union as it was, Lincoln enforced the arrest, albeit reluctantly.

The Vallandigham incident, the most dramatic example of Lincoln's use of presidential power to suppress hostile speech, has attracted much attention but has not been placed in the cultural context of the Puritan-Cavalier divide that many at the time said was the basis of the war. Six years before the Civil War, Vallandigham had praised the Constitution for forging a compromise between "the Puritan Roundhead of New England and the Cavalier of Virginia." Southerners like George Washington, James Madison, John Rutledge, and Charles Pinckney had "joined hands in holy brotherhood" with Northerners like John Adams, Roger Sherman, Benjamin Franklin, and Oliver Ellsworth "to form a political union, so as to establish justice and to secure domestic tranquillity, the common defence, the general welfare, and the blessings of liberty to themselves and posterity."[16]

In Vallandigham's view, this constitutional compromise between the Puritan and the Cavalier had held up until evil abolitionism arose in the 1830s, when "the narrow, presumptuous, intermeddling, and fanatical spirit of the old Puritan element began to reappear in a form very much more aggressive and destructive than at first." John Quincy Adams gave antislavery reform his imprimatur, and "then every form and development of fanaticism sprang up in rank and most luxuriant growth, till abolitionism, the chief fungus of all, overspread the whole of New England first, and then the middle States, and finally every State in the Northwest." There were two types of Puritanism, Vallandigham said: the intolerant, persecuting type represented by the Pilgrims and the *Mayflower*; and the mild, tolerant type represented by Roger Williams. The Union could not be saved "until its worst and most mischievous development, Abolitionism, has been utterly extinguished" and "the Roger Williams element, as distinguished from the extreme Puritan or *Mayflower* and Plymouth Rock type of the New Englander," was cultivated.

As for the Civil War, Vallandigham insisted, it was pointless to continue it, because it resulted from a cultural division that would never heal. "This whole war," Vallandigham declared, "is not so much one of sections—least of all, between the slaveholding and non-slaveholding sections—as of races, representing not difference in blood, but mind and its development, and different types of civilization. It is the old conflict of the Cavalier and the Roundhead, the Liberalist and the Puritan; or, rather, it is a conflict, upon new issues, of the ideas and elements represented by those names."

CLEMENT VALLANDIGHAM   SAMUEL S. COX

Vallandingham's anti-Puritan argument was developed in a January 1863 speech in Cleveland by his colleague Samuel "Sunset" Cox, a fellow Ohio Democrat. Speaking on "Puritanism in Politics," Cox insisted that the "reptile" of Puritanism destroyed the Constitution, caused the war, and made the nation collapse into anarchy. Denouncing "the Constitution-breaking, negro-loving pharisaism of New England," Cox noted that Puritanism yielded "the propagandism of the higher law. . . . The history of Puritanism shows that it always sought to introduce the moral elements involved in slavery into politics." Cox explained, "This same tendency to make a moral reform society is observable in the laws punishing Quakers, against smoking tobacco, against making mince pies, and walking in the garden on Sunday. (Laughter.) The Maine liquor laws and tax laws against whiskey to stop its use, come from the same Puritan tendency to mix up politics and morals, to the detriment of both." There were many offshoots of Puritanism, including the "infidel" transcendentalism of Emerson and Parker. But the worst was abolitionism. Cox declared: "Abolition is, in the moral sense, the cause of the war. (Cheers.) It is the offspring of Puritanism." Worst of all, for Cox, Puritan-bred abolitionism had taken over the US government, in the form of the Lincoln administration. The Emancipation Proclamation was the most egregious example of moralistic Puritan meddling in the public sphere. Resorting to a racist metaphor, Cox intoned, "I cannot see any especial difference between the republicanism that sustains emancipation proclamations and the real genuine Congo abolitionism."[17]

Vallandigham and Cox became leading Peace Democrats—Northerners who opposed Lincoln's so-called "abolition war" and who called for a cessation of hostilities. Vallandigham coined the Copperhead catchphrase "To maintain the Constitution as it is, and to restore the Union as it was."[18] With their spurious version of American history, which traced an evil line from New England Puritanism to abolitionism and Republicanism, they exculpated the South for any responsibility for the war.

Lincoln set out to demolish this twisted reasoning.

Vallandigham was arrested on March 5, 1863, after giving an anti-administration speech at a Democratic rally in Mount Vernon, Ohio. He was taken into custody under Ambrose Burnside's General Order No. 38, which demanded the arrest of anyone in the Ohio Military District who habitually expressed sympathy with the enemy—what Burnside called "treason, expressed or implied."[19] At the rally, Vallandigham had said that he "spat upon" Burnside's order "trampled it under his feet."[20] He denounced the "injurious, cruel, and unnecessary war,—a war for the purpose of crushing out liberty, and establishing despotism,—a war for the freedom of the blacks and the enslaving of the whites." He said that his purpose was "to defeat an attempt to build up a monarchy on the ruins of our free government; that he believed the men in power were trying to establish a despotism."[21]

A military tribunal condemned Vallandigham to prison for the remainder of the war, but Lincoln commuted the sentence to exile to the Confederacy. Protests against Vallandigham's punishment broke out in many cities. Democrats portrayed Vallandigham as the victim of a tyrannical suppression of free speech. They tarred Lincoln with epithets like "dictator," "flatboat tyrant," "Caesar," and so on.[22] Although Lincoln had disagreed with Burnside's arrest of Vallandigham, he seized the opportunity to make a point about civil liberties and the war. Even before the incident, he had been preparing an explanation of his suspension of habeas corpus. Now was his moment to publicize it.

He took Anna Ella Carroll's approach. The South, not the North, had violated the Constitution. The South's disruption of the US government made necessary a suspension of certain constitutional rights. History validated the suspension of habeas corpus during wartime. The suspension was just a temporary emergency measure.

Lincoln made these points forcefully in his June 16 letter to Erastus Corning, the leader of a group of Albany, New York, Democrats who issued a resolution against the president. In his carefully worded reply, Lincoln agreed with Corning in his insistence on adhering to the Constitution. Corning in his letter had brought up the English civil wars of the 1640s, reminding Lincoln that the rights that the Puritans had fought for had also been pursued during the American Revolution. Lincoln countered by saying that the rights that the British and American revolutionaries had battled for came *after*, not *during* the wars. Lincoln wrote, "I too am devotedly for them *after* civil war, and *before* civil war, and at all times 'except when, in cases of Rebellion or Invasion, the public Safety may require' their suspension."[23] Cromwell and Washington had every right to defy statutes when necessary during wartime, just as Lincoln had to suspend certain laws during the Civil War.

These were concise renderings of points Anne Carroll had made, as were Lincoln's assurances about the temporary nature of his emergency measures. In her pamphlet on *The War Powers of the President*, Carroll wrote, "While the war continues the President must conduct [law enforcement] by the instrumentality of the military force, but when the war ceases, upon having accomplished its end, then ipso facto the functions of the war power cease and those of the judiciary are replaced in complete authority."[24]

Lincoln enlivened this argument through a striking metaphor drawn from medical culture. Many drugs in that era of heroic medicine were emetics. Like another favorite treatment, bloodletting—by which a vein was sliced or leeches were applied to draw out supposedly tainted blood—emetics like antimony and potassium tartrate were thought to expel bad liquids from the body. Lincoln compared his wartime suspension of constitutional rights to such disagreeable treatments. He said he could not believe Americans would expect to lose rights like habeas corpus, due process, and the freedom of speech and press "throughout the indefinite peaceful future which I trust lies before them, any more than I am able to believe that a man could contract so strong an appetite for emetics during temporary illness, as to persist in feeding upon them through the remainder of his healthful life."[25]

Like Carroll, Lincoln cited the historical example of Andrew Jackson's suspension of habeas corpus after the Battle of New Orleans. Lincoln's most memorable statement, however, drove home the malicious influence of antigovernment activism like Vallandigham's. Lincoln asked rhetorically, "Must I shoot a simple-minded soldier boy who deserts, while I must not touch a hair of a wiley [sic] agitator who induces him to desert?"[26]

By enlivening Carroll's arguments with pungent images, Lincoln

Lincoln in 1863 (photograph by Lewis Emory Walker)

snatched victory from apparent defeat. Many newspapers printed Lincoln's Corning letter, which was also widely distributed in pamphlet form. Republican politicians heaped praise on Lincoln, calling the letter "one of your best State Papers," "the best Campaign document we can have," "another Ten Strike. Full of points, . . . and all unanswerable," "complete and triumphant— . . . You have 'hit the nail on the head.'"[27]

It didn't hurt Lincoln's image that in the midst of the Vallandigham brouhaha he intervened judiciously in two civil liberties cases: he revoked an order by General Burnside that had shuttered a hostile newspaper, the *Chicago Times*; and he had persuaded Burnside to reverse the guilty verdict reached by a military court against Indiana politician Alexander J. Douglas, who had made disloyal comments in a speech.[28]

What, then, is the scorecard on Lincoln and civil liberties? Mark E. Neely Jr. argues persuasively that we should be sympathetic to the president in this regard. Neely concedes that the actions Lincoln took in the late summer and early fall of 1862 constituted the "lowest point for civil liberties in the North during the Civil War . . . and one of the lowest for civil liberties of all time in United States history."[29] But as Neely points out, most of the arrests took place in the politically ambiguous border states and involved matters such as smuggling, fraud, and running blockades. Also, Neely reminds us, Lincoln took exceptional care when adjudicating the fate of 303 Sioux Indians who were sentenced to death for slaughtering white settlers in Minnesota.[30] Lincoln sifted through trial records and, carefully weighing the evidence in each case, winnowed the number to be executed to thirty-nine. He also had a well-known tendency to pardon soldiers who had done wrong. His basic instincts were for mercy and fairness, not undue punishment.

He could thank Anne Carroll for supporting his position on the Constitution with her well-reasoned, history-based pamphlets. He could also thank her for the contributions she made to the Tennessee River campaign, which proved crucial to the Union cause.

THE TENNESSEE RIVER CAMPAIGN: "NOT ONLY A CIVILIAN BUT *A WOMAN*?"

In the fall of 1861, prospects for the Union military forces were bleak. Defeats at Bull Run, Big Bethel, Ball's Bluff, Lexington, and Wilson's Creek had shattered expectations of a short, easy war. In the East, General George McClellan was training troops skillfully, but he made no aggressive military moves; his tentativeness, caused by his chronic overestimation of enemy troop size, would continue to hobble him as a

A Pook Turtle

battlefield commander. In the West, General John Frémont, in the wake of Lincoln's revocation of his proclamation of emancipation in Missouri, was on a futile chase of Confederate troops that led to his removal from command on November 3. The Union had vague plans to advance down the Mississippi River from St. Louis and destroy the Confederate forts that controlled the river. Taking the Mississippi was a part of the so-called Anaconda Plan, devised by the aged, corpulent general Winfield Scott, who called for encircling the Confederacy on oceans and rivers.

A fleet of seven innovative gunboats was being built for the Union's river campaign. Designed by the famous St. Louis engineer James B. Eads, the slope-sided boats were called mud turtles or Pook Turtles (after Samuel Pook, the contractor who built them). Flat-bottomed paddle wheelers, the boats were formidable. Each was 175 feet long and 51 feet wide and carried thirteen large-caliber guns. Four of the boats were the first ironclads built in the United States; the other three were of wood.

The problem, as Anne Carroll saw it, was advancing down the heavily fortified Mississippi River from St. Louis. In November 1861, she traveled to Missouri, stopping along the way to meet with Union troops and generals, including Ulysses S. Grant and William Tecumseh Sherman. In St. Louis, while staying at the Everett House, she studied topographical maps and concluded that descending the Mississippi was inadvisable, because the river was shallow in some places and its current ran south. The heavy Pook Turtles were slow and could not move backward against a current. If crippled by enemy fire, they would float helplessly back into Confederate-held areas.

Anne thought about an alternate route of attack. She focused on the 652-mile Tennessee River, which flows from east Tennessee through Chattanooga and northern Alabama before running up through Tennessee and Kentucky, where it joins the Ohio River. She interrogated the pilot Charles M. Scott about the Tennessee River. A Southerner who had left the Confederacy and joined Brigadier General Grant as a pilot, Scott told her that he had often navigated the river and knew it to be of sufficient depth for the Pook Turtles. Anne decided that the Union force should not approach the rebel forts directly, on the Mississippi, but from the less-protected rear, by going up the Tennessee River and, where necessary, proceeding overland. This strategy would also allow for cutting the Memphis and Charleston Railroad, a main Confederate supply route. Anne envisaged a rapid move on to Vicksburg, the rebels' major stronghold on the Mississippi, and a simultaneous attack on Mobile, Alabama, via the Gulf of Mexico, followed by moving north through Alabama on the Tombigbee and Alabama Rivers.

On November 12, Anne wrote about her plan to Attorney General Bates and Assistant Secretary of War Thomas A. Scott. She also sent a note to Lincoln. Soon she was back in Washington, where she composed a concise but comprehensive summary of the plan. "The civil and military authorities," she wrote, "seem to be laboring under a great mistake in regard to the true key of the war in the Southwest. . . . Now all preparations in the West predicate that the Mississippi River is the point to which the authorities are directing their attention. . . . The Tennessee offers many advantages over the Mississippi."[31]

She described these advantages so persuasively that the Ohio senator Benjamin Wade, a Radical Republican who headed a congressional committee on the war, took her summary immediately to Lincoln. The president was diffident. How would his military commanders respond to this proposal from someone who was "not only a civilian but *a woman*?" he asked. Wade exclaimed, "Hang, damn, and otherwise blankety-blank, blank, blank the military. If it is a good plan, let us have it!" Lincoln mulled over the plan for days. When Anne met him at a social function in mid-December, she asked if he had considered her plan. She later recalled his reply: "I have been able to think of nothing else."

On January 14, 1862, Edwin Stanton replaced Simon Cameron as Lincoln's secretary of war. Stanton believed in the Tennessee River strategy, and he helped set it in motion. By early February, Ulysses Grant had taken Fort Henry on the Tennessee River. The Pook Turtles destroyed Confederate shipping and railway bridges. The Tennessee was now open to the Union. Grant's troops sloshed twelve miles east through mud to Fort Donelson, which they captured on the sixteenth. The long, grueling battle in wintry conditions earned the general his nickname, Unconditional Surrender Grant. His superior, General Henry Halleck, announced the next month that the Tennessee River "is now the great strategic line of the Western campaign."[32]

Fort Donelson was followed by what the *New York Times* called "A Deluge of Victories" in the West. Between February and May 1862, as James M. McPherson notes, "Union forces conquered 50,000 square miles of territory, gained control of 1,000 miles of navigable rivers, captured two state capitals and the South's largest city, and put 30,000 enemy soldiers out of action."[33] The South Carolina diarist Mary Boykin Chesnut lamented, "Battle after battle has occurred, disaster after disaster. . . . Down into the very depths of despair are we. New Orleans gone—and with it the Confederacy. . . . [N]othing to chronicle but disaster."[34]

Desperate times were ahead for the Union as well. Second Manassas, the Seven Days, Fredericksburg, Chancellorsville, Chickamauga, Cold Harbor—these and other Confederate victories caused the same kind of feelings among Northerners that Mary Chesnut experienced in 1862. There were moments when the South seemed poised to win the war.

But it is hard to envisage the Union's ultimate triumph without the success of the Tennessee River campaign. As Anne Carroll wrote in April 1865, the campaign "made the opening of the Mississippi River possible, broke the Confederate power throughout its great valley, and opened the gate for the great Sherman [to advance] into the South Atlantic States, enabling him to cooperate with General Grant in the siege of Petersburg and Richmond, and leaving Davis without a country in which to create another army."[35]

To be sure, Anne Carroll was not alone in perceiving the possible value of the Tennessee River as a military route. Lincoln and his generals appear to have been considering the idea before she offered it.[36] Grant's pilot, Scott, later contested Anne's claims for a government paycheck by saying that he came up with the idea and that Grant himself mulled it over in the fall of 1861. But Anne Carroll can be credited with studying the Tennessee River strategy closely, working out many of its details on maps and surveys, and explaining it in forceful prose that may have helped spur military action. Although Grant and Halleck deservedly received most of the praise for the Tennessee River campaign, it's hard to dispute Edwin Stanton's remark that Anne "did the great work that made the others famous." And she was quick to grasp the larger implications of the campaign. By recognizing Vicksburg, the

Confederacy's key stronghold on the Mississippi, as the most important target of Union forces in the West, she anticipated Grant's later capture of Vicksburg, a major turning point in the war.

Anne's support of forceful military action and strengthened executive power did not place her completely in Lincoln's camp. Her relationship with the president was sometimes testy. Once, when she approached him with a proposal he disliked, he said sharply, "We differ in a lot of things."[37] Although he subsequently apologized for this comment, he was being truthful.

Their main point of disagreement related to slavery. Even though she had freed between twenty and thirty enslaved people of her own, she persisted in believing that the Constitution did not permit interfering with slavery where it existed. Lincoln initially supported this idea, but fundamentally he loathed slavery and wished it to be abolished. Anne clung to the constitutional defense of slavery far longer than he did.

For a time she took advantage of his Old Whig conservatism, which he never completely shed. An ardent colonizationist, she worked to devise a viable plan for transporting blacks. Liberia, she argued, was too distant and not a welcoming place for African Americans, and Haiti was too small to accept a large number of émigrés. She proposed Central America—Honduras, in particular—as the preferred destination. Lincoln, who entertained the idea of colonization during the first two years of the war, supported the idea (which others proposed as well), and when the Panama region of Chiriquí emerged as the top choice, she studied it and reported on it to him. Lincoln offered a plan of voluntary colonization to a delegation of blacks who visited the White House in August 1862.

By then, however, he had already drafted the Emancipation Proclamation, a preliminary version of which he would issue the next month. Also, he had signed into law two Confiscation Acts, which called for the seizure of Confederate property, including enslaved persons, who became free when taken by Union troops. Anne Carroll initially opposed the confiscation of enslaved persons, which she considered against the rules of war. She wrote, "I do not think there is any grant in the Constitution, but rather an express inhibition upon the power of Congress to abolish slavery or confiscate the property of rebels."[38] If Lincoln permitted these unconstitutional acts, he would be the worst tyrant since Charles I or Charles II, who had persecuted Puritans like her seventeenth-century ancestor Thomas King.[39] In April 1862, she encouraged him to veto the bill abolishing slavery in the District of Columbia, and she initially opposed the idea of setting free the enslaved by proclamation. Eventually she supported emancipation by any means. Also, during Reconstruction she sided with the Radical Republicans who advocated fair treatment of African Americans in the South. But she was a latecomer to emancipation.

On slavery, she did not apply the laws of war in ways that influenced Lincoln. That task was left to others.

THE EMANCIPATION JUGGERNAUT

The force that first brought about the actual emancipation of large numbers of enslaved persons in the Civil War—military emancipation—has a rich history.[40] The seventeenth-century Dutch statesman Hugo Grotius had advanced the notion of a just war. In his view, war could be justified by human law, natural law, or divine law. A nation at war could appeal to God in battling for the right. "It is God's Will that certain wars should be waged," Grotius wrote. "No one will deny that whatsoever God will, is just. Therefore, some wars are just."[41] Grotius is also recognized as the father of natural law. But neither he nor his eighteenth-century follower John Locke, another influential advocate of just war and natural law, had progressive views on slavery. The main early publicist of natural law, Emmerich de Vattel, in his landmark 1758 book *The Law of Nations*, upheld the traditional notion that enslaved people captured by a foreign army during war must be returned to their rightful owners once the war was over.

An important reinterpretation of natural law came with the 1772 decision in *Somerset v. Stewart*. The judge in the case, Lord Mansfield, ruled that slavery was such a vile institution that it violated natural law and could only be *created* by positive (or statute) law.[42]

Military emancipation grew from a fusion of the notions of just war and post-*Somerset* antislavery natural law. In the American Revolution and the War of 1812, the British emancipated enslaved American blacks who fled to their lines. During the Seminole Wars of the 1830s, generals Thomas Jesup, Zachary Taylor, and Edmund P. Gaines awarded freedom to fugitives who assisted their military effort.

John Quincy Adams ardently defended military emancipation as a congressman. In 1836, addressing the emancipation of fugitives in the Seminole Wars, he distinguished between the peace power and the war power. The peace power, he said, "is limited by regulations and restricted by provisions prescribed within the Constitution." The war power, in contrast, "is limited only by the laws and uses of nations. This power is tremendous; . . . it breaks down every barrier so anxiously erected for the protection of liberty, of property, and of life."[43] Six years later, inspired by the emancipation of enslaved people in a war in Colombia, Adams repeated, "In a state of actual war the laws of war take precedence over civil laws and municipal institutions. I lay this down as the law of nations." He went so far as to say that during war "not only the President of the United States, but the Commander of the Army has the power to order the universal emancipation of the slaves."

Early in the Civil War, antislavery advocates felt empowered by this heritage of military emancipation to launch a full-scale defense of the Constitution as an antislavery document. William Lloyd Garrison, who had formerly criticized the Constitution for what he considered its proslavery implications, issued a pamphlet, *The Abolition of Slavery: The Right of the Government Under the War Power*, in which he cited

Adams as well as more recent defenders of military emancipation, such as the antislavery leaders Congressman Joshua Giddings and Senator Charles Sumner. These two went to the extreme of suggesting that civil law evaporates during war. Giddings in 1861 said, "By the laws of war, an invaded country has all its laws and municipal institutions swept by the board, and martial law takes the place of them."[44] Sumner argued that "the war power" is provided by the Constitution but, simultaneously, is "above the Constitution, because, when set in motion, like necessity, it knows no other law. For the time, it is law and Constitution. The civil power, in mass and in detail, is superseded, and all rights are held subordinate to this military magistracy." According to this radical outlook, the Civil War permitted the North's political leaders to take extreme measures to emancipate the South's enslaved millions.

Military emancipation got a huge boost from religion. Many Civil War soldiers thought they were fighting for the highest of higher laws: divine law.

Views of divine law changed during the first two years of the war. The North's leading general during the early phase, George McClellan, associated religion with civility and conservatism in war. He followed what he considered a civilized form of warfare. Not only should the South's enslaved population remain untouched, but its other property should be as well. War, he said, "should be conducted upon the highest principles known to Christian civilization. . . . Neither confiscation of property, political executions of persons, territorial organization of States or forcible abolition of slavery should be contemplated for a moment."[45] Although he opposed slavery, he wrote, "I confess to a prejudice in favor of my own race, & I can't learn to like the odor of either Billy goats or niggers."[46] He vowed to return fugitives to their owners and to suppress slave insurrections if he witnessed any. "Help me to dodge the nigger," he begged a Democratic politician; "we want nothing to do with him." He also loathed abolitionism. He stated flatly, "I will not fight for the abolitionists."

A more hard-nosed, progressive attitude toward war emerged, principally from two sources: the Puritan revolutionary Oliver Cromwell and the Prussian military strategist Carl von Clausewitz. During the Civil War, the Columbia University professor and Union military adviser Francis Lieber drew from both these sources and from the historical precedent of military emancipation, by which people held in slavery by the enemy were awarded freedom if they escaped or were taken in the course of war. With the approval of Lincoln's secretary of war, Edwin Stanton, Lieber codified his rules of war in *Instructions for the Government of Armies of the United States in the Field*, published by the War Department as General Order No. 100.

Lieber did not dispense wholly with the spirit of "civilized" war of the McClellan variety. There was a strong moral element to Lieber's code, one that has placed limitations on warfare ever since. "Men who take up arms against one another in public war," he wrote, "do not cease on this account to be moral beings, responsible to one another and to God."[47] For instance, Lieber discountenanced the use of poison, torture, assassination, and the violation of truce flags or agreements. But Lieber called for tough tactics and progressive ends. The seizure of enemy property, including enslaved persons, and the destruction of civilian infrastructure and food sources in hostile territory were permissible. Extreme violence was justified as long as it aimed toward a decisive victory.[48]

Lieber's views merged with Lincoln's in 1863, the third year of the war. By then, Lincoln had become frustrated by the tentative performances of generals like McClellan, Halleck, and Meade. He was furious when McClellan failed to pursue Lee's retreating army after the Battle of Antietam in the fall of 1862 and when Meade made the same mistake after Gettysburg the following July. Lincoln wrote disdainfully of war fought "with elder-stalk squirts [that is, squirt guns], charged with rose water."[49]

Both Lieber and Lincoln came under the influence of Oliver Cromwell, the Puritan warrior whose toppling of the British monarchy in the British civil wars was one of the inspirations for later battles against tyranny. Francis Lieber, a devout Christian, saw "wonderful greatness" in Cromwell and had special admiration for two of Cromwell's followers, John Pym, a harsh critic of Charles I, and John Hampden, who died in battle while fighting against the king's forces.[50]

Over the years, Oliver Cromwell's reputation had shifted notably. During the eighteenth-century Enlightenment, the Puritan leader was frowned on as a zealot who was overly fond of battle and (ironically for a man who helped to usher in human rights) dictatorial when he became the Lord Protector of England in the 1650s. Reviled by rationalists, including Thomas Jefferson, Cromwell was resurrected in the 1830s by Thomas Carlyle, who portrayed him as a stern but passionate fighter for principle. A Cromwell cult arose, fueled in part by popular biographies, especially Joel Tyler Headley's *The Life of Oliver Cromwell* (1848).

John Brown, a devout Calvinist who patterned himself after Cromwell, kept Headley's book on a shelf next to the Bible. In Brown's eyes, Cromwell was the ideal warrior for justice. When fighting proslavery forces in Kansas, Brown often repeated Cromwell's famous line, "Trust in God and keep your [gun]powder dry." Brown's contemporaries compared him to Cromwell more than to any other historical figure.[51] Thoreau, who revered Brown, said of him, "He died lately in the time of Cromwell, but he reappeared here. Why should he not? Some of the Puritan stock are said to have settled in New England." Brown's hard words about slaveholders were, Thoreau said, "like the speeches of Cromwell compared with those of an ordinary king," and his band of soldiers in Kansas missed being "a perfect Cromwellian troop" only because there was no clergyman worthy of joining it.[52]

Such praise, however, masked controversies that surrounded both Cromwell and Brown. Cromwell was notorious for his excesses in Ireland, where at towns like Drogheda and Wexford he ordered the slaughter by sword of thousands of civilians and priests. Brown, too, had killed in the name of a cause. In May 1856 he directed the slaying by sword of five proslavery settlers at Pottawatomie Creek, Kansas. Then came Brown's deadly antislavery raid on Harpers Ferry, which polarized the nation. Equally controversial were his views of race and war, which were the opposite of McClellan's. Brown saw slavery as a war against an entire race. He and his followers waged what they considered a holy war to emancipate America's enslaved millions. Brown's goal was the integration of black people into mainstream society, with full social and political rights awarded to them.

Few Americans—even committed antislavery Northerners—were ready to go as far as Brown did in his call for integration and racial equality. At the start of the war, most Northern volunteers were prepared to battle against Southern "traitors" but not for emancipation. In time, as James McPherson notes, the Northern soldiers assumed a more antislavery position.[53] Like them, initially Lincoln recoiled from the abolitionist Brown, whose courage he admired but whose violent tactics he at first rejected. Not only did he renounce Brown during his presidential run, but in the first year of the war, he decried a war for emancipation, which he associated with John Brown. As the *New York Herald* reported in December 1861: "The President is resolutely determined to veto schemes whatever, involving the emancipation of negroes in a manner that they are turned loose upon the Southern States on an equality with white occupiers of the soil. He, on Saturday evening, uttered the following words:—'Emancipation would be equivalent to a John Brown raid, on a gigantic scale.'"[54]

Distancing himself from John Brown, however, was not easy. A Southern newspaper, noting "a vein of coercion" beneath Lincoln's moderate exterior, announced, "In the body of Lincoln the spirit of John Brown lives."[55] A broadside of 1861 criticized "Old Abe Lincoln and his Abolition war—his Old John Brown raid against the South, and his usurpations and tyranny, and schemes of death and hell—rapine, plunder, murder, piracy."[56]

The alleged connection between Brown and Lincoln persisted through the war and beyond, as signaled by a pro-Southern editorial, published three months after Appomattox, that generalized bitterly: "The name of John Brown and Abraham Lincoln will indeed *go down to posterity together* . . . into the abyss of infamy and eternal shame . . . The administration of Abraham Lincoln was a John Brown raid on the grandest scale; and it was no more. That is the place it will occupy in history."[57]

Extreme as this statement is, it made sense from the South's vantage point in 1865. By then, Lincoln's war *had* become a war for emancipation, infused by a religious spirit. Shortly before his hanging, Brown had handed his jailer a note that read:

CHARLESTOWN, VA. 2ND, DECEMBER, 1859.

I John Brown am now quite *certain* that the crimes of this *guilty land: will* never be purged *away*; but with Blood. I had *as I now think: vainly* flattered myself that without *verry* [*sic*] *much* bloodshed; it might be done.[58]

Brown's conviction that "this *guilty land*" would be punished by God for its "crimes" was echoed in several of Lincoln's religious proclamations during the war. Though never a church member, Lincoln respected God's will and mysterious purposes. He was sensitive to religious groups who approached him, many of whom expressed their opinion that the Civil War was God's punishment of the nation for its sins. Scattered throughout Lincoln's nine religious proclamations were Calvinist images of sin and retribution. In August 1861 he proclaimed a day of prayer "to recognize the hand of God in this terrible visitation, and in sorrowful remembrance of our own faults and crimes as a nation and as individuals, to humble ourselves before Him, and to pray for His mercy,—to pray that we may be spared further punishment, though most justly deserved."[59] Similarly, in a proclamation of March 1863 he asked that because "we know that, by His divine law, nations like individuals are subjected to punishments and chastisements in this world, may we not justly fear that the awful calamity of civil war, which now desolates the land, may be but a punishment, inflicted upon us, for our presumptuous sins, to the needful end of our national reformation as a whole People?"[60]

Because Lincoln avoided identifying himself with contested historical figures, he did not openly embrace Cromwell or John Brown. But their presence was culturally inescapable during the war. Northern soldiers sang "John Brown's Body" as they marched, and they were frequently compared in the popular press with Cromwell's New Model Army, aka the Roundheads or Ironsides. Just after the war, one commentator noted, "The Union soldiers were often compared to the famous 'Ironsides' of Cromwell. The comparison was natural."[61]

Southerners viewed themselves as chivalric gentlemen in the vein of the British Cavaliers, while they denigrated the northern "Puritans" as lowly scum—"Roundheads," in the words of one paper, "these greasy mechanics, these vulgar tradesmen, this 'inferior race' . . . of the north, . . . arrayed against the very flower of the English aristocracy and their adherents."[62] In turn, democratic averageness became a badge of honor among the Northern troops, who could boast of fighting with Cromwellian passion against decadent Southerners who defended slavery.

A regiment from Lawrence County, Pennsylvania, an area originally settled by Cromwellian Covenanters, nicknamed itself the Roundheads. They were described by their captain as "men that will hold slavery to be a sin against God and a crime against humanity and will carry their bibles into battle," and by a reporter as "true and lion-hearted men of Puritanic times."[63] They fought in major battles of the Civil War and held regular reunions in the postwar decades.

Cromwell's main influence on the North's soldiers was his combination of piety and relentlessness in battle. A New England journalist noted, "Cromwell, it is well known, believed that those soldiers that pray fight best."[64] Sarah Emma Edmonds, who served as a man in the Union army, wrote, "Cromwell and his praying puritans were dangerous men to meet in battle. 'The sword of the Lord and of Gideon' was exceeding sharp, tempered as it was by hourly prayers."[65]

Lincoln continually cultivated religion and morality among the Union troops. By the second year of the war, the government had spent nearly $1.5 million for chaplains in military units.[66] Lincoln also encouraged the work of the United States Christian Commission, headed by the Philadelphia philanthropist George H. Stuart. A nongovernment agency made up of more than five thousand volunteer agents, the Christian Commission distributed religious literature and provided counsel, comfort, and food in military camps. Over the course of the war, Stuart reported, the commission distributed some two million free Bibles to army and navy men. It also handed out eighteen million copies of religious newspapers and eight million religious tracts like Newman Hall's *Come to Jesus* and William Reid's *The Blood of Jesus*.[67]

Lincoln met with George Stuart during the war, corresponded with him, and attended several Christian Commission events. When he could not attend, he sent supportive notes, as in February 1863, when he wrote that although his work prevented him from joining a commission meeting, "I can not withhold my approval of the meeting, and it's [sic] worthy objects. Whatever shall be sincerely, and in God's name, devised for the good of the soldier and seaman, in their hard spheres of duty, can scarcely fail to be blest."[68]

Among the works distributed by the Christian Commission was the American Tract Society's reissue of Oliver Cromwell's Bible, a short Bible for soldiers that Cromwell had started providing for his troops in 1643. Cromwell had selected military-oriented passages from the Geneva Bible (or Breeches Bible). The Geneva Bible, first published in 1560, five decades before the King James Version, was the Bible favored by Puritans like Cromwell, John Bunyan, and the *Mayflower* Pilgrims.

The Geneva Bible "continued to be used by the Puritans long after King James's version was published," a Massachusetts paper explained.[69] Cromwell's abridged version included Bible passages under headings like "A Souldier must not doe wickedly," "A Souldier must be valiant for Gods cause," "A soldier must denie his own," "A Souldier must pray before he goes to fight," and the ambiguous "A Souldier must love his enemies as they are his enemies and hate them as they are God's enemies."

The Cromwell Bible (reissued by the American Tract Society, 1861)

In September 1861 the American Tract Society issued a facsimile edition titled *Soldier's Pocket Bible, Issued for the Army of Oliver Cromwell.* Small and portable, it sold for $0.05 (or $3.50 per hundred). Promoted as "having been prepared in 1643 with the approbation of Cromwell and circulated extensively among his soldiers," it contained "extracts from various parts of the Bible suitable to all occasions of a soldier's life."[70] Twenty thousand copies of a facsimile of Cromwell's Bible were published in September 1861. By the following April, more than three hundred thousand copies of the book had been sent to Union soldiers.[71]

Lincoln reportedly received a copy of the Cromwell Bible. George Stuart told of going to the White House and presenting the book to the president, who "seemed so interested in its distribution that he arose from his seat and thanked me for presenting him with it."[72] Stuart later related the story to a German soldier who initially refused to accept the Bible, explaining that he was a disbeliever. Stuart tried Puritan persuasion on the soldier: "I told him it was what is called Cromwell's Bible, and I told him how Cromwell's soldiers read this book, and how it enabled them to fight so vigorously." The soldier remained unmoved until Stuart described his recent visit to the White House:

> When I went to see the President he was writing, and when I handed him a copy of Cromwell's Bible he stood up—and you know he was a very tall man and took a long time to straighten. He received the Bible, and made me a low bow, and thanked me; and now I shall have to go back and tell him that one of his soldiers who was fighting his battles refused to take the book which he had accepted so gladly. The German softened at once. He said, "Did the President take the book? Well, then, I guess I may take one too."

This is not to say soldiers and sailors read only Bibles and tracts; nor did Lincoln expect them to. Their reading covered a broad spectrum, from classics—Shakespeare, Dante, Milton, Dickens, and so on—all the way to yellow-covered sensational novels with titles like *The Pirate's Son* and *The Gold Fiend*. An Indiana soldier recalled that "miserable worthless . . . novels . . . were sold by the thousand," and men paid one dollar for "three worthless novelettes which contained a love story or some daring adventure by sea or land." Another soldier reported that "enticing literary productions, such as Beadle's novels, novelettes and other detestable works were received with popular favor."[73] Also popular in the camps were daily papers such as the *Herald* and the *Tribune*, illustrated papers like *Frank Leslie's Weekly*, literary magazines such as the *Atlantic* and *Harper's*, and comic weeklies, including *Phunny Phellow*, *Budget of Fun*, and *Nix-Nax*. Lincoln, eager to absorb the popular culture of the day, displayed equally eclectic reading tastes, which ranged from Shakespeare and serious poetry through newspapers to zany humorous books.

But both the president and his troops knew the special value of religion during wartime. "Strange feelings come over one when he is in battle and bullets are whizzing around one," a soldier wrote. "It is a wonderful place for one who is a Christian to test his faith."[74] Not only did Cromwellian piety steel soldiers for battle, but the overwhelming amount of death and suffering made the afterlife a daily preoccupation. Soldiers and sailors read far more religious material than did civilians. The volunteer religious agencies made such reading readily available, while they discouraged secular reading. Religious literature provided real consolation; it promised the eternal reward of a reunion with loved ones in heaven. The popular press teemed with pious stories like "The Soldier's All," in which a dying soldier in a camp hospital is asked if he wants "any books, or papers, or magazines" to read; he smiles, shakes his head, and holds up a well-worn Bible, saying that "he had no wants which his Bible could not supply."[75] In another story, a soldier named Charles promises his mother that he will read the Bible every day. He does, and he meets a dying veteran who confesses that he is a skeptic and a sinner. When Charles reads him Bible passages promising redemption through Christ, the veteran dies with the blissful assurance of heaven.[76]

Religion was also a powerful motivator for the Confederacy. The Constitution of the Confederate States, adopted in March 1861, invoked "the favor and guidance of Almighty God" in its preamble—a rebuff to the godless US Constitution.[77] The South had no problem defending slavery in the name of religion. To the contrary, it prided itself on preserving what it considered a God-ordained institution. The Confederacy's leading Episcopal bishop, Stephen Elliott, declared that Southerners had a holy mission to convert heathen Africans to Christianity. God, he said, "has caused the African race to be planted here under our political protection and under our Christian nurture."[78] Northern agitators, in contrast, had been the "fountain of evil whence have sprung all these bitter waters." Denouncing "these wretched infidels, the harbingers of war, of woe, and of anarchy," Elliott fumed: "I cannot conceive any thing more hateful to God than the infidelity which has revelled in the Eastern States for the last forty years, . . . especially in the philosophy of abolitionism."

Although the Confederacy did not have many religious publishing centers, Northern publishers shipped around 300,000 Bibles to the South, despite the ban on trade between the sections. A Richmond man smuggled 10,000 Bibles, 50,000 New Testaments, and 250,000 abridged Bibles to the South from England.[79]

In the course of the war, Jefferson Davis issued ten religious proclamations, one more than Lincoln. Revivals swept through Southern troops. Especially notable was the religious frenzy that overtook Lee's Army of Northern Virginia between September 1862 and May 1863, and even more strongly, from August 1863 through May 1864, known as "a high point in army evangelism."[80] At such times, the Southern soldiers felt that "no army in all history—not even Cromwell's 'Roundheads'—had in it as much of real, evangelical religion and devout piety as the Army of Northern Virginia."[81]

Moreover, the Confederates had a Cromwell in their midst: Thomas "Stonewall" Jackson. Other Confederate generals, such as J. E. B. Stuart, Nathan Bedford Forrest, and Robert E. Lee, were cut in the Cavalier mold of Southern agrarianism, chivalry, honor, and gentlemanliness. Jackson was different. A pious Presbyterian, he was sober, plainspoken, and devoted to Bible reading. On the battlefield he was as fearless and ruthless as Cromwell. A contemporary noted that while other Confederates resembled "the Cavaliers of Prince Rupert, . . . Jackson himself might have passed for a type of all that was best and worthiest in their Puritan enemies," with a bearing that was "decidedly of the Puritan stamp."[82] He was called "a typical Roundhead" and the "Cromwell of the Cavaliers."[83] Along with Robert E. Lee and John Wilkes Booth, Jackson had attended the hanging of John Brown in 1859. Although Jackson rejected Brown's views on slavery, he felt a kinship with the Puritan warrior. He prayed for Brown's soul on the night before the execution, and as he wrote his wife, when he witnessed Brown's "unflinching firmness" on the scaffold, "I sent up the petition that he might be saved."[84]

If Jackson had sympathy for an antislavery Northerner like Brown, many Northerners respected Jackson. When he died of pneumonia after being wounded by friendly fire at Chancellorsville in May 1863, there was an outpouring of grief throughout the South and homages in the North and in Europe. Herman Melville in a poem called Jackson "True to the thing he deemed was due, / True as John Brown or steel."[85] Lincoln's journalist friend John W. Forney wrote an article praising Jackson as a "great general, a brave soldier, a noble Christian, and a pure man," despite his dedication to a bad cause.[86] Forney sent his piece to the president, who replied, "I wish to lose no time in thanking you for the excellent and manly article in the Chronicle on 'Stonwall [sic] Jackson.'"[87]

STONEWALL JACKSON

MILITARY NECESSITY AND MORAL GRANDEUR: TOWARD THE EMANCIPATION PROCLAMATION

Although Lincoln saw religion as an important catalyst for battlefield vigor, he avoided references to divine law in his public pronouncements on slavery during the first two years of the war. He pursued emancipation indirectly and cautiously. He knew that slaveholders believed in God and the Bible as much as Radical Republicans did. He feared losing the border states and alienating the substantial number of political conservatives and moderates in the North. He stayed on his tightrope.

In a widely quoted article, the *New York World* remarked: "President Lincoln is a very Blondin in the art of political balancing. When in his elevated position a portion of the balancing pole is thrown out on the left side, he deftly projects an equal weight of it on the right. Thus he maintains his equilibrium."[88]

That is, he constantly adjusted his stance, now leaning toward the conservative and now toward the radical. He knew that if he shifted too strongly in either direction at the wrong moment, both he and the nation could fall.

He acted firmly in dealing with field commanders who issued emancipation orders in their districts. He revoked the emancipation edicts of General John Frémont in Missouri in August 1861 and of General David Hunter in Georgia, South Carolina, and Florida the following May. Such orders, he insisted, were "not within the range of *military* law, or necessity."[89] Only he, as commander in chief, had the power to issue an emancipation proclamation. His main concern was to restore the Union, and to do that he needed to retain the loyalty of the slave-holding border states—Kentucky, Maryland, Delaware, Missouri, and, from 1862 on, West Virginia. "I think to lose Kentucky is nearly the same as to lose the whole game," he wrote. "Kentucky gone, we can not hold Missouri, nor, as I think, Maryland. . . . We would as well consent to separation at once, including the surrender of this capitol."[90]

Although he strongly desired emancipation in the border states, he approached the issue gingerly. He spent much of the period between November 1861 and July 1862 promoting a program of compensated emancipation in those states. He drafted two such measures for Delaware, offering federal payment to slave owners who accepted a plan of gradual emancipation. When Delaware did not accept the plan, he sent to Congress a joint resolution offering to cooperate with any state that would agree to a plan of gradual, compensated emancipation. Congress passed the resolution, and Lincoln signed it on April 10, 1862. He tried to sell the plan to border state representatives in two meetings. They rejected it, despite his argument that they should accept the government's money while they could, because the signs pointed toward emancipation.

Dismissed by the border states, compensated emancipation succeeded in the District of Columbia. In April 1862, Congress passed a bill for the nation's capital similar to the one Lincoln had proposed in 1849. The Compensated Emancipation Act of 1862 liberated 3,200 enslaved persons in the District of Columbia, paying up to $300 per person and offering $100 for voluntary removal to Liberia or Haiti.[91]

Military emancipation, meanwhile, had begun early in the war. General Benjamin Butler was stationed at Fort Monroe in Virginia's Hampton Roads on May 23, 1861, when three fugitives arrived at his camp. Butler took the blacks in, sending away a Confederate officer who arrived under a flag of truce to reclaim them. Within a month, Butler had accepted five hundred fugitives. They were called "contraband of war" because they were considered stolen enemy property. Within a year, tens of thousands of fugitives had made their way behind Union lines. At first, blacks worked without pay for the Union military, but by the fall of 1861 the navy was paying ten dollars a month for their labor, and the army was paying eight dollars monthly to men and four dollars to women.

Lincoln found himself on an emancipation juggernaut. He signed two Confiscation Acts passed by Congress, the first in August 1861, which freed enslaved persons who worked for the Union military, and the second, in July 1862, emancipating all who came under military control. In March 1862 he signed a bill that prohibited the military from sending runaways back to their owners. In April, he told representatives of the Freedmen's Association, "I am entirely satisfied that no slave who becomes for the time free within the American lines will ever be re-enslaved. Rather than have it so, I would give up and abdicate."[92]

The issue that had catapulted Lincoln to national visibility—preventing the westward spread of slavery—was settled quietly on June 19, 1862, when Congress passed a bill outlawing slavery in the territories. That month also saw the diplomatic recognition of Haiti and Liberia as well as a strengthened treaty between the United States and England banning the international slave trade. Early in the year, Lincoln had ordered the execution of a convicted slave trader, Nathaniel Gordon.

All of these antislavery actions saw Lincoln leaning in a radical direction. But despite impressive military successes in the West, results on the battlefield were not keeping up with the advances on the antislavery scene. McClellan's peninsular campaign, designed to take Richmond from a southeastern position on the Virginia Peninsula, ended in the bloody standoff of the Seven Days' Battles against Lee's Army of Northern Virginia. In July, McClellan retreated to a base on the James River. He later moved north of Richmond but did little to aid the beleaguered John Pope, who suffered a devastating defeat at Second Manassas in late August. The Union forces moved to a defensive position around Washington.

Frustrated by the military losses in the East and by the unwillingness of the border states to accept compensated emancipation, Lincoln decided to take the dramatic step of issuing a presidential proclamation of emancipation. By July 1862 he had drafted a proclamation that he announced as "a fit and necessary military measure."[93] It freed the enslaved people held in rebellious states as of January 1, 1863. He discussed the matter with William Seward and Gideon Welles in a carriage ride on July 13. Nine days later, on July 22, he read the proclamation to his cabinet, whose reaction was mixed. He took the advice of Seward, who argued that he should not issue the proclamation until the Union had achieved a military victory. The wait was on.

Those who complain that the Emancipation Proclamation is a dry, legalistic document—having "all the moral grandeur of a bill of lading," as Richard Hofstadter famously wrote—ignore the fact that Lincoln knew that, to alienate the least number of people, such a proclamation must be presented as a purely military measure, not as a moral statement about slavery.[94] Lincoln also knew that outside of military necessity he lacked the authority under the Constitution to liberate the enslaved. By

The First Reading of the Emancipation Proclamation Before the Cabinet (engraving by Alexander H. Ritchie from the painting by Francis B. Carpenter). This 1864 engraving portrays the momentous cabinet meeting of July 22, 1862. Pictured, left to right, are Edwin M. Stanton, Salmon P. Chase, President Lincoln, Gideon Welles, Caleb B. Smith, William H. Seward, Montgomery Blair, and Edward Bates. The paintings on the wall show Simon Cameron and Andrew Jackson.

1862, there was great latitude under the laws of war by which emancipating the enemy's enslaved population could be justified as a means to gain military victory.

But Lincoln was aware that even if the proclamation appeared without moralizing, it would still shock conservatives. He felt he had to prepare for what he knew would be the stunning impact of the proclamation, which would immediately subject him to harsh attacks from the right. And so, in the period leading to issuing a proclamation, he put on a flamboyant show of centrism. Although he still hated slavery as much as any abolitionist, for now he would play the Old Whig.

He put on his best Old Whig performance when he talked with a delegation of African Americans on August 14, 1862.[95] The innovation of a president holding a serious discussion with black people in the White House—a first in American history—was buffered by what he said to them. He addressed them politely, but he delivered messages that could not have pleased them. The presence of black people in America, he said, was the reason for the current war. Innate racial differences and the indelible antiblack prejudice of whites forbade the two races from living on equal terms in America. It was best for blacks, once freed, to choose to leave the country. Central America, he told them, was a most desirable destination to which American blacks could move. A colony there would soon prosper, for that region was fertile and rich in coal.

He was tilting to the right to please conservatives, in preparation for the pending release of the Preliminary Emancipation Proclamation.

Abolitionists, predictably, denounced the president. William Lloyd Garrison described Lincoln's address to the black delegation as "insulting, . . . preposterous, . . . puerile, absurd, illogical, impertinent, untimely."[96] Black people, Garrison fumed, had as much right to live in America as whites, who had kidnapped them from Africa and had subjected them to slavery. Lincoln, Garrison said, callously ignored the immorality of slavery and racial prejudice. A black journalist in New Jersey sarcastically suggested that Lincoln and Vice President Hamlin should be shipped to Central America to dig coal.

Conservatives, in contrast, not only praised Lincoln for his colonization plan but exceeded him in their assertions of racial difference. The editor of the *Philadelphia Press*, for example, commended the president's "practical and humane" proposition and used the occasion to vent racism:

> Our people do not like the negro. He is not a congenial companion, nor an acceptable fellow-citizen. There must forever be an antagonism of race. . . . There can be nothing like an equality of race where the blue-veined Saxon exists. The tawny East Indians are crouching at his feet—the Chinaman cowers

in dismay—the Indian proudly and submissively moves on to oblivion and the setting sun, while the negro tills his fields, grows his cotton, digs his entrenchments, and gathers his food and raiment. . . .

The negro . . . cannot eat at my table, or sit in my parlor, or ride in my carriage, or lounge in my opera-box; he cannot be my partner in business, the friend of my social life, or the husband of my kinswomen. He is forever an inferior being.[97]

Such explicit bigotry makes us realize that Lincoln's words to his black visitors were not as reactionary as they initially seem. They were close in spirit to the rhetoric used by the black activist Martin Delany, who in his 1854 pamphlet *Political Destiny of the Colored Race on the American Continent* recommended that American blacks should move out of the country in order to flee the racial discrimination they faced in the United States.

If we compare Lincoln's proposal to his black visitors with Delany's words, we see similarities. Here is Lincoln: "Your race are suffering, in my judgment, the greatest wrong inflicted on any people," because "even when you cease to be slaves, you are yet far removed from being placed on an equality with the white race. . . . [O]n this broad continent, not a single man of your race is made the equal of a single man of ours. Go where you are treated the best, and the ban is still upon you."[98] Here is Delany: "[Free blacks in the North] occupy the very same position politically, religiously, civilly and socially (with but few exceptions,) as the bondman occupies in the slave States. . . . Denied an equality not only of political, but of natural rights, in common with the rest of our fellow citizens, there is no species of degradation to which we are not subject."[99] Lincoln: "The place I am thinking about having for a colony is in Central America. . . . The country is a very excellent one for any people, and with great natural resources and advantages." Delany: "Central and South America, are evidently the ultimate destination and future home of the colored race on this continent; the advantages of which in preference to all others, will be apparent when once pointed out."

It is understandable, given these similarities, that Delany's *Political Destiny of the Colored Race* was included as an appendix to the *Report of the Select Committee on Emancipation and Colonization*, 10,000 copies of which were published by the authority of the House of Representatives on July 16, 1862. It is also understandable that Delany approved of Lincoln's colonization proposal to the black delegation.[100]

Lincoln would soon stop speaking about colonization publicly. Within two months of his meeting with the black delegation, he terminated a government plan to transport some five hundred American blacks to Chiriquí Province (now Panama). In 1863 he withdrew support for the entrepreneur Bernard Kock's scheme of resettling a similar number to Vache Island, off Haiti—a disastrous scheme that ended with Lincoln sending a ship to Haiti that brought 453 black people back to America. Colonization for Lincoln had always been a voluntary decision to be made by black people themselves. He had long suspected it to be impracticable; even in his remarks to the delegation he noted that only twelve thousand American blacks had emigrated during the many decades since colonization had begun. His address to the blacks has the signs of being a sop to conservatives and a stalling tactic. At the end of the address, he told his visitors that the topic was so complicated that it merited careful deliberation. He suggested that they might need at least a month to think it over.

By then, he knew, he could have already announced the Preliminary Emancipation Proclamation.

For the time being, however, the antislavery press grew frantic over what appeared to be his apostasy. Horace Greeley in the *New-York Tribune* sent a public letter to Lincoln titled "The Prayer of Twenty Millions." The president, Greeley insisted, had betrayed his millions of supporters by taking a conservative stance on slavery. Lincoln was merely appeasing the South and kowtowing to the border states, not punishing the Confederate traitors by attacking slavery, as he should be doing.

Lincoln wrote a letter of reply, which was published as widely as Greeley's letter, in which he said that his chief goal was to save the Union, irrespective of slavery. "My paramount object in this struggle *is* to save the Union, and is *not* either to save or to destroy slavery. If I could save the Union without freeing *any* slave I would do it, and if I could save it by freeing *all* the slaves I would do it; and if I could save it by freeing some and leaving others alone I would also do that."[101]

HORACE GREELEY

This letter, of course, was disingenuous. By the time he wrote it many enslaved people had already been liberated through military emancipation, and several antislavery measures were in place. The letter to Greeley was President Blondin showing that he was right in the middle between allowing slavery to exist and banishing it altogether. As a nod to Greeley, he closed his note saying that "I intend no modification of my oft-expressed *personal* wish that all men every where could be free."

Some saw Lincoln's ambiguous letter as merely an attention-grabbing attempt to confuse the self-important Greeley. *The Independent* called it an example of "the president's wit," a "sensation *hit*" designed for the newspaper war between the *Tribune* and rival newspapers like the *Herald*. Showing his "keen eye . . . for the ludicrous," Lincoln was just toying with Greeley, a favorite target of other papers.[102]

Others valued what they saw as the moderation of the president's letter. *Frank Leslie's Weekly* commented, "It is proof of Mr. Lincoln's conservative tendencies that he has never yet been in advance of the nation on any question of public policy."[103]

Lincoln also shrewdly utilized his meeting with a group of Chicago ministers who visited him on September 13. The clergymen, from several denominations, came to advise him to issue a proclamation against slavery, which God proclaimed a sin. Lincoln cagily replied that if God intended to communicate such a message, surely He would send it to the president directly. He added, "These are not, however, the days of miracles, and I suppose it will be granted that I am not to expect a direct revelation. I must study the plain physical facts of the case, ascertain what is possible and learn what appears to be wise and right."[104]

Was he backing off from the preliminary proclamation of emancipation he had written and was waiting to publish?

Actually, he was inching publicly toward a radical position: slavery must be abolished, not only because of the laws of war but also because it was unjust and immoral. But he didn't say that directly. He clothed his radical antislavery position in the dress of military necessity:

[A]s commander-in-chief of the army and navy, in time of war, I suppose I have a right to take any measure which may best subdue the enemy. Nor do I urge objections of a moral nature, in view of possible consequences of insurrection and massacre at the South. I view the matter as a practical war measure, to be decided upon according to the advantages or disadvantages it may offer to the suppression of the rebellion.

At the same time, though, he pretended to back off. What good would an emancipation proclamation do? he asked the ministers. How could words from him abolish slavery in the South? They would be as effective, he joked, as a papal bull against a comet—a reference to the legendary story of the medieval Pope Callixtus III, who had excommunicated the "apparition" of Halley's comet in 1456.

As far as the Chicago ministers knew, he was an overly cautious president who was merely continuing the constitutional defense of slavery that he had initiated in his inaugural address. But he was just making a feint, awaiting the right moment to issue his proclamation.

The moment came four days after his equivocal remarks to the ministers. On September 17, George McClellan stopped Robert E. Lee's northward advance at Antietam Creek in Maryland. One of the bloodiest events in US history, the Battle of Antietam produced more than 22,000 dead, wounded, or missing. This was not the kind of victory Lincoln had hoped for. Lee's force was badly hurt, but it escaped across the border back into Virginia, thanks to McClellan's typical dilatoriness (which this time got him fired, although his replacement, Ambrose Burnside, proved to be even more ineffective).

However, Antietam was close enough to a win for Lincoln to use emancipation as a weapon against the South and a way of preventing Europe's involvement in the war. The Preliminary Emancipation Proclamation, issued on September 22, 1862, offered the rebel states a few months to weigh Lincoln's offer of a plan of gradual, compensated emancipation, to be paid for by federal funds. If the rebel states did not accept this offer, their enslaved people would be declared free, by executive order, in a final Emancipation Proclamation that would be issued on January 1, 1863. Always concerned about losing the border states, Lincoln left slavery alone there as long as they remained loyal to the Union.

The Preliminary Emancipation Proclamation shook Lincoln's tightrope more strongly than ever. Passionate responses to the Preliminary Emancipation Proclamation came from both sides.

The strong reactions were justified. Lincoln's document said that "all persons held as slaves" in any state still in rebellion against the United States as of January 1, 1863, "shall be then, thenceforward, and forever free."

The key word here was "forever." The question of whether or not enslaved persons seized in war became forever free or were only emancipated for the duration of military necessity had been a complex one during the Revolution and the War of 1812, and it remained so early in the Civil War. Congressional decisions of 1861 and 1862—especially the two Confiscation Acts and the 1862 bill forbidding military personnel from returning fugitives to their owners—purported to resolve the issue. Lincoln would support the Lieber Code of 1863, which would forever emancipate black fugitives who arrived behind Union lines. In 1863 and '64, he would continue to try to promote emancipation in the border states. But he knew that only a constitutional amendment that abolished slavery would be, in his words, "a King's cure for all the evils."[105]

The Preliminary Emancipation Proclamation was an important step toward that amendment. For a president to proclaim permanent emancipation in some states was a tremendously inspirational gesture.[106] Emerson called the Preliminary Emancipation Proclamation one of the rare "jets of thoughts into affairs," a huge "step in the history of political liberty," promising "a day which most of us dared not hope to see, an event worth the dreadful war, worth its costs and uncertainties." All doubts about Lincoln's virtuous goals, Emerson insisted, must now be dropped. With this proclamation, "He has been permitted to do more for America than any other American man."[107]

Many antislavery Northerners heaped similar praise on the Preliminary Emancipation Proclamation. *The Independent* asserted, "There can be no state paper imagined more noble than one which carries substantial liberty to millions of slaves. It is that very moral grandeur and sublime importance which makes us jealous of anything which threatens its certainty or diminishes its moral power."[108] The *Chicago Tribune* raved: "So splendid a vision has hardly shone upon the world since the day of the Messiah." William Lloyd Garrison held that while the proclamation did not go far enough, it was "an act of immense historic importance, and justified the almost universal gladness of expression and warm congratulation which it has simultaneously elicited in every part of the free states." Horace Greeley, who weeks before had attacked Lincoln as a lackey of the South, wrote of the proclamation: "It places our government distinctly, unequivocally, on the side of freedom as against slavery."

Greeley's perennial foe, James Gordon Bennett at the *Herald*, poked fun at Greeley for his about-face. "It is enough for us to dance with joy," Bennett wrote, to see Greeley's *Tribune*, "which has been cursing and abusing the President for some time past, indicting him for malfeasance in office, . . . accusing him of not executing the laws, . . . [saying] that it was the prayer of twenty million that he should resign," now "indulges in a wiggle-waggle, and exclaims, 'God bless Abraham Lincoln.'" After all, Greeley had said, "God do the other thing to Abraham Lincoln, a short while ago."[109]

But the Preliminary Emancipation Proclamation was no laughing matter for conservatives. "Mr. Lincoln has yielded to the radical pressure," the *Journal of Commerce* stated. "We have only anticipations of evil from it, and we regard it, as will an immense majority of the people of the North, with profound regret."[110] The *New York Express* declared that Lincoln's one aim now was "to execute the *programme* that *Puritan* abolitionism of New England demands of him."[111]

The *New York World* remarked angrily, "The president has swung loose from the constitutional moorings of his Inaugural address and . . . is fully adrift on the current of radical fanaticism. . . . This proclamation is made in pursuance of that higher law—that is to say, that open defiance of law—which distinguished the tribe of pestilent abolition agitators from the beginning."[112]

Adrift on a radical current. Given over to the higher law. Actually, Lincoln, like other Republicans, had long thought that the Constitution contained the higher law, since it embodied the egalitarian principles of the Declaration of Independence. But the war had pulled him from his initial position of protecting slavery where it existed. He was now prepared to challenge slavery by fiat. The war had opened up new possibilities for the nation.

The Lincoln White House

The war also opened up new vistas for Mary Todd Lincoln. We have often heard that she was a temperamental wife and a reckless spendthrift whose purchases for herself and the White House led to overspending and possibly corrupt practices. Her shifting moods indeed made her erratic, but they revealed a woman who enacted many female roles—some subversive, some entrepreneurial, some conventional—that had been gathering force in American culture for decades.

She was so unpredictable that she resisted easy categorization—or easy control by Lincoln. Her behavior, varied at best and chaotic at worst, provided him with home practice in the kinds of issues that he confronted publicly. He strove to maintain union and direction at home even as he tried to restore them to the nation. But the control was not all from his side. At key moments, she helped him focus on political and military issues that mattered most.

The picture that is generally drawn of their marriage is one of increasing separation during the White House years. It is true that the war pulled them apart to some extent, absorbing his energies even as Mary had dealings with men in her White House coterie. But the couple had long been accustomed to spaces in their togetherness ever since the Springfield years, when Lincoln was on the law circuit for months at a time.

Although the war changed their marriage, it did not alienate them from each other. In some ways, it brought them closer together. It forced Mary to choose between her Confederate relatives and her husband's cause. It stimulated the couple's shared hospitality to White House visitors. It also brought deaths that bonded them in tragedy—the ongoing casualties of the war and the devastating loss of their eleven-year-old son Willie, who died of typhoid in 1862. Willie's death resulted in her communicating with his spirit through mediums at séances that the president sometimes attended. He got surprising answers from spiritualists—not about the afterlife but about politics and the world around him.

LADY PRESIDENT

We understand the variety of roles Mary Lincoln played when we compare her to previous first ladies, who can be roughly separated into four groups: invalids, hostesses, apolitical wives, and political helpmates or advisers.

Among the invalids, the most reclusive ones were Letitia Tyler, largely restricted, after a paralytic stroke, to an upstairs room in the White House, and Jane Pierce, incapacitated by depression and catatonia after the death in a train accident of her only surviving son. (Hawthorne, a friend of the Pierces', called her "that death's head" in the White House.)[1] Depressive disorder also hobbled Louisa Catherine Adams, the wife of John Quincy Adams. Elizabeth Monroe was well enough to give receptions, but her snobbishness turned off visitors, and various illnesses—apparently rheumatoid arthritis, epilepsy, and gastrointestinal disease—curtailed her activities. Even the formidable Abigail Adams, that pioneering promoter of women's equality, was beset with maladies that kept her at home in Quincy, Massachusetts, away from John Adams's presidential residences in Philadelphia and then in Washington for all but eighteen months of his four-year term. Also, Abigail chafed against the public exposure of the role, which she compared to being "fastend up Hand and foot and Tongue to be shot as our Quincy Lads do at the poor Geese and Turkies."[2]

Martha Washington also felt trapped by publicity. She hosted presidential receptions but lamented, "I think I am a state prisoner more than anything else," explaining that although she occupied "a place with which a great many younger and gayer women would be prodigiously pleased," she would "much rather be at home."[3] Margaret (Peggy) Taylor, in effect, did stay home, even in the White House. She had not wanted Zachary to be the Whig nominee for the presidency, and when the Whigs chose him anyway, he joked that his wife prayed for his defeat in the election. During his abbreviated term, Peggy Taylor managed the enslaved workers in the White House, took care of the garden, attended church every day, and cared for her family. She refused to act as the hostess for receptions. She left that to her young daughter, Elizabeth Taylor Dandridge, popularly known as "Miss Betty."

This turning over social duties to a relative other than one's wife occurred among other presidents, including Andrew Jackson, who lost his wife shortly after the 1828 campaign and took on his capable niece Emily Donelson as a surrogate first lady; Martin Van Buren, whose wife had died in 1819 and whose young daughter-in-law Angelica Van Buren served as the White House hostess; John Tyler, whose daughter-in-law, an actress, stood in for the sickly Letitia until John married the sparkling Julia Gardiner; and the bachelor James Buchanan, whose niece, the blond, blue-eyed Harriet Lane, became a much photographed celebrity who enlivened the scene with parties and distinguished guests.

The gold standard among early first ladies was Dolley Madison. A warm hostess who made guests feel relaxed and at home, she also redecorated the Executive Mansion, did charity work for orphaned girls, and was a fashion doyenne who wore colorful dresses, a turban, and scarves. Dolley often guided political conversations. Nor was she alone among first ladies to do so: Emily Donelson, for instance, was not shy about standing up to Andrew Jackson, and even the aloof Peggy Taylor kept apprised of her husband's political doings.

How does Mary Lincoln compare with the earlier first ladies? She had things in common with many of them. Although she was never an invalid for long periods, she did remove herself from the public arena twice: in the months immediately following the death of Willie on February 20, 1862; and for about three weeks after she injured her head in a carriage accident on July 2, 1863. As a White House hostess, she shined. At the many events she hosted, she dressed elegantly and put to use her talkativeness and charm. Her cultured background gave her a worldly sparkle.

MARY TODD LINCOLN

The one group of former first ladies she bore little resemblance to were the apolitical ones. She often gave political advice to her husband, and she met regularly with Washington politicians. William Herndon remarked that she was like a toothache, keeping her husband "awake to politics day and night."[4]

To mention politics is to raise the issue of slavery. James Madison, Andrew Jackson, and Zachary Taylor, after all, were slaveholders, and their wives accepted slavery, as did those of other slaveholders, such as Washington, Jefferson, Monroe, Tyler, and Polk. (Sarah Childress Polk is an instance of a presidential wife who quietly but powerfully supported her husband's position as a slaveholder.)[5] Because twelve American presidents owned enslaved workers, eight of them while in office, it was rare that an early first lady did not condone the South's peculiar institution. Jane Pierce, who was from an abolitionist background, was an exception, but her timid, dour nature and her husband's resistance to abolition minimized her influence—in contrast to Mary Lincoln, who wrote, "I never failed to urge my husband to be an *extreme* Republican."[6] That is, she always pushed him toward a strongly antislavery position.

It is notable that one of Mary's closest friends in Washington was Elizabeth Keckly, her African American dressmaker. Formerly enslaved by a Virginian who manumitted her, Keckly, who was forty-three in 1861, had a light-complexioned son who enlisted as a white man in the Union army and died in battle in August of that year. A skilled tailor, Lizzy Keckly worked faithfully for Mary, making elaborate dresses and helping tend to the Lincolns' two boys. The kindly, intelligent Keckly was a ubiquitous presence, and Mary confided in her, especially in times of crisis. Mary also contributed to Keckly's Contraband Relief Association, which found housing, medical care, and clothing for freed people in Washington.

Among political figures in the capital, Mary's favorite was Charles Sumner, the fervently antislavery Republican senator from Massachusetts. A tall, handsome bachelor in his fifties, Sumner could be stiff, but

ELIZABETH KECKLY

the loquacious Mary drew him off his pedestal. She said she was pleased that this "cold & haughty looking man to the world . . . visited no other lady," and "we would have such frequent and delightful conversations & often late in the evening—my darling husband would join us."[7] Among the topics discussed were slavery and writings by Sumner's antislavery friends, including Whittier, Emerson, and Longfellow. Not only was Sumner a Radical Republican, but he was a famous antislavery martyr whom a Southern politician had beaten nearly to death in the Senate in 1856.

While friendly to Sumner, Mary did not feel the same about all the

CHARLES SUMNER

antislavery politicians she knew. She lashed out against competitors for her husband's position. She harshly criticized two ambitious cabinet members, Salmon Chase and William Henry Seward. Seeing Chase as a selfish politician, not a true patriot, she warned Lincoln "not to trust him too far."[8] And she called Seward "worse than Chase." When she heard Lincoln tell someone that he was appointing Seward as his secretary of state, Mary exclaimed, "Never! Never! Seward in the Cabinet!" She insisted that Seward would get the credit if things went right, while her husband would be blamed if they did not.[9] Lincoln told her, "Mother, you are mistaken; your prejudices are so violent that you do not stop to reason. Seward is an able man, and the country as well as myself can trust him."[10]

The dialogue was typical: Mary made a passionate outburst that prompted his rational reaction. As was often the case, Mary's tirade contained some truth. After all, Seward announced himself early on as the "Premier" of the government, and Chase schemed to run against Lincoln in 1864. She was also not far off when, in the midst of the cabinet upheaval of early 1863, she told Francis Blair Sr. "that there was not a member of the Cabinet who did not stab her husband & the Country daily" except his son Montgomery.[11] Lincoln, when warned about such "intermeddling" by his wife, explained that she was just that way, adding, "Tell the gentleman not to be alarmed, for I myself manage all important matters."[12]

Disputes also arose over generals. Lincoln probably came to agree with Mary that George McClellan was "a humbug" who "talks so much and does so little."[13] But he differed from her about Ulysses S. Grant. During the Overland campaign, Mary complained, "Grant is a butcher and is not fit to be at the head of an army." She insisted that if the war continued for four more years "and he should remain in power, he would depopulate the North." She added brashly, "I could fight an army as well myself"—prompting Lincoln's reply, "Well, Mother, supposing that we give you command of the army. No doubt you would do much better than any general that has been tried."

He said this with a smile, but he had made a similar remark when venting his own frustration after Meade let Lee's army escape after Gettysburg: "If I had gone up there, I could have whipped them myself."[14] He knew that Mary had strong enough feelings against the Confederacy to share his passing fantasies of military action. Some women, after all, did fight in the Civil War. About four hundred to seven hundred women disguised themselves as men and went to the war front.[15] The best-documented case of a female soldier, the Union volunteer Sarah Edmonds, gives us a clue about women who assumed military roles. Edmonds said she was inspired when as a girl she had read Maturin Murray Ballou's popular novel *Fanny Campbell, the Female Pirate Captain* (1845), about a woman sea captain who fights the British during the American Revolution.[16] Ballou emphasizes the traditionally manly capabilities of his heroine: "Fanny could row a boat, shoot a panther, ride the wildest horse in the province, or do almost any brave and useful act."[17] Fanny Campbell typified the bold, adventurous woman character of popular literature who took on male roles.[18] This character was featured in much of the writing of the period, from the novels of James Fenimore Cooper and Catharine Sedgwick to pulp adventure fiction to Whitman's *Leaves of Grass*, where the speaker extols women who "know how to swim, row, ride, wrestle, shoot, run, strike, retreat, advance, resist, defend themselves."[19] Sarah Edmonds, patterning herself after Fanny Campbell, volunteered for the Union army and in the course of the war donned eleven disguises, including that of a black contraband, in order to go to the battlefront.

Mary Lincoln, of course, did not seriously entertain volunteering for the army, but she probably knew of adventurous heroines from her wide-ranging reading. Also, she got a closer look at military life than had most previous first ladies. She got to know the Zouaves who stayed in the grand rooms of the White House early in the war. She met wounded veterans who lived at the Soldiers' Home, an enclave on the outskirts of Washington that became the Lincolns' summer retreat. She made visits to the war hospitals in Washington, handing out food, flowers, and reading material to wounded soldiers, and writing letters for them. She reviewed troops with her husband, often along with her excited boys, and she sometimes went to the front with him.

The male role Mary Lincoln was most commonly said to have assumed was that of Lady President. While she claimed that politicians like Chase and Seward were trying to take the place of her husband, journalists made the same point about her. As early as September 1861, five months into the war, the *Springfield Republican* reported that

"Mrs. Lincoln's political influences are the theme of all who returned from Washington"; she was "ambitious of having a finger in every government pie; being much in conversation with cabinet members, and holding correspondence with them on political matters; making the political fortunes of men; suggesting to the president some of his ideas and projects."[20]

All of this was true. Mary did have regular dialogues with politicians, and she often gave her husband advice. What was most surprising was that this political involvement by a woman did not raise more eyebrows than it did. After all, this was a time when women were expected to keep out of political discussions. Women's rights lecturers were roundly denounced, and even the popular Harriet Beecher Stowe shied from public speaking; when huge crowds greeted her on an 1852 tour after the publication of *Uncle Tom's Cabin*, she had her husband or brother speak for her.

What saved Mary Lincoln from wholesale public rejection were her seemingly ambiguous political views and her domestic and hostessing activities, which were at the time typed as "womanly." She was far removed from Lucy Stone, Susan B. Anthony, or other controversial women who preached radical reform. Mary's background as the daughter in a slaveholding family actually helped her. A reporter speculated that she was probably "neutral" politically because she was from the border state of Kentucky and had Confederate relatives.[21]

Such statements provided a cover for Lincoln, who wanted to avoid appearing as a dangerous abolitionist. Mary's Southern background, like his, helped shield him from being typed as an extremist. The Confederate sympathizers in Mary's family were often mentioned in the press, as in a widely reprinted article, "Mrs. Lincoln's Secession Relatives" (sometimes titled "Old Abe's Kentucky Relatives").[22] Through this article and similar ones, her Southern connections became familiar to the public. Of her seven half brothers and half sisters who were living at the time of the Civil War, all but one supported the Confederacy, as did their mother (Mary's stepmother). One of her Confederate half brothers, Sam, died at Shiloh in April 1862; another, Aleck, died that August by friendly fire near Baton Rouge; a third, David, was seriously wounded at Vicksburg. Her full brother George, another staunch Confederate, served as a surgeon in the Army of Northern Virginia and was with Lee at Gettysburg and other battles. Her brother-in-law, Benjamin Hardin Helm, having rejected Lincoln's offer to serve as paymaster for the Union army, fought for the South and was killed at Chickamauga in 1863.

Although these deaths were publicly known, Mary's reaction to them was not until it was revealed two years after the war. She did not make much of the deaths. In fact, she shocked a friend who visited her in the Executive Mansion by saying that she hoped her Confederate relatives would die or be captured, because "they would kill my husband if they could, and destroy our government—the dearest of all things to us."[23] As for Aleck, despite her past affection for him, she said, "He made his choice long ago. He decided against my husband, and through him against me. He has been fighting against us; and since he chose to be our deadly enemy, I see no special reason why I should bitterly mourn his death."[24] When the press reported that her half brother David Todd had tortured Union captives while in command of Richmond's Libby Prison, she remarked that "by no word or act of hers should he escape punishment for his treason against her husband and government."[25]

Her common references in these statements were her husband and his cause. Her love for Lincoln merged with her patriotic fervor, providing her—and him—with a sure anchor in a time of national crisis.

The death of Benjamin Hardin Helm hit the Lincolns especially hard. Ben had refused the president's offer of the paymastership reluctantly, feeling that his true loyalty was with the South. Lincoln was deeply disturbed by his choice, and when he received the news of Helms's death in battle, he said, "I feel as David of old did when he heard of the death of Absalom. 'Would God I had died for thee, O Absalom, my son, my son!'"²⁶ Lincoln invited Emilie Todd Helm, Ben's widow, to Washington, and she stayed in the White House for three weeks. "Little Sister" Emilie was dear to Mary; she and Abe tearfully embraced the widow and offered her and her three children a permanent home. She returned to Lexington, though, and by the next year she was blaming the Lincolns for the deaths of her husband and her half brother Levi. She told a Union general and Northern senator that if she had twenty sons "they would all be fighting yours."²⁷ In 1864, she wrote the Lincolns, begging for money and declaring, "I also would remind you that your Minnie bullets have made us what we are."²⁸ This statement ended the relationship. Mary never contacted her again.

The painful situation of a family torn by divided loyalties during the Civil War was not uncommon. Four of Henry Clay's grandsons fought for the Confederacy, and three others for the Union. Francis Lieber had one son who died while fighting for the South; two other sons served the North. One of Senator John J. Crittenden's sons was a Union general, another a Confederate one. D. W. Griffith would exploit the divided-family motif in his film *The Birth of a Nation* (1915).

However, loyalties were definitely *not* divided in the White House. The deaths in Mary's family, though sad, were vivid reminders that millions of Southerners were willing to die in order to defend slavery and destroy the Union—anathema to both of the Lincolns. In the end, it was an advantage to Lincoln to be married to a woman with Confederate relatives. If retaining Kentucky, a slaveholding border state, was, in his view, crucial to the North's success in the war, being married to a woman who chose the Northern cause over her Confederate relatives showed that antislavery commitment and loyalty to the Union could trump family ties.

MARY'S MANY ROLES

Mary's loyalty to her husband and his cause fed into her jealousy of potential rivals for his affection. Elizabeth Keckly considered her "extremely jealous," explaining that "if a lady decided to court her displeasure, she could select no surer way to do it than to pay marked attention to the President. These little jealous freaks were often a source of perplexity to Mr. Lincoln."[29] One evening when he asked her before a party whom he should talk with that night and mentioned a "Mrs. D.," she lambasted her as a "deceitful woman" who merely flattered him. When he inquired if there was anyone else he should talk with, she said that he should "not talk to anybody in particular," adding, "you know well enough, Mr. Lincoln, that I do not approve of your flirtations with silly women, just as if you were a beardless boy, fresh from school."

She had especially hard feelings toward the lovely young star of Washington society, Kate Chase. Tall, buxom yet svelte, with hazel eyes and lush auburn hair, Kate Chase was as sociable as Mrs. Lincoln and was politically involved, too: she was ambitious for her father, Salmon Chase, and she advantageously married the wealthy William Sprague, the governor of Rhode Island. At first she tried to use Mary to gain sway over President Lincoln, but when that failed, she backed off. Mary, for her part, grew suspicious and jealous of her. In the fall of 1863 she refused to attend the wedding of Kate Chase and William Sprague, and Lincoln attended it alone. In January 1864, Mary insisted that neither Kate nor her husband or father should be invited to a dinner for cabinet members. Lincoln erupted in anger. John Nicolay reported, "There soon arose such a rampage as the House hasn't seen for a year."[30]

A more public exhibition of Mary's possessiveness occurred in March 1865, when the Lincolns were visiting General Grant's headquarters at City Point, Virginia. One day Lincoln and others went ahead to visit the front. When she later arrived, Adam Badeau, one of

KATE CHASE

Grant's staff, mentioned in passing that Lincoln had permitted the young wife of one of the generals to remain there, unlike the other army wives. Furious, Mary exclaimed to Badeau, "What do you mean by that, sir? Do you mean to say that she saw the President alone? Do you know that I never allow the President to see any woman alone?"[31] The next day she showed up at a troop review to find that her husband had arrived on horseback alongside the wife of General Edward Ord. In front of others, Mary gave Mrs. Ord a tongue-lashing that drove the woman to tears. Then Mary turned on her husband. As she scolded him for his conduct, Badeau recalled, "he called her 'mother' with his old-time plainness; he pleaded with eyes and tones. . . . He bore it as Christ might have done; with an expression of pain and sadness that cut one to the heart, but with supreme calmness and dignity."

But if the war years intensified Mary's outbursts, they also opened up new avenues to creativity and power, as they also did for Emily Dickinson, the reclusive poet who peaked artistically during those years. For both women, the disruptions of war seemed to unleash their creative experimentation with many roles—Dickinson through her numerous imaginary poetic speakers, Mary through her real-life activities in redecorating the White House, designing fashionable clothes for public functions, shopping zealously, sharing wit and gossip with men in her Blue Room salons, and manipulating money behind the scenes.

Mary's purchases for the White House, while extravagant, were understandable. When the Lincolns moved into the mansion, many of its thirty-one rooms were in disrepair, with peeling wallpaper and damaged furniture. In an era when the general public was admitted freely into the White House, carpets and walls were dirty and spotted with yellowish-brown stains from tobacco juice. Rats infested the servants' quarters in the basement, which stank of mildew. One visitor compared the White House to a decaying Southern manor, another to "an old and unsuccessful hotel."[32]

Mary took it upon herself to restore the White House. She had the outside and inside repainted. On a trip to Philadelphia she ordered from William H. Carryl & Brothers many elegant items. By the end of 1861, she had transformed the Executive Mansion.[33] Colored satin curtains with gold fringes and tassels adorned the Blue Room, Green Room, and Red Room. The spacious East Room featured multicolored wallpaper patterned after Louis Napoleon's reception hall in the Tuileries as well as a five-thousand-square-foot carpet decorated with medallions. Furniture was revarnished, and satin coverings were installed on the sofas and chairs. A guest room named after the Prince of Wales, who had stayed there during an 1860 visit, was decked out with light purple wallpaper, a Wilton carpet, and a bed, eight feet long and nine feet wide, that had a carved rosewood headboard that was nearly three yards high.

Mary wanted to create an atmosphere of grandeur without losing sight of democratic nationality. To that end, she had the US seal—a shield of the Stars and Stripes on which were arrows and a stern-looking eagle—embroidered on curtains and furnishings. She also purchased a 190-piece purple porcelain set decorated with the national seal and a border of intertwined gilt lines that stood for the North and the South, symbolizing the restored Union for which the North fought. And to promote her own devotion to the cause while defying the Confederate Todds, Mary had *ML* (without the *T* in the middle) inscribed on a Limoges china set that she ordered for private use.

The upstairs bedrooms—those of the president, Mary, Willie, Tad, and the usually absent Robert—were tastefully redecorated, as was the upstairs library and the small rooms used by Lincoln's secretaries, Hay and Nicolay. The one upstairs room left unfinished was Lincoln's office, on the opposite end of the hall from the bedrooms. Although the office was repapered, its rickety furniture remained: Lincoln's old desk under a window overlooking the Potomac; a large wooden table for cabinet meetings in the center of the room; maps arranged on racks; a picture of Andrew Jackson above a fireplace—everything made the room look, in William Stoddard's words, like a "historic cavern" with "less space for the transaction of the business of his office than a well-to-do New York lawyer."[34] A journalist reported jauntily, "Mr. Lincoln don't complain, because it resembles so much the dingy old room he occupied and familiarized himself with in the State House at Springfield, from the time he was elected until he left for Washington."[35]

Lincoln had always been accustomed to humble environments. He cared as little about elegant home decorations as he did about what he ate for dinner. He considered Mary's beautification of the White House wasteful at a time when the economy was unstable and the troops were undersupplied.

His anger flared when she approached him indirectly through Benjamin B. French, the commissioner of public buildings. For the upkeep of the White House, Congress had appropriated $6,000 a year, targeted mainly for repairs of plumbing, heating, and so on. In her very first year at the White House, Mary exhausted the entire amount Congress had reserved for Lincoln's four-year term. She wanted yet more funds for purchases, but she was afraid to approach her husband about them. She persuaded French to make her case to him. The president bristled at French's request, explaining, "It can never have my approval—I'll pay it out of my pocket first—it would stink in the nostrils of the American people to have it said that the president of the United States had approved a bill overrunning an appropriation of $20,000 for *flub dubs*, for this damned old house, when soldiers cannot have blankets!!" The White House, he added, was "furnished well enough, better than any one we ever lived in."[36]

He knew from long experience the political importance of identifying with common people, a lesson that he had learned in Harrison's Log Cabin campaign and that had helped him in his own run as the Illinois Rail-splitter in 1860. Filling the White House with costly decorations had nothing to do with average Americans, especially with soldiers on the battlefield or seamen in the navy.

Predictably, opposition newspapers had a field day with the White House improvements, which made Lincoln seem like a king showing off his power and wealth. "It did not take Mr. Lincoln long after his inauguration as President to become a despot," the *Charleston Mercury* fulminated in a piece titled "The Despotism at Washington—The Palace of Abraham." At a time when "thousands upon thousands of his people" were dying, Lincoln was "gradually bringing around him the usual insignia and trappings of royalty," including "exact imitations from the palace of the French Emperor."[37]

There was also the issue of Mary's expenditures on clothes. Altogether, she went on eleven buying expeditions to the North during the

MARY TODD LINCOLN

war years, shopping in Philadelphia, New York, and Boston and sometimes while vacationing in New Jersey or New England. When she wasn't buying household items, she purchased apparel or cloth from which Lizzy Keckly made her dresses.

Mary's attitude toward clothing was the opposite of Henry David Thoreau's. Advocating spartan simplicity, Thoreau in *Walden* (1854) launched stinging attacks on fashion. He remarked of his contemporaries: "We don garment after garment, as if we grew like exogenous plants by addition from without."[38] "We worship not the Graces, . . . but Fashion. . . . The head monkey at Paris puts on a traveller's cap, and all the monkeys in America do the same."

Mary felt that she needed fancy dresses, scarves, gloves, shoes, and other apparel for state functions. She added ribbons, flounces, bows, and tucks to the dresses, and a decorative hat or floral wreath often adorned her head. All told, she attended 105 events in Washington from March 1861 to April 1865 that called for special apparel.[39] She insisted on dressing for the occasion, often with boldly colored, patterned dresses that trailed behind her and had a deep décolletage. She won praise from many journalists, including one who wrote, "Her dress was, of course, decolleté and with short sleeves, displaying the exquisitely moulded shoulders and arms of our fair 'Republican Queen,' the whiteness of which were absolutely dazzling."[40] But some were shocked by her exposed skin. A senator who attended government parties commented that she liked "to exhibit her milking apparatus to public gaze."[41] Even Lincoln once remarked, "Whew, our cat has a long tail tonight. . . . Mother, it is my opinion, if some of that tail were nearer the head, it would be in better style."[42]

Some severely criticized Mary's showy clothing. The abolitionist author Lydia Maria Child, who thought that the short, thick-waisted Mary looked "more like a dowdy washerwoman" than "the 'representative of fashion,'" complained that the first lady cared only for "flattery, and dress, and parties."[43] When she learned of Mary's shopping trips, she declared, "So *this* is what the people are taxed for! To deck out this vulgar doll with foreign frippery."

To be sure, Mary's purchases could seem frivolous, and they left her with a debt of between $6,000 and $20,000 by the end of the war. It's hard to explain rationally her buying eighty-four kid gloves in a single month or $3,200 worth of jewelry toward the end of the war.[44]

It's true that many women saw fashion and shopping as real avenues to power and self-expression. As early as 1790, Judith Sargent Murray had commented that women had the same mental capacities as men but were frustrated on all sides and therefore manifested creativity in selecting fashionable clothing. Murray wrote: "Observe the variety of fashions . . . which distinguish and adorn the female world: . . . Now what a playfulness, what an exuberance of fancy, what strength of inventive imagination, doth this continual variation discover?"[45]

By the mid-nineteenth century, America saw a proliferation of fashion periodicals, most notably *Godey's Lady's Book*, one of Mary's favorite magazines. The latest fashions were put on display in the nation's first department stores, including New York's Lord & Taylor (which opened in 1826), Jordan Marsh (1841), A. T. Stewart's (1848), Macy's (1858), and B. Altman (1865). For women, shopping at such stores was a means of appearing in public and exercising choice. *Godey's* announced that shopping "might almost be called one of the fine-arts. As our fair ladies are not altogether destitute of talent, and have no other means of exhibiting it, it is natural that they should seek the only avenue open for a useful and agreeable employment of the faculties which their Creator has bestowed." The streets of America's cities, the writer continued, were full of women "happy in their favorite pursuit. They purchase, and purchase, and purchase everything recommended by the ineffable young men making their *ko-tows* . . . behind the counter, until their purses are emptied, and the patience of their husbands exhausted; but this does not dampen their ardor in the least."[46] The suffragist and author Laura Curtis Bullard noted that every spring "the largest and most fashionable shops" sent invitations to women known to have made recent purchases, and "nearly every lady accepts the invitation."[47] Women flocked to the stores and engaged in "the fascinating occupation of shopping and buying, of selecting and buying beautiful goods." Bullard explained, "Every womanly woman has a taste for dress." Attractive garments and jewelry answered the "love for the beautiful" in women, who were "perfectly right in buying the pretty costumes and stuff which they crave for their personal adornment." Ready-made dresses were rarely available; the stores exhibited styles and sold material for dresses that were made at home or by a skilled seamstress. The latter, Bullard said, was hard to find at any cost. Lizzy Keckly solved that problem for Mary.

Mary especially enjoyed going to A. T. Stewart's, which held its first "fashion shows" in its Ladies' Parlor in 1848 and then opened its immense six-story Iron Palace on New York's Broadway. America's largest store, Stewart's exhibited the full range of European fashions, and for a woman like Mary who appeared constantly in public, the trip north from Washington was always worthwhile, for it resulted in her acquiring dresses and other clothing in the latest styles and patterns. In April 1862, not long after the loss of the Lincolns' beloved son Willie, Mary filled her letters with precise requests for this-or-that kind of pattered cloth, hat, or fine lace, as though choosing styles provided therapy in a time of shattering grief.

Lincoln, while he disapproved of Mary's excessive purchases for the White House, was more tolerant of her buying clothes. For the tastes of the day, her elaborate attire made her look elegant—and, in his eyes, beautiful. At one reception, he watched her as she greeted guests and said, "My wife is as handsome as when she was a girl and I, a poor nobody then, fell in love with her; and what is more, I have never fallen out."[48]

It was to his advantage for his well-clothed wife to get positive reviews. There's evidence that he helped this happen. More than 130 articles between 1860 and 1865 appeared in seven newspapers, including two Washington ones, that merit special attention because, as Michael Burlingame and Douglas Warren Hill show, they were written by Lincoln's secretary John Hay, who used a number of pseudonyms, including "An Idler."[49]

Hay penned glowing reports of Mary Lincoln and the Executive Mansion. He paid homage to Mary's home decorating skills, describing socialites flocking to a presidential reception because "all had heard how magnificently the White House had been refurnished."[50] Hay also nodded to Mary's political power, telling readers that "we shall run no risk of saying that the mistress of the White House possesses more influence over its master than any other lady, or any masculine either, for that matter, excepting one of his Cabinet members."[51]

Hay often praised Mary's charm and graciousness. Her appearance at one event inspired this rave: "The ladies all admired Mrs. Lincoln's dress, which one of them described as a rich, delicately-shaded purple silk, trimmed with black velvet and fringe, with a rare lace neck tie, and a pearl brooch at the throat . . . I can say that Mrs. Lincoln never appeared to greater advantage, or received her visitors and friends with more affability."[52] Another event prompted Hay to comment, "Her headdress was of white and black flowers, with jet and pearl ornaments. Her gloves were white, stitched with black. The effect of all was in fine taste, very rich and beautiful." Hay portrayed Mary as the ideal hostess and the renovated White House as the perfect setting, as here: "Mrs. Lincoln, as usual, was surrounded by a crowd of admiring ladies. . . . The reception was a most perfect success—the charming kindness of the hostess, the beautiful bouquets adorning the rooms, and the inspiring music discoursed by the marine band in attendance, beguil[ed] and enchant[ed] the refined tastes of the guests until the close of the levee."

What made Hay's public praise of Mary remarkable is that he privately loathed her. Writing to his fellow secretary John Nicolay, he called her "the 'enemy,'" the "Hellcat," the daughter of "the devil." At one point he complained, "The Hellcat is getting more Hellcattical, day by day."[53] He expressed animosity as early as November 1861, when Mary, realizing that she was overrunning Congress's appropriation for purchases, tried to get him to siphon money to her from other funding sources—a strategy she would try with others.

The cloying compliments Hay showered on Mary in his journalism, therefore, were all about public relations. And the president may have guided his secretary. Lincoln had long recognized the value of positive press. Doubtless it was through him that Hay got connected with the

National Republican and the *Daily Morning Chronicle*, the Washington newspapers in which his most lavish celebrations of Mary appeared.[54] Both papers were government funded. The *Chronicle*, considered the organ of the White House, was edited by Lincoln's friend John W. Forney, who appreciated the president's help in getting him elected as the secretary of the US Senate. The *Chronicle* promoted the policies of Lincoln, who had ten thousand copies of the newspaper distributed to the Army of the Potomac daily.

Lincoln wanted Mary to appear in the best possible light. John Hay, burying his real feelings about her, helped make that happen.

So did the popular author and journalist Nathaniel P. Willis, whom Hay praised as "the pen-portrayer of our best society."[55] Tall and dandyish—Poe dismissed him as "a graceful trifler"—Willis purveyed gossip and novelty about public figures, including the Lincolns, whom he sometimes visited.[56] Dubbed "the inevitable Nat" and "a born lion," Willis wrote effusive sketches in his *Home Journal* about the Lady President and her husband.[57] In one, he emphasized the "thorough good nature and covert love of fun, which are the leading qualities of our lady President"; he cited her vacations and shopping tours in the North and her creativity in fashions.[58] In another, he reported that "the president-ess has returned to the White House," which will "now become a very joyous place," because "the joyous '*Reine d'Illinois*' will again dress splendidly and receive splendidly and do her best to make everybody happy."[59]

La Reine and the Republican Queen of the White Palace became Mary's nicknames among those who attended the salons that she held in the Executive Mansion. Willis was a regular, as were a number of men skilled in glib repartee and surrounded by an aura of the illicit. What she called "my beau monde friends of the Blue Room" included Henry "Chev" Wikoff, a multilingual womanizer and dilettante who had been jailed for kidnapping his fiancée in Italy and who used his connection with Mary to steal Lincoln's 1861 message to Congress for publication in the *New York Herald* (for which he also went to prison); his friend Daniel "Cap" Sickles, notorious for having killed his wife's paramour (he escaped punishment by pleading temporary insanity); and Oliver "Pet" Halsted, a swaggering lawyer businessman who tried to sell arms to the Union and after the war was murdered by a love rival.[60]

In this shady group, Mary must have felt somewhat like what I've called elsewhere the feminist criminal of sensation novels: the woman who, feeling thwarted in a patriarchal society, takes revenge by becoming either actively criminal herself or the leader of other wrongdoers.[61]

Mary's own petty crimes related to buying. She colluded with the White House gardener, John Watt, who padded expense accounts to help pay for her redecorating bills, and then with a doorkeeper and watchman, Thomas Stackpole, through whom she evidently distributed government travel or trading permits in exchange for cash.[62] Lincoln reportedly heard of her shenanigans and became "very indignant, and refunded what had been thus filched from the government out of his private purse."

PARENTING AND LOSS

Whatever conflicts arose between the Lincolns melted in their shared devotion to their boys and the overwhelming grief they suffered when the eleven-year-old Willie died in 1862.

During the White House years, Abe and Mary maintained their relaxed attitude toward parenting. The boys had the run of the White House and its grounds. An early Lincoln biographer noted, "The boys had their own way with their father; and while their mother was sometimes disposed to chide them for undue mischief, even she gave them quite as much liberty as was good for them."[63] The boys court-martialed their Zouave doll, Jack, for desertion or sleeping at his post, found him guilty, executed him, and buried him in the rose garden. They did this so many times that John Watt saw his garden being ruined. He complained, and the boys went to their father, who wrote a pardon for the doll, upon which they promised never to punish Jack again—though within a week they hanged him on a tree branch after convicting him of being a spy. On the roof of the White House the boys built a crude structure that was alternately a fort and the deck of a man-of-war, armed with old condemned muskets and a small log that served as a cannon. With friends, they formed a colorfully clad military company called "Mrs. Lincoln's Zouaves," which the president and first lady reviewed with great ceremony. Missing the snow in Illinois, Willie and Tad gathered thousands of guest cards left by visitors, ripped them up, and created blizzards by tossing them around in the attic.

The boys also loved playing with their pets. The south lawn of the Executive Mansion was a menagerie of horses, ponies, donkeys, and a pair of pet goats, Nanny and Nanko. Willie and Tad created a ruckus when they converted kitchen chairs into sleighs and attached them to the goats, who dragged them around the White House and its lawns. Lincoln enjoyed the goats. In the tense spring of 1862, when his wife was away on a trip with Tad, Lincoln sent an affectionate telegram: "Tell Tad the goats and father are very well—especially the goats."[64] To Elizabeth Keckly, he said one day, "Come here and look at my two goats. I believe they are the kindest and best goats in the world."[65] Lincoln had reluctantly left his dog, Fido, behind in Illinois when he came to Washington, but in the White House he doted over the family's pet cats, Tabby and Dixie. When during a state dinner he fed Tabby with a gold fork left over from James Buchanan's term, his wife called his behavior "shameful." He replied that "if the gold fork was good enough for Buchanan I think it is good enough for Tabby."[66]

In March 1861, shortly after the Lincolns arrived in Washington, Willie and Tad had met children who lived nearby—Julia ("Julie) Taft and her brothers Horatio ("Bud") and Halsey ("Holly") Taft—who became regular playmates. Bud was twelve, a year older than Willie, and Holly was eight, Tad's age. The four boys became good friends. Not only did they spend many days playing, but on Sundays the Lincoln boys attended the Tafts' Presbyterian church instead of the New York Avenue Church, which Mary (and sometimes Abe) attended. The boys found the Tafts' church lively because Confederate parishioners frequently stood up and left in a noisy huff when prayers were said for the president.[67]

Sixteen-year-old Julie often talked with Mary or the president, and both told her they wished they had had a girl like her. Mary listened to Julie's teenage chatter and asked her to play pieces on the piano, especially "Colonel Ellsworth's Funeral March." Lincoln enjoyed taking Julie on his knee and telling her stories. He called her a "flibbertigibbet." When she asked what it meant, he expressed shock that she didn't know. After much teasing, he winked and defined the word as "a small, slim thing with curls and a white dress and a blue sash who flies instead of walking."[68]

Tad remained the most mischievous of the Lincoln boys—a contrast to the stuffy Robert and the self-controlled Willie. In a typical prank, Tad stole from his mother's drawer the blood-stained Confederate flag she had been given in remembrance of Elmer Ellsworth, who had been killed just after he had taken it down in his raid on Alexandria, Virginia. Tad waved the hated flag behind his father, who was reviewing troops from the portico of the White House, to the shock of all below. Lincoln scolded him for making light of the flag, but reprimands were few and far between from the tolerant father. Tad was playfully dismissive of learning. When he was twelve, his mother showed him a picture of an ape and asked him what "a-p-e" spelled. "Monkey," he answered. He stubbornly repeated the mistake despite Mary's corrections.[69] Born with a cleft lip and probably a cleft palate, he had a vocal defect that made him hard to understand.[70] Lincoln had real affection for him, and he put up with his antics. It was not unusual for Tad to break into a

Tad Lincoln

cabinet meeting and sit on his father's lap or climb onto his shoulders. Tad longed for a "real revolver."[71] His father gave him one but then feared he would find ammunition and fire it. He wrote Mary when she was out of town with the boy. "Think you better put Tad's pistol away. I had an ugly dream about him."[72]

Willie, by all reports, was extraordinary. He romped with Tad and the Taft boys but was also studious and thoughtful. Julie Taft recalled him as "the most lovable boy I ever knew, bright, sensible, sweet-tempered, and gentle-manned."[73] He designed maps and train schedules. Like Tad, he called his father Paw, in his western accent, and he retained the candor and freshness of his background in small-town

WILLIE LINCOLN

Illinois. He said he wanted to be a teacher or a clergyman. He was also a budding poet. His moving eulogy to his father's friend Edward Baker, killed at the Battle of Ball's Bluff, was published in a Washington newspaper in October 1861.

Two of the poem's verses reveal the young Willie's awareness of the meaning of the Civil War:

> There was no patriot like Baker,
> So noble and so true;
> He fell as a soldier on the field,
> His face to the sky of blue. . . .

No squeamish notions filled his breast,
The Union was his theme;
'No surrender and no compromise,'
His day-thought and night's dream.[74]

The poem must have deeply affected Lincoln, who had had a long kinship with Baker. In Illinois, the two had served together in the Black Hawk War, in the state legislature, and on the law circuit. They had engaged in the musical-chairs political arrangement whereby Lincoln succeeded Baker in the US Congress. They enjoyed competing at fives, a form of handball. The two became so close that Lincoln named his second son Edward Baker Lincoln. Baker subsequently moved to California, where he practiced law and promoted the Free Soil cause, and then to Oregon, where he was elected as a Republican US senator. While serving in the Senate in 1860–61, he spoke out eloquently against secession and on behalf of Lincoln and the Union. He was chosen to introduce Lincoln at the president's first inauguration.

Lincoln was devastated when he heard of Baker's death at Ball's Bluff. He got the news in the telegraph office and left "with bowed head, and tears rolling down his furrowed cheeks, his face pale and wan, his heart heaving with emotion." He "almost fell as he stepped into the street" and walked with his hands across his chest, stumbling into the White House without returning the salute of a sentinel at the door.[75] Lincoln said that Baker's death "smote him like a whirlwind from a desert."[76]

When Lincoln read Willie's affecting verses about Baker, he could not know that an even more terrible whirlwind was about to strike. A few months after writing the poem, Willie himself was gone.

It appears that the boy died of typhoid fever, perhaps caused by water pumped into the White House from the Potomac River, which was contaminated by fecal matter from soldiers' camps that lacked latrine trenches. Also near the White House was a fetid marsh where human waste and animal carcasses were deposited.

EDWARD D. BAKER

In January 1862, Willie, who had turned eleven the month before, became feverish and was confined to an upstairs room. The Lincolns had planned a ball for February 5, and they sent out hundreds of invitations. But they grew apprehensive over Willie's condition, and by the end of the month Mary wanted to cancel the event. However, Dr. Robert Stone reported that Willie's condition had improved. The party was on, with the president's caveat that there would be no dancing.

The evening was spectacular. Some five hundred guests came: politicians, military figures, diplomats, and social figures. Lincoln's cabinet members arrived, as did congressmen and generals, including George McClellan and John Frémont, along with Frémont's wife, Jessie. Salmon

The Grand Presidential Party at the White House, February 5, 1862
(*Frank Leslie's Illustrated News*, February 22, 1862)

Chase attended with his daughter Kate, whose blue satin dress competed for fashion-worshippers' attention with Mary's flowered Parisian headdress, pearl necklace, and low-cut white gown with black flounces and ribbons. Also attending was "the inevitable Nat" Willis, who, as a journalist commented, "was in full force, saying witty things and graceful things in equal proportion."[77] Heaped platters offered duck, turkey, beef, quail, foie gras, oysters, and cakes of different designs, including a Swiss cottage and Fort Pickens. Desserts of spun sugar represented a war helmet, a temple surmounted by the Goddess of Liberty, beehives, and the frigate *Union* supported by cherubs that were decorated by the Stars and Stripes. It was not a temperance evening. Champagne and wine flowed, and other liquor was available, including a rum-and-champagne punch in an enormous Japanese bowl. The Marine Band played songs, starting with "The President's March" and ending with "The Mary Lincoln Polka," composed for the occasion.

Upstairs in Willie's sickroom, the distant music came "in soft, subdued murmurs, like the wild, faint sobbing of far-off spirits," according to Lizzy Keckly, who watched anxiously over the boy.[78] Mary's mind was on her son. She left the party several times to go upstairs and check on him.

Over the next two weeks, the gala became a glittering memory. Willie grew delirious and weak, then fell into a coma. He died on February 20, 1862, at 5:00 p.m.

Standing over Willie's body, Lincoln heaved with tears. He said, "My poor boy, he was too good for this earth. God has called him home. I know that he is much better off in heaven, but then we loved him so. It is hard, hard to have him die!"[79] He walked down the hall, stopped at his secretary's office, and said, "Well, Nicolay, my boy is gone—he is actually gone!"[80] He burst into tears, entered his own office, and shut the door.

Mary went into convulsions of grief. She stayed in bed for days, until her sister Elizabeth Edwards arrived from Illinois and persuaded her to go to church. Lincoln, seeing that Mary was in no condition to tend to Tad, who had also fallen ill, had a hospital nurse, Rebecca Pomroy, stay at the White House until the boy recovered.

Lincoln had sobbing sessions alone in his bedroom. Unlike Mary, who was incapacitated by grief, he attended Willie's funeral and burial, which were arranged by the president's Illinois friend Orville Browning. The funeral followed the era's conventions of the Good Death. Willie was embalmed, and his body lay in the Green Room for viewing. Lying in a faux-rosewood metallic coffin, Willie wore his usual brown pants and jacket, with white socks and low shoes, and his white shirtsleeves turned over his jacket cuffs. Wreaths lay on his chest and at his feet. His hands were folded over a bouquet on his chest, and flowers surrounded his body.[81]

The funeral service was held in the crepe-draped East Room. Dignitaries, many of whom had been at the ball earlier in the month, somberly assembled in the room and heard the sermon of the Reverend Phineas Gurley of the New York Avenue Presbyterian Church. Pallbearers carried Willie's coffin to the hearse, which led a long, slow procession to Oak Hill Cemetery in Georgetown for interment. Oak Hill was one of the nineteenth century's rural cemeteries, like Mount Auburn in Massachusetts or Green-Wood in Brooklyn. Dr. Gurley conducted another service in the cemetery chapel, and Willie's coffin was placed in a crypt, available for later removal and reburial in Illinois.

For three months, Mary alternated between paroxysmal sobbing and passive depression. She wore black for a year. She could not bear to enter the upstairs guest room, where Willie had died, or the Green Room, where he'd been embalmed. She was so distraught that reportedly Lincoln at one point looked out a window to the distant St. Elizabeths, a mental hospital, and warned Mary that she might have to be sent there unless she brought herself under control.

To newspaper readers, however, she seemed to be observing the decorum of the Good Death, which called for grief restrained by faith and resignation. A month after Willie's death, the White House's publicist in chief John Hay, as the Idler, reported:

> All of our readers will be pleased to learn, we doubt not, . . .
> that Mrs. Lincoln is slowly recovering from the effects of her
> sad bereavement and her unceasing motherly care. Her sister,
> Mrs. Edwards, is now with her, and has had the melancholy
> satisfaction of gazing on the lifeless yet lifelike remains of
> little Willie, which are temporarily deposited in the pictur-
> esque Oak Hill Cemetery, at Georgetown.[82]

Mary had lost her beloved Willie. But she had not given up on seeing him again. American culture offered her a ready means of doing so.

THE LINCOLNS IN THE BARDO

Spiritualism—direct communication with the dead—had roots in biblical times, and more recently in the mysticism of the eighteenth-century philosopher Emanuel Swedenborg. Spiritualism gained real popularity in America in 1848, after two sisters in the village of Hydesville, New York, Margaret and Catherine Fox, heard rapping sounds in their home allegedly produced by a ghost they called Splitfoot. Maggie and Kate Fox soon became celebrities, sought after for their powers as spiritualist mediums, with a special capacity for receiving messages from the afterlife.

Within two years the spiritualist movement had gained traction, and by 1867 the movement claimed eleven million adherents in America.[83] Among the notables who took up with spiritualism were William Lloyd Garrison, Sojourner Truth, Fanny Fern, Thomas Wentworth Higginson, Parker Pillsbury, Benjamin Wade, and Joshua Giddings. Others who attended séances included James Fenimore Cooper, Horace Greeley, Harriet Beecher Stowe, and Walt Whitman. A number of people in Mary Lincoln's circle turned to spiritualism, including Lizzy Keckly, Chev Wikoff, and Gideon Welles's wife, Mary Jane, one of Mary's closest friends.

Books promoting the new craze appeared, including Judge John W. Edmonds's two-volume tome *Spiritualism* and Robert Dale Owen's *Footfalls of the Boundary of Another World*. Consoling novels about the afterlife included Elizabeth Stuart Phelps's bestselling trilogy *The Gates Ajar, Beyond the Gates*, and *The Gates Between* and George S. Woods's *The Gates Wide Open; or, Scenes in Another World*.

Apparent miracles became commonplace among spiritualists. Groups typically sat around a table at which a medium, often a young woman, served as a vehicle for communication with the dead, who sent messages through raps, musical sounds, ghostly hands, and the lifting of tables, chairs, pianos, and so on. Sometimes a person in the room would float upward while seated in a chair, ostensibly supported by invisible arms. Spiritualist mediums took on extraordinary powers. For instance, Judge Edmonds's daughter, thirteen-year-old Laura, reportedly played sophisticated Beethoven pieces while in a trance, even though she had never previously touched a piano.[84] Edmonds also told of mediums who knew only English but spoke Greek, Italian, Arabic, Chinese, German, and other languages fluently while under spiritual influences. Spirits directed the writing of books—they were literally ghostwriters. Starting in 1861, spirit photographs were taken, in which the ghosts of the departed appeared in the company of the living.

It was not unusual, then, for Mary Lincoln to consult spiritualists after the death of Willie. She held séances in the White House. She also went to a number of séances at the home of Cranston Laurie in Georgetown. Laurie had a daughter, Belle Miller, who was reputedly a gifted medium. Not only could she talk with the departed, but, while entranced, she also played wonderful piano pieces while the piano itself pitched and rocked in rhythm to the music. Lincoln, who sometimes accompanied Mary to séances, allegedly sat on the waltzing piano and conceded that its movement might result from "invisible power."[85]

At the Lauries' home, Mary met another young medium, Nettie Colburn, who gave communications from what she called a Congress of Spirits, which included Pinkie (an Aztec princess who had died five hundred years before), Bright Eyes (a diminutive squaw), Priscilla (John Alden's wife), and Dr. Bamford (a physician from Colburn's Connecticut childhood). Dr. Bamford, with his Yankee twang, became Lincoln's favorite spirit. Not only did Lincoln witness Colburn in spiritual trances, but he received from his good friend Joshua Speed, a believer in spiritualism, a recommendation of Nettie and another young woman as "mediums & believers in the spirits" who were "very choice spirits themselves."[86]

Spiritualists tended to be radically antislavery, and it was not unusual that Nettie Colburn approached Lincoln at a séance and told him that the Congress of Spirits said "the world is in universal bondage; it must physically set free." She reportedly lectured Lincoln for an hour on "the importance of emancipating the slave, saying that the war could not end until slavery was abolished: That all men should be free to rise to their destined status."[87] The spirits had told her that Lincoln should stand firm and not waver in issuing the Emancipation Proclamation, which would be "the *crowning event of his administration and his life.*"[88]

Lincoln with the spiritualist medium Nettie Colburn

Mary came under the spell of a spiritualist who proved to be especially controversial: Lord Colchester. Claiming to be the illegitimate son of an English duke, Colchester gave séances that featured musical sounds supposedly played by spirits. After hearing that Mary had been impressed by him, the journalist Noah Brooks attended one of his séances and exposed him by opening a curtain that revealed Colchester sitting with drums, a horn, and bells. Brooks got into a fistfight with Colchester and warned him to leave Washington and never return.[89]

Spiritualism provoked fierce criticism among those who saw it as un-Christian or dangerous. Newspapers like the *New York Times* and the *Washington Intelligencer* berated the movement. But even such critics gave credence to it. After all, it was the age of miraculous new technology, notably the telegraph. If communications could travel thousands of miles within seconds, why could not the "spiritual telegraph" connect the living and the dead through what was thought to be invisible electromagnetic fluid?

Eventually, spiritualism came into disrepute. In the 1880s the Fox sisters turned against the movement, which they now dismissed as "an absolute falsehood from beginning to end, . . . the flimsiest of superstitions, . . . one of the greatest curses that the world has ever known."[90] Splitfoot, they revealed, referred to sounds they had made by cracking their toe joints under their dresses. Later, in the 1920s, when Arthur Conan Doyle and others championed spiritualism, Harry Houdini campaigned against it, proving that an illusionist could easily produce many of its manifestations.

But in Mary Lincoln's lifetime, spiritualism was viable and growing. For believers, the spirits of the dead were always available for contact. A leading spiritualist wrote, "Our city streets are thronged with an unseen people who flit about us, jostling us in thick crowds, and in our silent chambers, our secret closets."[91] It was in the privacy of her bedroom that Mary had her most vivid spiritualistic experiences. When her half sister Emilie Todd visited the White House in 1863, Mary spoke to her of nightly visits from Willie. Her eyes wide and shining, Mary exclaimed:

> He lives, Emilie! He comes to me every night, and stands at the foot of my bed with the same sweet, adorable smile he has always had; he does not always come alone; little Eddie is sometimes with him and twice he has come with our brother Alec, he tells me he loves his Uncle Alec and is with him most of the time. You cannot dream of the comfort this gives me.[92]

Mary said to Charles Sumner, "a very slight veil separates us, from the 'loved & lost' and to me, there is comfort, in the thought, that though unseen by us, they [the spirits of loved ones] are very near."[93] After her husband was killed, she entered a long period of mourning that was relieved somewhat when she went to William Mumler, a spiritual photographer who produced a photo of her with the ghostly Lincoln behind her. This was an era when, Arthur Conan Doyle claimed, "thousands of spirit photographs" were taken—doctored, obviously, but comforting to those like Mary who believed that spirits could be tangibly sensed and even photographed.[94]

Mary's infatuation with spiritualism casts light on the long-debated issue of her mental health. A main reason that her staid son Robert had her committed to an asylum in 1875 was that she reported having the sensation that a tiny Native American woman was inside her head. Today, such a symptom might be attributed to psychosis, bipolar disorder, or severe trauma. But it should be noted that such delusions were common among spiritualists. Her seeing a squaw was no different from Nettie Colburn's seeing Pinkie, Bright Eyes, and Dr. Bamford—or from Harriet Beecher Stowe's hearing a distant guitar and casually asking her husband which of their dead sons was strumming the instrument. In 1875, Mary Lincoln found herself in the position of the famous Elizabeth Ware Packard, the Illinois spiritualist whose husband, alarmed by her visions, had committed her in 1860 to the Jacksonville Insane Asylum, where she remained for three years. After her release, Packard publicly impugned her husband for committing her merely because of a difference in religious beliefs. She told her harrowing tale in books with titles like *Marital Power Exemplified, or Three Years Imprisonment for Religious Belief by the Arbitrary Will of a Husband* (1864) and *The Prisoners' Hidden Life, Or Insane Asylums Unveiled* (1868).[95]

Actually, for most of the time in the seventeen years after her husband's death, Mary Lincoln had her wits about her. She fought successfully for the reburial of her husband in an Illinois rural cemetery and then for a widow's pension from Congress that she believed she deserved. She maintained a circle of friends and family. Her four months in the asylum were uneventful. She lived calmly there, and she then returned to normal life.[96] As for her hallucinations, they came in the period after the untimely death in 1871 of her eighteen-year-old son Tad, with whom she had grown very close. Within a decade, Mary had suffered the loss of the three people very dear to her—Willie, Abe, and Tad. She had also experienced the deaths of Todd family members in the war, and she responded with deep emotion to the national bloodletting, which she compared to butchery. There was good reason why novels like *The Gates Ajar* and *The Gates Wide Open* became bestsellers after the war and why millions turned to spiritualism. Making direct contact with the spirits of loved ones was the nation's way of alleviating the trauma of a war that took the lives of 750,000 Americans.

How did Abraham Lincoln feel about spiritualism?

He had closer connections to it than is generally realized. He told Mariah Vance, his black housekeeper in Springfield, that after the death of Eddie in 1851, he and Mary consulted "three good women who are in

touch with the spirit world, and can straighten us out."⁹⁷ In 1860, when
he went east before his presidential nomination, he reportedly had at
least two sittings with a New York medium named J. B. Conklin, who
saw him later in Cleveland on his trip from Springfield to Washington.
Conklin recognized Lincoln as a client who had consulted him during
his New York visit about a deceased person, "K." This encounter with
the medium was reported in a widely reprinted newspaper story, "The
President Elect a Spiritualist."⁹⁸ After Edward Baker's death at Ball's
Bluff, J. B. Conklin sent Lincoln a spirit letter allegedly written by Baker's spirit, who assured Lincoln that death was "a happy reality—a glorious change" and that he, "like millions of other disembodied spirits,"
was grateful that Lincoln was committed to sustaining "the Union."⁹⁹

In 1863, the linkages between President Lincoln and spiritualism
strengthened. Newspapers reported Lincoln as having attended a séance led by a Charles E. Shockle in which the president received advice
on war strategy from the spirits of Washington, Lafayette, Franklin,
Napoleon, and others. (Lincoln joked that these great souls seemed just
as confused about how to conduct the war as his cabinet was.) Soon
a paper flatly stated, "We have an administration controlled by Spiritualism." The report charged Lincoln with getting advice from noted
spiritualists such as John Edmonds and Robert Dale Owen. Since spiritualism was considered one of the devilish offshoots of Puritanism,
the writer affirmed that "no Puritan—no *Spiritualist,* has ever been
arrested—none ever will" under Lincoln. "Has it come to this!" the
writer exclaimed. "A great country governed by ghosts, spirits, hob-
goblins, table-turnings, rappings, &c. Be not deceived; this is the nim-
bus of the administration."¹⁰⁰

These charges were made far more stridently in a pamphlet of 1863
by an Ohioan, David Quinn, titled *Interior Causes of the War: The Nation Demonized, and Its President a Spirit-rapper.* Under the command
of spirits, Quinn wrote, the despotic Lincoln had launched a bloody war

to liberate "the negro," a "passive and dependent" creature whose "little dark eyes, flat nose, thick lips, bullet head, and animal expression . . . show, at a glance, his inferior nature." Quinn drew a straight line from the fanatical Puritans of early New England to devilish modern spiritualists, whose leader was President Lincoln. The "spiritualist element," Quinn wrote, infected the North, where "the puritanic blood most flowed":

> At one period, we find her burning witches, at another, hanging Quakers; and now, when she claims a higher development of civilization, we find her rallying all her forces to murder six millions of white people because she discovers them to be the owners of negro slaves. These things show a tendency to spiritual distempers or that fanaticism is natural to the Yankee mind.[101]

Although Lincoln was not a New Englander, Quinn argued, he typified the Puritan-Yankee spirit more than anyone. Quinn wrote: "Mr. Lincoln, we are well assured, is as confirmed a spiritualist as there is in the United States; has full faith in the communications." He had "in a secret hole in the White House, a rapping table" by which he received regular instructions from Caesar, Washington, Jefferson, Napoleon, Jackson, and other past leaders. Lincoln was "a spiritualist of the abolitionist school . . . and has been, from the beginning of his term, directing the war under the direction of spirit rappings" with the aid of such mediums as "Robert Dale Owen, of Indiana, Judge Edmonds, of New York," who "are said to be almost constantly around him, advising him from the spirit world, and urging him onward in his abolition, death-dealing policy."

Some of Quinn's claims were ludicrous. There's no evidence of a "rapping table" in a "secret hole" of the White House. Nor would the rationalist Lincoln have allowed spirits to control him. He constantly received otherworldly advice but ignored it. He got "almost daily" letters, as William Stoddard reported, from "The Angel Gabriel," who wrote him in blood (actually cheap red ink) with advice from George Washington, Thomas Jefferson, John Adams, among others.[102] During the war years, he attended four or five séances with Mary; his attitude toward spiritualism wavered between amused interest and genial skepticism.[103]

Quinn was on surer ground when he said that Robert Dale Owen and Robert Edmonds, two leading spiritualists, advised Lincoln. Of the two, Edmonds was the pushiest on spiritual matters. Declaring that "we should have a Spiritualist as a President," Edmonds wrote him in 1863 saying that he had "heard & read in various ways" that Lincoln was "so far interested in the subject, as to have entered upon its investigation."[104] Edmonds sent two of his own spiritualist books to the president, who replied tactfully, through a senator, "Please present my compliments to Judge Edmonds, & say to him the books will be gratefully accepted by me."[105]

Despite his spiritualist beliefs, Edmonds apparently made no pretense of giving the president instructions directly from the spirit world. Lincoln knew well that Edmonds was a serious-minded man who had a history as a lawyer, legal scholar, and New York politician. In 1861, Edmonds made the sensible proposition to Lincoln that he appoint the New York antislavery editor and author William Cullen Bryant as secretary of state. Two years later, the abolitionist Sydney H. Gay made a strong argument that the president appoint Edmonds as the administration's representative to investigate causes of the New York City draft riots. Lincoln considered the proposal seriously before deciding against sending a representative.

Robert Dale Owen was far closer to the heart of Lincoln's vision than Edmonds. Short, thin, and blond haired, Owen was the son of the famous Scotch reformer Robert Owen, whose experimental

ROBERT DALE OWEN

socialist community New Harmony in the 1820s was near to Lincoln's Indiana home during his adolescence. The elder Owen had been a holdover Enlightenment rationalist who turned to spiritualism in the years before his death in 1857. His son Robert Dale Owen entered Indiana state politics before serving in the US House of Representatives from 1843 to 1848. Following his father's example, he was converted to spiritualism. His advocacy of the movement was neither naive nor ahistorical. In his books on spiritualism, he detailed the historical background of the movement over time in many religions. The miracles of modern spiritualists were to him demonstrable, not delusionary.

When it came to dealing with the harsh realities of the Civil War, Owen put aside his spiritualist speculations and fixed his attention on political and social facts. He met with Lincoln, advised him, and wrote letters to him and members of his cabinet. The advisory letters that Owen wrote to Lincoln were deliberate, reasoned, and persuasive. Before the war, Owen argued, the North had no constitutional rationale for interfering with Southern slavery. The war, however, abrogated the South's constitutional rights. The most effective weapon that Lincoln had was a proclamation abolishing slavery. Such a proclamation, Owen affirmed, would strip the South, at least on paper, of its most valuable and treasured resource: enslaved people. In fact, Owen penned a draft of an emancipation proclamation that he hoped would serve as a template for the president. He sent the draft to Lincoln on September 17, 1862. Emphasizing that time was of the essence, he urged Lincoln to issue such a proclamation within a week. Five days later, on September 22, Lincoln released his own Preliminary Emancipation Proclamation.

Owen's template was similar in sentiment to Lincoln's proclamation, although Owen's was more radical because it called for the abolition of slavery not only in the rebel states and not just for military reasons. It declared that "to hold and use Human Beings as property" was "always morally wrong" and that, "as essential to the salvation of the Republic[,] the condition of slavery is hereby forever abolished throughout the United States and every one of them."[106] Lincoln was as openly radical as Owen in one respect. Both declared enslaved people *forever* free. Neither of their proclamations promised the return of the South's chattels once peace was restored.

Antislavery passion was the key quality that spiritualists had in common with Lincoln. Most spiritualists—from Garrison to Higginson to Owen—were, like him, strongly opposed to slavery. In the run-up to the 1864 presidential election, spiritualists put themselves at the forefront of pro-Lincoln campaigning. A nationwide spiritualist convention held in Chicago in August 1864 passed resolutions backing

Lincoln's antislavery war effort in the firmest terms. At a time when Peace Democrats called for a negotiated truce that would include maintaining slavery in the South, the spiritualists demanded that the war must continue, "no matter how long the struggle, how great the cost, or how fearful the sacrifice" in order to ensure the abolition of slavery.[107] Southerners and Copperheads who attacked Lincoln, the spiritualists declared, merely advertised their cruelly callous attitude toward the "enslavement of millions of the human family and their posterity, herding them with the beasts that perish, and trafficking in their bodies and souls." On the other side, radical abolitionists who called Lincoln too slow on emancipation failed to appreciate that the president "has never taken a step backward, but has steadily proceeded onward in the right direction, striking at the root of the rebellion, and seeking to secure the unity of our now dismembered Republic upon the basis of universal freedom and justice, without which there can be no peace." Abraham Lincoln alone, the convention affirmed, was capable of leading a war to end slavery. His effectiveness as commander lay in his unique moral stature. In the words of one of the convention's resolutions: "Abraham Lincoln stands before this nation, and before all Europe, as the political embodiment of the spirit and principle of freedom and free institutions, and as the political representative of the anti-slavery sentiment of the nation." His reelection, then, was crucial.

Predictably, Lincoln's opponents slammed the spiritualist convention, calling it another sign that Lincoln was the idol of those who fell for all the wild isms. One critic wrote: "It must be some solace to the Ancient Joker, that he can rely on the loyalty of the strong-minded women and weak-minded men who have been representing the 'spheres' in the convention of spiritualists held at Chicago during the last few days. It is well known that the infidels, atheists, free-thinks, free-lovers, spiritualists, and 'progressive Christians' have always been ardent admirers of Mr. Lincoln and his policy."[108] But the isms charge didn't carry as much weight as it once had. The spiritualist convention, after all, was organized and orderly. Its pro-Lincoln resolutions were rationally presented statements, not mystical messages that arrived from above. The war, as directed by Lincoln, had brought under control some of the zanier aspects of spiritualism. Reformers, historically opposed to structured institutions, had found a new kind of institution, one they could believe in: a US government and a disciplined war effort led by a firm antislavery president.

Lincoln, in short, had the same kind of steadying influence on the isms as he did on his family, with the severe traumas it faced. He had a similarly stabilizing impact on many other disordered aspects of American politics and society.

"O Captain!"

Ralph Waldo Emerson, the Civil War era's leading thinker, and Walt Whitman, its preeminent poet, understood Lincoln and his relationship to the Civil War better than most commentators of the time. Both had personal contact with Lincoln: Emerson twice visited the White House while on a lecture tour that took him to Washington in early 1862; and Whitman later that year moved from Brooklyn to Washington, where he worked for several years as a volunteer nurse in the war hospitals and frequently saw Lincoln riding about. Sometimes the president and the poet exchanged bows.

Emerson and Whitman observed that Lincoln, through his character and his actions, successfully balanced the competing forces of the individual and the mass, powerful leadership and democratic outreach, and a belief in a strong central government along with a respect for the rights of states and individuals.

Emerson, having long preached self-reliance, admired the president for speaking "in his own thought and style"—an impression confirmed when Lincoln greeted him at the White House by exclaiming, "O Mr. Emerson, I once heard you say in a lecture, that a Kentuckian seems to say by his air & manners, 'Here am I; if you don't like me, the worse for you.'"[1]

Frontier toughness characterized many of Lincoln's actions. In the months before the war, he once became so angry about the South's secession that a visitor reported that Lincoln's "Kentucky blood is up, he means *fight*."[2] A sculptor who made a bust of Lincoln noted that as chief executive he acted "as he did in all his rough-and-tumble encounters in the West."[3] The president showed his strength in his sheer endurance of the prolonged agony of Civil War, which caused periodic depression but not physical collapse, as noted by a friend who remarked that "a man of less iron frame would have sunk under the enormous burdens laid upon him during four years, marked by Executive cares that have no parallel in history."[4] In a famous incident, while on a ship carrying him to meet General McClellan on the Virginia Peninsula, he seized a heavy axe and held it out horizontally with one hand for a long time—a feat that no other man on board could match.

More significant than Lincoln's physical strength, in Emerson's view, was his mental sturdiness, which grew from his immersion in the lives of ordinary Americans. Emerson pointed out that Lincoln—"Kentuckian born, working on a farm, a flatboatman, a captain in the Black Hawk War, a country lawyer, a representative in the rural legislature of Illinois"—had "what farmers call a long head; was excellent in working out the sum for himself; in arguing his case and convincing you fairly and firmly."[5]

Whitman saw in Lincoln a special combination of individualism and averageness. On the one hand, Whitman wrote, Lincoln "went his own lonely road, disregarding all the usual ways—refusing the guides, accepting no warnings—just keeping his appointment with himself every time." While "flexible, tolerant, almost slouchy" on "minor matters," he exhibited "great firmness (even obstinacy) . . . involving great points."[6] At the same time, Whitman noted, Lincoln was the everyday American, with his barnyard humor, his carelessness about niceties, his "somewhat rusty and dusty" appearance.[7]

Whitman and Emerson believed that the Civil War brought meaning and order to an America that had previously been corrupt, fragmented, and demoralized. Taking a comprehensive view of the era, they sometimes came close to romanticizing the war. Whitman wrote that the government had previously been full of "the meanest kind of bawling and blowing office-holders, office-seekers, pimps, malignants, conspirators, slave catchers, pushers of slavery, . . . bribers, compromisers, . . . policy backers, money dealers, . . . crawling, serpentine men."[8] The war, in Whitman's view, was a cleansing storm. He wrote in a poem, "War! an arm'd race is advancing! The welcome for battle, no turning away; / War! be it weeks, months, or years, an arm'd race is advancing to welcome it."[9] Later, Whitman immortalized Lincoln in his poem "O Captain! My Captain!," hailing the president as the principled leader who guided "the victor ship" through its "fearful trip."

For Emerson, the war did not just cleanse the nation: it reorganized it. In Emerson's words, "War ennobles the Country; searches it; fires it; acquaints it with its resources; . . . concentrates history into a year, invents means; systematizes everything. We began the war in vast confusion; when we end it, all will be in system."[10] Leading this escape from confusion was Lincoln. Emerson said in his eulogy to Lincoln after the assassination, "His mind mastered the problem of the day; and, as the problem grew, so did his comprehension of it. Rarely was man so fitted to the event."[11]

Since his youth, Lincoln had been accustomed to taming the wild; as president, he handled confusion or wildness on many levels. In the early part of the war, Lincoln faced disorder of many varieties: conflicts within his administration, threatening signs from other nations, an unstable economy, Indian uprisings, and widespread corruption. Lincoln confronted these problems with great inventiveness. He was like a tremendous funnel, open fully to anarchic currents that he channeled, condensed, and redirected in positive ways.

By flexing his centripetal muscles at the right moments, Lincoln greatly increased the central government's strength, organizational structure, and commitment to human rights.

CONTROLLING THE CABINET

One of Lincoln's accomplishments was corralling the energies of his cabinet. In creating what Doris Kearns Goodwin calls his "team of rivals"—a cabinet made up largely of former political opponents—he fashioned a balanced slate politically and geographically.[12] He chose three former Democrats: Gideon Welles of Connecticut for the Navy Department, Montgomery Blair of Maryland as postmaster general, and Pennsylvania's Simon Cameron as secretary of war. Former Whigs included New York's William H. Seward as secretary of state, Salmon P. Chase of Ohio at the Treasury, Edward Bates of Missouri as attorney general, and Caleb Blood Smith of Indiana as secretary of the interior.

It was a motley group. Salmon Chase—tall, broad-shouldered, with regular features and blue eyes—was pious, cold, and steady; he harbored resentment for not having won the nomination for president, and, while he liked Lincoln, he felt superior to him and wanted to take his place. Montgomery Blair, well read but cantankerous, offended many with his abrasive personality; tall and thin, he had deep-set eyes that gave him "a rat-like expression," as a reporter described it.[13] The sixty-eight-year-old Edward Bates, whose white-bearded, rugged face gave him a Mosaic look, was a dour, reticent man who would work behind the scenes as attorney general to enforce Lincoln's policies on slavery and civil liberties. The stodgy Gideon Welles looked so odd in his curled, flowing wig and long white beard that cartoonists and journalists gave him nicknames—most commonly Father Neptune, but also Grandmother Welles, Rip Van Winkle, and Marie Antoinette.[14] The derisive names belied his energetic leadership of the Navy Department.

The balding, stocky Caleb Smith, appointed for having helped Lincoln win Indiana at the 1860 convention, proved to be an inefficient secretary of the interior; he mishandled Indian affairs, led the failed effort to transport blacks to Panama, and opposed Lincoln's plans for emancipation. Sickly, he left the government in December 1862 because of his opposition to the Emancipation Proclamation. He was replaced at Interior by John Palmer Usher, another thickset Indianan with receding hair. Simon Cameron, like Caleb Smith, was a poor choice for the cabinet. Thin-lipped and gray-haired, with close-set eyes and a prominent nose, Cameron had a record of alleged corruption, but Lincoln awarded him the War Department in order to repay him for bringing Pennsylvania to Lincoln's side at the Chicago Wigwam convention. In January 1862, Lincoln removed Cameron for mismanagement and replaced him with Edwin M. Stanton of Ohio, a highly disciplined but nervous and irritable man with a long dark beard and gold-rimmed glasses that magnified his large eyes.

Jealousies, infighting, and self-promotion abounded. The former Jacksonian Democrat Welles loathed the ex-Whig Seward, who also had rocky relationships with Bates, Blair, and, particularly, Chase. Seward told Lincoln that "there were differences between himself and Chase which rendered it impossible for them to act in harmony."[15] At one point, Lincoln was reported to be "very much agitated" by the different opinions hurled at him from various quarters.[16] When an Ohio congressman asked him if he did not think "the elements of the Cabinet are too strong and in some respects too conflicting," Lincoln replied, "it may be so, but I think they will neutralize each other."[17] "I have been pulled this way and that way," he remarked. "I have poised the scales, and it is my province to determine, and now I'm going to be master."[18]

His comment about the cabinet members neutralizing one another suggests that he saw the cabinet as a whole forming a Blondin-like group that was ideologically balanced. While everyone in the cabinet

EDWARD BATES

opposed slavery and its extension, there was a range of outlooks, from the conservatism of Blair to the radicalism of Chase. In general, Lincoln succeeded in keeping the group in balance. As Nicolay and Hay wrote, "In weaker hands, such a Cabinet would have been a hotbed of strife; under him it became a tower of strength."[19]

Lincoln dealt with his cabinet self-reliantly. He weathered the feuds among the various department chiefs. He listened to their advice, but he alone made final decisions. He was self-reliant enough to put up with one-upmanship or disagreement. He judged each cabinet member according to his contribution to saving the Union and ensuring social justice.

A strong call for social justice came, surprisingly, from one of the formerly conservative cabinet members, Edward Bates. Once a staunch Old Whig, Bates, apparently inspired by Lincoln's antislavery war, wrote a pamphlet in late 1862 that argued for black citizenship in wording that refuted the Dred Scott decision and anticipated the Fourteenth and Fifteenth Amendments. Presented in the form of a letter from Bates to Salmon Chase, the pamphlet asked, "Is a man legally incapacitated to be a citizen of the United States by the sole fact that he is a colored, and not a white man?"[20] Bates answered his own question: "The Constitution says not one word, and furnishes not one hint, in relation to the color or to the ancestral race of the 'natural-born citizen.'" Bates paraphrased the Citizenship Clause of the Constitution by affirming that "every person born in the country at the moment of birth is *prima facie* a citizen," regardless of race. Then Bates made a radical assertion: "I give it as my opinion that the *free man of color*, . . . if born in the United States, is a citizen of the United States." "Color," by implication, extended to people of all ethnicities.

This remarkably forward-looking argument was, predictably, sharply attacked, as in a Missouri newspaper that said it would "produce regret and disappointment in the minds of those who revere the Constitution as our fathers made it."[21] But it boldly anticipated later constitutional amendments and Supreme Court decisions. Significantly, Bates's radical opinion was understood to be Lincoln's as well. A leading journal, averring that Bates's pamphlet had "a legal and a moral significance that can hardly be overestimated," said that it carried "the moral weight of the Administration—for it is constructively the opinion of the President."[22]

If Bates moved from conservatism to uncharted territory on race, Montgomery ("Monty") Blair remained stuck in a reactionary position. To be sure, as postmaster general, Blair performed well. He regularized the postal system by issuing a standard postage stamp, improving registered mail, introducing the return receipt to verify delivery, pioneering the money-order system through the post office, and establishing rules for international postal service. Also, along with his father, the veteran politician Francis Blair Sr. of Maryland, and his brother, the Missouri senator Francis (Frank) Blair Jr., Monty Blair helped keep the border states of Missouri and Maryland in the Union.

MONTGOMERY BLAIR

But the Blairs' racial views clashed with Lincoln's increasing progressiveness. The Blairs were Negrophobes who clung to the belief that black people had no place in American society. The elder Blair, whose twenty-some enslaved workers served him at his estate in Silver Spring, Maryland, until they were emancipated by the Thirteenth Amendment, called for "the deportation or extermination of the African race from among us."[23] Monty Blair, an ardent colonizationist, declared in October 1863 that the continued presence of blacks in America would produce "a hybrid race," "a hybrid government," and "abortive generations."[24] There is no record of Lincoln's response to this statement by his postmaster general. But he had moved beyond viewing colonization as a viable option for African Americans. Nor did he share Blair's fear of miscegenation. In 1864, he fired Blair and replaced him with Ohio governor William Dennison Jr., a strongly abolitionist Republican who had led his state's anti-Copperhead coalition.

While Lincoln gave the cabinet members great latitude in supervising their departments, he put his foot down at key moments. When Simon Cameron in 1861 proposed arming blacks to fight in the war, Lincoln thought it was too early to do so and said, "That is a question that belongs exclusively to me!"[25] In August 1862, when several cabinet members planned to resign should Lincoln reinstate General McClellan, the president reappointed him anyway, stating, "[T]he order was mine; and I will be responsible for it to the country."[26] Later, when Radical Republicans in Congress tried to gain domination of the government by causing the dismissal of everyone in the cabinet except Chase and Stanton, he handled the situation with aplomb. He received the resignation of Seward and arranged a White House meeting with the disgruntled congressmen and the rest of the cabinet. Salmon Chase, exposed as a participant in the revolt against the administration, was so abashed that he also handed Lincoln a letter of resignation. The president refused to accept it, and he called back Seward, who reassumed his position in the State Department. Lincoln knew that it was important to maintain a Blondin cabinet, with both Chase and Seward kept in place. The frontier custom of riding to market with two pumpkins evenly balanced on the horse came to Lincoln's mind. "I can ride on now," he quipped; "I've got a pumpkin in each end of my bag!"[27]

He kept the pumpkins adroitly balanced. Under his direction, Seward and Chase made important contributions to the Union effort, even though they posed formidable challenges: Seward initially acted as though he were the rightful president, and Chase schemed to take Lincoln's place in 1864. Lincoln handled these talented but self-important politicians with firmness and judgment.

WILLIAM H. SEWARD

The gray-haired William Seward was, in Henry Adams's memorable account, "a slouching, slender figure; a head like a wise macaw; a beaked nose; shaggy eyebrows; unorderly hair and clothes; hoarse voice; offhand manner; free talk, and a perpetual cigar."[28] A convivial wine drinker and raconteur, Seward eventually grew close to Lincoln. But in the months leading up to Fort Sumter, he sometimes overreached his position. Evidently, he still held a grudge over having lost the Republican nomination in 1860. He told a European diplomat that Lincoln was like a hereditary monarch, a mere figurehead in a government whose true leader, Seward himself, was equivalent to a prime minister. Charles Francis Adams Jr. recalled that Seward, who viewed Lincoln as "a clown, a clod," planned to "steer . . . the nerveless president" by "subtle maneuvering, astute wriggling & plotting."[29] From Washington, Seward wrote to his wife, "I am the only *hopeful, calm, conciliatory* person here."[30]

Despite his outward calmness, Seward's alarm over the imminence of civil war led to his frustrated words in an April 1 memo to Lincoln titled "Some thoughts for the president's consideration." Seward wrote, "We are at the end of a month's administration, and yet without a policy, either domestic or foreign."[31] Seward confusingly recommended that Lincoln surrender Fort Sumter to the Confederates but reinforce other US forts in the South. Seward also proposed a quixotic plan to rally the South to unified military action with the North by declaring war against France, Spain, and possibly other European nations that were making incursions into the western Caribbean. If the president could not undertake the task, Seward added, the president should "devolve it on some member of his cabinet." Lincoln answered the secretary of state by restating his intention, formerly supported by Seward, of holding all the federal forts, including Fort Sumter. He ignored Seward's suggestion about entering into a war with Europe. He did not want to quarrel with Seward, whose presence in the administration he valued greatly. For one thing, he knew that Seward was an unswerving antislavery radical who was enlightened on race. In 1861, Seward started issuing passports to American blacks in the belief that they were American citizens.[32]

And he was useful to Lincoln in other ways. He became the main enforcer of the president's policy of suspending habeas corpus in cases of Northerners arrested on suspicion of disloyalty to the Union. Despite Seward's bravado just before the war, he went on to treat international affairs with sensitivity and nuance. He performed sensibly when many Americans called for the retention and punishment of Confederate envoys who had been taken from a British schooner, the *Trent*, in December 1861. So much tension arose from the seizure of the envoys that England was poised for war with the United States, while Northerners called for a trial of the captured Confederates. Seward thought carefully about the situation and decided that permitting the Southern envoys to make their trip to England was the best course of action—an argument that won over Lincoln and indeed proved to be a judicious decision.

It was largely due to Seward's negotiating skills that neither England nor France became involved in the Civil War. Also, in 1862, Seward worked out with England the Lyons-Seward Treaty, which laid down strong measures aimed at ending the international slave trade. He had other major achievements as well: he prevented England from continuing to build ships like the *Alabama*, the *Florida*, the *Georgia*, and the *Shenandoah*, Confederate commerce raiders that wreaked havoc on the Union's merchant fleet; he dealt deftly with France over its attempted intervention in Mexico; and he developed a farsighted Latin American policy. He also opened vistas by airing an idea about a canal across Central America and by advancing the open-door policy to the Far East. Later, under Andrew Johnson, he famously managed the acquisition of Russian America (Alaska) and began negotiations for reparations from England for its shipbuilding for the Confederacy, leading to a $15.5 million settlement.

Seward became Lincoln's boon companion. Warm and outgoing, Seward lived in a home diagonally across Lafayette Square from the White House. He led virtually a bachelor's life in Washington because his wife, Frances, who disliked the frenetic social scene in the capital, had remained home in Auburn, New York. Seward regularly dropped in to see the president, who returned the visits, spending many an evening relaxing in Seward's parlor. Lincoln loved stretching his long legs before Seward's fire while the effervescent secretary sipped wine and puffed cigars. The friends discussed many subjects and traded stories and jokes, frequently off-color ones. During Emerson's weekend in Washington, Seward, despite Lincoln's warning to avoid being "smutty," told Emerson a story with the punchline "I can't say I have carnal knowledge of him," which the staid philosopher called an "extraordinary exordium."[33] On another occasion, Lincoln was in a carriage whose driver cursed vehemently. Lincoln asked what church he attended. When the driver said Methodist, Lincoln replied, "Oh, excuse me, I thought you must be an Episcopalian, for you swear just like Secretary Seward, and he's a church-warden!"[34]

Lincoln's closeness to Seward, however, created some difficulties. It was commonly thought that the New Yorker had succeeded in his original plan of becoming the "Premier" of the Lincoln administration, acting as the puppeteer of the president. Some of the bitterness the other cabinet members felt toward Seward signaled envy of his friendship with Lincoln. Also annoyed was Mary Todd Lincoln, who saw Seward as a power-hungry schemer who wanted to supplant her husband. She went so far as to avoid driving by Seward's house in her carriage rides.

Treasury secretary Salmon Chase, who lived a mile from the White House and whose stiff personality stymied warm relationships, especially resented the easygoing Seward's intimacy with the president. Lincoln had to exercise far more forbearance with the aggressive Chase than with the gregarious Seward.

After his victory in the 1860 election, Lincoln had been warned by the Springfield businessman John W. Bunn against appointing Salmon Chase to his cabinet. Lincoln asked, "Why do you say that?" Bunn replied, "Because he thinks he is a great deal bigger than you are." For someone less sure of himself than Lincoln, this statement would have raised red flags about Chase's possible disloyalty. But Lincoln asked Bunn, "Well, do you know of any other men who think they are bigger than I am?" Bunn: "I do not know that I do, but why do you ask me that?" Lincoln: "Because I want to put them all in my Cabinet."[35]

SALMON P. CHASE

Humorless and reserved, Salmon Chase never surrendered his sense of superiority over Lincoln. Senator Benjamin F. Wade remarked: "Chase is a good man, but his theology is unsound. He thinks there is a fourth person in the Trinity."[36] Chase's desire for the presidency led to his attempt to become the Republican presidential nominee in 1864. On learning of his effort, Lincoln told a story about him and his stepbrother once trying to plow a cornfield with a lazy horse. Lincoln swept a stinging chin-fly off the horse's neck, but his stepbrother objected, saying, "Why, that's all that made him go." "Now," said Lincoln, "if Mr. Chase has a presidential chin-fly biting him, I am not going to knock him off, if it will only make his department go."[37]

Actually, Lincoln had great respect for Chase, who had been a path blazer in the fight against slavery. As a Cincinnati lawyer known for the pro bono counsel he gave to runaway blacks and Underground Railroad agents, he earned a reputation as the Attorney General for Fugitive Slaves. He was associated successively with the Whigs, the Liberty Party, the Free Soil Democrats, and the Republican Party, under whose mantle he served as the governor of Ohio and then as a US senator from that state. He coined the famous Republican slogans "Free Soil, Free Labor, and Free Men" and "Freedom is national; slavery only is local and sectional."[38] Lincoln deeply appreciated Chase's vigorous campaign speeches on his behalf in the 1858 Senate race in Illinois against Douglas. Chase's well-reasoned interpretation of the Constitution as antislavery in spirit anticipated Lincoln's Cooper Union Address. During the war, Chase objected when his financier friend Jay Cooke opened a Washington streetcar line from which black people were banned.

Lincoln also admired Chase's competence as a Treasury secretary. The president said he thought that Chase's maneuvering for the presidency "was very bad taste, but that he had determined to shut his eyes to all these performances: that Chase made a good Secretary and that he would keep him where is: if he becomes Presdt., all right. I hope we may never have a worse man." Lincoln added: "I am entirely indifferent as to his success or failure in these schemes, so long as he does his duty as the head of the Treasury Department."[39] Chase indeed performed his Treasury duties competently, but his strategizing for the presidency in time soured his relationship with Lincoln, who in June 1864 accepted his offer to resign. However, Lincoln sought to keep Chase's radical voice alive by appointing him chief justice of the Supreme Court in December 1864.

FINANCING THE WAR

Chase's greatest contribution came in an area in which he entered the Civil War with little previous experience: economics. By applying his native intelligence and adapting to the rapidly changing conditions of war, Chase, with regular input from Lincoln, established a government-backed fiscal structure that proved to be a major factor in the North's victory.

Lincoln inherited a weak economy. His predecessor, James Buchanan, had begun his administration in March 1857 with a surplus in the Treasury of $1.3 million and a modest debt of $28.7 million. Wasteful spending and corruption during his presidency led to a large deficit and a debt of $76.4 million by the time Lincoln took office.[40] American currency was in a state of "paper anarchy"—what amounted to financial centrifugalism. Many varieties of paper currency were issued in the states by individual banks, creating what has been called "a crazy quilt of money." By 1861 there were no fewer than seven thousand different legitimate bills in circulation, more than 80 percent of which had been successfully counterfeited.[41]

Given the depleted Treasury and the chaotic currency, how was the Union to pay for the sudden military buildup in the months just after Fort Sumter?

This was the dire situation that confronted Lincoln's Treasury secretary, Salmon Chase. With his background in the law and antislavery politics, Chase did not have much preparation in fiscal matters. Confronted with the fiscal confusion of the opening months of the Civil War, he took economic action that was repellent to him. He had always been devoted to metallic currency. He confessed to "a great aversion to making anything but coin a legal tender in payment of debts."[42] Nonetheless, he quickly realized that funding must come from somewhere, and so he turned to paper money. With the help of an association of eastern bankers led by the Philadelphia financier Jay Cooke, Chase devised issuances of government bonds, securities, and legal tender that provided much needed revenue for the Union. In August 1861 came demand notes, so called because they could be exchanged on demand for gold or silver. When the supply of hard currency ran out at the end of the year, Chase argued for cash backed by government promises rather than specie. The Legal Tender Act, passed by Congress on February 25, 1862, authorized the printing of $150 million in government money as bills known as greenbacks. In the course of the war, some $500 million of greenbacks (about $7 billion today) were printed. Chase did not feel comfortable with them, and in fact as chief justice of the Supreme Court in 1869 he ruled that paper money was unconstitutional, a decision that was later overturned. But he considered greenbacks a wartime necessity.

Lincoln did, too, especially because many state banks continued to issue their own currency. When in January 1863 Lincoln approved a fresh printing of greenbacks, he predicted that "continued issues of United States notes, without any check to the issues of suspended banks," could have "disastrous consequences."[43] Despite his qualms about paper money, he saw the need for a national currency, and he recognized its value for cultural stability and cohesion. He implemented another of Chase's ideas, a national banking system, in May 1863. This system required state banks to hold federally produced currency. In December 1864 Lincoln reported to Congress that 584 national banks (many of them converted state banks) had been established during the past year. "The national banking system," he declared, "is proving to be acceptable to capitalists and to the people. . . . [I]t is hoped that, very soon, there will be in the United States, no banks of issue not authorized by Congress, and no bank-note circulation not secured by the government. . . . The national system will create a reliable and permanent influence in support of the national credit, and protect the people against losses in the use of paper money."[44]

Also important to the Northern economy were the interest-bearing government bonds sold by Chase's financier friend Jay Cooke. Known as five-twenties and seven-thirties because of their differing interest rates and maturity periods, the bonds became a symbol of patriotism and democracy. Cooke's many agents fanned out through the North, appearing in cities, towns, and villages, where they promoted the purchase of the bonds as an act of patriotism. Newspaper ads, signs, and broadsides invited Northerners of all social grades to buy government bonds in order to fund the military and the government. A typical advertisement announced, "Money is the great power in war and will conquer at last, and he who contributes his money to aid his country in her hour of danger may thereby evince as much patriotism as he who marches to the battle field."[45] Outside Cooke's Washington office was an American flag and a banner that read:

> The Bravery of our Army
> The Valor of our Navy
> Sustained by our Treasury
> Upon the Faith and
> Substance of
> A Patriotic People.[46]

One problem with so much paper currency was that it accelerated inflation. An item that cost one dollar in the North in 1860 had risen to $1.75 by the end of the war. However, the economic situation in the South was far worse. There, an item that was one dollar in 1860 cost ninety-two dollars in 1865—an astounding 9,000 percent inflation rate over the course of the war.[47] Seven series of Confederate banknotes were issued, with no backing in hard currency. Because the greybacks, as they were called, were credit notes that promised payment to bearers once peace came and the Confederacy was firmly established as an independent nation, the notes became virtually worthless by early 1865, as the South's defeat loomed. Counterfeiting the greybacks was easy and widespread. Relatively speaking, then, the North was in strong fiscal shape, thanks in part to the work of Salmon Chase, under Lincoln.

Notably, the Treasury under Chase also oversaw the first national income tax in US history. In August 1861 Lincoln authorized a 3 percent tax on annual income above $800. The following July he signed a bill that lowered the exemption to $600 and raised the tax on income above $10,000 to 5 percent, including moneys earned from property, rents, dividends, or other sources. In 1864 there came another graduated tax, which taxed incomes between $800 and $10,000 at 5 percent, then 7.5 percent for incomes between $10,000 and $25,000, and 10 percent above that.[48] The income tax was seen as a people's tax, for it did not affect many Americans in a time when the average annual wage was around $600 for skilled workers and $400 for laborers.[49] Also democratic were excise taxes imposed during the war on luxury items such as jewelry, watches, refined sugar, and carriages.

Lincoln's administration, therefore, centralized and standardized currency and banking in ways that did not lose sight of average Americans. The greenback was the ancestor of today's dollar, and government bonds would continue to have a vibrant place in the US economy. Chase and Lincoln also played lead roles in introducing types of taxation that were adopted, in revised form, by later administrations.

DEMOCRATIZING COLLEGE EDUCATION AND LAND IMPROVEMENT

If these initiatives raised revenue for the war, another program under Lincoln opened the way to practical education for generations of Americans. It is often forgotten that Lincoln was the president who authorized land grant colleges and universities. Before his presidency, there had been efforts toward federally funded higher education, but none had gained traction. In 1857, Senator Justin Morrill of Vermont had introduced a bill that would allocate federal land to each state for the development of institutions of higher learning in agriculture and mechanics. His bill passed Congress two years later, but President Buchanan vetoed it.

During Lincoln's first term, Senator Morrill reintroduced his bill, which was approved by Congress and signed by the president on July 2, 1862. The Morrill Land-Grant Colleges Act distributed public land for the endowment of colleges devoted primarily to "agriculture and the mechanic arts" but "without excluding other scientific and classical studies, . . . in order to promote the liberal and practical education of the industrial classes in the several pursuits and professions in life."[50] In 1890, a second Morrill Act expanded the program and stipulated that race must not be a factor in admission to the state colleges. Over time, more than three hundred land grant institutions were founded, among them Cornell, Ohio State, Michigan State, Penn State, Texas A & M, the University of California, and many historically black and Native American colleges and universities. Land grant colleges reflected Lincoln's deep interest in agriculture, which fit economic reality in an age when more than half of all Americans lived on farms.

Given Lincoln's interest in merging technological advance with economic prosperity, it is fitting that in 1862 he created the Department of Agriculture, committed to improving farming techniques, gathering statistics, and performing experiments that might lead to agricultural progress. "The creation of this department," Lincoln told Congress, "was for the more immediate benefit of a large class of our most valuable citizens; and I trust that . . . [it will] become the fruitful source of advantage to all our people."[51] He viewed the department as an earth-centered symbol of democracy. "It is peculiarly the people's department," he declared, "in which they feel more directly concerned than in any other."[52] He appointed as the commissioner of the department Isaac Newton, a Quaker farmer from Pennsylvania, who submitted regular reports that provided information showing, in Newton's words, "that Agriculture is the grand element of our progress in wealth, stability and power."[53]

Also in 1862, Lincoln oversaw the passage of the Homestead Act, which he signed into law in March. This bill awarded 160 acres of public land to any head of family who paid a small registration fee and settled on the land. The acreage was given free to those who occupied the land for five years; alternatively, it was available for purchase at $1.25 an acre after six months. Distribution of public land had long been the dream of working-class champions like George Henry Evans and Horace Greeley. The Homestead Act eventually led to the distribution of 10 percent of the continental United States to more than 1.5 million people, including free blacks. Few in 1862, however, could predict that a large portion of the offered land would be bought by speculators who saw that government projects would pass through it, principally the transcontinental railroad, funded by the Pacific Railway Acts of 1862 and 1864 and completed in 1869.

Conservation is not usually associated with Lincoln, who rose to popularity partly for his skill in cutting down trees and who directed a war that ravaged portions of the American countryside. Notably, however, he became the first president to sign into law a bill to protect a unique area of public land—the first step in what became the national parks system.

The conservation movement has been traced to several of Lincoln's contemporaries, including the transcendentalists Emerson and Thoreau, the Hudson River school artists, the nature photographer Carleton Watkins, and the Vermont politician and scholar George Perkins Marsh. Of these, Marsh and Watkins had the most direct relationship with Lincoln. George Perkins Marsh and Lincoln served together as Whig congressmen in the 1840s, when both opposed the Mexican War. Marsh became a loyal Republican, and in 1861 Lincoln appointed him minister to Italy, a post he held until his death in 1882. As early as 1847, when both he and

Mirror Lake, Yosemite (photograph by Carleton Watkins)

Lincoln were in Congress, Marsh gave a lecture before an agricultural society in Vermont in which, with amazing prescience, he predicted global warming due to damage inflicted by humans on the earth; the lecture carried the seeds of Marsh's pioneering 1864 book *Man and Nature: Physical Geography as Modified by Human Action.*

On June 30, 1864, Lincoln signed a bill giving Yosemite Valley and the nearby Mariposa Big Tree Grove to the state of California as a nature reserve to "be held for public use, resort, and recreation . . . inalienable for all time."[54] He appears to have been inspired by a swelling chorus of cultural voices bringing attention to Yosemite's grandeur, which had first been impressed on Americans in the mid-1850s through the lithographs of Thomas A. Ayers and was soon known worldwide through woodcuts, engravings, the oil paintings of Albert Bierstadt, and the photographs by Carleton Watkins. Not only were Watkins's photographs widely displayed during the 1860s, but Lincoln reportedly saw them up close through his California friend Senator John Conness. The bill Lincoln signed anticipated the National Park Service, especially because of its influence on John Muir, whose time living in the government-protected Yosemite during the 1870s inspired his path-blazing contributions to land preservation, which eventually earned him the nickname "Father of the National Parks."

THE GREAT FATHER AND HIS CHILDREN

Much of the territory Lincoln opened up to homesteaders or railroaders was west of the Mississippi and was occupied by Native Americans, the tragic victims of westward expansion.

As many have noted, Lincoln had a blind spot where Indians were concerned.[55] This was not surprising, given his personal history. His ancestors had been on the cusp of westward migration that kept them on the front line of violent encounters with Native Americans. The Lincolns had been very close to the Boones, the most famous of whom, Daniel Boone, had hunted Indians who had killed several of his friends and family members. The murder of Lincoln's grandfather and namesake, Abraham Lincoln, by an Indian affected Abe's attitudes. Lincoln's participation in the Black Hawk War, though it did not involve killing on his part, pitted him against native tribes who were fighting against whites over land.

There were larger cultural factors, as well. Prejudice against Indians was stamped on the DNA of generations of white Americans from the seventeenth century onward. Historians have coined phrases—the anti-Indian sublime, the metaphysics of Indian hating, regeneration through violence, and so on—to describe the fierce anti-Indian sentiment that permeated the psyche of whites and produced the long, ugly history of Indian removals and the demonization of natives in popular culture.[56] Persistent efforts by whites to "civilize" various tribes had only mixed results, while attempts by some to romanticize indigenous peoples as noble savages yielded euphemistic racial stereotyping. Nor did it help matters that during the Civil War four times as many Native Americans—a portion of them slaveholders—fought for the Confederacy than for the Union.[57]

There were moments, however, when Lincoln's innate fairness overcame his emotional distance from Indians. During the Black Hawk War, an old Indian man wandered into an area where Lincoln and his troops were camped. The Indian showed a pass that, he claimed, General Lewis Cass had given him because of his previous service to whites. Lincoln's men dismissed the paper as a forgery. Thinking that the Indian was a spy, they leveled their muskets and prepared to shoot him. Lincoln intervened. The Indian's story, he said, was credible. When his men called Lincoln a coward, he declared, "If any one doubts my courage let him try it."[58] He "swore [that] if [the] Indian was slaughtered it must be done over his dead body."[59]

If Lincoln saved one Indian then, he saved more than 260 natives in a dramatic incident in the Civil War.

In August 1862, desperate Minnesota Sioux, driven to near starvation by withheld annuities and poor crops, rose up and massacred hundreds of whites. A 5-man military tribunal tried 392 Sioux and condemned 303 to death. Prejudice against indigenous people was so strong among Americans that there were strident calls for the deaths of all 303. Cries for mob action against the Sioux arose—exactly the kind of vigilante justice Lincoln had warned of in his 1838 lyceum lecture and in some of his homicide cases as a lawyer. Newspapers swelled the chorus for vengeance.

So did a Minnesota doctor, Thaddeus Williams, who wrote Lincoln a long letter describing alleged atrocities committed by the Minnesota natives, including the rape of a sixteen-year-old girl by "23 painted savages [who] satiated their lust on her" for three days, and "human beings, butchered, their entrails torn out, & their heads cut off & put between their lifeless thighs, or hoisted on a pole; their bodies gashed & cut to strips, & nailed or hung to trees; mothers with sharp fence rails passed through them & their unborn babes; children with hooks stuck through their backs & hung to limbs of trees."[60]

Especially telling is Williams's remark, "This is no fancy sketch, such as Cobb or Cooper might concoct for the Ledger or a novel; it is a scene written on the broad prairies of Minnesota." Actually, Williams in his letter presented the Sioux uprising to Lincoln through the lens of popular sensational fiction. Williams had in mind novels like James Fenimore Cooper's *The Last of the Mohicans*, which fictionalized the 1757 massacre of hundreds of whites by drunken Indians near Lake George, New York, or the blood-soaked adventure fiction by the novelist Sylvanus Cobb Jr., who often published in the pulp newspaper the *New York Ledger*, which in a typical issue advertised a story that was "by far the most ABSORBING and THRILLING TALE of LIFE AMONG THE INDIANS ever published" [capitalization in the original]. The ad gives titillating suggestions of rape: "The Heart-rending Trials, Sufferings, and Privations, of the lovely heroine, BLANCHE BERTRAND, whose life was in constant peril, and who suffered more than pen can relate, during her captivity, will enlist the SYMPATHIES of every reader."[61]

Lincoln had long been accustomed to reacting against such sensationalism in popular culture. This time, he sympathized with those who argued that the Minnesota Sioux had acted with justifiable vindictiveness and must therefore be treated mercifully. That was the plea of the Reverend Henry B. Whipple, the Episcopal bishop of Minnesota, who visited Lincoln in Washington and explained the real causes of the massacre: "the corruption of agents and traders, the lack of government protection for the Indians, and examples of how the corruption led directly to bloody war." Lincoln reportedly told a friend that the bishop "came here the other day and talked with me about the rascality of this Indian business until I felt it down to my boots." Lincoln promised the bishop, "If we get through this war, and I live, *this Indian system shall be reformed!*"[62]

Lincoln never got the opportunity to pursue the Indian reforms he envisaged. But he did put his pardoning power to use when adjudicating the cases of the 303 condemned Sioux Indians. He asked for the court records along with "a careful statement" about uncertain cases.[63] He and two others went through the documents and decided that only 39 natives deserved to be executed. Thirty-eight Sioux were hanged (one received a last-minute reprieve) on December 26, 1862, in Mankato, Minnesota. This stands as the largest mass execution in American history, but it would have been far larger had Lincoln not intervened.

Having commuted the sentences of 265 of the convicted Sioux, he explained his action in Blondin-like fashion: "Anxious to not act with so much clemency as to encourage another outbreak on the one hand, nor with so much severity as to be real cruelty on the other, I caused a careful examination of the records of trials to be made, in view of first ordering the execution of such as had been proved guilty of violating females. Contrary to my expectations, only two of this class were found."[64]

Thaddeus Williams's charges of mass rape, then, were bogus. Williams had responded to the Sioux uprising as someone who had read too many racy Sylvanus Cobb novels and perfervid *New York Ledger* stories. Many others had reacted that way, too. Lincoln, in contrast, responded with the judiciousness of a seasoned lawyer.

But Lincoln's intervention in the case did not improve the lot of the

Minnesota Sioux. What was widely regarded as his undue clemency toward the natives fueled a demand for their total removal from the state. Indian removals had occurred under several presidents, who acted on Thomas Jefferson's advice about the natives: "[W]e shall be obliged to drive them with the beasts of the forest into the stony [that is, Rocky] mountains."[65] The removals, which in retrospect have the marks of ethnic cleansing, were then championed as the inevitable victory of civilization over savagery. In February and March 1863 Congress authorized the deportation of the Minnesota Sioux to the barren, wretched Crow Creek reservation in Dakota Territory, where they stayed for three years before being moved to another location near the mouth of a river in Nebraska.

Few Americans in 1863 would have pitied the displaced Sioux. And few would have taken umbrage at the portrait of Lincoln's attitudes toward Indians as depicted in one of that year's bestsellers, *The Pioneer Boy, and How He Became President*, a fictionalized biography of the president by the popular Boston author William M. Thayer. *The Pioneer Boy*, designed as a novel for young readers but popular among older ones as well, focused on Lincoln's frontier childhood and young manhood. Thayer began his book with the young Abe listening to the tale, told by his father Thomas, of the killing of grandfather Abraham Lincoln by a native. "The Injins were very cruel," Thomas tells Abe, "and sometimes they attacked a family and killed them all with a tomahawk."[66] Thayer invented episodes of Indian cruelty, including the story that the grandfather was not only murdered but scalped. According to Thayer, the feelings Abe absorbed as a boy shaped his attitude when, at twenty-three, he captained a troop in the Black Hawk War. Thayer had Lincoln call Black Hawk "one of the most treacherous Indians there is, . . . a cunning, artful warrior, and determined to massacre all the whites he can." Doubtless, many readers approved of this supposed statement by Lincoln, which was part of a conversation in the book in which he said of Black Hawk, "I hope he will be shot."

Barring fresh evidence, we'll never know what Lincoln thought of Thayer's imaginary portrait of him, but we do know that the president was so focused on the main military theaters during the Civil War that he did not attend carefully to Indian problems in the West.[67] These problems were badly mishandled by the Bureau of Indian Affairs, whose commissioner, William P. Dole, was an Illinois associate of Lincoln's. The bureau was part of the Department of the Interior, headed by Caleb B. Smith, who became ill and was replaced in early 1863 by John P. Usher. These were politically motivated appointments filled by men with backward views on race. They sent a large number of federal agents throughout lands inhabited by Indians. The agents, along with opportunistic traders, engaged in massive corruption. They pilfered government annuities slated for the natives, ignored treaties, plied the natives with alcohol, and otherwise maltreated them. Military officials assumed a harsh stance toward the natives. During the Sioux uprising, Lincoln sent west General John Pope, who had recently met defeat at Second Bull Run. Shortly after his arrival in Minnesota, Pope wrote to a state politician, "It is my purpose utterly to exterminate the Sioux if I have the power to do so. . . . They are to be treated as maniacs or wild beasts, and by no means as people with whom treaties or compromises can be made."[68]

Despite the inadequacies of Lincoln's Indian policies, there are indications that Native Americans had warm feelings about the president. Augustus Wattles, a Kansas abolitionist who had been a friend of John Brown's and who knew several western tribes intimately, discovered "one remarkable emotion among the destitute Indians he visited." He reported, "Their veneration for the President is very profound, and their awe, when speaking of his power, is like that which children feel when listening to ghost stories." These people believed "that if the ear of the Great Father can be reached, all will be well with them."[69]

In March 1863, the Great Father's ear was reached when a delegation of fourteen Indian chiefs, along with two squaws, responded to an invitation from Washington by visiting the White House. Dressed in full regalia, the natives were taken to the East Room, where they squatted in a semicircle as the president talked with them. Cabinet members and others observed the discussion. Lincoln was friendly and receptive but at times condescending. He dealt with the chiefs as though they were all hunter-gatherers, which was true of the five nomadic Plains tribes represented that day (Apache, Arapaho, Cheyenne, Comanche, and Kiowa) but not of the sixth, the southwestern Caddo tribe, which raised crops. Through an interpreter, Lincoln told the chiefs that Indian preference for hunting was ill founded. Whites outpaced Indians economically, he explained, because they engaged in agriculture. He said, "The pale-faced people are numerous and prosperous because they cultivate the earth, produce bread, and depend upon the products of the earth rather than wild game for a subsistence."[70]

Lincoln told the chiefs that he could not advise them whether "to maintain the habits and customs of your race, or adopt a new mode of life." But he had trouble explaining whites' ongoing betrayals of Native Americans. "It is the object of this Government," he assured them, "to be on terms of peace with you, and with all our red brethren. . . . We make treaties with you, and will try to observe them; and if our children should sometimes behave badly, and violate these treaties, it is against our wish." The "children" here were the government agents and traders who, as Lincoln knew, often acted treacherously. Lincoln said, "You know it is not always possible for any father to have his children do precisely as he wishes them to do."

Despite his apparent efforts to sympathize with his guests, the president made a ham-handed statement: "Although we [whites] are now engaged in a great war between one another, we are not, as a race, so much disposed to fight and kill one another as our red brethren." This remark, which typified whites' view of the Indian character at the time, was unwittingly ironic, given the bloody war Lincoln was then directing.

Six of the fourteen Native Americans who visited the White House, March 27, 1863
(photographic print on carte de visite mount: albumen. Photograph by Mathew B.
Brady). Among those standing in the background are, on the left, the interpreter
John Simpson Smith; next to him, agent Samuel G. Colley; in the middle, Lincoln's
secretary John G. Nicolay. The woman at the right is thought to be Mary Todd
Lincoln. Within eighteen months of the taking of this photograph, three of the
natives sitting in the front row were killed by whites in the West.

In any case, the chiefs reportedly responded to him positively.
According to a witness of the meeting, "The President's remarks were
received with frequent marks of applause and approbation. 'Ugh,' 'Aha'
sounded along the line as the interpreter proceeded, and their counte-
nances gave evident tokens of satisfaction."

Whether or not the chiefs truly appreciated Lincoln's comments to
them, they must have been mystified when their eastern visit became a
mass spectacle. Phineas T. Barnum, ever alert to curiosities, invited
them through their agent to New York and put them on display for ten
days in his museum. On April 8, he placed a typically hyperventilated
ad in the *New York Times*:

TODAY

EXTRAORDINARY SIGHT IN NEW YORK

First Appearance of the

GREAT INDIAN CHIEFS AND WARRIORS

who have just arrived from Washington where they

were on a visit to their "Great Father," the

PRESIDENT OF THE UNITED STATES

all of them being fully attired in their

WAR-PAINT, WAMPUM AND FEATHERS

and presenting the most attractive features of the

REDMAN IN HIS NATIVE GRANDEUR

fresh from the hunting grounds and

WIGWAMS OF HIS WILD ABODES.[71]

By early May, the natives were back in their western locations, but several met sad ends.[72] The Cheyenne chiefs War Bonnet and Standing in Water died in the Sand Creek Massacre of November 1864, when US troops under the Indian hater Colonel John Chivington killed and mutilated between seventy and five hundred Arapaho and Cheyenne people. Another White House visitor, the Cheyenne chief Lean Bear, was shot in May 1864, even though he carried a note signed by Lincoln saying that he was peaceful and friendly to whites; his murderers were Colorado troops who had been ordered by Chivington to kill any Indian they encountered on the Plains.

Lincoln, known by the natives as the Great Father, had heard their plea, but he could not protect them against his disobedient children.

SHODDY

Lincoln had been expected to clean up governmental corruption. When he won the Republican nomination in 1860, Joshua R. Giddings told him "that to my certain knowledge your selection was made upon two grounds 1 That you are an *honest* man. 2nd That you are not in the hands of Corrupt or dishonest men."[73] Lincoln replied that he would try to defend "the cause of truth, justice, and humanity" but added, "I am not wanting in the purpose, . . . though I may fail in the strength, to maintain my freedom from bad influences."[74]

He did *not*, thankfully, fail in strength. He gained resolve from the crookedness that had permeated Washington in the 1850s.[75] In an interview, he "spoke with great freedom of corruption in high places. He regarded it as the bane of our American politics; and said he could not respect, either as a man or a politician, one who bribed or was bribed."[76] He pointed to political colleagues who "were bribed by the Buchanan corruption fund" and "were bought and sold like hogs are sold in the market."[77] When a Washington journalist assured him that his administration would be "a reign of steel," Lincoln quipped, "Why don't you add that Buchanan's was the reign of *stealing*?"[78]

Although the Civil War quickly hurled his administration into a morass of financial corruption—caused mainly by venal contractors who supplied the Union military—to a great degree he succeeded in pulling it out of the morass by appointing skilled people who shared his devotion to the war effort and the Union.

The corruption he encountered was mainly a by-product of the massive mobilization effort in the North during the opening months of the war. Because America's regular army was so small at the time of Fort Sumter—fewer than 17,000 officers and troops—no government structure was in place to supply a huge military force. Having called up 75,000 militia in April 1861, Lincoln asked for 500,000 troops in his address to Congress on July 4. In the speech he said, "One of the greatest perplexities of the government, is to avoid receiving troops faster than it can provide for them."[79] Perplexities indeed. By August 3, 485,640 three-year men were under arms. The rate of this early buildup was nearly ten times as rapid as that in the opening months of World War I and four times faster than in the year leading up to World War II.[80]

A tremendous strain was placed on the Quartermaster's Department and the War Department, which faced the challenge of supplying an immense number of troops with munitions, clothing, food, tents, blankets, and transportation. After Quartermaster General Joseph E. Johnston left for the Confederacy on April 22, Lincoln and Seward supported the experienced army engineer Montgomery Meigs to replace him. But the secretary of war, Simon Cameron, waffled for several weeks before appointing Meigs. By the time he did, on June 13, the Northern military force was rapidly expanding. After the Union loss at Bull Run in July, the buildup far outpaced the ability of the government to provide supplies. At the time, there were few government-run military factories. The staffs of government purchasing agencies included people of doubtful loyalty to the Union. A large percentage of supplies were acquired through ostensibly reliable private contractors, who, as it turned out, frequently overcharged the government, engaged in bribery, skimmed money, or provided inferior matériel.

Those in the Lincoln administration most closely connected with corrupt practices were War Secretary Cameron, Secretary of the Navy Gideon Welles, and John Frémont, commander of the Department of the West. Of the three, Welles was the least culpable. The rapid military buildup led him to arrange early purchases of vessels through his brother-in-law, George D. Morgan, a wholesale grocer with little previous expertise in ships. Morgan took a commission of 2.5 percent, earning him in five months $90,000 (the equivalent of about $2.3 million today).[81] When the hiring of Morgan was blasted as "reprehensible" nepotism, Welles publicly defended himself in a long statement, explaining that he had been "forced into the open market to make sudden and prompt purchases, on a large scale," and that his relative seemed like a plausible buyer.[82] Welles's reasoning was sound. Morgan purchased eighty-nine vessels, mostly merchant ships slated to be modified for military use, for $3.5 million—a fair price, for the time.[83]

Simon Cameron was on far shakier ground. Cameron, whose "very name," Lincoln himself conceded, "stinks in the nostrils of the people for corruption," was a poor choice as secretary of war.[84] He was awarded the post because he was an ex-Democrat (thus counterbalancing ex-Whigs in the cabinet) and because of his help in winning Pennsylvania's delegates for Lincoln at the 1860 Republican convention. Cameron, who raised all kinds of red flags among politicians who warned Lincoln against appointing him, was not so much corrupt in office as he was incompetent. He ordered the purchase of rifles at $15 apiece that the government had previously rejected and had sold for $2; after Cameron repurchased the rifles, they proved worthless to the army and were sold for $3.50 to private speculators. He hired as his main purchasing agent a friend, the newspaper editor Alexander Cummings, who made bizarre purchases, such as straw hats and linen pants; seventy-five thousand pairs of shoes at the high price of $2.50 a pair; and senseless items like Scotch ale, port wine, herring, and twenty-three barrels of pickles.[85]

Cameron favored his home state, Pennsylvania, as when he arranged for one thousand cavalry horses to be bought from two Pennsylvanians at more than three times the prevailing price. Nearly half of the horses proved to be unusable. Cameron's cronyism extended to his appointees to the War Department, a quarter of whom were from Pennsylvania.

Cronyism, of course, was hardly limited to Cameron. Other cabinet heads also exercised patronage, as did Lincoln. The president, however, reserved his most important uses of patronage for the cause of winning the war and ending slavery, as in his backroom maneuvering to gain votes for the Thirteenth Amendment, which abolished slavery.

Abolishing slavery was also the goal of General John Frémont in Missouri, but he overstepped the boundaries of his military position by proclaiming freedom to enslaved persons in the Western Department. Lincoln's revocation of Frémont's local emancipation order, controversial in his day and ever since, has understandably garnered great attention from historians. There is now little doubt that Lincoln took this action because of his fear over losing the border states. There was also the constitutional issue of a field general taking the kind of action reserved for the president.

It should be noted, however, that Lincoln did not dismiss Frémont because of his emancipation order. Frémont made public his order on August 30, 1861, and was not fired until early November. That two-month period witnessed evidence not only of Frémont's weakness as a military leader but also his inefficiency in supplying troops. With government money, he purchased at $22 apiece the very rifles that Cameron had sold cheaply to speculators—rifles so defective that they were liable to cause severe accidents for those who fired them. Also, Frémont was surrounded by officials of doubtful reputation who saw the sudden infusion of government funds as a means of making quick money. Profiteering and bribery thrived under Frémont. Lincoln, who described Missouri as a place where "every foul bird comes abroad, and every dirty reptile rises up," got direct word of the shenanigans in Frémont's department when he sent his longtime friend, the Illinois congressman Elihu B. Washburne, to investigate the situation there.[86] In mid-October 1861, Washburne telegrammed the president from St. Louis that "the robberies, the frauds, the peculations in the govt. which have already come to our knowledge, are absolutely frightful."[87]

Had double-dealing been confined to a handful of people, Lincoln could have rapidly snuffed it out, but it was widespread in the opening phase of the war. Supplying the troops was a chaotic process. Most military supplies came from individual states, often from individual localities and local contractors who were not under the eye of government inspectors. Contractors' fraud created confusion and suffering for Northern military volunteers. The New York congressman Charles H. Van Wyck condemned corrupt contractors as "worse than traitors in arms. . . . [They] feast and fatten on the misfortunes of the nation, while patriot blood is crimsoning the plains of the south and bodies of their countrymen are mouldering in the dust."[88] There was hardly any aspect of a soldier's daily life that was unaffected. Rifle shells were frequently filled with sawdust rather than gunpowder. As one historian notes, "For sugar, [military purchasers] often got sand; for coffee, rye; for leather, something no better than brown paper; for sound horses and mules, spavined beasts and dying donkeys; and for serviceable muskets and pistols . . . the refuse of shops and foreign armories."[89]

Military suppliers produced enormous quantities of low-quality cloth. Because Southern cotton was scarce and the supply of Northern wool was uncoordinated, many uniforms manufactured early on were made of shoddy, a flimsy material consisting of multicolored scraps and rags ground to a pulp, glued, and pressed to create a cheap material that ripped quickly and became the bane of soldiers early in the war. Sellers of uniforms thrived on shoddy, for it was inexpensive to produce. There was an instant market—the rapidly expanding Union military—and a product very easy to supply at a huge profit. The result was cloth of highly inferior quality. (Oddly enough, Brooks Brothers in New York produced lots of shoddy.) Uniforms, tents, and blankets made of shoddy quickly tore or fell apart in poor weather.

Shoddy prompted jokes among popular humorists. In a widely re-printed squib, "Doesticks on 'Shoddy,'" the humor character Q. K. Philander Doesticks (one of Lincoln's favorites) assumed the persona of an Ellsworth Zouave dressed in a coat blown into rags by a gentle wind and breeches that disintegrated quickly, so that he went into battle "dressed only in a bayonet."[90] There also appeared a comic verse about a regiment in "shoddy uniforms" on parade:

> "March," said the colonel, "Forward march!"
> Crack went the seams in halves;
> A hundred steps, a hundred men
> Showed just two hundred calves.[91]

Henry Morford's 1863 book *The Days of Shoddy. A Novel of the Great Rebellion in 1861* described a swindling textile manufacturer who got rich on selling inferior cloth and tried to seduce the wife of an employee who was off serving in the military. In the novel, shoddy is not just cheap material but a symbol for rampant corruption among war contractors, whom Morford calls "an evil spawn of men," leeches who have "fastened upon the blood of the nation, and . . . will not let go until the victim has the last drop sucked away."[92] Morford writes, "Every shoddy contractor . . . has been a national murderer."

Newspapers of the time fulminated against "shoddy" contractors, who allegedly raked in money while the poor fought the war.

Opponents of Lincoln's administration used shoddy as a nickname for Republicans. The term became especially prominent in the presidential election year, 1864, when Democrats used it to brand the Republicans as corrupt. One Democratic journalist wrote, "The Lincoln Administration with its coterie of shoddy contractors and office-holders are prepared to do anything to retain power and patronage."[93] The typical Republican, declared a Democratic congressman, "may sing unending hosannas to the President of the U S, he may bow down to the shrine of shoddy and worship the ebony idol of Abolitionism; nay, Mr. Speaker, he may even be an apostle of the new gospel of 'Miscegenation;' but, sir, he is no friend of the Union—he is rather an insidious and implacable enemy."[94] Lincoln's presidency was labeled "a shoddy despotism," and the convention that nominated him for reelection was called "the Baltimore Shoddy Republican Convention."[95]

Nor was it just Democrats who used the word to denigrate Lincoln: Radical Republicans did, too. There was rich irony in John Frémont, who had overseen a swamp of corruption in Missouri, being touted as pure when Radicals backed him for the presidency in 1864. A speaker at a Frémont rally said that the choice between Frémont and Lincoln was the choice "between a gentlemen and a buffoon, between decent Fremont and indecent Lincoln—between principles and shoddy."[96] Another speaker at the rally announced, "I am ready to join with all honest, all sincere, and all earnest . . . American citizens who will defeat shoddy and shoddy's defenders."

The shoddy charge, however, was largely false after the first year of the war. By January 1862, the national government had taken over most military purchases from the states. From that time forward, corruption diminished notably.

Lincoln made wise appointments toward that goal. In January 1862 he replaced Cameron with Edwin Stanton, who was intent on cleaning up government purchasing. Disciplined and businesslike, despite his irascible nature, he launched a program to nationalize purchasing, most of which was placed under government inspection and control. Throughout the remainder of the war, he was ably assisted in this effort by Montgomery Meigs, Lincoln's quartermaster general.

The Quartermaster's Department, which before the war had been led for forty-two years by Thomas Jesup, had long dominated government spending, and its importance became even more pronounced under Meigs. In the course of the war, Meigs's department spent more than $1 billion, more than twice the amount of the combined spending of the Ordnance and Subsistence Bureaus and far more than the Navy Department, which spent $300 million.[97] Just as important, the Quartermaster's Department was staffed by a small army of Blondins—that is, people who were politically centrist. They were not blinded by ideology and thus not susceptible to being pulled left or right in the war effort. They had their noses to the purchasing grindstone. They led the effort to improve and regularize outfitting and transporting troops. At the same time, private production of military supplies gave way largely to nationalization. Government-run factories, arsenals, and bakeries multiplied. Centrifugal production was replaced in large part by centripetal production and purchasing. Spending by the federal government increased from just 2 percent of the total economy in 1860 to 20 percent in 1865, with 90 percent of that amount spent on the military.

Corruption declined not only because of increasing federal oversight of war expenses but also because of legislation backed by Lincoln. A congressional committee led by Charles H. Van Wyck prepared two reports of more than a thousand pages, each exposing the frauds committed by the government agents during the first year of the war. In reply, Lincoln gave a speech to Congress in which he explained that in the months just after Fort Sumter, government purchasing agencies could not be fully trusted because they harbored many Confederate-leaning officials. With "so large a number of disloyal persons" in these agencies, Lincoln said, the cabinet members assigned many purchasing duties to "citizens favorably known for their ability, loyalty, and patriotism."[98]

The famous sign on President Harry Truman's desk that read "The Buck Stops Here" describes Lincoln's taking responsibility for his subordinates' dealings with contractors.[99] Throughout the speech he declared that he had "authorized and directed" various cabinet members to hire questionable contractors such as George D. Morgan, Alexander Cummings, and New York bankers hired by Secretary of Treasury Salmon Chase, even though there's no evidence he was closely connected to the hirings.

Lincoln took antifraud action by creating a three-man board consisting of his campaign manager David Davis, the St. Louis merchant Hugh Campbell, and Joseph Holt of Kentucky, a former Democrat turned Radical Republican. The reform activity spearheaded by the board and by Charles Van Wyck's committee led to the passage of the False Claims Act, designed to "prevent and punish frauds upon the Government of the United States." Passed by Congress on March 2, 1863, and signed by Lincoln on the same day, the act allowed people unaffiliated with the government to file actions against contractors on behalf of the government. Also known as the Lincoln Law or the Whistleblower Law, the False Claims Act during the Civil War led to the courts-martial and imprisonment of private contractors and military personnel involved in procurement. The Whistleblower Law, which has been expanded and toughened over the years, proved to be one of the most potent legal legacies of Lincoln's administration. In recent times, it has led to the recovery of billions of dollars in fraudulent claims involving government spending programs such as the military and health care.[100]

One of the unexpected results of Lincoln's encounters with corruption was the degree to which they contributed to his antislavery agenda. Two officials he dismissed, Frémont and Cameron, were associated with both fraudulent purchasing and antislavery activity—Frémont with his emancipation order in Missouri and Cameron with his call for arming blacks. Although Lincoln considered these antislavery actions premature, it is notable that he did not treat these men harshly after he fired them. He appointed Frémont as the head of the Mountain Department, and he reassigned Cameron as minister to Russia. Lincoln appeared to know that proclaiming emancipation and arming African Americans were measures he would soon adopt.

The fight against fraudulent purchasing brought him ever closer to taking positive action toward emancipation. The antifraud warrior Charles Van Wyck was fiercely antislavery—so much so that he nearly got into a duel with a Southern congressman who "spoke of Massachusetts burning witches in the ancient times." Van Wyck declared, "Does he not know that your own people burn slaves at the stake, and it seems to awaken no horror in your minds?"[101] Van Wyck avoided assassination only because a notebook and newspaper he carried in his breast pocket shielded his heart from a bowie knife thrust into him when three thugs assaulted him near the Capitol.

By far the most important antislavery figure linked with anticorruption reform was the Michigan senator Jacob M. Howard, who was a principal congressional advocate of the False Claims Act and a leading voice for emancipation. An unofficial member of Lincoln's kitchen cabinet, Howard advised the president to refuse peace overtures from the South during the war, and he wrote Lincoln saying that the Emancipa-

James M. Ashley

tion Proclamation was "mighty." He added, "It is a terrible weapon, & for one I hope & trust it will never be recalled,—never!"[102] He worked closely with Lincoln on promoting the Thirteenth Amendment and is credited with contributing to its language. After Lincoln's death, he was a major force behind the Fourteenth Amendment, granting citizenship to those born in the United States, and the Fifteenth Amendment, which gave the vote to African American males.

The issue of corruption and antislavery activism also surrounded another of Lincoln's allies, the Ohio representative James M. Ashley. In Ashley's case, questionable ethics on financial matters came with an unyielding devotion to emancipation. Ashley obtained the surveyor generalship of Colorado for a political contact, Francis M. Case, from whom he hoped to gain insider information about the future sale of land through which the Pacific Railroad would pass. "I will probably be chairman of the Committee on Territories," Ashley wrote Case, "and then I will know all the proposed expenditures in the Territories, and post you in *advance*."[103] But Case, upon assuming office, did not engage in land speculation, and Ashley did not make his fortune in real estate.

If wire-pulling failed Ashley in this situation, it aided him in pushing the Thirteenth Amendment through Congress. Patronage promises, arm-twisting, and, it seems, hard cash were tools Ashley used. Lincoln worked closely with Ashley and others on the amendment. Dedicated to abolishing slavery definitively, Lincoln may have turned a blind eye here to shady practices. In any case, he had lengthy talks in the White House with wavering congressmen, to whom he said that passing the amendment would end the war. Enough Democrats were persuaded to vote for the amendment that it passed the House on January 31, 1865. Although presidential verification was not required, Lincoln broke with tradition and emphasized his association with the historic amendment on February 1, when he signed the resolution submitting it to the states for ratification, which occurred on December 6, 1865.

The statement that "the greatest measure of the nineteenth century was passed by corruption, aided and abetted by the purest man in America," attributed by David Donald and others to Thaddeus Stevens, who utters it in Steven Spielberg's film *Lincoln*, is almost surely apocryphal.[104] But unlike many ersatz Lincoln stories, it contains a germ of truth.

By 1865, it was clear that the war, under Lincoln's guidance, had brought order and discipline in many areas: economic policy, international diplomacy, mail delivery, and control of government spending. Although Emerson exaggerated when he had written that the war systematized "everything," it did systematize much, in ways that changed

American governance forever. And Emerson was wholly accurate in calling Lincoln the man exactly appropriate for the occasion.

Effective handling of the economy and the government, however, was important only if it was matched by skill in overseeing the Union military effort. At the same time that Lincoln struggled with administrative challenges, he tackled even stiffer military ones. The captain of the ship of state also learned how to be an innovative commander in chief.

Commander in Chief

Military success results from interacting factors, including weaponry, war strategy, battlefield tactics, the ability of officers to train and motivate troops, and contingency. The latter includes chance occurrences and the response of troops to what is known as the fog of war (that is, the confusion of battle). Among chance occurrences of the Civil War, perhaps most important was McClellan's discovery before Antietam of Lee's battle plan, which had been written on a paper that was used to wrap three cigars discarded by a Confederate soldier and found by a Union one. As for the fog of war, both sides suffered greatly. Civil War battles raged in a haze—the dense smoke produced by exploding gunpowder from rifles and cannon. As a Union volunteer explained, "Soldiers do not take aim after the first shot because the smoke is so thick, but they only bring the gun to the Shoulder & and then pull."—seconded by a Virginia veteran who reported that in battle "we couldn't see a thing, but away we fired as fast as we could load, blazing away in every direction."[1]

Chance and confusion aside, Lincoln's leadership was crucial to the Northern war effort. Unlike his Confederate opponent, the West Pointer Jefferson Davis, Lincoln was a military tyro at the start. But he was a quick learner. He became an expert in military matters and, in several areas, was well ahead of his officers and government advisers.

The fact that several of his subordinates disagreed with him politically or personally did not influence his dealings with them. Winning the war was his goal, and he did not allow incidental insubordination or petty insults to interfere with reaching it. When he did not see success, he prodded and pushed. When success came, as in the cases of Ulysses S. Grant and William Tecumseh Sherman, he backed off and gave his generals rein to follow their instincts.

Despite the North's superiority to the South in manpower and, eventually, firepower, things often went badly for the Union, and there were moments when it seemed quite possible that the Confederacy would win the war.

It was Lincoln's persistence in pursuing effective weapons, strategy, and officers that made the key difference in the North's victory.

WEAPONS WORRIES

Lincoln had frustrating experiences with weapons. Just before the war, James Buchanan's secretary of war, John B. Floyd of Virginia, seeing that a national crisis was approaching, transferred thousands of rifles from Northern arsenals to Southern ones, diminishing the North's weapons supply in the early months of the war. Although the North had advantages over the South in raw materials, factories, and skilled workers, it had to play catch-up in weapons production because of Floyd's action. The North went with tried-and-true weapons that could be readily manufactured. The overwhelming majority of the nearly three million small arms provided by the Union's Ordnance Department for military service during the Civil War were muskets that were cumbersome to load, prime, and fire.

This is not what Lincoln wanted. He had a penchant for engineering that fed his fascination with new munitions. Advances in weaponry rarely escaped his eye. When he learned of a newly designed weapon, he usually made a point of watching it tested.

But few of the new weapons saw battlefield use. There were major impediments to their adoption. A main one was the head of the Ordnance Department, Brigadier General James W. Ripley. Largely forgotten today, Ripley had a big impact on the Civil War. Age sixty-six when he was made a lieutenant colonel and appointed as the chief of ordnance on April 23, 1861, he was averse to innovations in weaponry. During the war, it was difficult to mass-produce novel weapons. But Ripley's resistance to the new went well beyond the challenges of wartime production. Ripley was old-fashioned. He lived up to his nickname, "Ripley Van Winkle." As the military historians Clayton Newell and Charles Shrader note, Ripley "had many doubts about the wisdom of adopting new weapons," and he proved "resistant to the appeals of inventors, contractors, and their supporters in Congress and the executive branch."[2]

Lincoln's attitude was exactly the opposite. He was radically open to fresh ideas about weapons.

To appreciate his attitude, it is useful to review rifles and guns available for widespread use at the time. Those who had fought in the American Revolution had used smoothbore muskets that were hard to load and often inaccurate when fired. Loading a musket was a multistep process that involved, among other actions, tearing open a paper cartridge with one's teeth, pouring the black gunpowder it contained down the gun barrel, inserting a round bullet into the barrel, drawing a steel ramrod from its groove, ramming the charge to the bottom of the barrel, withdrawing the rammer, returning it to its holder, pulling the gun's hammer to full cock, and firing. Loading and firing took around a minute for neophytes and about fifteen seconds for very experienced soldiers.

Improvements came in the first half of the nineteenth century when muskets were rifled—a term that referred to grooves cut inside the gun barrel so that the bullet, which was now cylindro-conoidal instead of round, spun when shot, thereby flattening its trajectory and greatly improving range and accuracy. Most Civil War soldiers carried the rifled musket into battle. Though more deadly than its eighteenth-century predecessor, the rifled musket still took time to load and fire. The powder container, the ramrod, the muzzle-loaded bullet, and the rest were still required. In the frenzy of battle, miscues in loading resulted in many unfired guns. After Gettysburg, for example, among the 27,574 muskets the US Army recovered on the battlefield, nearly half contained undischarged bullets due to errors in loading caused by nervousness, battle fright, or inexperience. A fifth of the muzzles contained three to ten unused rounds.[3]

An attractive alternative to the muzzle loader was the breech-loading rifle, which permitted a cartridge or shell to be loaded into a gun's breech, a chamber near the trigger. The advantage of the breechloader was that it permitted rapid firing. The single-shot Sharps breechloader was introduced by Christian Sharps in 1859, followed the next year by the Spencer repeater, which held seven shells, and the Henry repeater, which held sixteen. Lever operated, the Spencer and Henry repeating rifles could fire twenty to thirty rounds per minute.

However, the percentage of breechloaders used in the Civil War was relatively small due to limitations in weapons production and the persistence of reactionary attitudes in the Ordnance Department. In the course of the war only about one in six soldiers carried breechloaders, which were reserved mainly for the cavalry. The typical soldier on both sides was armed with a single-shot muzzle-loading musket. But Lincoln pushed hard for breechloaders, and his support for them paid off. His favorite weapon, the durable seven-shot Spencer repeater, was, as James McPherson notes, the best shoulder weapon of the war and gave the Union cavalry a distinct advantage in the final fifteen months of the war.[4]

Lincoln promoted other weapons, too. One of his prize discoveries was the so-called coffee mill gun, capable of shooting fifty rounds a minute—a fraction of the firing rate of today's assault rifles, but still impressive. After seeing the coffee mill tested twice in 1861, Lincoln ordered ten of the guns for McClellan. Over the course of the war, the president ordered fifty more, some of which were used briefly in battle. But at more than $1,000 apiece, the coffee mills were not only prohibitively expensive (a musket cost, on average, $20, a breechloader, $36); they also met with the usual huffiness from the Ordnance Department.[5] It would not be until after the war that the coffee mill, in the improved version of the Gatling gun, was officially adopted by the US Army.

Lincoln kept up his keen interest in discoveries. He considered many forms of arms: light and heavy artillery, submarines, mines, rockets, iron-clad ships, explosives, observation balloons, and flame throwers. He was quick to go to the Navy Yard or a nearby field to see weapons tested, some of them successfully, others not. His interest in the new products was frequently technical. For example, when his curiosity was piqued by a new kind of gunpowder proposed by Isaac M. Diller, he asked seventeen probing questions about its ignition, weight, durability, and performance in battle.[6]

Military innovations in the Navy took hold, particularly the development of ironclads and the use of long-range shells, which were of great use in the bombardment of Vicksburg and Charleston in 1863. But given the possibilities of weapons Lincoln judged, he must have been disappointed by the backwardness of many weapons being used. It may well be, as some contend, that the war would have ended as early as 1862 had most of the Union army moved beyond muskets.

POLITICAL GENERALS AND WEST POINTERS

In his choice of generals, Lincoln tried to create unity out of diversity. His generals fell into two main groups: ones from the regular army, many of them West Pointers, and others called political generals because they represented some voting bloc or ethnic group, useful for recruiting volunteer soldiers from different regions and different backgrounds.

The relationship between the two groups of generals was testy. The West Pointers often looked down on the political generals as amateurs, while the political generals put themselves in the common-man tradition of the citizen soldier that reached back to the Battle of New Orleans, when Andrew Jackson defeated the British with a ragtag group of average types.

Besides this overall tension between the two groups, there was a good amount of disagreement or one-upmanship among individual generals. In the Carolinas, generals David Hunter and J. G. Foster feuded over who should lead certain regiments. In Missouri, General John G. Schofield became so angry when his commanding officer, Samuel Curtis, did not allow him to go on the offensive that he threatened to resign his commission. A similar threat came from a leading German American general, Franz Sigel, who felt he was being drastically shortchanged in troops and supplies. Another German American general, Carl Schurz, quarreled bitterly over strategy with General Oliver O. Howard. In an ongoing controversy, General John A. McClernand of Illinois, who had recruited many regiments, boiled with resentment over playing second fiddle to Grant and Sherman in the West.

Lincoln tried to rise above such "*family* controversies," as he called them.[7] His eye was trained on winning the war. This is not to say he made no mistakes; he did, as when he stuck too long with generals like John McClernand or Nathaniel Banks. But, by and large, he did not espouse either an anti–West Point view or an anti-citizen soldier view. Just as his embrace of culture went from top to bottom, so did his survey of generals. He shied from emphasizing one political group in choosing generals. He made sure to appoint both Republicans and Democrats in an effort to create a Blondin-like balance in the military, comparable to the balance in his cabinet. His Illinois friend Leonard Swett recalled, "In his conduct of the war he acted upon the theory that but one thing was necessary, and that was a united North. He had all shades of sentiments and opinions to deal with, and the consideration was always presented to his mind, How can I hold these discordant elements together?"[8]

A main way to do so was to inspire a shared devotion to the Union war effort. He was confident that the war would seal officers and soldiers alike. In this respect, he differed from a previous war president, James Polk, who during the Mexican War selected commanders on a partisan basis—ones who were either loyal Democrats, like Jefferson Davis and Franklin Pierce, or were then unaffiliated with a party, like Zachary Taylor.[9] (Polk's strategy backfired when the Whig Party chose Taylor as its presidential candidate in 1848.) Lincoln's choices, unlike Polk's, were notable for their heterogeneity.

The political generals have, understandably, a poor reputation among historians. Many of them proved to be inept on the battlefield. But Lincoln believed he had good reason to utilize political generals, who numbered more than one hundred in the course of the war. By avoiding partisanship, he responded to a political landscape whose complexity he appreciated. He also put up with shifts and dodges of his political generals. Some who began the war as strong Democrats ended up as antislavery Republicans, and vice versa.

He looked for battlefield achievement, not political loyalty, from his generals. When General Carl Schurz argued that Lincoln needed more Republicans like himself as officers, and fewer Democrats, Lincoln wrote, "I must say I need success more than I need sympathy, and that I have not seen the so much greater evidence of getting success from my sympathizers, than from those who are denounced as the contrary," including some generals who "have been bitterly, and repeatedly, denounced to me as secession sympathizers."[10]

This political open-mindedness put him into conflict with Radical Republicans in Congress. Because the first two major battles of the war,

Bull Run, on July 21, 1861, and, three months later, Ball's Bluff, had been lopsided defeats, Congress created the Committee on the Conduct of the War, designed to investigate the ongoing Union military effort, including officers, war strategy, supplies, and other matters. Four of the committee's seven members—senators Benjamin F. Wade of Ohio and Zachariah Chandler of Michigan, representatives George W. Julian of Indiana and John Covode of Pennsylvania—were Radical Republicans. Because General George McClellan, a Democrat, had been ultimately responsible for the Ball's Bluff debacle, the committee took umbrage with him and everything he stood for: the Democratic Party, West Point, generals from the regular army, and a war not aimed at emancipation. Throughout the war, the committee criticized West Pointers and promoted political generals of a particular variety: hard-nosed abolitionists devoted to the war against slavery.

Lincoln, however, knew that a commitment to abolitionism was not a prerequisite for effective generalship. As he wrote to Frank Blair, some of those who were most sympathetic to his antislavery views were the least effective on the battlefield. By the same token, a general who was distanced from his views might well help rescue the Union.

That is how he initially regarded George B. McClellan, who held hidebound views on race and slavery. To this day, many wonder how Lincoln could have put up with McClellan's dilatory battlefield tactics and his insults (the general loathed Lincoln and let him know it). The answer lies in McClellan's undeniable magnetism and his professional record. McClellan had the perfect résumé: second in the class of 1846 at West Point; creditable service in the Mexican War; knowledge of military engineering and tactics; useful information from observing the Crimean War in the 1850s; and four years of leadership as a railroad executive in Illinois and Ohio, in which capacity he once dealt with a lanky Sucker lawyer who would later be his commander in chief. As the major general of the Ohio Volunteers in June and July 1861, McClellan defeated Confederate forces in western Virginia, earning him the nickname the Young Napoleon and paving the way for the admittance in 1863 of West Virginia as the nation's thirty-fifth state. A man below middle height whose clipped mustache, square jaw, and direct eyes gave him an appealing look, Little Mac had a taste for crisp uniforms with gold buttons and epaulettes.

GEORGE B. McCLELLAN

On July 22, 1861, the day after the defeat at Bull Run, Lincoln summoned McClellan to Washington. When the general arrived at the capital four days later, he found the Union officers and soldiers discouraged and disorganized. Many of them frequented the saloons and whorehouses of Washington, a city in peril of Confederate attack. "All was chaos," McClellan later recalled, "and the streets, hotels, and bar-rooms were filled with drunken officers and men absent from their regiments without leave—a perfect pandemonium."[11] McClellan issued an order banning his men from leaving camp except on rare occasions. He instituted regular drills and exercises. By the fall he had transformed "a collection of raw, dispirited, and disorganized regiments" into "a hundred thousand men, trained and disciplined, organized and equipped, animated by the highest spirit and deserving of the fond name of The Grand Army of the Potomac."[12]

On November 1, 1861, McClellan took the place of the aging Winfield Scott as general in chief of the Northern armies. During the winter of 1861–62, McClellan contracted typhoid, which delayed major action on the part of his army, as did the terrible snows that year. Lincoln, increasingly restive, ordered a major move by all Union armies on February 22, 1862, Washington's birthday. The order was answered in the West by Halleck's armies, which had already been winning battles, but in the East the war prospects remained murky.

On March 11, Lincoln, dissatisfied with McClellan's performance as general in chief, dismissed him from the position and restricted him to the command of the Army of the Potomac. McClellan, who had learned at West Point the strategy of seizing key enemy locations in major battles, had previously proposed a master war plan by which he would first take Richmond, the Confederate capital, and then sweep south and take other cities in succession. That plan having been rejected as quixotic, McClellan now proposed to take Richmond from below by circling south by sea to Fort Monroe and then proceeding seventy miles northwest up the Virginia Peninsula to Richmond. Lincoln, who wanted McClellan to keep his force between Washington and Richmond, cast doubt on the plan, but when it was approved by eight of twelve generals who voted on it, he reluctantly gave in.

An armada of nearly four hundred ships carried more than 120,000 men, along with 15,000 horses, and vast quantities of weapons and supplies to the Peninsula, where McClellan spent three months moving slowly to the outskirts of Richmond. His sluggishness enabled the Confederates to amass there and repulse his army in a series of battles known as the Seven Days, a bloody standoff that resulted in his ignominious retreat down the Peninsula. To make matters worse, he stalled on the Peninsula for two weeks instead of following orders on August 4 to travel north immediately to reinforce General John Pope, who was under threat of an imminent attack by Robert E. Lee's Army of Northern Virginia near Manassas. It appears that McClellan, sour over his recent losses, intentionally procrastinated. The Young Napoleon wrote Lincoln that one of his options was "to leave Pope to get out of his scrape."[13] That, essentially, is what he did by not promptly bolstering Pope, who later insisted that he could have defeated the rebels "if General McClellan had been in the least energetic or had had any genuine purpose to push his army to support mine." Second Manassas (or Second Bull Run) became as great a disaster for the Union as the first battle there had been. The North was demoralized once more.

At this point, Lincoln did something puzzling. He retained McClellan as the head of the Army of the Potomac. Many—especially Radical Republicans—harshly criticized his decision, which has been questioned ever since. But it's hard to gainsay Lincoln's own explanation: no better general was then available. He told his secretary John Hay, "Unquestionably [McClellan] has acted badly toward Pope! He wanted him to fail. That is unpardonable. But he is too useful just now to sacrifice."[14] Lincoln explained to Gideon Welles, "I must have McClellan to reorganize the army and bring it out of chaos."[15] *Chaos* was an apt word in the wake of Second Bull Run. No Union general was as capable of organizing and inspiring troops as McClellan.

He also had cutting-edge knowledge. McClellan introduced aeronautics to the US armed services by using gas-filled balloons to make observations near Washington and on the Peninsula. Like Lincoln, he showed keen interest in the latest weapons, although red tape and manufacturing issues made most of them unavailable. He was the first

American general to send regular telegraphs from the battlefield—a technological advance that eventually contributed to concerted action by the North; eight thousand miles of military telegraph lines were installed by 1865.[16] McClellan sent his messages by a freshly devised cipher. Lincoln, who spent much of his time in the telegraph office, learned the cipher and became the first president to witness war in what came close to real time.[17]

McClellan was also an expert in the tactics of both defensive war, involving trenches and piled logs, and frontal attacks. He used the frontal attack, albeit clumsily, on October 17, 1862, at Antietam, which proved to be a major turning point in the war. Having prior knowledge of Lee's battle plan, McClellan threw forces against the rebel army to stop its advance through Maryland. The battle was hardly the "glorious and complete victory" that he boasted of, but it halted Lee's northern invasion.[18] It enabled Lincoln to issue his Preliminary Emancipation Proclamation, and it made European powers think twice about interfering in the Civil War on the South's behalf.

Lincoln, however, was not satisfied. McClellan did not try to finish off Lee's army by pursuing him vigorously. A week after Antietam, McClellan telegrammed the excuse that nearly half of his horses were incapacitated. The president responded sharply, "I have just read your despatch about sore tongued and fatiegued [sic] horses. Will you pardon me for asking what the horses of your army have done since the battle of Antietam that fatigue anything?" Surely Lincoln was not pleased with McClellan's explanation that "my cavalry has been constantly employed in making reconnaissances, scouting, and picketing" and in fact "has performed harder service since the battle than before."[19]

The time had now come to remove McClellan from command. Despite his skills, he had chronic problems as a general. For one, he usually overestimated the size of the enemy by about 100 percent.[20] His fearful imagination, along with faulty reconnaissance by his detective scout Allan Pinkerton, often inflated the enemy's army, which in fact was far smaller than his own army in almost all situations. His many requests for additional troops led Lincoln to compare him to a monkey in a comic story whose ever-growing tail threatened to wrap around and smother him.[21]

In McClellan's eyes, however, it was Lincoln who was the simian. He called the president "the 'Gorilla'" and "nothing more than a well meaning baboon."[22] Infuriated by Lincoln's acerbic telegram after Antietam, he wrote his wife, "[T]he good of the country requires me to submit to all this from men whom I know to be greatly my inferiors socially, intellectually & morally! There was never a truer epithet applied to a certain individual than that of 'Gorilla.'"

The comment typified McClellan's arrogance. More than once, he indicated that he was the de facto leader of the nation. When he first arrived in Washington, he wrote his wife: "I find myself in a new & strange position here—Presdt, Cabinet, Genl Scott & all deferring to me—by some strange operation of magic I seem to have become *the* power of the land. I almost think that were I to win some small success now I could become Dictator or anything else that might please me[.]"[23]

A graduate of elite Philadelphia schools and the University of Pennsylvania, and fluent in three foreign languages, McClellan dismissed Lincoln as "an idiot," "destitute of refinement—certainly in no sense a gentleman," and "'an old stick'—& of pretty poor timber at that."[24] McClellan's view of the president as uncouth and vulgar went along with his admiration of the Southern Cavaliers he faced in battle. Generals like Robert E. Lee and Jeb Stuart followed the Southern code of honor that were part of the aristocratic Cavalier ideal—an ideal often rooted in family history, as in the case of Lee, who was descended from Richard Lee, a supporter of Charles I who had fled to Virginia in 1641 and had pledged to keep the colony loyal to the Crown. McClellan admired Lee, who in turn called McClellan the Union's greatest general "by all odds."[25] One historian has argued that the battlefield timidity of several Union generals resulted from combined envy and fear of imposing

Southern commanders; with McClellan, at least, there seems to be truth to the idea, especially in light of his disdain for the shambling, humble Lincoln.[26]

The president felt his contempt. Once, when he, William Seward, and John Hay visited McClellan in his Washington home, they were told to sit in the parlor to await McClellan's return from a wedding. When the general arrived an hour later, he went directly upstairs. The president and his party waited for another half hour only to be told by an orderly that McClellan had gone to bed and would see no one.

The snub didn't ruffle the self-confident Lincoln. What he wanted was results, regardless of personal loyalty. He did not get the results he expected from McClellan, whom he fired on November 5, 1862, just after the Republicans fared poorly in the midterm elections—a sign, Lincoln thought, that voters wanted a more vigorous prosecution of the war. Lincoln replaced McClellan with Ambrose Burnside as the commander of the Army of the Potomac.

The choice proved mistaken. Burnside directed what became a horrendous fiasco at Fredericksburg, Virginia, where thousands of his soldiers charged up Marye's Heights and were mowed down by Confederates who were protected by a stone wall.[27] In January he led the notorious Mud March, in which his troops were stopped by foul weather while pursuing the enemy. Burnside offered his resignation, which Lincoln accepted, putting General Joseph Hooker in command of the eastern army.

The appointment was surprising because Hooker had denounced Lincoln and his administration as "imbecile and 'played out.'" The North, Hooker insisted, needed "a dictator, and the sooner the better."[28] As usual, Lincoln wanted results, and he was willing to test out the self-confident Hooker, who had performed competently under McClellan. He wrote Hooker, assigning him to the command of the Army of the Potomac. Lincoln praised Hooker's bravery and ambition but added, "I have heard, in such way as to believe it, of your recently saying that both the Army and the Government needed a Dictator. Of course it was not *for* this, but in spite of it, that I have given you the command. Only those generals who gain successes, can set up dictators. What I now ask of you is military success, and I will risk the dictatorship."[29]

Six feet tall and erect in posture, the sandy-haired, blue-eyed Hooker had the kind of charisma and enthusiasm that appealed to soldiers. In the first month of his command, Hooker succeeded in getting the Army of the Potomac into excellent shape through drills and discipline. His nickname, Fighting Joe, assigned to him by a journalist, gave him an aura of indomitable toughness (but he disliked the name, which, he thought, made him sound like Fighting Fool).[30] In early April 1863, Lincoln and a few others, including his son Tad and the journalist Noah Brooks, visited Hooker's Virginia camp, opposite Fredericksburg. The president was impressed by Hooker's army, but he balked when the general kept repeating, "When I get to Richmond," or "After we have taken Richmond." Lincoln told Brooks with a sigh, "That is the most depressing thing about Hooker. It seems that he is over-confident."[31]

That was an understatement. Hooker was sure that he would easily handle Lee. He boasted to fellow officers: "I have the finest army the sun ever shone on. . . . My plans are perfect, and when I start to carry them out, may God have mercy on General Lee, for I will have none."[32] As it turned out, God had mercy on General Lee. Hooker devised a flanking strategy against Lee at Fredericksburg that ended up with Hooker being surprised by Stonewall Jackson near the village of Chancellorsville, where Lee's army, though less than half as large as Hooker's, launched a multipronged attack that forced Fighting Joe to retreat. Chancellorsville was another disheartening loss for the North, which gained only moderate relief from the fact that Stonewall Jackson was accidentally killed by friendly fire there. Hooker soon resigned from his command, but not altogether from the army; he later served well in the western theater under Grant at Lookout Mountain and Chattanooga and under Sherman in the Atlanta Campaign.

Lincoln next gave the command of the Army of the Potomac to the thin, hatchet-faced George Meade, whose men called him "a damned old goggle-eyed snapping turtle" or "a four-eyed old devil" because of his ever-present glasses and his hot temper.[33] Meade's assignment was to stop Lee's post-Chancellorsville invasion of the North, which he did magnificently in early July at Gettysburg, Pennsylvania. Lincoln, like the rest of the North, exulted over the victory, but his joy rapidly faded when Meade failed to destroy Lee's retreating army. Enraged, Lincoln said at a cabinet meeting, "There is bad faith somewhere. Meade has been pressed and urged, but only one of his generals was for an immediate attack, was ready to pounce on Lee; the rest held back. What does it mean? . . . Great God! What does it mean?"[34] He penned a letter to Meade in which he praised the Gettysburg victory but added, "[M]y dear general, I do not believe you appreciate the magnitude of the misfortune involved in Lee's escape." The war, he wrote, would have "ended" but now "will be prolonged indefinitely." He added, "Your golden opportunity is gone, and I am distressed immeasureably because of it."[35]

Painful words, but Meade, apparently, never knew of them, for Lincoln did not send the letter—a typical act of tactful restraint on Lincoln's part, who often held back letters he thought might be inflammatory or hurtful. Not given to holding grudges, Lincoln wrote to another Union officer a week later that he was "profoundly grateful for what was done [at Gettysburg], without criticism for what was not done." He praised Meade as "a brave and skillful officer, and a true man."[36]

HALLECK, LIEBER, AND THE TURN TO HARD WAR

A major reason for the insufficiency of many Union generals in 1862–63 was the indecisiveness of Lincoln's general in chief, Henry W. Halleck.

As with McClellan, Lincoln has been questioned over the years about his utilizing for the long term Henry Halleck, who served as general in chief from July 1862 to March 1864. Once again, stellar credentials help provide an explanation. Like McClellan, Halleck had had an outstanding record at West Point. In 1846 he published a book on army strategy, fortification, and tactics called *Elements of Military Art and Science*, which became a standard text in American military theory. During the Mexican War, he was the military secretary of California and a main author of the state's constitution. He stayed on there and became a highly successful lawyer and businessman. In 1861, he published a tome of nearly a thousand pages on international law.

Impressed by this record, Lincoln in November 1861 had General McClellan appoint Halleck to replace John Frémont as commander of the Department of Missouri, which included Missouri, Wisconsin, Illinois, Arkansas, Iowa, and western Kentucky. McClellan informed Halleck that he was to assume not only military command but also "the far more difficult task of reducing chaos to order, . . . and of reducing to a point of economy consistent with the interests and necessities of the State a system of reckless expenditure and fraud perhaps unheard of before in the history of the world."[37]

Halleck brought some stability to Missouri and oversaw Grant's victories at Fort Henry and Fort Donelson. Halleck was quick to take credit for Grant's successes and to magnify his own leadership in the occupation of the strategically located city of Corinth, Mississippi. With a tremendous force of 100,000, three of Halleck's generals, Don Carlos Buell, George H. Thomas, and John Pope, advanced slowly on Corinth—so slowly that the outnumbered rebel soldiers there, having much advance warning, vacated the city before the arrival of the Union army. There were few casualties on either side.

Corinth made Halleck seem brilliant, justifying his sobriquet Old Brains. A balding man with protruding eyes, a double chin, and a paunch, Halleck was nervous and irritable. He habitually rubbed his

HENRY W. HALLECK

elbows when under pressure. But in the spring of 1862, he was a hero throughout the North. Lincoln summoned him east in June, when McClellan was still tangled up with Lee on the Peninsula. In his new job as general in chief, Halleck gave military advice and acted as a buffer between Lincoln and his generals. In the latter capacity, Halleck proved useful. He took over administrative details involved in reassigning, appointing, and firing generals. He dealt with quarrels between officers, of which there were many.

As an adviser on military tactics and strategy, however, Halleck was only moderately successful. His main problem was that he shrank from giving generals explicit directions. He behaved as though officers on the battlefield knew far more about their situation than he did, and so he would leave immediate military decisions up to them. Halleck's effectiveness as commanding general diminished not long after he assumed the position, in the summer of 1862. Although he ordered McClellan out of the Peninsula, Little Mac's delay in carrying out the order, followed by Pope's loss at Second Bull Run, caused Halleck to collapse emotionally. Lincoln later remarked that after that battle Halleck "broke down—nerve and pluck all gone" and became "little more since that [time] than a first-rate clerk."[38] Unlike Lincoln, Halleck was not mentally tough enough to take devastating disappointment. Psychological and physical problems plagued him intermittently until Grant replaced him as general in chief in March 1864.

Because Lincoln himself, along with Secretary of War Stanton, took over much of the work of directing war strategy, why was Halleck kept on? For one thing, he adapted to the shifting direction of the war. He joined the movement toward hard war that in the end would yield the hammer and anvil campaign of Grant and Sherman.

By making this turn, Halleck participated in a transition in warfare that had implications not only for America but internationally. The transition is captured in a military historian's statement that "the story of Civil War strategy is one of general movement away from the Jominian to the Clausewitzian."[39] That is, an emphasis on maneuvering to seize key locations was largely replaced by one of assaulting enemy armies. Halleck and other West Pointers had been trained in the strategies and tactics of the Swiss military theorist Antoine Henri de Jomini, who argued for large armies putting intense pressure on strategic enemy points. Applying Enlightenment rationalism to war, Jomini devised a geometry of battlefield lines, vectors, triangles, and so on in an effort to make war a science. Halleck's 1846 *Elements of Military Art and Science*, which was full of geometrical references, owed much to Jomini.

The war had begun in Jominian fashion, with an emphasis on taking certain locations. McClellan caught the "On to Richmond!" bug early on, and his vision of sweeping through the South and seizing key cities resonated with Jomini's ideas about massed forces concentrating on strategic points. The same was true of Halleck's siege of Corinth with a huge army.

Massed armies directed at strategic places made sense in earlier wars, when the inaccuracy and short range of flintlock muskets forced soldiers to line up and fire together in the hope that some bullets would reach their targets. But in the era of more powerful weapons—the rifled musket, the minié ball, improved artillery, and on occasion, the repeating breechloader—greater distances and more dispersed formations became effective. Also, the "civilized," chivalric form of war stressed by the eighteenth-century theorists gave way in the nineteenth century to a tougher form of war.

The main advocate of hard war was the Prussian military author Carl von Clausewitz. His classic work, *On War*, was published in German in 1832. Although the first English translation did not appear until 1873, some of the book's arguments were made available to Civil War leaders and soldiers through the writings of Francis Lieber.

Born in Berlin around 1798, Lieber fought in the Prussian army in the Napoleonic Wars before fleeing first to England and then to America, where he arrived in 1827. An intellectual fascinated by politics, social issues, and especially military matters, he wrote prolifically and entered academe. From 1835 to 1856 he taught at South Carolina College. In 1857, he moved to New York and assumed a professorship at Columbia College. In New York, during the 1840s Lieber became friendly with Henry Halleck. Their friendship blossomed during the Civil War and resulted in a professional association that would influence history.

Indeed, Halleck's most lasting achievement was his nurturing of Francis Lieber during the Civil War. In 1861–62, Halleck noticed a series of eight lectures that Lieber had given on guerrilla warfare, a matter of grave concern for Union generals, who were harassed by bands of partisan soldiers who had broken off from the Confederate army. Halleck asked Lieber to write a set of rules for dealing with guerrillas. After Lieber finished the project, he offered to be on a committee, under Halleck, that would write a general set of principles to structure the North's military efforts. Along with Edwin Stanton, Halleck commissioned the Prussian émigré and four generals to write a code of rules of war, to be distributed to Union military leaders.

Lieber was the main author of *Instructions for the Government of Armies of the United Stated in the Field*, which Lincoln authorized and issued as General Orders, No. 100. This publication, which contained 157 succinct articles, was simultaneously compassionate and tough, fair-minded and fierce. Its compassionate elements included its discouragement of torture, poison weapons, and needless cruelty toward noncombatants. It also mandated a respect for flags of truce, and it outlined ways of properly treating enemy prisoners. These restraints on war formed the basis of later military agreements, notably the Geneva Convention.

The tough side of Lieber's code related to the Clausewitzian recommendation of the use of great force in waging war. Lieber writes, "The more vigorously wars are pursued the better it is for humanity. Sharp wars are brief" (Article 29). Clausewitz had offered a similar idea in his *On War* of 1832: "Kind-hearted people might of course think there was some ingenious way to disarm or defeat an enemy without too much bloodshed. . . . Pleasant as it sounds, it is a fallacy that must be exposed: war is such a dangerous business that the mistakes which come from kindness are the very worst."[40]

That Lincoln approved General Orders, No. 100 and had it distributed among his officers reflects the fact that by 1863 he had developed ideas about war that were strikingly similar to Lieber's. The code quickly became associated with the president—so much so that at an international conference in Brussels in July 1874, Antoine Henri de Jomini announced, "The rules of President Lincoln to lessen the sufferings of war are fresh in the memories of us all. International struggles have an incontestable analogy to the civil war which rent the American Union."[41]

If Jomini felt the influence of Lincoln, the president had learned from Jomini early in the war, when he had read Halleck's book and other Jominian military manuals. In a letter to a French correspondent, Lincoln discussed the challenge of the South's having the advantage of holding interior lines because it was defending its own territory.[42] He came to realize, however, that this Jominian model need not stymie the Union effort. For one thing, the problem of communications on exterior lines was minimized by the telegraph, a new technology in war, just as transportation of troops and supplies were greatly enhanced by the railroad. Then, too, the recent weapons technology altered battlefield tactics.

In a larger sense, Lincoln could observe the effect that certain Northern strategies had on the South. The blockade of Southern ports had created immense shortages in the Confederacy, whose people suffered greatly even as their economy collapsed. Militarily, the North had the inherent advantage of superior numbers. Repeatedly, Lincoln or Congress called up large numbers of volunteers—400,000 on July 4, 1861; 500,000 more on July 22, the day after Bull Run; 300,000 on July 2, 1862, and the same number on August 4; and 500,000 on July 18, 1864.

In addition, the Enrollment Act of March 1863 instituted the draft, which made the 3.1 million Northern men between the ages of twenty and forty-five eligible for conscription. One could buy oneself out of the draft by paying $300 (about three quarters of a year's salary for an unskilled worker) or by hiring a substitute. Conscription, however, was handled ineffectively. The provision that allowed drafted men to buy their way out of military service made the North's effort appear as a poor man's war. Coming on the heels of the Emancipation Proclamation, the situation made the poorer soldiers feel like they shouldered the burden of military duty merely to liberate enslaved blacks, about whom racist sentiment was endemic.

Antidraft passions boiled over in New York City in mid-July 1863, when thousands of working-class people, largely Irish, rampaged for two days through the city, murdering blacks, attacking businesses and newspaper offices, and burning the homes of the rich. Francis Lieber, who lived in an area affected by the rioting, reported to Halleck that "Negro children were killed in the street, like rats with clubs."[43] A contingent of Meade's army, along with the New York police force and the state militia, quelled the riots. But more than one hundred had been killed and three hundred wounded. The riots fueled a lingering resentment of the draft. In the end, only 7 percent of those whose names were listed in the draft saw military service, due to desertions, draft dodging, buying substitutes, or paying the commutation fee. Volunteers made up the bulk of Union soldiers and sailors throughout the war.

Irrespective of the draft, the North, with its large population, was able to put far greater numbers on the battlefield than did the South. Superior numbers, of course, do not guarantee victory. It was the way Lincoln used that manpower that made the real difference in the Civil War.

Increasingly, Lincoln replaced the strategy of targeting locations with one of attacking enemy armies simultaneously on several fronts. In his words, "I state my general idea of this war to be that we have the *greater* numbers, and the enemy has the *greater* facility of concentrating forces upon points of collision; that we must fail, unless we can find some way of making *our* advantage an over-match for *his*; and that this can only be done by menacing him with superior forces at *different* points, at the *same* time."[44]

Rejecting war pursued with squirt guns "charged with rose water," Lincoln assumed an approach to war that was visceral, elemental, rooted in physical combat and the natural world.[45] Here his youthful exposure to ferocious, eye-gouging fights on the frontier came into play. He expressed his anger over Lee's escape after Gettysburg by declaring, "If I had gone up there, I could have whipped them myself."[46]

Lincoln's unblinking courage sometimes bordered on recklessness.

In July 1864, he stood in his stovepipe hat on the parapet of a fort near Washington to witness Jubal Early's army, which was threatening the capital. When an enemy sniper's bullet struck an army surgeon near him, someone ordered him to leave the parapet. According to the most reliable account of the incident, it was Major General Horatio G.

Lincoln on January 8, 1864 (photograph by Mathew B. Brady)

Wright. When the president resisted, Wright declared that he would have to be removed forcibly. In Wright's words, "The absurdity of the idea of sending off the President under guard seemed to amuse him; but, in consideration of my earnestness in the matter, he agreed to compromise by sitting behind the parapet instead of standing upon it." But that did not end the matter. Wright wrote, "After he left the parapet he would persist in standing up from time to time, thus exposing nearly one-half of his tall form to the bullets."[47]

Lincoln often talked of war matters in animal metaphors. He warned Joseph Hooker in June 1863 that if he tried to cross the Potomac while chasing the enemy, he would risk "being entangled upon the river, like an ox jumped half over a fence, and liable to be torn by dogs, front and rear, without a fair chance to gore one way or kick the other."[48] He also noted to Hooker that Lee's army was stretched out, commenting that "the animal must be very slim somewhere. Could you not break him?"

If his view of war was related in part to the physical world, so was his belief in the Union. The continent, like the Union under the Constitution, was indivisible—which explains his fury over Meade's boast after Gettysburg that he had driven Lee "from our soil."[49] For Lincoln, there was no "our" or "their" in the continental United States, just as there was none in the American Union.

But in order to restore national unity, Lincoln realized, the earth must be torn by war. One of the corollaries of hard war was physical devastation.[50] According to the Clausewitz-Lieber view, sources of enemy supplies, food, and transportation were fair game. Anything that might weaken the enemy, barring wanton violence against private property or noncombatants, was permissible. This attitude was distant from McClellan's statement to Lincoln that the war must follow "the highest principles known to Christian civilization" and must avoid "the subjugation of the people of any state" or any "confiscation of property, . . . or forcible abolition of slavery."[51] The confiscation acts, the acceptance of contrabands behind Union lines, and the Emancipation Proclamation all justified the military liberation of the enslaved, as did Lieber's code. The code also stipulated that destruction of property and territory useful to the enemy was justified in war. Military necessity, Lieber wrote, "allows of all destruction of property, and obstruction of the ways and channels of traffic, travel, or communication, and

ULYSSES S. GRANT

of all withholding of sustenance or means of life from the enemy; of the appropriation of whatever an enemy's country affords necessary for the subsistence and safety of the army" (Article 15).

This view of war was carried out by Generals Ulysses S. Grant and William Tecumseh Sherman. Like Lincoln, they had an elemental view of war. They carried on a war of annihilation and of exhaustion.[52]

The middle-sized, chestnut-haired Grant, a sloppily uniformed, cigar-puffing general who kept his alcoholism generally under control during the war, had risen to national notice in the Tennessee River campaign of early 1862, when he took Forts Henry and Donelson. At Donelson, he got a memorable nickname, Unconditional Surrender Grant, when he was asked by his Confederate opponent about his terms. "No terms," Grant replied, "except an unconditional and immediate surrender can be accepted."[53] After the stunning Confederate attack at Shiloh, General Sherman said, "Well, Grant, we've had the devil's own day, haven't we?" Grant drew on his cigar and replied, "Yes, lick 'em tomorrow though."[54] He did just that.

Real fame came to Grant when, through shrewd tactics, a patient siege, and unrelenting force, he captured Vicksburg, the last Confederate bastion on the Mississippi River. Grant's victory at Vicksburg came on July 4, 1863, the day after Meade's triumph at Gettysburg. But Meade's dilatory behavior after the battle contrasted strikingly with Grant's trademark doggedness. Lincoln called the Vicksburg campaign "one of the most brilliant in the world" and wrote, "Grant is my man, and I am his the rest of this war."[55] "He has the *grit* of a bulldog!" the president said. "Once let him get his 'teeth' *in*, and nothing can shake him off."[56] Grant made relentless attacks on Confederate armies with the aim of destroying them.

Another grizzled, plain-uniformed, cigar-loving general, William Tecumseh "Old Billy" Sherman, had a similarly aggressive attitude. Sherman intended, in his words, to "make the interior of Georgia feel the weight of war."[57] That meant foraging widely in the country and laying waste to infrastructure, places of business, warehouses, and so on. Although he warned his soldiers to avoid inflicting unnecessary harm on noncombatants, the people of Georgia and the Carolinas felt what he called "the hard hand of war." Sherman explained, "War is cruelty, and you cannot refine it."

Grant and Sherman proved that personal loyalty to the president or acceptance of his views were not requirements for outstanding military performance. Grant had seen Lincoln debate Douglas at Freeport, and he confessed that he was "by no means a 'Lincoln man' in that contest; but I recognized then his great ability."[58] Grant oversaw some enslaved people his wife had inherited. He disliked abolitionism, but he realized

WILLIAM TECUMSEH SHERMAN

that slavery threatened to destroy the Union, which he wanted to save. Once he was in place as an officer in the Northern army, he devoted his energy to preserving the nation. Part of that devotion included an openness to using African American troops.

Sherman was a different story. Early in the war, he said he believed that black people were better off enslaved. If they were freed, he thought, they would either murder their former masters or would become extinct because of an inability to survive.[59] He wanted to use contrabands as workers but not as soldiers. "I would prefer to have this a white man's war," he wrote. "I won't trust niggers to fight yet."[60]

In a published letter, he opined that "the negro is in a transition state, and is not equal of the white man" and added, "I prefer some negroes for pioneers, teamsters, cooks, and servants," with others assigned to light service, such as garrison duty.[61]

Ironically enough, because of the contingencies of war, the racist Sherman became a great hero among blacks. When he marched through Georgia, swarms of freedmen trailed his army, hailing him as a godlike liberator.[62] Even more unexpected, Sherman was responsible for one of the most progressive measures of the Civil War. Henry Louis Gates Jr. describes it as "astonishingly radical for its time, proto-socialist in its implications."[63] In his Special Field Order No. 15, issued in January 1865, Sherman gave freedmen in coastal Carolina, Georgia, and Florida forty acres of land apiece; he later offered the use of army mules. The main motive for Sherman's order was to punish the former Confederates, but the prospect of "forty acres and a mule" opened vistas of economic self-sufficiency for emancipated blacks—promising, in Eric Foner's words, "a transformation of Southern society more radical even than the end of slavery."[64] (However, the hidebound president Andrew Johnson revoked Sherman's order, and the land went back to its former owners.)

Sherman's attitude toward Lincoln was ambivalent. Initially, he regarded Lincoln and other Northern politicians as inept in military strategy. As the war advanced, Sherman gained respect for the president, about whom he wrote in 1862, "I think Mr. Lincoln is a pure-minded, honest and good man. I have all faith in him."[65] But as the 1864 election approached, his senator brother John Sherman, who dismissed Lincoln as "our Monkey President" and "an honest clown," urged William to vote for McClellan. Sherman equivocated, writing, "I almost despair of a popular Government, but if we must be so inflicted I suppose Lincoln is the best choice, but I am not a voter."[66]

Lincoln, who did not ask for political support from his leading generals, was apparently unbothered by Sherman's distaste for politics.

Actually, this distaste was a military advantage in Sherman's case. He had no distraction, no larger agenda, other than a fleeting, hopeless idea of establishing a military dictatorship in order to get rid of politicians. For Sherman, the debate over slavery was irresolvable. He came to see that slavery was wrong, but he considered abolition equally bad. Politics were mired in confusion. War channeled Sherman's excessive nervous energy: it gave him concentration and focus. What appeared to him as chaotic politics was brought under control by the commitment to methodical, inexorable war.

In Grant and Sherman, Lincoln could feel confident that he had found self-reliant generals who could bring order out of chaos and could usher the North's superiority in manpower and technology toward military success.

But Lincoln knew that success on the battlefield was only part of the problem he faced. Once the initial war fever that unified the North early in the war had worn away, Northern society and politics fractured. Although Lincoln never expected complete social and political unity, he actively sought ways to bring together competing factions by affirming cultural unity wherever he could find it.

He found it in surprising places.

Forging Cultural Unity

Even as Lincoln was controlling his cabinet and his military, he made powerful efforts throughout the war to unify the cultural scene, which was more fractured and unruly than ever.

No president has had as many face-to-face conversations with ordinary Americans as Lincoln. At least twice a week, except for times when he was indisposed or overly busy, he greeted hundreds of visitors at the White House. In that era, average folk had access to the president. Unlike previous presidents, Lincoln put this opportunity to good use.

He typically went to bed between ten and eleven p.m., unless war affairs kept him up later. He was a restless sleeper. In the summer, while staying in the Soldiers' Home on the outskirts of Washington, he typically rose early, had for breakfast an egg, toast, and coffee, and got to the White House by eight a.m. The rest of the year, he usually slept with Tad, his close companion after Willie's death, and stayed in bed later. On visiting days, he opened his office at around ten to greet those who wanted to see him. By that time, people had long been waiting in the anterooms and halls.

The crowds drove his secretaries, John Nicolay and John Hay, to distraction. So did Lincoln's unpredictable schedule. Hay reported,

"He was extremely unmethodical; it was a four years' struggle on Nicolay's part and mine to get him to adopt some systematic rules. He would break through every regulation as fast as it was made."[1] But the scene was, in general, orderly. At noon, Lincoln lunched lightly—a biscuit and milk in the winter, fruit in the summer—and then resumed the meetings.

He called these greeting sessions his "public-opinion baths."[2] The bath metaphor was apt. He literally immersed himself in the public. He told the army officer and popular humorist Charles G. Halpine, "Though the tax on my time is heavy, no hours of my day are better employed than those which thus bring me again within the direct contact of our whole people." John Hay remarked, "Anything that kept the people themselves away from him he disapproved—although they nearly annoyed the life out of him by unreasonable complaints & requests."[3] When a soldier approached him about a petty matter, he told the man to take it up with an officer, declaring, "Now, my man, go away! I cannot attend to all these details. I could as easily bail out the Potomac with a spoon."[4] Someone asked his permission to distribute ale to the troops, eliciting his remark, "Look here! What do you take me for, anyhow? Do you think I keep a beer shop?"[5] A delegation requested his help in finding new equipment for a fire department; he said drily, "It is a mistake to think that I am at the head of the fire department of Washington. I am simply the President of the United States."[6]

Despite his anger over small requests and his frustration with countless office seekers, he usually lent a sympathetic ear. He showed special compassion for those with a relative in the military who was threatened with severe punishment for a relatively minor offense, in which case he often issued a pardon.

The meetings fulfilled his impulse to identify with the popular mind. They gave him a firsthand look at the attitudes, tastes, and feelings of the masses. The quality that, in Emerson's view, made him unique—his embrace of all levels of culture, from the highest to the lowest—was manifested during the war as his promotion of cultural phenomena brought many Americans together. These phenomena included religion, theater, literature, music, and humor.

TAPPING INTO THE RELIGIOUS SPIRIT

During the half century after Lincoln's death, no topic was more hotly contested than his religion. On one side were biographies, from Josiah Gilbert Holland's 1866 *The Life of Abraham Lincoln* through William Barton's *The Soul of Abraham Lincoln* (1920), that argued that he was a devout Christian.[7] On the other side were several biographers, especially his law partner William Herndon and his bodyguard Ward Hill Lamon, who contended that he was an agnostic, if not an atheist.[8] Both sides agreed that he was superstitious. Seizing on that quality and linking it to his sometime attendance at séances, others tagged him as a spiritualist.[9] Recent historians have offered more nuanced interpretations.[10]

The Civil War and deaths in his family definitely drove Lincoln closer to religion than his previous experiences had. He received comfort from Christian ministers, and he defended the Bible to a skeptical friend. Finally, though, he clung to his conviction about the unknowability of God and the inadequacy of any single church. The South, he realized, laid claim to God's favor as strongly as did the North. He saw that once any religion claims to contain the whole truth to the exclusion of all other religions, conflict arises, and war can result.

He had no patience with visiting clergymen who tried to convert him to their faith. When a minister showed up saying he simply wanted to pay his respects, the president grasped his hand warmly and declared, "My dear sir, I am very glad to see you. I am very glad to see you indeed. I thought you came to preach to me!"[11]

Religion was most important to him as a means of repairing the

Union—not only by combating secession but also by healing divisions in the North. As president, he tried to promote a nondenominational, creedless religion in order to foster national unity.

He pursued this nationalization of religion in distinct ways: through proclamations, through a refurbishing of religious holidays, and through references to God in public statements, currency, and documents. From all this religious activity, it might seem that he violated the cherished American doctrine of the separation of church and state. But he did not push any particular church or religion—he tried to appeal to the religious spirit in order to inspire a broad swath of Americans in a divided time.

Issuing religious proclamations had a mixed history in America. The Continental Congress, with John Hancock as president, had proclaimed two days of fasting and prayer, the first in July 1775 and the second in May 1776. President John Adams proclaimed two fast days in the late 1790s, and James Madison followed with three during the War of 1812.[12] Thomas Jefferson, the arch opponent of any association between government and religion, was careful to avoid any such proclamations because, in his words, "the Constitution has precluded them."[13] When the growing divisions over slavery split several national churches, presidents backed off from declaring days of fasting or prayer.

The Civil War brought a sudden urgency to the political use of religion, which became a potent cultural weapon for both sides. The Confederate Constitution, issued in early 1861, aimed to be a pious alternative to the "godless" US Constitution; it invoked in its preamble "the favor and guidance of Almighty God."[14] A Confederate officer declared, "No God was ever acknowledged in the Constitution of the old United States. We have acknowledged 'the Almighty God' in our Constitution—the God of the Bible, the only living and true God—as our God. . . . And moreover, under the old Constitution of the United States we never had a Christian President."

During the war, leading Christians in the North demanded a religious amendment to the Constitution. The Reverend Ezra Adams called it "monstrous" that the US Constitution did not directly pay homage to God, whereas the Confederacy's constitution did.[15] The respected minister and theologian Horace Bushnell held the deistic founding fathers responsible for the Civil War because of their "godless theorizing"; he called for putting God into the preamble of the Constitution by an amendment.[16]

This sentiment gathered force. On February 10, 1864, a delegation of ministers from the newly formed National Reform Association met with Lincoln to request a Christian amendment. The clergymen proposed the addition of this phrase to the Constitution: "We the people of the United States, humbly acknowledging the Almighty God as the source of all authority and power in civil government, and the Lord Jesus Christ as the Ruler among nations, his revealed will as the supreme law of the land, in order to constitute a Christian government. . . ."[17] Surprisingly, given the caution of the Founders to exclude religious references other than the vague "year of our Lord," Lincoln seriously considered the ministers' proposal. "The general aspect of your movement," he said, "I cordially approve. In regard to particulars I must ask time to deliberate, as the work of amending the Constitution should not be done hastily." The proposal gained the support of senators Charles Sumner, B. Gratz Brown, and John Sherman, who proposed it to Congress. But it did not come to a vote. Later efforts toward a Christian amendment, in 1874, 1896, and 1910, also failed in Congress.

But if Lincoln did not add God to the Constitution, he did sign into law another landmark infusion of religion into American life: the printing of "In God we trust" on American coins. Salmon Chase, the most pious member of Lincoln's cabinet, made the decision to put the motto on currency. In the fall of 1861, Chase received letters from Americans who insisted that the nation must respond to God's punishment by recognizing His name on currency. The Pennsylvania minister M. R. Watkinson wrote Chase, "I have felt our national shame in disowning God as not the least of our present national disasters." Were the United States destroyed by the war, the minister argued, history would remember it as a heathen nation. Watkinson suggested the words "God, liberty, law" for the patriotic seal on coins. "This would relieve us from the ignominy of heathenism," he wrote. "This would place us openly under the Divine protection we have personally claimed."[18]

Two weeks later, Chase asked James Pollock, the director of the United States Mint, to pursue the matter. Chase wrote, "No nation can be strong except in the strength of God, or safe in His defense. The trust of our people in God should be declared on our national coins." Pollock, a Pennsylvania judge and politician who had served with Lincoln as a Whig representative in the 1840s, was a devout Presbyterian. An acquaintance called him an "extreme Roundhead," and a biographer described him as "extremely puritanical in his attitude towards cards and liquor"—just the person to oversee the imprinting of a religious phrase on money.[19] In 1863 Pollock offered Chase the slogans "Our country; our God" and "God our trust" before the two agreed on "In God we trust," which was approved by Congress in coinage acts of April 1864 and March 1865.[20] The phrase first appeared on coins in 1864, and eventually on other currency as well. In the mid-1950s, under President Eisenhower, it became the national motto—America's spiritual response to the atheistic Soviet Union during the Cold War. In the same spirit, Congress in 1954 added "under God" to the 1892 Pledge of Allegiance.

Why "In God we trust" instead of another religious slogan? If we look back before the Civil War, we see that the phrase symbolized national unity. It had been popular among the Odd Fellows, the fraternal organization founded in England in the early eighteenth century. In America, the Independent Order of Odd Fellows was established in Baltimore in 1819. It spread quickly and by mid-century had male, female, and African American lodges in most states and territories. In time, the Odd Fellows became the world's largest fraternal organization and included notable members such as Ulysses S. Grant, Rutherford B. Hayes, and Franklin D. Roosevelt. "In God we trust" was commonly inscribed on signs and banners at Odd Fellows lodges.[21] In November 1860, just after the election of Lincoln, Salmon Chase had spoken at an Odd Fellows lodge in Kentucky in which he emphasized the president-elect's unswerving devotion to the Union. "I have no doubt he will do right," Chase said of Lincoln.[22] By promoting the religious motto during the war, Chase advanced the spirit of togetherness of sections, races, and genders that the Odd Fellows had advanced.

"In God we trust" also had antislavery overtones. It had been used in antislavery contexts, from the early 1840s, when the *National Era* published a poem with the lines "Let the far West repeat the strain; / The East and North—and South disdain / On Freedom's soil to forge a chain! / 'In God we trust,'" to an 1859 memorial service in Concord, Massachusetts, for the antislavery martyr John Brown, where a dirge was sung with the lines "Like him, in God we trust, / And though our eyes with tears are dim, / We know that God is just."[23]

Lincoln also added religion to the Emancipation Proclamation and the Gettysburg Address. At the suggestion of Salmon Chase, he inserted an appeal to "the gracious favor of Almighty God" into the Emancipation Proclamation.[24] His religious addition to the Gettysburg Address appears to have been spontaneous. The first two drafts of the address, written in Lincoln's hand, made no mention of God. He added "under God" as he was speaking. In news reports, and in the three later copies of the speech that Lincoln wrote out, the final line resolves "that this nation, under God, shall have a new birth of freedom—and that government of the people, by the people, for the people, shall not perish from the earth."[25]

This merging of the nation, God, and the government of people was a rhetorical reminder of the sanctity of the Union. Lincoln did not specify the Northern people or government. Instead, he aligned the United States as a whole with God and with the democratic government created by the Founders.

PROCLAIMING GOD, ADVANCING UNITY

The same spirit of national unity guided Lincoln's nine proclamations of prayer, thanksgiving, and fasting during the war. Jefferson Davis also issued such proclamations, but his had a wholly different tone from Lincoln's. Davis repeatedly asked for God's help in defeating the South's enemy. His proclamations were sectional, feeding division and conflict, whereas Lincoln's strained toward unity and national togetherness.

We see these differences in tone if we compare some of Davis's proclamations with a sampling of Lincoln's. In his proclamation of "humiliation and prayer" for November 15, 1861, Davis urged Southerners to appeal to God "that He may set at naught the efforts of our enemies, and humble them to confusion and shame."[26] In a March 1863 religious proclamation, he declared that "an enemy, with loud boasting of power, of their armed men and mailed ships, threaten us with subjugation, and with evil machinations seek, even in our homes and at our own firesides, to pervert our men servants and our maid servants into accomplices of their wicked designs." When things went well on the battlefield, Davis asked God to "continue his merciful protection over our cause; . . . scatter our enemies and set at naught their evil designs." When they went poorly, as after Sherman's March to the Sea and Grant's victories over Lee in Virginia, he prayed that "the trials and sufferings which have so long borne heavily upon us may be turned away by His merciful love" and "that the Lord of Hosts will be with our armies, and fight for us against our enemies."[27]

Lincoln's religious proclamations generally contain little of this vilification of the enemy. His earliest proclamation of "a day of public humiliation, prayer, and fasting," issued in August 1861, came shortly after the unexpected disaster of First Bull Run, which ended the North's hopes for a short war. The darkest of Lincoln's religious proclamations, this one urged Americans "to bow in humble submission to [God's] chastisements; to confess and deplore their sins and transgressions in the full conviction that the fear of the Lord is the beginning of wisdom; and to pray, with all fervency and contrition, for the pardon of their past offences." Lincoln asked his fellow citizens "to recognize the hand of God in this terrible visitation" and to have "sorrowful remembrance of our own faults and crimes as a nation and as individuals."[28]

This emphasis on sin and God's judgment harks back to New England Calvinism of the Jonathan Edwards variety, though Lincoln emphasizes America's "crimes as a nation"—a reference to slavery—as much as he does individual sin. Neither here nor in his later religious proclamations does he mention the wickedness of the enemy, as Davis was wont to do. Even in talking about sin, he includes the whole nation. This national outreach becomes even more pronounced in his later, more optimistic religious proclamations. In a typical one, he prays that "the united cry of the Nation will be heard on high and answered with blessings, no less than the pardon of our national sins, and the restoration of our now divided and suffering Country, to its former happy condition of unity and peace."[29]

By far his most important use of religion for affirming national unity was his proclamation of a national Thanksgiving in 1863. Before the Civil War, he had called attention to the importance, for all humans, of "occasions of recreation," of "holidays" that "bring us together, and thereby make us better acquainted, and better friends than we otherwise would be."[30] By proclaiming the first national Thanksgiving during the war, he not only tried to answer this "positive need of occasional recreation" but also to summon the entire nation to prayer.

He was not the first American leader to proclaim a Thanksgiving: Henry Laurens had done it in 1777 as president of the Continental

SARAH JOSEPHA HALE

Congress, and George Washington had done so twice, in 1789 and 1795, as had John Adams (1798 and 1799) and James Madison (1814 and 1815). Otherwise, however, Thanksgiving had been a state holiday that occurred mainly in New England. Beginning in the 1840s, Sarah Josepha Hale, the editor of *Godey's Lady's Book*, started promoting the nationalization of Thanksgiving. Most commonly remembered as the author of "Mary Had a Little Lamb," Hale had an impact on Lincoln and the future of the nation that has not been fully appreciated.

Hale regarded Thanksgiving as a holiday that could bind together people of different sections. At the time, Hale noted, the United States had only two truly national holidays, Washington's birthday and the

Fourth of July, but the latter was increasingly controversial due to the slavery crisis. (By the 1850s, Frederick Douglass considered the celebration of July 4 a mockery of the nation's ideal of human equality, as did Lincoln, who wrote sarcastically in 1855, "The fourth of July has not quite dwindled away; it is still a great day—*for burning firecrackers!!!*")[31]

In 1847, Hale noted that twenty-one of the twenty-nine states celebrated Thanksgiving, but they held it at different times in November. She suggested that "from this year, henceforth and forever, as long as the *Union* endures, the *last Thursday in November be the* DAY set apart by every state for its annual *Thanksgiving.*"[32] The boost to national unity, she argued, would be immense. Nine years later, she was still insisting that in order "to make [Thanksgiving] a national festival, the time of holding it must be fixed by circumstance, by custom, and by statute."[33]

Her emphasis on Thanksgiving as a source of union became increasingly stronger as the slavery crisis intensified. The effect of the holiday, she wrote, would be to "strengthen the bond of union that binds us brothers and sisters in that true sympathy of American patriotism."[34] By 1859, she was calling the holiday "A THANKSGIVING UNION FESTIVAL!"[35] In 1860, she happily announced that all the states and territories with one exception, Virginia, celebrated Thanksgiving, which, she maintained, "contributes to bind us into one vast empire together, to quicken the sympathy that makes us feel from the icy North to the sunny South that we are one family, each a member of a great and free Nation."[36]

The Civil War made her even more adamant in pushing Thanksgiving, which she now envisaged as a worldwide holiday, one that would proclaim that "all nations are one brotherhood, under the fostering care of one beneficent Father of humanity."[37]

She took her campaign directly to Lincoln. She wrote him a letter pleading that he must have "the *day of our annual Thanksgiving made a National and fixed Union Festival.*" She told him that by announcing

"this union Thanksgiving," the president could ensure that "the permanency and unity of our Great American Festival of Thanksgiving would
be forever secured."[38]

Lincoln had already proclaimed a local thanksgiving for Washington's government and municipal employees in November 1861, and the
following April he had announced a day of thanksgiving to "Almighty
God" for "victories to the land and naval forces engaged in suppressing
an internal rebellion."[39] But it was not until 1863 that he proclaimed a
national Thanksgiving. First came his announcement after the victories
at Gettysburg and Vicksburg of August 6 as the day of "National
Thanksgiving, Praise and Prayer." His proclamation did not emphasize
defeating the enemy. Instead it thanked God for giving "augmented
confidence that the Union of these States will be restored."[40]

On October 3, 1863, shortly after receiving Sarah Hale's letter, Lincoln issued a carefully worded Thanksgiving statement, which he worked
on with William Seward, in which he combined political ecology, economics, and religion in an effort to create a national holiday that might
truly contribute to restoring the Union. He named the last Thursday of
November as the day when God would be thanked "as with one heart
and one voice by the whole American People" by "my fellow citizens in
every part of the United States, and also those who are at sea and those
who are sojourning in foreign lands."[41] Lincoln gave thanks for "the blessings of fruitful fields and healthful skies" as well as productivity in agriculture, manufacturing, and mining—all of which showed that "harmony
has prevailed everywhere except in the theatre of military conflict." He
asked for "the Almighty Hand to heal the wounds of the nation and to
restore it as soon as may be consistent with the Divine purposes to the
full enjoyment of peace, harmony, tranquillity and Union."

In this proclamation, Lincoln effaced the violent, disturbing details
of the Civil War almost as much as he would in another famous public
statement that he made that fall, the Gettysburg Address, which he
delivered just a week before America celebrated its first presidentially

authorized Thanksgiving of many, right up to Franklin Roosevelt, who made the day an official national holiday.

It was difficult for Lincoln to avoid sectionalism in his Thanksgiving proclamation, not only because of the war but also because 1863 was a year in which especially vehement anti–New England and anti-Puritan rhetoric raged. Copperhead politicians like Samuel S. Cox and Clement Vallandigham viciously denounced Puritanism as the Constitution-destroying spirit behind the North's "evil" isms and behind the Lincoln administration.[42] Another Copperhead, the Ohioan David Quinn, that year published his pamphlet characterizing Lincoln as a fanatical, tyrannical spirit rapper whose ideas could be traced back to wicked New England Puritanism.[43] Moreover, the direct connection between Thanksgiving and early New England Puritanism had been solidified by William Bradford's *History of Plymouth Plantations*, which was published for the first time in the mid-1850s. Bradford gave vivid details of the Puritans celebrating the first Thanksgiving in Plymouth.

For Lincoln to advance Thanksgiving, therefore, was both progressive, because it had historical associations with Puritan-related reforms such as abolitionism, and risky, since it gave credence to the political smear that he was in the tradition of New England fanatics.

A pro-Lincoln essayist, in a brilliant caricature of Copperhead attitudes toward Lincoln, published in *Harper's Weekly* a mock "Study for a Copperhead Editorial" in the fall of 1863. Repeating all the Copperhead clichés about Lincoln, the essayist pilloried the president as a "gorilla," a "drunken ape" who destroyed law and order, changing the North into a "huge Bastille" and directing a "Yankee horde" that caused "massacre, rape, and fire" in the South. And now, the essayist continued, came Lincoln's most nefarious act: his declaration of a national Thanksgiving—the quintessence of Puritan tyranny over the nation:

> The final damning proof of the utter subserviency of the present imbecile Administration to the rankest Puritan fanaticism

is the proclamation of Thanksgiving! What is Thanksgiving? It is a Yankee, Puritan, Roundhead, sniveling, shuffling, canting, hypocritical institution. It smells of baked beans, roast turkey, and Indian pudding, not to say pumpkin pie and soft custards. Bah! . . . It is an outrageous and illegal ebullition of that Roundhead spirit of Phariseeism which incessantly bloats New England conceit. . . . Is not this Thanksgiving notoriously a State institution? And shall we, without a murmur, see the Washington tyranny sweep this poor state right away? Awake, freemen! Arise, ye oppressed! . . . [Let us say] to Lincoln and his minions . . . that the people of this country have had enough of Yankee fanaticism, of Puritanism, and of cant, and are resolved to vindicate the majesty of State rights.[44]

This piece of comic exaggeration mimicked the growing animosity of Copperheads and Peace Democrats against Puritan-rooted New England. In 1863 Lincoln received notice from Indiana's governor, Oliver P. Morton, that anti–New England sentiment was gaining ground in the Midwest. Morton wrote, "Every democratic paper in Indiana is teeming with abuse of New England and it is the theme of every speech; . . . they allege that New England has brought upon us, the War by a fanatical crusade against Slavery."[45]

There was a real danger that the rising anti–New England furor would undermine the Union cause and turn the 1864 election against Lincoln. Indeed, parts of the North greeted his nationalization of Thanksgiving as a great antislavery victory for New England. An abolitionist newspaper responded to Lincoln's Thanksgiving proclamation by crowing: "The People have asserted the sublime idea of Undivided Nationality for Freedom!" Thanksgiving, created by the New England Puritans, has now "gone forth with her children to all the continent, and now not another holiday is more universally observed over all the land than the Thanksgiving!" The writer continued: "Slavery offered us all the Kingdoms of the Earth if we would fall down and worship it. But this loyal people, . . . true to the faith of Liberty has said 'Get thee behind me, Satan!' . . . America was never, in popular sympathies, so near to her original ideas of liberty as to-day!"[46]

Although Lincoln carefully tailored his Thanksgiving proclamation to emphasize the theme of national unity and made no direct mention of the North's cause, he was subtly and powerfully nationalizing a holiday that was by its nature associated with New England, the seat of abolitionism. The proclamation accomplished for Puritan-based notions of liberty what the Gettysburg Address did for the doctrine of human equality in the Declaration of Independence: it merged progressive American ideals with the very definition of the nation.

Besides nationalizing Thanksgiving, Lincoln reportedly started what would eventually become an American tradition: pardoning the White House turkey. The journalist Noah Brooks reported that when a turkey was sent to the White House as a gift for a holiday dinner in late 1863, Tad Lincoln grew attached to the bird, which he named Jack, and, upon learning that it was to be killed, stormed into a cabinet meeting demanding that it be saved. The president paused in his business and signed a note of reprieve for the turkey, just as he had previously pardoned Tad's delinquent soldier doll (also named Jack).[47] The next fall, Lincoln saw the turkey watching voters walking toward a polling booth. He grinned and asked Tad, "Does he vote?" Tad replied, "No, he is not of age."[48]

SANTA CLAUS LINCOLN

If Thanksgiving was weighted toward New England, Christmas had historical associations with the South. For generations, Southerners proudly followed the Anglican Church calendar, which retained a number of the Catholic saint days, including Christmas, with its patron saint, Nicholas. The main impulse on Christmas Day for Southerners was not the religious one of celebrating Christ's birth but the genial one of enjoying the holiday by feasting and drinking. Christmas celebrations varied from plantation to plantation, but there were the common denominators of relaxation and merrymaking. The Christmas holiday validated the institution of slavery. Southerners plied their chattels with alcohol and allowed them to let off steam. In the words of one slave owner: "The Southern Negro, like the child, has a reverence for Christmas. . . . Slavery then put on its holiday garb. . . . The bondsmen for the time forgot their bondage, and for a week gave themselves up to the rollicking enjoyment in which Sambo distances all competitors."[49] Frederick Douglass hated the Christmas drunkenness because he saw it as merely an escape valve for the enslaved workers' trapped energies contrived by masters as another form of oppression. Slaveholding Southerners, for their part, felt that they were giving a rare treat to the enslaved people and carrying on the old Anglican tradition of a festive Christmas of the kind that Oliver Cromwell had ended in England but that they carried on in America.

Cromwell had indeed put a damper on Christmas, which he and the other Puritans considered a heathen ritual left over from Catholicism. His rise to power in the 1640s dealt a "staggering blow" to Christmas during his reign.[50] Business and government remained open on Christmas Day from 1648 to 1652, and in the latter year, a minister could be imprisoned for preaching the Nativity on that day. Puritans in New England shared Cromwell's mistrust of Christmas. For them, the Sabbath was holy, as ordered by the Bible, but Christmas and other Anglican saints' days were pagan. Governor John Winthrop did what he could to suppress Christmas celebrations in the Massachusetts Bay Colony. Increase Mather, who pointed out that there was no proof that Christ was born on December 25, wrote in his diary that "men dishonor Christ more in the 12 days of Christmas than in all the 12 months beside. . . . The manner of Christmas-keeping, as generally observed, is highly dishonourable to the Name of Christ."[51] As the nineteenth-century historian George Curtis recalled, "The Puritans . . . frowned on Santa Claus as Antichrist" and viewed Christmas a relic of "popery."[52]

The Civil War era brought a sea change in Northern attitudes toward Christmas. Lincoln played an unexpected role in it.

The first significant steps toward the reorientation of Christmas came from the author Washington Irving. In his *Knickerbocker's History of New York* (1809), Irving mentioned the Dutch legend of Saint Nicholas's flying above trees in a wagon and leaving presents by fireplaces for children. Irving subsequently lived for five years in England, where he witnessed rural Christmas customs that he enlivened in tales in his 1820 volume *The Sketch-Book*, where Christmas became a time of festive gatherings, carol singing, and kissing under the mistletoe. It was left to the poem "A Visit by St. Nicholas," first published anonymously in an upstate New York newspaper in 1823, to introduce to a wide American audience the sleigh-riding Santa Claus making his rooftop visits. It is commonly believed that Irving's acquaintance Clement Clarke Moore, a New York professor and landowner, wrote the poem, though some identify its author as Henry Livingston Jr., another New Yorker. Driven by lilting anapests—" 'Twas the night before Christmas, and all through the house"—the poem portrayed a jolly Saint Nicholas arriving on his reindeer-pulled sleigh, alighting on a roof, coming down the chimney to deliver his gifts, and then departing with a cheerful "and to all a good night." Over the next three decades, this Saint Nicholas merged with two European mythical figures, Christkindl (or Kris Kringle), who traveled around giving presents, and Belsnickel, who rewarded good children but punished bad ones with his switch.

There was a widespread yearning to establish Christmas as a communal holiday that would bring the family together and contribute to national unity by providing a generally shared custom. But the actual practice of Christmas was often marked by gun shooting, rowdiness, and roving mobs—what a folklorist calls a "temporary plunge into chaos" and a historian describes as "free-form holiday mayhem."[53]

An increasing spirit of unity replaced such disorder, as raucous celebration lost favor with the rising middle class and "at least a fictive sense of harmony and common focus with neighbors of different religions, nationalities, and classes" emerged.[54] In 1850, however, Christmas could still be considered a neglected holiday, as evidenced by an article in Lincoln's hometown paper, the *Illinois Daily Journal*. The writer of the article wrote of Christmas: "[O]ur puritan forefathers acted not wisely in interdicting or discouraging its observance" merely because some would "pervert it from sacred to profane uses." The writer hoped that Americans who regarded Christmas "as more a heathenish, than a Christian custom" would "come more generally to favor the observances of this festival, and will cheerfully lend their aid in rescuing it from the neglect into which it has fallen, and the desecration to which it has been subjected."[55]

Steadily, Christmas grew more domestic, peaceful, and pious. The Christmas tree was introduced to America by Hessian soldiers during the American Revolution, though it did not become commonplace in the United States until later.[56] By the 1830s, it was a custom among German Americans. Initially the tree met with some resistance. The author Lydia Maria Child confessed, "The puritan blood still flows too briskly in my veins to allow me relish over much the Christmas tree."[57] By the 1850s, when Christmas trees were sold commercially, they appeared in many American households. Franklin Pierce in 1856 began the tradition of the White House Christmas tree. Several now-familiar Christmas carols also arrived on the cultural scene. The year 1840 brought "Oh Come All Ye Faithful," "Deck the Halls," and Mendelssohn's "Hark, the Herald Angels Sing." American composers wrote "It Came upon a Midnight Clear" (1850), "Jingle Bells" (1857), "We Three Kings of Orient Are" (1857), and "O Little Town of Bethlehem" (1865).

The first American-produced Christmas card
(Albany, NY: R. H. Pease, c. 1850)

The first Christmas card known to be produced in America, by the Albany printer and variety store owner R. H. Pease, was issued around 1850. The card pointed both to the past and to the future. It shows a family—a mother, father, and three children—together on Christmas morning as an African American woman behind them sets the table for Christmas dinner. A reminder of the tradition of Christmas festivities appears in the wine bottles and heaped food in the card's right foreground and the partying people in its upper left corner. Commercialism trumps religion. A church, barely seen through a window, is minimized by the banner ad for Pease's store, the Temple of Fancy, whose building looms in the upper right of the card. There is no Christmas tree in the scene.

During the Civil War, the North made tremendous strides in appropriating Christmas. The illustrator Thomas Nast, best known for creating the Republican elephant and popularizing the Democratic donkey and Uncle Sam, also introduced popular pictures of what came to be the modern Santa Claus: the white-bearded, roly-poly, red-suited man with a pipe. Nast, an ardent abolitionist and a wholehearted supporter of Lincoln and the Union, not only depicted Santa: in some pictures, he politicized him. One of his first distinctive Santas, shown on the cover of *Harper's Magazine* in January 1863—the month Lincoln issued the Emancipation Proclamation—showed Santa delivering presents to Union soldiers at the front. Nast's Santa is, quite literally, an embodiment of the North: he is clad in stars and stripes, he is surrounded by cheering Union soldiers, some of them Zouaves, and he holds in his hand a toy puppet of Jefferson Davis being hanged by the neck—a reminder of the improvised line in "The John Brown Song," "We'll hang Jeff Davis from a Sour Apple Tree."

Small wonder, given Nast's support for the Northern cause, that Lincoln said, "Thomas Nast has been our best recruiting sergeant. His emblematic cartoons have never failed to arouse enthusiasm and patriotism, and have always seemed to come just when these articles were getting scarce."[58] When Ulysses Grant was asked who was "the foremost figure in civil life developed by the rebellion?" he averred, *"I think, Thomas Nast."*

Not only did Nast politicize Christmas; he domesticated it. In an affecting 1862 montage, *Christmas Eve*, he juxtaposed a Union soldier, sitting alone near a battlefield looking at photographs of his family, and his wife at home, praying as she gazes sadly out a window, with their children asleep behind her. The next year, in *Christmas 1863*, Nast created the first montage that fully captured Christmas as we know it today. A joyful picture of a family reunited during a Union soldier's furlough, the picture features images of Santa bending over two sleeping children, a Nativity scene, the opening of presents on Christmas morning, the Christmas dinner, and relatives arriving, with a Christmas tree topped by the stars and stripes in the background. While

Thomas Nast, *Santa Claus in Camp*
(*Harper's Weekly*, January 3, 1863)

Detail of Santa presenting to Union
soldiers a dancing puppet of Jefferson
Davis, who is hanged by the neck.

pro-Northern, this Christmas scene held nonsectional appeal with its comforting domesticity.

Thomas Nast, *Christmas 1863* (*Harper's Weekly*, December 26, 1863)

Other cartoons were bolder in linking Christmas specifically to the Union cause. The comic weekly *Phunny Phellow* in 1863 ran a picture of Lincoln dressed in a Santa costume and stuffing a Christmas stocking with presents, each bearing the title of a Union victory—Gettysburg, Vicksburg, Port Hudson, etc. The next year, *Harper's* featured a picture of "Santa Claus Lincoln" thumbing his nose at the sleeping Jefferson Davis, whose peace efforts were negated by Lincoln's reelection. This picture illustrated a common sentiment in the North during the Civil War: the South, once the main celebrant of Christmas, no longer had a right to celebrate the day. A Northern journalist published a story in which Santa appears and says to Southerners, "I am not permitted to travel in your rebel States. . . . Ah, the brave old Christmas times in the

South are over until the war is over. The hearthstones there are desolate."[59]

Lincoln himself appears to have supported an effort to appropriate Christmas for the North. John Hay, the ever-active public relations person for the White House, in December 1863 boasted in one of his Idler pieces for the *National Republican* that the celebration of Christmas in Washington had improved greatly now that Southerners had lost control of the capital. "Right merry was our Christmas," Hay wrote. "The weather was genial, 'gifts' were generously bestowed, the churches were well attended, . . . and there was far less drunkenness than in former years, when foaming bowls of egg-nog were seen in almost every house. Taken all in all, the Yankees really seem to know how to keep Christmas better than all the descendants of the FFVs [First Families of Virginia] who used to reign supremely here."[60]

Hay—with Lincoln's support, we may surmise—also tried to usher another holiday, Easter, into the Northern camp. In an April 1862 Idler essay, he began by noting that Russians celebrated Easter by saying, "Christ has risen!" Hay then connected the Christian resurrection with America's rebirth under Lincoln. Hay did not hold back his piously patriotic rhetoric: "Might not we as a people, while devoutly remembering the glorious resurrection of our Lord, also congratulate each other that since last April *the American people have risen*?" He wrote, "Thanks to . . . our gallant regular army and to our navy directed by President Lincoln, the stars and stripes have been uplifted, justice has been asserted, the national honor has been vindicated, and rebellion is well-nigh crushed out. . . . '*Jubilate!*'"[61] Hay, of course, was overly optimistic; it would take three more years of grueling war to crush the rebellion. But his association of the nation under Lincoln with the risen Christ lends pious meaning to the "new birth of freedom" that the president would speak of in the Gettysburg Address the next year.

A stronger merging of national holy days and the Union cause would come in December 1864. William Tecumseh Sherman intentionally timed his note to Lincoln about his capture of Savannah so that it would arrive by telegraph by Christmas. Indeed, Lincoln received Sherman's telegram—"I beg to present you as a Christmas gift the city of Savannah."—on December 25. Lincoln immediately replied, "Many, many, thanks for your Christmas-gift—the capture of Savannah."[62] Newspapers ran exuberant headlines like "SAVANNAH OURS. Christmas Gift to the Nation."[63] The North came alive with gratification to Sherman and Lincoln for this unprecedented Christmas present. Because this was an extremely important moment for the Thirteenth Amendment, which was about to work its difficult way through Congress, Sherman's landmark Christmas present gave a last-minute boost to the abolition of slavery.

With victory now in sight, Lincoln now regarded Christmas, like other holidays, not as a time to revel in the South's defeat but to reaffirm the Union. No one saw this more clearly than Thomas Nast did. If his previous Christmas pictures had been pro-Northern, his 1864 Christmas cartoon used the holiday as a metaphor for reunion with the South. His engraving *The Union Christmas Dinner* showed the tall, dignified Lincoln standing at the open door of the White House and welcoming Southerners to a holiday feast at a long table. Northerners occupy the chairs on one side of the table; the opposite side of the table is empty, soon to be filled with Southerners who will take chairs labeled with abbreviations of the names of their respective states (NC, SC, GA, etc.). The picture has religious themes: the words "Peace on Earth and Good Will Toward Men" stretch above Lincoln, and a small image of the Prodigal Son returning to his father appears in the upper right corner of the picture. By having Lincoln invite Southerners to resume their seats at the national table in a Christmas context, Nast was projecting the president's compassionate attitude to all Americans.

Thomas Nast, *The Union Christmas Dinner*
(*Harper's Weekly*, December 31, 1864)

ALL THE WORLD'S A STAGE

Just as in his religious proclamations Lincoln tried to embrace all Americans, so in his taste for plays, poems, songs, and jokes he reached out to the broadest public possible.

He enjoyed plays ranging from popular potboilers and burlesques to Shakespeare. For example, between March 1863 and March 1864, he attended performances of Shakespeare's *Othello, Henry IV, Hamlet, Richard III, Julius Caesar, The Merry Wives of Windsor,* and *The Merchant of Venice.*[64] In the same period he saw forgettable comedies and farces (including *Pocahontas, Handy Andy, A Lesson for Husbands, Fanchon, The Cricket*) and melodramas (such as *The Duke's Motto; The Sea of Ice, or A Mother's Prayer;* Edward Bulwer-Lytton's *Richelieu;* and two plays by Tom Taylor, *The Fool's Revenge* and *The Ticket-of-Leave Man*).[65]

He appreciated actors, no matter the material. His response to the popular John Wilkes Booth was typical. The son of the legendary Junius Brutus Booth (Walt Whitman's favorite actor) and the brother of the renowned Edwin Booth, John Wilkes Booth lacked their exceptional talents but was flexible enough to act in the various kinds of plays Lincoln loved. In 1863, the president saw him in Shakespeare's *Richard III* and in Charles Selby's melodrama *The Marble Heart*. He saw the latter play in the recently opened Ford's Theatre in Washington on November 9, 1863, ten days before he gave the address at Gettysburg. We don't know how Lincoln responded to this improbable play about a sculptor's interactions with ancient Greek statues who came to life, but he admired John Wilkes Booth's performance in the lead role. Lincoln would see Booth act several times again in Washington. The president enjoyed meeting performers, and Booth was no exception. Through a friend, he invited Booth a few times to the White House, but Booth, a proslavery Southerner who detested Lincoln, ignored the invitations. When he heard that the president liked his acting, Booth, a thoroughgoing racist, snarled that "he would rather be applauded by a negro."[66]

Leonard Grover, the proprietor of Grover's National Theatre in Washington, claimed that Lincoln attended Grover's at least one hundred times as president and may have gone to the two rival theaters, Ford's Theatre and Washington Theatre, just as frequently.[67] Although this number seems exaggerated, Lincoln did enjoy seeing plays of all kinds, and, according to Noah Brooks, he often slipped away from the White House unannounced to escape visitors and to relax.

The fact that Shakespeare was by far his favorite playwright might seem to have distanced him from the popular audience. Actually, though, the opposite is true: his affection for Shakespeare connected him with the people. Unlike later on in America, when Shakespeare came to be known as an elite dramatist, in the mid-nineteenth century his plays were truly popular cultural phenomena.[68] They were tremendous draws that provoked mass enthusiasm and passion. Shakespeare opened up the prospect of cultural unity because Americans of all classes enjoyed him.

Shakespeare was not only popular; he was also, potentially, a military force. That was the message of a whimsical 1863 piece in the nation's most widely read newspaper, James Gordon Bennett's *New York Herald*. Shakespeare had depicted the perils of civil rebellion more powerfully than anyone had, the essayist noted. Why not, then, send the nation's two most popular Shakespearean actors, the stentorian tragedian Edwin Forrest and the skilled comedian James Hackett, to the South, where they would destroy the Confederacy by spouting Shakespeare, with each actor using his specialized tone? The essayist explained: "Hackett and Forrest on alternate nights would bring the whole confederacy to dust. Hackett would make them roar and Forrest would roar at them. One would split their sides with laughter and the other would split their heads with noise or their hearts with pathos."[69]

This rhetorical spoof actually revealed a truth. Culture *can*, after all, have a powerful impact in divided times. For Americans of that era, Shakespeare transcended the sectional divide; he had devoted fans in both the South and the North. The fact that a Marylander like Junius Brutus Booth could stir a Northern Free-Soiler like Walt Whitman or that Booth's proslavery son John Wilkes Booth attracted the Republican Lincoln showed how cross-sectional culture could be.

However, culture alone does not build bridges. One's *view* or *use* of it does that. John Wilkes Booth carried his Southern views into his acting. One story has it that while performing he once walked close to the president and pointed at him angrily. Lincoln said, "He looks pretty sharp at me!"[70] The tale may be apocryphal, but it is known that when Booth's character in *The Marble Heart* was charged with supporting emancipation, he yelled, "Death and dishonor!" and moved threateningly toward the character who said it. The fact is, Booth not only hated what Lincoln stood for but also identified with vindictive, murderous roles he played onstage. Tragically, he played out these roles when he shot Lincoln, whom he considered a hateful tyrant.

For Lincoln, in contrast, culture was a great equalizer, a joiner. It put kings and commoners, presidents and the people on the same level. It punctured pomp, ripped away false appearances, and brought alive fundamental passions and desires. That's how he saw Shakespeare.

His relationship with the Shakespearean actor James Hackett was telling. Hackett had risen to fame by playing the frontier screamer character Nimrod Wildfire in *The Kentuckian*, a play full of adventurous incidents of the sort Lincoln had known in his youthful days on the frontier. Hackett subsequently took on Shakespearean roles. He came to be best known as Falstaff, the fat, rollicking con man in several of Shakespeare's history plays. In April 1863, Hackett sent Lincoln a book he had written on actors and acting. He included a note to the president, who replied several months later saying he had seen Hackett play Falstaff once and looked forward to seeing the performance again. Lincoln gave his opinion of Shakespeare. He admitted he had not read some of the Bard's plays, "while others I have gone over perhaps as frequently as any unprofessional reader." Among the latter were *King Lear*, *Hamlet*, *Richard III*, *Henry VIII*, and, as he wrote, "especially Macbeth. I think nothing equals Macbeth. It is wonderful."[71]

Hackett, delighted with the note, showed it to his son, who, without permission, sent it to the press. Newspapers weighed in on Lincoln's abilities as a drama critic. The *New York Herald* wrote, with tongue in cheek, "Mr. Lincoln's genius is wonderfully versatile. No department of human knowledge seems to be unexplored by him." He discussed religion with preachers, military campaigns with generals, constitutional law with Vallandigham sympathizers, and now he showed himself to be "a dramatic critic of the first order."[72] Other papers were less kind. One noted that Lincoln's letter to Hackett proved that the president had "a partiality to Shakespeare's lunatics and despots," including

JAMES HENRY HACKETT AS FALSTAFF

"the ambitious and bloody-minded Macbeth, and the hump-backed ty-rant of York."[73] A Virginia paper noted sardonically, "King Abraham I asserts that Macbeth is 'Shakespeare's masterpiece.'"[74]

Hackett, embarrassed that he had leaked the president's letter, wrote Lincoln an apologetic note. Good-naturedly, Lincoln replied:

My note to you, I certainly did not expect to see in print; yet I have not been much shocked by the newspaper com-ments upon it. Those comments constitute a fair specimen of what has occurred to me through life. I have endured a great deal of ridicule without much malice; and have received a great deal of kindness, not quite free from ridicule. I am used to it.[75]

Why wasn't Lincoln more upset that his private letter had been published? Actually, his connection with Shakespeare was something he wanted to publicize. Newspapers often announced his theatergoing, as on April 4, 1864, when a Washington paper ran a notice that "The president, with Mrs. Lincoln and Sec. Seward and family, will visit Ford's Theatre this evening to witness Edwin Forrest's grand impersonation of King Lear."[76]

Lincoln found that Shakespeare's universal appeal lay in his depiction of shared human qualities. Disloyalty, jealousy, revenge, hatred, madness, self-destructiveness, tomfoolery, devotion, faith, depression—they were all there in Shakespeare's plays, delivered in language so carefully calibrated that they remained under artistic control.

The president sometimes paused in a conversation to read or recite a Shakespearean passage. In particular, Shakespeare's dark passages reflected the agony he experienced during the war. Of all the forms of chaos Lincoln faced, the inner demons that sometimes overtook him were the most painful. These demons were especially harsh when he witnessed death, both in his family and in the Union military. But in Lincoln's case, depression was not a crippling factor for long periods. Melancholy Shakespearean passages provided him with relief. They offered structured, resonant versions of gloom. They organized sad topics and made them meaningful. Reciting dark writings aloud let him project his depression outward so that it was filtered through the improving lens of poetry. The rhythms and images of verse crystallized his private experience in a manner similar to the way his finest speeches crystallized and uplifted the national experience.

Take his reading from *Macbeth* after the Battle of the Wilderness, the grinding standoff in May 1864 between Grant and Lee in the woods of northern Virginia. When told of the battle's high casualty count, he cried, "My God! my God! Twenty thousand poor souls sent to their final account in one day. I cannot bear it! I cannot bear it!" His pallid face, disheveled hair, and dark rings under his eyes gave him a ghastly look. He found solace in one of the gloomiest passages in literature. He picked up a Shakespeare volume and leafed to Macbeth's most famous soliloquy. He said, "I cannot read it like [Edwin] Forrest, but it comes to me to-night like a consolation." The haunting words came forth slowly in Lincoln's high-pitched voice:

> Tomorrow, and tomorrow, and tomorrow,
> Creeps in this petty pace from day to day,
> To the last syllable of recorded time;
> And all our yesterdays have lighted fools
> The way to dusty death. Out, out, brief candle!
> Life's but a walking shadow, a poor player,
> That struts and frets his hour upon the stage,
> And then is heard no more. It is a tale
> Told by an idiot, full of sound and fury,
> Signifying nothing.[77]

This passage held special poignancy for Lincoln because it translated into beautiful language the universal fact of human mortality, a fact driven home with painful frequency during the Civil War.

Another Shakespearean passage that especially moved him was King Claudius's guilt-ridden speech in *Hamlet* about killing his brother, the king of Denmark. Claudius has committed the murder out of a thirst for power; now he tries to gain expiation by praying, but he finds he cannot do so because fratricide is too great a crime for God to forgive. Calling this passage "one of the finest touches of nature in the world," Lincoln recited all forty lines of the soliloquy—from "O my offence is rank!" to "All may be well!"—to the artist Francis Carpenter.[78] "He repeated this entire passage from memory," Carpenter remarked, "with a feeling and appreciation unsurpassed by anything I ever witnessed upon the stage."

Next, Carpenter recalled, the president recited Richard III's soliloquy that begins "This is the winter of our discontent." Most actors, Lincoln told Carpenter, delivered the lines too bombastically. The tone must be bitterly satirical because Richard is scheming to seize power from those he serves with outward loyalty. Lincoln delivered Richard's speech, in Carpenter's words, "with a degree of force and power that made it seem like a new creation to me."

Doubtless, there were personal associations for Lincoln in such passages. Like Richard, Claudius, or Macbeth, Lincoln wrestled with the complexities of political power. He fought against a cruel form of oppression, slavery, with strong executive actions that themselves were at times called despotic—and that, in the end, got him killed (John Wilkes Booth regarded him as an evil "king"). Within his own administration, Lincoln confronted would-be usurpers, such as Salmon Chase or William Henry Seward, who may have reminded him of Shakespeare's power-hungry schemers. There were also analogies between the personal and political crimes in Shakespeare's plays and America's fratricidal struggle over the national sin of slavery.

Politics also helps explain Lincoln's attraction to the comic figure of Falstaff. Although debauched, vain, and deceptive, Falstaff is also an unwitting voice for democracy in the history plays. Based on the fifteenth-century Lollard rebel martyr Sir John Oldcastle, Falstaff mocks pretensions of the sort that, later on, chivalric American Southerners held dear. The Confederacy was built largely on the Southern code of honor—pride in the Cavalier traditions of gentility, independence, and hierarchical order. In a famous passage, Falstaff demolishes honor:

> What is honour? A word. What is in that word "honour"?
> What is that "honour"? Air. A trim reckoning! Who hath it?

He that died o' Wednesday. Doth he feel it? No. Doth he hear it? No. 'Tis insensible then? Yea, to the dead. But will it not live with the living? No. Why? Detraction will not suffer it. Therefore I'll none of it. Honour is a mere scutcheon. And so ends my catechism. (*Henry IV,* part 1, 5.1.129–39)

Falstaff here deconstructs the kind of ersatz honor that became the underpinning of Southern culture. The historian William Robert Taylor writes of the South, "The right of a state to secede . . . could not be questioned. The honor of the South demanded that Southerners stand up and be counted; it required that they not retire cowering from the field of action."[79] Falstaff calls honor merely "air," a "word" that people die for. Applied to the Civil War, the South's fighting to defend the institution of slavery in the name of honor was a sham.

Both the North and the South could see themselves reflected in Shakespeare. But as in other forms of culture, Lincoln sought possibilities for unity, not division, in the Bard of Avon, who captured all human motivations and passions in characters and language that spoke to many Americans of his day.

FEELING THE POPULAR PULSE

He felt the same way about other writers. His was an era when poetry had a far wider audience than it has had in our era. Experimental poets like Whitman and Dickinson were too far ahead of the time to be widely appreciated. The public loved more conventional versifiers, especially the Fireside Poets—Longfellow, Whittier, James Russell Lowell, and Oliver Wendell Holmes Sr.—as well as female poets such as Lydia Huntley Sigourney.

Although Lincoln did not have time for extensive reading as president, books were readily available to him. During his time in office, he borrowed some 1,215 books from the Library of Congress.[80] Mary Lincoln, an avid reader, made major additions to the White House library, which was then located in a well-upholstered oval room above the Blue Room. Before Millard Fillmore's administration, the Executive Mansion was said to have been "entirely destitute of books."[81] Abigail Fillmore, a teacher, wanted books around her. Her husband, who had formerly been her student, got an appropriation from Congress to buy volumes that included Shakespeare, Milton, Dr. Johnson, Jefferson, *Aesop's Fables*, and Tocqueville's *Democracy in America*. Presidents Pierce and Buchanan added little to the book collection. Mary Lincoln applied her shopping expertise in 1861 and 1862 toward large purchases of books, including eight volumes of Longfellow, twenty-one volumes of Irving, and books of poetry by Sigourney, Bryant, and Felicia Hemans, along with books about travel and history and novels by Harriet Beecher Stowe, Cooper, and Scott. In all, she bought 153 volumes at a price of nearly $500.

Of course, neither Lincoln's Library of Congress borrowings nor Mary's additions to the White House library tell us with certainty about specific authors he read. But from various sources, we can make confident statements about his preferences in reading and music. He liked simple, direct poems and songs that were either melancholy, patriotic, sentimental, or comically nonsensical.

His longtime attraction to poems about death and transience grew during the war. N. P. Willis recalled riding once with the president and the first lady when Lincoln suddenly recited lines from Willis's "Parrhasius," a bleak poem about an enslaved Greek man who was taken to an artist who had the man tortured so that he could capture his torment on canvas. The artist declares, "Old man! we die / Even as the flowers, and we shall breathe away / Our life upon the chance wind, even as they!"[82] Everything humans hold dear—money, love, friendship, the hope of heaven—are vain, the artist says, and *"what thrice-mocked fools are we!"*

Lincoln found the full range of tones he enjoyed, from gloomy to comic, in the verse of Thomas Hood. "The Haunted House," a Hood poem of more than 350 lines that he read aloud to a White House visitor, is a Poe-like piece about a deserted mansion, overrun by vegetation, insects, bats, and rats, that gives rise to thoughts of those who have died there—a meditation on human death in the ever-changing physical world.[83] Also among the president's favorites was Hood's "The Lost Heir," in which a comically ill-spoken woman of back alleys frantically searches for her missing son, whom she praises extravagantly until she finds him, at which point she promises to break every bone in his body.

He discovered a similarly attractive mix of gloom and levity in Oliver Wendell Holmes Sr. The president frequently recited from memory Holmes's "The Last Leaf," about a once-robust man who has become a tottering figure with a cane on the street. Holmes had based the poem on Herman Melville's paternal grandfather, Thomas Melvill, a Revolutionary War hero who declined notably over the years. A bittersweet reflection on the passage of time, the poem makes much of the transition from healthful youth to infirm old age. The speaker says that he cannot help but grin at the old man's three-cornered hat and old-fashioned breeches, vestiges of an earlier time. Predicting his own demise, the speaker remarks that when he, too, someday becomes "The last leaf upon the tree, / . . . Let them smile, as I do now, / At the old forsaken bough / Where I cling."[84] Holmes is suggesting that everyone is a leaf on the tree of life, initially green and finally crumbling. This was the same dust-to-dust theme, negating pretensions that lay behind Lincoln's attraction to other poems about impermanence, such as William Knox's "Mortality" or William Cullen Bryant's "Thanatopsis."

Like Shakespeare, Holmes could be comical to the point of absurdity. "September Gale," another Holmes poem Lincoln enjoyed, describes a man driven to a frenzy when a windstorm rips his clothes from a laundry line and carries them heavenward, making the man have a wild dream about his favorite breeches being ripped apart when a huge flying demon puts them on.

Even such nonsense implies that all humans are subject to larger forces, whether storms, illness, or death. From such poems, Lincoln got a laugh and a lesson in humility. He did not, as did Melville or Dickinson, look into the abyss and respond with premodernistic relativism that verged on nihilism. Without shrinking from mortality, he retained his faith in vigorous human effort aimed at justice. We're frail beings, he saw, but that does not negate our efforts to bring about change. Each of us must try to make our contribution, no matter how lowly our sphere.

This is the message of another Holmes poem he liked, "The Chambered Nautilus." The poem describes the beautiful spiral-shaped shell of a mollusk, the nautilus, which the speaker finds on a beach. The speaker imagines the life of the small creature: its time of youth in the sea, its arrival on the shore, and its death. The nautilus, however, leaves behind a pearl-like shell, each spiral chamber of which speaks to the mollusk's unceasing effort, while alive, to build its tiny, lovely home.

Lincoln was moved by this theme of humble work wherever he found it, as in "Your Mission," a song he heard performed by the "singing evangelist" Philip Phillips at the third annual meeting of the United States Christian Commission, held in the House of Representatives in January 1865. Lincoln was supportive of the Christian Commission and its leader George H. Stuart, who gave him a Cromwell Bible and kept in touch with him during the war. Some five thousand volunteer agents of the commission had distributed millions of Bibles, hymnbooks, and religious newspapers to soldiers and seamen. Phillips's song validated Lincoln's belief that even the lowliest worker merits respect. One can be a common sailor, the song says, and not a captain, a laborer in the valley instead of a mountain climber, a person doing menial work rather than a millionaire, and yet still make a significant contribution to the world. Lincoln enjoyed the song so much that he scribbled a note to George Stuart:

Near the close let us have "Your Mission" repeated by Mr. Philips. Dont say I called for it. LINCOLN[85]

Phillips, delighted by the president's request, later sent him a letter of thanks along with a hymnbook containing the lyrics of "The Mission."

Lincoln had also requested a repeat performance of a song at the previous year's Christian Commission meeting. A chaplain's singing of "The Battle Hymn of the Republic" stirred him so much that his eyes moistened and he shouted, "Sing it again!"[86] Lincoln was responding, indirectly, to the example of the martyred John Brown, for, as everyone at the time knew, Julia Ward Howe had written "The Battle Hymn" in 1862 after hearing troops sing "John Brown's Body." She borrowed from the song its melody and the chorus "Glory, glory hallelujah," replacing the image of Brown's soul marching on with that of God's truth marching on. Her husband, Samuel Gridley Howe, had been one of the Secret Six who had funded Brown's abolitionist activities. Her anthem, with its memorable words about God fighting for the Union with his "terrible swift sword," recalled John Brown's battles against slavery in Kansas, where he used swords to slay proslavery settlers, and at Harpers Ferry, Virginia, where he had seized guns at a federal arsenal in an attempt to trigger a slave rebellion. It is hard to imagine that Lincoln didn't have John Brown in mind when he requested the repetition of "The Battle Hymn" at the Christian Commission event.

He responded with equal emotion to other pro-Northern poems and songs. Henry Wadsworth Longfellow's poem "The Building of the Ship" moved him to tears when the journalist Noah Brooks recited it to him. The antislavery Longfellow had written the poem in 1849, a moment of national crisis over slavery in the western territories taken in the Mexican War. In Longfellow's first version, the poem was pessimistic; it depicted inspired shipbuilders (the nation's founders) working long and hard to construct a beautiful, sturdy ship, the *Union*, which now seemed destined to be "Wrecked upon some treacherous rock, / Or rotting in some noisome dock."[87] When Charles Sumner objected to this negative ending, Longfellow rewrote it and had the passengers say at the end: "Our hearts, our hopes, are all with thee, / Our hearts, our hopes, our prayers, our tears, / Our faith triumphant o'er our fears, / Are all with thee,—are all with thee!"

These passionate words overwhelmed Lincoln. Brooks recalled, "As he listened to the last lines, . . . his eyes filled with tears, and his cheeks were wet. He did not speak for some minutes, but finally said, with simplicity: 'It is a wonderful gift to be able to stir men like that.'"[88]

He also embraced antislavery songs. In early 1862, he invited to the White House the Hutchinson Family singers, the ardently antislavery group from New Hampshire whose songs included "Get off the Track," about the unstoppable train of abolition roaring through the nation, and "Lincoln and Liberty," which had Lincoln slaying "the slaveocrats' giant," Stephen Douglas. Lincoln, who had heard the Hutchinsons when they visited Springfield in the 1850s, was so pleased by their White House performance that he encouraged them to sing to General McClellan's troops in Virginia. They got a pass and traveled to the Union camps, where they sang, among other songs, John G. Whittier's militant "We Wait Beneath the Furnace Blast," which urged Northern troops to fight against "the demon, . . . SLAVERY!"[89] Word of the performance reached McClellan, who disapproved of any connection between the war and emancipation. He revoked the Hutchinsons' pass and issued an order saying, "They will not be allowed to sing to the troops."[90] The group returned to Washington and called on the treasury secretary Salmon Chase, who read Whittier's abolitionist hymn to Lincoln. The president remarked, "I don't see anything very bad about that. If any of the commanders want the Hutchinsons to sing to their soldiers, and invite them, they can go."

The Hutchinson Family Singers

Lincoln's enjoyment of antislavery music was in line with his attraction to pro-Northern songs like "Battle Cry of Freedom," an instant success when it appeared in 1862. Also known as "Rally 'Round the Flag," the song, written by James Root, described Union soldiers vowing to "hurl the rebel crew from the land that we love best / Shouting the battle cry of Freedom."[91] An amusing incident happened in relation to Root's song and another popular Civil War anthem also written that year, "We Are Coming Father Abraham." A poem by James Sloan Gibbons that was set to music by L. O. Emerson, "Father Abraham" described "300,000 more" troops coming to fight for Lincoln from every

755

part of the North. One evening when Lincoln took Tad to see a play at Grover's Theatre, the boy went down to meet the actors, as he often did. One of them dressed him in an ill-fitting soldier's wardrobe shirt and cap. Soon Tad was onstage with the actors, one of whom handed a flag to the boy, who waved it vigorously as the actor sang lines that mixed the two patriotic songs:

> We are coming Father Abraham, three
>   hundred thousand more,
> Shouting the battle cry flag of
>   freedom!

The audience, recognizing Tad as the president's son, pitched in and sang the patriotic words. Lincoln, at first flummoxed by Tad's impromptu performance, laughed and hugged the boy when he returned to his seat.[92]

It is fully understandable that Lincoln would appreciate songs promoting the North and abolition, but what explains his enthusiasm for "Dixie"?

He had first heard "Dixie" in March 1860, when he went with a friend to a minstrel show in Chicago where the song, then new, was performed. Lincoln went wild when he heard it. He clapped along, stomped his feet, and was loudest in crying, "Let's have it again! Let's have it again!"[93] Lincoln once remarked that music was the one thing God created to produce sheer pleasure. The songs Lincoln loved were folk based and communal, created by the people and for the people, capable of passing from generation to generation and singer to singer. They fostered unity of sections and nations, and of successive generations—as they did for Whitman, the self-styled "bard" who saw poetry as music that bound together people of all nations and all times.

It is difficult to think of "Dixie" as a unifying song, because it became the National Anthem of the Confederacy, but delight in it was widespread during the Civil War.[94] A Northerner had written "Dixie," which then became the South's signature song while remaining popular among Northerners, too. All the while, it went through variations in lyrics. Despite its Southern emphasis, Northerners reveled in the song's idealistic nostalgia, as captured in its opening lines:

> I wish I was in de land ob cotton,
> Old times dar am not forgotten;
> Look away! Look away! Look away!
>   Dixie Land.[95]

A Maine newspaper reported in 1861, "This lively tune has in our cities become as popular as the most ravishing airs of operatic composition. Its effect on the hearer is wonderful, magical."[96] The New York *Commercial Advertiser* noted, "'Dixie' has become an institution. . . . Even those whose souls are so dead as to have no love for music, cannot refrain from an expression of pleasure as the bewitching strains strike the ear, while those who always love anything lively and sweet, fairly leap with joy whenever and wherever they hear it."

As president, Lincoln frequently requested bands to play the song, as when he greeted serenaders from a White House window on April 10, 1865, the day after Appomattox and four days before his death. He said to the group, "I have always thought 'Dixie' one of the best tunes I have ever heard. . . . I now request the band to favor me with its performance."[97] He got a laugh from the crowd when he said that he thought the North had "fairly captured" the song after "our adversaries over the way attempted to appropriate it." He knew that "Dixie" had nationwide appeal. Culture, for him, was national, not sectional, and music above all embodied the pleasure that culture could bring.

Just as significant as his cross-sectional devotion to "Dixie" was his love of sentimental songs that held appeal on both sides. Among the sentimental songs popular in the Confederacy were "Rock Me to Sleep,

Mother," "My Wife and Child," "O, Come to Me, Love, in a Beautiful Dream," "O! Touch Not My Sister's Picture," "Mother Is the Battle Over," and "Who Will Care for Mother Now." Similar-themed songs on the Union side included "Mother on the Brain," "Mother I Am Going," "Soldiers Wife," "When This Cruel War Is Over," "Our Sweet-hearts at Home," "Mother Kissed Me in My Dream," and "Tell Mother I Die Happy."

The most popular sentimental song of the Civil War was the classic "Home, Sweet Home." With a wistful melody written by the British composer Henry Rowley Bishop and lyrics by the American actor/dramatist John Howard Payne, the song, which first appeared in an 1823 opera, is egalitarian and universal; it says that even the humblest home, with its simple pleasures and memories, is preferable to palaces or exotic pleasures.

The song created unexpected comradeship on the war front. The camps of the opposing armies were sometimes separated only by a hundred yards or so, and regimental bands gave evening performances. Before one battle in April 1863, a Union band struck up "Dixie," eliciting cheers from Confederate soldiers camped just across the Rappahannock River. The Confederate band followed with a Northern song, "Yankee Doodle," and the federal soldiers cheered. Then came "Home, Sweet Home," which made both sides cheer. On December 30, 1862, the evening before the Battle of Murfreesboro (or Stones River), the forces of Braxton Bragg and William Rosecrans enjoyed a similar moment of musical amity. One regiment's band played "Home, Sweet Home," and soon all regimental bands in both armies were playing the song, with the Union and Confederate soldiers singing the plaintive lyrics in unison.[98]

Lincoln, too, responded fervently to the song. In 1862, the nineteen-year-old Italian singer Adelina Patti visited the White House. Born in Spain to Italian parents who had moved to America, Patti had been a child prodigy and by her teenage years was a famous singer of both operatic and popular vocal music. In the Red Room, she performed for the president and the first lady, who were still grieving over Willie's death. After her first song failed to impress them, Lincoln asked her to sing "Home, Sweet Home." She did, and, as she recalled, "when Mr. Lincoln thanked me his voice was husky and his eyes were full of tears. By that time I was so wrought up over the situation myself that I was actually blubbering when we were taking leave of the recently bereaved parents."[99]

JESTER IN CHIEF

On one memorable occasion, Lincoln's taste for popular songs got him into trouble. After the Battle of Antietam, he went to the front to review McClellan's troops. His bodyguard and friend Ward Hill Lamon, whom Lincoln had appointed as the marshal of the District of Columbia, accompanied him on the trip, along with others.[100] The party arrived in the Antietam area on October 1, 1862, two weeks after the battle. Lincoln joined McClellan and others who reviewed the army over the following days. At one point, the president, who was riding in an army ambulance distant from the battlefield, asked Lamon to sing a song. Lamon, capturing the sober spirit of the aftermath of the battle, chose what he knew to be Lincoln's melancholy favorite, "Twenty Years Ago," about time's passage and the death of loved ones. Then someone present (reportedly not Lincoln) asked for more. Lamon came out with a few ditties, including "Picayune Butler," a popular minstrel song about a banjo-strumming black man who was said to be "coming to town." The chorus went: "Picayune Butler, coming, coming, / Picayune Butler come to town. / Ahoo, ahoo, ahoo, ahoo, ahoo!"

A journalist leaked the incident, which the press immediately distorted. Sensational journalists invented the story that the president, when surveying the ghastly remains of those who had fallen at Antietam, had requested "Picayune Butler," to the disgust of McClellan, who allegedly refused to hear a song that he considered an example of callous levity in the face of real tragedy. In the words of the *New York World*, "The ambulance had just reached the neighborhood of the old stone bridge, where the dead were piled highest, when Mr. Lincoln, suddenly slapping Marshal Lamon on the knee, exclaimed: 'Come, Lamon, give us that song about Picayune Butler; McClellan has never heard it.' 'Not now, if you please,' said General McClellan, with a shudder; 'I would prefer to hear it some other place and time.'"[101]

Among satirical cartoons about the incident was one in which Lincoln is pictured standing amid the dead and the severely wounded at Antietam. He looks calm, while Lamon's back is turned and his hand covers his eyes, as though he is crying. Lincoln coolly says, "Now, marshal, sing us 'Picayune Butler,' or something else that's funny."[102]

The way Lincoln dealt with the controversy tells us much about his character. Lamon wrote an explanation of the incident that he intended to release to the press, but Lincoln found it too aggressive and produced a more moderate version in which he wrote, truthfully, that he was miles away from the battlefield when Lamon sang "Twenty Years Ago" and then, at someone's request, "Picayune Butler" and other songs. He also noted that he and the rest of his party had seen neither a corpse nor a grave during their time in the region.

It was a thoroughly convincing memorandum, but he did not release it. He told Lamon that he accepted Sir Walter Scott's dictum that if one's motives were good, they needed no explanation; if they were bad, they could never be convincingly defended.[103] Lincoln advised his friend:

There has already been too much said about this falsehood. Let the thing alone. If I have not established character enough to give the lie to this charge, I can only say that I am mistaken in my own estimate of myself. In politics, every man must skin his own skunk. These fellows are welcome to the hide of this one. Its body has already given forth its unsavory odor.

However, Lincoln's holding back of a written response, a common habit for him, appears to have been a mistake in this case. The Antietam controversy put him in a worse political position than he may have realized, for it made him politically vulnerable to George McClellan, whom he would soon fire. Lincoln's critics said, in short: you dismissed the general who won the battle that saved the nation, and you defamed him by requesting a flippant song at the battle site, and then, after his successor led the disastrous effort at Fredericksburg, you told a humorous story.

Anti-Lincoln poems and cartoons fanned the controversy. When McClellan ran for the presidency in 1864, his supporters published a widely reprinted poem that included lines about Lincoln's allegedly heartless tomfoolery:

> Abe may tell his jolly jokes,
> O'er blood fields of stricken battle,
> While yet the ebbing life-tides smokes
> From men that die like butchered cattle;
> He, ere yet the guns grow cold,
> To pimps and pets may crack his stories, [etc.][104]

Always known for his humor, Lincoln now seemed to some as a mere clown, with no real sympathy for those who had sacrificed their lives for the Union. "A year ago we laughed at the Honest Old Abe's grotesque genial Western jocosities," George Templeton Strong wrote in December 1862, "but they nauseate us now."[105] Lincoln was even known to repeat jokes about himself, such as one about a Quaker woman who told a friend that she thought that the Confederate president Jefferson Davis would succeed in the war because "he is a praying man." The friend comments, "Abram is a praying man [too]." The reply: "Yes, but the Lord will think Abram is joking."[106]

The impression of Lincoln as jester in chief spawned humor books with "Abe" or "Lincoln" in the title. The first of them, *Old Abe's Joker* (1863), was a silly collection that actually contained few of his own jokes but many by others—all presented under his name.

Such misrepresentation generated similar accusations against him. In 1864, the presidential election year, his chances for reelection dimmed because of his reputation as a joker.[107] Two ostensibly serious people, the pious Salmon Chase and the self-important George McClellan, were running against him. Chase withdrew from the race in March after support for him failed to materialize, but he lurked in the background as an available candidate should the need arise. McClellan, the Democratic Party's nominee, pushed the antijester theme. Signs at his rallies read "No Vulgar Joker for President," "Old Abe Can't See This Joke," "Old Abe's Jokes Have Operated for Little Mac Since Antietam."[108]

Lincoln's position was further damaged by an editorial in James Gordon Bennett's *Herald* that announced, "President Lincoln is a joke incarnated. The idea that such a man as he should be President of such a country as this is a very ridiculous joke." His traveling from Harrisburg to Washington in disguise was a joke, as was his inaugural address, whose promises he did not keep. The editorial continued: "His Cabinet is and always has been a standing joke. All his State papers are jokes. . . . His emancipation proclamation was a solemn joke." Then there were Lincoln's "stupendous military jokes," such as removing Little Mac after Antietam and resorting to humor and storytelling after it. The editorial concluded sarcastically, "If President Lincoln is going to try for another election, we advise him to collect and publish his jokes . . . issued in pamphlet and book form."[109]

Actually, two joke books related to Lincoln did appear in 1864. One of them, *Lincolnania; or, the Humors of Uncle Abe. A Second Joe Miller* was a kind of zigzag comic biography, featuring humorous incidents that involve him, many fictional, some not.[110] The other, *Old Abe's Jokes, Fresh from Abraham's Bosom*, was a campaign document. Far from blasting Lincoln's humor, this volume promoted it and combined it with serious content. As in the other books, some of the jokes or stories were not Abe's. But many of them were. Also, they were prefaced by a pro-Lincoln biography and comments on the need for humor in anxious times.

The Abe of *Old Abe's Jokes* was no heartless clown. The book emphasized that he felt the pain of the war deeply. For instance, after Fredericksburg, the president declared, "If there is a man out of Hell that suffers more than I do, I pity him."[111] His facial wrinkles, his pallid skin, and the dark rings around his eyes revealed a man who had "suffered more and deeper," in Harriet Beecher Stowe's words, than anyone. His jokes and stories helped relieve that pain, for him and for the nation. The book pointed out that Lincoln spent many hours a week welcoming ordinary Americans to the White House, and "the simple and natural manner in which he delivers his thoughts makes him appear to those visiting him like an earnest, affectionate friend." An important part of his naturalness was his readiness to tell good jokes and stories.

Scattered throughout the book were reminders of Lincoln's compassion (as in a sketch in which he comforted wounded soldiers) and eloquence (in a piece praising the Gettysburg Address). A main theme of the book was that his humor and anecdotes were healthy; they proved that he had qualities that McClellan and Chase lacked, such as warmth, humility, and flexibility. One sketch in the book had the telling title "Salmon the Solemn vs. Abe the Jocular."[112] The book directly called Abe "the National Joker" and argued that he was precisely the president America needed in a time of national bloodletting—someone who, through the worst, still saw the bright side of life. Gifted with a unique popular touch, Lincoln told the kinds of stories that average Americans loved.

Trying to reach a wide audience, the book's publisher, T. R. Dawley of New York, issued the book as a cheap pamphlet that was available at street bookstalls and railway stations. Newspaper ads announced that it contained "THE ESSENCE OF PRESIDENT LINCOLN'S LIFE." The volume, according to the ads, could be bought "together with all the late dime publications," including sensational pulp thrillers like *Ocean Rover, Guerillas of the Osage*, and *Maud of the Mississippi*.[113]

Did John Hay write *Old Abe's Jokes* at Lincoln's behest? That was the suspicion of an Indiana newspaper that noted that Hay's publicity techniques seemed visible in the book and that doubtless the president knew of this venture.[114] This may be true because parts of the book, especially the accounts of Lincoln's daily behavior in the White House and his private comments on the war, are things that only someone close to Lincoln could have known.

At any rate, we do know that Hay considered humor a significant part of the 1864 campaign. In June, as the Idler, he wrote a long article insisting that laughter was normal and healthy in a time of war. He wrote, "We have no sympathy with the solemn cant of those who would suppress all cheerfulness, banish all recreation, and compel everyone to sit down in sackcloth and ashes. . . . It is not in human nature to be perpetually sorrowful." As for the president, "mirthfulness is the recuperative agency by which nature preserves his energies."[115]

As the election approached, Hay wrote that "humorous documents" were important to the campaign.[116] He brought special attention to a recent pamphlet, *Lights and Notes: By a Looker-on in Vienna*, that hilariously satirized George McClellan. Hay insisted that all Republicans should get this book, which contained comic pictures and jokes caricaturing Little Mac. The pamphlet's author, Norman Wiard, was a Canadian-born gun inventor and proprietor of a New Jersey arms factory who became a close adviser to Lincoln in 1864. He wrote the president long letters on weapons, the economy, and the soldier vote. Devoted to Lincoln, he told him that "your enemies are the enemyies [sic] of the

Country."[117] That Wiard would pen a joke book attacking McClellan was understandable, as was John Hay's hyperbolic praise of Wiard as "a genius of the first order" and his pamphlet as a "a stunner" that "ought to be circulated both in the army and every northern state."[118]

Similar anti-McClellan humor appeared in the *Only Authentic Life of Geo. Brinton McClellan, alias Little Mac*, a yellow-covered, five-cent paperback that portrayed McClellan as a laughably inefficient, cowardly general and a waffling politician.[119] This pamphlet featured cartoons of a befuddled Little Mac that showed him during the Seven Days campaign, enjoying his first-through-seventh "victories" while gazing helplessly toward the distance beneath a sign that pointed "To Richmond." Then, as his "final act," came a cartoon of McClellan standing astride two galloping horses, one called War, the other one Peace—a reference to the division in the Democratic Party between those who called for defeating the South, with slavery left alone, and those who wanted immediate peace, with the Confederacy established as a separate nation.

Another popular anti-McClellan piece was the poem "Tardy George," printed during the 1864 campaign in many Northern newspapers, including Washington's *Daily National Republican*, the official government organ that featured John Hay's writings. Highlighting McClellan's chronic indecisiveness, the poem asked, "What are you waiting for, George, I pray?," followed by, "Are you waiting for your hair to turn, / Your heart to soften, your bowels to yearn / A little more towards 'our Southern friends' . . . / . . . whom you hold so dear / That you do not harm and give no fear, / As you tenderly take them by the gorge? / What are you waiting for, tardy George?"[120] Journalists often referred to Little Mac as "tardy George" until the end of the nineteenth century.

Even as backers of the opposing presidential candidates weaponized stories and jokes, Lincoln found entertainment and political use in bestselling humorists of the day. Noah Brooks recalled that during the war years, "Mr. Lincoln's reading was with the humorous writers. He liked to repeat from memory whole chapters from these books, and on such occasions he always preserved his own gravity though his auditors would be convulsed with laughter. He said that he had a dread of people who could not appreciate the fun of such things."[121]

Among the president's favorites were Artemus Ward, Orpheus C. Kerr, and Miles O'Reilly. Not only did they provide him with diversion in painful moments, but they also performed cultural work that helped his political program. Most of them contributed toward his goal of unifying the nation. Humorous stories in periodicals had wide appeal in nineteenth-century America. As the cultural historian Walter Blair notes, "The newspapers were active in carrying this humorous material into every part of the nation."[122] A journalist of the day observed, "Far and wide, daily, weekly, and monthly publications issue from the press to face us with at least one feature smiling."[123] Periodically, the humorists collected their newspaper squibs and published them in books, some of which became huge sellers.

Several of the humorists positioned themselves near the center, between extremes, which explains why they appealed both to Lincoln and to Americans of different sections. Valuably for the president, they attacked popular isms that had diverted much discussion away from what for him was the main issue of the war: slavery.

Artemus Ward (the pen name of Charles Farrar Browne) is best remembered for the fact that Lincoln read his comic sketch "High-handed Outrage at Utica" to his puzzled, silent cabinet just before he read the Preliminary Emancipation Proclamation. What was Ward's importance to Lincoln? If we look at his writings, we see that he performed a sizable cultural role. As a popular author and lecturer, he took many of the controversial isms of the period and put them on comic display, stripping them of the seriousness that they had for many Americans, who learned from Ward to laugh at them. We saw that Stephen Douglas had tried to tar the Republicans with the charge of espousing fanatical reform movements, and Lincoln critics like the Copperhead Samuel S.

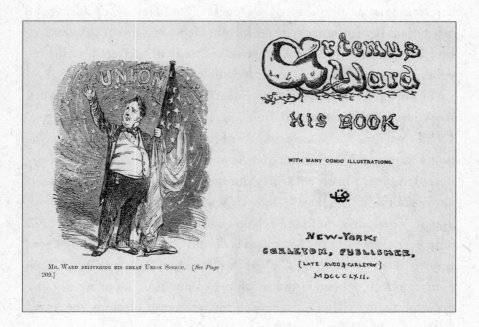

Mr. Ward delivering his great Union Speech. [*See Page* 209.]

Artemus Ward
His Book

WITH MANY COMIC ILLUSTRATIONS.

New-York:
Carleton, Publisher,
[late Rudd & Carleton]
MDCCCLXII.

[Charles Farrar Browne], *Artemus Ward. His Book* (1862)

Cox ramped the charge up during the Civil War. Artemus Ward helped to defang the isms by reducing them from social threats to funny exhibits in his "museum."

Ward was the P. T. Barnum of American humor. He called himself a showman who was engaged in "show bizniss," displaying animals like his "Boy Constructor" and "wax figgers" of notables from Jesus to Andrew Jackson.[124] In his sketches, Ward presented himself as a roving entertainer who went places where popular movements or fads were practiced, like a free-love community or spiritualist séance, and deflated these movements with his humor. Mormons, spiritualists, free lovers, sensational and sentimental novelists, feminists, intemperate temperance reformers—Ward lanced them all as ludicrous.

Ward provided an answer to critics who associated the Republicans with threatening isms, which, in Ward's hands, proved to be not so threatening after all. Formerly a Douglas Democrat, Ward during the war became a firm supporter of Lincoln. He was a kind of cultural ice-breaker, bursting through a range of crazes that interfered with Lincoln's goals: restoring the Union and abolishing slavery.

From this perspective, the president's reading of an Artemus Ward story just before reading the Emancipation Proclamation made sense. Of all the Civil War humorists, Ward had the largest appeal. His columns were widely reprinted, and *Artemus Ward. His Book*, which appeared in 1862, quickly sold forty thousand copies. Ward placed himself above politics. In his sketch "Interview with Abraham Lincoln," Ward, asked by the president for advice on choosing a cabinet, declared, "Fill it up with showmen, sir! Showmen is devoid of politics. . . . They know how to cater for the public."[125] By reading from Artemus Ward, Lincoln, in effect, was inviting his cabinet to put aside momentarily any political qualms they might have in the interest of reaching the broad public that Ward attracted. Anticipating (correctly) a backlash against the proclamation, Lincoln selected the humorist known to be enjoyed by many Americans—not just conservatives and moderates but also radicals, who laughed at Ward's odd malapropisms even when they disagreed with his politics. Lincoln distanced himself from overt radicalism and from Puritan worship in order to avoid seeming sectional or divisive. By preceding his controversial proclamation with an Artemus Ward joke, he made the humorist an unlikely compatriot in emancipation.[126]

The Ward story that Lincoln chose described the showman going with his animals and wax figures to Utica, where a man attacked a wax figure of Judas Iscariot. The showman yelled to the man, "You egrejus ass, that air's a wax figger—a representashun of the false 'Postle." The man beat the wax Judas to a pulp anyway, and Ward sued him, informing us that "the Joory brawt in a verdick of Arson in the 3d degree."[127]

This inane sketch suggested how convictions misled some irrational people. The enraged man who mistook a wax statue for a human and then pummeled it was analogous to the deception and falsity that permeated the Barnumesque culture of the era, including lies that surrounded the war itself. Just after reading this story of misdirected passion, Lincoln got to the true heart of the war by reading aloud the Preliminary Emancipation Proclamation. There, in that proclamation, was something solid and unmistakable. All too often, politicians of various stripes attacked false enemies—wax Judases, in effect. The time for deception was over, Lincoln was saying. The greatest enemy was slavery. The Founders, Lincoln believed, had put it on the path to extinction. Lincoln would hasten it down that path by issuing the Emancipation Proclamation and later pushing hard for the constitutional amendment that would abolish it forever.

If Artemus Ward mocked many of the movements that were distracting many Americans of the day, Orpheus C. Kerr (Robert Henry Newell) and Miles O'Reilly (Charles G. Halpine) made the Civil War itself the subject of humor. When Montgomery Meigs told Lincoln he had not read Kerr's comic pieces, the president exclaimed, "Why, have you not read those papers? They are in two volumes; any one who has not read them must be a heathen."[128] It was Kerr's story about the monkey that asked endlessly for "more tail" that Lincoln used to describe ever-delaying General McClellan. Lincoln conceded that sometimes Kerr's jibes against himself hit too close to home, but he laughed heartily at hits at others, such as Kerr's comparison of Gideon Welles to a grandmother who tried to replicate Noah's Ark for use in the navy.[129] Kerr represented the kind of lighthearted treatment of the war that provided respite for the often-tormented president.

Kerr also bolstered Lincoln's centrism by pillorying secessionist fire-eaters, self-styled "chivalric" Southern Cavaliers, and complacent Copperheads. Kerr even made comic mincemeat of the colonizationist scheme Lincoln pushed for a time early in the war. Kerr riffed on

Lincoln's interview with black leaders in August 1862, in which he called for the voluntary emigration of African Americans. Kerr, impersonating a government official, absurdly invited black people to volunteer to emigrate to Nova Zembla, a frigid, uninhabitable island off the northeast coast of Canada that, in Kerr's words, "has great resources for ice-water, and you will be able to have ice cream every day."[130] Lincoln, who had long been aware of severe problems surrounding colonization, might have learned by laughing at Kerr's farcical proposal. At any rate, he soon dropped the colonization scheme, which had been mainly a sop to conservatives of the Monty Blair stripe for whom colonization was *the* solution to slavery. Once Lincoln put himself firmly on the path to permanent, legal abolition of slavery, colonization waned in his mind, and he turned toward the progressive idea of citizenship for African Americans.

Miles O'Reilly was the pseudonym of Charles G. Halpine, who fought for the Union in an Irish regiment and wrote comic sketches that were published in periodicals and then in books. Lincoln not only considered Halpine "a most capable and deserving officer" but also enjoyed his writings.[131] As Private Miles O'Reilly, Halpine wrote funny ballads about episodes and figures in the war. In his comic narrative, the president pardons him for a small offense he has committed, and O'Reilly subsequently becomes a big Lincoln booster. O'Reilly accepts Lincoln as a jokester and storyteller and, far from criticizing him for it, wants the president to hire him to transform his western anecdotes into a popular book. O'Reilly writes, "No doubt such a volume—the materials and anecdotes furnished by Mr. Lincoln and the verses by the Bard of Erin—will be equal to anything in the same line since the day of Aesop's fables, translated by the poet Gray."[132] O'Reilly praises his humor and says that the president's epitaph should read:

Though thraitors treated him vilely,
He was honest an' kindly, he loved a joke,
An' he pardoned Miles O'Reilly!

As much as Lincoln liked these humorists, in his own writing and speaking he created a style that departed from their directionlessness and sometime racism.

In noticing that the "chief characteristic" of American humor was "grotesqueness and extravagance," he caught the wacky, presurrealistic elements of the American style that led to the tall tale, a genre Mark Twain perfected after the Civil War.[133] In "How to Tell a Story," Twain explained, "To string incongruities and absurdities together in a wandering and sometimes purposeless way, and seem innocently unaware that they are absurdities, is the basis of the American art."[134] One of Lincoln's favorite humorists, Artemus Ward, strongly influenced Twain, who noted that Ward in his lectures spoke with no apparent logic or forethought, stringing together non sequiturs. As another commentator explained, "Grave and apologetic, [Ward] would appear to be drifting helplessly from one idea to another as if his mind were floating along a natural current of thought which he was unable to check. . . . As he drifted about ineptly in search of words and phrases, he would become ensnared in verbal traps of his own making."[135]

Lincoln had long been reacting against this popular centrifugal style in his own jokes and anecdotes. Emerson praised the president as "the author of a multitude of good sayings, so disguised as pleasantries that it is certain they had no reputation at first but as jests; and, only later, by the very acceptance and adoption they find in the mouths of millions, turn out to be the wisdom of the hour."[136] Lincoln added form and point to the kinds of popular humor that were often formless. He "bounced off" the stylistic disconnectedness he saw around him and offered a meaningful alternative to it. Not only was his humor more focused than its popular counterparts, but his mature style as a speaker—pithy, condensed, and balanced—was worlds apart from the disconnectedness of the popular style.

The other difference between Lincoln and the humorists pertained to race. Most Northern humorists could expose racism among slaveholding Southerners, but they backed off from describing its pervasiveness in their own section. Orpheus Kerr, in a typical piece, impersonated a Southerner who cried, "Oh! for a nigger, and oh! for a whip; / . . . Oh! for a captain, and oh! for a ship; / Oh! for a cargo of niggers each trip."[137] Kerr also mocked certain Union generals, like Halleck and McClellan, who refused to accept contrabands into their camps. However, he went no further than that.

Nor did Artemus Ward. Although Ward was hard on secessionists, he also attacked radical abolitionists, and he was not above making racist jokes, as when he proclaimed in his odd vernacular, "Feller Sitterzuns, the Afrikan may be Our Brother. Sevral hily respectyble gentlemen, and sum talentid females tell us so, & fur argyment's sake I mite be injooced to grant it, tho' I don't b'leeve it myself. But the Afrikan isn't our sister & our wife & our uncle."[138] He also ridiculed the abolitionists' veneration of the Puritan fathers. Insisting that he would not cater to the fashion of tracing "the growth of Ameriky frum the time when the Mayflowers cum over in the Pilgrim and brawt Plymmuth Rock with them," he attacked the Puritans as "peple which hung idiotic wimmin for witches, burnt holes in Quaker's tongues and consined their feller critters to the treadmill and pillery on the slightest provocashun."[139]

Ward and the other Northern humorists were like sponges that soaked up cultural dross and emitted it as what a historian of journalism of the time described as "Odds and Ends," "Flashes of Fun," "Twinklings," and "Sparks."[140] In that sense, they served Lincoln's goal of cultural unity because they converted controversial topics into rib-tickling humor with wide appeal.

On the issue of race, however, these humorists were of little use politically. On that thorny topic, Lincoln received cultural help from a humorist who was less an absorptive sponge than an abrasive scouring pad. David Ross Locke, under the name Petroleum V. Nasby, launched a wholesale assault on racial prejudice that energized Lincoln's political battles and contributed to his evolving views on race.

Politics, Race, and the Culture Wars

S uddenly the master politician stopped politicking—party politicking on the stump, that is. During the Civil War, Lincoln avoided the kind of pointed political argumentation that had previously been his forte. From his slasher-gaff attacks on opponents in the Illinois legislature through his anti-Polk diatribes in the US Congress to his brilliant debates with Stephen Douglas in the 1850s, he had proved himself a virtuoso party politician. During the war, however, his overt jousting with political opponents on the hustings ceased. As Mark E. Neely Jr. notes, a reason the Republicans fared poorly in the 1862 midterms was Lincoln's failure that year to enter the political fray.[1]

Why did he not campaign as a Republican partisan? Actually, he *did* campaign, but he did so indirectly, through proclamations, public letters, and, especially, through his leadership of the increasingly antislavery war. To assault his political enemies head on through party-driven speeches would have damaged his goal of fostering cultural togetherness. In a time of national division, he saw, a president who vituperated political opponents could only deepen the rift. Paradoxically, as Lincoln adopted harsher tactics in the military field, his political activity was deliberately toned down as he looked to the project of restoring the nation to unity in the peace to follow.

As the war went on, his most vigorous efforts went toward restoring union on the basis of justice for African Americans. For his opponents, this notion of justice was totally *un*just—it violated the rights of white Americans. This is why his presidency was the target of some of the nastiest political campaigning in American history. Starting in late 1862, and intensifying exponentially in the next two years, anti-Lincoln rhetoric surged among Northern Democrats, who branded him as a despotic defier of the Constitution who was a mere tool of Negro-loving abolitionists.

The racial theme was central to the Democratic argument. The Confiscation Acts, the abolition of slavery in the District of Columbia, the Emancipation Proclamation—these and other antislavery measures, in the eyes of Democrats, threatened to let loose an ignorant, inferior race that would mix with white Americans and lead to racial mongrelization and, ultimately, the destruction of the nation.

Lincoln, meanwhile, was moving in the opposite direction on race. Despite his occasional strategically conservative behavior, as in the weeks leading up to his bombshell announcement of the Preliminary Emancipation Proclamation on September 22, 1862, he progressed steadily toward an enlightened view of race, stimulated by his personal encounters with African Americans and his genuine respect for the courage and heroism of black troops. At the end of the war, he became the first president to publicly advocate the vote for blacks.

How was he able to counter Democratic racism without confronting it directly? Here he relied largely on popular culture. In the face of an avalanche of racist literature published by Democrats, the Ohio journalist David Ross Locke, masquerading as the comically ill-spoken Copperhead Petroleum V. Nasby, impersonated Democratic attitudes with such satirical brilliance that he served as a one-person battering ram against racial prejudice. Commentators of the day credited Locke with contributing to the fall of slavery. Among them was President Lincoln, who admired Locke's humorous Nasby papers so much that he remarked that he would gladly trade places with the Ohioan if he could learn to write like him.

Only by probing cultural racism and the reactions to it on the part of Locke and Lincoln do we understand the dynamics behind the 1864 election, which restored Lincoln to power and made possible the passage of the Thirteenth Amendment, the first of several landmark steps toward civil rights in America. And only by probing Lincoln's responses to the outstanding performance of African American troops and to his personal interchange with black people, especially Frederick Douglass and Martin Delany, do we see the complete falsity of the charges of innate racism that some have leveled at him over the years.

VARIETIES OF CIVIL WAR RACISM

Lincoln's attitudes toward race must be measured against those of the surrounding culture. Only then can we responsibly come to a conclusion about this crucial topic.

The lowest baseline for cultural views of race during the Civil War was the Southern outlook. Slavery was racist at its core. Science, religion, history—the South invoked them all in defense of its peculiar institution. When combined with the region's hostility to the allegedly "Puritan" North and the Constitution-defying Lincoln, Southern racism yielded a truly toxic combination captured in an anonymously published mock article called "Contents of a Secesh Journal." The article pointedly coupled "Abe Lincoln" with "niggers," "John Brown," and "Puritan intolerance." Here's part of the parody:

> Nigger, niggers more nigger, big nigger, little nigger, abolition, John Brown, Stonewall Jackson's grave, nigger, black

nigger, yeller nigger; C-o-n-s-t-i-t-u-t-i-o-n; . . . confiscation, and abomination; nigger, lots of nigger, cords of nigger; Puritan intolerance; abridgment of our sacred liberties; . . . God bless Jeff. Davis, d—d Abe Lincoln; nigger, no end to the nigger; more about Stonewall Jackson's grave, Puritan intolerance and religious persecution; nigger, sleek, well-fed nigger slaves at the South, and poor starving white slaves at the North; despotism, anarchy and rain stare us in the face; down with the fratricidal Abolition Administration at Washington; nigger, nigger, n-i-g-g-e-r; and go on *ad infinitum*.[2]

The point of the parody was that the rampantly racist Confederacy associated Abe Lincoln, the Puritan North, and the legacy of John Brown with an unnatural, unconstitutional respect for black people; the Lincoln administration was a despotism designed to force this perverse view on slaveholders.

The parody shattered the glossy veneer of honor and chivalry that coated the inhumanity of the Southern slave system. However, while the parody was accurate in spirit, rarely did Southerners express the truth so boldly. They wanted to put a positive spin on the treatment of blacks held in slavery, which they presented as a noble institution sanctioned by the Bible and confirmed by racial science. A typical euphemism was Alexander Stephens's announcement of "the great physical, philosophical, and moral truth" that slavery held an innately inferior people in natural "subordination to the superior race."[3] The Virginia author Edward A. Pollard went so far as to say that "there is no such thing" as slavery in the South; rather there was "a system of African *servitude*" in which "the negro . . . has, by the *law* of the land, his personal rights recognized and protected, and his comfort and 'right' of 'happiness' consulted." This benign institution, Pollard wrote, "elevates a savage, and rests on the solid basis of human improvement."[4]

When blatant racism did appear in Southern publications, it was often delivered through humorous writings.

Take Charles Henry Smith, the most popular Southern humorist of the Civil War. A Georgia lawyer and Confederate officer, Smith, under the pseudonym Bill Arp, wrote a syndicated column that appeared in newspapers throughout the Civil War and well into Reconstruction. Like others, Arp traced the Civil War to the New England Puritans, but his take was distinctly pro-Southern. In his telling, "Old Pewrytan went off one day with sum ships and . . . bought up a lot of kaptured niggers from the Hottentotts, or sum other totts, and stole a few more on the kost of Afriky and brought em over" to the North. But "the cold winds and kodfish airs of New England didn't agree with nigger, and so they begun to slide em down South as fast as possible." But then Northerners "jind the church and bekum sanktifide about slavery," and later on "they was a stealin from five to fifty [enslaved people] a day, and kuverin their karkasses over with nigger larseny, and a smuglin the konstitution into an abolishun mush."[5] Next, "Kolonel Federlist" attacked "Gen. States Rights," and the war began. "Linkhorn" did his devilish best "to xtend the egis of freedom over all creashun—over things animate and inanimate—over bull bats and skreech owls, grub worms and grind-stones, niggers and alligators." His "proklamation," Arp says, "hav entailed Afrika upon us so strong that you can aktually smell it," and with the Thirteenth Amendment, "old Abe's Kongress hav finaly and forever set all the niggers free." But "What does it all amount to?" Arp boasts that he can buy "a chunk of a *free* nigger as eny other . . . I don't keer a darn about his bein free, if I can subjergate him."

Racism, while predictable coming from a Confederate author, was surprisingly common in the North as well. William Lloyd Garrison had said in 1829 that "the prejudices of the north are stronger than those of the south."[6] By the 1850s, those prejudices had diminished, largely due to the publication of powerful slave narratives and other antislavery writings, particularly *Uncle Tom's Cabin*, that showed enslaved blacks to be oppressed human beings deserving of compassion. But racism persisted. In 1862, Orestes Brownson estimated that while three fourths of Northern voters were antislavery, at least as many were antiblack.[7]

Working-class whites sometimes aired resentment about risking their lives by fighting a "Negro war." A Union soldier after Antietam wrote that his fellows "do not wish to think that they are fighting for Negroes, but to put down the Rebelion [*sic*]. We must first conquer & then it is time enough to talk about the *dam'd niggers*." He explained, "I came out to fight for the restoration of the Union and to keep slavery as it is without going into the territories & not to free the niggers."[8] Such remarks about African Americans were common in the diaries and letters of Northern soldiers. The deadly New York City draft riots of July 1863 provided a violent outlet for Northern racism.

The riots, however, were more than an explosion of working-class prejudice. They reflected an increasing racist trend on the part of Democratic politicians in the North. The riots were fanned by Democrats who assailed Lincoln's "tyrannical" act of drafting Americans merely to fight in his "abolition war." New York's Democratic governor, Horatio Seymour, and the ex-president Franklin Pierce provided encouragement to the riots through their denunciations of conscription, which they considered illegal. Abolitionists held Seymour in particular responsible for the violence, because he addressed the rioters as "my friends." Frederick Douglass wrote, "Had Governor Seymour been loyal to his country, . . . he would have burned his tongue with a red hot iron sooner than allow it to call these thugs, thieves, and murderers his 'friends.'"[9] Also involved in the antidraft movement was Fernando Wood, the suave ex-mayor of New York who had gone so far as to propose that New York City secede from the Union like the South.

Several Democrats launched public battles against "Puritan" Northerners and the "abolition administration." Speeches by Samuel S. Cox and Clement Vallandigham were laced with insults about African

Americans and their abolitionist supporters. Cox, in his address "Puritanism and Politics," lambasted the typical antislavery New Englander, who "makes the negro part of himself" and "holds him to be his equal."[10] Denouncing "the Constitution-breaking, law-defying, negro-loving Phariseeism" of antislavery Republicans, Cox added that he saw little difference between "the republicanism that sustains emancipation proclamations and the real old genuine Congo Abolitionism. [Cheers]. They are two separate links of the same Bologna made out of the same canine original. [Great and continued applause and laughter]."

Copperheads—the nickname (referring to the poisonous snake) that Republicans applied to Northern Peace Democrats—became organized and prolific. Many, including Vallandigham, joined an organization devoted to advancing Southern views. Formed in 1854 as the Knights of the Golden Circle (referring to an envisioned "circle" of slave states, to include Mexico, Central America, and the West Indies), the group was later renamed the Order of American Knights and then the Sons of Liberty. Although concentrated in the South, the group had branches in Northern states. Joseph Holt, Lincoln's judge advocate general of the army, investigated the organization and reported in 1864 that it had at least half a million members in the Union states, mainly Indiana, Illinois, Ohio, Missouri, Kentucky, Michigan, and New York.[11] The group did what it could to stop the war and bring back the Union as it was, including the restoration of Southern slavery.

Though secret, the group publicized its views widely. According to Holt's report, through a network of agents it "circulated throughout the country a great quantity of treasonable publications, as a means of extending its power and influence, as well as of giving encouragement to the disloyal and inciting them to treason." Pro-Southern publications, tailored to the popular audience, streamed from the Copperhead press. The nation was seized, in the words of a Democratic New York paper, by "the rage for pamphlets."[12]

These publications were a kind of shotgun blast at the Lincoln administration. The pellets fired represented different popular genres, including the religious tract, the trial pamphlet, the history book, the city-mysteries story, the faux-biblical poem, and allegedly scientific ethnology. The common theme was that the Constitution-breaking, tyrannical Lincoln was waging an abolition war in order to elevate the African race to an abnormal position of equality or superiority to whites.

Among tracts, the most popular was *The Lincoln Catechism: Wherein the Eccentricities & Beauties of Despotism Are Fully Set Forth: A Guide to the Presidential Election of 1864.* This racist pamphlet had Lincoln's supporters pledging their loyalty to him in dialogues such as:

> By whom has the Constitution been made obsolete?
> By Abraham Africanus the First . . . [so] that he can make
>   himself and his people the equal of negroes.[13]
> What is a President?
> A general agent for negroes. [. . .]
> What are the Ten Commandments?
> Thou shalt have no other God but the negro.
> Is amalgamation the true doctrine of *negro equality* as
>   taught by Mr. Lincoln in his debates with Mr. Douglas?
> It is.

Conservative Democrats also publicized their argument through history books, most notably Edward A. Pollard's *A Southern History of the War.* A Virginia journalist and historian, Pollard, the editor of the *Richmond Examiner,* is most famous for coining a famous Confederate moniker in the title of his 1866 book *The Lost Cause: A New Southern History of the War.* In the spring of 1863, Pollard brought out the first volume of his *Southern History,* which described the war's first year and its historical backgrounds. In 1864 came his book on the second year of the war. The book in its different editions was among the most-ballyhooed publications of the time. Democratic newspaper ads in the North blared, "Read the Other Side!," "BUY AND READ! A Thrilling Narrative." *"MOST IMPORTANT WORK ON THE WAR!"*[14]

Joseph Holt included Pollard's book on his list of "treasonous" publications. Doubtless, the book seemed threatening because Pollard was a skillful writer and, as it then seemed, a solid historian. He lent ostensible substance to the popular idea that the seventeenth-century Puritan-Cavalier conflict lay behind the Civil War. "There could be no congeniality," he wrote, "between the Puritan exiles who established themselves upon the cold and rugged and cheerless soil of New England, and the Cavaliers who sought the brighter climate of the South, and drank in the baronial halls in Virginia confusion to round heads and regicides."[15] From the seventeenth century onward, he argued, Southerners possessed qualities associated with the Cavaliers: chivalry, refinement, hospitality, and a love of adventure. These qualities shone in the South's lifestyle and its gallant Civil War generals. Slavery placed a naturally inferior race under the compassionate care of Southern masters. In stark contrast, the descendants of the Puritans, Pollard argued, were heartless, intrusively moralistic persecutors. Intolerant Northerners, spearheaded by the fanatic John Brown, seized power when the Black Republican Lincoln won an unfair election in which he did not receive a majority of the popular vote. The South then fell victim to despotism, persecution, and bloody war. Lincoln, in Pollard's rendering, was a dictatorial, fanatical jester whose uncouth appearance and vulgar character were aptly captured in the epithet "the Illinois Ape."[16]

For readers who preferred timely articles to history books, there was the Copperhead essay collection *The Washington Despotism Dissected*. This volume, which quickly went through five printings, included an article on Lincoln's "military despotism," which "made the liberty of the white man only of secondary importance to that of the negro"; another against emancipation, which would "flood the labor markets of the North with black competitors against the interests of the white industrial classes"; a third assailed Lincoln's enlistment of black troops, called here "a fiendish expedient with which to make war upon the defenseless women and children of the South"; and a piece titled "Grounds of Impeachment of the President."[17]

Trial pamphlets, which had a long history of popularity in America, were represented by *Trial of Abraham Lincoln by the Great Statesmen of the Republic.* The premise of the pamphlet was that "the present unworthy successor of Washington, the Abolition President, Abraham Lincoln, had become a convert to spiritualism, and that he had recently held a conversation in the White House with the departed spirits of certain great men of the Revolution."[18] At the trial, the Spirit of the Constitution charges Lincoln with "treasonable intent, purposes, and designs" for having opposed secession, suspended habeas corpus, violated freedom of the press, issued the Emancipation Proclamation, and committing other "crimes." The witnesses against Lincoln include the spirits of Washington, Jefferson, Hamilton, Hancock, Patrick Henry, Andrew Jackson, Henry Clay, and others. At the end of the trial, there arises a "grand phantasmagory" of victims of the Civil War: soldiers with their brains oozing out or their limbs torn off, orphans longing for their fathers, and widows crying for their slain husbands. The Spirit of the Constitution finds Lincoln guilty as charged.

The *Metropolitan Record*, a Catholic newspaper that was the official organ of Archbishop John Hughes of New York, published both *The Washington Despotism Dissected* and *Trial of Abraham Lincoln.* The newspaper's ceaseless campaign against Lincoln's emancipation policy raises the thorny issue of American Catholicism and slavery. With few exceptions, such as Orestes Brownson and Archbishop John Baptist Purcell of Cincinnati, American Catholics either condoned slavery or remained silent about it. This attitude was predictable in the South; the Catholic archbishop of Baltimore typically excoriated the "horrible and detestable" Emancipation Proclamation, which, he insisted, was "letting loose from three to four millions of half civilized Africans to murder their Masters and Mistresses!"[19]

But we should note that Northern Catholics, by and large, shared this attitude. The *Metropolitan Record* warned that the "disgraceful" Emancipation Proclamation, by liberating many blacks and admitting them into the military, changed the whole character of the war, which "is no longer to be a war between white men; it is St. Domingo massacres inaugurated on our own soil under the sanction, approval, and encouragement of the Government of the United States." Lincoln, the paper asserted, had opened the way for "an ordeal of carnage and fiendish outrage" that "will hardly be surpassed in the history of ancient or modern warfare."[20]

The fact that the *Metropolitan Record* represented Archbishop Hughes made its anti-Lincoln stance especially complicated. Hughes, although opposed to emancipation, supported the Union and was a sometime adviser to the president.[21] In late 1862 and early 1863, he served as an envoy to France and the Vatican. As Carl Sandburg notes, "the Archbishop became one the President's personal agents with full powers to set forth the Union cause in Europe."[22] Lincoln asked Hughes for recommendations of Catholic priests to administer to wounded and dying soldiers in military hospitals. Reportedly, the president even wrote the Pope, hinting that he should consider appointing the archbishop as America's first cardinal.[23]

Despite Hughes's connections with Lincoln, his organ, the *Metropolitan Record*, challenged the president's emancipationist goals, as did other Catholic periodicals. Not only was the *Record* the publisher of *Trial of Abraham Lincoln* and *Washington Despotism*, but it promoted other anti-Lincoln works as well. It hailed Alexander del Mar's *Abraham Africanus I*, as "one of the most extraordinary and mirth provoking squibs we remember to have seen," claiming that "it can hardly be delivered fast enough for the demand of book sellers and agents."[24]

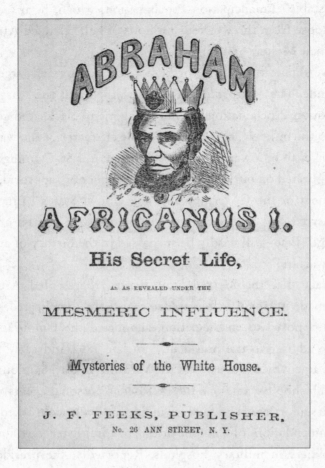

ABRAHAM

AFRICANUS I.

His Secret Life,

AS AS REVEALED UNDER THE

MESMERIC INFLUENCE.

Mysteries of the White House.

J. F. FEEKS, PUBLISHER,
No. 26 ANN STREET, N. Y.

[Alexander del Mar], *Abraham Africanus I*

The author of *Abraham Africanus I*, Alexander del Mar, was a New York–based financial journalist and historian who fiercely opposed the Civil War and Lincoln's policies. After the war, del Mar was slated to be the secretary of the treasury under the Democrat Horatio Seymour, who campaigned against Ulysses S. Grant under the motto: "This is a White Man's Country; Let White Men Rule."[25]

A similar view informs *Abraham Africanus I*. For two decades, readers had gobbled up pulp fiction about the "mysteries" of American cities, which sensationalized debauchery and wickedness behind the closed doors of the rich and famous. *Abraham Africanus I* offered, in the words of its subtitle, *Mysteries of the White House*. The fifty-seven-page pamphlet, which sold for fifteen cents, blended common elements of the mysteries genre—hidden corruption, substance abuse, demonic conspiracies—and pointed them at Lincoln. The novella has Lincoln, here called Bram, drinking liquor by his fireplace when, in an alcoholic daze, he sees Satan, who puts him into a mesmeric trance. Bram signs a contract in his own blood whereby he exchanges his soul for the guarantee of another presidential term. He agrees to prevent peace by stirring up "this all-fired nigger question," waging an illegal war, violating the Constitution, telling vulgar stories, and using outward honesty as a cover for "false promises" and "every imaginable form of low cunning."[26] Satan says, "YOU AGREE TO BRING TO DEATH ONE MILLION OF HUMAN BEINGS; and I'll agree to give you the Presidency." The devil assures Bram that the two of them will tell jokes to each other in "a hotel down in hell," as opposed to Stephen Douglas, who has gone to heaven. Bram willingly surrenders himself to Satan, who tells him, "A slave you are, and though much bigger, / As much a slave as any nigger."

No scattered literary blast against Lincoln would be complete without a faux biblical narrative. The nineteenth century was full of revisions of the Bible, from the Book of Mormon through Whitman's *Leaves of Grass* (which the poet called "*the New Bible*") to *Ben-Hur*, by the ex-Union general Lew Wallace.[27] Lincoln himself, as seen earlier, had participated in the genre at twenty in Indiana with his spoof "Chronicles of Reuben."

Two satirical biblical rewrites praised in the Copperhead press— *Book of the Prophet Stephen, Son of Douglas* and *Revelations; A Companion of the "New Gospel of Peace," According to Abraham*—pamphlets written in pseudo-biblical language and numbered passages, presented racist themes in a mock-formal way.

Revelations describes an ancient city, Repuplicanus, whose citizens "were not like other men; for they believed *black* was *white*, only more so."[28] The "*devil*" they were possessed by "means Niggero in the original." The people erected an altar in which they placed "the figure of our god, even a molten Niggero, and fall down and worship it in the sight of all the people." They sing praise to "our Great Potentate" (Lincoln). Among his preachers are "Philip the Amalgamator" (the abolitionist Wendell Phillips), who "may have taken his wife from among the daughters of Niggero," and "Cheeverite" (the antislavery minister George B. Cheever), "who calleth Niggero his better."

The other popular biblical narrative, *Book of the Prophet Stephen, Son of Douglas*, appeared in 1863, followed by a *Second Book* in 1864. It took as its premise that Lincoln had violated the principle laid down before the war by his Illinois opponent Stephen Douglas: "*I hold that this Government was made on the* WHITE BASIS, *by* WHITE MEN, *for the benefit of* WHITE MEN, *and their* POSTERITY, *forever.*"[29] The book tells of King Abraham, who grew furious when certain people in his kingdom—those in Sunland (the South) and members of the Copperhead "tribe"—failed to bow down to his Black Idol and instead wanted to continue worshipping white idols. Following the command of the god Woolly Dragon, King Abraham (nicknamed King of the Woollyheads) waged war on the harmless people of Sunland. During the bloody war, the king issued a proclamation that declared the Bible invalid because it endorsed slavery. He also revoked the Constitution and all existing laws, for he wanted his Black Idol alone to be worshipped, and he wished whites to marry Negroes. In the Second Book, the Woollyhead King becomes a strong advocate of miscegenation.

The latter topic gained notoriety from the anti-Republican pamphlet that introduced the term to the language, *Miscegenation: The Theory of the Blending of the Races, Applied to the American White Man and Negro.* A spurious mix of ethnographical lingo and idealistic visions of racial improvement, the pamphlet pretended to reveal that miscegenation (a neologism from the Latin *miscere*, to mix, and *genus*, race) would in time yield a superior new race. Two writers associated with the Democratic paper the *New York World*, managing editor David Goodman Croly and reporter George Wakeman, masqueraded as Republican champions of the theory. On Christmas Day 1863, they mailed the pamphlet to antislavery leaders, requesting blurbs. Several abolitionists took the bait and showered praise on it. In a long, enthusiastic review in the *National Anti-Slavery Standard*, Parker Pillsbury declared that the pamphlet had "cheered and gladdened a winter morning" that had begun "in cloud and shadow." Predicting that there would be "a progressive intermingling," as "black and white are disposed to seek each other in marriage," Pillsbury wrote, "We are sure that many will agree with us in finding the pamphlet interesting and instructive, and in thanking the unknown author for it."[30] Henry Ward Beecher's response was also positive: "We believe the whole human race are one family," and "whites and blacks should intermarry if they wish."[31]

Others, such as Lucretia Mott, sniffed deception, but the pamphlet was not revealed as a hoax until after the November election. The *World* then boasted that "the doctrine of 'Miscegenation,' conceived as a satire, was received as a sermon" and as "a glad tidings of great joy" by antislavery devotees.[32]

The pamphlet had indeed exploited a position actually advocated by antislavery reformers and politicians, some of whom had fought for years against state bans on interracial marriages. Such bans reached back to colonial times, when Massachusetts and six other colonies outlawed interracial marriage under British law.[33] After independence, existing bans remained and others arrived when new states entered the Union. Pennsylvania canceled its ban in 1880, but it was the exception to the rule of ongoing local antimiscegenation laws. The longevity of such laws varied from state to state: examples of the lifespans of laws include Rhode Island (1798–1881), Michigan (1838–1883), California (1850–1948), and Indiana (1818–1965). The record holders for longevity were Virginia and Maryland, which imposed bans, respectively, in 1691 and 1692 that lasted until 1967, the year the Supreme Court in *Loving v. Virginia* ruled that state bans on interracial marriage violated the Fourteenth Amendment. *Loving v. Virginia* ended the antimiscegenation laws in sixteen states, all of them in the South.

Abolitionists had made it part of their program to challenge marriage restrictions based on race. They succeeded in Massachusetts, where they won a cancellation of the ban in 1843. Partly as a result of this success, antislavery politicians, including Lincoln, were accused of advocating interracial marriage. Lincoln had faced pressure on the issue in Illinois in the 1850s, where amalgamation, as it was then called, had been legally proscribed in 1829—a ban that lasted in the state until 1874.

In his political battles of the 1850s, Lincoln danced around the issue. Why were Democrats so eager to defend the law banning racial intermarriage? he asked. Was Stephen Douglas so tempted to marry a black woman that he had to be restrained from doing so by law? Amalgamation, Lincoln pointed out, most frequently occurred in the slaveholding South, whose growing mulatto population revealed the sexual violation of enslaved women. As for the charges leveled at Republicans, he remarked that the "one distinguished instance" of amalgamation that he knew of was that of a Democrat, "Judge Douglas's old friend Colonel Richard M. Johnson" (Martin Van Buren's vice president, who reportedly had a black common-law wife by whom he'd sired two children).[34] In what became Lincoln's most widely quoted statement on the topic, he said, "I do not understand that because I do not want a negro woman for a slave I must necessarily want her for a wife. [Cheers and laughter.]" This statement, leavened by what then passed for humor, positioned Lincoln squarely among the great bulk of the population of the North who opposed slavery without believing in political or social equality.

Did he ever express his actual view of miscegenation? It would seem so. When in October 1858 he was asked what he thought of the Illinois law banning interracial marriage, he replied, "The law means nothing.

I shall never marry a negress, but I have no objection to anyone else doing so. If a white man wants to marry a negro woman, let them do it—if the negro woman can stand it."[35]

In the 1860 presidential race, the *New York Herald* told readers that the choice was between white rule under Democrats or Negro rule under Black Republicans. "Vote against Lincoln and negro suffrage," the paper advised; it warned that "the millennium of Republican rule" would be "African amalgamation with the fair daughters of the Anglo Saxon, Celtic, and Teutonic races."[36]

Such warnings about Lincoln reached a fever pitch in the 1864 presidential race, during the furor over miscegenation. Four more years of Lincoln, opponents declared, would bring the twin horrors of black citizenship and interracial marriage.

In a desperate effort to topple Lincoln, Democrats launched miscegenation as a political weapon. A Democratic broadside, *Black Republican Prayer*, transformed the Lord's Prayer into an anti-Lincoln diatribe. The prayer began in sarcastic reverence—"Abraham Lincoln—who art in the White House—gloried be thy name"—and went on to praise the "Royal Highness" who had spurned the Constitution in order to "free dear Sambo—that he may become white and equal to ourselves." The prayer continued as an homage to "the patriarch Abraham, sent on earth for the salvation of poor Sambo." The concluding benediction predicted the racially mixed America Lincoln would create:

> May the blessings of emancipation extend throughout our unhappy land—and the illustrious sweet-scented Sambo nestle in the bosom of every Abolition woman—that she may be quickened by the pure blood of the majestic African—and the spirit of Amalgamation shine forth in all its splendor and glory—that we may be a regenerated nation of half breeds, mongrels, and the distinction of color be forever consigned to oblivion—and that we may live in beds of fraternal love,

union and equality with the Almighty Nigger—henceforward now and forever—Amen.[37]

In a speech in the House of Representatives titled "Miscegenation or Amalgamation," the Copperhead Samuel Cox lamented that Attorney General Bates had "declared the African to be a citizen," Secretary of State Seward had granted him a passport, and "the President of the United States calls him an American citizen of African descent." The Senate, moreover, had been "discussing African equality in street cars." With the Republican Party "moving steadily forward to perfect social equality of black and white," Cox fulminated, Lincoln's presidency could "only end in this detestable doctrine of—Miscegenation!"[38]

Lincoln unwittingly mired himself in the miscegenation controversy even more deeply by making a statement that he thought would foster unity but in fact stimulated a torrent of right-wing criticism. On March 21, 1864, while accepting an honorary membership given him by the New York Workingmen's Democratic Republican Association, Lincoln told his largely Irish audience that workers of all races should sympathize with one another. Noting that the draft riots the previous summer had witnessed "the hanging of some working people by other working people," he chided, "It should never be so." Workers, he advised, should "beware of prejudice, . . . division and hostility among themselves. . . . The strongest bond of human sympathy, outside of the family relation, should be one uniting all working people, of all nations, and tongues, and kindreds."[39]

To his critics, these remarks were an open call for miscegenation. When the authors of "Miscegenation" sent him their pamphlet for his comments, they said they were inspired to do so by "your speech to the New-York workingmen, in which you recognize the social and political equality of the white and colored laborer." Lincoln did not respond to the pamphlet. A Copperhead newspaper ranted, "Mr. Abraham Lincoln deliberately . . . classes labouring white men with negroes. . . . In this brief sentence we have the new doctrine of 'miscegenation' or amalgamation officially announced."[40] A pamphlet titled *Miscegenation Indorsed by the Republican Party* pointed to Lincoln's workingmen's speech as evidence that "miscegenation is but another pet object of the Lincoln party, of the same stamp with emancipation, confiscation, and subjugation."[41] The *New-York Freeman's Journal* averred that the "beastly doctrine of the intermarriage of black men with white women" was now "openly and publicly avowed and indorsed and encouraged by the President of the United States. . . . Filthy buck niggers, greasy, sweaty, and disgusting, now jostle white people and even ladies everywhere, even at the President's levees."[42]

This theme of Lincoln's personal closeness to blacks became an obsession of Dr. John H. Van Evrie, editor of the *Day-Book and Weekly Caucasian* (New York). Van Evrie, who in 1856 had coined the term *white supremacy*, was an advocate of polygenesis, the theory that blacks and whites were not different types of humans but rather were different *species*.[43] Because he considered blacks innately inferior, their proper condition was slavery. Van Evrie's newspaper proudly proclaimed its guiding principle: "It is absolutely certain that this Government was made by White Men, for White Men and their posterity forever."[44] Van Evrie asserted that Lincoln, in his March address to the New York workers, had insulted "every white workingman by including him in the category of negroes, or, in other words, calling him a nigger!"[45]

In July 1864, Van Evrie advertised a twenty-five-cent lithograph, *Miscegenation, or The Millennium of Abolitionism*, that pictured Lincoln and other antislavery leaders consorting with blacks in a park. In the cartoon, Charles Sumner introduces "Miss Dinah, Arabella, Aramintha Squash" to Lincoln, who bends down and says to her, "I shall be proud to number among my intimate friends any member of the Squash family, especially the little Squashes." The woman replies, "Ise 'quainted wid Missus Linkum I is, washed for her 'fore de hebenly Miscegenation times was cum. Dont do nuffin now but gallevant 'round

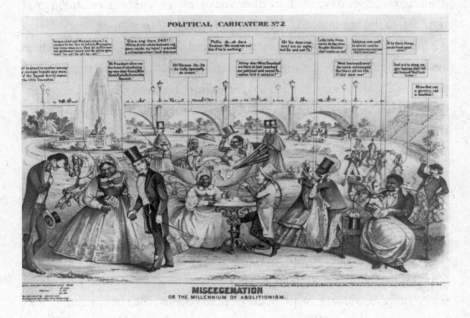

Miscegenation, or The Millennium of Abolitionism
(lithograph by G. W. Bromley, 1864)

Among the figures pictured is Lincoln, who tells a black woman, Dinah Arabella Aramintha Squash, that he would be proud to count the Squash family among "my intimate friends." At the right, Republican editor Horace Greeley shares ice cream with a black woman, to whom Greeley says, "Ah! my dear Miss Snowball we have at last reached our political and social Paradise. Isn't it extatic?" Near them, a white woman embraces a black man and declares, "Oh! You dear creature. I am so agitated! Go and ask Pa." He replies, "Lubly Julia Anna, name de day, when Brodder Beecher [abolitionist clergyman Henry Ward Beecher] shall make us one!" Also pictured is a white woman who sits on a black man's lap and invites him to attend her forthcoming lecture, and a black family in a carriage driven by a white man and attended by two white footmen.

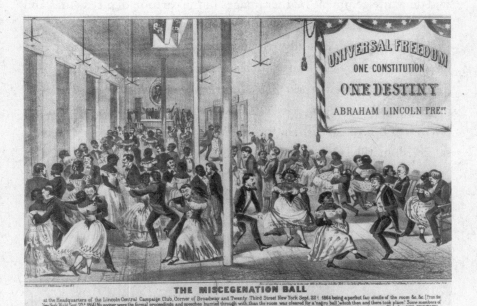

The Miscegenation Ball (lithograph by G. W. Bromley, 1864)

Pictures an interracial ball that allegedly took place in a large hall after a Republican
meeting of the Lincoln Central Campaign Club at Broadway and Twenty-third
Street in New York on September 22, 1864. At the ball, white men dance and flirt
with black women. Those present include members of the "'Central Lincoln Club,' . . .
the accredited leaders of the Black Republican party, . . . Republican Office-Holders,
and prominent men of various degrees, and at least one Presidential Elector On The
Republican Ticket."

wid de white gemmen!" Other images in the cartoon depict whites and blacks in various phases of intimate contact.[46]

In October, Van Erie advertised a similar cartoon, this one based on a dance attended by African American women at the Lincoln campaign headquarters in New York. *The Miscegenation Ball* showed white men dancing with or making passes at black women. In the background is a portrait of Lincoln and, in the foreground, a banner proclaiming "Universal Freedom, One Constitution, One Destiny. Abraham Lincoln Prest."[47]

Miscegenation, however, was actually too tame for Van Evrie, who published a revised version of an early book and titled it *Subgenation: The Theory of the Normal Relation of the Races: An Answer to "Miscegenation."* Since Van Evrie assumed that Lincoln, along with all other Republicans, accepted miscegenation, he tried to make a firm case for the restoration of slavery. "Miscegenation is Monarchy; Subgenation [that is, slavery] is Democracy," Van Evrie wrote. "When Lincoln issued his Miscegenation Proclamation, he proclaimed a monarchy."[48]

One might want to dismiss Van Evrie, who found even Copperheads too mild, as an aberration, but similar themes fueled the mainstream Democratic presidential campaign effort in 1864. At a huge McClellan rally in September in Cincinnati, campaign placards featured the usual anti-Lincoln thrusts ("Picayune Butler" sung in the presence of the Antietam dead; "Abraham 1st" dedicated to "shoddy"; "Old Ape Lincoln, and a figure of an ape's head"; "Old Abe, a fine specimen of an Illinois guerilla"; the president a spirit rapper, and the like) along with many virulently racist signs. Among them was one showing Lincoln riding a black man to the White House, another picturing a black man perched on Lincoln's shoulders, a third illustrating "Massa Bob Lincoln and His Chosen Bride," which showed Robert promenading "with a negress on his arm." Lincoln's goals were summed up on a sign that read "Abolition platform: emancipation, miscegenation, and amalgamation."[49]

Perhaps the most remarkable phenomenon of the 1864 race was Lincoln's silence in the face of constant racist assaults. His only extant comment on miscegenation was his remark to two journalists who in August asked him, "Now Mr P[resident] are you in favor of miscegenation[?]" He answered, "That's a democratic mode of producing good Union men, & I dont propose to infringe on the patent."[50]

This wasn't just another evasive joke about a testy issue. It had a kernel of truth: he did, after all, want "good Union men" coming from anywhere, including from "the democratic mode" of interracial relationships. A good number of the formerly enslaved people then serving in the Union military were from such relationships, and Lincoln considered them vital to the war effort. In any case, his reluctance to engage in open battles against his racist opponents reflected his confidence that such battles were being carried on, with signal success, by his favorite popular humorist.

PETROLEUM VESUVIUS NASBY TO THE RESCUE

Largely forgotten today, David Ross Locke was regarded in the nineteenth century as a strong influence on the fall of slavery. As the humor character Petroleum V. Nasby, Locke took on the Democratic horde. If cultural battles largely replaced open political ones for Lincoln during the war years, Locke emerged as perhaps the strongest anti-Democratic soldier on the cultural front. His immensely popular writings, it was said, were as responsible for the North's victory as were Sherman's troops. The Massachusetts politician George S. Boutwell, secretary of state under President Grant, declared in a speech at Cooper Union that "the crushing of the Rebellion could be credited to three forces: the Army, the Navy, and the Nasby Letters."[51] Charles Sumner affirmed, "Unquestionably [the Nasby letters] were among the influences and agencies by which disloyalty in all its forms was exposed, and public opinion assured upon the right side. It is impossible to measure their value. Against the devices of slavery and its supporters, each letter was like a speech or one of those songs that stir the people."[52] When Locke died in 1888, his obituary recalled of his Civil War writings, "They were copied into newspapers everywhere, quoted in speeches, read around camp fires of union soldiers, and exercised enormous influence in molding public opinion north in favor of vigorous prosecution of the war."[53] The *New York Herald* remarked of Nasby, "He was the most quoted man of letters in the country, and his oddities were repeated by statesmen, soldiers, the clergy—everybody."[54]

Among those who repeated them was Lincoln, who read the Nasby sketches as they appeared in periodicals and books from 1861 onward.

Born in 1833 in Vestal, New York, near Binghamton, David Ross Locke came from an abolitionist family. His father, the tanner and shoemaker Nathaniel R. Locke, was a devout Methodist who strongly opposed slavery—"one of the original anti-slavery men of the country," as a biographical sketch described him.[55] David went to work at twelve for local newspapers and eventually found his way to Ohio, where he became a newspaper publisher and editor. In March 1861, he made his first appearance as the anti-Confederate Petroleum Nasby in an Ohio newspaper. He went on to become the editor of the Findlay (Ohio) *Jeffersonian* and then the *Toledo Blade*, where many other Nasby sketches appeared. The pieces were reprinted in countless newspapers throughout the North.

Locke and Lincoln admired each other immensely. They met twice in the 1850s, when the journalist Locke was in Illinois reporting on candidate Lincoln. They had an especially friendly meeting in Quincy, Illinois, in October 1858, just after the sixth Lincoln-Douglas debate. The two joked and talked politics. Later, Locke respected Lincoln's performance as president. He was, Locke said, "The greatest man, in some respects, who ever lived, and in all respects the most lovable—a man whose great work gave him the heart of every human being—with a heart—throughout the civilized world."[56]

During the Civil War, Lincoln enjoyed Locke's writings so much

David Ross Locke

that he shared them with others, even in pressing situations. He committed to memory several of the sketches, which he recited spontaneously at key moments. When he didn't have one stored in his brain, he pulled out a Nasby book and read from it. As Locke recalled, "He kept a pamphlet which contained the first numbers of the [Nasby] series in a drawer in his table, and it was his wont to read them on all occasions to his visitors, no matter who they might be, or what their business was."

On a typical evening, a group of politicians and citizens appeared in the president's office with a pile of official papers for him to consider. He eyed the documents wearily and pushed them aside. He asked one of the party, "Have you heard of Nasby? . . . There is a chap out in Ohio

797

who has been writing a series of letters in the newspapers over the signature of 'Petroleum V. Nasby.' . . . I am going to write to 'Petroleum' to come down here, and I intend to tell him if he will communicate his talent to me, I will *'swap'* places with him."[57] He pulled from his drawer a Nasby pamphlet and read one of the sketches aloud. He periodically broke out into an explosive laugh, of which a witness said, "The 'neigh' of a wild horse on his native prairie is not more undisguised and hearty." Once he was done reading, he put down the pamphlet, resumed a serious look, and went back to work.

Locke said that in 1863 he received a letter from Lincoln, who wrote, "Why don't you come to Washington and see me? Is there no place you want? Come on and I will give you any place you ask for—that you are capable of filling—and fit to fill."[58] The Ohioan went to Washington and spent "a delightful hour" with the president, though a government appointment did not result (which may have been just as well for Lincoln; Locke's penchant for alcohol was as strong as that of his humorous persona, Nasby).[59] Locke was back in Washington the next year, this time asking Lincoln to pardon an Ohio soldier who had deserted the army and gone home to save his relationship with a woman, who had started seeing someone else. The soldier won her back but faced execution for desertion. Lincoln extended a pardon, which Locke found characteristic: "No man on earth hated blood as Lincoln did, and he seized eagerly upon any excuse to pardon a man when the charge could possibly justify it. . . . He was as tender-hearted as a girl."

What was it about David Ross Locke that made him unique in Lincoln's eyes? In a word, Locke performed crucial cultural work for the president and the Republican Party. He fought political battles with an intensity and viciousness that Lincoln, as a unifying president, avoided. Locke's mission as a humorist was to expose the racism and fundamental amorality of the growing number of Northern Democrats who took advantage of war weariness and complacency on slavery by calling for a peaceful compromise with the South, regardless of slavery.

Appalled by the reactionary drift of the Democrats, Locke appeared in newspapers as Petroleum V. Nasby, the ill-spoken, drunken lout who impersonated Democratic views. By grossly exaggerating these views, Locke made them laughably monstrous. If Lincoln loved American

PETROLEUM VESUVIUS NASBY

humor for its "grotesqueness," Locke gave him that in spades, along with a sharp political message that sliced through Democrats. As the *Detroit Tribune* remarked, "During the war, Nasby's pen was 'mightier than the sword.' Probably no such cheer came from any other pen to the Union soldier as came from his. To the enemy it was a rapier keen and dreaded."[60]

Rarely in the cultural annals has political satire been taken to such caustic extremes as in the Nasby papers. Petroleum Vesuvius Nasby was as inflammable as his first name, as explosive as his middle name, and as nasty as his surname sounds.

To us, it's shocking that Lincoln's favorite humor character used the N-word liberally. Coming from Petroleum Nasby, however, the word was scathingly ironic—an ugly reflection of the racism Locke saw among conservatives. The Nasby character exposed the stupidity of Lincoln's proslavery enemies.

In absurdly inept prose, full of misspellings and non sequiturs, Nasby, the quintessential Copperhead, calls for permanent white rule. His motto is "Ameriky for white men!" Declaring that "the crude, undeodorizd Afrikin is a disgustin obgik," he is enraged by the increasing number of free blacks in the North.[61] He yells, "Fellow-whites, arouse! The enemy is onto us! Our harths is in danger! When we hev a nigger for judge—niggers for teachers—niggers in pulpits—when niggers rool and controle society, then will yoo remember this warnin!" Well before the miscegenation controversy, Nasby asserted that rule by Republicans would give rise to interracial marriages. Insisting in that "the alarmin amalgamashun uv the races must be prohibbytid," he asks, "Do yoo want to marry nigger wenches? Do yoo want yoor gushin daughters tied by indissoluble ties to disgustin buck niggers?"[62] In 1864 he announced that he had learned "to spell and pronounce Missenegenegenashun." "It's a good word," he wrote, if you want to knock down "a man uv straw that yoo set up yerself."

Continuing to lampoon the proslavery crowd, Nasby has the Lincoln administration inevitably leading to black citizenship. He demanded: "Do yoo want a buck nigger to march up to the poles with yoo to vote? Do yoo want their children mixt with yoors in skools? Do yoo want em on juries and holdin offis in yoor township? My God! think uv it!"

In his frantic effort to prevent such "horrors," Nasby calls for the revoking of the Emancipation Proclamation and the reinstatement of slavery. As the *"Paster uv the Church uv the Noo Dispensayshun,"* he bolsters his racism with scriptural evidence, such as the curse of Ham and Saint Paul's return of an enslaved man to his owner. He has his Ohio congregation sing a hymn he has written: "Shel niggers black this land possess, / And mix with us up here? / Oh, no, my friends, we rather guess / We'll never stand that 'ere."[63]

Abandoning the pulpit, Nasby is drafted into the Union army and is shocked when he learns that he is fighting to emancipate "niggers." He deserts his regiment and joins the Confederate army, only to find his pay, clothing, and food wretchedly poor. And so he deserts again, this time marrying a Southern woman, who, to his revulsion, turns out to be an octoroon (that is, one-eighth black). He leaves her and returns to Wingerts Corners, Ohio, where he devotes himself to Democratic politics.

Locke castigates the Copperheads by making them Nasby's heroes. Nasby praises Clement Vallandigham ("the grate Vallandigum"), Fernando Wood ("Fernandywood, . . . that Sterlin Patryot and unkorruptible chrischen gentleman"), Samuel Cox ("the elegant Samcox"), the Ohio editor Samuel Medary ("Sammedary"), and Franklin "Peerse" ("that hi-toned man and wool-dyed Dimokrat").[64] He at first objects to the Democrats' choice of "Micklellan," a War Democrat, as their presidential candidate, but supports the ticket because of Little Mac's running mate, the Copperhead George H. Pendleton. At one point, Nasby has a dream of a future utopian society in which blacks have been exterminated, Jefferson Davis is emperor, and Copperheads are royalty (Nasby is excited to find himself the "DOOK DE NASBY!").

Utterly opposed to the war, which he says was "conseevd by John Brown and innoggeratid by A. Linkin," Nasby goes to Washington and sees the president. Introducing himself as "a free-born Dimocrat," who knows "that you er a goriller, a feendish ape, a thirster after blud," Nasby says, "I speek."[65] He tells Lincoln he will back the war only if the president follows his commands to "revoak the Emansipashen proclamashen, . . . protect our dawters frum nigger eqwality, disarm yoor nigger soljers, and send back the niggers to ther owners to conciliate them." Incensed by Lincoln's unresponsiveness to these requests, Nasby leaves in a huff, saying, "Linkin! Goriller! Ape! I hev dun."

Given Locke's actual affection and respect for Lincoln, it must have been very hard for him to maintain the outrageous Copperhead pose. But maintain it he did. Petroleum Nasby announces his misery when

Lincoln wins the 1864 election and becomes apoplectic when in early April 1865 Richmond and Petersburg fall to the Union:

> Lee surrenderd! Why, this ends the biznis. Down goes the curtain. The South is *conkered*! CONKERED!! CONK-ERED!!! Linkin rides into Richmond! A Illinois rale-splitter, a buffoon, a ape, a goriller, a smutty joker, sets hisself down in President Davis's cheer, and rites despatchis![66]

The one time Locke dropped the Nasby mask was just after the Lincoln assassination. In reporting the event, Nasby comes close to calling Lincoln "the Goriller" and John Wilkes Booth "a patriot," but he checks himself:

> The nashen mourns! The hand uv the vile assassin hez bin raised agin the Goril—the head uv the nashen, and the people's Father hez fallen beneath the hand uv a patr—vile assassin.

Immediately, however, Locke reassumes the Nasby persona; he has his bigoted rube regret that the president had not been killed in 1862, before the damage to Southern slavery had been done.

Lincoln's enjoyment of Locke's humor reveals that below his veil of moderation and caution lay a radically progressive self. Within the political centrist on his tightrope lurked a leftist abolitionist who loathed racism and wanted dramatic social change. Or to point to Petroleum V. Nasby's middle name, Vesuvius, Lincoln was what Emily Dickinson called "a reticent Volcano," "Vesuvius at Home"—phrases that captured the politically cautious but inwardly radical antiracist Lincoln. These Dickinson phrases could be applied as well to the outwardly conventional but rebellious Mary Todd Lincoln.

Because Locke's words as Nasby were in exact reverse to his real meaning, we see the future America that Locke (and, by association,

Lincoln) envisaged—an integrated nation in which people of color enjoyed full citizenship rights, and interracial marriage was permitted.

Because Locke's writings were far more popular than those produced by Copperheads or Southerners, we can glean that the Northern public was more forward thinking on race than is customarily believed. While the publication of scurrilous and racist material about Lincoln by his political opponents points to a depth of feeling among those hostile to him and his problack policies, Nasby could never have been so successful unless there was a large number of Northerners who found the racists' claims absurd and repellent. Nasby's popularity points to a broad sympathy in the North toward the humanity of enslaved people and rejection of the racial ideas put forward to justify slavery.

This became increasingly true over the course of the war. A major reason for the public's enlightenment on race was Lincoln's embrace of black participation in the war.

AFRICAN AMERICANS
AS SOLDIERS AND HUMANS

Early on, Lincoln ignored calls from Frederick Douglass, Charles Sumner, Simon Cameron, and others to enlist black troops. He feared that doing so would cause one or more of the border slave states to bolt to the Confederacy. When in March 1862 General David Hunter raised the First Carolina Colored Regiment by inducting contrabands, Lincoln refused to support it, just as he rejected Hunter's decree of emancipation for Georgia, Florida, and South Carolina. However, the Second Confiscation Act of July 1862 permitted the president to use contrabands in any military capacity, and in August, he authorized the creation of the First South Carolina Volunteer Infantry, a black regiment that by November was commanded by Colonel Thomas Wentworth Higginson. Having been a member of John Brown's Secret Six of supporters, Higginson later recalled, "I had been an abolitionist too long, and had known and loved John Brown too well, not to feel a thrill of joy at last on finding myself in the position where he only wished to be."[67] (Not only was Higginson one of the most radical people of the era, but he had a head for language. He was the first to publish Emily Dickinson's poetry, and he helped preserve Negro spirituals and the Gullah dialect in his book *Army Life in a Black Regiment*.) Higginson declared that "the key to the successful prosecution of this war lies in the unlimited employment of black troops."

The Emancipation Proclamation in January 1863 freed the enslaved in rebel states and announced that "such persons of suitable condition, will be received into the armed service of the United States to garrison forts, positions, stations, and other places, and to man vessels of all sorts in said service."[68] The proclamation gave Lincoln confidence to recruit black troops. Recruit he did, with pent-up enthusiasm. He wrote letters, made appointments, and issued calls for African American volunteers. Within seven months, the War Department had raised more than thirty black regiments.[69] Each regiment consisted of one thousand black soldiers, led by white officers.

The payoff came soon. In May, during the siege of Port Hudson, Louisiana, on the Mississippi River, eight Negro regiments took part in the assault on the Confederate fort there. The black troops "fought & acted superbly," a captain wrote home. "The theory of Negro inefficiency is . . . at last thoroughly exploded by facts."[70] Another officer reported that the black soldiers "fought splendidly; could not have done better. They were far superior in discipline to the white troops, and just as brave."[71]

In early June, at Milliken's Bend, Louisiana, two African American regiments resisted a Confederate attack on the fort they were guarding on the Mississippi River. Though raw and untrained, these formerly enslaved men stood their ground despite withering enemy fire and hand-to-hand combat. They suffered many casualties. Union gunboats saved the day. The war reporter Charles A. Dana averred, "The bravery of the blacks in the battle of Milliken's Bend completely revolutionized the army with regard to the employment of negro troops."[72]

In July 1863 came the battle of Fort Wagner, South Carolina, which still lives in the national memory, thanks in part to the film *Glory*. The Fifty-fourth Massachusetts Regiment, under the command of Robert Gould Shaw, led the attack on the Confederate fort at dusk, sweeping across an exposed beach and clambering up the sides of the fort, receiving heavy fire from above. A group of African American soldiers reached the parapet and took over part of the fort until the Confederates drove them back into the night. Shaw died in the attack and reportedly was buried in an impromptu grave. Confederates boasted, "We buried him below his niggers!"[73] Although the attack was ill planned, the courage of Shaw and his black troops became legendary.

Other sterling performances by African American troops followed, including the Battle of Olustee, or Ocean Pond, in Florida on February 20, 1864. Though heavily outnumbered, Union soldiers, led by the newly recruited Eighth United States Colored Troops from Pennsylvania, rushed into the battle. "The black man stood to be killed or wounded," an officer said.[74] Other black regiments that fought bravely at Olustee were the Thirty-fifth United States Colored Infantry and the famed veterans of the Fifty-fourth Massachusetts.

The stellar performance by black troops was especially remarkable because of the many obstacles they faced. They typically were armed with inferior guns, such as old-style smoothbore muskets that were inaccurate, hard to load, and erratic in performance. The commanding officer of the Ninety-second United States Colored Infantry declared that his regiment was armed with smoothbores "of very inferior and defective quality; many of them becoming useless at the first fire."[75] Raw troops, such as those at Port Hudson and Olustee, frequently had to quit firing and fight the advancing enemy with bayonets or rifle butts.

Another problem was the racism of white officers. Although officers such as Higginson and Shaw treated their black troops respectfully, others, such as General Truman Seymour, who served with Shaw at Fort Wagner, saw the African Americans as cannon fodder. Seymour declared, "Put those damned niggers from Massachusetts in the advance; we may as well get rid of them one time as another."[76] This problem could have been alleviated by the promotion in rank of blacks, but that happened rarely. Around 7,000 white officers served as leaders of the nearly 187,000 African Americans who enlisted in the war; at various times about 100 blacks held commissions, which were, in the main, lieutenancies, with the notable exception of Martin R. Delany, who in February 1865 was appointed as a major of infantry.[77]

Then there was the issue of low pay. The Militia Act of July 1862 set the monthly wage for the black soldier at $10 a month, of which $3 could be applied toward clothing, in contrast to his white private's $13 a month plus a clothing allowance of $3.50.[78] Vehement complaints arose among black troops and their champions, such as Frederick Douglass. The Fifty-fourth Massachusetts, in which Douglass's sons Charles and Lewis served, refused the paltry government pay for more than a year and adopted an ironic battle cry: "Three cheers for Massachusetts and seven dollars a month!"[79] Such protests led to the equalization of the pay in June 1864, retroactive to January 1, 1864.

Grimmer than all these challenges were the ones that faced blacks who were captured by the rebels. They were likely to be either killed on the spot or sold into slavery. Their white officers faced execution.

Lincoln was anguished over injustices against black troops, which became a main talking point in antislavery periodicals and in letters sent to him. He felt, however, that the twin bombs of emancipation and black enlistment that he had dropped on January 1, 1863, were, for the time being, the most powerful advances he could propose for African Americans without sacrificing a large portion of the support of the American public.

He explained his position to Frederick Douglass, who visited him on August 10, 1863. Nine days earlier, Douglass had temporarily stopped

FREDERICK DOUGLASS

recruiting blacks for the military in protest against what he regarded as the government's slowness in responding to the unequal treatment of African Americans. Having greeted Douglass warmly, Lincoln said he had read in the papers of Douglass's complaints about being "tardy" and "hesitating" in his policies.[80] Lincoln admitted that he was sometimes slow to take action for blacks but added that once he had made a commitment to them, he stuck to it. The charge of vacillation was therefore inaccurate. He told Douglass that if he acted too swiftly, a racist public reaction might overwhelm any gains he had made. As Douglass later recalled, "He felt that the colored man throughout this country was a despised man, a hated man," and that if he went too far too fast "all the hatred that is poured upon the head of the negro race would be visited upon his Administration." Lincoln said that he had hesitated to that point because "the country was not ready for it." He declared that the "preparatory work had now been done," thanks to the performance of blacks who had proved their military capabilities irrefutably. "Remember this, Mr. Douglass," Lincoln said; "remember that Milliken's Bend, Port Hudson and Fort Wagner are recent events, and that these were necessary to prepare the way for this very proclamation of mine."

The proclamation he referred to was his recent order of retaliation against the Confederates for their treatment of black prisoners. In the order, which he had issued on July 30, Lincoln denounced the Confederate policy as "a relapse into barbarism, and a crime against the civilization of the age."[81] The president stipulated that for every Union prisoner the rebels killed or enslaved, a captured Confederate would be sent into hard labor for the duration of the war. This call for recognition of the POW status of captured black soldiers followed the provisions of the Lieber Code, except for its harsher penalty of death for those committing reenslavement.

Unfortunately, Lincoln's attempt to protect his black soldiers led to misery for captured white soldiers. In the summer of 1863, in reaction to the South's summary execution and/or reenslavement of captured black soldiers, the Lincoln administration announced it would cease exchanging prisoners until the South complied. The suspension of the prisoner cartel led to misery for the white Union POWs, whose privations in captivity were extended to make Lincoln's point about racial egalitarianism. Union soldiers were dying at the rate of one hundred a day in the notorious Andersonville prison camp in Georgia. The humanitarian price of not exchanging prisoners was paid by Confederates as well, as their prisoners were stranded in prison camps in the North. All in all, 55,000 captured soldiers of both sides were kept prisoner instead of being exchanged and freed due to the North's principle. The suspension of prisoner exchanges is thus another example of Lincoln's commitment to blacks, even at great political cost to himself as well as injury to whites. It further belies the charges of these critics that Lincoln was really a racist or indifferent to the plight of blacks. Not only did Lincoln consider the recruitment of black soldiers as crucial to the Union army, but he respected their humanity enough to realize that blacks would not enlist if they thought the Union would not protect them.

Lincoln's effort to protect blacks by suspending prisoner exchanges did not end the atrocities, as evidenced by two infamous massacres in April 1864: at Poison Spring, Arkansas, where Confederate soldiers murdered and mutilated members of the First Kansas Colored Infantry; and at Fort Pillow, Tennessee, where Southern troops slaughtered more than three hundred blacks and their white officers after they had surrendered. But the president's order, along with the Lieber Code, did reduce the number of such outrages, which in fact fired up black troops, who now had new battle cries: "Remember Poison Spring!" and "Remember Fort Pillow!"[82]

Lincoln's order of retaliation also enforced the idea that the life of a black person was just as valuable as that of a white one. Equality, after all, was an implied message of the inclusion of African Americans in the military. The issues of race and slavery came down, ultimately, to the question of the humanity of blacks and other ethnic minorities. By displaying valor, skill, and patriotism in battle, soldiers gave undeniable proof that they were human beings. As the Republican congressman Thomas Williams declared in the House of Representatives in April 1864, the black man "has a musket in his hand, and stands revealed as a soldier and a man, of higher physical and moral type than his persecutors themselves. . . . The flesh that fed and crisped and crackled in the flames of [Port Hudson and Fort Wagner] . . . has turned out to be human, and the blood that was licked up by the devouring element, to be as red and warm as our own, the physiologists and philosophers to the contrary notwithstanding."[83]

Here Williams cut through racial pseudoscience and sham proslavery apologia and pointed to the sheer *physical* basis of shared humanity: as he put it, the black man's flesh "has turned out to be human," his blood is "as red and warm as our own." By saying that the African American soldier is "of higher physical and moral type than his persecutors," he also was testifying to the ethical and psychological soundness of African Americans.

This association of the universally human with both the physical and the mental was a point Walt Whitman had made in the 1855 poem eventually titled "I Sing the Body Electric." Picturing a man and a woman at auction, Whitman invites us to consider people of different races, bonded by the sameness of their bodies and their minds:

> Examine these limbs, red, black, or white, [. . .]
> Within there runs blood,
> The same old blood! the same red-running
> blood!
> There swells and jets a heart, there all passions,
> desires, reachings, aspirations.[84]

Blacks who fought for the Union put on a powerful display of their humanity that gave Lincoln a fresh opportunity to air his views on race. Although he still avoided radical statements, he made his progressive views clear.

In August 1863, the same month he met with Douglass, Lincoln received from an Illinois friend, James C. Conkling, an invitation to attend a mass meeting of "unconditional Union men of all parties" in Springfield on September 3. A longtime law associate of Lincoln's who had married a close friend of Mary Todd Lincoln's, Conkling hoped Lincoln would use this opportunity to defend his policies against attacks from Democrats, who had held a huge rally in Springfield on June 7. The Democrats were calling for a peaceful restoration of the Union as it had been before the war, with slavery in place. Lincoln declined Conkling's invitation, citing other duties, but wrote him a long letter that he asked to be read at the meeting.

In the carefully worded missive of August 26, Lincoln backed into the issue of race by covering other topics first. The Democrats said they wanted peace and objected to the Emancipation Proclamation and the use of blacks in the military. Lincoln replied saying that he also wanted peace, but that could only be restored by applying vigorous military pressure on the South. A compromise was beyond reach because the Confederacy's survival depended on its army. Once the rebel army was defeated, peace could be restored. Recent Union victories, such as at Gettysburg and Murfreesboro, portended well.

Continuing to address the Democrats, Lincoln wrote, "[Y]ou are dissatisfied with me about the negro. Quite likely there is a difference of opinion between you and myself upon that subject. I certainly wish that all men could be free, while I suppose you do not."[85] After this jab, he eased into the racial issue by mentioning the proslavery view of blacks. Even if we say that "slaves are property," he wrote, "is there— has there ever been—any question that by the law of war, property, both of enemies and friends, may be taken when needed? And is it not needed whenever taking it, helps us, or hurts the enemy?" Here was a defense of the Confiscation Acts that even—or especially—those who saw blacks as things would have to admit.

The Democrats called the Emancipation Proclamation invalid. So what? Lincoln asked. Even symbolically, it was a powerful weapon against the South. He said that commanders in the field, including those unassociated with abolition, had told him that "the emancipation policy, and the use of colored troops, constitute the heaviest blow yet dealt to the rebellion; and that at least one of those important successes could not have been achieved when it was, but for the aid of black soldiers."

Now to the human side of the question. On the guarantee of freedom for blacks who served in the military, Lincoln appealed to shared humanity: "[N]egroes, like other people, act upon motives. Why should they do any thing for us, if we will do nothing for them? If they stake their lives for us, they must be prompted by the strongest motive—even the promise of freedom. And the promise being made, must be kept."

His message was forceful and unmistakable: blacks are *people*. They act on motives and desires, like everyone else. We must respect them as fellow humans. If we promise them something, we are obliged to give it to them.

It was a masterful, quietly radical declaration. Conkling soon reported to Lincoln that he read the letter to the enthusiastic crowd at the meeting and sent it to newspapers. He assured the president that it was "a document that will occupy an important position in the history of our country," one that would invigorate "the war power" and the push toward "universal liberty," so that "when peace arrives, there can be no question as to the condition and rights of 'American citizens of African descent.'"[86]

Lincoln knew that millions would see the letter. Indeed, newspapers across the nation printed it.

He repeated similar ideas in a letter he wrote a year later, in August 1864, in response to a note from the Wisconsin newspaper editor Charles D. Robinson, a War Democrat who was disturbed by what he saw as a radical turn in Lincoln's emancipation policy. Lincoln had recently made a strong antislavery pronouncement. In response to Horace Greeley's proposal in early July to meet with Confederate commissioners for a peace conference at Niagara Falls, Lincoln had written a terse statement saying he would entertain a peace deal that included the South's "abandonment of slavery."[87] Fully aware that the Confederates would reject his terms, he sent his message through Greeley and John Hay, who met three Confederates at Niagara on July 18. The conference quickly collapsed. Newspapers were filled with reports of Lincoln's insistence on an abolitionist war.

To Charles Robinson, the president's position seemed like a betrayal of the Emancipation Proclamation, in which, Robinson said, emancipation was merely a military tool, not the unequivocal goal of the war. Robinson insisted that Lincoln's statement about the Niagara Falls meeting "puts the whole war question on a new basis, and takes us War Democrats clear off our feet, leaving us no ground to stand upon."[88]

In his reply to Robinson, Lincoln denied the accuracy of his charge. He referred to physical force. The Emancipation Proclamation opened the way to peace "by inducing the colored people to come bodily over from the rebel side to ours." Black soldiers, seamen, and laborers, whom Lincoln numbered at between 130,000 and 150,000, had made the big difference in the war because of the sheer strength they brought to the Union cause. Lincoln wrote, "It is not a question of sentiment or taste, but one of physical force, which may be measured, and estimated as horsepower, and steam power, are measured and estimated."[89] Take that force away and give it to the enemy, Lincoln argued, and the war would be lost.

Nor did Lincoln neglect the human and ethical dimensions. He referred to the Conkling letter, in which he had said the blacks act from motives "like other people." If they were not motivated by the promise of emancipation, why would they fight for the North? "As a matter of morals, could such treachery by any possibility, escape the curses of Heaven, or of any good man?" Lincoln asked.

He worked carefully on the letter, writing two drafts of it and showing it to others, including Frederick Douglass. But he didn't send it. That in itself was not unusual for him. But why did he hold this letter back? Wouldn't it have been another publicity coup for him, as the Conkling letter had been a year earlier?

For the answer, we must look at his situation in August 1864. It was much different from that of the previous August. At that time he was able to refer to recent military victories. Now progress on the main military fronts—Virginia, Georgia, and the Gulf of Mexico—was murky. Extreme war weariness gripped the nation.

From the right, Copperheads had been pummeling Lincoln mercilessly with their demands that he achieve peace by disbanding African

American troops, canceling the Emancipation Proclamation, and reenslaving freedmen. From the left, Radical Republicans were furious over his pocket veto in July of the Wade-Davis Bill, which would have imposed stiff terms on the South for Reconstruction, in contrast to the more lenient ones he had proposed. Salmon Chase, who had resigned as treasury secretary in June, wrote during the summer, "There is great and almost universal dissatisfaction with Mr. Lincoln among all earnest men. They doubt he can be reelected."[90]

The presidential election was just ten weeks away. From New York, the Republican mastermind Thurlow Weed wrote William Seward on August 22 that he had recently informed Lincoln that his reelection was "an impossibility. . . . [N]obody here doubts it; nor do I see any body from other States who authorises the slightest hope of success." Many in the North now seemed ready to compromise with the South. Weed wrote, "The People are wild for Peace. They are told that the President will only listen to terms of Peace on condition Slavery be 'abandoned.' . . . That *something* should be done and promptly done, to give the Administration a chance for its life, is certain."[91]

Even antislavery friends of the president urged compromise. Henry Raymond, editor of the *New York Times*, opined that if something dramatic was not done, "all is lost." He recommended that peace commissioners be sent to Richmond to make a deal to restore the Union.

The immense pressures on Lincoln at this moment were captured in a cartoon, *The Political Blondin*, that appeared in *Frank Leslie's Budget of Fun* on September 1, 1864. In the cartoon, the president's position on the tightrope is more precarious than ever. A glum-looking Lincoln pushes a wheelbarrow stuffed with the American flag (the nation). On his shoulders, he carries two worried-looking cabinet members, Secretary of War Stanton and Secretary of the Navy Welles (representing the uncertain Union military prospects in the summer of 1864). A third member, the departed Chase, has tumbled off Stanton's shoulders. From the galleries, on opposite sides, are Union leaders, including Grant and

The Political Blondin (*Frank Leslie's Budget of Fun*, September 1, 1864)

Sherman, and Confederate ones, including Robert E. Lee and Jefferson Davis. Also present is John Bull (Great Britain) and Napoleon III (France), foreign voices in the war. The cartoon's caption tells us that the spectators are assailing Lincoln with contradictory advice to move "slower," "faster," "more North," "more to the South." The president looks down at a wounded soldier who pathetically waves a crutch at him.[92]

Those close to the president had serious doubts about the forthcoming election. "Everything is darkness and doubt and discouragement," wrote John Nicolay on August 25. The election hopes were so poor, Nicolay wrote, that "weak-kneed d—d fools like Chas. Sumner are in the movement for a new candidate—to supplant the Tycoon."[93]

Which gets us back to the letter to Charles Robinson that Lincoln chose not to send. Although he was in extreme political peril when he drafted the letter, his mind was mainly fixed on saving the nation, not on his own personal political fortunes. Instead of sending the political letter, he wrote a memorandum on August 23 to his cabinet stating that the chances of his reelection were slim, and he looked forward to working with his successor to help rescue the nation. He wrote:

> This morning, as for some days past, it seems exceedingly probable that this Administration will not be re-elected. Then it will be my duty to so co-operate with the President elect, as to save the Union between the election and the inauguration; as he will have secured his election on such ground that he can not possibly save it afterwards.[94]

He sealed the note in an envelope that he had his cabinet members sign. It remained unopened until a week after he was reelected. He then explained to the cabinet that he had written it when he "seemed to have no friends." He said he had known that any Democratic successor would not fight to end slavery.

As it turned out, Sherman's capture of Atlanta in September, following fast on Farragut's victory at Mobile Bay, reinvigorated Northern enthusiasm for the war. Soon positive news came from Grant and cavalry commander Philip Sheridan in the Shenandoah Valley as well. The Democrats, meanwhile, hobbled themselves by nominating the War Democrat McClellan for the presidency and the Copperhead Pendleton as his running mate. John Nicolay now wrote, "We have encouraging news from all quarters," and: "If things continue as favorable as they seem today we shall beat Little Mac very handsomely."[95] The prediction proved accurate. Momentously, on November 4, Lincoln was reelected, winning the popular vote convincingly and the electoral college overwhelmingly.

Looking back at Lincoln's behavior in August 1864, when reelection seemed unlikely, we see his real character. He thought about the nation, not himself.

His selflessness came out vividly in meetings he had that month with John Eaton, an Ohio Republican who was serving in Louisiana as the commissioner of contraband there. Having just come from Toledo, where he had heard Frederick Douglass attack Lincoln for the alleged weakness of his retaliation policy against Confederate atrocities, Eaton went straight to the White House. He found Lincoln surprisingly unconcerned about his political enemies.

Over the next week, Eaton visited Lincoln several times at the president's request. During one conversation, the two heard distant musket fire. The president went to the open window, stared into the distance, and then turned to Eaton. His eyes were filled with tears. He said, "This is the day when they shoot deserters. I am wondering whether I have used the pardoning power as much as I ought. I know some of our officers feel that I have used it with so much freedom as to demoralize the army and destroy the discipline."[96] The punishment of soldiers should take into account extenuating circumstances, he said. Every case must be judged on its own.

What especially struck Eaton during his visits was Lincoln's earnest concern for the blacks who remained in slavery and were apparently uninformed about the Emancipation Proclamation. Eaton found that "the President's grasp of the situation was astonishing, especially in view of the many and serious problems that lay upon his mind." Lincoln, Eaton noted, manifested "in his talk with me the deepest interest in all the elements of the Negro character which had been revealed to our officers in the course of our association with the freedmen."

Eaton mentioned Frederick Douglass's recent speech in which he criticized the president's lenient proposal for Reconstruction and his failure to endorse suffrage for blacks. In response, Lincoln read Eaton a letter of March 13, 1864, in which he had encouraged Louisiana governor Michael Hahn to extend the vote to "some of the colored people . . . —as, for instance, the very intelligent, and especially those who have fought gallantly in our ranks. They would probably help, in some trying time to come, to keep the jewel of liberty within the family of freedom."[97] Coming from the cautious Lincoln, this was a ringing endorsement of the vote for blacks.

The president's immediate concern, given the unlikelihood of his reelection, was spreading the news of emancipation to the millions of blacks still held in slavery. They must hear of their liberation and be urged to flee behind Union lines before the election. No Democratic successor would care about the matter, which therefore must be addressed soon. But how could the word be spread among the enslaved? Lincoln had thought deeply on the topic.

The person on his mind was John Brown. As Eaton recalled, Lincoln "alluded to John Brown's raid," which had been designed to disseminate freedom by infiltrating Southern plantations.[98] Brown's effort in 1859, the president told Eaton, had been ill timed—a point he had made in his Cooper Union speech, where he described Brown's single-handed effort to liberate millions of enslaved people as quixotic because of the absence of ready communication between the blacks. Now he asked: What if such communication could be established? The war opened new options for creating a "grapevine telegraph," Lincoln said. "The war [is] upon us," he declared, and the North must be "considering every possible means by which the Negro could be secured in his freedom"—including a strategy somewhat reminiscent of John Brown's.[99]

HIS SOUL WAS MARCHING ON

By combining emancipation with hard war, Lincoln had already established a cultural atmosphere friendly to the memory of John Brown. Frederick Douglass considered the Emancipation Proclamation a John Brown document that made the Union's military effort comparable to a large-scale John Brown's raid. In a speech on the proclamation at Cooper Union, Frederick Douglass declared, "Good old JOHN BROWN [applause] was a madman two years ago, now the whole nation is as mad as he. [Applause.] Every honest soldier who marches into Virginia goes there to carry out the object that led JOHN BROWN to Harper's Ferry. [Applause.]"[100] At some of his recruitment rallies, Douglass led his black audience in singing "John Brown's Body," with its stirring words, "He's gone to be a soldier in the Army of the Lord, . . . His soul is marching on."[101] Douglass inspired his listeners by mentioning two of Brown's African American soldiers: "Remember Shields Green and [John Anthony] Copeland [Jr.], who followed noble John Brown, and fell as glorious martyrs." While recruiting for what became the intrepid Massachusetts Fifty-fourth Regiment, Douglass worked closely with the antislavery millionaire George Stearns, who had been one of John Brown's Secret Six.[102] As the Fifty-fourth Massachusetts marched through New York on its way south, crowds cheered as it lustily sang the John Brown song.

After his interview with John Eaton, Lincoln summoned Douglass to Washington. In a meeting on August 19 that left Douglass stunned, the president proposed that Douglass gather a force of blacks that would spread through the South and funnel enslaved people to freedom. Douglass listened with "the deepest interest and profoundest satisfaction" as Lincoln asked him to organize "a band of scouts, composed of colored men, whose business should be somewhat after the original plan of John Brown, to go into the rebel States, beyond the lines of our armies, and carry the news of emancipation, and urge the slaves to come within our boundaries."[103] This was Brown's Subterranean Pass Way on a grand scale. It solved the problem of noncommunication in Brown's plan that Lincoln had mentioned at Cooper Union. It established a network of African American agents, under Douglass's direction, throughout the South. Douglass eagerly accepted the assignment, which, as it turned out, was canceled after news of the Union victories came the next month.

The second part of Lincoln's plan—creating an African American army of liberation—surfaced when the black physician and reformer Martin R. Delany visited the White House the next February. Widely regarded as the father of black nationalism and an inspirer of Marcus Garvey and Malcolm X, Delany in a newspaper article praised "our glorious Chief Magistrate, President Lincoln" and felt he was in the presence of "an able and master spirit" during the White House meeting.[104]

Delaney, the grandson of Africans who had been brought to America and enslaved there, Martin Delany was born a free black in Charles Town, Virginia, in 1812. As a child, he had moved with his family to Pennsylvania, where he received a strong education. He explored many subjects at Jefferson College, worked for black newspapers (including Frederick Douglass's *North Star*), and briefly studied medicine at Harvard before leaving the school amid protests over his presence aired by white students. Thereafter, Delany doubled as a physician and an antislavery reformer. A well-built man of middle height whose eyes flashed with determination, he took pride in his extremely dark skin. A contemporary wrote, "His great boast is, that there lives none blacker than himself."[105] In the 1850s, he spearheaded an emigration movement that called for African Americans to relocate to a country where they would enjoy full rights: at different times he proposed Africa, Central America, and South America. Colonizationists in the Lincoln administration cited his 1852 book *The Condition, Elevation, Emigration, and Destiny of the Colored People of the United States, Politically Considered*. Delany, having moved to Canada in 1856, endorsed slave rebellions in the United States. He aided John Brown in the preparation for Harpers Ferry and wrote *Blake, or the Huts of America* (1859), about a black man who roamed through the South attempting to incite slave insurrections.

Insurrections were on his mind when he visited Lincoln on February 9, 1865. It turned out that they were on Lincoln's mind, too. In his interview with the president, Delany pointed out that black troops were demoralized by the paucity of officers of color and by the condescension expressed by many white officers. Delany proposed that more blacks be commissioned as officers to lead an African American army through the South, liberating enslaved people along the way and enlisting them in the Union army. This ever-growing black force would strike terror in the Confederacy.

Lincoln was not just receptive to the idea; he told Delany that he had pondered a similar plan for more than two years. He declared, "This is the very thing I have been looking and hoping for; but nobody offered it. I have thought it over and over again. I have talked about it; I hoped and prayed for it; but till now it has never been proposed."[106] He exclaimed, "Won't this be a grand thing? When I issued my Emancipation Proclamation, I had this thing in contemplation." He said he had expected that word of the proclamation would spread and cause enslaved people to rise up against their masters. He had been disappointed that the uprising had not happened, he explained, which is why he found Delany's proposal so appealing. Such a plan had been the dream of John Brown, who had never gotten the opportunity to advance southward into slave territory and raise a black army of liberation.

Delany accepted Lincoln's offer to take on the leadership of the African American force. He became the first black major of infantry in the Union army. He organized a regiment in Charleston, South Carolina, that missed action only because it entered the war too late. (Delany took command of his troops on April 11, two days after Appomattox.)

The bonding between the president and these two militant African American leaders, Frederick Douglass and Martin Delany, puts to rest any doubts about Lincoln's underlying radicalism on race. His meetings with them were in the spirit of John Brown, the man about whom Douglass said, "I could live for the slave, but he could die for him."[107] If Lincoln at Cooper Union had criticized John Brown's plan as unrealistic, the Civil War gave him the means of making certain aspects of such a plan workable, albeit in a wholly different context. Fomenting slave resistance and forming an ever-expanding army of freedmen had been denied to John Brown but seemed plausible to Lincoln, who sought the leadership of two

MAJOR MARTIN R. DELANY

African Americans who had been close to Brown: Douglass, who had supported Brown for a dozen years before Harpers Ferry; and Delany, who had organized the convention in Chatham, Canada, where Brown had outlined his planned invasion of the South.

Douglass sometimes wavered on Lincoln, especially early on, but there was one quality in the president that stood out for him: a genuine dedication to human equality. Douglass remarked, "In all my interviews with Mr. Lincoln I was impressed with his entire freedom from popular prejudice against the colored race. He was the first great man that I talked with in the United States freely, who in no single instance reminded me of the difference between himself and myself, of the difference of color, and I thought that all the more remarkable because he came from a State where there were black laws."[108]

Delany felt the same way. He was impressed by Lincoln's openness toward him. The president greeted Delany with "a generous grasp and shake of the hand" and placed himself "at ease, the better to give me a patient audience." Lincoln's respect for Delany came through in a note of introduction he sent to Edwin Stanton: "Do not fail to have an interview with this most extraordinary and intelligent black man. A. LINCOLN."[109]

Douglass and Delany were hardly alone. Lincoln's personal warmth to black people extended from ones he had known in Springfield, such as William Florville and William K. Donnegan, to ones he met in the White House years.

Among them was the aged abolitionist and feminist Sojourner Truth. Intent on meeting Lincoln before she died, Truth journeyed in October 1864 from her home in Michigan to Washington, where she met with the president on the twenty-ninth. When interviewed later about the visit, she reported that as she entered the White House she saw the tall Lincoln in the midst of a group of visitors, two of them black women. His behavior astonished her. She commented, "He showed as much kindness to the colored persons as to the whites,—if there was any difference, more."[110] Her meeting with the president was emotional. She told him, "You are the best President who has ever taken the seat." Addressing her as "Auntie Truth," Lincoln showed her the Bible that the black delegation from Baltimore had given him. She found the Bible "beautiful beyond description" and noted the extraordinary fact that black people had given it to the head of "the government [that] once sanctioned laws that would not permit its people to learn enough to enable them to read this Book." The president signed her autograph book: "For Auntie Sojourner Truth, October 29, 1864. A. Lincoln." All told, Truth recalled, "I never was treated by any one with more kindness and cordiality than was shown me by that great and good man, Abraham Lincoln."

SOJOURNER TRUTH

Lesser-known African Americans were touched by Lincoln's openness to them as well. Mary Lincoln's dressmaker and companion Lizzy
Keckly, whom Lincoln called "Madam Elizabeth," always felt Lincoln's
warmth.[111] Rebecca Pomroy, the black nurse brought into the White
House after Willie Lincoln's death, likewise enjoyed a relationship of
mutual respect with the president. Pomroy once invited the president for
a visit to the Washington hospital where she worked and introduced him
to the staff, including the black cooks and servants. He spoke to them
kindly. The incident infuriated Pomroy's white colleagues, who berated
her for doing "such a mean, contemptible trick as to introduce those d—
niggers to the President." Pomroy later asked Lincoln if he had been hurt

when she introduced him to the blacks. "Hurt? No, indeed!" he exclaimed. "It did my soul good. I'm glad to do them honor."[112]

Among the many African Americans who had little or no personal contact with Lincoln, he attained mythic stature. Witness the African American response to the Emancipation Proclamation. While all historians recognize the importance of the proclamation, it has been slighted in some circles because of its morally neutral tone, its partial application (to the rebel states alone), and its apparent belatedness, as it came after several previous military and legal steps toward emancipation.

True enough. But we must not forget the enormously exuberant response to Lincoln's proclamation. As the news of it spread, Lincoln became a demigod among black people. The artist Francis Carpenter recalled, "By the Act of Emancipation, Mr. Lincoln built for himself the first place in the affections of the African race on this continent. The love and reverence manifested for his name and person on all occasions during the last two years of his life, by this down-trodden people, were always remarkable, and sometimes of a thrilling character."[113] Carpenter told of South Carolina freedmen whose term for God was "Massa Linkum." A black preacher asserted to his listeners, "Massa Linkum, he ebrywhar. He know ebryting . . . *He walk de earf like de Lord*!"

The combination of interracial respect and black-centered militancy that Lincoln displayed fueled proslavery comparisons between Lincoln and John Brown, one of the least racist white people in American history. The Copperhead Charles Chauncey Burr later wrote, "The administration of Abraham Lincoln was a John Brown raid on the grandest scale, and it was no more. That is the place it will occupy in history." From Burr's perspective, the spectacle was nightmarish. Union soldiers had made cities "hideous as hell by singing '*John Brown's souls is marching on!*' Words that also surged "from the brazen throats of negro-worshipping mobs." The war, Burr wrote, had unleashed "the insane gibberish and fantastic dance of negroes, of both white and black complexion, making night and day hideous with infernal delight."[114]

Despite Burr's wildly racist distortions, his comments made the accurate point that Lincoln had ended up leading a war for the liberation of blacks, which had been John Brown's dream.

There were, however, important differences between the two versions of antislavery war. John Brown followed a higher law in the name of human justice, starting with the emancipation of America's four million enslaved people. Because Brown knew that many Americans interpreted the Constitution as proslavery, he wrote an explicitly antislavery document—his "Provisional Constitution and Ordinances for the People of the United States"—as the foundation for the new society he envisaged.[115] He also wrote a new version of the Declaration of Independence that overtly affirmed equality for all, with specific emphasis on the marginalized and oppressed. Confronted with a government whose proslavery laws and court rulings he called "wicked, cruel, and unjust enactments," he took individual action to circumvent that government.[116] He infiltrated the South with a small band of armed followers in order to trigger events that would lead to emancipation. His actions were deemed treasonous, and he and six followers were hanged.

Although Lincoln shared Brown's goals, he thought Brown's strategy was lawless. Lincoln worked within the political system and the laws. As for the Constitution, he tried to respect it. Before the war, he argued persuasively that it was antislavery in spirit. When the war came, he resorted to methods such as suspending habeas corpus that he believed were among the war powers assigned to him as president during periods of rebellion or invasion.

As the war progressed, Lincoln came to realize that the Constitution must be changed in order to ensure the permanency of freedom. To make this happen, he came to adopt some of John Brown's methods, which by 1864, in Lincoln's capacity as commander in chief, were the actions of a democratically elected president, not the extralegal strategies of an inspired individual. Like Brown, Lincoln wanted to appoint African Americans as leaders of the emancipation effort. The reason Frederick

Douglass and Martin Delany did not get the chance to carry out their assigned roles in that effort was that the Union military, including its strong African American contingent, defeated the Confederacy first.

John Brown's raid was a vigilante effort, motivated by the higher law that deepened the national divide. Lincoln, in contrast, directed a Constitution-backed war that never lost sight of restoring the entire nation and putting it on a just basis.

Justice came, at long last, with the three war amendments. Through brilliant finagling on the part of Lincoln and congressional Republicans, the Thirteenth Amendment, which the Senate had approved the previous year, passed the House on January 31, 1865. Nine days later, Lincoln quietly backed Martin Delany's emancipation plan. That the president put this plan into action even after Congress had passed the amendment reflected his John Brown–like eagerness to make emancipation arrive as quickly as possible. But Delany's plan was rendered moot by Lee's surrender to Grant on April 9. By the end of 1865, the required number of states had ratified the amendment, which abolished slavery. Within the next five years came the Fourteenth Amendment, affirming birthright citizenship, and the Fifteenth Amendment, which gave black males the vote (women would wait another half century for it).

Lincoln's long-term goal of citizenship for black people, therefore, came to fruition. Frederick Douglass had sometimes doubted the president's position on the issue and had actually in the spring of 1864 backed the Radical Republican candidate, John Frémont. But he regained faith in Lincoln when he visited the White House in August and when, the following April, the president called publicly for limited suffrage for African Americans.

Douglass and Delany would both pay moving homage to Lincoln after his death. Douglass called Lincoln "unsurpassed by any for his interest in the white man" but at the same time "emphatically the black man's President: the first to show any respect to their rights as men. He was the first of the long line [of presidents] to show any respect to the rights of the black man, or to acknowledge that he had any rights the white man ought to respect."[117]

Major Martin Delany, for his part, would make a public plea for a national monument to be erected in Lincoln's honor. Delany's memorial was never built, but it was an astonishing idea that would have projected African Americans' reverence for the president. Delany said the monument could be paid for if four million black Americans each contributed a penny. In describing the monument, Delany did not mention how Lincoln would be portrayed, but he gave a precise account of what he envisioned as a figure to accompany the president on the monument: a sculpture of "Ethiopia stretching forth her hands unto God." An African woman, draped in flowing robes, would kneel next to an urn, with one leg bent up before her and her face looking heavenward. Sculptured tears would fall down her face into the urn. The "distinct teardrops," Delany instructed, "shall be so arranged as they represent the figures of 4,000,000 (four million), which shall be emblematical not only of the number of contributors to the monument, but the number of those who shed tears of sorrow for the great and good deliverer of their race from bondage in the United States."[118]

Delany left no doubt as to the distinct racial character of the proposed statue. He wrote, "This figure is neither to be Grecian, Caucasian, nor Anglo-Saxon, Mongolian nor Indian, but *African—very African*—an ideal representative genius of the race, as Europa, Britannia, America, or the Goddess of Liberty, is to the European race."

Lincoln, however, ultimately reached a position where he was beyond any ethnic or national category, except an inclusive American one.

During his presidency, he built his own monuments—majestic oratorical ones—to people of all races and nationalities: the Gettysburg Address and the Second Inaugural Address. Those landmark speeches enshrined him in world memory.

Democratic Eloquence

In the Lincoln Memorial in Washington, DC, the Gettysburg Address and the Second Inaugural Address are etched in stone. The memorial has three chambers. The central one features the statue of the seated Lincoln. The other two present the two famous speeches. In the South Chamber, the 272-word Gettysburg Address appears on a wall in a single panel. In the North Chamber, the 698-word Second Inaugural Address is reproduced in three panels side by side.

Given the windiness of political speeches (especially nineteenth-century ones), it is astonishing that two of the greatest speeches of all time are short enough to fit on a wall and can be read in a matter of minutes. The marvelous brevity of the speeches shows that Lincoln was a master of what the neuroscientist Jean-Pierre Changeux calls parsimony in art—that is, explaining much with little, finding a pattern in the midst of apparent disorder. In art, Changeux detects "a certain economy of means revealed as a bold line, a convincing brushstroke, a contrasting juxtaposition of colors, all creating sensory consonance, and endowing a work of quality with its own unique harmony."[1]

We find the "bold line," the "juxtaposition of colors," and "unique harmony" in both of Lincoln's finest speeches, whose rhythmic sentences are literary brushstrokes that deliver timeless truths about human equality, justice, and charity. The speeches are prime examples of what might be called political parsimony. They reduce many progressive concepts to fundamental egalitarian principles that still survive in the world's collective consciousness.

Reading the Gettysburg Address and the Second Inaugural today, one is tempted to view them as statements by a sage who looked beyond and above his era. They were not. They gained transcendent power because Lincoln responded attentively to the America of his time and absorbed its most enlightened currents. The speeches were extracts of cultural and social forces, produced by the most receptive and principled president America has had.

THE GETTYSBURG ADDRESS IN CONTEXT

The progress from the Battle of Gettysburg in early July 1863 to the Gettysburg Address on November 19 was a journey from chaos and death to Lincoln's affirmation of order, justice, and national regeneration.

First, the chaos and death. The Battle of Gettysburg produced the most casualties of any Civil War battle—more than 23,000 dead, missing, or wounded on each side. The three-day engagement epitomized the firestorm that was the Civil War. Robert E. Lee's post-Chancellorsville invasion of the North, with its uncharacteristic miscues; the collision of the rebels and the federals at the Pennsylvania crossroads town of Gettysburg; on the first day, the clashes that pushed the federals from north of the town to the hills south of it; on the second and third days, the assaults by Lee's forces on the entrenched enemy; the fights to the death at the Peach Orchard, Devil's Den, the Wheat Field, Culp's Hill, and Little Round Top; the desperate charge of 15,000 yelling rebels under George Pickett on the Union center at Cemetery Ridge, followed by the frenzied Confederate retreat and Meade's bungled pursuit of Lee—all are part of Civil War lore.

Then the horrific aftermath of this Northern victory. South and west of Gettysburg, the corpses of soldiers and horses stretched for miles. One witness reported, "All was a trodden, miry waste, with corpses at every step, and the thick littered *débris* of battle."[2] For days, bodies decayed in the summer rain and sun. Vultures swarmed, and hogs rooted at the bodies. The sickening stench of rotting flesh filled the town. All the houses, stores, barns, and other structures in the area became hospitals, including the four-story building of the Pennsylvania College of Gettysburg. The dying and wounded received care from selfless women of the Sanitary and Christian Commissions, but doctors were in short supply.

Burying the dead was grueling. The bodies of Confederates were dumped by the hundreds into trenches and covered with earth. The Union fallen received careful attention. Letters, receipts, diaries, and other personal items assisted in identifying the dead. At first an effort was made to ship bodies that could be identified in coffins to soldiers' families, but after several hundred shipments this gruesome task ceased. Instead, federal soldiers were buried where they lay in shallow graves marked by rough boards on which their names were scribbled in pencil.

Someone recognized the inadequacy of these temporary graves and had the idea of turning the battle site into a national cemetery. David Wills, a Gettysburg lawyer who supervised the postbattle activities, got the approval of Pennsylvania authorities and Lincoln himself to develop the cemetery. Wills purchased for the state some twenty-two acres in a boot-shaped area on a slope about a half mile south of the town, where the Union dead would be interred. In the cemetery, designed by landscape gardener and horticulturist William Saunders, the bodies were buried in sections for the eighteen states where the soldiers had come from. Those states contributed funds to the project, as did the

Corpses of Union soldiers after the Battle of Gettysburg,
July 1–3, 1863 (photograph by Timothy H. O'Sullivan)

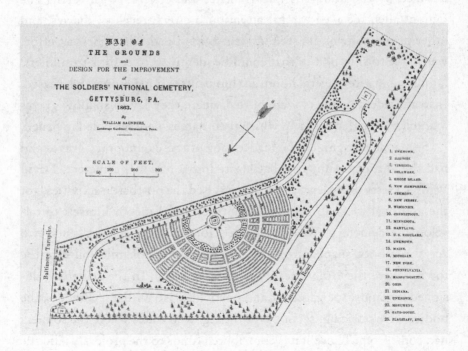

Plan of the Soldiers' National Cemetery at Gettysburg

federal government. Transferring the dead from the battlefield to the cemetery began in October and ended in March 1864; in all, 3,512 bodies were buried, about a third of them in two large sections called Unknown.[3]

The cemetery symbolized the unification of Northern states around a common cause. Lincoln met with Saunders and was "much pleased" with the layout, commenting that it "differed from the ordinary cemetery."[4] Unlike the dispersed, natural design of rural cemeteries, with their groups of graves clustered separately by individual families, the Gettysburg Cemetery placed the dead in parallel rows of half circles with a sixty-foot statue of the Genius of Liberty at their center. The headstones were arranged in symmetrical arcs of short granite blocks, with names and ranks inscribed on them, creating a democracy in death that subsumed individuality to the goals of Union and Liberty. "The cemetery at Gettysburg," Drew Gilpin Faust notes, "was arranged so that every grave was of equal importance; William Saunders's design, like Lincoln's speech, affirmed that every dead soldier mattered equally regardless of rank or station."[5]

In August 1863, Pennsylvania governor Andrew Curtin began organizing a dedication ceremony in honor of those killed at Gettysburg. The speaker who first came to mind was Edward Everett. He was a natural choice. Over the years, the distinguished Everett had been a Unitarian minister, the president of Harvard College, a US congressman and senator, secretary of state under Millard Fillmore, and the running mate of Constitutional Union Party presidential candidate John Bell in 1860. Above all, Everett was an orator, prepared to speak at important events of all kinds. After his death in 1865, a eulogist asked, "On what occasion of honor to the living and the dead,—at what commemoration to the glorious past,—in what exigency of the present moment,—have those lips ever been mute?"[6]

Many considered Everett a modern-day Demosthenes. His moderate position on slavery helped him appeal to a varied audience. On

EDWARD EVERETT

September 23, David Wills invited him to be the main speaker at Gettysburg. The silver-haired, sixty-nine-year-old Everett accepted, with the caveat that he would not be available until November 19. The date was thus set. Organizing the ceremony was put under the command of Lincoln's close friend Ward Hill Lamon, the US marshal for the District of Columbia, and Major General Darius N. Couch.

Lincoln was expected to participate in this important event. Governor Curtin visited him in late October, and on November 2 Wills sent the president a note asking if he might like to give "a few appropriate remarks" at the ceremony.[7] Lincoln accepted the invitation.

Lincoln on November 8, 1863 (photograph by Alexander Gardner)

He spent the two and half weeks before his trip to Gettysburg carrying on his usual duties as war president and otherwise occupying himself. Twice he visited the photographic studios of Alexander and James Gardner to have his portrait taken. On November 9, he went to Ford's Theatre and saw John Wilkes Booth in the lead role as a Greek sculptor in *The Marble Heart*. Three days later, he went alone to the wedding of Kate Chase and William Sprague (Mary, who hated the lovely, wasp-waisted Kate, stayed away). On November 17, the California senator John Conness presented Lincoln with a cane that had been a gift from his predecessor, the tough-fisted b'hoy politician David C.

Broderick. Lincoln said he had never met Broderick but had heard enough good things about him to say that receiving a memento of Broderick's was "a fact he would remember through all the years of his life."[8]

Meanwhile, he mulled over his speech. He wanted to deliver a message about the meaning of the war. He had hinted the message in some impromptu words he had spoken on July 7, just after the victories at Gettysburg and Vicksburg. He told a crowd of serenaders, "How long ago is it—eighty odd years—since on the Fourth of July for the first time in the history of the world a nation by its representatives, assembled and declared as a self-evident truth that 'all men are created equal.'" He added, "Gentlemen, this is a glorious theme, and the occasion for a speech, but I am not prepared to make one worthy of the occasion."[9]

He was so excited about having halted Lee's northern advance that on July 19 he scribbled a giddy verse he called "Gen. Lees invasion of the North written by himself":

> In eighteen sixty three, with pomp,
> and mighty swell,
> Me and Jeff's Confederacy, went
> forth to sack Phil-del
> The Yankees they got arter us
> and giv us particular hell
> And we skedaddled back again
> and didn't sack Phil-del.[10]

Here, like his favorite humorist, Petroleum Nasby, he impersonated the enemy in order to debunk him. His tone was not as caustic as Nasby's, but he used the same techniques—vernacular language, misspellings, the assault on Southern chivalry—that were staples of David Ross Locke's humor.

Like Locke, Lincoln delivered a serious message in a humorous format. Unlike Locke, he possessed another gift: the capability of expressing serious ideals in truly memorable language. The invitation to the Gettysburg ceremony offered him the opportunity he had been waiting for. The legend that he scribbled his address on an envelope on his train ride to Gettysburg is just that—a legend—as is the story that he composed it spontaneously just before he gave the speech. Several days before Gettysburg, Simon Cameron visited Lincoln, who showed him the speech, written in pencil on commercial note paper, saying he had taken "great pains in writing it."[11] Around the same time he told the journalist Noah Brooks, "I have written it over, two or three times, and I shall have to give it another lick before I am satisfied."[12] The speech was substantially done by the time he left for Gettysburg on November 18.

The president's train was scheduled to leave Washington at noon that day. But Tad had fallen ill, and Mary was panicking over the boy's condition. Lincoln delayed going to the station in order to attend to his wife and son. James Fry, the official who picked him up at the White House at eleven thirty, tried to speed him up. Lincoln answered Fry by telling him the story of a convicted man in Illinois who was on the way to the gallows and, seeing crowds rushing ahead to see him hang, called out, "Boys, you needn't be in such a hurry to get ahead, *there won't be any fun until I get there.*"[13]

The special train had four cars; its locomotive was festooned with patriotic bunting and streamers. Lincoln sat in a section of the rear car. Also on board were three cabinet members—Seward, Blair, and Usher—along with other government officials and citizens. The train reached Gettysburg at sundown. Lincoln was taken to the home of David Wills, who had invited him to stay the night. Wills held a dinner attended by thirty-eight luminaries, including a foreign diplomat and a French admiral. In the evening, the town's usually quiet streets were alive with shouting, singing, and laughter from the crowds who had come to attend the ceremony. Liquor flowed, and pickpockets plied their trade. Serenades by a military band and glee clubs wafted through the night.

Calls rang out for Lincoln and Seward. The president appeared at a window and waved. He said he did not want to speak that evening, adding that it was important as president that he "not say any foolish things." Someone cried, "If you can help it," to which he replied, "It very often happens that the only way to help it is to say nothing at all."[14] The crowd laughed and cheered. Seward gave a brief, bland speech as Lincoln retired to his room. The president looked over his speech and at eleven made his way, under guard, next door, where Seward was staying, so that the secretary of state could read it as well.

The next morning, Lincoln accompanied Seward on a tour of the battleground north of town where the clashes between the armies had occurred on the first day. At ten, Lincoln was escorted to the diamond-shaped town center, where a procession was forming that would go to the cemetery south of the town for the ceremony. The crowd yelled, "Hurrah for Old Abe!," "We are coming Father Abraham!," and "God save the President!"[15] He mounted a bay horse so small that his long legs nearly reached the ground. Waiting for the parade to begin, Lincoln sat on his horse, shook hands with well-wishers, and was cheered by a telegram reporting good news from Grant in Tennessee and another one saying that his son Tad was better. The procession soon started moving. It included cabinet members, state governors, military officers, civic societies, and bands. Citizens and journalists took up the rear.

Passing through the town, the paraders could see houses and walls pocked with bullet holes and children selling battle relics. Outside of town, there appeared a ravaged landscape. Trees had been peeled by musket fire or reduced to splintered trunks by shells. Strewn about were the skeletons of horses, muddy knapsacks, old shoes, canteens, cartridge boxes, and scraps of uniforms. Here and there lay a human skull. Even in this grim surrounding, socializing and chatter abounded.

Crowds gathering at Gettysburg, November 19, 1863

Thousands had come for the ceremony, and many strolled through the historic battlefield, gathering souvenirs, talking politics, and courting.

The crowd of fifteen thousand quieted down when it gathered to watch the dedication ceremony, which began at 11:30 a.m. Many officials in the parade took seats arranged in three rows on a low twelve-foot-by-twenty-foot platform. Lincoln sat on an old, cushionless settee between Everett and Seward. A chaplain's long opening prayer was followed by Everett's oration. Then Lincoln spoke.

The two speeches responded to the same event—the Battle of Gettysburg and its soldier-heroes—but were vastly different from each other.

Four years earlier, a perceptive Chicago journalist had contrasted the oratorical styles of Everett and Lincoln. The journalist wrote that Lincoln, with "the vigor of his rhetoric, . . . is at once the equal and the opposite of Mr. Everett. The latter excels in lengthy sentences of most musical flow." Everett's style "is rather cloying than satisfying. There is diffusion, not concentration of idea"; it is "truthful to a fault, overladen with detail, overcrowded with elaborate ornament." The essayist continued, "Mr. Lincoln belongs to another school. His style is broad and sketchy, accomplishing at a stroke that to which Mr. Everett devotes an hour, and gaining in force and expression all that is lost in minuteness of execution." The essayist said of Lincoln, "*Terse* is the term which describes his language. It is eminently direct."[16]

Nowhere was the contrast between the two styles more obvious than at Gettysburg. Everett recited from memory his 13,000 words over the course of two hours. Lincoln read his speech, fewer than 300 words long, from a written draft in just over two minutes. Everett's speech was flowery, pretentious. Lincoln's was succinct, direct.

Everett meandered through world history, from the distant past to the present. He discussed funeral rituals in ancient Athens. He mentioned the Puritan civil wars in England as a backdrop to the American experience. "The Puritans of 1640," he declared, "rebelled against arbitrary power to establish constitutional liberty," as opposed to the Confederacy, which rejected a federal government that "favored equal rights." The British civil wars proved "that it is just and proper to rebel against oppressive governments," whereas the Southern rebellion criminally established a slave society.[17] Coming up to date, Everett described the Battle of Gettysburg: its background, its highlights, its participants. He re-created the chaos and confusion of war. He traced the strategizing of Confederate and Union forces during Lee's northward advance, and he carefully described the shifting fortunes of the Gettysburg battle over three days, including chance occurrences, such as Lee's odd delay on the second day in attacking the federals.

Everett came to no conclusion about the Civil War except that the South had committed a crime by seceding in the name of state sovereignty. Toward the end of the speech, he proclaimed national unity. He declared, "The heart of the People, North and South, is for the Union."

Lincoln's speech did not just *proclaim* unity: it *was* unity—a demonstration of political parsimony, a radically condensed statement about the nation's purpose.

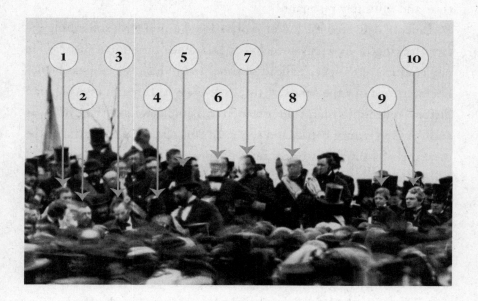

Photograph of Lincoln at Gettysburg on November 19, 1863. The figures on the crowded speakers' platform include the hatless Lincoln (number 3) and Secretary of State William Seward (number 4). Evidence indicates that others in the picture are Lincoln's private secretaries John Hay (number 1) and John Nicolay (number 2), Edward Everett (number 6), the chief marshal Ward Hill Lamon (number 5), Lamon's aide Benjamin B. French (number 8), the Gettysburg attorney David Wills (number 7), and Andrew Curtin, the governor of Pennsylvania (number 10) with his twelve-year-old son (number 9).

THE NATION, SUCCINCTLY DEFINED

Like the gnomic, suggestive poems that Emily Dickinson was then writing in Amherst, Massachusetts, the Gettysburg Address compressed tremendous meaning into a small number of words. About three quarters of the speech's words have just one syllable. There are only seven words of four syllables and thirteen of three. A two-syllable word, *nation*, is used five times, making the point of unified nationhood repeatedly. The ten sentences of the speech are rhythmic and balanced, crystal clear and infinitely resonant.

Lincoln delivered the message of national union with something utterly lacking in Everett's speech—an insistence on human justice. He had read Everett's speech ahead of time, and in his own address he deliberately left out the kinds of things Everett featured: non-American history, reflections on revolution and secession, details of the Civil War and the Gettysburg battle, and so on. In contrast, he demonstrated the meaning of a single historical text: the preamble to the Declaration of Independence.

Like many antislavery advocates, Lincoln had long viewed the Declaration's proclamation of human equality as the most powerful moral law America had produced. He had always considered the Declaration's spirit to be inherent in the Constitution, as had his fellow Republicans, who in their party platforms of 1856 and 1864 had stated that the Constitution "embodied . . . the principles promulgated in the Declaration of Independence."[18] In 1862, two significant works had claimed that black people were citizens under the Constitution. Lincoln's attorney general Edward Bates had argued persuasively that the Constitution was color-blind. People born in the United States merited rights as citizens, no matter their race. George Livermore's book *An Historical Research Respecting the Opinions of the Founders of the Republic, on Negroes as Slaves, as Citizens, and as Soldiers*, a copy of which Charles Sumner gave to Lincoln, made a similar argument. Livermore explored the Articles of Confederation and the Constitutional Convention and concluded that the egalitarian, antislavery spirit of the Declaration of Independence permeated them. The Constitution, Livermore pointed out, of necessity made concessions to the slave power, but those concessions did not abrogate the fundamental commitment on the part of the majority of the Founders to freedom and equality.

By 1863, Lincoln was directing a war of emancipation, a war that would soon lead to rights for African Americans under an amended Constitution.

At Gettysburg, he affirmed equality through images of religion, the earth, and the body. With laser-like focus, he fused these images in his opening sentence: "Four score and seven years ago our fathers brought

Address delivered at the dedication of the cemetery at Gettysburg.

Four score and seven years ago our fathers brought forth on this continent, a new nation, conceived in Liberty, and dedicated to the proposition that all men are created equal.

Now we are engaged in a great civil war, testing whether that nation, or any nation so conceived and so dedicated, can long endure. We are met on a great battle field of that war. We have come to dedicate a portion of that field, as a final resting place for those who here gave their lives that that nation might live. It is altogether fitting and proper that we should do this.

But, in a larger sense, we can not dedi-

cate— we can not consecrate— we can not
hallow— this ground. The brave men, living and dead, who struggled here, have consecrated it, far above our poor power to add
or detract. The world will little note, nor
long remember what we say here, but it can
never forget what they did here. It is for us
the living, rather, to be dedicated here to
the unfinished work which they who four-
ght here have thus far so nobly advanced.
It is rather for us to be here dedicated to
the great task remaining before us— that
from these honored dead we take increased
devotion to that cause for which they gave
the last full measure of devotion— that
we here highly resolve that these dead shall
not have died in vain— that this nation,
under God, shall have a new birth of freedom— and that government of the people,

by the people, for the people, shall not perish from the earth.

                                        Abraham Lincoln.

November 19. 1863.

The Gettysburg Address (final version), in Lincoln's hand

forth on this continent, a new nation, conceived in Liberty, and dedicated to the proposition that all men are created equal."[19]

The line was packed with cultural firepower. The pedestrian "eighty-odd years" of his July 7 speech became at Gettysburg the resonant "four score and seven years." Here he directed American culture's impulse toward biblical rewriting into a phrase that updated Psalms 90:10: "The days of our *years* are threescore *years and ten*; and if by reason of strength they be *fourscore years*, yet is their strength labour and sorrow"—a biblical dictum that commonly appeared in Civil War sermons and speeches. In July 1861, Galusha Grow, the newly elected Speaker of the House, had declared, "Fourscore years ago, fifty-six bold merchants, farmers, lawyers and mechanics" had "met in convention to found a new empire, based on the inalienable rights of man."[20]

Lincoln's next phrase—"our fathers"—revealed a key point Lincoln was making about the American past. He differed on this matter from Everett and many other New Englanders. For the New England–bred Everett, the nation's original fathers were the *Mayflower* Pilgrims. Although Everett, of course, paid homage to the Revolutionary generation, he traced the roots of liberty to the Pilgrims. As early as 1824, he had addressed a Forefathers' Day celebration in Plymouth, and he gave later speeches on the Puritans and the launching of the *Mayflower*. "The Pilgrim settlers of New England," he asserted, "put everything at once on a footing of broad downright political and religious equality."[21] One of his best-known speeches was "The Pilgrim Fathers," in which he praised the Puritans for introducing the "grand idea" of liberty, with "a purpose to establish civil government on the basis of republican equality."[22] Even in his speech at Gettysburg, in which he tried to be national rather than sectional, he could not resist contrasting Oliver Cromwell's Puritan revolution, which he considered a worthy example of rebellion, with the South's revolt against the federal government.

Everett was hardly alone among prominent Northerners who in 1863 affirmed that the New England settlers were the true fathers of the nation. Lincoln's friend Charles Sumner, whose Pilgrim ancestors included Plymouth Colony founder William Bradford, wrote a widely reprinted letter to the New England Society in which he insisted that there were two fundamental historical referents in America: the *Mayflower*, which carried "the Pilgrim Fathers, consecrated to Human Liberty," and the English warship that carried more than twenty enslaved Africans to Virginia around the same time. "In the holds of those two ships," Sumner wrote, "lay the germs of the present direful war, and the simple question now is between the Mayflower and the slave ship. Who that has not forgotten God can doubt the result? The Mayflower must surely prevail."[23]

By contrast, Lincoln at Gettysburg wanted to implant the radically egalitarian principles of Revolutionary fathers deep in the national soil. The date he fixed as the nation's Ur moment was neither 1620, when the *Mayflower* landed, nor 1787, when the Constitutional Convention met, but 1776, when the Declaration of Independence was signed.

Lincoln's phrase "brought forth on this continent, a new nation, conceived in Liberty" anchored American liberty in the body and nature. (One reviewer, seeing sexual connotations in the words "conceived" and "birth of freedom," mocked the address as "Obstetrics.")[24] The continent of the United States was a symbol of unbreakable unity for Lincoln, as in his 1862 message to Congress, where he called the continent "our national homestead," which "demands union, and abhors separation."[25] By referring in the Gettysburg Address to liberty as "brought forth on this continent," he grounded the very meaning of the United States in the indissoluble land itself. In a masterfully concise piece of earth-based rhetoric, Lincoln wiped out the rationale behind secession and slavery.

In the last phrase of the first sentence—"dedicated to the proposition that all men are created equal"—he used a word that established equality as a mathematical law. The evening before, he had shown his address to William Henry Seward, who objected to his using the word "proposition." But Lincoln insisted on keeping it.[26] Here his mathematical instinct came through. Founders like Thomas Paine had considered geometry as the true theology; the principles of the triangle were as true in the distant reaches of the universe as they were on earth. Lincoln had learned from Euclidian geometry that things equal to the same thing are equal to each other. In his use of the Euclidian term "proposition" at Gettysburg, he presented a striking political syllogism: all humans are equal; blacks are human; therefore, blacks are equal to whites.

In 1858, when fighting for a Senate seat against Stephen Douglas, he had said he believed that "the negro is included in the word 'men' used in the Declaration of Independence" and that "'all men are created equal' is the great fundamental principle upon which our free institutions rest."[27] At the same time, in an effort to win votes in a state in which free blacks were not permitted to settle and interracial marriage was outlawed, Lincoln added the obligatory disclaimer that he had no "intention to produce social and political equality between the white and black races."

Any such disclaimer is absent from the Gettysburg Address, which highlights the Declaration's announcement of human equality without qualification.

Although Lincoln made no explicit reference to race in the address, he did not have to. He had gone on record in his August letter to James Conkling that the military service of blacks proved that they were human. The public letter had inspired abolitionists. One supportive paper reduced the Conkling letter to its basic antislavery message: "Is the slave a man? Then we throw the flag over him, and he can speak as a man."[28]

For the Lincoln of 1863, African Americans were absolutely part of the Founders' "proposition" of human equality. His supporters saw this, and so did his critics, who pounced on him for it. Even his offhand public comment that at the Battle of Gettysburg "those who opposed the doctrine of human equality *took tail* and ran" prompted an attack on him in a Democratic paper, which said the remark showed that "Republicanism naturally runs into Abolitionism," which in turn "leads to *negro equality* and *amalgamation*, just as naturally as a duck takes to water."[29]

A Democratic critic in the *Chicago Times* denounced the Gettysburg Address in similar terms. Objecting to "the introduction of Dawdleism [political partisanship] in a funeral sermon," the writer called the address "an insult" to the Gettysburg dead and "a perversion of history so flagrant that the most extended charity cannot regard it as otherwise than willful." The writer contrasted Lincoln's "proposition" of equality with three proslavery clauses in the Constitution—about three-fifths representation, the return of fugitives from labor, and the slave trade—and charged Lincoln with violating the Constitution. The writer declared that those who died at Gettysburg gave their lives for the Union, not for the rights of black people. The critic blasted Lincoln in racial terms: "How dared he, then, standing on their graves, misstate the cause for which they died, and libel the statesmen who founded the government? They were men possessing too much self-respect to declare that negroes were their equals, or were entitled to equal privileges."[30]

Such attacks pointed out Lincoln's increasingly public progressiveness on race, which struck his opponents as despicable. In the thirty words of the Gettysburg Address's opening sentence, Lincoln integrated the ideal of racial justice into the fabric of democratic America, which, as he had called it the year before, was "the last best hope of earth."[31] If his words at Gettysburg "remade America," as some argue, they did so because they proved that liberty and equality, announced in 1776, were transcendent (echoing the Bible), bound to the flesh and the earth (they were "conceived" on "the continent"), and as certain as a geometric proposition.[32]

In the rest of the address, Lincoln continued to apply his longstanding oratorical strategies to making sense of the Civil War and its relation to the nation. His logical side emerged again in the sentence in which he said that the war was "testing" if "any nation so conceived and dedicated, can long endure." If the nation's survival was a test, it was one that must be pursued to an egalitarian solution by living Americans. First, however, he addressed those who died at Gettysburg. He simultaneously honored them and put them in the past. He had often uttered concepts in negatives ("A house divided against itself can*not* stand," "We must *not* be enemies," etc.), and he did so here as well: "we can *not* dedicate—we can *not* consecrate—we can *not* hallow—this ground [italics added]." The brave men who fought at Gettysburg did so "far above our poor power to add or detract." Here Lincoln, who often utilized humility rhetorically, projected his humble persona on his Northern audience—the "we" with "our poor power."

He then made the transition to the future: "It is rather for us to be here dedicated to the great task remaining before us—that we take increased devotion to that cause for which they gave the last full measure of devotion." That "cause," as Lincoln had established in his first line, was human equality.

The cause, if attained, would bring about national regeneration. If Americans worked hard, "this nation, under God, shall have a new birth of freedom," so "that government of the people, by the people, for the people, shall not perish from the earth."

Lincoln's image of a "new birth of freedom" revived the spirit of unified commitment that had brought political opponents together in the weeks just after Fort Sumter, when a journalist wrote, "Regenerated as by a new birth of freedom, and purified by trial, we shall emerge from the clouds which at present surround us to a career of glory and prosperity never dreamed of before."[33] It also caught the patriotic emotion of a *New York Times* reporter who had lost his son in the Battle of Gettysburg and had written, "Oh, you dead, who at Gettysburgh [*sic*] have baptized with your blood the second birth of Freedom in America, how you are envied!"[34]

No fewer than twelve sources for the phrase "of the people, for the people, by the people" have been suggested.[35] The most likely ones, given Lincoln's preferences, were either Daniel Webster, who in his Second Reply to Hayne (which Lincoln had committed to memory) praised "the People's Government; made for the People; made by the People; and answerable to the People," or Lincoln's favorite minister, Theodore Parker, in a sermon Lincoln was said to have marked in 1858: "Democracy is direct self-government, over all the people, by all the people, for the people." Whatever its source, the final line made the democratic process timeless through its controlled language. Lincoln's fluid trochees—"*of* the *people, by* the *people, for* the *people*"—gave wings to the rhythmically bumpy phrases of Webster and Parker. Turning their platitudes into poetry, Lincoln drove home his belief that the goal of human equality, proclaimed by the Declaration of Independence, could be approached only through a democratically elected government, as established by the Constitution.

Not only do the closing phrases soar; they also return us to humanity—"the people"—and to the physical world: "shall not perish from *the earth*" [italics added]. Lincoln had long accepted cosmic democracy, by which people and the physical world were linked in the larger view of things. The Gettysburg Address grounded its vision in the physical. Democracy for Lincoln was a tangible reality, subject to either renewal, through careful cultivation and ethical action, or destruction, as a result of reckless trampling on justice or equality.

Democracy was also holy for him. His speech invested democracy with religious meaning through words like "consecrated" and "hallow." Nor can we forget the phrase he apparently added extemporaneously in the last line: "under God." Since early in the war, he had made religious proclamations in order to foster cultural unity. At Gettysburg, cultural religion merged with personal faith. There is evidence that Lincoln made a personal religious turn connected to Gettysburg. He told a general that one day during the battle, he went into a room at the White House, got down on his knees, and asked God to avert another Fredericksburg or Chancellorsville. According to the general,

Lincoln told him, "I then and there made a solemn vow to Almighty God that if he would stand by our boys at Gettysburg I would stand by him. And he did, and I will."[36]

The president allegedly had another religious experience when he visited Gettysburg in November. He was so moved by the signs of human self-sacrifice on the battlefield, the story went, that he responded to a question about his religion by saying that he embraced Christ.[37] The report got into the papers, prompting an Iowan to write Lincoln expressing "my joy, (& I doubt not the joy of every Christian heart throughout our land), at the statement recently made in the religious press that you have sought & found the Saviour, that you 'do love Jesus.'"[38] The story of Lincoln's Gettysburg "conversion," however, is unsubstantiated and probably apocryphal. A more measured assessment came from Mary Lincoln, who said that the death of Willie and the emotions surrounding Gettysburg turned his mind to the spiritual. Mary said, "he felt religious More than Ever about the time he went to Gettysburg: he was not a technical Christian: he read the bible a good deal about 1864."[39]

There are conflicting accounts of the crowd's immediate reaction to the Gettysburg Address. A few papers reported that the audience maintained a reverent silence during Lincoln's speech, while others, such as the *New York Times*, said that applause broke out several times as he spoke. Benjamin French, who helped organize the ceremony, wrote in his diary, "Anyone who saw & heard as I did, the hurricane of applause that met his every movement at Gettysburg would know that he lived in every heart. It was no cold, faint, shadow of a kind reception—it was a tumultuous outpouring of exultation, from true and loving hearts, at the sight of a man whom everyone knew to be honest and true and sincere in every act of his life, and every pulsation of his heart. It was the spontaneous outburst of heartfelt confidence in *their own* President."[40]

Edward Everett realized he had lost the battle of the speeches. He wrote Lincoln, "I should be glad, if I could flatter myself that I came as near to the central idea of the occasion, in two hours, as you did in two minutes."[41]

After the ceremony, Lincoln attended a luncheon at David Wills's house, followed by a public reception, with lots of hand shaking. French wrote, "He received all who chose to call on him, and there were thousands that took him by the hand."[42]

Among those he greeted was a local celebrity he had asked to meet, John L. Burns, a seventy-year-old Gettysburg shoemaker who had spontaneously joined the Battle of Gettysburg. When the Confederates attacked his town in July, Burns, a veteran of the War of 1812 and the Mexican War, ventured forth in his old-fashioned clothing carrying his flintlock musket. He came upon a wounded Union soldier who gave him an Enfield rifle. He then approached an officer, asking to join the battle. He was placed in a relatively safe place in the woods, from which he served as a sharpshooter. He received several wounds in the battle but managed to survive by convincing Confederates he was a noncombatant.

Burns met up with the president at the reception, and the two walked to the town's Presbyterian church, where they heard an address on the war delivered by Ohio lieutenant governor-elect Charles Anderson, the brother of Robert Anderson, the hero of Fort Sumter.

When Lincoln left that evening on the train to Washington, he was feverish and headachy. He stretched out on chairs arranged to hold his long body. It turned out that he had a mild case of smallpox, which laid him up for two weeks in the White House. He remarked that people were always asking him for something, and *"now he has something he can give them all."*[43]

The quip unwittingly applied to the speech he had given that day at Gettysburg. He had indeed given something to all: a gem of political wisdom—one approached in beauty and cultural meaning only by the speech he would give sixteen months later, at his second inauguration.

JOHN L. BURNS

THE MILITARY BUILDUP TO
THE SECOND INAUGURAL

If the Gettysburg Address made enduring statements about human
equality and American democracy, the Second Inaugural Address proclaimed that war, no matter how vigorously pursued, was just if its goal
was awarding human rights to all. Lincoln made the transition to the
open antislavery militancy of the Second Inaugural by participating in
a major shift toward hard war between 1863 and 1865.

The Battle of Gettysburg had been a great victory for the North, but it was also, in some ways, a painful lesson of how *not* to fight the Civil War. The negatives in Lincoln's address—"we can not dedicate—we can not consecrate—we can not hallow—this ground"—offer humble praise to the fallen but, at the same time, may have reflected his underlying frustration with the Union performance at Gettysburg.

Lincoln's chief disappointment was with his generals. Leading up to the battle, he was exasperated when Joseph Hooker failed to stop Lee's invasion of Pennsylvania. After the battle, when George Meade allowed Lee to cross the Potomac and head back to Virginia, Lincoln was reminded of "an old woman trying to shoo her geese across the creek."[44]

Lincoln now turned to his "bulldog," U. S. Grant, who had proved himself at Fort Donelson, Shiloh, and Vicksburg. In recognition of Grant's battlefield prowess, Lincoln in March 1864 promoted Grant to lieutenant general, a high post that had not been held by anyone since George Washington. Over the next six months, Grant tenaciously pursued Lee in Virginia, sometimes with disappointing results, as in the Battle of the Wilderness, a bloody slugfest that left a total of 28,000 killed, wounded, or missing. But Grant's stubborn declaration "I propose to fight it out on this line, if it takes all summer" inspired Lincoln to repeat it publicly.[45] Lincoln's faith in Grant was amply repaid when the disheveled general, aided by the cocky, foul-mouthed general Philip Sheridan, hounded Lee in Virginia, leading finally, in April 1865, to the fall of the Confederate capital, Richmond.

In the meantime, William Tecumseh Sherman was advancing confidently through Georgia. By September 1864 Sherman had captured Atlanta, a central supply hub, where his army burned many public buildings, businesses, and private residences. His victory came on the heels of the Union victory at Mobile, Alabama, by a fleet that braved enemy mines in Mobile Bay, reportedly inspired by Admiral David Farragut's words: "Damn the torpedoes! ... Full speed! ... Go ahead!"[46]

The triumphs strengthened the North's support of the war and helped Lincoln get elected to a second term.

Shortly after the election, Sherman and his army of 60,000 began their famous March to the Sea. Sherman recalled, "Behind us lay Atlanta smoldering and in ruins, the black smoke rising high in the air and hanging like a pall over the ruined city." A band struck up "John Brown's Body," which the soldiers sang loudly. "Never before or since," Sherman wrote, "have I heard the chorus of 'Glory, glory, hallelujah!' done with more spirit, or in better harmony of time and place."[47] Sherman took Savannah the next month. He followed up with a campaign through the Carolinas that, in combination with Grant's victories in Virginia, shattered the Confederacy.

The hard-nosed military approach of Grant and Sherman matched that of Lincoln and Francis Lieber, the Union's leading military theorist.

But Lieber also brought an extra dimension that he shared with Lincoln: antislavery commitment. Lieber's code supported military emancipation and included a concise statement of antislavery doctrine, distinguishing between things/property and humans, between local law and natural law: "Slavery, complicating and confounding the ideas of property, (that is of a *thing*,) and of personality, (that is of *humanity*,) exists according to municipal or local law only. The law of nature and nations has never acknowledged it."[48] Giving an abolitionist twist to Clausewitz's famous principle that war is an extension of politics, Lieber aligned the Civil War directly with emancipation.

Which brings us back to Puritanism and Lincoln's pathway to the Second Inaugural Address. The address's religiosity, combined with its militant demand for human rights, was commonly said to recall the spirit of the Puritan warriors Oliver Cromwell and his American successor John Brown. We've seen that Lieber revered Cromwell and his followers and that Lincoln had John Brown on his mind in the final phase of the Civil War, as expressed in his White House interviews with Frederick Douglass and Martin Delany.

Having pointed the principles of 1776 toward civil rights in the Gettysburg Address, Lincoln now aimed to channel the moral energy of Puritanism in the same direction.

FACING TWO NATIONS

He showed how he intended to redirect this energy when in November 1864 he was asked to attend a Forefathers' Day festival to celebrate the New England Pilgrims. The politician and philanthropist Joseph Hodges Choate invited him to the event, which was to be held the next month by the New England Society of New York. Lincoln declined the request. He wrote Choate that he was honored by "your kind invitation to be present at the annual festival of the New England Society to commemorate the landing of the Pilgrims." He explained that his duties prevented him from attending, but he congratulated "you and the country ... upon the spectacle of devoted unanimity presented by the people at home, the citizens that form our marching columns, and the citizens that fill our squadrons on the sea—all animated by the same determination to complete and perpetuate the work our fathers began and transmitted." He told Choate that he recognized the nation's debt to the New England forefathers but concluded his letter by saying, "The work of the Plymouth emigrants was the glory of their age. While we revere their memory, let us not forget how vastly greater is our opportunity."[49]

The spirit of liberty, Lincoln was saying, must be constantly updated to accord with evolving concepts of human rights. The destruction of slavery and the unification of the nation were "vastly greater" aims than those sought by the New England Puritans.

Having proposed at Gettysburg that the egalitarian ethos of 1776 should become the unifying spirit of the nation, Lincoln hoped to put the Puritan/Cavalier conflict completely in the past. That was no easy task. The hoary conflict persisted during the Civil War, and even intensified. The actual separation of the South from the Union impelled each side to rally around its long-standing cultural traditions.

The North's belief that it was fighting a holy war against the slave power in the spirit of the Puritan rebellion yielded many cultural offshoots, including the Cromwell Bible, the ubiquitous John Brown song, and popular poems like "The Stolen Stars," by General Lew Wallace. The future author of *Ben-Hur* struck a chord with his often-reprinted poem, which pictures Uncle Sam as having two sons: "The name of one was Puritan; / The other Cavalier." Uncle Sam had a flag whose original thirteen stars increased to thirty-four before eleven of them were wickedly stolen by Cavalier (the South) from Puritan (the North). This crime by Cavalier—a would-be aristocrat who has "A thousand niggers up aloft, / And a thousand down below"—creates a fight with Puritan, who sends "a million Northern boys" to fetch the pilfered stars.[50]

Pro-Northern pamphlets appeared, such as William H. Whitmore's *The Cavalier Dismounted*, which debunked the idea that settlers of the Southern colonies were of "nobler blood" than the Puritans or formed what the Confederate leader Robert Toombs called "a nation of gentlemen." Whitmore argued that "so far as there was any superiority of *character, purpose* and *impulse*, the advantage at the outset was with the Puritan stock of New England."[51]

Southern propagandists promoted the opposite view. A Louisville journalist wrote, "The Norman cavalier cannot brook the vulgar familiarity of the Saxon Yankee, while the latter is continually devising some plan to bring down his aristocratic neighbor to his own detested level."[52] Similarly, a Georgia newspaper announced in 1863 that Confederates would "see to it that no terms are made with the enemy that pollutes our soil, save only the unconditional independence of our land, and the perpetual separation of the Cavalier and Puritan races of this continent."[53] Samuel S. Cox's speech "Puritanism in Politics," which described

Puritanism as a "reptile" that had eroded the mound of the Constitution and let loose a horde of intrusively moralistic higher-law fanatics, was issued as a popular pamphlet, priced at four cents.[54] Clement Vallandigham's statement that the Civil War was actually between "different types of civilization," between "the Cavalier and the Roundhead . . . Puritan," ricocheted in the press.[55]

The Cavalier myth helped synthesize the Confederate states under words like "civilization" and "nation." The South's leading journal, *DeBow's Review*, announced: "No civil strife is this; . . . but a war of alien races, distinct, nationalities, and opposite, hostile, and eternally antagonistic governments. Cavalier and Roundhead no longer designate parties, but *nations*."[56]

This historically defined distinction influenced the Confederacy's president, Jefferson Davis, who was known as "the model cavalier."[57] One newspaper noted "the contrast between Lincoln and Davis—the Puritan and the Cavalier."[58] The February 1865 Hampton Roads peace conference between Lincoln and three of Davis's commissioners can be best understood when placed against the background of Davis's acceptance of the Cavalier myth. In Davis's view, Southerners were refined gentlemen, while Northerners were lowly money seekers and meddling moralists. As he expressed it, Confederate people were "essentially aristocratic, their aristocracy being based on birth and education; while the men of the North were democratic in the mass, making money the basis of their power and standard to which they aspired."[59] He argued that the North's ethos stemmed from "the hard, grasping, money-grubbing, pitiless and domineering spirit of the New England Puritans."

Davis believed that the profound cultural dissimilarities between the North and the South would forever prevent their reunion. He declared, "We can never, never reunite with the North, the people whose ascendants Cromwell had gathered from the bogs of Scotland and Ireland."[60] Given his culturally defined hostility to the North, it is no wonder that peace efforts late in the Civil War proved fruitless. Lincoln foresaw the failure of any negotiations. In his December 6, 1864, annual message to Congress, he declared that "no attempt at negotiation with the insurgent leader could result in any good," because Davis "would accept nothing short of severance of the Union." Lincoln stated flatly, "Between him and us the issue is distinct, simple, and inflexible. It is an issue which can only be tried by war, and decided by victory."[61]

JEFFERSON DAVIS

Lincoln's words proved accurate, as was shown when the seventy-three-year-old political veteran Francis P. Blair Sr. took it upon himself to go to Richmond, Virginia, where on January 12, 1865, he negotiated informally with Jefferson Davis. Trying to establish terms for peace, Blair proposed that the South join up with the North to enforce the

Monroe Doctrine by expelling France from Mexico, where Napoleon III had made incursions. Although Davis showed little interest in the idea, he remained hopeful about achieving an armistice with the North. The South was in disarray: its military effort was flagging, its economy was in shambles, and its people were demoralized. An attempted peace deal would at least allow Davis to stall for time.

However, Davis remained firm about the South's not reuniting with the North. Through Blair, he sent Lincoln a message stating that he was willing to start negotiations "with a view to secure peace to the two countries."[62] Southern independence, as Lincoln had predicted, was Davis's sine qua non for peace. Lincoln sent Davis a carefully worded reply saying that he would discuss ways of "securing peace to the people of our one common country."[63]

When Lincoln, along with Secretary of State William Seward, met with Davis's three representatives—Alexander Stephens, John A. Campbell, and Robert M. T. Hunter—in the steamer *River Queen* at Hampton Roads, Virginia, on February 3, he made the South's reunion with the North one of his three demands. His other demands were the disbanding of all forces hostile to the federal government and the South's acceptance of all presidential proclamations and congressional legislation on slavery up to the president's December 1864 address to Congress.

On January 31, three days before the Hampton Roads conference, Congress took decisive action on slavery by passing the Thirteenth Amendment, which abolished slavery and involuntary servitude—the nation-changing goal that Lincoln had now reached. The amendment proceedings and the Hampton Roads peace efforts were closely related. When rumors flew that Confederate peace commissioners were in Washington, ready to talk with the North, Lincoln wrote a canny and perhaps deceitful note to the Republican congressman James M. Ashley: "So far as I know, there are no peace commissioners in the city, or likely to be in it."[64] The key words were "in the city." Had the three

Confederate representatives been permitted to go to Washington, as they had requested, the Thirteenth Amendment may not have won the two-thirds majority of votes required for House approval. Wavering congressmen may have withheld support for the amendment to see what came of the negotiations, though they probably would have passed the amendment once the peace talks had failed.

Fail they did, in an atmosphere that was amicable, even jovial, though ultimately glum for the Southerners. On the *River Queen*, Lincoln talked about old times with his erstwhile congressional Whig colleague Alexander Stephens, whose short, thin body looked smaller than ever. Lincoln later joked about the diminutive Stephens emerging from his ample overcoat. "Was there ever such a nubbin after so much shucking?" the president asked.[65] For nearly four hours, the two sides discussed terms for peace, to no avail because the Confederates rejected Lincoln's three stipulations. Although Lincoln said he would explore securing federal money to compensate the South for its enslaved people he would not retreat on emancipation or reunion with the South under the Constitution.

One of the Southerners, R. M. T. Hunter, reportedly tried to make the Confederate case by citing the English civil wars, when King Charles I had agreed to negotiate with the Puritan rebels who had taken up arms against him. Why couldn't Lincoln do the same? The president replied, "Upon questions of history I must refer you to Mr. Seward, for he is posted in such things, and I don't pretend to be bright. My only distinct recollection of the matter is, that Charles lost his head."[66] Not only was this a witty comeback to the Confederates, but it may have been a gentle slap to his friend Seward, who had once said in a New England Society speech, "I know no better rule of conduct than the Puritans," whose rebellion had led to the execution of Charles I.[67]

It was this kind of section-specific partisanship that Lincoln was determined to overcome. After Congress's approval of the Thirteenth

Amendment and the Hampton Roads conference, he was in a stronger position than ever to achieve the political and cultural unity he had long sought. At the request of Congress, on February 10 he issued a record of the peace negotiations, including all relevant documents. His handling of the negotiations won enthusiastic approval throughout the North. Just before the conference, Radical Republicans like Thaddeus Stevens and Benjamin Wade had feared that he would be too lenient with the South. His unyielding insistence on his three main terms pleased the Radicals, as did his instructions to Grant to continue the war even as the peace talks proceeded. Copperheads such as Samuel Cox and Fernando Wood, for their part, were encouraged by the talks, which at least showed Lincoln's willingness to discuss peace with the rebels. Even the *New York Herald*, known to be harsh on Lincoln, now praised him as "one of the shrewdest diplomats of the day," commenting that at Hampton Roads "Old Abe . . . was a giant among the pigmies."[68] Another paper noted the unifying effect of Hampton Roads, whose effect "will be to unite the North and to divide the South."[69]

Indeed, there seemed to be justification for the congratulatory note Henry Ward Beecher sent Lincoln on February 4. "No man on earth," Beecher wrote, "was ever before so *impregnably* placed, as you are." Beecher pointed to "the facts." First, "The south is exhausted and defeated. The military *result is sure*." Second, every step Lincoln had taken "toward emancipation & national liberty is now confirmed beyond all change." Last, Lincoln had ended "the most dangerous and extraordinary rebellion in history . . . without sacrificing *republican government*."[70]

But Lincoln, who had long known the wisdom of humility, was not as ready as Beecher was to exult in success. Although he saw the same positive signs Beecher did, he had a sense of unfinished business. What was going to happen with the Thirteenth Amendment? He called the amendment "a King's cure for all the evils," but it would not take effect until it was ratified by three quarters of the states.[71] For this reason, in

Lincoln on January 8, 1864 (photograph by Mathew B. Brady)

February he took John Brown–like action to speed up emancipation by appointing Martin Delany as the army's highest-ranking black officer, with the plan of infiltrating behind rebel lines into the Deep South and liberating enslaved blacks through military action. Also, he continued to urge the armies under Grant, Sherman, and others, and the fleets under naval commanders like William A. Parker and David Porter, not to let up the military pressure now that peace was in sight.

But there was a larger issue than the military one. He wanted to drive home the antislavery meaning of the war and to demonstrate how inclusive American democracy could be. That opportunity came on March 4, 1865, the day of his second inauguration.

A SACRED EFFORT

Inauguration Day witnessed American democracy at its ethical best and its directionless worst. On that day, a unique kind of moral centripetalism—in the form of the short but resonant Second Inaugural Address—was offered to the nation, providing inspiration for Lincoln's contemporaries and for later generations.

Lincoln's long-standing belief in cosmic democracy, rooted in natural forces, was enforced by the extreme weather conditions. Inside the Capitol Building, where the Thirty-eighth Congress was wrapping up its term, early morning found senators, some of them nodding off after an all-night session, being startled awake by a burst of wind and rain that shook the building. Outside, throngs who had come to Washington from around the nation to celebrate the inaugural faced miserable conditions. It had been raining for days, and the city's streets, most of them unpaved, were a quagmire many inches deep. A reporter noted, "Washington was, as usual, all mud and marble—the grandest architecture on the continent and the dirtiest streets. . . . Myriad of patriots [were] hopelessly enslaved in mud, whom no emancipation proclamation could set free."[72] The Washington mud was yellowish-brown, tinted by the waste matter of roving farm animals—cows, hogs, goats, sheep—and by privies that spilled over during floods.[73]

But spirits soared on that momentous day. Not only was Lincoln being reinstalled, but the news from the Union armies and naval forces was promising. The mud only added to the festivity. A journalist wrote, "Particles of this yellow material added to the holiday appearance of the people, marking them with gay and festive spots from head to heel. . . . All the world floundered about in it, and swore at it, and laughed at it."[74]

The rain tapered off during the morning, and at 11:10, the inaugural parade started down Pennsylvania Avenue, from the White House to the Capitol, under a blanket of clouds, with streaks of blue sky in the west. The parade offered new examples of public democracy. Along with the military presence—soldiers, marine bands, artillery on display, a pasteboard model of the ironclad *Monitor*—were several companies of firemen with their equipage, a wagon carrying a printing press, and a Temple of Liberty on which boys sang war tunes like "Rally Round the Flag" and "The Battle Cry of Freedom."

A remarkable aspect of the scene was the large presence of African Americans. The antislavery newspaper the *New-York Tribune* hailed the event as "The Negro in a New Character" and reported, "One distinguishing feature of the procession and of the assemblage was the presence of the negro as a citizen and as a soldier."[75] Not only did the parade include black troops, an African American brass band, and "delegations of colored Odd Fellows," but African American men and women were everywhere among the spectators. The racially mixed crowd was fitting in light of Lincoln's status among blacks, for whom he was the messiah of emancipation. The *National Anti-Slavery Standard* hailed the African American presence as one of the "unmistakable signs of the mighty revolution that the war has wrought in the minds and hearts of the American people."[76]

If the imposing number of African Americans in the celebration was a novelty, the discussions of racial issues inside the Capitol were even more so. The day before, Lincoln had signed the landmark Freedmen's Bureau Act, with its provisions for land, labor contracts, medical care, and education for the nation's millions of emancipated blacks. That law was the US government's boldest foray yet into social welfare. Equally bold was a commerce bill taken up by the Senate on inauguration morning. The bill stipulated that no American, regardless of color, could be excluded from any railroad car, omnibus, steamboat, or other conveyance. The abolitionist senator John Hale of New Hampshire requested an added clause that would also prohibit discrimination at public places like churches, hotels, and restaurants.

Senator Charles Sumner called for a vote, but the bill died amid a distraction in the Senate chamber. At 11:00 a.m., the east door of the Capitol was opened to admit spectators to the swearing in of Vice President Andrew Johnson, scheduled for noon. Johnson, the Tennessee Democrat whom Republicans had chosen as Lincoln's second-term running mate because he had remained loyal to the Union even though his state joined the Confederacy, was to be sworn in by the outgoing vice president, Hannibal Hamlin of Maine. Crowds of men and women, soaked and mud spattered, rushed into the Senate galleries, which came alive with their chatter. Amid the noise, the fatigued senators relocated to the one side of the chamber to make room for other government officials and visiting foreign dignitaries, who entered and took seats.

Then came an exhibition of democratic speechmaking at its worst. As soon as Andrew Johnson was escorted into the Senate by Hannibal Hamlin, something seemed wrong. The five-foot-ten Johnson leaned unsteadily on the taller Hamlin's arm. Johnson's face was flushed, and his eyes were bleary. As he sank into a chair, it was obvious that he was drunk. Earlier that morning he had gulped down three glasses of straight whiskey to steady his nerves and fight a fever. Hamlin briefly introduced Johnson, who wobbled to the rostrum to give an inaugural speech that was supposed to last about seven minutes but instead went three times that long before someone pulled him away.

The idea that Lincoln had concisely expressed at Gettysburg in the phrase "a government of the people, by the people, for the people" came out of the inebriated Johnson as a string of platitudes. Gesticulating wildly and veering between whispers and roars, Johnson declared, "I'm a-going to tell you [*yoo*, he drawled] here to-day—yes, to-day, in this

ANDREW JOHNSON

place—that I am a plebeian—glory in it—Tennessee has never gone out of the Union [a whiskey-fueled lie]—I am a-going to talk two minutes and a half on that point—I want you to hear me. Tennessee was always loyal—we all derive our power from the people. Yes, I am a plebeian. The people—yes, the people of the United States, the great people—have made me what I am; and I am a-going to tell you here to-day—yes, to-day in this place—that the people are everything. We owe all to them." He then turned to Chief Justice Salmon Chase, Secretary of State William Seward, and other officials in the room, pointed at each of them successively, and said, "You [giving the name] derive your power from the people." When he came to Gideon Welles, he bent down and asked someone, "Who is the Secretary of the Navy?" He got the answer, pointed at Welles, and assured him that he, too, was a "creature of the people."[77]

Lincoln, who had been detained signing congressional bills into law, took a seat in the chamber about halfway through Johnson's speech. He instantly grasped the situation, and his gaunt, creased face took on a sorrowful expression. Chase, meanwhile, looked like stone. Seward closed his eyes serenely. Welles was expressionless. Charles Sumner covered his face with his hands. Some guffaws broke out. Most listeners squirmed in agony.

What they were witnessing was a reprise, in caricature, of the kind of alcohol-laced oratory that was widespread among American politicians of the era. In the 1820s, John Randolph gave long, directionless harangues in the Senate as he swigged malt liquor or brandy. Even the respectable Whigs Daniel Webster and Lincoln's ideal statesman Henry Clay were often in their cups.[78] During the Civil War, notoriety surrounded many politicians, such as the bibulous proslavery Delaware senator Willard Saulsbury Sr., who only days before Lincoln's second inauguration was so drunk that when he spewed "a tirade of abuse on New England and all who favored prosecution of the war against the 'noble and chivalrous' south" he had to be hauled off to a cloak room, where he passed out.[79] On the same day, the amiably smashed California senator James A. McDougall drifted about the Senate chamber mumbling incoherently. Other "notorious drunkards," as a reporter described them, included senators Zachariah Chandler (Michigan), Richard Yates (Illinois), James Lane (Kansas), and James Nye (Nevada).[80] A Cincinnati paper commented that Andrew Johnson's "inaugural speech may prove to be the most effective temperance lecture ever delivered in the country," for it would serve as an "Awful Example" to "a Congress of drunkards," where "it is rather expected of a 'great man' . . . that he shall consume a large ration of whisky."[81]

Even when sober, politicians frequently gave declamatory speeches full of personal pronouns, rambling reflections, or sensational effects. The teetotaler Lincoln had sometimes used this style early in his political career. The extent to which he had abandoned this style was discussed in newspaper responses to the inauguration. A reporter for the *New York Herald* remarked that Johnson's speech "might have been appropriate at some hustings in Tennessee; but it was . . . not only a ninety-ninth rate stump speech, but disgraceful in the extreme."[82] Another newspaper noted that the ex-tailor Johnson and the frontiersman Lincoln were both from humble backgrounds, but they had gone in different directions. No one, the reporter wrote, thought the worse of Lincoln because he was once "a rail-splitter and a boatman," but "if, as President of the U. S., he behaved like a rail-splitter, spoke like one, drank like one, and could not import into the higher sphere of his new life anything but the vulgar manners and gross habits of the old, it would be impossible for any one to forget his origin." Johnson, in contrast, reminded his listeners only that he represented "the dregs of society . . . His behavior was that of an illiterate, vulgar, and drunken rowdy."[83]

Johnson was tugged away by his coattails from the lectern, but he was not done. When Hamlin administered the oath of office, Johnson seized the Bible, held it to his lips, and, facing the audience, cried theatrically, "I kiss this Book in the face of my nation the United States."[84] In his tipsy state he evidently thought the Bible belonged to him. As vice president, it was his duty to swear in the new senators, but he played a cat-and-mouse game of motioning them away whenever one of them tried to put his hand on the Holy Book. Finally, a clerk relieved him of the swearing-in duty. Lincoln warned a marshal, "Don't let Johnson speak outside."[85]

The transition to Lincoln's speech that day seemed providential, in more ways than one. When the convocation moved to the east steps of the Capitol, where Lincoln was to give his speech, the thousands who had been awaiting his appearance let forth with thunderous applause and shouts. As Lincoln stepped up to the podium that had been set up in the middle of the steps, sunlight flooded the scene. "Did you notice that sunburst?" Lincoln said to his journalist friend Noah Brooks the next day. "It made my heart jump."[86] The superstitious Lincoln saw the sunlight as a good omen.

Nature was smiling on one of the most majestic moments in American history. Lincoln's inaugural address—a mere 698 words that took about seven minutes to deliver—was everything Johnson's was not. If Johnson's speech was a sieve that collected a few loose cultural and personal bits while allowing vital juices to flow away, Lincoln's was a funnel that brought together a range of cultural forces in a rich, concentrated mixture.

Minimizing the personal, Lincoln's address was directed at the entire nation. Focused, elegantly balanced, suggestive in every phrase, it was light-years distant from Johnson's fragmented, egocentric speech. More than anything, it offered healing to a nation ravaged by four years of bloody war. It did so by assigning meaning to the war without sounding partial or smug.

In a masterwork of rhetorical centripetalism, matched only by the Gettysburg Address, Lincoln avoided digressions or rambling. He explained that his first inaugural speech had demanded details; now, he said, "there is less occasion for an extended address than there was at the first," because the nation had endured "four years, during which public declarations have been constantly called forth on every point and phase" of the war. He did not harp on what a more egocentric president would have emphasized: his own skilled handling of the war. The most he said about the war was: "With high hope for the future, no prediction in regard to it is ventured," though he trusted that the recent news from the battlefront was "reasonably satisfactory and encouraging to all."[87]

Having established his strategy of concentration and concision, he turned to his main themes: the need for national unity and for an unending pursuit of human rights.

He avoided one-upmanship in his rhetoric. He did not speak for one side. He made no mention of South or North, Democrat or Republican. He talked about "all" and about the "parties" involved. Four years ago, "all thoughts" were turned toward war; "All dreaded it—all sought to avert it." "Both parties deprecated war; but one of them would *make* war rather than let the nation survive; and the other would *accept* war rather than let it perish. And the war came [underlining added]."

The collective pronouns helped to detach the war from a particular section or party. *All* Americans, he was saying, dreaded war; but "the war came," like an inexorable force. Even in describing the war itself, Lincoln used the rhetoric of unity: both sides expected a short war, both sides prayed to the same God, and the prayers of neither were fully answered.

He directed this language of unity toward a clever debunking of those who evaded the fact that slavery was the actual cause of the war. Pointing out that enslaved people made up about an eighth of the US population in 1861, he said, "These slaves constituted a peculiar and powerful interest. All knew that this interest was, somehow, the cause of the war [underlining added]." Lincoln was reminding his listeners that this was a fundamental truth some tried to evade. Although the original secession documents, beginning with South Carolina's, had emphasized the protection of slavery as justification for leaving the Union, many Southerners liked to attribute the war to other factors—the incompatibility of Cavaliers and Puritans, the sovereignty of the states, and so on. A Louisville newspaper typically insisted that "the slavery question is merely a pretext not the cause of this war," which in fact resulted from "the hereditary hostility, the sacred animosity and eternal antagonism between the two races engaged."[88] Lincoln, by saying that "all knew" the war was about slavery, was discarding such evasions and returning to the real cause of the war.

Abe

But slavery did not only cause the war, he insisted; it was an unjust institution that must be fought to the bitter end, under God's direction.

References to religion permeated the Second Inaugural, which contained fourteen mentions of God (including God-related pronouns and synonyms), three references to prayer, and four quoted or paraphrased Bible passages. Lincoln had long been wary about proclaiming publicly an antislavery higher law for fear of alienating moderates, but he now felt confident to do so because the war had opened up the probability that emancipation would soon be integrated into the Constitution. The Second Inaugural Address definitively promoted an antislavery religion.

In an era of biblical rewriting, when countless authors and orators offered revised versions of the Bible to push their agendas, Lincoln's antislavery adaptation of the Bible was especially forceful. In the address, Lincoln cited scriptural passages that drove his point home with visceral force. Giving an antislavery take on Genesis 3:19, where God tells Adam that he must earn his bread through sweaty labor, Lincoln declared, "It may seem strange that any men should dare to ask a just God's assistance in wringing their bread from the sweat of other men's faces; but let us judge not that we be not judged." If the bread-sweat image graphically indicted Southern slavery, the phrase "let us judge not," taken from Matthew 7:1, enforced Lincoln's notion that the North, which had formerly been commercially involved with the South, bore some responsibility for slavery.

But the address left no question about which side was chiefly culpable. Americans who invoked God and the Bible to defend slavery, he indicated, were simply wrong. The proslavery higher law was nonsense. Quoting Matthew 18:7—"Woe to the world because of offenses . . . and that man by whom offenses cometh!"—he declared that "we shall suppose that American Slavery is one of those offenses" that God "now wills to remove." We can "fondly" hope and "fervently" pray, he continued, that "this mighty scourge of war may speedily pass away," but, if God wills that it continue "until all the wealth piled by the

872

bond-man's two hundred and fifty years of unrequited toil shall be sunk, and until every drop of blood drawn with the lash, shall be paid by another drawn with the sword, as was said three thousand years ago, so still it must be said 'the judgments of the Lord, are true and righteous altogether.'"

The very long time periods Lincoln mentions—the 250-year history of American slavery, the indefinite future when the slaveholders' wealth "shall be sunk," and, in the quotation from Psalms 19:9, the judgment made by God "three thousand years ago"—gave remarkable range and depth to Lincoln's antislavery pronouncement. In this rhythmically rippling sentence, Lincoln converted huge swaths of history—past, present, and future—into a history of slavery and its evils.

He did not simply tell his listeners about slavery's injustice. He made them *see* it and *feel* it, as though it were a bodily sensation. For centuries, bondsmen had been subjected to torture and dehumanizing exploitation. Their "toil" had gone "unrequited"; it was used merely to "pile" up "wealth" for slave owners. Now the moment had come for "every drop of blood drawn with the lash" to "be paid by another drawn with the sword."

In effect, Lincoln was saying that the fate of countless enslaved people like Uncle Tom, who was whipped to death in Stowe's novel, must be avenged in the spirit of John Brown, who had used swords in Kansas to slay proslavery settlers.

"With malice toward none; with charity for all; with firmness in the right, as God gives us to see the right"—the flowing phrases, made resonant by Lincoln's use of parallelism, are so fixed in the national memory that it is difficult to hear how they must have sounded in March 1865. If "malice toward none" and "charity for all" may have meant that Lincoln was willing to be fair to Southerners during Reconstruction, "firmness in the right" suggested that, whatever happened, he would not bend in his devotion to civil rights. The "all" in "charity for all" resembled his "men" in the statement on equality at Gettysburg—it referred to *all* humans, regardless of race. The "him" in "to care for him who shall have borne the battle" reaches out to all soldiers, regardless of which side, North or South, they fought for. The phrases radiated a democratic expansiveness matched only, in that era, by Walt Whitman's poetry. In the last sentence of the speech, Lincoln invited Americans "to bind up the nation's wounds," to care for soldiers, widows, and orphans, and "to do all which may achieve and cherish a just and lasting peace among ourselves, and with all nations." Here, all-embracing compassion merged with a demand for human rights; the peace Lincoln envisaged was not only "lasting" but also "just."

Given the progressive thrust of the speech, it is no wonder that those who responded to it most passionately were African Americans. A kind of political sermon, the address had the call-and-response rhythms of an evangelical service. Standing behind and above Lincoln on the Capitol steps were black people who murmured "Bless the Lord!" after almost every sentence.[89]

Among the African Americans in the audience was Frederick Douglass. During the inauguration ceremony, Andrew Johnson spotted Douglass in the crowd and gave him an instinctive look of "bitter contempt and aversion," which he quickly tried to cover up with "a bland and sickly smile." Douglass muttered to a friend who stood nearby, "Whatever Andrew Johnson may be, he certainly is no friend of our race."[90] Lincoln made an altogether different impression on Douglass that day. At a White House reception that evening, Douglass made his way to Lincoln, despite having trouble getting past entrance guards because of his color. The president called out, "Here comes my friend Douglass." The two grasped hands, and Lincoln told Douglass he had seen him in the audience during his address. The president said, "There is no man in the country whose opinion I value more than yours. I want to know what you think of it?" Douglass replied, "Mr. Lincoln, that was a sacred effort."[91]

Sacred for African Americans—but how about for others who heard

The second inauguration of
Lincoln, March 4, 1865

Lincoln delivering the Second
Inaugural Address

the address or read it in one of its many newspaper reprintings? The overall response was glowing, though some sharply attacked the address. Lincoln knew that it would not sit well with everyone. He wrote, "I expect [the speech] to wear as well—perhaps better than—any thing I have produced; but I believe it is not immediately popular. Men are not flattered by being shown that there has been a difference of purpose between the Almighty and them."[92]

Antislavery reviewers were ecstatic. The *National Anti-Slavery Standard* raved, "Every year Abraham Lincoln grows stronger and stronger in the Anti-Slavery faith. His Inaugural this time is what might fall from the lips of a Garrison." Garrison's newspaper, *The Liberator*, which had once denounced Lincoln because of his apparent caution on slavery, described the Second Inaugural as a singular event in American history:

> For once, a President of the United States . . . quotes from Scripture in the interest of justice. He imitates so closely the language and reasoning of the Abolitionists, that the American Anti-Slavery Society itself might suspect him of plagiarism, and search its records for identical utterances. All honor to Abraham Lincoln, that on the day of his re-inauguration, he contemplates but two objects in the universe—the slave and his Maker. All honor and long life![93]

And so Lincoln, who had once criticized Garrisonian abolitionists as extreme, by 1865, when a nation without slavery seemed imminent, allowed his long-standing hatred of slavery to come out in a way that delighted the Garrisonians. If Garrison had once publicly burned a copy of the Constitution because he considered it a proslavery document, Lincoln had directed a hard war that opened the way to the amendment that made the Constitution unequivocally antislavery.

The Second Inaugural Address possessed the combined piety and human-rights advocacy of Oliver Cromwell and other Puritan revolutionaries, along with a gentle quality they lacked. The *New York Times* described a common response to the Second Inaugural: "Many pronounced it a Cromwellian speech, but it had one peculiarity, which Cromwell's speeches never had—a tone of perfect kindness and good will to all, whether enemies or political opponents."[94]

There were some, however, who did not approve the antislavery passion and humaneness of the Second Inaugural. The *New-York Freeman's Journal*, a leading Catholic newspaper, bitterly castigated the reinstalled Lincoln as the "greatest official in the new Puritan Nation," whose administration was merely a "Puritan, Bare Bones, Rump concern" and whose drunken buffoon of a vice president was well suited "to preside over this Puritan Senate."[95] The *New York World* found Lincoln's pairing of divine justice with antislavery fervor in his speech as a revival of the nefarious ideals of that latter-day Puritan, John Brown. The *World* reporter confessed that he read the speech "with a blush of shame," saying it was a pity that a "divided, suffering nation" was "mocked at in its calamity by a prose parody of 'John Brown's Hymn' from the lips of its chosen Chief Magistrate."[96]

Undergirding such criticism was racism. A California newspaper said that "these puritans" who again "called to the bloody throne" their war mongering president had perverse racial attitudes: "In their passion and frenzy they hug the negro with renewed affection, treat him with profound respect, and give him position in the highest and most sacred tribunals of our nation."[97]

Racism had raised its head during the inauguration ceremony. The fervent response by blacks to Lincoln's address riled some white members of the crowd. After the speech, there was a chaotic milling in which blacks were injured. "It is a wonder no one was killed there," the *New York Herald* reported. "The darkey suffered most. Soldiers knocked negro women roughly about and called them very uncomplimentary names. . . . Every negro boy got an extra push on account of his color."[98]

Also ominous that day were portents of assassination. Frederick Douglass had been so worried about the possibility of Lincoln's being murdered that during the parade he watchfully followed the presidential carriage, unaware that Mrs. Lincoln was inside it without her husband, who had gone earlier to the Capitol to sign bills. Douglass later reported, "I felt then that there was murder in the air, and I kept close to his carriage on the way to the Capitol, for I felt that I might see him fall that day. It was a vague presentiment."[99]

Douglass's fears were justified. In the audience at Lincoln's inaugural address was a twenty-six-year-old actor who loathed Lincoln's message. John Wilkes Booth had been plotting against Lincoln for at least nine months. His original plan of kidnapping the president and taking him South in order to exchange him for Confederate prisoners had been recently obviated by General Grant's restoration of prisoner exchanges. Booth had murder on his mind. He and some of his fellow conspirators were present at Lincoln's speech. At one point the movement of the crowd had brought him within striking distance of the president. Booth later said, "What a splendid chance I had to kill the President on the 4th of March!"[100]

A Southern loyalist and a white supremacist, the Maryland-born Booth regarded Lincoln as a devilish tyrant whose reelection presaged a horrid racial reversal in America. These views were common among Lincoln haters. Why did Booth cling to them so obsessively, and how was he able to act on them with deadly success in a Washington theater six weeks after the second inauguration?

Without understanding the context of the Lincoln assassination—its immediate background and its cultural repercussions—we can't fully understand Lincoln's meaning for America.

Lincoln on February 5, 1865 (photograph by Alexander Gardner)

Union, Tragedy, and Legacy

The last six weeks of Lincoln's life, which brought military victory for the North, saw the president come close to achieving what he had long sought: union on different levels. Bonds within his family tightened. Connections also strengthened between the president and his larger family: those who served in the army and navy. The winding down of the war brought the president far closer to African Americans than he had ever been before. Culturally, Lincoln enjoyed the full range of genres during these weeks, from opera and Shakespeare to sentimental poetry to popular music and satirical humor. Most important, he set the stage for a reunited nation that, as he envisaged it, would include a reconstructed South based on freedom and justice.

During the weeks just after the March 4, 1865, inauguration, Lincoln made political appointments for his new administration and watched the military news as it came in from the front. For two days, he was laid up with the flu and held cabinet meetings in his bedroom. In three successive weeks in March, he and Mary saw operas—Friedrich von Flotow's *Martha*, Mozart's *The Magic Flute*, and Francois-Adrieu Boieldieu's *La Dame Blanche*—at Grover's Theatre.

On March 20, General Grant invited the president to visit his headquarters at City Point, Virginia, writing, "I think the rest will do you good."[1] On Thursday, March 23, Lincoln, Mary, and Tad, accompanied by a bodyguard and an army officer, set off on the steamer *River Queen* to City Point, where they arrived the next evening. The family met up with Robert, who was now a captain under Grant. Over the next sixteen days, Lincoln visited battlefields and mingled with Union soldiers, sailors, and officers. He reviewed troops and went to field hospitals. In his memorable tour of the Depot Field Hospital, a sprawling array of tents and barracks covering two hundred acres, he walked from cot to cot, greeting thousands of soldiers—so many that by the end of the day his hand ached badly.[2]

The high point of his trip was his visit to Richmond on April 4, the day after it had fallen to Union troops. (Significantly, General Godfrey Weitzel's Twenty-fifth Army Corps, composed of all black troops, was the first unit to invade the city.) April 4 was Tad's twelfth birthday. A naval rowing barge, manned by twelve oarsmen, took the father and son on the James River from a navy steamer to the Richmond shore. Once on land, Lincoln took Tad by the hand and walked through the city. The day was unusually warm. Dust rose from the dry streets, and the air reeked with the acrid smoke of the burning structures and provisions that the rebels had torched before they vacated the city. The president and his son proceeded under a light guard to the house of Jefferson Davis, where the perspiring Lincoln sat in Davis's leather-covered easy chair, had a glass of water, and met for a time with General Weitzel and a Southern representative, John A. Campbell. After spending about an hour in the house, Lincoln and Tad were taken by carriage to other parts of the city and finally to a wharf, where a rowboat took the president out to the USS *Malvern*, where he and his son stayed the night.

The most notable aspect of Lincoln's Richmond visit was the response of the city's black people, who greeted the president with frenzied enthusiasm. A freedwoman spotted the tall Lincoln in his long overcoat and stovepipe hat. When someone told her, "There is the man who made you free," she jumped up and down, yelling, "Glory! Glory! Glory!"[3]

Soon her words were taken up by a mass of the formerly enslaved, who were swept up in ecstasy. To them, Lincoln was a liberating god. Hats, handkerchiefs, and scarves waved in the air, as the freed people cheered and shouted: "Glory to God! glory! glory! glory!"; "I thank you, dear Jesus, that I behold President Lincoln!"; "Bless the Lord, there comes the Messiah. There is Massa Abram Lincoln sure enough!" At one point, Lincoln paused and told his formerly enslaved listeners that they were now as free as air—as free as he was. An elderly black man walked up to Lincoln and prayed aloud for his safety. To the shock of a white person present, Lincoln raised his hat and bowed to the man.

John Chester Buttre, *Abraham Lincoln Entering Richmond, April 3d. [sic], 1865* (Boston: B. B. Russell & Co., 1866)

The joyful blacks pressed so close to Lincoln that it took a full hour for him, Tad, and their military escorts to walk from the shore to Davis's house, a distance of only a mile. When he and his son emerged from the house and got into a waiting carriage, the African Americans were still there, and they followed him for the rest of his Richmond tour, beyond a statue of Washington and the Libby Prison to the wharf, to be rowed out to the *Malvern*.

Lincoln's tour was exhilarating for him but anxiety producing for officers assigned to him, who feared he would be assassinated at any moment. The unrestrained enthusiasm of Richmond's blacks made the situation especially volatile because the white Southerners who remained in the city were disgusted by the sight of the Yankee president being worshipped and touched by black people. As a reporter noted, "Abraham Lincoln was walking their streets; and, worst of all, that plain, honest-hearted man was recognizing the 'niggers' as human beings by returning their salutations!"[4] Later that day, Lincoln confronted this hostile attitude when an old political acquaintance, the Jacksonian Democrat Duff Green, visited him on the *Malvern*. Lincoln smiled and extended his hand to Green, who refused to take a hand "red with blood," which had "cut the throats of a thousand of my people."[5] Green hissed, "I do not know how God and your conscience will let you sleep at night after being guilty of the notorious crime of setting the niggers free."[6] Green continued to vilify the president, who, according to one observer, berated Green harshly, although another witness said that Lincoln remained silent and dismissed Green from his presence.[7] (Given Lincoln's customary behavior, the latter account seems probable.)

Reportedly, there was another man that evening who wanted to see the president. Lincoln was informed that there was a man on the shore who wanted to be brought by boat out to the *Malvern* in order to deliver a military dispatch from a general to the president. But the man, who insisted on seeing Lincoln in person, had no military credentials. Highly suspicious, the commander of the *Malvern*, Admiral David Dixon Porter, ordered sailors to bring the man out to the ship and, once aboard, to handcuff him. Sailors rowed to fetch the man, but by the time they reached shore, he had fled. Porter, who had seen the man through his binoculars, later testified that the man was "without a doubt" John Wilkes Booth.[8]

Whether or not Porter was correct, we do know that Booth, who shared Duff Green's attitude toward Lincoln, would have been horrified by the intimacy exhibited that day between the president and African Americans. Booth had already missed the chance to kill Lincoln at the inauguration on March 4. He was pursuing his goal relentlessly.

Another chance came soon enough. This time, Booth would not bungle it.

LINCOLN'S LAST DAY

April 14, 1865. Good Friday that year. Washington, DC, was giddy with triumph. It had been exactly four years since the Confederates had seized Fort Sumter. With Lincoln's advice from a distance, a four-year anniversary ceremony was held that day in South Carolina, in which General Robert Anderson, who had surrendered to the rebels in 1861, raised the US flag over the fort before a large crowd.

In the capital city, Lincoln reconnected that day with his immediate family and planned for his and the nation's future.

Always affectionate to Tad, he had recently shown extra kindness to the boy. Having taken Tad with him on the trip to City Point, after their return to Washington on April 10, he requested military souvenirs for him from cabinet members. "Tad wants some flags. Can he be accommodated[?]" he wrote Edwin Stanton, and to Gideon Welles: "Let Master Tad have a Navy sword."[9] On the fourteenth he would give Tad a special treat by letting him to go to Grover's Theatre to see *Aladdin and His Wonderful Lamp*.

Lincoln's twenty-one-year-old son, Captain Robert Lincoln, visiting Washington from the Virginia front, breakfasted with the president on the fourteenth, and told him details of Lee's surrender to Grant at

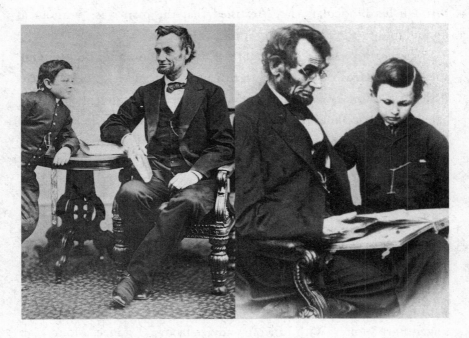

TAD AND ABRAHAM LINCOLN

Appomattox Court House. One can almost hear Robert's account: the dignified, white-bearded fifty-eight-year-old Lee, in full Confederate regalia, rode up on his gray horse Traveller, dismounted, entered Wilmer McLean's brick house, talked terms with the cigar-puffing, forty-two-year-old Grant, who was shabbily dressed and wearing dirty boots. After three hours, the defeated but proud Lee emerged from the building, mounted Traveller, soberly tipped his cap after Grant and other officers had lifted their hats to him, and rode off. After his son had told the story, Lincoln looked at a portrait of General Lee that Robert had brought with him and remarked, "It is a good face. It is the face of a noble, brave man. I am glad that the war is over at last."[10]

If he bonded that day with his son, Lincoln also enjoyed special happiness with Mary. On an afternoon carriage ride around the city, she said she had never seen him so "supremely happy." She remarked,

Robert Lincoln

"Dear Husband, you almost startle me, by your great cheerfulness." He replied, "And well I may feel so, Mary, I consider this day, the war has come to a close. We must both be more cheerful in the future—between the war & the loss of our darling Willie—we have both been very miserable."[11] Happy memories poured forth. The Springfield home, the law office, his adventures on the law circuit, the green bag in which he used to carry his papers—familiar images from the past revived the warmth between the husband and wife.[12] Looking to the future, they agreed they would travel, perhaps to Europe or out to California.[13]

California also came up in a meeting he had that day with the Indiana congressman Schuyler Colfax, who planned to visit the Golden

State soon. Lincoln told Colfax that the mines of California could help pay off the nation's war debt. The president gave the congressman a message for the miners. "Visit all the mining regions," he said. "Tell the miners I have not forgotten them or their interests—tell them that I look to them to redeem this nation from its great debt— . . . that the government will do all it can to hasten the development of the vast wealth hid in their mountain sides and along their valleys."[14] The president who had fostered economic nationalism by creating a big-spending government during the war was thinking about bolstering the nation's specie reserves.

He was also thinking about the reconstruction of the South. One of the unknowns of history is how Lincoln would have handled Reconstruction had he lived. Once toward the end of the war he gave out a conservative signal, but it turned out to be a momentary anomaly.

His interest in restoring the Union quickly led him in early April to hint to the Virginian John Campbell that the state's former Confederate legislature, which now was in flight, could be brought back to Richmond to help terminate Southern military activities. The prospect of a reconvened Confederate legislature appalled Lincoln's cabinet, especially Edwin Stanton. Lincoln realized he had taken precipitate action. Campbell had already begun to call back the Virginia lawmakers when Lincoln sent instructions to General Weitzel in Richmond that he had not meant that he would recognize the Confederate legislature as "a *rightful* body," with the power to "settle all differences with the federal government." Lincoln said he had only allowed "the gentlemen who have *acted* as the legislature of Virginia in support of the rebellion" to stifle Southern resistance to Union forces.[15] Lincoln quickly withdrew his offer to Campbell.

The war, overall, had radicalized Lincoln's view of future race relations in America. On the surface, his stated plan for Reconstruction seemed more conservative than that of Radical Republicans, because he asked that only 10 percent of registered Louisiana voters swear loyalty to the Union before the state was readmitted to the Union, while radicals like Benjamin F. Wade and Henry Winter Davis demanded that 50 percent of Louisianans take the loyalty oath. But his plan, which mandated emancipation, accorded with his goal of restoring union with freedom as efficiently as possible. His attorney general had argued in 1862 that American-born blacks were citizens under the Constitution. Lincoln took important strides toward calling for black citizenship in his March 1864 letter to the Louisianan Michael Hahn, saying that giving blacks the vote would help "keep the jewel of liberty within the family of freedom," and in his last speech, on April 11, 1865, in which he called publicly for limited suffrage for African Americans.[16]

His lack of programmatic statements on Reconstruction reflected his experimental approach. He was ready to adapt to developing circumstances. By April 1865 he had reached a progressive place on Reconstruction. There can be little doubt that he would *not* have followed the pattern of his successor, Andrew Johnson, who at first seemed tough on ex-Confederates but then quickly reversed course, issuing numerous pardons to white Southerners and restricting the rights of African Americans. An ex-slaveholder and an unapologetic white supremacist, Johnson resuscitated states' rights after the war and held that the federal government had no business forcing black citizenship on the South.[17]

Lincoln, in contrast, saw the complexity of reconstruction and possessed a deep social conscience that Johnson lacked. For his entire political life, Lincoln had been forging unity and direction out of apparent chaos. He had done so with the fragmented Illinois Whig Party, with the political shards that became the Republican Party, and, as president, with his diverse cabinet and generals. He faced another muddle in Reconstruction, which was, he said in his last speech, "fraught with great difficulty" because "we must begin with, and mould from, disorganized and discordant elements."[18] Not only were there conflicting views of it within his own party (conservatives called for leniency to the

South, radicals for vindictive punishment), but as Lincoln said, "so great peculiarities pertain to each state; and such important and sudden changes occur in the same state" that "no exclusive, and inflexible plan can safely be prescribed as to details and colatterals [*sic*]." He was certain of one thing: the resolution must come from above—that is, from the federal government. He and the congressional radicals agreed on this point, though he assigned principal power to the executive branch, while the Radicals emphasized Congress's role. He and they agreed on what he called "the restoration of the national authority throughout all the States."[19] Indeed, he literally equated a powerful central government with Reconstruction in his last speech, where he said the problem of the day was "the re-inauguration of the national authority—reconstruction." Because in the same speech he recommended that "the elective franchise" be given at least to blacks who were "very intelligent" or who had served in the military, we see that he was prepared to flex the government's muscles in order to guide the nation toward civil rights.

That is how the antislavery radicals who were present at his last cabinet meeting, held in the early afternoon of April 14, interpreted his attitude. His attorney general, James Speed, wrote that Lincoln "very cheerfully" took up Reconstruction, admitting that he had been wrong in bringing up the reconvening of Virginia's legislature and that he now wanted to treat the South strictly. Speed wrote his fellow radical Salmon Chase, "He never seemed so near our views."[20] Edwin Stanton, also present at the meeting, believed that the president now fully supported suffrage for blacks.[21]

Other radicals felt the same way. The abolitionist Lydia Maria Child, a former critic of Lincoln's, wrote around that time, "I think we have reason to thank God for Abraham Lincoln," noting that "he has grown continually."[22] Senator Charles Sumner, who had once complained of Lincoln's slowness on civil rights, wrote, "The more I have seen of the Prest the more his character has risen in certain respects."

Although we cannot know for certain how Lincoln would have

acted in the postbellum years, it is significant that Schuyler Colfax, with whom he discussed Reconstruction at length on his final day, was a strong advocate of rights for African Americans.

Colfax, who would become vice president under U. S. Grant, was an ardent supporter of citizenship for blacks and a leader of Radical Reconstruction. As early as 1850, as a Whig speaker at Indiana's state constitutional convention, he had denounced legislators who "declare the negro a brute, by excluding him from the commonest, the poorest, the humblest privileges of human beings"; he insisted that his associates must treat blacks "with humanity, and not to crush them as you would vermin out of your sight."[23] As Speaker of the US House of Representatives between 1863 and 1869, Colfax played a prominent role in the passage of the Thirteenth Amendment and in the impeachment proceedings against President Johnson. At a time when the House Speaker did not customarily cast votes for congressional bills, he demanded that his vote be counted on behalf of the Thirteenth Amendment, the Civil Rights Act of 1866, and the Fourteenth Amendment.[24]

Dedicated to improving the Constitution, Colfax also shared Lincoln's reverence for the Declaration of Independence. In November 1865 he went so far as to say, "The Declaration of Independence must be recognized as the law of the land, and every man, alien and native, white and black, protected in the inalienable rights of 'life, liberty, and the pursuit of happiness.' The blacks must be protected in their rights of person and property, to sue in court and to testify."[25] Like Lincoln, Colfax believed that the Constitution embodied the Declaration's ideal of human equality. General Lew Wallace called Colfax's 1865 speech "the greatest act of Colfax's life," because "it was at once accepted by Republicans in Congress as their programme of Reconstruction." Wallace added, "If Abraham Lincoln earned immortality as the great Emancipationist, Schuyler Colfax should share the glory, for it was he who first moved to protect the freeman in his freedom."[26] Colfax himself, however, gave the glory to Lincoln. In a eulogy to the murdered president, he declared that Lincoln would "live in the grateful hearts of the dark-browed race he lifted from under the heel of the oppressor to the dignity of manhood."[27]

Schuyler Colfax

Such themes probably came up in Lincoln's conversation with Colfax on April 14, when Lincoln indicated his firm position on the South. Lincoln rejected the idea of a blanket pardon for ex-Confederates. According to a witness that day, "He believed there could be no restoration of peace or order with the leading rebels in the country, and proposed to have our generals 'skeer' them out by intimating to them that they would not be pursued, but would be punished for their crimes if they remained."[28] Lincoln put special emphasis on rights for the oppressed. In the words of the witness, "He spoke with great impressiveness of his determination to secure liberty and justice to all, with full protection for the humblest, and to re-establish on a sure foundation the unity of the Republic after the sacrifices made for its preservation."

Before parting with Colfax, Lincoln asked the congressman to come back to the White House early in the evening. He invited Colfax to accompany him and Mary to Ford's Theatre that evening to see the comedy *Our American Cousin*. He explained that Mary had invited General Grant and his wife, Julia, to go with them, but the Grants were traveling north to New Jersey to see their daughter. (Actually, Julia was avoiding Mary Lincoln because of the first lady's haughty behavior at City Point in March.) Colfax politely declined the invitation, explaining that he had other plans but that he would stop by briefly at 7:30 p.m.

The president sought out other companions. Ward Hill Lamon, who often served as Lincoln's bodyguard, was away in Richmond on political matters. Before he left, he had warned the president not to attend public events.

So had Lincoln's secretary of war, Edwin Stanton. Nonetheless, on the morning of April 14, Lincoln went to the War Department and asked Stanton whether his muscular assistant secretary Thomas T. Eckert would go with him and Mrs. Lincoln to the theater. Hoping to quash the theater plan, Stanton refused the president's request. Lincoln countered by saying that Eckert was so strong that he once broke five iron pokers over his arm—he was the perfect bodyguard. Continuing to try to discourage Lincoln, Stanton said he had an important job for Eckert to do that evening. Lincoln then approached Eckert himself, who knew of Stanton's feelings and told the president he was very busy and could not go.[29]

At the cabinet meeting he held in the afternoon, he reported having had the previous night an oft-recurring dream that he had had at important moments in the war. In it, he found himself "in a singular and indescribable vessel" that was "moving with great rapidity toward a dark and indefinite shore."[30] Those who heard Lincoln describe the dream later considered it a prophecy of the tragedy that occurred that night at Ford's Theatre.

Union was at the forefront of Lincoln's mind on April 14. He wrote a letter to General James H. Van Alen in which he said he would try to "restore the Union" in ways that would make it "a Union of hearts and hands as well as of States."[31] He took presidential action on behalf of both the North and the South. He pardoned a soldier who had been condemned to death for desertion. "Well, I think the boy can do us more good above ground than under ground," he remarked.[32] He responded to a Southern soldier's petition to be released from a Northern prison by scribbling, "Let it be done."[33] When asked whether he agreed with Secretary Stanton that Jacob Thompson, a fleeing Confederate secret service agent, should be arrested before he boarded a ship to England, Lincoln drawled, "Well, I rather guess not. When you have an elephant on your hands, and he wants to run away, better let him run."[34]

He was also in the mood that day to relax by reading his favorite humorist, David Ross Locke. In the late afternoon, after returning to the White House from his carriage ride with Mary, he read aloud several chapters of Locke's *The Nasby Papers* to two Illinois friends, Governor Richard J. Oglesby and General Isham N. Haynie, who had come for a visit. Doubtless the group laughed often as the president read the words of the whiskey-swigging, racist Petroleum Nasby, with his fulminations against "Linkin! Ape! Goriller!"[35] For the moment, Lincoln was too entertained by Nasby to think of anything else. Oglesby recalled, "They kept sending for him to come to dinner. He promised each time to go, but would continue reading the book." Finally, a "peremptory order" to "come at once" drew him away.[36]

It was tragically ironic that Lincoln was reading Petroleum Nasby only hours before he was shot by a real-life Petroleum Nasby—a pro-Southern Lincoln hater with a low opinion of black people and a penchant for strong liquor.

JOHN WILKES BOOTH

THE ASSASSIN AND THE PRESIDENT

Lincoln had long faced the threat of assassination. He received so many written death threats that he had a file in his desk marked "Assassination Letters."[37] In late summer 1864, someone fired at him while he was riding between the White House and the Soldiers' Home. The bullet missed high, making a hole in his top hat. Lincoln often had a cavalry guard when riding about, but he was known to be lax even about taking that precaution. John Wilkes Booth banked on his negligence; on March 7, 1865, he and his coconspirators planned to intercept the president when he was riding outside of town, kidnap him, take him south, and ransom him for Confederate prisoners who were held in the North. The plot was foiled by Lincoln's change of his plans for the evening.

A famous actor, Booth had virtually abandoned his stage career in August 1864. He devoted much of his time from then until the next April to scheming against Lincoln.

What accounts for Booth's unusual persistence?

At a young age, Booth declared, "I must have fame! fame!"[38] In worldly terms, he achieved it. By the early 1860s, he was a popular leading man whose acting engagements brought in a substantial income. But as the South's prospects sank during the war, Booth dreamed of a different kind of fame. In the months leading up to the assassination, he told several people he would do "something which the world would remember for all time."[39]

In physique and temperament, the actor and the president were very different. Lincoln, commonly considered homely, joked about his own appearance. By April 1865, the cragged face of the fifty-six-year-old president had a pallid look, with sunken, furrowed cheeks and dark circles under the deep-set eyes. Booth, in contrast, was outwardly attractive but inwardly warped. Five feet eight and physically fit, Booth had dark hair, regular features, perfect teeth, and soulful eyes. Starstruck women flocked to his performances, and men found his personal magnetism irresistible. On the morning of the assassination, the brother of the manager of Ford's Theatre saw the nattily dressed Booth approach and remarked, "Here comes the handsomest man in America."[40]

"[I] have loved the Union beyond expression," wrote John Wilkes Booth in a letter of 1864.[41] The Union he worshipped, however, was the one that had existed before the Civil War, when slavery was in place. He held Northern abolitionists and Southern secessionists responsible for destroying the Union and causing a horrible war. The abolition "fanatics," he declared, were especially culpable.[42]

Booth professed to love blacks. He had grown up among enslaved people, some of whom worked on his father's farm near Bel Air, Maryland. He claimed, "Heaven knows *no one* would be willing to do *more* for the negro race than I."[43] But racial bias governed Booth's feelings toward African Americans, who, he insisted, were luckiest when they were held in slavery. He wrote of enslaved people, "Witness their elevation and happiness and enlightenment above the race, elsewhere."[44] Booth saw slavery as a marvelous gift from the founding fathers. He intoned, "[L]ooking upon *African slavery* from the same stand-point held by those noble framers of our Constitution, I for one have ever considered *it* one of the greatest blessings (both for themselves [that is, blacks] and us) that God ever bestowed upon a favored nation." Black people, he believed, had no place in mainstream society. He was repulsed when he saw Southern soldiers being guarded by black troops. "We are all slaves now," he declared. "If a man were to go out and insult a nigger now, he would be knocked down by the nigger, and nothing would be done to the nigger."[45] He wrote, "This country was formed for the *white* not for the black man."[46] If blacks were set free, as Lincoln and the Republicans wanted, they would inevitably die out. "Lincoln's policy is only preparing the way for their total annihilation," he argued, because free blacks were incapable of surviving on their own.

John Wilkes Booth took immense pride in the fact that he had participated in the execution of John Brown. On November 19, 1859, he left an acting engagement in Richmond, joined a militia company, and traveled west to Charles Town, Virginia, to help guard the jail where John Brown and six followers were being held.[47] For two weeks, Booth took on quartermaster duties, distributing food and supplies to his militia unit. On December 2, as a member of the troops overseeing Brown's execution, he was only feet away from Brown, who stood above him on the scaffold. Booth stared at Brown with combined contempt for the old man's antislavery convictions and admiration for his unflappable courage. Awed, Booth got a piece of wood from the box that contained Brown's coffin and later gave pieces of it to friends and associates.

For Booth, John Brown showed the capacity of a powerfully motivated individual to change society. Booth wrote, "John Brown was a man inspired, the grandest character of the century!"[48] It might seem strange that Booth, who detested abolitionists, would praise Brown, the most fervent abolitionist of all. But Brown's courage under pressure impressed his Southern foes, such as Virginia governor Henry Wise, who called him "a bundle of the best nerves I ever saw, . . . cool, collected, and indomitable."[49] One of Brown's slaveholding hostages at Harpers Ferry, Lewis Washington, a descendant of the nation's first president, testified that Brown "was the coolest and firmest man he ever saw in defying danger and death."[50] Another descendant of the first president, the Virginia militia officer B. B. "Bird" Washington, gave Booth one of the knife-pointed pikes that Brown had distributed among enslaved people as he liberated them. On the pike's handle were the words, scrawled in ink, "Major Washington to J. Wilkes Booth."[51]

Although Booth, at his mother's request, never volunteered for the Confederate army, he prided himself on his courage. In youth, he had been, for a time, a typical b'hoy, given to street brawls and running with fire engines. As he matured, he became an athlete, skilled at fencing, shooting, boxing, and other sports. As an actor, he was known for his physical feats. His twelve-foot leap to the Ford's Theatre stage after he shot Lincoln was not unusual for someone who enjoyed doing daring entrances into Shakespearean scenes, such as his leap from a tall rock ledge in the witches' scene in *Macbeth*.

Booth saw himself as a soldier for justice who would single-handedly alter history. If John Brown proclaimed, "No man sent me here; it was my own prompting and that of my Maker," Booth called himself *"A Confederate doing duty on his own responsibility."*[52] If Brown said that to die fighting against slavery was "the greatest service a man can render to God," Booth told his mother that he was ready to sacrifice his life in "struggling for such holy rights" as the South's "sacred" cause.[53] After the assassination, he reportedly wrote of Lincoln, "Our country owed all its troubles to him, and God simply made me the instrument of his punishment."[54] When he was cornered at the end by federal troops near Port Royal, Virginia, in Richard Garrett's barn, Booth declared that he would fight to the death rather than surrender, which led to his being shot by Thomas H. "Boston" Corbett. To the bitter end, he wanted to exhibit courage with single-minded intensity like John Brown's.

But he badly misinterpreted the man he called "that rugged old hero."[55] Booth wrote, "If Brown were living I doubt whether he *himself*, would set slavery, against the Union." In other words, he thought that Brown, had he lived, would not have supported Lincoln's aggressive war against slavery if it meant destroying the Union. Here, as in other matters, Booth was exactly wrong. Brown, just before he was hanged, had written a note saying that the crime of slavery would be purged away only with very much bloodshed.[56] He had declared several times that a whole generation of Americans might have to die in order for slavery to be uprooted.

Booth regarded Lincoln with sneering condescension: "This man's appearance, his pedigree, his low coarse jokes and anecdotes, his vulgar similes, his frivolity, are a disgrace to the seat he holds. He is standing in the footprints of old John Brown, but no more fit to stand with that rugged old hero—Great God! No."[57] Lincoln, Booth continued, was merely "the tool of the North to crush out, or try to crush out slavery, by robbery, rapine, slaughter, and bought armies." He was "overturning this blind Republic and making himself a king"; his new term "will be a reign."

Booth's hatred of Lincoln and his party resembled that of Lincoln's favorite humor character, Petroleum Nasby, the quintessential Copperhead. Though Southern-born, Booth spent most of his time from 1860 to 1865 in the North, where most acting opportunities were. Though the

North made Booth a stage star, he was wretched there. In the summer of 1864 he wrote his mother, "For four years I have lived (I may say) a slave in the north—a favored slave, it's true, but no less hateful to me on that account."[58] Every principle he believed in was considered treasonous by those around him. He argued furiously with Lincoln supporters like his brother Edwin. A theater manager remarked that John Wilkes Booth "was very vitriol in his talk as to Pres't Lincoln, and called the Union soldiers all manner of evil names." At a social gathering, he performed a Copperhead song, "Then and Now," which lamented the decline of liberty and the unnatural rise of black people that Booth thought Lincoln had brought about. One of the song's verses went:

> Ab'rm wants to free the nigger,
> And we let him have his way;
> Our chance for Liberty
> Is hardly worth a d—n,
> But there's a nigger kingdom coming.
> And the king is Abraham!

The charge that Lincoln was a horrid, Negro-loving despot was common among Copperheads and Southerners. Booth, a journalist noted, was "a good sample of Copperheadism" who wanted only "to curse the nigger and curse the Lincoln Government."[59] Booth's anxiety spiked after Lincoln won reelection. Because there were no presidential term limits at the time (they came with the passage of the Twenty-second Amendment in 1947), it seemed possible that Lincoln's presidency would continue indefinitely—a nightmare for Booth, who asked a friend, "He can be president as long as he lives, do you suppose?" When the friend replied, "Yes," Booth said, "There is no help that I can see as long as Lincoln lives."[60]

It was not just Lincoln who must die. As Booth's anger grew, he planned the deaths of officials around the president. Just as Petroleum

Nasby envisaged killing Abe's cabinet members along with Abe himself, Booth, a real-life Nasby, targeted not just Lincoln but other leaders as well. The plan, as finalized on April 14, was that he would kill Lincoln and General Grant (who was reportedly scheduled to attended Ford's Theatre with the president), while one coconspirator, Lewis Powell (aka Payne), would murder Secretary of State William Seward at his home on Lafayette Square and another one, George Atzerodt, would assassinate Vice President Johnson in his room at the Kirkwood House.

What was it about Booth that drove him to commit the act that others only contemplated? After all, assassination plots were common, and there were plenty of Nasbys around.

Booth alone among would-be assassins had long been immersed in an identifiably American style of intense acting—what today might be called exaggerated method acting. The complete identification with the role one plays was a technique Booth inherited from his father, Junius Brutus Booth. Walt Whitman said of Junius Booth, "His genius was to me one of the grandest revelations of my life, a lesson of artistic expression."[61] Junius Booth did not just inhabit a role; he took it to emotional limits. Whitman said of Junius Booth, "The words fire, energy, *abandon*, found in him unprecedented meanings. . . . When he was in a passion, face, neck, hands, would be suffused, his eye would be frightful—his whole mien enough to scare audience, actors; often the actors *were* afraid of him."

They had reason to be, for Junius Booth often carried his acting too far.[62] One night he became so overwrought as Othello that he had to be pulled away when he nearly suffocated Desdemona with a pillow. In a swordfight scene, Booth once drove his opponent out of the theater and continued the fight on the streets. Another time, he nearly killed the actor playing his rival, who said, "It seemed as if all hell was raging in his heart; his eyes displayed the fierceness of a tiger's, and his thrust at me, I verily believe, would have been fatal had I not stepped aside to avoid it."[63] Junius Booth's disfigured nose came from an incident in a

Junius Brutus Booth in theatrical costume

hotel room where he was rehearsing *Othello* with an actor who became so terrified by Booth's vehement emotions that he smashed Booth's face with an iron poker in self-defense. Junius Booth carried theatrical roles into daily life. Known as "the Mad Tragedian," he would walk the streets in costume as Shylock or Richard or Cardinal Richelieu, distributing coins to strangers.

Of the three Booth children who became prominent actors—Edwin, John Wilkes, and Junius Jr.—only John adopted their father's tempestuous style. A Boston reviewer said that John "had more of the native fire and fury of his great father than any of his family."[64] John relished violent stage roles. As a child, he had gotten perverse pleasure out of

The Booths—John Wilkes, Edwin, and Junius Jr.—in Shakespeare's
Julius Caesar, 1864

shooting stray cats—unlike Lincoln, who avoided hunting because he
did not want to hurt animals.[65] As an actor, John Wilkes Booth struck
Whitman "a queer fellow; had strange ways."[66] Whitman didn't like
Booth's version of the American style, which lacked finesse. For instance, John carried the sword fight scene in *Richard III* to sadistic
lengths. "The Richard of Mr. [John Wilkes] Booth," commented a reviewer in 1863, "is an impossible personage." He made Shakespeare's
character someone one "who loved murder for murder's sake alone."
With an "almost demoniac look," Booth's Richard "dabbles in blood;
sprinkles it on the stage after the murder of Henry; wipes his sword on

his mantle (a very vulgar and disgusting thing for a nobleman to do), and revels in it from beginning to end."⁶⁷ Once, when Booth departed from the script by refusing to die in a sword fight, the actor playing his opponent edged close to him and whispered, "For God's sake, John, die! Die! If you don't, I shall!"⁶⁸ In another performance, John wielded his sword so vigorously that his foe fell off the stage into the orchestra pit. A month before he assassinated Lincoln, while playing an evil duke in Richard Lalor Sheil's tragedy *The Apostate*, Booth was so realistic when he tortured a woman on the wheel that a spectator was truly frightened by "the hideous, malevolent expression of his distorted countenance, the fierce glare and ugly roll of his eyes," as he gleefully boasted about his "masterpiece" of cruelty.⁶⁹

For John Wilkes Booth, the extreme American acting style led to a merging of stage characters with real life. He often played rebels who rose up against tyrants, such as Major Gough, the Puritan rebel in William Bayle Bernard's play *The Wept of Wish-ton-Wish* who signed the death warrant of King Charles I; Brutus, the virtuous nobleman in Shakespeare's *Julius Caesar* who joined conspirators against the would-be Roman emperor Caesar; William Tell, the fourteenth-century Swiss huntsman who in Friedrich Schiller's play of that name killed an oppressive governor; and one of the conspirators involved in the plot to murder Venetian officials in Thomas Otway's tragedy *Venice Preserved*.

Booth didn't just identify with these stage assassins; he *became* one of them. America itself was now his stage, and Lincoln was the targeted tyrant. When asked shortly before the assassination why he no longer acted, he answered that "the only play he cared to present was *Venice Preserved*"—an unsubtle reference to the real-life murderous drama he was soon to act out, in imitation of Otway's play about conspiratorial violence against a government.⁷⁰ Assassinating the "despot" Lincoln in a theater would be Booth's ultimate sensational performance. A couple of hours before he shot Lincoln, he recommended to a hotel clerk that he go to Ford's Theatre that evening, saying, "There is to be some splendid acting there tonight." The Lincoln assassination was the American acting style taken to the hilt. As a contemporary remarked, "It was so theatrical in plan and performance—the conspiracy—the dagger—the selection of a theater—the brandishing of the weapon—the cry 'sic semper tyrannis' to the audience—all was exactly that a madman brought up in the theater might have been expected to conceive."[71]

Even Booth's most private thoughts, as recorded in a diary he kept while he was fleeing south after the assassination, ran to stage roles he had played. While being hunted through the cold swamps and woods, he scribbled these words: "I am here in despair. And why; For doing what Brutus [in Shakespeare's *Julius Caesar*] was honored for. What made Tell [in Schiller's *William Tell*] a Hero. And yet I for striking down a greater tyrant than they ever knew am looked upon as a common cutthroat. My action was purer than either of theirs."[72]

The same cultural factors that led Booth toward right-wing vigilantism carried Lincoln toward democratic openness and dedication to a nation based on justice for all. The example of John Brown impelled Lincoln not toward anarchistic violence but toward a vision of emancipation through infiltration of the Deep South, to be directed by the highest-ranking African American officer, Martin Delany. Lincoln's higher law was a world apart from Booth's. Not only was his Second Inaugural Address a religion-saturated demand for black freedom, but two days after Robert E. Lee surrendered, Lincoln, in the same speech in which he called for African American suffrage, declared, "He, from Whom all blessings flow, must not be forgotten. A call for a national thanksgiving is being prepared, and will be duly promulgated."[73] God and civil rights had joined in Lincoln's mind.

While Booth aimed to sow discord and chaos, Lincoln was thinking of cultural and social unity. While visiting General Grant's headquarters at City Point, Virginia, he surprised a military band by calling for

"Dixie." The South's signature song, he said, was now federal property, and people of either section could enjoy it unabashedly.[74] He called for it again when he delivered his last speech on April 11.

Lincoln shared Booth's interest in literature about death or murder, but for different reasons. One might think that after having visited the fallen Confederate capital of Richmond and sitting in Jefferson Davis's vacated chair, he would gloat over the North's victory. Not so. On the boat trip from City Point back to Washington on April 9—the day of Lee's surrender to Grant—Lincoln ignored Charles Sumner's pleas to discuss the war or Reconstruction and focused instead on literature. According to the Marquis de Chambrun, a French ambassador who was traveling with the president, "That whole day the conversation dwelt upon literary subjects."[75] Lincoln recited from memory Longfellow's "Resignation," a poem about the universality of death, with brief references to heaven. Doubtless Lincoln had on his mind his own lost loved ones and those of hundreds of thousands in the war-ravaged nation when he recited Longfellow's words, "The air is full of farewells to the dying, / And mournings for the dead." And surely he found comfort in the poet's assurance that this life "is but a suburb of the life elysian, / Whose portal we call Death."[76]

Besides poetry, Chambrun wrote, "Mr. Lincoln read to us for several hours passages taken from Shakespeare," among them Macbeth's speech about one of his murder victims, Duncan (*Macbeth*, act 3, scene 2).[77] Obsessed by the passage, Lincoln read it several times. In the speech, Macbeth meditates on the fact that his murdered victim is fortunate because he has escaped the ills of this world. Duncan "after life's fitful fever sleeps well," and neither "steel, nor poison, / Malice domestic, foreign levy, nothing," can now touch him. Macbeth, in contrast, is left with a devastating sense of guilt.

In his reaction to literary culture, we see a key difference between Lincoln and Booth. The difference becomes clear if we consider Herman Melville's distinction between a thoughtful response to Shakespeare and that of the mere thrill seeker. Melville contrasted "those mistaken souls, who dream of Shakespeare as a mere man of Richard-the-Third humps, and Macbeth daggers," with the contemplative reader, who was unconcerned with "blood-besmeared tragedy" for its own sake and attended instead to "those deep far-away things" in the Bard of Avon, "those occasional flashings-forth of the intuitive Truth in him; those short, quick probings at the very axis of reality . . . that make Shakespeare, Shakespeare."[78] John Wilkes Booth responded to the "blood-besmeared tragedy" and "Macbeth daggers" in Shakespeare; Lincoln responded to the playwright's deeper, universal meanings. For Booth, Shakespeare and other dramatists provided a recipe for spectacular murder in support of a political agenda. For Lincoln, literature told truths about the human condition that bound all people together.

THE CLIMAX

The Lincolns were about an hour late in leaving for the theater that night. After dinner, Lincoln had met with George Ashmun and Schuyler Colfax—his political past and future, so to speak, because Ashmun, a former congressman from Massachusetts, had chaired the Chicago Wigwam convention that had nominated him in 1860 and Colfax would go on to carry his message of civil rights into Reconstruction. Neither Mary nor Lincoln wanted to go out. She had had a headache all day, he was weary, and the weather was raw and gusty. Rain threatened. But the Lincolns felt obliged to go. The papers had announced their attendance, and the people were expecting them. Tad was sent with a chaperone to see *Aladdin and the Wonderful Lamp*, which was playing at Grover's Theatre, while they set off to Ford's to catch the famous Laura Keene in Tom Taylor's *Our American Cousin*, a costume drama involving a boorish but good-natured American who creates havoc in stuffy British drawing rooms.

John Wilkes Booth had planned for this moment. As an actor, he received his mail at Ford's Theatre, and when he appeared there on the morning of the fourteenth, he learned that the Lincolns and the Grants would be attending the play there in the evening. At noon, Booth went to a livery stable and rented a spirited bay mare. He gave the horse a test run, then returned it to the stable, saying he would call for it at around 3:00 p.m. After lunch, he set his plan in motion. Over several months, he had gathered a circle of at least eight conspirators, all of whom shared his love for the South and loathing for Lincoln. One of them, Lewis Powell, was a big, muscular man who was deeply embittered because he had lost two Confederate brothers in the war. He responded enthusiastically when Booth met with him in the early afternoon and gave him the task of going that evening to William Seward's home to kill the secretary of state. Later on, Booth encountered another conspirator, George Atzerodt, a boozy, German-born ferryman who had joined Booth's team reluctantly. Booth assigned him to kill Vice President Andrew Johnson in his room at the Kirkwood House. Shocked at the idea, Atzerodt told Booth he had prepared for kidnapping, not murder. After a heated back-and-forth, Booth threatened to kill him if he didn't follow orders. Atzerodt glumly fell into line.

In Booth's mind, a new, updated version of *Julius Caesar* or *Venice Preserved* was about to appear on the grandest stage of all: America. And he would be the star.

After picking up his horse at the stable, Booth met a fellow actor, John Matthews, who asked him if he had seen the group of Confederate troops that had just passed by under the guard of Northern soldiers. Booth had indeed seen them and was stunned. He put his hand to his forehead and exclaimed, "Great God! I have no longer a country!"[79] He gave Matthews a letter he had written, asking him to send it for publication in a Washington newspaper. The letter never appeared; Matthews, who apparently destroyed it, later described it as a typical Copperhead editorial.

Matthews pointed to a carriage passing by and said to Booth, "Why, Johnny, there goes Grant. I thought he was going to the theater this evening with the president." Booth galloped after the carriage and approached it, to the irritation of Julia Grant, who recognized Booth as one of a group of men who had looked menacingly at them that day at lunch from across a hotel dining room.[80]

Booth circled back to Ford's, where he left the horse in a stable behind the theater. With some theater employees he went to the nearby Taltavull's Star Saloon and had drinks. Returning to Ford's, Booth traced his route up to the presidential box, above stage left. He apparently went into the vestibule behind the box, boring a peephole through its door and putting on the floor a board to be used as a door brace to prevent intrusion once he had attacked Lincoln.

Booth returned to his hotel and armed himself with a small .44 caliber pistol, made by Henry Deringer of Philadelphia, and a large Bowie knife, which he stuck in his boot. He went to another hotel and met with Powell, Atzerodt, and David Herold, coordinating the murders for 10:15 p.m. and instructing them to meet up with him at the Navy Yard Bridge. Herold would lead Powell to Seward's home, and Atzerodt would finish off Johnson at Kirkwood House.

By 9:30 p.m. Booth was back at Ford's Theatre. He got his horse from the stable and asked Ned Spangler, a stagehand, to hold it for him in the alley behind the theater. Busy changing sets, Spangler turned the task over to the young Joseph "Peanuts" Burroughs. Booth went next door to Taltavull's Star Saloon and ordered a bottle of whiskey and some water.

The Lincolns had arrived at Ford's at around 9:00 p.m. On the way, they had picked up their last-minute invitees, Major Henry R. Rathbone, a government disbursement officer, and his fiancée Clara Harris, the daughter of New York senator Ira Harris.

As was usual when Lincoln went to the theater, the security detail was light. He was accompanied by a White House valet, Charles Forbes.

The president's guard for the night, the Washington policeman John F. Parker, walked in the drizzle to the theater because there was no room for him in the carriage, and he greeted the Lincolns there. Parker escorted the Lincoln party to the presidential box and then left, either to watch the play or to have drinks. Charles Forbes sat alone in the hall outside the president's box.[81]

The Lincolns had caused a stir when they entered the theater. When the president appeared in his box, an actor onstage ad-libbed, "This reminds me of a story, as President Lincoln would say." The orchestra broke out with a rousing "Hail to the Chief." Lincoln smiled and bowed as the audience stood and cheered. He then settled into the velvet-covered rocking chair that the theater manager had put there for him. To his right was Mary, and beyond her sat Clara Harris and Henry Rathbone.

Our American Cousin, which Lincoln had seen before, was the sort of frothy fare he enjoyed when he wanted to forget everything. He and Mary laughed their way through the silly confrontations between the play's crude Vermonter and his snooty British relatives. Mary leaned close to Lincoln and whispered, "What will Miss Harris think of my hanging on to you so?" He replied with a smile, "She won't think anything about it."[82]

They were being watched. John Wilkes Booth, spiked with whiskey, had entered the theater at about 10:00 p.m. He went up the stairs to the dress circle and walked down the corridor, ignoring two acquaintances who greeted him. When he reached the door outside the president's box, he handed a visiting card to the valet Charles Forbes, an unsuspecting man who let Booth pass. Booth pushed open the door that led to the passageway that adjoined the president's box. He jammed the door behind him with the board that had been left on the floor. Through the peephole he had made, he could see Lincoln. Booth knew *Our American Cousin* well, for he had acted in it twelve times. He was waiting for a really funny moment when he knew the audience would be distracted.

That moment came at around 10:13 p.m., in act 3, scene 2 of the

Ford's Theatre

Lincoln's box at Ford's Theatre

play, when the play's bumpkin hero declares, "Well, I guess I know enough to turn you inside out, old gal—you sockdologizing old man-trap." As the audience exploded in laughter, a loud shot was heard. Booth had approached Lincoln from behind and fired at him from about four feet away.

Lincoln, shot through the brain, slumped forward, senseless, as though dozing, as he often did at the theater. Mary looked at him and shrieked. Henry Rathbone spotted Booth and lunged at him. The two grappled. Booth slashed Rathbone's left arm with his knife, wounding it badly. Booth mounted the rail of the box and jumped twelve feet down to the stage. He landed awkwardly; he would claim that he broke his left leg in the fall, although the snapping of his left fibula may have happened later, when his horse fell.[83] He walked across the stage and exited on the left. Partway across, he turned to the audience and, his eyes glaring, raised his knife, which glittered like a diamond in the stage lights. Some heard him hiss the Virginia state motto: "Sic semper tyrannis!" ["Thus always to tyrants!"][84] Heading toward the rear exit, Booth was intercepted by the orchestra leader, William Withers Jr. Booth slashed him with his knife, pushed through the stage door to the alley, grabbed his horse's reins from Peanuts Burroughs, and, apparently with difficulty because of his bad leg, mounted the mare, which wheeled violently before galloping away.

The theater became sheer mayhem. Some in the audience surged forward, tumbling over seats toward the stage. Others rushed out of the theater. Cries of "Stop him!" "Hang him!" "Burn the theater!" rang out.[85] Several, including two doctors and the actress Laura Keene, went directly to Lincoln's box, bursting into it after Rathbone removed the door brace. The actress cradled Lincoln's head in her lap. Mary Lincoln, hysterical at the sight of the blood-stained dress of Clara Rathbone, shrieked, "My husband's blood!," unaware that Lincoln's wound bled little because a clot had quickly formed; the blood she saw came from Rathbone's slashed artery.

The assassination of Lincoln

Lincoln never regained consciousness. He was carried across Tenth Street to the house of William Petersen, a German tailor. Taken to a small room at the end of the front hall, the president was laid out on a bed diagonally because of his seventy-six-inch length; even then, his feet rested on the bottom bed board, which could not be removed from the frame. His clothes were taken off. An army blanket and colored wool coverlet were thrown over him. When doctors pulled down the covers to hear his lungs and heart, witnesses were astonished by the lean muscularity of his body. The rail-splitter and wrestling champion from New Salem was still in fine trim.

All night he was attended by physicians, and the room was visited by many people—cabinet members and other politicians as well as ordinary citizens. Mary kissed her husband and tried to get him to respond by showering him with endearments. For nine hours she watched

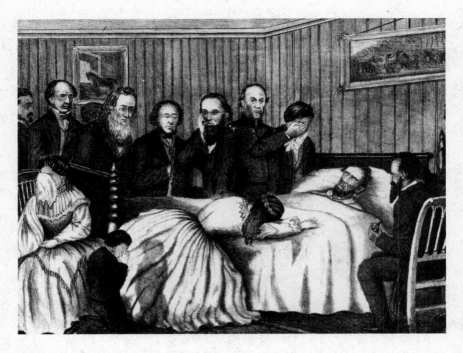

The deathbed of Lincoln, 453 Tenth Street,
Washington, DC, April 14–15, 1865

her husband die. She intermittently left, going to an adjoining room where she let loose her grief. Robert stood for long periods by his father's side, crying. Booth's bullet, a lead ball, had entered Lincoln's skull behind the left ear and settled in the brain behind the right eye, around which the skin darkened. Trying to remove the bullet, doctors probed the wound with a long instrument, but they reached only a few bone fragments. Lincoln's breathing and heart rate wavered throughout the night and finally stopped altogether at 7:22 in the morning of April 15. Edwin Stanton, who had been by Lincoln's side through the night and who had wept uncontrollably, said, according to John Hay, "Now he belongs to the ages."[86] Outside, it was pouring.

John Wilkes Booth met up with David Herold and made his way south through Maryland over the next twelve days but was tracked to a

Virginia farm and killed there when he tried to fight his pursuers when cornered. Lewis Powell forced his way into William Seward's home and stabbed but did not kill the secretary, whose bodyguard and two other men managed to shove Powell out of the house; Seward's son Frederick was badly wounded in the attack. George Atzerodt made no attempt on Andrew Johnson at the Kirkwood House. Instead, he drank at the hotel bar and then went out, threw his knife in a gutter, pawned his guns in Georgetown, and traveled to Germantown, Maryland, where he was arrested six days later. Although he had not carried out his murderous assignment, he was too deeply involved in the conspiracy to escape punishment. The seven-week trial of the Lincoln conspirators resulted in the hanging of Atzerodt, Powell, Herold, and, controversially, Mary Surratt, who ran a boardinghouse where the conspirators sometimes stayed. Two other conspirators were sentenced to prison for life and another one was jailed for six years.

Several people directly involved in the tragedy had dark fates. Clara Harris saved Henry Rathbone's life that evening by improvising a tourniquet for his badly hurt arm. The two were married in 1867. They went on to have three children. Henry, obsessed by the question of whether or not he could have saved Lincoln, sank into depression. He also came to suspect his wife of infidelity. In 1883, after the family had moved to Germany, he murdered Clara by stabbing and shooting her, and attempted suicide by stabbing himself several times in the chest. He survived, but he spent the rest of his days in a German hospital for the criminally insane.

Mary Lincoln was prostrated by grief. For forty days she mainly lay in bed. Because she refused to stay in any familiar room in the White House, Lizzy Keckly and Elizabeth Dixon (a Connecticut senator's wife) chose for her a small, little-used "summer room."[87] Lizzy Keckly, who took care of her, never forgot "the wails of a broken heart, the unearthly shrieks, the terrible convulsions, the wild, tempestuous outbursts of grief from the soul."[88] Mary did not attend the funeral service held in the White House on April 19; of the immediate family, only

Robert went. Mary was so indifferent about her surroundings that strangers walked in and out of the White House at will, taking away silver, china, pieces of carpet, and even heavy furniture.[89]

In late May, Mary gathered herself sufficiently to leave the White House and move to Chicago, where she lived, initially with Robert and Tad and eventually with Tad alone. She wore black widow's clothes for the rest of her life. She wrote on mourning stationery bordered in black. Hard-pressed for money, she created a scandal by selling many of her White House dresses. She continued to take comfort from spiritualism and was delighted when William Mumford took a spirit photograph of her with Lincoln standing behind her. She was devastated, however, when in 1866 William Herndon, publicized the claim that Lincoln had always loved Ann Rutledge, not Mary; and when, two years later, Lizzy Keckly published her White House tell-all *Behind the Scenes*. The offended Mary never again spoke to the dressmaker she had called her *"best living friend."*[90]

When Tad heard that his father had been shot, he was inconsolable for a day, but on Easter Sunday, he awoke to a beautiful spring morning. During the day, he asked a White House visitor if he thought his father was now in heaven. The stranger assured him, "I have not a doubt of it." Tad said, "I am glad he has gone there, for he was never happy after he came here [to Washington]. This was not a good place for him!"[91] Tad went on to become a decent student and a responsible young man. However, he died of pneumonia or tuberculosis at eighteen—another terrible blow for Mary.

Robert Lincoln became estranged from his mother. Appalled by what he considered her strange behavior, some of it associated with her spiritualist visions, he committed her to a Batavia, Illinois, asylum, the upscale Bellevue Place, in 1875. Her four months there were uneventful. All told, her nineteen years of life after Lincoln's death saw her struggling to maintain mental stability and to avoid a financial meltdown that was, given her sizable assets, a chimera produced by her anx-

Mary Todd Lincoln with her husband's spirit
(Photograph by William Mumford)

ieties. Toward the end, suffering from illnesses, she confined herself in
a room in a relative's home in Springfield with the shades always drawn,
even in sunny weather. She died of a stroke at age sixty-three in July
1882. Robert, a lawyer and businessman, went on to serve as secretary

917

of war under James A. Garfield and Chester Arthur and as an ambassador to England under Benjamin Harrison.

Lincoln's death on April 15, 1865, prompted an outpouring of mourning throughout the North and even in much of the South.[92] Sorrow seized the nation's capital. On Tuesday, the eighteenth, the president, whose body had been embalmed, lay in state in the East Room of the White House, where at least twenty thousand mourners, including many African Americans, solemnly walked by his body. The next day, after a funeral service in the East Room, Lincoln was taken by hearse in a procession a mile and a half to the Capitol Rotunda for another public viewing. African American troops, who arrived late, met the procession head on, and, turning around, took its lead fortuitously; they were followed by white military regiments, government officials, and dignitaries. Gun salutes crackled, cannon boomed, and bells tolled.

On Friday, the twenty-first, Lincoln's funeral train set out on a ceremonial journey to Springfield, Illinois, the president's home city, where he would be buried. Also on the train was the exhumed body of Willie Lincoln, to be interred along with his father. Robert Lincoln was on the train, but Mary Lincoln, incapacitated by grief, was still back in the White House with Tad. The funeral train proceeded on a circuitous 1,700-mile, 12-day journey through 180 cities and towns in 7 states. Nearly the entire way, mourners lined the route, standing silently with their heads uncovered as the train passed. The train stopped many times, and there were processions and viewings of the body in Philadelphia, New York, Albany, Cleveland, Chicago, and many other places.

Walt Whitman, in his sonorous eulogy to Lincoln "When Lilacs Last in the Dooryard Bloom'd," described the president's last train journey in grief-laden lines:

> Coffin that passes through lanes and streets, . . .
> With processions long and winding and the
>   flambeaus of the night,

With the countless torches lit, with the silent
     sea of faces and the unbared heads,
With the waiting depot, the arriving coffin, and
     the sombre faces,
With dirges through the night, with the
     thousand voices rising strong and solemn,
With all the mournful voices of the dirges
     pour'd around the coffin,
The dim-lit churches and the shuddering
     organs—where amid these you journey,
With the tolling tolling bells' perpetual clang,
Here, coffin that slowly passes,
I give you my sprig of lilac.[93]

During that journey, Lincoln's decomposing corpse, growing ever darker and more shrunken, required constant powdering by his embalmer, who was among the some three hundred people who were on the funeral train.

In the middle of the Civil War, Lincoln had written, "Springfield is my home, and there, more than elsewhere, are my life-long friends."[94] On May 3, 1865, Lincoln arrived home. For twenty-four hours, his body lay for viewing in Springfield's state house. The next day at around 11:00 a.m., the president's casket was put into a lavish hearse drawn by six black horses and taken in a procession to Oak Ridge Cemetery, two miles away.[95] General Joseph Hooker led the procession, which was headed by two army divisions, followed by the hearse, behind which, in carriages or on foot, came state and federal officials, fraternal groups, and average citizens—some ten thousand in all. The only blood relatives in attendance at the funeral were Robert Lincoln and John Hanks, the president's first cousin once removed, who had helped create the Abe image in 1860, when he publicly presented fence rails once split by Lincoln.

Lincoln's Springfield home, draped in black, on May 4, 1865, the day of
his funeral and burial. In front of the home is Old Bob, Lincoln's
horse, attended by the African American ministers Harry Brown (left)
and William C. Trevan (right).

Just behind the hearse, the African American ministers Harry
Brown and William C. Trevan led Lincoln's horse, Old Bob. Lincoln's
longtime barber and friend William Florville witnessed the funeral
along with thousands of other blacks, some of whom joined the immense procession that followed the casket.

At the cemetery, the Baptist preacher Andrew C. Hubbard conducted a religious service, which included a reading of the Second
Inaugural Address. At least five other ministers participated as well,
including the Methodist bishop Matthew Simpson, who delivered an
hour-long eulogy. Lincoln and Willie were laid to rest in a large vault.
At last, the father and his beloved son were reunited.[96] Over the years,
they would be joined by Mary, Tad, and Eddie. Robert Lincoln, who
died at eighty-two in 1926, was buried at Arlington National Cemetery.

AFTERMATH AND LEGACY

What did John Wilkes Booth hope to gain through his murderous plot? We get a clue from a conversation he had with John Coyle, a book-keeper at the anti-Lincoln *National Intelligencer*, on the morning of his crime. He asked Coyle what would happen if Lincoln was killed. Coyle told him Andrew Johnson would then become president. And how about if Johnson was killed as well? Coyle said vaguely that Americans would be left with "anarchy or whatever Constitution provides."[97] Louis Weichmann, a War Department clerk who knew Booth and later wrote a book about the assassination, was horrified by the thought of what would have happened had Booth and his cohorts succeeded in killing Lincoln, Johnson, Seward, and Grant. According to the Consti-tution's line of succession, the presidency would go to the president pro tempore of the Senate, Lafayette Foster of Connecticut, until a new president was chosen under the due forms of law. Weichmann stated that this was all that "would have stood between our government and absolute anarchy or destruction. The human mind recoils in horror at the contemplation of the possibility of the success of such a scheme."

Anarchy, destruction. That's what Booth hoped for. Ironically, his effort to create chaos by murdering Lincoln had the opposite effect. No death in history did more to unify Americans than did that of Abraham Lincoln.

That was Walt Whitman's point in his lecture "The Death of Abra-ham Lincoln," which he delivered often between the Civil War and his death in 1892.[98] A nation, Whitman noted, is defined by its deaths. Whenever a great person dies, that person becomes a strong unifying force. The "final use," Whitman wrote, "of a heroic-eminent life—especially of a heroic-eminent death—is its indirect filtering into the nation and the race, and to give . . . a cement to the whole people, subtler, more underlying, than anything in written constitution, or courts or armies—namely, the cement of a death identified thoroughly with that people." The "heroic-eminent death" has the greatest power of all to "condense—perhaps only really lastingly condense—a Nationality."

This does not mean that all Americans came together in grief over Lincoln's death. As Martha Hodes shows, the immediate reactions were remarkably varied, ranging from sincere grief to vindictive glee.[99] Those who welcomed the grim news included the South Carolina diarist Mary Boykin Chesnut, who called the assassination "a warning to tyrants," and the former Virginia governor Henry Wise, who considered John Wilkes Booth an avenging angel who had killed "an inhuman monster."[100] Robert H. Crozier, a former Confederate colonel, in his 1869 book *The Bloody Junto, or The Escape of John Wilkes Booth,* likened Booth to one of "ancient semigods," who was "providentially ordered, to save an already ruined country from the lowest depths of political and social degradation."[101] There is a tradition of Booth worshipping, from avid relic gatherers just after the assassination to the Confederate veteran Joseph Pinkney Parker, who in 1904 erected a monument with the words "In honor of John Wilks [*sic*] Booth / For killing old Abe Lincoln," to Izola Forrester, allegedly the granddaughter of Booth, who wrote in a 1937 book that "you cannot but feel a deep love for [Booth]," to the Southern radio host and former Rand Paul aide Jack Hunter, who said that he personally raised a toast on every May 10, Booth's birthday, to Lincoln's assassin, about whom Hunter declared, "John Wilkes Booth's heart was in the right place."[102]

A corollary tradition, Lincoln hating, has been kept alive by some Americans, mainly right-wing neo-Confederates, who view Lincoln as a violent despot and a flouter of the Constitution who initiated a dangerous ascendancy of black people, destroying the idyllic Old South in the process.[103]

Nor did Lincoln's death repair social or cultural division for everyone. The Puritan-Cavalier myth fed into the conflicts of Reconstruction. Radical Northerners said that now that victory was theirs, the Puritan force ruled America. "The rebellion is crushed!" announced a Boston paper. "It is settled that Plymouth, and not Jamestown, is to be the nation's watchword; the Puritan and not the Cavalier, to be master and pilot here."[104] A Maine preacher declared, "The Puritan has conquered the Cavalier."[105] Such Puritan rhetoric bolstered the Radical Republican program of taking stiff measures against ex-Confederates while supporting emancipated blacks in the South. Opponents of the Radicals answered in kind. The Copperhead Samuel Cox declared that "the Puritan element . . . made war" and now will not permit national unity: "It denounces [Andrew] Johnson as it did Jackson and Jefferson."[106] The president of the South Carolina state convention asked Southerners to "resolve before high heaven that the land which was once the home of the Huguenot and the Cavalier shall never be ruled by the Puritan and the African!"[107]

The Puritan/Cavalier distinction diminished over time; by the end of the nineteenth century it was largely discarded in the spirit of reunion between the North and the South. The memory of Lincoln was a key factor in the reunion; he was thought to blend the values of the North and the South. Henry Grady's 1886 speech announcing that the quintessentially average American had been Abraham Lincoln—"the sum of the Puritan and Cavalier," with "the virtues of both"—opened the way for others who used Lincoln as a model for Grady's idea that "people of all sections" now saw themselves as "citizens of the same country, members of the same government,— . . . all united now, and united forever."[108] This outlook echoed Whitman's point that Lincoln's death provided a "cement to a whole people" more fundamental than "constitutions." To this day, there is no president who is as more beloved or respected than Lincoln. People on opposite sides of the political spectrum embrace him.

As the Jim Crow period showed, however, there is a danger in political opponents joining together in reverence for Lincoln. A homogenized, nonsectional Lincoln fit all too easily into the mentality of

Jim Crow. Henry Grady and other New South spokespersons were white supremacists who placed the apparently moderate Lincoln firmly in their own camp. D. W. Griffith's virulently racist film *The Birth of a Nation* (1915) likewise said that with the death of Lincoln the South had lost its "best friend," resulting in the Radical Republicans' bringing on a nightmarish period of black supremacy during Reconstruction until the KKK and the Southern redeemers came to the rescue.

This reactionary appropriation of Lincoln was highly misleading. We should recall that in Lincoln's day the Republicans were, in most respects, the progressive party, while the Democrats were the conservatives. Although Lincoln was not as outwardly radical as Republicans such as Thaddeus Stevens or Charles Sumner, inwardly he was just as progressive as they were. He realized that a president, in order to effect change in a deeply divided time, must strike a balance publicly between the left and the right. To avoid deepening an already gaping political and cultural rift, the president must maintain a moderate public position and move at a cautious pace—unless, that is, an immediate crisis such as the secession of eleven states calls for decisive use of presidential war powers. By launching military attacks and periodically suspending habeas corpus, Lincoln did act decisively. But on the issue of slavery, the president waited to act until he felt that the majority of citizens were ready for dramatic change. A lawyer friend of Lincoln's, Christopher C. Brown, said, "Lincoln was a radical—fanatically so—& yet he never went beyond the People. Kept his views & thoughts to himself.—ie he never told all he felt."[109]

"He never went beyond the People." Brown was hardly alone in pointing out Lincoln's very close attention to the popular will. Herndon said similarly, "As a politician and a statesman he took no steps in advance of the great mass of our people." Before acting, he "made observations, felt the popular pulse; and when he thought that the people were ready he acted, and not before."[110] He did not go beyond the people because, in his very soul, he was one of them. He knew them

well—their lives, their tastes, their hopes. The people *respected* him as Father Abraham, but they *loved* him as Abe. Honest Abe. Uncle Abe. Old Abe. The epithets were interchangeable. Average folk lined up to see Abe in the White House. He made regular visits to wounded and dying soldiers in the war hospitals. "Uncle Abe is very popular—a shrewd, firm, clear & strong man," wrote a clergyman in 1862.[111] Even the snobby George Templeton Strong admitted in 1863, "Uncle Abe is the most popular man in America today. The firmness, honesty, and sagacity of the 'gorilla despot' may be recognized by the rebels themselves sooner than we expect, and the weight of his personal character may do a great deal toward restoration of our national unity."[112] When the president visited a field hospital during his visit to City Point shortly before his assassination, it was Abe whom the wounded soldiers recognized. A Pennsylvania soldier wrote, "Old Abe passed through on a shake hands with all the patients."[113] A New Yorker reported, "Uncle Abe gave us each a word of cheer."

"Never told all he felt." Silence and restraint were Lincoln's ways of not inflaming already heated political passions. Underneath, he was, in Christopher Brown's words, "fanatically radical," but at all costs, he avoided flagrant pronouncements, insults, and one-upmanship. Instead, he used constitutional means of achieving his goals.

One of these goals was to create an activist government that would help Americans economically. With all his faith in free enterprise and self-help, he wrote that the government must do not only what people "can not do, *at all*" but also what they "can not, *so well do*, for themselves—in their separate, and individual capacities."[114] This is a remarkably expansive vision of governmental power. In Illinois in the 1830s, he had backed huge government projects for roads, canals, and railroads—what today would be called infrastructure. As president, he applied his vision of government-funded infrastructure to the nation by signing into law the Pacific Railway Act of 1862. The transcontinental railroad was completed when the Central Pacific and Union Pacific railroads were joined at Promontory Summit, Utah Territory, in May 1869. Another of his governmental interventions was the Homestead Act, which opened up tremendous expanses of federal land for inexpensive settlement—a virtual handout of real estate, designed especially for the poor. Yet another government project he signed into law was funding for land grant colleges, which over the years have provided higher education for millions of Americans, many of them people of color. The False Claims Act of 1863 (aka Whistleblower Law or the Lincoln Law) provided a powerful legal weapon over the years that has enabled whistleblowers to expose fraud and corruption in the government. The National Currency Act of 1863 and the National Banking Act of 1864 centralized and regularized the American financial system. The Revenue Act of 1861 introduced the federal income tax. A fair tax from the start, because it did not affect the lower or lower-middle classes, it became truly progressive in 1864 by creating two brackets with increasingly higher tax rates for annual incomes above $5,000 and $10,000 (substantial incomes for that time).

Lincoln's activist government drove the war effort. A main reason government spending increased tenfold between 1861 and 1865 was the cost of funding a war that rose from $1.5 million a day in 1861 to $3.5 million daily by 1865.[115] Despite waste and a certain amount of corruption, the Union war machine worked efficiently, as Lincoln's cabinet, despite infighting, proved capable of sustaining the Union's forces on land and at sea. Lincoln and other officials tried out a series of less-than-stellar generals before arriving at the powerful Grant-Sherman-Farragut triad of 1864–65. Lincoln made advances toward civilized war by distributing copies of Francis Lieber's war code, which anticipated the Geneva Convention by prohibiting cruelty, protecting prisoners of war, and insisting on the emancipation of enslaved persons when encountered.

If Lieber's code brought a moral dimension to the practice of war, Lincoln brought a similar spirit to the presidency. He dedicated himself to restoring the Union not only through economics, war, and politics but through culture. The humor and storytelling for which he was famous struck his critics as unpresidential but won the hearts of millions and showed that American humor, usually formless or grotesque, could be ethical and instructive. Religion was high on his list for cultural cohesion. He approved "In God We Trust" for American currency, placed the nation "under God" at Gettysburg, and considered adding a religious amendment to the Constitution. Along with a respect for religion went a remarkable tolerance. He embraced people of all faiths and little faith, from the Jewish podiatrist Issachar Zacharie to the Methodist bishop Matthew Simpson and the Quaker Eliza Gurney to the freethinker/spiritualist Robert Dale Owen. Though he personally embraced no church or creed, Lincoln read the Bible, was consoled by it, and tapped it for images that gave his speeches unusual resonance. Responding to the collective agony of war, he issued more proclamations of religion or thanksgiving than any other president. His 1863 proclamation of National Thanksgiving initiated a yearly family ritual in late November that became official when Franklin Roosevelt signed the Thanksgiving Holiday Bill in 1941. Domesticity also permeated Christmas in new ways during Lincoln's presidency, in large part because the popular illustrator Thomas Nast invented the modern Santa Claus and used the pathos of war to accentuate the joy of family togetherness during soldiers' furloughs.

Nast also featured family life in perhaps his most stirring Civil War picture: *The Emancipation of the Negroes, January 1863—the Past and the Future.* A celebration of the Emancipation Proclamation, the picture is separated into three sections. In the left portion, Nast shows the horrors of slavery: fugitives running through a swamp, an enslaved man being sold away from his family, a female being whipped, and a man being branded. The right side of the illustration shows the benefits of emancipation and imagines the lives of freedmen after the war. One group of African Americans sends its children to a public school, another group lines up at a cashier to pick up paychecks, while others

Thomas Nast, *The Emancipation of the Negroes, January 1863–the Past and the Future* (*Harper's Weekly*, January 24, 1863)

befriend their former master or reunite with a lost child. At the heart of Nast's picture is the African American family, with the mother cooking, the father playing with his baby while four siblings surround them. Lincoln appears in a superimposed portrait in the foreground and in a picture on the wall behind the family—a testament to the fact that his Emancipation Proclamation, though issued under the aegis of military necessity, had tremendous moral and emotional impact on African Americans. Nast's black people are not caricatures or stereotypes. They are fully human—respectable, dignified, and, most important, together in freedom.

The shared humanity that suffused Nast's picture also impelled Lincoln to direct his presidency toward equality and justice. In no area was his government as active as in the area of slavery and race. Lincoln's military commanders led the way in emancipation by accepting fugitive blacks as contraband as early as 1861—followed soon by Congress's passage of the Confiscation Acts of 1861 and 1862. James Ashley and other congressional Republicans opened the way to Radical Reconstruction with a bill in 1862. During the next two years, Lincoln established a progressive reconstruction policy in his suggestions for the readmission of Louisiana to the Union without slavery and with citizenship and education for African Americans. He publicized his radical position on slavery and race in language so carefully regulated and persuasive that it did not offend most people. His public letters on Copperheadism and African Americans in the military were so precisely worded that they made their liberal point firmly yet without much controversy. His Gettysburg Address highlighted equality through winning eloquence, and his Second Inaugural aligned the fight against slavery with God's justice. At challenging points in the war, he ordered John Brown–like infiltrations of the South in order to forcibly liberate the enslaved. Amending the Constitution to abolish slavery absorbed much of his energy as the war proceeded. Even Congress's approval of the Thirteenth Amendment in January 1865 did not lead him to abandon his vigorous military pursuit of emancipation. Meanwhile, his personal bonding with African Americans such as Frederick Douglass, Martin Delany, Sojourner Truth, and Elizabeth Keckly reflected the genuine humanity behind his antislavery activism.

In 1865, Martin Delany proposed a Lincoln monument that would feature the figure of a kneeling African woman shedding millions of tears for the murdered Great Emancipator. Although Delany's monument, to be funded solely by blacks, was never constructed, the efforts of other African Americans led to the construction of a far less mournful Lincoln monument, the Emancipation Memorial (aka the Freedman's Memorial or the Emancipation Group).

Shortly after the Lincoln assassination, Charlotte Scott, an Ohio washerwoman who had been formerly enslaved in Virginia, contributed five dollars, her first earnings as a free woman, as seed money for a Lincoln statue to be paid for only by black people. Contributions poured in from thousands of African Americans, many of them former Union soldiers, until $1,700 was raised—enough for the Western Sanitary Commission to hire a sculptor, Thomas Ball, to build a statue.

Ball's first version of the statue was rejected because it did not give enslaved people enough agency in their own emancipation. It showed Lincoln with one hand holding the Emancipation Proclamation and the other extended to a formerly enslaved man who was kneeling and wearing a conical freedom cap, a traditional symbol of liberty. The man was, in the words of a contemporary account, "perfectly passive, receiving the boon of freedom from the hand of the great liberator."[116] Criticized for this statue, Ball revised it "to bring the presentation near to the historical fact, by making the slave an agent in his own deliverance" and to give him "a far great degree of dignity and vigor." In the final version, a muscular black man, breaking chains from his wrists, looks upward and begins to rise on the balls of his feet, like a runner preparing to take position on the starting block.

The dedication ceremony of the Emancipation Memorial in Washington, DC, in April 1876 was mainly an African American affair. It was organized by John Mercer Langston, the grandfather of Langston Hughes and one of the few blacks to win office during Jim Crow. Most of the some 20,000 attendees of the ceremony were African Americans. A bishop of the African Methodist Church gave the opening prayer. The black civil rights activist William E. Matthews read an eighty-line poem, "Lincoln," written for the occasion by the black attorney and author Cordelia Ray. After President Grant unveiled the statue, Frederick Douglass gave a speech in which he captured the unique political tact that had enabled Lincoln to save the Union. Douglass declared, "Viewed from the genuine abolition ground, Mr. Lincoln seemed tardy, cold, dull, and indifferent; but measuring him by the sentiment of his country, a sentiment he was bound as a statesman to consult, he was swift, zealous, radical, and determined."[117]

Lincoln would have agreed with this statement, which captured the Blondin-like quality that allowed the president to push steadily for emancipation while avoiding disruptive extremes. Lincoln, who while entering Richmond in April 1865 had told a black man not to kneel to him, would probably have also agreed with Douglass's call, a few days after the ceremony, for another statue that would show a black person standing erect to symbolize citizenship. In any case, Lincoln would have appreciated the heartfelt recognition by African Americans that the Emancipation Memorial represented.

He also would have embraced the theme of national unity affirmed by a later monument constructed in Washington, DC, the Lincoln Memorial, which was designed by the architect Henry Bacon and opened in 1922. Inspired by the Athenian Parthenon, the ancient seat of democracy, the Lincoln Memorial has thirty-six Doric columns that stand for the number of states in 1865. Its terrace is made of Massachusetts granite, the upper steps and outside façade of Colorado marble, the inner walls and columns of Indiana limestone, the ceiling tiles of Alabama marble, and the Lincoln statue of Georgia marble.[118]

With its neoclassical columns, three inner chambers, and huge marble statue of the seated Lincoln, who would measure twenty-eight feet if standing, the Memorial delivers a message of grandeur. It suggests Father Abraham.

But the statue itself gives a different impression. The tousled hair, the overarching brows and wrinkled, hollow cheeks; the mole on the edge of the right cheek; the odd lips, thin on top, bulging on the bottom right; the rumpled clothing and rough boots, the oversize ears and hands and feet—this is the ordinary, approachable Lincoln in a typical state of thoughtful abstraction, caught expertly by the sculptor Daniel Chester French. This is Abe, thinking things over and ready to burst out with a joke or a story—or with an enduring speech like the Gettysburg Address or the Second Inaugural, inscribed on the walls of the Memorial.

Langston Hughes memorably captured the spirit of the statue in his 1926 poem "Lincoln Monument: Washington":

> Let's go see Old Abe
> Sitting in the marble and the moonlight,
> Sitting lonely in the marble and the moonlight,
> Quiet for ten thousand centuries, old Abe.
> Quiet for a million, million years.
> Quiet—
> And yet a voice forever
> Against the
> Timeless walls
> Of time—
> Old Abe.

Martin Luther King's "I Have a Dream" speech, delivered before a quarter of a million people from the steps of the Lincoln Memorial on August 28, 1963, guided Old Abe's voice toward the future. "Five score years ago," King said, "a great American, in whose symbolic shadow we stand today, signed the Emancipation Proclamation."[119] Lincoln's decree "came as a joyous daybreak" for millions of enslaved people. But since then, America had betrayed Lincoln's ideals. Injustice still prevailed. King envisioned a time when "all of God's children, black men and white men, Jews and Gentiles, Protestants and Catholics, will be able to join hands and sing in the words of the old Negro spiritual, 'Free at last! Free at last! Thank God Almighty, we are free at last!'" Affirming national unity, King declared, "With this faith, we will be able to transform the jangling discords of our nation into a beautiful symphony of brotherhood."

These inspiring words bring us back to Lincoln. At America's most divided time, Lincoln pushed hard toward justice while keeping the whole nation foremost in his mind. He progressed cautiously, shrewdly,

The exterior of the Memorial, patterned after a Doric temple

Statue of Lincoln (Daniel Chester French)

inexorably. With honesty. With humility. With winning humor. And in the end, with his thoughts on all Americans, regardless of party, religion, or race.

His principled vision and his disarming modesty remain an inspiration to everyday Americans and political leaders alike.

Freedom. Equality. Justice for everyone—even for the most marginalized or oppressed—contained within one nation.

This was *Abe*, in his democratic fullness.

ACKNOWLEDGMENTS

This book began with a paragraph on Lincoln in a book proposal I had written on a different topic. Scott Moyers, the vice president and publisher of Penguin Press, thought that the paragraph had the seeds of a book. He encouraged me to develop my ideas on Lincoln by considering the president's connections with nineteenth-century American culture, a subject I'd been mulling over for decades. I quickly realized that a book on Lincoln had long been buried inside me, just waiting to be written. Scott has been the ideal editor—insightful, patient, and reassuring. I also thank my agent, Lynn Nesbit, who first contacted Scott on my behalf and who has been wonderfully supportive of my project.

Anyone who writes about Lincoln owes a tremendous debt to past and current biographers, historians, and other commentators on America's sixteenth president. While a good number of them are mentioned in this book, it has been impossible to mention by name all those who contributed to the bedrock of my knowledge of Lincoln and his era. Among those who directly helped me were James Oakes and David Waldstreicher, my esteemed colleagues at the Graduate Center of the City University of New York. Both read my manuscript with a critical eye; their generous comments were immensely helpful, as were those of Douglas L. Wilson, who gave me crucial feedback on several biographical questions. I also profited from the input of Mason I. Lowance Jr. of the University of Massachusetts at Amherst. Very special thanks go to Richard Salomon, who brought his acute judgment to his readings of my manuscript. Also, Rick and I had stimulating discussions about Lincoln with Tom Klingenstein.

Two Lincoln-specific websites created by the Gilder Lehrman Institute of American History—Abraham Lincoln's Classroom and Mr. Lincoln's White House—are a godsend to all who have an interest in Lincoln. I have frequently consulted these websites, which feature a wealth of political, social, cultural, and personal information related to Lincoln.

Staff members at the Abraham Lincoln Presidential Library in Springfield, Illinois, and the Lincoln Financial Foundation Collection in the Allen County Public Library in Fort Wayne, Indiana, helped me locate and explore material from their remarkable collections. Also of assistance were the staffs at the Houghton Library, the John Hay Library, the American Antiquarian Society, the Library of Congress, the New York Public Library, the Northern Illinois University Libraries, the National Portrait Gallery, the University of Illinois-Urbana Library, the Lilly Library at Indiana University-Bloomington, the Chicago History Museum, the Oregon Historical Society Library, the University of Iowa Library, the Huntington Library, and the Harriet Beecher Stowe Center Library. I appreciate the help I've received from Sara Gabbard, the executive director at the Friends of the Lincoln Collection of Indiana and the editor of *Lincoln Lore*.

A big shout-out goes to my students at the CUNY Graduate Center who assisted me in my research over the past several years. They include Eva Gordon-Wallin, Michael Druffel, Yu-yun Hsieh, Paul Fess, Christina Katopodis, Cary Fitzgerald, Weiheng Sun, Andreea Scarlat, and Paul Hebert. I've had rewarding dialogues with these and other

CUNY students, including Andrew Lang, Evan Turiano, Jaja Tantirungkij, Ladi Dell'aira, and Howard Levi. The Office of the Provost at the Graduate Center provided me with an annual research and travel fund that went toward this project.

I've had the delightful experience of writing this book while my wife, Professor Suzanne Nalbantian, was working on her latest book, on the subject of creativity in relation to the humanities and neuroscience. Along the way we've shared our scholarly experiences, from the frustrating to the exhilarating. I'm deeply grateful to Suzanne for her thoughtful reading of my manuscript, which led me to revise it in several places. Her love and support have meant the world to me, as has the encouragement I've received from our daughter, Aline Reynolds, and Suzanne's brother, Haig Nalbantian.

ABBREVIATIONS

ALP *Abraham Lincoln Papers at the Library of Congress.* Manuscript Division (Washington, DC: American Memory Project, 2000–2010). At https://www.loc.gov/collections/abraham-lincoln-papers.

CW *The Collected Works of Abraham Lincoln.* Edited by Roy P. Basler, Lloyd A. Dunlap, and Marion Dolores Pratt. 8 vols. (New Brunswick, NJ: Rutgers University Press, 1953–55). At https://quod.lib.umich.edu/l/lincoln.

EK Elizabeth Keckly, *Behind the Scenes, or, Thirty Years a Slave and Four Years in the White House* (New York: G. W. Carleton & Co., 1868).

FC Francis B. Carpenter, *Six Months at the White House with Abraham Lincoln* (New York: Hurd and Houghton, 1866).

HI *Herndon's Informants: Letters, Interviews, and Statements About Abraham Lincoln.* Edited by Douglas L. Wilson and Rodney O. Davis (Urbana: University of Illinois Press, 1998).

HL *The Hidden Lincoln. From the Letters and Papers of William H. Herndon.* Edited by Emanuel Hertz (New York: Viking, 1938).

HOL William H. Herndon, *Herndon on Lincoln: Letters.* Edited by Douglas L. Wilson and Rodney O. Davis (Urbana: University of Illinois Press, 2016).

HW William Henry Herndon and Jesse William Weik, *Herndon's Lincoln: The True Story of a Great Life.* 3 vols. (1889; Springfield, IL: Herndon's Lincoln Pub. Co., c. 1921).

IM Rufus Rockwell Wilson, *Intimate Memories of Abraham Lincoln* (Elmira, NY: Primavera Press, 1945).

JH *Inside Lincoln's White House: The Complete Civil War Diary of John Hay*. Edited by Michael Burlingame and John R. Turner Ettlinger (Carbondale: Southern Illinois University Press, 1999).

JMN *The Journals and Miscellaneous Notebooks of Ralph Waldo Emerson*. Edited by William H. Gilman et al. 16 vols. (Cambridge, MA: Harvard University Press, 1960–82).

JN *An Oral History of Abraham Lincoln: John G. Nicolay's Interviews and Essays*. Edited by Michael Burlingame (Carbondale: Southern Illinois University Press, 2006).

JT Justin G. Turner and Linda Levitt Turner, *Mary Todd Lincoln: Her Life and Letters* (New York: Alfred A. Knopf, 1972).

LGC Walt Whitman, *Leaves of Grass. Comprehensive Reader's Edition*. Edited by Harold Blodgett and Sculley Bradley (New York: New York University Press, 1965).

LJ *Lincoln's Journalist: John Hay's Anonymous Writings for the Press, 1860–1864*. Edited by Michael Burlingame (Carbondale: Southern Illinois University Press, 2014).

LL William H. Townsend, *Lincoln and Liquor* (New York: The Press of the Pioneers, 1934).

LPAL *The Law Practice of Abraham Lincoln: Complete Documentary Edition*, 2nd ed. Edited by Martha L. Benner, Cullom Davis, et al. (Springfield: Illinois Historic Preservation Agency, 2009). At http://www.lawpracticeofabrahamlincoln.org/Reference.aspx?ref=Reference%20html%20files/NarrativeOverview.html.

LSW *Lincoln's Selected Writings. A Norton Critical Edition*. Edited by David S. Reynolds (New York: W. W. Norton, 2015).

LY Louis A. Warren, *Lincoln's Youth: Indiana Years, Seven to Twenty-One, 1816–1830* (New York: Appleton, Century, Crofts, Inc., 1959).

PW Walt Whitman, *Prose Works, 1892* (vol. 1, *Specimen Days* [1963]; vol. 2, *Collect and Other Prose* [1964]). Edited by Floyd Stovall (New York: New York University Press).

RAL *Reminiscences of Abraham Lincoln: By Distinguished Men of His Time*. Edited by C. Allen Thorndike Rice (New York: North American Publishing Co., 1886).

TDC Thomas D. Clark, *The Rampaging Frontier: Manners and Humors of Pioneer Days in the South and the Middle West* (Indianapolis: Bobbs-Merrill, 1939).

W Henry C. Whitney, *Life on the Circuit with Lincoln* (Boston: Estes and Lauriat, 1892).

Z *Abe Lincoln's Legacy of Laughter: Humorous Stories by and About Abraham Lincoln*. Edited by Paul M. Zall (Knoxville: University of Tennessee Press, 2007).

NOTES

PREFACE

1. See Henry C. Whitney's discussion of his preference in names in W 53. Whitney writes, "We spoke *of* him as '*Uncle Abe*'; but *to* his face we called him 'Lincoln.' He *very* much disliked to be called 'Mr. President.' This I knew, and I never called him so once. He didn't even like 'Mr.' He preferred plain 'Lincoln.'"

2. JN 41.

3. Leo Tolstoy, interview with Count S. Stakeberg, in *The Lincoln Anthology: Great Writers on His Life and Legacy from 1860 to Now*, edited by Harold Holzer (New York: Library of America, 2009), 386; Karl Marx and Friedrich Engels, *The Civil War in the United States* (1937; New York: International Publishers, 2016), 166.

4. See further David S. Reynolds, *John Brown, Abolitionist: The Man Who Killed Slavery, Sparked the Civil War, and Seeded Civil Rights* (New York: Alfred A. Knopf, 2005), 9, and David S. Reynolds, "Why I Write Cultural Biography: The Backgrounds of *Walt Whitman's America*," in *Leaves of Grass: The Sesquicentennial Essays*, edited by Susan Belasco, Ed Folsom, and Kenneth M. Price (Lincoln, University of Nebraska Press, 2007), 378–401. What I call cultural biography is similar to what some describe as microhistory. As Jill Lepore explains, microhistorians "have particular nonbiographical goals in mind: even when they study a single person's life, they are keen to evoke a period, a mentalité, a problem" and to show "how that individual's life serves as an allegory for broader issues affecting the culture as a whole" (Jill Lepore, "Historians Who Love Too Much: Reflections on Microhistory and Biography," *The Journal of American History*, 8.1 [June 2001]: 132, 133).

5. David Herbert Donald, *Lincoln* (New York: Simon & Schuster, 1995), 14. The quotation in the next paragraph is also from this page.

6. D. H. Donald *Lincoln's Herndon* (New York: Alfred A. Knopf, 1948), 185.

7. Noah Brooks, "Personal Recollections of Abraham Lincoln," *Harper's New Monthly Magazine* 31.182 (July 1865): 228.

8. R. W. Emerson, "Shakespeare; or, the Poet," in *The Collected Works of Ralph Waldo Emerson,* vol. 4, *Representative Men,* edited by Jean Ferguson Carr (Cambridge, MA: Harvard University Press, 1987), 110.

9. R. W. Emerson., "Eloquence," in *The Collected Works of Ralph Waldo Emerson,* vol. 8, *Letters and Social Aims,* edited by Ronald A. Bosco, Glen M. Johnson, and Joel Myerson (Cambridge, MA: Harvard University Press, 2010), 66.

10. R. W. Emerson, "Greatness," in *The Collected Works of Ralph Waldo Emerson,* vol. 8, *Letters and Social Aims* edited by R. A. Bosco, G. M. Johnson, and J. Myerson, 176.

11. IM 17.

12. L. Swett, quoted in RAL, 227, and Swett's speech "The Life of Lincoln," delivered at the dedication of St. Gaudens's statue of Lincoln in Chicago, *Chicago Times,* October 23, 1887.

13. HOL 238. The quotation in the next sentence is from p. 339.

14. CW 7: 282.

15. CW 3: 27.

16. JMN 10: 79–80.

17. Henry David Thoreau, *Walden* (1854), in *A Week on the Concord and Merrimack Rivers, Walden; or, Life in the Woods, The Maine Woods, Cape Cod* (New York: Library of America, 1985), 584.

18. Alexis de Tocqueville, *Democracy in America,* edited by J. P. Mayer (1935; Garden City, NY: Doubleday, 1969), 432.

19. CW 1: 111.

20. Walt Whitman, "Nationality—(And Yet)," PW 2: 514.

21. LGC: 79.

22. CW 4: 268.

23. Lincoln to James H. Van Alen, CW 8: 413.

24. PW 1: 98.

CHAPTER I
THE LINCOLN TREE

1. HI 57.

2. CW 3: 511.

3. G. Welles, "Administration of Abraham Lincoln," *The Galaxy* 23 (January 1877): 15.

4. Joel Chandler Harris, ed., *Life of Henry W. Grady, Including His Writings and Speeches* (New York: Cassell, 1890), 86.

5. *New York Herald,* March 22, 1861.

6. Parmenas Taylor Turnley, *Reminiscences of Parmenas Taylor Turnley* (Chicago: Donohue & Henneberry, 1892), 287.

7. Mark Twain, *Life on the Mississippi,* in *Mississippi Writings* (New York: Library of America, 1982), 501.

8. Quoted in George C. Rable, *Damn Yankees! Demonization and Defiance in the Confederate South* (Baton Rouge: Louisiana State University Press, 2015), 11.

9. "Speech by Chilton A. White of Ohio Before the House of Representatives, January 19, 1864," in *Crisis* (Columbus, OH), March 9, 1864.

10. N. Hawthorne, "Chiefly About War-Matters. By a Peaceable Man," *Atlantic Monthly* 10 (July 1862): 44; in LSW, 389.

11. *New-York Tribune*, October 6, 1866.

12. Henry Watterson, *"Marse Henry": An Autobiography* (New York: George H. Doran, 1919), 1: 134.

13. O. S. Fowler, *Hereditary Descent . . .* (1844), reprinted as O. S. Fowler, *Hereditary Descent: Its Laws and Facts Applied to Human Improvement* (New York: Fowlers and Wells, 1848), 48. The next quotation in this paragraph is from p. 201.

14. HOL 238, 286. The next quotation in this paragraph is from p. 339.

15. HOL 204, 100.

16. O. S. Fowler, *Hereditary Descent*, 210.

17. HW 1: 13; HL 343; LY 56–57.

18. See especially Paul H. Verduin, "New Evidence Suggests Lincoln's Mother Born in Richmond County, Virginia, Giving Credibility to the Planter Grandfather Legend," *Northern Neck of Virginia Historical Magazine* 38 (December 1988): 2354–89.

19. HOL 100.

20. William H. Herndon, "Nancy Hanks," notes written in Greencastle, Indiana, ca. August 20, 1887, Herndon-Weik Papers, Library of Congress; HOL 307.

21. HOL 100.

22. Eleanor Atkinson, "Lincoln's Boyhood: Reminiscences of His Cousin and Playmate, Dennis Hanks," *American Magazine*, 65 (February 1908), 363.

23. HOL 264.

24. Scholars have found that Southerners were unified by "an exaggerated sense of honor. . . . Indeed, the concept of honor was an article of the Cavalier code most easily appropriated by Southern men, regardless of their precise standing in Dixie's hierarchy. . . . The idea of personal honor was esteemed by white men of all classes" (Ritchie Devon Watson Jr., *Yeoman Versus Cavalier: The Old Southwest's Fictional Road to Rebellion* [Baton Rouge: Louisiana State University Press, 1999], 118). See also Bertram Wyatt-Brown, *Southern Honor: Ethics and Behavior in the Old South* (New York: Oxford University Press, 1982). For an analysis of Lincoln's honor and its Southern roots, see especially Orville Vernon Burton, *The Age of Lincoln: A History* (New York: Hill and Wang, 2007).

25. HI 120.

26. HI 509.

27. James Oakes, *The Scorpion's Sting: Antislavery and the Coming of the Civil War* (New York: W. W. Norton, 2014), 61.

28. CW 3: 81, CW 8: 333.

29. O. S. Fowler, *Hereditary Descent*, 201.

30. S. S. Cox, "Puritanism in Politics," *The Plain Dealer* (Cleveland), January 1, 1863.

31. CW 3: 255.

32. O. S. Fowler, *Hereditary Descent*, 201.

33. CW 4: 16, 20. The next quotation in this paragraph is from CW 2: 492.

34. HI 5.

35. HI 97; HI 503; J. Henry Lea and J. R. Hutchinson, *The Ancestry of Abraham Lincoln* (Boston: Houghton Mifflin, 1909), 134.

36. W 23.

37. Solomon Lincoln to Artemas Hale, Hingham, March 2, 1848, photostatic copy, Lincoln Miscellaneous Collection, University of Chicago.

38. CW 1: 456.

39. Solomon Lincoln to Abraham Lincoln, February 26, 1849; ALP.

40. See HW 1, chap. 10.

41. James Grant Wilson, "Recollections of Lincoln," *Putnam's Magazine* 5 (February 1909): 515.

42. Hartley in early 1860 traveled to Springfield to seek Lincoln's lawyerly advice about a criminal case. As Hartley later recalled, "As soon as he learned that I had come straight from England his thin face with its high cheek bones lighted with the greatest interest, and he shook my hand warmly. Then he ran his fingers through his coarse black hair and with almost boyish eagerness asked me a number of questions about England, informing me at the same time that his ancestors were English and he hoped sometime to visit the land of their birth" (IM 318).

43. For background on Samuel Lincoln's religious contexts, see *Hingham: A Story of Its Early Settlement and Life* (Hingham, MA: Old Colony Chapter of the Daughters of the American Revolution, 1911). Also useful are Ida Minerva Tarbell, *Abraham Lincoln and His Ancestors* (1924; Lincoln: University of Nebraska Press, 1997) and J. Henry Lea and J. R. Hutchinson, *The Ancestry of Abraham Lincoln* (Boston and New York: Houghton Mifflin), 1909.

44. "Abraham Lincoln, Descendant of Puritanical Line Bust of the Emancipator Looks Down Upon the Worshipers," *Oregonian* (Portland), February 6, 1921.

45. Arthur C. W. Upcher, *History of Hingham, Norfolk, and Its Church of St. Andrew* (East Dereham, UK: A. F. Mason, 1921), 27.

46. W. D. Howells, *Life of Abraham Lincoln* (New York: Judd & Carleton, 1860), 6.

47. Bradley R. Hoch, *The Lincoln Trail in Pennsylvania: A History and Guide* (University Park: Pennsylvania State University Press, 2001), 26. See also I. M. Tarbell, *Abraham Lincoln and His Ancestors*, 21–22.

48. R. Hoch, *The Lincoln Trail in Pennsylvania*, 17.

49. CW 3: 511.

50. See, for example, CW 4: 60.

51. A legend long persisted that Mordecai Lincoln Jr. was a Quaker who was buried in a Friends burial ground in Pennsylvania near several Boones, who were known to be Quakers. Not only is this story difficult to validate, because the burial land was sold and many graves were reinterred elsewhere, but when Anne Boone, a Quaker, married Mordecai Jr.'s posthumously born son Abraham, she was chastised by the Friends for marrying a non-Quaker. As a genealogist writes of the Boone family in Pennsylvania: "The Lincolns were Congregationalists and the Boones Quakers, consequently Anne Boone's marriage to Abraham Lincoln was 'out of meeting,' and considered a disorderly act. For this she was disciplined by the Exeter Monthly Meeting, and acknowledged her error to the meeting on August 27, 1761" (Ella Hazel Spraker, *The Boone Family: A Genealogical History of the Descendants of George and Mary Boone Who Came to America in 1717; Containing Many Unpublished Bits of Early Kentucky History* [Rutland, VT: Genealogical Publishing Company, 1922], 91–92). Furthermore, Mordecai Jr.'s daughter Sarah married the Quaker William Boone in 1748, having joined the Quakers

a year earlier, because she "appears not to have been a member with Friends by birth," a genealogist explains (*The Lincoln Family Magazine: Genealogical, Historical and Biographical*, edited by William Montgomery Clemens, vol. 1 [January 1916–April 1917]: 27). A close genealogical study of the Pennsylvania Lincolns concludes, "The Lincolns were not Quakers, as has been stated by the biographers of President Lincoln" (*Notes and Queries Historical and Genealogical, Chiefly Relating to Interior Pennsylvania*, Volume 3, edited by William Henry Egle [Harrisburg, PA: Harrisburg Publishing Company, 1896], 480).

52. See Louis A. Warren, "Lincoln's Baptist Background," *Lincoln Lore*, no. 1042, March 28, 1949.

53. Quoted in Mark A. Noll, *The Civil War as a Theological Crisis* (Chapel Hill: University of North Carolina Press, 2006), 27. The quotation in the next sentence is from p. 28.

54. CW 3: 310.

55. *DeBow's Review*, 15.2 (August 1853): 173, 182. For the political and religious significance of the Middle Colonies, see Michael Zuckerman, "Puritans, Cavaliers, and the Motley Middle," in *Friends and Neighbors: Group Life in America's First Plural Society*, edited by M. Zuckerman (Philadelphia: Temple University Press, 1982), chap. 1.

56. *DeBow's Review* 23.4 (October 1857), 383.

57. *The Life and Public Services of Hon. Abraham Lincoln, of Illinois, and Hon. Hannibal Hamlin, of Maine* (Boston: Thayer & Eldridge, 1860), 13.

58. Reuben Vose, *The Life and Speeches of Abraham Lincoln, and Hannibal Hamlin* (New York: Hilton, Gallaher, & Co., 1860), xxiii.

59. *The Life, Speeches, and Public Services of Abram Lincoln: Together with a Sketch of the Life of Hannibal Hamlin* (New York: Rudd & Carleton, 1860), 7.

60. John Locke Scripps, *Life of Abraham Lincoln* (Peoria, IL: Edward J. Jacob, 1860), 1; David S. Bartlett, *The Life and Public Services of Hon. Abraham Lincoln* (Cincinnati: Moore, Wilstach, and Baldwin, 1864), 11.

61. James Quay Howard, *The Life of Abraham Lincoln* (Columbus, OH: Follett, Foster, & Co., 1860), 3.

Chapter 2
Child of the Frontier

1. HW 1: ix.

2. HI 57. As John Stauffer discusses, it was as useful for Lincoln to promote the self-made image as it was for Frederick Douglass to; see J. Stauffer, *Giants: The Parallel Lives of Frederick Douglass and Abraham Lincoln* (New York: Twelve [Hachette Book Group], 2014). Paul Kendrick and Stephen Kendrick make a similar comparison in *Douglass and Lincoln: How a Revolutionary Black Leader and a Reluctant Liberator Struggled to End Slavery and Save the Union* (New York: Walker, 2008).

3. Madison Clinton Peters, *Abraham Lincoln's Religion* (Boston: Richard G. Badger, 1909), 3. More recent commentators, however, have noticed that Lincoln's early contexts were more favorable than was once thought. See, for example, Kenneth J. Winkle, *The Young Eagle: The Rise of Abraham Lincoln* (Dallas: Taylor

Trade Publishing, 2001) and William W. Freehling, *Becoming Lincoln* (Charlottesville: University of Virginia Press, 2018).

4. RAL 468.

5. W. Wilson, *Division and Reunion: 1829–1889* (New York: Longmans, Green and Co., 1893), 216–17.

6. "Reminiscences of John E. Roll," *Chicago Times-Herald*, August 25, 1895.

7. HI 28.

8. HI 28; Ward Hill Lamon and Chauncey F. Black, *The Life of Abraham Lincoln* (Boston: J. R. Osgood & Co., 1872), 8.

9. HI 96.

10. HI 37, 28.

11. HI 37.

12. HI 115.

13. In addition to HI, HW, and LY the main sources I've tapped for information about Thomas Lincoln are Willard Mounts, *The Pioneer and the Prairie Lawyer: Boone and Lincoln Family Heritage, Biographical and Historical, 1603–1985* (Denver: Ginwill Publishing, 1991); Louis A. Warren, *Lincoln's Parentage and Childhood: A History of the Kentucky Lincolns Supported by Documentary Evidence* (New York: Century Co., 1926); Michael Burlingame, *The Inner World of Abraham Lincoln* (Urbana: University of Illinois Press, 1997); R. Gerald McMurtry, *The Lincolns on Mill Creek* (Harrogate, TN: Lincoln Memorial University, 1939); and Louis A. Warren, "Lincoln's Pioneer Father," in *New England Genealogical and Historical Register* 83 (October 1930): 389–400.

14. Mrs. Thomas D. Winstead, "Thomas Lincoln: 'A Man Who Didn't Drink An' Cuss None,'" *The Register of the Kentucky Historical Society* 71.2 (April 1973): 191.

15. R. G. McMurtry, *The Lincolns on Mill Creek*, 49.

16. CW 4: 61. The quotation in the first sentence of the next paragraph is from CW 4: 61–62.

17. Quoted in Paul W. Gates, "Tenants of the Log Cabin," *The Mississippi Valley Historical Review* 49.1 (June 1962): 4. The Marshall quotation in the next sentence is also from this page.

18. John S. C. Abbott, *Daniel Boone, Pioneer of Kentucky* (New York: Dodd, Mead and Co., 1898), 269–70. Boone was, understandably, outraged and baffled by the loss of his land, because as Abbott notes, "He regarded Kentucky almost as his own by the right of discovery." Abbott concludes, "The deed was so cruel that thousands since, in reading the recital, have been agitated by the strongest emotions of indignation and grief," 270.

19. CW 3: 511.

20. Albert J. Beveridge, *Abe Lincoln in Indiana* (Fort Wayne: Public Library of Fort Wayne and Allen County, 1958), 20.

21. See Thomas H. Greer, "Economic and Social Effects of the Depression of 1819 in the Old Northwest," *Indiana Magazine of History* 44.3 (September 1948): 227–43.

22. RAL 457.

23. James Hall, *Notes on the Western States; Containing Descriptive Sketches of Their Soil, Climate, Resources and Scenery* (Philadelphia: Harrison Hall, 1838), 174–75.

24. LY 96.
25. HI 454.
26. Quoted in LY 194.
27. Robert H. Browne, *Lincoln and the Men of His Time* (Chicago: Blakely-Oswald, 1907), 1: 82–83.
28. John J. Hall, in Eleanor Gridley, *The Story of Abraham Lincoln, or The Journey from the Log Cabin to the White House* (n.p.: Juvenile Publishing Co., 1908), 62.
29. Alice Felt Tyler, *Freedom's Ferment: Phases of American Social History to 1860* (Minneapolis: University of Minnesota Press, 1944), 318. The statistic cited in the next sentence is from p. 312 of Tyler's book. See also David S. Reynolds, *Waking Giant: America in the Age of Jackson* (New York: HarperCollins, 2008), 175–80.
30. CW 1: 274.
31. L. A. Warren, *Lincoln's Parentage and Childhood*, 169.
32. LL 7.
33. HI 66.
34. Quoted in a speech by William H. Herndon, in Jesse William Weik, *The Real Lincoln: A Portrait* (Boston: Houghton Mifflin, 1922), 111.
35. HI 97.
36. LY 85.
37. Rev. J. Edward Marr, "He Knew Lincoln's Neighbors," in Bess V. Ehrmann, *The Missing Chapter in the Life of Abraham Lincoln . . . in Spencer County, Indiana, Between 1816–1830 and 1844* (Chicago: Walter M. Hill, 1938), 97. The quotations in the next sentence are from HI 240 and LY 85, successively.
38. Sara E. Quay, *Westward Expansion* (Westport, CT: Greenwood Press, 2002), 26.
39. HI 41.
40. Mark Friedberger, "Country Schooling in the Heartland," review of Paul Theobald's "Call School: Rural Education in the Middle West to 1918," *American Journal of Education*, 104.2 (February 1996): 150.
41. One rural preacher boasted, "Yes, bless the Lord, I are a poor, humble man and I doesn't know a single letter in the ABC's and couldn't read a chapter in the Bible nohow you could fix it, bless the Lord. I jist preach like old Peter and Poll, by the spirit. Yes, we don't ax pay in cash nor trade neither for the gospel, and aren't no Hirelin's like them high-flowered college-larned [Presbyterian] sheep-skins but as the Lord freely gives us, we freely give our fellow critturs" (TDC 146–47).
42. As Paul Theobald notes, "Free state school systems headed by Calvinist clerics were often fiercely resisted by Methodists and Baptists." See Theobald, "Rural Education," in *The American Midwest: An Interpretive Encyclopedia*, edited by Andrew R. L. Cayton, Richard Sisson, Chris Zacher (Bloomington: Indiana University Press, 2006), 800.
43. HI 107–8.
44. Lincoln quoted by Leonard Swett in RAL, 458.
45. Noah Brooks, *Abraham Lincoln and the Downfall of American Slavery* (New York: G. P. Putnam's Sons, 1894), 21.
46. See James A. Peterson, *In Re Lucey Hanks* (Yorkville, IL: n.p., 1973), 26–35.
47. HOL 84.
48. HI 113.
49. HI 37; HOL 264; HI 126.

50. Usher Linder and Joseph Gillespie, *Reminiscences of the Early Bench and Bar of Illinois* (Chicago: The Chicago Legal News Co., 1879), 39–40.

51. William M. Thayer, *The Pioneer Boy, and How He Became President* (Boston: Walker, Wise and Co., 1863), 82–83.

52. CW 7: 542.

53. HI 106, 107. The next quotation in this paragraph is from p. 37.

54. HI 37.

55. JMN 10: 178.

56. F. Trollope, *The Domestic Manners of the Americans* (1832; New York: Alfred A. Knopf, 1949), 108.

57. Quoted in L. A. Warren, *Lincoln's Parentage and Childhood*, 232.

58. L. A. Warren, *Lincoln's Parentage and Childhood*, 244.

59. Dr. James LeGrande, paraphrasing remarks he heard from his mother, Sophie Hanks; undated interview with Arthur E. Morgan, Morgan Papers, Library of Congress.

60. David S. Reynolds, *Beneath the American Renaissance: The Subversive Imagination in the Age of Emerson and Melville* (New York: Alfred A. Knopf, 1988), chap. 1. See also D. S. Reynolds, "From Doctrine to Narrative: The Rise of Pulpit Storytelling in America," *American Quarterly* 32.5 (Winter 1980): 479–98.

61. John H. Spencer, *A History of Kentucky Baptists. From 1769 to 1885*, vol. 1 (Cincinnati: J. R. Baumes, 1886), 493.

62. J. L. Scripps, *Life of Abraham Lincoln*, 16.

63. Leonard W. Volk, "The Lincoln Life-Mask and How It Was Made," *Century Magazine* 23 (1881): 226.

64. HI 102.

65. Quoted in Raymond Warren, *Abe Lincoln, Kentucky Boy* (Chicago: Reilly & Lee, 1931), 116.

66. HI 109.

67. HI 127 and William Eleazer Barton, *The Soul of Abraham Lincoln* (New York: George H. Doran Company, 1920), 81.

68. Alexander K. McClure, *"Abe" Lincoln's Yarns and Stories* (New York: Western W. Wilson, 1901), 149–50.

69. HI 172.

70. Z 46.

71. FC 277.

72. CW 1: 1.

73. The journalist was James Matlock Scovel; IM 525.

74. M. M. Bakhtin, *The Dialogic Imagination: Four Essays*, edited by Michael Holquist, translated by Caryl Emerson and Michael Holquist (Austin: University of Texas Press, 1981), 281–82, 425.

75. HI 108. The next quotation in this paragraph is from p. 99; the next quotation after that is from p. 108.

76. Quoted in A. J. Beveridge, *Abe Lincoln in Indiana*, 42.

77. Much of the biographical information about Sarah in this paragraph and succeeding ones is from HI, LY (especially pp. 60 ff.), and W. Mounts, *The Pioneer and the Prairie Lawyer*.

78. Quoted in LY, 60. The anecdote in the next sentence about the removal of the bullet is also from this source.
79. HI 126, 99.
80. HW 1: 26.
81. HI 41.
82. Interview with Austin Gollaher by J. C. M., *Cincinnati Tribune*, March 24, 1895; HI 113, 126.
83. Redmond Grigsby, correspondence to the *Evansville* [Indiana] *Journal-News*, October 1, 1902.
84. A. J. Beveridge, *Abe Lincoln in Indiana*, 43.
85. HI 109.
86. LY 153.
87. CW 2: 16.
88. HI 137; W 22–23.
89. Information and quotations about these and other alleged Indiana romances are in LY 156–57.
90. LY 154.

Chapter 3
Foundations of Presidential Character

1. HI 107.
2. *Recollected Words of Abraham Lincoln*, compiled and edited by Don E. Fehrenbacher and Virginia Fehrenbacher (Stanford, CA: Stanford University Press, 1996), 189.
3. Information about Lincoln's schools derives in part from R. Warren, *Abe Lincoln, Kentucky Boy*; Michael Burlingame, *Abraham Lincoln: A Life*, vol. 1 (Baltimore: Johns Hopkins University Press, 2008), chaps. 1 and 2; and Ronald C. White Jr., *A. Lincoln: A Biography* (New York: Random House, 2009), chaps. 2 and 3.
4. CW 3: 510.
5. CW 2: 459.
6. HI 193.
7. LGC 88.
8. An illuminating study of Lincoln's life in relation to his reading is Fred Kaplan, *Lincoln: The Biography of a Writer* (New York: HarperCollins, 2008).
9. Thomas Dilworth, *Dilworth's Spelling-Book, Improved: A New Guide to the English Tongue* (Philadelphia: John McCulloch, 1796), 45.
10. HW 1: 34.
11. CW 1: 315.
12. Z 68.
13. Robert C. Bray, *Reading with Lincoln* (Carbondale: Southern Illinois University Press, 2011), 22.
14. The earliest known narrative, by Joshua Gee, was written in 1680 but was not published until the twentieth century. See *Narrative of Joshua Gee of Boston, Mass., While He Was Captive in Algeria of the Barbary Pirates, 1680–1687*

(Hartford: n.p., 1943). See also Jennifer Costello Brezina, "A Nation in Chains: Barbary Captives and American Identity," in *Captivating Subjects: Writing Confinement, Citizenship, and Nationhood in the Nineteenth Century*, edited by Jason Haslam and Julia M. Wright (Toronto: University of Toronto Press, 2005).

15. James Riley, *An Authentic Narrative of the Loss of the American Brig Commerce, Wrecked on the Western Coast of Africa, in the Month of Aug., 1815* (New York: T. & W. Mercein, 1817), 531.

16. CW 5: 537.

17. William Grimshaw, *History of the United States: From Their First Settlement as Colonies, to the Cession of Florida, in Eighteen Hundred and Twenty-one* (Philadelphia: Benjamin Warner, 1821), 271.

18. CW 4: 235.

19. Mason Locke Weems, *The Life of George Washington; With Curious Anecdotes* (Philadelphia: n.p., 1809), 26.

20. James Grant Wilson, "Recollections of Lincoln," *Putnam's Magazine* 5 (February 1909): 516. The Illinois judge Samuel H. Treat told Lincoln he had heard this from George Washington Parke Custis, the first president's stepgrandson and ward.

21. David Ramsay, *The Life of George Washington* (New York: Hopkins & Seymour, 1809), 420. The quotations in the next two paragraphs are from pp. 373 and 331–32, successively.

22. M. L. Weems, *The Life of George Washington*, 18. The subsequent quotations in this paragraph are from pp. 156 and 170, successively.

23. See James A. Haught, *2000 Years of Disbelief: Famous People with the Courage to Doubt* (Amherst, NY: Prometheus, 2010), 99–100, and Barry Schwartz, *George Washington: The Making of an American Symbol* (New York: The Free Press, 1987), 174–75.

24. *Memoirs of the Life and Writings of Benjamin Franklin*, vol. 1 (Philadelphia: William Duane, 1818), 60.

25. T. Jefferson, First Inaugural Address, *The Papers of Thomas Jefferson*, vol. 33, 17 February to 30 April 1801 (Princeton: Princeton University Press, 2006), 148–51.

26. FC 190. The Golden Rule (Matthew 7:12) is: "Therefore all things whatsoever ye would that men should do to you: do ye even so to them: for this is the law and the prophets."

27. *Memoirs of the Life and Writings of Benjamin Franklin*, vol. 1, 89. The subsequent quotations from Franklin's list of virtues are also from this page.

28. HI 104.

29. Among the most penetrating studies of Lincoln and the power of language are Ronald C. White Jr., *Lincoln's American Eloquence* (New York: Random House, 2005) and Douglas L. Wilson, *Lincoln's Sword: The Presidency and the Power of Words* (New York: Vintage, 2007).

30. T. Dilworth, *Dilworth's Spelling-Book*, 121; the quotation in the next sentence is from William Scott, *Lessons in Elocution, or Selections of Pieces in Prose and Verse for the Improvement of Youth in Reading and Speaking* (Montpelier, VT: E. P. Walton, 1820), 93.

31. HI 127.
32. HW 2: 44.
33. John George Nicolay and John Hay, *Abraham Lincoln: A History*, vol. 4 (New York: Century Co., 1890), 70.
34. D. H. Donald, *Lincoln's Herndon*, 210.
35. HI 171.
36. HI 238.
37. HI 108.
38. W. Scott, *Lessons in Elocution*, 59; the quotation in the next sentence is from L. Murray, *Murray's English Reader*, 43.
39. George Tuthill Borrett, *Letters from Canada and the United States* (London: J. E. Adlard, 1865), 255.
40. L. Murray, *Murray's English Reader*, 40; W. Scott, *Lessons in Elocution*, 92, 183.
41. W. Scott, *Lessons in Elocution*, 92; Noah Webster, *The American Spelling Book: Containing the Rudiments of the English Language, for the Use of Schools in the United States* (Hartford, CT: Hudson & Goodwin, 1809),158.

Chapter 4
The Powers of Nature

1. W. Whitman, "The Eighteenth Presidency!" (1856), PW 2: 535.
2. R. W. Emerson, "Europe and European Books," *Essays and Lectures* (New York: Library of America 1983), 1250.
3. H. D. Thoreau, "Walking," in *"Wild Apples" and Other Natural History Essays*, edited by William John Rossi (Athens: University of Georgia Press, 2002), 75.
4. *American Big-Game Hunting: The Book of the Boone and Crockett Club*, edited by Theodore Roosevelt and George Bird Grinnell (New York: Forest and Stream Pub. Co., 1893), 15; "Tributes Paid to Lincoln at His Old Kentucky Home. Impressive Ceremonies Held at the Birthplace," *The Daily Picayune* (New Orleans), February 13, 1909.
5. T. Roosevelt, *Theodore Roosevelt: An Autobiography* (New York: Macmillan and Co., 1913), 96; CW 3: 339.
6. *The Maine Woods* (1864) in H. D. Thoreau, *A Week . . . , Cape Cod*, 645–46.
7. H. D. Thoreau, "Walking," 64.
8. See Leo Marx, *The Machine in the Garden: Technology and the Pastoral Ideal in America* (New York: Oxford University Press, 1964), chap. 5.
9. The most comprehensive study of the Whig sensibility is Daniel Walker Howe, *What Hath God Wrought: The Transformation of America, 1815–1848* (New York: Oxford University Press, 2007). See also Daniel Walker Howe, *The Political Culture of the American Whigs* (Chicago: University of Chicago Press, 1979); Gabor Boritt, *Abraham Lincoln and the Economics of the American Dream* (Memphis, TN: Memphis State University Press, 1978); and O. V. Burton, *The Age of Lincoln*.
10. John Filson and Daniel Boone, *The Discovery . . . of Kentucke . . . to Which Is Added an Appendix Containing . . . The Adventures of Col. Daniel Boon* (Wilmington: J. Adams, 1784), 3.

11. Charles Humphreys, *A Compendium of the Common Law in Force in Kentucky* (Lexington, KY: William Gibbes Hunt, 1922), 107.

12. CW 3: 511.

13. Quoted in A. J. Beveridge, *Abe Lincoln in Indiana*, 7.

14. HI 217, 235.

15. A. J. Beveridge, *Abe Lincoln in Indiana*, 8.

16. CW 4: 62.

17. John James Audubon, "The Wild Turkey," *American Turf Register and Sporting Magazine* 9 (January 1838): 437.

18. *Walden* (1854), in H. D. Thoreau, *A Week . . . Cape Cod*, 401.

19. H. D. Thoreau, journal entry of May 28, 1854, in *The Writings of Henry David Thoreau*, edited by Bradford Torrey and Franklin Benjamin Sanborn (Boston: Houghton Mifflin, 1906), 12: 311.

20. HI 27.

21. The historian Jon Grinspan notes, "Nineteenth-century boys were killing machines. Squirrels, frogs, rabbits, quail, and deer died by the thousands, pursued by boys roaming the countryside" (J. Grinspan, *The Virgin Vote: How Young Americans Made Democracy Social, Politics Personal, and Voting Popular in the Nineteenth Century* [Chapel Hill: University of North Carolina Press, 2016], 28.)

22. HI 39. The quotation in the next sentence is from p. 217.

23. *American Big-Game Hunting*, edited by T. Roosevelt and G. B. Grinnell, 9. The quotation in the next sentence is from p. 338.

24. William Riley McLaren, "Reminiscences of Pioneer Life in Illinois," quoted in John Mack Faragher, *Sugar Creek: Life on the Illinois Prairie* (New Haven: Yale University Press, 1988), 153.

25. HI 109. The remaining quotations in this paragraph are from pp. 112 and 94, successively.

26. Ward Hill Lamon, *Recollections of Abraham Lincoln, 1847–1865*, edited by Dorothy Lamon Teillard (Washington, DC: n.p., 1911), 101.

27. Joshua Fry Speed, *Reminiscences of Abraham Lincoln. Notes of a Visit to California. Two Lectures* (Louisville, KY: Bradley & Gilbert Co., 1896), 25.

28. James Ernst Gallaher, *Best Lincoln Stories, Tersely Told* (Chicago: Donohue Brothers, ca. 1898), 17.

29. HOL 100. The remaining quotations in this paragraph are from the same page.

30. Francis Marion Van Natter, *Lincoln's Boyhood: A Chronicle of His Indiana Years* (Washington, DC: Public Affairs Press, 1963), 68.

31. William D. Nowlin, *Kentucky Baptist History 1770–1922* (Louisville, KY: Baptist Book Concern, 1922), 190.

32. J. W. Weik, *The Real Lincoln*, 25.

33. W. Mounts, *The Pioneer and the Prairie Lawyer*, 109.

34. LY 25.

35. Z 26.

36. JH 103.

37. Helen Nicolay, *Personal Traits of Abraham Lincoln* (New York: Century Co., 1912), 33.

38. HI 189–90; and "Reminiscences of John Watkins," as told to Thomas P. Reep in an interview of 1890, quoted in Reep's interview with Joseph F. Booton, Petersburg, IL, October 18, 1934, typescript, 19–21, Abraham Lincoln Presidential Library, Springfield, IL.

39. Shelby Foote, *The Civil War: A Narrative. Red River to Appomattox* (New York: Random House, 1974), 864.

40. JH 99.

41. Z 68.

42. N. Brooks, "Personal Recollections of Abraham Lincoln," 228.

43. For a description of the fight narrative in popular humor, see Joseph J. Arpad, "The Fight Story: Quotation and Originality in Native American Humor," *Journal of the Folklore Institute* 10.3 (December 1973): 141–72.

44. *The Crockett Almanacks. Nashville Series, 1835–1838*, edited by Franklin J. Meine (Chicago: Caxton Club, 1955), xxx.

45. James Kirke Paulding, *Letters from the South* (New York: James Eastburn & Co., 1817), 2: 90.

46. *A Treasury of American Folklore: Stories, Ballads, and Traditions of the People*, edited by B. A. Botkin (New York: Crown, 1944), 14.

47. *Crockett's Almanac, 1848* (Boston: James Fisher, 1848).

48. HI 442–43; HL 385.

49. HI 442–43.

50. Z 79.

51. Z 77; HI 676.

52. HI 174.

53. Z 78.

54. HL 399.

55. This point has been confirmed by folklorists who in a comparative investigation of American and foreign storytelling found that 95 percent of the nearly four thousand American folk stories they studied fell into the tall tale category, while less than 1 percent of the British, Scottish, Irish, and Welsh ones did, demonstrating that "the tall tale is an overwhelmingly American form" (Ernest W. Baughman, *A Type and Motif-Index of the Folk-Tales of England and North America* [The Hague: Mouton, 1966], xvii).

56. *Humor of the Old Southwest*, edited by Hennig Cohen and William B. Dillingham (Boston: Houghton Mifflin, 1964), 253; George Washington Harris, *Sut Lovingood*, edited by Brom Weber (New York: Grove, 1954), 171–72.

57. FC 235.

58. H. Nicolay, *Personal Traits of Abraham Lincoln*, 18.

59. IM 94.

60. HW 1: 113–14.

61. TDC 184–85.

62. F. M. Van Natter, *Lincoln's Boyhood*, 41.

63. CW 1: 274.

64. Charles Augustus Murray, *Travels in North America During the Years 1834, 1835, 1836* (New York: Harper & Brothers, 1839), 153–54. See Elliott J. Gorn, "'Gouge and Bite, Pull Hair and Scratch': The Social Significance of Fighting in

the Southern Backcountry," *The American Historical Review* 90.1 (February 1985): 18–43.

65. Timothy Flint, *Recollections of Ten Years* (Boston: Cummings, Hilliard, & Co., 1826), 98; T. Flint, in *Early Western Travels, 1748–1846,* edited by Reuben Gold Thwaites (Cleveland: Arthur H. Clark Co., 1904), 9: 138.

66. T. Flint, *Recollections of Ten Years,* 98.

67. TDC 34.

68. Clara Stillwell, "A Few Lincoln-in-Indiana Stories," typescript, 4–5, Lincoln Papers, Lilly Library, Indiana University, Bloomington; "The Early Life of Abe Lincoln," *The Plain Dealer* (Cleveland), July 19, 1860.

69. HW 1: 47.

70. The fullest account of these trips is Richard Campanella, *Lincoln in New Orleans: The 1828–1831 Flatboat Voyages and Their Place in History* (Lanham, MD: Garrett County Press, 2012).

71. Anna Caroline Roby Gentry, the wife of Allen Gentry, told this to her grandson, E. Grant Gentry; in Francis Marion Van Natter's report of two interviews (on January 21 and February 10, 1936); Van Natter Papers, Vincennes University, Vincennes, IN.

72. HI 457.

73. HI 162.

74. CW 4: 62.

75. M. Twain, *Life on the Mississippi,* 238. For a discussion of the origins of the half-horse, half-alligator image, see Michael Allen, *Western Rivermen, 1763–1861: Ohio and Mississippi Boatmen and the Myth of the Alligator Horse* (Baton Rouge: Louisiana State University Press, 1994).

76. E. Bennett, *Mike Fink: A Legend of the Ohio* (Cincinnati: Robinson & Jones, 1848), 28.

77. F. M. Van Natter, *Lincoln's Boyhood,* 36.

78. Joseph Gentry, in an interview with Anna C. O'Flynn (ca. 1895); Anna C. O'Flynn Papers, Vincennes University.

79. HI 124. The quotation in the next sentence is from the same page.

80. Otto R. Kyle, *Abraham Lincoln in Decatur* (New York: Vantage Press, 1957), 15. Some of the information about Lincoln's time in Macon County period is from this book.

81. T. G. Onstot, *Pioneers of Mason and Menard Counties* (Peoria, IL: J. W. Franks & Sons, 1902), 135.

82. Eleanor Atkinson, "The Winter of the Deep Snow," *Transactions of the Illinois State Historical Society for the Year 1909* (Springfield: Illinois State Historical Society, 1909), 49–50.

83. Richard Lawrence Miller, *Lincoln and His World* (Mechanicsburg, PA: Stackpole Books, 2006), 1: 98.

84. TS 1: 79. See also HI 12 and HI 80.

85. HI 439.

86. Charles H. Coleman, *Abraham Lincoln and Coles County, Illinois* (New Brunswick, NJ: Scarecrow Press, 1995); and at http://www.rootsweb.ancestry.com /~ilcoletp/history/abraham_lincoln.htm#1.

CHAPTER 5
THE SCHOOL OF EVENTS

1. *The Liberator* (Boston), January 1, 1831.
2. David Grimsted, *American Mobbing, 1828–1861: Toward Civil War* (New York: Oxford University Press, 1998), 3. See also Michael Feldberg, *The Turbulent Era: Riot and Disorder in Jacksonian America* (New York: Oxford University Press, 1980).
3. CW 1: 111.
4. FC 225.
5. CW 8: 333.
6. John Moses, *Illinois: Historical and Statistical* (Chicago: Fergus, 1892), 1: 390–91.
7. See Thomas P. Reep, *Lincoln at New Salem* (Petersburg, IL: Old Salem Lincoln League, 1924), and Josephine Craven Chandler, "New Salem: Early Chapter in Lincoln's Life," *Journal of the Illinois State Historical Society* (1908–1984) 22.4 (January 1930): 501–58.
8. Much of the information in this section about Graham is derived from Kunigunde Duncan and D. F. Nickols, *Mentor Graham, the Man Who Taught Lincoln* (Chicago: University of Chicago Press, 1944).
9. K. Duncan and D. F. Nickols, *Mentor Graham*, 35.
10. K. Duncan and D. F. Nickols, *Mentor Graham*, 138.
11. T. P. Reep, *Lincoln at New Salem*, 31. A further complication here is that William Greene's brother, Lynn McNulty Greene, claimed to have been the grammar teacher. He told Herndon, "In the summer after he came home from the Black Hawk War he got possession of one of Kirkham's Grammars & began studying it on the hill sides of old Salem. I spent several days giving him instruction in this manner. In fact all the instruction he ever had in Grammar he rec'd from me as above indicated" (HI 80).
12. Samuel Kirkham, *A Compendium of English Grammar* (1823); reprinted as *English Grammar in Familiar Lectures* (Rochester, NY: Marshall & Dean, 1834), 14. The remaining quotations in this paragraph are from p. 15.
13. HI 384. The quotation in the next sentence is from p. 385.
14. Quoted in Douglas L. Wilson, *Honor's Voice: The Transformation of Abraham Lincoln* (New York: Alfred A. Knopf 1998), 93. The first two quotations in the next sentence are from p. 71; the third one is from p. 90.
15. Theodore Calvin Pease, *The Centennial History of Illinois*, vol. 2, *The Frontier State, 1818–1848* (Chicago: A. C. McClurg, 1922), 23.
16. HW 1: 125. The quotation in the next sentence is from HW 2: 149.
17. HI 107.
18. K. Duncan and D. F. Nickols, *Mentor Graham*, 143.
19. *The Age of Reason*, in *The Writings of Thomas Paine*, edited by Moncure Daniel Conway (New York: G. P. Putnam's Sons, 1894), 4: 24. The quotations in the rest of this paragraph are from pp. 31 and 22, successively.
20. HI 472.
21. HI 577.

22. See Benjamin Franklin, *Autobiography*, in *The Works of Benjamin Franklin*, vol. 1, *Autobiography, Letters and Misc. Writings 1725–1734*, edited by John Bigelow (New York: G. P. Putnam's Sons, 1904), 205.
23. HOL 78.
24. CW 1: 382.
25. HI 432.
26. HI 576–77; HOL 330.
27. William Knox, *The Lonely Hearth. The Songs of Israel, Harp of Zion, and Other Poems* (London: John Johnstone, 1847), 97.
28. *Poems of William Cullen Bryant* (London: Oxford University Press, 1914), 12.
29. See Drew Gilpin Faust, *This Republic of Suffering: Death and the American Civil War* (New York: Alfred A. Knopf, 2001), and David S. Reynolds, *Faith in Fiction: The Emergence of Religious Literature in America* (Cambridge, MA: Harvard University Press, 1981).
30. Brian R. Dirck discusses Lincoln and the Good Death in *The Black Heavens: Abraham Lincoln and Death* (Carbondale: Southern Illinois University Press, 2019), especially chap. 1.
31. *The Centenary Edition of the Works of Nathaniel Hawthorne*, edited by Thomas Woodson and Bill Ellis (Columbus: Ohio State University Press, 1997), 22: 163.
32. Walter B. Stevens, *A Reporter's Lincoln* (St. Louis: Missouri Historical Society, 1916), 12.
33. *The Poetical Works of Lord Byron* (London: William P. Nimmo, 1875), 61.
34. See John Bickle, *Philosophy and Neuroscience: A Ruthlessly Reductive Account* (Dordrecht, The Netherlands: Kluewer Academic Publishers, 2013).
35. CW 1: 79. The fullest account of Lincoln and depression is Joshua Wolf Shenk, *Lincoln's Melancholy: How Depression Challenged a President and Fueled His Greatness* (New York: Houghton Mifflin Harcourt, 2005).
36. *The Centenary Edition of . . . Hawthorne*, 22: 163.
37. LGC 28.
38. D. H. Donald, *Lincoln*, 41; C. Sandburg, *Abraham Lincoln: The Prairie Years* (New York: Harcourt Brace, 1927), 97; A. J. Beveridge, *Abraham Lincoln, 1809–1858*, vol. 1 (Boston: Houghton Mifflin, 1928), 135.
39. HI 528; the quotation in the next sentence is from p. 390.
40. W 110; *At Lincoln's Side: John Hay's Civil War Correspondence and Selected Writings*, edited by Michael Burlingame (Carbondale: Southern Illinois University Press, 2006), 137.
41. W. Whitman, "Robert Burns as Poet and Person," PW 2: 567. The remaining quotations in this paragraph are on pp. 567, 561, and 562, successively.
42. R. Burns, "Tam O'Shanter," *The Oxford Edition of the Works of Robert Burns*, vol. 1 (New York: Oxford University Press, 2014), 199. The quotation from "Holly Willie's Prayer" in this paragraph is from p. 185.
43. Quoted in D. L. Wilson, *Honor's Voice*, 73–74. The quotation in the next sentence is from p. 74.
44. Noah Brooks, *Washington in Lincoln's Time* (New York: Century Co., 1895), 295.
45. HW 2: 302.
46. *At Lincoln's Side*, edited by M. Burlingame, 137.

47. *The Collected Works of Ralph Waldo Emerson,* vol. 8, *English Traits,* edited by Alfred Riggs Ferguson, Joseph Slater, and Jean Ferguson Carr (Cambridge, MA: Harvard University Press, 1971), 43.

48. George Alfred Townsend, *Lincoln Miscellany: The Real Life of Abraham Lincoln. A Talk with Mr. Herndon, His Late Law Partner* (New York: Bible House, 1867), 5.

49. HI 498. The next quotation in this paragraph is from p. 497.

50. Information about the frontier roughs, including the Clary's Grove Boys in this and subsequent paragraphs is derived mainly from T. G. Onstot, *Pioneers of Mason and Menard Counties; History of Sangamon County, Illinois* (Chicago: Inter-state Publishing 1881), 210–11; and Benjamin P. Thomas, *Lincoln's New Salem* (Chicago: Lakeside Press, 1934), 27–35.

51. CW 4: 65; Josiah Gilbert Holland, *The Life of Abraham Lincoln* (Springfield, MA: Gurdon Bill, 1866), 54.

52. Thomas Ford, *A History of Illinois from Its Commencement as a State in 1818 to 1847,* vol. 1 (1854; Chicago: R. R. Donnelley & Sons, 1945), 119.

53. Josephine Craven Chandler, "New Salem: Early Chapter in Lincoln's Life," *Journal of the Illinois State Historical Society* 22.4 (January 1930): 509.

54. HI 369.

55. HI 386.

56. Alonzo Rothschild, Lincoln, *Master of Men: A Study in Character* (Chicago: Lincoln Centennial Association 1912), 50.

57. HI 353; and John Todd Stuart, in an 1875 interview with John G. Nicolay, in JN 9.

58. HI 6–7.

59. Risdon M. Moore's record of a conversation with Lincoln in Springfield in August 1860: R. M. Moore, "Mr. Lincoln as a Wrestler," *Transactions of the Illinois State Historical Society* 9 (1904): 433–34.

60. Benjamin Perley Poore, in RAL 219.

61. HI 339.

62. John Todd Stuart, May 1860 interview with James Q. Howard, copied by John G. Nicolay, John Hay Papers, Brown University, Providence, RI.

63. HI 48.

64. HI 362.

65. HI 372.

66. HI 18.

67. T. C. Pease, *The Frontier State, 1818–48,* 172. The next quotation in this paragraph is also from this page.

68. *The Crockett Almanacks. Nashville Series, 1835–1838,* edited by Franklin J. Meine and Harry J. Owens (Chicago: Caxton Club, 1955), xvi. The quotation in the next sentence is from p. vii.

69. HI 171.

70. HI 51.

71. CW 1: 6. The quotation at the end of this paragraph is from CW 1: 7.

72. *Southern and South-western Sketches. Fun, Sentiment, and Adventure* (Richmond, VA: J. W. Randolph, 1850), 10–11.

73. Lincoln's 1,500-word article appeared as a letter to the editor, with the heading "New Salem, Sept. 7th, 1834," in the *Beardstown Chronicle* on November 1, 1834; see Douglas L. Wilson, *Lincoln Before Washington: New Perspectives on the Illinois Years* (Urbana: University of Illinois Press, 1997), 63–66, and Robert Bray, *Peter Cartwright: Legendary Frontier Preacher* (Urbana: University of Illinois Press, 2005), 143–52.

74. W. H. Lamon and C. F. Black, *The Life of Abraham Lincoln*, 195.

75. K. Duncan and D. F. Nickols, *Mentor Graham*, 95.

76. CW 1: 5.

77. Thomas Ford, *A History of Illinois from Its Commencement as a State in 1818 to 1847*, vol. 1 (1854; Chicago: R. R. Donnelley & Sons, 1945), 146.

78. William Butler, in an 1875 interview with John G. Nicolay, in JN 20.

79. HI 450.

80. B. P. Thomas, *Lincoln's New Salem*, 75.

81. W 33.

82. HI 15.

83. *Illinois Register*, November 23, 1839.

84. *Journal of the House of Representatives of the Ninth General Assembly of the State of Illinois* (Vandalia, IL: J. Y. Sawyer, 1835), 311.

85. Paul M. Angle, *"Here I Have Lived": A History of Lincoln's Springfield, 1821–1865* (Springfield, IL: The Abraham Lincoln Association, 1935), 40.

86. *Abraham Lincoln Association Bulletin*, November 1, 1928.

87. T. Ford, *A History of Illinois* . . . vol. 1, 289, and *Illinois State Register* (Vandalia), July 20, 1838.

88. Quoted in D. L. Wilson, *Honor's Voice*, 153.

89. LL 42–43.

90. *Sangamo Journal*, January 29, 1841.

91. Merton L. Dillon, "Abolitionism Comes to Illinois," *Journal of the Illinois State Historical Society* 53.4 (Winter 1960): 401.

92. CW 1: 347.

93. J. F. Speed, *Reminiscences of Abraham Lincoln*, 20–21.

94. *The Letters of William Cullen Bryant: 1809–1836* (New York: Fordham University Press, 1975), 345; *The Letters of Ralph Waldo Emerson*, edited by Ralph Rusk (New York: Columbia University Press, 1941), 345.

95. John J. Duff, *A. Lincoln, Prairie Lawyer* (New York: Rinehart, 1960), 40.

96. Much of the information about Springfield here is paraphrased from P. M. Angle, *"Here I Have Lived,"* 41–52.

97. *Illinois Herald*, October 1, 1815.

98. Eudora Ramsay Richardson, "The Virginian Who Made Illinois a Free State," *Journal of the Illinois State Historical Society* 45.1 (Spring 1952): 12.

99. Richard E. Hart, "Springfield's African-Americans as a Part of the Lincoln Community," *Journal of the Abraham Lincoln Association* 20.1 (Winter 1999): 41–42.

100. Elmer Gertz, "The Black Laws of Illinois," *Journal of the Illinois State Historical Society* (1908–1984), 56.3 (Autumn 1963): 454–73.

101. *The Liberator*, March 29, 1834.

102. *History of Sangamon County, Illinois* (Chicago: Inter-state Publishing Co., 1881), 251.

103. CW 1: 76, n. 2.

104. CW 1: 75.

105. Thomas Ford, *A History of Illinois from Its Commencement as a State in 1818 to 1847*, vol. 2 (1854; Chicago: R. R. Donnelley & Sons, 1945), 33.

106. The quotations from the lyceum address are from CW 1: 108–15.

107. As he wrote a young man who wanted to study law, "Begin with Blackstone's Commentaries, and after reading it carefully through, say twice, take up Chitty's Pleading, Greenleaf's Evidence, & Story's Equity &c. in succession. Work, work, work, is the main thing" (CW 4: 121).

108. As Blackstone writes, "The punishment of unlawful assemblies, if to the number of twelve . . . may be capital, according to the circumstances that attend it; but from the number of three to eleven is by fine and imprisonment only." In Sir William Blackstone, *Commentaries on the Laws of England in Four Books. . . . In Two Volumes* (Philadelphia: J. B. Lippincott & Co., 1893), vol. 2 [first published in 1753], 378.

109. CW 1: 111.

110. See Howard L. Lubert, "Sovereignty and Liberty in William Blackstone's 'Commentaries on the Laws of England,'" *The Review of Politics* 72.2 (Spring 2010): 271–97.

111. *Sangamo Journal*, June 16, 1838.

Chapter 6
Turmoil and Sensations

1. Tocqueville wrote that the "anarchy" of "democratic states"—with their "fierce hatreds, conflicting interests, and contending factions"—must be restrained by a central government that was strong enough to harness such disruption but that did not fall into the hands of an unprincipled or despotic president who could misuse the power of the executive office (Alexis de Tocqueville, *Democracy in America*, edited by J. P. Mayer, 259, 677).

2. *Emerson in His Journals*, edited by Joel Porte (Cambridge, MA: Harvard University Press, 1982), 433; *The Journal of Henry David Thoreau*, edited by Bradford Torrey and Francis H. Allen (New York: Dover, 1962), 4: 267.

3. HOL 197.

4. Edgar Lee Masters, *The Spoon River Anthology* (New York: Macmillan, 1931), 219.

5. James G. Randall, "Sifting the Ann Rutledge Evidence," an essay appended to Randall's *Lincoln the President: Springfield to Gettysburg* (New York: Dodd, Mead and Co., 1945), 2: 321–42.

6. See especially Douglas L. Wilson, "Abraham Lincoln, Ann Rutledge, and the Evidence of Herndon's Informants," originally in *Civil War History* 36 (December 1990): 301–24, reprinted in Douglas L. Wilson, *Lincoln Before Washington: New Perspectives on the Illinois Years* (Chicago: University of Illinois Press, 1997), 74–98; and John Y. Simon, "Abraham Lincoln and Ann Rutledge," *Journal of the Abraham Lincoln Association* 11 (1990): 13–22. For critical critiques of

Wilson's rehabilitation of the Ann Rutledge story, see David Herbert Donald, *"We Are Lincoln Men": Abraham Lincoln and His Friends* (New York: Simon & Schuster, 2003), 20–24; C. A. Tripp, *The Intimate World of Abraham Lincoln* (New York: Free Press, 2005), 67–90; and Lewis Gannett, "'Overwhelming Evidence' of a Lincoln-Ann Rutledge Romance? Reexamining Rutledge Family Reminiscences," *Journal of the Abraham Lincoln Association* 26 (Winter 2005): 28–41. Michael Burlingame accepts Wilson's recovery of the Rutledge romance in his biography *Abraham Lincoln: A Life*, vol. 1, 97–101. Like Burlingame, I find Wilson's argument, as well as the primary evidence from *Herndon's Informants*, convincing.

7. Jean H. Baker, *Mary Todd Lincoln: A Biography* (New York: W.W. Norton & Co., 2008); Catherine Clinton, *Mrs. Lincoln: A Life* (New York: HarperCollins, 2009).

8. W. Blackstone, *Commentaries on the Laws of England in Four Books*, vol. 1, 442.

9. Barbara Welter, "The Cult of True Womanhood: 1820–1860," *American Quarterly* 18.2 (Summer 1966): 151–74.

10. CW 1: 48.

11. HOL 346.

12. HI 470.

13. Quoted in J. H. Baker, *Mary Todd Lincoln*, 93.

14. CW 1: 117. The subsequent quotations in this paragraph are from CW 1: 118–19.

15. These assessments of Mary Owens appear in HI on pp. 243, 530, 126, and 610, successively.

16. "New Salem Community Activities: Documents," edited by Fern Nance Pond, *Journal of the Illinois State Historical Society* 48 (1955): 100

17. HI 262. The quotation in the next sentence is from p. 256.

18. HI 263.

19. *Report of the Special Committee Appointed to Investigate the Troubles in Kansas* (Washington, DC: Cornelius Wendell, 1856), 30.

20. Much of the biographical information about the Rutledges in this and the next paragraph is derived from H. Donald Winkler, *Lincoln's Ladies: The Women in the Life of the Sixteenth President* (Nashville, TN: Cumberland House, 2004), chap. 3.

21. HI 242.

22. A number of New Salem residents described Lincoln's extreme reaction to Ann's death. Hardin Bale recalled: "It was said that after the death of Miss Rutledge & because of it, Lincoln was locked up by his friends—Saml Hill and others, to prevent derangement or suicide—so hard did he take her death" (HI 13). Robert B. Rutledge said, "The effect [of Ann's death] upon Mr Lincoln's mind was terrible; he became plunged in despair, and many of his friends feared that reason would desert her throne" (HI 383). Thompson Ware McNeely recalled "the immediate associates & friends of Mr Lincoln [said] that he had been insane—that his Mind had been shaken—that disappointed love was the cause—Her name Miss Rutledge" (HI 397).

23. HI 21.

24. Nancy Rutledge Prewitt, in an interview conducted by E. E. Sparks, *Los Angeles Times*, February 14, 1897.

25. Virgil Thomson, *A Virgil Thomson Reader* (Boston: Houghton Mifflin, 1981), 17. See also Kiri Miller, *Traveling Home: Sacred Harp Singing and American Pluralism* (Urbana: University of Illinois Press, 2008).

26. Allen D. Carden, *The Missouri Harmony: A Choice Collection of Psalm Tunes, Hymns and Anthems* (1820; Cincinnati: Morgan and Sansay, 1834), 62, 32.

27. For Lincoln's knowledge of the songs discussed in this paragraph, see HI 168 and 215. See also John Lair, *Songs Lincoln Loved* (New York: Duell, Sloan, and Pearce, 1954).

28. W. H. Lamon, *Recollections of Abraham Lincoln*, edited by D. L. Teillard, 155.

29. W. Knox, *The Lonely Hearth*, 97.

30. HW 1: 130.

31. HI 21. The next quotation in this paragraph is from p. 440.

32. W. H. Lamon, *Recollections of Abraham Lincoln*, edited by D. L. Teillard, 21.

33. HI 443. The quotations in the next three sentences are from pp. 623, 63, and 63, successively.

34. HOL 197.

35. J. H. Baker, *Mary Todd Lincoln*, 83.

36. For a discussion of Presbyterianism and slavery, see Joseph S. Moore, "Covenanters and Antislavery in the Atlantic World," *Slavery & Abolition* 34.4 (2013): 539–61; and W. Melancthon Glasgow, *History of the Reformed Presbyterian Church in America* (Baltimore: Hill & Harvey, 1888).

37. See Kenneth J. Winkle, *Abraham and Mary Lincoln* (Carbondale: Southern Illinois University Press, 2011), 16 ff.

38. JT 8.

39. William H. Herndon and Jesse W. Weik, *Herndon's Lincoln*, edited by Douglas L. Wilson and Rodney O. Davis (Urbana: University of Illinois Press, 2006), 134.

40. JT 200.

41. Mary Edwards Raymond, *Some Incidents in the Life of Mrs. Benjamin S. Edwards* (n.p.: n.p., 1909), 11–12.

42. Sarah Rickard (sister of Mrs. William Butler of Springfield) in an interview in the *Kansas City Star*, February 10, 1907; see also Elizabeth L. Norris to Emilie Todd Helm, Garden City, Kansas, September 28, 1895, Elizabeth L. Norris Papers, Abraham Lincoln Presidential Library, Springfield, IL.

43. Frederick Marryat, *Second Series of A Diary in America: With Remarks on Its Institutions* (Philadelphia: T. K. & P. G. Collins, 1840), 58.

44. *Walt Whitman of the New York Aurora: Editor at Twenty-Two*, edited by Joseph J. Rubin and Charles J. Brown (Westport, CT: Greenwood Press, 1950), 115.

45. See David S. Reynolds, *George Lippard* (Boston: Twayne, 1982) and *George Lippard, Prophet of Protest: Writings of an American Radical, 1822–1854*, edited by David S. Reynolds (New York: Peter Lang, 1986).

46. Kenneth Cmiel, *Democratic Eloquence: The Fight over Popular Speech in Nineteenth-Century America* (Berkeley: University of California Press, 1990), chap. 2. See also Todd Vogel, *Rewriting White: Race, Class, and Cultural Capital*

in Nineteenth-Century America (New Brunswick, NJ: Rutgers University Press, 2004), 20.

47. *The Diary of Philip Hone, 1828–1851*, edited by Allan Nevins (New York: Dodd, Mead, and Co., 1927), 2: 143.

48. HI 451. The next quotation in this paragraph is also from this page.

49. Sidney Blumenthal, *A Self-Made Man: The Political Life of Abraham Lincoln, Vol. 1, 1809–1849* (New York: Simon & Schuster, 2016), 189.

50. CW 2: 283.

51. Henry C. Whitney, *Lincoln the Citizen* (New York: Current Literature Publishing Co., 1907), 127–28.

52. CW 8: 429.

53. *Sangamo Journal*, July 16, 1836.

54. *Sangamo Journal*, July 15, 1837. The editors of *The Collected Works of Abraham Lincoln* note that the six letters signed "Sampson's Ghost," which appeared in the *Journal* on June 17, 24, and July 8, 15, 22, and 29, 1837, "in view of subsequent developments seem possibly to have been the work of Lincoln and his colleagues, Edward D. Baker, Stephen T. Logan, and John T. Stuart" (CW 1: 90). In the *Collected Works* the editors reproduce only Lincoln's cowritten comments on James Adams and "Sampson's Ghost," which appeared in the *Journal* on September 6, 1837 (CW 1: 95–9).

55. CW 1: 244.

56. CW 1: 178.

57. For a discussion of dark reform and its influence on pre–Civil War American literature, see D. S. Reynolds, *Beneath the American Renaissance*, chaps. 2–5.

58. George Lippard, *The Quaker City, Or, The Monks of Monk Hall: A Romance of Philadelphia Life, Mystery, and Crime*, edited by David S. Reynolds (1845; Amherst: University of Massachusetts Press, 1995), 372–93.

59. Herman Melville, "Hawthorne and His Mosses" (1850), in *The Piazza Tales and Other Prose Pieces, 1839–1860*, edited by Harrison Hayford, Alma A. MacDougall, and G. Thomas Tanselle (Evanston, IL: Northwestern University Press, 1987), 243; Herman Melville, *Moby-Dick, Or The Whale*, sixth volume of the Scholarly Edition, edited by Harrison Hayford, Hershel Parker, and G. Thomas Tanselle (1851; Evanston, IL: Northwestern University Press, 1988), 79.

60. The suicide poem appeared in the *Sangamo Journal* on August 25, 1838. Quotations from the poem here are from this source.

61. The story of the lovers' suicide appeared in the *Sangamo Journal* on March 23, 1833; the one about the four sisters who kill themselves was in the *Journal* on July 20, 1833; the report of the woman who swallows arsenic was published in the *Journal* on June 18 1833; and the story about the world's "most extraordinary suicide" appeared in the *Journal* on June 13, 1835.

62. CW 1: 229; HI 133; and Jane D. Bell to Anne Bell, Springfield, January 27, 1841, copy, "Wife" folder, Lincoln files, Lincoln Memorial University, Harrogate, Tennessee.

63. See Paul Simon, *Lincoln's Preparation for Greatness: The Illinois Legislative Years* (Urbana: University of Illinois Press, 1971), 232–36.

64. HI 472. The next quotation in this paragraph is from p. 47.

65. *Sangamo Journal*, February 23, 1839.

66. Gary M. Walton and Hugh Rockoff, *History of the American Economy* (Mason, OH: South-Western Cengage Learning, 2014), 182.

67. Richard Allen Sauers, *Nationalism* (New York: Chelsea House, 2010), 87.

68. HW 1: 172. The next quotation in this paragraph is also from this page.

69. T. Ford, *A History of Illinois . . .* Volume I, 308. See Robert Bray, "'The Power to Hurt': Lincoln's Early Use of Satire and Invective," *Journal of the Abraham Lincoln Association* 16.1 (Winter 1995): 39–58.

70. Statement made by the Illinois governor Richard Yates; in U. Linder and J. Gillespie, *Reminiscences*, 235.

71. CW 1: 62.

72. Albert Taylor Bledsoe, "Lamon's Life of Lincoln," *The Southern Review* (April 1873): 333. The next quotation in this paragraph is also from p. 333.

73. U. Linder and J. Gillespie, *Reminiscences*, 249.

74. CW 1: 211, n. 2. The next quotation in this paragraph is also from this page.

75. Newspaper clipping, "Temperance" folder, Abraham Lincoln Association reference files, Abraham Lincoln Presidential Library, Springfield, IL.

76. His Springfield neighbor John B. Weber recalled, "I remember Lincolns temperance Speeches well: he & I used to go to the Country together in his buggy: he had a horse & buggy & I had none: . . . Speeches &c. from 1841 to 1849, according to my recollections" (HI 389). Another neighbor, James Gourley, said, "Lincoln was a great temperance man during the time of the Washingtonians—he would go a foot 5 or ten miles to talk. . . . He was a good temperance man—he Scarcely Ever drank" (HI 452).

77. CW 2: 188.

78. CW 6: 487.

79. CW 1: 275, 273.

80. W. Scott, *Lessons in Elocution*, 64.

81. George Pullen Jackson, *Spiritual Folk Songs of Early America* (1937; Locust Valley, NY: J. J. Augustine, 1953), p. 39.

82. John Allen, letter to Eleazar Baldwin, May 5, 1832, New Salem Museum, copied in "John Allen Residence," p. 31, typescript in the Sangamon Valley Collection, Abraham Lincoln Presidential Library, Springfield, IL.

83. K. Duncan and D. F. Nickols, *Mentor Graham*, 139.

84. Thomas J. Nance, untitled address to the New Salem Temperance Society, February 26, 1834, Abraham Lincoln Presidential Library, Springfield, IL.

85. LL 28.

86. See D. S. Reynolds, *Beneath the American Renaissance*, 145.

87. R. Warren, *Abe Lincoln, Kentucky Boy*, 23.

88. J. H. Spencer, *A History of Kentucky Baptists*, 1: 163–64, 336.

89. J. H. Baker, *Mary Todd Lincoln*, 267.

90. C. H. Coleman, *Abraham Lincoln and Coles County, Illinois*, 115.

91. Allen D. Spiegel, *A. Lincoln, Esquire: A Shrewd, Sophisticated Lawyer in His Time* (Macon, GA: Mercer University Press, 2002), 83.

92. Ralph Emerson Twitchell, *Old Santa Fe: The Story of New Mexico's Ancient Capital* (Santa Fe: Santa Fe New Mexican Press, 1925), 351.

93. FC 247.

94. *Boston Statesman*, May 2, 1835.

95. *New York Times*, reprinted in the *New Hampshire Patriot and State Gazette*, July 27, 1835.
96. *Lowell Patriot*, March 20, 1835.
97. CW 1: 274. The subsequent quotations in this paragraph are from pp. 272–73.
98. CW 1: 273–79. The subsequent quotations in this paragraph are from CW 1: 278–79.
99. HI 452.
100. CW 4: 271 and CW 7: 21.
101. See C. A. Tripp, *The Intimate World of Abraham Lincoln,* especially chapt. 7.
102. A judicious study of male same-sex love that, in most cases, did not involve sex is E. Anthony Rotundo, *American Manhood: Transformations in Masculinity from the Revolution to the Modern Era* (New York: Basic Books, 1993). See also David S. Reynolds, *Walt Whitman's America: A Cultural Biography* (New York: Alfred A. Knopf, 1995). Sodomy or bestiality, when discovered and brought to trial, were punished quite severely. See Jonathan Ned Katz, *Love Stories: Sex Between Men Before Homosexuality* (Chicago: University of Chicago Press, 2001). See also Charles Shively, *Loving Comrades: Walt Whitman's Homosexual Loves* (New York: Taylor and Francis, 1995); Michael Bronski, *A Queer History of the United States* (Boston: Beacon, 2011); and David R. Greenberg, *The Construction of Homosexuality* (Chicago: University of Chicago Press, 1988).
103. HI 350. The quotations in the next two sentences are from HI 617 and HL 247, successively.
104. HI 719.
105. HOL 334.
106. Speed to Holland, June 22, 1865; in Allen C. Guelzo, "Holland's Informants: The Construction of Josiah Holland's 'Life of Abraham Lincoln,'" *Journal of the Abraham Lincoln Association* 23 (2002): 1–55. A thorough portrait of the Lincoln-Speed relationship is provided in Charles B. Strozier, *Your Friend Forever, A. Lincoln: The Enduring Friendship of Abraham Lincoln and Joshua Speed* (New York: Columbia University Press, 2016).
107. RAL 241.
108. C. Sandburg, *Abraham Lincoln: The Prairie Years,* 264.
109. Margaret Fuller, *Woman in the Nineteenth Century* (1843; New York: Greeley & McElrath, 1845), 103.
110. HI 561. The next quotation in this paragraph is from p. 507.
111. HI 475.
112. CW 4: 546.
113. CW 1: 265.
114. CW 1: 266.
115. CW 1: 303.
116. CW 1: 278. The quotations in the next two sentences are from CW 1: 279.
117. CW 1: 268, 270.
118. CW 1: 266.
119. JT 27.
120. Quoted in Kate H. Winter, *Marietta Holley: Life with "Josiah Allen's Wife"* (Syracuse, NY: Syracuse University Press, 2005), 43.
121. CW 1: 293. The remaining quotations in this paragraph from Lincoln's Rebecca piece are from CW 1: 295–96.

122. *Sangamo Journal*, September 9, 1842. The subsequent quotation from this Rebecca piece is also from this source.
123. *Sangamo Journal*, September 16, 1842.
124. U. Linder and J. Gillespie, *Reminiscences*, 64–65.
125. HW 260.
126. William H. Condon, *Life of Major-General Shields* (Chicago: Blakely, 1900), 21.
127. CW 2: 97.
128. HI 596.
129. RAL 468.
130. HI 597.
131. CW 2: 16.
132. Quoted in J. H. Baker, *Mary Todd Lincoln*, 89.
133. CW 1: 305.
134. JT 504, 49–50.
135. HI 327.
136. HI 35. The quotation in the next sentence is from p. 181.
137. Quoted in J. H. Baker, *Mary Todd Lincoln*, 120. The next quotation in this paragraph is from pp. 120–21.
138. JT 251.
139. HOL 287, 202. Michael Burlingame in *An American Marriage: The Untold Story of Abraham Lincoln and Mary Todd* (New York: Pegasus Books, 2021) uses Herndon's comments and other evidence to paint a highly negative picture of the Lincolns' marriage.
140. JT 21; and quoted in J. H. Baker, *Mary Todd Lincoln*, 88.
141. *Boston Traveler*, December 2, 1825.

CHAPTER 7
LAW AND CULTURE

1. Quoted in J. J. Duff, *A. Lincoln, Prairie Lawyer*, 37.
2. CW 1: 159. The quotation in the next sentence is from CW 1: 158.
3. Robert J. Johnson, "Trial by Fire: Abraham Lincoln and the Law" (PhD diss., CUNY Graduate Center, 2007), 84.
4. J. F. Speed, *Reminiscences of Abraham Lincoln*, 34; H. C. Whitney, *Lincoln the Citizen*, 174.
5. HI 167; Gibson William Harris, "My Recollections of Abraham Lincoln," *Woman's Home Companion*, January 1904, 13.
6. For an account of Lincoln's law offices and other Lincoln-related locales in Springfield, see "Lincoln's Law Offices in the Tinsley Building," *Lincoln Lore* 1579 (September 1969), 1–4.
7. S. T. Logan, in July 1875 interview with John G. Nicolay, JN 35. The subsequent quotations in this paragraph are from p. 38.
8. *Memorials of the Life and Character of Stephen T. Logan* (Springfield, IL: H. W. Rokker, 1892), 17. For a judicious discussion of Lincoln's role as a peace-making lawyer, see R. C. White Jr., *A. Lincoln: A Biography,* chap. 10.
9. CW 2: 81. The next Lincoln quotation in this paragraph is also from this page.
10. *Memorials of . . . Stephen T. Logan*, 48.

11. CW 2: 81. The quotation in the next sentence is also from this page.
12. *San Francisco Bulletin*, December 17, 1855.
13. *Litchfield Republican*, December 25, 1851.
14. CW 2: 82.
15. Albert A. Woldman, *Lawyer Lincoln* (Boston: Houghton Mifflin, 1936), 45.
16. JN 19.
17. HOL 21, 49, 88. The quotation in the next sentence is from p. 35.
18. Quoted in D. H. Donald, *Lincoln's Herndon*, 54.
19. Quoted in D. H. Donald, *Lincoln's Herndon*, 112.
20. "The Profession of the Law," *Western Law Journal* 7 (1849): 109.
21. G. W. Harris, "My Recollections of Abraham Lincoln."
22. CW 2: 81; W. H. Herndon to Ward Hill Lamon, March 6, 1870, Lamon Papers, Huntington Library, San Marino, CA; HW 2: 1.
23. H. Melville, "Bartleby, the Scrivener," in *The Piazza Tales: and Other Prose Pieces*, edited by H. Hayford and M. M. Sealts, 14. The subsequent quotations in this paragraph are from pp. 18–19.
24. W 404.
25. HOL 237. The first quotation in the next paragraph is also from this page.
26. HW 3: 313.
27. HOL 216.
28. *San Francisco Daily Evening Bulletin*, April 22, 1865.
29. CW 2: 81.
30. H. D. Thoreau, *Walden*, in *A Week . . . Cape Cod*, 377; H. Melville, Letter to Lemuel Shaw, October 6, 1849, in Melville, *Correspondence*, edited by Lynn Horth (Evanston, IL: Northwestern University Press, 1993), 139.
31. For a revealing account of Lincoln's business habits as a lawyer, see W. W. Freehling, *Becoming Lincoln*, chapters 6 and 11.
32. *Abe Lincoln Laughing: Humorous Anecdotes from Original Sources by and About Abraham Lincoln*, edited by Paul M. Zall (Berkeley: University of California Press, 1982), 118–19.
33. CW 5: 501.
34. W 55.
35. L. Swett, "An Old Friend's Recollections of David Davis," *Globe-Democrat* (St. Louis), June 27, 1888 (reprinted from the *Chicago Mail*).
36. W. H. Lamon, *Recollections of Abraham Lincoln*, edited by D. L. Teillard, 16–17.
37. Quoted in M. Burlingame, *Abraham Lincoln: A Life*, vol. 1, 326.
38. W 40–41.
39. J. H. Buckingham, quoted in Harry E. Pratt, "Illinois as Lincoln Knew It . . . in 1847," *Papers in Illinois History and Transactions for the Year 1937* (Springfield: Illinois State Historical Society, 1938), 139–40.
40. Willard L. King, *Lincoln's Manager: David Davis* (Cambridge, MA: Harvard University Press, 1960), 77, 75, 82.
41. HOL 156.
42. Quoted in M. Burlingame, *Abraham Lincoln: A Life*, vol. 1, 326.
43. HI 350.
44. Quoted in C. Sandburg, *Abraham Lincoln: The Prairie Years*, 297.

45. HI 349.

46. Quoted in J. J. Duff, *A. Lincoln, Prairie Lawyer*, 179.

47. W. H. Herndon to Truman Bartlett, July 19, 1887, Bartlett Papers, Massachusetts Historical Society.

48. *Alton Telegraph* (Alton, IL), August 20, 1847.

49. R. W. Emerson.,"Greatness," in *The Collected Works of Ralph Waldo Emerson*, vol. 8, edited by R. A. Bosco, G. M. Johnson, and J. Myerson, 176.

50. "David Davis Pays Tribute to Abraham Lincoln" (1865 lecture), in IM 69.

51. Usher Linder, "Reminiscences of the Late President Lincoln," *Washington Sunday Chronicle*, April 23, 1865.

52. HW 2: 325.

53. Hiram W. Beckwith, "Lincoln: Personal Recollections of Him, His Contemporaries and Law Practice in Eastern Illinois," *Chicago Tribune*, December 29, 1895; and A. K. McClure' "'Abe' Lincoln's Yarns and Stories," 93.

54. "David Davis Pays Tribute to Abraham Lincoln," in IM 76.

55. HL 100–101.

56. Quoted in Clark E. Carr, *The Illini, a Story of the Prairies* (Chicago: McClurg, 1905), 186.

57. W 75.

58. HI 648.

59. N. Brooks, "Personal Recollections of Abraham Lincoln," 228; W 52.

60. J. W. Weik, *The Real Lincoln*, 78–79.

61. Jane Martin Johns, *Personal Recollections of Early Decatur, Abraham Lincoln, Richard J. Oglesby and the Civil War* (Decatur, IL: Decatur Chapter Daughters of the American Revolution, 1912), 65–66.

62. HW 2: 322.

63. W. H. Lamon, *Recollections of Abraham Lincoln*, edited by D. L. Teillard, 150.

64. J. Lair, *Songs Lincoln Loved*, 70.

65. J. Lair, *Songs Lincoln Loved*, 29.

66. HI 146–48.

67. Lyman Abbott, "The Religion of Abraham Lincoln," *The Outlook* 124 (January–April 1920): 656.

68. W 497.

69. W 44–45; HI 643.

70. Z 92. The next quotation in this paragraph is from p. 101.

71. HI 146–47. The song Hanks refers to is titled "None Can Love Like an Irishman."

72. *The American Minstrel: Being a Choice Collection of Original and Popular Songs, Glees, Duetts, Choruses, Etc.* (Philadelphia: H. F. Anners, 1844), 76.

73. HW 1: 65.

74. Thomas Carr, *The Much Admired and Popular Song of Miss Lucy Long* (Philadelphia: George Willig, 1842).

75. J. Lair, *Songs Lincoln Loved*, 44–45.

76. J. Lair, *Songs Lincoln Loved*, 39. The remaining quotations in this paragraph are also from this page.

77. Thomas Birch, *Zip Coon* (New York: Atwill's Music Saloon, 1834), at http://utc .iath.virginia.edu/minstrel/zipcoonfr.html.

78. George Washington Bungay, *Hutchinson's Republican Songster, for the Campaign of 1860* (New York: O. Hutchinson, 1860), 71–72.

79. Samuel L. Forcucci, *A Folk Song History of America: America Through Its Songs* (Englewood Cliffs, NJ: Prentice-Hall, 1984), 131.

80. Joseph Hopkinson, *Hail Columbia: The Favorite New Federal Song* (1798; Washington, DC: Library of Congress, 2002).

81. HI 146.

82. Henry B. Rankin, *Personal Recollections of Abraham Lincoln* (New York: Putnam, 1916), 120.

83. HOL 329.

84. HOL 180.

85. HOL 342.

86. CW 2: 437. The quotations in the next paragraph are also from this page. On Lincoln's two-part lecture, see especially Wayne C. Temple, "Lincoln the Lecturer, Part II ," *Lincoln Herald* 101.3 (Fall 1999): 94–110, and W. C. Temple, "Lincoln the Lecturer, Part I," *Lincoln Herald* 101.4 (Winter 1999): 146–63.

87. CW 3: 356–63.

88. HI 519.

89. HI 519, n. 2.

90. CW 4: 51.

91. CW 1: 367–68.

92. Fitz-Greene Halleck, "Burns," *The Poetical Writings of Fitz-Greene Halleck: With Extracts from Those of Joseph Rodman Drake* (New York: D. Appleton, 1882), 28; CW 7: 18. The first quotation in the next paragraph is from CW 7: 17.

93. FC 315. The remaining quotations in this paragraph are also from this page. For the influence of Euclid on Lincoln, see David Hirsch and Dan Van Haften, *Abraham Lincoln and the Structure of Reason* (New York: Savas Beatie, 2012) and Jordan Ellenberg, "What Honest Abe Learned from Geometry," *Wall Street Journal*, May 22, 2021.

94. HI 350.

95. W 109.

96. CW 7: 17.

97. Quoted in Manisha Sinha, *The Slave's Cause: A History of Abolition* (New Haven, CT: Yale University Press, 2017), 200.

98. W. D. Howells, *Life of Abraham Lincoln*, 31–32.

99. HI 519.

100. HW 2: 319.

101. E. A. Poe, "The Purloined Letter," in *Poetry and Tales* (New York: Library of America, 1984), 692.

102. CW 1: 368–69.

103. CW 1: 387–89.

104. Among the most detailed studies of Lincoln's law practice are Brian R. Dirck, *Lincoln the Lawyer* (Urbana: University of Illinois Press, 2009) and Mark E. Steiner, *An Honest Calling: The Law Practice of Abraham Lincoln* (DeKalb: Northern Illinois University Press, 2009).

105. W 41.

106. HOL 238.

107. HW 2: 1.

108. See D. S. Reynolds, *Beneath the American Renaissance*, chap. 6, and D. S. Reynolds, *Walt Whitman's America*, chap. 7.

109. Declaration in *Torrence v. Galloway* (1847–48), LPAL, case file #L01595. See A. D. Spiegel, *A. Lincoln, Esquire*, 167.

110. For bestiality involving a dog, see plea in *Thompson v. Henline* (1851–52), LPAL, case file #L01689; for ones involving cows, see plea in *Davidson v. McGhilton* (1852), LPAL, case file #L01753, and plea in *Thompson v. Patton* (1851), LPAL, case file #L01691.

111. *Martin v. Underwood* (1857–58), LPAL, case file #L01953 (narration, p. 5).

112. Declaration in *Cantrall v. Prim* (1849), LPAL, case file #L03010.

113. *Mitchell et ux. v. Mitchell* (1852), LPAL, case file #L00673.

114. George R. Dekle Sr., *Prairie Defender: The Murder Trials of Abraham Lincoln* (Carbondale: Southern Illinois University Press, 2017), 187.

115. The case was *People v. William Fraim* (1839), LPAL, case file # L01846.

116. *People v. Goings* (1859), LPAL, case file #L01800. George Dekle points out that while the report that Lincoln told this joke is unsubstantiated, the joke itself did circulate in Illinois law circles at the time; see G. Dekle, *Prairie Defender*, 139.

117. *People v. William Fraim* (1839), LPAL, case file #L01846.

118. *People v. William Duff Armstrong* (1858), LPAL, case file #L00800.

119. *People v. Truett* (1838), LPAL, case file #L04327.

120. *Sangamo Journal*, March 17, 1838.

121. *Recollected Words of Abraham Lincoln*, D. E. Fehrenbacher and V. Fehrenbacher, 242.

122. FC 338.

123. Quoted in J. J. Duff, *A. Lincoln, Prairie Lawyer*, 80.

124. *Quincy Whig*, April 15, 1846.

125. The quotations in this paragraph are from CW 1: 373–75.

126. CW 1: 111. The quotation in the next sentence is also from this page.

127. *People v. Delny* (1853), LPAL, case file #L01235.

128. Article in the *Cleveland Leader*, copied in the *Independent Democrat* (Concord, NH), June 7, 1860, the *Coos Republican*, June 19, 1860, and other newspapers.

129. HW 2: 27–28.

130. HI 213.

131. For example, his early biographers John Nicolay and John Hay claimed that Lincoln did not defend cases he considered morally unjust. This idea was in line with that of Judge David Davis, who described Lincoln as "a good Circuit Court lawyer, . . . if he thought he was right" (HI 347). The lawyer Samuel C. Parks recalled that "at the bar when he thought he was wrong he was the weakest lawyer I ever saw" (HI 239). Joseph Gillespie insisted that "it was not in his nature to assume or attempt to bolster up a false position. He would abandon his case first" (HI 182).

132. W. Blackstone, *Commentaries on the Laws of England in Four Books*, vol. 2, 358.

133. Letter from Benjamin Franklin to Benjamin Vaughan, March 14, 1785, *The Papers of Benjamin Franklin*, vol. 42, at https://franklinpapers.org/framedVolumes .jsp?vol=42&page=712.

134. "Adams' Argument for the Defense: 3–4 December 1770," Founders Online, National Archives, last modified November 26, 2017, http://founders.archives.gov /documents/Adams/05-03-02-0001-0004-0016.

135. Schuyler Colfax, in RAL, 333–34.

136. The statistics in this and the following paragraphs are derived from "The Law Practice of Abraham Lincoln: A Statistical Portrait," LPAL, at http://www.law practiceofabrahamlincoln.org/Reference/Reference%20html%20files/Statisti calPortrait.html.

137. See Daniel W. Stowell, *In Tender Consideration: Women, Families, and the Law in Abraham Lincoln's Illinois* (Champaign: University of Illinois Press, 2002).

138. *Address to Females* (New York: George S. Sickels, 1831), 11.

139. H. Melville, *Moby-Dick; or, The Whale*, 485.

140. *Lloyd v. Lloyd* (1839), LPAL case file #L04044.

141. *McDaniel v. McDaniel* (1842), LPAL case file #L04006.

142. *Jones v. Jones* (1852), LPAL, case file #L03722.

143. *Klein v. Klein* (1859), LPAL, case file #L03929.

144. *Hill v. Hill* (1852), LPAL, case file #L02511.

145. *Hook v. Denton* (1859), LPAL, case file #L03579.

146. *Ray v. Ray* (1856), LPAL, case file #L04414.

147. HI 510. The remaining quotations in this paragraph are also from this page.

148. Judge Joseph Holt, quoted in JN, 69.

149. Quoted in Jonathan M. Bryant, *Dark Places of the Earth: The Voyage of the Slave Ship* Antelope (New York: W. W. Norton, 2015), 229–30.

150. *Argument of John Quincy Adams, Before the Supreme Court of the United States: In the Case of the United States, Appellants, vs. Cinque, and Others, Africans, Captured in the Schooner* Amistad (New York: S. W. Benedict, 1841), 126.

151. S. P. Chase, *Reclamation of Fugitives from Service. An Argument for the Defendant, Submitted to the Supreme Court of the United States, at the December Term, 1846, in the Case of Wharton Jones vs. John Van Zandt* (Cincinnati: R. P. Donogh & Co., 1847), 93.

152. William O. Douglas, *Mr. Lincoln and the Negro* (New York: Atheneum, 1963), 23. See Carl Adams, "Lincoln's First Freed Slave: A Review of Bailey v. Cromwell, 1841," *Journal of the Illinois State Historical Society* 101 3/4 (Fall–Winter 2008): 235–59.

153. The closeness between Lincoln and Florville comes through in letters such as one Lincoln sent to the attorney M. W. Packard in which Lincoln said, "*William Florville*, a colored barber here, owns four lots in Bloomington, on which I have been paying the taxes for him several years." Saying that he neglected to pay Florville's most recent tax, Lincoln asked Packard to "pay all taxes due, and send me the receipt, or receipts" (CW 3: 518). Florville deeply appreciated Lincoln's help. During the Civil War he wrote the president, expressing "an irrisisteble feeling of gratitude for the kind regards Shown, and the manifest good wishis exhibited towards me" by Lincoln, whom Florville hailed as "the truly great Man [who] regards with corresponding favor the poor, and down troden of the Nation, to those more favored in Color, position, and Franchise rights" (William Florville to Abraham Lincoln, Sunday, December 27, 1863; ALP).

154. *In Re Bryant et al.* (1847), LPAL, case file #L00714.

155. Quoted in Jesse W. Weik, "Lincoln and the Matson Negroes," *Arena Magazine* 17 (April 1897): 755.

156. O. B. Ficklin, "A Pioneer Lawyer," *Tuscola Review*, September 7, 1922.

CHAPTER 8
ECONOMY AND POLITICS

1. For instance, in the 1840 presidential race, which pitted the Whig William Henry Harrison against the Democrat Martin Van Buren, the voter turnout was 80.2 percent, of which 37.5 were new voters. See Reginald Horsman, "William Henry Harrison: Virginia Gentleman in the Old Northwest," *Indiana Magazine of History* 96.2 (June 2000): 125–49.
2. CW 1: 491.
3. LPAL, "A Statistical Portrait," at http://www.lawpracticeofabrahamlincoln.org /reference/reference%20html%20files/statisticalportrait.html#Common. See also A. D. Spiegel, *A. Lincoln, Esquire*, especially pp. 23–25.
4. CW 1: 163. The next quotation in this paragraph is from CW 1: 178.
5. Michael F. Holt, *The Rise and Fall of the American Whig Party: Jacksonian Politics and the Onset of the Civil War* (New York: Oxford University Press, 2003), 61.
6. William Herndon reported that "Carey's political economy" was one of the books he owned that Lincoln had looked into (HL 117). It's possible, however, that Herndon was referring to Matthew Carey's 1822 book *Essays on Political Economy*. See Robert Bray, "What Abraham Lincoln Read: An Evaluative and Annotated List," *Journal of the Abraham Lincoln Association* 28.2 (Summer 2007): 43; Stewart Winger, "Lincoln's Economics and the American Dream: A Reappraisal," *Journal of the Abraham Lincoln Association* 22.1 (Winter 2001): 50–80.
7. CW 1: 408–409.
8. See Introduction, *George Lippard, Prophet of Protest*, edited by D. S. Reynolds.
9. LGC 77.
10. *Recollected Words of Abraham Lincoln*, edited by D. E. Fehrenbacher and V. Fehrenbacher, 242.
11. HL 116.
12. Francis Wayland, *The Elements of Political Economy* (New York: Leavitt, Lord, & Co., 1837), 107.
13. CW 1: 411.
14. Lincoln declared, "It may seem strange that any men should dare to ask a just God's assistance in wringing their bread from the sweat of other men's faces; but let us judge not that we be not judged" (CW 8: 333).
15. CW 7: 368.
16. Henry C. Carey to Abraham Lincoln, June 20, 1861; ALP.
17. CW 2: 357.
18. CW 2: 383.
19. *Illinois Daily Journal* (Springfield), June 17, 1851.
20. *The Weekly Herald* (New York), October 15, 1844.
21. William Dean Howells, *A Boy's Town, Described for "Harper's Young People"* (New York: Harper & Bros., 1890), chap. 11.
22. For instance, at least 87 percent of those who voted for the Whig presidential candidate in 1840 did so again in 1844, while 95 percent of Democratic voters in 1840 remained loyal in 1844. See Sean Wilentz, "The Bombshell of 1844," in

America at the Ballot Box: Elections and Political History, edited by Gareth Davies and Julian E. Zelizer (Philadelphia: University of Pennsylvania Press, 2015), 54.

23. CW 1: 185.
24. As Sean Wilentz notes, in 1840 "a rising group of new school Whig managers crush[ed] the Democrats with their Log Cabin campaign, which carried party organization to the county, township, and ward level throughout the country" (S. Wilentz, "The Bombshell of 1844," in *America at the Ballot Box*, edited by G. Davies and J. E. Zelizer, 37).
25. CW 1: 205.
26. CW 1: 180.
27. J. Grinspan, *The Virgin Vote*, 88.
28. W. D. Howells, *A Boy's Town*, 127–28.
29. CW 1: 320.
30. CW 1: 491.
31. CW 1: 497, 499.
32. CW 1: 491.
33. CW 2: 130.
34. Studies of antislavery politics include Richard H. Sewell, *Ballots for Freedom: Antislavery Politics in the United States, 1837–1860* (New York: Oxford University Press, 1976); Reinhard O. Johnson, *The Liberty Party, 1840–1848: Antislavery Third-Party Politics in the United States* (Baton Rouge: Louisiana State University Press, 2009); and Corey M. Brooks, *Liberty Power: Antislavery Third Parties and the Transformation of American Politics* (Chicago: University of Chicago Press, 2016). Also useful are earlier studies such as Dwight L. Dumond, *Antislavery Origins of the Civil War in the United States* (Ann Arbor: University of Michigan Press, 1939) and Dwight L. Dumond, *Antislavery: The Crusade for Freedom in America* (Ann Arbor: University of Michigan Press, 1961).
35. CW 1: 347. His point about the Free Soil Party, cited in the next sentence, is found in CW 2: 3.
36. CW 1: 206.
37. CW 1: 210.
38. *Illinois State Register* (Springfield), July 17 and January 25, 1840.
39. *The Ohio Statesman*, March 5, 1841.
40. CW 1: 347.
41. CW 1: 315. The quotations in the next paragraph are also from this page.
42. CW 1: 307.
43. CW 1: 319. The remaining quotations in this paragraph are from CW 1: 325 and 323, successively.
44. CW 1: 382.
45. CW 1: 319.
46. CW 1: 391.
47. RAL 16. The remaining quotations in this paragraph are also from this page.
48. *History of Cook County, Illinois . . . from the Earliest Settlement to the Present Time*, vol. 1, edited by Weston Arthur Goodspeed and Daniel David Healy (Chicago: Goodspeed Historical Association, 1909), 181.
49. *Chicago Evening Journal*, July 6, 1847.

50. *Cincinnati Daily Gazette*, July 22, 1847. The quotations in the next paragraph are also from this source.

51. PW 1: 98.

52. Quoted in *History of Cook County, Illinois*, 14. The quotations by Polk's critics in the next paragraph are also from this page.

53. See James K. Polk, "Veto Message, Read to the US House of Representatives on December 15, 1847," The American Presidency Project, at http://www.presidency.ucsb.edu/ws/index.php?pid=67965.

54. Quoted in R. C. White Jr., *A. Lincoln: A Biography*, 136.

55. Quoted in *New York Herald*, July 14, 1847.

56. *Illinois Journal* (Springfield), October 28, 1847.

57. Quoted in Ruth Painter Randall, *Mary Lincoln: Biography of a Marriage* (Boston: Little, Brown and Co., 1953), 106.

58. *Speech of Henry Clay, at the Lexington Mass Meeting, 13th November, 1847: Together with the Resolutions Adopted on that Occasion* (New York: G. F. Nesbitt, 1847), 9, 12. The subsequent quotations in this paragraph are from p. 11.

59. *Daily Ohio Statesman*, February 3, 1848; D. H. Donald, *Lincoln*, 125. For the political debates over the Mexican War, see especially Amy S. Greenberg, *A Wicked War: Polk, Clay, Lincoln, and the 1846 U.S. Invasion of Mexico* (New York: Alfred A. Knopf, 2012).

60. C. Dickens, *American Notes* (1842; New York: Modern Library, 1996), 149, 154.

61. Scott W. Berg, *Grand Avenues: The Story of Pierre Charles L'Enfant, the French Visionary Who Designed Washington*, Part 3 (New York: Knopf Doubleday, 2009), 68. For a comprehensive discussion of the nation's capital as Lincoln knew it, see Kenneth J. Winkle, *Lincoln's Citadel: The Civil War in Washington, DC* (New York: W. W. Norton, 2014).

62. Samuel C. Busey, *Personal Reminiscences and Recollections of Forty-six Years' Membership in the Medical Society of the District of Columbia* (Washington DC: n.p., 1895), 26–27, 25. For a thorough account of Lincoln's years as a congressman, see Chris DeRose, *Congressman Lincoln: The Making of America's Greatest President* (New York: Threshold Editions, 2013).

63. RAL 218.

64. John J. Hardin to David Allen Smith, January 23, 1844, Hardin Family Papers, Chicago History Museum.

65. Elihu B. Washburne, in RAL 18.

66. For a comparative analysis of Lincoln, Adams, and other antislavery figures, see Fred Kaplan, *Lincoln and the Abolitionists: John Quincy Adams, Slavery, and the Civil War* (New York: HarperCollins, 2017).

67. *The Diary of James K. Polk During His Presidency, 1845 to 1849*, vol. 4 (Chicago: A. C. McClurg & Company, 1910), 128.

68. CW 1: 488.

69. Joanne B. Freeman, *The Field of Blood: Violence in Congress and the Road to Civil War* (New York: Farrar, Straus & Giroux, 2018).

70. Washington correspondence in *The Eagle* (Maysville, Kentucky), reprinted in the *Indiana State Journal* (Indianapolis), April 30, 1849.

71. Quoted in Michael Burlingame, *Abraham Lincoln: A Life*, Unedited Manuscript Chapters, pdf document online, chap. 8, 756, at https://www.knox.edu/about

-knox/lincoln-studies-center/burlingame-abraham-lincoln-a-life. The quotation in the next sentence is also from this page.

72. Joshua R. Giddings, *Speeches in Congress (1841–1852)* (Boston: J. P. Jewett, 1853), 213–14. The remaining quotations in this paragraph are from pp. 218 and 203, successively.

73. CW 2: 130.

74. CW 1: 421. The next quotation in this paragraph is from CW 1: 433.

75. CW 1: 439. The remaining quotations in this paragraph are from CW 1: 440 and 441, successively. The quotation in the next paragraph is from CW 1: 441–42.

76. CW 1: 508. The remaining quotations in this paragraph are also from this page.

77. CW 1: 509. The remaining quotations in this paragraph are from CW 1: 510 and 516, successively.

78. *Baltimore American*, copied in the *Illinois State Journal* (Springfield), August 13, 1848.

79. Benjamin Perley Poore, in RAL, 221.

80. CW 1: 505.

81. Quoted in J. J. Duff, *A. Lincoln, Prairie Lawyer*, 74.

82. A. T. Bledsoe, "Lamon's Life of Lincoln," *The Southern Review* 12–14 (April 1873): 364.

83. *The Lincoln Memorial: Album-immortelles*, edited by Osborn Hamiline Oldroyd (New York: G. W. Carleton & Company, 1882), 241.

84. HI 186.

85. CW 1: 448.

86. CW 1: 439.

87. *Speech of Mr. Stephens, of Georgia, on the War and Taxation* (Washington, DC: J. & G. S. Gideon, 1848), 7. The next quotation in this paragraph is from p. 14. The quotations in the next paragraph are from pp. 3, 14, 15, and 13, successively.

88. Richard Malcolm Johnston and William Hand Browne, *Life of Alexander H. Stephens* (Philadelphia: J. B. Lippincott & Co., 1883), 237. The remaining quotations in this paragraph are from pp. 237, 247, 248, and 243, successively.

89. LGC 79, 347.

90. PW 2: 535.

91. CW 1: 505.

92. *Speech of Mr. W. W. Wick, of Indiana, on the Privilege of Members and the Subject of Slavery: Delivered in the House of Representatives, April 25, 1848* (Washington, DC: Towers, 1848), 14. The remaining quotations in this paragraph are on pp. 14–15.

93. CW 1: 465. The next two quotations in this paragraph are from CW 1: 465 and 466, successively.

94. CW 1: 478.

95. CW 2: 3. The next quotation in this paragraph is from CW 2: 5.

96. *Boston Daily Advertiser*, September 14, 1848; *Taunton Gazette*, September 23, 1848; HI 690.

97. Arthur P. Rugg, *Abraham Lincoln in Worcester* (Worcester, MA: Belisle, 1914), 6.

98. CW 2: 7.

99. CW 2: 6.

100. Account taken from *Bristol County Democrat*, September 29, 1848; CW 2: 6–9.

101. HW 2: 297.
102. CW 2: 10–11.
103. CW 2: 32.
104. CW 2: 51.
105. CW 2: 66.
106. Nathaniel G. Wilcox recollection, Abraham Lincoln Papers, University of Chicago, Chicago. See also Nathaniel G. Wilcox to Abraham Lincoln, June 6, 1864, ALP, where Wilcox recalls Lincoln in 1849 reading to him his letter "setting forth the 'Claims of the Center' &c. &c.," and objecting to Butterfield "chiefly upon the ground of his locality in the north part of the State."
107. One of Lincoln's political associates noted that there was "a very powerful N. York, & Yankee influence" behind Butterfield, whose supporters, another associate wrote, were a "Yankee clique." See William H. Henderson to Abraham Lincoln, Sunday, May 13, 1849, ALP; Josiah M. Lucas to Anson G. Henry, May 22, 1849, ALP.
108. CW 2: 54.

Chapter 9
Antislavery Emergence

1. CW 2: 320.
2. CW 1: 260.
3. CW 2: 320.
4. On the impact of Stowe's novel on popular attitudes toward slavery, see David S. Reynolds, *Mightier Than the Sword:* Uncle Tom's Cabin *and the Battle for America* (New York: W. W. Norton, 2011), especially chap. 3.
5. F. Douglass, *The Anti-slavery Movement: A Lecture Before the Rochester Ladies' Anti-slavery Society* (Rochester, NY: Lee, Mann, 1855), 40.
6. *The Speeches of Frederick Douglass: A Critical Edition*, edited by John R. Mc-Kivigan, Julie Husband, and Heather L. Kaufman (New Haven, CT: Yale University Press, 2018), 568. An especially perceptive study of Lincoln's antislavery constitutionalism is James Oakes's *The Crooked Path to Abolition: Abraham Lincoln and the Antislavery Constitution* (New York: W. W. Norton, 2021); my thanks to James Oakes for providing me with an advance copy of the book. Also essential are Sean Wilentz's *No Property in Man: Slavery and Antislavery at the Nation's Founding* (Cambridge, MA: Harvard University Press, 2018), William M. Wiecek's *The Sources of Antislavery Constitutionalism in America, 1760–1848* (Ithaca, NY: Cornell University Press, 1977), and James Oakes, *Freedom National: The Destruction of Slavery in the United States, 1861–1865* (New York: W. W. Norton, 2014).
7. Annie Fields, *Life and Letters of Harriet Beecher Stowe* (Boston: Houghton Mifflin, 1897), 269. According to Fields, it was Stowe's daughter Harriet, who went along with her younger brother Charles and their mother to the White House, who reported this statement by Lincoln.
8. See the June 16, 1862, entry in *The Lincoln Log: A Daily Chronology of the Life of Abraham Lincoln*. Lincoln Sesquicentennial Commission, at http://www.thelincolnlog.org/Home.aspx.
9. IM 305.

10. Letter by HBS to Eliza Lee (Cabot) Follen, December 16, 1852; E. Bruce Kirkham Collection at the Harriet Beecher Stowe Center Library, Hartford, CT.

11. James T. Hickey, "Lincolniana: Robert S. Todd Seeks a Job for His Son-in-Law, Abraham Lincoln," *Journal of the Illinois State Historical Society (1908–1984)* 72.4 (November 1979): 273–76.

12. See William H. Townsend, *Lincoln and the Bluegrass* (Lexington: University Press of Kentucky, 1989), 176–91.

13. See Marion Brunson Lucas, *A History of Blacks in Kentucky: From Slavery to Segregation, 1760–1891* (Lexington: University Press of Kentucky, 2003), 89–90; John Dean Wright, *Lexington: Heart of the Bluegrass* (Lexington: University Press of Kentucky, 1982), 76; and Randolph Hollingsworth, *Lexington, Queen of the Bluegrass* (Charleston, SC: Arcadia, 2004), 47.

14. Gertrude Pettus, "The Issues in the Kentucky Constitutional Convention 1849–1850" (MA Thesis, University of Louisville, 1941), 31. The quotation in the next sentence is also from this page.

15. Richard White, *The Republic for Which It Stands: The United States During Reconstruction and the Gilded Age, 1865–1896* (New York: Oxford University Press, 2017), 479. Although tuberculosis is usually identified as the cause of Eddie's death, other causes have been suggested, including diphtheria and medullary thyroid cancer, associated with the genetic disorder multiple endocrine neoplasia type 2B (aka MEN2b).

16. Quoted in R. P. Randall, *Mary Lincoln*, 141.

17. CW 2: 77.

18. CW 1: 465–66.

19. See Samuel P. Wheeler, "Solving a Lincoln Literary Mystery: 'Little Eddie,'" *Journal of the Abraham Lincoln Association* 33.2 (Summer 2012): 34–46.

20. On cultural attitudes toward the Good Death, see D. G. Faust, *This Republic of Suffering*, and Mark Schantz, *Awaiting the Heavenly Country: The Civil War and America's Culture of Death* (Ithaca: Cornell University Press, 2013). On Lincoln and the Good Death, see B. R. Dirck, *The Black Heavens*, chap 1.

21. E. Grey, *Sunset Gleams from the City of the Mounds* (New York: John F. Trow, 1852), 68–69.

22. Robert J. Havlik, "Abraham Lincoln and the Reverend Dr. James Smith: Lincoln's Presbyterian Experience in Springfield," *Journal of the Illinois State Historical Society* 92.3 (Autumn 1999): 222–37.

23. HI 119.

24. R. Bray, "What Abraham Lincoln Read," 70.

25. CW 2: 97.

26. Sidney Blumenthal, *Wrestling with His Angel: The Political Life of Abraham Lincoln, Vol. II, 1849–1856* (New York: Simon & Schuster, 2017), 125.

27. George M. Stroud, *A Sketch of the Laws Relating to Slavery in the Several States of the United States of America* (Philadelphia: Kimber and Sharpless, 1827), 22–23. The quotation in the previous sentence is also from these pages.

28. Matthew P. Deady to Benjamin Simpson, July 28, 1857, Matthew P. Deady Papers, Oregon Historical Society Library.

29. *National Eagle* (Claremont, NH), May 12, 1843. For Douglass's bitter accounts of the South's treatment of enslaved people as things, see David W. Blight,

Frederick Douglass, Prophet of Freedom (New York: Simon & Schuster, 2018), especially chap. 8.

30. S. P. Chase, *Reclamation of Fugitives from Service . . . in the Case of Wharton Jones vs. John Van Zandt*, 93. The quotation in the next sentence is also from this page.

31. The *Richmond Daily Dispatch*, August 25, 1852.

32. *The Democrat* (Cambridge, MD), April 29 and May 20, 1857.

33. Florine Thayer McCray, *The Life-work of the Author of* Uncle Tom's Cabin (New York: Funk & Wagnalls, 1889), 106.

34. CW 3: 18.

35. HL 95.

36. CW 2: 492.

37. R. M. Johnston and W. H. Browne, *Life of Alexander H. Stephens*, 243.

38. CW 2: 137. The next quotation in this paragraph is from CW 2: 157.

39. For a revealing account of the congressional debates that produced the Compromise of 1850, see Fergus M. Bordewich, *America's Great Debate: Henry Clay, Stephen A. Douglas, and the Compromise That Preserved the Union* (New York: Simon & Schuster, 2012).

40. CW 2: 137.

41. See "Voter Turnout in Presidential Elections: 1828–2012," *The American Presidency Project*, at http://www.presidency.ucsb.edu/data/turnout.php.

42. D. S. Reynolds, *Beneath the American Renaissance*, and D. S. Reynolds, *Walt Whitman's America*.

43. PW 2: 429.

44. CW 2: 87. The subsequent quotations in this paragraph are from CW 2: 89, as is the first quotation in the next paragraph.

45. Holman Hamilton, *Zachary Taylor: Soldier in the White House* (New York: Bobbs-Merrill, 1951), 46.

46. CW 2: 123. The quotation in the next sentence is from CW 2: 125.

47. *Speech of Henry Clay, at the Lexington Mass Meeting, 13th November, 1847* (New York: G. F. Nesbitt, 1847).

48. CW 2: 131. The subsequent quotations in this paragraph are from CW 2: 130–31.

49. T. W. Weld, *American Slavery as It Is: Testimony of a Thousand Witnesses* (New York: American Anti-slavery Society, 1839), 9.

50. George Bourne, *Slavery Illustrated in Its Effects Upon Woman and Domestic Society* (Boston: Isaac Knapp, 1837), 27.

51. W. Phillips, "The Philosophy of the Abolition Movement" (1853), *Speeches, Lectures, and Letters*, Volume 1 (Boston: Lee and Shephard, 1894), 108.

52. *The Liberator* 18 (January 21, 1848): 10.

53. D. Nelson, "Slavery a System of Licentiousness," *The Anti-Slavery Record* 2 (October 1836): 6.

54. Carol Lasser, "Voyeuristic Abolitionism: Sex, Gender, and the Transformation of Antislavery Rhetoric," *Journal of the Early Republic* 28.1 (Spring 2008): 83–114; D. S. Reynolds, *Beneath the American Renaissance*, chap. 2.

55. W. L. Garrison, "No Compromise with Slavery" (1854), in *Against Slavery: An Abolitionist Reader*, edited by Mason I. Lowance (New York: Penguin, 2000), 126.

56. W. Phillips, "The Philosophy of the Abolition Movement" (1853), *Speeches, Lectures, and Letters*, 135.

57. William Henry Seward, *The Works of William H. Seward*, vol. 1, edited by George E. Baker (New York: Redfield, 1853), 74.

58. Studies of efforts to rescue runaways and otherwise defy fugitive slave enactments include Andrew Delbanco, *The War Before the War: Fugitive Slaves and the Struggle for America's Soul from the Revolution to the Civil War* (New York: Penguin, 2018); Eric Foner, *Gateway to Freedom: The Hidden History of the Underground Railroad* (New York: W. W. Norton, 2015); Karolyn Smardz Frost, *I've Got a Home in Glory Land: A Lost Tale of the Underground Railroad* (New York: Farrar, Straus and Giroux, 2007); Fergus M. Bordewich, *Bound for Canaan: The Underground Railroad and the War for the Soul of America* (New York: Amistad, 2005); and Albert J. Von Frank, *The Trials of Anthony Burns: Freedom and Slavery in Emerson's Boston* (Cambridge, MA: Harvard University Press, 1999).

59. F. Douglass, "Literary Notices. Uncle Tom's Cabin, or Life Among the Lowly," *Frederick Douglass's Paper*, April 8, 1852.

60. *New Englander* 10 (November 1852): 590.

61. *Southern Literary Messenger* 18 (December 1852): 721; *Democratic Review*, 33 (June 1854): 301.

62. CW 4: 50. The subsequent quotations in this paragraph are from CW 2: 156.

63. R. M. Johnston and W. H. Browne, *Life of Alexander H. Stephens*, 313.

64. *Alexander H. Stephens, in Public and Private: With Letters and Speeches, Before, During, and Since the War*, edited by Alexander Hamilton (Philadelphia: National Publishing Co., 1866), 721.

65. Fanny Fielding, "The Southerner's Dream: A Christmas Story," *The Old Guard* 4 (December 1866): 740.

66. R. W. Emerson, "The Fugitive Slave Law" (1854), in *The Later Lectures of Ralph Waldo Emerson, 1843–1871*, vol. 1, edited by Ronald A. Bosco and Joel Myerson (Athens: University of Georgia Press, 2010), 342.

67. Douglas quoted in Albert Taylor Bledsoe, *An Essay on Liberty and Slavery* (Philadelphia: J. B. Lippincott & Co., 1856), 311.

68. Henry M. Flint, *Life of Stephen A. Douglas* (New York: Derby & Jackson, 1860), 44–201.

69. CW 3: 28–29.

70. Robert Henry Browne, *Abraham Lincoln and the Men of His Time* (Cincinnati, OH: Jennings & Pye, 1901), 1: 517.

71. CW 2: 268.

72. CW 2: 320.

73. "MUST RUNAWAY SLAVES BE DELIVERED BACK?" Whitman asked in his 1856 prose tract "The Eighteenth Presidency!" His answer: "They must . . . By a section of the fourth article of the Constitution" (W. Whitman, *Complete Poetry and Collected Prose*, [New York: Library of America, 1982], 1320).

74. Lerone Bennett, *Forced into Glory: Abraham Lincoln's White Dream* (Chicago: Johnson, 2000), 66. For a balanced discussion of Lincoln and racism, see Michael Lind, *What Lincoln Believed: The Values and Convictions of America's Greatest President* (New York: Doubleday, 2005).

75. *Chicago Times*, August 2, 1861, and October 2, 1858.

76. Quoted in D. W. Blight, *Frederick Douglass, Prophet of Freedom*, 273.

77. Quoted in David L. Smiley, *Lion of White Hall: The Life of Cassius M. Clay* (Madison: University of Wisconsin Press, 1962), 56. See Eugene H. Berwanger, "Negrophobia in Northern Proslavery and Antislavery Thought," *Phylon* 33.3 (3rd Qtr., 1972): 266–75.

78. *Congressional Globe*, 37th Congress, 2nd session, 944 (February 25, 1862).

79. Quoted in Kenneth M. Stampp, *The Imperiled Union: Essays on the Background of the Civil War* (New York: Oxford University Press, 1980), 109.

80. *The Independent* (New York), September 20, 1860.

81. *New-York Tribune*, February 29, 1860.

82. See M. Sinha, *The Slave's Cause*, 331.

83. *Martin R. Delany: A Documentary Reader*, edited by Robert S. Levine (Chapel Hill: University of North Carolina Press, 2003), 191. The quotation in the next sentence is from M. Sinha, *The Slave's Cause*, 578.

84. Theodore Parker, *The Effect of Slavery on the American People* (Boston: W. L. Kent & Co., 1858), 5. HW 2: 396.

85. Lincoln's longtime Illinois law associate and political supporter Jesse W. Fell reported that in the 1850s he sent Lincoln the Unitarian William Ellery Channing's *Complete Works* as well as Theodore Parker's writings, and "they were generally much admired and approved by him" (HI 579). Fell said that if Fell were to choose an author "whose views most nearly represented Mr Lincoln's on this Subject [of religion], I would say that author was Theodore Parker" (HI 580).

86. Theodore Parker to S. J. May, Theodore Parker Papers, Massachusetts Historical Society. See Michael Fellman, "Theodore Parker and the Abolitionist Role in the 1850s," *The Journal of American History* 61.3 (December 1974), 666–84. The statistics about Parker's lectures, cited later in this paragraph, are from this Fellman article, 668.

87. M. Fellman, "Theodore Parker and the Abolitionist Role in the 1850s," 668.

88. William H. Herndon to Theodore Parker, May 13, 1854; Herndon Papers, Abraham Lincoln Presidential Library, Springfield, IL.

89. *John Brown: The Making of a Revolutionary*, edited by Louis Ruchames (1969; New York: Grosset & Dunlap, 1971), 259.

90. T. Parker, *St. Bernard and Other Papers* (Boston: American Unitarian Association, 1911) 275.

91. Herndon to Theodore Parker, February 20, 1858; Herndon Papers, Abraham Lincoln Presidential Library, Springfield, IL.

92. CW 3: 399.

93. See Nicholas Guyatt, *Bind Us Apart: How the First American Liberals Invented Racial Segregation* (New York: Basic Books, 2016).

94. Richard H. Sewell, *Ballots for Freedom*, 176, 336.

95. CW 2: 222–23.

96. See D. S. Reynolds, *Beneath the American Renaissance*, especially 90–91, 120–23, 135–37.

97. An especially revealing study of this speech is Lewis E. Lehrman, *Lincoln at Peoria: The Turning Point* (Mechanicsburg, PA: Stackpole, 2008).

98. CW 2: 255–56.

99. CW 1: 272.
100. HI 648–49.
101. CW 2: 282. The quotations in the next sentence are from CW 2: 270–71.
102. CW 2: 255.
103. CW 3: 235. The remaining quotations in this paragraph are from CW 4: 182 and CW 4: 171, successively.
104. CW 2: 255.
105. Quoted in Robert Walter Johannsen, *The Frontier, the Union, and Stephen A. Douglas* (Urbana: University of Illinois Press, 1989), 86.
106. CW 3: 115.
107. *Liberty, Equality, Power: A History of the American People*, edited by John M. Murrin, Pekka Hämäläinen, Paul E. Johnson et al. (Boston: Cengage Learning, 2015), 365.
108. *Selections from the Speeches and Writings of Hon. Thomas L. Clingman, of North Carolina* (Raleigh, NC: J. Nichols, 1877), 569.
109. *The Crime Against Kansas. Speech of Hon. Charles Sumner, of Massachusetts. In the Senate of the United States, May 19, 1856* (New York: Greeley & McElrath, 1856), 3; *The Speeches of Frederick Douglass*, edited by J. R. McKivigan, J. Husband, and H. L. Kaufman, 81, 87.
110. CW 2: 255. The quotation in the next sentence is also from this page.
111. CW 4: 271 and 8: 333.
112. H. B. Stowe, *Uncle Tom's Cabin*, 6.
113. CW 2: 264.
114. Betty Wood, *Slavery in Colonial America, 1619–1776* (Lanham, MD: Rowman & Littlefield, 2005), 4.
115. CW 2: 298–99; CW 3: 362.
116. Historians have long probed the paradoxical combination of antislavery and proslavery strands in the Constitution. Some have emphasized the Founders' antislavery intentions while others have highlighted their concessions to slavery. See debates over the issue in S. Wilentz, *No Property in Man: Slavery and Antislavery at the Nation's Founding*; David Waldstreicher, *Slavery's Constitution: From Revolution to Ratification* (New York: Hill and Wang, 2009); Paul Finkelman, *Slavery and the Founders: Race and Liberty in the Age of Jefferson* (New York: Routledge, 2014); and Akhil Amar, *America's Constitution: A Biography* (New York: Random House, 2005). James Oakes points out that Lincoln's antislavery view of the Constitution had roots in antislavery politics from the nation's founding onward; see J. Oakes, "'No Such Right': The Origins of Lincoln's Rejection of the Right in Property in Slaves," in *Lincoln's America*, edited by Joseph R. Fornieri et al. (Carbondale: Southern Illinois University Press, 2008), chap. 7. See also "'No Property in Man': An Exchange. Sean Wilentz and James Oakes Reply to Nicholas Guyatt," *The New York Review of Books*, June 27, 2019.
117. *Quincy Whig*, October 11, 1852.
118. CW 2: 253. The quotations in the next sentence and in the next paragraph are from CW 2: 264.
119. CW 2: 281.
120. *Quincy Whig*, October 11, 1852.
121. CW 2: 275.
122. CW 2: 248.

CHAPTER 10
THE ISMS AND THE WOOLLY HORSE

1. *The Republican Party Going to the Right House* (New York: Currier & Ives, 1860). Library of Congress, at http://www.loc.gov/pictures/item/2003674590.
2. CW 2: 468.
3. *The Crisis* (Columbus, OH), October 22, 1862.
4. *Proceedings of the First Three Republican National Conventions of 1856, 1860 and 1864*, edited by Horace Greeley (Minneapolis, MN: C. W. Johnson, 1893), 18.
5. CW 3: 471. The quotation at the end of this paragraph is from CW 2: 385.
6. *The Plain Dealer* (Cleveland, OH), June 27, 1856.
7. Article reprinted from the *Richmond Enquirer*, in the *Daily Journal* (Wilmington, NC), July 12, 1856.
8. *Independent Democrat* (Concord, NH), October 16, 1856.
9. Phineas Taylor Barnum, *The Life of P. T. Barnum* (London: Samson Low, 1855), 350.
10. *Daily Telegraph* (Jersey City, NJ), June 20, 1856.
11. *Daily Ohio Statesman*, September 11, 1856.
12. *Campaign Democrat* (New York, NY), August 11, 1856.
13. CW 2: 370–71. The subsequent quotations in this paragraph are from CW 2: 378.
14. *Lowell Daily Citizen and News*, October 5, 1860.
15. *New York Herald*, August 30, 1860.
16. CW 2: 188.
17. LL 66.
18. LL 75, 88.
19. W. Herndon to T. Parker, October 30, 1855, Herndon Papers, Abraham Lincoln Presidential Library, Springfield, IL.
20. J. J. Duff, *A. Lincoln, Prairie Lawyer*, 108.
21. LL 97.
22. Cases in which he defended prohibition advocates include *People v. Shurtliff et al.* (1854), *McClatchy and Sits v. Roney* (1854), and *Pearl & Pearl v. Graham et al.* (1855). He represented liquor sellers in cases such as *People v. Stafford* (1837), *People v. Capps* (1837), *People v. Hinkle* (1852), *Pearl & Pearl v. Graham et al.* (1855), *People v. Matheny* (1856), *People v. Yount* (1856), and *People v. Sandusky* (1857).
23. Daniel H. Whitney to Abraham Lincoln, December 19, 1854; ALP.
24. Milton C. Sernett, review of Tyler Anbinder's *Nativism and Slavery: The Northern Know Nothings and the Politics of the 1850s*, *Church History* 63.1 (March 1994): 136.
25. D. Grimsted, *American Mobbing*, 226.
26. CW 2: 234–35.
27. CW 2: 322.
28. PW 2: 429.
29. LGC 64; *In Re Walt Whitman*, edited by Horace Traubel, Richard Maurice Bucke, and Thomas B. Harned (Philadelphia: David McKay, 1893), 19.
30. W. Whitman, *Complete Poetry and Collected Prose*, 1308.
31. CW 2: 316.

32. *Transactions of the McLean County Historical Society, Bloomington, Illinois* (Bloomington: Pantagraph, 1856), 90. The quotation in the next sentence is from p. 161. See Bruce Levine, "'The Vital Element of the Republican Party': Antislavery, Nativism, and Lincoln," in *Abraham Lincoln and Liberal Democracy*, edited by Nicholas Buccola (Lawrence : University Press of Kansas, 2016), 139–63.

33. CW 2: 373.

34. CW 3: 380.

35. Leonard Dinnerstein, *Antisemitism in America* (New York: Oxford University Press, 1995), 24. The rabbi's statement about American antisemitism quoted in this paragraph is also from this page.

36. *We Called Him Rabbi Abraham: Lincoln and American Jewry, a Documentary History*, edited by Gary Phillip Zola (Carbondale: Southern Illinois University Press, 2014), 5.

37. Among the Jews who worked for his election were the Prussian-born lawyer Lewis Naphtali Dembitz, the Springfield clothing merchant Julius Hammerslough, the Missouri abolitionist Moritz Pinner, the Wisconsin journalist Marcus Otterbourg, and the New York attorney Abram J. Dittenhoefer.

38. CW 3: 517.

39. CW 4: 86.

40. CW 1: 337–38.

41. H. C. Whitney quoted in David Davis to Lincoln, July 28, 1860; ALP.

42. See *Ethnic Voters and the Election of Lincoln*, edited by Frederick C. Luebke (Lincoln: University of Nebraska Press, 1971).

43. Quoted in *We Called Him Rabbi Abraham*, edited by G. P. Zola, 20.

44. Much of the discussion of Irish Americans in this chapter is influenced by Niall O'Dowd's book *Lincoln and the Irish: The Untold Story of How the Irish Helped Abraham Lincoln Save the Union* (New York: Skyhorse Publishing, 2018).

45. CW 2: 499–500.

46. Seneca Falls Convention, "Declaration of Sentiments" (1848), in *History of Woman Suffrage*, edited by Elizabeth Cady Stanton, Susan B. Anthony, and Matilda Joslyn Gage (Rochester, NY: Charles Mann, 1889), 70.

47. Much of the information here about the Jessie cult is from *The Letters of Jessie Benton Frémont*, edited by Pamela Herr and Mary Lee Spence (Urbana: University of Illinois Press, 1993), 67. See also Steve Inskeep, *Imperfect Union: How Jessie and John Frémont Mapped the West, Invented Celebrity, and Helped Cause the Civil War* (New York: Penguin Books, 2020); Sally Denton, *Passion and Principle: John and Jessie Frémont, the Couple Whose Power, Politics, and Love Shaped Nineteenth-Century America* (New York: Bloomsbury, 2007); and John Bicknell, *Lincoln's Pathfinder: John C. Frémont and the Violent Election of 1856* (Chicago: Chicago Review Press, 2017).

48. *Frank Leslie's Weekly*, October 25, 1856.

49. *Boston Herald*, August 11, 1856. The quotation from the Pittsburgh journalist in the next sentence is also from this article.

50. Elizabeth R. Varon, *We Mean to Be Counted: White Women & Politics in Antebellum Virginia* (Chapel Hill, NC: University of North Carolina Press, 2000), 100–101.

51. Quoted in Michael D. Pierson, *Free Hearts and Free Homes: Gender and American Antislavery Politics* (Chapel Hill: University of North Carolina Press, 2003), 109.

52. Sally Denton, *John and Jessie Frémont: The Couple Whose Power, Politics, and Love Shaped Nineteenth-Century America* (New York: Bloomsbury USA, 2007), 47–48.

53. *Conversations with Lincoln*, edited by Charles M. Segal (New Brunswick, NJ: Transaction, 1961), 133.

54. *The Springfield Republican*, quoted in the *New York Herald*, October 24, 1861.

55. *Frank Leslie's Weekly*, October 25, 1856.

56. J. H. Baker, *Mary Todd Lincoln*, 181.

CHAPTER 11
THE SPRINGFIELD FAMILY

1. J. H. Baker, *Mary Todd Lincoln*, 124.

2. Horace Bushnell, *Christian Nurture* (1847; New York: Scribner, Armstrong & Co., 1876), 339.

3. HOL 111.

4. N. Brooks, *Washington in Lincoln's Time*, 281. For an overview of Lincoln's relationship to his children, see Alan Manning, *Father Lincoln: The Untold Story of Abraham Lincoln and His Boys—Robert, Eddy, Willie, and Tad* (Guilford, CT: Rowman & Littlefield, 2016).

5. Quoted in Jason Emerson, *Giant in the Shadows: The Life of Robert T. Lincoln* (Carbondale: Southern Illinois University Press, 2012), 25. The information about Robert in this paragraph and the next one is largely from this book.

6. See J. H. Baker, *Mary Todd Lincoln*, chaps. 5–6.

7. Robert Todd Lincoln to J. G. Holland, Chicago, June 6, 1865, Robert Todd Lincoln Papers, Library of Congress.

8. *Collected Works of Abraham Lincoln: Second Supplement, 1848–1865*, edited by Roy B. Basler et al. (New Brunswick, NJ: Rutgers University Press, 1990), 14.

9. HI 453.

10. JT 17. The quotation in the next sentence is from p. xv.

11. For a concise look at same-sex love among nineteenth-century women, see Carroll Smith-Rosenberg, "The Female World of Love and Ritual," *Signs: Journal of Women in Culture and Society* 1.1 (1975): 1–30.

12. JT 58–59, 56.

13. Quoted in J. H. Baker, *Mary Todd Lincoln*, 283.

14. Seneca Falls Convention, "Declaration of Sentiments" (1848), in *History of Woman Suffrage*, edited by E. C. Stanton, S. B. Anthony, and M. J. Gage, 70.

15. *Illinois State Journal,* April 24, 1858.

16. *The Ottawa Free Trader* (Ottawa, IL), August 8, 1857.

17. *The Ottawa Free Trader*, September 8, 1855.

18. CW 4: 195.

19. FC 274.

20. Katherine Todd Helm, *The True Story of Mary, Wife of Lincoln: Containing the Recollections of Mary Lincoln's Sister Emilie (Mrs. Ben Hardin Helm)* (New York: Harper & Brothers, 1928), 110–11.

21. HI 435.
22. Quoted in J. H. Baker, *Mary Todd Lincoln*, 230.
23. See John G. Sotos, "'What an Affliction': Mary Todd Lincoln's Fatal Pernicious Anemia," *Perspectives in Biology and Medicine* 58.4 (Autumn 2015): 419–43. For the diabetes diagnosis, see W. A. Evans, *Mrs. Abraham Lincoln: A Study of Her Personality and Her Influence on Lincoln* (New York: Knopf, 1932). On Mary's possibly having had both diabetes and syphilis, see Norbert Hirschhorn and Robert G. Feldman, "Mary Lincoln's Final Illness: A Medical and Historical Reappraisal," *Journal of the History of Medicine and Allied Sciences* 54.4 (October 1999): 511–42. For an overview, see Jen Christensen, "What Was Behind Mary Todd Lincoln's Bizarre Behavior?" CNN, July 6, 2016, https://www.cnn.com /2016/07/06/health/mary-todd-lincoln-pernicious-anemia/index.html.
24. For a weighing of the evidence about Mary's mental condition, see especially Jason Emerson, *The Madness of Mary Lincoln* (Carbondale: Southern Illinois University Press, 2007).
25. H. Schwartz, "Abraham Lincoln and the Marfan Syndrome," *The Journal of the American Medical Association* 187 (February 15, 1964): 473–79. For a comprehensive analysis of theories about the mental and physical health issues of Abraham Lincoln and his wife, see John G. Sotos, *The Physical Lincoln Complete* (Mt. Vernon, VA: Mt. Vernon Book Systems, 2008).
26. Robert G. Feldman and Ian A. Greaves, "Abraham Lincoln's Blue Pills: Did Our 16th President Suffer from Mercury Poisoning?" *Perspectives in Biology and Medicine* 44.3 (Summer 2001): 1315–332; HI 632.
27. See especially J. W. Shenk, *Lincoln's Melancholy.*
28. HI 474. The next quotation in this paragraph is from p. 473.
29. M. A. Burlingame, *The Inner World of Abraham Lincoln*, 291–92.
30. John A. Sylvester, quoted in Wayne Calhoun Temple, *By Square and Compasses: The Building of Lincoln's Home and Its Saga* (Bloomington, IL: Ashlar Press, 1984), 274–75.
31. HI 407.
32. Quoted in J. H. Baker, *Mary Todd Lincoln*, 107.
33. Eliza Leslie, *Miss Leslie's House Book or Manual of Domestic Economy for Town and Country* (Philadelphia: Carey & Hart, 1845), 227.
34. Quoted in J. H. Baker, *Mary Todd Lincoln*, 107. The information about servants in the next paragraph is also from this page. See also N. O'Dowd, *Lincoln and the Irish*, chap. 2.
35. See *Mary Todd Lincoln, Servants. Excerpts from Newspapers and Other Sources* (Fort Wayne, IN: Lincoln Financial Foundation Collection, 1942).
36. JT 46. The quotation in the next paragraph is also from this page.
37. Quoted in JT 145.
38. Bonnie E. Paull and Richard E. Hart, *Lincoln's Springfield Neighborhood* (Charleston, SC: The History Press, 2015), 74.
39. Much of the information about Johnson in this paragraph is from Richard E. Hart, *The Early African-American Population of Springfield, Illinois (1818–1861)*, Spring Creek Series (Springfield, IL: n.p., 2008), 169.
40. CW 4: 275, 288.

41. For Florville and his relationship to Lincoln, see especially Brian Dolinar, *The Negro in Illinois: The WPA Papers* (Urbana: University of Illinois Press, 2013), 37–39. The quotations in this paragraph, except for the final one, are from these pages.
42. The cases discussed in this paragraph include *Florville v. Stockdale et al.* (1849), *Florville v. Allin et al.* (1853), and *Lincoln Paid Taxes as Agent for Florville* (1860).
43. William Florville to Abraham Lincoln, December 27, 1863; ALP.
44. D. H. Donald, *Lincoln*, 167.
45. Benjamin Quarles, *Lincoln and the Negro* (New York: Oxford University Press, 1962), 40.
46. *Illinois State Journal*, February 18, 1858. See R. E. Hart, "Springfield's African-Americans as a Part of the Lincoln Community."
47. Richard E. Hart, "Springfield's Underground Railroad, Part 2," *For the People: A Newsletter of the Abraham Lincoln Association* 8.2 (Summer 2006). The quotations in this paragraph are from this source.
48. B. E. Paull and R. E. Hart, *Lincoln's Springfield Neighborhood*, 95–96.
49. *The Liberator*, June 22, 1860.
50. CW 2: 320.
51. The cases discussed in this paragraph include *Ex Parte Warman* (1845), *People v. Pond* (1845), *People v. Scott* (1847), *People v. Kern* (1847), and *McElroy v. Clements* (1857). For a discussion of Lincoln's fugitive slave cases, see especially R. L. Miller, *Lincoln and His World*, 3: 89, 151.
52. *Illinois State Journal*, August 1, 1857.
53. CW 2: 404.
54. See Thomas D. Morris, *Free Men All: The Personal Liberty Laws of the North, 1780–1861* (Union, NJ: The Lawbook Exchange, 2001), chap. 1.
55. B. Dolinar, *The Negro in Illinois*, 22.
56. CW 4: 492.
57. Zebina Eastman to Abraham Lincoln, December 6, 1864; ALP.
58. The case was *Thomas v. Wright* (1846).
59. "Two Old Letters," *Journal of the Illinois State Historical Society* 2.4 (January 1910): 46; CW 4: 134.
60. CW 7: 366.
61. CW 2: 288.
62. W. L. King, *Lincoln's Manager: David Davis*, 112–13; CW 3: 347; S. Blumenthal, *All the Powers of Earth: The Political Life of Abraham Lincoln, Vol III: 1856–1860* (New York: Simon & Schuster, 2019), 199–204.
63. Owen Lovejoy, *His Brother's Blood: Speeches and Writings, 1838–64* (2004), edited by William Frederick Moore and Jane Ann Moore (Urbana: University of Illinois Press, 2004), 178.
64. CW 7: 366.
65. One of the most convincing rebuttals of this claim about Lincoln's alleged racism is James Oakes's *The Radical and the Republican: Frederick Douglass, Abraham Lincoln, and the Triumph of Antislavery Politics* (New York: W. W. Norton, 2007).
66. CW 4: 264.
67. The statistics in this paragraph are from P. M. Angle, *"Here I Have Lived,"* 165.
68. CW 4: 121.

69. *The Collected Works of Abraham Lincoln: Supplement 1832–1865*, edited by Roy P. Basler (Westport, CT: Greenwood Press, 1974), 19.
70. CW 3: 478–79. The next quotation in this paragraph is from CW 4: 24–25.
71. CW 2: 437.
72. The information about Springfield in this and the next two paragraphs is from P. M. Angle, *"Here I Have Lived,"* chaps. 8 and 9.
73. See Erika Holst, "When Springfield Got Gas," *Illinois Times* (Springfield, IL), January 9, 2014.
74. CW 2: 483.
75. Quoted in the *Illinois State Journal*, October 29, 1856. The quotation in the next sentence is also from this source.
76. F. Douglass, "The Slavery Party" (speech in New York City, May 1853), in *My Bondage and My Freedom* (New York: Miller, Orton & Mulligan, 1855), 453.
77. See M. Sinha, *The Slave's Cause*, chap. 10.

CHAPTER 12
THE HOUSE DIVIDED AND THE LINCOLN-DOUGLAS DEBATES

1. Horace Traubel, *With Walt Whitman in Camden*, vol. 1 (New York: Rowman & Littlefield, 1905), 223.
2. O. Lovejoy, *His Brother's Blood: Speeches and Writings, 1838–64*, edited by W. F. Moore and J. A. Moore, 282.
3. See Carrie Prudence Kofoid, "Puritan Influences in Illinois Previous to 1860" (MA thesis, University of Illinois, 1903).
4. Sydney E. Ahlstrom, *A Religious History of the American People* (1972; New Haven, CT: Yale University Press, 2004), 129.
5. *New York Times*, December 21, 1860.
6. *National Anti-Slavery Standard*, June 17, 1854.
7. Ritchie Devon Watson Jr., *Normans and Saxons: Southern Race Mythology and the Intellectual History of the American Civil War* (Baton Rouge: Louisiana State University Press, 2008), 125.
8. JMN 14: 93.
9. *The Collected Works of Ralph Waldo Emerson* vol. 8, *English Traits*, edited by A. R. Ferguson, J. Slater, and J. F. Carr (Cambridge, MA: Harvard University Press, 1994), 176.
10. JMN 2: 197 and 6: 53.
11. R. W. Emerson, "John Brown," in *Emerson's Antislavery Writings*, edited by Len Gougeon and Joel Myerson (New Haven, CT: Yale University Press, 1995), 123.
12. *The Fanaticism of the Democratic Party: Speech of Hon. Owen Lovejoy, of Illinois, Delivered in the House of Representatives, February 21, 1859* (Washington, DC: Buell and Blanchard 1859), 5–6.
13. Algernon Sidney, *Discourses Concerning Government* (London: n.p, 1698), 380.
14. The quotations in this and the next paragraph are from W. H. Seward, "The Pilgrims and Liberty" (1855), in *The Works of William H. Seward*, vol. 4, edited by George E. Baker (Boston: Houghton Mifflin, 1861), 189–92.
15. *The Liberator*, January 2, 1857.
16. D. W. Blight, *Frederick Douglass, Prophet of Freedom*, 316.

17. "New England and the Union. From the South," *The Liberator*, April 23, 1858. The quotations in this paragraph are from this article. For a discussion of the designs of the Southern-controlled US government to annex the West Indies during the 1850s, see Matthew Karp, *This Vast Southern Empire: Slaveholders at the Helm of American Foreign Policy* (Cambridge, MA: Harvard University Press, 2016).

18. *The Worship of the North*, cartoon (ca. 1861) by the Confederate political satirist Adalbert Johann Volck of Baltimore. See George M. Anderson, *The Work of Adalbert Johann Volck, 1828–1912, Who Chose for His Name the Anagram V. Blada, 1861–1865* (Baltimore: Schneidereith & Sons, 1970). See also Adam Arenson, "Lampooning the Union," *New York Times*, July 27, 2012.

19. The quotations in this paragraph are from the *Illinois State Journal*, December 24, 1856.

20. CW 3: 3.

21. CW 2: 288.

22. See Victor B. Howard, "The Illinois Republican Party: Part II, The Party Becomes Conservative, 1855–1856," *Journal of the Illinois State Historical Society* 64.3 (Autumn 1971): 285–311; and Reinhard H. Luthin, "Abraham Lincoln Becomes a Republican," *Political Science Quarterly* 59.3 (September 1944): 420–38.

23. CW 2: 321.

24. Walter B. Stevens, *A Reporter's Lincoln* (St. Louis: Missouri Historical Society, 1916), 35.

25. Quoted in Mitchell Snay, "Abraham Lincoln, Owen Lovejoy, and the Emergence of the Republican Party in Illinois," *Journal of the Abraham Lincoln Association* 22.1 (Winter 2001): 92.

26. William F. Moore and Jane Ann Moore, *Collaborators for Emancipation: Abraham Lincoln and Owen Lovejoy* (Urbana: University of Illinois Press, 2014), 43.

27. George Fitzhugh, *Cannibals All!, or, Slaves Without Masters*, edited by C. Vann Woodward (1857; Cambridge, MA: Harvard University Press, 1988), 103.

28. George Fitzhugh, *Sociology for the South, or the Failure of Free Society* (Richmond, VA: A. Morris, 1854), 197–98.

29. CW 2: 361.

30. CW 2: 385.

31. CW 2: 461.

32. CW 2: 391.

33. CW 2: 318.

34. This statement was preceded by the observation that "social forms so widely differing as those of domestic slavery and (attempted) universal liberty cannot long coexist in the great Republic of Christendom" (*Richmond Enquirer*, May 6, 1856). For Lincoln's references to this article, see CW 3: 205, 431, 451, and 4: 6–7, 23. On Lincoln's use of the house divided image, see especially S. Blumenthal, *All the Powers of Earth*, chap. 23.

35. Harold Holzer, Introduction to *The Lincoln-Douglas Debates: The First Complete, Unexpurgated Text*, edited by H. Holzer (New York: Fordham University Press, 2004), 20. Some of my factual information about the debates is derived from Holzer's edition.

36. Quoted in *The Lincoln-Douglas Debates of 1858*, edited by Edwin Erle Sparks (Springfield: Illinois State Historical Library, 1908), 503. See Gillian Silverman,

"'The Best Circus in Town': Embodied Theatrics in the Lincoln-Douglas Debates," *American Literary History* 21.4 (Winter 2009): 757–87; reprinted in LSW, 467–75.

37. CW 3: 14 and 118. The quotations in the next paragraph are from CW 3: 35.

38. CW 2: 344. The quotations in the next paragraph are from CW 3: 171 and 263, successively.

39. See J. Oakes, *The Radical and the Republican* and J. Stauffer, *Giants: The Parallel Lives of Frederick Douglass and Abraham Lincoln*.

40. Quoted in *The Life and Work of Susan B. Anthony: Including Public Addresses, Her Own Letters and Many from Her Contemporaries During Fifty Years*, edited by Ida Husted Harper (Indianapolis: Bowen-Merrill Company, 1899), 1: 215.

41. *Indiana State Sentinel* (Indianapolis), July 22, 1858.

42. CW 3: 483–84. The quotations in the next two sentences are from CW 3: 446 and 425, successively.

43. CW 3: 9. The quotations in the next paragraph are from CW 3: 145.

44. Quoted in J. David Hoeveler, *The Evolutionists: American Thinkers Confront Charles Darwin, 1860–1920* (Lanham, MD: Rowman & Littlefield, 2007), 57.

45. CW 3: 16.

46. H. C. Bradsby, *History of Bureau County, Illinois* (Chicago: World Publishing Co., 1885), 226.

47. Owen Lovejoy, *Human Beings Not Property: Speech of Hon. Owen Lovejoy, of Illinois; Delivered in the House of Representatives, February 17, 1858* (Washington, DC: Buell & Blanchard, 1858), 6–7.

48. CW 3: 113. The quotation in the next paragraph is from CW 3: 10.

49. CW 3: 309.

50. O. Lovejoy, *Human Beings Not Property: Speech of Hon. Owen Lovejoy*, 1.

51. Owen Lovejoy, *The Barbarism of Slavery. Speech of Hon. Owen Lovejoy, of Illinois. Delivered in the House of Representatives, April 5, 1860* (Washington, DC: Buell & Blanchard, 1858), 8.

52. CW 3: 18. The quotation in the next paragraph is from CW 3: 181.

53. *The Weekly Pioneer and Democrat* (St. Paul, MN), December 2, 1858.

54. CW 3: 27.

55. CW 4: 17. The quotations in the next two paragraphs are from CW 3: 315.

56. *Proceedings of the First Three Republican National Conventions*, 19.

57. O. Lovejoy, *His Brother's Blood*, edited by W. F. Moore and J. A. Moore, 145.

58. CW 3: 315.

59. W. L. King, *Lincoln's Manager: David Davis*, 125.

60. William H. Herndon to Theodore Parker, Springfield, October 30, 1858, Herndon-Parker Papers, University of Iowa.

61. CW 3: 329–30.

62. W 467.

63. *Cincinnati Commercial*, January 12, 1859.

64. CW 3: 339; Anson G. Henry to Abraham Lincoln, February 16, 1859; ALP.

65. RAL 441. The subsequent quotations in this paragraph are from pp. 441 and 442, successively.

66. RAL 442.

67. Quoted in Z 11.

68. RAL 440.

NOTES TO PP. 452–65

69. RAL 444. The subsequent quotations in this paragraph are from pp. 444, 445, and 440, successively.
70. The subsequent quotations in this paragraph are from CW 3: 184, 279, and 228, successively.

CHAPTER 13
BLONDIN, BARNUM, AND B'HOYS

1. CW 3: 471. The remaining quotations in this paragraph are from pp. 429–30.
2. *New York Evangelist*, August 11, 1859.
3. Harold Holzer, *Lincoln at Cooper Union: The Speech That Made Abraham Lincoln President* (New York: Simon & Schuster, 2004).
4. CW 2: 10.
5. For contemporary accounts of Blondin's Niagara crossings, see *Illinois State Journal*, July 2 and August 20, 1859; *New York Clipper*, September 10, 1859; *Vincennes Gazette*, July 23, 1859; and *The Liberator*, September 23, 1859. See also George Linnæus Banks, *Blondin: His Life and Performances* (New York: Routledge, Warne & Routledge, 1862).
6. JN 48–49.
7. FC 257–58.
8. *Vanity Fair*, June 9, 1860. See Gary L. Bunker, *From Rail-Splitter to Icon: Lincoln's Image in Illustrated Periodicals, 1860–1865* (Kent, OH: Kent State University Press, 2001), 39.
9. *Harper's Weekly* 4 (August 25, 1860), 544.
10. *The Liberator*, June 10, 1864.
11. CW 7: 243.
12. *Abraham Lincoln! And His Doctrines, Examined and Presented in a Concise Form, from His Own Speeches* (n.p., 1858); pamphlet in Houghton Library.
13. LGC 88.
14. CW 3: 384. The remaining quotations in this paragraph are from pp. 390–91.
15. Thoreau said: "Some eighteen hundred years ago Christ was crucified; this morning perchance John Brown was hung. These are two ends of a chain which I rejoice to know is not without its links." In "A Plea for Captain John Brown" (lecture given at the Concord Town Hall on October 30, 1859), H. D. Thoreau, *Cape Cod, and Miscellanies* (Boston: Houghton Mifflin, 1906), 438.
16. R. W. Emerson, "Courage" (lecture given at the Music Hall in Boston on November 8, 1859), *New-York Tribune*, November 8, 1859. For an account of the growth of the John Brown legend, see D. S. Reynolds, *John Brown, Abolitionist*, chaps. 16–18.
17. Quoted in Joseph Fort Newton, *Lincoln and Herndon* (Cedar Rapids, IA: Torch Press, 1910), 264–65.
18. Charles H. Ray to Abraham Lincoln, October 31, 1859; ALP.
19. *Republican Vindicator* (Staunton, VA), November 18, 1859.
20. *Rise and Progress of the Bloody Outbreak at Harper's Ferry* (New York: New York Democratic Vigilant Association, 1859), 16.
21. *Louisville Daily Courier*, October 24, 1859. The quotation in the next sentence, from the *New York Herald*, is also from this source.

22. *John Brown*, edited by Richard Warch and Jonathan F. Fanton (Englewood Cliffs, NJ: Prentice-Hall, 1973), 129–30.
23. *Recollected Words of Abraham Lincoln*, edited by D. E. Fehrenbacher and V. Fehrenbacher, 154.
24. William Harlan Hale, *Horace Greeley: Voice of the People* (New York: Harper and Bros, 1950), 210.
25. CW 3: 496, 502.
26. CW 3: 496.
27. See James Grant Wilson, "Recollections of Lincoln," *Putnam's Magazine* 5 (February 1909): 515; IM 318.
28. CW 3: 512.
29. HW 3: 454.
30. CW 3: 530. The quotations in the next sentence are from p. 545.
31. CW 3: 541. The quotation in the next paragraph is from p. 542.
32. H. Holzer, *Lincoln at Cooper Union*, 149–50.
33. CW 3: 555.
34. Mark W. Delahay to Abraham Lincoln, March 26, 1860; ALP.
35. *Chicago Press and Tribune*, February 27, 1860.
36. CW 3: 517.
37. William Baringer, *Lincoln's Rise to Power* (Boston: Little, Brown and Co., 1937), 182–83. See Mark A. Plummer, "Richard J. Oglesby, Lincoln's Rail-Splitter," *Journal of the Illinois State Historical Society* 80.1 (Spring 1987): 2–12; and James T. Hickey, "Oglesby's Fence Rail Dealings and the 1860 Decatur Convention," *Journal of the Illinois State Historical Society* 54.1 (Spring 1961): 5–24.
38. Wayne C. Temple, "Lincoln's Fence Rails," *Journal of the Illinois State Historical Society* 47 (1954), 26; W. Baringer, *Lincoln's Rise to Power*, 184–85.
39. HI 462–63.
40. Emerson David Fite, *The Presidential Campaign of 1860* (Port Washington, NY: Kennikat Press, 1911), 123.
41. *Proceedings of the First Three Republican National Conventions*, edited by Horace Greeley (Minneapolis, MN: Charles W. Johnson, 1893), 131.
42. CW 4: 51.
43. Memo by Kellogg Fairbank, April 7, 1926, enclosed in a letter by Janet Fairbank to Albert J. Beveridge, April 9, 1926, in Beveridge Papers, Library of Congress; quoted in J. J. Duff, *A. Lincoln, Prairie Lawyer*, 184.
44. "all the hogs": Murat Halstead, in the *Cincinnati Commercial*, May 21, 1860; "a thousand steam whistles": Leonard Swett to Josiah H. Drummond, May 27, 1860, quoted in the *Evening Express* (Portland, ME, n.d.), copied in the *New York Sun*, July 26, 1891.
45. *Missouri Democrat*, copied in the *Illinois State Journal* (Springfield), June 8, 1865.
46. *Memoirs of Gustave Koerner, 1809–1896*, edited by Thomas J. McCormack (Cedar Rapids, IA: Torch Press, 1909), 2: 93–94.
47. CW 4: 51.
48. CW 4: 75.
49. "Observations by the author Sara Jane Lippincott (aka Grace Greenwood)," in *Abraham Lincoln: Tributes from His Associates, Reminiscences of Soldiers,*

Statesmen and Citizens, edited by William Hayes Ward (New York: Thomas Y. Crowell, 1895), 111.

50. D. S. Reynolds, *Waking Giant*, 276–77.

51. See D. S. Reynolds, *Beneath the American Renaissance*, 450–52.

52. *Salem Register* (Salem, MA), June 16, 1862.

53. N. Hawthorne, from "Chiefly About War-Matters. By a Peaceable Man," in LSW 388–89.

54. Z 24 and HI 85.

55. IM 435.

56. *The Civil War Papers of George B. McClellan: Selected Correspondence, 1860–1865*, edited by Stephen W. Sears (New York: Houghton Mifflin Harcourt, 1989), 135–36.

57. HOL 155. The quotation in the next sentence is also from this page.

58. *New-York Tribune*, February 28 and March 6, 1860; *New York Herald*, February 28, 1860.

59. *The Diary of George Templeton Strong* (vol. 3, *The Civil War, 1860–1865*), edited by Allan Nevins and Milton Halsey Thomas (New York: Octagon, 1974), 188, 204.

60. *Boston Evening Transcript*, May 19, 1860.

61. Quoted in the *Salem Register* (Salem, MA), May 24, 1860. The quotation in the next sentence is from the same source.

62. *The Life, Speeches, and Public Services of Abraham Lincoln*, 11–12.

63. P. T. Barnum, *The Humbugs of the World* (New York: Carleton, 1866), xi.

64. CW 2: 247. The subsequent quotations in this paragraph are from CW 2: 355, 509, and CW 3: 18, successively.

65. *Phunny Phellow*, November 1860; see G. L. Bunker, *From Rail-Splitter to Icon*, 49.

66. *An Heir to the Throne, or The Next Republican Candidate* (New York: Currier & Ives, 1860).

67. Quoted in Roy Meredith, *Mr. Lincoln's Camera Man, Mathew B. Brady* (1946; Garden City, NY: Dover, 1974), 68.

68. *Proceedings of the First Three Republican National Conventions*, edited by H. Greeley, 149.

69. G. W. Bungay, *Hutchinson's Republican Songster, for the Campaign of 1860*, 72.

70. "Last Rail Split by Honest Old Abe," *Momus*, June 2, 1860; see G. L. Bunker, *From Rail-Splitter to Icon*, 35.

71. Julia Taft Bayne, *Tad Lincoln's Father* (Boston: Little, Brown and Co., 1931), 165.

72. JN 103.

73. HOL 49; JT 71.

74. *Wabash Express*, quoted in the *Independent Democrat* (Concord, NH), May 31, 1860.

75. Michel F. Holt, *The Political Crisis of the 1850s* (New York: W. W. Norton, 1978), 214.

76. Quoted in J. M. McPherson, *Battle Cry of Freedom: The Civil War Era* (1988; New York: Ballantine Books, 1989), 227.

77. *New York World*, n.d., copied in *The Liberator*, July 13, 1860.

78. *The Republican Party Going to the Right House* (1860).

79. G. Foster, *New-York by Gas-Light* (New York: De Witt & Davenport, 1850), 101.

80. These descriptions of Whitman are, successively, from the *New York Daily News* (February 27, 1856), the *New York Examiner* (January 19, 1882), and the *Washington Daily National Intelligencer* (February 18, 1856). Another reviewer, Charles A. Dana, similarly noted that Whitman's poems reflected "the extravagance, coarseness, and general 'loudness' of Bowery boys" ("New Publications: Leaves of Grass," *New-York Tribune*, July 23, 1855).
81. *Brooklyn Daily Eagle*, January 9, 1847.
82. CW 1: 491.
83. *Illinois Daily Journal*, June 17, 1851; *Chicago Times*, April 17, 1856.
84. *The Constitution* (Washington, DC), September 15, 1860.
85. *New-York Tribune*, reprinted in the *National Anti-Slavery Standard*, August 1853.
86. *Philadelphia Sunday Dispatch*, September 11, 1853.
87. *Young America Fremont Journal*, August 9, 1856. For an insightful discussion of the 1856 campaign, see S. Blumenthal, *All the Powers of Earth*, chap. 17.
88. *The Independent* 12 (November 15, 1860): 1.
89. CW 3: 356. The subsequent quotations in this paragraph are from CW 3: 357, 362, and 363, successively.
90. CW 2: 459, 511.
91. CW 3: 16.
92. *The Plain Dealer* (Cleveland), July 19, 1860.
93. *Abraham Lincoln: Tributes from His Associates*, edited by W. H. Ward, 183. On the Wide Awakes, see especially Adam Goodheart, *1861: The Civil War Awakening* (New York: Alfred A. Knopf, 2011), chap. 1, and LeeAnna Keith, *When It Was Grand: The Radical Republican History of the Civil War* (New York: Hill and Wang, 2020), chap. 9. Lincoln did not originate the political use of "wide awake," which had been applied, for instance, to youthful supporters of John Frémont in 1856, as in a campaign song that contained the lyrics "Providence Boys Are Wide Awake, . . . / They'll elect Fremont, there's no mistake." [*New London Daily Chronicle*, September 12, 1856]).
94. See Joshua Zeitz, *Lincoln's Boys: John Hay, John Nicolay, and the War for Lincoln's Image* (New York: Penguin, 2014).
95. LJ 4–5.
96. *Illinois State Journal*, August 9, 1860.
97. *Illinois State Journal*, August 16, 1860.
98. *Illinois State Journal*, September 15, 1860.
99. *St. Louis Democrat*, quoted in the *San Francisco Bulletin*, November 24, 1860.
100. IM 329–30.
101. IM 327. The next two quotations in this paragraph are from IM 537 and 329.
102. Report by Henry C. Bowen, editor of *The Independent*, in *Abraham Lincoln: Tributes from His Associates*, edited by W. H. Ward, 32.
103. IM 330.

CHAPTER 14
CHALLENGING SECESSION

1. J. D. B. DeBow, "Presidential Candidates and Aspirants," *DeBow's Review* 29 (July 1860): 101.

2. CW 4: 160.

3. H. Cleveland, *Alexander H. Stephens, in Public and Private*, 721.

4. Joseph R. Long, "Tinkering with the Constitution," *Yale Law Journal* 24.7 (May 1915): 579.

5. CW 4: 172, 153.

6. HI 137.

7. James G. Randall, *Mr. Lincoln*, edited by Richard N. Current (New York: Dodd, Mead, and Co., 1957), 130.

8. *Illinois State Journal*, February 9, 1861. For a lively, detailed account of Lincoln's trip east, see Ted Widmer, *Lincoln on the Verge: Thirteen Days to Washington* (New York: Simon & Schuster, 2020).

9. CW 4: 195.

10. *Albany Evening Journal*, February 15, 1861.

11. *New-York Tribune*, February 16, 1861.

12. *The Plain Dealer* (Cleveland), February 12, 1861

13. *The Daily Constitutionalist* (Augusta), February 19, 1861.

14. Richmond, Virginia, correspondent, *Charleston Mercury*, February 16, 1861.

15. *Charleston Mercury*, February 19, 1861.

16. CW 4: 211. The next quotation in this paragraph is from CW 4: 216.

17. CW 4: 204. The subsequent quotations in this paragraph are from CW 4: 243.

18. CW 4: 230.

19. CW 4: 219. The next quotation in this paragraph is from CW 4: 242.

20. JN 112.

21. CW 4: 219.

22. PW 2: 501.

23. *New York Herald*, February 21, 1861.

24. The quotations in this and the next paragraph are from CW 4: 240–41.

25. *Indiana State Guard*, March 2, 1861.

26. John G. Nicolay, *A Short Life of Abraham Lincoln: Condensed from Nicolay & Hay's Abraham Lincoln* (New York: Century Co., 1902), 533.

27. Anonymous to Lincoln, February 20, 1861, Lincoln Collection, Chicago History Museum.

28. A. G. Frick to Lincoln, February 14, 1861, Lincoln Collection, Chicago History Museum.

29. William O. Stoddard, *Inside the White House in War Times* (New York: Charles L. Webster, 1890), 33.

30. For detailed accounts of the Baltimore plot, see especially Daniel Stashower, *The Hour of Peril: The Secret Plot to Murder Lincoln before the Civil War* (New York: Minotaur, 2013) and Michael J. Kline, *The Baltimore Plot: The First Conspiracy to Assassinate Abraham Lincoln* (Yardley, PA: Westholme, 2008).

31. *Cincinnati Gazette*, n.d., copied in the *Illinois State Register*, February 25, 1861.

32. *The Weekly Vincennes Western Sun* (Indiana), March 9, 1861.

33. *Missouri Republican*, March 1, 1861.

34. *Louisville Courier*, n.d., copied in *The Weekly Vincennes Western Sun*, March 2, 1861.

35. See Daniel W. Crofts, *Lincoln and the Politics of Slavery: The Other Thirteenth Amendment and the Struggle to Save the Union* (Chapel Hill: University of North Carolina Press, 2016), chap. 6.

36. Some details from this paragraph are derived from David Zarefsky, "Philosophy and Rhetoric in Lincoln's First Inaugural Address," *Philosophy & Rhetoric* 45.2 (2012): 165–88.

37. G. Washington, *The Writings of George Washington, (vol. 13*, 1794-1798), edited by Worthington Chauncey Ford (New York: G. P. Putnam's Sons, 1892), 287, 297.

38. D. Webster, *The Webster-Hayne Debate on the Nature of the Constitution: Selected Documents* (1830; Indianapolis: Liberty Fund, 2000), 124.

39. A. Jackson, "Nullification Message" (January 16, 1833), *The Addresses and Messages of the Presidents of the United States . . . ,* (vol. 2), edited by Edwin Williams (New York: E. Walker, 1849), 817.

40. CW 4: 266.

41. CW 4: 243.

42. CW 4: 264.

43. CW 4: 264. The remaining quotations in this paragraph are from CW 4: 253.

44. CW 4: 268–69.

45. CW 4: 258. The quotation in the next paragraph is from CW 4: 259.

46. CW 4: 192. The quotation in the next paragraph is from CW 4: 260.

47. CW 4: 268.

48. CW 4: 268.

49. CW 4: 262–63. The next block quotation is from CW 4: 271.

50. *New York Illustrated News*, March 23, 1861.

51. John F. Marszalek, "The Old Army and the Seeds of Change," in *Exploring Lincoln: Great Historians Reappraise Our Greatest President*, edited by Harold Holzer, Craig L. Symonds, and Frank J. Williams (New York: Fordham University Press, 2015), 38. See also *The Oxford Companion to American Military History*, edited by John Whiteclay Chambers II (New York: Oxford University Press, 1999), 741.

52. CW 4: 291.

53. Edward Bates to Abraham Lincoln, Thursday, April 18, 1861; ALP.

54. Elizabeth Brown Pryor, *Six Encounters with Lincoln: A President Confronts Democracy and Its Demons* (New York: Penguin, 2017), 47. For a more sympathetic account of Ellsworth, see B. R. Dirck, *The Black Heavens*, chap. 4.

55. Charles A. Ingraham, "Col. Elmer E. Ellsworth, The First Hero of the Civil War," *Wisconsin Magazine of History* 1.4 (June 1918): 5. Much of the biographical information on Ellsworth in these paragraphs derives from Ingraham's piece.

56. C. A. Ingraham, "Col. Elmer E. Ellsworth," 15.

57. For pictures of Ellsworth's Zouaves performing exercises see *Frank Leslie's Weekly*, July 28, 1860.

58. IM 247.

59. HW 2: 319.

60. C. A. Ingraham, "Col. Elmer E. Ellsworth," 20.

61. *Commercial Advertiser* (New York), May 8, 1861.

62. LJ 64.

63. *Wisconsin Daily Patriot*, May 20, 1861.

64. See *Lowell Daily Citizen and News*, June 1, 1861; *Providence Evening Press*, June 1, 1861; and *New York Clipper*, June 15, 1861.

65. LJ 63.

66. C. A. Ingraham, "Col. Elmer E. Ellsworth," 22.
67. Quoted in William Howard Russell, *My Diary North and South* (Boston: T. O. H. P. Burnham, 1863), 236.
68. *Illinois State Journal*, May 29, 1861.
69. Quoted in LJ 356, note 30.
70. CW 4: 385.
71. The information in this paragraph is from J. T. Bayne, *Tad Lincoln's Father*, 38–39.
72. LJ 67.
73. *At Lincoln's Side*, edited by M. Burlingame, 10.
74. *New York Herald*, May 25, 1861.
75. *The Oxford Companion to American Military History*, edited by J. W. Chambers II, 741.
76. *Illinois State Journal*, May 28, 1861.
77. *Lowell Daily Citizen and News*, July 22, 1861.
78. *Charleston Mercury*, July 27, 1861
79. *Commercial Advertiser*, May 25, 1861.
80. "Remember Ellsworth," envelope, American Broadsides and Ephemera, Series I, no. 26698, Archive of Americana, 1861.
81. J. T. Bayne, *Tad Lincoln's Father*, 131
82. RAL 437.
83. Robert H. Newell, *The Orpheus C. Kerr Papers* (New York: Blakeman & Mason 1862), 47–49.
84. "Reminiscences by J. B. Magruder," in *Philadelphia Weekly Times*, December 28, 1878.
85. CW 4: 438.
86. Raleigh Banner, clipped in *The Liberator*, May 17, 1861. The remaining two quotations in this paragraph, clipped from the *Norfolk Day Book* and the *Richmond Dispatch*, successively, are also from this issue of *The Liberator*.
87. *The Goose Hangs High* (Boston: Horace Partridge, 1861).

CHAPTER 15
THE HIGHER LAWS OF WAR

1. John Jay Chapman, *William Lloyd Garrison* (New York: Moffat, Yard, and Co., 1913), 243. Prominent among "the Anti-slavery people of the country" were Radical Republicans in Congress and on the political fringes who contributed strongly to the fall of slavery. On this subject, see especially Fergus M. Bordewich, *Congress at War: How Republican Reformers Fought the Civil War, Defied Lincoln, Ended Slavery, and Remade America* (New York: Alfred A. Knopf, 2020) and L. Keith, *When It Was Grand*.
2. *Civil Liberties and the State: A Documentary and Reference Guide*, edited by Christopher Peter Latimer (Santa Barbara: ABC-CLIO, 2010), 89.
3. CW 4: 430. The quotations in the next two sentences are from CW 4: 450 and 430, successively.
4. CW 4: 426.
5. *Official Opinions of the Attorneys General of the United States, Advising the President and Heads of Departments in Relation to Their Official Duties* (vol.

10), edited by J. Hubley Ashton (Washington, DC: W. H. and O. W. Morrison, 1868), 90. The first quotation in the next paragraph is also from this page.

6. Harold Holzer, *Lincoln and the Power of the Press: The War for Public Opinion* (New York: Simon & Schuster, 2014), 356.

7. The quotations in this paragraph are from the *Speech of Hon. John C. Breckinridge, of Kentucky, on Executive Usurpation, July 16, 1861* (Washington, DC: Congressional Globe Office, 1861).

8. E. B. Pryor, *Six Encounters with Lincoln*, 226; Walter P. Armstrong "The Story of Anna Ella Carroll: Politician, Lawyer and Secret Agent," *American Bar Association Journal* 35.3 (March 1949): 199.

9. Lincoln quoted by the Republican Indiana congressman William Mitchell before the House of Representatives, May 13, 1862, in *Miscellaneous Documents of the House of Representatives, 44th Congress, 1st Session*, Misc. Doc. 179, Vol. 285 (Washington, DC: U.S. Government Printing Office, 1876), 33.

10. Reply to the "Speech of Hon. J. C. Breckinridge, Delivered in the U.S. Senate, June 16, 1861," in *Life and Writings of Anna Ella Carroll*, vol. 2, (Washington, DC: Judd & Detweiler, 1895), 33. The quotation in the next sentence is also from this page. The quotations in the next three paragraphs are from pp. 39–40 and 43.

11. Edward Bates to Anna Ella Carroll, September 21, 1861, in Sarah Ellen Blackwell, *A Military Genius: Life of Anna Ella Carroll, of Maryland* (Washington, DC: Judd & Detweiler, 1891), 41.

12. Mary Livermore, *Story of the War: A Woman's Narrative of Four Years' Personal Experience* (Hartford, CT: A. D. Worthington and Co., 1889), 174.

13. CW 5: 381.

14. Elizabeth Brown Pryor, *Six Encounters with Lincoln*, 238.

15. CW 6: 34.

16. Clement L. Vallandigham, *Speeches, Arguments, Addresses, and Letters of Clement L. Vallandigham* (New York: J. Walter, 1864), 101. The quotations in the next two paragraphs are from pp. 443–44 and 441, successively.

17. S. S. Cox, "Puritanism in Politics," *The Plain Dealer* (Cleveland), January 17, 1863.

18. C. L. Vallandigham, *Speeches, Arguments, Addresses*, 365.

19. A. Burnside, General Order No. 38, Ohio History Central, at http://www.ohio historycentral.org/w/General_Order_No._38.

20. John Sherman, *Recollections of Forty Years in the House, Senate, and Cabinet* (Chicago: Werner, 1895), 332.

21. *Wisconsin Daily Patriot*, May 7, 1863.

22. Frank L. Klement, *The Limits of Dissent: Clement L. Vallandigham and the Civil War* (Lexington, University Press of Kentucky, 1970), 179.

23. CW 6: 262.

24. *Life and Writings of Anna Ella Carroll*, vol. 2, 69.

25. CW 6: 267.

26. CW 6: 266.

27. These quotations are, successively, from letters to Lincoln, in ALP: Edwin D. Morgan to Lincoln, June 15, 1863; Roscoe Conkling to Lincoln, June 16, 1863; George F. Train to Lincoln, June 16, 1863; and John C. Ten Eyck to Lincoln, June 16, 1863.

28. For the *Chicago Times* incident, see especially H. Holzer, *Lincoln and the Power of the Press*, 428; on Douglas, see Stephen E. Towne, "Worse Than Vallandigham: Governor Oliver P. Morton, Lambdin P. Milligan, and the Military Arrest and Trial of Indiana State Senator Alexander J. Douglas During the Civil War," *Indiana Magazine of History* 106.1 (March 2010): 1–39.

29. Mark E. Neely Jr., *The Fate of Liberty: Abraham Lincoln and Civil Liberties* (New York: Oxford University Press, 1992), chap. 3.

30. Mark E. Neely Jr., *Lincoln and the Democrats: The Politics of Opposition in the Civil War* (New York: Cambridge University Press, 2017), 182–83.

31. Sydney Greenbie and Marjorie Barstow Greenbie, *Anna Ella Carroll and Abraham Lincoln* (Tampa, FL: University of Tampa Press, 1952), 293. The quotations in the next paragraph are from pp. 301 and 303, successively.

32. *The War of the Rebellion: A Compilation of the Official Records of the Union and Confederate Armies,* Series 1, Vol. 10 (Washington, DC: Government Printing Office, 1884), 24.

33. J. M. McPherson, *Battle Cry of Freedom*, 422.

34. Mary Boykin Miller Chesnut, *A Diary from Dixie, Electronic Edition* (Chapel Hill: Academic Affairs Library, University of North Carolina at Chapel Hill, 1997), 157–58, 161.

35. *National Intelligencer* (Washington, DC, April 12, 1865) in S. Greenbie and M. B. Greenbie, *Anna Ella Carroll and Abraham Lincoln*, 421. The quotations in the next two paragraphs are on pp. 314 and 350, successively.

36. See Kenneth P. Williams, "The Tennessee River Campaign and Anna Ella Carroll," *Indiana Magazine of History* 46.3 (September 1950): 221–48. For a concise discussion of Carroll's disputed claim to have originated the Tennessee River campaign, see *Notable American Women, 1607–1950: A Biographical Dictionary, Volume 2,* edited by Edward T. James, Janet Wilson James, and Paul S. Boyer (Cambridge, MA: Harvard University Press, 1971), 289–92.

37. In S. Greenbie and M. B. Greenbie, *Anna Ella Carroll and Abraham Lincoln*, 350.

38. *Life and Writings of Anna Ella Carroll*, vol. 2, 100.

39. Anna Ella Carroll to Abraham Lincoln, July 14, 1862; ALP.

40. The fullest discussion of military emancipation during the Civil War is J. Oakes's *Freedom National: The Destruction of Slavery in the United States, 1861–1865.*

41. Hugo Grotius, *De iure praedae commentarius (Commentary on the Law of Prize and Booty),* edited by G. L. Williams et al. (1603; Oxford: Oxford University Press, 1950), chap. 3.

42. See J. Oakes, *The Scorpion's Sting*, 61.

43. Quoted in William Lloyd Garrison, *The Abolition of Slavery: The Right of the Government Under the War Power* (Boston: R. F. Wallcut, 1862), 7. The subsequent quotations in this paragraph are from p. 5.

44. W. L. Garrison, *The Abolition of Slavery*, 4. The subsequent quotations in this paragraph are from p. 20.

45. Hiram Ketchum, *General McClellan's Peninsula Campaign: Review of the Report of the Committee on the Conduct of the War Relative to the Peninsula Campaign* (n.p.: n.p., 1864), 63.

46. Stephen W. Sears, *George B. McClellan: The Young Napoleon* (New York: Ticknor & Fields 1988), 116. The subsequent quotations in this paragraph are from pp. 128 and 117, successively.

47. *Instructions for the Government of Armies of the United States in the Field, prepared by Francis Lieber, promulgated as General Orders, No. 100 by President Lincoln, April 24, 1863* (repr., Washington, DC: Government Printing Office, 1898); The Avalon Project: Documents in Law, History, and Diplomacy, Yale Law School, at https://avalon.law.yale.edu/19th_century/lieber.asp#sec1.

48. See John Fabian Witt, *Lincoln's Code: The Laws of War in American History* (New York: Free Press, 2012). Recent discussions of Lieber's code and other restraining factors complicate the once-dominant theory that the Civil War was initially limited and later turned into total war. From the beginning of the war, extreme violence was frequently interspersed with restraint; this mixture even characterized Sherman's Georgia campaign in 1864. See Aaron Sheehan-Dean, *The Calculus of Violence: How Americans Fought the Civil War* (Cambridge, MA: Harvard University Press, 2018). For other accounts of the mixed texture of the war, see Charles Royster, *The Destructive War: William Tecumseh Sherman, Stonewall Jackson, and the Americans* (New York: Alfred A. Knopf, 1991) and *Weirding the War: Stories from the Civil War's Ragged Edges*, edited by Stephen Berry (Athens: University of Georgia Press, 2011).

49. CW 6: 346.

50. *The Life and Letters of Francis Lieber*, edited by Thomas Sergeant Perry (Boston: James R. Osgood, 1882), 138.

51. See D. S. Reynolds, *John Brown, Abolitionist*, 164–66.

52. H. D. Thoreau, "A Plea for Captain John Brown" (lecture of 1859), in H. D. Thoreau, *Cape Cod, and Miscellanies*, 412, 414.

53. James M. McPherson, *For Cause and Comrades: Why Men Fought in the Civil War* (New York: Oxford University Press, 1997). As Gary Gallagher notes, preserving the Union was also a strong motivation for Northern soldiers (G. Gallagher, *The Union War* [Cambridge, MA: Harvard University Press, 2012]). Elizabeth R. Varon argues that a widely shared motive for the Civil War was the longing for "deliverance"—that is, Northerners' desire for deliverance from the slave power, Southerners' drive for deliverance from Yankee domination, and the hope of deliverance from bondage among the South's enslaved millions (E. R. Varon, *Armies of Deliverance: A New History of the Civil War* [New York: Oxford University Press, February 13, 2019]). Peter S. Carmichael reminds us that many soldiers on both sides were driven not by ideology but by a pragmatic effort to handle the day-to-day challenges of the war (P. S. Carmichael, *The War for the Common Soldier: How Men Thought, Fought, and Survived in Civil War Armies* [Chapel Hill: University of North Carolina Press, 2018]). These challenges are portrayed with special vividness in D. G. Faust, *This Republic of Suffering*, in Michael C. C. Adams, *Living Hell: The Dark Side of the Civil War* (Baltimore: Johns Hopkins University Press, 2014), in *Weirding the War*, edited by S. Berry, in chapters on the war years in Allen C. Guelzo, *Fateful Lightning: A New History of the Civil War and Reconstruction* (New York: Oxford University Press, 2012), and in Brenda Wineapple, *Ecstatic Nation: Confidence, Crisis, and Compromise, 1848–1877* (New York: HarperCollins, 2014).

54. *New York Herald*, December 10, 1861.

55. *Charleston Mercury*, February 25, 1861.
56. "Julien," *Old Abe Lincoln and His Abolition War!* (New York: n.p., 1861); broadside at the Houghton Library, Harvard University.
57. "History of Old John Brown," *The Old Guard* 3 (July 1865), 324, 330.
58. *John Brown: The Making of a Revolutionary*, edited by L. Ruchames, 167.
59. CW 4: 482.
60. CW 6: 156.
61. Lemuel Moss, *Annals of the United States Christian Commission* (Philadelphia: J. B. Lippincott & Co., 1868), 578.
62. "Roundhead and Cavalier," *North American and United States Gazette* (Philadelphia), July 26, 1861.
63. "One Hundredth Pennsylvania, Veteran Volunteer Regiment, 'The Roundheads,'" newspaper article titled "Odd War Nicknames, Crack Regiments with High Sounding Adopted Titles, SOME WERE WON IN BATTLE." From Col. N. J. Maxwell Scrapbook, Author's Collection at http://www.100thpenn.com; *Washington Reporter*, October 10, 1861.
64. *Portsmouth Journal of Literature and Politics* (Portsmouth, NH), September 21, 1861.
65. *Memoir of Sarah Emma Edmonds*, in *Nurse and Spy in the Union Army* (Hartford, CT: W. S. Williams & Co., 1865), 278.
66. "Religion in the Army," *Hampshire Gazette* (Northampton, MA), October 8, 1861.
67. L. Moss, *Annals of the United States Christian Commission*, 283.
68. CW 6: 114.
69. *Boston Evening Transcript*, August 16, 1861. The subsequent quotations in this paragraph are also from this article.
70. *The World* (New York), August 31, 1861.
71. *Christian Mirror*, April 1, 1862.
72. George H. Stuart, *The Life of George H. Stuart, Written by Himself* (Philadelphia: J. M. Stoddard and Co., 1890), 178. The subsequent quotations in this paragraph are from pp. 353–54.
73. Bell Irvin Wiley, *The Common Soldier in the Civil War* (1951; New York: Grosset & Dunlap, 1952), 155–56.
74. B. I. Wiley, *The Common Soldier in the Civil War*, 73.
75. *Congregational Journal* (Boston, MA), November 27, 1862.
76. *The Presbyter* (Cincinnati), January 20, 1864.
77. Constitution of the Confederate States, March 11, 1861, The Avalon Project, at http://avalon.law.yale.edu/19th_century/csa_csa.asp.
78. Stephen Elliott, *Our Cause in Harmony with the Purposes of God in Christ Jesus: A Sermon* (Savannah, GA: John M. Cooper 1862), 10. The subsequent quotations in this paragraph are on pp. 22–23.
79. Mark A. Noll, "The Bible and Slavery," *Religion and the American Civil War*, edited by Randall M. Miller, Harry S. Stout, and Charles Reagan Wilson (New York: Oxford University Press, 1998), 48.
80. George C. Rable, *God's Almost Chosen Peoples: A Religious History of the American Civil War* (Chapel Hill: University of North Carolina Press, 2010), 303.
81. J. William Jones, *Christ in the Camp: or, Religion in Lee's Army* (Richmond, VA: B. F. Johnson & Co., 1887), 90.

82. *Saturday Review of Politics, Literature, Science and Art* 22 (October 20, 1866): 488–89.

83. Quoted in *The Confederate Image: Prints of the Lost Cause*, edited by Mark E. Neely Jr., Harold Holzer, and Gabor S. Boritt (Chapel Hill: University of North Carolina Press, 2000), 107; *Sacramento Weekly Union*, May 16, 1863.

84. Quoted in *The Confederate Image*, edited by M. E. Neely Jr., H. Holzer, and G. S. Boritt, 108.

85. H. Melville, "Stonewall," *The Poems of Herman Melville*, edited by Douglas Robillard (Kent, OH: Kent State University Press, 2000), 71.

86. *Washington Chronicle*, May 13, 1863.

87. CW 6: 214.

88. *The World*, copied in *The Liberator*, October 3, 1862, and in several other newspapers.

89. CW 4: 531. The next quotation in this paragraph is from CW 4: 532.

90. CW 4: 532.

91. Kenneth J. Winkle, "Mining the Compensated Emancipation Petitions," in *Civil War Washington: History, Place, and Digital Scholarship*, edited by Susan C. Lawrence (Lincoln: University of Nebraska Press, 2015), 80.

92. *New-York Tribune*, April 15, 1862.

93. "Emancipation Proclamation—First Draft," CW 5: 336–37; see also LSW 280–81.

94. Richard Hofstadter, *The American Political Tradition and Those Who Made It* (1954; New York: Alfred A. Knopf, 1962), 131.

95. "Address on Colonization to a Deputation of Negroes," CW 5: 370–75.

96. *The Liberator*, August 22, 1862. The comment at the end of this paragraph by the black New Jerseyan cited in the next sentence, whose remarks about Lincoln appeared in the *Paterson Guardian*, is also from this issue of *The Liberator*.

97. Article from the *Philadelphia Press*, reprinted in the *National Anti-Slavery Standard*, August 30, 1862.

98. CW 5: 371–72. The next Lincoln quotation in this paragraph is from CW 5: 373.

99. *Martin R. Delany: A Documentary Reader*, edited by Robert S. Levine (Chapel Hill: University of North Carolina Press, 2003), 191. The Delany quotation at the end of this paragraph is from p. 206.

100. See Victor Ullman, *Martin R. Delany: The Beginnings of Black Nationalism* (Boston: Beacon, 1971), 272–73. For a discussion of Lincoln's views on colonization from 1862 onward, and an analysis of the relevant scholarship, see Phillip W. Magness, "Benjamin Butler's Colonization Testimony Reevaluated," *Journal of the Abraham Lincoln Association*, 29.1 (Winter 2008): 1–28.

101. CW 5: 388. The quotation in the next paragraph is from p. 389.

102. *The Independent*, copied in the *National Anti-Slavery Standard*, August 30, 1862.

103. *Frank Leslie's Weekly*, September 6, 1862.

104. CW 5: 420. The block quotation at the end of the next paragraph is from CW 5: 421.

105. CW 8: 254.

106. The fullest history of the period leading up to the Emancipation Proclamation is Louis P. Masur, *Lincoln's Hundred Days: The Emancipation Proclamation and the War for the Union* (Cambridge, MA: Belknap Press, 2012).

107. R. W. Emerson, "The President's Proclamation," *Atlantic Monthly* 10 (November 1862): 638–42; in LSW 396–99.

108. Article from *The Independent* (New York), copied in the *National Anti-Slavery Standard*, October 4, 1862. The remaining quotations in this paragraph, copied from different newspapers, are also from this source.

109. Article in the *New York Herald*, copied in the *National Anti-Slavery Standard*, October 4, 1862.

110. Article from the *Journal of Commerce* (New York), copied in the *Connecticut Courant* (Hartford), September 27, 1862.

111. Article from the *New York Express*, copied in the *National Anti-Slavery Standard*, October 4, 1862.

112. *The World*, September 24, 1862.

CHAPTER 16
THE LINCOLN WHITE HOUSE

1. Quoted in Ludwig M. Deppisch, *The Health of the First Ladies: Medical Histories from Martha Washington to Michelle Obama* (Jefferson, NC: McFarland, 2014), 54. Much of the information in this paragraph is gleaned from this book.

2. Abigail Adams to John Adams, December 23, 1796, *Adams Family Papers: An Electronic Archive*, Massachusetts Historical Society, at http://www.masshist.org/digitaladams/archive.

3. Martha Washington to Fanny Bassett, October 23, 1789, *Washington's Mount Vernon*, at https://www.mountvernon.org; Martha Washington to Mercy Otis Warren, December 26, 1789, *Martha Washington: A Life*, Item #25, at http://marthawashington.us/items/show/25.

4. Quoted in J. H. Baker, *Mary Todd Lincoln*, 152.

5. See Amy S. Greenberg, *Lady First: The World of First Lady Sarah Polk* (New York: Alfred A. Knopf, 2019).

6. JT 447.

7. JT 185.

8. EK 128. The quotation in the next sentence is from 131.

9. George B. Lincoln to Gideon Welles, April 25, 1874, in "New Light on the Seward-Welles-Lincoln Controversy," *Lincoln Lore* #1718 (April 1981): 2–3.

10. EK 131.

11. *Wartime Washington: The Civil War Letters of Elizabeth Blair Lee*, edited by Virginia Jeans Laas (Urbana: University of Illinois Press, 1991), 231.

12. Henry B. Stanton, *Random Recollections* (New York: Harper & Brothers, 1887), 221.

13. EK 132. The remaining quotations in this paragraph are from EK 133–34.

14. From John Hay's diary, in *Recollected Words of Abraham Lincoln*, edited by D. E. Fehrenbacher and V. Fehrenbacher, 228.

15. Larry G. Eggleston, *Women in the Civil War: Extraordinary Stories of Soldiers, Spies, Nurses, Doctors, Crusaders, and Others* (Jefferson, NC: McFarland, 2015), 2.

16. DeAnne Blanton and Lauren Cook, *They Fought Like Demons: Women Soldiers in the American Civil War* (Baton Rouge: Louisiana State University Press, 2002), 42.

17. M. M. Ballou, *Fanny Campbell, The Female Pirate Captain* (New York: Samuel French, 1845), 12.

18. D. S. Reynolds, *Beneath the American Renaissance*, 345–51.

19. LGC 102.
20. *Springfield Republican* (Massachusetts), October 11, 1861.
21. *Springfield Republican*, October 11, 1861.
22. This article first appeared in the *Cincinnati Commercial* and was reprinted in the *New Hampshire Patriot and State Gazette* (Concord) on November 6, 1861; the *Boston Traveler* on October 15, 1861; and in several other newspapers.
23. JT 155.
24. EK 135–36.
25. Stephen Berry, *House of Abraham: Lincoln and the Todds, a Family Divided by War* (Boston: Houghton Mifflin Harcourt, 2009), 92.
26. Quoted in M. Burlingame, *The Inner World of Abraham Lincoln*, 83.
27. J. H. Baker, *Mary Todd Lincoln*, 224.
28. Quoted in S. Berry, *House of Abraham*, 174.
29. EK 124. The remaining quotations in this paragraph are from EK 124–25.
30. J. G. Nicolay, *With Lincoln in the White House: Letters, Memoranda, and Other Writings of John G. Nicolay, 1860–1865*, edited by Michael Burlingame (Carbondale: Southern Illinois University Press, 2006), 124.
31. Adam Badeau, *Grant in Peace: From Appomattox to Mount McGregor. A Personal Memoir* (Hartford, CT: S. S. Scranton & Company, 1887), 357. The next quotation in this paragraph is from p. 360.
32. W. O. Stoddard, *Inside the White House in War Times*, 49.
33. For descriptions of the White House as refurbished by Mary Lincoln, see the *New York Herald*, January 10, 1862, and J. H. Baker, *Mary Todd Lincoln*, 187–88.
34. William O. Stoddard, "White House Sketches, No. IV," *New York Citizen*, September 8, 1866.
35. *New York Herald*, January 10, 1862.
36. Quoted in M. Burlingame, *The Inner World of Abraham Lincoln*, 299.
37. *Charleston Mercury*, January 22, 1862.
38. H. D. Thoreau, *Walden*, in *A Week . . . Cape Cod*, 341. The quotation in the next sentence is from p. 342.
39. Betty Boles Ellison, *The True Mary Todd Lincoln: A Biography* (Jefferson, NC: McFarland, 2014), 139.
40. *Frank Leslie's Illustrated Newspaper*, February 22, 1862.
41. J. H. Baker, *Mary Todd Lincoln*, 196.
42. EK 101.
43. Quoted in M. Burlingame, *Abraham Lincoln: A Life*, 272. The quotation in the next sentence is also from this page.
44. Mark E. Neely Jr. and R. Gerald McMurtry, *The Insanity File: The Case of Mary Todd Lincoln* (Carbondale: Southern Illinois University Press, 1993), 15.
45. J. S. Murray, "On the Equality of the Sexes," in Sheila L. Skemp, *Judith Sargent Murray: A Brief Biography with Documents* (Boston: Bedford/St. Martin's 1998), 177.
46. "Lucy in the City," *Godey's Lady's Book*, January 1858.
47. *Auburn Daily Bulletin*, May 21, 1872.
48. JT 114.
49. See Introduction, LJ xi–xxviii; and Introduction, *An Idler: John Hay's Social and Aesthetic Commentaries for the Press During the Civil War, 1861–1865*, edited by Douglas W. Hill and Helmut Relsig (Bethesda, MD: Academica Press, 2006), 1–32.

50. *An Idler*, edited by D. W. Hill and H. Relsig, 35.

51. LJ 113.

52. *An Idler*, edited by D. W. Hill and H. Relsig, 254. The subsequent quotations in this paragraph are from pp. 262 and 386, successively.

53. See J. Zeitz, *Lincoln's Boys*, chap. 7.

54. This and some other information in this paragraph is from the Introduction to *An Idler*, edited by D. W. Hill and H. Relsig, 6.

55. *An Idler*, edited by D. W. Hill and H. Relsig, 40.

56. *The Letters of Edgar Allan Poe*, vol. 1, edited by John Ward Ostrom (New York: Gordian Press, 1966), 246.

57. "The President's Levee—Mrs. Lincoln—The Hutchinsons—The Inevitable Nat," *Hartford Daily Courant*, January 25, 1862.

58. N. P. Willis, *Home Journal*, quoted in the *New York Herald*, October 24, 1861.

59. N. P. Willis, *Home Journal*, quoted in the *Springfield Republican*, October 19, 1861; the *New York Herald*, October 24, 1861; and several other newspapers.

60. J. H. Baker, *Mary Todd Lincoln*, 231.

61. See D. S. Reynolds, *Beneath the American Renaissance*, 363–67.

62. See Michael Burlingame, "Mary Lincoln's Unethical Conduct as First Lady," in *At Lincoln's Side*, edited by M. Burlingame, Appendix 2; and Daniel Mark Epstein, *The Lincolns: Portrait of a Marriage* (New York: Ballantine, 2008), 381–82. The quotation in the next sentence, from an 1862 diary entry by Orville H. Browning, is in *At Lincoln's Side*, edited by M. Burlingame, 187.

63. William E. Barton, foreword to J. T. Bayne, *Tad Lincoln's Father*, ix. The information in this and the following two paragraphs is from Bayne's book.

64. CW 7: 320.

65. EK 197.

66. *Reminiscences of Mary Miner Hill*, 1923, Small Collection 1985, Abraham Lincoln Presidential Library, Springfield, IL.

67. J. T. Bayne, *Tad Lincoln's Father*, 32–33.

68. J. T. Bayne, *Tad Lincoln's Father*, 13.

69. EK 217–19.

70. See John M. Hutchinson, "What Was Tad Lincoln's Speech Problem?," *Journal of the Abraham Lincoln Association* 30.1 (Winter 2009): 35–51.

71. J. T. Bayne, *Tad Lincoln's Father*, 130.

72. CW 6: 255.

73. J. T. Bayne, *Tad Lincoln's Father*, 7.

74. EK 99–100.

75. RAL 176.

76. N. Brooks, "Personal Recollections of Abraham Lincoln," 228.

77. *Evening Star* (Washington), February 6, 1862.

78. EK 102.

79. EK 103.

80. J. G. Nicolay, *With Lincoln in the White House*, edited by M. Burlingame, 71.

81. *National Republican* (Washington), reprinted in the *Providence Evening Press*, February 27, 1862.

82. *Washington Sunday Morning Chronicle*, March 23, 1862, in *An Idler*, edited by D. W. Hill and H. Relsig, 45.

83. Emma Hardinge, *Modern American Spiritualism: A Twenty Years' Record of the Communion Between the Earth and the World of Spirits* (New York: n.p., 1870), 13.

84. John W. Edmonds and George T. Dexter, *Spiritualism* (New York: Partridge & Brittan, 1853), 1: 86. The account in the next sentence of multilingual mediums is also from this page.

85. Nettie Colburn Maynard, *Was Abraham Lincoln a Spiritualist?* (Philadelphia: R. C. Hartranft, 1891), 91.

86. From Joshua F. Speed to Abraham Lincoln, October 26, 1863; ALP.

87. James Joseph Fitzgerrell and Benjamin Fish, *Lincoln Was a Spiritualist* (Los Angeles: Austin, 1924), 69.

88. N. C. Maynard, *Was Abraham Lincoln a Spiritualist?*, 41.

89. N. Brooks, *Washington in Lincoln's Time*, 64–66.

90. Reuben Briggs Davenport, *The Death-blow to Spiritualism: Being the True Story of the Fox Sisters, as Revealed by Authority of Margaret Fox Kane and Catherine Fox Jencken* (New York: G. W. Dillingham, 1888), 76. See also the *New York Herald*, October 9 and 22, 1888.

91. E. Hardinge, *Modern American Spiritualism*, 33.

92. K. Helm, *The True Story of Mary, Wife of Lincoln*, 227.

93. JT 256.

94. Arthur Conan Doyle, *The History of Spiritualism*, vol. 2 (London, UK: Cassell and Co., 1925), 142.

95. See Barbara Sapinsley, *The Private War of Mrs. Packard* (New York: Paragon House, 1991).

96. See J. H. Baker, *Mary Todd Lincoln*, 335–36; M. E. Neely Jr. and R. G. McMurtry, *The Insanity File: The Case of Mary Todd Lincoln*; and J. Emerson, *The Madness of Mary Lincoln*.

97. Quoted in Mark A. Lause, *Father Abraham: Free Spirits: Spiritualism, Republicanism, and Radicalism in the Civil War Era* (Champaign: University of Illinois Press, 2016), 67.

98. *The Plain Dealer* (Cleveland), reprinted in the *Waukesha Freeman* (Wisconsin), March 12, 1861.

99. J. B. Conklin to Abraham Lincoln, December 28, 1861 (spiritual communication with Edward D. Baker); ALP.

100. *The Argus* (Burlington, IA), reprinted in several newspapers, including the *Weekly Patriot and Union* (Harrisburg, PA), May 7, 1863.

101. David Quinn, *Interior Causes of the War: The Nation Demonized, and Its President a Spirit-rapper* (New York: M. Doolady, 1863), 50. The quotations in the next paragraph are on pp. 101, 94, and 6, successively.

102. IM 230.

103. Jay Monaghan, "Was Abraham Lincoln Really a Spiritualist?" *Journal of the Illinois State Historical Society* 34.2 (June 1941): 209–32.

104. John W. Edmonds to Abraham Lincoln, June 1, 1863; ALP.

105. CW 7: 133.

106. Robert Dale Owen to Abraham Lincoln, September 17, 1862; ALP.

107. Quotations in this paragraph are from resolutions passed by the Chicago convention of spiritualists are from *The Liberator*, August 26, 1864. Not all spiritualists,

however, supported Lincoln; a spiritualist convention in early June 1864 passed resolutions written by "a concourse of departed spirits" calling for a peace candidate for the presidency (see F. Bordewich, *Congress at War*, 288).

108. *Illustrated New Age* (Philadelphia), August 19, 1864.

Chapter 17
"O Captain"

1. "in his own thought and style": R. W. Emerson, "American Civilization," *Atlantic Monthly* 9 (April 1862), 511; "O Mr. Emerson": *JMN* 15: 187. For a thoughtful discussion of Emerson's visit to the White House, see Stephen Cushman, "When Lincoln Met Emerson," *The Journal of the Civil War Era* 3.2 (June 2013): 163–179.

2. James H. Van Alen to Horace Greeley, St. Louis, December 21, 1860, Greeley Papers, New York Public Library.

3. IM 407–408.

4. HI 386.

5. R. W. Emerson, "Abraham Lincoln," *The Complete Works of Ralph Waldo Emerson: Miscellanies*, vol. 11 (Boston: Houghton Mifflin, 1904), 330–31. The next quotation in this paragraph is from p. 334.

6. PW 2: 602–604. The first two quotations in the next paragraph are also from these pages.

7. W. Whitman, *The Correspondence*, edited by Edwin Haviland Miller (New York: New York University Press, 1961), 1: 82.

8. PW 2: 428.

9. W. Whitman, "First O Songs for a Prelude," LGC 281.

10. JMN 15: 453.

11. LSW 424.

12. Doris Kearns Goodwin, *Team of Rivals: The Political Genius of Abraham Lincoln* (New York: Simon & Schuster, 2006).

13. W. H. Russell, *My Diary North and South* 43.

14. William E. Gienapp and Erica L. Gienapp, "Brief Biography of Gideon Welles," *The Civil War Diary of Gideon Welles, Lincoln's Secretary of the Navy* (Urbana: University of Illinois Press, 2014), xvii.

15. *Diary of Gideon Welles, Secretary of the Navy Under Lincoln and Johnson* (Boston: Houghton Mifflin, 1911), 2: 391.

16. See *New York Times*, February 28, March 1, 3, and 4, 1861.

17. "Reminiscences of George B. Loring," *New-York Tribune*, August 9, 1885.

18. *Philadelphia Inquirer*, March 4, 1861.

19. *Abraham Lincoln: The Observations of John G. Nicolay and John Hay*, edited by Michael Burlingame (Carbondale: Southern Illinois University Press, 2007), 27.

20. Edward Bates, *Opinion of Attorney General Bates on Citizenship* (Washington, DC: Government Printing Office, 1863), 3. The subsequent quotations in this paragraph are from pp. 8, 12, and 27, successively.

21. *Daily Missouri Republican*, January 21, 1863.

22. *The Congregationalist*, January 2, 1863.

23. "Blair," *Lincoln Lore*, No. 1708 (June 1980): 3.

24. *Speech of the Hon. Montgomery Blair (Postmaster General), on the Revolutionary Schemes of the Ultra Abolitionists, . . . Delivered at the Unconditional Union meeting, Held at Rockville, Montgomery Co., Maryland, on Saturday, October 3, 1863* (New York: D. W. Lee, 1863), 4.

25. FC 136.

26. W. H. Lamon, *Recollections of Abraham Lincoln*, edited by D. L. Teillard, 204.

27. Frederick W. Seward, *Seward at Washington as Senator and Secretary of State . . . 1846–1861* (New York: Derby and Miller, 1891), 148.

28. Henry Adams, *The Education of Henry Adams: An Autobiography* (Boston: Houghton Mifflin, 1918), 104.

29. Charles Francis Adams Jr. to Frederic Bancroft, October 11, 1911, Allan Nevins Papers, Columbia University.

30. F. W. Seward, *Seward at Washington*, 497.

31. CW 4: 316. The next quotation in this paragraph is from CW 4: 317.

32. See Eric Foner, *The Fiery Trial: Abraham Lincoln and American Slavery* (New York: W. W. Norton, 2011), 234.

33. JMN 15: 188.

34. James Grant Lincoln, "Recollections of Lincoln," *Putnam's Magazine* 5 (February 1909): 524.

35. *Abraham Lincoln by Some Men Who Knew Him*, edited by Paul M. Angle (Chicago: Americana House, 1950), 114–15.

36. John C. Waugh, *Reelecting Lincoln: The Presidential Election of 1864* (New York: Crown, 1998), 38.

37. Z 29–30.

38. *The Salmon P. Chase Papers: Correspondence, 1823–1857*, edited by John Niven (Kent, OH: Kent State University Press, 1993), xvi; Eric Foner, *Free Soil, Free Labor, Free Men: The Ideology of the Republican Party before the Civil War* (New York: Oxford University Press, 1995), 83.

39. JH 93.

40. Jane Flaherty, "'The Exhausted Condition of the Treasury' on the Eve of the Civil War," *Civil War History* 55.2 (June 2009): 33. The quotations in the next two sentences are both from p. 116. The statistic about counterfeit bills in the last sentence of this paragraph is from p. 113.

41. Wesley C. Mitchell, *A History of the Greenbacks: With Special Reference to the Economic Consequences of Their Issue* (Chicago: University of Chicago Press, 1903), 62. See also F. Bordewich, *Congress at War*, 76 ff.

42. Quoted in W. C. Mitchell, *A History of the Greenbacks*, 62.

43. CW 6: 60–61.

44. CW 8: 143.

45. Quoted in Max M. Edling, *A Hercules in the Cradle: War, Money, and the American State, 1783–1867* (Chicago: University of Chicago Press, 2014), 203.

46. Heather Cox Richardson, *The Greatest Nation of the Earth: Republican Economic Policies During the Civil War* (Cambridge, MA: Harvard University Press, 2009), 63.

47. See Mark R. Wilson, *The Business of Civil War: Military Mobilization and the State, 1861–1865* (Baltimore: Johns Hopkins University Press, 2006), 228, and J. M. McPherson, *Battle Cry of Freedom*, 447. Yearly inflation rates in the Confederacy swung wildly, varying with the South's money supply; see "Confederate

Inflation Rates (1861–1865): Confederate Inflation During the Civil War," InflationData.com, at https://inflationdata.com/articles/confederate-inflation.

48. See Sheldon D. Pollack, "The First National Income Tax, 1861–1872," *Tax Lawyer* 67.2 (Winter 2014): 1–20; and Christopher Michael Shepard, *The Civil War Income Tax and the Republican Party, 1861–1872* (New York: Algora, 2010).

49. *Wages and Earnings in the United States 1860–1890*, edited by Clarence D. Long (Princeton, NJ: Princeton University Press, 1960), 94–108.

50. US Code § 304—"Investment of Proceeds of Sale of Land or Scrip," Legal Information Institute, Cornell Law School, at https://www.law.cornell.edu/uscode/text/7/304.

51. CW 5: 526–27.

52. CW 8: 147–48.

53. Isaac Newton to Abraham Lincoln, 1862, "Annual Report of the Department of Agriculture"; ALP. The Department of Agriculture would gain cabinet status in 1889 under Grover Cleveland.

54. *Global Americans: A History of the United States*, edited by Maria Montoya et al. (Boston: Cengage Learning, 2016), 456.

55. Elizabeth Brown Pryor, for example, writes, "By almost any measure, the Lincoln administration was catastrophic for Native Americans" (E. B. Pryor, *Six Encounters with Lincoln*, 217).

56. See Peter Silver, *Our Savage Neighbors: How Indian War Transformed Early America* (New York: W. W. Norton, 2008); Richard Drinnon, *Facing West: The Metaphysics of Indian-Hating and Empire-Building* (Norman: University of Oklahoma Press, 1997); Richard Slotkin, *Regeneration Through Violence: The Mythology of the American Frontier, 1600–1860* (Middletown, CT: Wesleyan University Press, 1974); and Jill Lepore, *The Name of War: King Philip's War and the Origins of American Identity* (New York: Alfred A. Knopf, 1998). Among other studies of the conflict between Native Americans and white colonizers are, to mention a few highlights, Pekka Hämäläinen, *Comanche Empire* (New Haven, CT: Yale University Press, 2009); Roxanne Dunbar-Ortiz, *An Indigenous Peoples' History of the United States* (Boston: Beacon, 2015); Ari Kelman, *A Misplaced Massacre: Struggling Over the Memory of Sand Creek* (Cambridge, MA: Harvard University Press, 2015); Christine DeLucia, *Memory Lands: King Philips War and the Place of Violence in the Northeast* (New Haven, CT: Yale University Press, 2018); and the sections on Native Americans in Jill Lepore, *These Truths: A History of the United States* (New York: W. W. Norton, 2019).

57. E. B. Pryor, *Six Encounters with Lincoln*, 203.

58. Statement by Royal Clary, a soldier in Lincoln's company, in HI 372.

59. Statement by the Illinois lawyer John Quay Howard, in Roy P. Basler, "James Quay Howard's Notes on Lincoln," *Abraham Lincoln Quarterly* 4.8 (December 1947): 398–99.

60. Thaddeus Williams to Abraham Lincoln, November 22, 1862; ALP.

61. *New York Ledger* ad, in *The National Era*, May 13, 1858.

62. Henry Benjamin Whipple, *Lights and Shadows of a Long Episcopate* (New York: Macmillan, 1899), 137.

63. CW 5: 493.

64. CW 5: 551.

65. *The Works of Thomas Jefferson, Federal Edition* (New York and London, G.P. Putnam's Sons, 1904–5), 11: 255.

66. W. M. Thayer, *The Pioneer Boy*, 24. The subsequent quotations in this paragraph are from p. 245.

67. In 1864, Lincoln received a letter praising Thayer's book from a New Hampshire man who wrote, "I think the history of your early struggles & success is not the least of the influences by which you are distined [*sic*] to bless the world—Every boy in the land ought to read it [that is, *The Pioneer Boy*]." A. K. Merrill to Abraham Lincoln, March 19, 1864; ALP.

68. Quoted in Francis Paul Prucha, *The Great Father: The United States Government and the American Indians* (Lincoln: University of Nebraska Press, 1986), 145. Over time, however, Pope, as a commander in the West until his retirement in 1886, advocated humane treatment of the western tribes (see Richard N. Ellis, *General Pope and U.S. Indian Policy* [Albuquerque: University of New Mexico Press, 1970]).

69. Quoted in David Allen Nichols, *Lincoln and the Indians: Civil War Policy and Politics* (Champaign: University of Illinois Press, 1999), 24.

70. The quotations in this and the following three paragraphs are from CW 6: 151–52.

71. *New York Times*, April 8, 1863, quoted in Stan Hoig, *The Peace Chiefs of the Cheyennes* (Norman: University of Oklahoma Press, 1990), 74.

72. See Clifford Krainik and Michele Krainik, "Photographs of Indian Delegates in the President's 'Summer House,'" The White House Historical Association, at https://www.whitehousehistory.org/photographs-of-indian-delegates-in-the -presidents-summer-house.

73. Joshua R. Giddings to Abraham Lincoln, May 19, 1860; ALP.

74. CW 4: 51.

75. See Mark W. Summers, *The Plundering Generation: Corruption and the Crisis of the Union, 1849–61* (New York: Oxford University Press, 1997).

76. *New York Herald*, June 27, 1860, copied in the *New-York Tribune*, July 9, 1860.

77. HL 265.

78. Simon P. Hanscom quoted in Benjamin Perley Poore, "Reminiscences of the Great Northern Uprising," *Youth's Companion*, July 26, 1883, 301.

79. CW 4: 432.

80. Russell F. Weigley, "M. C. Meigs, Builder of the Capital and Lincoln's Quartermaster General. A Biography" (Diss., University of Pennsylvania, 1956), 418.

81. See George D. Morgan, printed list of vessels purchased, 1861; ALP.

82. "Purchases for the Navy," *New York Times*, January 17, 1862.

83. John Mooney, "Gideon Welles's Role in Lincoln's Cabinet," ConnecticutHistory .org, at https://connecticuthistory.org/gideon-welles-role-in-lincolns-Cabinet.

84. JN 28.

85. Fred A. Shannon, *The Organization and Administration of the Union Army, 1861–1865* (Cleveland: Arthur H. Clarke, 1928), 62; and Erwin Stanley Bradley, *Simon Cameron, Lincoln's Secretary of War: A Political Biography* (Philadelphia: University of Pennsylvania Press, 1966), 196–98.

86. CW 6: 500.

87. Elihu B. Washburne to Abraham Lincoln, October 17, 1861; ALP.

88. *Report of the Committee on Government Contracts*, March 3, 1863, House of Representatives, 37th Congress, 3rd Session, Report No. 50, 47. Van Wyck's declaration is often wrongly attributed to Lincoln.

89. F. A. Shannon, *The Organization and Administration of the Union Army*, 56.

90. *Weekly Wisconsin Patriot*, September 21, 1861.

91. *Salem Observer*, July 27, 1861.

92. H. Morford, *The Days of Shoddy. A Novel of the Great Rebellion in 1861* (Philadelphia: T. B. Peterson & Brothers, 1863), 174, 177. The quotation in the next sentence is from p. 198.

93. The *Weekly Vincennes Western Sun*, September 24, 1864.

94. *The Age* (Philadelphia), April 11, 1864.

95. Speaker at the Democratic National Convention, August 29, 1864, quoted in *The Liberator*, September 30, 1864; *New York Herald*, May 8, 1864.

96. "The Fremont Ratification Meeting," *The Liberator*, July 8, 1864. The quotation in the next sentence is from the same article.

97. M. R. Wilson, *The Business of Civil War*, 57. The information in the following sentences about the politics of employees of the Quartermaster's Department is also on p. 57. The statistics on federal spending cited at the end of this paragraph are from p. 1.

98. CW 5: 242. The information in the next paragraph is from CW 5: 241–42.

99. Harry S. Truman: *1951: Containing the Public Messages, Speeches, and Statements of the President, January 1 to December 31, 1951* (Washington, DC: Office of the Federal Register, National Archives and Records Services, 1965), 132.

100. Between 1987 and 2013, for example, the government recovered $38.9 billion under the Lincoln Law. ("U.S. Department of Justice, Fraud Statistics, Overview 2" [2013], cited in Ryan T. Andrews, "The Plausibility Standard and the False Claims Act," *George Mason Law Review* 22.5 [2015–16]: 1290). Allison Stanger discusses the Lincoln Law in her concise history *Whistleblowers: Honesty in America from Washington to Trump* (New Haven: Yale University Press, 2019), chap. 2.

101. C. H. Van Wyck, *True Democracy—History Vindicated. Speech of Hon. C. H. Van Wyck of New York. Delivered in the House of Representatives, March 7, 1860* (Washington, DC: Republican Executive Congressional Committee, 1860), 12.

102. Jacob M. Howard to Abraham Lincoln, July 8, 1863; ALP.

103. Quoted in Allan G. Bogue, *The Congressman's Civil War* (New York: Cambridge University Press, 1989), 90.

104. D. H. Donald, *Lincoln*, 554. The statement evidently first appeared in an article by James M. Scovel in *Lippincott's Monthly Magazine* in April 1898, three decades after Stevens's death. It was printed as factual in Fawn Brodie's *Thaddeus Stevens: Scourge of the South* (1959) and repeated in several books since then.

CHAPTER 18
COMMANDER IN CHIEF

1. Quoted in Jonathan M. Steplyk, *Fighting Means Killing: Civil War Soldiers and the Nature of Combat* (Lawrence: University Press of Kansas, 2018), 47.

2. Clayton R. Newell and Charles R. Shrader, *Of Duty Well and Faithfully Done: A History of the Regular Army in the Civil War* (Lincoln: University of Nebraska Press, 2011), 8–9.
3. J. M. Steplyk, *Fighting Means Killing*, 60.
4. James M. McPherson, *Tried by War: Abraham Lincoln as Commander in Chief* (New York: Penguin, 2008), 191.
5. On the price of the coffee mills, see George B. McClellan to Abraham Lincoln (copy in Lincoln's hand with endorsement by Lincoln), December 19, 1861; ALP. On the prices of the other guns, see John K. Mahon, "Civil War Infantry Assault Tactics, *Military Affairs* 25.2 (Summer 1961): 58.
6. CW 6: 560.
7. CW 6: 70.
8. HI 165.
9. David Work, *Lincoln's Political Generals* (Urbana: University of Illinois Press, 2009), chap. 2.
10. CW 5: 509–10.
11. George B. McClellan, *McClellan's Own Story* (New York: C. L. Webster, 1887), 66–67.
12. James Havelock Campbell, *McClellan: A Vindication of the Military Career of General George B. McClellan* (New York, Neale, 1916), 30.
13. *The Military Memoirs of General John Pope*, edited by Peter Cozzens and Robert I. Girardi (Chapel Hill: University of North Carolina Press, 1998), 163. The quotation in the next sentence is from p. 145.
14. JH 38–39.
15. *Diary of Gideon Welles*, 1: 113.
16. David Hochfelder, *The Telegraph in America, 1832–1920* (Baltimore: Johns Hopkins University Press, 2012), chap 1.
17. William R. Plum, *The Military Telegraph During the Civil War in the United States*, vol. 1 (Chicago: Jansen, McClurg, 1882), 45. For Lincoln's experience with military telegraphs, see David Homer Bates, *Lincoln in the Telegraph Office: Recollections of the United States Military Telegraph Corps During the Civil War* (New York: Century Co., 1907).
18. G. B. McClellan, *McClellan's Own Story*, 612.
19. CW 5: 474–75.
20. Lloyd Lewis, "Lincoln and Pinkerton," *Journal of the Illinois State Historical Society* 41.4 (December 1948): 373.
21. RAL 324.
22. *The Civil War Papers of George B. McClellan*, edited by S. W. Sears, 515, 106. The quotation in the next sentence is from p. 515.
23. *The Civil War Papers of George B. McClellan*, edited by S. W. Sears, 70.
24. "an idiot" and "an old stick": in *The Civil War Papers of George B. McClellan*, edited by S. W. Sears, 85. "Destitute of refinement": quoted in Stephen W. Sears, *George B. McClellan: The Young Napoleon* (New York: Ticknor & Fields, 1988), 59.
25. Robert Edward Lee, *Recollections and Letters of General Robert E. Lee* (New York: Doubleday, Page, 1904), 416.
26. Michael C. C. Adams, *Our Masters the Rebels: A Speculation on Union Military Failure in the East, 1861–1865* (Cambridge, MA: Harvard University Press, 1978).

27. An especially vivid account of the battle is George C. Rable, *Fredericksburg! Fredericksburg!* (Chapel Hill: University of North Carolina Press, 2011).
28. Quoted in Stephen W. Sears, *Chancellorsville* (Boston: Houghton Mifflin, 1996), 21.
29. CW 6: 78–79.
30. W. F. G. Shanks, *Personal Recollections of Distinguished Generals* (New York: Harper & Brothers, 1866), 189.
31. N. Brooks, *Washington in Lincoln's Time*, 47, 52.
32. John Bigelow, *The Campaign of Chancellorsville: A Strategic and Tactical Study* (New Haven, CT: Yale University Press, 1910), 108.
33. Gamaliel Bradford, *Union Portraits* (Boston: Houghton Mifflin, 1916), 88; *Pennsylvania at Gettysburg: Ceremonies at the Dedication of the Monuments . . .* (Harrisburg, PA: W. S. Ray, 1914), 233.
34. *Diary of Gideon Welles*, 1: 370.
35. CW 6: 327–28.
36. CW 6: 341.
37. *The War of the Rebellion*, Series 1, Volume 5 (Washington, DC: Government Printing Office, 1881), 37.
38. JH 191–92.
39. James Turner Johnson, *Just War Tradition and the Restraint of War: A Moral and Historical Inquiry* (Princeton, NJ: Princeton University Press, 1981), 284.
40. Carl von Clausewitz, *On War*, translated and edited by Michael Howard and Peter Paret (New York: Oxford University Press, 2013), 75.
41. Quoted in Ernest Nys, "Francis Lieber—His Life and His Work," *The American Journal of International Law* 5.2 (April 1911): 392. It's also notable that the definitive study of General Order No. 100, by J. F. Witt, is titled *Lincoln's Code: The Laws of War in American History*.
42. CW 5: 356.
43. Quoted in J. F. Marszalek, *Commander of All Lincoln's Armies*, 184.
44. CW 5: 98.
45. CW 5: 546.
46. CW 6: 329.
47. George T. Stevens, *Three Years in the Sixth Corps* (New York: D. Van Nostrand, 1870), 382.
48. CW 6: 249. The quotation in the next sentence is from CW 6: 273.
49. JH 62.
50. Analyses of the devastation inflicted by the war on the environment include Mark Fiege, *The Republic of Nature: An Environmental History of the United States* (Seattle: University of Washington Press, 2012), chaps. 4–5; Megan Kate Nelson, *Ruin Nation: Destruction and the American Civil War* (Athens, GA: University of Georgia Press, 2012); Jack Temple Kirby, "The American Civil War: An Environmental View," National Humanities Center, *Nature Transformed: The Environment in American History*, rev. 2001, http://nationalhumanitiescenter.org/tserve/nattrans/ntuseland/essays/amcwar.htm; Lisa M. Brady, *War upon the Land: Military Strategy and the Transformation of Southern Landscapes During the American Civil War* (Athens: University of Georgia Press, 2012), and Franny Nudelman, *John Brown's Body: Slavery, Violence, and the Culture of War* (Chapel Hill: University of North Carolina Press, 2004).

51. George B. McClellan to Abraham Lincoln, July 7, 1862; ALP.

52. For a discussion of the military strategies of annihilation and exhaustion, see J. T. Johnson, *Just War Tradition and the Restraint of War*, 281–326.

53. *The Papers of Ulysses S. Grant*, edited by John Y. Simon et al. (Carbondale: Southern Illinois University Press, 1985), 4: 218.

54. Quoted in Ron Chernow, *Grant* (New York: Penguin Press, 2017), 205.

55. CW 6: 409, 230.

56. FC 283.

57. *Memoirs of General William T. Sherman* (New York: D. Appleton & Co., 1891), 2: 157. The subsequent quotations in this paragraph are from pp. 227 and 126, successively.

58. Quoted in R. Chernow, *Grant*, 103

59. *Home Letters of General Sherman*, edited by M. A. De Wolfe Howe (New York: Charles Scribner's Sons, 1909), 229.

60. Quoted in Michael Fellman, *Citizen Sherman: A Life of William Tecumseh Sherman* (New York: Random House, 1995), 156.

61. *The War of the Rebellion*, Series 1, Volume 36, Part 1, 306.

62. *Home Letters of General Sherman*, edited by M. A. De Wolfe Howe, 319.

63. Henry Louis Gates Jr., "The Truth Behind '40 Acres and a Mule,'" *The African-Americans: Many Rivers to Cross*, at https://www.pbs.org/wnet/african-ameri cans-many-rivers-to-cross/history/the-truth-behind-40-acres-and-a-mule.

64. Eric Foner, *Reconstruction: America's Unfinished Revolution, 1863–1877* (New York: HarperCollins, 2011), 71.

65. *Sherman's Civil War: Selected Correspondence of William T. Sherman, 1860–1865*, edited by Brooks D. Simpson and Jean V. Berlin (Chapel Hill: University of North Carolina Press, 1999), 217.

66. G. Boritt, *Lincoln's Generals*, 127; *Sherman's Civil War*, edited by B. D. Simpson and J. V. Berlin, 733.

CHAPTER 19
FORGING CULTURAL UNITY

1. *At Lincoln's Side*, edited by M. Burlingame, 109.

2. Charles G. Halpine, in *Recollected Words of Abraham Lincoln*, edited by D. E. and V. Fehrenbacher, 194. The next quotation in this paragraph is also from this page.

3. *At Lincoln's Side*, edited by M. Burlingame, 109.

4. J. Hay, "Life in the White House in the Time of Lincoln," *Century Magazine* 41 (1890): 33–34.

5. *New York Evening Post*, October 21, 1865.

6. William Bender Wilson, *A Few Acts and Actors in the Tragedy of the Civil War in the United States* (Philadelphia: n.p., 1892), 109–10.

7. Josiah Gilbert Holland, *The Life of Abraham Lincoln* (Springfield, MA: Gurdon Bill, 1866); W. E. Barton, *The Soul of Abraham Lincoln* (New York: George H. Doran Company, 1920).

8. See W. H. Lamon and C. F. Black, *The Life of Abraham Lincoln*. William Herndon's arguments in several periodicals that Lincoln was a skeptic or an atheist

influenced the Lamon biography and books like John Eleazer Remsburg's *Abraham Lincoln: Was He a Christian?* (New York: The Truth Seeker Co., 1893).

9. See especially N. C. Maynard, *Was Abraham Lincoln a Spiritualist?*

10. Thoughtful studies of Lincoln's religious and philosophical views include Allen C. Guelzo, *Abraham Lincoln: Redeemer President* (Grand Rapids, MI: Wm. B. Eerdmans, 1999); William Lee Miller, *Lincoln's Virtues: An Ethical Biography* (New York: Alfred A. Knopf, 2002); Richard J. Carwardine, *Lincoln* (London: Pearson Longman, 2003); Stewart Winger, *Lincoln, Religion, and American Cultural Politics* (Dekalb: Northern Illinois University Press, 2003); Mark Noll, "Lincoln's God," *The Journal of Presbyterian History* 82.2 (Summer 2004): 77–88; M. Lind, *What Lincoln Believed*; Stephen Mansfield, *Lincoln's Battle with God: A President's Struggle with Faith and What It Meant for America* (Nashville, TN: Thomas Nelson, 2012); John Burt, *Lincoln's Tragic Pragmatism: Lincoln, Douglas, and Moral Conflict* (Cambridge, MA: Harvard University Press, 2013); Joseph R. Fornieri, *Abraham Lincoln, Philosopher Statesman* (Carbondale: Southern Illinois University Press, 2014); Ferenc Morton Szasz and Margaret Connell Szasz, *Lincoln and Religion* (Carbondale: Southern Illinois University Press, 2014); Samuel W. Calhoun and Lucas E. Morel, "Abraham Lincoln's Religion: The Case for His Ultimate Belief in a Personal, Sovereign God," *Journal of the Abraham Lincoln Association* 33.1 (Winter 2012): 38–74; and Harold K. Bush, *Continuing Bonds with the Dead: Parental Grief and Nineteenth-Century American Authors* (Tuscaloosa: University of Alabama Press, 2016), chap. 2. See also David S. Reynolds, "God Above, America Beneath: Abraham Lincoln and Religion," in *Above the American Renaissance: David S. Reynolds and the Spiritual Imagination in American Literary Studies*, edited by Harold K. Bush and Brian Yothers (Amherst: University of Massachusetts Press, 2018), 275–92.

11. *New York Evening Post*, November 1, 1864.

12. See James S. Kabala, *Church-State Relations in the Early American Republic, 1787–1846* (London: Routledge, 2015), 41.

13. Quoted in Derek H. Davis, *Religion and the Continental Congress, 1774–1789: Contributions to Original Intent* (New York: Oxford University Press, 2000), 90.

14. Quoted in Harry S. Stout, *Upon the Altar of the Nation: A Moral History of the Civil War* (New York: Penguin, 2007), 46. The quotation in the next sentence is from p. 97.

15. Ezra E. Adams, *The Temple and the Throne* (Philadelphia: H. C. Peck & T. Bliss, 1861), 9.

16. Horace Bushnell, *Reverses Needed* (Hartford, CT: L. E. Hunt, 1861), 21.

17. *Proceedings of the National Convention to Secure the Religious Amendment of the Constitution of the United States* (Philadelphia: Christian Statesman Association, 1874), 7. The next quotation in this paragraph is on p. 8.

18. Quoted in Louis Fisher and Nada Mourtada-Sabbah, "Adopting 'In God We Trust' as the U.S. National Motto," *Journal of Church & State* 44.4 (Autumn 2002): 672. The first quotation in the next paragraph is also from this page.

19. Quoted in Tyler Anbinder, *Nativism and Slavery: The Northern Know Nothings and the Politics of the 1850s* (New York: Oxford University Press, 1992), 58.

20. Quoted in L. Fisher and N. Mourtada-Sabbah, "Adopting 'In God We Trust,'" 673.

21. For accounts of "In God We Trust" displayed at Odd Fellows events, see the *Charleston Courier* (South Carolina), June 20, 1843; the *Portland Advertiser* (Maine), September 3, 1844; and the *Baltimore Sun*, September 19, 1846.
22. *New York Evening Post*, November 5, 1860.
23. *National Era*, quoted in the *Daily Cincinnati Gazette*, July 4, 1840; Osborne P. Anderson, *A Voice from Harper's Ferry* (Boston: n.p., 1861), 72.
24. FC 89.
25. CW 7: 17–23.
26. William Peters, *The Confederate Army Navy Prayer Book* (Chattanooga, TN: C. S. Printing Office, 2014), 89–90. The quotations in the next two sentences are from pp. 93–94.
27. *The War of the Rebellion*, series 4, volume 3 (Washington, DC: Government Printing Office, 1902): 1037.
28. CW 4: 482.
29. CW 6: 156.
30. CW 3: 472. The next quotation in this paragraph is also from this page.
31. CW 2: 318.
32. *Godey's Lady's Book*, January 1847.
33. *Godey's Lady's Book*, September 1856.
34. *Godey's Lady's Book*, November 1857.
35. *Godey's Lady's Book*, July 1859.
36. *Godey's Lady's Book*, February 1860.
37. *Godey's Lady's Book*, November 1861.
38. Sarah Josepha Hale to Abraham Lincoln, September 28, 1863; ALP.
39. CW 5: 185.
40. CW 6: 332.
41. CW 6: 497. The remaining quotations in this paragraph are from CW 6: 496–97.
42. S. S. Cox, "Puritanism in Politics" and C. L. Vallandigham, *Speeches, Arguments, Addresses*, 365.
43. D. Quinn, *Interior Causes of the War*.
44. *Harper's Weekly*, October 17, 1863.
45. Oliver P. Morton to Abraham Lincoln, February 9, 1863; ALP.
46. *The Farmer's Cabinet* (Amherst, NH), November 26, 1863.
47. F. F. Browne, *The Every-day Life of Abraham Lincoln*, 642–43.
48. N. Brooks, *Washington in Lincoln's Time*, 217.
49. "Christmas at the South," *New York Times*, December 25, 1867.
50. Penne L. Restad, *Christmas in America: A History* (New York: Oxford University Press, 1995), 7. The information in the next sentence is also from this source. Some of the information in my discussion of Christmas is derived from Restad and from Stephen Nissenbaum, *The Battle for Christmas* (New York: Alfred A. Knopf, 1996).
51. Quoted in P. L. Restad, *Christmas in America*, 14.
52. George Curtis, "Christmas," *Harper's New Monthly Magazine* 68 (December 1883): 6.
53. See P. L. Restad, *Christmas in America*, 38.
54. See P. L. Restad, *Christmas in America*, 37–38.
55. *Illinois Daily Journal*, December 25, 1851.

56. In England, the Christmas tree was introduced in 1800 by Queen Charlotte, the German wife of George III. Thereafter, the tree slowly became a custom in British homes. See Alison Barnes, "The First Christmas Tree," *History Today* 56.2 (December 12, 2016), at https://www.historytoday.com/archive/first-christmas-tree.

57. P. L. Restad, *Christmas in America*, 61.

58. Quoted in Albert Bigelow Paine, "'Harper's Weekly' and Thomas Nast," *Harper's Weekly* 51 (January 5, 1907): 16. The quotation in the next sentence is also from this page.

59. *New York Herald*, December 24, 1864.

60. *An Idler*, edited by D. W. Hill and H. Relsig, 247.

61. *An Idler*, edited by D. W. Hill and H. Relsig, 79.

62. CW 8: 181–82.

63. *Easton Gazette* (Maryland), December 24, 1864.

64. I've derived this information from the record of Lincoln's daily activities in *The Lincoln Log: A Daily Chronology of the Life of Abraham Lincoln*. See also Michael A. Andregg, *Lincoln and Shakespeare* (Lawrence: University Press of Kansas, 2015).

65. Information about Lincoln's attendances at performances is gleaned from *The Lincoln Log: A Daily Chronology of the Life of Abraham Lincoln*.

66. See Terry Alford, *Fortune's Fool: The Life of John Wilkes Booth* (New York: Oxford University Press, 2015), 139–40.

67. Gordon Samples, *Lust for Fame: The Stage Career of John Wilkes Booth* (Jefferson, NC: McFarland, 1982), 125.

68. See Lawrence W. Levine, *Highbrow/Lowbrow: The Emergence of Cultural Hierarchy in America* (Cambridge, MA: Harvard University Press, 2009), chap. 1.

69. *New York Herald*, November 17, 1863.

70. T. Alford, *Fortune's Fool: The Life of John Wilkes Booth*, 140. The quotation in the next sentence is also from p. 140.

71. CW 6: 392.

72. *New York Herald*, September 17, 1863.

73. *The Newark Journal*, quoted in the *Wisconsin Daily Patriot*, October 15, 1863.

74. *Southern Illustrated News*, October 31, 1863.

75. Abraham Lincoln to James H. Hackett, November 2, 1863, ALP.

76. *Evening Star* (Washington), April 8, 1864.

77. John W. Forney, *Anecdotes of Public Men* (New York: Harper & Brothers, 1881), 2: 180. See H. Holzer, *Lincoln and the Power of the Press*, 519.

78. FC 50. The remaining quotations in this paragraph and the next one are from pp. 51–52.

79. W. R. Taylor, *Cavalier and Yankee*, 226.

80. James S. Sweet, "Libraries in Lincoln's Time" (1959); unpublished typescript in files of the Lincoln Financial Foundation Collection, Allen County Public Library, Fort Wayne, IN.

81. Louis A. Warren, "A. Lincoln's Executive Mansion Library," *Antiquarian Bookman* 5 (February 11, 1950): 569–70. Much of the information in the rest of this paragraph, including statistics on book purchases, are from this article and from James B. Conroy, *Lincoln's White House: The People's House in Wartime* (Lanham, MD: Rowman & Littlefield, 2016), 38.

82. N. P. Willis, *The Poems, Sacred, Passionate, and Humorous, of Nathaniel Parker Willis* (New York: Clark and Austin, 1847), 105. The next quotation in this paragraph is from p. 108. For an account of Lincoln's recitation of the poem, see FC 115.

83. For an account of Lincoln's recitation of this poem to Orville Browning, see JN 129, n. 15.

84. O. W. Holmes, *The Poems of Oliver Wendell Holmes* (Boston: Ticknor & Fields, 1863), 61.

85. CW 8: 245.

86. John Stauffer and Benjamin Soskis, *The Battle Hymn of the Republic: A Biography of the Song That Marches On* (New York: Oxford University Press, 2013), 94.

87. H. W. Longfellow, *The Building of the Ship and Other Poems* (Boston: Houghton Mifflin, 1906), 22. See Brook Thomas, *Civic Myths: A Law-and-Literature Approach to Citizenship* (Chapel Hill: University of North Carolina Press, 2007), 92–94.

88. Noah Brooks, "Lincoln's Imagination," *Scribner's Monthly* 18 (August 1879): 585.

89. J. G. Whittier, *We Wait Beneath the Furnace Blast* (Boston: Oliver Ditson & Co., 1862).

90. Charles Carleton Coffin, *Abraham Lincoln* (New York: Harper & Brothers, 1892), 295. The next quotation in this paragraph is also from this page.

91. George F. Root, *The Battle Cry of Freedom* (Chicago: Root & Cady, 1862).

92. Kenneth A. Bernard, "Lincoln and the Music of the Civil War," *Civil War History* 43 (September 1958): 274–75.

93. W 157. The point in the next sentence about the pleasure of music is from W 156.

94. *Macon Telegraph*, April 6, 1861.

95. Dan W. Emmett, *Dixie's Land* (New York: Firth, Pond & Co., 1859).

96. *Republican Journal* (Belfast, ME), April 12, 1861. The quotation copied from the *Commercial Advertiser* in the next sentence is also from this source.

97. CW 8: 393. For insights into "Dixie," as well as an overview of other Civil War–era songs, see Jon Meacham and Tim McGraw, *Songs of America: Patriotism, Protest, and the Music That Made a Nation* (New York: Random House 2019), chaps. 3–4. See also Kenneth A. Bernard, *Lincoln and the Music of the Civil War* (Caldwell, ID: Caxton Printers, 1966).

98. Tim McNeese, *Life in the Civil War: Soldiers and Battles* (Dayton, OH: Milliken, 2003), 66.

99. Adelina Patti, in an interview in the *Montgomery Advertiser*, February 12, 1911; quoted in David Rankin Barbee, "The Musical Mr. Lincoln," *The Abraham Lincoln Quarterly* (December 1949), 437–39.

100. For documents related to this episode, see CW 7: 548–50.

101. *New York World*, September 9, 1864; CW 7: 550.

102. "The Commander-in-Chief Conciliating the Soldier's Votes on the Battle Field," Library of Congress, at http://www.loc.gov/pictures/collection/app/item/2008 661672.

103. This comment and the block quotation that follows are from W. H. Lamon, *Recollections of Abraham Lincoln*, edited by D. L. Teillard, 144–45.

104. *New York World*, September 9, 1864; CW 7: 550.

105. *Diary of George Templeton Strong*, vol. 3, edited by A. Nevins and M. H. Thomas, 281–82.

106. Z 13.

107. See Todd Nathan Thompson, *The National Joker: Abraham Lincoln and the Politics of Satire* (Carbondale: Southern Illinois University Press, 2015).

108. *Newark Daily Advertiser*, September 21, 1864.

109. *New York Herald*, reprinted in the *Columbian Register* (New Haven), February 27, 1864.

110. [Andrew Adderup], *Lincolnania; or, the Humors of Uncle Abe. A Second Joe Miller* (Springfield, IL: J. F. Feeks, 1864).

111. *Old Abe's Jokes, Fresh from Abraham's Bosom* (New York: T. R. Dawley, 1864), 35. The subsequent quotations in this paragraph are from pp. 35 and 32–33, successively.

112. *Old Abe's Jokes*, 104. The quotation in the next sentence is from p. 74.

113. *The Washington Examiner*, April 28, 1864.

114. *The Weekly Vincennes Western Sun*, April 9, 1864.

115. *An Idler*, edited by D. W. Hill and H. Relsig, 424.

116. *An Idler*, edited by D. W. Hill and H. Relsig, 434. The quotations at the end of this paragraph are also from this page.

117. Norman Wiard to Abraham Lincoln, September 3, 1864; ALP.

118. *An Idler*, edited by D. W. Hill and H. Relsig, 434.

119. *Only Authentic Life of Geo. Brinton McClellan, alias Little Mac* (New York: American News Co., 1864).

120. *Boston Evening Transcript*, September 30, 1864.

121. N. Brooks, "Personal Recollections of Abraham Lincoln," 229.

122. Walter Blair, *Essays on American Humor: Blair Through the Ages*, edited by Hamlin Hill (Madison: University of Wisconsin Press, 1993), 28.

123. *North American Review* 102 (April 1866): 589.

124. [Charles Farrar Browne], *Artemus Ward. His Book* (New York: Carleton, 1862), 185.

125. [C. F. Browne], *Artemus Ward. His Book*, 185–86.

126. Frederic Hudson, *Journalism in the United States from 1690 to 1872* (New York: Harper and Brothers, 1873), 695.

127. [C. F. Browne], *Artemus Ward. His Book*, 85.

128. *Diary of Gideon Welles*, 1: 333. The description in the next sentence of Lincoln's reaction to Kerr's story about the demanding monkey is also from this page.

129. Noah Brooks, "Personal Reminiscences of Abraham Lincoln," *Scribner's Monthly* 15 (February 1878): 563–64.

130. Robert H. Newell, *The Orpheus Kerr Papers*, Series 2 (New York: Carleton, 1862), 133.

131. CW 6: 490.

132. Charles G. Halpine, *The Life and Adventures, Songs, Services, and Speeches of Private Miles O'Reilly [pseud.] (47th Regiment, New York Volunteers)* (New York: Carleton, 1864), 53. The next quotation in this paragraph is from p. 61.

133. N. Brooks, "Personal Recollections of Abraham Lincoln," 228.

134. Samuel L. Clemens, *How to Tell a Story, and Other Essays* (New York: Harper & Brothers, 1897), 8. Clemens's response to Artemus Ward, summarized in the next two sentences, is also in *How to Tell a Story*.

135. John Quincy Reed, "Artemus Ward: A Critical Study" (PhD diss. University of Iowa, 1855), 204.

136. R. W. Emerson, "Abraham Lincoln," *The Living Age* 85 (April–June 1865): 283.

137. Robert H. Newell, *The Orpheus C. Kerr Papers*, Series 1 (New York: Blakeman & Mason, 1862), 31.

138. *Vanity Fair* 3 (January 26, 1861), 37.

139. *Vanity Fair* 4 (July 13, 1861), 15.

140. Frederic Hudson, *Journalism in the United States, from 1690–1872* (New York: Harper & Brothers, 1873), 695.

Chapter 20
Politics, Race, and the Culture Wars

1. See M. E. Neely Jr., *Lincoln and the Democrats.*

2. *Sierra Democrat*, reprinted in *The Liberator*, April 22, 1864.

3. H. Cleveland, Alexander H. Stephens, in *Public and Private*, 721.

4. E. A. Pollard, *Southern History of the War* (New York: C. B. Richardson, 1866), 202.

5. [C. H. Smith], *Bill Arp's Peace Papers* (New York: G. W. Carleton & Co., 1873), 137–38. The subsequent quotations in this paragraph are from pp. 57, 32, 30, and 105, successively.

6. W. L. Garrison, "Park Street Address," July 4, 1829, American Antiquarian Society; *The Black Abolitionist Papers*, edited by C. Peter Ripley (Chapel Hill: University of North Carolina Press, 1991): 4: 202.

7. *Washington Evening Star*, August 27, 1862.

8. Quoted in B. I. Wiley, *The Common Soldier in the Civil War*, 42.

9. *Life and Times of Frederick Douglass, Written by Himself* (Boston: De Wolfe & Fiske, 1892), 433.

10. S. S. Cox, "Puritanism and Politics." The subsequent quotations in this paragraph are also from this speech.

11. [Joseph Holt], *Report of the Judge Advocate General on "The Order of American Knights," alias "The Sons of Liberty": A Western Conspiracy in Aid of the Southern Rebellion* (Washington, DC: Chronicle Print, 1864), 5. The first quotation in the next paragraph is from p. 11.

12. *Metropolitan Record and New York Vindicator*, March 12, 1864.

13. *The Lincoln Catechism: Wherein the Eccentricities & Beauties of Despotism Are Fully Set Forth: A Guide to the Presidential Election of 1864* (New York: J. F. Feeks, 1864), 3. The next three quotations are from pp. 3, 12, and 29, successively.

14. *Boston Evening Transcript*, May 2, 1863; *Hartford Daily Courant*, May 28, 1863.

15. E. A. Pollard, *The Lost Cause: A New Southern History of the War of the Confederates* (New York: E. B. Treat & Co., 1866), 49.

16. E. A. Pollard, *The Lost Cause*, 101.

17. *The Washington Despotism Dissected in Articles from the Metropolitan Record* (New York: Office of the Metropolitan Record, 1863), 8, 14, 23, 29.

18. *Trial of Abraham Lincoln by the Great Statesmen of the Republic: A Council of the Past on the Tyranny of the Present; The Spirit of the Constitution on the Bench—Abraham Lincoln, Prisoner at the Bar, His Own Counsel* (New York: Office of the Metropolitan Record, 1863), 3. The subsequent quotations in this paragraph are from pp. 5 and 28, successively.

19. Diary of Archbishop Martin J. Spalding, January 1, 1863, in Kenneth J. Zanca, "Baltimore's Catholics and the Funeral of Abraham Lincoln," *Maryland Historical Magazine* 98.1 (2003): 94.

20. *Metropolitan Record and New York Vindicator*, January 3 and January 10, 1863.

21. See, for example, these letters on the ALP website: John Hughes to William H. Seward, October 15, 1861, at https://www.loc.gov/item/mal1247000; John Hughes to Lincoln, January 23, 1863, at https://www.loc.gov/item/mal2132800; and Lincoln to John Hughes, Monday, October 21, 1861, at https://www.loc.gov/item/mal1256600.

22. C. Sandburg, *Abraham Lincoln: The War Years* (New York: Harcourt Brace, 1939), 2: 508.

23. Rena Mazyck Andrews, "Archbishop John Hughes and the Civil War" (PhD diss., University of Chicago, 1935), 10.

24. *Metropolitan Record and New York Vindicator*, March 12, 1864.

25. Horatio Seymour campaign badge, 1868; Schomberg Collection, New York Public Library.

26. [Alexander del Mar], *Abraham Africanus I: His Secret Life, as Revealed Under the Mesmeric Influence: Mysteries of the White House* (New York: John F. Feeks, 1864), 11. The subsequent quotations in this paragraph are on pp. 47, 56, and 57, successively.

27. Walt Whitman, *Notebooks and Unpublished Prose Manuscripts*, edited by Edward F. Grier (New York: New York University Press, 1984), 1: 353.

28. *Revelations; A Companion of the "New Gospel of Peace," According to Abraham* (New York: M. Doolady, 1863), 6. The subsequent quotations in this paragraph are on pp. 4, 14, and 35–36, successively.

29. *Book of the Prophet Stephen, Son of Douglas* (New York: Feeks & Bancker, 1863), 12.

30. *National Anti-Slavery Standard*, January 16 and 30, 1864.

31. *The Independent*, February 25, 1864. For a useful discussion of the miscegenation controversy and many other aspects of nineteenth-century racism, see Henry Louis Gates Jr., *Stony the Road: Reconstruction, White Supremacy, and the Rise of Jim Crow* (New York: Penguin Press, 2019). For additional insights into the 1864 race, see Sidney Kaplan, "The Miscegenation Issue in the Election of 1864," *The Journal of Negro History* 34.3 (July 1949): 274–343.

32. *The World*, November 18, 1864.

33. Much of the information in this paragraph is from Peggy Pascoe, *What Comes Naturally: Miscegenation Law and the Making of Race in America* (New York: Oxford University Press, 2009).

34. CW 3: 146. The quotation in the next sentence is also from this page.

35. *Recollected Words of Abraham Lincoln*, edited by D. E. Fehrenbacher and V. Fehrenbacher, 303.

36. *New York Herald*, November 6, 1860.

37. *Black Republican Prayer*, anonymously published broadside, ca. 1864; Houghton Library.

38. *Miscegenation or Amalgamation: Fate of the Freedman. Speech of Hon. Samuel S. Cox, of Ohio, Delivered in the House of Representatives, February 17, 1864* (Washington, DC: Office of the Constitutional Union, 1864), 10.

39. CW 7: 259.

40. *The Jeffersonian* (West Chester, PA) quoted in S. Kaplan, "The Miscegenation Issue in the Election of 1864," 318.

41. *Miscegenation Indorsed by the Republican Party* (New York: n.p., 1864), 9.

42. *New-York Freeman's Journal and Catholic Register*, April 30, 1864.

43. Van Evrie described the "natural law of white supremacy and Negro subordination" (*New York Day-Book*, May 5, 1856). Mark E. Neely Jr. rightly says that Van Evrie's extreme racism did not characterize the mainstream Democratic Party in the lead-up to the election of 1862 (see M. E. Neely Jr., *Lincoln and the Democrats*). However, opposition to Lincoln's increasingly emancipationist policies fanned Democratic racism in 1863 and especially 1864, as argued here.
44. *New-York Caucasian*, May 2, 1863.
45. Quoted in S. Kaplan, "The Miscegenation Issue in the Election of 1864," 322.
46. *Political Caricature. No. 2, Miscegenation or the Millennium of Abolitionism* (New York: G. W. Bromley & Co., 1864).
47. *Political Caricature. No. 4, The Miscegenation Ball* (New York: G. W. Bromley & Co., 1864).
48. J. H. Van Evrie, *Subgenation: The Theory of the Normal Relation of the Races* (New York: John Bradburn, 1864), 65.
49. *The Daily Ohio Statesman*, September 22, 1864.
50. CW 7: 508.
51. *Jackson Citizen* (Jackson, MI), February 21, 1888.
52. Quoted in "D. R. Locke," *Queries: Devoted to Literature, Art, Science, Education* 411 (November 1888): 350.
53. *Jackson Citizen* (Jackson, MI), February 21, 1888.
54. *New York Herald*, February 16, 1888.
55. *Jackson Citizen*, February 21, 1888.
56. RAL 448. The quotation in the next paragraph is on p. 447.
57. The quotations in this paragraph are from FC 150–51.
58. *The Table Talk of Abraham Lincoln*, edited by William O. Stoddard (1894; rpt., New York: Frederick A. Stokes, 1909), 48.
59. RAL 448. The quotation at the end of this paragraph is from p. 451.
60. Quoted in the *Daily Inter Ocean* (Chicago), February 18, 1888.
61. David Ross Locke, *The Struggles (Social, Financial and Political) of Petroleum V. Nasby* (Boston: Lee and Shepard, 1893), 42. The next two quotations in this paragraph are also from this page.
62. D. R. Locke, *The Nasby Papers. Letters and Sermons Containing the Views of Petroleum V. Nasby* (Indianapolis: C. O. Perrine & Co., 1864), 6; D. R. Locke, *The Struggles . . . of Petroleum V. Nasby*, 210. The remaining quotations in this paragraph and the one in the next paragraph are from D. R. Locke, *The Struggles . . . of Petroleum V. Nasby*, 210.
63. *Washington Reporter* (Washington, PA), August 5, 1863.
64. D. R. Locke, *The Nasby Papers*, dedication page; D. R. Locke, *Divers Views, Opinions, and Prophecies of Yoors Trooly Petroleum V. Nasby* (Cincinnati: R. W. Carroll & Co., 1866), 182.
65. D. R. Locke, *The Nasby Papers*, 45. The subsequent quotations in this paragraph are from pp. 46–47.
66. D. R. Locke, *Divers Views, Opinions, and Prophecies*, 301. The block quotation after the next paragraph is from p. 304.
67. Thomas Wentworth Higginson, *Army Life in a Black Regiment* (Boston: Fields, Osgood, & Co., 1870), 4. The Higginson quotation at the end of this paragraph is from *The War of the Rebellion: A Compilation of the Official Records of the*

Union and Confederate Armies, Series 1, Vol. 14, edited by Robert N. Scott (Washington, DC: Government Printing Office 1885), 198.

68. CW 6: 30.

69. Dudley Taylor Cornish, *The Sable Arm: Negro Troops in the Union Army, 1861–1865* (1956; New York: W. W. Norton, 1966), 95. For a discussion of many aspects of African American participation in the war, see James M. McPherson, *The Negro's Civil War: How American Blacks Felt and Acted During the War for the Union* (1965; New York: Knopf Doubleday, 2008). See also Manisha Sinha, "Allies for Emancipation? Lincoln and Black Abolitionists," in *Our Lincoln: New Perspectives on Lincoln and His World*, edited by Eric Foner (New York: W. W. Norton, 2009), chap. 7.

70. Captain Robert F. Wilkinson, quoted in Lawrence Lee Hewitt, *Port Hudson, Confederate Bastion on the Mississippi* (Baton Rouge: Louisiana State University Press, 1994), 176.

71. *National Intelligencer* (Washington), August 24, 1863.

72. C. A. Dana, *Recollections of the Civil War* (New York: D. Appleton and Co., 1902), 85.

73. *Coos Republican* (Lancaster, NH), March 15, 1864.

74. Colonel J. R. Hawley, quoted in Booker T. Washington, *The Story of the Negro* (1909; Philadelphia: University of Pennsylvania Press, 2005), 330.

75. Quoted in Herbert Aptheker, "Negro Casualties in the Civil War," *The Journal of Negro History* 32.1 (January 1947): 31.

76. Quoted in H. Aptheker, "Negro Casualties in the Civil War," 37.

77. D. T. Cornish, *The Sable Arm*, 95.

78. See J. M. McPherson, *The Negro's Civil War*.

79. Quoted in J. Matthew Gallman, "In Your Hands That Musket Means Liberty," in *Wars Within a War: Controversy and Conflict over the American Civil War*, edited by Joan Waugh and Gary W. Gallagher (Chapel Hill: University of North Carolina Press, 2009), 102.

80. F. Douglass, "Our Work Is Not Done," speech at the annual meeting of the American Anti-slavery Society, Philadelphia, December 3–4, 1863, *Proceedings of the American Anti-slavery Society at Its Third Decade, Held in the City of Philadelphia, Dec. 3d and 4th, 1864 [that is, 1863]* (New York: American Anti-slavery Society, 1864), 117. The remaining quotations in this paragraph are also from this page.

81. CW 6: 357.

82. D. T. Cornish, *The Sable Arm*, 177.

83. *Speech of Hon. Thomas Williams, of Pennsylvania, on the Restoration of the Union: Delivered in the House of Representatives, April 28, 1864* (Washington, DC: W. H. Moore, 1864), 7.

84. W. Whitman, "I Sing the Body Electric," LGC 98–99.

85. CW 6: 407. The subsequent quotations in this and the following two paragraphs are from CW 6: 408–409.

86. James C. Conkling to Abraham Lincoln, September 4, 1863; ALP.

87. CW 7: 451.

88. Charles D. Robinson to Abraham Lincoln, August 7, 1864; ALP.

89. CW 7: 500. The quotations in the next paragraph are also from this page.

90. *The Salmon P. Chase Papers: Correspondence, April 1863–1864*, edited by John Niven et al. (Kent, OH: Kent State University Press, 1993), 419.
91. CW 7: 514–15, n. 1. The quotation in the next paragraph is from CW 7: 515, n. 1.
92. *The Political Blondin, Frank Leslie's Budget of Fun*, September 1, 1864, 8–9, at https://elections.harpweek.com/1864/cartoon-1864-Medium.asp?UniqueID =43&Year=1864.
93. J. G. Nicolay, *With Lincoln in the White House*, edited by M. Burlingame, 152.
94. CW 7: 515. The quotation in the next paragraph is from CW 7: 515, n. 1.
95. J. G. Nicolay, *With Lincoln in the White House*, edited by M. Burlingame, 158, 155.
96. John Eaton, *Grant, Lincoln, and the Freedmen: Reminiscences of the Civil War* (New York: Longmans, Green, and Co., 1907), 180. The quotations in the next paragraph are on pp. 168 and 172, successively.
97. CW 7: 243.
98. J. Eaton, *Grant, Lincoln, and the Freedmen*, 173. The next two quotations in this paragraph are from pp. 178 and 179, successively.
99. J. Eaton, *Grant, Lincoln, and the Freedmen*, 178–79. For the convergence of some of the ideals of Lincoln and John Brown toward the end of the Civil War, see D. S. Reynolds, *John Brown, Abolitionist* and H. W. Brands, *The Zealot and the Emancipator: John Brown, Abraham Lincoln, and the Struggle for American Freedom* (New York: Doubleday 2020).
100. *New York Times*, February 7, 1863.
101. See D. W. Blight, *Frederick Douglass, Prophet of Freedom*, 393. The next quotation in this paragraph is from p. 395. For analysis of the growing linkages between Douglass and Lincoln, see Blight's book as well as J. Oakes, *The Radical and the Republican*; J. Stauffer, *Giants: The Parallel Lives of Frederick Douglass and Abraham Lincoln*; and P. Kendrick and S. Kendrick, *Douglass and Lincoln*.
102. For an account of the recruitment of black soldiers for the Union by Douglass, Stearns, and others, see James M. McPherson, *The Struggle for Equality: Abolitionist and the Negro in the Civil War and Reconstruction* (Princeton, NJ: Princeton University Press, 1964), especially chap. 9.
103. *Life and Times of Frederick Douglass, Written by Himself*, 434.
104. Quoted in V. Ullman, *Martin R. Delany*, 293–94.
105. Frank A. Rollin, *Life and Public Services of Martin R. Delany* (Boston: Lee and Shepard, 1883), 22.
106. F. A. Rollin, *Life and Public Services of Martin R. Delany*, 169. The next quotation in this paragraph is also from this page.
107. *John Brown, An Address by Frederick Douglass, at the Fourteenth Anniversary of Storer College, Harper's Ferry, West Virginia, May 30, 1881* (Dover, NH: Morning Star, 1881), 9.
108. RAL 193.
109. CW 8: 272.
110. FC 201. The subsequent quotations in this paragraph are on pp. 202–203. The White House visit was differently described by Truth's friend Lucy Colman, who said that the president that morning kept his female visitors waiting for more than three hours while he chatted with a group of men, and that, though cordial during his interview with Truth, he was guarded when discussing emancipation

with her (Nell Irvin Painter, *Sojourner Truth: A Life, A Symbol* [New York: W. W. Norton, 1997] 204–209).

111. EK 156–57. For insights into many aspects of the relationship between the Lincolns and Keckly—including the correct spelling of Lizzy (not "Lizzie," as Mary Lincoln spelled it) and Keckly (not the commonly used "Keckley")—see Jennifer Fleischner, *Mrs. Lincoln and Mrs. Keckly* (New York: Broadway Books, 2003).

112. Anna L. Boyden, *Echoes from Hospital and White House: A Record of Mrs. Rebecca R. Pomroy's Experiences in War-Times* (Boston: Lothrop, 1884), 97–98.

113. FC 196–97. The subsequent quotations in this paragraph are on p. 209.

114. C. C. Burr, "History of Old John Brown," *The Old Guard*, July 1865; reprinted in LSW 430–31.

115. For a discussion of the "Provisional Constitution," see D. S. Reynolds, *John Brown, Abolitionist*, 249–55.

116. Franklin Benjamin Sanborn, *The Life and Letters of John Brown: Liberator of Kansas, and Martyr of Virginia* (Boston: Roberts Brothers, 1891), 585.

117. These words are from Douglass's eulogy to Lincoln, delivered before a largely black audience on June 1 at Cooper Union, in the hall where Lincoln had given his landmark speech five years earlier (*National Anti-Slavery Standard*, June 10, 1865). Nine years later, after the failure of Reconstruction, Douglass would speak more ambiguously, calling Lincoln "preeminently the white man's president," although, on a positive note, he pointed out that Lincoln, who appeared to be tardy on abolition, actually held himself back in order to maintain public support, all the while being "radical, zealous, determined" underneath about rights for African Americans (F. Douglass, oration in Washington, DC, April 14, 1876, in LSW 436–38).

118. F. A. Rollin, *Life and Public Services of Martin R. Delany*, 207. The quotation in the next paragraph is also from this page.

CHAPTER 21
DEMOCRATIC ELOQUENCE

1. Jean-Pierre Changeux, *The Good, the True and the Beautiful: A Neuronal Approach* (2008; New Haven, CT: Yale University Press, 2012), 63. Changeux's notion of parsimony is adapted in part from the economist Herbert Simon.

2. "The Battlefield of Gettysburg," *Frank Leslie's Popular Monthly* 26.2 (August 1888): 130.

3. *Revised Report Made to the Legislature of Pennsylvania, Relative to the Soldiers' National Cemetery, at Gettysburg* (Harrisburg, PA: Singerly & Myers, 1867), 161, 177.

4. Quoted in Martin P. Johnson, *Writing the Gettysburg Address* (Lawrence: University of Kansas Press, 2013), 51.

5. D. G. Faust, *This Republic of Suffering*, 100. See also Mark S. Schantz, "Death and the Gettysburg Address," in *The Gettysburg Address: Perspectives on Lincoln's Greatest Speech*, edited by Sean Conant (New York: Oxford University Press, 2015), 107–25.

6. *A Memorial of Edward Everett, from the City of Boston* (Boston: City Council, 1865), 48.

7. David Wills to Abraham Lincoln, November 2, 1863; ALP. See D. L. Wilson's *Lincoln's Sword*, 208.

8. CW 7: 13.

9. CW 6: 319–20.

10. LSW 315.

11. Louis A. Warren, *Lincoln's Gettysburg Declaration: "A New Birth of Freedom"* (Fort Wayne, IN: Lincoln National Life Foundation, 1964), 54.

12. *The Nation*, 26 (January 24, 1878): 61.

13. RAL 403.

14. CW 7: 16–17.

15. *The Press* (Philadelphia), November 21, 1863. Much of the information in these paragraphs about Lincoln's visit to Gettysburg is from this article and from Philip B. Kunhardt Jr., *A New Birth of Freedom: Lincoln at Gettysburg* (Boston: Little, Brown and Co., 1983).

16. *Chicago Press and Tribune*, June 13, 1860.

17. Edward Everett, "Address at the Consecration of the National Cemetery at Gettysburg, 19th November, 1863," *Orations and Speeches on Various Occasions*, vol. 4 (Boston: Little, Brown and Co., 1872), 644–45. The quotation at the end of the next paragraph is from pp. 657–58.

18. *Proceedings of the First Three Republican National Conventions*, 43, 131.

19. The Lincoln quotations here and in the following paragraphs are from "Address Delivered at the Dedication of the Cemetery at Gettysburg," CW 7: 18–19.

20. "The Independence Day Election of Pennsylvania representative Galusha A. Grow as Speaker of the House, July 4, 1861," *History, Art, & Archives, United States House of Representatives*, at https://history.house.gov/Historical-Highlights/1851 -1900/The-Independence-Day-election-of-Pennsylvania-Representative-Galu sha-A--Grow-as-Speaker-of-the-House. See Allen C. Guelzo, "Lincoln and the Murk of Myth at Gettysburg," in *The Gettysburg Address*, edited by S. Conant, 147–72.

21. E. Everett, *Orations and Speeches on Various Occasions*, vol. 2 (Boston: Little, Brown and Co., 1865), 157.

22. "The Pilgrim Fathers" (speech at the Plymouth Festival, August 1, 1853, to celebrate embarkation of the Pilgrims), in *Orations and Speeches on Various Occasions*, vol. 3 (Boston: Little, Brown and Co., 1865), 242.

23. *The Dollar Newspaper* (Philadelphia), December 30, 1863. Similarly, in a speech at Plymouth Rock in Plymouth, Massachusetts, on August 1, 1853, Sumner had compared the early American Puritans with "our Antislavery Puritans" as "champions of liberty" and people of "true grandeur" (C. Sumner, "Finger-point from Plymouth Rock," in *Charles Sumner: His Complete Works* [Boston: Lee & Shepard, 1900], 73, 79).

24. *The Union Democrat* (Manchester, NH), December 8, 1863.

25. CW 5: 529.

26. Michael Angelo Musmanno, *The Glory and the Dream: Abraham Lincoln, Before and After Gettysburg* (New Canaan, CT: Long House, 1967), 19; and P. B. Kunhardt Jr., *A New Birth of Freedom*, 120. See also Gabor S. Boritt, *The Gettysburg Gospel: The Lincoln Speech That Nobody Knows* (New York: Simon & Schuster, 2006).

27. CW 3: 328. The subsequent quotation in this paragraph is also from this page.
28. *The Press* (Philadelphia), September 3, 1863.
29. *The Crisis* (Columbus, OH), January 27, 1863.
30. *Chicago Times*, November 23, 1863; review reprinted in LSW 407–408.
31. CW 5: 537.
32. See especially Garry Wills, *Lincoln at Gettysburg: The Words That Remade America* (New York: Simon & Schuster, 1992). Another fine study of Lincoln's debt to the Declaration of Independence is Richard Brookhiser, *Founders' Son: A Life of Abraham Lincoln* (New York: Basic Books, 2016).
33. *The Christian Era*, April 26, 1861.
34. *New York Times*, July 6, 1863; see H. Holzer, *Lincoln and the Power of the Press*, 434.
35. P. B. Kunhardt Jr., *A New Birth of Freedom*, 61. The quotations in this paragraph are, successively, from D. Webster, *The Webster-Hayne Debate on the Nature of the Constitution*, ed. H. Belz, 126, and T. Parker, *The Effect of Slavery on the American People*, 5. Also, Parker in an 1854 speech had praised democracy as "the government of all, for all, and by all" (T. Parker, *A Sermon of the Dangers Which Threaten the Rights of Man in America* [Boston: B. B. Mussey & Co., 1854], 28).
36. *Abraham Lincoln: Tributes from His Associates*, edited by W. H. Ward, 23.
37. See Sean A. Scott, *A Visitation of God: Northern Civilians Interpret the Civil War* (New York: Oxford University Press, 2011), 257.
38. Benjamin Talbot to Abraham Lincoln, December 21, 1864; ALP.
39. HI 360.
40. Benjamin B. French, *Witness to the Young Republic: A Yankee's Journal, 1828–1879* (Hanover, NH: University Press of New England, 1989), 436.
41. CW 7: 25.
42. B. B. French, *Witness to the Young Republic*, 436.
43. *Chicago Tribune*, December 15, 1863; in JH 328.
44. William A. Croffut, *An American Procession, 1855–1914: A Personal Chronicle of Famous Men* (Boston: Little, Brown and Co., 1931), 102.
45. N. Brooks, *Washington in Lincoln's Time*, 149; CW 7: 395.
46. Quoted in Chester G. Hearn, *Mobile Bay and the Mobile Campaign: The Last Great Battles of the Civil War* (Jefferson, NC: McFarland, 2010), 91.
47. *Memoirs of General William T. Sherman*, 2: 179.
48. Article 42, *Instructions for the Government of Armies of the United States in the Field*.
49. CW 8: 171.
50. In Alfred Burnett, *Incidents of the War, Humorous, Pathetic, and Descriptive* (Cincinnati: Rickey & Carroll, 1863), 302.
51. *Salem Observer*, November 12, 1864. See W. H. Whitmore, *The Cavalier Dismounted* (Salem: G. M. Whipple & A. A. Smith, 1864).
52. *Louisville Journal*, quoted in the *Christian Mirror*, May 26, 1863.
53. *Daily Constitutionalist* (Augusta), September 29, 1863.
54. *New-York Caucasian*, January 31, 1863.
55. *The Washington Examiner*, January 29, 1863.
56. J. Quitman Moore, "The Belligerents," *DeBow's Review* 31.1 (July 1861): 73.
57. W. H. Whitmore, *The Cavalier Dismounted*, 6.

58. *Salem Observer*, June 3, 1865.
59. John Joseph Craven, *Prison Life of Jefferson Davis: Embracing Details and Incidents in His Captivity* (London: Carleton, 1867), 112. The next quotation in this paragraph is from p. 86.
60. William Edward Dodd, *Jefferson Davis* (Philadelphia: G. W. Jacobs, 1907), 297.
61. CW 8: 151.
62. CW 8: 275.
63. CW 8: 221.
64. CW 8: 248. See James B. Conroy, *Our One Common Country: Abraham Lincoln and the Hampton Roads Peace Conference of 1865* (Guilford, CT: Lyons Press, 2014).
65. W. H. Lamon, *Recollections of Abraham Lincoln*, edited by D. L. Teillard, 128.
66. Z 41.
67. *National Anti-Slavery Standard*, December 29, 1855.
68. *New York Herald*, February 8, 1865.
69. *The Washington Chronicle*, quoted in the *New-York Tribune*, February 7, 1865.
70. CW 8: 318.
71. CW 8: 254.
72. *The Press* (Philadelphia), March 6 1865.
73. In 1868, an estimated twenty thousand animals infested the city streets. The city didn't take action to impound the animals until the 1870s, and even then the problem lingered, due to its magnitude. See Robert Harrison, *Washington During the Civil War and Reconstruction* (New York: Cambridge University Press, 2011), 237. A western journalist described the "fearful condition" of Washington's streets during heavy rains: "They are seas or canals of liquid mud, varying in depth from one to three feet" (in R. Harrison, *Washington During the Civil War*, 157). Besides the ubiquitous animal waste, effective plumbing and sewage removal were nonexistent, and so human waste was thrown into pits or privies that flowed onto the streets during storms (see Jeff Dickey, *Empire of Mud: The Secret History of Washington, DC* [Guilford, CT: Lyons Press, 2014], 207).
74. *New York Herald*, March, 6, 1865. See also the *Washington Evening Star*, March 4, 1865.
75. *New-York Tribune*, March 6, 1865.
76. *National Anti-Slavery Standard*, March 11, 1865.
77. *Illustrated Times* (London), March 25, 1865.
78. For Webster and alcohol, see Jonathan M. Chu, "The Demon and Daniel Webster: Drinking in the Antebellum Senate," *Nineteenth Century American History* 1.2 (2000): 97–104. For Clay, see, for example, Robert V. Remini, *Henry Clay: Statesman for the Union* (New York: W. W. Norton, 1993), 23.
79. *Newark Daily Advertiser*, March 4, 1865. The McDougall incident described in the next sentence is also from this source.
80. *Weekly Union* (Manchester, NH), March 14, 1865.
81. "Case of Andrew Johnson," *Cincinnati Daily Commercial*, reprinted in the *Daily Milwaukee News*, March 23, 1865, and *The Liberator*, April 7, 1865.
82. *New York Herald*, March, 6, 1865.
83. *Illustrated Times* (London), March 25, 1865. The details in the next paragraph are from the reports in the *Illustrated Times* and the *New York Herald*. Although

the negative comments about Johnson's performance on March 4 were fully justified, it should be noted that Johnson, when he planned his speeches and remained sober, could be an effective speaker. The reports about Johnson's drinking are mixed. Lincoln said a few days after the inaugural, "I have known Andy Johnson for many years; he made a bad slip the other day, but Andy ain't a drunkard" (in Hugh McCulloch, *Men and Measures of Half a Century: Sketches and Comments* [New York: C. Scribner's Sons, 1888], 373). That seems to have been true, but a friend of Johnson's reported that Johnson "did take three or four glasses of Robertson County whisky on some days; some days less and some days and weeks no liquor at all" (in Gary L. Donhardt, *In the Shadow of the Great Rebellion: The Life of Andrew Johnson, Seventeenth President of the United States (1808–1875)* [New York: Nova Science Publishers 2009], 165). Another observer said that Johnson had developed a "habit of denunciatory declamation which he had formed in his bitter contests in Tennessee" that could make him seem drunk even when he wasn't (H. McCulloch, *Men and Measures*, 374).

84. N. Brooks, *Washington in Lincoln's Time*, 238.
85. Quoted in William C. Harris, *Lincoln's Last Months* (Cambridge, MA: Harvard University Press, 2009), 139.
86. Quoted in Frances Fisher Browne, *The Every-day Life of Abraham Lincoln* (New York: N. D. Thompson, 1886), 680. See also Noah Brooks, "Lincoln's Re-election," *The Century Magazine* 49 (April 1895): 871.
87. Quotations from the Second Inaugural Address are from CW 8: 332–33. For revealing details about the Second Inaugural, see Edward Achorn, *Every Drop of Blood: The Momentous Second Inauguration of Abraham Lincoln* (New York: Atlantic Monthly Press, 2020) and Ronald C. White, *Lincoln's Greatest Speech: The Second Inaugural* (New York: Simon & Schuster, 2020). Also illuminating are R. C. White, *A. White: A Biography*, chap. 26, and M. Burlingame, *Abraham Lincoln: A Life*, chap. 35.
88. *The Louisville Journal*, quoted in the *Christian Mirror*, May 26, 1863.
89. *New York Herald*, March 6, 1865.
90. *Life and Times of Frederick Douglass, Written by Himself*, 442.
91. *Life and Times of Frederick Douglass, Written by Himself*, 444–445.
92. CW 8: 356.
93. *The Liberator*, March 17, 1865.
94. *New York Times*, April 17, 1865; in LSW 417.
95. *New-York Freeman's Journal and Catholic Register*, May 18, 1865.
96. *The World*, March 6, 1856.
97. *Daily California Express* (Marysville, CA), quoted in the *Sacramento Daily Union*, March 8, 1865.
98. *New York Herald*, March 6, 1865.
99. RAL 191.
100. In T. Alford, *Fortune's Fool: The Life of John Wilkes Booth*, 227.

CHAPTER 22
UNION, TRAGEDY, AND LEGACY

1. Ulysses S. Grant to Abraham Lincoln, March 20, 1865; ALP.

2. See Noah André Trudeau, *Lincoln's Greatest Journey: Sixteen Days That Changed a Presidency, March 24–April 8, 1865* (El Dorado Hills, CA: Savas Beatie, 2016), 235–37.

3. Charles Coffin, "Scenes in Richmond," *Boston Journal*, April 10, 1865. The remaining quotations in this paragraph are also from this article. For an account of Lincoln's day in Richmond, see Michael D. Gorman, "A Conqueror or a Peacemaker? Abraham Lincoln in Richmond," *The Virginia Magazine of History and Biography* 123.1 (2015): 2–88. See also N. A. Trudeau, *Lincoln's Greatest Journey*, chap. 12. Jay Winik in *April 1865: The Month That Saved America* (New York: HarperCollins, 2001) ably describes the Richmond episode as well as many other important Lincoln-related events that month.

4. Charles Coffin, "Late Scenes in Richmond," *Atlantic Monthly* 15 (1865): 753–55.

5. David D. Porter, *Incidents and Anecdotes of the Civil War* (New York: D. Appleton and Co., 1886), 307.

6. William Henry Crook, *Through Five Administrations: Reminiscences of Colonel William H. Crook* (New York: Harper, 1910), 56–57.

7. See D. D. Porter, *Incidents and Anecdotes of the Civil War*, 308, and W. H. Crook, *Through Five Administrations*, 56.

8. D. D. Porter, *Incidents and Anecdotes of the Civil War*, 303–304.

9. CW 8: 395.

10. F. F. Browne, *The Every-day Life of Abraham Lincoln*, 701.

11. Letter from Mary Lincoln to F. B. Carpenter, November 15, 1865, in *Conversations with Lincoln*, edited by Charles M. Segal (New York: Putnam, 1961), 396; see also FC 293.

12. F. F. Browne, *The Every-day Life of Abraham Lincoln*, 103.

13. Hilton Obenzinger, *American Palestine: Melville, Twain, and the Holy Land Mania* (Princeton, NJ: Princeton University Press, 1999), chap. 9.

14. *Springfield Republican*, May 13, 1865.

15. CW 8: 406–407.

16. CW 7: 243. LaWanda Cox persuasively argues that Lincoln, despite his outward caution, deeply sympathized with Radical Republican attitudes toward Reconstruction; see L. Cox, *Lincoln and Black Freedom: A Study in Presidential Leadership* (Columbia: University of South Carolina Press, 1981). For a detailed account of Lincoln's dealings with Louisiana, see Peyton McCrary, *Abraham Lincoln and Reconstruction: The Louisiana Experiment* (Princeton, NJ: Princeton University Press, 1978).

17. Among the landmark studies of Reconstruction are W. E. B. Du Bois, *Black Reconstruction in America: An Essay Toward a History of the Part Which Black Folk Played in the Attempt to Reconstruct Democracy in America, 1860–1880* (New York: Russel & Russel, 1935); John Hope Franklin, *Reconstruction* (Chicago: University of Chicago Press, 1961); Eric Foner, *Reconstruction: America's Unfinished Revolution* (Boston: Houghton Mifflin, 2010); E. Foner, *The Second Founding: How the Civil War and Reconstruction Remade the Constitution* (New York: W. W. Norton, 2019); Edward H. Bonekemper III, *The Myth of the Lost Cause: Why the South Fought the Civil War and Why the North Won* (Washington, DC: Regnery, 2015); D. W. Blight, *Frederick Douglass, Prophet of Freedom*; and H. L. Gates Jr., *Stony the Road: Reconstruction, White Supremacy, and the Rise of Jim Crow*. On President Johnson in the context of Reconstruction, see

especially Brenda Wineapple, *The Impeachers: The Trial of Andrew Johnson and the Dream of a Just Nation* (New York: Random House, 2019).

18. CW 8: 400–401. The quotation in the next sentence is also from these pages, as are the quotations in the last two sentences of this paragraph.

19. CW 8: 386.

20. *Inside Lincoln's Cabinet: The Civil War Diaries of Salmon P. Chase*, edited by David Donald (New York: Longmans, Green, 1954), 268.

21. Benjamin Platt Thomas and Harold Hyman, *Edwin M. Stanton: The Life and Times of Lincoln's Secretary of War* (New York: Alfred A. Knopf, 1962), 355.

22. Quoted in Herman Belz, *Reconstructing the Union, Theory and Policy During the Civil War* (Ithaca, NY: Cornell University Press, 1969), 308. The Sumner quotation in the next sentence is also from this page.

23. Ovando James Hollister, *Life of Schuyler Colfax* (New York: Funk & Wagnalls, 1886), 59.

24. See Willard H. Smith, "Schuyler Colfax and Reconstruction Policy," *Indiana Magazine of History* 39.4 (December 1943): 323–44.

25. *Hartford Daily Courant*, November 20, 1865.

26. Lew Wallace, speech at South Bend, Indiana, March 15, 1898; quoted in W. H. Smith, "Schuyler Colfax and Reconstruction Policy," 327.

27. Willard H. Smith, *Schuyler Colfax: The Changing Fortunes of a Political Idol* (Indianapolis: Indiana Historical Bureau, 1952), 208–209.

28. O. J. Hollister, *Life of Schuyler Colfax*, 253. The next quotation in this paragraph is also from this page.

29. D. H. Bates, *Lincoln in the Telegraph Office*, 366–68.

30. *Diary of Gideon Welles*, 2: 282–83. See also F. W. Seward, *Reminiscences of a War-Time Statesman and Diplomat 1830–1915*, 255; W. H. Lamon, *Recollections of Abraham Lincoln*, edited by D. L. Teillard, 118–20.

31. CW 8: 413.

32. F. F. Browne, *The Every-day Life of Abraham Lincoln*, 704.

33. CW 8: 412.

34. F. F. Browne, *The Every-day Life of Abraham Lincoln*, 704.

35. Edwin C. Haynie, "At the Death-bed of Lincoln," *Century Magazine* 51 (April 1896): 954.

36. K. Helm, *The True Story of Mary, Wife of Lincoln*, 256.

37. William M. Thayer, *A Youth's History of the Rebellion: From the Massacre at Fort Pillow to the End* (Boston: Walker, Fuller, and Co., 1866), 339.

38. Quoted in G. Samples, *Lust for Fame: The Stage Career of John Wilkes Booth*, 20.

39. *New York Clipper*, April 29, 1865. See T. Alford, *Fortune's Fool: The Life of John Wilkes Booth*, 249–50.

40. Louis J. Weichmann, *A True History of the Assassination of Abraham Lincoln and the Conspiracy of 1865* (New York: Alfred A. Knopf, 1975), 136.

41. A. B. Clarke, *John Wilkes Booth: A Sister's Memoir*, 106.

42. T. Alford, *Fortune's Fool: The Life of John Wilkes Booth*, 97.

43. A. B. Clarke, *John Wilkes Booth: A Sister's Memoir*, 107.

44. *Right or Wrong, God Judge Me: The Writings of John Wilkes Booth*, edited by John Rhodehamel and Louise Taper (Urbana: University of Illinois Press, 2000), 125. The next quotation in this paragraph is also from this page.

45. T. Alford, *Fortune's Fool: The Life of John Wilkes Booth*, 257.

46. *Right or Wrong, God Judge Me*, edited by J. Rhodehamel and L. Taper, 125. The next quotation in this paragraph is also from this page.

47. For an account of Booth's visit to Charles Town and Harpers Ferry, see T. Alford, *Fortune's Fool: The Life of John Wilkes Booth*, 73–82.

48. *Right or Wrong, God Judge Me*, edited by J. Rhodehamel and L. Taper, 129.

49. "Speech of Governor Wise," *Richmond Enquirer*, October 25, 1859.

50. L. Washington, quoted in "Speech of Governor Wise," *Richmond Enquirer*, October 25, 1859.

51. T. Alford, *Fortune's Fool: The Life of John Wilkes Booth*, 81.

52. John Edwin Cooke, *The Life, Trial, and Execution of Captain John Brown* (New York: Robert M. De Witt, 1859), 46; L. J. Weichmann, *A True History of the Assassination of Abraham Lincoln*, 10.

53. J. E. Cooke, *The Life, Trial, and Execution of Captain John Brown*, 47; T. Alford, *Fortune's Fool: The Life of John Wilkes Booth*, 199–200.

54. Quoted in Michael W. Kauffman, *American Brutus: John Wilkes Booth and the Lincoln Conspiracies* (New York: Random House, 2004), 272.

55. *Right or Wrong, God Judge Me*, edited by J. Rhodehamel and L. Taper, 129. The quotation in the next sentence is from p. 125.

56. *John Brown, the Making of a Revolutionary*, edited by L. Ruchames, 167.

57. *Right or Wrong, God Judge Me*, edited by J. Rhodehamel and L. Taper, 129. The remaining quotations in this paragraph are also from this page.

58. T. Alford, *Fortune's Fool: The Life of John Wilkes Booth*, 5. The next quotation in this paragraph is from p. 169. The quotation from the poem "Then and Now" is from p. 192.

59. *Chicago Tribune*, April 17, 1865.

60. L. J. Weichmann, *A True History of the Assassination of Abraham Lincoln*, 95.

61. PW 2: 597. The next quotation in this paragraph is also from this page.

62. The incidents described in this paragraph are from Jacob Larwood, *Theatrical Anecdotes, or Fun and Curiosities of the Play, the Playhouse, and the Players* (London: Chatto and Windus, 1882); Jody Enders, *Death by Drama and Other Medieval Urban Legends* (Chicago: University of Chicago Press, 2005); and Stephen M. Archer, *Junius Brutus Booth: Theatrical Prometheus* (1992; Carbondale: Southern Illinois University Press, 2010). See also D. S. Reynolds, *Walt Whitman's America*, chap. 6.

63. J. Larwood, *Theatrical Anecdotes*, 259.

64. Quoted in M. W. Kauffman, *American Brutus: John Wilkes Booth and the Lincoln Conspiracies*, 127.

65. T. Alford, *Fortune's Fool: The Life of John Wilkes Booth*, 22.

66. Horace Traubel, *With Walt Whitman in Camden*, vol. 4, (1953; Carbondale: Southern Illinois University Press, 1959): 485.

67. *The Press* (Philadelphia), March 5, 1863.

68. T. Alford, *Fortune's Fool: The Life of John Wilkes Booth*, 168.

69. L. J. Weichmann, *A True History of the Assassination of Abraham Lincoln*, 119.

70. L. J. Weichmann, *A True History of the Assassination of Abraham Lincoln*, 131. The next quotation in this paragraph ("splendid acting") is from p. 141.

71. Adam Badeau, quoted in T. Alford, *Fortune's Fool: The Life of John Wilkes Booth*, 7.

72. *Right or Wrong, God Judge Me*, edited by J. Rhodehamel and L. Taper, 154.

73. CW 8: 399–400.

74. Adolphe de Pineton, marquis de Chambrun, "Personal Recollections of Mr. Lincoln," *Scribner's Magazine* 13 (January 1893): 28.

75. A. de Pineton, "Personal Recollection of Mr. Lincoln," 35.

76. Henry Wadsworth Longfellow, *Longfellow's Poetical Works* (London: George Routledge and Sons, 1883), 48.

77. A. de Pineton, "Personal Recollection of Mr. Lincoln," 35.

78. H. Melville, "Hawthorne and His Mosses," in *Pierre . . . Uncollected Prose*, 1159–60.

79. T. Alford, *Fortune's Fool: The Life of John Wilkes Booth*, 261.

80. *The Personal Memoirs of Julia Dent Grant (Mrs. Ulysses S. Grant)* (Carbondale: Southern Illinois University Press, 2016), 155–56.

81. E. Lawrence Abel, *A Finger in Lincoln's Brain: What Modern Science Reveals About Lincoln, His Assassination, and Its Aftermath* (Santa Barbara, CA: Praeger, 2015), 57. The quotation in the next paragraph is also from this page. My discussion of Lincoln's assassination in the following pages is based on primary sources and on historical accounts such as W. Emerson Reck, *A. Lincoln: His Last 24 Hours* (1967; Jefferson, NC: McFarland, 2006); Edward Steers Jr., *Blood on the Moon: The Assassination of Abraham Lincoln* (Lexington: University Press of Kentucky, 2001); James L. Swanson, *Manhunt: The 12-Day Chase for Lincoln's Killer* (New York: William Morrow, 2006); J. L. Swanson, *Lincoln's Assassins: Their Trial and Execution* (New York: Harper Perennial, 2008); and *The Lincoln Assassination. The Evidence*, edited by William C. Edwards and Edward Steers Jr. (Urbana: University of Illinois Press, 2009).

82. Mary Lincoln, letter to Anson G. Henry, quoted in R. P. Randall, *Mary Lincoln*, 382.

83. Booth wrote, "In jumping I broke my leg." But Michael Kauffman argues persuasively for the horse theory. See M. W. Kauffman, *American Brutus: John Wilkes Booth and the Lincoln Conspiracies*, 272–73.

84. Kathryn Canavan, *Lincoln's Final Hours: Conspiracy, Terror, and the Assassination of America's Greatest President* (Lexington: University Press of Kentucky, 2015), 79.

85. L. J. Weichmann, *A True History of the Assassination of Abraham Lincoln*, 154.

86. J. Nicolay and J. Hay, *Abraham Lincoln: A History*, vol. 10, 302. However, one of Lincoln's deathbed physicians, Charles Sabin Taft, recalled that Stanton said, "Now he belongs to the angels." See C. S. Taft, "Abraham Lincoln's Last Hours," *Century Magazine* 45 (1893): 635.

87. Elizabeth Dixon, *The Assassination of Lincoln. Excerpts from Newspapers and Other Sources* (Fort Wayne, IN: Lincoln Foundation Association, 1866).

88. EK 191.

89. JT 224.

90. JT 472.

91. FC 293.

92. Some of the details here about the funerals and commemorations for Lincoln are derived from Martha Hodes, *Mourning Lincoln* (New Haven, CT: Yale University Press, 2015) and Richard Wightman Fox, *Lincoln's Body: A Cultural History* (New York: W. W. Norton, 2015).

93. Quotations from the poem are from LGC 328–37.

94. CW 6: 275.

95. Several details in this paragraph are derived from "Two Days in May: The Funeral of Abraham Lincoln," Sangamon Link, April 22, 2015, at http://sangamon countyhistory.org/wp/?p=7141.

96. Among the more thorough newspaper accounts of the funeral are those in the *Chicago Daily Tribune*, May 6, 1865, and *The World* (New York), May 5, 1865.

97. L. J. Weichmann, *A True History of the Assassination of Abraham Lincoln*, 138. The next quotation in this paragraph is from p. 7.

98. PW 2: 508. The quotations in this paragraph are from this page.

99. See M. Hodes, *Mourning Lincoln*, especially chap. 3.

100. M. B. M. Chesnut, *A Diary from Dixie: Electronic Edition*, 380; J. Wise quoted in Merrill D. Peterson, *Lincoln in American Memory* (New York: Oxford University Press, 1994), 45.

101. Robert H. Crozier, *The Bloody Junto, or The Escape of John Wilkes Booth* (Little Rock, AR: Woodruff & Blocher, 1869), 11, 96.

102. Stewart Winning McClelland, *A Monument to the Memory of John Wilkes Booth* (n.p.: n.p., 1951), 5; Izola L. Forrester, *This One Mad Act: The Unknown Story of John Wilkes Booth and His Family* (Boston: Hale, Cushman & Flint, 1937), 135; Michael Tomasky, "The John Wilkes Booth Wing of the Republican Party," *The Daily Beast*, July 9, 2013.

103. See John McKee Barr, *Loathing Lincoln: An American Tradition from the Civil War to the Present* (Baton Rouge: Louisiana State University Press, 2014).

104. *The Congregationalist*, December 8, 1865.

105. *Boston Evening Transcript*, December 30, 1865.

106. *Cincinnati Daily Enquirer*, March 4, 1866.

107. *The Independent*, October 1, 1868.

108. *Life of Henry W. Grady*, edited by J. C. Harris, 86.

109. HI 438.

110. HOL 345.

111. Henry W. Bellows to Joseph Bellows, February 1, 1862, Bellows Papers, Massachusetts Historical Society.

112. *The Diary of George Templeton Strong*, edited by A. Nevins and M. Halsey, 3: 379.

113. This quotation and the one in the next sentence are from N. A. Trudeau, *Lincoln's Greatest Journey*, 234.

114. CW 2: 220.

115. John Steele Gordon, "The High Cost of War," *Barron's*, April 9, 2011, at https://www.barrons.com/articles/SB50001424052970203990104576191061207786514.

116. *Inaugural Ceremonies of the Freedmen's Memorial Monument to Abraham Lincoln: Washington City, April 14, 1876* (Saint Louis: Levison & Blythe, 1876), 8. The quotation in the next sentence is from p. 9.

117. F. Douglass, oration in Washington, DC, April 14, 1876, in LSW 436–38.

118. "Lincoln Memorial Builders," Lincoln Memorial, at https://www.nps.gov/linc /learn/historyculture/lincoln-memorial-design-individuals.htm.

119. Quotations in this and the following paragraphs are from *The Essential Martin Luther King, Jr.: "I Have a Dream" and Other Great Writings* (Boston: Beacon, 2013), chap. 10.

ILLUSTRATION CREDITS

p. 178, p. 527, p. 537, p. 552, p. 577, p. 726, p. 799, p. 832 (bottom), Courtesy of the American Antiquarian Society

p. 186, Collection of the Speed Art Museum, Louisville, Kentucky

p. 200 (bottom), p. 411, p. 843, p. 844, Courtesy of the Abraham Lincoln Presidential Library and Museum

p. 213, "Prairie Lawyer," *Illiniwek* 7.3 (May–June 1969), p. 24; from archive.org

p. 352, p. 391, p. 648, p. 903, Courtesy of the National Portrait Gallery

p. 457 (left), *Charles Blondin.* Zip Lexing; Alamy Stock Photo

p. 457 (right), *Charles Blondin (1824–1897) carries his manager Harry Colford over the gorge of the Niagara River in 1859.* Pictorial Press Ltd.; Alamy Stock Photo

p. 460 (left), p. 490 (right), p. 501, p. 518 (left), p. 738, p. 815, Courtesy of Richard West

p. 484, University of Illinois-Urbana Rare Book and Manuscript Library

p. 490 (left), Courtesy of the Chicago History Museum

p. 491, *The Rail Splitter* (Chicago, September 1, 1860); from archive.org

p. 532, From Charles Anson Ingraham, "Colonel Elmer E. Ellsworth, First Hero of the Civil War," *Wisconsin Magazine of History*, 1.4 (June 1918), opposite p. 16; from archive.org

p. 632, From Nettie Colburn Maynard, *Was Abraham Lincoln a Spiritualist?* (Philadelphia: Rufus C. Hartranft, 1891), opposite p. 74; from archive.org

p. 735, Manchester Metropolitan University Special Collections

p. 767, Charles Farrar Browne, *Artemus Ward. His Book* (New York: Carleton, 1862), frontispiece and title page; from archive.org

p. 822, United States Army Heritage and Education Center, Carlisle, PA

p. 883, James E. and Joan Singer Schiele Print Collection, Washington University (Saint Louis, MO)

p. 933, Carol M. Highsmith's America, Library of Congress, Prints and Photographs Division

INDEX